CORPORATE FINANCE

Principles and Practice

GARY W. EMERY
University of Oklahoma

ADDISON-WESLEY

An imprint of Addison Wesley Longman, Inc.

Reading, Massachusetts • Menlo Park, California • New York • Harlow, England
Don Mills, Ontario • Sydney • Mexico City • Madrid • Amsterdam

Senior Editor: Denise Clinton
Associate Editor: Julie Zasloff
Editorial Assistant: Emily Meehan
Development Editor: Ann Sass
Supplements Editor: Joan Twining
Marketing Manager: Jodi Fazio
Cover Designer: Jeannet Leendertse
Senior Production Supervisor: Nancy Fenton
Project Coordination and Text Design: Elm Street Publishing Services, Inc.

Library of Congress Cataloging-in-Publication Data
Emery, Gary W.
   Corporate finance : principles and practice / Gary W. Emery.
     p.   cm.
   Includes bibliographical references and index.
   ISBN 0-321-01455-3
   1. Corporations—Finance.   I. Title.
HG4026.E473   1998
658.15—dc21   97-18709
                                                 CIP

ISBN 0-321-01455-3

Printed in the United States of America.

1 2 3 4 5 6 7 8 9 10—DOC—01 00 99 98 97

PREFACE

Critics of management education have challenged instructors to prepare students to work in real businesses without neglecting their quantitative skills and understanding of financial theories. Finance faculty have responded to this challenge, although existing textbooks do not effectively support their efforts. I wrote *Corporate Finance: Principles and Practice* to help faculty meet this challenge by making financial theory accessible to students and by using practical examples that integrate production, marketing, management, accounting, and finance.

GUIDING PHILOSOPHY

Three precepts guided my work as I wrote this book. First, I was committed to providing the rigorous treatment of fundamental theories that faculty expect in a modern corporate finance textbook. The reason is familiar to all of us. Students who thoroughly understand fundamental principles can apply the best financial practices now and learn new financial practices as they are developed in the future.

Second, I was committed to helping students intuitively understand financial theories. Instructors want students to use financial principles to make sense of a complex world and to critically examine proposed solutions to management problems. This requires that students develop their intuition and not simply learn financial principles as formal statements and mathematical formulas. Fulfilling this commitment helps students recognize the truth of Albert Einstein's statement that "(t)he whole of science (finance) is nothing more than the refinement of everyday thinking."[1]

Third, I was committed to showing students how to use their knowledge of financial theories to solve realistic management problems. Faculty have often been asked to respond to critics who say that students lack knowledge of the real world and do not understand how one functional area relates to another.[2] Instructors know how to meet this challenge but need a supportive textbook to fine-tune an existing course or to teach in an integrated curriculum.

KEY FEATURES

The key features of *Corporate Finance: Principles and Practice* reflect the precepts that have guided my work.

---

[1] *Bartlett's Familiar Quotations,* Boston, Little, Brown and Company, 1992, p. 635.
[2] See Lyman Porter and Lawrence McKibbin, *Management Education and Development: Drift or Thrust Into the 21st Century?* New York, McGraw-Hill, 1988.

Focus on Fundamental Principles

I focus on the financial principles widely considered to be fundamental to every management student's education. These are: discounted cash flow and option valuation, the role of financial markets, and financial policy, including dividends and capital structure. These fundamental principles provide the foundation that production, marketing, management, and accounting students need to understand finance's role in a modern corporation, and that finance students need to study advanced topics.

Development of Intuition

I use a variety of techniques to make financial principles accessible to students without diminishing the theories in any way. At every opportunity, I use real data to illustrate the theories, especially when discussing interest rates; exchange rates; diversification; and the valuation of debt, equity, and options. Where I couldn't use real data, I have used the simplest hypothetical examples possible while still conveying the essential ideas embodied in the theories. Finally, throughout the text I use simple language and examples drawn from common experiences to help students intuitively understand the principles.

Use of Practical Applications

I use a variety of examples to illustrate how to use financial principles to solve realistic management problems. A detailed, realistic example integrates production, marketing, accounting, and finance to describe the capital budgeting process. I examine innovative production systems—such as just-in-time—from a financial perspective by using market imperfections and asymmetric information to explain their costs and benefits. I demonstrate how to use option pricing to value real options in operations as well as capital budgeting. These examples illustrate an idea that all faculty have professed: Financial principles are applicable to *all* business decisions.

INTENDED AUDIENCE

I wrote this textbook for the introductory corporate finance course for MBAs and for the advanced corporate finance course for undergraduates. I have successfully taught both courses using the class notes on which this book is based. This book may also be appropriate for instructors who want to offer a challenging introductory course at the undergraduate level.

I assume that students using this book have studied accounting, economics, and statistics. Prior or concurrent enrollment in these courses is desirable but not strictly necessary. To compensate for variation in students' backgrounds, I carefully explain the use of accounting information for financial decision making and how to calculate and interpret key statistical measures.

PEDAGOGICAL FEATURES

Not all students are inherently interested in finance, and not all learn the same way. Therefore, I incorporate a variety of pedagogical features to arouse and maintain students' interest and to accommodate different learning styles.

Chapter Opening Examples

Every chapter begins with a brief story about a real company or business situation. For example, the dividend chapter begins with a discussion of the market reaction to McDonnell-Douglas's announcement that it would split its stock, raise its dividend, and repurchase shares. Chapter opening examples get students involved right away by demonstrating that the topic is of more than just "academic" interest.

"In the News" Features

Every chapter has at least one—most chapters have two or three—boxed features excerpted from business periodicals and, occasionally, academic journals. For example, Chapter 5, on diversification, has an excerpt from a *Forbes* article entitled "Egg Basket Analysis." These features maintain students' interest by reminding them of the practical importance of the topic at hand.

Worked-out Exercises

Every chapter except Chapters 1 and 14 has several worked-out exercises that give students an opportunity to practice what they have just learned and to receive immediate feedback. These exercises provide a bridge between the examples used to present the material within the text and the end-of-chapter questions and problems.

Key Terms

Every chapter's key terms are printed in boldface type where they first appear and are defined. Key terms are also listed with a page reference after each chapter's summary and defined in a glossary at the end of the book.

Additional Readings

Every chapter has an annotated list of books and articles for readers who desire more information. These readings almost always include the classic articles on the subject as well as recent works accessible to most students.

End-of-Chapter Questions and Problems

Every chapter ends with a large number of class-tested questions and problems. Many of these questions and problems use real data, and some require students to use the Internet to obtain financial information. Answers to selected problems are provided at the end of the book.

Part-Ending Mini-Cases

An integrative mini-case concludes each of the book's four parts. Students must apply their knowledge of production, marketing, management, accounting, and finance to prepare these cases. Consequently, they learn that corporate finance is more than a collection of formulas and techniques and that managers must integrate their knowledge of several functional areas to solve realistic problems.

ORGANIZATION

Corporate Finance: Principles and Practice begins with an introductory chapter followed by 19 chapters organized in four parts: Valuation Principles, Investments and Operations, Financial Policy and Planning, and Restructuring.

In Part 1, the economic logic, intuition, and procedures of financial valuation principles are carefully developed. Chapter 2 reviews financial statements, emphasizing the differences between cash flow and income, and market and book values. Chapter 3 discusses the time value of money, including its theoretical foundation, Fisher-separation. Chapter 4 explains the level and structure of foreign and domestic interest rates, while Chapters 5 and 6 cover diversification and asset pricing. Valuation principles are applied to debt and equity in Chapter 7 and to options in Chapter 8. I introduce options at this early point in the book in order to discuss the analysis of real options in several subsequent chapters.

I demonstrate how to apply finance valuation principles to realistic investment and operating decisions in Part 2. Chapter 9 integrates valuation principles with concepts from marketing, production, cost accounting, and international finance to estimate the market values of long-term assets. Chapters 10 through 12 show how to use finance principles to estimate the market value of routine operating decisions. Chapter 10 sets the stage for this discussion by describing the association between a company's operating policies and operating cash flows. Chapters 11 and 12 then show how to estimate the market values of various production, payment, and collection policies. Chapter 13 demonstrates how to determine the market values of a variety of real options in capital budgeting and operations.

Part 3 describes the principles that shape companies' financial policies and the procedures they use to anticipate financing shortages and surpluses. Chapter 14 provides the background by explaining how companies obtain financing from private investors and the public. Chapters 15 and 16 describe the factors companies must consider when choosing the proportion of financing to obtain from retained earnings, debt, and common stock. Chapter 17 explains how companies recognize the effect of this financing choice in investment analysis. Chapters 18 and 19 conclude Part 3 by describing how to use free cash flow and financial cash flow statements for financial planning.

Part 4 comprises a single chapter on acquisitions, divestitures, and buyouts and restructurings in financial distress. This chapter emphasizes that these dramatic events take place when managers do not continuously restructure a company by making sound investment, operating, and financing decisions.

ACKNOWLEDGMENTS

At this point in the preface it is customary for an author to acknowledge those who contributed to the development of his or her textbook. These acknowledgments have a great deal of meaning to me now. I know better than anyone that my family, teachers and professors, students, colleagues, and publishers made this book much better than it would have been had I worked alone. For their kind and generous support I am indebted to the following individuals.

The following colleagues unselfishly devoted their time when reviewing various drafts of this project. Their insights and suggestions undoubtedly improved my original vision for the text. I particularly thank Russ Ezzell for his reviews of the interaction of investment and financing decisions in Chapter 17.

Roger P. Bey
University of Tulsa

Maclyn L. Clouse
University of Denver

Arnold R. Cowan
Iowa State University

Charles M. Cox
Brigham Young University

Michael E. Edleson
Infinity Financial Technology

John R. Ezzell
Pennsylvania State University

James Harris
University of North Carolina, Wilmington

Michael L. Hemler
University of Notre Dame

Ned C. Hill
Brigham Young University

John Kensinger
University of North Texas

Dean Kiefer
University of Southern Illinois—Carbondale

Dennis E. Logue
Dartmouth College

Michael S. Long
Rutgers University at Newark

Ileen B. Malitz
Rutgers University at Newark

Kenneth J. Martin
New Mexico State University

Stanley A. Martin
University of Colorado, Boulder

Michael A. Mazzeo
Michigan State University

William T. Moore
University of South Carolina

Robert A. Taggart
Boston College

Nikhil P. Varaiya
San Diego State University

Joe Walker
University of Alabama at Birmingham

David J. Wright
University of Wisconsin—Parkside

J. Kenton Zumwalt
Colorado State University

I also thank Samir Barman, Dipankar Ghosh, Jae Ha Lee, Scott C. Linn, Duane R. Stock, and G. Lee Willinger, my colleagues at the University of Oklahoma, who read various chapters and recommended improvements.

Students at the University of Oklahoma also played an important role in the development of this textbook. Undergraduate finance majors and MBA students used the book when it was still in manuscript form. Their comments helped me improve its pedagogy. Doctoral students in accounting and finance read chapters and assisted in the development of end-of-chapter problems. I thank J. Scott Chaput, Susan J. Crain, and Lori M. Mason for this help.

Editors at three publishing companies brought this project to fruition. Kirsten Sandberg at HarperCollins College Publishers was my original sponsoring editor. Her enthusiasm convinced me to go ahead with the project. Joan Cannon and Arlene Bessenoff provided continuing support when Kirsten took another job. HarperCollins was acquired by Addison Wesley Longman and my project was placed in the very capable hands of Associate Editor Julie Zasloff and Senior Production Supervisor Nancy Fenton. During the production phase of the project, other talented individuals stepped in, including Barbara Campbell and Phyllis Crittenden of Elm Street Publishing Services. To these individuals I owe a special thanks for their unfailing ability to keep the project on schedule even when I failed to meet deadlines.

Ann Sass, my developmental editor, deserves special mention. Ann assembled the talented review panel described above, helped me incorporate their suggestions in ways that preserved my intentions for the book, and provided invaluable continuity as the project moved from one publisher to another and through the various stages of the process. Her phone calls, invariably begun with a cheerful "Hey, Gary," were always a welcome break from writing.

Over the years, teachers and professors not only taught me their subjects, but by their examples, taught me the joys of teaching. I hope Lee Dodson, Robert Stapleford, Charles Beall, and Maurice Joy recognize their influence on this book.

Finally, I owe a great deal to my family. My father taught me to work hard, and I learned to enjoy reading from my mother. Perhaps it was inevitable that I would write a book given these influences. Even with all the aforementioned help, I could not have finished the project without my wife's and daughters' patience and understanding.

Gary W. Emery

BRIEF CONTENTS

CONTENTS

Part 2

INVESTMENTS AND
OPERATIONS *361*

Part 3

FINANCIAL POLICY AND
PLANNING   573

Part 4
RESTRUCTURING   *823*

CHAPTER 20

RESTRUCTURING A COMPANY'S
ASSETS AND CLAIMS   *825*

INTRODUCTION TO CORPORATE FINANCE

The allure and excitement of finance are perfectly illustrated by the story of Xylan Corporation, a California-based, high-technology company.[1] Steve Kim and Yuri Pikover used their own money to establish the company in 1993 to design and manufacture communications equipment for computer networks. The company did not earn a profit until the fourth quarter of 1995 but its bright future prospects attracted other investors. Brentwood Associates, a company that provides financing to start-up ventures, invested $4 million.

Xylan sold common stock to the general public for the first time on March 17, 1996, in an offering managed by the New York investment banking firm, Morgan Stanley & Company. The stock's official offering price was $26 per share but it quickly moved to $55, giving the company a market value of $2.3 billion. The 6.46 million shares owned by Chief Executive Steve Kim and his family were immediately worth $360 million, which dwarfed his 1995 salary of $112,500. Brentwood Associates' profits were nearly $400 million, a 5,000 percent annual rate of return on its investment.

Many others also benefitted from the formation and subsequent public financing of Xylan Corporation. The *Los Angeles Times* noted that Calabasas, California, where Xylan is located, now has more employment opportunities for its citizens and a higher tax base due to both the company's activities and the owners' wealth. These employment and tax benefits may multiply if Xylan's success attracts other high-tech companies to the area. In addition, Brentwood Associates was acting on behalf of other investors, mainly pension funds, when it invested $4 million in Xylan. These pensioners will have more money to spend during retirement because, as *Fortune* put it, they received "the kind of return you can usually get only from a winning lottery ticket."

---

[1]Patrice Apodaca, "Xylan Shares More Than Double in 1st Day of Trading," *Los Angeles Times,* March 13, 1996, p. D1; Tom Petruno, "Xylan Could Be a Windfall for Calabasas," *Los Angeles Times,* March 18, 1996, p. D9; and Shawn Tully, "How to Make $400,000,000 in Just One Minute," *Fortune,* May 27, 1996, pp. 84–92.

Xylan Corporation's story is a spectacular example of what happens in new and established companies every day. Companies invest money to design and produce new products and services to meet society's needs. Those that develop successful products they can produce at a profit attract additional financing from financial institutions and other investors who become owners. This financing permits the companies to expand operations, which in turn creates jobs in the community and wealth for the owners. Coca-Cola is a prominent *established* company that followed these steps to create nearly $60 billion of wealth for its owners since 1981 under the leadership of chief executive officer (CEO) Roberto Goizueta.[2]

High-profile entrepreneurs and CEOs such as Kim, Pikover, and Goizueta receive help creating jobs and wealth from senior and subordinate managers who efficiently use the financial resources that investors entrust to them. These managers fulfill this responsibility by ensuring that their unit's activities provide enough cash to cover the company's costs *and* pay the owners an acceptable rate of return on their investment. Ensuring that investments and methods of operation meet this standard of performance is a vital task in all areas of business, including production, marketing, and administration. Consequently, an understanding of the principles and practices of corporate finance is a prerequisite to becoming an effective manager of any function.

This book will prepare you to apply fundamental finance principles in production, planning, customer service, or wherever your management career may lead you. It also will prepare you for advanced study if you decide to become a finance specialist. Either way, this book will prepare you to learn new principles and practices—as they are developed in the future—by giving approximately equal attention to financial principles, concentrated in the first half of the book, and financial practices that are based on these principles, concentrated in the last.

This chapter is both an introduction to and summary of the book. The following sections provide an overview of the major topics you will study later. Read this chapter now as you would a map before a trip to get a general idea of where you are going and how to get there. Return to it periodically to reorient yourself, to relate a current topic to topics that came before and the topics that will follow. Finally, reread this chapter after you have finished the book: It will be more meaningful to you then because you will understand the details of the topics that are merely introduced here.

1.1   FINANCIAL MANAGEMENT AND FINANCIAL MANAGERS

Managers practice *financial* management when they (1) obtain cash from investors, (2) use that cash to buy productive assets, (3) operate those assets to produce additional cash, and (4) return cash to the investors. The first and fourth activities are part of the process of financing a business while the second and third are concerned with its investments and operations. Managers may be responsible for large amounts of cash when they perform these activities as illustrated by Merck & Co.'s 1995 results, which are shown in Table 1.1.

---

[2]Terence P. Pare, "The Champ of Wealth Creation," *Fortune,* September 18, 1995, pp. 131–132.

MERCK & COMPANY'S NET CASH FLOWS FOR 1995 (IN MILLIONS)		Table 1.1

Sources of Cash

Cash obtained from investors	$1,873.6
Cash provided by operations	2,944.2
Total	$4,817.8

Uses of Cash

Cash used to purchase assets	$1,542.8
Cash returned to investors	3,275.0
Total	$4,817.8

Merck is a prominent pharmaceutical company that is regularly listed among the most profitable and admired companies in the United States. The company obtained $1.9 billion of cash from investors in 1995 and generated an additional $2.9 billion of cash from operations. Merck used $1.5 billion of cash to purchase new assets and returned the remainder, $3.3 billion, to the investors. Merck's finance specialists made some of the decisions that produced these cash flows, but the company's scientists, engineers, plant managers, sales managers, etc. made other decisions. The company's owners apparently approved of these financial decisions because they valued Merck's stock at $80.8 billion at the end of 1995—an increase of $32.8 billion from 1994.

Alternative Ways to Organize and Finance a Business

Merck is a very large company with approximately 47,000 employees and more than 240,000 owners.[3] A company this size must be organized differently than an owner-operated business such as a neighborhood pharmacy. We will briefly review the alternative ways to organize and finance a business before describing who makes a corporation's financial decisions.

Sole Proprietorships and Partnerships   A sole proprietorship is a business with an identity that is inseparable from the identity of its individual owner. The business's assets, liabilities, and income are the owner's assets, liabilities, and income under the law and according to the rules of the U.S. Internal Revenue Service. There are several implications of this relationship between the business and its owner. First, the owner is fully responsible for any judgments against the business if it fails to pay its debts or if someone is injured on its property or by one of its products. In other words, the owner has *unlimited liability*. Second, most proprietorships cease to exist when the owner

---

[3]Source: January 1, 1996 edition of Value/Screen III, Value Line Publishing Inc., copyright 1993.

dies or withdraws from the business. Third, the owner must pay taxes on the proprietorship's income even if he or she does not withdraw the income from the business, however, the proprietorship itself is not taxed.

General **partnerships** are like sole proprietorships in every important respect except that there are two or more owners rather than one. Nevertheless, each owner has unlimited liability, the partnership is dissolved when one owner dies or withdraws for any reason, and each must pay taxes on his or her share of the partnership's income.

The main disadvantage of sole proprietorships and general partnerships is their relatively poor access to new financing. Potential owners may be unwilling to invest in a proprietorship or partnership because (1) they are reluctant to accept unlimited liability, (2) there is no assurance the business will survive its current owners, or (3) they cannot foresee how they will transfer their equity to someone else. These factors also limit the amount of financing available from lenders who cannot closely examine the company or hold the loan until it matures. As a result, most proprietorships and partnerships only have access to short- and intermediate-term loans from private lenders and banks. Nevertheless, many businesses begin as proprietorships or partnerships because they are easy to form, the owner can exercise direct control, and limited access to new financing is not a serious problem initially.

Corporations   A **corporation** is a business with an identity that is distinct from the identities of its owners. The business's assets, liabilities, and income are its own under the law and according to the rules of the U.S. Internal Revenue Service. A corporation's status as an individual in the eyes of the law is established by its *articles of incorporation*, which describe the company's purpose and how it is governed. A company's articles of incorporation are on file or registered in a particular state and must comply with that state's laws no matter where the company conducts business or maintains its corporate offices.

A corporation's owners receive shares of common stock that describe their claim on the company's assets and income. Owners are entitled to a proportionate share of the assets that remain after liabilities are paid in a liquidation but the company is not obligated to distribute assets to them otherwise. Owners also are entitled to a proportionate share of dividends paid but the company is not obligated to pay dividends. Owners who want to withdraw from the business or create a "homemade dividend" may do so by selling some or all of their shares of stock. A large volume of shares are traded for these reasons every day. For example, 9,014,900 shares of IBM's common stock were traded on July 25, 1996.[4]

The distinction between a corporation and its owners has several implications. First, the corporation is responsible for judgments against the business that result from default or injury. The owners' equity may become worthless if the company loses a judgment, but their personal assets are shielded by the "corporate veil."[5] In other words, the corporate form of organization provides the owners with *limited liability*. Second, a cor-

---

[4]*The Wall Street Journal,* July 26, 1996, p. C2.

[5]Owners can give up this protection by accepting personal responsibility—to obtain a loan, for example—or they can lose it if the courts determine they attempted to use it fraudulently.

poration survives if an owner dies or withdraws from the business. Third, a corporation pays taxes on its own income and the owners pay taxes again on the portion of the corporation's income that is distributed to them as dividends.

The advantages of the corporate form of organization are substantial. Limited liability permits investors far removed from the business to become owners by buying shares of common stock because, knowing they have not risked all their personal assets, they do not insist on exercising daily control. The ease of transferring ownership permits investors who cannot provide financing indefinitely to become owners because they can sell their stock to others when they want their money back. The greater amount and permanence of ownership capital available to a corporation makes lenders willing to loan it money on the merits of its business and future income rather than on the basis of its owners' characteristics. Consequently, a corporation's size is limited only by the demand for its products or services and the quality of its management. These advantages are so significant that most large businesses are organized this way even though a corporation's income is taxed twice.

As they grow, many companies that began as proprietorships or partnerships become private or closely held corporations to obtain the benefits of limited liability and better access to financing. Eventually, they may seek financing from the general public, as Xylan Corporation did, by selling common stock in an *initial public offering*. We will discuss this process in more detail when we describe financing decisions in Chapter 14.

Hybrid Forms of Organization   The advantages and disadvantages of proprietorships, partnerships, and corporations are summarized in Exhibit 1.1. You can see that their strengths and weaknesses are complementary. A proprietorship or partnership's income is taxed only once, but a business organized in this way has poor access to new financing. A corporation's income is taxed twice but it has good access to new financing. Hybrid forms of organization are designed to provide the advantages of proprietorships, partnerships, and corporations without the corresponding disadvantages.

A *limited partnership* comprises general and limited partners. The general partners manage the business and have unlimited liability while the limited partners do not participate in management but are liable only to the extent of their investment. Limited partners usually can sell their interest in the partnership to someone else without forcing the partnership to dissolve, but general partners cannot. The partnership's income is taxed as personal income so, from the limited partners' perspective, a limited partnership has some of the features of a corporation and a partnership.

A *master limited partnership (MLP)* is a limited partnership in which the limited partners' interests are publicly traded. The limited partners' ability to transfer their ownership interests makes an MLP even more like a corporation. Congress made this gambit less effective in 1987 by permitting the Internal Revenue Service to tax most newly formed master limited partnerships as corporations.

A *limited liability company (LLC)* is a limited partnership with no general partners, that is, all the owners have limited liability. Management may be centralized, as in a limited partnership, but the owners cannot freely transfer their ownership interests and the business must be re-organized when an owner departs. An LLC must maintain the latter two features to be taxed as a partnership.

Exhibit 1.1

**ADVANTAGES AND DISADVANTAGES OF ALTERNATIVE
WAYS TO ORGANIZE A BUSINESS**

Form	Advantages	Disadvantages
Sole proprietorship	*Easy to establish	*Owner has unlimited liability
	*Business income not taxed	*Owner pays taxes on the business's profits even if he does not withdraw them
		*Business has a limited life
		*Difficult to transfer ownership to another person
		*Financing limited by the amount of the owner's wealth and how much he can borrow
Partnership	*Same as sole proprietorship	*Same as sole proprietorship*
Corporation	*Owners have limited liability	*Double taxation: Business pays taxes on its profits and owners pay taxes on the business's profits that are distributed to them
	*Business has an unlimited life	
	*Easy to transfer ownership	
	*Financing only limited by the corporation's future business prospects	

This book will concentrate on financial management in corporations because the corporation is the dominant form of organization. This focus does not limit our discussion very much, however, because owners and managers must make the same types of investment, financing, and operating decisions in all businesses—no matter how they are organized or financed.

Financial Decision Making in Corporations

Large corporations are managed by professionals who make or approve financial decisions. Senior managers, especially the chief executive officer (CEO) and president, are responsible to the owners through the owners' representatives who sit on the board of directors. The board delegates most financial decisions to these senior managers but reserves the right to distribute earnings to the owners as dividends and to approve the sale of new securities. Senior managers in turn delegate financial decisions to subordinates, some of whom are finance specialists.

The most senior finance specialist in large corporations is the **chief financial officer (CFO)**, a member of the senior management team who often sits on the board of directors. Consequently, the CFO plays a key role in establishing and directing a company's overall financial strategy.

The treasurer and controller are senior finance specialists who report to the CFO. These officers typically are responsible for a company's external and internal financial

I N   T H E   N E W S

FINANCE STAFF ALIGNED WITH OPERATIONS AT FORD MOTOR COMPANY

FORD MOTOR CO. is shaking up its once all-powerful finance staff, subordinating much of it to operating executives. Ford said a new automotive-operations finance organization, led by Murray Reichenstein, vice president and controller, will report to Edward Hagenlocker, the president of Ford automotive operations. Mr. Reichenstein also will continue to report on a functional basis to Stanley Seneker, executive vice pres-

ident and chief financial officer. Ford created more than a dozen new positions under Mr. Reichenstein, mostly having to do with controllers' activities at various operating units, as well as financial planning, profit analysis, and accounting.

"The finance staff used to be absolutely omnipotent," acknowledges one Ford official. Now, the official adds, it will "be more of an assistant than an adversary."

Source: Robert L. Simison and Neal Templin, "Ford Motor Co. Shakes Up Staff of Finance Unit," *The Wall Street Journal*, June 14, 1994, p. A3. Reprinted by permission of *The Wall Street Journal*, © 1994 Dow Jones & Company, Inc. All rights reserved worldwide.

relationships, respectively. **Treasurers** are generally responsible for obtaining new financing, managing the cash flows a company pays and receives, making interest and principal payments and disbursing dividends, and using financial products (such as insurance) to manage a company's risk. In contrast, **controllers** are usually responsible for preparing financial statements and administering financial procedures that managers use to plan, coordinate, and control a company's investments and operations. The treasurer's and controller's functions are complementary because a company must manage its investments and operations to achieve the financial objectives required by its external investors.

The positions occupied by the stockholders, board of directors, and senior managers are shown in the typical organization chart in Exhibit 1.2.

Treasurers are assisted by a small staff of finance specialists who usually work at the corporation's headquarters. The controller's work is performed in part by a larger, full-time staff of finance and accounting specialists and in part by scientists, engineers, and production, marketing, sales, and human resource managers who periodically make investment proposals and prepare and analyze operating budgets and financial reports. Some of the controller's staff may work at the corporation's headquarters but many work at remote production facilities, distribution centers, etc. where they help the local managers with financial management. With or without the assistance of a finance specialist, the scientists, engineers, and managers who periodically make financial decisions must understand financial controls and their importance to outside investors. This is necessary to justify their requests for financial resources, to effectively use those resources, and to convincingly report their results.

The organization chart in Exhibit 1.2 does not show that operating managers also make financial decisions. However, the excerpt from *The Wall Street Journal* article (see "In the News") describes how Ford Motor Company recently changed their organizational structure to facilitate cooperation between its operations and finance departments.

Exhibit 1.2

TYPICAL ORGANIZATION CHART

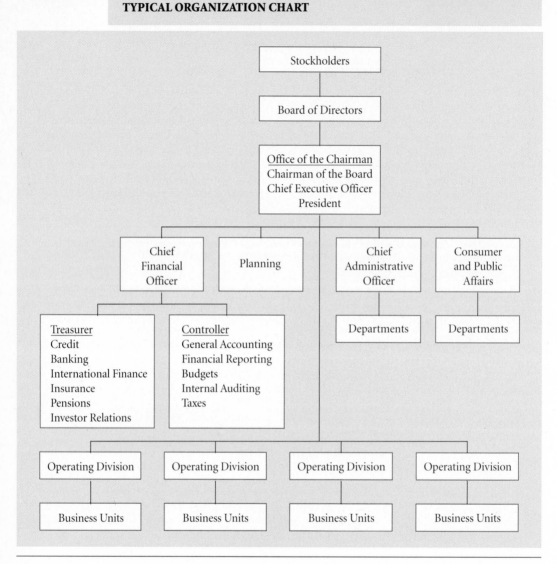

Changes such as this intensify the need for managers in all areas to understand financial principles and practices.

Owner–Manager Conflicts in Corporations

The senior managers who exercise daily control over most corporations often have only a small ownership stake in the business. They are, in effect, agents who make decisions on behalf of the owners, who are principals. In the same way, subordinate managers

I N   T H E   N E W S

AGENCY COSTS AND ALL THAT JAZZ

BORLAND INTERNATIONAL INC.'s chief executive officer charged the company for personal expenses, according to Borland's latest proxy statement sent to shareholders in anticipation of its annual meeting on August 30. Some of the expenses come from Philippe Kahn's previously reported use of company funds to produce three compact discs featuring jazz musicians. The spokesman also said that some of the repaid expenses covered Mr. Kahn's personal use of an airplane that Borland had until recently leased for Mr. Kahn. The rest of the money was for personal expenses related to Mr. Kahn's travel. The proxy didn't specify the amount of the expenses. Mr. Kahn, the CEO, doesn't owe Borland any money, the software company said, because it withheld bonuses owed him.

Source: G. Pascal Zachary, "Borland Paid for Personal Expenses of Its Chief, Proxy Statement Shows," *The Wall Street Journal,* August 18, 1994, p. B9. Reprinted by permission of *The Wall Street Journal,* © 1994 Dow Jones & Company, Inc. All rights reserved worldwide.

are agents for the senior managers who delegate tasks to them. This system generally works well because neither the owners nor the senior managers have the time or the specialized knowledge required to closely supervise every financial decision.

The separation of ownership and control and the separation of responsibility and control within a corporation presents a problem, however, when there is a disparity between the information available to the principal and his or her agent. Then, the owners may not have enough information to hold senior managers accountable for their actions and senior managers may not have enough information to hold subordinate managers accountable for their decisions. This situation, known as **asymmetric information**, creates an opportunity for managers to make decisions in their *own* interests rather than the owners'.

The losses caused by actual and potential conflicts of interest between a principal and his or her agent are called **agency costs**. These are the costs of organizing a business in any way that does not permit the owners to exercise direct control, however, these costs are of particular concern to corporations. Spending more than necessary for dinner when using an expense account is a common and usually trivial agency cost. Distorting a company's investment and financing policies to enhance the safety of one's job is a serious one. Vigilant corporations try to control these costs, as the article from *The Wall Street Journal* attests (see "In the News").

One way companies reduce agency costs is by converting managers from agents to principals by making them owners. Some companies give their managers options to buy stock so they will begin to think and act as the owners would. Others require board members and senior managers to purchase shares of the company's stock on their own. Lockheed took this approach when it recently began requiring its top 1,400 employees to own common stock equal to as much as five times their annual salary. Lockheed chairman, Daniel M. Tellep, said this requirement will motivate the management team to maximize shareholder value (see "In the News" on page 10).

DEFENSE CONTRACTOR TAKES THE OFFENSIVE ON MANAGEMENT OWNERSHIP OF STOCK

DEFENSE GIANT LOCKHEED Martin Corp. said yesterday it will require its 1,400 top employees to buy shares in the company to increase their stake in "enhancing shareholder value." Company Chairman Daniel M. Tellep eventually will have to own stock worth five times his salary, while President Norman R. Augustine must own shares worth four times his base pay. Most of the others will be required to own stock equivalent to two or three times what they make. Based on Tellep's 1994 base salary of $820,000, when he headed Lockheed Corp. before it merged with Martin Marietta, he would have to own about $4.1 million worth of Lockheed Martin stock.

Shareholder activists applauded the move, as they do most plans to get stock in executives' hands. "There's nothing like putting your money on the line . . . to improve the chances you'll work harder, smarter, and longer term at a company," said Sarah Teslik, executive director of the Washington-based Council of Institutional Investors, which advocates stockholder's interests.

Tellep agreed. "By asking our key employees to take a significant ownership position in the corporation," he said, "we further motivate our management team to continuously achieve superior performance, the highest quality products and services, and maximum shareholder value."

1.2 THE GOAL OF FINANCIAL MANAGEMENT

Another way to reduce agency costs is to give managers a clear goal and hold them accountable for accomplishing it. This goal must serve the owners' interests and also should help society solve the basic economic problem that resources are scarce but people's wants are unlimited. Market economies solve this problem by using prices to direct resources to their most productive use. Companies and their owners prosper when the procedure they use to allocate capital internally is compatible with the market's approach. The key to establishing a compatible procedure is to choose a financial management goal that is a practical version of the market's abstract goal.

The Abstract Goal: Maximize Economic Profit

Economic theory tells us that market economies achieve their goals when businesses maximize economic profit, which equals cash revenues minus cash costs minus the opportunity cost of using the owners' resources elsewhere. Cash revenues reflect the value society places on a business's product or service while cash costs reflect the value society places on the resources the business consumes. The opportunity cost measures the value of the financial resources the owners devote to the business. A company that earns a positive economic profit produces goods or services that society values more highly than all the resources consumed in production. Consequently, the amount of economic profit a business earns reveals society's opinion about its net contribution to the stock of goods and services available to the economy.

In a free market economy, the owners of businesses are entitled to employ their economic resources in their self-interest. Therefore, we can expect them to expand the production of products and services that provide positive economic profits and vice versa. By this method, a business's privately owned resources are directed to their most productive use as determined by the public.

A Practical Goal: Maximize the Owners' Wealth

Telling managers to maximize economic profit does not provide much direction for real decision making. Managers might reasonably ask, "How do I measure economic profit?" "Should I maximize current economic profit or future economic profit?" "Should I advance the owners' interests or balance them against the interests of other stakeholders such as customers, employees, suppliers, and creditors?" These are serious questions to a person whose job performance will be judged by the outcome of his or her decisions.

Fortunately, we can restate this goal in practical terms by telling managers to maximize the owners' wealth, which equals the market value of the owners' investment in the company. This goal has several desirable features.

First, maximizing the owners' wealth is pragmatic because most owners prefer to have more money rather than less. Maximizing the owner's wealth is almost certain to be the goal pursued by the owner of a sole proprietorship and owners who decide to organize their business as a corporation cannot be expected to abandon this objective. The owners appoint a corporation's managers and expect the managers to pursue this objective for them.

Second, maximizing the owners' wealth is socially responsible because it helps society use scarce resources efficiently. Here's how: Investors provide financing to companies they believe will increase their wealth and withhold it from the rest. Managers compete for this capital by increasing the net cash flow the company earns for the owners or by reducing the owners' opportunity cost. For example, a product design and marketing team may improve a product's features to increase cash revenues while an engineering and production team may adopt an innovative manufacturing technique to reduce cash costs. These are actions a company would take to increase economic profit. Consequently, maximizing the owners' wealth is equivalent to maximizing economic profit, which directs resources to their most productive use.

Third, managers can pursue the goal of maximizing the owners' wealth without explicitly balancing the interests of customers, employees, suppliers, and creditors because the owners are paid *last*. Customers' requirements for a product worthy of the price, employees' requirements for competitive wages, and suppliers' and creditors' requirements for timely payment of amounts owed them must be met before a single dollar of profit is available to the owners. This means we can interpret an increase in the owners' wealth as evidence that a company has met the needs of its other stakeholders and is producing a product or providing a service that is valued by society.

Finally, the market price of a company's common stock provides a public record of the managers' success at maximizing the owners' wealth.

Of course, maximizing the owners' wealth does not benefit society or indicate that a company's other stakeholders have been served if managers behave inappropriately. Illegal behaviors undermine the moral foundation of the goal of financial management as do unethical behaviors although ethical standards are not as clear as legal ones. Imposing costs on third parties—by polluting the environment or seeking unwarranted subsidies, for example—is another way managers can advance the owners' narrowly defined interests to the detriment of society.

Throughout this book, we will assume managers do not engage in illegal or unethical acts but instead, pursue the goal of maximizing the owners' wealth within the bounds established by society. From time to time, we will discuss the ethical issues that arise in the context of specific financial decisions.

1.3   FINANCIAL INSTRUMENTS AND MARKETS

Financial instruments and markets play a vital role in helping companies direct resources to their most productive use. They make it easier for corporations to raise capital and provide ways for investors to monitor the corporations to ensure they use the capital productively. As a result, managers throughout the firm must adopt a broader perspective than they would if they were permitted to focus on narrow, locally defined performance objectives.

The Role of Financial Instruments

Owners and creditors who provide capital to a large, perhaps distant, corporation require some evidence of their investment. Financial instruments, such as common stocks, promissory notes, and bonds, are securities that are used for this purpose. Owners receive shares of common stock while creditors receive promissory notes and bonds.

These financial instruments describe the terms and conditions under which the investor will be repaid. Bondholders are owed a debt that must be paid first and stockholders receive an owner's share of remaining profits after all other obligations are met. The money available to pay stockholders varies from year to year according to the company's profitability. The income from common stock is therefore less certain or more risky than the income from bonds.

Owners receive compensation for their additional risk in two ways. First, they expect to receive a higher average return than the creditors. Second, they elect the board of directors who can replace the managers and change the company's policies if the common stock does not provide a return commensurate with its risk.

These differences between common stocks and bonds permit investors to choose securities that provide the amount of income, risk, and control that is important to them. With so many alternatives, nearly everyone can find an investment that suits their preferences. This is one of the reasons corporations have better access to capital than sole proprietorships and partnerships.

The Role of Financial Markets

Even if investors find an acceptable match on income, risk, and control, there are several reasons why some may be reluctant to purchase a stock or bond. First, the investors may be uninformed and worry that the owners or managers will sell them stocks or bonds for more than they are really worth. Second, they may be unable to commit their capital to the company for the amount of time it is needed. Third, the securities may be sold in larger denominations than investors can afford.

Financial markets diminish these problems. The mere existence of a financial market means there are market prices for stocks and bonds that investors can use as benchmarks. In an *ideal* market, these prices summarize the information known by everyone and thereby place all investors on equal terms. A financial market also provides a place for investors to sell their stocks and bonds to other investors so they can get their money back before the company is required to pay them. Finally, financial institutions tailor financial instruments to fit particular needs. For example, banks accept small, short-term savings deposits from individuals and make large, intermediate-term loans to businesses.

Individuals are willing and able to save and invest more because financial markets and institutions provide these financial services. This makes more capital available to businesses, especially corporations that issue stocks and bonds.

Implications for Financial Managers

Financial markets make it easier for corporations to raise capital but also subject them to greater scrutiny. Banks and other financial institutions have a greater interest in and more time for closely monitoring a corporate borrower than a part-time investor who has purchased only a few bonds or shares of stock. Financial institutions also have more financial expertise, which narrows the information disparity between the company and its investors. A company therefore must pay careful attention when financial institutions express concern about its profitability and risk and this benefits all the company's investors. Pension funds have been especially effective monitors (see "In the News" on page 14).

The financial market also provides greater scrutiny because security prices quickly reflect the market's expectation about the outcome of the managers' decisions. A favorable announcement, that the company will sell an unprofitable subsidiary for example, is likely to cause the stock price to increase immediately. This enables the company to obtain more financing at lower cost from both owners and creditors. An unfavorable announcement has the opposite effect. Recent events had exactly these effects on Zenith Electronics Corporation and Valence Technology Incorporated (see "In the News" on page 15).

This daily, public posting of the managers' performance ratings in terms of the company's stock price puts constant pressure on them to make sound decisions. Senior managers, particularly the CEO and finance specialists, understand this process very clearly. They are directly responsible to the board of directors, which represents the owners and may be rewarded with bonuses or punished by losing their jobs when the stock price

IN THE NEWS

PENSION FUNDS ARE ACTIVE INVESTORS

AN INFLUENTIAL GROUP representing many of the nation's biggest pension funds is targeting 20 businesses as underachievers that need to bolster shareholder value. The Council of Institutional Investors plans to release its annual list of poor performers at a meeting here today. The council's 100 member pension funds, whose combined assets exceed $800 billion, often use the target list (or their own lists) as a bargaining lever with managements. "Managements [now] understand that when shareholders have concerns, they should resolve those concerns," observed Kurt Schacht, general counsel of the Wisconsin State Investment Board.

This kind of corporate-governance activity increasingly appears to pay off for investors, according to an analysis of the 97 targets on the council's 1991, 1992, and 1993 lists. The year after being listed, such businesses experienced an average total return (share-price appreciation plus reinvested dividends) of 21.1%. The gain briskly outpaced the S&P 500's increase by 11.6 percentage points, the study found. "There's no way anyone can prove that this is due to the council [list]," conceded Tim Opler, a co-author of the study and assistant finance professor at Ohio State University's business school. But "it looks like the activities of these institutional investors are having a strong effect," he added.

Source: Joann S. Lubin, "Pension Funds Take Aim Again at Weak Stocks," *The Wall Street Journal,* October 2, 1995, p. A4. Reprinted by permission of *The Wall Street Journal,* © 1994 Dow Jones & Company, Inc. All rights reserved worldwide.

goes up or down. Subordinate managers also must attend to the market's concerns because their decisions affect the company's stock price as well. Failure to do so eventually imperils the company's future and their jobs.

1.4 VALUATION PRINCIPLES

Managers make sure their investment, financing, and operating decisions meet market-wide standards of financial performance by applying the same valuation techniques within the company that investors use in the financial market. These techniques use opportunity costs measured by percentage rates of return to determine the current value of future cash flows given their risk.

Cash Flows and the Time Value of Money

Investors provide *cash* that companies use to acquire productive assets and conduct operations and expect to be repaid with cash produced by these activities. Consequently, managers must base their investment, operating, and financing decisions on the amounts and timing of the cash flows they use and provide. The chairman of AlliedSignal Corporation understood this principle very well when he asked his managers to "make cash flow a top priority" (see "In the News" on page 16).

Investors expect to receive cash payments that are larger than their original investment as compensation for the income they could have earned by using their money else-

IN THE NEWS

THE PUBLIC POSTING OF
MANAGERS' PERFORMANCE

Good News at Zenith

ZENITH ELECTRONICS CORP. shares surged on news that the company won a $1 billion contract to manufacture digital television set-top boxes for Americast, the budding cable-entertainment consortium. In heavy New York Stock Exchange composite trading, the TV-maker's shares soared $5.50, or 48%, to $16.875. Zenith was the Big Board's most-active stock, with more than 9.7 million shares changing hands. Yesterday's announcement "sends a strong message to the entire industry that Zenith is back," a company official said.

Bad News at Valence

Valence Technology, Inc. said it is delaying commercial production of its new lithium battery because of manufacturing problems—an announcement that caused its stocks to plunge 36%. The company said Friday that it can't meet the specifications of Hewlett-Packard Co. for a potential $3.5 million order. And Valence earlier announced similar problems filling a potential $100 million order from Motorola Inc. Valence's stock fell $2.188 to close at $3.813 in heavy Nasdaq Stock Market trading Friday. The stock is off 84% from its 52-week high of $23.75, reached last October.

Sources: James P. Miller, "Zenith Shares Surge as It Wins a $1 Billion Digital-TV Contract," *The Wall Street Journal,* August 23, 1996, p. B3 and Christian Hill, "Valence Stock Falls on Delay in New Battery," *The Wall Street Journal,* June 20, 1994, p. B10.

where. In other words, the additional money they require must cover their opportunity cost, and the amount must be larger the longer they wait to be repaid. This requirement that a dollar invested today must return more than a dollar in the future is what gives money time value. Managers must account for the time value of money when they evaluate the cash flows their investment, operating, and financing decisions use and provide.

Required Rates of Return and Risk

We use percentage rates of return to represent investors' opportunity costs in finance. These opportunity costs are the rates of return that the owners can earn by investing their money elsewhere. Investors apply higher opportunity costs to riskier investments because it is more difficult to predict their outcomes. Managers must measure the risk that is of concern to the owners to compute the rate of return they expect to be paid on their investment.

Valuation

Investors evaluate a company's stocks and bonds by using risk-adjusted opportunity costs to value the cash flows these securities provide. They will purchase a share of stock or a bond only if its value is greater than or equal to its cost. The results determine whether capital is allocated to or away from each company.

CHAIRMAN OF ALLIED-SIGNAL
EMPHASIZES CASH FLOW

"WE HAVE A serious issue in cash flow and need your immediate attention and focus," AlliedSignal Chairman Lawrence Bossidy wrote to his unit general managers and sector presidents in a June 13 internal memo obtained by this newspaper. In order to meet the company's 1996 cash-flow target of $400 million, Mr. Bossidy continued, second-half cash flow will have to reach $650 million.

The one-page memo concluded: "Cash flow is a critical issue for the company. Not only is it the fuel for our growth, but it is an indication of operational efficiency. Our second-quarter cash flow, coupled with the results of the first quarter, may cause the analysts who follow AlliedSignal to question our performance. . . . Please make cash flow a top priority."

Source: Amal Kumar Naj, "AlliedSignal Is Targeting Cash Flow," *The Wall Street Journal,* July 10, 1996, p. C1. Reprinted by permission of *The Wall Street Journal,* © 1996 Dow Jones & Company, Inc. All rights reserved worldwide.

Managers should use the same valuation principles to make investment, operating, and financing decisions within their firm. This is the surest way for them to increase the owners' wealth, attract the capital their company needs for expansion, and thereby contribute to the efficient allocation of society's scarce resources.

1.5 ORGANIZATION OF THIS BOOK

Part 1 of this book carefully develops the financial valuation principles that owners and managers use to make investment, operating, and financing decisions. You will learn how to estimate cash flows in Chapter 2, how to account for the time value of money in Chapter 3, and how the level of interest rates and risk affect opportunity costs in Chapters 4 through 6. Then you will apply these principles—as investors do—to the valuation of a company's bonds, common stock, and options in Chapters 7 and 8.

Part 2 describes how to use finance valuation principles to manage a company's investments and operations. You will learn how to evaluate proposals to invest in new plant and equipment in Chapter 9, how to manage the short-term assets that support production and sales in Chapters 10 through 12, and how to closely examine the investment and operating decisions that can secure or jeopardize a company's future in Chapter 13.

Part 3 describes financing decisions. You will learn more about the role of financial instruments and markets in Chapter 14, theories of how managers establish long-term financing policies in Chapters 15 and 16, and how these policies affect the owners' opportunity cost in Chapter 17. These chapters will strengthen your understanding of the company's dependence on the financial market. Chapters 18 and 19, which describe how managers anticipate their requirement for new financing, conclude Part 3.

DUPONT'S CFO INTEGRATES FINANCE AND OPERATIONS

THE GOALS AND concerns of the new generation of chemical industry CFOs indicate an alignment of purpose with operating managers: To consistently earn returns on assets in excess of the cost of capital, building value for shareholders.

Jerry Henry, senior v.p. and CFO at DuPont for eight months, joined DuPont 30 years ago as a process engineer and spent much of his career in the businesses. That is a big switch for the conservatively managed DuPont where "senior finance people have always come out of the finance operations," Henry says. "Many never even worked in a business."

For example, only about 20% of DuPont's current financial managers have operating experience.

That is changing on Henry's watch. He spends about half his time working with the people who run the businesses, taking an active role in acquisition and divestiture, and wants 100% of financial managers to have operating experience. He also wants to move finance people into product management and sales. "If our best financial people are running the businesses, they won't need as much help," saving costs at headquarters, Henry says.

Source: Emily S. Plishner, "CFOs and Business Managers Pull in Same Direction," *Chemical Week*, March 30, 1994, pp. 18–19.

Part 4 contains a single chapter that describes the mergers and restructurings that take place when companies' investment, operating, or financing policies do not meet the owners' requirement for a competitive rate of return on their investment.

The finance principles and practices you will learn here are robust. They are applicable to all areas of management, as the boxed article about DuPont's new CFO reveals (see "In the News" above), and they are spreading to Europe, as the article about America's challenge to European businesses warns (see "In the News" on page 18). You will be a better manager for knowing them no matter where your management career may lead you.

1.6 SUMMARY

Every manager who has a say in how a company's resources are used makes financial decisions that affect the company's investments, operations, and financing. Owners/managers in sole proprietorships and partnerships may make or approve all crucial financial decisions while most are delegated to others in corporations. Some of these decisions are delegated to senior finance specialists, including the chief financial officer, treasurer, and controller. Other financial decisions are delegated to engineers, production managers, and marketing, sales, and human resource managers who manage some part of a company's investment or operating cash flows.

Managers should make financial decisions to maximize the owners' wealth. This goal is necessary because the managers are responsible to the owners and it is appro-

I N   T H E   N E W S

THE SPREAD OF AMERICA'S BRAND OF CAPITALISM

EUROPE IS FACING a new American challenge as an aggressive new-world capitalism spreads all over the old world. The changes mostly concern management technique and business organization. In most continental European countries, strong business relationships are highly valued; the "European model" fosters long-term ties between managers, owners, and workers. In contrast, in America and Britain, firms are more influenced by shareholders who rely not on personal ties but on published accounts, staightforward ownership structures, and clear goals for managers.

Many Europeans fear that (these changes) spell the end of Europe's business civilization. But in lamenting the move from one system to another, critics are mistaking the symptom for the disease—the underlying weakness of the existing system. Remember that Europeans are adopting these ideas willingly. They know something is badly wrong with the "European model."

Source: "Showing Europe's Firms the Way," *The Economist,* July 13, 1996, p. 15. Copyright © 1996, The Economist, Ltd.

priate because it contributes to society's welfare and implies that the needs of the company's other constituents (customers, employees, creditors) have been met. Managers must behave legally and ethically to maintain this connection between the maximization of the owners' wealth and the welfare of others.

Corporations have an advantage at raising capital in financial markets in part because these markets provide mechanisms by which the owners can monitor the managers to ensure they use the capital productively. As a result, companies must meet world-class standards of financial performance when they choose investment projects, operating policies, and methods of financing.

The surest way for managers to meet these standards is to apply the same decision rules within the company that investors use when they evaluate financial instruments. This requires them to estimate future cash flows, adjust these cash flows for the effect of time and risk, and compare the result to the amount of cash required to implement the decision. Managers should proceed with opportunities that pass this test and abandon the others because the owners would do the same.

Companies that apply this decision process successfully attract additional capital and can expand; those that don't may fail. By this process, private decisions allocate real and financial resources to the activities most desirable to society.

- **KEY TERMS**

Sole proprietorship *3*	Chief financial officer	Controllers *7*
Partnerships *4*	(CFO) *6*	Asymmetric information *9*
Corporation *4*	Treasurer *7*	Agency costs *9*

- ## QUESTIONS AND PROBLEMS

1. Briefly answer each of the following questions.

   (a) What are the principal tasks in financial management?

   (b) Which financial management tasks are performed by the treasurer and her staff? The controller and his staff?

   (c) Which financial management tasks are performed by nonfinancial managers such as plant managers, sales managers, and human resource managers?

2. Owners have several alternatives for organizing a business.

   (a) What are the advantages and disadvantages of organizing the business as a sole proprietorship, a partnership, and a corporation?

   (b) How do hybrid forms of organization provide the advantages of proprietorships, partnerships, and corporations without the corresponding disadvantages?

3. Why do corporations have better access to financing than proprietorships or partnerships?

4. Large corporations are usually controlled by professional managers who may own only a very small portion of the business.

   (a) How do the owners benefit from entrusting daily control of their business to professional managers?

   (b) What costs may the owners incur from entrusting daily control of their business to professional managers?

5. You reluctantly conclude it is time to paint your house and are considering two alternatives. You can paint it yourself by working every Saturday and Sunday for the next four weekends or you can hire professional painters. The painters will work during the week while you are at your office.

   (a) Describe the actual costs and benefits of each alternative.

   (b) What are some potential agency costs of hiring the professional painters?

6. Many companies give their managers stock options or require them to purchase common stock on their own in an attempt to reduce agency costs.

   (a) Why do they expect these policies to reduce agency costs?

   (b) Should they expect these policies to *eliminate* owner–manager conflicts (such as the tendency to spend more for dinner when using the company's expense account)?

7. The discussion in your sociology class turns to the evils of corporations, their profits, and the stock market. Everyone knows you are in the business school and expects you to respond. Gather your thoughts and explain why:

   (a) Maximizing economic profit is beneficial to society.

   (b) Maximizing the owners' wealth, as represented by the market price of a company's common stock, is consistent with maximizing economic profit.

   (c) Managers *must* pursue the owners' interests as a practical matter.

   (d) Those sociologists are persistent and claim that corporations that attempt to maximize the owners' wealth are inclined to act illegally or unethically and to ignore the interests of other stakeholders. How do you respond?

8. Corporations have better access to financing partly because they issue securities that are traded in public financial markets.

(a) How do the differences in income, risk, and control provided by bonds and common stocks make investing in a corporation more appealing to a wide range of potential investors?

(b) What additional benefits do investors obtain when securities are traded in a public financial market?

9. Operating managers rarely, if ever, have any contact with their company's stockholders, bondholders, and banks. Does this mean these managers can safely ignore these investors' interests and concerns? Why or why not?

10. Joe Sliderule was very proud of himself. His careful engineering analysis convinced the vice-president of production that adopting stricter quality standards was just not worth the cost. Joe figured this decision saved the company at least $25 million. A few weeks later, Joe's company failed to win an important contract because it couldn't meet the customer's quality requirements. The market price of the company's stock fell by $1.25 upon the announcement. There were 40 million shares of stock outstanding at the time.

(a) What was the financial market's opinion of Joe's recommendation and the production vice-president's decision?

(b) Identify some factors Joe may have overlooked that are important to the financial market.

(c) What should companies do to ensure that operating managers do not overlook any of these factors?

11. Answer the following questions about valuation as best you can given the information in this chapter. Return to these questions and your answers after you have studied valuation principles in detail (Chapters 2–8) to see how much your understanding has improved.

(a) Discuss the three components of finance valuation principles.

(b) How are these components related to economic profit? To the owners' wealth?

12. Visit Coca-Cola's Internet site at http://www.cocacola.com/co/ and click on "Mission and Profile."

(a) What is the company's mission?

(b) What are the key assets it must use efficiently to accomplish this mission? How many of these assets appear to be the direct responsibility of financial managers? Operating managers?

(c) Does Coca-Cola apparently believe that only financial managers are responsible for maximizing the owners' wealth? Explain your answer.

VALUATION PRINCIPLES

Chapter 1 described financial management as the *financial* part of the process by which managers equip, operate, and obtain funding for a business. All of a company's managers are involved in one or more of these activities, which means all of them function as financial managers when they perform their jobs. Managers must base their financial decisions on fundamental principles to ensure they meet marketwide standards of performance.

The fundamental principles managers use to make their decisions can be stated simply: For example, managers should choose the alternatives that maximize the owners' wealth. However, this simple description of the goal of financial management belies the difficulty of actually estimating the values of the alternatives so the best ones can be chosen.

Part 1 provides a step-by-step development of the principles managers must use to estimate the value of investment, operating, and financing alternatives. Chapter 2 describes how to use ordinary accounting statements to perform the first step— estimating the cash flows used or provided by each alternative. Chapter 3 explains how to adjust these cash flows for differences in timing and risk. This adjustment reveals whether an alternative provides enough cash to cover the owners' opportunity cost, which is the rate of return they could earn by investing their money elsewhere. Chapters 4 through 6 describe how to estimate opportunity costs by considering the level of foreign and domestic interest rates and an alternative's risk.

Cash flows, opportunity costs, and adjustments for time and risk are brought together in Chapters 7 and 8 to estimate the market value of financial assets. The valuation principles are applied to debt and equity in Chapter 7 and options in Chapter 8. Learning how to value these financial assets is worthwhile in its own right. In addition, these assets are prototypes for routine and strategic investment, operating, and financing alternatives that we'll examine in Parts 2 and 3.

Part 1 is the most important part of this book for several reasons. First, Part 1 lays the groundwork for Parts 2 and 3. Once you have mastered the financial principles in Part 1, you will be very well prepared to study and apply these practices yourself in the next two parts. Second, many companies expect all managers to make decisions that maximize the owners' wealth. A solid understanding of financial principles will enable you to connect your day-to-day activities in production, human resources management, or marketing to changes in the company's stock price. Finally, as a successful manager, you are likely to accumulate personal wealth that you will hold as stocks, bonds, and other investments. Knowledge of the financial principles described in Part 1 will help you understand the risks and rewards you can expect from alternative investment and retirement strategies.

FINANCIAL STATEMENTS AND CASH FLOW

Apple Computer Incorporated was profitable but in trouble at the end of 1995. The company's net income increased from $84 million in 1993 to $424 million in 1995 but its future prospects looked bleak. Apple was losing market share to its IBM PC rivals, key executives were resigning to work for other firms, and the company suspended its dividend payments for the first time. Some analysts even speculated that Apple would not survive as an independent company. *Business Week* described Apple's condition in its February 5, 1996, cover story, "The Fall of an American Icon."

How could a company that reported nearly one-half billion dollars of net income be viewed so negatively? There are two explanations. First, net income is an accounting number that may bear very little relationship to the actual amount of cash a company paid or received. Second, financial reports describe the past rather than the future. Consequently, reported net income may be a poor predictor of a company's *future* cash flows. Exhibit 2.1 underscores these differences. You can see that the price of the company's common stock rose and fell as its cash flow rose and fell even though net income increased over the period.

The existence of a strong association between cash flows and the value of a company's assets and claims is why we begin this section on valuation principles by discussing financial statements. We will review the format and preparation of the cash statement, income statement, and balance sheet. We also will describe how to analyze these statements to extract more information.

You have probably seen some of the material in this chapter in prior accounting courses. Nevertheless, it will still be worth your time to study this chapter carefully because we will emphasize the difference between cash flow and net income as measured by accrual accounting and historical costs. Managers must understand this difference to plan, coordinate, and control their company's financial resources. Investors also must understand the difference between cash flow and net income to make reliable inferences about a company's financial performance.

Section 2.4 is especially important. Here, you will learn how to use the indirect method to prepare a cash statement. This method clearly shows the reasons for the

Exhibit 2.1

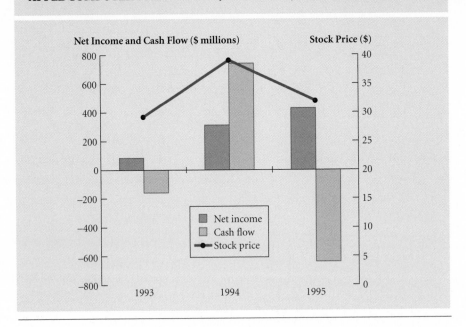

APPLE COMPUTER'S NET INCOME, CASH FLOW, AND STOCK PRICE

difference between cash flow and net income. You also will learn how to rearrange a cash statement into free cash flow and financial cash flow statements to improve its usefulness for planning and analysis. We will use these revised statements repeatedly throughout the book.

2.1   THE CASH STATEMENT

The **cash statement** describes a company's or unit's sources and uses of cash. Cash flows from current operations, investment, and financing are shown separately in addition to total net cash flow, which is the change in the company's or unit's cash balance for the period. Companies prepare internal statements on a pro forma basis for planning purposes and as reports to describe the results of a prior period's activities. The familiar cash budget is an example of a cash statement that nearly all companies prepare internally to anticipate cash surpluses and deficits.

Companies were not required to prepare external cash statements to report to their investors until the Financial Accounting Standards Board (FASB), accounting's rule-making body, issued its *Statement of Financial Accounting Standards No. 95, Statement of Cash Flows* in 1987. This pronouncement set forth the rules for preparing an external cash statement and required that companies include the statement with their other financial reports.

Exhibit 2.2

FORMAT OF A TYPICAL CASH STATEMENT

CASH FLOWS PROVIDED BY AND USED FOR OPERATIONS

Cash inflows from customers from the sale of goods and services and the collection or sale of accounts receivable

Cash outflows to suppliers for the purchase of materials, supplies, labor, and other services and payments on accounts payable

Cash inflows from interest and dividends received

Cash outflows and inflows from governments for taxes, fines, refunds, etc.

Cash inflows and outflows from miscellaneous sources: lawsuits, insurance settlements, refunds, etc.

CASH FLOWS PROVIDED BY AND USED FOR INVESTMENT

Cash outflows and inflows from the purchase and sale of the company's own property, plant, and equipment

Cash outflows and inflows from the purchase and sale of other companies' debt and equity

CASH FLOWS PROVIDED BY AND USED FOR FINANCING

Cash inflows and outflows from issuing and retiring the company's own debt and equity

Cash outflows from paying dividends

CASH FLOWS CLASSIFIED DIFFERENTLY IN INTERNAL AND EXTERNAL STATEMENTS

Cash outflows for interest paid

Format of the Cash Statement

The format of a cash statement is described in Exhibit 2.2. Cash flows provided by and used for operations are those associated with the production, distribution, and sale of the company's products and services. The main components of this category are cash collected from current and credit sales and cash paid for current and credit purchases of materials, labor, services, and taxes. Cash flows from miscellaneous transactions related to operations are also included here.

Cash flows provided by and used for investment are those associated with the purchase and sale of the company's own capital equipment and the securities issued by others. You must be careful about this category because a transaction may or may not belong here depending on the company's line of business. For example, a fork-lift truck is inventory to a heavy equipment dealer and capital equipment to a company that operates a warehouse. Consequently, the purchase of a fork-lift truck should be classified as an operating cash flow by the dealer and an investment cash flow by the warehouse owner. Similarly, buying and selling securities are operating transactions for securities dealers and investment transactions for other companies.

Cash flows provided by and used for financing are those associated with issuing and retiring the company's own debt and equity and the payment of dividends. All sources of financing except accounts payable and accrued wages and taxes are included here. These exceptions are included in operating cash flows as described above.

The FASB required that cash outflows for interest paid be included among operating cash flows in external cash statements. Saying that these cash transactions are the result of operating activities is controversial. After all, interest paid is payment for debt financing in the same way that dividends are payment for equity financing. This suggests these transactions should be classified as financing cash flows. Three members of the Financial Accounting Standards Board actually preferred this alternative but their opinions did not prevail. Consequently, companies must classify cash outflows for interest paid as operating cash flows when they prepare external cash statements.

Companies are not bound by the FASB's definitions of operating, investing, and financing cash flows when they prepare cash statements for their own, internal use. Then, cash outflows for interest paid should be classified as financing cash flows. This ensures that cash flows provided by and used for operations include only those transactions associated with the production, distribution, and sale of the company's products and services. A cash statement prepared this way is more useful for separately evaluating operating and financial performance and, as we will see later, for analyzing investment proposals and formulating financial plans.

Preparing a Cash Statement

There are two ways to prepare the cash flow from operations section of a cash statement. This section of a *direct method* statement looks very similar to Exhibit 2.2 with amounts, in dollars or another currency, entered after each cash flow component. An *indirect method* cash statement computes operating cash flows by adjusting net income for the effects of noncash transactions rather than by separately listing actual cash receipts and payments. The two methods are the same in all other respects.

The additional information about the components of operating cash flows in a direct method cash statement gives investors and managers more knowledge of the company's operating plans and performance. This makes a cash statement prepared this way closer to an internal document than any other financial statement. The FASB encouraged companies to use the direct method in their financial reports for this reason although they did not require it. The Chicago Pacific Railroad uses the direct method to prepare cash statements, however, because the managers consider it more useful for planning analysis. (See "In the News.")

Throughout this chapter, we will refer to a fictitious gift shop called Something Special to illustrate the various financial statements. We'll begin by looking at the development of the gift shop's direct method cash statement, using their internal reports. First, however, we need to quickly review the following information about the firm.

A company that manufactures several lines of collectible ceramic figures established a small gift shop, Something Special, in an outlet mall near its plant. The company pro-

IN THE NEWS

CHICAGO CENTRAL ENGINEERS ITS FINANCIAL GOALS WITH THE DIRECT CASH FLOW REPORT

CHICAGO CENTRAL'S REPORTING of cash receipts, disbursements, and daily cash balances was understood by the accounting department only. While the data were useful as a daily and weekly cash management tool, the company needed a report that summarized the detailed information and could be used for long-term cash management. The decision to develop a direct cash flow report was based on several factors.

First, the cash flows would determine whether Chicago Central had a future and could service sufficient debt in order to avoid liquidation. Second, the company needed a report that could be understood readily and explained to operating managers required to deal with the cash impact of their decisions. Finally, direct cash flow reporting facilitates variance analysis. The cash budget information can

be tied into the cash flow report, thereby drawing attention to the real source of any problems.

Chicago Central adopted the FASB's definitions of operating, investing, and financing activities to classify the cash flows in their direct format cash statement. However, "for purposes of analysis and discussion, Chicago Central adjusts interest out of the operating cash flows" as we did.

The new direct cash flow report provided operating managers with clear information about cash inflows and outflows that enabled them to act more effectively. Financial managers now were able to quantify some of their intuitive feelings regarding the actual cash flows. Based on the response from its management team, the company recommends (the direct cash flow statement) to other firms.

Source: R. Kevin Trout, Margaret M. Tanner, and Lee Nicholas, "On Track with Direct Cash Flow," *Management Accounting*, published by Institute of Management Accountants, Montvale, NJ, July 1993, pp. 23–27.

vided $54,000 of equity financing and gave the shop some fully depreciated display racks to be used or sold at the manager's option. The gift shop borrowed an additional $12,000 from two local financial intermediaries. Most of the $66,000 in cash was used to rent and furnish the space at the mall, pay salaries, and acquire a merchandise inventory. The display shelves were sold for $750 cash.

Something Special receives its merchandise shipment from its parent company on the first Wednesday of each month. The shop must pay cash for high-demand items but may pay for the remainder in 30 days. The gift shop prices its ceramic figures at cost plus 25% and sells them at this price for cash or on credit. Credit sales are collected in 30 days and there are no bad debts.

Interest on the gift shop's loans is paid monthly, and the principal is due at maturity. Something Special distributes earnings to its parent company, that is, it pays a dividend at the end of each quarter.

An internal quarterly report that summarizes these and other operating and financing transactions during the shop's first three months in business is presented in Table 2.1. Now that we have this background information, we will use it to prepare Something Special's direct method cash statements, which are shown in Table 2.2.

Table 2.1   SOMETHING SPECIAL'S INTERNAL QUARTERLY REPORTS

Panel A: Operating Transactions

	October	November	December
Sales of merchandise			
Cash	$11,250	$18,750	$15,000
Credit	17,500	31,250	30,000
Total	$28,750	$50,000	$45,000
Purchases of merchandise			
Cash	$35,000	$10,000	$ 7,000
Credit	20,000	31,000	28,000
Total	$55,000	$41,000	$35,000
Merchandise inventory			
Beginning balance	$ 0	$32,000	$33,000
Purchases	55,000	41,000	35,000
Ending balance	32,000	33,000	32,000
Cost of goods sold	$23,000	$40,000	$36,000
Salaries	$ 4,000	$ 4,000	$ 4,000
Rent	$ 1,000	$ 1,000	$ 1,000
Capital equipment			
Sell display racks	$ 750	$ 0	$ 0
Buy new fixtures and improvements	30,000	0	0
Net expenditures	$29,250	$ 0	$ 0

Panel B: Financing Transactions

	October	November	December
Equity issued	$54,000	$ 0	$ 0
Debt issued			
One-year, 9% bank loan	$ 4,000	$ 0	$ 0
Five-year, 12% term loan	8,000	0	0
Total	$12,000	$ 0	$ 0
Interest paid	$ 110	$ 110	$ 110
Dividend paid	$ 0	$ 0	$ 1,000

Cash sales are collected at the time of the transactions and credit sales become accounts receivable, which are collected in full the following month. Therefore, merchandise sales in October produced cash inflows from customers of $11,250 and $17,500 in October and November, respectively. Adding November's cash sales of $18,750 to the $17,500 gives the second month's total cash received from customers of $36,250.

Cash payments for merchandise are treated similarly. Cash purchases are paid for at the time of the transactions and credit purchases become accounts payable, which are paid in full the following month. Therefore, merchandise purchased in October was paid for with cash outflows of $35,000 and $20,000 in October and November, respec-

SOMETHING SPECIAL'S CASH STATEMENTS (DIRECT METHOD)   **Table 2.2**

	October	November	December
Cash Flow Provided by (Used for) Operations			
Cash received from customers	$ 11,250	$ 36,250	$ 46,250
Cash paid to suppliers	(35,000)	(30,000)	(38,000)
Salaries and rent	(5,000)	(5,000)	(5,000)
Taxes	(400)	(1,800)	(1,400)
Net cash flow	$(29,150)	$ (550)	$ 1,850
Cash Flow Provided by (Used for) Investment			
Sale of display racks	$ 750	$ 0	$ 0
Purchase fixtures and improvements	(30,000)	0	0
Net cash flow	$(29,250)	$ 0	$ 0
Cash Flow Provided by (Used for) Financing			
Pay interest	$ (66)	$ (66)	$ (66)
Pay dividends	0	0	(1,000)
Issue equity	54,000	0	0
Issue debt	12,000	0	0
Net cash flow	$ 65,934	$ (66)	$ (1,066)
Increase (Decrease) in Cash Balance	$ 7,534	$ (616)	$ 784

tively. Adding November's cash purchases of $10,000 to the $20,000 gives the second month's total cash paid to suppliers of $30,000.

Salaries and rent were paid in cash so these amounts are entered directly on the cash statement. Taxes paid are computed at the company's marginal tax rate of 40%. (We'll discuss taxes later when we review the income statement.)

The sum of these cash flows for each month is the net cash flow provided by or used for operations. Something Special's monthly net operating cash flows ranged from a low of –$29,150 in October to a high of $1,850 in December.

There are only two entries in the investment section of the gift shop's cash statements. The manager sold the old display racks for $750 and paid $30,000 for new fixtures and improvements when the shop was established. Therefore the net amount of cash used for investments in October was $29,250.

Finally, the financing section shows the amount of cash the gift shop obtained from and paid to investors. The parent company's $54,000 equity investment and the financial intermediaries' $12,000 loans are entered for October. The $66 interest payment equals the total of the monthly after-tax interest for each loan, $(0.09 \times \$4,000 + 0.12 \times \$8,000) \times (1 - 0.40)/12$. The parent company's share of the shop's quarterly earnings, $1,000, is entered as a cash outflow for dividends in December.

The cash statement shows that the total amount of cash provided by operations and financing in October exceeded the amount used for investment by $7,534. This excess cash was retained by the gift shop as a cash balance. November's activities depleted this cash balance by $616; December's activities replenished it by $784.

EXERCISE

2.1 **PREPARING A DIRECT FORMAT CASH STATEMENT**

Prepare revised direct format cash statements for Something Special under the assumption that the labels for cash and credit sales were inadvertently switched.

Under this assumption, sales and cash received from customers each month are:

	October	November	December
Sales			
Cash	$17,500	$31,250	$30,000
Credit	11,250	18,750	15,000
Total	$28,750	$50,000	$45,000
Cash received from customers			
Cash sales	$17,500	$31,250	$30,000
Collection of prior month's credit sales	0	11,250	18,750
Total	$17,500	$42,500	$48,750

Substitute these amounts into the operating section to obtain the revised direct format cash statement.

SOMETHING SPECIAL'S REVISED CASH STATEMENTS (DIRECT METHOD)

	October	November	December
Cash Flow Provided by (Used for) Operations			
Cash received from customers	$ 17,500	$ 42,500	$ 48,750
Cash paid to suppliers	(35,000)	(30,000)	$(38,000)
Salaries and rent	(5,000)	(5,000)	(5,000)
Taxes	(400)	(1,800)	(1,400)
Net cash flow	$(22,900)	$ 5,700	$ 4,350
Cash Flow Provided by (Used for) Investment			
Sale of display racks	$ 750	$ 0	$ 0
Purchase fixtures and improvements	(30,000)	0	0
Net cash flow	$(29,250)	$ 0	$ 0
Cash Flow Provided by (Used for) Financing			
Pay interest	$ (66)	$ (66)	$ (66)
Pay dividends	0	0	(1,000)
Issue equity	54,000	0	0
Issue debt	12,000	0	0
Net cash flow	$ 65,934	$ (66)	$ (1,066)
Increase (Decrease) in Cash Balance	$ 13,784	$ 5,634	$ 3,284

Improperly classifying cash and credit sales makes a substantial difference in the company's cash flows provided by operations.

● ———————— ●

The cash statement is an important management tool because it describes the actual amount of cash paid and received during an accounting period. We will see that managers can use this report to plan, coordinate, and control their company's operating, investment, and financing activities.

2.2 THE INCOME STATEMENT AND STATEMENT OF RETAINED EARNINGS

The **income statement** describes a company's sources and uses of revenue. Operating and nonoperating revenues and costs and financing revenues and costs are shown separately and on a net basis as net income. In this limited sense, the income statement is similar to the cash statement although the former is based on revenue and the latter is based on cash. The statement of retained earnings simply shows how much of net income is retained by the company as part of the owners' equity.

Differences between Net Income and Cash Flow

There may be significant differences between the income and cash statements when a company or unit uses the *accrual method of accounting* to recognize income and costs. This method assigns revenues and costs to the accounting period in which a transaction takes place rather than the period when cash is received or paid. Consequently, net income does not equal net cash flow when there are credit sales or purchases or when expenses that did not use cash are allocated to the period. You can see exactly how this difference arises by carefully examining each line of an income statement.

Consider the operating section of the income statement first. Net sales do not equal the cash received from customers because credit sales are recognized at the time of the transactions rather than when the accounts are collected. Cost of goods sold does not equal the cash paid to suppliers because some of the merchandise sold from inventory may have been purchased and paid for in prior periods while some may have been recently purchased and not yet paid for. Finally, some selling and administrative expenses (such as an office lease and depreciation) are accrued expenses that are allocated to each period even though the cash was paid to the lessor or was used to buy the equipment earlier.

Now consider the miscellaneous and financing and tax sections of the income statement. The other income and expense category is based on the book values of the assets sold and not on the amount of cash paid or received. To illustrate, suppose a company owns an airplane with a book value of $2.5 million and sells it for $2 million cash. Then the rules of accrual accounting require them to enter a $500,000 loss in the other income and expense category of the income statement even though they received $2 million cash. Finally, interest and taxes also are accrued expenses that are allocated to the period whether the actual cash outflow was paid earlier or will be paid later.

The net effect of these accounting rules is that net income is sometimes greater than and sometimes less than cash flow, as illustrated by the Apple Computer example. You will see this difference again when we examine Something Special's income statements. Importantly, you will see that the indirect method of preparing a cash statement, which we will discuss in Section 2.4, is specifically designed to remove these effects from a company's accrual-based income statement.

Something Special's Income Statements

Something Special's income statements and statements of retained earnings are presented in Table 2.3. The information in the company's internal quarterly report and cash statements was used to construct these statements. You can see the differences between net income and cash flow by comparing these income statements to the gift shop's cash statements.

Net sales for October equal total cash and credit sales for the month: $28,750. Note that this figure exceeds cash received from customers by the amount of October's credit sales. Net sales are less than cash received from customers in December because November's large amount of credit sales were collected then.

Table 2.3   SOMETHING SPECIAL'S INCOME STATEMENTS AND STATEMENTS OF RETAINED EARNINGS

Panel A: Income Statements

	October	November	December
Net sales	$28,750	$50,000	$45,000
Cost of goods sold	23,000	40,000	36,000
Gross profit	5,750	10,000	9,000
Selling expenses	5,000	5,000	5,000
Depreciation	500	500	500
Net operating income	250	4,500	3,500
Other income	750	0	0
Interest expense	110	110	110
Taxable income	890	4,390	3,390
Taxes	356	1,756	1,356
Net income	$ 534	$ 2,634	$ 2,034

Panel B: Statements of Retained Earnings

	October	November	December
Beginning balance	$ 0	$ 534	$ 3,168
Plus net income	534	2,634	2,034
Minus dividends	0	0	1,000
Ending balance	$ 534	$ 3,168	$ 4,202

Cost of goods sold equals beginning inventory plus purchases minus ending inventory. For October, this is $0 + $55,000 − $32,000 = $23,000. This value does not equal cash paid to suppliers because some purchases were on credit and the level of inventory changed. These two factors caused cost of goods sold to exceed cash paid to suppliers in October but they had the opposite effect in December.

Salaries and rent were the company's only selling expenses. These amounts were paid in cash so the values entered on the income statements equal the corresponding values on the cash statements.

The gift shop used straight-line depreciation and a five-year life to depreciate its store fixtures and improvements. This means there are 60 months in the assets' lives, so the monthly depreciation deduction was $30,000/60 = $500.

Net sales minus cost of goods sold, selling expenses, and depreciation equals net operating income. Net operating income does not equal net cash flow from operations in any month but the difference is greatest in October. Someone who does not understand the distinction between cash and accrual accounting may be surprised by this difference. This could be very costly to a company if this surprises the manager responsible for financing cash deficits. For this reason, cash statements are much more useful than income statements for financial planning and analysis.

The $750 gain from selling the old display racks in October was the gift shop's only other income. Interest was paid in cash so the entries for the cash and income statements are the same. Taxes are computed here, for purposes of illustration, at a 40 percent rate. These deductions left a net income of $534 in October.[1]

No dividends were paid in October so the entire $534 was added to retained earnings. Because $1,000 of earnings was distributed to the parent company as dividends, $1,034 was added to retained earnings in December.

EXERCISE

2.2

PREPARING AN INCOME STATEMENT

You had to revise Something Special's cash statements in Exercise 2.1 because the labels on cash and credit sales were switched. Is it necessary for you to make any changes to the company's income statements?

The answer is no. Accountants recognize revenues and costs at the time the sales take place. The earlier mistake did not change the total amount of the company's sales so it has no effect on the income statements.

---

[1]Notice that taxes shown on the income statement are accounted for in two separate places on the internal cash statement in Table 2.2. The tax on earnings before deducting interest is treated as an operating cash flow ($1,000 × 0.40 in October). The tax savings obtained by deducting interest expense is treated as a financing cash flow because only the after-tax interest is entered in the financing section of the cash statement ($110 × 0.40). Combining the tax portion of each of these entries, $1,000 × 0.40 − $110 × 0.40, gives the amount of taxes shown on the income statement.

2.3   THE BALANCE SHEET

The **balance sheet** describes a company's assets and how they were financed. Assets and claims are recorded at book value, which equals the amount of money exchanged at the time of the initial transaction. Book value may not equal market value because historical cost accounting does not recognize all the factors that can affect an asset's value.

Differences between Book and Market Values

The use of historical costs misrepresents the values of both the assets and claims recorded on the balance sheet; it also affects the income statement. Consider the asset side of the balance sheet first. Some assets may be worth less than their book values if changes in customers' preferences or technology have made them obsolete. For example, action figures related to *last year's* hit movie may have a market value of considerably less than their book value. Other assets may be worth more than their book values if inflation has made it more expensive to replace them. Many forest product companies acquired their logging rights more than 50 years ago, and these rights now are almost certainly worth more than their original cost.

The income statement is distorted when assets are incorrectly valued on the balance sheet. Deductions from inventory for cost of goods sold are too high if the inventory is obsolete and too low if its value has been increased by inflation. Deductions from gross fixed assets for depreciation are too high or too low for similar reasons. These distortions affect reported net income and, more importantly, the amount of taxes a company must pay.

Another problem caused by historical cost accounting is that some assets are omitted from the balance sheet because there is no specific transaction that determines when they were acquired and what they cost. Brand names and associated trademarks, such as McDonald's golden arches, are prime examples of assets that are valuable to their owners but do not appear on the companies' balance sheets. Companies incur expenses to register and protect these symbols but their real cost is the companies' investments in quality, service, and "mystique." Most accounting systems do not separately measure these costs.

Now consider how historical costs distort the claims side of the balance sheet. One problem is that debt claims are not adjusted for the effect of inflation. As an illustration of how this affects the balance sheet, suppose a company obtains a one-year, $10,000 loan at 10 percent interest. This loan will appear as a $10,000 liability on the company's balance sheet and requires a $1,000 interest payment that will be recorded as an interest expense in its income statement. Now suppose unforeseen inflation causes the price level to increase by 100 percent shortly after the company receives the loan. Then each dollar used to repay the loan is worth only $0.50, so the real amount of principal and interest paid is $5,500 ($11,000/2). Historical cost accounting does not permit an adjustment for these effects, so the book value of a company's debt claims overstates its liabilities and interest expense in the presence of inflation.

Another problem is that some claims are omitted from the balance sheet because no transaction or event has established their cost. Examples are future obligations to clean up hazardous wastes and recall unsafe products. Payments for these purposes have priority over payments to the owners, which gives them the characteristics of a senior claim on a company's cash flows. Historical cost accounting does not recognize these types of claims on the balance sheet although they may be described in explanatory notes to the statements.

Finally, a balance sheet must balance, which means claims' values are automatically misrepresented when assets' values are misrepresented due to the effects described above. This is only one reason that the book values of a company's securities usually do not equal their market values.

The distortions caused by historical cost accounting are more serious the longer an asset's or claim's life. There are two reasons: First, a company's shortest-lived assets are cash and accounts receivable, which are monetary assets that are immune from the effects of obsolescence. Second, short-lived assets and claims are resistant to the effects of inflation because they are converted into cash before the price level can change very much.

Even if all the problems mentioned above could be corrected, historical cost accounting would still misrepresent the value of assets and claims because it focuses on the past rather than the future. The true value of a company's assets is determined by the amount, timing, and risk of the future cash flows they provide. Similarly, the true value of the securities issued to purchase those assets is determined by the share of the cash flows that will be paid to each claimant. These true values can only be determined by referring to market prices.[2] Professional investors now pay less attention to book value because of these problems as described by the article "In the News."

A company's assets, particularly its intangible assets such as brand names, may not be traded in a public market but some of its securities probably are. This means we can calculate the true or market value of its securities by simply multiplying the number outstanding by their market prices. Furthermore, the balance sheet identity, *assets = claims,* allows us to estimate the true or market value of its assets by simply adding up the market values of these securities. Market value is larger than the book value for successful companies with promising futures and is a better representation of the economic resources available to the company and owned by its claimants.

Table 2.4 gives the average book value of assets and market value of assets for selected industries and for selected companies in the miscellaneous retail industry. The book values are from the companies' balance sheets, while the market values equal the book values of their debt plus the market values of their common stock. You can see that the market values are generally larger than the book values although there is some variation, particularly among companies in the miscellaneous retail industry. Two companies, General Hosts and Michaels Stores, had market values that were less than their book values, indicating that the financial market did not think their future prospects were very good.

---

[2]If you are unsure about this, answer the following multiple choice question. "What value would you place on a gold bar that you found, (a) its cost, which is $0; or (b) its market price?" Please contact me immediately if you find a gold bar and your answer was (a).

PROFESSIONAL INVESTORS SAY
BYE-BYE TO BOOK VALUE

MONEY MANAGERS ARE closing the book on the book value of equity.

Bargain-hunting investors used to pay a lot of attention to the book value of equity, namely a company's assets minus its liabilities. But now even die-hard fans concede that this measure of a company's worth has lost much of its meaning because of new accounting rules, share buybacks, and write-offs.

"I was a big proponent of book value," says Richard Fontaine, a Towson, Maryland, stock-picker with $270 million under management. "But it's very difficult to use it as a yardstick anymore. The distortions have gotten so big that it's got rid of most of the value."

Last year, for instance, General Motors' book value shrank to $8.47 a share from $42.89, in large part because of new accounting rules regarding retiree benefits. At Dayton Hudson, book value fell between 1986 and year-end 1989, as the retailer bought large chunks of its own stock. In recent years, International Business Machines' book value has shriveled as the computer giant took write-offs to cover its restructuring.

"Book-value measurements have gone through so many changes as to be almost meaningless," says Wayne Nordbert, partner in charge of equity investments at New York's Lord Abbett & Co. "We look at it. But it doesn't occupy the same position in our analytical process as it did five or 10 years ago."

Source: Jonathan Clements, "Book Value Is More Rarely Required Reading Now," *The Wall Street Journal*, September 10, 1993, p. C1. Reprinted by permission of *The Wall Street Journal*, © 1993 Dow Jones & Company, Inc. All rights reserved worldwide.

Something Special's Balance Sheets

The information in Something Special's internal quarterly report, cash statements, and income statements was used to construct the balance sheets in Table 2.5. This hypothetical company does not have a market value that we can use for comparison, but you can see the effect of accrual accounting and historical costs by examining the structure of these balance sheets.

The gift shop's current assets are cash, accounts receivable, and inventory. The cash balance is computed from the shop's cash statements. Beginning at zero, the cash balance increased to $7,534 in October; decreased by $616 to $6,918 in November; and increased by $784 to $7,702 in December. Accounts receivable equals the previous month's balance plus credit sales minus payments. All accounts are paid in full in 30 days, so the entries for October and November are $17,500 ($0 + $17,500 − $0) and $31,250 ($17,500 + $31,250 − $17,500), respectively. Ending inventory is taken straight from the shop's internal operating report.

Gross fixed assets equal the value of the fixtures and improvements recorded at cost, $30,000. Something Special recognized depreciation expense of $500 per month on its income statements and accounted for it here in accumulated depreciation. The value of net fixed assets therefore declined to $28,500 by the end of December.

The gift shop's current liabilities are accounts payable and a bank loan. Accounts payable equals the previous month's balance plus credit purchases minus payments. They

BOOK AND MARKET VALUES OF SELECTED INDUSTRIES AND COMPANIES   Table 2.4

Panel A: Selected Industries

Industry (Sample Size)	Average Book Value of Assets	Average Market Value of Assets*
All manufacturing (736)	$ 4,626	$ 7,839
Food and kindred products (58)	7,128	13,865
Apparel and textiles (28)	806	1,128
Chemicals and allied products (121)	3,772	8,967
Petroleum and coal products (30)	21,987	31,543
Industrial machinery (162)	2,145	4,519
Electrical equipment (76)	2,806	6,252
All retail (129)	2,740	4,166
Miscellaneous retail (50)	977	1,562

Panel B: Selected Companies in Miscellaneous Retail Industry

	Book Value of Assets	Market Value of Assets*
General Host	$465	$436
Lillian Vernon	138	154
Michaels Stores	686	650
Pier 1 Imports	489	680
Sanhome, Inc.	512	801

*Market value of assets equals book value of debt plus market value of equity.

Source: January 1, 1996 edition of Value/Screen III, Value Line Publishing, Inc., copyright 1993.

pay their bills in full in 30 days, so the entries for October and November are $20,000 ($0 + $20,000 – $0) and $31,000 ($20,000 + $31,000 – $20,000), respectively. The principal of the bank loan, $4,000, is the amount of this liability.

Long-term financing comprises the term loan, with a principal of $8,000, and common equity. The parent company's initial equity investment of $54,000 is recorded under common stock. Additions to the equity account from retained earnings are taken from the shop's statements of retained earnings presented at the end of its income statements. Beginning at zero, retained earnings increased to $534 in October; increased by $2,634 to $3,168 in November; and increased again by $1,034 to $4,202 in December.

● EXERCISE
2.3

PREPARING A BALANCE SHEET

Prepare Something Special's balance sheets given the mislabeling of cash and credit sales described in Exercise 2.1.

Table 2.5   SOMETHING SPECIAL'S BALANCE SHEETS

	October	November	December
Assets			
Cash	$ 7,534	$ 6,918	$ 7,702
Accounts receivable	17,500	31,250	30,000
Inventory	32,000	33,000	32,000
Total current assets	57,034	71,168	69,702
Gross fixed assets	30,000	30,000	30,000
Accumulated depreciation	500	1,000	1,500
Net fixed assets	29,500	29,000	28,500
Total assets	$86,534	$100,168	$98,202
Claims			
Accounts payable	$20,000	$ 31,000	$28,000
Bank loan	4,000	4,000	4,000
Total current liabilities	24,000	35,000	32,000
Term loan	8,000	8,000	8,000
Common stock	54,000	54,000	54,000
Retained earnings	534	3,168	4,202
Total equity	54,534	57,168	58,202
Total claims	$86,534	$100,168	$98,202

The revised cash statements in Exercise 2.1 show that Something Special's cash balance increased each month. Accumulating these changes gives the company's cash balance as it appears on each month's revised balance sheet.

	October	November	December
Beginning cash balance	$ 0	$13,784	$19,418
Increase in cash balance (from Exercise 2.1)	13,784	5,634	3,284
Ending cash balance	$13,784	$19,418	$22,702

The company's revised accounts receivable balance is computed similarly.

	October	November	December
Beginning accounts receivable balance	$ 0	$11,250	$18,750
Plus credit sales	11,250	18,750	15,000
Minus payments	0	11,250	18,750
Ending accounts receivable balance	$11,250	$18,750	$15,000

All the other balance sheet accounts are unaffected. Therefore, you only need to make these changes to cash and accounts receivable to obtain the company's revised balance sheets.

SOMETHING SPECIAL'S REVISED BALANCE SHEETS

	October	November	December
Assets			
Cash	$13,784	$ 19,418	$22,702
Accounts receivable	11,250	18,750	15,000
Inventory	32,000	33,000	32,000
Total current assets	57,034	71,168	69,702
Gross fixed assets	30,000	30,000	30,000
Accumulated depreciation	500	1,000	1,500
Net fixed assets	29,500	29,000	28,500
Total assets	$86,534	$100,168	$98,202
Claims			
Accounts payable	$20,000	$ 31,000	$28,000
Bank loan	4,000	4,000	4,000
Total current liabilities	24,000	35,000	32,000
Term loan	8,000	8,000	8,000
Common stock	54,000	54,000	54,000
Retained earnings	534	3,168	4,202
Total equity	54,534	57,168	58,202
Total claims	$86,534	$100,168	$98,202

2.4 MORE ABOUT THE CASH STATEMENT

This section describes the indirect format cash statement and the free cash flow and financial cash flow statements. These statements provide much the same information as a direct format cash statement but they are often more useful for financial management.

The Indirect Format Cash Statement

Now that you have a better understanding of income statements and balance sheets, we can prepare a cash statement using the indirect method. This approach uses information in the income statement and balance sheet to remove the effects of accrual accounting from net income. The indirect method is simpler to use than the direct method because detailed operating information is not required, however, it is also less informative for the same reason.

An indirect method cash statement begins with net income, which is adjusted for the effect of transactions that did not provide or use cash. First, depreciation expense is added to net income because it was subtracted at an earlier stage in the income statement even though it did not use cash. Second, the change in accounts receivable is subtracted from net income because credit sales were included in accrued revenue even though they did not provide cash. Similarly, the change in inventory is subtracted because purchases for inventory used cash even though they were not included in cost of goods sold. Third, the change in accrued expenses and accounts payable are added to net income because the costs of wages and materials were subtracted as part of cost of goods sold at an earlier stage in the income statement even though credit purchases of these inputs did not use cash. Finally, revenue and costs related to investment and financing transactions are removed from net income so they can be assigned to the correct category. Gains and losses on the sale of assets are reassigned to the investment category while *after-tax* interest expense is reassigned to the financing category.

Net income plus (and minus) these adjustments equals net cash flow from operations. The net amount, if not the entries used to calculate it, is the same whether the direct or indirect method is used. The investment and financing sections are identical under both methods.

Something Special's indirect method cash statements are presented in Table 2.6. For October, the shop's net income and depreciation, $534 and $500, respectively, were taken from the income statement. Accounts receivable increased in October from zero to $17,500 while inventory increased from zero to $32,000 for a total change of

Table 2.6   SOMETHING SPECIAL'S CASH STATEMENTS (INDIRECT METHOD)

	October	November	December
Cash Flow Provided by (Used for) Operations			
Net income	$ 534	$ 2,634	$ 2,034
Plus depreciation expense	500	500	500
Minus change in receivables and inventory	49,500	14,750	(2,250)
Plus change in payables	20,000	11,000	(3,000)
Minus gain on sale of asset	750	0	0
Plus interest expense	66	66	66
Net cash flow	$(29,150)	$ (550)	$ 1,850
Cash Flow Provided by (Used for) Investment			
Sale of display racks	$ 750	$ 0	$ 0
Purchase fixtures and improvements	(30,000)	0	0
Net cash flow	$(29,250)	$ 0	$ 0
Cash Flow Provided by (Used for) Financing			
Pay interest	$ (66)	$ (66)	$ (66)
Pay dividends	0	0	(1,000)
Issue equity	54,000	0	0
Issue debt	12,000	0	0
Net cash flow	$ 65,934	$ (66)	$(1,066)
Increase (Decrease) in Cash Balance	$ 7,534	$ (616)	$ 784

$49,500. Accounts payable went from zero to $20,000. The $750 gain from selling the old display racks is transferred from the operating to the investment section, and the after-tax interest expense, $110 $\times$ (1 – 0.40), is transferred to the financing section. The result is –$29,150 net cash flow from operations, which is the same as computed directly in Table 2.2.

EXERCISE

2.4

PREPARING AN INDIRECT FORMAT CASH STATEMENT

Prepare revised indirect format cash statements for Something Special given the afore-mentioned error in identifying cash and credit sales.

The revised indirect format cash statements are based on Something Special's income statements, which were not affected by the error, and its revised balance sheets. By using these statements and following the line-by-line instructions in the cash statement, you obtain the revised indirect format cash statements given below.

SOMETHING SPECIAL'S REVISED CASH STATEMENTS (INDIRECT METHOD)

	October	November	December
Cash Flow Provided by (Used for) Operations			
Net income	$ 534	$ 2,634	$ 2,034
Plus depreciation expense	500	500	500
Minus change in receivables and inventory	43,250	8,500	(4,750)
Plus change in payables	20,000	11,000	(3,000)
Minus gain on sale of asset	750	0	0
Plus interest expense	66	66	66
Net cash flow	$(22,900)	$ 5,700	$ 4,350
Cash Flow Provided by (Used for) Investment			
Sale of display racks	$ 750	$ 0	$ 0
Purchase fixtures and improvements	(30,000)	0	0
Net cash flow	$(29,250)	$ 0	$ 0
Cash Flow Provided by (Used for) Financing			
Pay interest	$ (66)	$ (66)	$ (66)
Pay dividends	0	0	(1,000)
Issue equity	54,000	0	0
Issue debt	12,000	0	0
Net cash flow	$ 65,934	$ (66)	$(1,066)
Increase (Decrease) in Cash Balance	$ 13,784	$ 5,634	$ 3,284

The Cash Statement and Free Cash Flow

The cash statement format we have discussed so far was designed for reporting and explaining the results of a company's activities. Net cash flows from operations, investing, and financing are added together to obtain a company's overall net cash flow, which equals the increase or decrease in its cash balance. In this format, the cash statement explains the change in cash from one period to the next in the same way that an income statement explains the change in dividends and retained earnings. This cash statement format is summarized by Equation 2.1:

$$\begin{matrix} \text{Cash flow} \\ \text{provided by} \\ \text{operations} \end{matrix} + \begin{matrix} \text{Cash flow} \\ \text{provided by} \\ \text{investing} \end{matrix} + \begin{matrix} \text{Cash flow} \\ \text{provided by} \\ \text{financing} \end{matrix} = \begin{matrix} \text{Change} \\ \text{in cash} \\ \text{balance.} \end{matrix} \qquad \textbf{[2.1]}$$

Managers plan, coordinate, and control operating, investing, and financing activities as well as report them. They also manage cash and do not allow the balance to simply fluctuate in response to the company's other activities—as the format of the ordinary cash statement suggests. Instead, they view cash and securities as *planned* temporary investments or **financial slack** that is held to meet unexpected requirements for funds.[3]

We can rearrange the format of the cash statement to account for the active management of financial slack by subtracting the change in the cash balance from both sides and renaming it "cash flow provided by financial slack." (This entry is a negative number if the company plans to *increase* its financial slack.) The result is given by Equation 2.2:

$$\begin{matrix} \text{Cash flow} \\ \text{provided by} \\ \text{operations} \end{matrix} + \begin{matrix} \text{Cash flow} \\ \text{provided by} \\ \text{investing} \end{matrix} + \begin{matrix} \text{Cash flow} \\ \text{provided by} \\ \text{financial slack} \end{matrix} + \begin{matrix} \text{Cash flow} \\ \text{provided by} \\ \text{financing} \end{matrix} = 0. \qquad \textbf{[2.2]}$$

The first three terms in Equation 2.2 equal the net cash flow provided by or used for an asset or business. The components of this cash flow are the net cash flow from operating the asset, the net cash flow from purchasing or selling the asset, and the net cash flow retained as financial slack to support its operations. The sum of these terms is known as **free cash flow** because it equals the net amount of cash flow available after all the asset's own cash requirements are met.

Positive free cash flow is the amount of surplus that can be paid *to* investors while negative free cash flow is the amount of shortage that must be financed *by* investors. The last term in Equation 2.2 is the **financial cash flow** to or from investors that offsets these surpluses or shortages. Here's a simple illustration:

---

[3]The amount of financial slack a company should hold depends on the opportunity cost of investing in cash and securities rather than productive assets and the anticipated costs of unexpected requirements for funds. We will examine some ways to estimate the requirement for financial slack when we discuss short-term financial planning in Chapter 19.

Majluf Manufacturing has a production facility that is expected to provide $4,500,000 of operating cash flow next year. The company will modernize one of the facility's production lines at a cost of $1,250,000 and increase its cash and temporary investments by $250,000 to provide for unforeseen events. Cash not reinvested in this facility is returned to the parent company. The facility's pro forma cash statement is

Cash flow provided by (used for) operations	$ 4,500,000
Cash flow provided by (used for) investment	
Modernize production line	(1,250,000)
Cash flow provided by (used for) financing	
Cash returned to parent	(3,000,000)
Increase (decrease) in cash balance	$ 250,000

The same information, presented in the free cash flow and financial cash flow format, is

Free Cash Flow

Cash flow provided by (used for) operations	$ 4,500,000
Cash flow provided by (used for) investment	
Modernize production line	(1,250,000)
Cash flow provided by (used for) financial slack	
Increase cash and temporary investments	(250,000)
Net free cash flow	$ 3,000,000

Financial Cash Flow

Cash flow paid to parent	$(3,000,000)
Net financial cash flow	$(3,000,000)

These free cash flow and financial cash flow statements are ideally suited for use in planning, coordination, and control by managers in different areas and at different levels of the company. Business unit managers are usually responsible for their unit's operations and investments and therefore can focus on free cash flow. They can use free cash flow forecasts to predict an asset's profitability and ensure that it is likely to meet minimum standards of financial performance before they approve the investment and to analyze the results afterwards. Corporate staff are responsible for obtaining and repaying financing and therefore can focus on financial cash flow surpluses and deficits to plan financing. We will use the free cash flow and financial cash flow statements repeatedly throughout this book for these purposes.

Table 2.7 shows Something Special's free cash flow and financial cash flow statements for October and November. Starting the gift shop in October required $36,784: $29,250 for improvements and fixtures plus $7,534 for financial slack. Operations used $29,150, so the shop had a free cash flow deficit of $65,934 ($36,784 + $29,150). The parent company and loans from two financial institutions financed this deficit as shown in panel B of the table. The gift shop ran a much smaller operating deficit in November and, by reducing its financial slack, produced a small positive free cash flow.

Table 2.7 SOMETHING SPECIAL'S FREE CASH FLOW AND FINANCIAL CASH FLOW STATEMENTS

Panel A: Free Cash Flow

	October	November
Cash flow provided by (used for) operations	$(29,150)	$(550)
Cash flow provided by (used for) investment	(29,250)	0
Cash flow provided by (used for) financial slack	(7,534)	616
Net free cash flow	$(65,934)	$ 66

Panel B: Financial Cash Flow

	October	November
Pay interest	$ (66)	$ (66)
Pay dividends	0	0
Issue equity	54,000	0
Issue debt	12,000	0
Net financial cash flow	$ 65,934	$ (66)

EXERCISE 2.5

PREPARING FREE CASH FLOW AND FINANCIAL CASH FLOW STATEMENTS

How much free cash flow did the gift shop produce in December? How was this free cash flow used?

Rearrange the company's cash statement to determine its free cash flow and financial cash flow. The result is:

	December
Free Cash Flow	
Cash flow provided by (used for) operations	$ 1,850
Cash flow provided by (used for) investment	0
Cash flow provided by (used for) financial slack	(784)
Net free cash flow	$ 1,066
Financial Cash Flow	
Pay interest	$ (66)
Pay dividends	(1,000)
Net financial cash flow	$(1,066)

Something Special produced $1,066 of free cash flow in December and used this money to pay interest and dividends.

We will use free cash flow and financial cash flow statements as the basis for evaluating operating, investment, and financing decisions throughout this book. By applying financial valuation principles to these cash flows, managers can make decisions that maximize the owners' wealth.

2.5 FINANCIAL STATEMENT ANALYSIS

Managers and investors analyze a variety of financial statements to extract more information from them. Managers analyze budgets to determine if a company or unit's plans will meet minimum financial performance standards and they analyze reports to determine the causes of favorable and unfavorable variances from their expectations. Investors analyze financial reports to identify a company's strengths and weaknesses and to forecast their future cash flows. Analysts may focus separately on the income statement or balance sheet or examine the relationship between them. In either case, they use the company's plans and past performance and competitors' performance as benchmarks.

Common-Sized Financial Statements

Common-sized financial statements are prepared by dividing each line in the income statement by net sales and each line in the balance sheet by total assets or claims. The results are financial statements expressed in percentage terms rather than a unit of currency. An analyst can look at these percentages and quickly determine where a company's or unit's financial performance differs from the benchmark.

Something Special's common-sized financial statements are given in Table 2.8. These statements show October differed from November and December, probably because it was the company's start-up month.

Ratio Analysis of the Income Statement and Balance Sheet

The income statement and balance sheet are examined jointly in slightly more complicated forms of financial statement analysis. The objective is to measure how profitably or actively a company's financial resources were used by forming ratios of balance sheet and income statement items. Analysts usually begin their investigation by computing return on equity (ROE) because it is a comprehensive measure of financial performance. They then compute supplementary ratios to examine the determinants of ROE.

Calculation and Analysis of Return on Equity   Return on equity (ROE) is defined as net income divided by common equity or net worth.[4] Because it is based on accounting statements, ROE measures the accounting rate of return on the book value of the owners' equity. A high ROE suggests the owners' money was invested profitably although this conclusion is subject to the limitations of accounting statements.

ROE is a comprehensive measure of financial performance for two reasons. First, it describes the owners' rate of return after deducting all operating costs, financing costs, and taxes. That is, ROE relates a company's *residual income* to the amount of investment by its *residual claimants.* Second, ROE is determined by the joint outcome of a company's main activities: cost and asset management and financing choice. This is easy to see if we factor ROE into its constituent parts. The result is

---

[4]Income available to common stockholders should be used in place of net income in the numerator of this ratio if the company has preferred stock outstanding.

Table 2.8   SOMETHING SPECIAL'S COMMON-SIZED FINANCIAL STATEMENTS

Panel A: Income Statements

	October	November	December
Net sales	100.0%	100.0%	100.0%
Cost of goods sold	80.0	80.0	80.0
Gross profit	20.0	20.0	20.0
Selling expenses	17.4	10.0	11.1
Depreciation	1.7	1.0	1.1
Net operating income	0.9	9.0	7.8
Other income	2.6	0.0	0.0
Interest expense	0.4	0.2	0.2
Taxable income	3.1	8.8	7.6
Taxes	1.2	3.5	3.0
Net income	1.9%	5.3%	4.6%

Panel B: Balance Sheets

Assets

	October	November	December
Cash	8.7%	6.9%	7.8%
Accounts receivable	20.2	31.2	30.6
Inventory	37.0	32.9	32.6
Total current assets	65.9	71.0	71.0
Net fixed assets	34.1	29.0	29.0
Total assets	100.0%	100.0%	100.0%

Claims

	October	November	December
Accounts payable	23.1%	30.9%	28.5%
Bank loan	4.6	4.0	4.1
Total current liabilities	27.7	34.9	32.6
Term loan	9.2	8.0	8.1
Total equity	63.0	57.1	59.3
Total claims	99.9%	100.0%	100.0%

Note: Totals may not equal 100.0% due to rounding.

$$\text{ROE} = \frac{\text{Net income}}{\text{Equity}} = \frac{\text{Net income}}{\text{Sales}} \times \frac{\text{Sales}}{\text{Total assets}} \times \frac{\text{Total assets}}{\text{Equity}} \quad [2.3]$$

$$= \text{Net profit margin} \times \text{Total asset turnover} \times \text{Leverage ratio}$$

Equation 2.3 shows that ROE is the product of three ratios. The first two, net profit margin and total asset turnover, describe the amount of net income obtained from each dollar of sales and the amount of sales obtained from each dollar of assets. Their product, net income divided by total assets, equals **return on assets (ROA)**. Companies earn

---

ANALYSIS OF SOMETHING SPECIAL'S RETURN ON EQUITY (ROE)   **Table 2.9**

	ROE*	=	Profit Margin	×	Total Asset Turnover	×	Leverage
October	$\dfrac{\$534}{\$54,534}$	=	$\dfrac{\$534}{\$28,750}$	×	$\dfrac{\$28,750}{\$86,534}$	×	$\dfrac{\$86,534}{\$54,534}$
	0.98%		1.86%		0.33 times		1.59
November	4.61		5.27		0.50		1.75

---

*Due to rounding, return on equity may not equal the product of profit margin, total asset turnover, and leverage.

high profit margins by controlling their costs, and they achieve high asset turnover ratios by using their assets productively. Therefore, the ROA ratio reflects the quality of a company's overall cost and asset management.

The third term, called simply the leverage ratio, describes how many dollars of assets a company obtained for each dollar the owners invested. A leverage ratio equal to 1.0 (assets = equity) means a company used only equity financing; a ratio greater than one means it used both equity and debt. Even though it increases ROE, a high leverage ratio is not necessarily desirable because debt financing also increases risk. Consequently, return on equity reflects a company's financing choice although the leverage ratio itself does not reveal whether that choice was good or bad.

Factoring return on equity into the profit margin, total asset turnover, and leverage ratios is sometimes called *DuPont analysis* because the DuPont company pioneered the use of these ratios to evaluate its operating divisions. We will apply DuPont analysis to business units later in this section. A recent article "In the News" used DuPont analysis to explain the currently high values of ROEs.

The analysis of Something Special's return on equity is presented in Table 2.9. Its ROE improved significantly in November, primarily because its net profit margin improved: The company earned higher profits because its selling expenses remained constant at $5,000 even though its sales nearly doubled from $28,750 to $50,000.

● ———————————————————————————————————— ●   EXERCISE

ANALYSIS OF RETURN ON EQUITY   2.6

Calculate and interpret Something Special's return on equity for December. Use the company's original income statements from Table 2.3 and its balance sheets from Table 2.5.

ROE	=	Profit Margin	×	Total Asset Turnover	×	Leverage ratio
$\dfrac{\$2,034}{\$58,202}$	=	$\dfrac{\$2,034}{\$45,000}$	×	$\dfrac{\$45,000}{\$98,202}$	×	$\dfrac{\$98,202}{\$58,202}$
3.49%		4.52%		0.46 times		1.69

IN THE NEWS

ROES ENTER UNCHARTED TERRITORY

THERE'S NEVER BEEN anything like it. By any number of measures, return on shareholder equity, traditionally the single most important and widely noted benchmark of corporate performance, has sprinted over the past several years to its loftiest level in U.S. history. Look at a few different ROE numbers and gape in wonder: The S&P 400 index of industrials sports a dizzying ROE of 22 percent. The 30 companies that make up the Dow Jones Industrial Average finished with a year-end return of 20.5 percent. There is no precedent for ROE anywhere like this, says James Gipson, president of Pacific Financial Research, a money management firm in Beverly Hills.

The big question is: Are U.S. businesses's racy ROE numbers sustainable? The short answer: probably not, certainly not forever. But to understand why, you have to smoke out the several factors that have been driving ROE. Back in 1903, an E.I. DuPont de Nemours senior accounting executive, Donaldson Brown, came up with a concept that helps do just that. He figured that return on equity can be arrived at by multiplying profit margin (profits as a percent of sales) and turnover (sales as a percent of assets, or, to put it another way, the rate at which a company's resources are turned into sales). Later, DuPont accountants discovered that another variable, leverage (assets as a multiple of equity), could be added to the formula to factor in the effect of financing costs on returns. Apply the overall formula today and you find all sorts of salutary tidings for the nation's ROE: Leverage and turnover are high, and profit margins are going as wild as sophomores on spring break.

Today's big news is that the current strong profits are largely a result of powerfully expanding mar-

gins. Look at this data from Investors Management Group, a Des Moines money management firm: So far in the 1990s, the growth in profits, at 11.5 percent, has far outstripped the growth in sales, shuffling along at just 5.6 percent.

What's happening with turnover today—the second part of the DuPont formula? Just-in-time inventory practices are still having their beneficent effect, allowing companies to rev sales higher with fewer assets. Here's proof: The turnover of *Fortune*'s top ten corporations rose from 0.757 in 1990 to 0.796 in 1995. Sounds like small potatoes? Bear in mind that with this type of equation, the percentage change in ROE will equal the percentage rise in any one of its variables. Thus, that 5.1% change in the ratio would have raised a 10 percent ROE to 10.5%—not a negligible number when you consider that the difference between a 10 percent and 15 percent ROE spells the difference between mediocrity and stardom.

The last part is leverage, or assets divided by stockholders' equity. Assets have been rising modestly, as you'd expect in a slow-growing economy. But equity is going in the other direction, as vast amounts get scorched off the balance sheets of corporate America through restructuring, accounting charges, and stock buybacks. Result: Higher leverage.

Can the ROE run-up continue? Some very smart people say it can and will: Strategists and economists, brokers and buy-siders alike, are proclaiming a sea change in America's corporate tidings, and nowhere is it written that they can't be right. But a more conservative—and more realistic—approach would be to simply enjoy it while it lasts, and to remember that ROE, like the market itself, can go down as well as up.

Source: Richard S. Teitelbaum, "What's Driving Return on Equity," *Fortune*, April 29, 1996, pp. 271–276. © 1996 Time, Inc. All rights reserved.

Something Special's return on equity was lower in December because its profit margin, total asset turnover, and leverage were lower.

Supplementary Ratios   Equation 2.3 shows that ROE is a comprehensive measure of financial performance and suggests which ratios to examine next. For example, an analyst should focus on the income statement if she determines that a low net profit margin caused a company to have a low return on equity. Alternatively, she should focus on the balance sheet to learn more about how well a company manages its assets and claims if the total asset turnover or leverage ratios were unusual.

A wide variety of supplementary ratios can be used at subsequent stages of financial statement analysis. Appendix 2A provides a brief introduction to some of these ratios now, but you will know more about how to interpret them after you have studied the principles of financial management. Consequently, we will revisit these ratios from time to time as we discuss the financial management of assets and claims.

Incorporating Market Information in Financial Statement Analysis

You know by now that financial statements misrepresent the values of assets and claims because the statements are based on accrual accounting and historical costs. Their true values can only be determined by referring to market prices. Analysts often combine market and financial statement information to address this deficiency. Once again, we can factor return on equity into separate parts to identify two ratios commonly used for this purpose.

$$\text{ROE} = \frac{\text{Net income}}{\text{Book value of equity}}$$

$$= \frac{\text{Net income}}{\text{Market value of equity}} \times \frac{\text{Market value of equity}}{\text{Book value of equity}} \qquad [2.4]$$

$$= \text{Earnings/Price ratio} \times \text{Market-to-book ratio}$$

The first term on the right-hand side of Equation 2.4, the **Earnings/Price ratio (E/P)**, is an estimate of the current rate of return on the *market value* of the owners' equity.[5] This ratio is so well known and widely used that *The Wall Street Journal* reports daily the value of its reciprocal, the P/E ratio, for each stock.

Despite its popularity, the E/P ratio is a poor estimate of the rate of return on the market value of the owners' equity for several reasons. First, net income is based on accrual accounting and therefore subject to all the limitations described earlier. Second, most companies do not pay 100% of their earnings as dividends so the E/P ratio would overstate the owners' current return even if net income equaled net cash flow per share. Both of these objections are overcome by replacing the numerator with

---

[5]This ratio is usually calculated on a per share basis, earnings per share divided by price per share, but the result is the same as the expression in Equation 2.4 because the number of shares outstanding appears in both the numerator and denominator. That is:

$$\text{E/P} = \frac{\text{Earnings per share}}{\text{Price per share}}$$

$$= \frac{\text{Net income divided by number of shares outstanding}}{\text{Market value of equity divided by number of shares outstanding}}$$

$$= \frac{\text{Net income}}{\text{Market value of equity}}$$

dividends, which are paid in cash. *The Wall Street Journal* also reports daily this measure of rate of return, called the **dividend yield**, for each stock. Even the dividend yield has limited value because it still measures the owners' current rate of return, which is less than their total return if the company has investment opportunities that will provide higher future dividends. You will learn how to calculate a better measure of the rate of return on the market value of the owners' equity when we discuss the valuation of common stock in Chapter 9.

The second term on the right-hand side of Equation 2.4, the **market-to-book ratio**, describes how much more than book value investors are willing to pay for a company's common stock. A ratio of 1.3, for example, means investors place a 30 percent premium on the stock. This premium is an estimate of the value a company has created for its shareholders. The market-to-book ratio must be interpreted with care, however, because the denominator of the ratio is based on historical costs. Consequently, a high market-to-book ratio may reveal a genuine market premium or that the company's equity is seriously undervalued by historical costs.

Benchmarks for Financial Statement Analysis

Analysts compare a company's financial ratios to benchmarks to determine which are abnormal. They must choose and interpret the benchmark financial ratios carefully, however, because absolute standards for financial ratios do not exist. This is because successful companies may organize production differently; that is, one company may use more capital equipment than another and therefore have a lower total asset turnover ratio but a higher net profit margin. Another reason for the lack of absolute standards is that equally successful companies can have very different financial statements due to the effects of accrual accounting and historical costs and because they account for the same transactions differently.

For example, consider the alternatives for using depreciation to allocate capital costs to a particular accounting period. The depreciation deduction in internal financial statements may be based on the number of hours equipment is operated if managers believe actual use is the best description of how soon the equipment must be replaced. At the same time, the managers may use accelerated depreciation in the company's tax statements to minimize taxable income early in an asset's life and straight-line depreciation in its annual report to maximize reported income. A similar range of alternatives is available to account for inventories and the cost of goods sold. To complicate matters further, similar companies may use different methods of accounting in their external financial reports.

These potential differences among statements prepared for distinct purposes and by different companies means they must be used with care. Managers must consider these differences when they compare their internal statements to a benchmark company's external statements. Investors and analysts must recognize that external statements provide an imperfect picture of a company's actual financial performance.

These differences across industries and within Something Special's industry—miscellaneous retail—are apparent in Table 2.10.[6] Note that the ranges show there can

---

[6]We cannot compare Something Special's monthly financial ratios to those in Table 2.10, which are based on annual financial statements.

FINANCIAL RATIOS FOR SELECTED INDUSTRIES AND COMPANIES   **Table 2.10**

Panel A: Selected Industries

Industry (sample size)	Profit Margin ×	Total Asset Turnover ×	Leverage =	Return on Equity =	Earnings/ Price Ratio ×	Market-to-Book Ratio
All manufacturing (736)	0.052	0.969	3.136	**0.16**	0.050	3.178
Food and kindred products (58)	0.059	1.061	3.245	**0.20**	0.050	4.067
Apparel and textiles (28)	0.043	1.325	2.235	**0.13**	0.067	1.892
Chemicals and allied products (121)	0.090	0.897	2.582	**0.21**	0.046	4.556
Petroleum and coal products (30)	0.042	1.000	3.097	**0.13**	0.055	2.346
Industrial machinery (162)	0.058	1.047	2.643	**0.16**	0.041	3.925
Electrical equipment (76)	0.082	1.052	2.261	**0.20**	0.052	3.776
All retail (129)	0.029	1.644	3.212	**0.15**	0.058	2.672
Miscellaneous retail (50)	0.036	1.864	2.123	**0.14**	0.063	2.270
Range	0.061	0.967	1.122	**0.08**	0.026	2.664

Panel B: Selected Companies in Miscellaneous Retail Industry

	Profit Margin ×	Total Asset Turnover ×	Leverage =	Return on Equity =	Earnings/ Price Ratio ×	Market-to-Book Ratio
General Host	0.009	1.222	3.953	**0.04**	0.057	0.750
Lillian Vernon	0.061	1.612	1.250	**0.12**	0.107	1.150
Michaels Stores	0.040	1.450	1.927	**0.11**	0.125	0.900
Pier 1 Imports	0.046	1.457	2.172	**0.15**	0.079	1.850
Sanhome, Inc.	0.056	1.543	1.900	**0.16**	0.079	2.070
Range	0.052	0.390	2.703	**0.12**	0.068	1.320

Source: January 1, 1996 edition of Value/Screen III, Value Line Publishing, Inc., copyright 1993.

be more variation in ratio values within a single industry than there is across industry averages.

Using industry average as a benchmark is a time-honored but not always sound approach because of this variability and because both strong and weak companies are included in the average. In addition, each industry average probably includes diversified companies that bear little resemblance to the company or unit being examined. The sources listed in panel A of Exhibit 2.3 provide a wide variety of industry averages for analysts who want to use them as benchmarks in spite of these limitations.

Knowledgeable industry analysts can always construct their own benchmark ratios using only the strongest and most similar competitor or a group of the stronger and more similar ones. Either approach excludes weak and highly diversified companies while the latter approach averages minor differences among the companies to emphasize what they have in common. The sources listed in panel B of Exhibit 2.3 provide complete or partial financial statements for individual companies and can be used to make custom financial ratio benchmarks.

Perhaps the best benchmark available to external analysts is past values of a company's or unit's own financial ratios. Although a company may change its accounting method over time, there should be fewer differences than there are between two or more

Exhibit 2.3

SOURCES FOR BENCHMARK FINANCIAL RATIOS

PANEL A: INDUSTRY AVERAGE FINANCIAL RATIOS

Dun and Bradstreet Industry Norms and Key Business Ratios. Common-sized financial statements and 14 financial ratios for more than 800 industries. Upper and lower quartile and median values are reported separately.

Federal Trade Commission Quarterly Financial Report. Aggregate financial statements for 50 industries. Values for small and large firms are reported separately.

Robert Morris Associates Annual Statement Studies. Sixteen financial ratios for 400 industries. Upper and lower quartile and median values are reported separately.

PANEL B: COMPANY FINANCIAL STATEMENTS

U.S. Securities and Exchange Commission EDGAR Database of Corporate Information (http://www.sec.gov/index.html). U.S. Securities and Exchange Commission filings in electronic format. The SEC's form 10-K contains much of the same information as a company's annual report.

Compact Disclosure. U.S. Securities and Exchange Commission filings by more than 9,000 companies in CD-ROM format.

Moody's Manuals. Excerpts from annual reports and other public disclosures.

Q-Data Corporation SEC-File. Microform copies of financial statements filed with the Securities and Exchange Commission.

Standard & Poor's Corporation Records. Excerpts from annual reports and other public disclosures.

Value Line Investment Survey. Partial financial statements for more than 1,600 companies. Available in print and computer-accessible formats.

---

separate companies. A company or unit also may change its method of production over time, for example, by using more capital equipment. However, detecting and evaluating these changes is a legitimate objective of financial statement analysis.

Finally, internal analysts can use their company's operating and financial plans as a benchmark against which to evaluate its actual financial performance. Variations from this benchmark help managers determine the causes of favorable and unfavorable performance.

Analysis of Business Units

Analyzing business units is more difficult than analyzing an entire company because the units often do not control all the factors that affect their financial performance. They seldom make independent financing decisions and may not control their own investment, revenues, or costs. DuPont analysis adapts financial ratios to these different situations so managers are evaluated only on the elements of financial performance they control. Even with these modifications, the analysis of business unit financial statements is subject to all the limitations previously mentioned.

Independent companies that become business units after they are acquired by another firm may be evaluated by return on equity if the unit's managers retain some control of its financing decisions. The parent company's investment is the unit's equity financing but the managers may still have the authority to negotiate bank loans and lease equipment. These forms of debt financing provide financial leverage, which affects the rate of return on the parent company's equity as shown in Equation 2.3. In this situation, ROE is a valid measure of net financial performance for a business unit.

Business units, whether formerly independent or not, often must obtain 100 percent of their financing from their parent companies. These units may be evaluated by ROA if their managers control all other aspects of their financial performance: Investment, revenues, and costs. ROA, as defined by the product of the first two terms on the right-hand side of Equation 2.3, may be used for this purpose if no interest expenses were allocated to the unit and deducted from revenues to determine its net income. However, if financing costs were assessed against the unit, then they should be removed because the managers did not control them. Financing costs are removed from the return on assets ratio by using the after-tax operating profit margin rather than net profit margin for the first term. The result, sometimes called **return on invested capital (ROIC)** is given by Equation 2.5. This version of return on assets is completely free of financing effects and is therefore a valid measure of net financial performance for business units that control their investment, revenue, and costs.

$$
\begin{aligned}
\text{ROIC} \quad &= \quad \frac{\text{After-tax operating income}}{\text{Total assets}} \\[2mm]
&= \quad \frac{\text{After-tax operating income}}{\text{Sales}} \times \frac{\text{Sales}}{\text{Total assets}} \qquad\qquad \textbf{[2.5]} \\[2mm]
&= \quad \text{After-tax operating profit margin} \times \text{Total asset turnover}
\end{aligned}
$$

By now, you can probably guess that the after-tax operating profit margin is an acceptable measure of net financial performance for business units that control their own revenues and costs but not their level of investment.

There are no simple financial ratios that summarize the performance of business units that control their revenues or costs but not both. This is a particularly troublesome situation when some of the revenues or costs are due to intracompany sales at negotiated prices. A high transfer price shifts the evidence of favorable financial performance from the business unit that buys the commodity to the business unit that sells it and vice versa. With and without complications due to transfer pricing, business units that control either their revenues or costs are often evaluated by comparing their results to their plans.

Some companies now analyze business units by measuring the amount of economic profits they produce. This is a superior approach because it is based on market values and should be affected by fewer of the distortions present in accounting statements. Although no special techniques are required to measure economic profit, many companies use the procedure known as Economic Value Analysis (EVA), which was popularized by a prominent consulting firm.[7] We will closely examine this popular technique in the next chapter when we discuss the time value of money.

---

[7]G. Bennett Stewart III, *The Quest for Value,* HarperBusiness, 1991.

2.6 SUMMARY

The cash statement is the most important financial statement for financial managers and investors because it describes the amount of *cash* paid and received rather than the amount of income allocated to the period. A direct format cash statement describes cash inflows and outflows; an indirect format statement removes the effects of accrual accounting from net income to determine net cash flow. Both types of cash statements have separate entries for cash flows from operations, investment, financing, and net cash flow, which equals the increase or decrease in the cash balance.

Cash statements can be rearranged to recognize the fact that increases and decreases in the cash balance are *planned* changes in financial slack that use and provide cash flows. This rearrangement produces two statements that describe a company's free cash flows and financial cash flows. Free cash flow is the cash flow provided by operations minus the cash used for investments and financial slack. Positive free cash flows can be paid to investors; negative free cash flows require additional financing from them. Financial cash flow is the net cash flow from the financial transactions undertaken to use free cash flow surpluses or to cover free cash flow deficits. Managers use these statements to plan, coordinate, and control their company's financial resources and investors use them to make inferences about a company's financial performance.

Companies also prepare income statements and balance sheets to plan and report their activities. Most income statements are prepared using the accrual method of accounting, which allocates revenues and costs to the accounting period in which a transaction takes place rather than when cash is paid or received. As a result, net income does not equal net cash flow if there were transactions that did not provide or use cash during the period. Managers and investors cannot use the income statement by itself to measure a company's past cash flows or to anticipate its future cash flows for this reason.

Balance sheets measure the book values of a company's assets and claims. Book values are based on historical costs, which may differ greatly from market values. Assets' book values do not equal their market values because financial statements do not account for the effects of obsolescence and inflation and omit assets, such as brand names, that were not created by specific transactions. Inflation and omitted claims, such as future product liability judgments, also distort the book values of claims, which means that managers and investors cannot use the balance sheet to determine a company's or business unit's value.

The cash statement is more informative than either of these other financial statements precisely because the effects of accrual accounting and historical costs are removed.

Finally, managers and investors analyze financial statements to (1) see if the company's plans meet minimum financial performance standards, (2) identify the causes of favorable and unfavorable variances from their expectations, and (3) forecast future cash flows. This analysis often includes some type of ratio analysis with the results compared to benchmarks such as industry averages. The results of financial statement analysis must be interpreted with care because they are subject to all the limitations of accounting statements prepared using accrual accounting and historical costs.

KEY TERMS

Cash statement *24*

Income statement *31*

Balance sheet *34*

Financial slack *42*

Free cash flow *42*

Financial cash flow *42*

Return on equity (ROE) *45*

Return on assets (ROA) *46*

Earnings/Price ratio (E/P)
   49

Dividend yield *50*

Market-to-book ratio *50*

Return on invested capital
   (ROIC) *53*

QUESTIONS AND PROBLEMS

1. Norman Manufacturing Company produces wheel bearings. Assign each of the following transactions to the proper category of the company's direct format June 30 quarterly cash statement.

   (a) Cash dividend paid to common stockholders on April 5.

   (b) Cash purchase of used computer-controlled lathe on May 15.

   (c) Cash sale of wheel bearings on June 20.

   (d) Cash payment of principal and interest to Everyone's Bank on June 15.

   (e) Cash purchase of 20 acres of adjoining property for expansion on April 18.

   (f) Credit sale of wheel bearings on June 29; payment due on July 9.

   (g) Wages paid to machinists on May 30.

   (h) Receipt of cash from selling mortgage bonds on May 20.

   (i) Credit purchase of bearing flanges on June 15; payment due July 15.

2. Stelton David may purchase a metal finishing company in Pennsylvania. The current owners gave Stelton a copy of the company's most recent income statement and balance sheet but he is concerned these statements don't reveal the company's actual performance.

   (a) For what reasons might the company's net sales not equal the cash received from customers?

   (b) For what reasons might the company's cost of goods sold not equal the cash paid to suppliers and employees?

   (c) How should Stelton use the information in the company's balance sheet to correct these discrepancies?

3. The book value of a company's assets usually does not equal the market value of those assets.

   (a) What are some reasons for this discrepancy?

   (b) Why is the discrepancy usually larger for accounts receivable than for cash? For inventory than for accounts receivable? For fixed assets than for inventory?

4. Choose a prominent company and identify some plausible assets and claims that are unlikely to be recognized on its balance sheet.

5. Inflation is one reason historical costs misrepresent the values of assets and claims.

   (a) Explain why inflation causes historical costs to misrepresent the values of inventories and fixed assets.

   (b) Explain why inflation causes historical costs to misrepresent the value of debt.

   (c) Can we ignore the effect of inflation since it misrepresents the values of both assets and claims?

6. Briefly explain the purpose of each step used to prepare an indirect format cash statement.

7. The free cash flow and financial cash flow statements are similar to but different from an ordinary cash statement.

    (a) What are the differences between the free cash flow and financial cash flow statements on one hand and an ordinary cash statement on the other?

    (b) Why are the free cash flow and financial cash flow statements more useful than an ordinary cash statement for financial decision making?

8. How can managers and investors use DuPont analysis to focus their attention on a company's investment, operating, or financing performance?

9. Suppose you manage one division of a large consumer goods company. Suppose also that you are responsible for the division's product mix, pricing, production, and investment in capital equipment but must obtain financing from corporate headquarters. Would you prefer that the CEO evaluate your performance on the basis of the division's:

    (a) Return on equity or return on assets?

    (b) Return on assets or return on invested capital?

10. Can you conclusively determine a company's strengths and weaknesses by comparing its financial ratios to industry averages? Why or why not?

11. Joe and Susan Edwards opened the Old Town Antique Mall on January 2, 1997. They financed this business with $35,000 of their own money and borrowed an additional $4,000 from a bank. The bank loan is due in three years but the interest, computed at 9 percent per year, is paid monthly. The Edwards pay $1,500 a month to rent the building and its fixtures and $300 a month for utilities. They sublet part of the building to other antique dealers for $4,000 per month. Joe and Susan's only capital equipment is a covered trailer they use to transport furniture. They paid $6,000 cash for this trailer on January 2 and will depreciate it over a five-year life using straight-line depreciation. They pay themselves a monthly salary of $3,000.

    The Edwards bought another antique shop's inventory for $30,000 cash on January 2. Subsequently, they purchased furniture, glassware, and old books at auctions and estate sales for $9,000 cash in January, $5,000 cash in February, and $7,000 cash in March. Cash sales in these months were $9,500, $4,200, and $1,800, respectively. Credit card sales, which are collected the following month, were $6,000 in January, $9,500 in February, and $6,700 in March. Tax payments, computed at the rate of 40 percent, were $1,392, $1,326, and $1,137 for the first three months of operation.

    A summary of these operating and financing transactions is given below.

OLD TOWN ANTIQUE MALL QUARTERLY REPORT

Panel A: Operating Transactions

	January	February	March
Sales of merchandise			
Cash	$ 9,500	$ 4,200	$ 1,800
Credit	6,000	9,500	6,700
Total	$15,500	$13,700	$ 8,500
Purchases of merchandise			
Cash	$39,000	$ 5,000	$ 7,000
Credit	0	0	0
Total	$39,000	$ 5,000	$ 7,000

	January	February	March
Merchandise inventory			
Beginning balance	$ 0	$27,909	$23,454
Purchases	39,000	5,000	7,000
Ending balance	27,909	23,454	25,727
Cost of goods sold	$11,091	$ 9,455	$ 4,727
Rental income	$ 4,000	$ 4,000	$ 4,000
Rent and utility expense	$ 1,800	$ 1,800	$ 1,800
Salaries	$ 3,000	$ 3,000	$ 3,000
Capital equipment			
Buy new trailer	$ 6,000	$ 0	$ 0

Panel B: Financing Transactions

	January	February	March
Issue equity	$35,000	$ 0	$ 0
Issue debt			
3-year, 9% term loan	$ 4,000	$ 0	$ 0
Pay interest	$ 30	$ 30	$ 30

(a) Prepare the Old Town Antique Mall's cash statements for January, February, and March using the direct method. Assign the after-tax interest expense to the financing category.

(b) Prepare the Mall's income statements and balance sheets for January, February, and March.

(c) Did net cash flow equal net income each month? Explain why or why not.

12. Billy Bilko imports hand-crafted ladies' bags from Turkey and Afghanistan. Each quarter, he prepares a pro forma cash statement to anticipate cash surpluses and deficits. Billy's forecast for the third quarter of 1998 is given below.

BILKO'S BAGS, INC., CASH STATEMENT

	July	August	September
Net cash flow provided by			
(used for) operations	$5,100	$6,900	$ 4,700
Net cash flow provided by			
(used for) investment	(8,200)	0	3,000
Net cash flow provided by			
(used for) financing	4,100	(4,900)	(8,700)
Planned increase			
(decrease) in cash balance	$1,000	$2,000	$(1,000)

(a) Convert these pro forma cash statements into free cash flow and financial cash flow statements.

(b) In which months does Billy expect a free cash flow deficit? A free cash flow surplus?

13. The treasurer of Two Step Boots Corporation must prepare her financing plans for the second half of 1997. The company's actual income statement and balance sheet for the six months

ending June 1997 and its pro forma income statement and partial balance sheet for the six months ending December 1997 are given below. Two Step's tax rate is 40 percent.

TWO STEP BOOTS CORP. INCOME STATEMENTS

	Six Months Ended:	
	June 30, 1997	**December 31, 1997**
Net sales	$95,130	$77,760
Cost of goods sold	57,078	46,656
Gross profit	38,052	31,104
Selling and administrative expenses	4,770	5,690
Depreciation	7,000	8,000
Net operating income	26,282	17,414
Interest expense	2,700	1,850
Taxable income	23,582	15,564
Taxes	9,433	6,226
Net income	$14,149	$ 9,338

TWO STEP BOOTS CORP. BALANCE SHEETS

	Six Months Ended:	
	June 30, 1997	**December 31, 1997**
Assets		
Cash	$ 1,710	$?
Accounts receivable	20,060	9,980
Inventories	19,050	15,540
Total current assets	40,820	?
Net fixed assets	38,930	50,930
Total assets	$79,750	$?
Claims		
Accounts payable	$11,050	$11,420
Notes payable	17,350	?
Total current liabilities	28,400	?
Long-term debt	24,360	24,360
Common stock	14,930	14,930
Retained earnings	12,060	?
Total equity	26,990	?
Total claims	$79,750	$?

(a) How much cash flow does the treasurer expect operations to provide or use during the last six months of 1997? (Assign after-tax interest expenses to the financing category.)

(b) The production manager told the treasurer that December's net fixed assets include $20,000 of new capital equipment the company will buy for cash during the last six months of the year. In addition, the treasurer intends to increase the company's financial slack by $2,000. How much free cash flow does the treasurer expect to have at the end of 1997?

(c) The treasurer will use the free cash flow to pay the last six months' after-tax interest expense and to pay $5,000 of dividends. She will use any free cash flow that remains to repay all or part of the notes payable. What is the balance of retained earnings and notes payable at the end of 1997 after these transactions?

(d) Complete the balance sheet for the last six months of 1997 given your answers to parts (a) through (c). The treasurer's financial plan is viable if total assets equal total claims.

14. Only Natural, Incorporated produces organic vegetables and dairy products. CEO Jethro LaFrance is conducting a periodic review of the dairy division, known as Hazel Farms Dairy. The dairy division's balance sheets and income statements for the past three quarters are given below. The division did not purchase or sell any capital equipment during this period nor did it obtain any new external financing. Accounts receivable and accounts payable on December 31 were $13,900 and $14,200, respectively. The company's tax rate is 40 percent.

HAZEL FARMS DAIRY INCOME STATEMENTS

	Quarter Ending:		
	March 31	June 30	September 30
Net sales	$86,500	$91,700	$100,600
Cost of goods sold	69,200	73,360	79,480
Gross profit	17,300	18,340	21,120
Selling expenses	8,500	8,000	9,500
Depreciation	8,000	8,000	8,000
Operating income	800	2,340	3,620
Interest expense	700	700	700
Taxable income	100	1,640	2,920
Taxes	40	656	1,168
Net income	$ 60	$ 984	$ 1,752
Minus dividends	0	0	1,500
Addition to retained earnings	$ 60	$ 984	$ 252

HAZEL FARMS DAIRY BALANCE SHEETS

	Quarter Ending:		
	March 31	June 30	September 30
Assets			
Cash	$10,800	$20,350	$ 15,466
Accounts receivable	15,700	19,700	39,200
Total current assets	26,500	40,050	54,666
Gross fixed assets	75,000	75,000	75,000
Accumulated depreciation	8,000	16,000	24,000
Net fixed assets	67,000	59,000	51,000
Total assets	$93,500	$99,050	$105,666

	March 31	June 30	September 30
Claims			
Accounts payable	$15,700	$20,266	$ 26,630
Total current liabilities	15,700	20,266	26,630
Bank loan	9,500	9,500	9,500
Term loan	19,000	19,000	19,000
Common stock	9,075	9,075	9,075
Retained earnings	40,225	41,209	41,461
Total equity	49,300	50,284	50,536
Total claims	$93,500	$99,050	$105,666

(a) Prepare Hazel Farms Dairy's cash statements for these three quarters using the indirect method. Assign the after-tax interest expense to the financing category.

(b) Convert the division's cash statements into free cash flow and financial cash flow statements. Assume the increase in the cash balance was planned. Should Jethro be pleased or disappointed by the change in the division's performance over these three quarters?

(c) Prepare Hazel Farms Dairy's common-sized financial statements. Can Jethro use these statements to determine the reasons for the change in the dairy's performance?

(d) Calculate the dairy's return on equity for each quarter. What explains the change in the division's ROE according to DuPont analysis?

(e) Should Jethro LaFrance place more weight on what he learned from the free cash flow and financial cash flow statements, the common-sized financial statements, or DuPont analysis?

15. Financial ratios that summarize the Ocean Transport Company's performance for 1998 are given below. Use these ratios to reconstruct the company's income statement and balance sheet given its total assets of $10,000. Be as complete as you can.

Net profit margin	14.0%
Total asset turnover	1.8 times
Leverage	2.5

16. Information from Ajax Valve Company's current financial statements and some industry average ratios are given below.

Ajax Valve Company		Industry	
Sales	$1,000	Return on equity	0.181
Cost of sales	700	Net profit margin	0.065
Selling and admin. expense	200	Total asset turnover	1.46
Interest expense	10	Return on assets	0.095
Taxes	26	Assets/equity	1.90
Cash	50		
Receivables	150		
Inventory	200		
Plant and equipment	325		
Total assets	725		
Current liabilities	150		
Long-term bonds	150		
Common equity	425		

(a) Calculate Ajax's return on equity and the three main ratios used in DuPont analysis.

(b) Compare Ajax's ratios to the industry averages and briefly describe the company's apparent strengths and weaknesses.

17. Elizabeth Bakker, executive vice-president and division manager, was preparing for a meeting with the company's CEO. The purpose of the meeting was to review her division's 1997 performance compared to benchmark companies. Elizabeth knew her division had not performed as well as expected but she hoped to mute the CEO's criticism by offering a plan for improvement. Some of the division's financial results and benchmark financial ratios for 1997 are given below.

Division's Results		Benchmark Ratios	
Sales	$20,500	After-tax operating profit margin	13.0%
Cost of sales	13,325	Total asset turnover	2.0
Selling expenses	3,390	Return on invested capital	26.0%
Taxes	1,325		
Total assets	10,000		

(a) Determine the division's ROIC and decompose it into its component parts to explain why it is less than the benchmark ROIC.

(b) What favorable results and future plans should Elizabeth emphasize in her meeting with the CEO?

(c) Suppose Elizabeth can maintain the division's total asset turnover at its current level. To what level must she improve the division's after-tax operating profit margin to match the benchmark companies' performance?

(d) How much must Elizabeth reduce the division's costs (cost of goods sold, selling expenses, or both) to reach the profit target you computed in part (c)?

• ADDITIONAL READING

A good reference on the basics of financial accounting is:
   Gary A. Porter and Curtis L. Norton, *Financial Accounting: The Impact on Decision Makers,* The Dryden Press, 1995.

A comprehensive book on financial statement analysis is:
   George Foster, *Financial Statement Analysis,* 2nd edition, Prentice-Hall, 1986.

You also can apply financial analysis to the cash statement. Two suggestions for how to do so are:
   Terry S. Maness and James W. Henderson, "A Framework for Analyzing the Statement of Cash Flows," *Journal of Cash Management,* May/June 1989, pp. 19–24.
   Brian Belt, "Leverage on the Cash Flow Statement," *Journal of Cash Management,* March/April 1993, pp. 52–58.

APPENDIX 2A

SUPPLEMENTARY FINANCIAL RATIOS

Equation 2.3 showed that return on equity (ROE) is a comprehensive measure of financial performance and suggests which ratios to examine next. For example, an analyst should focus on the income statement to learn more about a company's net profit margin. Alternatively, she should focus on the balance sheet if a company's total asset turnover or leverage ratios are abnormal. This appendix describes some common financial ratios that are often used at this secondary stage of analysis. The ratios we will discuss are defined in Exhibit 2A.1.

INCOME STATEMENT RATIOS

Analysts sometimes compute a company's gross profit margin and operating profit margin to examine the income statement in more detail. Cost of goods sold is the only expense deducted to compute gross profit which means the gross profit margin provides an indication of how well a company controls these costs. Selling and administrative expenses also are deducted to determine operating profit. The operating profit margin therefore describes the profitability of a company's overall operations. Unlike the net profit margin, this ratio is not affected by interest expense and nonoperating profits and losses.

The times interest earned and fixed charge coverage ratios describe a company's ability to pay its financing costs. The times interest earned ratio measures how many times a company's periodic interest expense is covered by the earnings stream from which interest is paid. This earnings stream is sometimes called earnings before interest and taxes although it may be the same as operating profit. Companies often have other financing costs, such as lease payments, that are every bit as obligatory as interest payments. Lease payments and other mandatory costs are included in the denominator of the fixed charge coverage ratio. The larger the value of these ratios, the more comfortably a company can meet its interest or total fixed charges.

Something Special's supplementary income statement ratios for December are computed below.

$$\text{Gross profit margin} = \frac{\$9,000}{\$45,000} = 20.00\%$$

$$\text{Operating profit margin} = \frac{\$3,500}{\$45,000} = 7.78\%$$

$$\text{Times interest earned} = \frac{\$3,500}{\$110} = 31.82 \text{ times}$$

Exhibit 2A.1

SUPPLEMENTARY FINANCIAL RATIOS

INCOME STATEMENT RATIOS

$$\text{Gross profit margin} = \frac{\text{Gross profit}}{\text{Sales}}$$

$$\text{Operating profit margin} = \frac{\text{Net operating income}}{\text{Sales}}$$

$$\text{Times interest earned} = \frac{\text{Earnings before interest \& taxes}}{\text{Interest expense}}$$

$$\text{Fixed charge coverage} = \frac{\text{Earnings before interest \& taxes}}{\text{Interest expense plus other fixed charges}}$$

BALANCE SHEET RATIOS: ASSETS

$$\text{Fixed asset turnover} = \frac{\text{Sales}}{\text{Net fixed assets}}$$

$$\text{Inventory turnover} = \frac{\text{Cost of goods sold}}{\text{Inventory}}$$

$$\text{Days' cost in inventory} = \frac{\text{Inventory}}{\text{Cost of goods sold per day}}$$

$$\text{Receivables turnover} = \frac{\text{Sales}}{\text{Accounts receivable}}$$

$$\text{Days' sales outstanding} = \frac{\text{Accounts receivable}}{\text{Sales per day}}$$

$$\text{Current ratio} = \frac{\text{Current assets}}{\text{Current liabilities}}$$

$$\text{Quick ratio} = \frac{\text{Current assets minus inventory}}{\text{Current liabilities}}$$

BALANCE SHEET RATIOS: CLAIMS

$$\text{Payables turnover} = \frac{\text{Cost of goods sold}}{\text{Accounts payable}}$$

$$\text{Days' payables outstanding} = \frac{\text{Accounts payable}}{\text{Sales per day}}$$

$$\text{Debt/Equity ratio} = \frac{\text{Total debt}}{\text{Common equity}}$$

$$\text{Debt/Total assets} = \frac{\text{Total debt}}{\text{Total assets}}$$

$$\text{Long-term debt/Assets} = \frac{\text{Long-term debt}}{\text{Total assets}}$$

$$\text{Market value debt ratio} = \frac{\text{Total debt}}{\text{Market value of equity}}$$

BALANCE SHEET RATIOS: ASSETS

Most supplementary balance sheet ratios are turnover ratios that are similar to total asset turnover. In each case, these ratios are used to determine the amount of sales activity a company generates from its investment in a particular category of assets. Fixed asset turnover relates sales to net fixed assets while accounts receivable turnover relates sales to accounts receivable. The inventory turnover ratio is similar, but cost of goods sold is used in the denominator because the inventory's value does not include the company's mark-up to selling price.

Variations of the inventory and receivables turnover ratios are expressed in terms of time rather than frequency. Days' cost in inventory (DCI) is an estimate of the amount of time goods are held in inventory. This ratio is calculated by dividing inventory by the cost of goods sold per day or by dividing the number of days in the period by the inventory turnover ratio. Days' sales outstanding (DSO), sometimes known as the average collection period, is an estimate of the amount of time it takes to collect credit sales. This ratio is calculated by dividing accounts receivable by sales per day or by dividing the number of days in the period by the accounts receivable turnover ratio. Analysts can easily evaluate DCI and DSO by comparing them to the length of the company's production process and credit terms, respectively.

Finally, the current and quick ratios are used to determine the extent to which current liabilities are covered by current assets. The current ratio equals total current assets divided by total current liabilities, but inventory is excluded from the numerator of the quick ratio because it is not as liquid as cash, securities, and receivables. Some analysts believe companies are less likely to become insolvent the higher the value of these ratios. We will see later that the current and quick ratios are not reliable solvency measures, however, because they omit cash flow.

Something Special's supplementary balance sheet ratios for December are calculated below.

$$\text{Fixed asset turnover} = \frac{\$45,000}{\$28,500} = 1.58 \text{ times per month}$$

$$\text{Inventory turnover} = \frac{\$36,000}{\$32,000} = 1.125 \text{ times per month}$$

$$\text{Days' cost in inventory} = \frac{\$32,000}{\$36,000/31 \text{ days}} = 27.56 \text{ days}$$

$$= \frac{31 \text{ days}}{1.125 \text{ times per month}} = 27.56 \text{ days}$$

$$\text{Accounts receivable turnover} = \frac{\$45,000}{\$30,000} = 1.50 \text{ times per month}$$

$$\text{Days' sales outstanding} = \frac{\$30,000}{\$45,000/31 \text{ days}} = 20.67 \text{ days}$$

$$= \frac{31 \text{ days}}{1.5 \text{ times per month}} = 20.67 \text{ days}$$

$$\text{Current ratio} = \frac{\$69{,}702}{\$32{,}000} = 2.18$$

$$\text{Quick ratio} = \frac{\$37{,}702}{\$32{,}000} = 1.18$$

BALANCE SHEET RATIOS: CLAIMS

The accounts payable turnover ratio is similar to the accounts receivable turnover ratio except that it describes how many dollars of costs are supported by the company's accounts payable. The days' payables outstanding ratio is a variation that describes this information in terms of days rather than frequency. Something Special's payables ratios are:

$$\text{Accounts payable turnover} = \frac{\$36{,}000}{\$28{,}000} = 1.286 \text{ times per month}$$

$$\text{Days' payables outstanding} = \frac{\$28{,}000}{\$36{,}000/31 \text{ days}} = 24.11 \text{ days}$$

$$= \frac{31 \text{ days}}{1.286 \text{ times per month}} = 24.11 \text{ days}$$

Two supplementary balance sheet ratios that are widely used to examine a company's financial structure are merely variations of the leverage ratio. The debt/equity ratio is simply the leverage ratio minus 1.0:

$$\frac{\text{Total assets}}{\text{Equity}} - 1 = \frac{\text{Debt} + \text{Equity} - \text{Equity}}{\text{Equity}} = \frac{\text{Debt}}{\text{Equity}}$$

The debt/total assets ratio is the debt/equity ratio divided by the leverage ratio:

$$\frac{\text{Debt}}{\text{Equity}} \times \frac{1}{\text{Total assets/Equity}} = \frac{\text{Debt}}{\text{Total assets}}$$

These supplementary ratios therefore provide the same information, in slightly different terms, as the basic leverage ratio.

There are a number of ways to modify these leverage ratios to obtain slightly different information. Long-term debt can be substituted for total debt in the debt/total assets and debt/equity ratios and the market value of the equity can be substituted for the book value of the equity when it appears by itself or in total assets. The latter modification is particularly useful when a company's common stock is worth considerably more than its book value.

Something Special's supplementary leverage ratios for December are computed below.

$$\text{Debt/Equity ratio} = \frac{\$40{,}000}{\$58{,}202} = 0.69$$

$$\text{Debt/Total assets} = \frac{\$40{,}000}{\$98{,}202} = 0.41$$

$$\text{Long-term debt/total assets} \quad = \quad \frac{\$8,000}{\$98,202} \quad = \quad 0.08$$

ANALYZING THE SUPPLEMENTARY RATIOS

You must examine a company's financial ratios systematically to extract the maximum amount of information from them. The analytical structure described by the tree in Exhibit 2A.2 provides a good approach.

First, calculate return on equity because it measures overall performance. Second, compute the profit margin, total asset turnover, and leverage ratios because they are the determinants of ROE. Third, calculate the values of the income statement and balance sheet ratios to examine the profit margin, total asset turnover, and leverage ratios in more detail. Place each ratio in perspective by comparing it to a benchmark such as an industry average or the company's own past history. Finally, synthesize what you have learned about the determinants of the company's ROE. We will compare Something Special's performance in December and November for an illustration.

Something Special's ratios are shown in Table 2A.1. The ratios that appear most significant are marked with an asterisk. The following statement synthesizes and summarizes these results.

> A seasonal decline in sales reduced Something Special's operating and net profit margins because selling expenses were fixed at $5,000. Lower sales in December also

Exhibit 2A.2

ORGANIZATION OF FINANCIAL RATIOS

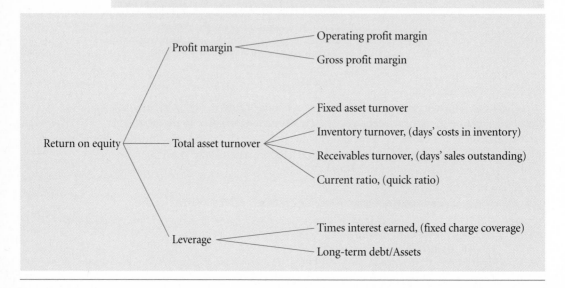

reduced fixed asset, inventory, and receivables turnover, which caused total asset turnover to fall. These factors combined to reduce the company's return on equity. Interest coverage, though lower because of reduced operating profits, is still very high.

Some analysts use ratio analysis to describe a company's strengths and weaknesses and even prescribe corrective actions. This is a little like recommending major surgery after only taking a patient's temperature—ratio analysis does not provide enough information to draw these conclusions. To take just one example, a company may have a low asset turnover ratio because it recently modernized its manufacturing facilities. This is not necessarily a weakness. A better approach is to use financial ratios in an exploratory analysis to decide what issues you want to investigate further. Judgments and recommendations must be based on thorough understanding of the company's situation and the application of sound finance principles.

SOMETHING SPECIAL'S FINANCIAL RATIOS   Table 2A.1

	November	December
Return on equity	4.61%	3.49%
Explanation of ROE		
* Net profit margin	5.27%	4.52%
* Total asset turnover	0.50 times	0.46 times
Leverage	1.75	1.69
Evaluation of Net Profit Margin		
Gross profit margin	20.00%	20.00%
* Operating profit margin	9.00%	7.78%
Evaluation of Total Asset Turnover		
* Fixed asset turnover	1.72	1.58
* Inventory turnover	1.21	1.13
* Receivables turnover	1.60	1.50
Current ratio	2.03	2.18
Evaluation of Leverage		
Long-term debt/Assets	0.08	0.08
Times interest earned	40.91	31.82

- QUESTIONS AND PROBLEMS

    1. The president of Aoki Manufacturing Company has asked you, his executive assistant, to evaluate the company's performance for 1996 and 1997 in comparison to its industry peers. The company's financial statements and some industry average financial ratios are given below.

AOKI MANUFACTURING COMPANY INCOME STATEMENTS

	1996	1997
Net sales	$29,000	$30,500
Cost of goods sold	19,500	20,960
Gross profit	9,500	9,540
Selling expenses	5,600	5,400
Depreciation	900	1,000
Net operating income	3,000	3,140
Interest expense	600	840
Taxable income	2,400	2,300
Taxes	816	782
Net income	$ 1,584	$ 1,518
Minus dividends	950	950
Addition to retained earnings	$ 634	$ 568

AOKI MANUFACTURING COMPANY BALANCE SHEETS

	1996	1997
Cash	$ 800	$ 120
Accounts receivable	3,200	3,800
Inventories	4,050	6,250
Total current assets	8,050	10,170
Gross fixed assets	12,500	13,300
Accumulated depreciation	3,600	4,600
Net fixed assets	8,900	8,700
Total assets	$16,950	$18,870
Accounts payable	$ 1,250	$ 1,350
Accruals	350	502
Notes payable	600	200
Total current liabilities	2,200	2,052
Bonds	5,500	7,000
Common stock	4,250	4,250
Retained earnings	5,000	5,568
Total equity	9,250	9,818
Total claims	$16,950	$18,870

INDUSTRY AVERAGE FINANCIAL RATIOS

Profit margin	6.6%
Gross profit margin	33.8%
Operating profit margin	12.8%
Total asset turnover	1.67 times
Fixed asset turnover	3.68 times
Inventory turnover	3.23 times
Receivables turnover	8.47 times
Leverage	1.86
Long-term debt/Total assets	0.35
Current ratio	4.86
Times interest earned	4.64 times
Return on equity	20.6%

(a) Perform a DuPont analysis of Aoki for 1996 and 1997. Which areas warrant further investigation?

(b) Compute Aoki's supplementary financial ratios, organizing your results as shown in Exhibit 2A.2. Highlight the factors that seem to explain the change in the company's performance from 1996 to 1997.

(c) Write a one-paragraph report to the president summarizing your conclusions.

2. The U.S. Securities and Exchange Commission (SEC) requires public companies to file 10-K reports that contain their financial statements and other information. Many of these reports are available on the Internet at the SEC's site, http://www.sec.gov/index.html. Visit this site and click on "EDGAR Database of Corporate Information."

(a) Choose two companies from the same industry and retrieve their 10-K reports from the EDGAR Database.

(b) Perform a complete ratio analysis of each company, organizing your work as shown in Exhibit 2.5.

(c) Synthesize your results and succinctly explain why the companies' ROEs are different.

THE TIME VALUE OF MONEY

The *Wall Street Journal* reported on January 12, 1994, that the Mellon Bank Corporation will refund all the interest paid over 20 years by consumers who use its CornerStone MasterCard.[1] The bank said the rebate would equal $8,667 for the average cardholder who pays 17.9 percent annual interest on an outstanding balance of $2,421. Gerri Detweiler, executive director of the Bankcard Holders of America, was quoted in the article as saying, "Consumers are going to love it." As a result, "Mellon's going to get a quick hit in gathering accounts and building balances at a high rate of interest," said James Daly, editor of the trade journal *Credit Card News*.

How can consumers determine whether or not they should love this credit card? How can Mellon Bank determine the cost of the rebate and its effect on the rate of return the bank will earn on its credit card loans? We will answer these questions later after you have mastered the techniques for analyzing the time value of money. You can look ahead to page 106 now to check the answer, but it is best to wait so you will understand the calculations and see how easy they really are.

The preceding example relates to personal finance and banking but time value of money problems arise in all areas of finance. Using time value of money techniques to estimate the value of an asset is the most fundamental of all finance problems. Operating and financial managers in manufacturing and service companies confront this problem when they evaluate investment proposals and consider alternative ways to finance their companies' assets. Similarly, investment and portfolio managers must estimate the values of stocks and bonds to decide which to buy or sell.

The financial approach to valuation is based on the assumption that real and financial assets are valued for the free cash flows they provide. The reasoning is simple: You cannot "consume" a machine, but you can operate the machine to generate cash flows that can be used to pay for any type of consumption such as food, shelter, clothing, entertainment, etc. Valuing these cash flows is difficult because they occur at different

---

[1]Valerier Reitman, "Want Interest Back on Your Credit Card after 20 Years' Use?" *The Wall Street Journal*, January 12, 1994, p. B2.

points in time and with varying degrees of certainty. This chapter explains how to deal with the first problem by accounting for the time value of money; Chapters 4, 5, and 6 describe how uncertainty and other factors affect the rates of return used in time value of money analysis.

The main valuation procedure we'll develop here and use throughout the text is net present value analysis. This procedure directs resources to their most productive use and measures how much an asset contributes to its owner's current wealth. Importantly, net present value analysis is a decision rule that can be delegated to others with the assurance that, if they apply the rule correctly, they will make the same decisions as the owners. This enables owners to hire professional managers and permits managers to decentralize decision making within their firms.

Sections 3.1 and 3.2 of this chapter provide the conceptual foundation for time value of money analysis. Understanding these concepts is essential to fully appreciate the benefits of valuation based on finance principles. Sections 3.3 and 3.4 show how to apply net present value analysis and other techniques to realistic problems. You will learn how to calculate the amount of savings required for retirement, how to compute effective annual interest rates, how to determine the net present value of investments, and how to amortize a loan, among other applications.

3.1   THE BASICS OF TIME VALUE OF MONEY ANALYSIS

Time value of money analysis is based on the simple principle that a dollar that can be spent or invested today is worth more than a dollar that cannot be spent or invested until later. We will use this principle in this section to perform elementary future value and present value analyses. By beginning at a basic level, you will clearly see the principle at work and learn the building blocks for performing more complicated analyses later.

Why Money Has Time Value

Cash that is available today is worth more than the same amount of cash that is available later because today's cash can be invested to earn income. For example, $1,000 invested at a 12 percent rate of return for one year will earn $120 and thereby grow to $1,120 ($1,000 × 1.12). Therefore, $1,000 today is worth $120 more than $1,000 in one year when the rate of return is 12 percent. The difference between these amounts reflects the time value of money.

This simple illustration of the time value of money has all the elements of more complicated, realistic problems. These elements are the amounts and timing of the cash flows ($1,000 now and $1,200 in one year) and the rate of return that relates the cash flows to one another (12 percent). The $1,000 is the **present value (PV)** and the $1,120 is the **future value (FV)** at time t (FV_t).

The rate of return (r) in time value of money problems is the investor's **opportunity cost** because it is the amount, stated in percentage terms, that the investor loses if he cannot take advantage of his next best opportunity. In the current example, an investor who is paid $1,000 in one year incurs a $120 opportunity cost because he cannot invest the money today to earn a 12 percent rate of return. We could measure this opportunity cost in absolute terms, $120, but we usually will use the rate of return itself, 12 percent, because it is not affected by the size of the investment.

The rate of return we use as an opportunity cost in time value of money calculations must be the company's or investor's next best alternative. This opportunity cost may be the rate of return that can be earned by purchasing another investment or the interest rate that can be saved by repaying a loan. In either case, the opportunity cost must reflect market-wide standards of financial performance to ensure the best comparable investment or repayment opportunities are considered. We will discuss in detail the factors that affect the opportunity cost in Chapters 4, 5, and 6.

Computing Future Values

You have already successfully computed the future value of a cash flow if you followed the illustration of why money has time value. A formal description of the calculation is given by Equation 3.1.

$$FV_1 = CF_0 \times (1 + r) \qquad \text{[3.1]}$$
$$= \$1,000 \times (1.12) = \$1,120$$

We will extend this equation later to compute future values more than one period away.

Before leaving our simple example, we will use it to demonstrate how to draw a *cash flow time line,* which depicts the amounts and timing of a project's cash flows and their present or future values. A typical example of a time line is given in Exhibit 3.1. Time 0 is today when cash flow 0 (CF_0) is paid or received, time 1 is the end of the first time period when cash flow 1 (CF_1) is paid or received, and so on. The length of each time period is determined by how frequently interest is computed. For example, the time periods are one year in length if interest is computed annually.

The cash flow time line for the current example is provided in Exhibit 3.2. The $1,000 cash flow at time 0 has a future value of $1,120 at the end of period 1, given a rate of return of 12 percent per year.

Exhibit 3.1

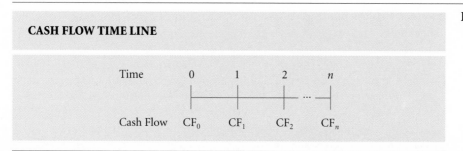

CASH FLOW TIME LINE

Time	0	1	2	n
Cash Flow	CF_0	CF_1	CF_2	CF_n

Exhibit 3.2

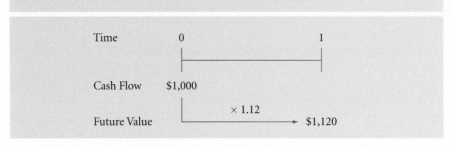

FUTURE VALUE OF $1,000 AT 12 PERCENT INTEREST

Time	0	1

Cash Flow $1,000

× 1.12

Future Value $1,120

EXERCISE

3.1   **COMPUTING FUTURE VALUES**

Constitutional Vending Company must post a $10,000 bond to sell souvenirs at the city convention center. They receive the money back plus 3 percent interest after 12 months. Diagram this problem on a cash flow time line and determine how much cash the company will receive in 12 months.

$10,000 $?

Future value = $10,000 × 1.03 = $10,300.

The convention center will return $10,300 to Constitutional Vending Company in one year.

Computing Present Values

Calculating the present value of a future cash flow is simple because it is the exact opposite of calculating a future value. Compare the equation for present value, given below, to Equation 3.1.

$$PV = CF_1/(1 + r)$$

Dividing a future cash flow by one plus the rate of return to determine its present value is called *discounting*. For this reason, the rate of return or opportunity cost is sometimes called the discount rate.

Determining the present value of a future cash flow may seem unfamiliar, but it is a common form of time value of money analysis. Banks perform this analysis to determine the principal of a loan that will be repaid with interest and individuals do the same

Exhibit 3.3

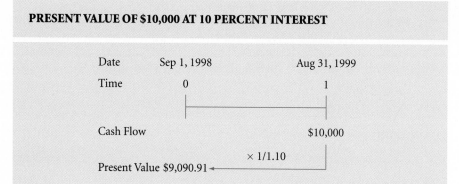

PRESENT VALUE OF $10,000 AT 10 PERCENT INTEREST

to determine how much they must deposit to reach a future savings goal. We'll look at examples of each of these problems.

A bank that will be paid $10,000 when a one-year loan matures cannot give the borrower $10,000 when the loan is initiated if it intends to earn interest. Instead, it can only lend the borrower the *present value* of $10,000 computed at the interest rate on the loan. Assuming the interest rate is 10 percent, the present value of the loan is

$$PV = \$10,000/1.10 = \$9,090.91.$$

The bank can lend the borrower exactly $9,090.91 because the future $10,000 cash flow is exactly enough to repay the principal of the loan ($9,090.91) plus 10 percent interest on the principal ($909.09). The cash flow time line for this loan is shown in Exhibit 3.3. The $10,000 cash flow at time one has a present value of $9,090.91, given an opportunity cost of 10 percent per year.

An alternative explanation for the discounting process is that the bank knows that the cash flow at the end of year 1 must cover both the principal (P) and interest (I) of the loan. The interest is the amount of the principal multiplied by the bank's interest rate, r. The bank knows the amount of the future cash flow and the interest rate so it can solve for the amount of the principal.

$$P + I = CF_1$$
$$P + P \times r = CF_1$$
$$P \times (1 + r) = CF_1$$
$$P = CF_1/(1 + r)$$
$$= \$10,000/1.10 = \$9,090.91$$

The principal of the loan is the present value of the future cash flow, as determined above.

Parents who must have $20,000 on August 31, 1999, to pay their daughter's college tuition must perform a similar analysis to determine how much to deposit on September 1, 1998. They want their deposit plus one year's interest on their deposit to equal $20,000.

$$\text{Deposit} \times (1 + r) = \$20,000$$

If the interest rate on their savings account is 8 percent per year, then they must deposit $18,518.52 ($20,000/1.08) on September 1, 1998, to have $20,000 in the account on August 31, 1999. The interest they earn on their deposit, $1,481.48, makes up the difference between their $18,518.52 and the $20,000 they need.

EXERCISE • —————————————————————————— •

3.2   **COMPUTING PRESENT VALUES**

Joel Shank must have $120,000 in one year to remodel his dry cleaning business. Diagram this problem on a cash flow time line and determine how much cash he must deposit today if his account earns 9 percent interest per year.

$$\text{Present value} = \$120,000/1.09 = \$110,091.74$$

Joel must deposit $110,091.74 today to have $120,000 in one year if his account earns 9 percent interest.

• ———— •

Computing and Interpreting Net Present Values

Most business projects have cash flows that occur today *and* in the future. We analyze this type of project by computing the present value of its future cash flow and adding the cash flow at time 0. The result is the project's **net present value** (**NPV**). The NPV of a typical investment project, which has a cash inflow at time 1 and a cash outflow at time 0, as described by Equation 3.2.

$$\text{NPV} = \text{CF}_1/(1 + r) - \text{CF}_0 \qquad \text{[3.2]}$$

Suppose Mark Lane can purchase 20 cows today for $13,000 and sell them in one year for $16,120 cash. What is the net present value of his investment if the rate of return on his next best alternative (raising pigs) is 15 percent per year? The answer is computed below and diagrammed on the cash flow time line in Exhibit 3.4.

$$\text{NPV} = \$16,120/1.15 - \$13,000 = \$1,017.39$$

A logical interpretation is attached to this $1,017.39 net present value. Stated in present value terms, it is the amount by which the cattle project's future cash flow exceeds Mark's opportunity cost. Here's why: If Mark bought pigs to earn his next best 15 percent rate of return, his $13,000 would grow to $14,950 ($13,000 × 1.15) at time 1. The cattle project actually provides $16,120 of cash, which is an excess of $1,170 ($16,120 − $14,950). The present value of this excess cash flow is $1,017.39 ($1,170/1.15), the project's NPV.

Exhibit 3.4

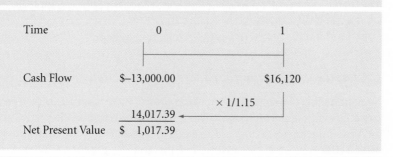

NET PRESENT VALUE OF MARK LANE'S INVESTMENT

Time	0	1

Cash Flow $-13,000.00 $16,120

× 1/1.15

14,017.39

Net Present Value $ 1,017.39

A project that has a positive net present value provides cash flows that more than cover its opportunity cost. Such a project should be undertaken because it is more profitable, in present value terms, than the investor's or company's next best alternative. In contrast, investors and companies should avoid projects that have negative NPVs because they do not cover their opportunity costs. For example, suppose Karla Allen can buy a coin collection from an estate for $8,500 and sell it next year for $9,200. She will pay for the coins by cashing in a certificate of deposit that earns 9 percent per year. Is this a good investment? The answer is no because at Karla's opportunity cost of 9 percent per year, the net present value of investing in the coin collection is negative.

$$NPV = \$9,200/1.09 - \$8,500 = \$-59.63$$

The reason this investment has a negative NPV is easy to see. By leaving the $8,500 in the certificate of deposit, Karla will have $9,265 next year ($8,500 × 1.09). This is $65.00 more than she can get by selling the coin collection then. The present value of her $65 opportunity loss is $-59.63, the net present value of investing in the coin collection.

COMPUTING NET PRESENT VALUES

EXERCISE

3.3

Modern Foliage Supply purchases 10,000 small shrubs annually for $125,000, allows them to grow an additional year, and then wholesales them to nurseries for $145,000. Diagram this project on a cash flow time line and determine its net present value if the company's opportunity cost is 12 percent. Are the shrubs a good investment?

Net present value = $145,000/1.12 − $125,000

Net present value = $4,464.29

The shrubs are a good investment project for Modern Foliage Supply because the net present value is positive.

● ———————— ●

Computing and Interpreting Internal Rates of Return

Sometimes it is convenient to evaluate a project by comparing its own rate of return to the investor's opportunity cost. This is usually an acceptable alternative to computing an NPV if the rate of return is calculated in a specific way called the **internal rate of return (IRR),** which is the discount rate that causes a project's NPV to equal zero. For a one-period investment project, such as we are considering in this section, the solution is

$$\text{NPV} = 0 = \frac{\text{CF}_1}{(1 + \text{IRR})} - \text{CF}_0. \qquad [3.3]$$

Rearranging terms, the IRR of a one-period project is:

$$\text{IRR} = \frac{\text{CF}_1 - \text{CF}_0}{\text{CF}_0}. \qquad [3.4]$$

This equation says that a one-period project's internal rate of return equals its cash profit divided by its initial cost. In other words, the IRR measures a project's cash profitability per dollar of investment. This is the ordinary way to calculate and interpret the rate of return on a one-period investment so the IRR has a familiar explanation even if the terminology is new. Companies and investors should accept projects that have IRRs greater than the opportunity cost.

The IRR of Mark Lane's investment in cows is:

$$\text{IRR} = \frac{\$16,120 - \$13,000}{\$13,000} = 0.2400, \text{ or } 24.00\%.$$

The 24 percent rate of return provided by investing in cattle is greater than the 15 percent rate of return that Mark can earn on his next best alternative of raising pigs. Therefore, the cow project more than covers Mark's opportunity cost, and he should pursue this venture.

We should arrive at the opposite conclusion if we compare the coin collection's internal rate of return to Karla Allen's opportunity cost. The IRR of this investment is:

$$\text{IRR} = \frac{\$9,200 - \$8,500}{\$8,500} = 0.0824, \text{ or } 8.24\%.$$

This rate of return is less than the 9 percent Karla can earn by keeping her certificate of deposit so she should not buy the coin collection as we expected.

COMPUTING INTERNAL RATES OF RETURN

Compute the IRR of Modern Foliage Supply's investment in shrubs described in Exercise 3.3.

First, set the project's net present value equal to zero.

$$\text{NPV} = \${-}125{,}000 + \$145{,}000/(1 + \text{IRR}) = 0$$

You can use algebra to solve this equation because there are only two cash flows.

$$\text{IRR} = \frac{\$145{,}000 - \$125{,}000}{\$125{,}000} = 0.1600, \text{ or } 16.00\%$$

The internal rate of return is greater than the company's opportunity cost, which indicates the shrubs are a good investment.

It is no coincidence that the NPV and IRR calculations lead to the same conclusion about these investment projects. Net present value expresses the amount by which the project's cash flows more than cover the opportunity cost in dollars, and the internal rate of return expresses this difference in percentage terms. The consistency between the NPV and IRR is assured when you evaluate single-period projects.

Perhaps the best way to see the consistency between NPV and IRR is to prepare a *net present value profile*, a graph of a project's NPV as a function of the opportunity cost.[2] The easiest way to prepare an NPV profile is to use the graphing function in a spreadsheet program. If you must prepare one by hand, it helps to know how to compute the vertical and horizontal intercepts. The vertical intercept, the project's NPV at $r = 0$, is simply the sum of the project's cash flows:

$$\text{NPV} = \text{CF}_0 + \text{CF}_1/(1 + r) = \text{CF}_0 + \text{CF}_1$$

where $r = 0$.

The horizontal intercept, the rate of return at which the project's NPV is zero, is simply its IRR. You determine the coordinates of other points on the graph by computing the project's NPV at various discount rates.

The NPV profile for Mark Lane's cattle project is shown in Exhibit 3.5. You can see that the project's NPV is positive only if Mark's opportunity cost is less than the IRR.

---

[2]Another way to see the consistency between NPV and IRR is to subtract Equation 3.3 from Equation 3.2 and rearrange terms.

$$\text{NPV} - 0 = \frac{\text{CF}_1}{(1 + r)} - \text{CF}_0 - \left[\frac{\text{CF}_1}{(1 + \text{IRR})} - \text{CF}_0 \right]$$

$$= \frac{\text{CF}_1(\text{IRR} - r)}{(1 + r) \times (1 + \text{IRR})}$$

The second equation shows that a project's NPV is greater than, equal to, or less than zero only if its IRR is greater than, equal to, or less than the opportunity cost.

Exhibit 3.5

NET PRESENT VALUE PROFILE OF MARK LANE'S INVESTMENT PROJECT

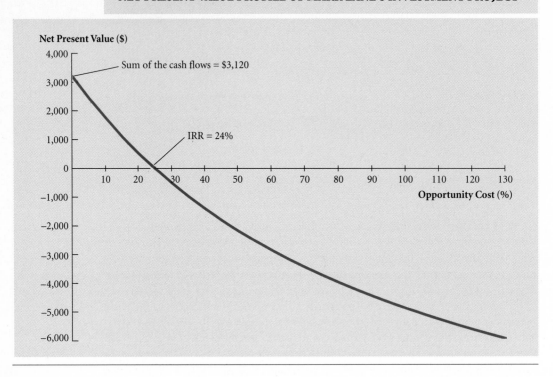

EXERCISE

3.5   PREPARING A NET PRESENT VALUE PROFILE

Prepare the net present value profile for Modern Foliage Supply's shrub project.

The vertical intercept of the project's NPV profile is the sum of the cash flows, $20,000. The horizontal intercept is the project's internal rate of return, calculated as 16.00 percent in Exercise 3.4. The project's NPV at some other opportunity costs are:

Opportunity Cost	Net Present Value
0.00%	$20,000.00
5.00	13,095.24
10.00	6,818.18
16.00	0
20.00	−4,166.67
30.00	−13,461.54

Plotting these points and connecting them with a smooth line gives the project's net present value profile.

NPV PROFILE OF MODERN FOLIAGE SUPPLY'S SHRUB PROJECT

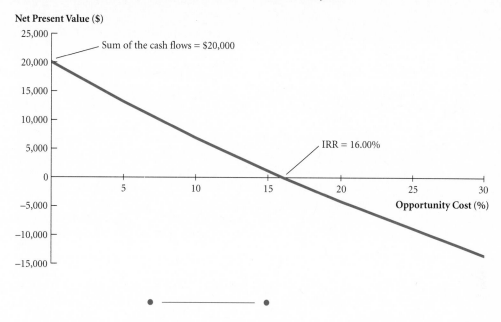

3.2 PRINCIPLES OF TIME VALUE OF MONEY ANALYSIS

So far, you have learned how to use NPV or IRR to determine whether a project's cash flows cover a company's or investor's opportunity cost. This idea, that a project is acceptable only if it is better than the company's or investor's next best alternative, is certainly reasonable. But there is more to it than that. This section shows that choices based on net present value analysis direct resources to their most productive use and that NPV measures the increase in a company's or investor's wealth. Given these characteristics, NPV analysis is a method of making financial decisions that can be delegated to professional managers.

Net Present Value and Economic Profit

We discussed economic profit and maximization of the owners' wealth qualitatively in Chapter 1 and concluded they are one and the same. Now we can quantitatively establish this connection. You will see that the NPV of an investment or financing choice equals the present value of the economic profits it creates. You also will see that NPV measures a decision's effect on the owners' wealth. Consequently, we can rely on NPV to direct society's resources to their most productive use and to meet the needs of the owners for a competitive rate of return on their investment.

   Remember that economic profit is defined as revenue minus actual costs minus opportunity costs. We can adapt this definition to our use by working with cash rather than accounting revenues and costs. The result is

$$\text{Economic profit} = \text{Cash revenue} - \text{Cash costs} - \text{Opportunity costs}$$
$$= CF_1 - CF_0 - r \times CF_0$$
$$= CF_1 - CF_0 \times (1 + r)$$

where CF_1 = net free cash inflow at time 1
  CF_0 = net free cash outflow at time 0
  r = opportunity cost stated as a rate of return.

Economic theory says that a company should adopt a project with a positive economic profit because the value of the goods and services it provides (CF_1) is greater than the value of the goods and services it uses ($CF_0 \times (1 + r)$). Conversely, economic theory says that companies should not adopt a project with a negative economic profit. Companies direct society's resources to their most productive use when they make decisions this way.

Economic profit is measured, as profits are, at the end of the period. It is a future value. Discounting economic profit at the opportunity cost expresses it in present value terms. The result is:

$$PV(\text{economic profit}) = \frac{CF_1 - CF_0 \times (1 + r)}{(1 + r)}$$

$$= \frac{CF_1}{(1 + r)} - CF_0$$

$$= NPV.$$

That is, the present value of economic profit equals net present value.

The fact that a project's NPV equals the present value of its economic profit is a very important relationship. It means that projects with positive NPVs provide positive economic profits and vice versa. Consequently, decisions based on net present value direct society's resources to their most productive uses. This relationship provides a basis for using NPV analysis that is more comprehensive than we obtain by focusing on the interests of individual investors and companies.

NPV and the Owner's Wealth

Net present value measures a project's worth in terms of current money even though some cash flows will not be received until later. Computing NPV is not simply an academic exercise, however, because the owner can obtain immediate access to this money by borrowing against the project's future cash flows in the financial market. The amount of additional cash the investor can obtain this way equals the project's NPV! Consequently, net present value not only indicates that a project provides for the efficient allocation of resources, but also measures the amount by which the project increases the owner's wealth. The following example illustrates this important relationship.

Jerrie Atrick owns 10 percent of Lamplighter Care, Inc., a company that provides home health care services to the elderly. The company's cash flows from operations, which are payments under a government contract on a cost-plus basis, are $100,000 at the end of 1998 and $125,000 at the end of 1999. Assuming the company will accept

---

JERRIE ATRICK'S INITIAL CASH FLOW PATTERN   **Table 3.1**

Panel A: Lamplighter Care, Inc.

	1998	1999
Free Cash Flow		
Cash flow provided by (used for) operations	$100,000	$125,000
Cash flow provided by (used for) investment	0	0
Cash flow provided by (used for) financial slack	0	0
Net free cash flow	$100,000	$125,000
Financial Cash Flow		
Pay dividends	$100,000	$125,000

Panel B: Jerrie Atrick's Cash Flows

	1998	1999
Dividends from Lamplighter	$ 10,000	$ 12,500

---

no new investments, its free cash flows equal the cash flows provided by operations. The company has no debt so it can distribute the free cash flows to the owners as dividends. Jerrie's share of these dividends is $10,000 and $12,500 at the end of 1998 and 1999. The company's situation and Jerrie's cash flows are described in Table 3.1.

The cash flow pattern described in Table 3.1 is only one among many possibilities available to Jerrie Atrick. She can, for example, issue a one-year $4,000 promissory note at the market rate of interest (say 10 percent) and use the proceeds to increase her 1998 cash flow to $14,000. Then, her 1999 net cash flow will be only $8,100 because she must repay the loan with interest ($8,100 = $12,500 – $4,000 × 1.1). Alternatively, Jerrie can buy a one-year $4,000 promissory note to shift her cash flows in the opposite direction. This transaction reduces her 1998 net cash flow to $6,000 but increases her 1999 net cash flow to $16,900 when the loan is repaid ($12,500 + $4,000 × 1.1).

Table 3.2 shows the results of Jerrie's transactions. Note that Lamplighter Care, Inc., does not have to change its policies to provide these alternative cash flow patterns to Jerrie. She can obtain them by conducting her own financial market transactions.

The three cash flow patterns we've examined and all other possibilities are described by the line in Exhibit 3.6. The slope of this line is $-(1 + r)$ or -1.10, which reflects the rate of interest at which Jerrie can exchange present for future cash flows. The line's vertical intercept is the maximum amount of cash flow she can obtain in 1999 by lending all of her 1998 dividends at the market rate of interest. The horizontal intercept is the maximum amount of cash flow she can obtain in 1998 by using all of her 1999 dividends to repay a loan. These extreme points, which are future and present values, are computed below.

$$FV_1 = \$10,000 \times 1.10 + \$12,500 = \$23,500$$
$$PV = \$10,000 + \$12,500/1.10 = \$21,364$$

Table 3.2   ALTERNATIVE CASH FLOW PATTERNS AVAILABLE TO JERRIE ATRICK

Panel A: Borrow to Increase Current Dividends

	1998	1999
Dividends from Lamplighter	$10,000	$12,500
Issue 1-year note at 10%	4,000	0
Repay note	0	(4,400)
Net cash flow	$14,000	$ 8,100

Panel B: Lend to Increase Future Dividends

	1998	1999
Dividends from Lamplighter	$10,000	$12,500
Buy 1-year note at 10%	(4,000)	0
Note is repaid	0	4,400
Net cash flow	$ 6,000	$16,900

The present value of the dividends Jerrie will receive from the company is a particularly important number because it equals her wealth—the cash equivalent of her ownership stake in the company. Maximizing *this* value is the goal of financial management.

Now suppose Lamplighter Care, Inc., learns it can obtain an additional government contract to deliver hot meals to the elderly. This business will require an investment of $75,000 at the end of 1998 and provide cash flow from operations of $91,300 at the end of 1999. Should the company accept this project? How will it affect Jerrie's wealth?

We answer the first question by computing the project's NPV using the market opportunity cost of 10 percent. The result is

$$NPV = \$91,300/1.10 - \$75,000 = \$8,000.$$

The positive NPV tells us that Lamplighter should accept this investment project.

We determine how this decision will affect Jerrie's wealth by revising Table 3.1 to incorporate the investment project's cash flows. The result is given in Table 3.3. Lamplighter's 1998 free cash flow is reduced to $25,000 because $75,000 of cash is used for investment. The following year's free cash flow is increased to $216,300, however, because the project provides an additional $91,300 of operating cash flows. These cash flows can be paid as dividends and Jerrie's share is $2,500 and $21,630 at the end of 1998 and 1999.

Jerrie Atrick's wealth is the present value of her dividends, or $22,164 ($2,500 + $21,630/1.1). This is an improvement in her wealth of $800 ($22,164 − $21,364), which exactly equals her 10 percent share of the project's net present value.

NPV and the Separation of Decision Making

At first, you may believe Jerrie's company cannot accept this project (even though it has a positive NPV and increases her wealth) because it reduces her 1998 dividend to only

Exhibit 3.6

ALTERNATIVE CASH FLOW PATTERNS AVAILABLE TO JERRIE ATRICK

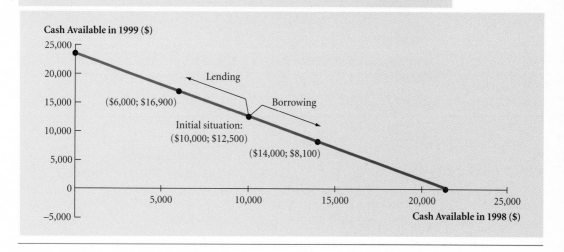

Cash Available in 1999 ($)

- ($6,000; $16,900)
- Lending
- Borrowing
- Initial situation:
  ($10,000; $12,500)
- ($14,000; $8,100)

Cash Available in 1998 ($)

Table 3.3

JERRIE ATRICK'S CASH FLOW PATTERN WITH HOT MEALS INVESTMENT PROJECT

Panel A: Lamplighter Care, Inc., with New Investment

	1998	1999
Free Cash Flow		
Cash flow provided by (used for) operations	$100,000	$216,300
Cash flow provided by (used for) investment	(75,000)	0
Cash flow provided by (used for) financial slack	0	0
Net free cash flow	$ 25,000	$216,300
Financial Cash Flow		
Pay dividends	$ 25,000	$216,300

Panel B: Jerrie Atrick's Cash Flows

Dividends from Lamplighter	$ 2,500	$ 21,630

$2,500. However, the company can accept the investment project and let Jerrie use the financial market to obtain the net cash flow that she requires. We will examine two of the many possibilities.

Table 3.4 describes two cash flow patterns that Jerrie can obtain if Lamplighter accepts the new investment project. One alternative is to borrow the $7,500 to maintain her 1998 net cash flow at $10,000. After repaying this loan with interest at the end

Table 3.4   ALTERNATIVE CASH FLOW PATTERNS AVAILABLE TO JERRIE ATRICK WITH NEW INVESTMENT

Panel A: Borrow to Maintain Current Dividends

	1998	1999
Dividends from Lamplighter	$ 2,500	$21,630
Issue 1-year note at 10%	7,500	0
Repay note	0	(8,250)
Net cash flow	$10,000	$13,380

Panel B: Borrow to Maintain Future Dividends

	1998	1999
Dividends from Lamplighter	$ 2,500	$21,630
Issue 1-year note at 10%	8,300	0
Repay note	0	(9,130)
Net cash flow	$ 10,800	$12,500

of 1999, she will have a net cash flow of $13,380 ($21,630 − $7,500 × 1.1). Her 1999 net cash flow is therefore $880 more than she would have if the company did not accept the hot meals project ($13,380 − $12,500). The $880 is the future value of Jerrie's share of the project's NPV ($800 × 1.1), so this plan transfers the increase in Jerrie's wealth to the future. Another alternative is for Jerrie to maintain her 1999 cash flow at $12,500 and borrow the rest to increase her 1998 net cash flow to $10,800. This $800 increase ($10,800 − $10,000) equals Jerrie's share of the project's NPV, which implies that she will spend the increase in her wealth immediately.

Exhibit 3.7 shows the effect of the company's investment decision and Jerrie's financing transactions. The difference between the horizontal intercepts of the new upper line and the original one equals the $800 increase in her wealth. The upper line describes all of Jerrie's possibilities for allocating her wealth between 1998 and 1999. No matter which pattern she chooses, the investment project has made her better off by $800—her share of its NPV.

We can conclude from this example that a company should accept any investment project with a positive NPV because this policy allocates resources to their most productive use and increases the owners' wealth. The actual pattern of the project's cash flows doesn't matter, however, because the company or its owners can use the financial markets to rearrange this pattern into one that fits the owners' preferences for current versus future spending. This idea, that investment and financing decisions can be made separately by separate individuals, is called the *separation principle.*

The separation principle is especially important in large companies with many owners because the owners can agree to accept positive NPV investment projects even though they cannot agree on when to spend the money the projects provide. They can separate their joint investment and individual spending decisions because each can borrow or lend in the financial market to obtain the precise mix of preferred current and future

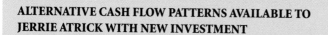

Exhibit **3.7**

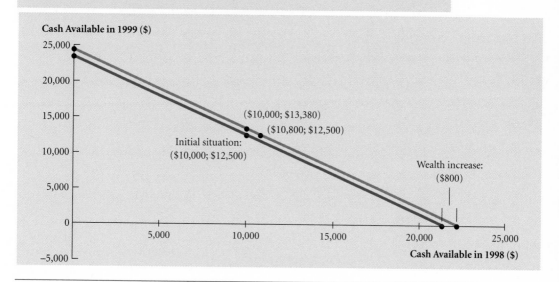

**ALTERNATIVE CASH FLOW PATTERNS AVAILABLE TO
JERRIE ATRICK WITH NEW INVESTMENT**

spending. The owners can even delegate these decisions to professional managers knowing that, if the managers base their decision on NPV analysis, they will select the same investments the owners would choose for themselves. This *separation of owner-ship and control* permits companies to obtain more financing and managerial skills than a single person can provide.

Net Present Value and Economic Value Added

Economic value added (EVA) and market value added (MVA) have become popular tools that managers use to identify decision alternatives that increase the owners' wealth.[3] The article by the consultant who developed EVA and MVA (see "In the News") shows that these popular performance measures are equivalent to economic profit and net present value, respectively. This means the generic versions of eco-nomic profit and NPV or their proprietary equivalents, EVA and MVA, can be used inter-changeably. The equivalency between these measures also means that this book will prepare you to knowledgeably apply NPV, MVA, or any other management tool that correctly describes how your decisions will affect the owners' wealth.

Application to Decision Making within Firms

The features of net present value analysis make it an attractive way to evaluate decisions within firms. Let's review these features before we describe how they apply to businesses. First, using NPV analysis ensures that resources are employed productively because only

---

[3]Shawn Tully, "The Real Key to Creating Wealth," *Fortune,* September 20, 1993, pp. 38–50.

IN THE NEWS

EVA: A TRADE-MARKED VERSION OF ECONOMIC PROFIT

IF WE ACCEPT that the prime financial objective of any company ought to be to maximize the wealth of the shareholders, and that NPV is the decision-making tool best suited to guide actions and strategies to that end, then a new question arises: How can the energies of operating people be directed most effectively to maximizing NPV? Stern Stewart developed EVA (Economic Value Added) with just this purpose in mind.

EVA is an estimate, however simple or precise, of a business's true economic profit. EVA thus differs from accounting profit in three principal respects.

- First, EVA is the residual income remaining after subtracting the cost of all the capital that has been employed to produce the operating profit. It thus integrates operating efficiency and balance sheet management in one measure accessible to operating people.

- Second, EVA is charged for capital at a rate that compensates investors for bearing the firm's explicit business risk.
- Third, EVA adjusts reported accounting results to eliminate distortions encountered in measuring true economic performance.

EVA, then, is a superior measure of performance because it charges management for using capital at an appropriate risk-adjusted rate and it eliminates financial and accounting distortions to the extent it is practical to do so. But besides being a superior measure of performance, EVA is also a superior measure of value. The final link in the chain of reasoning that provides the conceptual basis for EVA is this all-important relation: *the NPV of a project, strategy, or acquisition candidate, and what amounts to the same thing, the contribution to the MVA (Market Value Added) of the company, is by definition equal to the present value of the EVA it can be expected to generate in the future.*

Source: G. Bennett Stewart III, "EVA: Fact and Fantasy," *Journal of Applied Corporate Finance,* Summer 1994, pp. 71–84.

projects whose cash revenues exceed their cash and opportunity costs are accepted. Second, net present value equals the increase in the owner's wealth, wealth that can be spent immediately, reinvested in other productive projects, or loaned in the financial market for future spending. Finally, NPV analysis can be delegated to professional managers who can use it to make decisions in their specialized areas.

Now you can see why NPV analysis is an effective way to evaluate business decisions. The owners of a company and their board of directors want the company's financial resources to be directed to their most productive use. They know the opportunity cost of these financial resources, but neither they nor senior managers have the expertise or information needed to identify and evaluate the company's internal investment alternatives. Ideally, they can ensure that the company adopts its best alternatives by telling the management specialists in each business unit the opportunity cost of the company's funds and requiring them to use NPV analysis to evaluate their own particular investment opportunities. The effect is that business units compete for money in the company's internal capital market because projects with positive NPVs are funded and the remainder are not.

The net present value of the adopted projects is an immediate addition to the company's wealth. This wealth is available to the company or its owners by selling additional shares of common stock or borrowing against the projects' future cash flows. The owners, through the board of directors and senior managers, determine how these new financial resources are used. They may be distributed to the owners as dividends, reinvested in other projects proposed by the business units, or used to grant or repay a loan in the financial market.

Net present value analysis is an attractive, decentralized decision-making rule because, under ideal conditions, it meets the needs of both the company's owners and its business unit managers. The owners can exercise control over the employment of financial resources by mandating the use of NPV analysis, which ensures that business unit projects cover the opportunity cost of these resources. Business unit managers can compete on a fair basis for these scarce resources, however, because NPV analysis incorporates their special information about their projects' cash revenues and costs as well as the company's opportunity cost.

However, net present value analysis cannot be used effectively in a decentralized setting unless it is applied honestly—without any distortions introduced by managers advancing their personal interests or the narrow interests of their business unit. Unfortunately, these distortions are most likely to be introduced into the analysis under the very conditions that make decentralized decision making desirable (that is, when business unit managers have specialized skills and information not available to senior managers and the owners). This problem is an example of the principal–agent conflicts we discussed in Chapter 1. We will return to this problem several times throughout the book when we discuss how companies direct their financial resources to their most productive use.

The Crucial Assumption: Perfect Financial Markets

The separation of ownership and control, which requires the separation of investment and financing decisions, is possible only in a **perfect financial market.** Such a market is one in which there are no transaction costs (such as brokerage fees and floatation costs), no taxes, information is instantaneously and freely available to everyone, securities are infinitely divisible, and the market is competitive. A perfect market is necessary to ensure there is only one market rate of interest at which individuals, businesses, and the government can borrow or lend to meet their spending preferences. This guarantees that everyone places the same value on an investment—regardless of the time-pattern of its cash flows.

The interest rate paid for borrowing money exceeds the interest rate received from lending money in an imperfect financial market. The cost of performing financial transactions is one reason for this difference. Borrowers will not refinance a 12 percent loan when interest rates drop to 11 percent if the cost of refinancing is more than 1 percent. Similarly, lenders will not redirect their money from 11 percent loans to 12 percent loans if their reinvestment costs are greater than 1 percent. Borrowers pay 12 percent interest and lenders receive 11 percent interest; in this case, the difference is accounted for by transaction costs. Monopoly powers also can cause a difference between lending and borrowing rates of interest. Financial institutions that are protected from competition can charge borrowers a higher interest rate than they pay lenders and keep the difference as a monopoly profit.

A company's owners may not agree on the opportunity cost that should be used to evaluate investment alternatives when the borrowing rate of interest exceeds the lending rate of interest. Impatient owners who expect to borrow against the proceeds of their investment will want the company to use the market borrowing rate of interest as the opportunity cost. Patient owners who expect to lend the proceeds of their investment will want the company to use the market lending rate of interest. Managers may be unable to choose an investment alternative that will please everyone in this situation.

Of course, real financial markets are not perfect. There are fees for buying and selling securities, there are taxes, and entry into and exit from the financial services industry are regulated by state and national governments. Nevertheless, modern financial markets operate very efficiently. Therefore, we will take the NPV rule as a starting point for making decentralized decisions and modify it as necessary to accommodate the imperfections of reality.

3.3   MULTIPERIOD TIME VALUE OF MONEY COMPUTATIONS

Realistic time value of money problems come in many varieties and may not be as simple as the projects we've considered so far. Some projects provide only a single payment, like our examples, but this cash flow may occur more than one period in the future. Others provide multiple payments of equal or unequal amounts received at varying intervals. Fortunately, we can analyze all types of projects by merely extending the logic of the techniques we have already developed. We will examine multiperiod projects and multipayment projects separately in this section and the next.

Computing Future Values

Future values more than one period away are computed by extending Equation 3.1 to account for the fact that the investment earns interest-on-interest. The general form of the revised equation is

$$FV_t = CF_0 \times (1 + r)^t. \qquad [3.5]$$

To illustrate, suppose you buy a certificate of deposit for $10,000 and the interest, computed at 14 percent annually, is paid at maturity. At the end of two years, your certificate will be worth

$$FV_2 = \$10,000 \times (1.14)^2 = \$12,996.$$

The logic of this computation is easy to see by proceeding in steps. You know that $10,000 invested at 14 percent will grow to $11,400 ($10,000 × 1.14) at the end of one year. Reinvesting the entire $11,400 at 14 percent will increase its value to $12,996 ($11,400 × 1.14) at the end of the second year. The future value is more than two year's interest on the original $10,000 because the interest earned during the first year is reinvested to earn additional interest in the second year as shown below.

FUTURE VALUE FACTORS (EXCERPT FROM TABLE A.1)   **Table 3.5**

Number of Periods (*t*)	Rate of Return (*r*)		
	0.06	0.08	0.10
10	1.7908	2.1589	2.5937
15	2.3966	3.1722	4.1772
20	3.2071	4.6610	6.7275

Original principal	$10,000
Interest on original principal (2 × $1,400)	2,800
Interest on one year's interest ($1,400 × 0.14)	196
Future value	$12,996

Accounts or investments in which interest income is reinvested to earn additional interest are said to pay **compound interest.** Those that pay interest only on the original principal, the $2,800 interest payment in the present example, provide **simple interest.**

The interest factor in Equation 3.5, $(1 + r)^t$, is the **future value factor** at *r* percent for *t* periods ($FVF_{r,t}$). Table A.1 in the end-of-book appendix provides future value factors for various rates of return and time periods. These same values are often built into calculators and electronic spreadsheets or can be computed by using their exponentiation function. The following example illustrates their use.

Tyrone Weaks deposited $100,000 in an insured savings account to provide for his retirement. The account earns 8 percent compounded annually, and Tyrone will retire in 15 years. What amount of money will be available to him when he begins retirement?

We can use Equation 3.5 or the future value factor in column 2, row 2 of Table 3.5 (an excerpt from Table A.1) to compute the answer.

Using Equation 3.5,

$$FV_{15} = \$100,000 \times (1.08)^{15} = \$317,216.91.$$

Using the table,

$$FV_{15} = \$100,000 \times FVF_{0.08,15}$$
$$= \$100,000 \times 3.1722 = \$317,220.$$

At 8 percent interest, Tyrone's deposit of $100,000 will more than triple in value in 15 years.

COMPUTING FUTURE VALUES WITH SEVERAL COMPOUND PERIODS   EXERCISE 3.6

Recalculate the amount of money available to Tyrone Weaks upon retirement if his savings earn (a) 10 percent for 15 years or (b) 8 percent for 20 years.

Using Equation 3.5,

    (a) $FV_{15} = \$100{,}000 \times (1.10)^{15} = \$417{,}724.82$

    (b) $FV_{20} = \$100{,}000 \times (1.08)^{20} = \$466{,}095.71.$

Using the table,

    (a) $FV_{15} = \$100{,}000 \times FVF_{0.10,15}$

             $= \$100{,}000 \times 4.1772 = \$417{,}720$

    (b) $FV_{20} = \$100{,}000 \times FVF_{0.08,20}$

             $= \$100{,}000 \times 4.6610 = \$466{,}100.$

These results reveal that beginning early and earning a high rate of return are the keys to a comfortable retirement.

• —————— •

Computing Effective Annual Interest Rates

Tyrone would also have more money to spend during his retirement if the interest earned on his savings was added to the principal more frequently. This is actually what happens when the compounding period is shorter than one year. Then, the account earns more interest-on-interest and the **effective annual interest rate** is greater than the *stated annual interest rate.*

    Equation 3.6 is the formula for the effective annual interest rate.

$$\text{Effective annual interest rate} = (1 + r/m)^m - 1 \qquad \textbf{[3.6]}$$

where $r =$ stated annual interest rate

              $m =$ number of compounding periods per year

For example, 8 percent interest compounded semi-annually is an effective annual interest rate of

$$\text{Effective annual interest rate} = (1 + 0.08/2)^2 - 1$$
$$= 0.0816.$$

To understand this formula, note that the future value of $1,000 invested at 8 percent interest compounded semi-annually is

$$FV = \$1{,}000 \times (1.04)^2 = \$1{,}081.60.$$

The internal rate of return on this investment, expressed as an annual interest rate, is

$$IRR = \frac{\$1{,}081.60 - \$1{,}000}{\$1{,}000}$$

$$= \frac{\$1{,}000 \times (1 + 0.08/2)^2 - \$1{,}000}{\$1{,}000},$$

which equals $(1 + 0.08/2)^2 - 1$, our formula for the effective annual interest rate.

COMPUTING EFFECTIVE ANNUAL INTEREST RATES

Determine the effective annual interest rate for 8 percent compounded quarterly.

$$\text{Effective annual interest rate} = (1 + r/m)^m - 1$$
$$= (1 + 0.08/4)^4 - 1$$
$$= 0.0824, \text{ or } 8.24\%$$

The effective interest rate is higher because the investment earns interest-on-interest more often.

Table 3.6 gives the effective annual interest rates for various compounding intervals when the stated annual rate is 8 percent. You can see that shortening the compound period increases the effective annual percentage rate at a decreasing rate. This process reaches its limit when the compounding period is infinitesimally small, that is, when m is a very large number. This limit is known as **continuous compounding,** in which case Equation 3.6 simplifies to $e^r - 1$ where $e = 2.71828$.[4] We will use continuously compounded rates of return to value options in Chapter 8.

Once you have computed the effective annual interest rate, you can use it as you would any other rate of return. For example, if Tyrone can earn 8 percent compounded quarterly, then the amount he will have when he retires in 15 years is computed as

$$\text{Effective annual interest rate} = (1 + 0.08/4)^4 - 1 = 0.0824$$
$$FV = \$100{,}000 \times (1.0824)^{15} = \$327{,}960.$$

Note that quarterly compounding gives Tyrone $10,740 ($327,960 – $317,220) more than annual compounding because he earns interest-on-interest more frequently.

EFFECT OF THE COMPOUNDING PERIOD (STATED RATE EQUALS 8 PERCENT)   **Table 3.6**

Compounded	Effective Annual Interest Rate
Annually	8.00%
Semi-annually	8.16
Quarterly	8.24
Monthly	8.30
Weekly	8.32
Daily	8.33
Continuously	8.33

[4]The number of compounding periods per year, m, is infinite with continuous compounding. Taking the limit of $(1 + r/m)^m$ as m approaches infinity gives e^r, so Equation 3.6 simplifies to $e^r - 1$.

EXERCISE • ———————————————————————————————— •

3.8 COMPUTING FUTURE VALUES WITH FREQUENT COMPOUNDING

Determine the future value of Tyrone Weak's retirement savings if his account earns 8 percent compounded *monthly* for 15 years.

$$\text{Effective annual interest rate} = (1 + 0.08/12)^{12} - 1 = 0.0830$$

$$FV = \$100,000 \times (1.0830)^{15} = \$330,694$$

• ———————————— •

Computing Net Present Values

The present value of a cash flow that will be paid or received more than one period in the future is $CF_1/(1 + r)^t$ or $CF_1 \times 1/(1 + r)^t$. This calculation is the exact opposite of the one used to compute a future value. The term, $1/(1 + r)^t$, is the **present value factor** at r percent for t periods ($\mathbf{PVF}_{r,t}$). Therefore, the present value of the future cash flow is

$$PV = CF_t/(1 + r)^t = CF_t \times PVF_{r,t}. \qquad [3.7]$$

Table A.2 in the appendix provides present value factors for various rates of return and time periods. Note that each entry in this table is the reciprocal of the corresponding entry in Table A.1. These present value factors also are often provided in calculators and electronic spreadsheets or can be computed using their other mathematical functions.

Adding the present value of a future cash flow to a cash flow paid at time zero gives the net present value of a multiperiod investment project:

$$NPV = CF_t/(1 + r)^t - CF_0 \qquad [3.8]$$

Alternatively,

$$NPV = CF_t \times PVF_{r,t} - CF_0$$

Compare Equation 3.8 to Equation 3.2 and notice that the only difference is that we discount the future cash flow by $(1 + r)^t$ to remove t time periods of opportunity cost. The following example illustrates the use of these equations.

The Garza Real Estate Group has the opportunity to buy some undeveloped property near a proposed four-lane highway. The land costs $200,000, and the company expects to sell it for $1,000,000 in 10 years when the highway and other improvements are in place. What is the net present value of this investment if the company's opportunity cost is 14 percent?

We can use Equation 3.8 or the present value factor in column 2, row 2 of Table 3.7 (an excerpt from Table A.2) to compute the answer.
Using Equation 3.8,

$$NPV = \$1,000,000 \times 1/(1.14)^{10} - \$200,000 = \$69,743.81$$

Using the table,

PRESENT VALUE FACTORS (EXCERPT FROM TABLE A.2)   **Table 3.7**

Number of Periods (t)	Rate of Return (r)		
	0.12	0.14	0.16
8	0.4039	0.3506	0.3050
10	0.3220	0.2697	0.2267
12	0.2567	0.2076	0.1685

$$NPV = \$1,000,000 \times PVF_{0.14,10} - \$200,000$$
$$= \$1,000,000 \times 0.2697 - \$200,000 = \$69,700.$$

The \$69,700 net present value has the same interpretation as in simpler problems. It is the present value of the amount by which the \$1,000,000 exceeds the company's opportunity cost. Consequently, the Garza Real Estate Group should purchase the property because it increases the owners' wealth and allocates resources to their most efficient use.

EXERCISE

COMPUTING PRESENT VALUES WITH SEVERAL COMPOUNDING PERIODS   3.9

Recalculate the NPV of Garza's investment if (a) the company's opportunity cost is 12 percent and they sell the property for \$1,000,000 in 10 years or (b) the company's opportunity cost is 14 percent but they sell the property in 8 years.

Using Equation 3.8,

(a) $NPV = \$1,000,000 \times 1/(1.12)^{10} - \$200,000 = \$121,973.24.$

(b) $NPV = \$1,000,000 \times 1/(1.14)^{8} - \$200,000 = \$150,559.05.$

Using Table 3.7,

(a) $NPV = \$1,000,000 \times PVF_{0.12,10} - \$200,000$
$$= \$1,000,000 \times 0.3220 - \$200,000 = \$122,000.$$

(b) $NPV = \$1,000,000 \times PVF_{0.14,8} - \$200,000$
$$= \$1,000,000 \times 0.3506 - \$200,000 = \$150,600.$$

These results reveal that the NPV of the property is larger the lower the opportunity cost or the sooner the company can sell it for \$1,000,000.

Computing Internal Rates of Return

You learned in Section 3.1 that a project's internal rate of return is the discount rate that causes its NPV to equal zero. This definition applies to any project, but we must use Equation 3.8 to obtain the solution when more than one period separates the cash flows paid and received. That is, the IRR of a multiperiod investment project is the solution to the following equation:

$$\text{NPV} = 0 = \frac{\text{CF}_t}{(1 + \text{IRR})^t} - \text{CF}_0.$$

Rearranging terms,

$$(1 + \text{IRR})^t = \text{CF}_t/\text{CF}_0$$
$$\text{IRR} = [\text{CF}_t/\text{CF}_0]^{1/t} - 1. \qquad\qquad [3.9]$$

This expression for the internal rate of return has the same form as Equation 3.4. The only difference is that we must take the *t*-th root of the ratio of the two cash flows to account for the growth in value taking place over *t* time periods rather than one. Here is an example.

Jill Bohay purchased 100 shares of stock for $11,750 on June 1, 1994, and sold them on May 31, 1997, for $16,425. The stock did not pay any dividends during this period. What was the annual rate of return on her investment?

$$\begin{aligned}
\text{IRR} &= (\text{CF}_t/\text{CF}_0)^{1/t} - 1 \\
&= (\$16,425/\$11,750)^{1/3} - 1 \\
&= (1.3979)^{1/3} - 1 \\
&= 0.1181, \text{ or } 11.81\%
\end{aligned}$$

This was a good investment for Jill if her opportunity cost was less than 11.81 percent.

EXERCISE
3.10

DETERMINING THE INTERNAL RATE OF RETURN ON A MULTIPERIOD INVESTMENT

The Carlton Investment Company paid $7,850 for some government bonds that do not pay interest and sold them four years later for $10,000. Determine the internal rate of return on this investment.

$$\begin{aligned}
\text{IRR} &= (\text{CF}_t/\text{CF}_0)^{1/t} - 1 \\
&= (\$10,000/\$7,850)^{1/4} - 1 \\
&= (1.2739)^{1/4} - 1 = 0.0624, \text{ or } 6.24\%
\end{aligned}$$

An Irishman's discovery of some very old cigars (see "In the News") provides an interesting multiperiod time value of money problem.

I N   T H E   N E W S

COMMON STOCKS ARE ONLY INVESTMENTS BUT A GOOD CIGAR IS A SMOKE!*

THE WALL STREET Journal reported on May 20, 1996 that an American investor offered Sandy Perceval $1,000,000 for 500 cigars brought to Ireland around 1864 by Mr. Perceval's great-great-grandfather.† The price per cigar, $2,000, is an incredible amount by anyone's standards but we really must consider the time value of money to place it in perspective. We'll assume the cigars cost $0.05 each, or $25 for 500 in 1864 for our analysis.

First, let's find the internal rate of return on this 132-year investment.

$$IRR = (CF_{132}/CF_0)^{1/132} - 1$$
$$= (\$1,000,000/\$25.00)^{1/132} - 1$$
$$= 0.0836 \text{ or } 8.36\%$$

A rate of return of 8.36 percent seems good, but we can't be sure unless we consider the opportunity cost. We'll use the rates of return from investing in U.S. common stock given below for comparison.

Period	Number of Years	Average Annual Rate of Return‡
1864–1925	61	7.84%
1925–1996	71	10.50

Twenty-five dollars invested in common stocks in 1864 would have grown at 7.84 percent for 61 years. Left to grow for an additional 71 years at 10.5 percent, the total future value would have become

$$FV_{1996} = PV_{1864} \times (1.0784)^{61} \times (1.105)^{71}$$
$$= \$25 \times 99.9016 \times 1,198.7310$$
$$= \$2,993,879.93.$$

Had his great-great-grandfather invested in common stocks, Mr. Perceval would have nearly $2,000,000 more than he may get by selling that box of cigars! Many people who read *The Wall Street Journal* story probably wished their great-great-grandfathers had left them 500 cigars in a musty cellar. Perhaps they should wish for S&P 500 stock certificates instead.

*With apologies to Rudyard Kipling.
†Kyle Pope, "These Old Stogies Just Might Be Worth Some $2,000 Apiece," *The Wall Street Journal*, May 20, 1996, p. A1.
‡The average annual rate of return from 1864 to 1925 was obtained from G. William Schwert, "Indexes of U.S. Stock Prices from 1802 to 1987," *Journal of Business*, July 1990, pp. 399–426. The average rate of return from 1925 to 1996 was obtained from *Stocks, Bonds, Bills and Inflation 1996 Yearbook*, Ibbotson Associates, Chicago, Illinois, 1996.

3.4 MULTIPERIOD/MULTIPAYMENT TIME VALUE OF MONEY COMPUTATIONS

Multipayment time value of money problems are easy to solve because the value of a series of cash flows equals the sum of their individual values. We can simplify these calculations when all the cash flows are of equal amounts or when they grow at a uniform rate. Even then, we are merely applying the concepts you've already learned.

Unequal Cash Flows

The most general type of multipayment time value of money problem is a series of unequal cash flows. The future value of the series is calculated by applying Equation 3.5 to each payment and adding the results. Similarly, the present value of the series is calculated by applying Equation 3.7 to each payment and adding the results. Although you must take care to compound or discount each cash flow the correct number of periods, the actual calculations are the same as those for single payment problems.

Lakeside Lawn and Garden began a lawn care service in the fall of 1998. The company established the capacity to care for 55 lawns in 1999 and planned to add 15 new customers each year until they reach their target of 100 lawns in 2002. The manager expects the net cash flows provided by operations to be $400 per lawn per year. The manager wants to know the future and present value of the cash flows provided by operations during the first four years of the new business given the company's opportunity cost of 9 percent per year. Total cash flows provided by operations their first four years of business are

Year	Cash Flow Provided by Operations
1999	55 lawns × $400 = $22,000
2000	70 lawns × $400 = $28,000
2001	85 lawns × $400 = $34,000
2002	100 lawns × $400 = $40,000

The project's cash flows are placed on a cash flow time line in Exhibit 3.8 and its future value is calculated below. Note that the cash flow provided in 1999 earns interest for only three periods by the end of 2002, the cash flow provided in 2000 earns interest for only two periods, and so on.

$$FV_4 = CF_1 \times (1 + r)^3 + CF_2 \times (1 + r)^2 + CF_3 \times (1 + r)^1 + CF_4 \times (1 + r)^0$$

$$= \$22,000 \times (1.09)^3 + \$28,000 \times (1.09)^2 + \$34,000 \times (1.09)^1 + \$40,000 \times (1.09)^0$$

$$= \$28,490.64 + \$33,266.80 + \$37,060.00 + \$40,000.00$$

$$= \$138,817.44$$

Exhibit 3.8

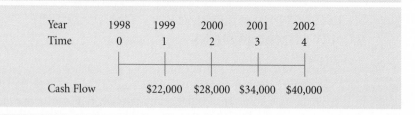

LAKESIDE LAWN AND GARDEN CASH FLOWS PROVIDED BY LAWN CARE PROJECT

Year	1998	1999	2000	2001	2002
Time	0	1	2	3	4
Cash Flow		$22,000	$28,000	$34,000	$40,000

Or, using future value factors,

$$FV_4 = CF_1 \times FVF_{0.09,3} + CF_2 \times FVF_{0.09,2} + CF_3 \times FVF_{0.09,1} + CF_4 \times FVF_{0.09,0}$$
$$= \$22,000 \times 1.2950 + \$28,000 \times 1.1881 + \$34,000 \times 1.09 + \$40,000 \times 1.0000$$
$$= \$28,490.00 + \$33,266.80 + \$37,060.00 + \$40,000.00$$
$$= \$138,816.80.$$

The present value of Lakeside Lawn and Garden's lawn care project is

$$PV = CF_1 \times 1/(1 + r)^1 + CF_2 \times 1/(1 + r)^2 + CF_3 \times 1/(1 + r)^3 + CF_4 \times 1/(1 + r)^4$$
$$= \$22,000 \times 1/(1.09)^1 + \$28,000 \times 1/(1.09)^2 + \$34,000 \times 1/(1.09)^3 + \$40,000$$
$$\times 1/(1.09)^4$$
$$= \$20,183.49 + \$23,567.04 + \$26,254.24 + \$28,337.01$$
$$= \$98,341.78.$$

Or, using present value factors,

$$PV = CF_1 \times PVF_{0.09,1} + CF_2 \times PVF_{0.09,2} + CF_3 \times PVF_{0.09,3} + CF_4 \times PVF_{0.09,4}$$
$$= \$22,000 \times 0.9174 + \$28,000 \times 0.8417 + \$34,000 \times 0.7722 + \$40,000$$
$$\times 0.7084$$
$$= \$20,182.80 + \$23,567.60 + \$26,254.80 + \$28,336.00$$
$$= \$98,341.20.$$

The present value calculations replaced the series of four cash flows with an equivalent amount, \$98,341, located at time period 0. This means we should be able to find the future value of this series by simply compounding its present value for four time periods. Multiplying \$98,341.00 by the $FVF_{0.09,4}$ equals \$138,818.16. This is the same answer, except for rounding, we obtained by compounding each cash flow individually. Finance problems more often are concerned with determining present value rather than future value, so we will restrict our attention to present values from now on. As this example showed, we can always determine a series' future value anyway, by simply computing its present value and multiplying the result by the appropriate future value factor.

EXERCISE

3.11

DETERMINING THE PRESENT VALUE OF A SERIES OF UNEQUAL CASH FLOWS

Sound and Fury Inc., a car stereo company, can buy a full-page ad in the regional newspaper's Sunday supplement for \$10,000. They expect the ad to generate operating cash flows of \$6,500 in one month, \$4,500 in two months, and \$1,000 in three months. Should Sound and Fury place this ad if its opportunity cost is 1.25 percent per month?

$$NPV = \$-10,000 + \$6,500/(1.0125) + \$4,500/(1.0125)^2 + \$1,000/(1.0125)^3$$
$$= \$-10,000 + \$6,419.75 + \$4,389.57 + \$963.42$$
$$= \$1,772.74$$

The company should place this ad in the Sunday supplement because the net present value is positive.

• ———————— •

Annuities

An **annuity** is a multipayment problem with equal periodic cash flows. Car and house payments, the interest payments on a government bond, and the proceeds from winning a state lottery are common examples of annuities. Annuities are easier to evaluate than ordinary multipayment problems because we can simplify the valuation equation by factoring out the equal cash flow.

Present Value of an Annuity   The general formula for the present value of multi-period cash flows is

$$PV = CF_1 \times PVF_{r,1} + CF_2 \times PVF_{r,2} + \ldots + CF_n \times PVF_{r,n}$$

$$= \sum_{t=1}^{n} CF_t \times PVF_{r,t}$$

All the cash flows are equal, $CF_1 = CF_2 = \ldots = CF_n = CF$, so we can factor out CF to obtain

$$PV = CF \times \sum_{t=1}^{n} PVF_{r,t} \qquad [3.10]$$

where $\sum_{t=1}^{n} PVF_{r,t} =$ the **annuity present value factor** at r percent for n periods ($APVF_{r,n}$).

Table A.3 in the appendix provides annuity present value factors for various rates of return and time periods. The entries in this table can be obtained by simply adding the appropriate entries from Table A.2, or they can be computed from Equation 3.11.[5]

$$APVF_{r,n} = \frac{1}{r} \times \left[1 - \frac{1}{(1+r)^n} \right] \qquad [3.11]$$

---

[5] $APVF_{r,n} = 1/(1+r)^1 + 1/(1+r)^2 + \ldots + 1/(1+r)^{(n-1)} + 1/(1+r)^n$ (A)
Multiply both sides by $(1+r)$ to obtain
$(1+r) \times APVF_{r,n} = 1 + 1/(1+r)^1 + \ldots + 1/(1+r)^{n-2} + 1/(1+r)^{n-1}$. (B)
Subtract A from B.
$r \times APVF_{r,n} = 1 - 1/(1+r)^n$.
Solve for
$APVF_{r,n} = \frac{1}{r} \times \left[1 - \frac{1}{(1+r)^n} \right]$.

Using the annuity present value factor, the present value of an annuity is

$$PV = CF \times \frac{1}{r} \times \left[1 - \frac{1}{(1+r)^n}\right] = CF \times APVF_{r,n.} \qquad [3.12]$$

Goban Manufacturing must pay disability benefits of \$1,000,000 each year for the next 10 years to a group of former employees. The first payment is due in one year. How much money must the company set aside now to provide for these future cash flows if the fund will earn 7 percent per year?

We solve this problem by determining the present value of an annuity of \$1,000,000 per year for 10 years at 7 percent interest. The interest factor we need is in column 2, row 2 of Table 3.8 (an excerpt from Table A.3).

$$PV = \$1,000,000 \times APVF_{0.07,10}$$
$$= \$1,000,000 \times 7.0236 = \$7,023,600$$

The difference between the amount of Goban's deposit, \$7,023,600, and the sum of the withdrawals is provided by the interest income on the account.

How much money must Goban set aside if the account earns 7 percent compounded monthly rather than annually? We can't use Table A.3 to find the answer, but we can compute it ourselves using the formulas we've developed already. Specifically, we must use Equation 3.6 to determine the effective annual interest rate, substitute the result in Equation 3.11 to compute our own annuity present value factor, and use it to find the present value of the annuity.

$$\text{Effective annual interest rate} = (1 + 0.07/12)^{12} - 1 = 0.0723$$

$$APVF_{0.0723,10} = \frac{1}{0.0723} \times \left[1 - \frac{1}{(1.0723)^{10}}\right]$$
$$= 6.9495$$
$$PV = \$1,000,000 \times 6.9495 = \$6,949,500$$

Goban can deposit \$74,100 less (\$7,023,600 − \$6,949,500) because the annuity earns more interest income when interest is compounded monthly.

ANNUITY PRESENT VALUE FACTORS (EXCERPT FROM TABLE A.3)   Table 3.8

	Rate of Return (r)		
Number of Periods (t)	0.06	0.07	0.08
9	6.8017	6.5152	6.2469
10	7.3601	7.0236	6.7101
11	7.8869	7.4987	7.1390

3.12   DETERMINING THE PRESENT VALUE OF AN ANNUITY

Malleable Metals pays Ellis Gas and Electric $20,000 per year for electricity no matter how much they use. Five years remain on this take-or-pay contract and the next payment is due in one year. What is the present value of Malleable Metals' electricity costs if the company's opportunity cost is 16 percent per year?

$$PV = \$20{,}000 \times APVF_{0.16,5}$$
$$= \$20{,}000 \times 3.2743 = \$65{,}486.$$

What is the present value if the company's opportunity cost is 16 percent compounded semi-annually?

$$\text{Effective annual interest rate} = (1 + 0.16/2)^2 - 1 = 0.1664$$

$$APVF_{0.1664,5} = \frac{1}{0.1664} \times \left[1 - \frac{1}{(1.1664)^5}\right]$$
$$= 3.2260$$
$$PV = \$20{,}000 \times 3.2260 = \$64{,}520.$$

The company's opportunity cost is higher with semi-annual compounding, which reduces the present value of its electricity costs.

● ─────── ●

Present Value of an Annuity Due   Occasionally, you must find the present value of an **annuity due**, which is a series of equal cash flows that are paid or received at the *beginning* of each period rather than at the end. Examples are rent and lease payments and insurance premiums. Some calculators and electronic spreadsheets have special functions to calculate the present value of an annuity due. These functions are unnecessary, however, because an annuity due is the same as an ordinary annuity with an additional cash flow at the beginning. This means we can determine the present value of an annuity due using our existing formulas.

George Wheellock rents a store in the local mall for $12,000 per quarter with each payment due at the beginning of the quarter. What is the present value of one year's rent if George's opportunity cost is 8 percent per year or 2 percent per quarter?

The cash flow time line that describes George's payments for rent is given in Exhibit 3.9. These payments comprise a single payment at time 0 plus an ordinary annuity of three payments. Consequently, the present value of the rent payments is

$$PV = CF + CF \times APVF_{0.02,3}$$
$$= CF \times (1 + APVF_{0.02,3})$$
$$= \$12{,}000 \times (1 + 2.8839)$$
$$= \$46{,}606.80.$$

The annual cost of George's rent in present value terms is $46,606.80.

Exhibit 3.9

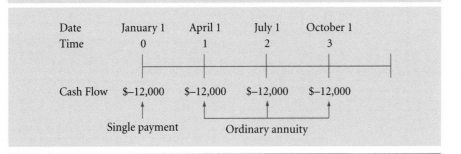

GEORGE WHEELLOCK'S RENT PAYMENTS

The term $(1 + \text{APVF}_{0.02,3})$ is the present value factor for an annuity due of four payments at 2 percent interest. This is the factor used by some calculators and spreadsheets, but now you know how to calculate it yourself using our tables or formulas.

EXERCISE 3.13

DETERMINING THE PRESENT VALUE OF AN ANNUITY DUE

The human resources manager of Gilson Manufacturing is negotiating a new health care contract for the company with The Poe Insurance Company. What is the present value of the cost of the insurance if the monthly premiums are $100,000 paid in advance and Gilson's opportunity cost is 12 percent per year?

This contract requires an immediate payment followed by an annuity of eleven payments. The company's opportunity cost is 1 percent per month, so the present value of the cost is

$$PV = \$100,000 + \$100,000 \times \text{APVF}_{0.01,11}$$
$$= \$100,000 \times (1 + 10.3676) = \$1,136,760.$$

See "In the News" for a description and analysis of Don Calhoun's annuity due.

Amortizing a Loan   Another important use for the annuity present value factor is the amortization of a loan, the process by which we determine the periodic payments that are necessary to repay a loan plus interest. Solving this problem is nothing more than solving an annuity problem in reverse. In this case, we already know the present value, which is the principal of the loan, and we seek the equivalent periodic cash flows. Consequently, the solution is obtained from Equation 3.12 written in terms of CF, the periodic cash flow. In symbols

I N   T H E   N E W S

W H A T   I S   H I S   (B A S K E T B A L L)   N E T   W O R T H ?

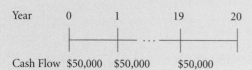

ON APRIL 14, 1993, Don Calhoun stepped onto the court during half-time at a Chicago Bulls basketball game and launched a shot from the free-throw line to the goal at the opposite end of the court.* When the ball swished through the net, he won $1,000,000 paid in 20 equal annual installments of $50,000. Was Don Calhoun's shot really worth one million dollars? Not in present value terms as the following calculations show.

A cash flow time line for Don's winnings is given below. This time line was constructed by assuming he received the first payment shortly after winning the contest and will receive each subsequent payment on the anniversary of the first.

Year	0	1	19	20
Cash Flow	$50,000	$50,000	$50,000	

These payments comprise an annuity due so the present value of Don's winnings is

$$PV = \$50,000 \times (1 + APVF_{r,19}).$$

Because we don't know his actual opportunity cost, we'll compute the present value of his winnings at three different discount rates. The results are

Opportunity Cost	$APVF_{r,19}$	Present Value
8%	9.6036	$530,180
10	8.3649	468,245
12	7.3658	418,290

Not bad for a few seconds of work—but not nearly $1,000,000.

*Frederick C. Klein, "Amateur Jocks Push and Swish to Top," *The Wall Stret Journal*, December 31, 1993, p. A5.

$$PV = CF \times APVF_{r,n}$$
$$CF = PV/APVF_{r,n}.$$

Replacing the symbols in this equation with the terminology of a loan,

$$Payment = Principal/APVF_{r,n}.$$

Kristy Brown will borrow $12,000 on August 31, 1998, to buy a quarter horse to ride in rodeos. She must repay the loan in three equal, annual installments; the first payment is due on August 30, 1999. What is the amount of each payment if the interest rate is 12 percent?

$$Payment = \$12,000/APVF_{0.12,3}$$
$$= \$12,000/2.4018 = \$4,996.25$$

Kristy must pay a total of nearly $15,000 (3 × $4,996.25) to repay the $12,000 plus interest.

We can verify that these payments will exactly repay the loan plus interest by preparing the amortization schedule in Table 3.9. The loan balance begins at $12,000, which

**AMORTIZATION OF KRISTY BROWN'S LOAN
(INTEREST RATE EQUALS 12 PERCENT)**

Table 3.9

Date	Payment	Interest Due	Applied to Principal	Loan Balance
1998				$12,000.00
1999	$4,996.25	$1,440.00	$3,556.25	8,443.75
2000	4,996.25	1,013.25	3,983.00	4,460.75
2001	4,996.04	535.29	4,460.75	0

means Kristy owes interest of $1,440.00 ($12,000 × 0.12) the first year. After subtracting the interest due from the first year's payment, $3,556.25 is applied to the principal, reducing it to $8,443.75. The entries for the year 2000 are prepared similarly. The payment for 2001 is adjusted for the effect of rounding.

EXERCISE
3.14

AMORTIZATION

Wesley Snider is a local office manager for a plate glass company. He receives an annual budget of $1,200 from which to pay his office's incidental expenses. How much can he spend for this purpose each month if he deposits the $1,200 in an account that earns 6 percent annual interest?

Wesley's monthly opportunity cost is 0.005 (0.06/12). Therefore,

$$PV = CF \times APVF_{r,n}$$
$$\$1,200 = \text{Monthly expenditure} \times APVF_{0.005,12}$$
$$\$1,200 = \text{Monthly expenditure} \times 11.6189$$
$$\text{Monthly expenditure} = \$1,200/11.6189 = \$103.28.$$

He can spend slightly more than the total amount divided by 12 because the balance remaining in his account continues to earn interest.

Several time value of money techniques are used to evaluate the Mellon Bank Corporation's interest rebate offer described in this chapter's opening example. See "In the News."

Present Value of a Growing Annuity   Some multipayment problems have cash flows that are not equal but change from year to year at a constant rate or a rate that is assumed constant for convenience. Examples are an increase in cash revenues due to either an increase in the number of units sold or an increase in prices caused by higher demand or inflation. These problems can always be solved by discounting each cash flow separately but this is tedious. Fortunately, we can modify the formula

IN THE NEWS

WANT INTEREST BACK ON YOUR CREDIT CARD AFTER 20 YEARS' USE?

NOW WE ARE in a position to evaluate Mellon Bank Corporation's offer. Based on the information in the article cited in footnote 1 at the beginning of this chapter, the average cardholder pays annual interest of $433.36 ($8,667/20) and will be entitled to a rebate of $8,667 in 20 years. The cardholder's cash flow time line is given below.

The present value of these cash flows at the cardholder's opportunity cost of 17.9 percent per year is

$$PV = \${-}433.36 \times APVF_{0.179,19} + \$8,233.64$$
$$\times 1/(1.179)^{20}$$
$$= \${-}433.36 \times 5.3420 + \$8,233.64 \times 0.0371$$
$$= \${-}2,315.01 + \$305.47 = \${-}2,009.54.$$

The effective amount of interest (I) the cardholder pays each year is determined by amortizing the $2,009.54 interest expense over the entire 20 years.

$$\${-}2,009.54 = I \times APVF_{0.179,20}$$
$$\${-}2,009.54 = I \times 5.3792$$
$$I = \${-}373.58$$

The effective annual interest rate equals the annual interest payment divided by the average balance, which the article says is $2,421.

Effective annual interest rate = $373.58/$2,421.00
= 0.1543, or 15.43%

The rebate program saves the average cardholder $59.78 ($433.36 – $373.58) per year in present value terms, which reduces the effective interest rate by 2.47 percent (17.9 percent – 15.43 percent). Ignoring the effect of taxes, the program costs Mellon Bank Corporation the same amounts.

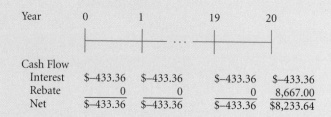

Year	0	1	19	20
Cash Flow				
Interest	$–433.36	$–433.36	$–433.36	$–433.36
Rebate	0	0	0	8,667.00
Net	$–433.36	$–433.36	$–433.36	$8,233.64

Source: Valerier Reitman, "Want Interest Back on Your Credit Card after 20 Years' Use?" *The Wall Street Journal*, January 12, 1994, p. B2.

for an annuity present value factor to incorporate the effect of constant growth. The result is

$$\text{APVF with growth} = APVF_{r,n,g} = \frac{1}{r-g} \times \left[1 - \frac{(1+g)^n}{(1+r)^n} \right]. \qquad [3.13]$$

The present value of the growing annuity is its *first* cash flow multiplied by this annuity present value factor.

$$PV = CF_1 \times \frac{1}{r-g} \times \left[1 - \frac{(1+g)^n}{(1+r)^n}\right] = CF_1 \times APVF_{r,n,g} \qquad \text{[3.14]}$$

Equation 3.13 will make sense to you if you set $g = 0$. Then, it reduces to Equation 3.11, the annuity present value factor for an ordinary annuity. College tuition is often cited as an expense that grows both in real terms and due to the effect of inflation, so let's use these expenses to illustrate the use of Equation 3.13.

Alice Johnson wants to set aside enough money to provide for her daughter's college expenses. The first year's expenses are due one year from today and will amount to $16,000. Alice expects these expenses to increase at 11 percent per year. How much money should she set aside today to provide for four years of expenses if her account earns 8 percent?

$$APVF_{r,n,g} = \frac{1}{r-g} \times \left[1 - \frac{(1+g)^n}{(1+r)^n}\right]$$

$$APVF_{0.08,4,0.11} = \frac{1}{0.08-0.11} \times \left[1 - \frac{(1.11)^4}{(1.08)^4}\right]$$

$$= 3.8609$$

$$PV = CF \times APVF_{0.08,4,0.11}$$

$$= \$16,000 \times 3.8609 = \$61,774.40$$

By depositing $61,774.40, Alice Johnson can withdraw the following amounts to pay her daughter's college expenses:

Year	Amount of Expenses
1	$16,000.00
2	$17,760.00 = $16,000.00 × 1.11
3	$19,713.60 = $17,760.00 × 1.11
4	$21,882.10 = $19,713.60 × 1.11

We can check our answer by determining the present value of these expenses, using individual present value factors.

$$PV = \$16,000.00 \times PVF_{0.08,1} + \$17,760.00 \times PVF_{0.08,2} + \$19,713.60$$
$$\times PVF_{0.08,3} + \$21,882.10 \times PVF_{0.08,4}$$
$$= \$16,000.00 \times 0.9259 + \$17,760.00 \times 0.8573$$
$$+ \$19,713.60 \times 0.7938 + \$21,882.10 \times 0.7350$$
$$= \$14,814.40 + \$15,225.65 + \$15,648.66 + 16,083.34$$
$$= \$61,772.05$$

This amount differs from the result we obtained using the revised annuity present value factor only because of rounding.

3.15   PRESENT VALUE OF A GROWING ANNUITY

Sally Treble just signed a five-year contract with workers at her concrete company that provides for annual pay of $27,000 the first year and an annual raise of 3 percent thereafter. Determine the present value of her labor costs if her opportunity cost is 12 percent per year. For simplicity, assume each employee's wages are paid at the end of the year.

$$PV = \$27,000 \times APVF_{0.12,5,0.03}$$

where

$$APVF_{0.12,5,0.03} = \frac{1}{0.12 - 0.03} \times \left[1 - \frac{(1.03)^5}{(1.12)^5}\right]$$

$$= 3.8022$$

$$PV = \$27,000 \times 3.8022 = \$102,659.40$$

Sally's labor costs, excluding any fringe benefits, are $102,659.40 per employee under the new contract.

● ──────── ●

Perpetuities

A perpetual annuity, one that goes on forever, is called a **perpetuity**. Such a long-lived annuity may seem unrealistic to you, but a consol (a British bond that pays a fixed amount of interest forever) is a real perpetuity. In addition, other investments are sometimes assumed to provide perpetual cash flows so that they can be valued easily. This is the approach we'll take to valuing preferred stock in Chapter 7.

Before we can find the present value of a perpetuity, we must modify our annuity present value factors to account for cash flows continuing forever. We do this by taking the limit as n, the length of the annuity, approaches infinity. This is easy in Equation 3.11 where there is no growth because n appears only in the denominator of the second term. The entire second term approaches zero as n approaches infinity, so the annuity present value factor for a level perpetuity, $APVF_{r,\infty}$, is

$$APVF_{r,\infty} = \frac{1}{r} .$$ [3.15]

Therefore, the present value of a level perpetuity is

$$PV = CF \times APVF_{r,\infty} = CF/r.$$ [3.16]

This is a sensible result because the payment an investor receives from a consol is entirely interest since the principal is never repaid, that is, it remains outstanding forever. Rearranging the formula for the present value of a level perpetuity gives exactly this result, $CF = PV \times r$; the periodic cash flow equals the amount of the principal multiplied by the rate of return.

KP Oil Exploration Company purchased a right-of-way from a rancher for an annual payment of $1,000 in perpetuity. What was the present value cost of the right-of-way if the company's opportunity cost is 12 percent?

$$\text{PV cost of right-of-way} = \$1{,}000 \times \text{APVF}_{0.12,\infty}$$
$$= \$1{,}000 \times 1/0.12$$
$$= \$1{,}000 \times 8.3333$$
$$= \$8{,}333.30$$

EXERCISE

3.16

PRESENT VALUE OF A PERPETUITY

A perpetuity goes on forever, but how long *is* forever? It actually depends on the opportunity cost. To see this, compute the APVF for 30 years and for infinity at opportunity costs of 2 percent and 20 percent.

At an opportunity cost of 2 percent,

$$\text{APVF}_{0.02,30} = \frac{1}{0.02} \times \left[1 - \frac{1}{(1.02)^{30}}\right] = 22.3965$$
$$\text{APVF}_{0.02,\infty} = 1/0.02 = 50.0000.$$

At an opportunity cost of 20 percent,

$$\text{APVF}_{0.20,30} = \frac{1}{0.20} \times \left[1 - \frac{1}{(1.20)^{30}}\right] = 4.9789$$
$$\text{APVF}_{0.20,\infty} = 1/0.20 = 5.0000.$$

A perpetuity is worth more than twice as much as a 30-year annuity at an opportunity cost of 2 percent because the distant cash flows are not discounted very much. Those distant cash flows are discounted very heavily when the opportunity cost is 20 percent, so a perpetuity and a 30-year annuity are virtually indistinguishable.

Modifying Equation 3.13 so we can apply it to a perpetuity is potentially more difficult because the length of the annuity affects both the numerator and the denominator. Consequently, the present value of the perpetuity may approach infinity unless there are some restrictions on growth. The usual approach is to assume that, if the growth is constant and continues forever, it must be at a rate that is less than the opportunity cost.

This assumption is both economically and mathematically appealing. First, the assumption is economically appealing because an investment that continued to grow at a compound rate that exceeded the opportunity cost would be the proverbial goose that lays golden eggs. Investors could borrow at rate r, earn profits of $g > r$, pay off the loan, and repeat the transaction indefinitely. This strategy would eventually produce infinite profits. Because such opportunities do not exist, the assumption that g is less than r is economically realistic. Second, the assumption that $g < r$ is mathematically appealing because the term $[(1 + g)/(1 + r)]^n$ approaches zero as n approaches infinity if $g < r$. Under this condition, the annuity present value factor for a growing perpetuity, $\text{APVF}_{r,\infty,g<r}$ is

$$\text{APVF}_{r,\infty,g<r} = \frac{1}{r-g} \tag{3.17}$$

and the present value of a growing perpetuity is

$$PV = CF_1 \times \text{APVF}_{r,\infty,g<r} = \frac{CF_1}{r-g}. \tag{3.18}$$

This too is a sensible result. Rearranging the formula for the present value of a growing perpetuity gives $r = CF_1/PV + g$. This expression says that the return investors earn on a growing perpetuity equals its current yield, CF_1/PV, plus growth, g. Investors who were not comfortable with the path we took to derive Equation 3.17 should be quite comfortable with the result stated this way. Here's an example that illustrates its use.

Salt-O, Inc. operates a mine from which they extract and sell 10,000 tons of rock salt annually. The supply of rock salt is inexhaustible but demand is limited to purchases by local governments for treating roads and bridges during the winter. Salt-O expects demand to increase at the same rate as motor vehicle miles traveled per year. What is the present value of their cash revenues if the price of rock salt next year is expected to be $7 per ton, the long-term growth rate of vehicle miles traveled per year is expected to be 2 percent, and Salt-O's opportunity cost is 6 percent.

$$PV(\text{growing perpetuity}) = \frac{\$70,000}{0.06 - 0.02} = \$1,750,000$$

The value of Salt-O's sales to local governments is $1,750,000.

EXERCISE ●───●

3.17   **THE PRESENT VALUE OF A GROWING PERPETUITY**

This exercise is a preview of how we'll estimate the value of common stock in Chapter 7. Snap-On, Incorporated is a New York Stock Exchange company that manufactures and distributes hand tools. The cash flow paid to the owners is the company's dividend, which was $0.72 in 1995. Investors' opportunity cost for this stock is approximately 12 percent. Estimate its stock price if its dividends grow forever at 10 percent per year.

$$\text{Stock price} = \frac{\text{Next dividend}}{r-g}$$

$$= \frac{\$0.72 \times 1.1}{0.12 - 0.10} = \$39.60$$

Snap-On's actual stock price varied from $27 to $33 in the first nine months of 1996, not far from your hastily prepared estimate.

●───────────────●

Internal Rates of Return

The internal rate of return has the same interpretation in single- and multiple-payment problems but the equation cannot be written down so neatly or the solution obtained so easily in the latter case. You must use a trial-and-error process to determine the IRR of a project with unequal cash flows, however, you can use present value tables if the project is an annuity.

The IRR of a Multipayment Project with Unequal Cash Flows   Determining the internal rate of return of a multipayment project is more difficult than finding the IRR of a single-payment project because the IRR is the root of a polynomial equation.[6] You may recall from algebra that there is no simple way to find the root of polynomials with powers of 3 and higher. Consequently, you must determine the IRR of a multipayment project by conducting a trial-and-error search for the discount rate that makes the NPV equal to zero. Here is a typical example.

The Hernandez Roofing Company can purchase a three-year license to install Plasto-Shakes, patented synthetic shake shingles. The license costs $50,000, and the manager of the company expects cash flows provided by operations to be $18,000, $24,000, and $30,000 at the end of years 1, 2, and 3. What is the project's IRR?

We will use a discount rate of 15 percent for trial 1.

$$NPV = \${-}50{,}000 + \$18{,}000/(1.15) + \$24{,}000/(1.15)^2$$
$$+ \ \$30{,}000/(1.15)^3$$
$$= \$3{,}525$$

Our next trial must use a rate of return larger than 15 percent to reduce the NPV. Let's try 20 percent.

$$NPV = \${-}50{,}000 + \$18{,}000/(1.20) + \$24{,}000/(1.20)^2$$
$$+ \ \$30{,}000/(1.20)^3$$
$$= \${-}972$$

The NPV must equal zero at a discount rate between 15 percent and 20 percent. The results of trials at discount rates in this interval are given below:

---

[6]This is apparent by writing out and rearranging the equation used to define the IRR of a three-year investment project.

$$- CF_0 + CF_1/(1 + IRR) + CF_2/(1 + IRR)^2 + CF_3/(1 + IRR)^3 = 0$$
$$- CF_0 \times (1 + IRR)^3 + CF_1 \times (1 + IRR)^2 + CF_2 \times (1 + IRR) + CF_3 = 0$$
$$- CF_0 \times X^3 + CF_1 \times X^2 + CF_2 \times X + CF_3 = 0$$
$$aX^3 + bX^2 + cX + d = 0$$

where
$$a = - CF_0$$
$$b = \ CF_1$$
$$c = \ CF_2$$
$$d = \ CF_3$$
$$X = (1 + IRR)$$

Discount Rate	NPV
15%	$3,525
16	2,573
17	1,648
18	750
19	−124
20	−972

These results indicate the IRR is slightly less than 19 percent.

The internal rate of return functions built into calculators and electronic spread-sheets determine the IRR by conducting this trial-and-error search for you. The result using the function in a typical financial calculator is IRR = 18.8568 percent.

EXERCISE

3.18   **DETERMINING THE IRR**

What is the IRR of an investment that costs $10,000 and provides free cash flows of $5,000, $4,000, and $3,000 in years one, two, and three?

Try a discount rate of 10 percent first.

$$\text{NPV} = \$-10,000 + \frac{\$5,000}{1.10} + \frac{\$4,000}{(1.10)^2} + \frac{\$3,000}{(1.10)^3}$$

$$= \$105$$

The NPV is greater than zero at 10 percent, so you must use a higher discount rate. Try 15 percent.

$$\text{NPV} = \$-10,000 + \frac{\$5,000}{1.15} + \frac{\$4,000}{(1.15)^2} + \frac{\$3,000}{(1.15)^3}$$

$$= \$-655$$

The NPV is less than zero at 15 percent, so the actual IRR is between 10 percent and 15 percent (and closer to 10 percent). Try 11 percent.

$$\text{NPV} = \$-10,000 + \frac{\$5,000}{1.11} + \frac{\$4,000}{(1.11)^2} + \frac{\$3,000}{(1.11)^3}$$

$$= \$-55$$

Now you know the IRR is between 10 percent and 11 percent. Additional trial-and-error searches (or a financial calculator) produce the answer: IRR = 10.6517 percent.

The IRR of an Annuity   Earlier we learned that annuities are simple to analyze because their equal cash flows can be factored out of the formula for net present value. This also makes it easy to determine the IRR of an annuity because we can solve the equation for the annuity present value factor and look up the rate of return in a table of annuity present value factors. The following example illustrates how to do this.

ANNUITY PRESENT VALUE FACTORS (EXCERPT FROM TABLE A.3)   **Table 3.10**

Number of Periods (t)	Rate of Return (r)		
	0.14	0.16	0.18
3	2.3216	2.2459	2.1743
4	2.9137	2.7982	2.6901
5	3.4331	3.2743	3.1272

Tracy Thonet paid \$1,000 for an annuity that will pay her \$450 each year for the next three years. What rate of return will she earn on this investment?

To find the IRR, we begin by setting the equation for the net present value of an investment that is an annuity equal to zero.

$$NPV = -CF_0 + CF \times APVF_{IRR,n} = 0$$

Next, we solve this equation for APVF.

$$APVF_{IRR,n} = CF_0/CF$$
$$APVF_{IRR,3} = \$1,000/\$450 = 2.2222$$

Finally, we refer to the row for a three-year annuity in Table 3.10 (an excerpt from Table A.3) and find that 2.2222 is between the 16 percent and 18 percent columns. This is close enough for many purposes, so we conclude Tracy's annuity has an internal rate of return of slightly more than 16 percent.[7]

● ── ●   E X E R C I S E

THE IRR OF AN ANNUITY   3.19

A \$10,000 loan must be repaid annually in five equal installments of \$2,915. Determine the implicit interest rate or IRR on this loan.

Set the loan's NPV equal to zero.

$$NPV = \$10,000 - \$2,915 \times APVF_{IRR,5} = 0$$

---

[7]You can use interpolation to get very close to the actual IRR. Here's how.

r	16%	?	18%
$APVF_{r,3}$	2.2459	2.2222	2.1743

0.0237
0.0716

The APVF we seek, 2.2222 is 1/3 (0.0237/0.0716) of the distance between the APVF for 16 percent and 18 percent, that is, the interest rate is approximately 1/3 of the distance between 16 percent and 18 percent or 0.0067 (0.02/3). Therefore, the IRR is approximately 16.67 percent (0.16 + 0.0067). Our estimate is fairly close because the actual IRR is 16.6487 percent.

Next, solve this equation for APVF.

$$APVF_{IRR,5} = \$10,000/\$2,915$$
$$= 3.4305$$

This value approximately equals the entry in Table 3.10 for a five-year annuity at 14 percent. Therefore, the IRR or implicit interest rate on this loan is 14 percent per year.

● ——————— ●

Some projects with multiple cash flows have more than one IRR. We will discuss this problem in Appendix 3A.

3.5 SUMMARY

A dollar available today is worth more than a dollar that is not available until later because today's dollar can be invested to earn income. Adding this income to a present dollar to determine its future value or removing it from a future dollar to determine its present value are two principal forms of time value of money analysis. Relating the future and present values to each other to determine their implied or internal rate of return is the third form.

The investor's opportunity cost—the rate of return on the next best alternative—is the rate of return to use in time value of money analysis. The opportunity cost also may be called the discount rate when it is used in present value problems. Whatever it is called, the rate of return used in time value of money analysis should be the best available considering market-wide opportunities for investing or repaying a loan.

Net present value analysis is a particularly important form of time value of money analysis. A project's net present value equals the sum of its discounted cash flows. Projects with positive net present values create economic profits and allocate resources to their most efficient use. Equivalently, they provide future cash flows that more than cover the investor's opportunity cost. These projects are beneficial to society as well as to their owners and should be adopted by them.

The availability of a financial market permits owners to delegate decisions to senior managers who in turn delegate them to subordinate managers who choose investments in their own areas of specialization. The managers will choose the same investments as the owners would choose if they apply net present value analysis honestly. Then, the owners can use the financial market to rearrange the timing of the cash flows the investments provide into a pattern that fits their individual needs. By these processes—called the separation of investment and financing and the separation of ownership and control—companies obtain more financing and more managerial skill than an individual can provide. Of course, these processes work perfectly only if the financial market is perfect.

Realistic time value of money problems come in many forms but only a few simple equations are needed to solve them. These equations were developed in this chapter and are summarized below.

Future value of a single cash flow:

$$FV_t = CF_0 \times (1 + r)^t = CF_0 \times FVF_{r,t} \tag{3.5}$$

Effective annual interest rate when stated rate is r and there are m compounding periods per year:

$$\text{Effective annual interest rate} = (1 + r/m)^m - 1 \qquad \text{[3.6]}$$

Present value of a single future cash flow:

$$PV = CF_t/(1 + r)^t = CF_t \times PVF_{r,t} \qquad \text{[3.7]}$$

Present value of n future cash flows:

$$PV = CF_1/(1 + r) + CF_2/(1 + r)^2 + \ldots + CF_n/(1 + r)^n$$

Present value of an annuity:

$$PV = CF \times \frac{1}{r} \times \left[1 - \frac{1}{(1 + r)^n}\right] = CF \times APVF_{r,n} \qquad \text{[3.12]}$$

Present value of an annuity with growth:

$$PV = CF_1 \times \frac{1}{r - g} \times \left[1 - \frac{(1 + g)^n}{(1 + r)^n}\right] = CF_1 \times APVF_{r,n,g} \qquad \text{[3.14]}$$

Present value of a perpetuity:

$$PV = CF/r \qquad \text{[3.16]}$$

Present value of a perpetuity with growth $g < r$:

$$PV = CF_1/(r - g) \qquad \text{[3.18]}$$

Net present value:

Present value minus cost

Internal rate of return:

Discount rate at which the net present value is zero

The future value factor in Equation 3.5 and the present value factors in Equations 3.7 and 3.12 are provided for various rates of return and time periods in Tables A.1, A.2, and A.3. These factors are also provided in many calculators and electronic spreadsheets or can be computed by using their other mathematical functions.

• **KEY TERMS**

Present value (PV) *72*	Compound interest *91*	Present value factor
Future value (FV) *72*	Simple interest *91*	(PVF) *94*
Opportunity cost *72*	Future value factor	Annuity *100*
Net present value	(FVF) *91*	Annuity present value
(NPV) *76*	Effective annual interest	factor (APVF) *100*
Internal rate of return	rate *92*	Annuity due *102*
(IRR) *78*	Continuous	Perpetuity *108*
Perfect financial	compounding *93*	
market *89*		

• QUESTIONS AND PROBLEMS

1. Your spring break trip to Las Vegas was great. You had no idea they had such a great library and you brought home $500 after expenses. A friend learned of your good fortune and asked you to lend him the money to buy a suit for interviews. He said he'll repay you $525 from his internship earnings in six months. Your friend is trustworthy and has good job prospects.

   (a) Given the following alternatives, what is your opportunity cost for this loan? Explain your answer.

   Repay a $500 school loan that is due in six months. The interest rate on the loan is 8.0 percent per year.

   Purchase a six-month certificate of deposit that earns 5.5 percent per year.

   Make two extra car payments. The interest rate on the loan is 7.5 percent per year.

   (b) Suppose you loan the money to your friend. How much better or worse off will you be in six months than if you had chosen your next best alternative? What is the net present value of the loan?

2. The president of Alex Industries has a dilemma. The company can build a venue for a world-class sporting event under a contract that will provide a 15 percent rate of return or construct the new county jail. The latter project's free cash flows are shown below. Alex Industries' cost of financing is 12 percent, so both projects look good but the company doesn't have enough skilled craftsmen to do both.

	1998	1999
Cash flow provided by (used for) operations		
Payment from county	$ 0	$15,000
Payments for labor and materials		(13,000)
Cash flow provided by (used for) investments	(1,650)	0
Free cash flow	$(1,650)	$ 2,000

   (a) What opportunity cost should Alex Industries use to evaluate the county jail project? Explain your answer.

   (b) Calculate the economic profit and NPV of building the county jail. Which construction project should the company accept?

   (c) The sports agency really wants Alex Industries to be the contractor for their venue. Can they persuade the company to build the venue by increasing the rate of return on their construction project to 18 percent? 24 percent? Why?

3. We have discussed a variety of future and present value factors in this chapter.

   (a) What is the mathematical relationship between future value factors and present value factors?

   (b) What is the mathematical relationship between present value factors and annuity present value factors?

   (c) Suppose you want to determine the *future* value of an annuity. Can you simply multiply the periodic cash flow by the reciprocal of the appropriate annuity present value factor? Explain your answer.

   (d) How can you determine the future value of an annuity using only an annuity present value factor and a future value factor?

4. What is the relationship between net present value and economic profit? Why is this relationship important?

5. What is the relationship between net present value and the owners' wealth? Why is this relationship important?

6. The ability to separate ownership and control has permitted the growth of the modern corporation.

   (a) How does the ability to separate ownership and control depend on the separation of investment and financing decisions?

   (b) Why does the separation of investment and financing decisions require a perfect financial market?

7. On August 15th, the partner who supervised your summer internship on Wall Street calls you in for a farewell chat and offers you a $5,000 signing bonus if you will accept full-time employment upon graduation. The bonus is payable on your first day of work, August 15th of the following year.

   (a) What is the cost of this bonus to your prospective employer if the company's opportunity cost is 15 percent per year?

   (b) What is the value of this bonus to you if your opportunity cost is 18 percent per year, the interest rate on your maxed-out credit cards?

   (c) Suppose you sign on with the Wall Street firm and learn that a nearby bank will extend you a loan tied to your signing bonus. What is the maximum amount you can borrow if the interest rate on the loan is 12 percent per year?

8. Bill White Bird owns and operates an automobile repair shop. A construction company with a contract to build a bridge near Bill's shop asked him to maintain the company's construction equipment for a one-time payment of $18,000, payable in one year. Mr. White Bird must spend his own money to buy the tools and supplies he'll need to service the equipment. This expenditure is required immediately.

   (a) Bill analyzed this opportunity and concluded it is acceptable. How much money does he expect to pay for tools and supplies if the internal rate of return on his investment is exactly 20.0 percent?

   (b) What is the net present value of this project at Bill's opportunity cost of 15 percent per year?

   (c) What is the maximum amount Bill can pay for tools and supplies to exactly cover his 15 percent opportunity cost?

   (d) Subtract your answer for part (a) from your answer to part (c) and compare the result with your answer to part (b). What does this comparison tell you about a project's NPV and IRR?

9. Critics of the goal of maximizing the owners' wealth sometimes claim it encourages companies to accept short-term projects at the expense of more profitable long-term projects because owners are impatient. Is this a valid criticism if the company's common stock is traded in a well-functioning financial market? Explain your answer.

10. In this book, several financial theories assume a perfect financial market.

    (a) Describe the characteristics of a perfect financial market.

    (b) In each of the following situations, which financial market is more likely to resemble the ideal of a perfect market? Explain each answer.

    The U.S. or Russian financial market in the mid-1990s?

A financial market with extensive or limited government regulation?

A financial market in which the banking industry is competitive or monopolistic?

11. A graph of future value as a function of time and the rate of return clearly shows the power of compound interest.

   (a) Graph the future value of $1,000 invested at a rate of return of 10 percent for 0, 5, 10, 15, 20, 25, and 30 years.

   (b) Rework part (a) for rates of return of 15 percent, 20 percent, and 25 percent. Plot all of your results on the same graph.

   (c) According to your graph, what is the best way to prepare for a comfortable retirement? Explain your answer.

12. You have determined that you'll need a $1,000,000 portfolio at the time you retire to live comfortably.

   (a) How much must you invest today if your portfolio's rate of return is 10 percent and retirement is 5, 10, 15, 20, 25, or 30 years away? Graph the results.

   (b) Rework part (a) for rates of return of 15, 20, and 25 percent. Plot all of your results on the same graph.

   (c) According to your graph, what is the best way to prepare for a comfortable retirement? Explain your answer.

13. Determine the NPV of the following cash flows at an opportunity cost of 10 percent.

Time	Cash Flow
0	$–1,000
1	500
2	500
3	500

   (a) Use your calculator or the appropriate present value factors.

   (b) Use the NPV function in a spreadsheet.

   (c) Was your answer $243.43 both times? You made a mistake if your answer to (a) was different. Your spreadsheet solved a different problem than the one described above if your answer to (b) was different. Read the spreadsheet's NPV function help file to be sure you know how to use it correctly in this case.

14. Consider an investment with projected cash flows of $660 at the end of year 1; $1,240 at the end of year 2; $480 at the end of year 3; and $2,060 at the end of year 4. Answer each question and provide a brief explanation.

   (a) Draw the project's cash flow time line and determine its present and future values using 5.25 percent as the rate of return.

   (b) Suppose each cash flow is received one year earlier. Does this increase or decrease the project's present value? Increase or decrease its future value?

   (c) Suppose the cash flows at years 2 and 3 are switched. Does this increase or decrease the project's present value? Increase or decrease its future value?

   (d) Suppose the rate of return increases to 7 percent. Does this increase or decrease the project's present value? Increase or decrease its future value?

15. Scientists at Blotto Corporation have discovered the company's face cream causes freckles and anticipate a class-action, product liability suit. The company's sales and marketing group

estimates that 10,000 customers used the offending formula and the company's legal staff estimates a court will award damages of $1,000 per plaintiff after a one-year trial.

(a) How much money should the company set aside today to provide for the eventual payment to the plaintiffs? The company will earn an 8 percent rate of return on this reserve for damages.

(b) In lieu of setting aside this money and going to trial, how much can the company afford to offer each plaintiff today for an out-of-court settlement?

(c) Blotto's chief attorney advises the board of directors that the company probably can delay the trial one year by hiring outside counsel, requesting additional tests, etc. She does not believe this tactic will change the eventual amount of the damages, it will just delay the payment by an additional year. What is the maximum amount of money Blotto can afford to spend on delaying tactics?

(d) What are some ethical problems in the chief attorney's proposal? Consider only the financial dimension of this problem.

16. Jason Argo, 35, works for Inter-Mac Transportation Corp. His normal job of loading trucks paid $12.00 per hour. While working, he suffered a back injury and was declared 50 percent disabled. To settle the disability claim, Inter-Mac offered Jason a job as a shipping clerk, which pays $6.00 an hour, plus a one-time payment of $105,000. Both jobs provide 2,000 hours of employment per year.

(a) Is the proposed settlement financially fair if the company's retirement age is 55 and Jason's opportunity cost is 10 percent?

(b) Suppose raises for unskilled workers in the trucking industry average 2 percent per year. Would this change your answer to part (a)? Explain your answer. (Don't do any calculations, just use your time value of money intuition.)

(c) Jason is tempted to take the company to court in an attempt to get a larger settlement. He estimates the suit will take one year and he knows it will create so much ill will he'll be unable to work for Inter-Mac as a shipping clerk. Under these circumstances, how large must the settlement be to justify going to court?

17. A compounding period that is shorter than one year permits you to earn interest on interest more frequently.

(a) Compute the effective annual interest rate for annual, semi-annual, monthly, daily, and continuous compounding when the stated annual interest rate is 6 percent.

(b) Rework part (a) with a stated annual interest rate of 12 percent.

(c) Under what circumstances is it more valuable to earn interest on interest more frequently? Does this make intuitive sense? Explain your answer.

18. Sally Hutchinson deposited $10,000 in an insured savings account.

(a) What will the balance of the account be after 5 years if it earns 9 percent compounded annually? Monthly?

(b) What will the balance of the account be after 20 years if it earns 9 percent compounded annually? Monthly?

(c) Under what circumstances is it more valuable to earn interest on interest more frequently? Does this make intuitive sense? Explain your answer.

19. Draw cash flow time lines for an ordinary annuity and for an annuity due. Refer to these time lines to explain how to use an annuity present value factor to determine the present value of an annuity due.

20. Here is a very simple annuity due:

Time Period	0	1	2
Cash Flow	$5,000	$5,000	$5,000

(a) Determine this annuity due's present value by discounting each cash flow for the appropriate number of time periods using an opportunity cost of 10 percent.

(b) Determine this annuity due's present value by adding the $5,000 cash flow at time 0 to the present value of an ordinary annuity of $5,000 for two periods at 10 percent. You may use the tables, the formula for an annuity present value factor, or the annuity function in your calculator.

(c) Determine this annuity due's present value by using the annuity function in your calculator *set for beginning of period payments.* Was your answer $13,677.69 using all three methods? You made a mistake if your answer to (a) or (b) was different. Your calculator solved a different problem from the one described by the time line if your answer to (c) was different. Carefully review your calculator's instruction manual in the latter case to learn how to set it up to solve this problem.

21. Justin Winslow manages a marina on behalf of the owner, Silas Melville. Justin has two alternatives for expanding the marina's boat storage business. The first alternative is to pave a vacant lot for storage at a cost of $10,000. The lot will produce an annual net cash flow of $6,000 for three years before it must be completely resurfaced. The second proposal is to install heated boat slips on one of the marina's docks so boats can be kept in the water year-round. This proposal also costs $10,000 and has a three-year life, but Justin expects to pre-lease for $12,500 the popular slips at the time construction begins. The proposals' net cash flows are summarized below.

Net Cash Flows

Time	Storage Lot	Heated Slips
0	$–10,000	$2,500
1	6,000	
2	6,000	
3	6,000	

(a) Silas Melville's opportunity cost is 14 percent per year. Which alternative for expanding the marina's boat storage business should Justin adopt? Why?

(b) Melville has always taken a hands-off approach to the business but Justin knows that he is impatient, has a lavish lifestyle, and prefers investments that permit greater current spending. Does this knowledge strengthen or weaken Justin's conclusion regarding which proposal is better? Explain your reasoning.

22. Judy Ann's uncle established a college trust account for her on her 18th birthday. She collected the third annual payment of $25,000 today and will collect the final payment of $25,000 in one year. Judy has always prepaid her tuition, books, and residence hall fees to avoid the temptation to spend the money on frivolous items. Statements that describe Judy's sources and uses of cash today and in one year if she continues this policy are given below.

Today			In One Year		
Sources of Cash			*Sources of Cash*		
Trust payment		$25,000	Trust payment		$25,000
Proceeds of loan		0	Investment payoff		0
Total		$25,000	Total		$25,000
Uses of Cash			*Uses of Cash*		
Investment cost	$	0	College expenses		$25,000
College expenses		25,000	Repay loan		0
Total		$25,000	Total		$25,000

Judy recently joined the business school's entrepreneur and investment clubs and is curious to know if she can improve her position by investing some of today's $25,000 rather than prepaying her expenses. She has identified the following investment opportunities.

Project	CF Today	CF in One Year
A	$-1,750	$1,900
B	-525	650
C	-950	1,200
D	-1,200	1,300

(a) Judy can borrow money from the student clubs at 9 percent interest. Determine each project's NPV using this interest rate as the opportunity cost. Which projects should Judy pursue? What is the total net present value of the acceptable projects?

(b) Enter the costs and payoffs of the good projects in Judy's sources and uses of cash statements. What is her total source of cash in one year? Her total uses of cash today?

(c) Suppose Judy will spend $25,000 on college expenses next year. How much money will be available to repay any loan she takes out today? How much money can she borrow today given the amount available for repayment and the interest rate of 9 percent?

(d) Add the principal of the loan to her sources of cash today. By what amount do today's sources of cash exceed her uses? (This is the additional amount of money she can spend today as a result of investing in the good projects.)

(e) Compare your answer to part (d) and the NPV of the accepted projects. What does net present value actually measure?

23. At the end of 1997 Riedel Holdings can purchase the mineral rights to a small oil field for $150,000. The company expects the field to produce oil for the next four years according to the schedule given below. Oil prices during this period are expected to remain constant at $16.00 per barrel. Production costs are $1.50 per barrel. State law requires the company to cap the well and clean the site when it is abandoned at the end of the fifth year. The cost will be $32,500.

Year	Oil Production (in Barrels)
1998	7,500
1999	7,000
2000	4,500
2001	1,250

(a) Should the company buy the mineral rights if its opportunity cost is 15 percent per year?

(b) Riedel's environmental compliance officer recommended that the company establish a fund to pay the fifth-year clean-up costs. What equal annual amount should the company deposit in this fund each year of the field's operation (1998–2001) to accumulate $32,500 by the end of year 2002? The fund will earn 15 percent per year.

(c) Subtract the amount of the deposit to the clean-up fund from each year's cash flow and recompute the oil field's NPV. What is the financial effect of the compliance officer's recommendation?

24. Consider the project described on the cash flow time line given below.

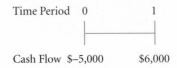

Time Period   0   1

Cash Flow $–5,000 $6,000

(a) Determine the project's net present value at opportunity costs of 0, 10, 20, 30, 100, 500, and 1,000 percent.

(b) Compute the project's internal rate of return.

(c) Draw the project's net present value profile. At what opportunity costs does this project have a positive net present value?

25. Andrea Little promised herself a luxury car as a reward for completing a difficult, two-year MBA program. She can't afford to buy one yet, but she can lease the car she wants for 36 monthly payments of $450, the first payment due upon signing the lease. The car must have a residual value of $15,000 at the end of the lease but Andrea is a low-mileage, low-impact driver and doesn't expect this requirement to be a factor in her decision.

(a) What is the cost of Andrea's lease if the interest rate on a new car loan is 9 percent per year?

(b) What is the total cost of the lease if she exceeds the mileage allowance and must pay an additional $750 when she returns the car after 36 months?

26. Consider the following projects.

Time	Project A	Project B	Project C
0	$2,500	$–1,000	$–2,000
1	0	445	1,129
2	0	445	854
3	–3,171	445	500

(a) Which are investment projects and which are loans?

(b) Determine each project's internal rate of return.

(c) Which projects are acceptable to a company that has a 15 percent opportunity cost?

27. A car dealer will sell the latest sport/utility vehicle for $35,000 cash or provide financing. The terms of the loan are $1,000 down and monthly payments of $718.22 for five years.

(a) What is the implicit interest rate on this loan?

(b) Prepare an amortization schedule for the first three months of this loan. On average, what percentage of the payment is used to pay interest and what percentage is applied to the principal of the loan?

28. Scott Lee will purchase a five-year, $12,000 certificate of deposit. He called several local banks and obtained the following quotes:

Good Bank	6% compounded annually
Better Bank	5.5% compounded semi-annually
Even Better Bank	5% compounded monthly
Best Bank	4.5% compounded continuously

    (a) What is the effective annual interest rate on each bank's CD?

    (b) How much will each CD be worth at maturity if Scott reinvests all the interest payments?

29. Construction Supply Inc. (CSI) leases equipment to contractors. The term of each lease is set equal to the life of the equipment. Lease payments are paid quarterly at the beginning of each quarter and are set to fully recover the equipment's cost.

    (a) CSI recently purchased a portable electric generator that cost $45,000 and has a life of two years. What will they charge to lease this generator if the company's opportunity cost is 15 percent per year?

    (b) CSI also will rent equipment monthly. How much must they charge per month to rent the portable electric generator if they know it will be out of service the last quarter of each year when bad weather slows construction work?

30. What amount must you deposit in an account each year for the next 5 years (starting one year from today) if you want to withdraw $15,000 per year for 5 years starting in year 6? The rate of return on the account is 13 percent per year.

31. The board of directors of Mighty-Lite Aluminum Products Company approved a personal loan of $250,000 to the company's president at an interest rate of 4 percent per year. The president will repay the loan in three equal annual installments, the first payment due in one year. How much interest income does the company earn each year of the loan's life?

32. Hanover Maple Works uses a cafeteria-style benefit plan to help its employees with college expenses. Plan options are described below. Each plan requires that the employee or his or her dependent make satisfactory progress toward a degree. A typical employee's opportunity cost is 8 percent per year.

    Plan A: Reimbursement of $1,500 of eligible expenses per year for four years.
    Plan B: $20,000 loan at 3 percent interest. Principal and interest due in five years.

    (a) Determine the present value of Plan A to a typical employee.

    (b) What amount will a typical employee owe under Plan B when the loan is due? Determine the present value of this amount at a typical employee's opportunity cost.

    (c) The present value you calculated in part (b) is the amount a typical employee normally could borrow. Subtract this amount from the $20,000 loan to determine the present value of the company's subsidized financing. Will a typical employee choose Plan A or Plan B?

    (d) Will employees with a higher opportunity cost tend to prefer Plan A or Plan B? Use your financial intuition to make a guess. Confirm your answer by reworking parts (a) through (c) with an opportunity cost of 10 percent.

33. Today is John Tardy's 45th birthday and, in spite of his finance professor's advice, he hasn't started to save for retirement. John can't believe time has passed so quickly. John wants to retire on his 65th birthday; mortality tables indicate his life expectancy is 85. Therefore, he will need a retirement fund that will sustain him for 20 years, or 240 months. John intends to completely deplete this fund by age 85, leaving nothing for his heirs.

(a) What amount of money must be in the retirement fund on John's 65th birthday if he will withdraw $5,000 then and every subsequent month? John will withdraw the last payment one month before his 85th birthday for a total of 240 payments. The rate of return on the retirement fund during this period is 0.75 percent per month.

(b) How much money must John save each month—beginning one month from today, his 45th birthday—to accumulate the necessary funds? The rate of return during this period is 1 percent per month.

(c) John would like to start saving right now, of course, but his 19-year-old daughter is about to start college at an exclusive eastern school and he hasn't saved for her tuition either. Suppose John can pay his daughter's expenses out of his current income but can't start saving for retirement until she graduates (she'll almost certainly take five years to finish). How much money must John save each month beginning one month after his 50th birthday to accumulate the necessary funds?

34. John Tardy, from the previous problem, thought that saving for retirement was going to be challenging but doable. However, *he forgot about the effect of inflation.* Suppose John wants each monthly retirement check to have the same value as $5,000 does at his current age, 45.

(a) What is the necessary amount for his first retirement check, withdrawn on his 65th birthday, if inflation is 0.25 percent per month?

(b) Rework problem 33 assuming inflation is 0.25 percent per month from John's 45th birthday until his 85th.

35. Carolyn Shaw is 27 and works as an accountant for an oil company. Her salary next year will be $40,000, and she expects to receive a 5 percent raise each year until she retires at age 65. Carolyn is considering a return to school to pursue an MBA degree. She expects the costs of books, tuition, and fees to be $21,000 the first year and $23,000 the second. These costs are paid at the beginning of the year (as you surely know). She will not work while in school. Graduates of the school Carolyn is considering receive starting salaries that average $60,000. Raises average 7 percent per year. Carolyn considers her opportunity cost to be 12 percent.

(a) Determine the present value of Carolyn's lifetime earnings if she does not return to school.

(b) Determine the present value of the cost of books, tuition, and fees.

(c) Determine the present value of Carolyn's lifetime earnings with an MBA degree. Remember, she won't start her new job for two years.

(d) What is the NPV of an MBA degree given Carolyn Shaw's assumptions?

(e) Suppose Carolyn can get a graduate assistantship that pays $8,000 cash at the beginning of her second year of school and permits her to pay in-state fees the second year, saving her an additional $4,000. What is the NPV of this assistantship? How much does it improve the NPV of the MBA degree?

- ## ADDITIONAL READING

A more advanced textbook discussion of net present value, internal rate of return, and the separation of decision making is provided in Chapters 1 and 2 of:

> Thomas E. Copeland and J. Fred Weston, *Financial Theory and Corporate Policy,* Addison Wesley Longman, Reading, Massachusetts, 1988.

Even more rigorous discussions of these topics are in two works by Jack Hirschleifer:

> Jack Hirschleifer, "On the Theory of Optimal Investment Decision," *Journal of Political Economy,* August 1958, pp. 329–352.
>
> Jack Hirschleifer, *Investment, Interest, and Capital,* Prentice-Hall, Englewood Cliffs, New Jersey, 1970.

An excellent discussion of net present value and shareholder wealth maximization is in Chapter 2 of:

> Ezra Solomon, *The Theory of Financial Management,* Columbia University Press, New York, 1963.

Economic value added and market value added are developed and explained in:

> G. Bennett Stewart III, *The Quest for Value,* HarperCollins Publishers, New York, 1991.

MULTIPLE INTERNAL RATES
OF RETURN

Unfortunately, some multipayment projects have more than one internal rate of return. This problem complicates the solution for and interpretation of the IRR and makes it unreliable for analyzing investment opportunities. This appendix explains why multiple IRRs arise and why they cannot be used for time value of money analysis.

Consider the projects shown in Exhibit 3A.1. Project A is a *simple investment project* because the initial cash flow to purchase the project is negative while all the subsequent cash flows produced by the investment are positive. Project A's NPV profile shows that its value decreases as the opportunity cost is raised because its future cash inflows are penalized by the increase in the time value of money. This project has a single IRR of 14.4 percent, found by trial and error.

Project B is a *simple financing project*; the initial cash flow when the loan is received is positive while all the subsequent cash flows to repay the loan are negative.

Exhibit 3A.1

NPV PROFILES

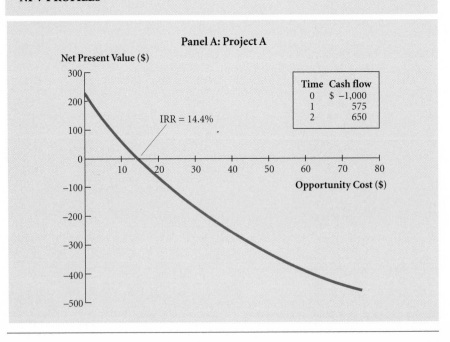

Panel A: Project A

Net Present Value ($)

IRR = 14.4%

Opportunity Cost ($)

Time	Cash flow
0	$ −1,000
1	575
2	650

NPV PROFILES

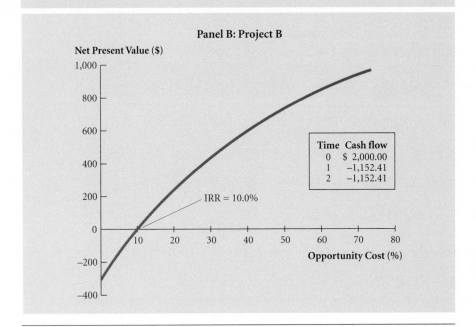

Panel B: Project B

Time	Cash flow
0	$ 2,000.00
1	−1,152.41
2	−1,152.41

IRR = 10.0%

Project B's NPV profile shows that its value increases as the opportunity cost is raised because its future cash outflows are penalized by the increase in the time value of money. Project B has a single IRR of 10.0 percent found by solving the equation below for $APVF_{IRR,2}$ and looking up the rate of return in Table A.3.

$$NPV(B) = 0 = \$2,000 - \$1,152.41 \times APVF_{IRR,2}$$
$$APVF_{IRR,2} = 1.7355$$
$$IRR = 10.0\%$$

Project C is a *mixed project* that starts out with a cash outflow to acquire an investment ($CF_0 < 0$) and ends with a cash outflow to repay a loan ($CF_2 < 0$). The cash flow at time 1 is partly a return of the investment undertaken at time 0 and partly the principal on the loan that is repaid at time 2. This mixture causes project C's NPV profile to exhibit the characteristics of both investment and financing projects. Project C therefore has two IRRs.[1] Project C's IRRs, which must be found by trial and error, are 19.8 percent and 380.0 percent.

---

[1]There is also a mathematical explanation for this problem. IRRs are the roots of a polynomial equation. Descartes' rule of signs tells us a polynomial equation may have as many roots as it has sign changes. A simple investment or financing project has only one sign change (− to + or + to −) and therefore is certain to have no more than one IRR. Mixed projects have more than one sign change (− + − for project C) and therefore many have multiple IRRs.

Exhibit 3A.1

NPV PROFILES

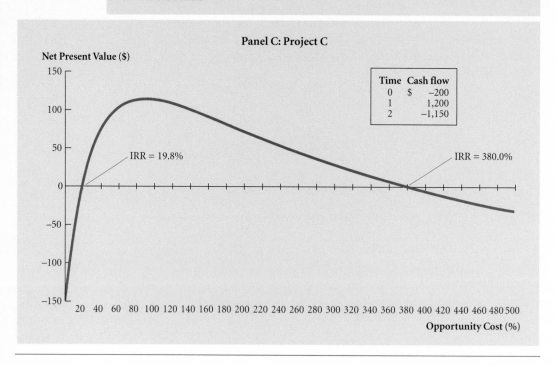

Panel C: Project C

The problem with multiple internal rates of return is that you cannot interpret them correctly. In Sections 3.2 and 3.4, you learned that a project's free cash flows more than cover its opportunity cost and its NPV is greater than zero if its IRR is greater than the investor's opportunity cost. This relationship does not hold for projects with multiple IRRs, however. For example, project C has a negative NPV at an opportunity cost of 8 percent even though both of its IRRs are greater than 8 percent. An investor with an 8 percent opportunity cost who adopted project C based on its IRRs would actually suffer an opportunity loss.

How can you escape this difficulty? The surest way is to avoid applying the IRR rule to mixed projects. Nonsimple projects *may* have a single IRR, but this is difficult for the novice to determine in advance. You can't even rely on the IRR functions in some calculators and electronic spreadsheets. Some of these functions will provide no solution at all, or, even worse, solve for the nearest IRR and never tell you that the cash flows have other IRRs that invalidate the usual interpretation of these returns. Therefore, it simply is best to use the net present value approach when analyzing mixed projects.

- # QUESTIONS AND PROBLEMS

1. Consider the following projects.

Time	Project A	Project B	Project C	Project D
0	$2,500	$–4,000	$–1,500	$–25,000
1	–300	30,000	829	31,000
2	–300	–29,000	654	–4,000
3	–2,800		445	

   (a) Which projects are investments? Loans? Mixed projects?

   (b) Determine each project's internal rate(s) of return. (You may use the quadratic formula for projects B and D.)

   (c) Suppose the investor's opportunity cost is 16 percent per year. Which projects appear to be acceptable based on their IRRs?

   (d) Graph each project's NPV profile.

   (e) Now which projects appear to be acceptable at an opportunity cost of 16 percent? Confirm your answer by computing each project's NPV using 16 percent as the discount rate.

2. A prominent city office building has been condemned due to the presence of asbestos. Richard Howell, a local real estate speculator, has learned he can buy the property for a mere $500,000 but must remove the asbestos before he can demolish the building and sell the land. The building does have a number of art nouveau architectural details, however, that Richard can sell to generate an interim cash flow. The anticipated cash flow schedule is given below. Howell's opportunity cost is 20 percent per year.

Year	Free Cash Flow	Explanation
1998	$ –500,000	Purchase building
1999	5,000,000	Salvage architectural features
2000	–13,000,000	Remove asbestos
2001	15,000,000	Sell the property

   (a) Can Howell base his investment decision on this project's IRR? (Hint: Prepare an NPV profile for opportunity costs between 0 and 100 percent to be sure of your answer.)

   (b) What is the project's NPV at the 20 percent opportunity cost? Should he buy the property?

3. Try to use the IRR function in your calculator and in a spreadsheet program to determine the internal rates of return of project C in Exhibit 3A.1.

   What is the result? (1) Both IRRs are identified? (2) You get an error message that tells you there may be more than one IRR? (3) One IRR is identified but you are not told there may be another? Use your calculator's or spreadsheet's IRR function with care if the result is (3).

CHAPTER 4

UNDERSTANDING INTEREST RATES

Many corporate treasurers probably opened *The Wall Street Journal* to page C24 on May 16, 1996, to review the interest rates reported there. Those who did saw the average yields on U.S. government and corporation debt summarized in panel A of Table 4.1. The preceding day, U.S. Treasury securities provided the lowest yields while low-quality corporation bonds provided the highest. Furthermore, the yields in each category were higher the longer the instruments' terms to maturity.

Panel B of Table 4.1 shows that the interest rate structure that existed on May 15, 1996, is typical of the long-term pattern of U.S. interest rates. Over a 70-year period, corporation bonds,

long-term government bonds, and U.S. Treasury bills, which are short-term government instruments, provided the highest rates of return—in that order.

The interest rate structure in Table 4.1 gives us our first clues about the determinants of investors' opportunity costs. They apparently require a higher rate of return the longer the term to maturity of the loan, and they require a higher rate of return on corporation debt than on government debt. Managers must understand how this interest rate structure is determined to make investment and financing decisions that cover these opportunity costs.

Knowledge of how interest rates are determined is important to both operating and financial managers. Operating managers must understand interest rates to fully comprehend how the financial market establishes the opportunity cost of their investments. Financial managers, especially treasurers, must understand how interest rates are determined to obtain financing at the lowest possible cost for a given amount of risk.

This chapter describes several economic theories that explain how the level and structure of interest rates are determined. You will learn the factors that affect the domestic and foreign supply and demand for loans; why loans of different maturities have different interest rates; and how the financial market incorporates tax, marketability, and default risk differences in interest rates. We will explore these issues individually for clarity, however, in reality, they simultaneously affect interest rates.

This chapter discusses interest rates, which is only part of the information necessary to fully understand opportunity costs. The remaining information is covered in Chapters 5 and 6 where we discuss how unavoidable risks affect investors' required rates of return. Together, the material in these three chapters provides the foundation for determining the opportunity cost of investing in financial assets such as stocks and bonds and real assets such as capital equipment.

4.1   The General Level of Interest Rates

The general level of interest rates depends on the supply and demand for loans, the expected rate of inflation, and the effect of foreign financial flows. We'll first restrict our attention to the domestic market and add foreign supply and demand later. For simplicity, we also will assume that there is only one type of loan and one interest rate. Before we are finished, we will explain the interest rates on all the types of debt instruments (loans) listed in Table 4.1.

The Supply of and Demand for Loans

Individuals, companies, and governments use the financial markets to borrow and lend. Some lend directly while others lend through financial intermediaries. The price of their loans is the interest rate at which the total amount of funds supplied by those with cash surpluses equals the total amount of funds demanded by those with cash deficits.

Table 4.1   THE STRUCTURE OF INTEREST RATES

Panel A: Yields on May 15, 1996

	Term to Maturity	
Issuer	**1 to 10 years**	**More than 10 years**
U.S. Treasury	6.19%	7.15%
U.S. government agencies	6.72	7.32
Corporation bonds		
High quality	6.86	7.67
Medium quality	7.08	7.99
Low quality		9.84

Panel B: Average Annual Rate of Return, 1926–1995

Long-term corporation bonds	6.0%
Long-term U.S. government bonds	5.5
Intermediate-term U.S. government bonds	5.4
U.S. Treasury bills	3.8

Sources: *The Wall Street Journal*, May 16, 1996, p. C24, and *Stocks, Bonds, Bills, and Inflation 1996 Yearbook*, Ibbotson and Associates, Inc., 1996.

Consequently, changes in the supply and demand for loans affect the level of interest rates. This is illustrated in Exhibit 4.1 where an increase in the demand for loans caused the equilibrium interest rate to increase from r_1 to r_2. Knowledge of the factors that affect the supply and demand for loans helps explain changes in the level of interest rates.

One of the more important factors affecting the supply and demand for loans is people's expectations about future economic conditions. An optimistic economic outlook increases consumer confidence and makes individuals more willing to deplete their savings and borrow money to increase current spending. Favorable expectations also increase business confidence, which causes companies to reduce their precautionary reserves and borrow money to increase their investment in plant and equipment. These factors decrease the supply of loans and increase the demand for loans and therefore cause an increase in the interest rate. Pessimism about the future has the opposite effect.

The age distribution of the population is also a factor. Families start out as net borrowers when they spend money to form their households and educate their children, become net savers when they reach middle age, and then deplete their savings during retirement. Therefore, the demand for loans to individuals decreases and the supply of loans first increases and then decreases as a population ages.

These inclinations to save or borrow are influenced by tax policies. For example, interest on home mortgages and business loans is a tax-deductible expense that lowers

Exhibit 4.1

THE SUPPLY AND DEMAND FOR LOANS

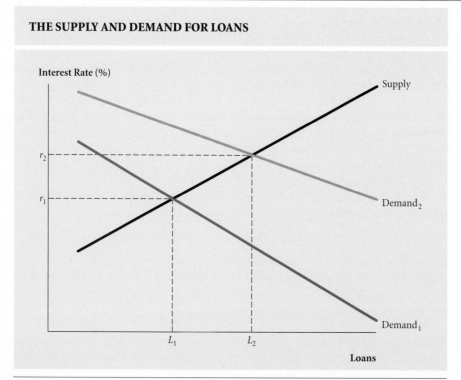

the cost of these forms of debt. These tax policies increase the demand for loans. At the same time, some programs permit individuals to defer the tax on income that is set aside for retirement. These programs make savings more attractive and thereby increase the supply of loans.

National and local governments also have an enormous effect on the demand and supply of loans. Local governments borrow money for public works such as roads, bridges, and schools and national governments borrow money to finance their budget deficits. Governments also may temporarily lend money when current tax collections exceed current expenditures, but they are net debtors overall. Factors that increase government spending such as the aging of the population (which causes an increase in spending for social programs), the aging of public works, and an increase in the threat of war therefore increase the demand for loans.

Finally, the central bank can change the amount of money available for lending by changing its monetary policy. The central bank expands the money supply by purchasing government securities or reducing the reserve ratio. This creates excess bank reserves that depository financial institutions can use as the basis for new loans. An expansionary monetary policy therefore increases the supply of loans and reduces the equilibrium interest rate. A contractive monetary policy, implemented by selling government securities or increasing the reserve ratio, has the opposite effect.

The Effect of Expected Inflation

Lenders require a higher interest rate on loans in the presence of inflation because they know they will be repaid with money that has less purchasing power. The best estimate of the premium they require is the expected rate of inflation. The inflation premium is incorporated in interest rates through changes in the supply and demand for loans. This is probably easiest to see with an example.

Suppose that on January 1, 1998, Jae Nayar invests $10,000 in a government security that will repay him $10,500 when it matures on December 31, 1998. The government security is riskless so Jae is certain to be repaid. However, whether he can actually buy $10,500 worth of goods and services with the money he receives depends on what happens to prices in 1998. Let's presume prices increase by 2 percent during the year. Then goods and services that cost $10,294.12 at the beginning of the year cost $10,500 at the end of the year ($10,294.12 $\times$ 1.02 = $10,500). In other words, Jae's $10,500 actually is worth only $10,294.12.

Two interest rates describe Jae's rate of return on this investment. The **real rate of interest**, i, is computed from the inflation-adjusted cash flow.

$$i = (\$10,294.12/\$10,000) - 1 = 0.0294 \text{ or } 2.94\%$$

This interest rate describes how much Jae really earned considering the change in his purchasing power. The **nominal interest rate**, r, is computed from the unadjusted cash flow.

$$r = (\$10,500 - \$10,000)/\$10,000 = 0.05 \text{ or } 5.0\%$$

The nominal interest rate describes how much Jae earned in name only. Only a little thinking should convince you investors are more concerned about their real rate of return than their nominal rate of return.

According to Irving Fisher, lenders protect themselves from a decline in purchasing power by requiring an interest rate on their loans that offsets the expected effect of inflation.[1] Here's how. Lenders who expect 2 percent inflation will require repayment of $10,200 to obtain compensation for the loss of purchasing power even before they calculate the interest on the loan. They then apply the real rate of interest, say 5 percent, to this amount to determine the total the borrower must repay when the loan is due. Consequently, the total amount due on a one-year, $10,000 loan is

$$\text{Amount due} = \$10,000 \times (1.02) \times (1.05) = \$10,710.$$

The nominal rate of interest on this loan is

$$r = \frac{\$10,710}{\$10,000} - 1 = \frac{\$10,000 \times (1.02) \times (1.05)}{\$10,000} - 1$$
$$= (1.02) \times (1.05) - 1 = 0.0710.$$

Generalizing from this example,

$$r = [1 + E(I)] \times [1 + i] - 1$$
$$= i + E(I) + i \times E(I) \qquad \qquad [4.1]$$

where
$$r = \text{nominal interest rate}$$
$$E(I) = \text{expected inflation rate}$$
$$i = \text{real interest rate}.$$

The relationship described by Equation 4.1 is known as the **Fisher effect**. This relationship says that the nominal rate of interest equals the real rate of interest plus premiums that compensate for the loss of purchasing power on the principal of a loan, $E(I)$, and on the interest income of a loan, $i \times E(I)$. The latter term is often omitted because its value is small at normal rates of inflation. Here's an example.

Laura Jennings must invest $10,000,000 of excess pension funds for one year. She intends to buy government bonds and hopes to earn a real rate of return of 3.5 percent. What nominal rate of return must she earn on the bonds if the expected rate of inflation is 2.75 percent?

According to the exact form of the Fisher effect,

$$r = [1 + E(I)] \times [1 + i] - 1$$
$$= [1.0275] \times [1.035] - 1 = 0.0635 \text{ or } 6.35\%.$$

According to the approximate form of the Fisher effect that omits the interaction term,

$$r = i + E(I)$$
$$= 3.50\% + 2.75\% = 6.25\%.$$

Laura must purchase bonds that provide a nominal rate of return of 6.35 percent (6.25 percent by the approximation method) to earn a real rate of return of 3.5 percent.

---

[1]Irving Fisher, *The Theory of Interest as Determined by Impatience to Spend Income and Opportunity to Invest It,* McMillan Company, New York, 1930.

EXERCISE ● ——— ●

4.1   **NOMINAL VERSUS REAL RATES OF RETURN**

Bob Starks can purchase a one-year government security that pays a certain nominal rate of return of 8 percent. Determine Bob's real rate of return if the expected rate of inflation is 1.9 percent.

Rewriting the exact form of the Fisher effect,

$$r = [1 + E(I)] \times [1 + i] - 1$$
$$i = [1 + r]/[1 + E(I)] - 1$$
$$= [1.08]/[1.019] - 1 = 0.0599 \text{ or } 5.99\%.$$

Rewriting the approximate form of the Fisher effect,

$$r = i + E(I)$$
$$i = r - E(I)$$
$$= 8.0\% - 1.9\% = 6.10\%.$$

Bob's real rate of return on the 8 percent bond is 5.99 percent (6.10 percent by the approximation method) if inflation is 1.9 percent.

● ——————————— ●

Changes in expectations about inflation are incorporated in interest rates through changes in the supply and demand for loans. The supply of loans decreases when lenders expect an increase in inflation because they expect to receive a lower real interest rate. At the same time, the demand for loans increases because borrowers expect to pay a lower real interest rate. These shifts in supply and demand cause the equilibrium nominal interest rate to increase, incorporating the market's expectation of higher rates of inflation. The change may not be the precise amount predicted by the Fisher effect, but Equation 4.1 provides a reasonable model of the direction and approximate magnitude of the change.

4.2   FOREIGN BORROWING AND LENDING

World financial markets are closely integrated. Information about interest rates in most countries is rapidly disseminated worldwide and financial institutions conduct around-the-clock global transactions. The availability of this information and these services enables individuals and companies to borrow and lend in the most favorable location. Consequently, the level of interest rates in a particular country reflects the foreign as well as the domestic supply and demand for loans.

The factors that affect the domestic supply and demand for loans also affect foreign supply and demand. These factors—expectations about future economic conditions, inflation, etc.—were described above. The rate at which one currency can be exchanged for another, the **foreign exchange rate**, is another factor that affects the foreign supply and demand for loans.

U.S./CANADIAN EXCHANGE RATES (MAY 15, 1996)   **Table 4.2**

	U.S. Dollar Equivalent	Currency per U.S. Dollar
Canadian dollar		
Spot rate	0.7310	1.3680
90-day forward rate	0.7321	1.3659
180-day forward rate	0.7329	1.3645

Source: *The Wall Street Journal*, May 16, 1996, p. C20.

Foreign exchange rates may seem mysterious but they are nothing more than the price of one currency stated in terms of another. Look at Table 4.2, which gives United States/Canadian foreign exchange rates for May 15, 1996. The **spot exchange rates** are the current costs for immediate delivery. The first column of the table says that on May 15, 1996, you could have purchased one Canadian dollar (C$) for 73.1 U.S. cents. The second column is simply the reciprocal of the first and says the cost of one U.S. dollar (US$) was a little more than C$1.36.

The **forward exchange rates** have the same interpretation but they are the current costs for delivery in 90 and 180 days. For example, the 90-day forward exchange rate states that US$73.21 was required on May 15, 1996 to purchase C$100 to be delivered 90 days later on August 13, 1996. You will see shortly how merchants engaged in international trade might use these forward exchange rates to protect themselves from changing currency prices.

We will use the Fisher effect and two new principles—purchasing power parity and interest rate parity—to see how inflation, foreign exchange rates, and international interest rates are interrelated.

Purchasing Power Parity

Purchasing power parity between two countries exists when identical products sell at the same price in each country after adjusting for the rate at which one country's currency can be exchanged for the other's. In other words, you should expect to pay the same price for a product if you use U.S. dollars to buy it in the United States or if you convert your U.S. dollars to Canadian dollars and buy it in Canada. Buyers will take actions that tend to restore purchasing power parity when it doesn't exist. Let's look at an example.

Suppose you own an outdoor clothing store in Detroit, which is directly across the border from Windsor, Ontario. Suppose also that you can buy identical rainsuits from a U.S. wholesaler for US$90 or a Canadian wholesaler for C$120. The Canadian wholesaler must be paid in Canadian dollars, so you must exchange your currency before you can buy from him. Using the spot exchange rate in Table 4.2, we see that you need only US$87.72 (C$120 × 0.7310) to purchase the 120 Canadian dollars you need to buy a Canadian rainsuit. Therefore, the Canadian wholesaler's price is lower and you should buy your rainsuits there.

This US$2.28 (US$90.00 – US$87.72) difference in the price of rainsuits will not persist because other store owners will respond similarly. The increase in demand for Canadian dollars to purchase Canadian rainsuits will cause the price of Canadian dollars (the exchange rate) to increase, the increase in demand for Canadian rainsuits will cause their price to increase, or the decrease in demand for U.S. rainsuits will cause their price to decrease. The precise combination of these changes that takes place cannot be predicted easily, but the final result must be that rainsuits sell at the same price in each country after adjusting for the exchange rate. Table 4.3 gives some possible outcomes of this process. Each case in panel B is in equilibrium because the U.S. price equals the exchange-rate-adjusted Canadian price. That is,

$$P_S^{US} = P_S^C \times S \qquad \qquad [4.2]$$

where P_S^{US} = U.S. spot price for the product
P_S^C = Canadian spot price for the product
S = spot foreign exchange rate.

Of course, purchasing power parity will not be completely restored if there are other costs to buy the Canadian rainsuits. Brokerage fees to purchase Canadian dollars, import tariffs, and expenses to transport the rainsuits to Detroit can reduce or even eliminate the US$2.28 savings. Then, the prices in the two countries will differ but only by the amount of these transaction costs.

You can use the prices of almost anything to check for purchasing power parity. See "In the News" (pages 140–141).

Table 4.3   PURCHASING POWER PARITY EQUILIBRIUM

Panel A: Original Situation

U.S. Price in US$	Canadian Price in C$	Exchange Rate	Canadian Price in US$
US$90.00	C$120.00	0.7310	US$87.72

Panel B: After Purchasing Power Parity Restored

U.S. Price in US$	Canadian Price in C$	Exchange Rate	Canadian Price in US$
US$90.00	C$120.00	**0.7500**	US$90.00
90.00	**123.12**	0.7310	90.00
87.72	120.00	0.7310	87.72
89.00	122.00	0.7295	89.00

Equilibrating factor is in bold type.

PURCHASING POWER PARITY

Suppose you also can buy the rainsuits in Mexico for 660 pesos. Determine the price of buying the suits there given the U.S. dollar equivalent exchange rate of 0.1348.

Price in US$ = Price in pesos × dollar equivalent exchange rate

= 660 × 0.1348 = $88.97

Does purchasing power parity hold if the cost of shipping four dozen suits from Juarez, Mexico, to Detroit is $50.00?

Cost of 48 suits purchased in Detroit = $90 × 48 = $4,320

Cost of 48 suits purchased in Juarez and shipped to Detroit = $88.97 × 48 + $50.00 = $4,320.56

Purchasing power parity holds because the prices of the rainsuits in Detroit and Mexico are nearly identical when transportation costs are considered.

Retail stores commonly order merchandise several months in advance to ensure supply and to lock-in the price. Your outdoor clothing store might place an order on May 15 for down jackets to be delivered on August 13, for example. You will need Canadian dollars on August 13 to pay for those jackets if you order them from Canada. You could always wait until August 13 to buy your Canadian dollars on the spot market but this is risky because you will suffer losses if the exchange rate has increased by then. A safer alternative that locks-in your *currency* costs is to buy the Canadian dollars now, on May 15, for delivery on August 13. The 90-day forward exchange rate in Table 4.2 says these dollars will cost you US$0.7321. By taking this approach, you are hedged against exchange rate movements and will have neither gains nor losses if these rates change.

Purchasing power parity applies to the forward market just as well as the spot market, so you should expect that the exchange-rate-adjusted price of Canadian down jackets delivered on August 13 will equal the price of U.S. jackets delivered then. That is,

$$P_F^{US} = P_F^{C} \times F \qquad \text{[4.3]}$$

where P_F^{US} = U.S. forward price for the product

P_F^{C} = Canadian forward price for the product

F = Forward foreign exchange rate.

Now, with just a little algebra, we can describe the relationship between the spot and forward exchange rates. First, we assume that the relationship between the spot and forward prices for the product in a particular country is determined by the expected inflation rate in that country. That is, $P_F^{US} = P_S^{US} \times [1 + E(I^{US})]$ and $P_F^{C} = P_S^{C} \times [1 + E(I^{C})]$. Second, we substitute these expressions into Equation 4.3, divide the result by Equation 4.2, and rearrange terms to obtain Equation 4.4:

I N   T H E   N E W S

McCURRENCIES: WHERE'S THE BEEF?

TEN YEARS ON, *The Economist's* Big Mac index is still going strong. Mad-cow disease notwithstanding, it is time to dish up our annual feast of burgernomics. The Big Mac index was devised as a lighthearted guide to whether currencies are at their "correct" level. It is not intended to be a predictor of exchange rates, but a tool to make economic theory more digestible.

Burgernomics is based upon the theory of purchasing-power parity (PPP). This argues that, in the long run, the exchange rate between two currencies should move toward the rate that would equalize the prices of an identical basket of goods and services in the two countries. Our basket is a McDonald's Big Mac, which is made to roughly the same recipe in more than 80 countries. The Big Mac PPP is the exchange rate that would make a burger cost the same in America as it does abroad. Comparing this with the actual rate is one test of whether a currency is under-valued or overvalued.

The first column of the table shows the local-currency prices of a Big Mac; the second converts them into dollars. The average price in America (including tax) is $2.36. However, bargain hunters should head for China, where a burger costs only $1.15. At the other extreme, the Swiss price of $4.80 is enough to make Big Mac fans choke on their all-beef patties. This implies that the yuan is once again the most undervalued currency, and the Swiss franc the most overvalued.

The third column shows Big Mac PPPs. For example, if you divide the Japanese price of a *Biggu Makku* by the American one, you get a dollar PPP of ¥122. The actual rate on April 22nd was ¥107, implying that the yen was 14% overvalued against the dollar. Similar sums show that the D-mark is overvalued by 37%. In general, the dollar is undervalued against the currencies of most big industrial economies, but overvalued against developing countries' ones.

Thanks partly to the dollar's recovery, the other rich-country currencies look less overvalued than a year ago. Adjustment to PPP can also come from changes in rela-tive prices rather than exchange-rate movements. The most dramatic example of this is Japan, where the price of a Big Mac was slashed by more than a quarter late last year. This reduced the yen's overvaluation from 100% to 14%.

The Big Mac index was originally introduced as a bit of fun. Yet it has inspired several serious studies over the past year. Li Lian Ong, an economist at the University of Western Australia, wrote her PhD thesis on the index.[*] She concludes that "the Big Mac index is surprisingly accurate in tracking exchange rates over the longer term." Another study, by Robert Cumby of Georgetown University in Washington, DC, also found that deviations from "McParity" are usually temporary.[**]

But a third study by Michael Pakko and Patricia Pollard of the Federal Reserve Bank of St. Louis, is more skeptical.[†] It concludes that "the Big Mac does as well— or as poorly—at demonstrating the principles and pitfalls of PPP as more sophisticated measures."

Their study concludes that although Big Mac PPP may hold in the very long run, currencies can deviate from it for lengthy periods. There are several reasons why the Big Mac index may be flawed:

- The theory of PPP falsely assumes that there are no barriers to trade. High prices in Europe, Japan, and South Korea partly reflect high tariffs on beef. Differences in transport costs also act as a trade barrier: shipping per-ishable ingredients such as lettuce and beef is dear.
- Prices are distorted by taxes. High rates of value-added tax in countries such as Denmark and Sweden exaggerate the degree to which their currencies are overvalued.
- The Big Mac is not just a basket of commodities: its price must cover rents and the cost of other non-traded inputs. Deviations of PPP may simply reflect differ-ences in such costs.
- Profit margins vary among countries according to the strength of competition. In the United States, the Big Mac has many close substitutes, but in other countries McDonald's is able to charge a premium.

---

[*]"Burgernomics: The Economics of the Big Mac Standard." University of Western Australia, November 1995.
[**]"Forecasting Exchange Rates and Relative Prices with Hamburger Standard: Is What You Want What You Get with McParity?" Georgetown University, July 1995.
[†]"For Here or To Go? Purchasing Power Parity and the Big Mac." Federal Reserve Bank of St. Louis, January 1996.
Source: *The Economist*, April 27, 1996, p. 82. Copyright © 1996, The Economist, Ltd.

In the News—Continued

Despite these weaknesses, which *The Economist* has long acknowledged, the Big Mac index still comes up with PPP estimates that are similar to those based on more sophisticated methods. Burgernomics has its methodological flaws, but our money is where our mouths are.

THE HAMBURGER STANDARD—HOW SERIOUSLY SHOULD YOU TAKE THE BIG MAC INDEX?

	Big Mac Prices				
	In Local Currency	In Dollars	Implied PPP* of the Dollar	Actual $ Exchange Rate 4/22/96	Local Currency under(−)/ over(+) Valuation,†%
United States‡	$2.36	2.36	—	—	—
Argentina	Peso3.00	3.00	1.27	1.00	+27
Australia	A$2.50	1.97	1.06	1.27	−17
Austria	Sch36.00	3.40	15.3	10.7	+43
Belgium	BFr109	3.50	46.2	31.2	+48
Brazil	Real2.95	2.98	1.25	0.99	+26
Britain	£1.79	2.70	1.32 ††	1.51 ††	+14
Canada	C$2.86	2.10	1.21	1.36	−11
Chile	Peso950	2.33	403	408	−1
China	Yuan9.60	1.15	4.07	8.35	−51
Czech Republic	CKr51.0	1.85	21.6	27.6	−22
Denmark	DKr25.75	4.40	10.9	5.85	+87
France	FFr17.5	3.41	7.42	5.13	+46
Germany	DM4.90	3.22	2.08	1.52	+37
Hong Kong	HK$9.90	1.28	4.19	7.74	−46
Hungary	Forint214	1.43	90.7	150	−39
Israel	Shekel9.50	3.00	4.03	3.17	+27
Italy	Lire4,500	2.90	1,907	1,551	+23
Japan	¥288	2.70	122	107	+14
Malaysia	M$3.76	1.51	1.59	2.49	−36
Mexico	Peso14.9	2.02	6.31	7.37	−14
Netherlands	Fl5.45	3.21	2.31	1.70	+36
New Zealand	NZ$2.95	2.01	1.25	1.47	−15
Poland	Zloty3.80	1.44	1.61	2.64	−39
Russia	Rouble9,500	1.93	4,025	4,918	−18
Singapore	S$3.05	2.16	1.29	1.41	−8
South Africa	Rand7.00	1.64	2.97	4.26	−30
South Korea	Won2,300	2.95	975	779	+25
Spain	Pta365	2.89	155	126	+23
Sweden	SKr26.0	3.87	11.0	6.71	+64
Switzerland	SFr5.90	4.80	2.50	1.23	+103
Taiwan	NT$65.0	2.39	27.5	27.2	+1
Thailand	Baht48.0	1.90	20.3	25.3	−20

*Purchasing-power parity: local price divided by price in the United States   †Against dollar
‡Average of New York, Chicago, San Francisco, and Atlanta   ††Dollars per pound

$$\frac{[1 + E(I^{US})]}{[1 + E(I^C)]} = \frac{F}{S} . \qquad [4.4]$$

In Equation 4.4, the ratio of forward-to-spot exchange rates is determined by the relative amount of expected inflation in the two countries. The spot and 90 day forward U.S./Canadian exchange rates in Table 4.2 indicate that the two countries were expected to have approximately the same rate of inflation from May 15 to August 13, 1996 because

$$[1 + E(I^{US})]/[1 + E(I^C)] = F/S$$
$$= 0.7321/0.7310 = 1.0015.$$

EXERCISE   ●——————————————————————————————————————●

4.3   DETERMINING IMPLIED INFLATION RATES

Use the foreign exchange rates in Table 4.2 to determine the relative rates of expected inflation in the United States and Canada from May 15 to November 11, 1996.

$$[1 + E(I^{US})]/[1 + E(I^C)] = F/S$$
$$= 0.7329/0.7310 = 1.0026$$

The United States and Canada were expected to have approximately the same rates of inflation during this 180-day period.

●————————————●

Interest Rate Parity

The Fisher effect (Equation 4.1) relates interest rates to inflation, while purchasing power parity (Equation 4.4) relates inflation to exchange rates. We can combine these two principles to obtain an expression for interest rate parity.

The Fisher effect is applied to the United States and Canada by Equations 4.5A and 4.5B:

$$1 + r^{US} = [1 + i^{US}] \times [1 + E(I^{US})] \qquad [4.5A]$$

$$1 + r^C = [1 + i^C] \times [1 + E(I^C)] \qquad [4.5B]$$

where r^{US}, r^C = nominal interest rate in the United States andCanada
i^{US}, i^C = real interest rate in the United States and Canada
$E(I^{US}), E(I^C)$ = expected inflation rate in the United States and Canada.

If real interest rates in the two countries are approximately equal, then we can divide Equation 4.5A by 4.5B to obtain

$$\frac{1 + r^{US}}{1 + r^C} = \frac{[1 + E(I^{US})]}{[1 + E(I^C)]}.$$

Substituting this result into Equation 4.4 gives

$$\frac{1 + r^{US}}{1 + r^{C}} = \frac{F}{S}.$$ [4.6]

The condition represented by Equation 4.6 is known as **interest rate parity**. This condition exists when identical loans provide the same yield in each country after adjusting for the rate at which one country's currency can be exchanged for the other's. In other words, you should expect to pay the same interest rate on a loan if you borrow U.S. dollars in the United States or if you borrow Canadian dollars in Canada and convert them into U.S. dollars. Borrowers and lenders will take actions that tend to restore interest rate parity when it doesn't exist. Let's look at another example.

Suppose a corporate treasurer has US\$1,000,000 that she wants to invest for 180 days. Her choices are to purchase U.S. or Canadian government securities with six-month yields of 2.65 percent and 2.38 percent. Which securities should she buy if the exchange rates are those given in Table 4.2? We must restate the interest rate on the Canadian securities in US\$ to answer this question. The calculations are shown in Table 4.4.

Table 4.4 gives the Canadian cash flows to be paid and received and their US\$ equivalents if the treasurer buys the Canadian government securities. Her US\$1,000,000 will buy 1,368,000 Canadian dollars according to the exchange rates in Table 4.2. This is the amount she can invest in Canadian government securities that will be worth C\$1,400,558 (C\$1,368,000 $\times$ 1.0238) at maturity. Based on the 180-day forward exchange rate, these Canadian dollars can be exchanged for US\$1,026,469 (C\$1,400,558 $\times$ 0.7329).

The interest rate on the Canadian government securities restated in US\$ is (US\$1,026,469/US\$1,000,000) $-$ 1 = 0.0265 or 2.65 percent. The treasurer can earn 2.65 percent for 180 days by investing in either U.S. or Canadian government securities because there is interest rate parity between the United States and Canada at these interest and exchange rates. Therefore, it doesn't matter which securities she buys.

We obtain the same conclusion by rewriting the interest rate parity condition, Equation 4.7, as follows:

$$r^{US} = [(1 + r^{C}) \times F/S] - 1.$$ [4.7]

The left-hand side is the U.S. interest rate and the right-hand side is the exchange-rate-adjusted Canadian interest rate. Substituting the interest and exchange rates available to the treasurer,

$$r^{US} = 2.65\%$$

$$\text{Adjusted } r^{C} = [(1 + r^{C}) \times F/S] - 1$$

CASH FLOWS AND INTEREST RATE FROM PURCHASING CANADIAN GOVERNMENT SECURITY   **Table** 4.4

	In US\$		Exchange Rate		In C\$
Amount invested	\$1,000,000	$\rightarrow$	1.3680	$\rightarrow$	C\$1,368,000
Value at maturity	1,026,469	$\leftarrow$	0.7329	$\leftarrow$	1,400,558
Effective interest rate	2.65%				2.38%

$$\text{Adjusted } r^C = (1.0238) \times 0.7329/0.7310 - 1$$
$$= 0.0265 \text{ or } 2.65\%.$$

The U.S. and exchange-rate-adjusted Canadian interest rates are equal, which means interest rate parity holds. This is an equilibrium in which there is no tendency for borrowers or lenders to seek loans in one country rather than the other. There will be no change in the foreign supply and demand for loans in either country as long as this situation persists.

We can use the formula for the exchange-rate-adjusted interest rate, adjusted $r^C = (1 + r^C) \times F/S - 1$, to easily see how violations of interest rate parity will cause changes in the foreign supply and demand for loans. Suppose the exchange-rate-adjusted Canadian interest rate falls from 2.65 percent to 2.50 percent. Then borrowers will be attracted to Canada and lenders will be attracted to the United States. This will reduce the demand and increase the supply of loans in the United States, which will tend to reduce U.S. interest rates. The process will end when interest rate parity is restored.

The formula for the exchange-rate-adjusted interest rate also shows us how the disequilibrium situation can arise. Continuing the example, the adjusted Canadian interest rate can decrease because the real rate of interest or the inflation rate decreased, because the forward exchange rate decreased, or because the spot exchange rate increased. Exchange rates respond to the demand for foreign currency to purchase real products so the foreign supply and demand for loans are also influenced by the level of trade between the two countries.

EXERCISE   ● ── ●

4.4 DETERMINING THE YIELD OF FOREIGN SECURITIES

Suppose a treasurer can purchase U.S. or Canadian government securities with 90-day yields of 1.60 percent and 1.50 percent. Use the exchange rates in Table 4.2 to determine the exchange-rate-adjusted yield on the Canadian securities. Should the treasurer invest in the United States or Canada? What will happen to interest and exchange rates if other treasurers follow suit?

$$\text{Adjusted } r^C = (1 + r^C) \times F/S - 1$$
$$= (1.015) \times 0.7321/0.7310 - 1$$
$$= 0.0165 \text{ or } 1.65\%$$

Because the exchange-rate-adjusted yield on Canadian government securities is higher than the yield on U.S. government securities (1.65 percent versus 1.60 percent), the treasurer should invest in Canada. Treasurers will buy Canadian dollars, causing the spot exchange rate to increase; they will buy Canadian government securities, causing their yields to decrease; and they will sell Canadian dollars on August 13, causing the forward exchange rate to decrease. If enough treasurers take these actions, interest rate parity will be restored.

● ────────── ●

4.3   THE TERM STRUCTURE OF INTEREST RATES

The **term structure of interest rates** describes the relationship between the spot interest rates on financial instruments and their terms to maturity. The term structure often is represented by a **yield curve**, a graph of bonds' yields versus maturity. *The Wall Street Journal* publishes a yield curve daily in its credit markets section. *The Wall Street Journal*'s yield curve for May 15, 1996 is reproduced in Exhibit 4.2. This is a normal yield curve because long-term interest rates usually exceed short-term rates. The yield curve is said to be *inverted* when short-term rates are higher than long-term rates.

You can construct your own yield curve from the yields on U.S. Treasury strips. *Treasury strips* are financial instruments that permit investors to buy separate claims on each interest and principal payment on U.S. Treasury notes and bonds. By separating these claims, Treasury strips convert an interest-bearing financial instrument into a pure-discount instrument, a security that pays a single cash flow at maturity. For example, a stripped 10-year Treasury bond becomes 21 pure-discount bonds: one bond for each semi-annual interest payment and one bond for the principal payment. The current yield on each pure-discount bond is the market interest rate for a riskless loan of exactly that length. Exhibit 4.3 is a yield curve constructed from the yields on U.S. Treasury strips on May 15, 1996.

Yield curves explicitly describe current **spot interest rates**—the yields on securities purchased for immediate delivery. For example, the yield curve in Exhibit 4.3 says that a one-year Treasury strip purchased on May 15, 1996 and held until maturity

---

U.S. TREASURY SECURITIES YIELD CURVE (MAY 15, 1996)

Exhibit 4.2

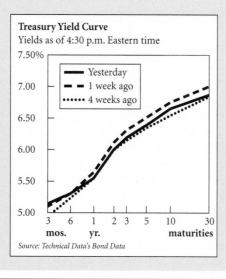

Source: *The Wall Street Journal,* May 16, 1996, p. C24.

Exhibit 4.3

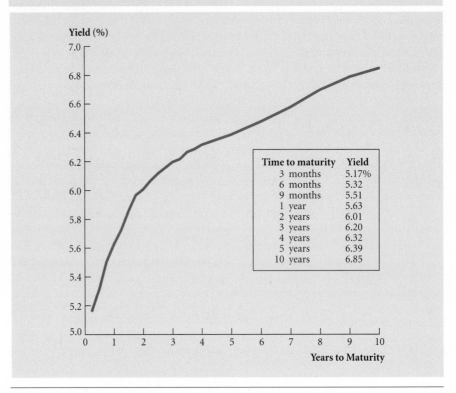

YIELD CURVE CONSTRUCTED FROM YIELDS ON TREASURY STRIPS (MAY 15, 1996)

Time to maturity	Yield
3 months	5.17%
6 months	5.32
9 months	5.51
1 year	5.63
2 years	6.01
3 years	6.20
4 years	6.32
5 years	6.39
10 years	6.85

Source: *The Wall Street Journal*, May 16, 1996, p. C26.

would earn 5.63 percent annual interest. Similarly, a two-year Treasury strip purchased on May 15, 1996 and held until maturity would earn 6.01 percent annual interest.

Yield curves also describe *implicit* **forward interest rates**—the yields on securities purchased for future delivery. Buying or selling a security for future delivery may seem like an unusual transaction, but it isn't. A common example is the loan commitment a person obtains to buy a home. The interest rate on the loan is set when the loan is approved even though the prospective homeowner doesn't actually borrow the money until the transaction is completed at closing perhaps 30 or 60 days later. This loan commitment is a forward transaction if both parties are obligated to complete the deal.

We will represent forward interest rates with the symbol, $_tf_n$, where f is the interest rate on a loan commencing at time t and due at time n. The present, as always, is time zero. Note that $n - t$ equals the length of the loan. To illustrate, suppose you know that one year from now you will need a two-year loan and arrange financing from your bank at 14.0 percent interest. Using our notation,

$$_1f_3 = 14.0\%.$$

You infer the forward interest rates implicit in the yield curve by setting the rate of return from buying a succession of short-term notes equal to the rate of return from buying a single long-term note that covers the same time period. Using one year as the length of our short-term period and two years as the length of our long-term period,

$$(1 + r_1) \times (1 + {}_1f_2) = (1 + r_2)^2 \qquad\qquad \textbf{[4.8]}$$

where r_1 = one-year spot interest rate
             r_2 = two-year spot interest rate
             $_1f_2$ = implied one-year forward interest rate.

Rearranging terms,

$$_1f_2 = (1 + r_2)^2/(1 + r_1) - 1.$$

You also can find the *approximate* value of the implied forward rate, $_1f_2$, using the arithmetic approximation,

$$r_2 = (r_1 + {}_1f_2)/2.$$

Rearranging terms,

$$_1f_2 = 2 \times r_2 - r_1.$$

Substituting the spot rates from Exhibit 4.3 for r_1 and r_2 gives the implied one-year forward interest rate on May 15, 1996. Using the exact method,

$$_1f_2 = (1 + r_2)^2/(1 + r_1) - 1$$
$$= (1.0601)^2/(1.0563) - 1$$
$$= 0.063914 \text{ or } 6.3914\%.$$

According to the arithmetic approximation,

$$_1f_2 = 2 \times r_2 - r_1$$
$$= 2 \times 0.0601 - 0.0563$$
$$= 0.06390 \text{ or } 6.39\%.$$

The exact result says that an investor who purchases a two-year Treasury strip on May 15, 1996 and holds it until maturity earns an implied rate of return during the second year of 6.3914 percent. At these rates ($r_1 = 5.63$ percent, $_1f_2 = 6.3914$ percent, and $r_2 = 6.01$ percent), the amount of interest paid or received on two consecutive one-year loans equals the amount of interest paid or received on a single two-year loan.

● ———————————————————————————————— ●   E X E R C I S E

DETERMINING IMPLIED FORWARD INTEREST RATES

4·5

Use the data in Exhibit 4.3 to determine the implied forward interest rate on a one-year loan commencing in two years, $_2f_3$.

$$_2f_3 = (1 + r_3)^3/(1 + r_2)^2 - 1$$
$$r_2 = 6.01\%, r_3 = 6.20\%$$

Therefore,

$$_2f_3 = [(1.0620)^3/(1.0601)^2] - 1$$
$$= 0.0658 \text{ or } 6.58\%.$$

The implied forward interest rate on a one-year loan commencing in two years is 6.58 percent.

• ——————— •

The Expectations Theory

The **expectations theory** of the term structure attaches special significance to the implied forward interest rates by stating that they must equal the spot interest rates borrowers and lenders anticipate in the future.[2] If this is true, current long-term spot interest rates are simply averages of the current short-term spot interest rates and expected future spot interest rates. You can see this relationship by substituting the expected future spot interest rate for the forward interest rate in Equation 4.8.

$$(1 + r_2)^2 = [1 + r_1] \times [1 + E(_1r_2)]$$

Solving for r_2,

$$r_2 = \{[1 + r_1] \times [1 + E(_1r_2)]\}^{1/2} - 1.$$

The arithmetic approximation is

$$r_2 = [r_1 + E(_1r_2)]/2. \tag{4.9}$$

where r_2 = two-year spot rate

r_1 = one-year spot rate

$E(_1r_2)$ = expected future one-year spot rate.

If the condition described by Equation 4.9 isn't satisfied, then the *expected* amount of interest on two consecutive short-term loans will not equal the amount of interest on a single long-term loan. Borrowers will prefer the loan with the lower interest payments and lenders will prefer the loan with the higher interest payments in this situation. Their divergent preferences shift the supply and demand for short- and long-term loans, which cause the interest rates to change. Equilibrium is restored when both types of loans have the same cost. By this process, borrowers' and lenders' expectations about the future interest rates are incorporated in the structure of current interest rates.

We can use the one-year spot rate of 5.63 percent and the two-year spot rate of 6.01 percent from Exhibit 4.3 to illustrate this process. These rates provide the initial equilibrium if we assume the expected future one-year spot rate equals the implied forward rate of 6.3914 percent. This situation is illustrated in panel A of Table 4.5 where the amount of interest paid or received is the same for short- and long-term loans.

Now suppose that expectations of increased government spending next year cause borrowers and lenders to revise their forecast of future spot interest rates from

---

[2]Irving Fisher, cited earlier, and Friedrich A. Lutz, "The Structure of Interest Rates," *Quarterly Journal of Economics,* November 1940, pp. 36–63.

HOW EXPECTATIONS ARE INCORPORATED IN THE TERM STRUCTURE   Table 4.5

Type of Loan	Amount of Loan (1/12/95)	Current 1-Year Spot Rate	Expected Future 1-Year Spot Rate	Current 2-Year Spot Rate	Expected Amount Due (1/11/97)	Effective Interest Rate
Panel A: Initial Equilibrium						
Two 1-year loans	$1,000,000	5.63%	6.3914%		$1,123,812	6.01%
One 2-year loan	1,000,000			6.01%	1,123,812	6.01
Panel B: Expected Future Spot Rate Increases to 7.0%						
Two 1-year loans	$1,000,000	5.63	7.00		1,130,241	6.31
One 2-year loan	1,000,000			6.01	1,123,812	6.01
Panel C: One Possible New Equilibrium						
Two 1-year loans	$1,000,000	5.50	7.00		1,128,850	6.2474
One 2-year loan	1,000,000			6.2474	1,128,851	6.2474

6.3914 percent to 7.00 percent. With no change in the one- and two-year spot rates, the expected amount of interest paid or received on two successive one-year loans is greater than the amount on a single two-year loan. Borrowers will therefore seek a two-year loan to avoid refinancing at the new, higher interest rate. This shifts the demand from short- to long-term loans, which causes short-term interest rates to fall and long-term interest rates to rise. At the same time, lenders will prefer to extend a one-year loan so they can reinvest after interest rates increase. This shifts the supply from long- to short-term loans, which also causes short-term interest rates to fall and long-term interest rates to rise. One possible conclusion to this process is shown in panel C. The implicit forward rate equals the expected future spot rate when $r_1 = 5.5$ percent and $r_2 = 6.2474$ percent, so this new equilibrium structure incorporates borrowers' and lenders' expectations about the future.

EXERCISE
4.6

FINDING A NEW EQUILIBRIUM SET OF INTEREST RATES

Beginning with $r_1 = 5.63$ percent, $r_2 = 6.01$ percent, and $_1f_2 = E(_1r_2) = 6.3914$ percent, find a new equilibrium set of interest rates if borrowers and lenders revise their forecast of future spot interest rates from 6.3914 percent to 5.75 percent.

The equilibrium condition is that

$$[1 + r_1] \times [1 + E(_1r_2)] \text{ must equal } [1 + r_2]^2.$$

Therefore, one possible equilibrium is

$$[1.0563] \times [1.0575] = [1 + r_2]^2$$
$$r_2 = \{[1.0563] \times [1.0575]\}^{1/2} - 1$$
$$= 0.0569 \text{ or } 5.69\%.$$

Using the arithmetic approximation,

$$r_2 = (5.63\% + 5.75\%)/2 = 5.69\%.$$

● ——————————— ●

The arithmetic approximation is often used for the general description of the expectations theory of the term structure of interest rates. Written to describe the interest rate on a loan of any maturity, *t*, this equation is

$$r_t = [r_1 + E(_1r_2) + E(_2r_3) + \dots + E(_{t-1}r_t)]/t. \qquad \textbf{[4.10]}$$

where $\quad r_t = $ *t*-year spot interest rate
$r_1 = $ current one-year spot interest rate
$E(_{t-1}r_t) = $ expected future one-year spot interest rate on a
loan commencing in $t-1$ years.

As an illustration, suppose the current one-year spot interest rate is 5.0 percent and the market's expectations are as described below.

$$E(_1r_2) = 5.40\%$$
$$E(_2r_3) = 5.50\%$$
$$E(_3r_4) = 5.55\%$$

Then, according to the expectations theory of the term structure of interest rates, the current spot rates for loans of two, three, and four years are

$$r_2 = [r_1 + E(_1r_2)]/2$$
$$= [5.00\% + 5.40\%]/2 = 5.20\%$$
$$r_3 = [r_1 + E(_1r_2) + E(_2r_3)]/3$$
$$= [5.00\% + 5.40\% + 5.50\%]/3 = 5.30\%$$
$$r_4 = [r_1 + E(_1r_2) + E(_2r_3) + E(_3r_4)]/4$$
$$= [5.00\% + 5.40\% + 5.50\% + 5.55\%]/4 = 5.36\%.$$

This yield curve is graphed in Exhibit 4.4. The positive slope results from the market's expectations that future short-term interest rates will increase. Exercise 4.7 assumes the market expects future short-term interest rates to decrease. Can you guess what shape this yield curve will have?

E X E R C I S E   ● ——————————————————————————————————— ●

4.7   **USING THE MARKET'S EXPECTATIONS
TO COMPUTE SPOT INTEREST RATES**

Use the market expectations given below to determine the current spot interest rate for loans of two, three, and four years.

Exhibit 4.4

HYPOTHETICAL YIELD CURVE

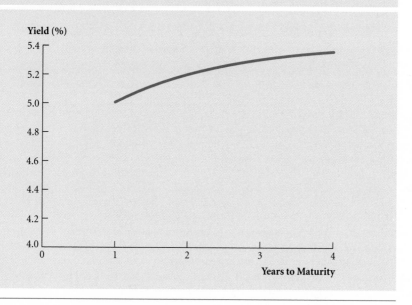

$r_1 = 6.0\%$

$E(_1r_2) = 5.70\%$

$E(_2r_3) = 5.50\%$

$E(_3r_4) = 5.40\%$

Using Equation 4.10,

$$r_t = [r_1 + E(_1r_2) + E(_2r_3) + \dots + E(_{t-1}r_t)]/t$$

$r_1 = 6.0\%$

$r_2 = [6.00\% + 5.70\%]/2 = 5.85\%$

$r_3 = [6.00\% + 5.70\% + 5.50\%]/3 = 5.73\%$

$r_4 = [6.00\% + 5.70\% + 5.50\% + 5.40\%]/4 = 5.65\%.$

This is an inverted yield curve, which reflects the market's expectations that interest rates will decline.

• ——— •

Economists use the yield curve to infer the market's expectations about future interest rates and other economic conditions such as the rate of inflation (see "In the News").

Interest Rate Risk

Borrowers and lenders lock-in the interest rate on a loan when they choose the term to maturity that matches the time period for which they have a cash deficit or surplus.

IN THE NEWS

USING THE YIELD CURVE FOR ECONOMIC FORECASTING

EIGHT MONTHS AGO the Treasury yield curve went nearly flat—an alarming shape for economists sensitive to signs of impending recession. Today this meaningful curve (which is a plot of the interest rates paid on U.S. securities ranging from 3-month bills to 30-year bonds) is nice and steep. This means, depending on who's talking: The economy is growing strongly; the economy is growing too strongly; interest rates and inflation may be headed up; the stock market will continue its bull run.

Apart from the yield curve's quick steepening, what's surprising about all this is that economists are paying attention to the yield curve at all. Only five years ago a lot of economic forecasters had dismissed many of the curve's signals as useless. It's taken a large body of research, but the yield curve's reputation has been rehabilitated. In fact, it may be the single best economic indicator forecasters have.

For most of its life, investors and market analysts used the yield curve to decide which Treasury bond or note offered the best interest rate deal. But in the 1980s, economists realized that the steepness of the curve might also predict inflation, interest rates, and even recessions. Their theories were based on the idea that investors usually demand higher interest rates on money tied up for longer periods to protect themselves against inflation and other risks. If investors think that the economy is healthy and that inflation won't take off, they'll demand only a modest premium for long-term bonds. Typically, 10-year notes yield between one and two percentage points more than 3-month bills, and the curve bends up. But if long-term rates fall below short-term rates, the curve inverts and arcs downward. This is bad. A yield-curve inversion means either that something (usually the Fed) is driving up short-term rates, which will slow economic activity, or that investors fearing a downturn have rushed to lock their money in long bonds, driving those yields down.

All that made sense to economist Frederic Mishkin, who wrote a series of articles a decade ago showing how the curve was a terrific predictor of inflation and interest rates. But Mishkin, who is now director of research at the Federal Reserve Bank of New York, soon began to question the curve's predictive powers. He, and many other economists, thought that it had failed to warn of the 1990 recession. Now, however, Mishkin and another researcher have published studies showing that the curve did flash a warning signal in 1989. Short rates crept slightly above long rates, inverting the curve for a brief period, so it wasn't much of an alert. (Then again, it wasn't much of a recession.) By the time the downturn hit, many experts, including Mishkin, had dismissed the curve's faint early warning sign.

But an inversion did happen, a recession followed, and today the yield curve is readorned with predictive prestige. Mishkin's newest research revisits the data and shows that the yield curve has been the best downturn predictor over the past 30 years: Every time the curve inverted, a recession followed a year or so later. It's little wonder, then, that a growing number of economists and stock pickers are heeding the yield curve.

However, their effective interest rate is uncertain when they choose a different term to maturity because they may have to renew the loan at higher or lower interest rates than they expected. This uncertainty about the effective yield on a loan is called **interest rate risk.**

THE EFFECT OF UNCERTAINTY ABOUT FUTURE INTEREST RATES **Table 4.6**

Change in Future 1-Year Rate	Amount of Loan (1/12/95)	Initial 1-Year Rate	1-Year Rate When Loan Is Refinanced	2-Year Rate	Amount Due (1/11/97)	Effective Interest Rate
Panel A: One 2-Year Loan						
Any change	$1,000,000			6.01%	$1,123,812	6.010%
Panel B: Two 1-Year Loans						
Decrease	1,000,000	5.63%	5.8357%		1,117,942	5.733
No change	1,000,000	5.63	6.3914		1,123,812	6.010
Increase	1,000,000	5.63	7.0000		1,130,241	6.313

Table 4.6 illustrates the effect of interest rate risk on borrowers and lenders who have a two-year time horizon. Each knows the final amount due on a two-year loan initiated on May 15, 1996 because the two-year interest rate applies to the entire term of the loan. The amount due, and therefore the effective interest rate of 6.01 percent, is fixed when the loan is arranged no matter what happens to one-year interest rates in the future.

DETERMINING THE PAYOFF FROM A TWO-YEAR BOND

EXERCISE 4.8

Otto Stock has $100,000 to invest on January 1, 1998. Determine the amount of cash he will have on December 31, 1999, if he buys two-year bonds given a spot two-year interest rate of 6.0 percent.

$$\text{Cash at maturity from 2-year bonds} = \$100,000 \times (1 + r_2)^2$$
$$= \$100,000 \times (1.06)^2$$
$$= \$112,360$$

Otto is certain to have $112,360 when his two-year bond matures.

The final amount due on two consecutive one-year loans will be more or less than $1,123,812, however, depending on whether the future one-year interest rate increases from 6.3914 percent to 7.00 percent or decreases to 5.8357 percent. Therefore, the effective interest rate over the entire two-year period may be as high as 6.313 percent or as low as 5.733 percent. The average of the effective interest rates is approximately 6.01 percent, but the actual rate that will be paid or received is uncertain when the loan is initiated on May 15, 1996. In other words, there is risk.

E X E R C I S E   ● ────────────────────────────────────── ●

4.9   ILLUSTRATION OF INTEREST RATE RISK

Otto also could buy one-year bonds and reinvest the proceeds at the interest rate that prevails on January 1, 1999. The current spot interest rates for one- and two-year loans are 5.5 percent and 6.0 percent. These rates imply a forward rate, $_1f_2$, of 6.5024 percent. How much cash will he have on December 31, 1999 if the interest rate on January 1, 1999 equals (a) the implicit forward rate, (b) 1.25 $\times$ the implicit forward rate, and (c) 0.80 $\times$ the implicit forward rate?

$$\text{(a)} \quad \text{Cash at maturity} = \$100{,}000 \times (1.055) \times (1.065024)$$
$$= \$112{,}360$$
$$\text{(b)} \quad \text{Interest rate on } 1/1/1999 = 6.5024\% \times 1.25 = 8.128\%$$
$$\text{Cash at maturity} = \$100{,}000 \times (1.055) \times (1.08128)$$
$$= \$114{,}075$$
$$\text{(c)} \quad \text{Interest rate on } 1/1/1999 = 6.5024\% \times 0.80 = 5.2019\%$$
$$\text{Cash at maturity} = \$100{,}000 \times (1.055) \times (1.052019)$$
$$= \$110{,}988.$$

Otto may have as much as \$114,075 or as little as \$110,988 on December 31, 1999 if he invests in one-year bonds. His future payoff is uncertain.

● ──────────── ●

The important point of the examples in Table 4.6 and Exercises 4.8 and 4.9 is this: Borrowers and lenders are not subject to interest rate risk unless they choose a loan with a term to maturity that does not match the period for which they have a cash deficit or surplus. The two-year loan was riskless and the one-year loan was risky in these examples because the borrower's and lender's time horizons were two years. These characterizations would be reversed if their time horizons were one year. We will have more to say about interest rate risk later.

Even the most experienced borrowers are tempted to accept interest rate risk by borrowing short term to meet long-term needs (see "In the News").

The Preferred Habitat Theory

The expectations theory of the term structure assumes borrowers and lenders ignore interest rate risk. Their assumed willingness to seek the loan with the most favorable interest rate regardless of its term to maturity is what incorporates their expectations into current yields. The theory's simple description of current interest rates as averages of expected future interest rates follows directly from this assumption. Unfortunately, the assumption that investors ignore risk is unrealistic and the term structure of interest rates is more complicated than the expectations theory suggests.

The complication arises because borrowers and lenders do care about risk and they can avoid risk entirely by choosing a loan with a term to maturity that exactly matches their time horizon or preferred habitat. For example, an electric utility's preferred habitat may be long-term loans because it is risky to refinance a power plant every few years. Conversely, a bank may prefer to extend short-term loans because its own liabilities are short term.

I N   T H E   N E W S

SUBSTITUTING BILLS FOR BONDS TO TRY AND SAVE A BUNDLE

STRAPPED WITH A debt of $4 trillion, Uncle Sam naturally wants to pay the lowest interest rates possible. In a move expected to save up to $16 billion over the next five years, the Treasury said it would shift a big chunk of its borrowing from long term to short term. The use of bonds and notes that mature in five years or more, which currently carry interest rates of roughly 5 percent to 7 percent, will be reduced 45 percent. More money will be raised with securities that mature in three years or less, on which the government has to pay only about 3 percent to 4 percent. The strategy makes sense now, but it's not foolproof. If inflation were to accelerate sharply, short-term interest rates could shoot higher than long-term rates. In that case, savings from the new plan could prove to be short term as well.

Source: "A Break for Uncle Sam," *Time*, May 17, 1993, p. 21. In *Time Almanac 1990s*, copyright Time Inc. Reprinted with permission.

The **preferred habitat theory** of the term structure of interest rates recognizes that investors have maturity preferences but asserts that these preferences may be overcome if interest rates include a premium that compensates them for the real and psychological costs of risk.[3] The addition to the interest rate that makes borrowers and lenders indifferent to loans of various maturities is called the **term premium**. Adding this premium to Equation 4.10 gives:

$$r_t = [r_1 + E(_1r_2) + E(_2r_3) + \dots + E(_{t-1}r_t)]/t + prem_t \qquad [4.11]$$

where

r_t = t-year spot interest rate

r_1 = current one-year spot interest rate

$E(_{t-1}r_t)$ = expected future one-year spot interest rate on a loan commencing in $t - 1$ years

$prem_t$ = term premium for loans that mature in t years.

Earlier, we determined that, according to the expectations theory, the spot interest rate for a two-year loan is 5.10 percent if $r_1 = 5.0$ percent and $E(_1r_2) = 5.20$ percent. Given the same assumptions plus a term premium of 1.0 percent, the spot interest rate on a two-year loan according to the preferred habitat theory is

$$r_2 = [r_1 + E(_1r_2)]/t + prem_2$$
$$= [5.0\% + 5.2\%]/2 + 1.0\%$$
$$= 5.1\% + 1.0\% = 6.1\%.$$

At these rates, borrowers and lenders are indifferent between one- and two-year loans because the higher interest rate on the two-year loan exactly compensates for its additional risk.

---

[3]John R. Hicks, *Value and Capital: An Inquiry into Some Fundamental Principles of Economic Theory*, Clarendon Press, Oxford, 1946.

EXERCISE ●

4.10   **ADDING A TERM PREMIUM TO THE TERM STRUCTURE**

Use the interest rate assumptions given above to determine the three-year spot interest rate according to the preferred habitat theory if $E(_2r_3) = 5.36$ percent and $prem_3 = 1.2$ percent.

$$r_3 = [r_1 + E(_1r_2) + E(_2r_3)]/3 + prem_3$$
$$= [5.00\% + 5.20\% + 5.36\%]/3 + 1.2\% = 6.39\%$$

The three-year spot interest rate is 6.39 percent.

● ─────── ●

In principle, the term premium can be positive, negative, or zero depending on the relative strength of borrowers' and lenders' preferences for a particular maturity. The term premium is positive when borrowers have stronger preferences for loans of a particular maturity because their demand for those loans increases the interest rate. Conversely, the premium is negative when lenders have stronger preferences for loans of a particular maturity because their supply of those loans decreases the interest rate. Nevertheless, term premiums have historically been positive and an increasing function of term to maturity. They are sometimes called *liquidity premiums* because they seem to reflect a net preference for short-term, more liquid or marketable securities.

Another theory of the term structure asserts that investors' preferences for particular maturities are absolute and cannot be overcome by paying them a risk premium. This theory, called the **segmented market theory**, implies there is no connection between current and expected future interest rates. Instead, the term structure of interest rates simply reflects the intersections of supply and demand for loans of various maturities. See J.M. Culbertson, "The Term Structure of Interest Rates," *The American Economic Review*, May 1966, pp. 178–197.

4.4   OTHER FACTORS THAT AFFECT THE STRUCTURE OF INTEREST RATES

The term structure of interest rates explains the difference between the yields on short- and long-term instruments in Table 4.1. Other differences, however, are attributable to the borrowers' characteristics or the *types* of financial instruments they use. The importance of these differences depends in part on whether the security is riskless or risky, so we will discuss these categories of financial instruments separately.

Premiums and Discounts on Riskless Debt

U.S. Treasury securities often are considered riskless because there is no danger that the U.S. government will default on its obligations.[4] The securities issued by U.S. government agencies such as the Federal Home Loan Bank also are generally considered to be riskless in this sense. Only a few agencies' debt is actually backed by the full faith and

---

[4]Don't forget that even government securities are subject to interest rate risk as we saw in the preceding section.

credit of the U.S. government, but no one really believes the Treasury would allow the other agencies to fail. Nevertheless, U.S. agency securities provide a higher yield than Treasury securities with the same maturity for two reasons.

One part of the yield premium on U.S. government agency securities compensates investors because these financial instruments are less marketable than Treasury securities. They are not less marketable because they have unique characteristics or because investors are unfamiliar with the government agencies. On the contrary, they are quite similar to the Treasury securities in these respects. The reason they are less marketable is that they are traded in less active markets. This difference is apparent by simply comparing the sizes of these markets; there was $3.292 trillion of U.S. Treasury bills, notes, and bonds outstanding at the end of 1995 but only $806.664 billion of agency securities outstanding.[5] Transaction costs are lower in larger, more active markets, which permits investors to buy and sell securities quickly without making a significant price concession. This is the essence of marketability.

The other part of the yield premium on U.S. government agency securities compensates investors because the income from some of these instruments is subject to state taxes. Suppose Treasury and agency securities are similar in every respect except taxes. Then investors may be satisfied with a similar after-tax yield on the securities, which implies their before-tax yield must be different. To illustrate, assume investors are subject to state income taxes that average 5 percent. Then equal after-tax yields on Treasury and agency securities require that their before tax yields are

$$r_{\text{agency}} \times (1 - 0.05) = r_{\text{Treasury}} \times (1 - 0)$$
$$r_{\text{agency}} = r_{\text{Treasury}}/0.95.$$

Tax-induced differences in interest rates also work in the opposite direction. Municipals or munies are bonds issued by cities and states and are exempt from U.S. government taxes. Assuming the marginal federal tax rate on individuals is 36 percent, the before-tax yields on munis should approximately equal:

$$r_{\text{muni}} \times (1 - 0) = r_{\text{taxable security}} \times (1 - 0.36)$$
$$r_{\text{muni}} = 0.64 \times r_{\text{taxable security}}$$

Premiums and Discounts for Attached Options

Bonds often are issued with attached options that give the borrower or lender the opportunity to exchange them for cash or another security. *Callable bonds* give the borrower the option to pay off the debt prior to maturity. Convertible bonds give the lender the option to convert the bonds into another security, usually common stock. These options are valuable and therefore have predictable effects on the yield of the securities to which they are attached.

Companies issue bonds with a call option attached to make it easy for them to refinance their debt when interest rates have declined. They can always buy their bonds back in the open market but this is expensive because bond prices increase when interest rates fall. Furthermore, buying the bonds back at their market price gives all the benefits of

---

[5]*Federal Reserve Bulletin,* Board of Governors of the Federal Reserve System, May 1996, Tables 1.41 and 1.44.

refinancing to the bondholders. When bonds are called at a price less than their market value, the company saves money; this permits the company's stockholders to obtain some of the benefits of refinancing.

The bondholders are quick to recognize that callable bonds are beneficial to the owners at their expense. In other words, they recognize that the call option is valuable to the common stockholders. The bondholders therefore protect themselves in several ways. One method of protection is to defer the call option for several years. This provision not only ensures the bondholders will continue to receive the contractual rate of interest, but may prevent the company from calling the bonds while interest rates are *temporarily* reduced.

Another method of protection is to require a call premium, an addition to the par value that must be paid when the bond is called. This premium raises the cost of calling a bond and makes it uneconomical for the company to refinance the debt when there is only a slight decrease in interest rates. Call premiums often equal one year's interest initially and decline over the life of the bond. In this sense, they also encourage the company to defer calling the debt.

With and without these protective devices, the interest rate on callable bonds is higher than the rate on similar noncallable debt. The higher interest rate compensates the bondholders for the greater variability in their yield to maturity because of the possibility the bond will be called. As you might expect, the differential in interest rates is smaller the longer the deferral period and the higher the call premium.[6]

Companies also issue *convertible bonds* that investors can exchange for another security, usually common stock, at their option. Companies issue these bonds because investors require a high interest rate or very restrictive bond covenants when they cannot easily assess a company's risk. This is necessary because their fixed claim limits their returns if the company does better than they expected but does not limit their losses if the company does worse. A convertible bond removes the limit on their returns when the company does well because the bondholders can convert their security to equity and share in the higher returns. Consequently, the bondholders can "afford" to accept a lower rate of return or less restrictive covenants without reducing their expected rate of return.

Accordingly, the interest rate on convertible bonds is lower than the rate on similar straight bonds of the same maturity. The more favorable the conversion privileges, the larger the interest rate differential.

Default Premiums on Risky Debt

Even the most financially sound companies are risky compared to sovereign governments. Governments can print money to make the interest payments on their debt and normally cannot be sued without their own consent. Companies do not have either of these powers, so there is always a risk that they may default on their debt obligations.

Investors require compensation for the risk of default, that is, the interest rate on risky debt has a default risk premium. Elaborate models explain the size of this premium, but we can see their main features in a simple example.

---

[6]Jess B. Yawitz and Kevin Maloney, "The Term Structure and Callable Bonds Yield Spreads," *Journal of Portfolio Management,* 1983, pp. 57–63.

A Simple Model of Default Premiums   Suppose a company issues a one-year bond with a par or face value of $\$F$. Suppose also that the probability this company will default on its obligation is p and that the market rate of interest on a one-year riskless bond is r_f. Then, if investors are indifferent to risk, they will view the *expected payoff* from the risky bond as equivalent to the payoff from a riskless bond, that is, its market price, B, equals:

$$B = \frac{\$F \times (1-p)}{1 + r_f}.$$ [4.12]

Now, $1 - p$ is approximately $(1 + p)^{-1}$ for small values of p. This permits us to write Equation 4.12 as

$$B = \frac{\$F}{(1 + r_f) \times (1 + p)} = \frac{\$F}{1 + r_f + p + r_f \times p}.$$

For small probabilities of default and normal interest rates, $r_f \times p$ is a small number that we can safely ignore. This means

$$B = \frac{\$F}{1 + r_f + p}.$$ (4.13)

Equation 4.13 says the market price of a risky bond is its face value discounted at an opportunity cost that equals the riskless rate of interest plus the probability of default. In other words, the interest rate on risky debt equals the riskless rate plus a default premium that depends on the probability of default.[7]

   In reality, Equation 4.13 is too simple for several reasons. First, investors are not indifferent to risk. They do not consider the expected payoff from a risky bond as equivalent to the certain payoff from a riskless bond, so we really should use an interest rate larger than r_f in Equation 4.12. How much larger that interest rate should be is not easily determined; it depends on the general attitude toward risk that prevails in the financial market. Second, there are varying degrees of default so bondholders can receive partial payments rather than all or nothing as this model assumes. Third, the risk of default changes over time in perhaps complicated ways, therefore this model is not easily extended to multi-period bonds.

   Accounting for only the first of these problems, we can rewrite Equation 4.13 as

$$P = \frac{\$F}{1 + r_d}$$ [4.14]

where $r_d > r_f + p$.

The expected rate of return on risky debt, r_d, depends on the market's overall sensitivity to risk and the amount of default risk in a particular issue. Almost certainly, this interest rate is greater than the riskless rate of interest plus the one-period probability of default.

---

[7]See Harold Bierman, Jr. and Jerome E. Hass, "An Analytical Model of Bond Risk Differentials," *Journal of Financial and Quantitative Analysis,* December 1975, pp. 757–773 for a similar model of default premiums on debt.

Exhibit 4.5

STANDARD & POOR'S CORPORATE RATING DEFINITIONS

AAA   Debt rated AAA has the highest rating assigned by Standard & Poor's. Capacity to pay interest and repay principal is extremely strong.

AA   Debt rated AA has a very strong capacity to pay interest and repay principal and differs from the higher-rated issues only in small degrees.

A   Debt rated A has a strong capacity to pay interest and repay principal although it is somewhat more susceptible to the adverse effects of changes in circumstances and economic conditions than debt in higher-rated categories.

BBB   Debt rated BBB is regarded as having an adequate capacity to pay interest and repay principal. Although it normally exhibits adequate protection parameters, adverse economic conditions or changing circumstances are more likely to lead to a weakened capacity to pay interest and repay principal for debt in this category than in higher-rated categories.

BB, B, CCC, CC, C   Debt rated BB, B, CCC, CC, and C is regarded, on balance, as predominantly speculative with respect to capacity to pay interest and repay principal in accordance with the terms of the obligation. BB indicates the lowest degree of speculation and C the highest degree of speculation. While such debt will likely have some quality and protective characteristics, these are outweighed by large uncertainties or major risk exposures to adverse conditions.

D   Debt rated D is in payment default. The D rating category is used when interest payments or principal payments are not made on the date due even if the applicable grace period has not expired, unless S&P believes that such payments will be made during such grace period. The D rating also will be used upon the filing of a bankruptcy petition if debt service payments are jeopardized.

Source: Standard & Poor's Bond Guide, p. 12.

Bond Ratings and Default Premiums   The ratings assigned to bonds by Standard & Poor's, Moody's, and other rating agencies help investors evaluate default risk. Standard & Poor's assigns bonds to one of 10 rating categories, ranging from AAA to D, according to the agency's assessment of the issuer's capacity to pay interest and repay principal. The agency also may attach a plus or minus sign to ratings from AA to CCC to further indicate the issue's relative position within the category. Standard & Poor's own description of the interpretation of these ratings is given in Exhibit 4.5.

Bonds rated BBB and above are known as *investment grade bonds* because banks regulated by the U.S. Comptroller of the Currency are permitted to purchase them as investments. Bonds rated BB and below are known as *speculative grade bonds*. Many of these were originally issued with higher ratings but were downgraded when the issuers' circumstances changed. Other speculative grade bonds, sometimes called *junk bonds* or *high-yield bonds*, were assigned low ratings when they were issued.

STANDARD & POOR'S RATING OF FLEMING COMPANIES,   **Table 4.7**
INC., SENIOR SUBORDINATED DEBT

Week of	Old Rating	New Rating	Explanation
July 25, 1994	BBB	BB+	$1.085 billion acquisition of Scrivner Co.
June 26, 1995	BB+	BB−	Less favorable conditions in food industry, reduced earnings from integration of Scrivner acquisition and reengineering.
October 2, 1996	BB−	B+	Award of damages to a Fleming's customer and 6 percent decrease in sales.

Source: *Standard & Poor's Creditweek* for the weeks indicated.

AVERAGE YIELDS ON BONDS RATED BY STANDARD   **Table 4.8**
& POOR'S (WEEK OF MAY 15, 1996)

	Average Yield	Yield Premium Relative to U.S. Government Bonds
Long-term U.S. government bonds	7.04%	0.00%
Corporation bonds		
AAA rating	7.37	0.33
AA	7.69	0.65
A	8.04	1.00
BBB	8.79	1.75
BB	9.19	2.15
B	10.91	3.87

The Fleming Companies Inc.'s experience with its senior unsecured debt illustrates why bond ratings are changed. Fleming is a large wholesale food distributor that had $800 million of rated debt outstanding in July 1994. Standard & Poor's rated the company's senior unsecured debt BBB (investment grade) at that time. Beginning that month, three events caused Standard & Poor's to reduce the rating of this debt. These events and their effects on Fleming's bond rating are summarized in Table 4.7.

Panel A of Table 4.1 showed that corporation bonds have higher yields the lower their quality. This effect is even more noticeable when quality is measured by bond ratings. The average yields on bonds rated by Standard & Poor's during the week of May 15, 1996 are given in Table 4.8. The higher yield premiums on lower-rated bonds reflect the market's perception that these bonds are less marketable and have more default risk than higher rated corporation bonds and U.S. government securities.

4.5 INTEREST RATES, OPPORTUNITY COSTS, AND MARKET VALUE

Now you know more about the level and structure of interest rates, but you may be asking yourself, "So what?" Good question. Here's a good answer: Interest rates affect opportunity costs and, through them, the value of the assets a company buys and the value of the bonds and common stock it issues. Therefore, managers must understand how interest rates are determined to make investment and financing decisions that maximize the owners' wealth.

Recall from Chapter 3 that the opportunity cost used in net present value analysis is the amount, stated in percentage terms, that investors lose because they cannot use the money to repay a loan or purchase alternative investments. An increase in the level of interest rates raises this opportunity cost by making loans more expensive and by causing the financial market to require a higher rate of return on alternative investments.[8] This increase in the opportunity cost reduces the net present value of current and prospective investment projects and may make some of them unacceptable. This is the financial market's way of telling the company and its owners to use less new financing to buy fewer investments. Managers must recognize this message when it comes and anticipate it if possible to make investment and financing decisions that maximize the owners' wealth. Here is a simple illustration.

Stanhouse Sports Equipment Company is considering the four long-term investment projects described in panel A of Table 4.9. CFO Jim Stanhouse has determined the net present value of each project using the company's opportunity cost of 10 percent at the current level of interest rates. For example, project A's NPV is

$$NPV(A) = \$-25{,}000 + \$6{,}730 \times APVF_{0.10,5}$$
$$= \$-25{,}000 + \$6{,}730 \times 3.7908 = \$512.$$

All four projects are acceptable because they have positive net present values. Stanhouse must obtain $34.5 million to finance these projects—which adds $1.444 million to the owners' wealth.

Now suppose Jim Stanhouse sees signs that interest rates may increase before he can obtain the funds needed to buy these projects. Specifically, he notes that the German central bank has raised interest rates to support the price of the mark. This will shift some of the demand for loans from Germany to the United States and some of the supply of loans from the United States to Germany and may increase U.S. interest rates. He also knows that a low unemployment rate in the United States is renewing concerns about inflation. Finally, he sees that both of these factors apparently are reflected in the yield curve that has a strong positive slope, indicating that the financial market expects higher future interest rates.

Given this outlook, Stanhouse decides to reexamine the investment projects under the assumption that higher interest rates cause the company's opportunity cost to

---

[8]To see the latter point, suppose the yield on U.S. Treasury bills is 3.5 percent and the expected rate of return on a share of common stock is 12 percent which provides a risk premium of 8.5 percent (12 percent − 3.5 percent). Now suppose an increase in government spending causes T-bill yields to increase to 5 percent. Unless investors' attitudes about risk also change, they will still require a risk premium of 8.5 percent, which means the expected rate of return on the common stock must increase to 13.5 percent.

INTEREST RATE CHANGES AND INVESTMENT AND FINANCING DECISIONS

Table 4.9

Panel A: Company's Plans When Opportunity Cost = 10 percent

Project	Description	CF_0	CF_{1-5}	NPV
A	Build new distribution center	$-25,000	$6,730	$ 512
B	Expand production line	-5,000	1,422	391
C	Upgrade management information system	-3,000	916	472
D	Build employee health and exercise facility	-1,500	414	69
Cost of acceptable projects		$-34,500		
NPV of acceptable projects				$1,444

Panel B: Company's Plans When Opportunity Cost = 11 percent

Project	Description	CF_0	$CF_{1-\infty}$	NPV
A	Build new distribution center	$-25,000	$6,730	$-127
B	Expand production line	-5,000	1,422	256
C	Upgrade management information system	-3,000	916	385
D	Build employee health and exercise facility	-1,500	414	30
Cost of acceptable projects		$ -9,500		
NPV of acceptable projects				$ 671

increase to 11 percent. The results are given in panel B of Table 4.9. Each project's NPV is smaller and project A is no longer acceptable. An increase in the company's opportunity cost from 10 percent to 11 percent, brought about by an increase in interest rates, will reduce the capital budget from $34.5 million to $9.5 million and reduce the amount of wealth created for the owners by more than 50 percent.

●————————————————————————● EXERCISE

REVISING THE CAPITAL BUDGET WHEN INTEREST RATES CHANGE

4.9

Determine Stanhouse Sports Equipment Company's capital budget and the amount of wealth created for the owners if higher interest rates cause the company's opportunity cost to increase to 12 percent.

You can ignore project A because it is already unacceptable when the opportunity cost is only 11 percent. For the other projects,

$$NPV = CF_0 + CF_1 \times APVF_{0.12,5}$$
$$NPV(B) = \$-5,000 + \$1,422 \times 3.6048 = \$126$$
$$NPV(C) = \$-3,000 + \$ 916 \times 3.6048 = \$302$$
$$NPV(D) = \$-1,500 + \$ 414 \times 3.6048 = \$-8.$$

Only projects B and C are acceptable if higher interest rates cause the company's opportunity cost to increase to 12 percent. This reduces the company's capital budget to $8.0 million and adds only $428,000 to the owners' wealth.

● —————— ●

These alternative capital budgets, based on opportunity costs of 10 percent, 11 percent, and 12 percent, are the company's investment plans given the level of interest rates. Stanhouse wouldn't even recognize the need to make these plans if he did not know how to interpret the signs that interest rates may increase.

4.6 SUMMARY

Several factors interact to determine the structure of interest rates. The general level of interest rates at any particular time depends on the supply and demand for loans. An increase in the demand for loans to offset anticipated cash flow shortages by individuals, companies, or governments causes interest rates to increase and vice versa. An increase in the supply of loans to offset anticipated cash flow surpluses has the opposite effect. People's expectations, the age distribution of the population, and fiscal and monetary policy all affect the supply and demand for loans.

Expected inflation also affects the level of nominal interest rates. Lenders must be compensated for the loss of purchasing power when prices increase and therefore add an inflation premium to the real rate of interest they require. Borrowers are willing to pay an interest rate premium because they know they will repay the loan with currency that has less value. The inflation premium is incorporated into interest rates through changes in the supply and demand for loans.

The general level of interest rates is affected by the foreign as well as the domestic supply and demand for loans. Purchasing power parity ensures that prices of real goods and services are equal in different countries and interest rate parity ensures that prices of money (interest rates) are equal in different countries. There is no net increase in the supply or demand for loans in a particular country when interest rate parity exists. A departure from parity, because of changes in the demand for goods, currency, or loans, will cause an increase in the demand for loans in the country with the lowest effective interest rates and vice versa.

Loans of different maturities are available at any given time and the relationship among the interest rates on these loans is known as the term structure of interest rates. Two widely accepted theories of the term structure of interest rates are the expectations theory and the preferred habitat theory. The expectations theory says that market forces will ensure the expected interest rate on a loan is independent of its maturity. Borrowers seeking the lowest cost loan and lenders seeking the highest yield loan will adjust the supply and demand for loans of different maturities to ensure this equilibrium condition is satisfied. In this situation, the term structure of interest rates merely reflects the market's consensus opinion about the future level of interest rates.

The preferred habitat theory says that borrowers and lenders are not indifferent to the maturity of their loans because of the risk of refinancing or reinvesting at unfavorable interest rates. They have preferred maturity habitats that they will not abandon for only a small improvement in the cost or return on their loan. According to this theory, the actual interest rate on a loan therefore includes the financial market's expectations plus a yield premium to induce borrowers and lenders to leave their preferred maturity. This term premium is normally positive which implies a net preference for short-term maturities in the financial market.

Taxes and marketability also affect interest rates. Financial instruments that provide tax-free interest payments have a lower yield than taxable instruments because of the tax savings they provide. Securities that are virtually identical with respect to term to maturity and the absence of risk, such as U.S. Treasury and agency securities, still have different yields because the former are traded in very liquid markets that make them more marketable than the latter.

Risky bonds have yield premiums that depend on the financial market's attitude toward risk and the risk of default inherent in a particular issue. Bond rating agencies assign bonds to classes according to their assessment of this risk. Highly rated bonds have only small yield premiums over U.S. government debt while low-rated bonds have larger premiums.

Financial instruments with attached options have yields that reflect the value of the options. Callable bonds have an option that is valuable to the issuer so they provide a yield premium over similar bonds that are not callable. Convertible bonds have an option that is valuable to the investor so their yield is smaller than the yield on similar nonconvertible bonds.

Managers must understand how these factors affect the level and structure of interest rates to make investment and financing decisions that maximize the owners' wealth. An increase in interest rates causes an increase in opportunity costs, which reduces the value of current and prospective investments and the value of the company's bonds and common stock. A decrease in interest rates has the opposite effect. Managers can prepare plans to adapt their company to the new conditions if they can interpret the signs that interest rates may change. The economic theories described in this chapter help managers make these interpretations.

KEY TERMS

- QUESTIONS AND PROBLEMS

1. Briefly describe how each of the following factors individually affects the domestic supply of or demand for loans.

   (a) A decrease in consumer confidence

   (b) An increase in the expected rate of inflation

   (c) A decrease in the unemployment rate

   (d) Realization by baby-boomers that they need to start preparing for retirement

   (e) A decision to replace 30 percent of the interstate highway system

   (f) An increase in U.S. exports

2. Use a chart similar to Exhibit 4.1 to show how a change in the expected rate of inflation affects the supply of and demand for loans. What happens to the nominal interest rate?

3. A coach-class airline ticket from New York City to London costs $459. A similar ticket on the same airline from London to New York costs 301.88 British pounds. What is the dollar–pound exchange rate assuming purchasing power parity holds?

4. Are you more likely to find a violation of purchasing power parity in the prices of:

   (a) Haircuts or hammers?

   (b) Bananas or briefcases?

   (c) Diamonds or coal?

   Explain each answer.

5. Are you more likely to see apparent violations of interest rate parity between the United States and Germany or the United States and Zaire? Explain your reasoning.

6. The treasurer of a small company was overheard to say, "We need a two-year loan but I refuse to pay the 12 percent interest when I can borrow for one year at 11 percent and simply renew the loan when it comes due." Do you think this treasurer understands the implications of the expectations theory of the term structure of interest rates?

7. Describe how an increase or decrease in interest rates affects the person in each situation given below. Which people are exposed to interest rate risk?

   (a) An investor with a one-year cash surplus purchases a six-month U.S. Treasury bill and will renew it at maturity.

   (b) A borrower with a two-year cash deficit takes out a two-year loan.

   (c) An investor with a two-year cash surplus purchases a 10-year U.S. Treasury bond and will sell it in two years.

   (d) A borrower with a 10-year cash deficit takes out a five-year loan and will renew it when it comes due.

8. Is the preferred habitat theory of the term structure of interest rates completely different from or merely an extension of the expectations theory? What about the segmented market theory?

9. Page B13 of the May 13, 1996 issue of *Investor's Business Daily* reported that 20-year U.S. Treasury and Federal National Mortgage Association (FNMA) bonds were yielding 7.10 percent and 7.31 percent, respectively, on May 12. The FNMA bonds are backed by the "full faith and credit" of the U.S. government, so why do they provide a higher yield than Treasury bonds?

10. The following bonds were listed on pages B12 and B13 of the May 13, 1996 issue of *Investor's Business Daily.* Each bond matures in June of the year 2000.

Issuer	Standard & Poor's Bond Rating	Yield
U.S. Treasury	Not applicable	6.40%
Federal National Mortgage Association	Not applicable	6.54
IBM	A	6.70
Ann Taylor Stores	B–	10.80

Explain the differences in the yields on these bonds.

11. The real rate of return on U.S. Treasury bills averaged approximately 0.6 percent from 1926–1995. Given this real rate of return:

   (a) Use the exact and approximate forms of the Fisher effect to compute the nominal interest rates on U.S. Treasury bills when the expected percentage rate of inflation is 2.5, 5.0, 10.0, and 20.0.

   (b) Repeat part (a) with a real rate of return of 2.5 percent.

   (c) Given the results of parts (a) and (b), under what circumstances is it reasonable to use the simpler, approximate form of the Fisher effect?

12. The October 26, 1996 issue of *The Economist* forecasted that U.S. consumer prices would increase by 3.0 percent in 1996 (p. 126). At the same time, the October 28, 1996 issue of *The Wall Street Journal* reported that the yield on 3-month U.S. Treasury bills was 5.02 percent on October 25 (page C1).

   (a) What was the real rate of return on U.S. Treasury bills given *The Economist*'s forecast?

   (b) The October 26, 1996 issue of *The Economist* also forecasted that U.S. consumer prices would increase by 3.2 percent in 1997 (p. 126). Assume the real rate of return you computed in part (a) is constant and forecast the nominal yield on U.S. Treasury bills in 1997.

13. The 30-speed mountain bike you so desperately want costs $1,500 on October 25, 1996 but you expect its price to increase to $1,650 next year. Page C24 of the October 28, 1996 edition of *The Wall Street Journal* reported that the yield on a one-year U.S. Treasury security on October 25, 1996 was approximately 5.60 percent.

   (a) What is the real rate of return on the U.S. Treasury security using the prices of the mountain bike to represent the effect of inflation? Use the approximate form of the Fisher effect.

   (b) Suppose you use your $1,500 to buy the Treasury security. How much will it be worth when it matures in one year? Is this enough money to buy the mountain bike?

   (c) How much additional money must you come up with to buy the bike? Divide this number by your original $1,500 to express it as a rate of return. Compare the result to your answer to part (a).

   (d) What does this exercise tell you about the meaning of a real rate of return?

14. Franklin Branch, a recent graduate of a prominent midwestern MBA program, is considering the purchase of a Mercedes-Benz E320. The cost of the car, delivered in Kansas City, Missouri, is $46,000. Franklin can take delivery of a similarly equipped car in Germany for 64,250 deutschemarks. Applicable spot and forward exchange rates are given on the following page.

	U.S. $ equivalent	Currency per U.S. $
Deutschemark		
Spot rate	0.7018	1.4249
30-day forward rate	0.7027	1.4231
90-day forward rate	0.7047	1.4190
180-day forward rate	0.7079	1.4126

(a) What is Franklin's dollar cost of taking delivery of the car in Germany given these exchange rates?

(b) What is the most he can pay to bring the car back to Kansas City under these circumstances?

(c) Suppose actual shipping costs are $750. Are the prices of E320s in Kansas City and Germany, the price of ocean transportation, and the price of marks in equilibrium? In which direction will each of the prices tend to move?

(d) Franklin has learned that shipping costs will decline by $300 in 90 days due to a seasonal surge in the supply of cargo space. Assume the price of E320s remains the same, that Franklin will buy marks now for delivery in 90 days, and that he will purchase the car in Germany then and ship it home to Kansas City. How much money does Franklin save in comparison to taking delivery of the car in Germany immediately?

(e) What additional prices can change given the opportunity to buy the E320 in the forward market? In which directions?

15. Brett Lockwood, treasurer of Western Products Inc., must borrow $10,000,000 for 180 days. He can obtain this loan from a consortium of U.S. banks for 6.0 percent annual interest or from a group of French banks for 5.2 percent annual interest. The spot and 180-day forward U.S.–French exchange rates are 0.1945 and 0.1948.

(a) Are the U.S. and French interest rates in parity?

(b) Rewrite the interest parity condition to determine the exchange-rate-adjusted French interest rate. Should Brett borrow in the United States or France?

(c) Prepare a table that shows the amounts received from and paid for the loan if Brett borrows in the United States and in France. Use the results to calculate the exchange-rate-adjusted interest rate on the French loan. How does the result compare with your answer to part (b)?

(d) What will happen to the U.S. and French interest rates and to the U.S.–French exchange rates if other treasurers follow Brett's example?

16. Page C24 of the October 28, 1996 edition of *The Wall Street Journal* reported that the yields on one- and two-year U.S. Treasury securities on October 25, 1996, were approximately 5.60 percent and 5.90 percent, respectively.

(a) Determine the implied one-year forward rate using the exact method and the arithmetic approximation.

(b) According to the expectations theory of the term structure, what one-year spot interest rate do investors expect to prevail in October 1997?

(c) Suppose that, after evaluating the government's plans for reducing the budget deficit, investors conclude that the future one-year spot interest rate will be 6.5 percent rather than the rate you computed in part (b). In which directions will the October 1996 one- and two-year spot rates move?

(d) Identify a new equilibrium of spot interest rates and investors' expectations. (There is no unique correct answer, but there is a unique relationship among the interest rates.)

17. Josh Barnes must invest $10,000 for two years. He can buy a two-year U.S. Treasury security and hold it until maturity or buy a one-year U.S. Treasury security and reinvest his money in another one-year security when the first one matures. The applicable one- and two-year spot interest rates on U.S. Treasury securities are 5.50 percent and 5.80 percent, respectively.

    (a) According to the expectations theory of the term structure, at what yield should Josh expect to reinvest his money in one year?

    (b) Calculate Josh's *expected* yield from buying two one-year Treasury securities in succession if his expectations are correct.

    (c) What is Josh's actual yield from buying two one-year U.S. Treasury securities in succession if the future one-year interest rate is 6.3 percent? What is his actual yield if the future one-year rate is 5.9 percent?

    (d) Is Josh exposed to interest rate risk if he buys a single two-year Treasury security? Two one-year Treasury securities? Explain your answer.

18. GMI, Incorporated manufactures road maintenance equipment in Tulsa, Oklahoma. A popular grader, used by many county governments to maintain gravel roads, sells for $200,000, f.o.b. the factory. The company recently began to seek foreign sales and compiled the following information about exchange rates, inflation rates, and interest rates in the United States and Japan.

	U.S. $ Equivalent
Japanese yen	
Spot rate	0.008818
90-day forward rate	0.008932

Source: *The Wall Street Journal,* 10/28/96, p. C23.

	United States	Japan
Three-month increase in producers' prices		
(stated in annual terms)	1.50%	0.10%
Yields on 90-day corporate securities		
(stated in annual terms)	5.38%	0.43%

Source: *The Economist,* 10/26/96, pp. 126–127.

    (a) GMI received an order for a grader from Otsu prefecture, Japan. The Japanese buyer offered to pay 23,000,000 yen for the machine, f.o.b. Osaka, payment due upon shipment. Should GMI accept this order if shipping, insurance, and import duties cost $3,000?

    (b) Kyoto prefecture also offered to buy a grader for 23,000,000 yen, f.o.b. Osaka, shipment and payment to take place in 90 days. Should GMI accept this order if all U.S. prices and costs are subject to inflation at the rate of increase in producers' prices? Ignore the time value of money.

    (c) Why did you come to different conclusions about the Otsu and Kyoto orders?

19. A Japanese contractor offered to buy one of GMI's road graders for 23,000,000 yen but wants to pay for it in 90 days with interest computed at the yield on Japanese corporate securities.

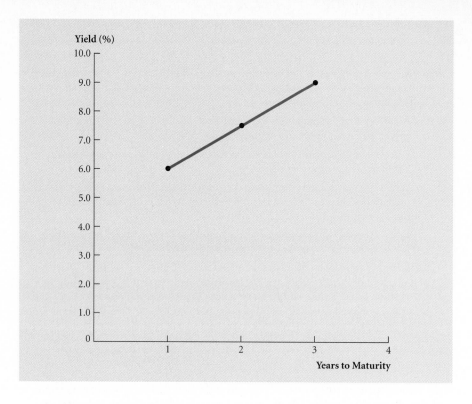

Should GMI accept this order if its next best alternative is to sell the machine in the United States for cash and invest the proceeds in 90-day U.S. corporate securities? The information about U.S. and Japanese financial markets provided in problem 18 also applies to this problem.

20. Sally Plains is a chocoholic who normally pays $22.00 per pound for imported chocolate truffles. Her friend will soon travel to Switzerland, where the truffles are made, so she gave him $100 to buy as much of the confection as he can. The truffles sell for 15.60 Swiss francs per pound and the dollar-Swiss franc exchange rate is 0.8013.

    (a) How many pounds of chocolate can Sally's friend bring back for her?

    (b) How many pounds can he bring back if the United States charges a 15 percent duty on imported chocolate? Sally's friend will pay the duty from her $100.

21. Use the yield curve shown above to determine the implied one-year forward rate at year 1 $(_1f_2)$ and the implied one-year forward rate at year 2 $(_2f_3)$.

22. The one-year spot rate is 4 percent and the five-year spot rate is 6 percent. What is the implied four-year forward rate $(_1f_5)$ at year 1?

23. Thomas Chavez needs $20,000 for five years to help pay his daughter's college expenses. The interest rate on a five-year loan is 8 percent while the interest rate on a one-year loan is 7.75 percent. Tom knows interest rates are likely to increase but he hopes he'll be able to renew his one-year loan each year at the following interest rates: 7.82 percent, 8.03 percent, 8.05 percent, and 8.10 percent.

    (a) Should Mr. Chavez use a five-year loan or the series of five one-year loans to obtain the $20,000 if his only concern is to pay the lowest expected cost?

(b) Should he use a five-year loan or the series of five one-year loans if his only concern is to have the least risk?

24. Suppose the financial market requires a term premium on two-year loans of 0.04 percent. Suppose also that the current one-year spot interest rate is 4.73 percent and the expected future one-year spot interest rate is 4.93 percent.

    (a) What is the current two-year spot interest rate according to the preferred habitat theory of the term structure of interest rates?

    (b) What will happen to the supply of and demand for two-year loans if the actual two-year spot interest rate is 4.85 percent rather than the rate you calculated in part (a).

    (c) Can you answer part (a) assuming the segmented market theory of the term structure is correct?

25. The yields on the municipal and U.S. Treasury securities described below were reported on pages C20 and C24 of the October 28, 1996 edition of *The Wall Street Journal.*

Issuer	Maturity	Yield
Denver, Colorado, Airport	2013	5.82%
U.S. Treasury	2013	6.75
Texas State Turnpike Authority	2023	5.78
U.S. Treasury	2023	6.92

    (a) Why do the municipal securities have lower yields than similar U.S. Treasury securities that are considered to be virtually riskless?

    (b) Determine the after-tax yields on these securities to an investor subject to 31 percent federal and 5 percent state tax rates. Do the after-tax yields fit the differences in risk more closely?

26. Visit the Federal Reserve Board's Internet site at http://www.bog.frb.fed.us/releases/h15/ for a list of interest rate reports.

    (a) Click on "current release" and record the yields on U.S. Treasury constant maturities from three-month to 30-years. (See the footnotes to this table for a description of the constant maturity series.) Use these yields to graph the U.S. Treasury yield curve.

    (b) According to the expectations theory of the term structure, does the financial market expect future interest rates to increase or decrease?

• ADDITIONAL READING

A textbook with much more information about interest rates and foreign exchange rates is:
   James C. VanHorne, *Financial Markets Rates and Flows,* Prentice Hall, Englewood Cliffs, New Jersey, 1994.

Another textbook with a wealth of information about government, agency, municipal, and corporate bonds is:
   Frank J. Fabozzi, *Bond Markets, Analysis and Strategies,* Prentice Hall, Englewood Cliffs, New Jersey, 1993.

For a description of how Standard & Poor's rates bonds, see:
   Hugh C. Sherwood, *How Corporate and Municipal Debt Is Rated,* Wiley, New York, 1976.

THE PRINCIPLES OF
DIVERSIFICATION

Nearly 1.5 million college teachers, staff members, and administrators are providing for their retirement by investing in a common stock portfolio called the College Retirement Equities Fund (CREF). Would you like to guess the market value of this portfolio? How broadly do you think this money is invested? In the shares of less than 500 companies? Between 500 and 1,000 companies? The answers may astonish you.

CREF's market value on December 31, 1995 was $70.7 *billion*, making it the largest common stock portfolio in the world. Ninety-eight percent of this money was invested in common stocks issued by approximately 3,800 different companies drawn from 60 industries in more than 30 countries. Table 5.1 provides some additional information about the extent of the fund's diversification.

How in the world can CREF's managers measure the rate of return and risk of such a large, complex portfolio? How can they possibly estimate the amount of risk an individual investment contributes to the total? With an infinite number of ways to invest $70.7 billion in 3,800 different companies, how can they be sure that *this* portfolio provides the least amount of risk for a given rate of return? Surprisingly simple financial principles provide the answers to these questions.

This chapter carefully develops the diversification principles used to manage large portfolios such as CREF and small portfolios such as you or I might construct for ourselves. Each principle is described graphically and mathematically to develop both your intuition and your technical skills. This approach, plus the use of numerical examples using real companies, will give you a thorough understanding of these crucial financial principles.[1]

---

[1]There are more equations in this chapter than there are in the other chapters of this book, but this is unavoidable. You may want to briefly review your textbook or notes from a prior statistics class if you are concerned about this. Simply refresh your knowledge of expected value, standard deviation, covariance, correlation, and regression analysis and you will be in good shape.

Table 5.1   COLLEGE RETIREMENT EQUITIES FUND PORTFOLIO (DECEMBER 31, 1995)

Panel A: Total Portfolio

	Market Value	Percent
Common stock (60 industries)	$68,603,839,557	97.72%
Short-term investments (9 types of instruments)	1,303,166,406	1.86
Preferred stock (32 industries)	227,536,959	0.32
Bonds		
Corporate (11 industries)	68,372,080	0.10
Government	416,406	0.00
Rounding	1,160	0.00
Total portfolio	$70,203,332,568	100.00%

Panel B: Industries in Which Common Stocks Are Held

	Market Value	Percent
Banks	$ 6,051,719,663	8.82%
Utilities-telephone	4,314,688,457	6.29
Healthcare-drugs	4,058,418,714	5.92
Petroleum-integrated	3,224,882,611	4.70
Electrical equipment	2,951,143,345	4.30
Utilities-electric	2,816,740,775	4.11
Retail-general merchandise	2,464,192,127	3.59
Financial-miscellaneous	2,371,489,727	3.46
Insurance-multiline, property & casualty	2,306,494,023	3.36
Office equipment	2,167,971,648	3.16
Other	35,876,098,467	52.29
Total	$68,603,839,557	100.00%

Panel C: Countries in Which All Securities Are Held

	Market Value	Percent
United States	$57,100,996,851	81.34%
Japan	3,997,122,609	5.69
United Kingdom	1,608,615,203	2.29
Hong Kong	1,036,978,787	1.48
Switzerland	721,646,454	1.03
Other	5,737,972,664	8.17
Total	$70,203,332,568	100.00%

Source: College Retirement Equities Fund 1995 Annual Report.

You may think you only need a superficial knowledge of these principles if you will work in a corporation, but this is incorrect. You may never manage a common stock portfolio, but each time your company buys an asset, it has the effect of adding a small proportion of that investment to the owners' personal portfolios. Consequently, you must understand how each investment will affect the risk and return of these portfolios to ensure that your decisions will increase the owners' wealth. This understanding requires a thorough knowledge of diversification principles, which is provided in this chapter, and the relationship between risk and return, which is provided in the next.

5.1   INTRODUCTION TO RETURN AND RISK

The analysis and valuation of any investment proposal requires predictions of its *future* performance. A company or business unit contemplating the purchase of a new manufacturing facility must forecast its future free cash flows to determine if they justify its current cost. Similarly, an investor considering the purchase of common stock must assess the prospects that its future dividends and growth will provide an adequate rate of return on his present investment. There are several ways to predict an investment proposal's future performance but none of them are prescient. Consequently, managers and individuals must assess both the rewards and the risks from investing in the presence of uncertainty.

Sources of Predicted Returns

Financial managers forecast an investment's rate of return by (1) assessing future economic and business conditions, (2) extrapolating the investment's own past performance, or (3) comparing the investment to a publicly traded benchmark. This forecast also helps describe an investment's risk by revealing the possibility that the managers' prediction will be wrong.

Fundamental Forecasts   Analysts often use fundamental forecasts to predict an investment's free cash flows but they also can use them to forecast rates of return. You prepare a fundamental forecast by projecting the investment's financial statements given assumptions about the condition of the general economy, the industry, the company, and the investment itself. You must prepare alternative versions of the forecast using a different set of assumptions for each version because you don't know which scenario will actually take place. You then use the predicted free cash flows to compute forecasted *holding period rates of return,* which are defined as $r = (CF_1 - CF_0)/CF_0$.[2] This process provides an estimate of the distribution of the investment's rate of return and thereby reveals the uncertainty inherent in predictions about the future. Here's a simple example.

Josey Graham operates several motels in the Ozark region of Missouri and Arkansas. She can buy a full-page ad in a regional travel guide for $10,000 and expects the outcome to depend on the condition of the economy. Her predictions of the net free cash flows from the additional business produced by the ad and the rates of return implied by these cash flows are given below.

---

[2]Compare this definition with Equation 3.4 and you will recognize that a holding period rate of return is the internal rate of return on a single-period investment.

	Weak Economy	Normal Economy	Strong Economy
CF_0	$–10,000	$–10,000	$–10,000
CF_1	7,000	12,000	15,000
r	–30.0%	20.0%	50.0%

This is a risky investment for Josey if she does not know exactly which economic condition will prevail.

Extrapolation Forecasts   You prepare an extrapolation forecast by projecting an investment's past performance into the future. You can base your prediction on simple measures such as the average of past performance or you can use more sophisticated methods such as time-series or regression analysis. The simpler techniques are appealing because they are easy to use and many studies have found that they are nearly as effective as the sophisticated ones.

A pitfall to using historical data, however, is hard for even experienced analysts to avoid. This hazard is the temptation to use the forecast uncritically because of an implicit assumption that history will repeat itself in the future. Of course, this may not happen because past performance was the result of business and economic conditions that may not occur in the same combination again. You can reduce this hazard by ensuring that the historical record you use encompasses a variety of business and economic conditions that are representative of what may happen in the future. This accomplishes the same purpose as using a range of favorable to unfavorable scenarios to prepare a fundamental forecast; it gives you an opportunity to see the amount of uncertainty in your prediction.

Benchmark Forecasts   You cannot use extrapolation to predict the rate of return on a new investment because it has no history. Consequently, it may seem that you must prepare a fundamental forecast even though this is a difficult and time-consuming process. You can avoid this difficulty, however, by using an existing enterprise as a benchmark and adapting a forecast of its rate of return to your needs. By this method, you avoid reinventing the wheel and may be able to use a forecast that represents the consensus of the entire financial market. One purpose of this chapter is to show you how to use financial market benchmarks to predict or assess return and risk.

There are two points to keep in mind no matter which forecasting method you use. First, you must focus on the future rather than on the past. Second, you cannot foresee the future with complete accuracy, so you should prepare multiple forecasts from which you can infer the amount of uncertainty in your prediction.

Computing Historical Common Stock Rates of Return   We'll use holding period rates of return computed from historical stock prices for all the illustrations in this chapter. Our example companies are The Gap and The Limited (clothing stores) and Kerr-McGee (an oil company). The holding period returns are calculated using Equation 5.1. The cash flows for each period are the profit or loss from buying and selling the stock plus any dividends received. Dividing these cash flows by the stock's purchase price expresses them as a rate of return.

CALCULATION OF THE GAP'S RATES OF RETURN   Table 5.2

Date	Price	Dividend	Rates of Return
December 31, 1990	$33.125	$0	
January 31, 1991	42.500	0	($42.50 − $33.125)/$33.125 = 0.2830
February 28, 1991	45.500	0	($45.50 − $42.50)/$42.500 = 0.0706
March 28, 1991	49.875	0.125	($49.875 − $45.50 + $0.125)/$45.50 = 0.0989

$$r_{j,t} = \frac{P_{j,t} - P_{j,t-1} + D_{j,t}}{P_{j,t-1}} \qquad [5.1]$$

where $r_{j,t}$ = rate of return on asset j for period t
$P_{j,t}$ = price of asset j at the end of period t (the sale price)
$P_{j,t-1}$ = price of asset j at the end of period $t-1$
(the purchase price)
$D_{j,t}$ = dividends on asset j received at the end of period t

The Gap's rates of return for January, February, and March 1991 are computed in Table 5.2. The rates of return for all three companies for January 1991 through December 1995 are given in Appendix 5A. We will treat these historical rates of return as the future rates of return an investor may earn by purchasing shares of stock in these companies.

● ——————————————————————————————————— ● E X E R C I S E

CALCULATING HOLDING PERIOD RATES OF RETURN   5.1

Suppose you owned some of The Gap's common stock in November and December 1995. What rate of return did you earn each month?

Date	Price	Dividend
October 31, 1995	$39.375	
November 30, 1995	45.125	$0.12
December 31, 1995	42.000	

$r_{\text{Gap,November}}$ = ($45.125 − $39.375 + $0.12)/$39.375
= 0.1491 or 14.91%

$r_{\text{Gap, December}}$ = ($42.000 − $45.125 + $0)/$45.125
= −0.0693 or −6.93%

You earned 14.91 percent and −6.93 percent on The Gap's common stock in November and December 1995.

● ——————— ●

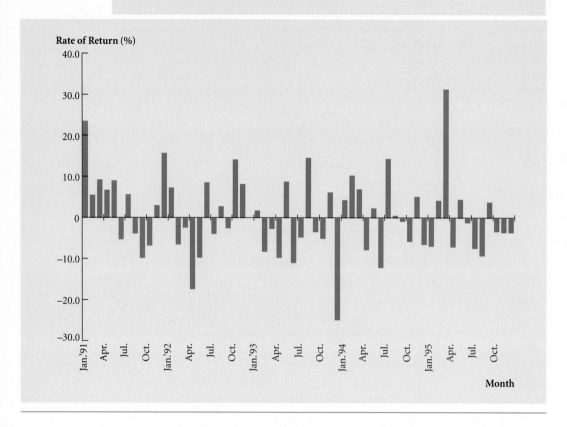

Exhibit 5.1

THE GAP'S MONTHLY RATES OF RETURN

The Gap's monthly rates of return also are graphed in Exhibit 5.1. This graph shows what values are typical and how much variability they have. A simple measure of this variability or risk is the range, −23.55 percent to 28.30 percent.

Summarizing Predicted Returns

A good forecast portrays the entire spectrum of possible rates of return but this distribution may be unwieldy. Suppose, for example, that an enthusiastic analyst placed one of the forecasting methods described above on a personal computer and produced a list of 1,000 possible rates of return for an investment proposal. The analyst's manager might reasonably ask him to summarize his results so she can grasp their significance. Familiar statistics such as mean, variance, and standard deviation of the distribution can be used for this purpose.

The mean is the average of the predicted returns and the variance is the average of the squared-deviations around the mean. The standard deviation is the square-root of the variance. The mathematical definitions of these statistics are

CALCULATION OF THE MEAN, VARIANCE, AND STANDARD DEVIATION OF THE GAP'S RATES OF RETURN

Table 5.3

Month	Actual Return r_t	Deviation from Mean $r_t - E(r)$	Squared Deviation $[r_t - E(r)]^2$
Jan 1991	0.2830	0.2609	0.0681
Feb	0.0706	0.0485	0.0024
Mar	0.0989	0.0768	0.0059
.	.	.	.
.	.	.	.
.	.	.	.
Oct 1995	0.0938	0.0717	0.0051
Nov	0.1491	0.1270	0.0161
Dec	−0.0693	−0.0914	0.0084
Sum	1.3271	0.0000	0.6906

$$E(r_{\text{Gap}}) = 1.3271/60 = 0.0221$$
$$\sigma^2(r_{\text{Gap}}) = 0.6906/60 = 0.0115$$
$$\sigma(r_{\text{Gap}}) = [0.0115]^{1/2} = 0.1072$$

$$E(r_j) = \sum_{t=1}^{T} r_{j,t}\text{Prob}_t \qquad [5.2]$$

$$\sigma^2(r_j) = \sum_{t=1}^{T} [r_{j,t} - E(r_j)]^2\text{Prob}_t \qquad [5.3]$$

$$\sigma(r_j) = [\sigma^2(r_j)]^{1/2} \qquad [5.4]$$

where
$E(r_j)$ = mean rate of return on asset j
$\sigma^2(r_j)$ = variance of rate of return on asset j
$r_{j,t}$ = rate of return on asset j for period t
Prob_t = probability of occurrence for $r_{j,t}$
T = number of observations.

The Gap's rates of return are used to illustrate these calculations in Table 5.3. Each rate of return is equally weighted so $\text{Prob}_t = 1/T$. The mean, variance, and standard deviation of the rates of return for our sample companies are shown in Table 5.4.

CALCULATING SAMPLE STATISTICS

EXERCISE 5.2

Suppose you owned some of The Gap's common stock in 1995. What was your average monthly rate of return and its standard deviation? The month-by-month rates of return are given in Appendix 5A.

Table 5.4   SUMMARY STATISTICS FOR THE RATES OF RETURN

	The Gap	The Limited	Kerr-McGee
Mean, $E(r)$	0.0221	0.0049	0.0109
Variance, $\sigma^2(r)$	0.0115	0.0091	0.0050
Standard deviation, $\sigma(r)$	0.1072	0.0954	0.0707

Month	Actual Return	Deviation from Mean	Squared Deviation
January	0.0661	0.0345	0.0012
February	0.0039	−0.0277	0.0008
March	0.1002	0.0686	0.0047
April	−0.1021	−0.1337	0.0179
May	0.0784	0.0468	0.0022
June	0.0145	−0.0171	0.0003
July	0.0000	−0.0316	0.0010
August	−0.0718	−0.1034	0.0107
September	0.1163	0.0847	0.0072
October	0.0938	0.0622	0.0039
November	0.1491	0.1175	0.0138
December	−0.0693	−0.1009	0.0102
Sum	0.3791	−0.0001	0.0739

Mean = 0.3791/12 = 0.0316 or 3.16%

Variance = 0.0739/12 = 0.0062

Standard deviation = $(0.0062)^{1/2}$ = 0.0787 or 7.87%

Your average monthly rate of return and standard deviation of rate of return were 3.16 percent and 7.87 percent.

● ———— ●

The mean of the distribution of predicted rates of return is a logical statistic to represent the *expected* rate of return because it is an unbiased summary of all the predictions. The standard deviation of the distribution of predicted rates of return is a logical statistic to represent the uncertainty in a forecast based on the mean because it measures the amount by which actual rates of return may differ from their expected value. In other words, the standard deviation is a measure of the potential error in a forecast based on the mean. The standard deviation is similar to the range in this respect because it also measures variability or dispersion. The standard deviation is different, however, because it takes into account all the deviations from the mean rather than only the two extremes.

Another difference is that we can use the standard deviation to quantify the amount of uncertainty in a forecast by constructing a confidence interval around the predicted value. You may recall from studying statistics that if a variable is normally distributed, then its actual value will fall within +/−1.96 standard deviations of the mean—95 percent of the time. Assuming the monthly returns are normally distributed and representative of the future, an analyst could state, "I predict The Gap's future monthly rate of return will be 2.21 percent, and I have 95 percent confidence that it will be between −18.80 percent and 23.22 percent (2.21 percent −/+1.96 × 10.72 percent)." Note that for this and any similar forecast, the confidence interval is larger, indicating more uncertainty about the forecast, the higher the standard deviation.

E X E R C I S E

5.3

CONSTRUCTING A CONFIDENCE INTERVAL

Based on the results for 1995 (calculated in Exercise 5.2), within what interval can you expect The Gap's monthly rate of return to fall with 95 percent confidence?

$$\text{Confidence interval} = E(r_{\text{Gap}}) \pm 1.96 \times \sigma(r_{\text{Gap}})$$
$$= 3.16\% \pm 1.96 \times 7.87\%$$
$$= -12.27\% \text{ to } 18.59\%$$

The 95 percent confidence interval for The Gap, based on its 1995 monthly rates of return, is from −12.27 to 18.59 percent.

Risk Aversion and the Standard Deviation of Returns

Most people are **risk averse,** that is, they must be paid to accept risk. In other words, given the choice between two investments with equal expected rates of return, risk-averse investors will choose the one with less risk. Or, equivalently, given the choice between two investments with equal risks, risk-averse investors will choose the one with a higher expected rate of return. In contrast, *risk-neutral* investors will choose the investment with the highest expected rate of return—without regard to its risk.

The idea that people are risk averse is easy to understand and accept when uncertainty is defined in terms of negative or unpleasant outcomes. Just about anyone would consider an investment where losses are possible as risky, for example. Finance theory has adopted a broader definition of risk, however, that includes *all* uncertainty whether it is favorable or unfavorable. There are several theoretical and expedient reasons for adopting this definition of risk. One of the simpler explanations is that investors suffer losses *whenever* the rate of return is different from what they expected.

Consider the analyst's prediction for The Gap once again. Someone who is willing to invest $10,000 in The Gap to earn an expected rate of return of 2.21 percent per month might not invest at all if he knew the return would be −18.80 percent, however, he might invest *more* than $10,000 if he knew its return would be 23.22 percent. Uncertainty makes the investor susceptible to a real loss in the first case and an opportunity loss in the second.

Using the standard deviation to measure uncertainty is consistent with the broad definition of risk because it includes outcomes that are both better and worse than expected. Furthermore, the standard deviation weights these deviations equally, implying that real and opportunity losses are equally undesirable.

Managing Risk

Exposure to risk is a cost of investing in the presence of uncertainty. Investors attempt to manage or control this cost as they would any other. Risk averse investors try to reduce risk without suffering a corresponding reduction in the expected rate of return. Three risk management techniques can be used for this purpose: diversification, allocation, and hedging. These techniques are described in this chapter and Chapters 6 and 8. A brief introduction now will help you keep the big picture in view as you study the details later.

Diversification   A natural way for investors to reduce risk is through diversification, which combines dissimilar investments in a portfolio. The basic idea is simple: Favorable deviations from the expected rates of return on some investments in the portfolio occur at the same time as unfavorable deviations from the expected rates of return on others. These deviations partially cancel out, leaving the entire portfolio with an actual rate of return that is close to its predicted rate of return. This reduction in the dispersion of a portfolio's rates of return is a reduction in risk.[3] The remainder of this chapter describes this idea precisely so we can apply it with skill.

Allocation   Forming a portfolio reduces—but does not eliminate—risk. Furthermore, the amount of risk that remains may be too much for some investors and not enough for others who want to earn a high rate of return. Both cautious and aggressive investors can achieve their objectives by dividing their wealth between safe assets (such as government securities) and a risky portfolio. The more wealth they allocate to government securities, the lower the risk of their personal portfolio. The more wealth they allocate to the risky portfolio, the higher the rate of return on their personal investment. Allocation thereby permits investors to obtain the exact amount of risk or return that is comfortable. We will discuss this risk management technique and its implications in Chapter 6.

Hedging   Finally, investors exposed to the possibility of unfavorable deviations from their expected rate of return can often buy or sell financial contracts that are *designed* to provide the favorable deviations that will cancel them. This risk management technique is called hedging. Hedging may seem similar to diversification, but differs because it targets a specific risk. Hedges may be constructed by buying or selling forward contracts (as we saw in Chapter 4) or by buying or selling options. We discuss hedging in the context of valuing options in Chapter 8.

---

[3]Diversification is properly called a natural process because we can find examples of diversification in nature. The descendants of plants and animals that reproduce sexually have more genetic diversity than descendants of plants and animals that reproduce asexually or by cloning. Greater genetic diversity improves the chances of survival (reduces risk), which is why sexual reproduction is more common in nature.

5.2   RETURN AND TOTAL RISK OF PORTFOLIOS[4]

We begin our discussion of diversification by describing how to measure the expected rate of return and risk of a portfolio. We'll form portfolios using our example companies but first, we need two equations that describe portfolio rates of return. The first, Equation 5.5, says that a portfolio's rate of return equals a weighted average of the rates of return on the individual assets in the portfolio.

$$r_{p,t} = \sum_{j=1}^{n} w_j r_{j,t} \qquad [5.5]$$

where $r_{p,t}$ = portfolio's rate of return for period t
w_j = proportion of the portfolio invested in asset j;

$$\sum_{j=1}^{n} w_j = 1.0$$

$r_{j,t}$ = rate of return on asset j for period t
n = number of assets in the portfolio

Equation 5.6 is obtained by taking the expected value of Equation 5.5. It says that a portfolio's expected rate of return equals a weighted average of the expected rates of return of the assets in the portfolio.

$$E(r_p) = \sum_{j=1}^{n} w_j E(r_j) \qquad [5.6]$$

where $E(r_p)$ = portfolio's expected rate of return
$E(r_j)$ = asset j's expected rate of return

Using Equation 5.6, the expected rate of return on a portfolio equally divided between The Gap and The Limited is

$$E(r_p) = w_{\text{Gap}} \times E(r_{\text{Gap}}) + w_{\text{Limited}} \times E(r_{\text{Limited}})$$
$$= 0.50 \times 2.21\% + 0.50 \times 0.49\% = 1.35\%.$$

EXERCISE
5.4

CALCULATING A PORTFOLIO'S EXPECTED RATE OF RETURN

Suppose you construct a portfolio that is 60 percent The Limited and 40 percent Kerr-McGee. What is your portfolio's expected rate of return?

$$E(r_p) = w_{\text{Limited}} \times E(r_{\text{Limited}}) + w_{\text{Kerr-McGee}} \times E(r_{\text{Kerr-McGee}})$$
$$= 0.60 \times 0.49\% + 0.40 \times 1.09\% = 0.73\%$$

The portfolio's monthly expected rate of return is 0.73 percent.

---

[4]The diversification principles described in this section were developed by Harry Markowitz who received the 1990 Nobel prize in economics for this work. See Harry Markowitz, "Portfolio Selection," *Journal of Finance*, March 1952, pp. 77–91.

We also can use Equation 5.6 to determine the composition of a portfolio that provides a target expected rate of return. For this illustration, let's assume a risk-averse investor wants to construct a portfolio that provides an expected rate of return of 1.60 percent. For a portfolio comprised of The Gap and The Limited,

$$E(r_{\text{Gap/Limited}}) = w_{\text{Gap}} \times 2.21\% + w_{\text{Limited}} \times 0.49\% = 1.60\%$$

$$w_{\text{Gap}} + w_{\text{Limited}} = 1.0.$$

Solving these two equations simultaneously, the portfolio weights are

$$w_{\text{Gap}} = 64.53\%, w_{\text{Limited}} = 35.47\%.$$

EXERCISE   ● ─── ●

5.5   DETERMINING THE COMPOSITION OF A PORTFOLIO TO ACHIEVE A TARGET EXPECTED RATE OF RETURN

What proportion of your wealth should you invest in The Gap and what proportion in Kerr-McGee to obtain a target expected rate of return of 1.60 percent?

$$E(r_{\text{Gap/Kerr-McGee}}) = w_{\text{Gap}} \times 2.21\% + w_{\text{Kerr-McGee}} \times 1.09\% = 1.60\%$$

$$w_{\text{Gap}} + w_{\text{Kerr-McGee}} = 1.0$$

The portfolio weights are

$$w_{\text{Gap}} = 45.54\%, w_{\text{Kerr-McGee}} = 54.46\%.$$

You should invest 45.54 percent of your wealth in The Gap and the remainder, 54.46 percent, in Kerr-McGee.

● ─────────── ●

The Gap/Limited and Gap/Kerr-McGee portfolios have identical expected rates of return. Therefore, our risk-averse investor will prefer the one with less risk or, equivalently, the one with better diversification. Here's a chance to test your understanding up to this point: which portfolio do you believe provides better diversification?

The Correlation Effect

You probably said the Gap/Kerr-McGee portfolio provides better diversification because The Gap and Kerr-McGee are in different industries. You are right. Companies in different industries are less likely to be affected by the same economic forces. Consequently, one company can have a favorable deviation from its expected rate of return when the other has an unfavorable deviation. The tendency for their fortunes to rise and fall separately provides many opportunities for one company's rate of return to compensate for the other's. In contrast, companies in the same industry are more likely to be affected by the same economic forces; they tend to have either favorable or unfavorable deviations from their expected rates of return at the same time. The

MONTHLY RATES OF RETURN

Exhibit 5.2

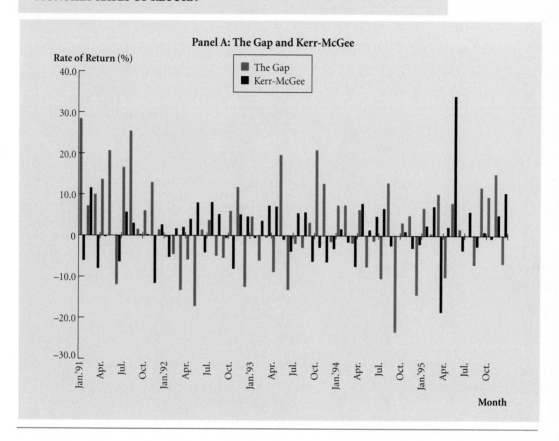

tendency for their fortunes to rise and fall together provides few opportunities for one company's rate of return to compensate for the other's.

The tendency for two companies' rates of return to rise and fall separately or together is described by their correlation. Two similar companies, such as The Gap and The Limited, have highly correlated rates of return. The correlation between the rates of return for two dissimilar companies, such as The Gap and Kerr-McGee, is low. We will incorporate the effect of correlation on risk mathematically, but it is instructive to first see the effect graphically.

Graphical Description of the Correlation Effect   You can see the differences between The Gap and Kerr-McGee and the similarities between The Gap and The Limited by plotting their monthly rates of return on the same graph. The Gap and Kerr-McGee are shown in panel A of Exhibit 5.2. This graph shows there were several months when one company's rate of return rose while the other's fell. The Gap's and The Limited's

Exhibit 5.2

MONTHLY RATES OF RETURN—*continued*

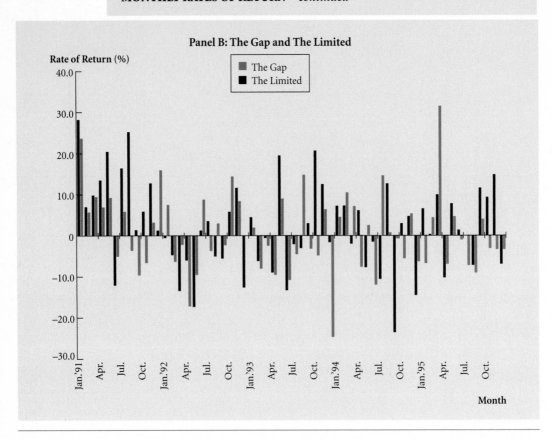

Panel B: The Gap and The Limited

rates of return are plotted in panel B. Note that their rates of return tended to rise and fall together. The difference between the patterns in panels A and B is evidence of the differences in the correlation between The Gap and Kerr-McGee and The Gap and The Limited, respectively.

The monthly rates of return for portfolios constructed using the proportions derived above are given in Appendix 5A. Equation 5.5 was used to compute the rates of return for each month. For example, the rate of return on the Gap/Kerr-McGee portfolio for January 1991 is 0.4554 × 28.30 percent + 0.5446 × −6.13 percent = 9.55 percent. The summary statistics for these portfolios also are given in Appendix 5A and repeated in Table 5.5. The mean and standard deviation of the rates of return were calculated by applying Equations 5.2 and 5.4 to the month-by-month portfolio returns. Note that the Gap/Kerr-McGee portfolio has a lower standard deviation of return (less risk) than the Gap/Limited portfolio. The graph of these rates of return in Exhibit 5.3 shows the same effect; the Gap/Kerr-McGee portfolio has a smaller range and lower overall variability.

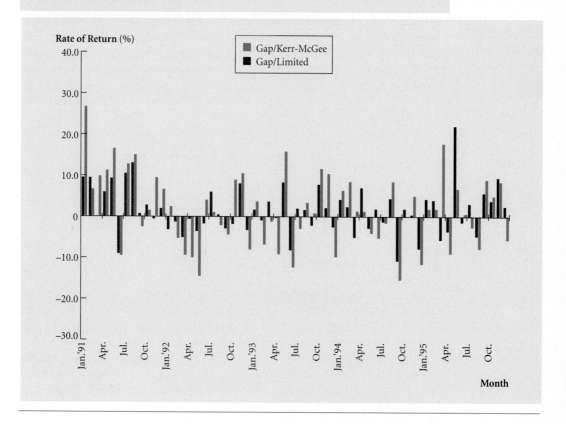

PORTFOLIO RATES OF RETURN

Exhibit 5.3

You may be tempted to think that the Gap/Kerr-McGee portfolio has less risk than the Gap/Limited portfolio because Kerr-McGee has a smaller standard deviation of return than The Limited. This difference is certainly a factor, but not the main one. The main reason the Gap/Kerr-McGee portfolio has less risk is that the correlation between The Gap and Kerr-McGee is lower than the correlation between The Gap and The Limited. Reiterating the important point, risk is reduced when individual investments that perform better than expected partially compensate for investments that perform

SUMMARY STATISTICS FOR THE PORTFOLIO RATES OF RETURN

Table 5.5

	Gap/Kerr-McGee	Gap/The Limited
Mean, $E(r)$	1.60%	1.60%
Standard deviation, $\sigma(r)$	5.74	8.83

worse than expected. Furthermore, the lower the correlation between the investments, the more frequently offsetting returns occur.

Using Covariance to Represent the Correlation Effect   We used Equation 5.4 to calculate the portfolio standard deviations in Table 5.5; however, it does not directly show the effect of correlation. An alternative equation for the standard deviation of a portfolio's rate of return directly shows the effect of correlation. It also is more convenient to use. Once again, we need some additional equations from statistics before we can proceed. The first is Equation 5.7, an expression for the **covariance** of the rates of return on two assets.

$$\text{Cov}(r_i, r_j) = \sum_{t=1}^{T} [r_{i,t} - E(r_i)] \, [r_{j,t} - E(r_j)] \, \text{Prob}_t \qquad [5.7]$$

The covariance is a measure of variability similar to the variance because each bracketed term in Equation 5.7 describes the amount by which an asset's actual rate of return differs from its expected value. Compare these terms to the corresponding term in Equation 5.3.[5] Covariance is a measure of *covariability*, however, because it describes how the assets' actual rates of return *simultaneously* deviate from their respective expected values.

The covariance is positive when both assets tend to have favorable or unfavorable deviations from their expected rates of return at the same time, that is, when $[r_{i,t} - E(r_i)]$ and $[r_{j,t} - E(r_j)]$ are both positive or both negative. Conversely, the covariance is negative when favorable deviations from the expected rate of return on one asset tend to occur at the same time as unfavorable deviations from the expected rate of return on the other (when either $[r_{i,t} - E(r_i)]$ or $[r_{j,t} - E(r_j)]$ is positive and the other is negative). In this way, Equation 5.7 shows that covariance captures the phenomenon that provides diversification, the tendency for two assets to have offsetting deviations from their expected rates of return.

These conclusions are reflected in the covariances of our example companies. The calculations to compute the covariance between The Gap's and Kerr-McGee's rates of return, –0.0011, are illustrated in Table 5.6. The covariance for The Gap and The Limited is 0.0041. These covariances indicate that better diversification is obtained by combining The Gap and Kerr-McGee as we saw in the preceding section.

EXERCISE

5.6   **CALCULATING THE COVARIANCE**

Did The Gap and Kerr-McGee tend to have similar or opposite deviations from their expected rates of return in 1995? Use the holding period rates of return in Appendix 5A to calculate the covariance between The Gap and Kerr-McGee's monthly rates of return for 1995.

---

[5]Note that an investment's covariance with itself equals its own variance. (You can see this by setting *i* equal to *j* in Equation 5.7.) We will make use of this fact shortly.

CALCULATION OF THE COVARIANCE BETWEEN THE GAP'S AND KERR-MCGEE'S RATES OF RETURN

Table 5.6

Month	The Gap Actual Return r_i	Deviation from Mean $r_{i,t}-E(r_i)$	Kerr-McGee Actual Return r_j	Deviation from Mean $r_{j,t}-E(r_j)$	Product of Deviations $[r_{i,t}-E(r_i)] \times [r_{j,t}-E(r_j)]$
Jan 1991	0.2830	0.2609	−0.0613	−0.0722	−0.0188
Feb	0.0706	0.0485	0.1154	0.1045	0.0051
Mar	0.0989	0.0768	−0.0804	−0.0913	−0.0070
.	.	.	.	.	.
.	.	.	.	.	.
.	.	.	.	.	.
Oct 1995	0.0938	0.0717	−0.0068	−0.0177	−0.0013
Nov	0.1491	0.1270	0.0499	−0.0390	0.0050
Dec	−0.0693	−0.0914	0.1043	0.0934	−0.0085
Sum					−0.0636

$Cov(r_{\text{Gap}}, r_{\text{Kerr-McGee}}) = -0.0636/60 = -0.0011$

Month	The Gap Actual Return	Deviation from Mean	Kerr-McGee Actual Return	Deviation from Mean	Product of Deviations
January 1995	0.0661	0.0345	0.0243	−0.0110	−0.0004
February	0.0039	−0.0277	0.0713	0.0360	−0.0010
March	0.1002	0.0686	−0.1861	−0.2214	−0.0152
April	−0.1021	−0.1337	0.0213	−0.0140	0.0019
May	0.0784	0.0468	0.3404	0.3051	0.0143
June	0.0145	−0.0171	−0.0359	−0.0712	0.0012
July	0.0000	−0.0316	0.0581	0.0228	−0.0007
August	−0.0718	−0.1034	−0.0263	−0.0616	0.0064
September	0.1163	0.0847	0.0091	−0.0262	−0.0022
October	0.0938	0.0622	−0.0068	−0.0421	−0.0026
November	0.1491	0.1175	0.0499	0.0146	0.0017
December	−0.0693	−0.1009	0.1043	0.0690	−0.0070
Sum					−0.0036

Covariance = −0.0036/12 = −0.0003

The negative covariance indicates The Gap and Kerr-McGee tended to have off-setting deviations from their expected rates of return in 1995.

The covariance provides a precise, quantitative link between the tendency for two assets to have offsetting deviations from their expected rates of return and the portfolio's risk. The covariance is difficult to interpret, however, because it is affected by each asset's own variability as well as the tendency to move together or separately. As a result, the unit of measurement is rate of return squared, and there is no upper or lower limit to covariance values.

Using the Correlation Coefficient to Represent the Correlation Effect   We eliminate the difficulty of interpreting the covariance by dividing it by each asset's standard deviation of rate of return. This scaling procedure removes the variance from covariance and leaves only the *co-* part; a measure of the assets' tendency to move together or separately. You saw the result when you studied statistics; it is the **correlation coefficient**, $\rho(r_i, r_j)$, which is defined by Equation 5.8.

$$\rho(r_i, r_j) = \text{Cov}(r_i, r_j)/\sigma(r_i)\sigma(r_j) \qquad [5.8]$$

The correlation coefficient is a good quantitative measure of the tendency for two assets to have offsetting deviations from their expected rates of return because it is "unitless" and must be less than or equal to the absolute v189alue of 1.0. Furthermore, correlation coefficients are easy to interpret: Two assets that have perfect positive correlation, $\rho = +1.0$, *always* have identical deviations from their expected values. Conversely, two assets that have perfect negative correlation, $\rho = -1.0$, *always* have exact opposite deviations from their expected rates of return. A positive value less than 1.0 means the assets *tend* to have similar deviations while a negative value means they *tend* to have different deviations. No association exists between the rates of return on two assets that have a correlation coefficient of zero.

The correlation coefficient captures the phenomenon that provides diversification just as well as covariance without the confounding information about each asset's own variability. The clarity this provides is apparent if we compare the correlation coefficients of our example companies. The correlation between The Gap and Kerr-McGee is

$$\rho(r_{\text{Gap}}, r_{\text{Kerr-McGee}}) = \text{Cov}(r_{\text{Gap}}, r_{\text{Kerr-McGee}})/\sigma(r_{\text{Gap}})\sigma(r_{\text{Kerr-McGee}})$$
$$= -0.0011/(0.1072 \times 0.0707)$$
$$= -0.1451.$$

EXERCISE •——————————————————————————•

5.7   CALCULATING THE CORRELATION COEFFICIENT

Does the correlation coefficient indicate that a portfolio of The Gap and The Limited will provide more or less diversification than a portfolio of The Gap and Kerr-McGee?

$$\rho(r_{\text{Gap}}, r_{\text{Limited}}) = \text{Cov}(r_{\text{Gap}}, r_{\text{Limited}})/\sigma(r_{\text{Gap}})\sigma(r_{\text{Limited}})$$
$$= 0.0041/(0.1072 \times 0.0954) = 0.4009$$

The Gap and The Limited have a larger correlation coefficient than The Gap and Kerr-McGee and therefore provide less diversification.

•——————————•

The Gap and Kerr-McGee have a negative correlation coefficient consistent with the pattern in panel A of Exhibit 5.2, which showed that there were several months when one company's rate of return rose while the other's fell. The Gap and The Limited have a positive correlation coefficient consistent with the pattern in panel B of Exhibit 5.2, which showed that their rates of return tended to rise and fall together. More precisely and more conveniently than industry membership, graphs, or covariance, the correlation coefficient indicates which investments provide better diversification.

We are now in position to see how the correlation between two assets' rates of return affects diversification and portfolio risk. Our alternative equation for the standard deviation of a portfolio's rate of return is

$$\sigma(r_p) = [\sum_{i=1}^{n} \sum_{j=1}^{n} w_i w_j \rho(r_i, r_j)\sigma(r_i)\sigma(r_j)]^{1/2}. \qquad [5.9]$$

For a two-asset portfolio, Equation 5.9 simplifies to

$$\sigma(r_p) = [w_1^2 \sigma^2(r_1) + w_2^2 \sigma^2(r_2) + 2w_1 w_2 \rho(r_1, r_2)\sigma(r_1)\sigma(r_2)]^{1/2}. \qquad [5.10]$$

Let's use Equation 5.10 to compute the standard deviation of the portfolio that is 64.53 percent invested in The Gap and 35.47 percent invested in The Limited.

$$
\begin{aligned}
\sigma(r_p) &= [w_{\text{Gap}}^2 \sigma^2(r_{\text{Gap}}) + w_{\text{Limited}}^2 \sigma^2(r_{\text{Limited}}) + 2w_{\text{Gap}} w_{\text{Limited}} \\
&\quad \times \rho(r_{\text{Gap}}, r_{\text{Limited}})\sigma(r_{\text{Gap}})\sigma(r_{\text{Limited}})]^{1/2} \\
&= [(0.6453)^2 \times 0.0115 + (0.3547)^2 \times 0.0091 + 2 \times 0.6453 \times 0.3547 \\
&\quad \times 0.4009 \times 0.1072 \times 0.0954]^{1/2} \\
&= 0.0884 \text{ or } 8.84\%
\end{aligned}
$$

This value differs from the standard deviation we computed from the portfolio's actual rates of return, $\sigma(r_p) = 8.83$ percent, only because of rounding.

EXERCISE

5.8

CALCULATING THE STANDARD DEVIATION OF A PORTFOLIO

What is the standard deviation of the portfolio that is 45.54 percent invested in The Gap and 54.46 percent invested in Kerr-McGee?

$$
\begin{aligned}
\sigma(r_p) &= [w_{\text{Gap}}^2 \sigma^2(r_{\text{Gap}}) + w_{\text{Kerr-McGee}}^2 \sigma^2(r_{\text{Kerr-McGee}}) + 2w_{\text{Gap}} w_{\text{Kerr-McGee}} \\
&\quad \times \rho(r_{\text{Gap}}, r_{\text{Kerr-McGee}})\sigma(r_{\text{Gap}})\sigma(r_{\text{Kerr-McGee}})]^{1/2} \\
&= [(0.4554)^2 \times 0.0115 + (0.5446)^2 \times 0.0050 + 2 \times 0.4554 \times 0.5446 \\
&\quad \times (-0.1451) \times 0.1072 \times 0.0707]^{1/2} \\
&= 0.0576 \text{ or } 5.76\%
\end{aligned}
$$

A portfolio that is 45.54 percent The Gap and 54.46 percent Kerr-McGee has a standard deviation of 5.76 percent.

Table 5.7   ILLUSTRATION OF RISK REDUCTION DUE TO CORRELATION EFFECT

	Portfolio	
	45.54% The Gap 54.46% Kerr-McGee	64.53% The Gap 35.47% The Limited
Expected rate of return	1.60%	1.60%
Standard deviation of rate of return		
If correlation equaled +1.0	8.73	10.30
Given actual correlation	5.76	8.84
Percent reduced by correlation effect	34.02	14.17

Equation 5.10 shows how the correlation effect works. Similar assets have a high correlation coefficient and contribute most of their individual risks to the portfolio through the third term on the right-hand side of the equation. Dissimilar assets have a low correlation coefficient and contribute less of their individual risks to the portfolio.

These conclusions are even clearer if we look closely at the extreme case of perfect positive correlation. Then, because $\sigma^2(r_i) = [\sigma(r_i)]^2$, Equation 5.10 can be rewritten as

$$\sigma(r_p) = \{[w_1\sigma(r_1) + w_2\sigma(r_2)] \times [w_1\sigma(r_1) + w_2\sigma(r_2)]\}^{1/2}$$
$$= \{[w_1\sigma(r_1) + w_2\sigma(r_2)]^2\}^{1/2}$$
$$= w_1\sigma(r_1) + w_2\sigma(r_2). \qquad [5.11]$$

That is, the standard deviation of a portfolio's rate of return is a weighted average of the standard deviations of the rates of return on the assets in the portfolio. Identical assets, with perfect positive correlation, contribute all their individual risks to the portfolio because there is no opportunity for offsetting returns. The standard deviation is less than a weighted average if the correlation is less than one, however. This difference is the risk reduction provided by a portfolio of assets that may simultaneously experience favorable and unfavorable rates of return.

Table 5.7 shows the effect of correlation on our example portfolios. The Gap/Kerr-McGee portfolio would have a standard deviation of 8.73 percent (0.4554 × 10.72 percent + 0.5446 × 7.07 percent) if the two companies were perfectly correlated. Its actual standard deviation, 5.76 percent, is 34.02 percent lower than the maximum value because the correlation between The Gap and Kerr-McGee is only −0.1451 rather than +1.0. The correlation effect provided only a 14.17 percent reduction in risk in the Gap/Limited portfolio because their correlation coefficient is much closer to one.

Let's review what you've learned and why it's important. You undoubtedly knew, at an intuitive level, that a portfolio of a clothing store and an oil company (The Gap and Kerr-McGee) would provide better diversification than a portfolio of two clothing stores (The Gap and The Limited).

You need more than good intuition, however, to describe the relationships among the investments in a large portfolio such as the College Retirement Equity Fund. Now you know that you can use the correlation coefficient to supplement or replace your intuition. This statistic is a precise, mathematical description of the similarity or

THE GAP/KERR-MCGEE OPPORTUNITY SETS   Table 5.8

| Percent Invested in | | $\sigma(r_p)$ if: | | |
The Gap	Kerr-McGee	$\rho = -.1451^*$	$\rho = +1.0^{**}$	$E(r_p)^{***}$
0.00	100.00	7.07	7.07	1.09
10.00	90.00	6.30	7.44	1.20
20.00	80.00	5.75	7.80	1.31
30.00	70.00	5.50	8.17	1.43
40.00	60.00	5.58	8.53	1.54
45.54	**54.46**	**5.76**	**8.73**	**1.60**
50.00	50.00	5.98	8.90	1.65
60.00	40.00	6.64	9.26	1.76
70.00	30.00	7.50	9.63	1.87
80.00	20.00	8.49	9.99	1.99
90.00	10.00	9.57	10.36	2.10
100.00	0.00	10.72	10.72	2.21

$^*\sigma(r_p) = [w_{Gap}^2\sigma^2(r_{Gap}) + w_{Kerr\text{-}McGee}^2 \sigma^2(r_{Kerr\text{-}McGee}) + 2w_{Gap}w_{Kerr\text{-}McGee}\,\rho(r_{Gap}, r_{Kerr\text{-}McGee})$
$\times \sigma(r_{Gap})\sigma(r_{Kerr\text{-}McGee})]^{1/2}$ [5.10]

$^{**}\sigma(r_p) = w_{Gap}\sigma(r_{Gap}) + w_{Kerr\text{-}McGee}\sigma(r_{Kerr\text{-}McGee})$ [5.11]

$^{***}E(r_p) = w_{Gap}E(r_{Gap}) + w_{Kerr\text{-}McGee}E(r_{Kerr\text{-}McGee})$ [5.6]

difference between two assets. Importantly, its value is determined by the tendency for two assets to have opposite deviations from their expected rates of return—the very phenomenon we rely on for diversification.

The Portfolio Opportunity Set

The set of all possible portfolios that can be constructed from a particular group of assets is called the **portfolio opportunity set**. Each portfolio in the set is identified by its expected rate of return and the standard deviation of its rate of return. The Gap/Kerr-McGee portfolio we've been examining, with $E(r_p) = 1.60$ percent and $\sigma(r_p) = 5.76$ percent, is one member of the Gap/Kerr-McGee opportunity set but there are an infinite number of others. A graph with standard deviation and expected return plotted on the x- and y-axes is the best way to describe an opportunity set. Opportunity sets plot as parabolas or straight lines on this graph depending on the correlation between the assets in the portfolios.

The coordinates of specific portfolios in two opportunity sets based on The Gap and Kerr-McGee are given in Table 5.8. The first opportunity set uses their actual correlation coefficient ($\rho = -0.1451$) to compute the standard deviations. The second uses the assumed correlation coefficient of $+1.0$ for comparison. The expected rates of return in each opportunity set are the same because $E(r_p)$ is not affected by the correlation coefficient (see Equation 5.6). The portfolios we've been examining are in bold print.

These two Gap/Kerr-McGee opportunity sets, plus another we'll discuss shortly, are graphed in Exhibit 5.4. The endpoints of each opportunity set are single-asset portfolios; 100 percent invested in Kerr-McGee for $E(r_p)$ = 1.09 percent, $\sigma(r_p)$ = 7.07 percent or 100 percent invested in The Gap for $E(r_p)$ = 2.21 percent, $\sigma(r_p)$ = 10.72 percent. The parabola connecting these single-asset portfolios is the actual Gap/Kerr-McGee opportunity given their correlation coefficient of −0.1451. The dotted line connecting the single-asset portfolios is what the opportunity set would look like if The Gap and Kerr-McGee were perfectly positively correlated. This opportunity set graphs as a straight line because the portfolios' expected returns and standard deviations of return are weighted averages of the corresponding values for The Gap and Kerr-McGee.

The parabola and the dotted line in Exhibit 5.4 are characteristic of opportunity sets that do and do not provide risk reduction through diversification. The distance between the curve and the line, whether measured horizontally or vertically, represents the diversification effect that results from a correlation coefficient less than one. The smaller the correlation coefficient, the greater this distance.

The dashed line in Exhibit 5.4 is what the opportunity set would look like if The Gap and Kerr-McGee were perfectly negatively correlated. They would be perfect opposites in this case, which means you could hold them in a combination that guaranteed one's favorable deviations would completely offset the other's unfavorable deviations. This combination would eliminate all risk. This is why the opportunity set touches the vertical axis in Exhibit 5.4. A portfolio constructed to eliminate all risk is called a *hedge portfolio*. As we will see later, investors can construct hedge portfolios in reality. Investors cannot combine The Gap and Kerr-McGee to form a hedge portfolio, however, because their actual correlation coefficient is not −1.0.

You can even get diversification benefits by dividing your money between two mutual funds. See "In the News."

The Portfolio Efficient Set

The Gap/Limited opportunity set is included along with the Gap/Kerr-McGee opportunity set in Exhibit 5.5. Four specific portfolios, labeled A, B, C, and D, are shown and

Exhibit 5.4

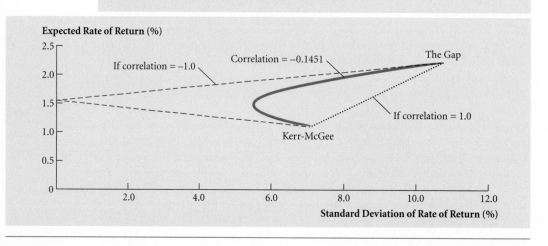

THE GAP/KERR-MCGEE OPPORTUNITY SET

their characteristics are described in the table. Clearly, risk-averse investors will consider some of these portfolios superior to others. Portfolio A dominates portfolio C, as we saw earlier, because both have an expected rate of return of 1.60 percent but the Gap/Kerr-McGee combination has less risk. Similarly, portfolio A dominates portfolio D because it has a higher expected rate of return for the same risk. Portfolio B dominates portfolio C for the same reason. Portfolio A does not dominate portfolio B, however, because it has *both* lower risk and a lower expected rate of return.

By extending this reasoning throughout the entire graph, you can see that the dominant portfolios are described by the green portion of the Gap/Kerr-McGee opportunity set. They are dominant because they provide a higher return for the same risk or a lower risk for the same return than all other alternatives. This set of dominant portfolios is called the **efficient set** because it provides the best available or most efficient trade-off between risk and return.

● —— ●   E X E R C I S E

IDENTIFYING DOMINANT PORTFOLIOS

5.9

Calculate the expected rate of return and standard deviation of the rate of return for portfolio X, which is 100 percent invested in Kerr-McGee, and for portfolio Y, which is 60 percent The Gap and 40 percent Kerr-McGee. Does portfolio A in Exhibit 5.5 dominate portfolio X or vice versa? Does portfolio A dominate portfolio Y or vice versa?

Portfolio X is 100 percent invested in Kerr-McGee so its expected rate of return and standard deviation equal Kerr-McGee's:

$$E(r_X) = E(r_{\text{Kerr-McGee}}) = 0.0109 \text{ or } 1.09\%$$
$$\sigma(r_X) = \sigma(r_{\text{Kerr-McGee}}) = 0.0707 \text{ or } 7.07\%.$$

Portfolio A has a higher expected rate of return, 0.0160, and a lower standard deviation, 0.0576, so portfolio A dominates portfolio X.

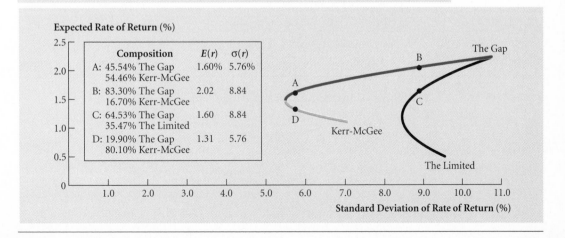

Exhibit 5.5

THE GAP/KERR-MCGEE, THE GAP/THE LIMITED OPPORTUNITY SETS

Composition	E(r)	σ(r)
A: 45.54% The Gap 54.46% Kerr-McGee	1.60%	5.76%
B: 83.30% The Gap 16.70% Kerr-McGee	2.02	8.84
C: 64.53% The Gap 35.47% The Limited	1.60	8.84
D: 19.90% The Gap 80.10% Kerr-McGee	1.31	5.76

I N   T H E   N E W S

ANALYZING THE BASKETS IN WHICH TO PLACE YOUR EGGS

DIVERSIFY. DON'T PUT all your eggs in one basket. We have all heard the wisdom, but few of us heed it in picking mutual funds. People who own the Fidelity Contrafund, say, may branch out to Fidelity Growth & Income with their next fund purchase, thinking they're diversifying. They aren't.

In the statistical scheme of things, these are two peas in a pod. They may both prove to be good funds, but the likelihood is that in a month when one goes up, the other will, too, and when one goes down, so will the other. You don't accomplish a lot by dividing your eggs between these two baskets. You might as well put all your money in the one blue-chip fund you like the most.

If you want true diversity, therefore, make sure you spread your money among funds that do not move in lockstep with each other. The Benham Treasury Note Fund and the Lexington Strategic Silver Fund are one such pair. When inflation perks up, so, most of the time, do silver prices and interest rates. That makes the T-note fund do badly and the Silver fund do well. The reverse is also true.

Heartland Value Fund and MFS World Governments-A bond fund are another intriguing pair. When one zigs, the other zags. These two funds are not mirror opposites, to be sure, but they really do travel on different wavelengths.

Here's yet another pair of funds that tend to veer off in different directions: GAM International Fund and Vanguard GNMA Fund.

How did we find these diversifications? With a computer. We fed it monthly returns since 1986 for 560 funds and asked it to calculate, for each pair, what statisticians call the correlation coefficient. That's a measure of how closely two data series track each other.

If you want to apply correlation analysis to your fund portfolio, try computer software from Value Line or Morningstar, two fund-rating companies. You feed the programs two or more fund names and they tell you the risk and return of each fund over the past several years, as well as the risk and return of a blend (see graphs).

Look at the Heartland Value/MFS World pair in the lower-right graph. The returns for the funds over the past ten years have averaged 14.3 percent and 11.8 percent, respectively. A blend would have earned you 13 percent, right in the middle. But the risk of the blend is below the average of the two funds' risk measures.

This, graphically, is what you gain by not putting all your eggs in one basket.

If you are going to use this software, understand its limits. It can give you a pretty good idea of which funds tend to move in lockstep and which ones don't. But it can't tell you which funds are going to go up the most.

So don't add Twentieth Century Ultra to your portfolio just because it went up a lot in the past. Add it if it complements another fund.

Source: Thomas Easton, "Egg Basket Analysis," *Forbes*, May 6, 1996, pp. 132–133. Reprinted by permission of *Forbes*, © Forbes, Inc. 1996.

Portfolio Y's expected rate of return and standard deviation are

$$E(r_Y) = w_{Gap} \times E(r_{Gap}) + w_{Kerr\text{-}McGee} \times E(r_{Kerr\text{-}McGee})$$
$$= 0.60 \times 0.0221 + 0.40 \times 0.0109 = 0.0176 \text{ or } 1.76\%$$

$$\sigma(r_Y) = [w_{Gap}^2\, \sigma^2(r_{Gap}) + w_{Kerr\text{-}McGee}^2\, \sigma^2(r_{Kerr\text{-}McGee}) + 2w_{Gap}w_{Kerr\text{-}McGee}$$
$$\times \rho(r_{Gap}, r_{Kerr\text{-}McGee})\, \sigma\,(r_{Gap})\sigma(r_{Kerr\text{-}McGee})]^{1/2}$$

$$= [(0.60)^2 \times 0.0115 + (0.40)^2 \times 0.0050 + 2 \times 0.60 \times 0.40 \times (-0.1451)$$
$$\times 0.1072 \times 0.0707]^{1/2}$$

$$= 0.0664 \text{ or } 6.64\%.$$

In the News—*Continued*

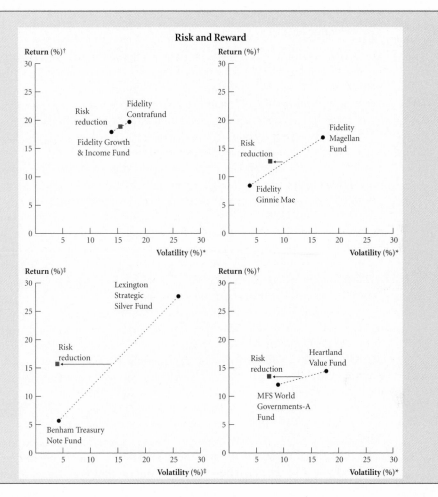

Risk and Reward

Balancing Funds. Start with upper left and go clockwise. FidelityContrafund + Fidelity Growth & Income: Two eggs, one basket. Less return, less risk. Gain from diversification? Zilch. Fidelity Magellan + Fidelity Ginnie Mae: Just a small gain from diversification. Heartland Value + MFS World Governments-A: Give up some return, but see the risk dramatically decline. Lexington Strategic Silver + Benham Treasury Note: Dramatic diversification. When one wiggles, the other waggles.

*Annualized standard deviation calculated over ten years.
†Compound annual return over ten years.
‡Three years.
■Fifty-fifty blend of two funds.
Source: Value/Screen III, January 1996. Copyright 1996 by Value Line Publishing, Inc.

Portfolio A has a lower expected rate of return, 0.0160 versus 0.0176, and a lower standard deviation, 0.0576 versus 0.0664, so it neither dominates nor is dominated by portfolio Y.

● ———————————— ●

The Number of Assets Effect

Forming a portfolio of two assets that are less than perfectly correlated reduces risk because favorable deviations from the expected rate of return on one asset partially compensate for unfavorable deviations from the expected rate of return on the other. Forming a portfolio of more than two assets that are less than perfectly correlated is even better. In fact, up to a point, a portfolio provides more diversification the larger the number of assets it contains. The explanation for this effect is simple: The more assets in a portfolio, the more sources of offsetting rates of return.

Think about our example companies again. In the two-asset portfolio, there was only one source of compensating returns, Kerr-McGee versus The Gap. Adding The Limited to make a three-asset portfolio provides three sources of compensating returns: Kerr-McGee & The Limited versus The Gap; The Gap & The Limited versus Kerr-McGee; and The Gap & Kerr-McGee versus The Limited. Of course, adding The Limited was useful only because its rate of return is less than perfectly correlated with the rates of return on the other two assets. This suggests another way to describe the number of assets effect: Increasing the number of assets in a portfolio provides more opportunities for the correlation effect to work.

The coordinates of specific portfolios in the efficient sets of two- and three-asset portfolios are given in Table 5.9. Equations 5.6 and 5.9 were used to calculate the coordinates of the Gap/Kerr-McGee portfolios. A mathematical technique that locates the portfolio with the minimum standard deviation for a given expected rate of return was used to calculate the coordinates of the Gap/Kerr-McGee/Limited portfolios.[6] Note that the three-asset efficient set dominates the two-asset efficient set.

The number of assets effect illustrated in Table 5.9 is a general result: The more assets in a portfolio, the lower the risk for a given rate of return. The graph in Exhibit 5.6 depicts this result when investors may choose from many assets. Then, the boundaries of the opportunity set are similar to the boundaries in Exhibit 5.5, but its interior is completely filled in by inefficient portfolios that may contain one, two, three, or even all the available assets.

The Limit to Diversification

The preceding discussion seems to imply that investors can totally eliminate risk by holding a large number of dissimilar risky assets in their portfolios. This inference is wrong. Portfolios do not entirely eliminate risk because you cannot find a large number of dissimilar assets. Refer to our example companies again. Kerr-McGee is different from both The Gap and The Limited, which implies The Gap and The Limited must be similar to each other.

---

[6]See Chapter 9 of Haim Levy and Marshall Sarnat, *Portfolio and Investment Selection: Theory and Practice,* Prentice-Hall International, Englewood Cliffs, New Jersey, 1984.

TWO- AND THREE-ASSET PORTFOLIO EFFICIENT SETS **Table 5.9**

	Standard Deviation of Rate of Return	
Expected Rate of Return	Gap/Kerr-McGee Portfolio	Gap/Kerr-McGee/ Limited Portfolio
1.50%	5.51%	5.45%
1.60	5.76	5.70
1.70	6.25	6.03
1.80	6.91	6.35
1.90	7.72	6.72
2.00	8.62	7.13
2.10	9.59	7.55
2.20	10.62	8.00

Exhibit 5.6

MULTI-ASSET PORTFOLIO OPPORTUNITY SET

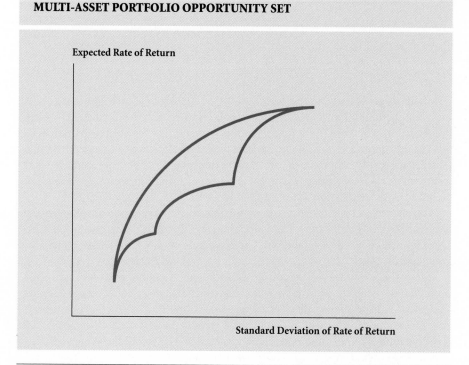

In reality, you won't run out of dissimilar assets so soon because you can choose from thousands of assets. Nevertheless, investors cannot find a large number of dissimilar assets because the vast majority are positively correlated with one another through their

Exhibit 5.7

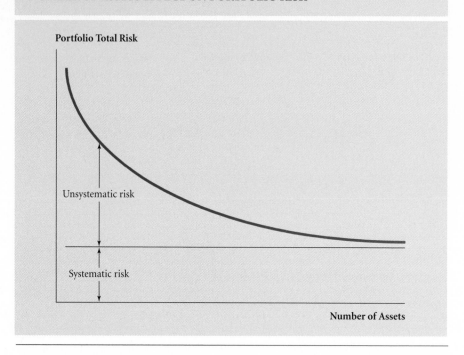

NUMBER OF ASSETS EFFECT ON PORTFOLIO RISK

sensitivity to general economic conditions. Consequently, a core amount of risk, caused by fluctuations in general economic conditions, cannot be eliminated through diversification. This core risk is pervasive or systematic, so it is called **systematic risk**.

The counterpart to systematic risk is the variation in an asset's rate of return that is unrelated to the variations in any other asset's rate of return. This uncertainty is called **unsystematic risk**. Unsystematic risk is the source of variation in rates of return that is reduced by diversification as we will clearly see later.

Fortunately, you don't need a large number of assets in a portfolio to reduce its risk to the core level. A recent study has found that, for all practical purposes, unsystematic risks are diversified away, and only the systematic or core risk remains in portfolios of approximately 30 to 40 assets.[7] Exhibit 5.7 graphically depicts the conclusion.

Given these results, you may wonder why CREF's portfolio is invested in the common stock issued by more than 3,800 different companies. One explanation is that CREF is too large to concentrate its investments in only 20 or 30 stocks. For example, the market value of the equity issued by the 20 largest companies in the Fortune 500 was approximately $935 billion on March 15, 1996.[8] CREF would own approximately 7.6 percent of each company on average ($70.7/$935) if it invested in only these large firms.

---

[7]Meir Statman, "How Many Stocks Make a Diversified Portfolio?" *Journal of Financial and Quantitative Analysis,* September 1987, pp. 353–363.

[8]*Fortune,* April 29, 1996, pp. F-1 and F-2.

It's time again to review the additional lessons you've learned about how diversification affects a portfolio's risk. We also need to recall why these lessons are important to managers.

Constructing a portfolio of assets that are not identical to one another, as measured by their correlation coefficients, reduces the portfolio's risk. More risk reduction is achieved by including more assets in the portfolio because there are more opportunities for them to have offsetting deviations from their expected rates of return. Risk is reduced at a decreasing rate, however, as it becomes increasingly difficult to find additional assets that are dissimilar from those already in the portfolio. Ultimately, the portfolio's risk cannot be reduced below a level that reflects what the assets have in common due to their sensitivity to general economic conditions. This limit is the portfolio's systematic risk. The risk eliminated by diversification is unsystematic risk.

Modern finance theory assumes that investors hold well-diversified portfolios and therefore are not affected by unsystematic risk. Consequently, managers can ignore unsystematic risk when determining how investment, operating, and financing decisions will affect the owners' wealth. Instead, they only need to consider systematic risk and its effect on the owners' opportunity cost or required rate of return. The remainder of this chapter shows how to measure systematic and unsystematic risk. Chapter 6 relates systematic risk to the owners' required rate of return.

5.3 DIVERSIFIABLE AND NONDIVERSIFIABLE RETURN AND RISK

Up to this point, we have used the entire distribution of predicted rates of return to compute an asset's mean and standard deviation. These are the appropriate summary statistics, but we assume that *any* outcome is possible when we compute their values this way. For example, a forecast that The Gap's expected monthly rate of return will equal its historical average of 2.21 percent assumes that all of the company's rates of return for 1991–1995 are equally likely to recur. The standard deviation is affected the same way. Even simple summary statistics such as the minimum and maximum rates of return are the smallest and largest values in the entire distribution rather than the smallest and largest given a particular set of circumstances.

We can improve our understanding of an asset's rate of return and risk by using additional information to describe the circumstances associated with each periodic rate of return. We might simultaneously record conditions in the economy, for example, so we can determine whether an asset performs best during strong or weak economic conditions. Using the additional information, we can make more specific predictions given the circumstances we expect to prevail in the future.

We will use variables that represent economic conditions to describe the circumstances associated with an asset's periodic rates of return. Taking economic conditions into account is a logical way to improve our predictions because there is an association between the performance of the economy and the performance of most assets. For example, companies that sell consumer goods such as automobiles and appliances tend to do well when the economy is healthy and vice versa. We still use the mean and standard deviation to describe an asset's expected rate of return and total risk, but their values are determined by the asset's relationship to economic conditions.

The Market Model

The **market model** uses the performance of a single, large, well-diversified portfolio to represent economic conditions.[9] Ideally, every asset in the economy is included in this portfolio in proportion to its market value. For example, if the market value of IBM's common stock is 1 percent of the total market value of all assets (it isn't), then IBM's stock would have a weight of 1 percent in this portfolio. A portfolio constructed this way is called the **market portfolio**.

The construction of the market portfolio ensures that it represents general economic conditions. All assets are included and diversification is complete. Events that affect only one asset (unsystematic risks) do not affect the portfolio's performance; they are diversified away. Instead, the portfolio's performance is affected only by events the assets have in common (systematic risks). The breadth of assets in the portfolio ensures the only events they *all* have in common are general economic conditions.

Unfortunately, we cannot construct the actual market portfolio because many important assets are not traded. This means we do not have reliable estimates of their market values. Examples of nontraded assets are human capital (the value of training and experience), many types of real estate, and art and collectibles. The way we get around this problem is to use a broad-based portfolio of traded assets as a proxy or **market index**. Standard & Poor's Index of 500 Stocks is often chosen for this purpose. Although using a market index is a compromise, it's not too bad because these companies own or use a large variety of traded and nontraded assets whose values are reflected in their common stock prices.

Graphical Description of the Market Model   We'll use the market model with the rate of return on the S&P 500 stock index as the market index to explain The Gap's rates of return. The S&P 500's rates of return are holding period returns computed from the index's closing value each month. These monthly rates of return are given in Appendix 5A and coordinated with The Gap's returns in Exhibit 5.8.

The scatterplot of The Gap and market index rates of return shows that The Gap tends to perform better when the market index performs better and vice versa. This is apparent because most of the returns plot in the northeast and southwest quadrants of the graph. The positive association between The Gap's returns and economic conditions also is apparent from the positive slope of the **characteristic line,** which summarizes the central tendency of the plotted returns.

The graph also indicates how knowledge of the association between The Gap and S&P 500 rates of return can be used to explain The Gap's performance. Suppose we expect that conditions in the economy will produce a market index rate of return between 0.0 percent and 2.0 percent. The graph tells us that, under these circumstances, The Gap's rate of return has been as small as −17.27 percent and as large as 20.76 percent. This range, which is conditional on the economy's performance, is much narrower than the unconditional range of −23.55 percent to 28.30 percent we measured earlier.

---

[9]The market model was developed by William F. Sharpe to simplify portfolio analysis. See William F. Sharpe, "A Simplified Model for Portfolio Analysis," *Management Science,* January 1963, pp. 277–293.

Exhibit 5.8

GRAPHICAL DESCRIPTION OF THE MARKET MODEL

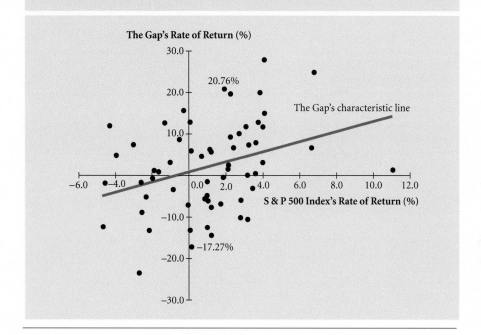

We also can use the association between The Gap and S&P 500 rates of return to make more precise statements about an asset's expected rate of return and standard deviation, but we need a mathematical description of the market model for this purpose.

Mathematical Description of the Market Model and Expected Rates of Return
The mathematical description of the market model is given in Equation 5.12.

$$E(r_j|r_I) = \alpha_j + r_I\beta_j \qquad [5.12]$$

where $E(r_j|r_I)$ = expected rate of return on asset j given the rate of return on the market index, r_I
   α_j = y-intercept of asset j's characteristic line
   β_j = slope of asset j's characteristic line

This equation provides an estimate of an asset's expected rate of return given the economy's performance. The first term, α_j or alpha, equals an asset's expected rate of return after the effect of economic conditions is removed, that is, when $r_I = 0$. The second term equals the addition to its expected rate of return that is due to economic conditions. The return on the market index, r_I, describes general economic conditions and the **beta** coefficient, β_j, describes how these conditions affect the asset in question. For example, a 1 percent improvement in the market index rate of return is expected to produce a 1.2 percent improvement in an asset's rate of return if that asset has a beta

I N   T H E   N E W S

BETAS AND COMMON SENSE

HERE ARE THE average betas of companies in selected industries. The demand for water and electricity does not depend on economic conditions so much as it does the size of the population so you might expect utilities to have small betas and they do. The demand for producer goods, such as office equipment and machine tools, depends on managers' expectations about economic conditions and companies in these industries have betas very close to one. Finally, consumer spending on airline tickets, housing, and stocks and bonds is highly discretionary. Therefore, we should expect the returns to companies in these industries to have strong associations with overall economic conditions (high betas) and they do.

Industry Name	SIC	Average Beta*
Water utilities	4941	0.59
Electric utilities	4900	0.69
Office equipment	3570	1.01
Machine tools	3540	1.10
Retail stores	5300	1.13
Air transport	4510	1.31
Home building	1521	1.46
Securities brokerage	6210	1.70

*Value/Screen III, Value Line Publishing, Inc. January 1996.

of 1.2. The higher an asset's beta, the more its rate of return is affected by economic conditions. Beta values usually make sense if you consider the nature of the demand for the industry's products. See "In the News."

You can use simple linear regression analysis to estimate the parameters of an asset's characteristic line. You also can use summary statistics, if you already have them, to calculate α_j and β_j directly. The equations are

$$\beta_j = \text{Cov}(r_j, r_I)/\sigma^2(r_I)$$
$$= \rho(r_j, r_I)\sigma(r_j)\sigma(r_I)/\sigma^2(r_I). \qquad [5.13]$$
$$\alpha_j = E(r_j) - E(r_I) \times \beta_j. \qquad [5.14]$$

Applying regression analysis to The Gap's historical returns, we obtain the following equation for the characteristic line in Exhibit 5.8.

$$E(r_{\text{Gap}}|r_I) = 0.89\% + r_I \times 1.2138$$

We also can calculate The Gap's alpha and beta directly. We already know that The Gap's expected rate of return is 0.0221. The S&P 500's expected rate of return over the sample period was 0.0109 and its variance was 0.0009; the covariance between The Gap and the S&P 500 was 0.0011. Substituting these values into Equations 5.13 and 5.14,

$$\beta_{\text{Gap}} = \text{Cov}(r_{\text{Gap}}, r_I)/\sigma^2(r_I) = 0.0011/0.0009 = 1.2222$$
$$\alpha_{\text{Gap}} = E(r_{\text{Gap}}) - E(r_I) \times \beta_{\text{Gap}}$$
$$= 0.0221 - 0.0109 \times 1.2222 = 0.0088 \text{ or } 0.88\%.$$

These estimates of The Gap's alpha and beta are different from the estimates obtained using regression analysis only because of rounding.

ESTIMATING ALPHA AND BETA

Use Equations 5.13 and 5.14 to estimate Kerr-McGee's alpha and beta and construct its characteristic line. Kerr-McGee's expected rate of return, which we calculated earlier, was 0.0109. The S&P 500's expected rate of return and variance were 0.0109 and 0.0009. The covariance between Kerr-McGee and the S&P 500 was 0.0007.

$$\beta_{\text{Kerr-McGee}} = \text{Cov}(r_{\text{Kerr-McGee}}, r_I)/\sigma^2(r_I) = 0.0007/0.0009$$
$$= 0.7778$$
$$\alpha_{\text{Kerr-McGee}} = E(r_{\text{Kerr-McGee}}) - E(r_I) \times \beta_{\text{Kerr-McGee}}$$
$$= 0.0109 - 0.0109 \times 0.7778$$
$$= 0.0024 \text{ or } 0.24\%$$

Kerr-McGee's characteristic line is therefore

$$E(r_{\text{Kerr-McGee}}|r_I) = 0.24\% + r_I \times 0.7778.$$

Using regression analysis to estimate Kerr-McGee's characteristic line gives a similar result,

$$E(r_{\text{Kerr-McGee}}|r_I) = 0.24\% + r_I \times 0.7812.$$

We will use these values for Kerr-McGee's alpha and beta in subsequent calculations.

The Gap's characteristic line provides an estimate of the company's expected rate of return given economic conditions as represented by the S&P 500's rate of return. For example, if the S&P 500's rate of return equals its historical average of 1.09 percent, then The Gap's expected rate of return is 0.89 percent + 1.09 percent × 1.2138 = 2.21 percent—The Gap's historical average. However, if the economy is expected to be better than average with an S&P 500 rate of return of 4.10 percent, then the prediction for The Gap is 0.89 percent + 4.10 percent × 1.2138 = 5.87 percent. The predicted improvement in The Gap's performance equals the improvement in the S&P 500's performance multiplied by The Gap's beta of 1.2138:

Change in The Gap's expected rate of return	=	Change in the market's expected rate of return × The Gap's beta
5.87% − 2.21%	=	(4.10% − 1.09%) × 1.2138
3.66%	=	3.65% (difference due to rounding).

This demonstrates that an asset's beta coefficient describes its sensitivity to changes in economic conditions.

EXERCISE

5.11   COMPUTING THE CONDITIONAL EXPECTED RATE OF RETURN

Given Kerr-McGee's characteristic line, what was Kerr-McGee's conditional expected rate of return for December 1995 when the rate of return on the S&P 500 index was 1.74 percent?

$$E(r_{\text{Kerr-McGee}}|r_I) = 0.24\% + r_I \times 0.7812$$
$$= 0.24\% + 1.74\% \times 0.7812 = 1.60\%$$

Given the performance of the S&P 500, Kerr-McGee's expected rate of return for December 1995 was 1.60 percent.

Exhibit 5.8 shows that The Gap's actual rate of return (each plotted point) is usually different from its expected rate of return given economic conditions (the characteristic line). For example, the rate of return on the S&P 500 was 4.10 percent in November of 1995 but The Gap's rate of return was 14.91 percent rather than 5.87 percent as predicted by the market model, a deviation of 9.04 percent. The favorable and unfavorable deviations from The Gap's expected rate of return are prediction errors defined as

$$\varepsilon_j = r_j - E(r_j | r_I)$$

where $\varepsilon_j =$ prediction error for asset j
$r_j =$ asset j's actual rate of return
$E(r_j | r_I) = \alpha_j + r_I \beta_j.$

EXERCISE

5.12   CALCULATING PREDICTION ERRORS

In Exercise 5.11, you determined that Kerr-McGee's expected rate of return for December 1995 was 1.60 percent. What was the amount of your prediction error if the company's actual rate of return for this month was 10.43 percent?

$$\varepsilon_j = r_j - E(r_j | r_I)$$
$$= 10.43\% - 1.60\% = 8.83\%$$

Kerr-McGee's rate of return for December 1995 was 10.43 percent, 8.83 percent higher than expected.

The Gap's prediction errors were caused by something other than the company's normal performance (represented by $\alpha_{\text{Gap}} = 0.89$ percent) or its relationship to general economic conditions (represented by $r_I \times 1.2138$). Possible explanations for the deviations are events that were favorable to (1) all retailing companies in the economy, (2) only retail clothing stores, or (3) only The Gap.

Importantly, the market model recognizes only the latter possibility because it assumes that deviations from an asset's conditional expected rate of return are caused by factors unique to that asset. In other words, the market model assumes there is no tendency for similar assets to have similar deviations from their conditional expected rates of return. They *may* have similar deviations from time to time, but purely by chance. In mathematical terms, the market model assumes that the deviations from one asset's conditional expected rate of return are uncorrelated with ($\rho = 0$) the deviations from every other asset's conditional expected rate of return.[10]

The assumption that the unexpected rates of return from different assets are uncorrelated implies the market model partitions an asset's rate of return into distinct systematic and unsystematic components. An asset's beta coefficient multiplied by the rate of return on the market index equals the systematic component of its return. This term also is called the *market component* of an asset's rate of return because its value is explained by the level of the market index and the asset's relationship to the index. An asset's alpha plus its error term equals the unsystematic component of its return. The alpha is a constant that accounts for expected performance, and the error term is a random variable that accounts for favorable and unfavorable surprises. These terms are said to comprise the *unique component* of an asset's rate of return because their values do not depend on market conditions; they are specific to a particular asset. Examples of activities and events associated with these return components are given in Table 5.10.

Mathematical Description of the Market Model and the Standard Deviation of Return   Equation 5.12 described how the market model partitions an asset's rate of return into its market and unique components. Equation 5.15 shows that the market model also partitions an asset's risk into these components. Equation 5.15 is easier to interpret if placed next to Equation 5.12.

$$E(r_j \mid r_I) = \alpha_j + r_I \beta_j$$
$$\sigma(r_j) = [\beta_j^2 \sigma^2(r_I) + \sigma^2(\varepsilon_j)]^{1/2} \qquad \text{[5.15]}$$

where $\sigma^2(\varepsilon_j)$ = the variance of the prediction errors for asset j

The first term on the right-hand side of Equation 5.15 measures the uncertainty in an asset's rate of return that is explained by its relationship to general economic conditions. The variability of the market index, $\sigma^2(r_I)$, is given so a particular asset's market risk is determined by its beta. The second term on the right-hand side of Equation 5.15 is the variance of the favorable and unfavorable deviations from an asset's conditional expected rate of return. These deviations are part of the unique component of an asset's rate of return so their variance measures unique risk. The y-intercept in Equation 5.12, α_j, is a constant so it does not contribute any risk to Equation 5.15.

We can use Equation 5.15 to compute the standard deviation of The Gap's rate of return. The Gap's beta, given above, is 1.2138. The variance of the S&P 500 stock

---

[10]Can you see where this is headed? Because the error terms are uncorrelated, they represent the part of an asset's risk that can be completely eliminated through diversification! We'll get to this soon.

Table 5.10   MARKET AND UNIQUE RETURN COMPONENTS

Activity or Event	Market or Unique	Return Component	Sign
Normal performance	Unique	α_j	Positive if performance creates value, negative otherwise
Increase in national unemployment rate	Market	$r_I\beta_j$	Negative
Improvement in U.S. budget deficit	Market	$r_I\beta_j$	Positive
Death of founder and CEO	Unique	ε_j	Negative
Company awarded patent on new computer chip	Unique	ε_j	Positive

index was 0.0009 and the variance of The Gap's prediction errors is 0.0102. Substituting these values into Equation 5.15,

$$\sigma(r_{\text{Gap}}) = [\beta_{\text{Gap}}^2 \sigma^2(r_I) + \sigma^2(\varepsilon_{\text{Gap}})]^{1/2}$$
$$= [(1.2138)^2 \times 0.0009 + 0.0102]^{1/2}$$
$$= 0.1074.$$

This value differs from the standard deviation we computed from The Gap's actual rates of return, $\sigma(r_{\text{Gap}}) = 0.1072$, only because of rounding.

EXERCISE

5.13   USING BETA TO COMPUTE THE STANDARD DEVIATION

Use the market model to compute Kerr-McGee's standard deviation of monthly rate of return. Kerr-McGee's beta is 0.7812, the variance of the market model prediction error is 0.0044, and the variance of the S&P 500 rate of return is 0.0009. How does the value of the standard deviation calculated this way compare to Kerr-McGee's standard deviation computed from its actual returns, 0.0707?

$$\sigma(r_{\text{Kerr-McGee}}) = [\beta_{\text{Kerr-McGee}}^2 \, \sigma^2(r_I) + \sigma^2(\varepsilon_{\text{Kerr-McGee}})]^{1/2}$$
$$= [(0.7812)^2 \times 0.0009 + 0.0044]^{1/2}$$
$$= 0.0704$$

There is only a small difference between the computed standard deviations, due to rounding.

Factor Models[11]

A **factor model** provides another way to describe economic conditions associated with an asset's periodic rates of return. Factor models differ from the market model in three respects. First, the market index is replaced by one or more factors thought to describe fundamental, general economic conditions such as inflation, gross national product, and interest rates. Second, factor models emphasize that an asset's rate of return changes only when the market receives *new* information, that is, information different from what was already expected. The factors are therefore defined as the deviations from their expected values. Third, a multivariate statistical technique, factor analysis, is used in place of regression analysis to estimate the values of the parameters (the α and βs) in factor models.

Equation 5.16 is an example of a factor model that uses interest rates and GNP to represent economic conditions.

$$E(r_j \mid F_1, F_2) = \alpha_j + F_1\beta_{j,1} + F_2\beta_{j,2} \qquad [5.16]$$

where $E(r_j|F_1,F_2)$ = conditional expected rate of return on an asset j
α_j = expected rate of return on asset j when there is no new information; when $F_1 = F_2 = 0$
F_1 = actual level of interest rates minus expected level of interest rates
$\beta_{j,1}$ = asset j's sensitivity to news about interest rates
F_2 = actual change in GNP minus expected change in GNP
$\beta_{j,2}$ = asset j's sensitivity to news about GNP

Although they are different, the market model and factor models are applied the same way as the following example demonstrates.

Suppose the factor model for the monthly rate of return on a share of stock in Ross Enterprises (RE) is described by Equation 5.16 with α_{RE} = 3.0 percent, $\beta_{RE,1}$ = −0.85, and $\beta_{RE,2}$ = 1.05. Suppose also that actual interest rates were 2 percent greater than expected and that the actual change in GNP was 1 percent less than expected. Then the conditional expected monthly rate of return on the stock would be

$$E(r_{RE} \mid F_1, F_2) = 3.00\% + 2.0\% \times -0.85 + (-1.00\%) \times 1.05 = 0.25\%.$$

If the stock's actual rate of return was 1.40 percent, then the prediction error, 1.15 percent (1.40 percent − 0.25 percent), is attributed to something other than Ross Enterprises's relationship to general economic conditions as represented by news about interest rates and the change in GNP.

For our purposes, the similarities between the market model and factor models are more important than their differences. Both recognize that economic conditions affect

---

[11]Most papers discuss factor models in the context of the arbitrage pricing theory (APT), which we describe in Chapter 6. Two of them are Adam Gehr Jr., "Some Tests of the Arbitrage Pricing Theory," *Journal of the Midwest Finance Association,* 1975, pp. 91–105 and Phoebus J. Dhrymes, Irwin Friend, Mustafa N. Gultekin, and N. Bulent Gultekin, "New Tests of the APT and Their Implications," *Journal of Finance,* July 1985, pp. 659–674.

an asset's rate of return, and both assume that everything one asset has in common with other assets is captured by its relationship to the variable(s) that represent economic conditions. Consequently, in both models, the beta coefficient(s) measure the systematic component of an asset's rate of return and risk. Both models assume that deviations from an asset's conditional expected rate of return are due only to activities or events that are unique to that asset. Therefore, the characteristics of these deviations measure the unsystematic component of an asset's return and risk in both models.

Either the market model or factor models can be used to describe diversifiable and nondiversifiable risk. We will use the market model for this purpose, however, because it is simpler.

Using the Market Model to Describe Diversifiable and Nondiversifiable Risks

The market model can be applied to portfolios just as easily as to individual assets. The result is described by Equation 5.15 with subscript j replaced by a p to emphasize that we are talking about portfolios. Furthermore, a portfolio is just a collection of individual assets, which means a portfolio's market and unique risks are determined by the market and unique risks of the assets in the portfolio. The appropriate expressions for these terms are

$$\beta_p = \sum_{j=1}^{n} w_j \beta_j \qquad\qquad [5.17]$$

$$\sigma^2(\varepsilon_p) = \sum_{j=1}^{n} w_j^2 \sigma^2(\varepsilon_j). \qquad\qquad [5.18]$$

Substituting these equations into equation 5.15 gives

$$\sigma(r_p) = \left[\left(\sum_{j=1}^{n} w_j \beta_j \right)^2 \sigma^2(r_I) + \sum_{j=1}^{n} w_j^2 \sigma^2(\varepsilon_j) \right]^{1/2}. \qquad\qquad [5.19]$$

Now that we have an equation that shows the market and unique components of a portfolio's risk, let's carefully think about what their values must be in a large, well-diversified portfolio. Consider the market risk first. This component represents how all the portfolio's assets are interrelated through their association with the market index. The source of this risk is the variability in the market index rate of return magnified or diminished by the portfolio's beta according to whether its value is greater or less than one. The variance of the market index is positive and the portfolio's beta is simply a weighted average of the betas of the portfolio's assets. There is no tendency for this average to approach zero as more assets are added to the portfolio because most assets have positive betas; negative betas are very rare. Consequently, a portfolio's beta remains positive no matter how many assets are in the portfolio; this means an investor cannot avoid a portfolio's market risk.

Now think about the unique risk. The sources of this risk are the favorable and unfavorable deviations from the expected rates of return on all the portfolio's assets. The market model assumes these deviations are uncorrelated, that is, with a large enough portfolio, there are always enough favorable deviations to offset unfavorable ones. In other words, they completely compensate for one another. This means that unique risks are eliminated from a well-diversified portfolio, leaving only the market risk. Consequently, Equation 5.19 reduces to

$$\sigma(r_p) = \beta_p \sigma(r_I)$$

$$= \sum_{j=1}^{n} w_j \beta_j \sigma(r_I). \qquad [5.20]$$

Equation 5.20 is a very important result because it says that even though investors may be concerned about the total risk of their portfolio, they are only concerned about the market risks of the portfolio's assets. This is true because these assets' individual unique risks are diversified away. Equation 5.20 permits us to shift our focus from the standard deviation of rate of return to beta because only market risk matters.

We can see these diversification effects by plotting the returns on the Gap/Kerr-McGee portfolio and the S&P 500 index and by using regression analysis to estimate the portfolio's characteristic line. The results are presented in Table 5.11. The first thing to note about these results is that the portfolio's characteristic line is simply a weighted average of The Gap and Kerr-McGee's characteristic lines. This result illustrates two important points made earlier: A portfolio's expected rate of return and *market risk* are weighted averages of the returns and market risks of the portfolio's assets. The second thing to note about these results is that the portfolio's unique risk, $\sigma(\varepsilon_p)$, is *less than* a weighted average of the unique risks of the assets in the portfolio. Taken together, these results confirm that it is unique risk and not market risk that is reduced through diversification.

These same conclusions are reflected in Exhibit 5.9, although the graph's most noticeable feature is that there is less dispersion of the portfolio's actual rates of return around its characteristic line than there was for The Gap in Exhibit 5.8. This reduction in dispersion indicates a reduction in the portfolio's unique risk, $\sigma(\varepsilon_p)$.

We've reached the end of our mathematical and intuitive descriptions of the principles of diversification. Let's make sure the last several points are clear before we move on.

Individual assets have both unsystematic and systematic risk. The favorable and unfavorable events unique to each asset are the sources of its unsystematic risk. This risk is eliminated in a fully diversified portfolio. These characterizations explain why unsystematic risk also is known as unique risk and diversifiable risk.

An asset's sensitivity to economic conditions is the source of its systematic risk. This risk cannot be eliminated from a fully diversified portfolio because it is caused by economy- or market-wide factors that all assets have in common. This is why systematic risk also is known as market risk and nondiversifiable risk.

An asset's sensitivity to economic conditions is measured by its beta coefficient in the market model or by its set of beta coefficients in factor models. Market risk determines the opportunity cost the owners apply to investment, operating, and financing decisions as we will see in the next chapter.

Table 5.11   RESULTS FROM APPLYING THE MARKET MODEL TO THE GAP/KERR-MCGEE PORTFOLIO

Panel A: Actual Regression Results for Portfolio

	Characteristic Line	$\sigma(\varepsilon)$
Gap/Kerr-McGee Portfolio[a]	$E(r_{\text{Gap/Kerr-McGee}} \mid r_{\text{S\&P500}}) = 0.54\% + r_I \times 0.9784$	5.00%

Panel B: Weighted Average of Actual Regression Results for The Gap and Kerr-McGee

	Characteristic Line		$\sigma(\varepsilon)$
The Gap	$E(r_{\text{Gap}} \mid r_{\text{S\&P500}})$	$= 0.89\% + r_I \times 1.2138$	10.11%
Kerr-McGee	$E(r_{\text{Kerr-McGee}} \mid r_{\text{S\&P500}})$	$= 0.24\% + r_I \times 0.7812$	6.67%
Average using portfolio weights[a]	$E(r_{\text{Gap/Kerr-McGee}} \mid r_{\text{S\&P500}})$	$= 0.54\% + r_I \times 0.9784$	8.24%

[a]Portfolio weights are 45.54 percent invested in The Gap and 54.46 percent invested in Kerr-McGee.

Exhibit 5.9

MARKET MODEL APPLIED TO THE GAP/KERR-MCGEE PORTFOLIO

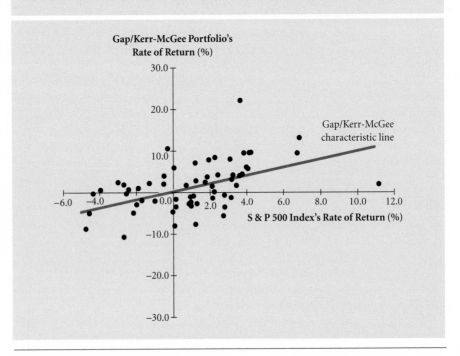

5.4   SHOULD *COMPANIES* DIVERSIFY?

Portfolio diversification reduces risk. Therefore, it is quite natural to believe that companies and their business units should diversify. You must think this through very carefully, however, to determine what the benefits are and who receives them. Let's look at this issue from the owners' perspective first and then from other points of view.

Owners do not receive any benefits from a company's diversification if the financial market is perfect. The reason is simple: With no transaction costs and infinitely divisible assets, anyone can construct a portfolio that includes every asset available in the economy. Even someone with only a small amount of money to invest could distribute that money among all assets. These fully diversified personal portfolios would completely eliminate unique risk at no cost, so it wouldn't matter if a particular company was undiversified and had unique risk itself.

Owners may not receive benefits from a company's diversification even if the financial market is imperfect. Transaction costs and indivisible assets may prohibit individuals from forming fully diversified portfolios, but pension and mutual funds are not affected the same way because these costs are insignificant to them. Most professionally managed portfolios are thoroughly diversified and therefore reduce unique risk to the extent that the funds' shareholders may only be concerned about the market risks of the companies they indirectly own. These market risks are the same whether the companies are diversified or not.

Owners *may* benefit from company diversification that gives them access to non-traded assets. This permits them to obtain a claim on assets they cannot purchase for themselves or that a financial intermediary cannot purchase for them. An example would be when a company acquires a foreign subsidiary whose stock is not traded in the domestic financial market. This type of acquisition is beneficial to the owners if the foreign subsidiary's returns are less than perfectly correlated with the returns on the assets in the owners' current portfolios.

Now let's look at this issue from the creditors' viewpoint. Creditors have a fixed claim on a company's cash flows. They are not paid more than the amount of their claim if the company performs better than expected, but they may be paid less if the company performs much worse than expected. Company diversification reduces the range of both favorable and unfavorable deviations from the expected value, but the net result is beneficial to the creditors. They don't receive a share of the favorable deviations anyway, and the reduction in the range of negative deviations from expected value decreases the likelihood of financial distress. Consequently, company diversification improves the safety of the creditors' claims to their advantage.

Finally, managers and employees benefit from company diversification for one of two reasons. Some managers and employees are similar to creditors because they are paid a fixed salary or wage. They do not receive a bonus if the company performs well, but they may lose their jobs if the company performs poorly. These types of managers and employees benefit from company diversification in the same way that creditors do because it improves the safety of their jobs.

Other managers are similar to owners because their pay is partially based on performance. They may be paid a cash bonus or receive stock options intended to align

USING REVERSE DIVERSIFICATION TO INCREASE SHAREHOLDER WEALTH

WHAT WAS IT that caused those AT&T shares to sprout wings on the day CEO Bob Allen announced the biggest voluntary breakup in history? To the company's 2.3 million shareholders, word of the grand triple spinoff quickly converted into an 11 percent jump in AT&T stock to $63.75, creating nearly $10 billion in market value in just hours. Allen's bold stroke was clearly a surprise, but in fact he was tapping a genie that has helped many CEOs breathe life into their stocks.

Not all spinoff plans deliver instant price appreciation, but they do tend to pay off for investors over time. Studies demonstrate that the stocks of spun-off businesses, and those of their parent companies, perform smartly in the years after a deal. Patrick Cusatis of Lehman Brothers and James Miles and J. Randall Woolridge of Penn State University analyzed 161 spinoffs over a 25-year period ending in 1990. The cumulative returns were robust: Shares of spun-off companies surged 51 percent in the two years after being distributed, and 76 percent in three years. More important, the shares generated hearty excess returns, meaning they outran the stock-market performance of their industry peers, by 33 percentage points over three years. Excess returns for parents were strong too.

Much of that lift comes from the altered dynamics of spun-off businesses and their parents. Freed from internal conflicts that often afflict conglomerates, managers in spun-off companies have the authority to get on with the pressing task at hand:

making money. And with their own stock price to watch, they have a visible barometer of their success or lack thereof.

The result? Performance revs up. According to the Penn State study, the operating income of spun-off companies and their parents improved significantly after separation. Says Forbes Tuttle, director of research at Hunstrete Group, a consulting firm in New York City that analyzes spinoffs for institutional clients: "It's almost impossible for spinoffs not to do well. They unleash earning power and allow the businesses to capitalize on inherent strengths."

With all this performance juice attributable to spinoffs, shouldn't shareholders be clamoring for—and getting—more of them? Notes G. Bennett Stewart III, senior partner of Stern Stewart & Co., the pioneers of EVA value-based management and accounting: "It is clearly one of the most under-utilized value-enhancing strategies in business." Many CEOs, he says, avoid spinoffs because they shrink the parent, and thereby the CEO's prestige. Indeed, the trend among managers is in the opposite direction. Companies in banking, media, and other industries are bulking up through megamergers and pricey acquisitions. Such growth does offer benefits, such as potential cost savings and the safety and predictability of size, but investors cherish these attributes less than raw growth. Says Stewart: "Diversification is something investors can get on their own, so they are not going to reward managers for doing it."

their interests with those of the common stockholders. These managers are similar to owners, but their fortunes are more closely tied to the company's success than the stockholders' fortunes are. They have a poorly diversified portfolio because their major asset is their human capital, which equals the present value of their salary and bonuses. Their human capital is a nontraded asset, which means these managers cannot undertake market transactions to diversify their personal portfolio. Therefore, they have an incentive to diversify the company to improve the safety of their jobs and the diversification of their personal portfolio.

Company diversification is clearly beneficial to creditors, managers, and employees and may benefit the owners. However, the pursuit of diversification may force a company to assign managers and employees to tasks outside their areas of expertise. Or a company may permit experts to manage the separate enterprises, but create and operate a bureaucracy to coordinate and control their activities. Either approach to managing a diversified company is costly. Consequently, managers must carefully consider whether the benefits of diversification justify the costs of diverting a company from its core competencies (see "In the News").

Recent studies indicate that the net effect of company diversification is negative.[12] Berger and Ofek found that the common stock value of diversified companies was 13 percent to 15 percent less than the common stock value of their separate business segments. Furthermore, Comment and Jarrell and John and Ofek found that companies with increased focus had higher common stock returns and were less likely to be subject to hostile takeovers. The results of these studies indicate that the market strongly prefers that companies and their business units not diversify.

5.5   SUMMARY

The analysis and valuation of any investment proposal requires a prediction about its future performance. No one can predict the future with perfect certainty, so investment decisions are subject to risk. Two familiar statistics, the mean and standard deviation of rate of return, are used to summarize these predictions. The mean represents an investment's expected reward and the standard deviation represents its risk. Using the standard deviation for this purpose implies investors are subject to a real loss if an asset's rate of return is less than expected and that they are subject to an opportunity loss if its rate of return is greater than expected. Furthermore, both real and opportunity losses are considered equally costly.

Investors manage risk by diversification, which combines dissimilar assets in a portfolio. Then, favorable deviations from the expected rates of return on some assets compensate for unfavorable deviations from the expected rates of return on others. The portfolio therefore experiences fewer deviations from its own expected rate of return, which means it has less risk. Diversification is more effective the more assets included in the portfolio and the lower the correlation between them. Constructing a portfolio reduces the risk due to each asset's unique characteristics but cannot reduce market risk, which is due to the characteristics the assets have in common.

The market model and factor models use an asset's sensitivity to general economic conditions to describe the characteristics it has in common with other assets. These models partition an asset's rate of return and risk into its market and unique

---

[12]Philip G. Berger and Eli Ofek, "Diversification's Effect on Firm Value," pp. 39–65, Robert Comment and Gregg A. Jarrell, "Corporate Focus and Stock Return," pp. 67–87, and Kose John and Eli Ofek, "Asset Sales and Increase in Focus," pp. 105–126, *Journal of Financial Economics,* January 1995.

components. The former are measured by the beta coefficient(s) and the latter is measured by the variance of the prediction errors. Investors and managers can use these models to more precisely measure and evaluate an asset's nondiversifiable (systematic or market) and diversifiable (unsystematic or unique) return and risk.

● **KEY TERMS**

● **QUESTIONS AND PROBLEMS**

1. You can never predict the future with perfect certainty, so you must construct forecasts that reveal the possibility for error.

   (a) How should you construct a fundamental forecast to ensure it reveals the uncertainty inherent in your predictions about the future?

   (b) Why is it important to ensure that the historical record you use as the basis of an extrapolation forecast includes periods of good and bad economic conditions?

2. Consider the following projections of cash flows for two investment projects:

	Project 1	Project 2
Year 0	$ −10,000	$ −10,000
Year 1		
Weak economy	11,000	10,500
Strong economy	12,000	12,500

   (a) Compute each project's rate of return in a weak economy and a strong economy.

   (b) Compute each project's expected rate of return and standard deviation of return assuming weak and strong economic conditions are equally likely.

   (c) Which project will a risk-averse investor prefer? Why?

3. Scott Banks purchased 100 shares of Briggs and Stratton Corporation's common stock on April 28, 1995, and sold it on June 30, 1995. The company paid a cash dividend of $0.25 per share in May. Briggs and Stratton's closing stock prices for April, May, and June were:

April 28	$35.125
May 31	35.50
June 30	34.50

   Assume the dividend was paid on May 31. What was Scott's monthly holding period rate of return for May? For June?

4. We use the standard deviation of an investment's rate of return as a measure of risk.

   (a) Is this measure of risk associated with the likelihood of unexpected losses, the likelihood of unexpected gains, or the likelihood of both?

   (b) How can we justify using the standard deviation of an investment's rate of return to measure risk given your answer to part (a)?

5. Use simple, intuitive language to explain each of the following diversification principles. Do not use mathematical terms or symbols. Instead, imagine you are talking to a person with average intelligence but no finance training.

   (a) The basic idea behind portfolio diversification.

   (b) The importance of forming a portfolio from *dissimilar* assets.

   (c) The benefit of including *many* assets in a portfolio.

   (d) Why portfolio diversification cannot completely eliminate risk.

6. If you saw the following patterns of returns for two stocks, what could you assume about (1) their correlation coefficient and (2) the diversification benefits of the 2-stock portfolio?

   (a)

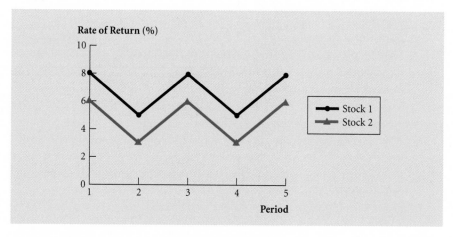

   (b)

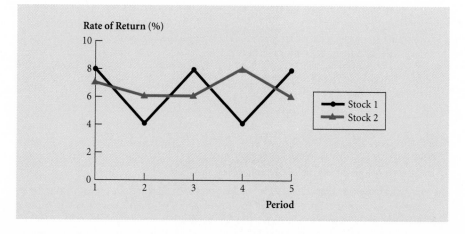

(c)

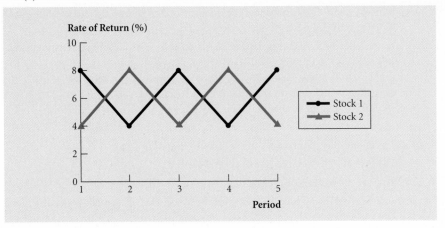

7. We can use covariance or the correlation coefficient to describe the amount of diversification obtained by combining two assets in a portfolio.

    (a) Exactly how does the covariance between two assets' rates of return measure the tendency for them to have offsetting deviations from their expected rates of return?

    (b) What is the relationship between covariance and the correlation coefficient? Why is the correlation coefficient easier to interpret?

8. Gene Hamilton's portfolio comprises investments in stocks 1 and 2, which have a correlation coefficient of $\rho(r_1,r_2) = +1.0$.

    (a) What can you say about the standard deviation of the rate of return of Gene's portfolio?

    (b) Would Gene obtain any diversification benefits by adding stock 3 to his portfolio if its correlation with stocks 1 and 2 are $\rho(r_1,r_3) = +1.0$ and $\rho(r_2,r_3) = +1.0$?

    (c) Repeat parts (a) and (b) with the correlation coefficients given below.

$$0 < \rho(r_1,r_2) \quad < +1.0$$
$$-1.0 < \rho(r_1,r_3) < \quad 0$$
$$-1.0 < \rho(r_2,r_3) < \quad 0$$

9. Compute the expected rate of return and standard deviation of return of an equally weighted portfolio of the following two stocks:

Stock	Expected Return	Standard Deviation
A	9.5%	5.0%
B	11.5	6.0

The correlation of their rates of return is 0.75.

10. Match the points on the multi-asset portfolio opportunity set shown below with the following choices: (1) a portfolio of General Motors stock, (2) a portfolio of General Motors, Microsoft, and Safeway, Inc., (3) a portfolio of General Motors and Ford Motor Co. stocks, or (4) a portfolio of General Motors, Ford Motor Co., and Wal-Mart. Explain your reasoning.

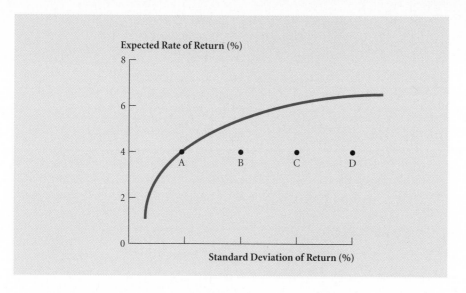

11. Investors can form a riskless portfolio by combining two risky assets with perfect negative correlation.

    (a) Why can't investors form a riskless portfolio from a combination of three or more risky assets?

    (b) How is your answer to part (a) related to the limit to diversification?

12. The expected rates of return, standard deviation of return, and correlation coefficients of three common stocks are given below.

	$E(r)$	$\sigma(r)$
Stock 1	6%	8%
Stock 2	4	6
Stock 3	3	4

$\rho(r_1,r_2) = 0.59$
$\rho(r_1,r_3) = -0.38$
$\rho(r_2,r_3) = -0.54$

Portfolio A contains 16 percent stock 1 and 84 percent stock 2.

Portfolio B contains 44 percent stock 1 and 56 percent stock 3.

Portfolio C contains 40.86 percent stock 1, 9.88 percent stock 2, and 49.26 percent stock 3.

    (a) Compute each portfolio's expected rate of return.

    (b) Without doing any calculations, rank the portfolios in order of least to most risk. Explain your answer.

    (c) Confirm your answer to part (b) by calculating each portfolio's standard deviation of return. The formula for the standard deviation of a three-asset portfolio, obtained by expanding Equation 5.9, is $\sigma(r_p) = [w_1\sigma^2(r_1) + w_2^2\sigma^2(r_2) + w_3^2\sigma^2(r_3) + 2w_1w_2\rho(r_1,r_2) \times \sigma(r_1)\sigma(r_2) + 2w_1w_3\rho(r_1,r_3)\sigma(r_1)\sigma(r_3) + 2w_2w_3\rho(r_2,r_3)\sigma(r_2)\sigma(r_3)]^{1/2}$.

13. The table on the following page describes an opportunity set of risky portfolios.

Expected Rate of Return	Standard Deviation Rate of Return
15%	20%
16	21
18	25
20	25
20	27
25	40

(a) Can you determine exactly which portfolio would be preferred by a risk-averse investor?

(b) Can you determine which portfolios *no* risk-averse investor would accept? What is the technical name of the portfolios that remain after you eliminate the unacceptable ones?

14. The equation and graph below describe an asset's characteristic line.

$$E(r_{asset} \mid r_{market}) = -0.0219 + r_{market} \times 2.1027$$

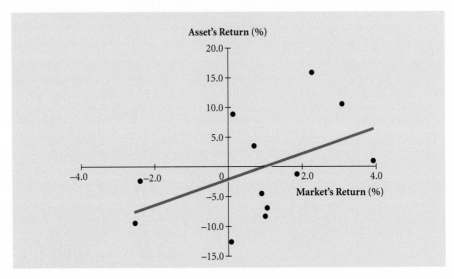

(a) Interpret each term on the left- and right-hand sides of the equation and associate them with the graph.

(b) Why do some of the asset's rates of return fall off the characteristic line?

15. Prepare a table that describes the similarities and differences between the market model and factor models.

16. Suppose the standard deviation of the market index's rate of return is 0.20. Which of the portfolio's described below are well-diversified? Explain your reasoning.

Portfolio	Beta	Standard Deviation
A	0.80	0.17
B	1.05	0.21
C	1.15	0.24
D	1.40	0.28

17. Based on a carefully conducted statistical study, a securities analyst predicts that the rates of return on asset X and asset Y will be 1.2 and 1.3 times the rates of return on the market index. The following rates of return are then observed.

Return on Market Index	Return on Asset X		Return on Asset Y	
	Predicted	Actual	Predicted	Actual
7.00%	8.40%	8.70%	9.10%	9.10%
15.60	18.72	19.75	20.28	20.27
13.00	15.60	16.08	16.90	17.00
4.40	5.28	3.45	5.72	5.61
$E(r)$ 10.00	12.00	12.00	13.00	13.00
$\sigma(r)$ 4.49	5.39	6.34	5.84	5.89

(a) How do you explain the inaccuracies in the securities analyst's forecast model? (Assume she made no statistical errors.)

(b) Should the analyst or risk-averse investors who hold well-diversified portfolios be concerned about these errors? Explain your reasoning.

(c) Which asset is more risky, X or Y? Why?

18. BARRA, Inc., is a company that produces investments research and software and provides consulting. Visit their site on the Internet at http://www.barra.com/. Click on "Market/Index Info" and then "Dow Jones Industrials" to see a list of the 30 companies in the Dow Jones Industrial Average, a stock market index similar to the S&P 500 index.

(a) Do the companies' betas make sense to you given their lines of business? Refer to some specific companies to explain your answer.

(b) Why do some companies' betas differ from their respective industry averages?

(c) Why do some companies' predicted betas differ from their historical betas? For help with your answer, read BARRA's description of how historical and predicted betas are computed. (Do you recognize the technique BARRA's is using to compute predicted betas?)

19. Suppose a food-processing company acquires a clothing company to diversify its product line. How does this decision affect each of the following groups?

(a) The owners.

(b) The creditors.

(c) The managers.

20. The following quotation is taken from "Hershey Craves Gumdrops, Hard Candy Amid Fat Fear," an article by Yumiko Ono that appeared on page B1 of the October 23, 1996 edition of *The Wall Street Journal*.

The candy business is dandy, as more consumers reach for jelly beans, gumdrops and other sweets without chocolate and its dreaded fat.

Just ask Hershey Foods Corp., the nation's largest chocolate maker. Last week Hershey agreed to pay $330 million for the North American confectionary operations of Leaf Inc., a unit of Finland's Huhtamaki Oy. The transaction gives Hershey a handful of venerable candy brands such as Jolly Rancher and Good & Plenty. And one big reason for the acquisition can be calculated in fat grams: zero for Jolly Rancher and Good & Plenty and 13 for a Hershey Milk Chocolate bar.

(a) Discuss Hershey's probable motive for this acquisition.

(b) Could Hershey's stockholders have accomplished the same result in their personal portfolios without Hershey's help? How?

(c) Would you expect investors to pay more for Hershey's common stock now that it has a more diversified product line? Why or why not?

Problems 21 through 26 are based on the end of month stock prices and dividends given below.

Month	Dow Jones & Co. Closing Price	Dividend	Mattel Inc. Closing Price	Dividend	Safeway Inc. Closing Price	Dividend	Winn-Dixie Stores Closing Price	Dividend	S&P 500 Index Closing Value
Dec. 94	$31.00		$25.125		$31.875		$51.375		459.27
Jan	32.875	$0.230	20.625		32.125		53.750	$0.130	470.42
Feb	35.375		22.375		35.875		56.000	0.130	487.39
Mar	37.875		24.500	$0.060	34.625		55.875	0.130	500.71
Apr	35.000	0.230	23.750		37.500		55.375	0.130	514.71
May	36.500		25.000		36.500		57.375	0.130	533.40
Jun	36.875		26.250	0.060	37.375		57.375	0.130	544.75
Jul	35.500	0.230	28.250		38.375		57.125	0.140	562.06
Aug	36.625		29.000		39.375		59.500	0.140	561.88
Sep	36.875		29.375	0.060	41.750		59.625	0.140	584.41
Oct	35.250	0.230	28.750		47.250		65.000	0.150	581.50
Nov.	38.375		28.000		46.500		64.125	0.150	605.37
Dec. 95	39.875		30.750	0.060	51.500		73.750	0.150	615.93

Source: Standard & Poor's Corporation, *Standard & Poor's Daily Stock Price Record, New York Stock Exchange*, 1995.

21. Use a calculator or spreadsheet to answer the following questions.

(a) Compute the monthly holding period rates of return for Dow Jones & Co. and the S&P 500 index and graph the results.

(b) Which appears to have more variability or risk? Does this result make sense given what you know about portfolio diversification?

(c) Compute the expected rate of return and standard deviation of return for Dow Jones & Co. and the S&P 500 index. Are the standard deviations consistent with your answer to part (b)?

22. Given below are the expected rates of return and standard deviations of return for Safeway, Mattel, and Winn-Dixie for 1995. Use your answers from problem 21 to complete the table.

Company	Expected Rate of Return	Standard Deviation of Return
Safeway	4.22%	5.47%
Mattel	2.07	7.53
Winn-Dixie	3.40	4.65
Dow Jones		
S&P 500		

Suppose a risk-averse woman will invest all of her wealth in Mattel, Winn-Dixie, or Dow Jones. Which one will she choose? Why?

23. The covariance and correlation between Safeway and Dow Jones's rates of return for 1995 are −0.0012 and −0.4436, respectively.

    (a) Do you expect the covariance and correlation between Safeway and Winn-Dixie to be lower or higher? Explain your answer.

    (b) Confirm your answer to part (a) by calculating the covariance and correlation between Safeway and Winn-Dixie's rates of return. These companies' monthly holding period rates of return for 1995 are given below.

Month	Mattel Inc.	Safeway Inc.	Winn-Dixie
Jan	−0.1791	0.0078	0.0488
Feb	0.0848	0.1167	0.0443
Mar	0.0977	−0.0348	0.0001
Apr	−0.0306	0.0830	−0.0066
May	0.0526	−0.0267	0.0385
Jun	0.0524	0.0240	0.0023
Jul	0.0762	0.0268	−0.0019
Aug	0.0265	0.0261	0.0440
Sep	0.0150	0.0603	0.0045
Oct	−0.0213	0.1317	0.0927
Nov	−0.0261	−0.0159	−0.0112
Dec 95	0.1004	0.1075	0.1524

24. The correlation coefficients between Safeway, Winn-Dixie, Dow Jones, and Mattel's rates of return for 1995 are given below. Use your answer from problem 23 to complete the table. The companies' expected rates of return and standard deviations of return are given in problem 22.

$$\rho(\text{Safeway, Winn-Dixie}) = (\text{insert your answer from problem 23})$$
$$\rho(\text{Safeway, Dow Jones}) = -0.4436$$
$$\rho(\text{Safeway, Mattel}) = 0.0802$$
$$\rho(\text{Winn-Dixie, Dow Jones}) = 0.0644$$
$$\rho(\text{Winn-Dixie, Mattel}) = 0.0865$$
$$\rho(\text{Dow Jones, Mattel}) = 0.0229$$

    (a) John Potter owns a portfolio that is 12.2 percent Safeway and 87.8 percent Winn-Dixie. Determine his portfolio's expected rate of return and risk as measured by its standard deviation of return.

    (b) Potter is considering a change in the composition of his portfolio. He hopes to obtain the same expected rate of return with less risk by substituting Dow Jones for Winn-Dixie. What proportion of his portfolio should Potter invest in Safeway and what proportion in Dow Jones to accomplish this objective? What is his new portfolio's standard deviation of return?

    (c) Potter liked the results so much that he decided to rearrange his portfolio again. This time, its composition will be 58.60 percent Safeway, 43.42 percent Dow Jones, and −2.02

percent Mattel. Calculate this portfolio's expected rate of return and standard deviation of return. The formula for the standard deviation of a 3-asset portfolio was given in problem 12.

(d) To what do you attribute the risk reduction Potter obtained in part (b)? In part (c)? Could John reduce his risk even more by adding some Winn-Dixie stock back to his portfolio? Explain your answers.

25. Compute the expected rate of return and standard deviation of return for each portfolio described below and use the results to answer the questions. The information you need is in problems 22 and 24.

Percent invested in

Dow Jones:	0%	10%	20%	30%	40%	50%	60%	70%	80%	90%	100%
Safeway:	100	90	80	70	60	50	40	30	20	10	0

(a) Graph this opportunity set.

(b) Without doing any calculations, add to your graph the opportunity set as it would look if Dow Jones' and Safeway's rates of return were perfectly positively correlated. Explain why the opportunity set appears as you drew it.

(c) Now use your graph to explain the diversification benefits provided by the actual Dow Jones-Safeway portfolios.

26. Suppose you may purchase Dow Jones & Company common stock. You computed the expected value and standard deviation of the company's total rate of return in problem 21. These values were $E(r_{\text{Dow Jones}}) = 2.46$ percent and $\sigma(r_{\text{Dow Jones}}) = 4.81$ percent. You may want to separate the company's total rate of return into its market and unique components, however, to better understand its risk.

(a) Estimate Dow Jones' characteristic line by using information from problem 21 in Equations 5.13 and 5.14. The correlation between the company's rate of return and the S&P 500 index rate of return for 1995 was 0.3159.

(b) Confirm your answer to part (a) by regressing the company's monthly holding period rates of return on the S&P 500 Index's monthly holding period rates of return for 1995.

(c) Use the company's characteristic line to compute the market and unique components of each month's rate of return. Determine the expected value and standard deviation of each component.

(d) Which components of Dow Jones' rate of return are added to your well-diversified portfolio? How do the expected values and standard deviations of these components compare with the expected value and standard deviation of the company's total rate of return?

(e) Use the results of part (d) to describe how portfolio diversification works.

27. Adam Stowe estimated the factor model shown below to explain the rate of return on Gehr Industries' (GI) common stock.

$$E(r_{\text{GI}} \mid F_1, F_2) = 4.0\% + F_1 \times -0.90 + F_2 \times 1.20$$

where F_1 = actual level of interest rates minus expected level of interest rates
F_2 = actual change in GNP minus expected change in GNP

(a) Determine the expected rate of return on Gehr Industries' common stock for the following quarters.

	Interest Rates			Change in GNP	
Quarter	Actual	Expected		Actual	Expected
1	4.95%	5.00%		1.15%	1.10%
2	5.10	5.05		0.98	1.00
3	5.30	5.10		0.45	0.60
4	5.05	5.25		0.32	0.20

Suppose the stock's actual rates of return each quarter were:

	Gehr Industries'
Quarter	Actual Rate of Return
1	4.00%
2	3.95
3	3.40
4	4.40

(b) Determine each month's prediction error.

(c) Suppose Adam Stowe's factor model is correct. What caused the prediction errors? Should Adam or any well-diversified investor worry about these errors? Explain your answer.

28. Jeannette Lau has invested her retirement funds in the portfolio described below. This is a well-diversified portfolio (has no unsystematic risk) even though it contains only four investments.

Stock	Investment Amount	$E(r)$	β
A	$30,000	15.20%	1.20
B	15,000	12.65	0.90
C	15,000	11.68	0.75
D	40,000	16.05	1.30

(a) Compute the expected rate of return, the beta, and the standard deviation of Jeannette's portfolio assuming the standard deviation of the market index's rate of return is 20 percent.

(b) Jeannette notes that market analysts are predicting the S&P 500 index will do 10 percent better than normal in the coming year. Exactly how will this improvement in economic conditions affect the rate of return on her portfolio? Suppose the analysts are wrong and the S&P 500 index does 10 percent worse than normal. How will this affect her portfolio's rate of return?

(c) Are the results of part (b) reflected in the standard deviation of the rate of return on Jeannette's portfolio? Explain your answer.

29. Dick Kosier, CEO of Adams Manufacturing, met with the board of directors' compensation committee. The subject of the meeting was the company's quarterly performance during the past year, and Kosier had expected to receive a bonus for each quarter's results except the third when the stockholders' return was an embarrassing –2.5 percent. He was very proud

of the fourth quarter's 4.3 percent rate of return, however. The stockholders' rates of return for all four quarters are given below.

Quarter:	1	2	3	4
Adams Mfg. equity return:	3.3%	3.8%	−2.0%	4.3%

Kosier left the meeting stunned and confused. The compensation committee reported they would recommend to the entire board that he receive a small bonus for the first quarter and a small bonus for the third quarter even though the owners' return was negative. They would recommend he receive no bonus for the second and fourth quarters, which were the best.

Explain the committee's decision to Kosier considering that the company's characteristic line is $E(r_{\text{Adams Mfg}} \mid r_I) = 1.0\% + r_I \times 1.1$ and that the quarterly market index rates of return were:

Quarter:	1	2	3	4
Market index return:	2.0%	3.0%	−3.0%	4.0%

• ADDITIONAL READING

Three advanced textbooks on the theory and practice of portfolio diversification are:

Gordon J. Alexander and Jack Clark Francis, *Portfolio Analysis*, Prentice-Hall, Englewood Cliffs, New Jersey, 1986.

Edwin J. Elton and Martin J. Gruber, *Modern Portfolio Theory and Investment Management*, John Wiley and Sons, New York, 1991.

Haim Levy and Marshall Sarnat, *Portfolio and Investment Selection: Theory and Practice*, Prentice-Hall International, Englewood Cliffs, New Jersey, 1984.

MONTHLY RATES OF RETURN

Month	The Gap	The Limited	Kerr-McGee	The Gap and Kerr-McGee	The Gap and The Limited	S&P 500 Index
Jan '91	0.2830	0.2361	−0.0613	0.0955	0.2664	0.0415
Feb	0.0706	0.0562	0.1154	0.0950	0.0655	0.0673
Mar	0.0989	0.0934	−0.0804	0.0012	0.0969	0.0222
Apr	0.1353	0.0683	−0.0029	0.0600	0.1115	0.0003
May	0.2053	0.0913	0.0000	0.0935	0.1649	0.0386
Jun	−0.1204	−0.0521	−0.0642	−0.0898	−0.0962	−0.0479
Jul	0.1649	0.0575	0.0568	0.1060	0.1268	−0.0029
Aug	0.2532	−0.0377	0.0300	0.1316	0.1500	0.0685
Sep	0.0143	−0.0976	0.0029	0.0081	−0.0254	−0.0191
Oct	0.0593	−0.0676	0.0029	0.0286	0.0143	0.0119
Nov	0.1280	0.0311	−0.1163	−0.0050	0.0936	−0.0439
Dec	0.0133	0.1586	0.0264	0.0205	0.0648	0.1116
Jan '92	−0.0047	0.0739	−0.0526	−0.0308	0.0232	−0.0199
Feb	−0.0469	−0.0648	0.0171	−0.0121	−0.0533	0.0096
Mar	−0.1339	−0.0235	0.0203	−0.0499	−0.0947	−0.0218
Apr	−0.0598	−0.1733	0.0400	−0.0055	−0.1001	0.0279
May	−0.1727	−0.0968	0.0801	−0.0350	−0.1458	0.0010
Jun	0.0133	0.0867	−0.0414	−0.0165	0.0393	−0.0174
Jul	0.0362	−0.0385	0.0813	0.0607	0.0097	0.0394
Aug	−0.0502	0.0286	0.0521	0.0055	−0.0222	−0.0240
Sep	−0.0554	−0.0247	−0.0055	−0.0282	−0.0445	0.0091
Oct	0.0586	0.1429	−0.0808	−0.0173	0.0885	0.0014
Nov	0.1168	0.0828	0.0516	0.0813	0.1047	0.0310
Dec	−0.1258	0.0000	0.0465	−0.0320	−0.0812	0.0101
Jan '93	0.0455	0.0185	−0.0056	0.0177	0.0359	0.0070
Feb	−0.0616	−0.0818	0.0363	−0.0083	−0.0688	0.0105
Mar	−0.0053	−0.0261	0.0729	0.0373	−0.0127	0.0187
Apr	−0.0895	−0.0969	0.0709	−0.0022	−0.0921	−0.0254
May	0.1957	0.0888	−0.0094	0.0840	0.1578	0.0227
Jun	−0.1326	−0.1094	−0.0385	−0.0813	−0.1244	0.0008
Jul	−0.0207	−0.0468	0.0550	0.0205	−0.0300	−0.0053
Aug	−0.0304	0.1472	0.0570	0.0172	0.0326	0.0344
Sep	0.0306	−0.0336	−0.0632	−0.0205	0.0078	−0.0100
Oct	0.2076	−0.0500	−0.0289	0.0788	0.1162	0.0194
Nov	0.1256	0.0627	−0.0644	0.0221	0.1033	−0.0129
Dec	−0.0156	−0.2486	−0.0321	−0.0246	−0.0982	0.0101
Jan '94	0.0730	0.0441	0.0166	0.0423	0.0627	0.0325
Feb	0.0734	0.1037	−0.0162	0.0246	0.0841	−0.0300

Month	The Gap	The Limited	Kerr-McGee	The Gap and Kerr-McGee	The Gap and The Limited	S&P 500 Index
Mar	−0.0193	0.0705	−0.0752	−0.0498	0.0126	−0.0457
Apr	0.0620	−0.0778	0.0783	0.0709	0.0124	0.0115
May	−0.0770	0.0242	0.0141	−0.0274	−0.0411	0.0124
Jun	−0.0144	−0.1210	0.0472	0.0192	−0.0522	−0.0268
Jul	−0.1053	0.1449	0.0663	−0.0118	−0.0166	0.0315
Aug	0.1273	0.0063	−0.0248	0.0445	0.0844	0.0376
Sep	−0.2355	−0.0081	0.0000	−0.1072	−0.1548	−0.0269
Oct	0.0304	−0.0573	0.0103	0.0195	−0.0007	0.0209
Nov	0.0478	0.0522	−0.0304	0.0052	0.0494	−0.0395
Dec	−0.1449	−0.0645	−0.0212	−0.0775	−0.1164	0.0123
Jan '95	0.0661	−0.0690	0.0243	0.0434	0.0182	0.0243
Feb	0.0039	0.0430	0.0713	0.0406	0.0178	0.0361
Mar	0.1002	0.3143	−0.1861	−0.0557	0.1761	0.0273
Apr	−0.1021	−0.0707	0.0213	−0.0349	−0.0910	0.0280
May	0.0784	0.0456	0.3404	0.2211	0.0668	0.0363
Jun	0.0145	−0.0112	−0.0359	−0.0129	0.0054	0.0213
Jul	0.0000	−0.0739	0.0581	0.0317	−0.0262	0.0318
Aug	−0.0718	−0.0920	−0.0263	−0.0470	−0.0790	−0.0003
Sep	0.1163	0.0392	0.0091	0.0579	0.0890	0.0401
Oct	0.0938	−0.0327	−0.0068	0.0390	0.0489	−0.0050
Nov	0.1491	−0.0351	0.0499	0.0951	0.0838	0.0410
Dec	−0.0693	−0.0352	0.1043	0.0253	−0.0572	0.0174
Minimum	−0.2355	−0.2486	−0.1861	−0.1072	−0.1548	−0.0479
Maximum	0.2830	0.3143	0.3404	0.2211	0.2664	0.1116
$E(r)$	0.0221	0.0049	0.0109	0.0160	0.0160	0.0109
$\sigma^2(r)$	0.0115	0.0091	0.0050	0.0033	0.0078	0.0009
$\sigma(r)$	0.1072	0.0954	0.0707	0.0574	0.0883	0.0300

CHAPTER 6

RISK AND THE REQUIRED RATE OF RETURN

Two investors, with $1 each, chose very different paths at the end of 1925. One investor wanted to eat well (earn a high rate of return) and used his dollar to purchase shares of a portfolio based on the Standard & Poor's stock index. The other investor wanted to sleep well (have safety) and purchased U.S. Treasury bills. Both allowed their portfolios to grow by reinvesting the income they received.

By the end of 1932, the Great Depression had taken its toll, reducing the value of the common stock portfolio to only $0.79. In contrast, the portfolio of Treasury bills was worth $1.21. The investors' positions were the opposite of what they expected, much to the dismay of the one who had chosen to invest in common stocks.

Common stocks made a big recovery in 1933, earning an annual rate of return that year of nearly 54 percent. This performance lifted the common stock portfolio's value from $0.79 to $1.21. The common stock and Treasury-bill portfolios were both worth $1.21 then; the two investors earned the same average compound rate of return over the 8-year period from 1926 to 1933.

What we think of as normal conditions returned in 1934 and persisted until the end of 1995. The investor who purchased common stocks earned more than the investor who purchased Treasury bills during 40 of the 62 years in this period. This performance more than compensated for the common stock portfolio's poor start, giving it an average compound rate of return from 1926–1995 of 10.5 percent. In contrast, the Treasury-bill portfolio's average compound rate of return was only 3.3 percent. The simple, arithmetic averages of their annual rates of return were 12.5 percent and 3.8 percent. The portfolios had a similar difference in risk with standard deviations of 20.4 percent for the common stock and 3.3 percent for the Treasury-bill portfolio.

The paths the two investors embarked upon in 1925 are shown in Exhibit 6.1. One dollar invested in common stocks eventually increased in value to $1,113.92, although the path had its ups and downs. One dollar invested in Treasury bills grew to only $12.87, barely keeping up with the rate of inflation, but the path was smooth and predictable. Exhibit 6.1 clearly shows that the investors' expectations about what one must do to eat well or sleep well were confirmed in the long run.

Exhibit 6.1

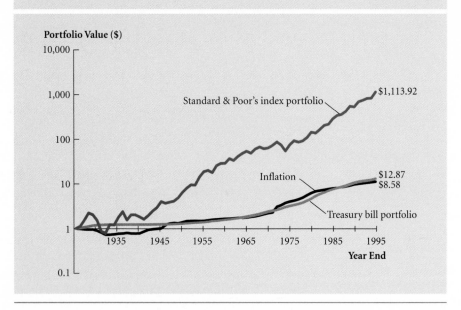

PERFORMANCE OF COMMON STOCK AND TREASURY-BILL PORTFOLIOS

Portfolio Value ($)

Standard & Poor's index portfolio — $1,113.92

Inflation — $12.87

Treasury bill portfolio — $8.58

Year End

Source: *Stocks, Bonds, Bills and Inflation, 1996 Yearbook,* Ibbotson Associates, 1996.

The investors in the preceding example were hypothetical—but the data were not. From 1926 to 1995, common stocks in the Standard & Poor's stock index *did* earn an average rate of return of 12.5 percent and had a standard deviation of rate of return of 20.4 percent. Similarly, a portfolio of U.S. Treasury bills earned an average rate of return of 3.8 percent and had a standard deviation of 3.3 percent.

These two portfolios are quite different from one another, but they probably didn't satisfy everyone in 1925 and are unlikely to satisfy everyone now. Some investors prefer a portfolio with more return than Treasury bills but less risk than the Standard & Poor's portfolio. Others prefer a very high rate of return and are willing to accept even more risk. Can investors construct the portfolios they prefer from the Standard & Poor's and Treasury-bill portfolios? The answer is *yes,* and Section 6.1 shows how. Most investors also want to know if the additional return they get from adding common stocks to their portfolios is worth the extra risk. Is there a benchmark they can use for comparison? The answer is *maybe,* and Section 6.2 discusses the theoretical models that have been developed for this purpose.

The majority of this chapter focuses on the owners rather than the corporation—and with good reason. Companies finance their investments and operations by issuing common stock to the owners, who then add these shares to their personal portfolios and require a rate of return that is appropriate for the additional risk they accept. Managers must know how their decisions affect this risk to determine the opportunity cost of using the owners' money. Then, the managers can use this opportunity cost to evaluate their alternatives and make the choice that maximizes the owners' wealth. Sections 6.3, 6.4, and 6.5 describe this application of investment principles to financial management.

6.1   RISK MANAGEMENT USING ALLOCATION[1]

You learned in Chapter 5 that forming a portfolio reduces but does not eliminate risk. Systematic risk, as measured by a portfolio's beta, remains—even in a completely diversified portfolio. Fortunately, investors can adjust the amount of risk they bear by allocating only part of their wealth to a risky portfolio and the remainder to a safe asset such as government securities. This process, **allocation**, permits them to expand the opportunity set to include portfolios with returns and risks not previously available.

The mathematics of allocation are simple, so we'll develop the graphical and mathematical descriptions simultaneously. Equations 5.6 and 5.17 are needed to compute the expected rate of return and beta of the new portfolios formed from a risky portfolio and a riskless asset. These equations are repeated here as Equations 6.1 and 6.2.

$$E(r_p) = w_x E(r_x) + (1 - w_x)r_f \qquad [6.1]$$
$$\beta_p = w_x \beta_x + (1 - w_x)\beta_f \qquad [6.2]$$

where
w_x = proportion of wealth allocated to risky portfolio x
$E(r_x)$ = expected rate of return on risky portfolio x
r_f = rate of return on riskless asset
β_x = beta of risky portfolio x
β_f = beta of riskless asset

The riskless asset has a beta of zero, so $\beta_p = w_x \beta_x$, which means $w_x = \beta_p/\beta_x$. Substituting this expression into the first equation and rearranging terms provides a single equation that relates a portfolio's expected rate of return to its risk:

$$E(r_p) = r_f + [E(r_x) - r_f]\beta_p/\beta_x \qquad [6.3]$$

Equation 6.3 says that the opportunity set of portfolios that can be constructed from a single risky portfolio and the riskless asset is a straight line. The endpoints of this line are the risky portfolio with $E(r_p) = E(r_x)$ (when $\beta_p = \beta_x$) and the riskless asset with $E(r_p) = r_f$ (when $\beta_p = 0$).

Exhibit 6.2 describes allocation. The parabola is an efficient set of risky portfolios from which investors can choose one portfolio to combine with the riskless asset. The rate of return on the risk-free asset, r_f, also is indicated in Exhibit 6.2. This interest rate plots on the vertical axis because the riskless asset's beta is zero. Finally, the solid lines connecting r_f with points K and M are the opportunity sets of new portfolios investors can construct by allocating their money between the riskless asset and portfolios K and M. These are segments of the straight lines described by Equation 6.3.

[1]The fact that investors can manage risk by allocating their wealth between a safe and a risky asset was first recognized by James Tobin in "Liquidity Preference as Behavior Toward Risk," *Review of Economic Studies,* February 1958, pp. 65–86.

Exhibit 6.2

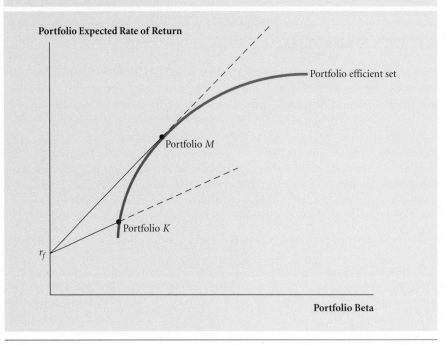

GRAPHICAL DESCRIPTION OF ALLOCATION

Investors form the portfolios represented by the solid lines connecting r_f to the efficient set by investing part of their money in a risky portfolio and lending the remainder at the riskless interest rate. They also can form portfolios represented by the extensions of these lines (shown as dotted lines in Exhibit 6.2) *if* they can borrow money at the riskless interest rate, combine it with their own wealth, and invest the total in the risky portfolio. Borrowing increases both expected rate of return and risk because investors receive the residual earnings when the risky portfolio is profitable but must make up the deficiency when the risky portfolio does not earn enough to cover the interest expense. Each point on the lines through r_f and K and r_f and M is a new portfolio with a combination of return and risk not previously available. An example should help clarify these points.

Benjamin's Boats provides a retirement program that permits each employee to designate how his or her funds are allocated between a U.S. Treasury-bill portfolio and a common stock portfolio with the characteristics described below.

	Treasury-Bill Portfolio	Stock Portfolio
$E(r)$	5.00%	10.25%
β	0	1.00

What is the expected rate of return and risk of Clarence Meggison's retirement fund if he allocates 25 percent to T-bills and 75 percent to common stocks?

The expected rate of return on his retirement portfolio is a weighted average of the rate of return on T-bills and the common stock portfolio.

$$E(r_{\text{Clarence's fund}}) = w_{\text{T-bills}} \times E(r_{\text{T-bills}}) + w_{\text{Stock}} \times E(r_{\text{Stock}})$$
$$= 0.25 \times 5.00\% + 0.75 \times 10.25\%$$
$$= 8.9375\%$$

The risk, measured by beta, is also a weighted average.

$$\beta_{\text{Clarence's fund}} = w_{\text{T-bills}} \times \beta_{\text{T-bills}} + w_{\text{Stock}} \times \beta_{\text{Stock}}$$
$$= 0.25 \times 0 + 0.75 \times 1.0$$
$$= 0.75$$

Therefore, Clarence can expect a rate of return of 8.9375 percent and a beta of 0.75.

Clarence's coworker, Dorothy McMillan, has accumulated $100,000 of retirement funds and can borrow an additional $25,000 at the 5 percent riskless interest rate by using her life insurance policy as collateral. What is the net return and risk of Dorothy's retirement fund if she allocates the entire $125,000 to the common stock portfolio? Note that –25 percent of Dorothy's equity is allocated to the riskless asset because she is borrowing—rather than lending—25 percent of her equity ($25,000/$100,000) at this interest rate. This financial transaction permits Dorothy to invest 125 percent of her equity ($125,000/$100,000) in the common stock portfolio. Therefore,

$$E(r_{\text{Dorothy's fund}}) = -0.25 \times 5.00\% + 1.25 \times 10.25\%$$
$$= 11.5625\%$$
$$\beta_{\text{Dorothy's fund}} = -0.25 \times 0 + 1.25 \times 1.0$$
$$= 1.25.$$

The return and risk of Clarence and Dorothy's retirement funds are graphed in Exhibit 6.3. The straight line connecting these portfolios to the company's Treasury-bill and stock portfolios describe all the alternatives available to them and the company's other employees. Importantly, Benjamin's Boats can meet any employee's needs by offering a retirement program built on a single risky portfolio and a single riskless portfolio.

EXERCISE 6.1

RETURN AND RISK FROM ALLOCATION

Robert Carl will allocate $10,000 of his retirement fund to Treasury bills and the remainder, $40,000, to common stocks. What is his expected rate of return and risk?

$$E(r_{\text{Robert's fund}}) = 0.20 \times 5.00\% + 0.80 \times 10.25\% = 9.20\%$$
$$\beta_{\text{Robert's fund}} = 0.20 \times 0 + 0.80 \times 1.0 = 0.80$$

His expected rate of return is 9.2 percent and the beta of his portfolio is 0.80.

Exhibit 6.3

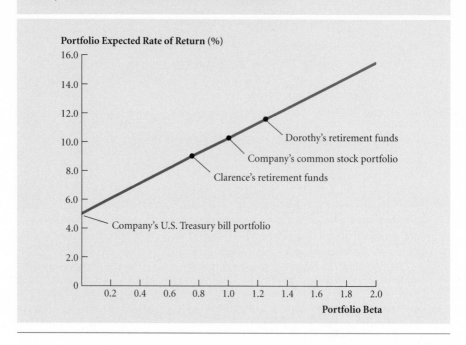

BENJAMIN'S BOATS RETIREMENT PROGRAM

Portfolio Expected Rate of Return (%) — Portfolio Beta

Dorothy's retirement funds

Company's common stock portfolio

Clarence's retirement funds

Company's U.S. Treasury bill portfolio

What is Robert Carl's return and risk if he borrows \$5,000 at the riskless rate of interest, adds it to his \$50,000 equity, and allocates the entire amount to common stocks?

$$w_{\text{riskless asset}} = \${-}5{,}000/\$50{,}000 = -0.10$$

$$w_{\text{stocks}} = \$55{,}000/\$50{,}000 = 1.10$$

$$E(r_{\text{Robert's fund}}) = -0.10 \times 5.00\% + 1.10 \times 10.25\% = 10.775\%$$

$$\beta_{\text{Robert's fund}} = -0.10 \times 0 + 1.10 \times 1.0 = 1.10$$

Using borrowed money increases Robert's expected rate of return to 10.775 percent, but also increases his beta to 1.10.

See "In the News" for some practical advice on how to allocate your own portfolio between stocks and bonds.

The examples we have examined so far demonstrate that investors can obtain a wide-range of returns and risks by allocating their wealth between safe and risky portfolios. Next, we will see that their ability to obtain these returns and risks on their own has important implications for the market-wide relationship between risk and return.

ASSET ALLOCATION IN PRACTICE

THIS ARTICLE WAS written as the Dow Jones Industrial Average stock market index approached a record high in early 1996.

Frightened by the giddy heights of the market and the sell-off of the last few days, you may feel the urge to sell your stocks, take your profits and get out. The only problem is where to put the proceeds. Into 10-year bonds, which earn 6 percent? Into a money-market fund yielding 5 percent? Into . . . what?

It's a tough question, but it's also the wrong question. You wouldn't have to agonize if you had something that most investors don't: An asset allocation strategy. That's a long-range plan on how to divide up your portfolio among stocks, bonds, and cash. In this case, "cash" means not dollar bills, but investments you can get your hands on quickly, such as short-term certificates of deposit, Treasury bills, and money-market funds.

Your allocation should depend on two factors:

- Your tolerance for risk. Some investors can't sleep at night, worrying about the fate of their shares. That's an expensive affliction, since stocks are the best-performing assets, by far. But I wouldn't shove a hydrophobe into a pool.
- Your own needs. How old are you? Do you require current income from your investments in the form of dividends and interest? When do you plan to use your savings? For retirement in 30 years? For a down payment on a house in three years?

The answers to questions such as these will determine how you should allocate your assets.

A good asset allocation strategy for a 30-year old who plans to retire at 65 might be: 100 percent stocks, zero percent bonds, zero percent cash. But, as this investor gets older, he should start to shift into bonds and cash. At retirement, the allocation might be: 40 percent stocks, 30 percent bonds, 30 percent cash.

Like stock-picking, asset allocation has no hard-and-fast rules, but the important thing is to stick to your strategy and let this plan—rather than your gut, or the last person you talked to—determine your key investment decisions.

Source: James K. Glassman, "Your Best Strategy Is Divide and Conquer . . . ," *The Washington Post,* February 18, 1996, p. H1.

6.2   THEORIES OF THE MARKET-WIDE RELATIONSHIP BETWEEN EXPECTED RETURN AND RISK

Finance scholars and professionals generally agree that the main ideas developed in Chapter 5 and up to this point in Chapter 6 are practical. Investors can form portfolios of assets that are less than perfectly correlated with one another to reduce risk, and they can allocate part of their wealth to a risky portfolio and part to a riskless asset to alter their personal return and risk. They also agree, although not as strongly, that the market model or factor models are practical methods for measuring the systematic and unique components of an asset's return and risk. Agreement about the practicality of these models is weakened by a recognition that the models' key assumption—that unexpected rates of return are uncorrelated—is probably violated in reality.

This section ventures into an area where the ideas are more speculative because they are based on theories for which we have both supportive and contradictory evidence. The objective of these theories is to provide a market-wide model of the relationship between expected rate of return and risk. These theories are sometimes called **asset pricing models** because they explain the price or value of risky assets.

The Capital Asset Pricing Model[2]

The **Capital Asset Pricing Model** (**CAPM**) says that an asset's expected rate of return must equal the riskless interest rate plus a risk premium determined by the asset's systematic risk. Specifically, the CAPM expected rate of return is computed from Equation 6.4, which is called the **Security Market Line** (**SML**).

$$E(r_j) = r_f + [E(r_m) - r_f]\beta_j \qquad \qquad \textbf{[6.4]}$$

where
$$
\begin{aligned}
E(r_j) &= \text{expected rate of return on asset } j \\
r_f &= \text{riskless interest rate} \\
E(r_m) &= \text{expected rate of return on market portfolio} \\
\beta_j &= \text{beta of asset } j
\end{aligned}
$$

The similarity between the SML and Equation 6.3, which describes the relationship between the return and risk of portfolios that can be constructed using allocation, is no coincidence. The CAPM was developed by considering the market- or economy-wide implications of risk management using diversification and allocation (as we will see). The SML is therefore a *general* description of the rates of return all investors can obtain by allocating their wealth between the market portfolio and the riskless asset.

Looking back at Exhibit 6.2, you can readily see that portfolios formed from combinations of the riskless asset and M dominate all existing risky portfolios because they have higher rates of return for the same levels of risk. Furthermore, portfolios formed from r_f and M dominate any portfolio that can be constructed using allocation such as portfolios on the r_f/K opportunity set. Portfolio M is therefore a dominant portfolio because, when combined with the riskless asset, it provides a higher expected rate of return for a given level of risk than any other actual or potential portfolio. Any risk-averse investor presented with the opportunities described in Exhibit 6.2 would prefer some combination of the riskless asset and portfolio M to all other alternatives.

The CAPM assumes that *all* investors are presented with the same opportunities and that *everyone* therefore prefers some combination of the riskless asset and portfolio M to all other alternatives. This assumption is justified if everyone can borrow and lend at the same riskless rate of interest and if everyone has the same information and expectations about the future, that is, they have the same efficient set. Under these circum-

---

[2]The Capital Asset Pricing Model was developed by William F. Sharpe and John Lintner. Sharpe won the 1990 Nobel prize in economics for this work. See William F. Sharpe, "Capital Asset Prices: A Theory of Market Equilibrium under Conditions of Risk," *Journal of Finance*, September 1964, pp. 425–442 and John Lintner, "Security Prices, Risk, and Maximal Gains from Diversification," *Journal of Finance*, December 1965, pp. 587–615.

stances, everyone will draw the same straight line through the same r_f tangent to the same efficient set at the same point M.

Only one specific portfolio is compatible with this result and equilibrium in the supply and demand for risky assets: The market portfolio, which includes every risky asset in proportion to its market value. To see why this is necessary, suppose some assets were included in portfolio M less than proportionately to their market values. Then the demand for these assets, through the demand for portfolio M, would be less than the supply of these assets and their prices would fall. Conversely, if some assets were included in portfolio M more than proportionately to their market values, then demand would exceed supply and their prices would rise. Supply will equal demand only if the risky assets are included in portfolio M in proportion to their market values, that is, portfolio M must be the market portfolio.

Now we can substitute $E(r_m)$ for $E(r_x)$ and β_m for β_x in Equation 6.3 to describe the market-wide relationship between return and risk. That is,

$$E(r_p) = r_f + [E(r_m) - r_f]\beta_p/\beta_m.$$

All we must do to complete our derivation of the SML is determine the beta of the market portfolio. This part is easy. Remember that an asset's beta is the slope of its characteristic line. This parameter is estimated by regressing the asset's rates of return on the market index's rates of return. Obviously, we get a perfect 45° line when we regress the market portfolio on itself, so $\beta_m = 1.0$. Substituting this result into $E(r_p) = r_f + [E(r_m) - r_f]\beta_p/\beta_m$ and replacing the subscript p with j (because beta is used to measure the risk of assets or portfolios) gives Equation 6.4—the Security Market Line.

$$E(r_j) = r_f + [E(r_m) - r_f]\beta_j \qquad\qquad [6.4]$$

The Security Market Line completely describes the rates of return all investors can obtain by allocating their wealth between the market portfolio and the riskless asset. We don't need to know the risks and returns of other portfolios, such as those on the parabola in Exhibit 6.2, because investors will not choose them. We also don't need to know the amount of money involved or whether an investor's position requires lending, borrowing, or neither. All we need to know to describe an investment's expected rate of return is its systematic risk as measured by its beta and the rates of return that determine the premium that the market expects for each unit of risk. The following example illustrates this simplification.

Wayne Jones Capital Corporation (WJCC) has $1,000,000 to invest for one year and may purchase a portfolio that has a beta of 0.70. What rate of return should the company expect to earn if $r_f = 6.5$ percent and $E(r_m) = 15.0$ percent? According to the CAPM,

$$E(r_p) = r_f + [E(r_m) - r_f] \times \beta_f$$
$$= 6.5\% + [15.0\% - 6.5\%] \times 0.70 = 12.45\%.$$

We can confirm that this is the rate of return WJCC should expect by comparing it to the rate of return they can get by using allocation to construct their own portfolio with a beta of 0.70. Using Equation 6.2,

$$\beta_p = w_m\beta_m + (1 - w_m)\beta_f$$
$$0.70 = w_m \times 1.0 + (1 - w_m) \times 0$$
$$w_m = 0.70.$$

WJCC must invest 70 percent of the $1,000,000 in the market portfolio and the remaining 30 percent in government bonds to construct its own portfolio with a beta of 0.70.

The expected net cash flow provided by this homemade portfolio equals the amount invested in market portfolio $\times E(r_m)$ plus the amount invested in government bonds $\times r_f$.

$$\text{Net cash flow} = \$700,000 \times 0.15 + \$300,000 \times 0.065$$
$$= \$105,000 + \$19,500 = \$124,500$$

The portfolio's expected rate of return is the expected net cash flow divided by the initial investment, $124,500/$1,000,000, or 12.45 percent. This is the same rate of return we computed in fewer steps using the CAPM.

E X E R C I S E ● ─── ●

6.2   **COMPARING THE CAPM AND HOMEMADE RATES OF RETURN**

Helen Sullivan has an opportunity to invest $50,000 in a portfolio with a beta of 0.60. Use the CAPM to determine her expected rate of return if $r_f = 6$ percent and $E(r_m) = 14.5$ percent. Confirm your answer by determining the rate of return she can earn by constructing a homemade portfolio.

The CAPM expected rate of return is

$$E(r_p) = r_f + [E(r_m) - r_f] \times \beta_p$$
$$= 6.0\% + [14.5\% - 6.0\%] \times 0.60 = 11.10\%.$$

The composition of the homemade portfolio is

$$\beta_p = w_m\beta_m + (1 - w_m)\beta_f$$
$$0.60 = w_m \times 1.0 + (1 - w_m) \times 0$$
$$w_m = 0.60.$$

Helen must invest $30,000 ($50,000 $\times$ 0.60) in the market portfolio and the remainder in government bonds.

The homemade portfolio's net cash flow is

$$\text{Net cash flow} = \$30,000 \times 0.145 + \$20,000 \times 0.06$$
$$= \$4,350 + \$1,200 = \$5,550$$

The homemade portfolio's expected rate of return is $5,550/$50,000 = 11.10 percent—the CAPM expected rate of return.

● ─────────── ●

Of course, the CAPM works just as well for portfolios with betas greater than 1.0. To illustrate this case, let's suppose Wayne Jones Capital Corporation may invest its $1,000,000 in a portfolio that has a beta of 1.25. According to the CAPM, the expected rate of return on this portfolio should be

$$E(r_p) = r_f + [E(r_m) - r_f] \times \beta_p$$
$$= 6.5\% + [15\% - 6.5\%] \times 1.25 = 17.125\%.$$

This portfolio must provide a higher expected rate of return because it has more risk.

Now let's see if WJCC would expect to earn the same rate of return by constructing a homemade portfolio with a beta of 1.25. Using Equation 6.2 again,

$$\beta_p = w_m \beta_m + (1 - w_m) \beta_f$$
$$1.25 = w_m \times 1.0 + (1 - w_m) \times 0$$
$$w_m = 1.25.$$

To construct a portfolio with a beta of 1.25, WJCC must invest 125 percent of its money ($1,250,000) in the market portfolio by borrowing $250,000 at the riskless rate of interest. This implies the proportion of the portfolio invested in government bonds is −0.25.

You compute the portfolio's expected net cash flow the same way as before: amount invested in market portfolio $\times E(r_m)$ plus the amount invested in government bonds $\times r_f$. Be sure to use the negative sign on the cash flow related to government bonds because the company will *pay* this interest.

$$\text{Net cash flow} = \$1,250,000 \times 0.15 - \$250,000 \times 0.065$$
$$= \$187,500 - \$16,250 = \$171,250$$

The portfolio's expected rate of return is $171,250/$1,000,000, or 17.125 percent. Once again, we get the same answer, but it was simpler to use the CAPM.

HOMEMADE RATES OF RETURN WITH LENDING

EXERCISE
6.3

Repeat Exercise 6.2 for a portfolio that has a beta of 1.40.

The CAPM expected rate of return is

$$E(r_p) = r_f + [E(r_m) - r_f] \times \beta_p$$
$$= 6.0\% + [14.5\% - 6.0\%] \times 1.40 = 17.90\%.$$

The composition of the homemade portfolio is

$$\beta_p = w_m \beta_m + (1 - w_m) \beta_f$$
$$1.40 = w_m \times 1.0 + (1 - w_m) \times 0$$
$$w_m = 1.40.$$

Helen must invest $70,000 ($50,000 × 1.40) in the market portfolio and borrow $20,000 ($50,000 × − 0.40) at the riskless rate of interest.

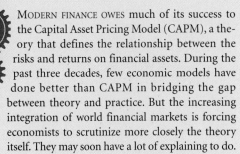

IN THE NEWS

INTERNATIONALIZING THE CAPM

MODERN FINANCE OWES much of its success to the Capital Asset Pricing Model (CAPM), a theory that defines the relationship between the risks and returns on financial assets. During the past three decades, few economic models have done better than CAPM in bridging the gap between theory and practice. But the increasing integration of world financial markets is forcing economists to scrutinize more closely the theory itself. They may soon have a lot of explaining to do.

The CAPM's power comes from the ease with which it can be applied. A company considering a new capital investment, for example, needs a benchmark to judge it against. By looking at the stock returns of similar companies with similar investments, the firm can estimate how sensitive the project's pay-off will be to market movements. This, in turn, allows it to estimate the market's expected return. If managers think the investment project can beat this return, they should go ahead.

Despite its many practical uses, however, the theory itself is far from solid. Its biggest drawback is its dependence on the notion of a "market portfolio." Technically, this should be the entire set of assets available in the world. Yet although it is a global model, investors and economists have until recently almost ignored its global implications. In testing the theory's validity, many researchers have looked only at America; others have examined several countries but have focused just on bonds and avoided equities. Furthermore, most countries' investors put only a small fraction of their equity investments into foreign stocks. As global markets become more integrated, research and applications that ignore the CAPM's international underpinnings look increasingly lame.

Source: "Time for the Chop?" *The Economist*, February 25, 1995, p. 72. Copyright © 1995, *The Economist*, Ltd.

The homemade portfolio's net cash flow is

$$\text{Net cash flow} = \$70,000 \times 0.145 - \$20,000 \times 0.06$$
$$= \$10,150 - \$1,200 = \$8,950$$

The homemade portfolio's expected rate of return is $8,950/$50,000 = 17.90 percent, the CAPM expected rate of return.

• ————— •

The CAPM expected rates of return are easier to calculate than those computed from expected net cash flows because we don't need information about the amount of money involved or whether there is borrowing or lending. More importantly, the CAPM describes market-wide expected rates of return because *anyone* can allocate his or her money between the riskless asset and the market portfolio to obtain the risk and return combinations described by this asset pricing model. This means we can use CAPM expected rates of return for opportunity costs.

The CAPM has been criticized on many grounds including the tendency to include only U.S. securities in the market index. (See "In the News.") Next, we will examine the Arbitrage Pricing Theory, a model of the relationship between risk and return, that is not subject to the same criticisms.

The Arbitrage Pricing Theory[3]

The **Arbitrage Pricing Theory** (APT) is an alternative to the CAPM that also predicts that the market-wide relationship between return and risk is linear. The APT is different, however, in two important respects. First, the APT requires fewer of the simplifying assumptions that may limit the CAPM's applicability to reality. The main assumption underlying the APT is that investors can construct a riskless portfolio without investing any of their own money—but this portfolio must have a zero rate of return. Earning profits without risk is called arbitrage, so this actually is a no-arbitrage assumption (should this model be called the *NAPT*?). You won't be too far off if you say the APT is based on the assumption that the financial market does not permit investors to get something for nothing. However, this is an attractive assumption, which is one reason for the APT's appeal.

The other difference between the Arbitrage Pricing Theory and the Capital Asset Pricing Model is that the APT admits the possibility of more than one component to systematic risk and that a market risk premium is associated with each component. Suppose systematic risk comprises sensitivity to unexpected changes in interest rates and sensitivity to unexpected changes in GNP as we assumed for the illustration of factor models in Section 5.3 in Chapter 5. Then, according to the APT, the expected rate of return the market requires of asset j is

$$E(r_j) = E(r_0) + [E(r_1) - E(r_0)]\beta_{j,1} + [E(r_2) - E(r_0)]\beta_{j,2} \qquad [6.5]$$

where
$E(r_j)$ = expected rate of return on asset j
$E(r_0)$ = expected rate of return on a portfolio with no systematic risk
$E(r_1)$ = expected rate of return on a portfolio with a return that is completely explained by its sensitivity to unexpected changes in interest rates
$\beta_{j,1}$ = asset j's sensitivity to news about interest rates
$E(r_2)$ = expected rate of return on a portfolio with a return that is completely explained by its sensitivity to unexpected changes in GNP
$\beta_{j,2}$ = asset j's sensitivity to news about GNP.

As an illustration of how to compute an APT expected rate of return, consider the Osage Orange Cabinet Company (OOCC), which makes kitchen cabinets for vacation homes. The sensitivity of the rate of return on the company's common stock to unexpected changes in interest rates is measured by its β_1, which equals –0.25 while the sensitivity of its rate of return to unexpected changes in gross national product is measured by its β_2, which equals 1.15. The market-wide expected rates of return for portfolios with no systematic risk and with sensitivity to only interest rates and GNP are

---

[3]The Arbitrage Pricing Theory was developed by Stephen A. Ross, "The Arbitrage Theory of Capital Asset Pricing," *Journal of Economic Theory*, December 1976, pp. 341–360.

$$E(r_0) = 6.0\%$$
$$E(r_1) = 7.0\%$$
$$E(r_2) = 15.0\%.$$

Given these values, the expected rate of return on OOCC's common stock is

$$E(r_{\text{Osage Orange}}) = 6.0\% + (7.0\% - 6.0\%) \times (-0.25) + (15.0\% - 6.0\%) \times 1.15$$
$$= 16.10\%.$$

This rate of return has the same interpretation as a CAPM expected rate of return, which is that the expected rate of return from buying a share of the OOCC's common stock equals the rate of return on an investment constructed by allocating money among the three portfolios with no systematic risk and with sensitivity to only interest rates and GNP.

EXERCISE   ●

6.4 **COMPUTING AN APT EXPECTED RATE OF RETURN**

The sensitivity of Grubstake Mining Company's common stock to unexpected changes in interest rates and gross national product is measured by betas of 0.85 and 0.20. What is the expected rate of return on the company's stock if market-wide expected rates of return for portfolios with no systematic risk and with sensitivity only to interest rates and GNP are

$$E(r_0) = 6.0\%$$
$$E(r_1) = 8.0\%$$
$$E(r_2) = 11.0\%?$$

Substituting these values into Equation 6.5, the expected rate of return is

$$E(r_{\text{Grubstake}}) = E(r_0) + [E(r_1) - E(r_0)]\beta_{j,1} + [E(r_2) - E(r_0)]\beta_{j,2}$$
$$= 6.0\% + (8.0\% - 6.0\%) \times 0.85 + (11.0\% - 6.0\%) \times 0.20$$
$$= 8.7\%.$$

The expected rate of return on Grubstake Mining Company's common stock is 8.7 percent.

● ────── ●

The APT's ability to use more than one component to represent the market premium for systematic risk is both its strength and weakness. This ability is a strength because it provides a richer description of how assets' rates of return are related to one another. It also is a weakness, however, because the theory does not identify the components that affect rates of return. Consequently, we don't know which unexpected changes in economic conditions are important or unimportant to the financial market. Unexpected changes in interest rates would certainly seem important, but this conclusion is based on intuition rather than theory.

Validity of the CAPM and APT

Empirical studies support and contradict the implications of both the CAPM and the APT. Early studies of the CAPM were supportive. For example, Fama and MacBeth examined the association between a portfolio's rate of return and its beta, beta-squared, and unique risk.[4] The intercept of their regression model was approximately equal to the riskless interest rate, the coefficient of beta was positive and significant, and the coefficients of beta-squared and unique risk were not significantly different from zero. These results imply the portfolios' rates of return fell on the Security Market Line as predicted by the CAPM.

Subsequent studies contradicted the CAPM because they found a regular association between an asset's rate of return and characteristics other than its beta. These studies found that the common stock issued by small companies and companies with low price/earnings ratios provided higher rates of return than appropriate for their systematic risk.[5] Fama and French conducted an important study in which they examined the association between a company's average rate of return and its beta, size, and market-to-book ratio.[6] There was no relationship between the returns and betas in their sample. However, smaller companies and those with smaller market-to-book ratios had the higher rates of return. These results have prompted scholars to search for sources of risk not recognized by the CAPM.

The APT has the potential to recognize other sources of risk because the statistical techniques used to estimate beta coefficients and test the model identify common factors in the sample used for the test. Studies have estimated that between three and five factors explain common stock returns, but the number identified differs from one study to another.[7] Furthermore, the statistical techniques do not assign names to these components of the risk premium. Consequently, we cannot be certain that each study has identified the same common factors. This makes it quite difficult to make general statements about the market-wide relationship between return and risk.

Developing an asset pricing model that accurately describes the market-wide relationship between return and risk is difficult. This is important, however, because the availability of an effective model permits investors and managers to plan and control their investments in risky assets. The difficulty and importance of this task explains why Harry Markowitz and William Sharpe shared the Nobel prize in economics for their

[4]Eugene Fama and John D. MacBeth, "Risk, Return, and Equilibrium: Empirical Tests," *Journal of Political Economy,* May 1973, pp. 607–636. See also Michael C. Jensen (ed.), *Studies in the Theory of Capital Markets,* Praeger, New York, 1972.

[5]Two studies of the size effect are R.W. Banz, "The Relationship between Return and Market Value of Common Stocks," *Journal of Financial Economics,* March 1981, pp. 3–18; and Marc R. Reinganum, "Abnormal Returns in Small Firm Portfolios," *Financial Analysts Journal,* March–April 1981, pp. 52–57. Two studies of the effect of price/earnings ratio are Sudipto Basu, "The Information Content of Price-Earnings Ratios," *Financial Management,* Summer 1975, pp. 53–64; and John W. Peavy III and David A. Goodman, "The Significance of P/Es for Portfolio Returns," *Journal of Portfolio Management,* Winter 1983, pp. 43–47.

[6]Eugene Fama and Kenneth R. French, "The Cross-Section of Expected Stock Returns," *Journal of Finance,* June 1992, pp. 427–465.

[7]Adam Gehr Jr., "Some Tests of the Arbitrage Pricing Theory," *Journal of the Midwest Finance Association,* 1975, pp. 91–105, and Phoebus J. Dhrymes, Irwin Friend, Mustafa N. Gultekin, and N. Bulent Gultekin, "New Tests of the APT and Their Implications," *Journal of Finance,* July 1985, pp. 659–674.

role in the development of portfolio theory and the CAPM. The difficulty and importance of this task also explain why the best scholars continue to search for an improved asset pricing model. Although the details of the new model may be different from either the CAPM or APT, it certainly will be based on the fundamental principles of allocation and diversification you learned here and in Chapter 5.

We will use the CAPM as our asset pricing model in the remainder of this book because it is simpler and more familiar. Nevertheless, all the applications we'll describe can be adapted to use the APT.

6.3   APPLYING THE CAPITAL ASSET PRICING MODEL

The Capital Asset Pricing Model describes an investment's expected rate of return as a function of its systematic risk. This rate of return is the minimum that any investor will accept because he or she can always obtain this rate by borrowing or lending and investing in the market portfolio. A CAPM expected rate of return is therefore a market-wide *required* rate of return, or opportunity cost that is tailored to an investment's risk. Importantly, this opportunity cost only depends on an investment's systematic risk and not on the investor's attitudes about risk and return.

Investors and managers can use CAPM required rates of return to evaluate entirely new risky assets. An asset with an expected rate of return greater than the CAPM required rate of return is an acceptable investment because it is more profitable than investors' market opportunities. Conversely, an asset with an expected rate of return less than the CAPM required rate of return is unacceptable.

You must specify the values of three parameters to use the CAPM to calcuate a required rate of return. These parameters are the riskless interest rate, r_f; the expected rate of return on the market portfolio, $E(r_m)$; and the investment's beta. You will learn how to estimate these values in Chapter 17 where we will compute the required rate of return for one of the business segments operated by a real company. In the meantime, we will simply assume these parameters are given. The following example demonstrates how to calculate and use a CAPM required rate of return—once you have obtained the necessary estimates.

James Michael, a wealthy investor with a well-diversified portfolio, has an opportunity to purchase a ski chalet that he will immediately lease to spectators at a winter carnival for $10,000 net of expenses. The chalet costs $200,000, and James expects to resell it one year later at the beginning of the next skiing season for $225,000. His expected free cash flows are therefore

$$CF_0 = \$-200{,}000 + \$10{,}000 = \$-190{,}000$$
$$CF_1 = \$\,225{,}000.$$

James will use the CAPM to determine his opportunity cost for this investment project. He estimates that the beta of vacation property is 1.20, the riskless interest rate is 6.0 percent, and the expected rate of return on the market portfolio is 14.5 percent. Given these estimates, his opportunity cost or required rate of return is

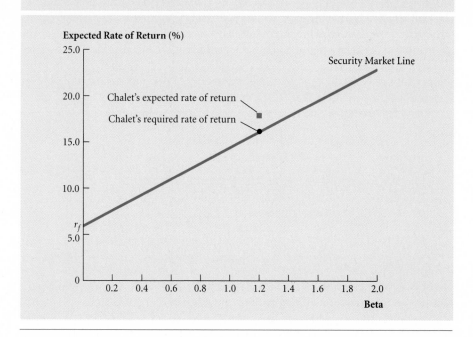

Exhibit 6.4

JAMES MICHAEL'S SKI CHALET

$$r_{chalet} = r_f + [E(r_m) - r_f]\beta_{chalet}$$
$$= 6.0\% + [14.5\% - 6.0\%] \times 1.20 = 16.2\%.$$

James's expected rate of return, computed from the chalet's expected free cash flows, is

$$E(r_{chalet}) = \frac{\$225,000 - \$190,000}{\$190,000} = 0.1842 \text{ or } 18.42\%.$$

The expected rate of return on the chalet is greater than its CAPM required rate of return, so James should buy the property. This result is depicted in Exhibit 6.4 where the chalet's expected rate of return is related to its required rate of return as determined by the CAPM.

We obtain the same conclusion by determining the net present value of the chalet's free cash flows using the CAPM required rate of return as the discount rate.

$$NPV = CF_0 + CF_1/(1 + r_{chalet})$$
$$= \$-190,000 + \$225,000/1.162$$
$$= \$3,631.67$$

This calculation tells us that the project is acceptable and will increase James' wealth by \$3,631.67.

NPV ANALYSIS WITH A CAPM REQUIRED RATE OF RETURN

Ron Gene, the production manager at Justafax Printing Company, wants to install equipment that recovers recyclable compounds from chemicals used to produce negatives for printing plates. The equipment costs $35,000 and has a one-year life. Ron believes the company can recover $41,500 of compounds, net of expenses. Should he buy this equipment if its beta is 1.10, r_f is 7 percent, and r_m is 15 percent? Assume the $41,500 is received at the end of the year.

The CAPM required rate of return for the recovery equipment is

$$r_{\text{recovery equip}} = r_f + [E(r_m) - r_f]\beta_{\text{recovery equip}}$$
$$= 7.0\% + [15.0\% - 7.0\%] \times 1.10 = 15.8\%.$$

The project's net present value at this required rate of return is

$$\text{NPV(recovery equipment)} = \text{CF}_0 + \frac{\text{CF}_1}{(1 + r_{\text{recovery equip}})}$$
$$= \$-35,000 + \$41,500/1.158$$
$$= \$837.65.$$

The NPV is positive at this discount rate, so Justafax Printing Company should purchase the recovery equipment.[8]

The CAPM has even been used in court to determine, among other things, the amount of damages to award in civil suits. (See "In the News.")

6.4   THE SEPARATION OF INVESTMENT AND FINANCING DECISIONS

The CAPM opportunity cost that applies to a particular asset only depends on its systematic risk. Whether the investor who may purchase the asset prefers low risk or high return has no effect. This means we can determine whether an investment is acceptable by considering only its own cash flows and risk. We need not consider the characteristics of its potential owners.

We can ignore the owners' characteristics because they can conduct financial transactions to transform an acceptable investment project into one that meets their preferences. Some owners, who value safety, may combine a risky investment and the riskless asset to reduce the risk of their personal portfolios. Others may use borrowed money to purchase a risky investment to increase the rate of return on their personal

[8]You obtain the same conclusion using the rate of return criterion because the equipment's expected rate of return, ($41,500 − $35,000)/$35,000 = 0.1857 or 18.57 percent, is greater than its CAPM required rate of return of 15.8 percent.

I N   T H E   N E W S

THE CAPM GOES TO COURT

THE NATURE OF the principal–agent relationship gives rise to many problems, especially when the agent has access to the principal's money. Similar to the conflict between shareholders and management is the friction between investor and broker. When an investor's portfolio is damaged by a broker's illegal conduct, some courts include as damages the loss suffered by the portfolio in relation to the market's performance. In particular, courts compute damages by determining how the account performed relative to the market's performance as measured by a market index.

In *Rolf v. Blyth, Eastman Dillon & Co.*, the investor had an account that, over the course of ten months, fell in value from $1,423,000 to $446,000. Rolf, the investor, was an aggressive stock trader who arranged to have his account overseen by both a broker and investment advisor with discretionary powers. Among other findings, the lower court determined that the defendant stockbroker had aided and abetted the investment advisor, who had violated the New York Stock Exchange's (NYSE) Know Your Customer Rule and the National Association of Securities Dealers' (NASD) Suitability Rule by investing Rolf in unsuitable stocks. The court held that damages should be determined by "tak[ing] the initial value of the [investor's] portfolio, adjust[ing] it by the percentage change in an appropriate index during the aiding and abetting period, and subtract[ing] the value of the portfolio at the end of the period."

Courts must be mindful of the connection between capital asset pricing and the value of risk when attempting to value damages connected to financial markets. By distinguishing systematic from nonsystematic risk, the CAPM allows for an intuitive means of understanding risks that an investor cannot avoid through diversification. Although the law should not be so lethargic as to lose sight of the fact that the CAPM is a theoretical financial model, the model still provides an instructive and comprehensive manner for valuing risk.

Source: Jeffrey S. Glaser, "The Capital Asset Pricing Model: Risk Valuation, Judicial Interpretation, and Market Bias," *The Business Lawyer*, February 1995, pp. 687–716. © 1995 American Bar Association. Reprinted by permission.

portfolios. In either case, they will allocate *some* money to an investment only if its expected rate of return meets or exceeds the market-wide opportunity cost appropriate for its risk.

You may recognize the preceding discussion as a restatement of the separation principle which we introduced in Chapter 3: There, you saw that individuals can choose investments without considering their preference for current versus future income because they can use the financial markets to allocate their additional wealth between current and future spending. Now we can extend this principle by saying investors can use the NPV rule to choose investments without considering their preference for return and risk because they can use the financial markets to allocate their additional wealth between safe and risky assets.

Let's return to James Michael's ski chalet project to see how this works. To recap, the project's free cash flows were $CF_0 = \$-190,000$ and $CF_1 = \$225,000$; its beta was 1.20; and its CAPM required rate of return was 16.2 percent based on $r_f = 6.0$ percent and

Table 6.1   JAMES MICHAEL'S SKI CHALET WITH LENDING

	Time 0	Time 1
Chalet's Free Cash Flow		
Cash flow provided by (used for) operations	$ 10,000.00	$ 0
Cash flow provided by (used for) investment	(200,000.00)	225,000.00
Cash flow provided by (used for) financial slack	0	0
Net cash flow	$(190,000.00)	$225,000.00
James's Personal Financial Cash Flow		
Extend one-year note at 6%	$ (64,543.89)	$ 0
Loan is repaid	0	68,416.52
Net cash flow	$ (64,543.89)	$ 68,416.52
James's Net Personal Cash Flow	$(254,543.89)	$293,416.52

$E(r_m) = 14.5$ percent. The NPV of the project's free cash flows at this required rate of return was $3,631.67, so we concluded it is an acceptable investment.

Now suppose James is conservative and prefers a beta of 0.90 for this real estate portfolio. Will he still consider this an acceptable investment project? The answer is yes because all he must do is simultaneously allocate money to the riskless asset to reduce the risk of the portfolio.

We use Equation 6.2 to determine how much wealth James should allocate to the chalet and how much to the riskless asset.

$$\beta_p = w_{chalet}\beta_{chalet} + (1 - w_{chalet})\beta_f$$
$$= w_{chalet} \times 1.2 + (1 - w_{chalet}) \times 0 = 0.90$$
$$w_{chalet} = 0.75$$

The chalet's *value*, before subtracting its cost, is $225,000/1.162, which equals $193,631.67. The chalet must account for 75 percent of James' real estate portfolio, so

$$w_{chalet} = \frac{\$193,631.67}{\text{total value of real estate portfolio}} = 0.75$$

Total value of real estate portfolio = $258,175.56.

The chalet is worth $193,631.67, which means James must lend $64,543.89 ($258,175.56 – $193,631.67) at the riskless interest rate.

Table 6.1 shows how James Michael's investment and financing transactions affect his wealth. The investment project uses $190,000 of free cash flow at time 0 and provides $225,000 of free cash flow at time 1. Extending the riskless loan uses $64,543.89 of financial cash flow at time 0 and provides $68,416.52 ($64,543.89 × 1.06) of finan-

JAMES MICHAEL'S SKI CHALET WITH BORROWING

Table 6.2

	Time 0	Time 1
Chalet's Free Cash Flow		
Cash flow provided by (used for) operations	$ 10,000.00	$ 0
Cash flow provided by (used for) investment	(200,000.00)	225,000.00
Cash flow provided by (used for) financial slack	0	0
Net cash flow	$(190,000.00)	$225,000.00
James's Personal Financial Cash Flow		
Borrow for one year at 6%	$ 50,000.00	$ 0
Repay loan	0	(53,000.00)
Net cash flow	$ 50,000.00	$(53,000.00)
James's Net Personal Cash Flow	$(140,000.00)	$172,000.00

cial cash flow at time 1 when the loan is repaid with interest. James's net cash flows are simply the sums of his free cash flows from buying the chalet and his personal financial cash flows from the riskless asset or $–254,543.89 and $293,416.52 at time 0 and time 1.

James has constructed his real estate portfolio to have a beta of 0.90, so its required rate of return is

$$r_p = 6.0\% + (14.5\% - 6.0\%) \times 0.90 = 13.65\%.$$

The NPV of James's real estate portfolio is

$$NPV = \$-254,543.89 + \$293,416.52/(1.1365)$$
$$= \$3,631.67,$$

which is exactly the same value we obtained by discounting the *chalet's* free cash flows at its own CAPM required rate of return.

To be sure you understand this process, let's compute the net present value of James Michael's real estate portfolio if he desires a high rate of return and borrows $50,000 at the riskless interest rate to purchase the chalet. Table 6.2 provides the revised net cash flows. The proceeds of the loan reduce his net cash outflow at time 0 by $50,000, and the repayment of principal and interest reduces his net cash inflow at time 1 by $53,000. The net cash flows from and to his real estate portfolio are therefore $–140,000 and $172,000 at time 0 and time 1.

We must use a CAPM required rate of return to discount these cash flows, which means we must calculate the beta of James's portfolio. The chalet's value is $193,631.67 (the same as before), so James's equity is $143,631.67 (the chalet's value minus the amount of financing provided by the loan). The proportions of his equity allocated to the project and the riskless asset are therefore

$$w_{\text{chalet}} = \$193{,}631.67/\$143{,}631.67 = 1.3481 \text{ or } 134.81\%$$
$$w_{\text{riskless asset}} = \$-50{,}000/\$143{,}631.67 = -0.3481 \text{ or } -34.81\%.$$

Using these weights, the beta of his real estate portfolio is

$$\begin{aligned}
\beta_p &= w_{\text{chalet}} \times 1.2 + w_{\text{riskless asset}} \times 0 \\
&= 1.3481 \times 1.2 + (-0.3481) \times 0 \\
&= 1.6177
\end{aligned}$$

and its required rate of return is

$$r_p = 6.0\% + (14.5\% - 6.0\%) \times 1.6177 = 19.75\%.$$

Using this opportunity cost as the discount rate, the NPV of James's portfolio—if he borrows money to finance the investment—is

$$\text{NPV} = \$-140{,}000 + \$172{,}000/1.1975 = \$3{,}632.57.$$

This is the same value, except for a $0.90 difference due to rounding, that we obtained by discounting the project's free cash flows at its own opportunity cost or by assuming James Michael would allocate some money to the riskless asset to reduce his risk.

EXERCISE   ● ── ●

6.6   **ILLUSTRATION OF SEPARATION OF INVESTMENT AND FINANCING**

Rework the James Michael example, assuming he prefers a portfolio beta of 0.80. Use Equation 6.2 to determine how much wealth James should allocate to the chalet and how much to the riskless asset.

$$\begin{aligned}
\beta_p &= w_{\text{chalet}}\beta_{\text{chalet}} + (1 - w_{\text{chalet}})\beta_f \\
&= w_{\text{chalet}} \times 1.2 + (1 - w_{\text{chalet}}) \times 0 = 0.80 \\
w_{\text{chalet}} &= 0.6667
\end{aligned}$$

Convert this proportion to dollars by dividing the chalet's value by the total value of James's portfolio.

$$w_{\text{chalet}} = \frac{\$193{,}631.67}{\text{total value of real estate portfolio}} = 0.6667$$

Total value of real estate portfolio = \$290,432.98

The chalet is worth \$193,631.67, which means James must lend \$96,801.31 (\$290,432.98 − \$193,631.67) at the riskless interest rate.

Use free cash flow statements to compute James's net personal cash flows.

	Time 0	Time 1
Chalet's Free Cash Flow		
Cash flow provided by (used for) operations	$ 10,000.00	$ 0
Cash flow provided by (used for) investment	(200,000.00)	225,000.00
Cash flow provided by (used for) financial slack	0	0
Net cash flow	$(190,000.00)	$225,000.00
James's Personal Financial Cash Flow		
Extend one-ear note at 6%	$ (96,801.31)	$ 0
Loan is repaid	0	102,609.39
James's Net Personal Cash Flow	$(286,801.31)	$327,609.39

Use the CAPM to determine the required rate of return on James's real estate portfolio. By design, its beta is 0.80.

$$r_{\text{James's portfolio}} = 6.0\% + (14.5\% - 6.0\%) \times 0.80 = 12.8\%$$

Discount James's net personal cash flows to determine the net present value.

$$\text{NPV} = \${-}286{,}801.31 + \$327{,}609.39/1.128 = \$3{,}632.55$$

This is the same answer we obtained earlier except for rounding.

• ———————— •

These results demonstrate that we can determine whether an investment is acceptable and how it will affect the owner's wealth by simply discounting its free cash flows at the market-determined required rate of return. We don't need to know the owner's current wealth, preference for risk and return, or whether she will borrow or lend. All we need to know are the asset's free cash flows, its systematic risk, and the parameters of the asset pricing model.

6.5 APPLICATION TO DECISION MAKING WITHIN FIRMS

Owners can use an effective asset pricing model to delegate investment decisions to professional managers because the managers only need to know the characteristics of the investment projects. This process directs the owners' resources to their most productive use if the managers follow a simple, three-step process: (1) estimate each project's free cash flows, (2) use an asset pricing model to determine the expected rate of return the financial market requires given each project's risk, and (3) accept each project with a positive NPV when its free cash flows are discounted at its own opportunity cost. The owners would accept the same projects if given the opportunity to make the decision themselves because positive NPV projects increase their wealth.

Senior managers can apply this process within the firm to delegate investment decisions to subordinate managers. Management specialists in each business unit have the information and expertise to perform the first step, estimating their projects' free

Table 6.3   DOUBLE-FELIX MANUFACTURING COMPANY'S INVESTMENT PROPOSALS

Project Code Name	Description	Free Cash Flows		Expected Rate of Return
		1998	1999	
CAT-1	*Mousy Nibbles* promotion	$-1,000,000	$1,140,000	14.00%
CAT-2	Adopt recyclable packaging	-2,000,000	2,265,000	13.25
CAT-3	Satellite communications link	-750,000	842,250	12.30
BIO-1	Multimedia computer network	-900,000	1,080,000	20.00
BIO-2	Photo-electric gene splicer	-1,200,000	1,410,000	17.50
BIO-3	Digital-sequencing software	-500,000	577,500	15.50

cash flows. They also may be able to determine their projects' betas and required rates of return, although these calculations may be performed by specialists at the corporate level. Managers at any level can perform the third step, computing projects' NPVs. We'll use the Double-Felix Manufacturing Company to illustrate this process.

The board of directors of the Double-Felix Manufacturing Company is planning the company's capital expenditures for 1998. The company has two divisions, cat food and bio-engineering. Experts on the chief financial officer's staff determined that the cat food division's beta is 0.80 and the bio-engineering division's beta is 1.30. In addition, they determined that the riskless rate of interest is 5.5 percent and the expected rate of return on the market portfolio is 14.0 percent. The CFO distributed these data to the division managers with instructions to analyze their own investment opportunities and forward those that meet their opportunity costs to the board for final approval.

Table 6.3 describes the investment proposals under consideration in each division. Each project's expected rate of return equals $(CF_1 - CF_0)/CF_0$. For example, CAT-1's expected rate of return is $(\$1,140,000 - \$1,000,000)/\$1,000,000 = 0.14$ or 14 percent. The division managers must evaluate these projects using CAPM opportunity costs or required rates of return (computed below).

$$r_{\text{cat food}} = 5.5\% + (14.0\% - 5.5\%) \times 0.80 = 12.30\%$$
$$r_{\text{bio-engineering}} = 5.5\% + (14.0\% - 5.5\%) \times 1.30 = 16.55\%$$

Using his opportunity cost of 12.30 percent, the manager of the cat food division determines the net present value of his investment opportunities are:

NPV of CAT-1 = $-1,000,000 + \$1,140,000/1.1230 = \$15,138$

NPV of CAT-2 = $-2,000,000 + \$2,265,000/1.1230 = \$16,919$

NPV of CAT-3 = $-750,000 + \$842,250/1.1230 = \$0$.

CAT-1 and CAT-2 have positive net present values at the division's opportunity cost of 12.30 percent, so the division manager forwards them to the board of directors for final approval. He *could* request approval of CAT-3 because it exactly covers its oppor-

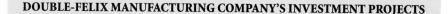

Exhibit 6.5

DOUBLE-FELIX MANUFACTURING COMPANY'S INVESTMENT PROJECTS

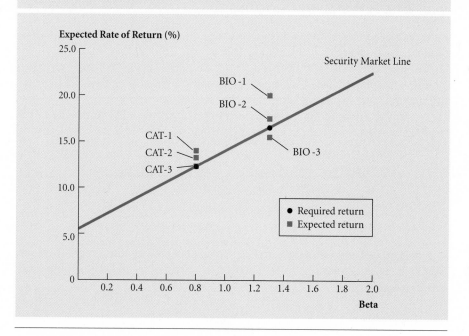

tunity cost. This, however, would be pointless because, with an NPV of zero, CAT-3 neither adds to nor subtracts from the owners' wealth.

The manager of the bio-engineering division performs a similar analysis using her opportunity cost of 16.55 percent. The results are

$$\text{NPV of BIO-1} = \${-}900{,}000 + \$1{,}080{,}000/1.1655 = \$26{,}641$$
$$\text{NPV of BIO-2} = \${-}1{,}200{,}000 + \$1{,}410{,}000/1.1655 = \$9{,}781$$
$$\text{NPV of BIO-3} = \${-}500{,}000 + \$577{,}500/1.1655 = \${-}4{,}505.$$

The bio-engineering manager forwards BIO-1 and BIO-2 to the board for final approval because they have positive net present values at the division's opportunity cost of 16.55 percent. She drops BIO-3 from further consideration, however, because it has a negative net present value and does not meet its opportunity cost.

Exhibit 6.5 describes these results by associating the investment projects with the Security Market Line (SML). Each project is plotted as a point with its beta and expected rate of return as coordinates. CAT-1, CAT-2, BIO-1, and BIO-2 plot above the line because their expected rates of return exceed the opportunity cost for investments with similar amounts of risk. This explains why these projects have positive NPVs and are acceptable investments. BIO-3 plots below the SML because its expected rate of return is less than its opportunity cost, which is why it has a negative NPV and is unacceptable. CAT-3 plots on the SML, indicating it exactly meets its opportunity cost and therefore has an NPV of zero.

EXERCISE

6.7

USING THE CAPM REQUIRED RATE OF RETURN IN INVESTMENT DECISIONS

An eccentric member of Double-Felix's board of directors proposes that the company produce genetically engineered cat food. His research indicates this project will require an investment of $5,000,000 and produce free cash flows of $650,000 per year in perpetuity. If this project's beta is a simple average of the betas of its cat food and bio-engineering divisions, should the other members of the board approve it?

To answer this question, compute the project's beta, use it to calculate its CAPM required rate of return, and discount its future free cash flows at this rate to determine its NPV.

$$\beta_{bio/cat} = 0.50 \times \beta_{cat\ food} + 0.50 \times \beta_{bio\text{-}engineering}$$
$$= 0.50 \times 0.80 + 0.50 \times 1.30 = 1.05$$
$$r_{bio/cat} = 5.5\% + (14.0\% - 5.5\%) \times \beta_{bio/cat}$$
$$= 5.5\% + (14.0\% - 5.5\%) \times 1.05 = 14.425\%$$

This project is a perpetuity, so the present value of its future free cash flows equals the annual amount of these cash flows divided by the opportunity cost. Therefore, its NPV is

$$\text{NPV} = CF_0 + CF_1/r_{bio/cat}$$
$$\text{NPV of bio/cat} = \$-5,000,000 + \$650,000/0.14425$$
$$= \$-493,934.14.$$

No, Double-Felix should not adopt the board member's proposal because producing genetically engineered cat food does not cover its opportunity cost.

You learned in Chapter 3 that financial market imperfections cause problems for the separation of ownership and control and decentralized investment decision making. Unfortunately, the same problems can arise here.

Suppose once again that the interest rate for borrowing money exceeds the interest rate for lending money. Then cautious stockholders, who expect to buy the riskless asset to reduce their risk, will want the company to use the lending rate of interest in the asset pricing model to compute investments' opportunity costs. More aggressive stockholders, who expect to borrow money to increase their rate of return, will want the company to use the borrowing rate of interest in the asset pricing model to compute opportunity costs. Managers may be unable to choose an investment alternative that will please everyone in this situation.

6.6 SUMMARY

Investors manage risk by allocating part of their wealth to a risky portfolio and the remainder to the riskless asset or by borrowing to increase their investment in the risky portfolio. The first strategy reduces their risk and return and the second increases them.

Allocation permits investors to construct combinations of return and risk not previously available. Investors can thereby use an efficient portfolio to construct a personal portfolio that meets their preferences about return and risk.

Asset pricing models provide a theoretical description of the market-wide relationship between expected rate of return and risk. Both the Capital Asset Pricing Model and the Arbitrage Pricing Theory assume investors only care about systematic risk because they hold well-diversified portfolios. The CAPM assumes there is only one source of systematic risk—represented by the market portfolio—while the APT permits many. Both models also assume that investors can costlessly buy and sell the safe asset and risky portfolios until there is a linear relationship between expected return and systematic risk. The detailed assumptions they use to reach this conclusion are quite different, but the results are similar. The CAPM is easier to understand and apply and therefore has been more widely used. Neither model has been conclusively supported by empirical tests, however, so you can expect further developments in the future.

Although not flawless, asset pricing models are used to support the separation of ownership and control and decentralized decision making. Delegation is accomplished by requiring the agent to discount an investment proposal's free cash flows using an estimate of the market-wide expected rate of return given the proposal's risk. The agent should accept proposals with positive NPVs because they provide a higher rate of return for their risk than the principal can obtain elsewhere. We will discuss ways to compensate for the problems caused by financial market imperfections and principal–agent conflicts as we proceed through the book.

- ## KEY TERMS

Allocation   *231*

Asset pricing models   *236*

Capital Asset Pricing Model
   (CAPM)   *236*

Security Market Line
   (SML)   *236*

Arbitrage Pricing Theory
   (APT)   *241*

- ## QUESTIONS AND PROBLEMS

1. Portfolio diversification is a powerful risk management technique but it has limitations.

   (a) What is the limitation of portfolio diversification from the viewpoint of extremely cautious investors? From the viewpoint of very ambitious investors?

   (b) How does the opportunity to allocate wealth between a risky portfolio and a safe asset, such as U.S. Treasury bills, overcome the limitations of portfolio diversification for both types of investors mentioned in part (a)?

2. Financial planners often recommend that young people allocate most of their retirement savings to common stocks and gradually increase the proportion of safe assets in their portfolios as they near retirement age. Carefully explain the reasoning behind this advice. You may find it helpful to refer to Exhibit 6.1 in your answer.

3. Joe Clayburn has an MBA degree and works as an independent investment advisor and portfolio manager. Joe's undergraduate degree was in resort management, so his focus is on the hotel and casino industry (SIC 7000) because he understands the business. He has managed

to completely diversify his portfolio even though it only contains stocks issued by companies in this industry.

(a) The hotel and casino industry is more risky than average. The January 1996 issue of Value Line Publishing Inc.'s ValueScreen III reported that the industry's average beta is 1.34. Has Joe unnecessarily limited the potential market for his investment advisory and portfolio management services by following only this high-risk industry? Explain your answer.

(b) How can cautious investors profit from Joe's expertise in the hotel and casino industry without being exposed to an unacceptable level of risk?

4. Refer to the efficient set of risky portfolios plotted in the following graph to answer this question.

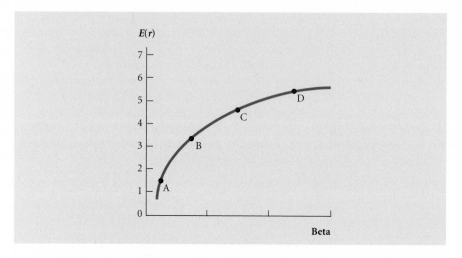

(a) Assume the portfolios in this efficient set are the only investments available (there is no riskless asset). Is there a single risky portfolio that will satisfy every risk-averse investor? If your answer is yes, identify the portfolio and explain why it is best. If your answer is no, explain why.

(b) Can owners delegate the investment decision to professional managers when there is no riskless asset? Explain your answer.

(c) Rework parts (a) and (b) assuming there is a riskless asset and its rate of return is 3.0 percent.

5. One of the Capital Asset Pricing Model's fundamental results is that anyone can construct a portfolio with the preferred amount of return and risk by allocating his wealth between only two investments: a riskless asset and the market portfolio.

(a) Exactly what is the market portfolio?

(b) What assumptions lead to the conclusion that the market portfolio is the only risky asset investors need to consider when deciding how to allocate their wealth?

(c) Can investors actually buy and sell the true market portfolio or only a proxy? Explain your answer.

6. Cathy Worker has an individual retirement account (IRA) that is invested in a portfolio with a beta of 1.5. Cathy is nearing retirement age and would like to reduce the risk of her retire-

ment savings to a beta of 0.75. Investing the IRA in a different portfolio is not an attractive alternative because she would have to fill out a lot of forms, pay some fees, and, if she's not careful, pay taxes. Describe how Cathy can reduce her risk without disturbing the IRA.

7. The expected rates of return and standard deviations of return of four assets are given below.

Asset	$E(r)$	$\sigma(r)$
A	10%	22%
B	18	34
C	16	30
D	6	0

   (a) Which is better, asset C or a portfolio that is 25 percent asset A and 75 percent asset B if the correlation between A and B is +1.0?

   (b) Which is better, asset C or a portfolio that is 25 percent asset A and 75 percent asset B if the correlation between A and B is +0.55?

   (c) Which is better: invest all your money in asset A or invest 40 percent of your money in the portfolio described in part (b) and the remainder in asset D?

   (d) Describe the risk management techniques illustrated by this problem.

8. Mycroft Holmes operates a consulting business and maintains a $100,000 portfolio as a form of disability self-insurance. The company that manages this money for him has invested it in a portfolio with a beta of 0.90. Last year's return on the portfolio, net of the management company's fee, was 12.5 percent.

   (a) Mycroft may manage the portfolio himself. How much of the $100,000 should he allocate to the market portfolio and how much to U.S. Treasury bills if he is satisfied with the portfolio's current level of risk?

   (b) Suppose Treasury bills and the market portfolio earned 6 percent and 14.5 percent last year. Should Mycroft be pleased or disappointed with the performance of his professional money managers?

9. Jake Smart manages a $12,000,000 retirement fund on behalf of the members of a local electricians' union. The older members, who were children during the Great Depression, are conservative and want their funds invested at low risk. The younger members are more concerned that their funds earn a high rate of return.

   (a) How can Jake satisfy the wide range of preferences among the union members without dividing their funds among an impractical number of different investments?

   (b) Suppose Jake decides to offer the members the opportunity to allocate their individual retirement funds between U.S. Treasury bills, which earn 5.0 percent, and a well-diversified common stock portfolio that has an expected rate of return of 14 percent. How much money should Jake advise Theodore Minelli and Shawn Robbins to allocate to each investment?

   Theodore Minnelli is 61, has $200,000 of retirement funds, and prefers portfolio risk equal to only 20 percent of the market average.
   Shawn Robbins is 26, has $30,000 of retirement funds, and prefers a portfolio expected rate of return of 125 percent of the market average.

10. Your wealthy aunt has a portfolio with an expected rate of return of 12 percent and a standard deviation of return of 25 percent. She is satisfied with the rate of return but will not

accept any additional risk. As her financial advisor, you have a challenging problem. You want to help her earn a high rate of return on her portfolio (because you'll probably inherit it), but you must maintain her confidence.

(a) Show her what a great financial advisor you are by using her existing portfolio and the two assets described below to construct a portfolio with a higher rate of return and less risk than her existing portfolio. You may use the assets in any combination you choose— but you must use all three.

	Asset A	Asset B
Expected rate of return	16.0%	8.0%
Standard deviation of return	40.0	0.0
Correlation with aunt's portfolio	0.35	0.0

(b) Explain to your aunt the financial principles you used to perform this seemingly impossible feat. Use simple, intuitive terms—she won't understand technical terms.

11. The Security Market Line (SML) is an equation that describes the rates of return the financial market expects of assets given their risks. What does that have to do with the *pricing* of assets as the name Capital Asset Pricing Model (CAPM) implies?

12. The investment committee of Hawthorne Holdings is fielding questions from the company's division managers. The manager of the electronic division angrily inquires why one of his proposals, with an expected rate of return of 18 percent, was rejected while a proposal from the food-processing division, with an expected rate of return of only 13 percent, was accepted. How should the committee respond?

13. Mother May I Corporation produces action figures associated with popular motion pictures. The producers of a forthcoming animated movie about the U.S. revolutionary war have offered the company the rights to produce and sell figures of George Washington, Ben Franklin, Paul Revere, Betsy Ross, and the like. Mother May I must pay $3.0 million for the rights to the figures and invest an additional $4.4 million for design, tooling, and molds. One year later, the company expects to receive a net cash flow of $9.6 million when they sell the figures to a major toy store chain. Should the company buy the rights to produce these figures if the beta of this project is 1.4, the risk-free rate of return is 4 percent, and the expected rate of return on the market index is 12.5 percent? Explain your answer.

14. Consider the investment opportunities described below.

	Beta	$E(r)$
Jelly Roll's	1.20	14.0%
Angels Unlimited	1.00	11.5
Video Viper	0.95	11.0
Shoe Lacers	0.70	9.0

(a) Plot these investments on the Security Market Line given $r_f = 3.5$ percent and $r_m = 11.5$ percent.

(b) Which of the investments are overpriced? Which have a positive NPV when their cash flows are discounted at the CAPM required rate of return? Explain your reasoning.

15. Viola Albina's niece asked her to invest $6,000 to produce cedar bird feeders. The pair will sell the bird feeders in one year and Viola's expected share of the free cash flows is $8,120.

(a) Determine the present value of the future cash flow and the net present value of the project if its beta is 1.2, the rate of return on U.S. Treasury bills is 4.0 percent, and the expected rate of return on the market portfolio is 14.0 percent. Should Viola help her niece?

(b) Viola really wants to help her niece with this project, but she is very conservative and prefers a personal portfolio beta of only 0.30. How much money must she allocate to U.S. Treasury bills to reach this risk target if she invests $6,000 in the bird feeder project?

(c) Determine the net cash flows at time 0 and time 1 for Viola's personal portfolio.

(d) Determine the CAPM required rate of return and NPV of Viola's personal portfolio. (Remember, the portfolio's beta is 0.30 by design.) Did Viola lose any value by using Treasury bills to make the risk of the birdhouse project acceptable to her? Explain your answer.

16. Carl K. Lutz is an ambitious investor who chooses stocks that provide high rates of return for his well-diversified portfolio. One of his favorite stocks is GenuineGene, a bio-tech company that tries to perfectly replicate specific plant genes. GenuineGene's expected rate of return is 24.0 percent, which is exactly the rate of return the financial market requires given its beta of 2.0 and current Treasury-bill and market index rates of return of 6.0 percent and 15.0 percent. Carl owns $100,000 of GenuineGene common stock.

The company just announced it will adopt less risky investment and financing strategies to reduce its beta from 2.0 to 1.5. Carl's initial reaction is disappointment because he believes in the company's future, but it will no longer meet his rate of return objectives. Subsequently, he remembers that he can borrow money at the riskless rate of return and invest it in GenuineGene to magnify the rate of return he earns on his own $100,000.

(a) How much money must Carl borrow and add to his own investment in GenuineGene to earn a 24 percent rate of return on his original $100,000?

(b) Describe the connection between the type of transaction Carl performed and managers' ability to make investment, operating, and financing decisions without considering the owners' preferences for risk and return.

17. Ben and Joyce Jacobean are antique dealers attending an estate sale to buy jewelry. They believe they can resell the jewelry at an upscale flea market next year for approximately $100,000, but the antique business is very cyclical with a beta of approximately 1.40.

(a) What is the maximum amount they can bid for these items if U.S. Treasury bills earn 5.0 percent and the market's *risk premium* is 8.7 percent?

(b) What is the NPV if they can buy the jewelry for only $80,000?

18. Several landscape companies have an opportunity to bid on 500 young fruit trees from an orchard that will be inundated by a new flood control reservoir in 15 months. The buyer must pay the orchard for the trees immediately but may leave them in place for 12 months. Then, the trees will be balled and burlapped and sold for an expected price of $40 per tree, net of all expenses. The beta of this investment project is 1.30, the rate of return on Treasury bills is 4.0 percent, and the expected rate of return on the S&P 500 index is 13.0 percent.

(a) Determine the CAPM required rate of return for this investment project.

(b) The opening bid was $16,000, which provides an expected rate of return of 25 percent and an NPV at the CAPM required rate of return of $1,286. This bid is associated with the Security Market Line in the chart below. The second and third bids were for $16,750 and $17,000. Determine the expected rate of return and NPVs of these bids and plot them on the chart.

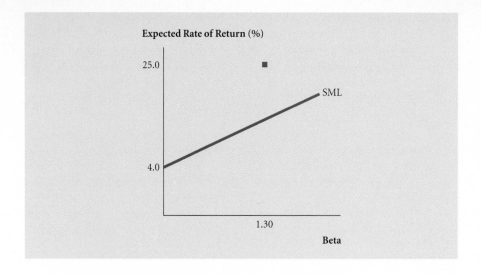

(c) What is the maximum amount the landscape companies can bid for the fruit trees? Plot this bid on the chart.

(d) Given the sequence of bids in this auction, where would you expect assets that are traded in open, competitive markets to plot relative to the Security Market Line? Explain your reasoning.

19. Tri-Corp, Inc., is planning its capital expenditures for the current year. The company has three operating divisions with the characteristics described below.

Division	Beta
Office equipment	1.00
Commuter airline	1.25
Real estate development	1.50

(a) Determine the CAPM required rate of return for each division if $r_f = 6.0$ percent and $E(r_m) = 14.0$ percent.

(b) Tri-Corp's division managers have submitted the following investment proposals to the company's investment committee for approval. Which should be approved and denied? Explain your recommendation.

	NPV (in millions) at:		
Proposal	14.0%	16.0%	18.0%
Build new shopping center	$6.5	$ 2.7	$ – 0.9
Develop fax/scanner	1.9	0.8	.3
Initiate air service between Tulsa and Dallas	0.8	– 0.2	– 1.2

20. Robertson Realty uses the APT to determine the required rate of return on its commercial properties. The company is developing a shopping center near a major interstate highway

and has determined its rate of return is sensitive to both unexpected changes in interest rates and unemployment. These sensitivities are represented by betas of 1.05 and 1.2.

(a) Determine the shopping center's APT required rate of return if the market-wide expected rate of return for portfolios with no systematic risk is 6.0 percent and the expected rates of return for portfolios with sensitivity to only interest rates and unemployment are 8.0 percent and 11.0 percent.

(b) The shopping center will be ready for occupancy in one year. Robertson expects to sell the property then and hopes to receive $11,000,000. What is its present market value?

● ADDITIONAL READING

An early but nevertheless still very good introduction to portfolio diversification and the CAPM is:

Franco Modigliani and Gerald A. Pogue, "An Introduction to Risk and Return, Concepts and Evidence," *Financial Analysts Journal*, March/April 1974, pp. 68–80 and May/June 1974, pp. 69–86.

Advanced textbooks on portfolio diversification and asset pricing include:

Gordon J. Alexander and Jack Clark Francis, *Portfolio Analysis*, Prentice-Hall, Englewood Cliffs, New Jersey, 1986.

Edwin J. Elton and Martin J. Gruber, *Modern Portfolio Theory and Investment Management*, John Wiley and Sons, New York, 1991.

Haim Levy and Marshall Sarnat, *Portfolio and Investment Selection: Theory and Practice*, Prentice-Hall International, Englewood Cliffs, New Jersey, 1984.

VALUING DEBT AND EQUITY

*T*he *Wall Street Journal* reports the prices of thousands of financial instruments every day. Among the prices included in its August 19, 1996, edition were the ones listed in Table 7.1. At first glance, these prices may appear to be incomprehensible, but they aren't. You actually can apply the fundamental financial valuation principles you studied in Chapters 2 through 6 to understand them.

We will build your understanding of market prices by developing valuation models that integrate what you learned about cash flows, the time value of money, and required rates of return. Then, we will use these models to estimate the market prices of each financial instrument in Table 7.1. We will not estimate these market prices without error, but you may be surprised at the accuracy of the estimates.

Company and business unit managers, investors, and the managers of financial institutions must understand how the financial market values financial instruments. The reason is simple: At one time or another, each of these parties buys or sells financial instruments and cannot be certain they pay or receive a fair price unless they know how prices are determined. Managers of corporations must understand how securities are priced to ensure their company receives the proper amount of financing from investors in return for the company's promise to pay future interest or dividends. Investors must understand how securities are valued to determine the proper price to pay for a company's debt or equity. Managers of financial institutions must understand how financial instruments are priced to determine a loan's value.

Managers and investors must know something about the valuation process even if they obtain price estimates from experts such as investment bankers or securities analysts. After all, they cannot monitor—let alone discipline—these experts to control agency costs if they do not understand the basis for their estimates.

Managers and investors also must know something about the valuation of financial instruments even if their securities are traded in competitive markets. Market prices reflect available information and change in response to new information. Managers who are the first to obtain new information can profit for their company's benefit by making financing and investment decisions in anticipation of the market's reaction. Investors can do the same for themselves. Managers and investors must understand how

Table 7.1   MARKET PRICES OF VARIOUS SECURITIES (AUGUST 16, 1996)

	Term to Maturity	Agency Rating of Company's Bonds*	Par Value	Market Price**
U.S. Treasury Bonds, Notes, and Bills				
Bill due November 21, 1996	93 days	NA	$10,000	$ 9,870.058
Bill due August 21, 1997	366 days	NA	10,000	9,461.167
9.25% note due August 1998	2 years	NA	10,000	10,609.375
4.75% note due August 1998	2 years	NA	10,000	9,771.875
6.25% note due August 2000	4 years	NA	10,000	10,000.000
U.S. Government Agency				
7.85% Federal National Mortgage Association (FNMA) bond due September 1998	25 months	NA	10,000	10,334.375
Corporate Bonds				
BellSouth Telecommunications 6.50% note due 2000	4 years	AAA	1,000	1,000.00
Best Buy Company 8.625% note due 2000	4 years	B	1,000	980.00
Preferred Stock				
Public Service Electric and Gas Company 4.08%		A–	100	55.00
Ohio Edison Company 4.44%		BBB–	100	57.50
Common Stock				
The Quaker Oats Company				34.00
The J. M. Smucker Company				17.25

Standard & Poor's Bond Guide, August 1996, various pages.

**The Wall Street Journal*, August 19, 1996, various pages.

the market values the new information, however, to correctly anticipate the new market price.

    Finally, managers must understand valuation to fully comprehend the financial market's reaction to their decisions. Knowledgeable managers are more likely to make decisions that meet market-wide performance standards that make more financial resources available to their company. The resulting opportunities to improve or expand their business is beneficial to the managers, the company's owners, and the entire economy.

    This chapter provides discounted cash flow models that managers and investors can use to value debt, preferred stock, and equity. These models are straightforward applications of the principles introduced in Chapters 2 through 6; a security's market price is estimated as the present value of its future cash flows using a discount rate that is appropriate for its risk. Some valuation models are simple and others are more complicated, but they are all fundamentally based on discounted cash flows. In fact, you will see that some of the models we'll use are identical to ones developed in Chapter 3 even though they were not used to value securities there.

We'll begin with the simplest models used to value a company's debt and preferred stock. We can use simple present value formulas from Chapter 3 to value these securities because creditors and preferred stockholders have a fixed claim on a company's cash flows. Next, we'll examine more complicated models used to value a company's equity. These models are more complicated because common stock dividends can vary from one year to the next. Finally, we will discuss the procedures securities analysts use to predict stock prices.

As you study this chapter, please keep in mind that its objective is to describe how the financial market values financial instruments—not to prepare you for trading bonds and stocks on Wall Street. Consequently, we can tolerate some errors in estimating the market values of the securities in Table 7.1 *if you learn something from these errors*. If you intend to trade bonds and stocks, you will need more training and experience than you can get from this chapter or from a single chapter of *any* finance textbook.

7.1   VALUING DEBT AND PREFERRED STOCK

The market value of a debt instrument such as a U.S. Treasury bill or note, a corporate bond, or a loan is determined by discounting each of its future interest and principal payments at a required rate of return that is appropriate for its term to maturity and risk. For U.S. Treasury securities, we obtain the required rate of return directly from the term structure as described in Chapter 4. The required rate of return we use to discount the cash flows from other fixed-income financial instruments must be larger to account for differences in marketability, default risk, and special features such as callability.

We first will use our valuation models to determine the market prices of U.S. Treasury securities because we can simply look up the required rates of return that apply to them. These rates are the yields on U.S. Treasury strips that are reported in *The Wall Street Journal*. We want to explain the August 16, 1996 market prices of the securities listed in Table 7.1 so we will use the yields on U.S. Treasury strips that prevailed on that day. These rates are given in Table 7.2. Subsequently, we will apply these rates of return to the government agency and corporate bonds in Table 7.1 so you can see the effect of the missing yield premiums.

Pure-Discount Instruments

The simplest security to value is a **pure-discount instrument** or **zero-coupon bond**. These securities are issued at a discount from face value to provide the investor with implicit interest income in lieu of explicit interest payments. U.S. Treasury bills and Treasury strips are examples of pure-discount instruments.[1] The amount of the discount from face value depends on the security's term to maturity and the market's required

---

[1]U.S. Treasury strips, which we discussed in Section 4.3 of Chapter 4, are Treasury notes that have been stripped of their periodic interest payments, leaving only the principal payments.

Table 7.2   **YIELDS ON U.S. TREASURY STRIPS (AUGUST 16, 1996)**

Maturity Date	Term to Maturity	Yield
November 1996	3 months	5.21%
February 1997	6 months	5.41
May 1997	9 months	5.53
August 1997	1 year	5.64
August 1998	2 years	5.95
August 1999	3 years	6.14
August 2000	4 years	6.25
February 2026	30 years*	6.68

*Actually, 29.75 years.

Source: *The Wall Street Journal*, August 19, 1996, p. C15.

rate of return for bonds with the same risk. We can easily derive an equation for the discount and use it to solve for a bond's price. The result will be very familiar to you.

For simplicity, let's assume an investor wants to determine the market price of a one-period, zero-coupon bond with a par value of P given a market interest rate of r_d per period. This investor will expect to buy the bond at a price, B, that is discounted from its face value exactly enough to provide implicit interest at the market interest rate on her investment of B. That is,

$$\text{Required discount} = \text{Interest income}$$

In symbols,

$$P - B = B \times r_d.$$

Solving this equation for the price of the bond gives

$$B = P/(1 + r_d) \tag{7.1}$$

where B = bond's price or market value
                P = bond's par value
                r_d = spot market interest rate for pure-discount bonds with the same risk and term to maturity.

You undoubtedly recognize this expression for the price of a one-year, zero-coupon bond as the present value of its future cash flow discounted at the market rate of interest. We'll use this model to explain the prices of U.S. Treasury bills in Table 7.1 shortly, but you must understand how the prices of U.S. Treasury securities are quoted before we can proceed.

The prices of U.S. Treasury bills are reported as a percentage discount from face value. For example, on August 16, 1996, bond dealers were offering to sell the 93-day bill described in Table 7.1 at a discount of 5.03 percent. This discount is computed using the following formula:

$$d = \frac{\text{Face value} - \text{Ask price}}{\text{Face value}} \times \frac{360 \text{ days}}{\text{Term to maturity}} \quad .$$

Rearranging this equation to solve for the asking price,

$$\text{Ask price} = \text{Face value} \times \left[1 - \frac{d \times \text{ Term to maturity}}{360}\right].$$

Substituting the values for the 93-day T-bill,

$$\text{Ask price} = \$10,000 \times [1 - (0.0503 \times 93)/360]$$
$$= \$9,870.058.$$

The dealers' asking price, \$9,870.058, on August 16 was used to represent the 93-day Treasury bill's market price in Table 7.1.

● ——————————————————————————————— ●   EXERCISE

ESTIMATING THE MARKET VALUE OF A T-BILL   7.1

On August 16, 1996, dealers were offering to sell the 366-day T-bill at a discount of 5.30 percent. What was the asking price?

$$\text{Ask price} = \text{Face value} \times \left[1 - \frac{d \times \text{ Term to maturity}}{360}\right]$$
$$= \$10,000 \times [1 - (0.0530 \times 366)/360]$$
$$= \$9,461.167$$

Dealers were asking \$9,461.167 for each T-bill, as shown in Table 7.1.

● ——————— ●

Now we can estimate the 93-day T-bill's market value and compare the result to its actual market price. The Treasury bill's par value is \$10,000 and the spot interest rate for three-month riskless debt on August 16, 1996 (from Table 7.2) was 5.21 percent per year. The discount rate for three months is therefore 1.303 percent (5.21 percent/4). Assuming the yield on a three-month T-bill also applies to one with 93 days until maturity, our estimate of the T-bill's market value is

$$B = P/(1 + r_f)$$
$$= \$10,000/(1.01303) = \$9,871.38.$$

Our estimate is greater than the market price of \$9,870.058 by only \$1.322, a difference of only 0.013 percent.

● ——————————————————————————————— ●   EXERCISE

ESTIMATING THE VALUE OF A PURE-DISCOUNT BOND   7.2

The treasurer of Flight-of-Fancy Travel Service intends to invest the company's surplus cash in the 366-day T-bill shown in Table 7.1. Is the dealers' asking price a fair one given the spot interest rate on one-year riskless debt shown in Table 7.2?

$$B = P/(1 + r_f)$$
$$= \$10,000/(1.0564) = \$9,466.11$$

Yes, the dealers' asking price, $9,461.167, is less than the treasurer's estimate of the Treasury bill's market value by only $4.943 or −0.05 percent.

● ——————— ●

You also can compare the yield on the 366-day T-bill to the spot interest rate on one-year riskless debt to determine if it's correctly priced. The calculation is

$$\text{Yield} = \frac{\text{Par value}}{\text{Market price}} - 1$$

$$= \frac{\$10,000}{\$9,461.167} - 1 = 0.0569 \text{ or } 5.69\%.$$

As we should expect, this yield is very close to 5.64 percent.

Coupon Bonds

Ordinary U.S. Treasury notes and bonds, U.S. government agency bonds, and corporate bonds are familiar examples of interest-bearing financial instruments. Coupon bonds are interest-bearing instruments that pay periodic interest, usually every six months, until the principal is repaid at maturity. The amount of the interest payment is determined by the bond's coupon rate, which is fixed when it is issued. The 9.25 percent U.S. Treasury note due August 1998 shown in Table 7.1 is an example. This note pays $925 of interest each year in semi-annual installments of $462.50 and repays the investor's $10,000 principal in August 1998.

We should recognize that interest is paid semi-annually when we estimate the value of a coupon bond, however, for simplicity, we will assume it is paid once a year. Given this simplification, the cash flows provided by the August 1998 U.S. Treasury note are

Date	Cash Flow
August 1997	$ 925
August 1998	10,925

Think about this note carefully and you will see that it comprises two pure-discount notes; the first pays $925 at the end of year 1 and the second pays $10,925 at the end of year 2. The financial market views interest-bearing notes and bonds this way rather than as a single financial instrument. In fact, Treasury strips were created just so investors can hold or trade these components separately.

A coupon instrument is easy to value once you recognize it as a collection of pure-discount bonds. You merely apply Equation 7.1, with the discount factor raised to the appropriate power, to each periodic payment and add the results. For a two-year coupon bond, the equation is

$$B = \text{Interest}/(1 + r_1) + (\text{Interest} + \text{Principal})/(1 + r_2)^2. \qquad [7.2]$$

Using the spot yields on one- and two-year riskless debt given in Table 7.2, the estimated market value of the 9.25 percent U.S. Treasury note is

$$B = \$925/(1.0564) + \$10{,}925/(1.0595)^2$$
$$= \$10{,}608.01.$$

The estimated value is less than the note's market price of $10,609.375 by only $1.365, a difference of 0.013 percent.

This note is worth more than its par value of $10,000 because its coupon rate of 9.25 percent is greater than the current spot market interest rates of 5.64 percent and 5.95 percent. Investors have bid up the price in pursuit of these higher than necessary interest payments. At a price of $10,608.01, investors earn the market rates of 5.64 percent on the amount invested for one year and 5.95 percent on the amount invested for the entire two years.

● ─────────────────────────────────────── ●   EXERCISE

ESTIMATING THE VALUE OF A COUPON BOND   7.3

Use the yields in Table 7.2 to estimate the market value of the 4.75 percent U.S. Treasury note that is due in August 1998. Assume interest is paid annually. This note provides cash flows of $450 and $10,450 in years 1 and 2. Therefore, its present value (estimated market value) is

$$B = \frac{\$475}{(1.0564)} + \frac{\$10{,}475}{(1.0595)^2} = \$9{,}781.15.$$

The estimate is close to the actual market price of $9,771.875.

● ───────── ●

The 4.75 percent Treasury note in Exercise 7.3 is worth less than its par value of $10,000 because its coupon interest rate is *less* than the current spot market yields of 5.64 percent and 5.95 percent. Investors have driven down the price of this bond so that they actually earn the prevailing yield on their investment.

We can use a bond's market price and future cash flows to compute its internal rate of return. The result, the **yield to maturity**, is a single interest rate that summarizes the rate of return on the bond over its entire life. You can probably guess that the 9.25 percent Treasury note's yield to maturity will be close to 5.95 percent because this note's largest component part is a two-year, pure-discount bond with this yield. Solving for the bond's IRR or yield to maturity (YTM) confirms this conjecture.

$$\$10{,}609.375 = \frac{\$925}{(1 + \text{YTM})} + \frac{\$10{,}925}{(1 + \text{YTM})^2} \qquad [7.3]$$

$$\$0 = \$-10{,}609.375 + \frac{\$925}{(1 + \text{YTM})} + \frac{\$10{,}925}{(1 + \text{YTM})^2}$$

By trial and error or by using a financial calculator or spreadsheet, the yield to maturity is 5.93 percent—very close to the yield on two-year bonds.

EXERCISE ● ─── ●

7.4   DETERMINING THE YIELD TO MATURITY

Determine the yield to maturity of the 4.75 percent U.S. Treasury note due in August 1998.

First, set the dealers' asking price equal to the present value of the note's future cash flows:

$$\$9,771.875 = \frac{\$475}{(1 + \text{YTM})} + \frac{\$10,475}{(1 + \text{YTM})^2}$$

$$\$0 = \$-9,771.875 + \frac{\$475}{(1 + \text{YTM})} + \frac{\$10,475}{(1 + \text{YTM})^2}$$

Next, solve for the YTM by trial and error, or by using a financial calculator or spreadsheet. The answer should be close to 5.95 percent—and it is. The yield to maturity of this note is 5.99 percent.

● ─────────── ●

If you compare Equations 7.2 and 7.3, you may be tempted to conclude it is easier to value a coupon bond by discounting its future cash flows at the yield to maturity. After all, this approach requires only a single interest rate and you can use an annuity present value factor and an ordinary present value factor to evaluate the periodic interest payments and principal repayment. One problem with this idea is that you don't know the yield to maturity *until* you know the price. Consequently, using the yield to maturity to determine a bond's price reverses the calculations performed to determine its yield to maturity.

You can eliminate the circularity problem by using one coupon bond's yield to maturity to value a similar bond. However, this is not a complete solution. A remaining problem is that the yield to maturity is a complicated average of the underlying spot rates. Consequently, the bond value obtained by using this average rather than the correct individual spot interest rates is wrong.

Let's use the 4.75 percent Treasury note's yield to maturity to estimate the market value of the 9.25 percent note. You'll see the estimate is not as good as the estimate we obtained using the spot rates.

$$B = \frac{\$925}{(1.0599)} + \frac{\$10,925}{(1.0599)^2} = \$10,597.77$$

This estimate is $11.61 less than the actual market price of $10,609.375. Remember, we were only off by $1.37 when we used the spot rates.

Before we leave the U.S. Treasury notes, take a look at the 6.25 percent note due in August 2000. The market price of this note equals its par value, $10,000. Can you tell why? The reason is that most of the note's cash flows occur four years in the future and the note's coupon exactly equals the Treasury strip yield for a loan with a four-year term to maturity. Estimate its market value using the yields in Table 7.2 if you need to practice one more time. Your answer should be $10,008.16.

Now it is time to consider why our estimated prices were different from the market prices represented by the bond dealers' asking prices. There are several reasons.

First, the dealers' quotations are *asking* prices—not necessarily the prices at which actual trades took place.[2] Second, the U.S. Treasury strip yields we used are measured as of 3:00 P.M. Eastern time, and the dealers' quotations are measured as of "mid-afternoon." Therefore, the yields and dealers' quotations may not apply to the same time periods. Finally, we assumed interest on notes is paid annually instead of semi-annually. Even considering these potential sources of error, our estimates were very close and should give you some confidence in using discounted cash flow models to value government bonds.

Now let's try estimating the market values of the government agency and corporate bonds listed in Table 7.1. The procedure is the same: Find the present value of each cash flow using the spot market interest rate for pure-discount bonds with the same risk and term to maturity.

You know from Chapter 4 that government agency bonds are not as marketable as Treasury bonds, so their yields must include a marketability premium. In addition, corporate bonds must provide a risk premium because there is a possibility of default. Therefore, the required rates of return for these bonds must be higher than the Treasury strip yields in Table 7.2.

We are going to apply the Treasury strip yields to our agency and corporate bonds—even though we know they are incorrect. We know in advance that our estimates of the bonds' market prices will be too high because our required rates of return are too low. The sizes of these errors will be directly related to the sizes of the yield premiums that we omit.

The estimated market price of the 7.85 percent FNMA bond due in September 1998 is

$$B_{\text{FNMA}} = \frac{\$785}{(1.0564)} + \frac{\$10,785}{(1.0595)^2} = \$10,350.76.$$

The estimated price of the 6.5 percent BellSouth bond due in 2000 is

$$B_{\text{BellSouth}} = \frac{\$65}{(1.0564)} + \frac{\$65}{(1.0595)^2} + \frac{\$65}{(1.0614)^3} + \frac{\$1,065}{(1.0625)^4} = \$1,009.46.$$

The estimated price of the 8.625 percent Best Buy bond due in 2000 is

$$B_{\text{Best Buy}} = \frac{\$86.25}{(1.0564)} + \frac{\$86.25}{(1.0595)^2} + \frac{\$86.25}{(1.0614)^3} + \frac{\$1,086.25}{(1.0625)^4} = \$1,082.95.$$

Panel A of Table 7.3 compares these estimated market values with the asking price of the FNMA bond and the actual closing prices of the two corporate bonds. We overestimated the values of all the bonds, and our errors became larger as we moved

---

[2]To see that this is an important distinction, suppose you are willing to trade your 1981 Monte Carlo for $20,000. This price is your *asking price,* but it isn't a 1981 Monte Carlo's *market price* unless you can actually make the trade for this amount.

Table 7.3   **ANALYSIS OF ERRORS FROM USING TREASURY YIELDS TO VALUE AGENCY AND CORPORATE BONDS**

Panel A: Price Comparisons

	Actual Market Price	Estimated Price Using Treasury Yields	Percentage Error
7.85% Federal National Mortgage Association (FNMA) bond due September 1998	$10,334.375	$10,350.76	0.16%
BellSouth Telecommunications 6.50% note due 2000	1,000.00	1,009.46	0.95
Best Buy Company 8.625% note due 2000	980.00	1,082.95	10.51

Panel B: Yield Comparisons

	Yield to Maturity Computed from Market Price	Yield to Maturity Computed from Estimated Price	Yield Premium in Market Prices
7.85% Federal National Mortgage Association (FNMA) bond due September 1998	6.03%	5.94%	0.09%
BellSouth Telecommunications 6.50% note due 2000	6.50	6.23	0.27
Best Buy Company 8.625% note due 2000	9.25	6.23	3.02

from the FNMA bond to the Best Buy bond. The explanation for this relationship is quite simple. By using the Treasury strip interest rates, we omitted a marketability premium from the FNMA bond and both marketability and default risk premiums from the corporate bonds. The BellSouth bond has Standard & Poor's highest rating, AAA, which means it has very little default risk.[3] That is why our additional error wasn't too large. The Best Buy bond is a speculative grade bond rated B, which means it has more default risk. Omitting its default risk premium had a significant effect

The bonds' yields to maturity, computed from their estimated prices and their actual market prices, are presented in panel B of Table 7.3. The difference between these yields is the amount of the omitted yield premium. You can see that FNMA's marketability premium was small but that Best Buy's marketability and default risk premiums were large. We will have more to say about the required rate of return that applies to a company's risky debt in Chapter 17 when we measure a particular company's cost of capital.

---

[3]See Chapter 4 to review the relationship between bond ratings and default risk.

Amortized Instruments

An amortized loan is repaid in equal periodic installments. Each installment payment is part repayment of the principal of the loan and part interest owed on the loan's outstanding balance. The amount of each payment is fixed when the loan is arranged and depends on its original principal and term to maturity and the prevailing market interest rate for loans of similar risk. Bank loans, leases, and home mortgages are familiar examples of amortized financial instruments.

Amortized instruments are annuities, but they should be valued the same way as a coupon bond. That is, the appropriate spot market interest rate should be used to discount each period's cash flow. Analysts often do not use these rates, however, and instead use the yield to maturity of a coupon bond with the same term as the loan for simplicity. This approach is illustrated in the following example.

The Producers and Farmers (P&F) Bank of Darnright, Oklahoma extended a $500,000, 5-year commercial loan at 8.5 percent interest to a local oil producer. The loan will be repaid in equal installments of $126,882.88 per year.[4] P&F Bank does not have enough capital to hold a loan this large until maturity, so they will sell it to the First National Bank of Maine (known to its depositors as ME First—only because of its U.S. Postal Service abbreviation). What price can P&F expect to receive for this loan if ME First requires a 9 percent rate of return on loans in the oil patch?

The loan is a five-year annuity so we can use an annuity present value factor to determine its present value or price.

$$\text{Price} = \$126,882.88 \times \text{APVF}_{0.09,5}$$
$$= \$126,882.88 \times 3.8897 = \$493,536.34$$

The P&F Bank can expect to sell the loan for $493,536.34.

E X E R C I S E

7.5

VALUING AN AMORTIZED LOAN

George Adams inherited some money and decided to pay off his home mortgage. His monthly payments for principal and interest are $1,200 and the interest rate on the mortgage is 7.5 percent with five years remaining in its life. What is the cost of paying off this mortgage?

The amount required to pay off Adams's mortgage is the present value of the 60 remaining monthly payments discounted at 7.5 percent per year, or 0.625 percent per month. Using the $\text{APVF}_{0.00625,60}$,

$$PV = \$1,200 \times \frac{1}{0.00625} \times \left[1 - \frac{1}{(1.00625)^{60}}\right]$$
$$= \$1,200 \times 49.9053 = \$59,886.36.$$

The difference between the total of his 60 payments, $72,000, and the amount required to pay off the loan, $59,886.36, is Adams's interest savings.

---

[4]See Section 3.4 of Chapter 3 for a review of how to amortize a loan.

Preferred Stock

A share of preferred stock has the characteristics of perpetual debt except the investor receives fixed dividend payments rather than interest. The amount of the dividend usually is stated as a percent of the stock's par value. For example, the Public Service Electric and Gas Company's preferred stock listed in Table 7.1 pays an annual dividend of $4.08, which equals 4.08 percent of its $100 par value. Some preferred stocks do not have a par value, so their dividends are directly stated in dollar terms. Preferred dividends usually are paid quarterly.

The price of a share of preferred stock is estimated by discounting its perpetual dividends. That is,

$$P = D/r_p \qquad\qquad [7.4]$$

where P = price of a share of preferred stock
D = annual dividend
r_p = required rate of return for this preferred stock.

Let's use this model to estimate the market value of Public Service Electric and Gas Company's 4.08 percent, $100 par value preferred stock. We will assume the company pays the entire $4.08 dividend annually, and we will use the 30-year Treasury strip interest rate as the required rate of return. We will overestimate the price of this stock because, as you know from our prior examples, we are omitting the marketability and risk premiums from its required rate of return. Given these simplifications, the stock's estimated market price is

$$P = D/r_p$$
$$= \$4.08/0.0668 = \$61.08.$$

The closing price of Public Service Electric and Gas Company's 4.08 percent preferred stock on August 16, 1996 was actually $55.00. Consequently, we made a $6.08 ($61.08 − $55.00) error by using the yield on 30-year Treasury strips as the required rate of return. We'll discuss this error shortly.

EXERCISE

7.6   VALUING PREFERRED STOCK

Use the yield on 30-year Treasury strips in Table 7.2 to estimate the market value of Ohio Edison Company's 4.44 percent, $100 par value bond. Assume the dividend is paid annually.

$$P = D/r_p$$
$$= \$4.44/0.0668 = \$66.47$$

The stock's actual closing price on August 16, 1996, was $57.50. Using the yield on 30-year Treasury strips as the required rate of return caused the $8.97 ($66.47 − $57.50) valuation error.

We overestimated the market value of both preferred stocks by using the yield on Treasury securities as the required rate of return. The percentage error was 11.05 percent ($6.08/$55.00) for Public Service Electric and Gas Company and 15.6 percent ($8.97/$57.50) for Ohio Edison. Do you know why the Ohio Edison error is larger? Public Service Electric and Gas Company's bonds are rated A− and Ohio Edison's are rated BBB−. Ohio Edison's bonds (and therefore its preferred stock) are riskier, so omitting the risk premium from its required rate of return had a larger effect.

You can see the same effect by calculating their dividend yield, defined as

$$r_p = \text{Dividend/Market price.}$$

Public Service Electric and Gas Company's dividend yield is 7.42 percent ($4.08/$55.00) and Ohio Edison's is 7.72 percent ($4.44/$57.50). These yields include risk premiums of 0.74 percent (7.42 percent − 6.68 percent) and 1.04 percent (7.72 percent − 6.68 percent), indicating the financial market believes Ohio Edison is riskier.

Note that both these stocks sold for less than their par values because the required rate of return is higher than it was when the stock's coupon rate was set. At their current market prices, these stocks' fixed dividends provide the rate of return the market expects.

Interest-Rate Risk

A financial instrument's market value changes when investors revise their predictions about its future cash flows or when the required rate of return changes. A change in the required rate of return is the main factor that affects the value of fixed income securities because their promised cash flows (interest and the repayment of principal or preferred dividends) are constant. We saw this effect in the preceding example: A share of preferred stock sold for less than its par value because the market's required rate of return had increased. This uncertainty about a fixed-income financial instrument's value due to variations in the required rate of return is called **interest-rate risk**.[5] All fixed-income financial instruments are subject to this risk. Even default-free government bonds are not immune as shown by the recent articles "In the News."

The amount of risk inherent in a fixed-income financial instrument depends on how long the investor must wait to receive the promised cash flows; the longer the wait, the greater the interest-rate risk. The explanation for this relationship is simple. A cash flow due in one day is discounted for the opportunity cost of just one day's interest. Consequently, there is not much change in the size of the discount factor, and therefore the present value of the next day's cash flow, when the market interest rate changes. A cash flow due in 10 years is discounted for the opportunity cost of 10 years' interest, so there is a substantial change in the discount factor when the interest rate changes. Table 7.4 illustrates the results when the interest rate doubles from 5 percent to 10 percent.

---

[5]Interest-rate risk was described as uncertainty about the effective yield on a loan in Chapter 4. These two definitions are equivalent because, given the cash flows, variations in value equal variations in yield.

IN THE NEWS

THINK TREASURY BONDS AREN'T RISKY?

FROM THE Wall Street Journal *September 16, 1996*
Bond investors bid farewell to the idea of an interest-rate increase by the Federal Reserve policymakers this month, sending Treasury prices soaring as much as 1-1/2 points Friday in their euphoria.

By late Friday, the 30-year bellwether bond had relinquished some of its earlier gain of 1-15/32 points, or $14.69 per $1,000 bond, on the day. The yield on the bond, which moves in the opposite direction to the price, fell back below the psychologically important 7 percent threshold, to 6.95 percent. Shorter-term bonds rose less than 1/2 point, but that was still enough to price out the possibility of an interest-rate increase that investors had been factoring into the yields for most of the last two months.

"I've never seen so many changes of view on what the Fed would do in such a short period of time," says Thomas Lynett, head of government-securities trading at Merrill Lynch.

From The Wall Street Journal *September 18, 1996*
Bond prices tumbled after the market changed its mind yet again about monetary policy prospects.

Sentiment—which had strongly favored no change in short-term interest rates—turned abruptly after a Reuter news-service report suggested that a majority of Federal Reserve district banks favor a rate increase. Bonds gave up nearly all of the price gains made Friday, when investors and traders had concluded that the Fed lacked compelling reasons to push rates upward. Late yesterday, the price of the benchmark 30-year Treasury bond was down nearly a point, or $9.38 for a bond with $1,000 face value, at 96-17/32.

Sources: Suzanne McGee, "Bond Prices Jump as Economic Data Suggest Rise in Interest Rates Is Unlikely," *The Wall Street Journal*, September 16, 1996, p. C1; and Jeffrey L. Hiday, "New Rate Fears, Stirred by Report on Fed Split Over an Increase, Send Bond Prices Tumbling," *The Wall Street Journal*, September 18, 1996, p. C20. Reprinted by permission of *The Wall Street Journal,* © 1996 Dow Jones & Company, Inc. All rights reserved worldwide.

Table 7.4   EFFECT OF MARKET INTEREST RATES ON SINGLE-PAYMENT DISCOUNT FACTORS

	Market Interest Rate		
	5%	10%	Percentage Change
One-day discount factor	0.9999	0.9997	−0.02%
Ten-year discount factor	0.6139	0.3855	−37.20

INTEREST-RATE RISK OF ONE- AND FIVE-YEAR   **Table 7.5**
$10,000 PURE-DISCOUNT BONDS

	Price	
Market Interest Rate	**1-Year Bond**	**5-Year Bond**
7%	$9,346	$7,130
9	9,174	6,499
11	9,009	5,935
Average price	9,176	6,521
Measures of price variability		
Standard deviation	138	488
Coefficient of variation	0.0150	0.0748

Table 7.5 illustrates the relationship between term to maturity and interest rate risk for one- and five-year pure-discount bonds. Two measures of price variability are calculated there, the standard deviation of price and the coefficient of variation of price, which equals the standard deviation divided by the average price. Both measures reveal that the one-year bond's value is less sensitive to changes in interest rates. Therefore, the one-year bond has less interest rate risk.

A security's term to maturity provides a good indication of its interest rate risk, but the relationship is a little more complicated for an amortized or interest-bearing financial instrument because these instruments provide intermediate payments of principal and interest. The present values of these nearby cash flows are less sensitive to changes in the market rate of interest than the terminal cash flow of a pure-discount bond with the same term to maturity. Consequently, amortized instruments have less interest rate risk than coupon bonds and coupon bonds have less interest-rate risk than pure-discount bonds of the same maturity. Table 7.6 illustrates these relationships.

Another way to think about these differences in interest-rate risk is that intermediate cash flows shorten a financial instrument's *effective* term to maturity. The amortized instrument has a shortened term to maturity because its principal and interest are paid periodically. The same is true to a lesser extent for the coupon bond because its interest is paid periodically. Only the pure-discount bond has an effective term to maturity of five years because no cash flows are paid before then.

The effective term to maturity of a fixed-income financial instrument is the weighted-average term to maturity of its individual cash flows. The weights are the proportions of the instrument's market value contributed by each cash flow. An effective term to maturity calculated this way is called an instrument's **duration** to distinguish it from the instrument's stated term. Table 7.7 calculates the duration of our example financial instruments. To clarify this procedure, we'll work step-by-step through the calculations for the 9 percent amortized instrument.

The present-value-weights that apply to each cash flow are computed in panel A of the table. A $10,000 loan at 9 percent annual interest is repaid in five installments of $2,571. The present value of the first payment, discounted for one year at 9 percent,

Table 7.6   INTEREST-RATE RISK OF FIVE-YEAR $10,000 FINANCIAL INSTRUMENTS

	Market Price		
Market Interest Rate	5-Year 9% Amortized Instrument	5-Year 9% Coupon Bond	5-Year Pure-Discount Bond
7%	$10,541	$10,820	$7,130
9	10,000	10,000	6,499
11	9,502	9,261	5,935
Average price	10,014	10,027	6,521
Measures of price variability			
Standard deviation	424	637	488
Coefficient of variation	0.0423	0.0635	0.0748

Table 7.7   DURATION OF FIVE-YEAR $10,000 FINANCIAL INSTRUMENTS

Panel A: Calculation of Present-Value Weights

	9% Amortized Instrument			9% Coupon Bond			Pure-Discount Bond		
Year	Cash Flow	Present Value	Percent of Market Value	Cash Flow	Present Value	Percent of Market Value	Cash Flow	Present Value	Percent of Market Value
1	$ 2,571	2,359	23.59%	$ 900	$ 826	8.26%	$ 0	$ 0	0.0%
2	2,571	2,164	21.64	900	757	7.57	0	0	0.0
3	2,571	1,985	19.85	900	695	6.95	0	0	0.0
4	2,571	1,821	18.21	900	638	6.38	0	0	0.0
5	2,571	1,671	16.71	10,900	7,084	70.84	10,000	6,499	100.0
Market price		$10,000			$10,000			$6,499	

Panel B: Calculation of Duration

	9% Amortized Instrument		9% Coupon Bond		Pure-Discount Bond	
Term	Present Value Weight	Term × PV Weight	Present Value Weight	Term × PV Weight	Present Value Weight	Term × PV Weight
1 year	0.2359	0.2359	0.0826	0.0826	0.0	0.0
2 years	0.2164	0.4328	0.0757	0.1514	0.0	0.0
3 years	0.1985	0.5955	0.0695	0.2085	0.0	0.0
4 years	0.1821	0.7284	0.0638	0.2552	0.0	0.0
5 years	0.1671	0.8355	0.7084	3.5420	1.0	5.0
Duration		2.8281		4.2397		5.0
Coefficient of variation of market price		0.0423		0.0635		0.0748

is $2,359; the present value of the second payment, discounted for two years at 9 per-cent, is $2,164; and so on. The market value of this instrument, $10,000, is the sum of the present values of its individual cash flows.[6] The cash flow received at the end of year 1 therefore contributes $2,359, or 23.59 percent, to this total.

The present-value weights are multiplied by the terms to maturity of the individual cash flows in panel B. A total of 23.59 percent of the amortized instrument has a term to maturity of one year, 21.64 percent has a term to maturity of two years, and so on. Consequently, the amortized instrument's effective term to maturity is only 2.8281 years. Similar calculations reveal that the coupon bond's duration is 4.2399 years, while the pure-discount bond's is 5 years as expected because it does not provide intermediate cash flows.

EXERCISE

7.7

DETERMINING A BOND'S DURATION

Determine the duration of a three-year, $1,000 par value, 10 percent coupon bond.

Year	Cash Flow	Present Value	Percent of Market Value	Term × PV Weight
1	$ 100	$ 90.91	9.091%	0.09091
2	100	82.64	8.264	0.16528
3	1,100	826.45	82.645	2.47935
		$1,000.00		2.73554

The bond's duration, or effective term to maturity, is 2.73554 years.

Note the close association between duration and interest-rate risk as measured by the coefficient of variation of an instrument's market price. The amortized instrument has the shortest duration and the least amount of interest-rate risk; the pure-discount bond has the longest duration and the greatest amount of interest-rate risk. The coupon bond's interest-rate risk is less than—but close to—the pure-discount bond's risk because its duration is similar.

7.2 VALUING EQUITY

Cash dividends are the only cash flows a company pays to investors who purchase its common stock. The stock is issued in perpetuity and the company makes no com-mitment to buy it back, so stockholders must sell their shares in the secondary market

---

[6]The loan's market value equals its par value because the market interest rate has not changed.

I N   T H E   N E W S

BOND'S DURATION IS HANDY GUIDE ON RATES

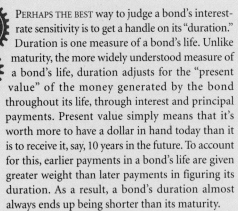

PERHAPS THE BEST way to judge a bond's interest-rate sensitivity is to get a handle on its "duration." Duration is one measure of a bond's life. Unlike maturity, the more widely understood measure of a bond's life, duration adjusts for the "present value" of the money generated by the bond throughout its life, through interest and principal payments. Present value simply means that it's worth more to have a dollar in hand today than it is to receive it, say, 10 years in the future. To account for this, earlier payments in a bond's life are given greater weight than later payments in figuring its duration. As a result, a bond's duration almost always ends up being shorter than its maturity.

The best thing about duration may be that it provides an extremely handy gauge of interest-rate risk in a given bond or bond fund. For instance, if rates go from 6 percent to 8 percent, a 10-year Treasury note with a duration of 7.4 will take a price hit of about 13.5 percent, or a bit less than two percentage points times the duration, according to Capital Management Sciences, a bond research company. A 30-year Treasury, meanwhile, with a duration of about 12.5, would be much more volatile. It would lose about 21 percent if rates rose two percentage points, or a bit less than the rate change times the duration. To figure out how much prices will move in response to rate changes, simply multiply the percentage change in rates by the duration of the bond or bond fund and, voila, you have a pretty good estimate of what to expect.

Source: Barbara Donnelly Granito, "Bond's Duration Is Handy Guide on Rates," *The Wall Street Journal*, April 19, 1993, p. C1. Reprinted by permission of *The Wall Street Journal*, © 1993 Dow Jones & Company, Inc. All rights reserved worldwide.

to recover their investment. Consequently, the price investors are willing to pay for a share of common stock depends on the dividends they expect to receive while they own the stock and the price they expect to receive when they sell it. We will see that the future sales price depends on dividends expected in the more distant future.

Common stock is the most difficult financial instrument to value because the dividend payments are neither fixed nor guaranteed. Consequently, the future dividends on a share of common stock can follow *any* conceivable pattern. A young company with opportunities to reinvest its cash flows at high rates of return may pay no dividends for a long period of time. Another company in a profitable but declining industry may pay a large portion of its free cash flows as dividends because it has few investment opportunities.

Companies tend to pay stable dividends once they initiate payments—but they are not required to do so. A company experiencing adversity may temporarily reduce or eliminate its dividend payments. Conversely, the managers of a company that is a takeover target may dramatically increase the company's dividends to reduce agency costs and maintain the owners' loyalties. This multitude of possibilities makes it difficult to estimate future dividends and impossible to use a single model to value all common stocks.

Valuing common stock would be simpler if investors had access to a company's pro forma cash statements. These statements describe the company's anticipated free cash flows and its financial cash flows, which include planned dividend payments. The planned dividend payments are management's best estimate of the amount of cash that will be distributed to the owners given the results of operations, the availability of reinvestment opportunities, and the availability of financing from other sources. Investors must make their own estimates of these values because these cash statements are unavailable to them. We shall discuss how investors gather and interpret information for this purpose later in the chapter when we describe security analysis.

A Single-Period Common Stock Valuation Model

An investor who buys a single share of common stock and holds it for one year has what appears to be the simplest valuation problem. This investor may receive one dividend payment from the company and will receive the proceeds from selling the stock.[7] We'll assume both cash flows occur at the same time exactly one year after she buys the stock. If the expected rate of return on stocks of similar risk is r_e, then the stock's present value is

$$P_0 = \frac{D_1}{(1 + r_e)} + \frac{P_1}{(1 + r_e)}$$

This model appears simple, but the valuation problem is merely displaced because the investor must estimate the price at which she can sell the stock in one year. We will describe a specific way to estimate that future price shortly but, for now, let's suppose she determines this company's stock has recently appreciated at an average annual rate of g percent. Furthermore, suppose she believes economic conditions make this an appropriate estimate of its future growth. Substituting $P_0 \times (1 + g)$ for P_1 and rearranging terms gives

$$P_0 = \frac{D_1}{r_e - g} . \qquad [7.5]$$

Note that the estimated growth rate must be less than the required rate of return for this model to give a sensible result.

Suppose Mariko Takana, a securities analyst for Kyodo Bank, predicts that the Nihon Mizu Company's dividends per share next year will be $4.35 and that the stock's price will appreciate by 7 percent. Given that the financial market expects a 12 percent rate of return on common stocks of similar risk, she estimates the market value of one share is $4.35/(0.12 − 0.07), or $87.00.

EXERCISE 7.8

USING THE SINGLE-PERIOD MODEL

Suppose an experimental purification process will permit the Nihon Mizu Company to increase next year's dividend to $4.50, cause the growth in its stock price to increase to 8 percent, and increase its required rate of return to 12.5 percent. Did these changes increase the owners' wealth?

---

[7]Dividends are normally paid quarterly, but it is customary to assume they are paid annually when developing a valuation model.

The new stock price is $4.50/(0.125 − 0.08) = $100.00. Yes, these changes increased the owners' wealth by $13.00 per share.

● ———————— ●

The way we derived the single-period dividend valuation model probably seems reasonable, but the final result may not have much meaning to you because it no longer looks like a present value equation. The result is actually very intuitive, however, as you can see by solving for r_e, the expected rate of return. The result is

$$r_e = \frac{D_1}{P_0} + g \; . \tag{7.6}$$

Equation 7.6 says that the rate of return from investing in common stock comes from two sources. One source is the dividend return—the amount of the dividend expressed as a percentage of the initial investment, D_1/P_0. The other source is the capital gain, which equals the percentage change in the stock's price from when it was purchased until it is sold one year later, g. This description of the rate of return from investing in common stock would be familiar and acceptable to any experienced investor whether or not she used Equation 7.5 to value the stock.

We will get an answer of 12 percent if we substitute D_1 = $4.35, P_0 = $87.00, and g = 7 percent in Equation 7.6 because we have just rearranged the terms. Alternatively, we can use Equation 5.1, repeated below, to calculate the holding period rate of return an investor will earn if Tanaka's predictions are correct. Then, next year's stock price will be $93.09 ($87.00 × 1.07) and r_e equals

$$r_e = \frac{P_1 - P_0 + D_1}{P_0} \tag{5.1}$$

$$= \frac{\$93.09 - \$87.00 + \$4.35}{\$87.00} = 0.12 \text{ or } 12\%.$$

Of course, the realized return will be different from 12 percent if the investor pays $87.00 for the stock and the dividend or future price estimate is wrong.

A Multiperiod Common Stock Valuation Model

An investor who buys a single share of common stock and holds it for n years may receive anywhere from zero to n dividend payments from the company, and will receive the proceeds from selling the stock to another investor. If the expected rate of return on stocks of similar risk is r_e, then the stock's present value is

$$P_0 = \sum_{t=1}^{n} \frac{D_t}{(1 + r_e)^t} + \frac{P_n}{(1 + r_e)^n} \tag{7.7}$$

This model has the same form as the single-period model except it recognizes that the investor receives up to n dividend payments and that the cash flow from selling the stock occurs in year n.

ESTIMATES OF THE QUAKER OATS COMPANY'S
FUTURE DIVIDENDS AND STOCK PRICE

Table 7.8

Year	Predicted Dividend	Predicted Stock Price	Source
1996	$1.14		Value Line
1997	1.14		Value Line
1998	1.195		Interpolation
1999	1.25	$30 to $45	Value Line

Equation 7.7 is a very versatile valuation model. An investor can apply this model to a company with any conceivable dividend pattern—no matter what his or her investment horizon. The price of this versatility is the necessity to estimate those individual dividend payments and the stock's final selling price. Investors sometimes simplify this task by assuming dividends follow a particular growth pattern, or they obtain estimates from an investment advisory service that uses simple or sophisticated forecasting models. Whatever method is used, the resulting price estimate is useful only if the assumptions are realistic. The following example illustrates this approach.

We'll use this multiperiod valuation model to explain the market price of The Quaker Oats Company's common stock on August 16, 1996, which was reported in Table 7.1 as $34.00 per share. The information we'll use is given in Exhibit 7.1, an August 16, 1996 report on The Quaker Oats Company prepared by the Value Line Investment Service. Quaker Oats is a New York Stock Exchange company that produces and sells foods and beverages. Value Line's report contains historical information about the company's financial position, dividend payments, and stock price.

We'll assume the investment horizon is four years and that annual dividends are paid at the end of each year. Therefore, the owner will receive four dividend payments (one at the end of each year from 1996 to 1999) and then sell the stock for the fifth cash flow—also at the end of 1999.[8]

Our first step is to extract Value Line's dividend and price predictions from the report. These predictions are summarized in Table 7.8. The investment service made explicit dividend forecasts for 1996, 1997, and 1999–2001, but there is no prediction for 1998. Consequently, we'll make our own estimate for 1998 by interpolating between the investment service's 1997 and 1999 estimates. Value Line provided both high and low estimates of the future stock price, so we'll use each one in turn.

Our second step is to estimate the rate of return the market expects for a stock with similar risk. Using the Capital Asset Pricing Model with a market risk premium of 8.5 percent, the current 3-month U.S. Treasury-bill yield of 5.21 percent (from Table 7.2), and the company's beta of 0.80, the market's expected rate of return is

---

[8]An investor who bought Quaker Oats stock on August 16, 1996 would receive only one-fourth of 1996's dividends. Therefore, we are introducing a small error when we use the entire 1996 dividend in our calculations.

Exhibit 7.1

VALUE LINE INVESTMENT SERVICE'S REPORT
ON THE QUAKER OATS COMPANY

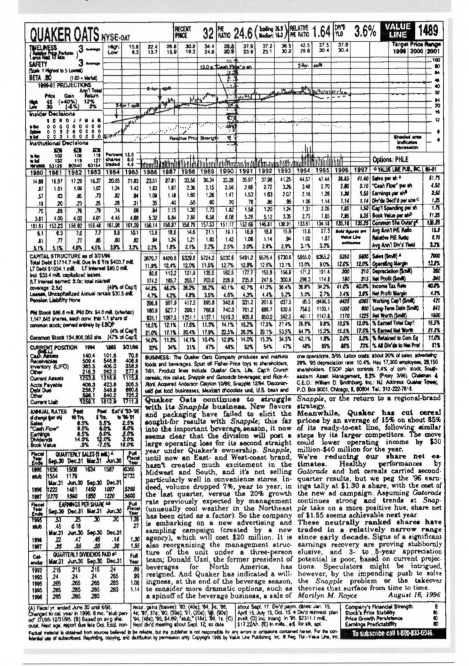

$$r_e = 5.21\% + 8.50\% \times 0.8 = 12.01\%.$$

Our third and final step is to use the predictions in Equation 7.7 to estimate Quaker Oats' market price.

Low estimate of market price:

$$P_0 = \frac{\$1.14}{(1.1201)} + \frac{\$1.14}{(1.1201)^2} + \frac{\$1.195}{(1.1201)^3} + \frac{\$1.25}{(1.1201)^4} + \frac{\$30.00}{(1.1201)^4}$$

$$= \$22.63$$

High estimate of market price:

$$P_0 = \frac{\$1.14}{(1.1201)} + \frac{\$1.14}{(1.1201)^2} + \frac{\$1.195}{(1.1201)^3} + \frac{\$1.25}{(1.1201)^4} + \frac{\$45.00}{(1.1201)^4}$$

$$= \$32.16$$

The Quaker Oats Company's actual closing stock price on August 16, 1996, was $34.00, just slightly above our high estimate.

USING THE MULTIPERIOD VALUATION MODEL

EXERCISE

7.9

Information about The J. M. Smucker Company from the Value Line Investment Service is given below. Use this information in the multiperiod valuation model to estimate the market price of Smucker's common stock on August 16, 1996.

Year	Predicted Dividend	Predicted Stock Price
1996	$0.54	
1997	0.56	
1998	0.63*	
1999	0.70	$20 to $30
beta	0.95	

*Obtained by interpolation

The J. M. Smucker Company's CAPM required rate of return is

$$r_e = 5.21\% + 8.5\% \times 0.95 = 13.28\%.$$

Low estimate of market price:

$$P_0 = \frac{\$0.54}{(1.1328)} + \frac{\$0.56}{(1.1328)^2} + \frac{\$0.63}{(1.1328)^3} + \frac{\$0.70}{(1.1328)^4} + \frac{\$20.00}{(1.1328)^4}$$

$$= \$13.92$$

High estimate of market price:

$$P_0 = \frac{\$0.54}{(1.1328)} + \frac{\$0.56}{(1.1328)^2} + \frac{\$0.63}{(1.1328)^3} + \frac{\$0.70}{(1.1328)^4} + \frac{\$30.00}{(1.1328)^4}$$

$$= \$19.99$$

The J. M. Smucker Company's actual closing stock price on August 16, 1996 was $17.25, very near the middle of our estimates.

● ———————— ●

Equation 7.7 is more complete than the single-period valuation model but still begs the important question of how to determine the *future* stock price. In the next section, we'll extend the logic we've used to this point to develop a model that makes future price estimates unnecessary.

The Constant Growth Dividend Valuation Model

The underlying principle of common stock valuation is that a stock's current price depends on the cash flows—future dividends and the future sales price—the owner will receive. Applying this principle to the future selling price adds another, similar equation to our model,

$$P_0 = \sum_{t=1}^{n} \frac{D_t}{(1+r_e)^t} + \frac{P_n}{(1+r_e)^n}$$

where

$$P_n = \sum_{t=n+1}^{2n} \frac{D_t}{(1+r_e)^t} + \frac{P_{2n}}{(1+r_e)^{2n}}.$$

Of course, we can simply combine these two equations because the second is just a continuation of the first. The result is

$$P_0 = \sum_{t=1}^{2n} \frac{D_t}{(1+r_e)^t} + \frac{P_{2n}}{(1+r_e)^{2n}}.$$

Applying the underlying valuation principle once again to obtain an estimate of P_{2n} and combining the results gives

$$P_0 = \sum_{t=1}^{3n} \frac{D_t}{(1+r_e)^t} + \frac{P_{3n}}{(1+r_e)^{3n}}$$

You can see that each price we must estimate is replaced by a dividend series and another future price that is pushed farther and farther into the future. This process continues until the future price is an infinite number of years away.

$$P_0 = \sum_{t=1}^{\infty} \frac{D_t}{(1+r_e)^t} + \frac{P_\infty}{(1+r_e)^\infty}$$

The present value of the future price in this equation is zero because the discount factor applied to it is infinite. Very large discount factors also are applied to the most distant dividend payments, but we cannot eliminate those terms yet. Therefore, our common stock valuation model for now is

$$P_0 = \sum_{t=1}^{\infty} \frac{D_t}{(1 + r_e)^t}.$$

[7.8]

Let's interpret this equation before we make it more practical. Our valuation model says a stock's price equals the discounted present value of *all* its future dividends. This makes perfect sense because the only benefit from owning common stock is to have a claim on the company's future cash flows. Particular investors hold the claim (the stock) for different lengths of time depending on their needs for cash and their expectations about the company's future. They buy the claim when they have surplus cash or high expectations and vice versa. The stock's value at any point in time is nothing more nor less than the price at which the buyer and seller are willing to exchange this claim on the company's future dividends. The prices of publicly traded stocks reflect the market's consensus about the opportunity cost of holding cash and the company's future.

Equation 7.8 is conceptually appealing but impractical because no one can estimate an infinite number of separate dividend payments. Myron Gordon simplified this model by assuming that dividends grow at a constant rate of *g* percent per year forever where *g* is less than r_e.[9] A company's dividends are a growing perpetuity given this assumption, and we learned how to value such cash flows in Chapter 3 using Equation 3.18. Applied to a company's dividends, the result is

$$P_0 = \frac{D_1}{r_e - g}.$$

[7.9]

To use this model, an analyst must estimate the values of only two variables, r_e and *g*. A separate estimate of next year's dividend payment is not required. The analyst can simply multiply the most recent dividend payment by the estimated dividend growth rate to obtain the predicted value of D_1.

Perhaps surprisingly, this infinite horizon, constant growth dividend valuation model is exactly the same as Equation 7.5, the single-period valuation model we began with. You might object that *g* represents the growth in stock price in Equation 7.5 and the growth in dividends in Equation 7.9, so they aren't really the same. However, we can use mathematics or economic logic to show that these two growth rates must be the same, therefore the models are the same.

Mathematically, the current price of a share of stock, P_0, and its price one year in the future, P_1 are

$$P_0 = \frac{D_1}{r_e - g}$$

$$P_1 = \frac{D_2}{r_e - g}$$

[9]Myron J. Gordon, "Optimal Investment and Financing Policy," *Journal of Finance,* May 1963, pp. 264–272.

One plus the growth in the stock's price is the ratio of P_1 to P_0, which equals one plus the growth in dividends.

$$1 + g_{\text{stock price}} = P_1/P_0 = D_2/D_1 = 1 + g_{\text{dividends}}$$

Consequently, the stock price and dividend growth rates must be equal. This result is a confirmation of the underlying economic logic of common stock valuation; if a stock's price equals the discounted present value of all its future dividends, then its price growth must equal its dividend growth.

Equation 7.9 requires estimates of the dividend growth rate, g, and the rate of return the market expects given an asset's risk, r_e. We can use the CAPM or APT to estimate r_e and we will use the **sustainable growth rate** to estimate g. A company's sustainable dividend growth rate is the annual amount by which it can increase dividends without changing its operating or financial policies. Retained earnings is the engine of this growth, which equals the current rate of return on past earnings that have been retained and profitably invested. That is,

$$g = \text{ROE} \times \text{RET} \qquad [7.10]$$

where   ROE = return on *beginning* equity
                = net income$_t$/net worth$_{t-1}$
          RET = earnings retention ratio
                = 1 − (dividends per share/earnings per share).

To see where this equation comes from, recall that one plus the dividend growth rate equals D_2/D_1. We know dividends equal the earnings on the previous year's net worth that are not retained by the firm so the dividend for any given year, t, is

$$D_t = \text{ROE} \times \text{Net Worth}_{t-1} \times (1 - \text{RET}). \qquad [7.11]$$

Substituting Equation 7.11 for D_2 and D_1 and simplifying gives

$$1 + g = D_2/D_1 = \frac{\text{ROE} \times \text{Net Worth}_1 \times (1 - \text{RET})}{\text{ROE} \times \text{Net Worth}_0 \times (1 - \text{RET})}$$

$$= \text{Net Worth}_1/\text{Net Worth}_0. \qquad [7.12]$$

A company's net worth at the end of year 1 equals its net worth at the end of year 0 plus the earnings retained during year 1. That is,

$$\text{Net Worth}_1 = \text{Net Worth}_0 \times (1 + \text{ROE} \times \text{RET}).$$

Substituting this equation into 7.12 and simplifying gives

$$g = \text{ROE} \times \text{RET}.$$

Let's return to The Quaker Oats Company and the information in Exhibit 7.1 and use the constant growth dividend valuation model to value their stock. Our first step is to estimate the company's sustainable growth rate as of 1995 using the sustainable growth model, $g = \text{ROE} \times \text{RET}$. The return on equity is calculated by dividing 1995's net income by 1994's net worth. The result is

$$\text{ROE} = \frac{\$174.8}{\$461.1} = 0.3791.$$

The company's retention rate in 1995 equals 1 minus the dividend payout ratio in 1995. The latter value also is given in the last line of the Value Line report, or you can calculate it yourself. The result is

$$\text{RET} = 1 - \$1.14/\$1.28 = 0.1094.$$

Consequently, our estimate of Quaker Oats' sustainable growth rate as of 1995 is

$$g = \text{ROE} \times \text{RET}$$
$$= 0.3791 \times 0.1094 = 0.0415.$$

Our new estimate of their 1996 dividend equals their most recent dividend, in 1995, multiplied by one-plus our estimated growth rate; $\$1.14 \times 1.0415 = \$1.1873$. We already have our estimate of the CAPM required rate of return, 12.01 percent. Entering all these estimates in Equation 7.9 gives our estimate of the company's market price:

$$P_0 = \frac{\$1.1873}{0.1201 - 0.0415} = \$15.11.$$

This estimate of the market value of Quaker Oats' common stock is less than our earlier estimates and less than its actual market price of $34.00. The financial market evidently does not believe that the company's required rate of return is 12.01 percent or that its future dividends will grow at 4.15 percent forever. Let's see if we can identify some causes of this difference.

First, let's determine the required rate of return implied by the market price given our estimate of the company's sustainable growth.

$$P_0 = \frac{\$1.1873}{r_e - 0.0415} = \$34.00$$

Solving for the implied required rate of return, $r_e = 7.64$ percent. Could the financial market believe that Quaker Oats' required rate of return is as low as 7.64 percent? Probably not because this interest rate is not much larger than the yield on 30-year U.S. Treasury strips on August 16, 1996. Quaker Oats has a relatively small beta but it is not riskless, so this is an unlikely reason that the market valued its common stock at $34.00 per share.

Now, let's determine the growth rate implied by the market price given our estimate that the company's required rate of return is 12.01 percent.

$$P_0 = \frac{\$1.14 \times (1 + g)}{0.1201 - g} = \$34.00$$

Solving this equation for the implied growth rate, $g = 8.38$ percent. Could the financial market believe that Quaker Oats' growth rate is as high as 8.38 percent? We may be able to answer this question by examining Quaker Oats' recent history. The necessary information is provided in Table 7.9.

Table 7.9   ANALYSIS OF QUAKER OATS' PAST GROWTH RATES

Year	Net Income	Net Worth Prior Year	ROE	Earnings per Share	Dividends per Share	RET	Growth
1994	$298.3	$562.5	53.03%	$2.16	$1.06	50.93%	27.01%
1993	300.8	850.0	35.39	2.07	0.96	53.62	18.98
1992	247.6	905.8	27.33	1.63	0.86	47.24	12.91
Averages			38.58			50.60	19.63

Table 7.9 shows that Quaker Oats' recent sustainable growth rates have ranged from 12.91 percent to 27.01 percent with an average of 19.63 percent. Therefore, a growth in dividends and net worth of 8.38 percent seems well within the company's capability. Of course, Quaker Oats must improve on its 1995 performance to meet this growth expectation. Let's see how much.

First, let's determine the ROE necessary to have 8.38 percent sustainable growth given 1995's retention rate of 10.94 percent.

$$g = \text{ROE} \times 0.1094 = 0.0838$$
$$\text{ROE} = 0.7660 \text{ or } 76.60\%$$

The financial market probably does not expect the company to improve its ROE to 76 percent because this is a large return on equity by any standard and well outside the limit of Quaker Oats' recent experience. Furthermore, the company's 1995 ROE (37.91 percent) is already approximately at its three-year average.

Now let's determine the RET necessary to reach the sustainable growth target given 1995's return on equity.

$$g = 0.3791 \times \text{RET} = 0.0838$$
$$\text{RET} = 0.2210 \text{ or } 22.10\%$$

The financial market may well believe this retention rate is an achievable goal because it is less than one-half the average of the company's recent RETs.

How can Quaker Oats improve its retention rate? In Chapter 15, you will learn that companies are very reluctant to reduce their dividend payments. (This preference is apparent in Quaker Oats' 1995 experience when they raised the dividend slightly even though earnings per share fell by nearly 50 percent.) Therefore, the market probably expects the company to improve its retention rate by improving earnings per share.

The text of the Value Line report notes the company has implemented a new advertising campaign to improve the sales of its Snapple business unit. If successful, this campaign will increase revenues, net income, and earnings per share. Value Line's report says the company will even consider selling this business if it remains unprofitable. We can conclude that the managers of the Snapple business bear a large part of the responsibility for improving Quaker Oats' performance. Our analysis indicates they must improve this performance to sustain the company's common stock price at its August 16, 1996 level of $34 per share.

APPLYING THE CONSTANT GROWTH DIVIDEND VALUATION MODEL

Given below is some additional information from the Value Line Investment Service about The J. M. Smucker Company. Use this information in the constant growth dividend valuation model to estimate the market value of the company's stock. The company's CAPM required rate of return, which you calculated in Exercise 7.9, is 13.28 percent.

1995 dividend/share	$ 0.52
1995 earnings/share	1.02
1994 net worth	258.0 (millions)
1995 net income	29.6

$$ \text{ROE} = \text{1995 net income/1994 net worth} $$

$$ = \$29.6/\$258.0 = 0.1147 $$

$$ \text{RET} = \frac{\text{1995 earnings per share} - \text{1995 dividends per share}}{\text{1995 earnings per share}} $$

$$ = (\$1.02 - \$0.52)/\$1.02 = 0.4902 $$

$$ g = \text{ROE} \times \text{RET} = 0.1147 \times 0.4902 = 0.0562 $$

Estimated 1996 dividend = 1995 dividend $\times (1 + g)$

$$ = \$0.52 \times 1.0562 = \$0.5492 $$

$$ P_0 = \text{1996 dividend}/(r_e - g) $$

$$ = \$0.5492/(0.1328 - 0.0562) = \$7.17 $$

This estimate is much lower than the actual market price of $17.25 but, again, that's because the financial market is using different assumptions about the required rate of return or the growth in dividends.

• —————— •

Combining Models to Value a Variety of Stocks

The constant growth dividend valuation model eliminates the necessity to estimate future prices or an infinite series of dividend payments but, once again, there is a cost: You must be willing to assume that dividends grow forever at a constant rate less than the market's expected rate of return on the stock. This assumption makes the model inapplicable to new companies that have not yet begun to pay dividends and to young and old companies whose dividend growth rates change according to the availability of profitable investments. Fortunately, we can combine the best features of the multiperiod and constant growth dividend valuation models to obtain one that will fit any of these situations.

The general form of the combined model is given by Equation 7.13.

$$P_0 = \sum_{t=1}^{H} \frac{D_t}{(1 + r_e)^t} + \frac{P_H}{(1 + r_e)^H}$$ [7.13]

where $$P_H = \frac{D_{H+1}}{r_e - g}$$

The investment horizon, H, is chosen to divide the future into two parts. The first part, from year 1 to year H, covers the period when the company's dividend growth rate is not constant or not less than the market's expected rate of return for the stock. These dividends are estimated individually using the growth pattern appropriate for the company. The second part, from year H to infinity, covers the period when the company's dividend growth rate has stabilized at a constant rate of $g < r_e$. Here are two examples that illustrate the combined model's versatility.

The After Dinner Video Company has grown rapidly by reinvesting its earnings to saturate major cities with videotape rental stores. As a result, they have paid no common stock dividends although they are expected to begin paying $1.00 per share in three years. These dividends are expected to grow at 12 percent per year for three years. After that, competition from new technology, especially transmission of programming over phone lines, is expected to reduce their dividend growth rate to 5 percent per year for the foreseeable future. What is the company's estimated stock price if the market's required rate of return is 11 percent?

The investment horizon that divides the video company's future into the proper two parts is six years; their dividend growth rate is neither constant nor less than r_e before year 6, but it is afterwards. We must calculate their dividends for seven years, however, because the dividend for year $H+1$ is used to determine the stock price at the end of the investment horizon. These projected dividends, computed using the company's anticipated growth rates, are given in Table 7.10.

The next step is to compute the stock's value at the end of the investment horizon, P_6. Using the constant growth dividend valuation model, this value is

$$P_6 = \frac{\$1.47}{0.11 - 0.05} = \$24.50.$$

Table 7.10   AFTER DINNER VIDEO COMPANY'S PROJECTED DIVIDENDS

Year	Dividend Growth Rate	Dividend
0		$0.00
1	0%	0.00
2	0	0.00
3	NA	1.00
4	12	1.12
5	12	1.25
6	12	1.40
7	5	1.47

LIL' BEAR PUBLISHING CORPORATION'S PROJECTED DIVIDENDS   Table 7.11

Year	Dividend Growth Rate	Dividend
0		$5.23
1	– 5%	4.97
2	– 5	4.72
3	– 5	4.48
4	– 5	4.26
5	– 5	4.05
6	0	4.05

The final step is to compute After Dinner's current market value by discounting this price and the first six dividend payments at the market's expected rate of return of 11 percent.

$$P_0 = \frac{\$0.00}{1.11} + \frac{\$0.00}{(1.11)^2} + \frac{\$1.00}{(1.11)^3} + \frac{\$1.12}{(1.11)^4} + \frac{\$1.25}{(1.11)^5} + \frac{\$1.40}{(1.11)^6} + \frac{\$24.50}{(1.11)^6} = \$16.06$$

The above example shows that you can use the combined valuation model to estimate the market value of a share of stock that has a changing but positive dividend growth rate. The next example shows that you can use this model to value stock that has a negative dividend growth rate.

The Lil' Bear Publishing Corporation publishes a popular line of children's books but their sales, profits, and dividends have declined over the years due to the falling birth rate. The company's most recent dividend was $5.23 per share but they expect to reduce these payments by 5 percent per year for the next five years until they reach a level they can maintain in perpetuity.

Five years is the proper investment horizon for Lil' Bear. The negative growth rate for years 1 through 5 and zero growth rate for year 6 (and beyond) were used to calculate the dividend payments in Table 7.11. Based on these dividends and the market's expected rate of return of 14 percent, Lil' Bear's projected stock price at the end of year 5 and their current stock price are

$$P_5 = \frac{\$4.05}{0.14 - 0} = \$28.93$$

$$P_0 = \frac{\$4.97}{1.14} + \frac{\$4.72}{(1.14)^2} + \frac{\$4.48}{(1.14)^3} + \frac{\$4.26}{(1.14)^4} + \frac{\$4.05}{(1.14)^5} + \frac{\$28.93}{(1.14)^5} = \$30.67.$$

● ——————————————————————————————— ●   E X E R C I S E

USING THE COMBINED MODEL   7.11

The Transcon Bus Company expects to pay a token annual dividend of $0.25 per share at the end of 1999, 2000, and 2001. The company has developed some new tours that are expected to increase Transcon's dividend by 8 percent per year thereafter. Determine the market price of the company's common stock at the end of 1998 if the required rate of return is 12 percent.

A three-year horizon is appropriate for Transcon because dividends are constant before this time period and the growth rate is constant thereafter. Therefore, determine P_3 and discount it and the first three years' dividends to 1998.

$$P_3 = \frac{\$0.25 \times 1.08}{0.12 - 0.08} = \$6.75$$

$$P_0 = \frac{\$0.25}{1.12} + \frac{\$0.25}{(1.12)^2} + \frac{\$0.25}{(1.12)^3} + \frac{\$6.75}{(1.12)^3}$$

$$= \$5.40$$

The market price of the company's stock is $5.40.

● ———————— ●

Why Not Value Earnings per Share?

Managers and investors are sometimes fascinated with earnings per share and the price/earnings (P/E) ratio. You learned in Chapter 2, for example, that the P/E ratio is widely reported in the financial press and can be used to incorporate market information into the analysis of a company's return on equity. The P/E ratio also is used to obtain an approximate estimate of the value of a company's common stock. This is accomplished by multiplying the company's projected earnings per share by its historical P/E ratio or the P/E ratio of similar companies. As an illustration, the approximate market value of a share of stock with projected earnings per share of $3.00 and a historical P/E ratio of 10 is $30.00 You can see the logic behind valuation based on the P/E ratio by writing the calculation differently:

$$\text{Price} = \text{EPS} \times \text{P/E} = \frac{\text{EPS}}{\text{E/P}} = \frac{\$3.00}{0.10} = \$30.00. \qquad \textbf{[7.14]}$$

Written this way, this valuation model clearly treats earnings per share as a perpetuity with the earnings price ratio as an estimate of the market's expected rate of return on the company's stock. The reasoning is that earnings belong to the shareholders and are valued by them whether they are paid as current dividends or reinvested by the company to provide future dividends.

There are two serious problems with this model. First, earnings are based on accrual accounting and are therefore a poor estimate of the cash flow available to the company and its shareholders. Second, although the earnings belong to the shareholders and are valued by them whether they are paid as dividends or reinvested, the relationship between current and future dividends and earnings per share is complicated and cannot be represented so simply. You can see the second problem if we rewrite our combined valuation model in terms of earnings per share, but it's best to begin with a numerical example. We'll assume that earnings per share are not distorted by the use of accrual accounting so that we can focus on the relationship between EPS and growth.

The Willinger Banjo Company manufactures and sells a traditional line of five-string banjos. Their instruments are very popular with traditional musicians who play bluegrass and Celtic music. There is virtually no growth in the demand for traditional banjos and these musicians are intolerant of innovations in banjo design. Under the circumstances, Willinger has adopted a policy of paying 100 percent of its earnings as dividends. The company's projected earnings per share are $8.00 per year in perpetuity.

Willinger's marketing manager has recommended the company use its manufacturing skills and distribution network to produce and sell traditional mandolins. The manager estimates this project will cost the company the equivalent of $5.60 per share for equipment and training and will generate $0.84 additional earnings per share in perpetuity. The additional earnings also will be paid as dividends because, beyond the initial investment, the traditional mandolin business provides no growth opportunities either.

The company's predicted dividend payments and the mandolin project's predicted cash flows are given in Table 7.12. The present value of each cash flow series at the expected rate of return for the traditional instrument business, 10 percent, is also given. The mandolin project's net present value is $2.55 on a per share basis so the company should accept the marketing manager's proposal. The project's NPV is an immediate addition to the market value of the company's stock, increasing its price from $80.00 to $82.55 per share. The company's stock price with the investment project was computed using the combined valuation model with an investment horizon of one year. That is,

$$P_1 = \frac{\$8.84}{0.10} = \$88.40$$

$$P_0 = \frac{\$2.40}{1.10} + \frac{\$88.40}{1.10} = \$82.55.$$

We can see how this price depends on the company's earnings per share by describing its dividend payments in these terms. Their first dividend equals 30 percent of earnings per share because 70 percent is retained to pay for the mandolin project.

$$D_1 = EPS \times (1 - RET) = \$8.00 \times .30 = \$2.40$$

VALUATION OF WILLINGER BANJO COMPANY   **Table 7.12**

Year	Dividends without Investment in Mandolin Project	Mandolin Project's Cash Flows per Share	Dividends with Investment in Mandolin Project
0	—	—	—
1	$ 8.00	$–5.60	$ 2.40
2 – ∞	8.00	0.84	8.84
Present value	$80.00	$ 2.55	$82.55

The dividends the company pays in years two through infinity equal the original earnings per share plus the additional earnings per share from the mandolin project. These additional earnings equal the project's return on equity of 15 percent ($0.84/$5.60) multiplied by the amount invested, which equals the old earnings per share multiplied by the retention rate.[10]

$$D_{2-\infty} = \text{EPS} + \text{ROE} \times \text{EPS} \times \text{RET}$$
$$= \text{EPS} \times (1 + \text{ROE} \times \text{RET})$$
$$= \$8.00 \times (1 + 0.15 \times 0.70)$$
$$= \$8.84$$

Substituting the definitions for the dividends rather than their amounts in the combined valuation model gives

$$P_1 = \frac{\text{EPS} \times (1 + \text{ROE} \times \text{RET})}{r_e}$$

$$P_0 = \frac{\text{EPS} \times (1 - \text{RET})}{(1 + r_e)} + \frac{\text{EPS} \times (1 + \text{ROE} \times \text{RET})}{r_e/(1 + r_e)}.$$

After simplifying this equation, the result is

$$P_0 = \frac{\text{EPS}}{r_e} \times \left[1 + \frac{\text{RET} \times (\text{ROE} - r_e)}{1 + r_e} \right] \qquad [7.15]$$

You can verify that Equation 7.15 is correct by substituting Willinger's earnings per share, retention rate, etc. and solving for its value with the investment. The answer will be $82.55, the same as we obtained earlier.

Look carefully at what this model tells us. It says a company's market value equals its earnings per share divided by the market's expected rate of return *plus* an adjustment for growth, $[\text{RET} \times (\text{ROE} - r_e)]/(1 + r_e)$. This adjustment factor is zero only if the company retains no earnings ($\text{RET} = 0$) or if it reinvests retained earnings in projects that do not provide an excess rate of return ($\text{ROE} - r_e = 0$). Consequently, these are the only two cases in which a company can be valued using the simple EPS model described by Equation 7.14. The omitted adjustment factor causes a valuation error in any other case.[11]

The way to avoid this problem is to value dividends rather than earnings per share. The dividend valuation models are simpler than a properly constructed earnings per share model and don't require any additional information. Given this, there is no reason to use the incorrect form described by Equation 7.14.

---

[10]Note that return on equity is an internal rate of return because we've assumed earnings per share are not distorted by the use of accrual accounting.

[11]The adjustment factor in Equation 7.15 is a special case for a one-time investment that produces a perpetual annuity. Nevertheless, the conclusion that $P_0 = \text{EPS}/r_e$ only if $\text{RET} = 0$ or $\text{ROE} - r_e = 0$ is a general result.

7.3 SECURITY ANALYSIS

Security analysis is the process of acquiring and analyzing information to estimate the market value of a financial instrument. The security may be debt or equity although there is a tendency to associate security analysis with the evaluation of common stock. Many people probably view security analysis in this way because common stock offers a wider scope for analysis due to its variable claim on earnings.

Types of Security Analysis

Fundamental analysis is the most widely practiced form of security analysis. Fundamental analysts study the economy and a company's industry to predict the company's earnings and cash flows. In effect, they prepare their own estimate of a company's pro forma free cash flow and financial cash flow statements. Then they use a discounted cash flow model or a price/earnings multiple to estimate the market price of a security. The models we've developed in this chapter are quite familiar to fundamental analysts.

Practitioners of **technical analysis** believe they cannot assimilate the vast amount of information that may affect a company's market price. Consequently, they look for clues about the market's collective evaluation of this information in a security's price history. Departures from the historical trend are interpreted as signals that the security's future price will rise or fall. The models we've developed in this chapter are known to technical analysts but they believe them to be too simple to be used in reality.

Sequence of Security Analysis

Not even professional securities analysts can follow and evaluate all common stocks so some process must be used to narrow the field to those worthy of detailed analysis. One procedure widely used for this purpose is economy-industry-company analysis, a process that uses analysis of (1) the general economy to form expectations about overall business conditions, (2) specific industries to determine which are likely to prosper under current and expected future business conditions, and (3) individual companies within the selected industries to identify potential investment candidates.

The rationale for this three-step process is implicit in the way we measure risk and in the results of studies that measured industry and general economic influences on common stock rates of return. First, the characteristic line, which we used to measure a stock's risk, assumes only general economic and company-specific factors affect its return. (Some analysts add the rate of return on an *industry* portfolio as an independent variable in this regression model and thereby estimate an industry beta.) Second, studies of stock prices have found that general economic conditions account for approximately 40 percent of a stock's rate of return, industry conditions account for an additional 15 percent, and company-specific factors account for the remainder.[12] Consequently, it is worthwhile to analyze the economy and industries prior to evaluating specific companies.

---

[12]Benjamin King, "Market and Industry Factors in Stock Price Behavior," *Journal of Business,* January 1966, pp. 139–190.

7.4 IMPLICATIONS FOR MANAGERS

Investors value a company's securities for the free cash flows distributed to them as interest payments, the return of the principal of a loan, or preferred or common dividends. There is no continuing source from which to pay them other than the cash flows provided by current operations minus the cash flows reinvested to support future operations. This simple fact—that free cash flow must equal financial cash flow—gives business unit managers a prominent role to play in determining the value of a company's securities. Their operating and investment decisions determine the amount and riskiness of the free cash flows available to investors each year. Consequently, the business unit managers' operating and investment decisions determine the value of their company's securities.

Because they represent the owners, the members of the board of directors are acutely aware of the links between free cash flows, financial cash flows, and the value of the company's securities. Senior managers also are normally aware of these links because they have frequent contact with the board, lenders, investment bankers, and securities analysts who represent investors or provide information to them. These senior managers, especially the CEO, CFO, and treasurer, hire investment bankers and make presentations to securities analysts to credibly convey their private information about the company's financial cash flows to investors. Managers and directors take these actions because they know that financial resources are allocated to companies that use them productively and away from companies that don't. The former can sell securities to obtain financing at rates of return that permit them to expand their operations while the latter cannot.

The board of directors and senior managers maintain or improve their company's access to this external financing by mandating the use of decision rules that mimic the financial market's valuation process. That is, they require business units to (1) estimate free cash flows, (2) apply the market's expected rate of return for projects with similar risk, and (3) choose the alternative with the highest net present value. A company whose business unit follows the market's rules is more likely to make operating and investment decisions that meet market-wide performance standards that will increase the value of the company's securities.

Business unit managers who understand and accept these links between their decisions and the value of the company's securities are more likely to propose acceptable projects. By doing so, they make more financial resources available to the company and their unit, which ultimately improves their job security. Furthermore, unit managers who ethically compete for these funds are less likely to cause principal–agent conflicts that discourage investors from buying the company's bonds and stocks.

7.5 SUMMARY

The models used to estimate the market price of financial instruments are applications of the principles introduced in Chapters 2 through 6. These principles state that the market price of any asset, real or financial, is the discounted present value of its future cash flows using a required rate of return that is appropriate for its unavoidable risk. Valuing debt and preferred stock is relatively simple because these securities provide a fixed claim on the company's future cash flows. Valuing equity is more difficult because future dividend payments are neither fixed nor guaranteed.

Pure-discount instruments, interest-bearing bonds, and amortized instruments should be valued by discounting each future cash flow at the required rate of return the financial market expects for a bond of the same maturity and risk. This means 20 separate rates may be needed to determine the market value of a 20-year bond. Once a debt instrument's value is determined this way, it is always possible to solve for its internal rate of return or yield to maturity—its average yield measured across its entire life.

All fixed-income financial instruments are subject to interest-rate risk. For a given term to maturity, amortized instruments have less interest-rate risk than coupon bonds and coupon bonds have less risk than pure-discount bonds. Pure-discount bonds have the most risk because they do not provide intermediate payments whose values are less sensitive to changes in interest rates. Duration, a present-value-weighted average term to maturity, accounts for these intermediate cash flows and therefore provides a better indication of an instrument's interest-rate risk.

The market price of a share of common stock equals the discounted present value of its future dividends and sales price. The future sales price depends on the dividends that will be paid in the more distant future. Consequently, the market price equals the present value of the future dividends to infinity. Investors cannot estimate an infinite number of separate dividend payments, so simplified models are required.

A widely used simplified model assumes dividends grow forever at a constant rate less than the market's expected rate of return for stocks with similar risk. This model is not applicable to companies that have not commenced dividend payments or companies with abnormally high-dividend growth rates. Therefore, a combination of equity valuation models must be used to estimate the market price of a share of common stock in this situation. The combination model is quite versatile because it can accommodate any conceivable dividend pattern. Simple models such as the price/earnings multiple approach are no substitute for discounting future cash dividends.

The debt and equity valuation models introduced in this chapter link a company's operating and investment decisions to the market price of its securities through the free cash flow and financial cash flow statements. Using similar valuation models to make decisions within the firm increases the likelihood that managers will choose alternatives that meet market-wide performance standards. Business unit managers who understand, accept, and ethically employ these procedures improve their company's ability to obtain financial resources, which is beneficial to themselves, the company's owners, and the entire economy.

- ### KEY TERMS

Pure-discount
   instrument   *265*
Zero-coupon bond   *265*
Yield to maturity   *269*

Interest-rate risk   *275*
Duration   *277*
Sustainable growth
   rate   *288*

Fundamental analysis   *297*
Technical analysis   *297*

• QUESTIONS AND PROBLEMS

1. We discussed U.S. Treasury strip securities in the context of the term structure of interest rates in Chapter 4 and in this chapter in the context of valuation.

   (a) What are U.S. Treasury strip securities?

   (b) Why should you use the yield on Treasury strips to estimate the market value of Treasury coupon instruments such as notes and bonds?

2. Ryan Healy, Cornought Manufacturing's pension fund manager, may invest some of the fund's money in a U.S. Treasury bond that pays interest semi-annually and matures in 5 years.

   (a) How many U.S. Treasury strip yields must he use to estimate the market price of this bond? Explain your answer.

   (b) Ryan noticed that the bond's yield to maturity is reported in the financial press. Why can't he simply use this yield to estimate the bond's market price?

3. Lauren Yoost manages temporary investments for the Painted Pear restaurant chain. The company's cash surplus on August 16, 1996 was nearly $100,000, and Lauren knew the company wouldn't need the money for approximately 90 days. Therefore, she planned to buy ten $10,000 par value U.S. Treasury bills that were due in 86 days on November 14, 1996. *The Wall Street Journal* (August 19, 1996, p. C15) reported that the dealers' ask discount for these bills on August 16th was 5.02 percent.

   (a) What price should Lauren expect to pay for each Treasury bill and in total for all 10 bills?

   (b) What is Lauren's yield on these Treasury bills if she holds them until they mature on November 14?

   (c) Why doesn't your answer to part (b) equal the bond dealers' ask discount of 5.02 percent?

4. Michael MacDaniel, treasurer of MacDaniel's Farms, has nearly $10,000 to invest for six months. The two U.S. Treasury bills he is considering are described below.

Maturity Date	Term to Maturity	Ask Discount
February 13, 1997	177 days	5.09%
May 29, 1997	282	5.23

   Source: *The Wall Street Journal*, August 19, 1996, p. C15.

   (a) What is the bond dealers' asking price for each T-bill?

   (b) What yields will Michael earn on these Treasury bills if he holds each one until it matures? Why does the May 29 T-bill have a higher yield to maturity?

   (c) On August 16, can Michael determine the holding period rate of return his company will earn if he buys the May 29 Treasury bill and sells it on February 13, 1997? Are both T-bills completely riskless if MacDaniel's Farms needs its money back on February 13? Explain your answer.

5. Gordon Young Personnel Services owns five $10,000 U.S. Treasury bills that mature on February 13, 1997. A bond dealer offered the company $48,740 for the T-bills on August 16, 1996 when 177 days remained until they matured. Is this a fair price if the yield on Treasury strips with 180 days until maturity on August 16 was 5.41 percent?

6. On August 16, 1996, *The Wall Street Journal* (page C15) reported the following bid and ask quotations on a U.S. T-bill and Federal National Mortgage Association (FNMA) bond. Both instruments had approximately 150 days until maturity.

	U.S. Treasury Bill Due January 16, 1997	5.07% FNMA Bond Due January 1997
Bid	$9,788.50	$9,987.50
Ask	9,789.33	9,993.75

Determine the dealers' spread on these financial instruments. Why does the FNMA bond have a larger dealer spread than the T-bill?

7. Compute the yield to maturity on an 8.75 percent, $10,000 par value U.S. Treasury note due August 2000 that was selling for $10,875 in August 1996.

   (a) Assume interest is paid annually.

   (b) Assume interest is paid semi-annually.

8. The August 19, 1996 edition of *The Wall Street Journal* reported the following quotations for $10,000 par value Treasury securities on page C15.

U.S. Treasury Note	Ask Price
6.00% note due Aug 99	$ 9,971.875
8.00% note due Aug 99	10,500.000

   (a) Why does the 6.00 percent note sell below and the 8.00 percent note sell above par value?

   (b) Use each note's ask price to compute its yield to maturity. Assume interest is paid annually.

   (c) Explain the yield to maturity on these notes by comparing them to the yields on U.S. Treasury strips given in Table 7.2.

9. Consider the two $10,000 par value U.S. Treasury notes whose August 16, 1996 ask prices are given below.

U.S. Treasury Note	Ask Price	Yield to Maturity
6.000% note due Aug 99	$ 9,971.875	6.11%
6.875% note due Aug 99	10,200.000	

Source: *The Wall Street Journal*, August 19, 1996, p. C15.

   (a) Use the yields on U.S. Treasury strips given in Table 7.2 to estimate the ask price of the 6.875 percent note.

   (b) Use the yield to maturity on the 6.000 percent note given above to estimate the ask price of the 6.875 percent note.

   (c) Which estimate is more accurate? Why?

10. Corporate treasurers temporarily invest surplus funds in marketable securities such as U.S. Treasury securities. Should treasurers be more concerned about the term to maturity or duration of the securities that they buy? Why?

11. Three financial instruments that provide an 8.0 percent rate of return are described below.

    A $10,000 loan at 8 percent interest, repaid in four equal annual installments of $3,019.21.

    A $10,000 4-year note at 8 percent interest paid annually. Principal repaid at maturity.

    A 4-year pure-discount bond that pays $10,000 at maturity. Current value is $7,350.30.

    (a) Determine each instrument's duration.

    (b) Which is more sensitive to interest-rate changes? Why?

12. Consider the $10,000 par value U.S. Treasury securities whose August 16, 1996 ask prices and yields to maturity are given below.

U.S. Treasury Security	Ask Price	Yield to Maturity
8.625% note due Aug 97	$10,287.50	5.59%
8.750% note due Aug 00	10,875.00	6.24
Treasury strip due Aug 00	7,825.00	6.25

Source: *The Wall Street Journal*, August 19, 1996, p. C15.

    (a) Use the yields on U.S. Treasury strips in Table 7.2 to estimate the ask price of these securities.

    (b) Rework part (a) after adding 1.00 percent to each yield in Table 7.2.

    (c) Which security's value declined the least in percentage terms? The most? Why?

    (d) Use each security's yield to maturity to compute its duration. Discuss the association between your answers to part (c) and these securities' durations.

13. On August 16, 1996, an 8.55 percent Federal National Mortgage Association (FNMA) bond due in August 1999 was selling for $10,643.375 (*The Wall Street Journal*, August 19, 1996, p. C15).

    (a) Use the yields on U.S. Treasury strips in Table 7.2 to estimate the market value of this bond. Assume interest is paid annually.

    (b) Compute the FNMA bond's yield to maturity using its actual market price and your estimated market price.

    (c) Why did the use of U.S. Treasury strip yields to discount the FNMA bond's future cash flows cause you to overestimate its market value and underestimate its yield to maturity?

14. The bond prices and U.S. Treasury strip yields given below were obtained from the February 16, 1996 issue of *The Wall Street Journal*.

    Federal National Mortgage Association 5.50 percent coupon bond due February 2001. Closing price $1,004.375.

    Safeway, Inc. 10.0 percent coupon bond due 2001. Standard & Poor's rating BB+. Closing price $1,146.25.

    Greyhound Lines, Inc. 10.0 percent coupon bond due 2001. Standard & Poor's rating CCC. Closing price $940.00.

Treasury Strip	Yield
February 1997	4.81%
February 1998	4.91
February 1999	5.00
February 2000	5.13
February 2001	5.24

(a) Use these Treasury strip yields to estimate the market value of each bond.

(b) Compare your estimates to the bonds' actual closing prices and explain the pattern of your valuation errors.

(c) Compute each bond's yields to maturity using your estimated market value and its actual closing price.

(d) Explain the difference between these yields for each bond. Why is the difference smallest for the FNMA bond? Why is it largest for the Greyhound bond?

15. Puget Sound Power and Light Company and Cleveland Electric Illuminating are two utilities with preferred stock traded on the New York Stock Exchange. Information about these companies and the preferred stocks from the January 3, 1997 issue of *The Wall Street Journal* and the December 1996 issue of *Standard and Poor's Bond Guide* is given below.

> Puget Sound 7.85 percent, $25 par value preferred stock. Closing price on January 2, 1997 $25.375. Standard & Poor's rating of the company's *bonds* A–.

> Cleveland Electric $7.40 no par value preferred stock. Closing price on January 2, 1997 $82.50. Standard & Poor's rating of the company's *bonds* BB.

(a) Use the 30-year U.S. Treasury strip yield on January 2, 6.59 percent, to estimate the market values of these preferred stocks.

(b) Compare your estimates to the stocks' actual closing prices and explain the pattern of your valuation errors.

(c) Compute each stock's dividend yields using your estimated market value and its actual closing price.

(d) Explain the difference between these yields for each bond. Why is the difference smaller for the Puget Sound preferred stock?

16. The treasurer of a small company was overheard to say, "My temporary investments are completely risk-free because I purchase only U.S. Treasury securities." Do you think this treasurer understands interest-rate risk? Explain your answer.

17. How can the manager of a portfolio comprising 30-year coupon bonds lengthen its effective term to maturity?

18. Smalltown Savings and Loan decided to sell a portfolio of nonperforming loans to a workout specialist. The portfolio's book value to the S&L was $600,000, but the highest bid they received was $400,000. Absent any defaults, the portfolio will provide free cash flows of $197,540.66 per year for four years.

(a) Determine the average interest rate the S&L charged on the loans in the portfolio.

(b) Determine the yield implicit in the workout specialist's bid.

(c) How do you explain the difference between these yields?

19. Millard Department Stores has a portfolio of credit card accounts that is expected to pay $1.2 million per quarter for the next two years. The company intends to borrow money using the cash flows from this portfolio to repay the loan. Past experience indicates the interest rate

on this loan will be 4 percent higher than the yield on U.S. Treasury strips of the same term to maturity.

(a) What is the maximum amount Millard can borrow given the annual yields on U.S. Treasury strips shown below?

Term to Maturity	T-strip Yield
0 to 6 months	5.10%
7 to 12 months	5.13
13 to 18 months	5.15
19 to 24 months	5.16

(b) What is the annual effective interest rate (yield to maturity) on Millard's loan?

20. According to the valuation models presented in this chapter, the market price of a share of common stock equals the discounted value of its future dividends. Are these models applicable to companies such as Digital Equipment Corporation that have never paid common stock dividends? Explain your answer.

21. Prepare an outline that describes the steps you would follow to estimate the market price of J.C. Penney Company's common stock using fundamental analysis. Make the steps in your outline specific to this company where possible.

22. Some analysts estimate the market value of a share of common stock by multiplying the company's earnings per share by its historical price-earnings ratio. Is this approach likely to lead to a larger error

(a) when valuing a public utility or a pharmaceutical company?

(b) when valuing a company with a low or high dividend payout ratio?

Explain your answers.

23. Pinegar Pixals is a computer graphics company that recently paid a common stock dividend of $2.35 per share. Pinegar's managers are considering a new investment program and want to assess the program's effect on the owners' wealth.

(a) Determine the current price of a share of Pinegar's common stock if its dividend growth rate is expected to be 7 percent per year forever and the owners' required rate of return is 12 percent.

(b) Adopting the new investment program will cause Pinegar to suspend dividend payments for the next three years but allow the company to pay a $3.25 dividend at the end of year 4 with future dividend growth at 8 percent. Should the company adopt the new investment program if the owners' required rate of return remains 12 percent? Should the company adopt the new investments if the required rate of return increases to 13 percent? Explain your answers.

24. Warren Buffalo is evaluating the stock of Genuinegene, Inc., a biotechnology company, to determine if it is a good investment at its current price of $35.00. Although the company has not yet paid dividends, Warren expects them to pay $1.00 per share next year. Furthermore, he anticipates that these dividends will grow at 12.5 percent per year for five years and then stabilize at a long-term constant growth rate of 8 percent. Should Warren purchase this stock at its current price if his required rate of return is 11 percent?

25. A securities analyst has compiled the following estimates about N. E. Buddy Can Company and the financial markets.

N. E. Buddy Can Company

Most recent dividend	$1.75
Profit margin	0.09
Asset turnover	1.05
Leverage	1.45
Retention ratio	0.70
Beta	1.25

Financial Markets

Return on T-bills	0.03
Return on market portfolio	0.115

(a) Determine the analyst's estimate of the market value of the company's common stock.

(b) Suppose the analyst's estimates are correct. What rate of return will you earn if you buy this stock at a price equal to its estimated market value? What rate of return will you earn if you buy this stock for $40 per share?

26. John Short and Jill Long independently arrived at the same conclusions about the future prospects for AnyTyme Herb Company's common stock. Their predictions are described below.

Most recent dividend payment	$3.00
Dividend growth rates	
1st year	12%
2nd year	10
3rd year	8
Subsequent years	5
Required rate of return	14

(a) John will buy the stock, hold it for two years, and then sell it at the prevailing market price at that time. Jill will follow a similar investment strategy but hold the stock for five years. Determine the current price each is willing to pay for the stock today.

(b) Given your answers to part (a), how important is the choice of investment horizon when estimating the market value of a share of common stock? Explain your answer.

27. Myra Gordon, a securities analyst with the Alexander Portfolio Management Company, must estimate the intrinsic value of Sharpe Bow Company's common stock. She compiled the financial information given below.

Sharpe Bow Co.		**Industry Average**		**Market**
Sales	$2,000	Profit margin	0.05	r_m 0.115
Net income	180	Asset turnover	1.50	r_f 0.03
Dividends	80	Leverage	1.30	
Total assets	1,250	Beta	1.00	
Common equity	750			
Shares issued	100			
Beta	1.1			

(a) Determine Sharpe's sustainable growth given its current financial condition and assuming its profit margin and asset turnover equal the industry average.

(b) Determine the owners' required rate of return given Sharpe's current risk and assuming its risk equals the industry average.

(c) What is Gordon's estimate of the value of Sharpe's common stock if she believes it will maintain its current condition for three years and then begin to resemble the industry averages as described in parts (a) and (b)?

28. Alcan Aluminum produces aluminum and aluminum products. The closing price of the company's common stock on August 2, 1996 was $30.50. A Value Line Investment Service report published the same day had the following information about Alcan.

Year	Predicted Dividend	Predicted Stock Price
1996	$0.60	
1997	0.75	
1998		
1999	1.20	$35 to $50
Beta 1.10		

(a) Use Value Line's predictions to estimate a range for the market value of Alcan's common stock on August 2, 1996. Use the yield on 3-month U.S. Treasury bills at that time, 5.1 percent, as the riskless rate of return and 8.5 percent as the market risk premium.

(b) The actual price of Alcan's common stock reflects the financial market's opinion about the company's future prospects. How do your estimates compare to the market's opinion?

29. Snap-On Incorporated manufactures hand tools and sells them to automobile mechanics. The closing price of the company's common stock on August 9, 1996 was $45.625. A Value Line Investment Service report published the same day had the following information about Snap-On.

Year	Net Worth	Net Income	Earnings per Share	Dividends per Share	Predicted Stock Price
1992	$ 664.7				
1993	701.7	$85.8	$1.34	$0.72	
1994	766.4	98.3	1.53	0.72	
1995	750.7	113.3	1.84	0.72	
1996*	830	131	2.15	0.76	
1997*	935	150	2.45	0.80	
1999*	1,400	220	3.50	1.00	$50 to $65
Beta 0.85					

*Predictions

(a) Use Value Line's predictions in the multiperiod valuation model to estimate a range for the market value of Snap-On's common stock on August 9, 1996. Use the yield on

3-month U.S. Treasury bills at that time, 5.1 percent, as the riskless rate of return and 8.5 percent as the market risk premium.

(b) What was Snap-On's sustainable growth rate at the end of 1995? Use this growth rate and Snap-On's 1995 dividend per share in the constant growth dividend valuation model to estimate the company's market value.

(c) Your estimate from part (b) almost certainly did not equal Snap-On's closing price on August 9th. Use your estimate of the company's sustainable growth rate and solve for the required rate of return implied by its actual stock price. What would the company's beta have to be to warrant this required rate of return?

(d) Use your original estimate of Snap-On's required rate of return and solve for the growth rate implied by its actual stock price. Assume your estimate of Snap-On's retention ratio from part (b) is accurate. What would the company's return on equity have to be to produce this rate of growth? How does this return on equity compare to the company's recent experience? How does this return on equity compare to a forecast computed from the company's 1995 net worth and Value Line's prediction of its 1996 net income?

(e) This problem is a limited example of common stock valuation. Nevertheless, use the results to explain the market price of Snap-On's common stock. Use clear and simple language.

30. Dow Chemical Company produces basic chemicals and plastics including such familiar products as Saran Wrap and Ziploc bags. The company's closing stock price on November 3, 1995 was $66.625. Information from a Value Line Investment Service report published the same day is given below.

Year	Predicted Dividend	Predicted Stock Price
1995	$2.80	
1996	3.00	
1997		
1998	3.00	$95 to $130
Beta 1.25		

(a) Use Value Line's predictions of Dow Chemical's dividends and low stock price to solve for the required rate of return implied by the company's actual stock price. Repeat your calculations using the high stock price. (Hint: You must solve for an internal rate of return.)

(b) Use Value Line's estimate of Dow Chemical's beta in the Capital Asset Pricing Model to estimate the company's required rate of return. Use the yield on 3-month U.S. Treasury bills at that time, 5.1 percent, as the riskless rate of return and 8.5 percent as the market risk premium.

(c) Compare the results of your answers to parts (a) and (b). Discuss some possible reasons for the differences.

• ADDITIONAL READING

Investment textbooks are the best places to learn more about valuing debt and equity from an investor's perspective.

A classic investments textbook that emphasizes fundamental analysis is:
    Benjamin Graham and David L. Dodd, *Security Analysis*, McGraw-Hill, New York, 1934.

Two modern, comprehensive investment textbooks with several chapters on valuing debt and equity are:
    Robert A. Haugen, *Modern Investment Theory*, Prentice-Hall, Englewood Cliffs, New Jersey, 1997.
    Frank K. Reilly, *Investment Analysis and Portfolio Management*, Dryden Press, Ft. Worth, Texas, 1996.

CHAPTER 8

VALUING OPTIONS

In 1994, Chemical Banking Corporation awarded every full-time employee options to buy 500 shares of the company's stock for $40.50 per share. Employees could use a portion of the options to buy stock when its price reached $50 and obtain an immediate gain of $9.50 ($50.00 − $40.50). Annie Hansley, a customer-service representative, said, "I hadn't been watching the stock price before. But once it hit 50, it was all we talked about in the morning."[1] On a much different scale, International Business Machines Corporation (IBM) gave Louis V. Gerstner Jr. options on 500 *thousand* shares of IBM stock when it hired him as chairman and CEO in 1993.

Do Hansley and Gerstner need to understand options? Absolutely, because stock options are an important part of their compensation. Do managers who are not paid with stock options need to understand them? Again, absolutely, because many business decisions are *optional*. For example, the companies that bid US$14.9 million for exploration rights in 558 square miles of Canada's Northwest Territories actually purchased an option on future natural gas production.[2] They will search for and produce natural gas if gas prices and exploration and production costs are favorable—but not otherwise.

Stock options, options on other types of financial assets, and implicit options on real assets are pervasive and are used to make managers think and behave like owners and to provide financial and operating flexibility. Employees and managers at all levels must understand options to make the right decisions for the owners, their companies, and themselves.

---

[1]Capell, Kerry, "Options for Everyone," *Business Week,* July 22, 1996, pp. 80–84.
[2]*The Wall Street Journal,* May 2, 1996, p. A10.

This chapter describes how to value options to buy or sell another asset. You can use the techniques you will learn here to value an option on a financial asset such as a share of common stock or a real asset such as property, plant, and equipment. We will use options on common stock for most of our examples, however, because this is the better context in which to learn option valuation principles. Nevertheless, some other applications are described in Section 8.4. Chapter 13 applies the lessons you learn here to the evaluation of options on real assets.

Option valuation models are different from the discounted cash flow models we used in Chapter 7. Those models assumed that once investors purchase a financial instrument, they must accept its good or bad payoffs—come what may. This is an acceptable assumption for stock and ordinary bonds because an individual investor cannot influence the payoffs from these investments. Options are different, however. An investor who purchases an option has the opportunity to buy another asset but is not required to do so. Consequently, she will buy the underlying asset if its payoff is favorable but not otherwise. We must use a different valuation procedure for these types of financial instruments because their risk isn't inherent; it depends on the investor's actions.

We will begin by describing option features and terminology and then derive and apply a simple model that will build your intuition. Finally, we will examine and apply the most widely used option pricing model, one developed by Fischer Black and Myron Scholes. You will see that it does a good job of explaining the prices of actual options on common stock.

8.1   ELEMENTARY PRINCIPLES OF OPTION VALUATION

Options have their own, somewhat arcane, features and vocabulary. They also are unusual in that their values are contingent on the values of other assets. Knowledge of these features and the relationship between the value of an asset and the value of an option on that asset provides a foundation for understanding formal option valuation models.

Option Features and Terminology

An option is a financial instrument that gives its owner the right to buy or sell another asset at a specified price within a specified period of time. The right to buy is called a **call option** because it is used to call in or gather the underlying asset.[3] The right to sell is called a **put option** perhaps because it is used to place the asset with another investor.

Someone who uses an option to make a purchase or sale is said to **exercise the option**. The transaction takes place at the **exercise price**, the price specified in the option contract. This price also may be called the **striking price** or simply *strike price*. Most options have a limited life and expire on a date specified in the option contract; **European options** cannot be exercised until this date while **American options** can be

---

[3]A similar interpretation is given to collecting assets in a different setting where politicians are sometimes said to *call in* their IOUs when they ask their associates to repay earlier favors.

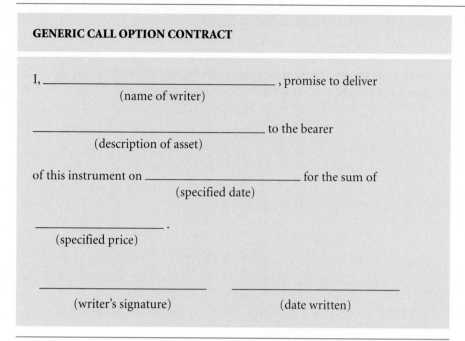

Exhibit 8.1

GENERIC CALL OPTION CONTRACT

I, _____ , promise to deliver
                (name of writer)

_____ to the bearer
            (description of asset)

of this instrument on _____ for the sum of
                          (specified date)

_____ .
      (specified price)

_____   _____
    (writer's signature)   (date written)

exercised then or earlier. (Were these names chosen because Americans have more free-dom or because they are less patient?)

An individual, company, or financial institution can create a call option simply by completing a contract similar to the one shown in Exhibit 8.1. The act of creating an option also is known as *writing an option* or *selling an option* because it is created for sale to other investors. The price the option writer or any subsequent owner receives when selling an option is called the **option premium**, which depends on the characteristics of the underlying asset and the terms of the option contract as we will see later.

The persons who own and write options have opposite rights and responsibilities. The owner of a call option has the right to buy the underlying asset at the exercise price but is not obligated to complete the transaction if the price is unfavorable. For example, an investor who has a call option that gives her the right to buy a share of common stock today for $35 will exercise the option if the stock's market price is greater than $35 but discard it otherwise. The option thereby enables her to obtain a gain equal to the difference between the market and exercise prices when this value is positive and avoid a loss when it isn't. A call option that provides a gain if it is exercised immediately (the asset's market price is greater than the option's exercise price) is said to be **in-the-money**.

The writer of a call option is in the opposite situation because he is obligated to sell the underlying asset at the exercise price even if this price is unfavorable. For example, suppose the $35 call option described above is exercised when the market price of the stock is $45. The option writer must supply a share of the stock for $35 by selling a share from his own portfolio at an opportunity cost of $45 or by purchasing a share in the financial market at a real cost of $45. The option writer's loss, $10, exactly equals the option owner's gain. The option writer's compensation for the possibility of such losses is the premium he received when he wrote and sold the call option.

The option owner and writer obtain complementary payoffs from this transaction because the call option partitions the underlying asset's risk. The owner buys the option and gets some of the underlying asset's variability while the writer sells the option and gets the rest. The price of the option therefore must reflect the underlying asset's risk and how the terms of the option contract divide this risk between the option owner and the writer. Mathematical models that describe the price in these terms are among the more successful developments in finance. We will examine some of these models after discussing the elementary principles on which they are based and the relationship between put and call prices.

Description of Listed Stock Options

Options to buy or sell shares of common stock are among the more widely and actively traded financial instruments in the world. One impetus for this activity was the formation of the Chicago Board Options Exchange (CBOE) in 1973. This exchange provided the first organized market in which to trade options in lieu of the over-the-counter markets available before that date. Options also are traded on the NYSE, AMEX, and some regional stock exchanges, but the CBOE still is predominant because it regularly accounts for more than 60 percent of trading volume.

The CBOE stimulated option trading by providing services that make trading more convenient. First, the exchange standardized option contracts. Standard contracts are for 100 shares of stock, expire on the first Saturday after the third Friday of the exercise month (usually January, April, July, or October), and have set exercise prices. Second, the CBOE formed the Options Clearing Corporation to match buyers and sellers on each trade and guarantee both sides of the transaction. Both of these services reduced information requirements and improved liquidity. Finally, the CBOE established listing requirements and trading rules and established procedures for self-regulation and enforcement of these rules.

Table 8.1 describes the options on Digital Equipment Corporation's (DEC's) common stock. Each row reports the strike or exercise price of a particular call and put option, when the option expires, the number of days until expiration, the closing price of a contract stated on a per share basis, and the number of contracts traded. For example, 83 Digital Equipment March 75 call option contracts were traded on February 7, 1996 with the last transaction at a price of $375.00 or $3.75 per share. This option was *at-the-money* when the market closed because the stock's closing price on that day, $75, equalled the option's exercise price. The July 50 call and the March and April 80 puts did not trade February 7.

The total volume of transactions in calls and puts on February 7, 1996 is shown in Table 8.2. Each option contract is for 100 shares of stock so this volume is equivalent to trading of 164 million shares. By comparison, the volumes on the New York and American stock exchanges that day were 455 million and 30 million shares. The trading of listed options has certainly become a major financial activity.

The establishment of the CBOE coincided with the publication of an option pricing model developed by Fischer Black and Myron Scholes. Their model has a rig-

---

**OPTIONS ON DIGITAL EQUIPMENT CORPORATION'S
COMMON STOCK (FEBRUARY 7, 1996)**   **Table 8.1**

Exercise Price	Expiration Date	Term	Call Closing Price	Call Volume	Put Closing Price	Put Volume
$50.00	July 20	164 days	$		$0.625	500
60.00	March 16	38 days	15.000	260	.250	4
65.00	April 20	73 days	12.000	16	1.750	72
70.00	February 17	10 days	4.500	372	0.438	171
75.00	February 17	10 days	1.813	236	2.625	230
75.00	March 16	38 days	3.750	83	4.250	54
75.00	April 20	73 days	5.500	14	5.250	137
80.00	March 16	38 days	2.000	475		
80.00	April 20	73 days	3.500	649		
80.00	July 20	164 days	6.125	111	9.750	10

The closing price of DEC's common stock on February 7, 1996 was $75.00.

Source: *The Wall Street Journal*, February 8, 1996, various pages.

orous economic and mathematical foundation but can still be used by ordinary investors to estimate an option's market value as a function of the characteristics of the underlying asset and the terms of the option contract. This benchmark undoubtedly made a significant contribution to investors' confidence in the validity of market prices, which provided an additional stimulus to trading.

The Value of a Call Option on the Expiration Date

You can learn about how options are valued by comparing the gains and losses on a stock and call option portfolio on the day the call option expires. We will use the Digital Equipment March 75 at-the-money call option to illustrate these concepts.

Suppose you have $6,375 on February 7, 1996 to invest in DEC common stock or DEC March 75 call options. You can buy 85 shares of stock ($6,375/$75 per share) or 17 call option contracts ($6,375/$3.75 × 100 shares per contract), which gives you effective control over 1,700 shares of stock (17 option contracts × 100 shares per contract). Thirty-eight days later when the options expire on March 16, the value of the stock and call option portfolios will depend on the stock's market price on that date.

The value of each share of stock in the common stock portfolio is, of course, simply the stock's market price. The value of an option on an individual share of stock also depends on the stock's market price because the option is worthless if the market price is less than the exercise price. In symbols,

$$C_T = S_t - E \text{ if } S_T > E$$
$$= \quad 0 \text{ if } S_T \leq E$$

Table 8.2 NUMBER OF PUT AND CALL CONTRACTS TRADED (FEBRUARY 7, 1996)

	Call Option Contracts	Put Option Contracts	Total Contracts	Percent of Total
Chicago Board Options Exchange	596,766	453,072	1,049,838	64.0%
American Stock Exchange	191,927	95,503	287,430	17.5
Pacific Stock Exchange	136,320	60,931	197,251	12.0
Philadelphia Stock Exchange	60,669	24,805	85,474	5.2
New York Stock Exchange	16,400	3,817	20,217	1.2
Total	1,002,082	638,128	1,640,210	99.9%

These volumes include options on indexes as well as options on common stocks.

Source: *The Wall Street Journal*, February 8, 1996, p. C13.

where C_T = value of an individual call option on the expiration date
S_T = market price of the stock on the option's expiration date
T = expiration date
E = option's exercise price.

Equation 8.1, an alternative description of an option's value on the expiration date, is more useful in calculations.

$$C_T = \text{Max}(S_T - E, 0) \qquad [8.1]$$

The corresponding formula for the value of a put on the expiration date P_T is:

$$P_T = \text{Max}(E - S_T, 0) \qquad [8.2]$$

For example, the value of a call option (if the market price of DEC's stock is $50 or $100 on the expiration date) is

$S_T = \$50:$ $C_T = \text{Max}(\$50 - \$75, 0) = \$0$

or

$S_T = \$100:$ $C_T = \text{Max}(\$100 - \$75, 0) = \$25.$

Option values computed from Equations 8.1 or 8.2 are called *intrinsic values* for reasons we will discuss later.

EXERCISE • ───────────────────────────────────── •

8.1 DETERMINING A CALL OPTION'S INTRINSIC VALUE

Call options on the common stock of Sun Microsystems with exercise prices of $35 and $60 expired on Saturday, July 20, 1996. The closing price of the company's common stock on Friday, July 19 was $55. Determine each option's intrinsic value on July 19.

For the July 35 option,

$$C_T = \text{Max}(S_T - E, 0)$$
$$= \text{Max}(\$55 - \$35, 0) = \$20$$

For the July 60 option,

$$C_T = \text{Max}(\$55 - \$60, 0) = \$0$$

The actual values of these call options on July 19 were $20.00 and $0.0625. The market values of these call options were very close to their intrinsic values because there was very little time remaining until expiration.

● ——————— ●

The values of the common stock and call option portfolios for these example stock prices are as follows.

Stock Price = $50

Value of stock portfolio = $50 × 85 shares   = $4,250
Value of option portfolio = $0 × 1,700 options = $0

Stock Price = $100

Value of stock portfolio = $100 × 85 shares   = $8,500
Value of option portfolio = $25 × 1,700 options = $42,500

These outcomes and others are given in Table 8.3. The gain or loss is the value of the portfolio minus the initial cost, $6,375, while the rate of return is the gain or loss as a proportion of this cost.

POSSIBLE PORTFOLIO VALUES AND RATES OF RETURN   **Table 8.3**

Price of DEC Common Stock	Stock Portfolio (85 shares)			Call Option Portfolio (17 March 75 contracts)		
	Value at Expiration	Gain or (Loss)	Rate of Return	Value at Expiration	Gain or (Loss)	Rate of Return
$ 55	$4,675	($1,700)	−26.7%	$ 0	($ 6,375)	−100.0%
60	5,100	(1,275)	−20.0	0	(6,375)	−100.0
65	5,525	(850)	−13.3	0	(6,375)	−100.0
70	5,950	(425)	− 6.7	0	(6,375)	−100.0
75	6,375	0	0	0	(6,375)	−100.0
80	6,800	425	6.7	8,500	2,125	33.3
85	7,225	850	13.3	17,000	10,625	166.7
90	7,650	1,275	20.0	25,500	19,125	300.0
95	8,075	1,700	26.7	34,000	27,625	433.3
100	8,500	2,125	33.3	42,500	36,125	566.7
Average rate of return			3.3%			100.0%
Standard deviation of rate of return			20.2%			253.4%

AN OPTION BY ANY OTHER NAME . . .

OPTIONS ARE LIKE those hidden figure drawings you may have played with as a child. Once you get used to looking, you can see the hidden rabbits, turtles, etc. very easily. Here are four cases that, at first glance, don't appear to involve options, but clearly do upon closer examination.

Have you borrowed money to purchase a car or house? If you have, then you don't own that asset, the mortgage company does. What *you* own is a call option on the car or house. To see this, suppose you have a $75,000 mortgage on your house and can sell it for $100,000 during a real estate boom or $55,000 during a real estate bust. You get to keep the $25,000 gain in the first case and can avoid the $20,000 loss in the second by defaulting on the loan and letting the mortgage company have the house. Your equity in this levered real estate portfolio therefore equals Max(house's value – loan amount, 0), which is the value of a call option at expiration as you know.

Managers have a similar opportunity when their company has issued callable bonds. These bonds have a call provision that gives the company the right but not the obligation to redeem its bonds at the call price prior to maturity. A company normally exercises this right when a decrease in interest rates causes the market price of its bonds to exceed the call price. This action provides the owners with an immediate gain equal to the difference between the market and call prices. The company will not call its bonds when the market price is less than the call price so the payoff from the call provision is Max(market price – call price, 0), which is the familiar expression for the payoff from a call option.

Managers can *create* options for their companies in both the common and technical senses by installing flexible production systems. Nalin Kulatilaka studied one case which involved the choice between installing a single- or dual-fuel steam boiler.* The cost of generating steam is uncontrollable when a company installs a single-fuel boiler but these costs can go no higher than the cost of the alternative fuel when the company can switch from oil to natural gas and vice versa. The opportunity to profit from the favorable variability of declining fuel prices and limit the losses from the unfavorable variability of increasing fuel prices is the hallmark of an option. Managers must understand the value of this option to determine whether the dual-fuel system's higher initial cost is justified.

Some environmentalists are dismayed that the economic value of immediate development almost always exceeds the economic value of preservation. They often make ethical or aesthetic appeals for preservation in these cases. Recently, other environmentalists have begun to describe and measure the option value of preservation.† They note that habitats may contain plant and animal species that have economic values we cannot recognize until our technology has improved. These environmentalists argue that these *potential* future values (the species' option values) should be added to the economic value of preservation for an accurate cost-benefit analysis of development.

---

*Nalin Kulatilaka, "The Value of Flexibility: The Case of a Dual-Fuel Industrial Steam Boiler," *Financial Management* 22 (Autumn 1993), pp. 271–280.

†Edward O. Wilson, *The Diversity of Life*, Cambridge, Massachusetts, The Belknap Press of Harvard University Press, 1992. Anthony C. Fisher and W. Michael Hanemann, "Option Value and the Extinction of Species," *Advances in Applied Micro-Economics*, 4, pp. 169–190, JAI Press, 1986.

The main point to observe in Table 8.3 is the difference between the rates of return on the common stock and call option portfolios. The common stock portfolio provides a rate of return between −26.7 percent and 33.3 percent, has a break-even rate of return (0 percent) when the stock price is $75, and an average rate of return of 3.3 percent. The call option portfolio provides a rate of return between −100.0 percent and 566.7 percent, has a break-even rate of return when the stock price is between $75 and $80 (actually at $78.75), and an average rate of return of 100.0 percent. Finally, the call option portfolio is riskier with a standard deviation more than ten times larger than the stock portfolio's.

The difference in the performance of the two portfolios is analogous to the difference between an all-equity investment in common stock and an investment partially financed with debt. As you know from Chapter 6, a levered portfolio provides a higher expected rate of return and has more risk than an unlevered one. These are the characteristics of the option portfolio, so we can think of it as analogous to buying DEC's common stock using borrowed money. We will make use of this interpretation later when we develop an option valuation model.

The Value of Combinations of Stock and Options on the Expiration Date

We obtain other insights into the valuation of options by calculating and graphing the per-share payoffs on the expiration date from buying and selling calls, puts, and combinations of calls and puts. Table 8.4 has the data we require. The payoff from buying

PAYOFFS FROM ALTERNATIVE INVESTMENT STRATEGIES   **Table 8.4**

Current stock price: $75   Exercise price for all options: $75

Price of DEC Common Stock: S_T	Buy Stock: S_T	Buy a Call: C_T	Sell a Call: $-C_T$	Buy a Put: P_T	Sell a Put: $-P_T$
$ 55	$ 55	$ 0	$ 0	$20	$−20
60	60	0	0	15	−15
65	65	0	0	10	−10
70	70	0	0	5	− 5
75	75	0	0	0	0
80	80	5	− 5	0	0
85	85	10	−10	0	0
90	90	15	−15	0	0
95	95	20	−20	0	0
100	100	25	−25	0	0

$C_T = \text{Max}(S_T - \$75, 0)$
$P_T = \text{Max}(\$75 - S_T, 0)$

Exhibit 8.2

PAYOFFS FROM VARIOUS FINANCIAL INSTRUMENTS

A: Buy One Share of Stock

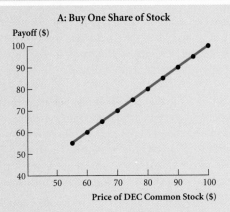

B: Buy One Call with Exercise Price = $75

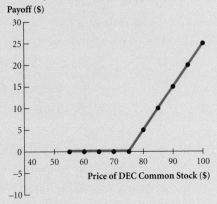

C: Sell One Call with Exercise Price = $75

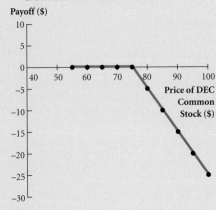

D: Buy One Put with Exercise Price = $75

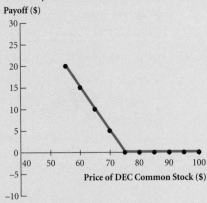

E: Sell One Put with Exercise Price = $75

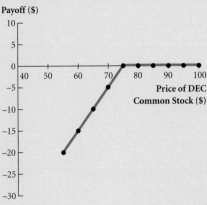

stock is the price of the stock on the expiration date. The payoffs from buying a call and a put are calculated from Equations 8.1 and 8.2, while the payoffs from selling these instruments is the negative of the payoff from buying them because an option owner's gain is the option writer's loss. These payoffs are graphed in Exhibit 8.2.

The graphs in Exhibit 8.2 vividly reveal how options partition the stock's risk so it can be borne by the investor most willing to do so. Consider the simple call option strategy first. An investor who owns a call option benefits from an increase in the stock price but does not lose from a decrease. The call option therefore functions as a type of insurance policy. Of course, this insurance policy is not free—the option owner must pay an insurance premium (the call option premium) to the option writer.

Now let's suppose you owned a share of DEC common stock on February 7, 1996 when its market price was $75 per share. We have just discovered that you could protect this $75 value by selling the stock and buying a call option with an exercise price of $75. Then, you would have $75 cash plus any gains you obtained on the call option (from $5 to $25 in the example in Table 8.4) when it expired.

This strategy ensures you will have a portfolio worth at least $75 (minus the cost of the call option) and possibly more, but it may be impossible to implement if you are unable to sell the underlying asset to lock in the $75. Suppose the asset is your home or your factory, for example. Then it isn't very realistic to periodically sell it and buy an option to repurchase it just to protect yourself from losses while preserving your opportunity for a gain.

Fortunately, we can put together a combination of these financial instruments that provides the same insurance-creating *profile* as a call option. Importantly, this profile is located at the same level as the value of the underlying asset, that is, you don't have to sell it to get the protection from losses and the opportunity for gains that a call option provides. Here's how to perform this feat of *financial engineering*.

First, look at the graph of the payoffs from owning the asset (see panel A of Exhibit 8.2). The payoffs go from $55 to $100 in our example but we want to eliminate payoffs below $75 and preserve payoffs above $75. That is, we want to add $20 in value when the stock price is $55, add $15 in value when the stock price is $60, and so on, but add or subtract nothing of value when the stock price is $75 or more. By looking at either Table 8.4 or the graphs in Exhibit 8.2, you can see that buying a put exactly fits the bill.

The payoffs on the combination—owning the asset and buying a put—are computed in Table 8.5 and graphed in Exhibit 8.3. The payoffs themselves, shown in column 4, have the familiar profile of a call option but are located $75 above where a simple call option would be located. This $75 is the exercise price of the option that we chose to avoid losses below this value. Many investors use this, and other option strategies, to protect the values of their portfolios (see "In the News").

This strategy, owning an asset and buying a put option on that asset, is a common insurance transaction. Suppose the underlying asset is an automobile worth $7,500 rather than shares of DEC common stock. Then a collision policy on this automobile is a put option with an exercise price equal to the face value of the policy. The automobile owner receives the benefits if the car increases in value, but receives a payment from the insurance company if it is damaged or destroyed. The amount of the payment is the difference between the face value of the policy, E, and the car's market value, S_T. The amount of the insurance premium is, of course, the put premium or cost.

Table 8.5   RELATIONSHIPS BETWEEN CALLS AND PUTS

Price of DEC Common Stock: S_T	Own Stock: S_T	+	Buy a Put: P_T	=	Total: $S_T + P_T$	−	Exercise Price: E	=	Own a Call: C_T
$ 55	$ 55		$20		$75		$75		$ 0
60	60		15		75		75		0
65	65		10		75		75		0
70	70		5		75		75		0
75	75		0		75		75		0
80	80		0		80		75		5
85	85		0		85		75		10
90	90		0		90		75		15
95	95		0		95		75		20
100	100		0		100		75		25

Exhibit 8.3   PAYOFF FROM BUYING ONE SHARE OF STOCK AND ONE PUT

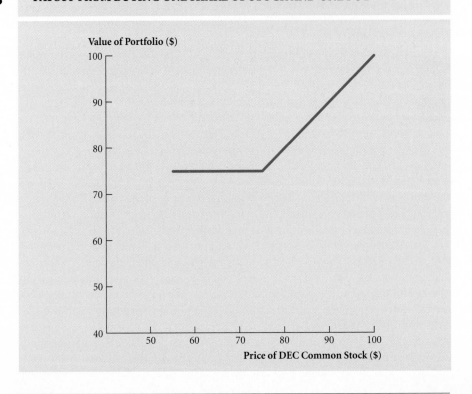

I N   T H E   N E W S

USING OPTIONS TO INSURE YOUR PORTFOLIO

How you use an investment sharply affects its risk. Selling options against shares you already own is one of the few options strategies that make sense for individual investors. Known as writing covered calls, this tactic is a conservative way of insuring part of your portfolio against a decline, according to Stephanie L. Ackler, a vice president at Tuckey Anthony, a financial services firm. Here's how it works.

Imagine you own 100 shares of XYZ Technology and you are worried its price will fall, either for company-specific reasons or due to a broad-market downturn. To soften the impact of such a drop, you sell an option to another investor to buy your stock. This "call" option gives the other person the right to buy your shares at a predetermined price, known as the strike price, within a certain period of time. One call covers 100 shares of stock. If XYZ is trading at $44, for example, imagine that you sell one November call at a strike price of $45. You get $300 for selling this right.

First, the $300 goes into your account and you keep that no matter what. Next, one of two things will take place. If the market falls and XYZ stock closes at, say $39 at some point before expiration, which occurs the third Friday in November, the option holder will have no interest in buying your stock at $45. The option will expire worthless. And, with the $300 you have pocketed you have cut in half the losses on your 100 shares due to the stock's decline. If the stock stays at $44, you have made money on the deal, to the tune of $300.

Suppose instead that the market rises and XYZ closes at $55 at the option's expiration. The defensive technique of writing covered calls doesn't work well in such a rise. The option holder will naturally elect to buy your 100 shares for $45 apiece. You do get the $300 from sale of the option, but that isn't nearly enough to make up for the $1,000 you lose in selling stock for $45 a share in a market where it is getting $55. Knowing that this can occur, you may want to consider selling calls on only half the number of XYZ shares in your portfolio. This way you won't miss out completely should the stock go up.

Source: Laura Pedersen, "An Options Strategy for Individual Investors," *The New York Times*, October 1, 1995, Section 3, p. F5.

Table 8.5 shows that it is possible to construct a call option by carrying out all the calculations in a given row. That is,

$$S_T + P_T - E = C_T.$$

This relationship is called **put-call parity** because it describes the transactions that make a put and call option equivalent. We will use this relationship to value a put option later.

● ————————————————————————————————————— ●   EXERCISE

USING PUT-CALL PARITY TO DETERMINE A CALL   8.2
OPTION'S INTRINSIC VALUE

Put options on the common stock of Sun Microsystems with exercise prices of $35 and $60 expired on July 20, 1996. The market values of these put options on Friday, July 19 were $0 and $5.25. Use put-call parity to determine the intrinsic values of the call options on the expiration date. Remember from Exercise 8.1 that the company's common stock price on July 19 was $55.

For the July 35 option,

$$C_T = S_T + P_T - E$$
$$= \$55.00 + \$0 - \$35.00 = \$20.00.$$

For the July 60 option,

$$C_T = \$55.00 + \$5.25 - \$60.00 = \$0.25.$$

The call options' actual values, $20.00 and $0.0625, respectively, were very close to their intrinsic values based on put-call parity because there was very little time remaining until expiration.

● —————————— ●

The Value of a Call Option Prior to the Expiration Date

The value of a call option on the expiration date is a function of only two variables: the price of the underlying asset (S_T) and the exercise price (E). Furthermore, the value of the option is a simple function of these variables because $C_T = S_T - E$ if this difference is positive and zero if it isn't. We'd all be option experts by now if this was all there was to determining their values.

Of course, the more significant problem is to determine the value of a call option *prior* to the expiration date. This problem has more practical significance because we buy and sell financial instruments before they expire, therefore we need a way to determine their values then. This problem also has more significance because the introduction of time means our option pricing model must account for those ubiquitous features of finance valuation problems: risk and the time value of money. Consequently, it is no surprise that a measure of the underlying asset's risk, the amount of time until expiration, and the market interest rate are the additional variables that affect a call option's value prior to the expiration date. We will examine the effect of these variables in intuitive terms in the remainder of this section before looking at them mathematically. For the time being, we will focus on American options and discuss the differences that apply to European options where appropriate.

Maximum and Minimum Call Option Values   Maximum and minimum call option values are enforced by investors who continually look for the opportunity to sell over-valued options and buy undervalued options to earn a riskless rate of return. These investors are, of course, arbitragers whom we've met before in the context of the level and term structure of interest rates and asset pricing.

A call option's maximum value at anytime prior to the expiration date is the price of the stock at that time, S. This limit is easy to understand. The cash outflow to purchase a share of stock using a call option is the cost of the option, C, plus the exercise price, E. The cash outflow to directly purchase the same share of stock at the same time is the price of the share, S. Clearly, no one will use a call option to purchase a share of stock if $C + E > S$. Therefore, C cannot be greater than S—even if the exercise price is 0.

How will arbitragers respond if the call option's price exceeds this limit? They will buy shares, which are undervalued relative to the call option, and sell call options, which are overvalued in relative terms. This pressure will cause the price of the stock to increase and the price of the call options to decrease until the upper limit is restored ($C \leq S$). These price changes produce the riskless profits the arbitragers seek when they initiate the process.

A call option's minimum value anytime prior to the expiration date is the value of the option if it is exercised immediately, $Max(S - E, 0)$. To see this, first suppose that the option is out-of-the-money, that is, $Max(S - E, 0) = 0$. Then C must be greater than or equal to 0 because the option price cannot be negative. Now suppose the option is in-the-money. The cost to acquire the stock using the option is $C + E$ compared to S buying it directly. No one will buy the stock directly if $C + E < S$ or if $C < S - E$. This means the option is undervalued at this price because it is less expensive to use it than not. Putting these two conditions together, the lower limit to a call option's value is $C \geq Max(S - E, 0)$. This lower limit is called an option's intrinsic value because factors related to the time until expiration have no effect.

Arbitragers will respond similarly to this situation. They will buy the undervalued call options, exercise them, and sell the overvalued stock. These actions will drive the price of the options up and the price of stock down until the lower limit is restored.

The limits on a call option's value prior to the expiration date are therefore given by inequality 8.3.

$$Max(S - E, 0) \leq C \leq S \qquad\qquad [8.3]$$

Let's apply these restrictions to a 75 call option on DEC common stock.

Stock Price = $50

Maximum value of option $= \$50$

Minimum value of option $= Max(\$50 - \$75, 0) = \$0$

Stock Price = $100

Maximum value of option $= \$100$

Minimum value of option $= Max(\$100 - \$75, 0) = \$25$

These points and all the others for stock prices between $0 and $175 are graphed in Exhibit 8.4.

The three 75 call options on DEC's stock listed in Table 8.1 expire on February 17, March 16, and April 20. The values of these call options on February 7 also are plotted in Exhibit 8.4. You can see that they fall within the limits on call option values that we have derived.

The value of the call option at a specific time prior to the expiration date must fall within the limits described by inequality 8.3 and graphed for DEC's common stock in Exhibit 8.4. Actions by arbitragers will enforce these limits. Whether the call option's value is closer to the minimum or maximum depends on the characteristics of the variables that become important with the introduction of time. These variables are the underlying asset's risk, the amount of time until expiration, and the market interest rate.

The Effect of the Underlying Asset's Risk   By far, the most important determinant of a call option's value prior to the expiration date is the underlying asset's volatility.

Exhibit 8.4

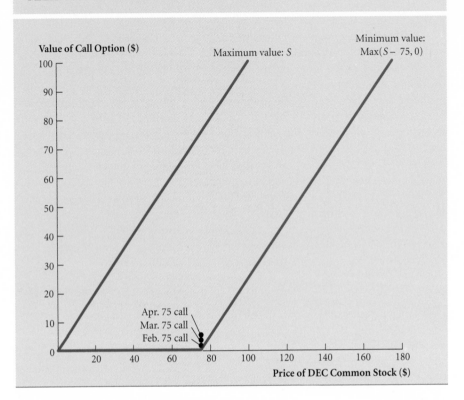

MAXIMUM AND MINIMUM OPTION VALUES

You may be surprised to learn that a call option is more valuable the more volatile or risky the underlying asset. Surprise is a common initial reaction to this statement because, up to this point, we have emphasized that most people are risk-averse. Consequently, they require a higher rate of return or, equivalently, pay a lower price for assets that have more risk.

Call options alter the relationship between an asset's risk and the option owner's payoffs, however. Although an investor who owns an asset directly is subject to all its variability, an investor who owns a call option on that asset accepts its positive variability and avoids its negative variability. The call option owner thereby obtains the benefits of unexpected increases in value without the offsetting costs of unexpected decreases in value.

The altered relationship between the asset's risk and the option owner's payoffs is reflected in our expression for the value of a call option on the expiration date: $C_T = Max(S_T - E, 0)$. An increase in the underlying asset's volatility makes the first parenthetical term larger but cannot make the second term smaller. This means an investor who owns an option on an asset can only benefit from an increase in that asset's risk. An example based on the March 75 call option on DEC's common stock illustrates volatility's favorable effect on an option's value.

The market price of DEC's common stock on March 17 when the March 75 call option expires can actually be any positive number, but we will assume only two prices are possible for this simplified example. These prices will be the February 7 market price of $75 plus and minus equally sized price changes. The low-volatility case is represented by allowing the price changes to be $10 and $ – 5. The price changes are $15 and $ – 10 for the high-volatility case. Assuming the plus and minus price changes are equally likely, their standard deviations in the low- and high-volatility cases are $7.50 and $12.50.

Exhibit 8.5 shows the values of the stock and the call option on the expiration date when the stock has low volatility (panel A) and high volatility (panel B).[4] The expected price change, stock price, and option value also are shown. You will note that the expected price change is $2.50 in both cases but that the expected value of the option on the expiration date is larger when the price change exhibits more variability. Furthermore, you can trace this increase in value to the higher payoff the option's owner receives when the option expires in-the-money ($15 versus $10) without a corresponding decrease in payoff when it expires out-of-the-money ($0 versus $0).[5]

An option with a higher value on the expiration date also has a higher value prior to expiration. Therefore, we can say that an increase in the volatility of the underlying asset places the value of an option on that asset nearer the top of the range described by inequality 8.3.

Summarizing our discussion to this point, the only characteristics of an asset that affect the value of an option on that asset are the asset's price and volatility. The higher the price, the larger the option's maximum and minimum values. The higher the volatility, the higher the option's value within these limits.

The Effect of the Exercise Price and the Amount of Time until Expiration   Now that we have established these relationships, we can turn our attention to how the terms of the option contract affect its value. The effect of the exercise price, E, is easy to understand. The difference between the asset's value and the exercise price, $S - E$, is the amount saved by using an option to acquire a share of stock when the option is in-the-money. The lower the exercise price, the larger the amount saved, so an option is more valuable when the price is lower.

The only other term of the option contract that affects its value is the amount of time until the option expires, t. The February, March, and April 75 options on DEC common stock graphed in Exhibit 8.4 showed that the effect is positive; the longer the time until expiration, the more valuable the option. Now we can explain this relationship.

A simple explanation for the effect of time on an option's value is that a longer option provides all the rights a shorter one does—plus more. The longer option

---

[4]The tree-structure used to portray these results is not really necessary for an option that has only one period until it expires but it will be helpful later when we examine options with more than one period until expiration.

[5]It would be convenient to discount the expected value of an option on the expiration date to determine its value prior to expiration but we can't. The reason is that we can't determine the required rate of return until we know how much unavoidable risk an option contributes to a portfolio. This problem stymied finance scholars until Fischer Black and Myron Scholes solved it in 1973. We will examine their solution and simpler solutions shortly.

Exhibit 8.5

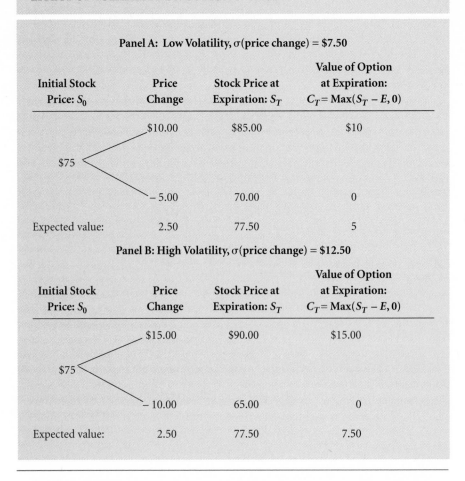

EFFECT OF VOLATILITY ON OPTION'S VALUE

Panel A: Low Volatility, σ(price change) = $7.50

Initial Stock Price: S_0	Price Change	Stock Price at Expiration: S_T	Value of Option at Expiration: $C_T = \text{Max}(S_T - E, 0)$
	$10.00	$85.00	$10
$75			
	−5.00	70.00	0
Expected value:	2.50	77.50	5

Panel B: High Volatility, σ(price change) = $12.50

Initial Stock Price: S_0	Price Change	Stock Price at Expiration: S_T	Value of Option at Expiration: $C_T = \text{Max}(S_T - E, 0)$
	$15.00	$90.00	$15.00
$75			
	−10.00	65.00	0
Expected value:	2.50	77.50	7.50

provides more options so it must be more valuable. This simplistic explanation is certainly true but it obscures a more fundamental reason a longer option is more valuable. The fundamental reason is that a longer time until expiration allows the underlying asset to express more volatility. The option's owner gains an advantage from this volatility without an offsetting cost—this is what makes the longer option more valuable.

Exhibit 8.6 re-examines the low-volatility option from panel A of Exhibit 8.5 assuming there are two periods until the expiration date. The stock price may change by $10 or $–5 with equal likelihood and the price changes in periods 1 and 2 are independent. The upper path—two successive price changes of $10—leads to a stock price and option value on the expiration date of $95 and $20. This is a much larger payoff than the best outcome ($10) when the option had only one period until expiration. The lower path—two successive price changes of $–5—leads to a stock price and option value of $65 and $0. The final stock price is lower than the worst outcome when there is only

---

Exhibit 8.6

EFFECT OF TIME UNTIL EXPIRATION ON OPTION'S VALUE

Initial Stock Price: S_0	Price Change at Time 1	Price Change at Time 2	Total Price Change	Stock Price at Expiration: S_T	Value of Option at Expiration: $C_T = \text{Max}(S_T - E, 0)$
		$10	$20	$95	$20.00
	$10				
		−5	5	80	5.00
$75					
		10	5	80	5.00
	−5				
		−5	−10	65	0
Expected value:			$ 5	$80	$ 7.50

one period until expiration, but the option's owner doesn't care because the option isn't exercised in either case. The intermediate paths produce intermediate values for the stock that leave the option in-the-money.

The expected value of the option on the expiration date is $7.50 in comparison to $5 when there was only one period until expiration. The difference is due to the positive effects of the larger payoffs produced by the additional volatility expressed over the two time periods. The favorable effects of this volatility are not offset by any unfavorable effects so the two-period option is more valuable.

The market interest rate also affects the value of an option prior to the expiration date because of the time value of money. The market interest rate's effect on an option's value is easier to see when we have an actual option pricing model, so we will examine this issue later.

The Effect of the Option's Type   Now we can determine how a call option's type affects its value. Remember that a European option can only be exercised on the expiration date and an American option can be exercised at that time or earlier. This means an American option must be worth at least as much as a European one. After all, both options provide the same opportunity (to buy the underlying asset) on the expiration date while an American option provides additional opportunities earlier. Therefore, an American option cannot be worth less than a European option.

Perhaps surprisingly, an American option is not worth *more* than a European option if the underlying asset does not provide interim benefits such as dividends or control prerogatives. This conclusion follows directly from the fact that the value of exercising an option prior to the expiration date is its *minimum* value at that time. The option's actual or market value is greater than or equal to this minimum because the underlying asset's volatility and the passage of time increase the likelihood that the option will be worth even more when it expires. Exercising an option prior to the expiration destroys the owner's opportunity to profit from this volatility and converts the option into a mere discount coupon. Consequently, an American option on an asset that provides no interim benefits should not be exercised prior to the expiration date; it should be treated as if it is a European option and will be valued accordingly.

You may wonder how you realize the value from an American option prior to the expiration date if you are supposed to treat it like a European option. That's simple. You sell the option and receive its market value, which is greater than or equal to the value you'd receive by exercising it. DEC's April 65 call option, described in Table 8.1, provides a good example. The market value of this option on February 7, 1996 was $12.00 but its value if exercised on that date was only $10 ($S_T - E = \$75 - \$65$). Therefore, it was clearly better to keep the option alive and sell it to someone else for $12.00 than to terminate it for a gain of $10.00.

The conclusion that an American call option should not be exercised prior to the expiration date and therefore has the same value as an otherwise identical European option changes if the underlying asset provides interim benefits. Then it may be worthwhile to exercise the option early to get those benefits which are an addition to the option's intrinsic value. Options on common stocks that pay dividends fall in this category as do options on real assets that provide interim cash flows (as we will see later).

As an illustration, suppose Maurice Pinches owns a call option on the common stock of the Gitman Bike Company that will pay a $1.00 dividend tomorrow. The current price of the common stock is $50 and the option's exercise price is $40, so its intrinsic value is $10. The option has 10 days until it expires, that is, its market value is at least $10, say $10.50. Maurice can sell the option for $10.50 or exercise it for a total gain of $11.00—its value if exercised immediately plus the value of the dividend. Clearly, Maurice should exercise the option early in this case and give up the potential gains from volatility in return for the certain gain from the imminent dividend payment.

8.2   A SIMPLE OPTION PRICING MODEL

Option pricing models can become very complicated. The more elaborate ones are based on principles borrowed from physics and use an esoteric branch of mathematics called stochastic calculus. The complexity of these models sometimes produces a kind of *option-phobia* that inhibits understanding of this important valuation process. This reaction is unnecessary, however, because even the simplest option valuation method relies on the same principles as the most complicated one *and* can be developed and explained in intuitive terms.

We will develop a simple option pricing model and your intuition in this section and apply these lessons to the best-known advanced option pricing model in the next. The simplified model is based on the assumption that there are only two possible values for the underlying asset on the date the option expires.[6] This is the same simplifying assumption we used for the illustrations in Exhibits 8.5 and 8.6.

The Relationship between the Value of a Call Option and the Value of a Levered Portfolio

Table 8.3 showed that a portfolio of call options on shares of common stock behaves in the same way as a portfolio of the shares themselves partially financed with debt. Both portfolios provide a higher expected rate of return and more risk than a portfolio of shares financed without debt. The similarity between these two investment alternatives is so strong that we can actually construct a levered portfolio of common stock that exactly replicates the payoffs from buying a call option. Because the replica portfolio and the call option have the same payoffs on the expiration date, arbitragers will ensure that they have the same value on the day they are formed. Consequently, we can simply refer to the market prices of the common stock and the riskless debt to determine the value of the call option on that date.

The key feature of the replica portfolio is that its payoff exactly matches the option's payoff in the *worse* case. Because the option's payoff can never be negative, this ensures that the value of the common stock in the levered portfolio is always greater than or equal to the value of the debt, which makes the debt riskless. This simple technique permits us to sidestep the complicated problem of determining how different debt levels—and therefore different costs of debt—might affect the value of the replica portfolio and the option.

We will illustrate and then derive an option pricing model using this replica portfolio approach. Once again, our example is loosely based on the March 75 call option on DEC's common stock. We will continue to assume the stock's market price on February 7 is $75 but that $70 and $85 are the only possible prices on March 16 when the option expires. The value of the $75 call option on the expiration date is therefore either $0 or $10. Contrary to the earlier example, we make *no* assumptions about the likelihood of these stock prices or option values.

Panel A of Table 8.6 presents the calculations used to construct a levered portfolio that exactly matches a March 75 call option. The payoff from the levered portfolio is the value of the owner's equity on the expiration date. The value of this equity equals the value of the assets, which is the number of shares of stock times the price per share, $n \times S_T$, minus the value of the debt that must be repaid, D_T. The owner's equity in our example is either $n \times \$70 - D_T$ or $n \times \$85 - D_T$.

The number of shares and amount of debt in the levered portfolio are chosen to match the option's payoffs. That is,

$$n \times \$70 - D_T = \$0$$
$$n \times \$85 - D_T = \$10.$$

---

[6]The model also assumes the financial markets are perfect, the stock does not provide any interim benefits, and the option cannot be exercised until the expiration date (it is a European option).

Table 8.6   USING A REPLICA PORTFOLIO TO VALUE A CALL OPTION

Panel A: Constructing the Levered Portfolio to Match the Option's Payoffs on March 16, 1996

Value of Levered Portfolio

Price of Stock at Expiration: S_T	Value of Assets at Expiration: $n \times S_T$	Value of Debt Owed at Expiration: D_T		Value of Equity at Expiration: $n \times S_T - D_T$	Value of Option at Expiration: C_T
$70	$n \times \$70$	D_T		$n \times \$70 - D_T$	$0
85	$n \times 85$	D_T		$n \times \ 85 - D_T$	10

Panel B: Determining the Value of the Levered Portfolio on February 7, 1996

Value of Levered Portfolio

Value of Stock: $n \times S_0$		Value of Debt: D_0		Value of Equity: $n \times S_0 - D_0$
$(2/3) \times \$75$		$\dfrac{\$46.67}{(1 + 0.0484/365)^{38}}$		$3.56

The solution to these two equations is $n = 2/3$ and $D_T = \$46.67$. A portfolio constructed this way exactly replicates the option's payoffs as shown below.

Value of Assets at Expiration	–	Value of Debt Owed at Expiration	=	Value of Equity at Expiration	=	Value of Option at Expiration
$(2/3) \times \$70 = \$46.67$		$46.67		$ 0		$ 0
$(2/3) \times \ 85 = \ 56.67$		46.67		10.00		10.00

EXERCISE ●
8.3   **DETERMINING THE COMPOSITION OF THE REPLICA PORTFOLIO**

Allison Richards wants to construct a levered portfolio that exactly matches the payoffs from a call option on the Foxworth Publishing Company's common stock. The stock's current price is $46 but may decrease to $43 or increase to $53 in 60 days. The call option has an exercise price of $45 and expires in 60 days. Determine the composition of Allison's levered portfolio.

Set the values of the equity in the levered portfolio at expiration, $n \times S_T - D_T$, equal to the values of the call option at expiration, $\text{Max}\,(S_T - E, 0)$.

For $S_T = \$43$: $n \times \$43 - D_T = \$0 = \text{Max}(\$43 - \$45, \$0)$

For $S_T = \$53$: $n \times \$53 - D_T = \$8 = \text{Max}(\$53 - \$45, \$0)$

Solve these two equations for n and D_T.

$$n = 0.80$$
$$D_T = \$34.40$$

A portfolio with eight-tenths of a share of Foxworth common stock financed in part with debt worth $34.40 in 60 days exactly replicates the payoff from the call option because

$$0.80 \times \$43 - \$34.40 = \$0 \text{ for } S_T = \$43$$
$$0.80 \times \$53 - \$34.40 = \$8 \text{ for } S_T = \$53.$$

● —————— ●

Panel B of Table 8.6 presents the calculations used to determine the value of the owner's equity in the levered portfolio when it was formed on February 7, 1996. This value of the assets is the number of shares of stock purchased times the price per share, $2/3 \times \$75.00 = \$50.00$. The debt is riskless by design so its value is the $46.67 future cash flow discounted at the market's riskless interest rate. The 3-month T-bill yield on February 7, 1996, was 4.84 percent and the option had 38 days until expiration so the amount of financing provided by the debt was $46.44 ($46.67/[1 + 0.0484/365]^{38}$). The owner's equity in the replica portfolio, the amount he or she must invest, is therefore $3.56 ($50.00 – $46.44).

The levered portfolio and the call option provide exactly the same payoffs on March 16 so they must have the same value on February 7. That is, the call option also must cost $3.56. Otherwise, arbitragers will sell the overvalued asset (the levered portfolio or the call) and buy the other one until their prices are identical and equilibrium is restored. Next we will demonstrate how arbitragers can execute these transactions without risk.

● ————————————————— ●   EXERCISE

DETERMINING THE COST OF THE REPLICA PORTFOLIO   8.4

How much of her own money must Allison Richards invest to construct the levered portfolio described in Exercise 8.3? The riskless interest rate is 5 percent.

Cost of stock $= 0.80 \times \$46 = \$36.80$

Minus financing provided by debt $= \dfrac{\$34.40}{(1 + .05/365)^{60}} = 34.12$

Allison's net investment $= \$ 2.68$

Allison can construct the levered portfolio that replicates the Foxworth call option with a net investment of $2.68. Therefore, the call option's value also must be $2.68.

● —————— ●

Construction and Performance of the Hedge Portfolio

In Chapter 5, we learned that investors can reduce risk by holding a portfolio of two or more assets that are less than perfectly correlated with one another. A portfolio reduces risk in this situation because a favorable deviation from the expected rate of return on one asset may offset an unfavorable deviation from the expected rate of return on the other. Portfolio diversification completely eliminates risk only if the two assets are perfectly negatively correlated. Then, two straight lines that intersect on the vertical axis comprise the opportunity set when it is graphed in terms of expected rate of return and standard deviation of return.

Now, the rates of return from buying common stock and call options on that stock are perfectly positively correlated. This association was demonstrated by the example in Table 8.6 where the payoffs (rates of return) from buying two-thirds of a share of stock were perfectly correlated with the payoffs (rates of return) from buying one call option on that stock. As we saw earlier, the payoffs from *selling* an option are exactly the opposite of the payoffs from buying an option. Consequently, the rates of return from buying two-thirds of a share of our example stock and *selling* one call option on that stock should be perfectly negatively correlated. This means the portfolio formed by these transactions should be riskless, that is, it should be a hedge portfolio like the one graphed in Exhibit 8.7.

Exhibit 8.7

OPPORTUNITY SET FOR BUYING STOCK AND SELLING CALL OPTION

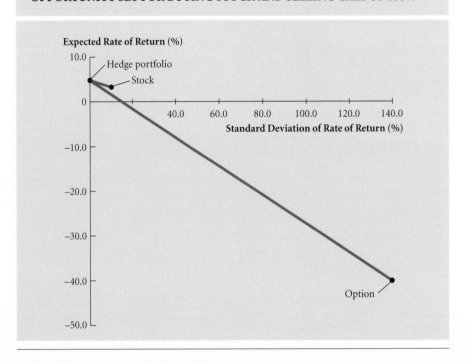

RATE OF RETURN ON THE HEDGE PORTFOLIO

Table 8.7

Cash Flow to Construct Hedge Portfolio on February 7, 1996			Cash Flow from Hedge Portfolio on March 16, 1996			
Buy 2/3 Share of Stock	Sell 1 Call Option	Net Cash Flow	Sell 2/3 Share of Stock	Payment to Owner of 1 Call Option	Net Cash Flow	Rate of Return
$-50.00	$3.56	$ - 46.44	$46.67	$ 0	$46.67	4.8%
			56.67	10	46.67	4.8

Table 8.7 demonstrates that the portfolio formed by buying two-thirds of a share of the example stock and selling one call option on that stock is a riskless hedge portfolio. An investor who forms this portfolio receives a net cash flow of $46.67 when the option expires—no matter what happens to the price of the underlying asset. The rate of return on this riskless portfolio is the value of *r* that satisfies the following equation.

$$(1 + r/365)^{38} = \$46.67/\$46.44$$

$$r = 4.8\%$$

The price of the call option causes the rate of return on the hedge portfolio to equal the market's riskless interest rate as it must to prevent arbitrage. Table 8.8 shows what happens if the price is different. Suppose first that the call option is overvalued with a market price of $3.80. Then the cost of the hedge portfolio on February 7 is $46.20 ($50 to buy two-thirds of a share of stock minus $3.80 from selling one call option). Whether the stock's value goes up or down, the net cash flow provided by the hedge portfolio on March 16 is still $46.67. The rate of return on the hedge portfolio is therefore a certain 9.7 percent. Arbitragers will form more hedge portfolios by selling more calls to earn this superior riskless rate of return. This increase in the supply of call options will cause their price to fall. An undervalued call option produces the opposite effect as arbitragers buy—rather than sell—calls to avoid the inferior riskless rate of return equal to 1.4 percent in the example. This pursuit of arbitrage profits forces the call option's price to equal $3.56.

The Binomial Option Pricing Model[7]

Appendix 8A derives the general form of the model we've been using by simply replacing the numbers in the example with symbols. This model is called the *binomial option pricing model* because the stock price changes are described by the binomial probability distribution. The result is given by Equation 8.4

---

[7]The option pricing model described in this section was originally developed in Richard J. Rendleman, Jr. and Brit J. Bartter, "Two-State Option Pricing," *Journal of Finance,* December 1979, pp. 1093–1110; and John C. Cox, Stephen A. Ross, and Mark Rubinstein, "Option Pricing: A Simplified Approach," *Journal of Financial Economics,* 1979, pp. 229–263.

Table 8.8   ARBITRAGE OPPORTUNITIES WHEN OPTIONS ARE INCORRECTLY VALUED

Option Price	Under- or Overvalued	Net Cash Flow to Construct Hedge Portfolio on February 7	Net Cash Flow from Hedge Portfolio on March 16	Rate of Return
$3.56	—	$ – 46.44	$46.67	4.8%
3.80	Over	– 46.20	46.67	9.7
3.40	Under	– 46.60	46.67	1.4

$$C_0 = S_0 \times \Phi_1 - \text{PV}(E) \times \Phi_2 \qquad [8.4]$$

where S_0 = current stock price

$\text{PV}(E)$ = present value of exercise price, E

= $E/(1 + r_f)^t$

r_f = riskless interest rate

t = number of time periods until expiration date

Φ_1 = $(C_T^+ - C_T^-)/(S_T^+ - S_T^-)$

Φ_2 = $(\Phi_1 \times S_T^- - C_T^-)/E$

S_T^+ = value of stock on expiration date if price increases

S_T^- = value of stock on expiration date if price decreases

C_T^+ = value of call option on expiration date if price of stock increases

= $\text{Max}(S_T^+ - E, 0)$

C_T^- = value of call option on expiration date if price of stock decreases

= $\text{Max}(S_T^- - E, 0)$

Let's use the binomial option pricing model to value March 75 calls and puts on the common stock of our example company modeled on DEC. First, calculate the values of the variables that enter Equation 8.4.

S_0 = $75, S_T^+ = $85, S_T^- = $70

E = $75

C_T^+ = $\text{Max}(S_T^+ - E, 0) = \text{Max}(\$85 - \$75, 0) = \$10$

C_T^- = $\text{Max}(S_T^- - E, 0) = \text{Max}(\$70 - \$75, 0) = \$0$

Φ_1 = $(C_T^+ - C_T^-)/(S_T^+ - S_T^-) = (\$10 - \$0)/(\$85 - \$70) = 2/3$

Φ_2 = $(\Phi_1 \times S_T^- - C_T^-)/E = (2/3 \times \$70 - \$0)/\$75 = 0.6222$

Now, substitute these values into Equation 8.4.

$$C_0 = S_0 \times \Phi_1 - \text{PV}(E) \times \Phi_2$$

$$= \$75 \times 2/3 - \frac{\$75.00}{(1 + 0.0484/365)^{38}} \times 0.6222$$

$$= \$3.57$$

The call option is worth \$3.56, the same value we obtained when we constructed and evaluated the replica portfolio.

EXERCISE
8.5

USING THE BINOMIAL OPTION PRICING MODEL

Use the binomial option pricing model to determine the value of the 60-day, \$45 call option on Foxworth Publishing Company common stock first mentioned in Exercise 8.3. Remember, the riskless rate of interest was 5 percent.

$$S_0 = \$46, S_T^+ = \$53, S_T^- = \$43$$
$$E = \$45$$
$$C_T^+ = \text{Max}(S_T^+ - E, 0) = \text{Max}(\$53 - \$45, 0) = \$8$$
$$C_T^- = \text{Max}(S_T^- - E, 0) = \text{Max}(\$43 - \$45, 0) = \$0$$
$$\Phi_1 = (C_T^+ - C_T^-)/(S_T^+ - S_T^-) = (\$8 - \$0)/(\$53 - \$43) = 0.80$$
$$\Phi_2 = (\Phi_1 \times S_T^- - C_T^-)/E = (0.80 \times \$43 - \$0)/\$45 = 0.7644$$
$$C_0 = S_0 \times \Phi_1 - PV(E) \times \Phi_2$$
$$= \$46 \times 0.80 - \frac{\$45.00}{(1 + 0.05/365)^{60}} \times 0.7644 = \$2.68$$

This is the same value that we computed using the replica portfolio.

Once you have the value of a call option, you can use put-call parity to determine the value of a put with the same exercise price and expiration date. Remember, put-call parity says that the value of a call option at expiration equals the value of the stock plus the value of a put minus the exercise price. That is,

$$S_T + P_T - E = C_T.$$

This relationship also must hold prior to the expiration date with the current values of the stock, put, and call and the present value of the exercise price substituted for the corresponding terms. The market value of a put option is therefore

$$P_0 = C_0 - S_0 + PV(E).$$

Applied to our example company,

$$P_0 = \$3.57 - \$75.00 + \frac{\$75.00}{(1 + 0.0484/365)^{38}}$$
$$= \$3.19.$$

The value of the March 75 put option for our example company is \$3.19.

8.6   USING PUT-CALL PARITY TO DETERMINE THE VALUE OF A PUT OPTION

Suppose Allison Richards also can purchase a put option on the Foxworth Publishing Company's common stock. Determine the value of a put option that expires in 60 days if its exercise price is $45.

You computed the value of a call option on Foxworth Publishing Company's common stock with these terms in Exercise 8.5 so you can use put-call parity to determine the put's value.

$$P_0 = C_0 - S_0 + PV(E)$$

$$= \$2.68 - \$46 + \frac{\$45}{(1 + 0.05/365)^{60}} = \$1.31$$

A put option on Foxworth Publishing Company's common stock is worth $1.31.

● ── ─────────── ── ●

The Effect of the Market Interest Rate on the Value of a Call Option Prior to the Expiration Date   Now you can see how the interest rate affects the value of a call option prior to the expiration date. In Equation 8.4, the value of the option equals the current stock price minus the present value of the option's exercise price (each term multiplied by the appropriate coefficient). An increase in the market interest rate reduces the effective price the option's owner pays for the stock, $E/(1 + r_f)$, and thereby increases the option's value.

Interpreting the Terms in the Binomial Option Pricing Model   The first point to note about the binomial option pricing model is that the current stock price is multiplied by $\Phi_1 = (C_T^+ - C_T^-)/(S_T^+ - S_T^-)$, which is two-thirds for our example company. We've seen this number before when we constructed the replica portfolio by purchasing two-thirds of a share of stock to make its payoffs equivalent to the call option's payoffs. We also bought two-thirds of a share of stock and sold one call option to construct the hedge portfolio.

The reappearance of this number in these contexts is not an accident. The term Φ_1 *always* tells us how many shares of stock to buy and how many call options to sell to construct the riskless or hedge portfolio. It is called the **hedge ratio** for this reason. Φ_1 also *always* tells us how many shares of the replica portfolio are equivalent to how many call options. The hedge ratio does not always equal two-thirds, but it has these interpretations—no matter what its value.

The hedge ratio and Φ_2 also can be interpreted as probabilities that describe the likelihood the call option will be exercised. We'll examine two extreme cases to see this interpretation.

Suppose first that the call's exercise price equals the stock's maximum value, $E = S_T^+$. The option can never expire in-the-money so its value should be zero. Substituting $E = S_T^+$ into the equations for Φ_1 and Φ_2,

$$C_T^+ = \text{Max}(S_T^+ - S_T^+, 0\ ) = 0$$

$$C_T^- = \text{Max}(S_T^- - S_T^+, 0) = 0$$

$$\Phi_1 = (C_T^+ - C_T^-)\ /\ (S_T^+ - S_T^-) = (0 - 0)/(S_T^+ - S_T^-) = 0$$

$$\Phi_2 = (\Phi_1 \times S_T^- - C_T^-)/E = (0 \times S_T^- - 0)/S_T^+ = 0$$

Interpreting these terms as probabilities, the option's value is zero because there is zero probability it will be exercised.

Now suppose that the call's exercise price equals the stock's minimum value, $E = S_T^-$. This option can never expire out-of-the-money. Substituting $E = S_T^-$ into the equations for Φ_1 and Φ_2,

$$C_T^+ = \text{Max}(S_T^+ - S_T^-, 0) = S_T^+ - S_T^-$$

$$C_T^- = \text{Max}(S_T^- - S_T^-, 0) = 0$$

$$\Phi_1 = (C_T^+ - C_T^-)\ /\ (S_T^+ - S_T^-) = (S_T^+ - S_T^-)\ /\ (S_T^+ - S_T^-) = 1$$

$$\Phi_2 = (\Phi_1 \times S_T^- - C_T^-)\ /E = (1 \times S_T^- - 0)\ /S_T^- = 1.$$

Interpreting these terms as probabilities again, exercise is certain and the option's value is

$$C_0 = S_0 - E/(1 + r_f).$$

The value of the option in this case equals the current stock price minus the present value of the price the investor will ultimately pay for the stock with certainty.

The structure of the more complicated option pricing model we'll examine in the next section is similar to Equation 8.4. Consequently, the lessons you've learned here about the relationship between call options and levered portfolios, about the opportunity to construct a riskless portfolio by purchasing stock and selling call options, and about the interpretation of the terms in the option pricing model as probabilities are applicable to that more complicated model.

The Risk-Neutral Form of the Binomial Option Pricing Model

We can rearrange the binomial option pricing model into another form that is sometimes more convenient to use. The result is given by Equation 8.5.

$$C_0 = \frac{C_T^+ \times q_T^+ + C_T^- \times (1 - q_T^+)}{1 + r_f} \qquad \text{[8.5]}$$

where C_T^+ = value of call option on expiration date if price of stock increases
    $= \text{Max}(S_T^+ - E, 0)$
    C_T^- = value of call option on expiration date if price of stock
        decreases
    $= \text{Max}(S_T^- - E, 0)$
    q_T^+ = Risk-neutral probability that the value of the asset increases
        (the call option will expire in-the-money)
    $= (1 + r_f - d)/(u - d);\ u = S_T^+/S_0,\ d = S_T^-/S_0$

The numerator of Equation 8.5 is the option's expected value on the expiration date. The option's market value, C_0, equals that expected future value discounted at the riskless rate of interest. This model is called the risk-neutral form because the discount rate does not include a risk premium; the option's value is computed *as if* investors are indifferent or neutral to risk.

The probabilities applied to the possible outcomes on the expiration date, C_T^+ and C_T^-, must be computed in a way that is consistent with the risk-neutral form of this model. Calculating q_T^+ as $(1 + r_f - d)/(u - d)$ provides this consistency, but other definitions of the probability that the option will expire in-the-money do not. For example, using the independently estimated probability that the stock price will increase for q_T^+ is wrong because stock prices are not actually established by investors who are indifferent to risk.

As an illustration, let's apply the risk-neutral form of the binomial option pricing model to our example based on DEC. The possible values of the option on the expiration date are

$$C_T^+ = \text{Max}(S_T^+ - E, 0) = \text{Max}(\$85 - \$75, 0) = \$10$$
$$C_T^- = \text{Max}(S_T^- - E, 0) = \text{Max}(\$70 - \$75, 0) = \$0.$$

The values of u and d are

$$u = S_T^+/S_0 = \$85/\$75 = 1.1333$$
$$d = S_T^-/S_0 = \$70/\$75 = 0.9333.$$

The risk-neutral probability that the option will expire in-the-money is

$$q_T^+ = (1 + r_f - d) / (u - d)$$
$$= [(1 + 0.0484/365)^{38} - 0.9333]/[1.1333 - 0.9333]$$
$$= 0.3588.$$

Therefore, the value of the call option is

$$C_0 = \frac{C_T^+ \times q_T^+ + C_T^- \times (1 - q_T^+)}{1 + r_f}$$
$$= \frac{\$10 \times 0.3588 + \$0 \times (1 - 0.3588)}{(1 + 0.0484/365)^{38}}$$
$$= \$3.57.$$

This is, of course, the same value we obtained earlier using the form of the binomial option pricing model described by Equation 8.4.

EXERCISE   •   ───   •

8.7   USING THE RISK-NEUTRAL FORM OF THE BINOMIAL OPTION PRICING MODEL

Use the risk-neutral form of the binomial option pricing model to determine the value of Allison Richards' call option on Foxworth Publishing Company first mentioned in Exercise 8.3.

The possible values of the call option on the expiration date are

$$
\begin{aligned}
C_T^+ &= \text{Max}(S_T^+ - E, 0) \\
&= \text{Max}(\$53 - \$45, 0) = \$8 \\
C_T^- &= \text{Max}(S_T^- - E, 0) \\
&= \text{Max}(\$43 - \$45, 0) = \$0.
\end{aligned}
$$

The values of u and d are

$$
\begin{aligned}
u &= S_T^+/S_0 = \$53/\$46 = 1.1522 \\
d &= S_T^-/S_0 = \$43/\$46 = 0.9348.
\end{aligned}
$$

The risk-neutral probability that the option will expire in-the-money is

$$
\begin{aligned}
q_T^+ &= (1 + r_f - d)/(u - d) \\
&= [(1 + 0.05/365)^{60} - 0.9348]/[1.1522 - 0.9348] \\
&= 0.3379.
\end{aligned}
$$

Therefore, the value of the call option is

$$
\begin{aligned}
C_0 &= \frac{C_T^+ \times q_T^+ + C_T^- \times (1 - q_T^+)}{1 + r_f} \\
&= \frac{\$8 \times 0.3379 + \$0 \times (1 - 0.3379)}{(1 + 0.05/365)^{60}} \\
&= \$2.68.
\end{aligned}
$$

This is the same answer you obtained in Exercise 8.5 because the risk-neutral approach is simply an alternative form of the binomial option pricing model.

One of the advantages to the risk-neutral form of the binomial option pricing model is that we can use it to value a put option directly without relying on put-call parity. Let's re-examine the March 75 put option on our example company that we valued earlier at $3.19. First, we must calculate the possible values of the put option on the expiration date.

$$
\begin{aligned}
P_T^+ &= \text{Max}(E - S_T^+, 0) \\
&= \text{Max}(\$75 - \$85, 0) = \$0 \\
P_T^- &= \text{Max}(E - S_T^-, 0) \\
&= \text{Max}(\$75 - \$70, 0) = \$5
\end{aligned}
$$

We already have the risk-neutral probabilities:

q_T^+ = Risk-neutral probability that the value of the asset increases (the put option will expire out-of-the-money)

= 0.3588.

Rewriting Equation 8.5 to apply to put options and substituting the above values,

$$P_0 = \frac{P_T^+ \times q_T^+ + P_T^- \times (1 - q_T^+)}{1 + r_f}$$

$$= \frac{\$0 \times 0.3588 + \$5 \times (1 - 0.3588)}{(1 + 0.0484/365)^{38}} = \$3.19.$$

Again, this is the same value we obtained earlier but with fewer steps.

E X E R C I S E

8.8   USING THE RISK NEUTRAL FORM OF THE BINOMIAL OPTION PRICING MODEL TO VALUE A PUT

Use the risk-neutral form of the binomial option pricing model to value the put option on Foxworth Publishing Company's common stock introduced in Exercise 8.6. The possible values of the put option on the expiration date are

$$P_T^+ = \text{Max}(E - S_T^+, 0)$$
$$= \text{Max}(\$45 - \$53, 0) = \$0$$
$$P_T^- = \text{Max}(E - S_T^-, 0)$$
$$= \text{Max}(\$45 - \$43, 0) = \$2.$$

The risk-neutral probabilities were calculated in Exercise 8.7.

q_T^+ = risk-neutral probability that the value of the asset increases
(the put option will expire out-of-the-money)

$= 0.3379$

Therefore, the value of the put option is

$$P_0 = \frac{P_T^+ \times q_T^+ + P_T^+ \times (1 - q_T^+)}{1 + r_f}$$

$$= \frac{\$0 \times 0.3379 + \$2 \times (1 - 0.3379)}{(1 + 0.05/365)^{60}} = \$1.31.$$

This is the same answer you obtained in Exercise 8.6 using put-call parity.

Another advantage of the risk-neutral form of the binomial option pricing model is that it is applicable to more than one time period. We will not explore these applications here but you can learn more about the model's use for this purpose by consulting the references at the end of the chapter.

8.3   THE BLACK-SCHOLES OPTION PRICING MODEL

We obtained a simple option pricing model by assuming there are only two possible values for the underlying asset on the date the option expires. This is, of course, a wide departure from reality because the asset's value may change many times during the option's life and there are a large number of possible values for any particular change. As a result, there may be virtually an infinite number of possible values for the underlying asset on the date the option expires.[8]

Admitting the possibility that the underlying asset's initial value evolves over time into a value that falls somewhere within an infinite range poses two serious problems for determining the option's price. First, we cannot use the simple four-step procedure described in Section 8.2 to establish the hedge portfolio. Remember, this procedure permitted us to sidestep the problem of determining the cost of debt in the replica portfolio. Second, even if we could establish the hedge portfolio at the time the option was written, the hedge ratio changes every time the stock's price changes. This means it is necessary to continually adjust the composition of the hedge portfolio as the option ages.

Fischer Black and Myron Scholes solved these problems.[9] They assumed that the natural log of the stock price is normally distributed and borrowed some principles from physics to obtain a pricing model analogous to Equation 8.4. The derivation of their option pricing model is beyond the scope of this textbook but its interpretation and use are well within your grasp. Therefore, we will focus on these aspects of the model in the remainder of this section.

The Valuation Equation

Equation 8.6 is the Black-Scholes Option Pricing Model.

$$C_0 = S_0 \times N(d_1) - PV(E) \times N(d_2) \qquad [8.6]$$

where
S_0 = current stock price
$PV(E)$ = present value of exercise price, E
$\quad = E/e^{rt}$ where e^{rt} = riskless rate of return, r, continuously compounded for t time periods
t = number of time periods until the expiration date
$N(d)$ = probability that the normally distributed random variable Z is less than or equal to d
$d_1 = \ln[S_0/PV(E)]/\sigma\sqrt{t} + (\sigma\sqrt{t})/2$
$d_2 = d_1 - \sigma\sqrt{t}$
σ = standard deviation per period of the asset's continuously compounded rate of return

Note that any unit of time can be used in the model as long as it is used consistently to describe r_f, t, and σ. Here's an illustration.

The current price of Dickson Motor Works' common stock is $59.375 per share. A call option on this stock has an exercise price of $55.00 and expires in 30 days. What

---

[8]To see this, suppose a stock's price could change only plus or minus 1 percent every five minutes. Then there would be $2^{12} = 4,096$ possible values for the stock's price at the end of one hour. The number of possible values at the end of one six-hour trading day would be $2^{72} = 4.7 \times 10^{21}$.

[9]Fischer Black and Myron Scholes, "The Pricing of Options and Corporate Liabilities," *Journal of Political Economy,* May–June 1973, pp. 637–654.

is the value of this call option if the standard deviation of continuously compounded rate of return on the stock is 0.2968 and the riskless rate of return is 5.0 percent per year?

First, express the time until the option expires in years.

$$t \text{ in years} = 30 \text{ days}/365 \text{ days} = 0.0822$$

Second, calculate the values of the other variables in Equation 8.5.

$$PV(E) = E/e^{rt} = \$55.00/e^{0.05 \times 0.0822} = \$54.774$$

$$d_1 = \ln[S_0/PV(E)]/\sigma\sqrt{t} + (\sigma\sqrt{t})/2$$

$$= \ln[\$59.375/\$54.774]/(0.2968 \times \sqrt{0.0822}) + (0.2968 \times \sqrt{0.0822})/2 = 0.9904$$

$$d_2 = d_1 - \sigma\sqrt{t}$$

$$= 0.9904 - 0.2968 \times \sqrt{0.0822} = 0.9053$$

Third, use a table for the standard normal distribution or the cumulative normal distribution function in a spreadsheet program to determine $N(d_1)$ and $N(d_2)$. From Table A.4,

$$N(0.9904) = 0.8390$$

$$N(0.9053) = 0.8173.$$

Finally, substitute these values into Equation 8.6.

$$C_0 = S_0 \times N(d_1) - PV(E) \times N(d_2)$$

$$= \$59.375 \times 0.8390 - \$54.774 \times 0.8173$$

$$= \$5.05$$

The call option is worth $5.05, slightly more than its value if it is exercised immediately, $4.375 ($59.375 − $55.00), as we should expect.

EXERCISE ●————————————————————————●

8.9   USING THE BLACK-SCHOLES OPTION PRICING MODEL

Determine the value of another call option on Dickson Motor Works stock that has an exercise price of $50 and expires in 45 days.

The amount of time until the option expires expressed in years is

$$t \text{ in years} = 45 \text{ days}/365 \text{ days} = 0.1233.$$

The values of the other variables are

$$PV(E) = E/e^{rt} = \$50.00/e^{0.05 \times 0.1233} = \$49.6927$$

$$d_1 = \ln[S_0/PV(E)]/\sigma\sqrt{t} + (\sigma\sqrt{t})/2$$

$$= \ln[\$59.375/\$49.6927]/(0.2968 \times \sqrt{0.1233}) + (0.2968 \times \sqrt{0.1233})/2 = 1.7602$$

$$d_2 = d_1 - \sigma\sqrt{t}$$

$$= 1.7602 - 0.2968 \times \sqrt{0.1233} = 1.6560.$$

From Table A.4, $N(d_1)$ and $N(d_2)$ are

$$N(1.7603) = 0.9608$$
$$N(1.6561) = 0.9511.$$

The value of the $50 call option that expires in 45 days is therefore

$$C_0 = S_0 \times N(d_1) - PV(E) \times N(d_2)$$
$$= \$59.375 \times 0.9608 - \$49.6927 \times 0.9511$$
$$= \$9.78.$$

This call option is worth more than the other Dickson Motor Works call option ($9.78 versus $5.05) because it has a lower exercise price and a longer time until expiration.

● ——————— ●

Interpreting the Terms in the Black-Scholes Option Pricing Model

The Black-Scholes option pricing model is more complicated than our simple model but has exactly the same structure. The value of a call option equals the current price of the stock multiplied by a probability, $N(d_1)$, minus the present value of the exercise price multiplied by another probability, $N(d_2)$, that is a function of the first. The probabilities are obtained from the standard normal distribution in this case but $N(d_1)$ is still the hedge ratio. These characteristics indicate the Black-Scholes model also is based on the principle that a call option is equivalent to a levered portfolio. Furthermore, $N(d_1)$ and $N(d_2)$ are similar to Φ_1 and Φ_2 in that they account for the effect of uncertainty on the option's value. Finally, the stock's expected rate of return and investors' attitude toward risk do not affect the option's value, as before.

Estimating the Values of the Parameters

An investor must estimate the values of only five parameters to use the Black-Scholes option pricing model. These variables are the current value of the underlying asset, S_0; the call option's exercise price, E; the number of periods until the option expires, t; the market's riskless rate of return per period, r_f; and the standard deviation per period of the underlying asset's continuously compounded rate of return, σ. For options on common stock, S_0 is the market price, available from a number of sources including *The Wall Street Journal*, while E and t are specified in the option contract. The current rate of return on U.S. Treasury bills is commonly used as an estimate of the riskless rate of return.

The standard deviation per period of the underlying asset's continuously compounded rate of return is the more difficult parameter to estimate. This value should be a *forecast* of the asset's risk over the term of the option contract; and accurate forecasts are notoriously difficult to prepare. Historical data are sometimes used for this purpose but must be adjusted to account for ways the future may differ from the past.

An alternative forecasting procedure is available for common stocks that have publicly traded options. *Assuming the Black-Scholes option pricing model is correct,* you set the call option's market value equal to the right-hand side of Equation 8.6 and solve for the implied standard deviation, $\hat{\sigma}$. Then, you can use the $\hat{\sigma}$ you obtain to price other call options on that stock given their exercise prices, expiration dates, and so on. Brenner and Subrahmanyam have shown that when the present value of the exercise price equals the current price of the stock, $S_0 = PV(E)$, an acceptable estimate of the implied standard deviation is[10]

$$\hat{\sigma} \cong (2.5 \times C_0)/(S_0 \times \sqrt{t}) \qquad [8.7]$$

As an illustration, suppose the current price of a share of Michael's Dairy Products common stock is $29.50, the riskless rate of return is 5 percent per year, and call options with the characteristics shown below are available.

Call Option	Exercise Price	Market Value	PV(E)
28 day	$30.00	$1.43	$30/e^{0.05 \times 28/365} = \$29.89$
91 day	30.00	2.45	$30/e^{0.05 \times 91/365} = \$29.63$

The present value of the exercise price for the 91-day call option, $29.63, is closer to the current stock price, $29.50, so it is the better choice to estimate the implied standard deviation. Substituting the characteristics of this option into Equation 8.7, the implied annual standard deviation of the continuously compounded rate of return on Michael's Dairy Products' common stock is

$$\hat{\sigma} \cong (2.5 \times C_0)/(S_0 \times \sqrt{t}) = (2.5 \times \$2.45)/(\$29.50 \times \sqrt{91/365})$$

$$\cong 0.4158.$$

You can use this implied standard deviation to estimate the values of other options on Michael's Dairy Products' common stock.

EXERCISE
8.10

ESTIMATING AN IMPLIED STANDARD DEVIATION

Determine the implied standard deviation of the continuously compounded rate of return on Kipling's Kampground's common stock if its current price is $21 per share and call options are available on this stock with the characteristics described below. The riskless rate of return is 5 percent.

Call Option	Exercise Price	Market Value
14 day	$22.50	$1.00
77 day	22.50	1.75

The present values of these options' exercise prices are

14-day option: $PV(E) = \$22.50/e^{0.05 \times 14/365} = \$22.46$

77-day option: $PV(E) = \$22.50/e^{0.05 \times 77/365} = \$22.26.$

---

[10]Menachem Brenner and Marti G. Subrahmanyam, "A Simple Approach to Option Valuation and Hedging in the Black-Scholes Model," *Financial Analysts Journal*, March–April 1994, pp. 25–28.

Use the characteristics of the 77-day option for your estimate because the present value of its exercise price, $22.26, is closer to the current stock price of $21.00.

$$\hat{\sigma} \cong (2.5 \times C_0)/(S_0 \times \sqrt{t}) = (2.5 \times \$1.75)/(\$21.00 \times \sqrt{77/365})$$

$$\cong 0.4536$$

The standard deviation of the continuously compounded rate of return on Kipling's Kampground's common stock is approximately 0.4536.

● ———————— ●

Comprehensive Example

Now let's put all your option pricing skills to work to estimate the market values of Digital Equipment Corporation's (DEC's) options. Table 8.1 shows DEC's stock price on February 7, 1996 and the exercise prices and expiration dates of the options on their stock. *The Wall Street Journal* reported the yield on three-month U.S. Treasury bills on that date was 4.84 percent so we will use this value as the market's riskless rate of return. The present value of the exercise price of the February 75 call option, $74.90 ($75.00/$e^{0.0484 \times 10/365}$), is closest to the current stock price of $75.00. Substituting the appropriate values for this option into Brenner and Subrahmanyam's approximation for the implied standard deviation,

$$\hat{\sigma} \cong (2.5 \times C_0)/(S_0 \times \sqrt{t})$$

$$\cong (2.5 \times \$1.8125)/(\$75.00 \times \sqrt{10/365})$$

$$\cong 0.3650.$$

The estimated values of the calls and puts are given in Table 8.9. The calculations for the March 60 options are given below.

$$t \text{ in years} = 38 \text{ days}/365 \text{ days} = 0.1041$$

$$PV(E) = E/e^{rt} = \$60.00/e^{0.0484 \times 0.1041} = \$59.698$$

$$d_1 = \ln[S_0/PV(E)]/\sigma\sqrt{t} + (\sigma\sqrt{t})/2$$
$$= \ln[\$75.000/\$59.698]/(0.3650 \times \sqrt{0.1041}) + (0.3650 \times \sqrt{0.1041})/2 = 1.9965$$

$$d_2 = d_1 - \sigma\sqrt{t}$$
$$= 1.9965 - 0.3650 \times \sqrt{0.1041} = 1.8787$$

From Table A.4,

$$N(1.9965) = 0.9771$$
$$N(1.8787) = 0.9699$$

$$C_0 = S_0 \times N(d_1) - PV(E) \times N(d_2)$$
$$= \$75.000 \times 0.9771 - \$59.698 \times 0.9699$$
$$= \$15.381.$$

Using put-call parity,

$$P_0 = C_0 - S_0 + PV(E)$$
$$= \$15.381 - \$75.000 + \$59.698 = \$0.079.$$

Table 8.9   USING THE BLACK-SCHOLES OPTION PRICING MODEL TO VALUE DIGITAL EQUIPMENT OPTIONS

Exercise Price	Expiration Date	Term	Call Option Value Actual	Call Option Value Estimate	Put Option Value Actual	Put Option Value Estimate
$50.00	July 20	164 days			$0.625	$0.241
60.00	March 16	38 days	$15.000	$15.381	0.250	0.079
65.00	April 20	73 days	12.000	11.690	1.750	1.064
70.00	February 17	10 days	4.500	5.357	0.438	0.264
75.00	February 17	10 days	1.813	1.856	2.625	1.757
75.00	March 16	38 days	3.750	3.705	4.250	3.328
75.00	April 20	73 days	5.500	5.225	5.250	4.502
80.00	March 16	38 days	2.000	1.784		
80.00	April 20	73 days	3.500	3.181		
80.00	July 20	164 days	6.125	5.936	9.750	9.215

Current date: February 7, 1996
Current stock price: $75.00
Standard deviation of stock's rate of return:* 0.3650
Riskless rate of return: 0.0484

*Inferred from actual value of February 75 call option using Brenner and Subrahmanyam's approximation, $\hat{\sigma} = (2.5 \times C_0)/(S_0 \times \sqrt{t})$.

Source: *The Wall Street Journal*, February 8, 1996, various pages.

The actual market values of these options on February 7, 1996 were $15.00 and $0.25. As you can see, the Black-Scholes option pricing model does a good job of estimating the market values of real call and put options. This is why the model and variations of it are widely used by options traders, investment bankers, and financial managers throughout the world.

8.4   RECOGNIZING AND EVALUATING MANAGEMENT OPTIONS

Managers are employed to use their knowledge, skills, and judgment to make decisions that increase the owners' wealth. Any real decision requires a choice among two or more options, which implies a manager's real job is to manage options in the owners' interests. Effective managers are those who recognize the options available to them and can accurately assess their value. Managers may not always be able to use option valuation principles to accomplish these tasks but knowledge of these principles can help.

The first step to applying option valuation principles in this context is identify the management options. These options exist *whenever* managers have the opportunity—

but not the obligation—to take some action. There are innumerable options in production. For example, the dual-fuel steam boiler described earlier provides options because the managers have the opportunity to switch fuels to reduce costs. The opportunity to switch between producing a component part or buying it from another company (outsourcing) is a similar, valuable option. Crosstraining workers provides options if they can be assigned to tasks that have the highest payoffs. Finally, a flexible process that can be switched from manufacturing one product to another provides comparable options on the output side.

There also are countless options in sales and marketing. An investment in research and development provides an option on a new product. Farther down the new product development path, an investment in test marketing provides an option on full-scale production and sales. Even the willingness to maintain a finished goods inventory has option-value because the company is not required to sell the product unless the price is favorable.

Once you have identified the management options, you can begin to evaluate them. It may be difficult to assign a dollar value to some of them; however, option valuation principles can at least tell you what factors to consider. For example, you have just learned that an option is more valuable the greater the volatility of the underlying asset. Consequently, the dual-fuel steam boiler is more valuable the greater the volatility of energy prices. Companies that manufacture and buy boilers must understand this relationship to assess single- and dual-fuel boiler prices. Similarly, the opportunities to outsource production or reassign cross-trained employees are more valuable the greater the uncertainty about demand. This knowledge is important to managers who want to keep these options open and to union representatives who may want to negotiate a contract that closes them. Both sides must know the option-value of these alternatives to make sound decisions. See "In the News" for a description of how Merck identifies and analyzes biotechnology options.

We will use option valuation principles to explicitly evaluate some management options in Chapter 13. There, you will learn that opportunities to expand, contract, accelerate, delay, and abandon a line of business should be viewed as options and evaluated accordingly. We also will examine outsourcing from an options perspective. In each case, you will see that the failure to recognize and evaluate a decision's option-value overlooks an important source of increase in the owners' wealth.

8.5 SUMMARY

Options play an increasingly important role in financial management. Companies give stock options to their managers and employees to help them adopt an owner's perspective so they will make decisions that maximize the owners' wealth. Companies also create their own financial and real options to improve their ability to adapt to uncertainty. They issue callable bonds that provide the option to refund debt when interest rates decrease and they install flexible manufacturing processes that enable them to limit their exposure to increases in operating costs. Virtually anyone may receive options or be responsible for managing them and therefore must understand their features and value.

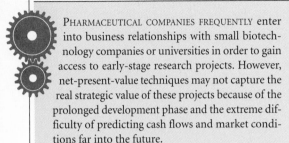

IN THE NEWS

OPTION ANALYSIS AT MERCK

PHARMACEUTICAL COMPANIES FREQUENTLY enter into business relationships with small biotechnology companies or universities in order to gain access to early-stage research projects. However, net-present-value techniques may not capture the real strategic value of these projects because of the prolonged development phase and the extreme difficulty of predicting cash flows and market conditions far into the future.

As a result, the business agreements are often structured so that the larger pharmaceutical company will make an up-front payment followed by a series of progress payments to the smaller company or university for research. These contingent progress payments give the pharmaceutical company the right—but not the obligation—to make further investments: for instance, funding clinical trials or providing capital for manufacturing requirements. This is known as an *option contract*.

The Financial Evaluation and Analysis Group at Merck was recently presented with just such an option contract—I'll call it Project Gamma. Under the terms of the proposed agreement, Merck would make a $2 million payment to Gamma over a period of three years. In addition, Merck would pay Gamma royalties should the product ever come to market. Merck had the option to terminate the agreement at any time if dissatisfied with the progress of the research.

Here was a project that clearly had option characteristics, an overwhelming potential upside with little current downside exposure. The group, therefore, chose to use the Black-Scholes option-pricing model to determine the project's option value. Five factors that influence an option's price are used in the Black-Scholes model. The finance group defined those factors as follows:

- The *exercise price* is the capital investment to be made approximately two years hence.
- The *stock price*, or value of the underlying asset, is the present value of the cash flows from the project.
- The *time to expiration* was varied over two, three, and four years because the option could be exercised in two years at the earliest but expired in four years.
- A sample of the annual standard deviation of returns for typical biotechnology stocks was obtained from an investment bank as a proxy measure for *project volatility*. A conservative range for the volatility of the project was set at 40 percent to 60 percent.
- A *risk-free rate of interest* of 4.5 percent was assumed.

The option value that the Financial Evaluation and Analysis Group arrived at from the above factors showed that this option had significantly more value than the up-front payment that needed to be invested.

The essential feature of an option is that it permits—but does not require—its owner to act. A call option permits its owner to buy another asset at a specified price within a specified period of time while a put option permits its owner to sell another asset under specified terms. Calls and puts are fundamental types of options that can be used to represent the value of a levered portfolio, insurance, and many other financial products and policy choices.

We determine an option's value by exploiting the association between a call option and a levered portfolio. We proceed by constructing a portfolio with payoffs that replicate the call option's payoffs on the expiration date. Because these terminal payoffs are equal, arbitrage ensures that the option's initial value must equal the portfolio's initial value, which is observable in market prices. This replica portfolio technique is the explicit approach used by the binomial option pricing model and this technique is implicit in the more complicated Black-Scholes model.

Both the binomial and Black-Scholes option pricing models reveal that an option's value depends on the value of the underlying asset, the price at which you can purchase the asset by exercising the option, the asset's risk, the amount of time until the option expires, and the market rate of interest. Somewhat surprisingly, an option's value is higher the riskier the asset and the higher market interest rates. These relationships arise because an option permits investors to accept favorable risk without accepting unfavorable risk and because the present value of the exercise price is lower at higher interest rates.

These option pricing models are among the more successful innovations in finance because they do a good job of explaining the prices of the options investors actually buy and sell. The models' effectiveness, combined with the development of organized options exchanges, has led to the rapid development of options markets, the design of new financial products to manage risk, and the application of option principles to a wide range of managerial choices. We will explore several of these applications in subsequent chapters.

- ## KEY TERMS

Call option *310*	Striking price *310*	In-the-money *311*
Put option *310*	European options *310*	Put-call parity *321*
Exercise the option *310*	American options *310*	Hedge ratio *336*
Exercise price *310*	Option premium *311*	

- ## QUESTIONS AND PROBLEMS

1. Briefly define each of the following terms.

    (a) Call and put options

    (b) Exercise an option

    (c) Exercise or strike price

    (d) American and European options

    (e) Writing an option

    (f) Option premium

2. Owning an option and writing or selling an option are distinctly different transactions.

    (a) How do the rights and responsibilities of option owners and option writers differ?

    (b) Illustrate your answer to part (a) by graphing a call option owner's and writer's payoffs on the expiration date. Assume the exercise price is $50 and ignore the option premium.

    (c) Redraw your graph assuming the option premium is $5. Explain why the option writer requires this payment and the option owner is willing to pay it.

3. A husband and wife who independently manage their retirement portfolios discovered one owns call options on Bull and Bear Pubs while the other sold exactly the same number of put options on this stock. Their options have identical exercise prices and expiration dates.

   (a) Will they have identical payoffs when these options expire? Explain your answer.

   (b) Graph the couple's net payoff from these options on the expiration date. What simple, direct transaction could they have jointly used to produce the same effect?

4. The following stock and option prices are from the February 26, 1996 issue of *The Wall Street Journal*. Classify each of the options as in-the-money, out-of-the money, or at-the-money.

   (a) A $12.50 October call option on AMD. The closing stock price was $13.875.

   (b) A $105 July put option on Microsoft. The closing stock price was $122.

   (c) A $7.50 December put option on Value Jet. The closing stock price was $8.9375.

   (d) A $35 August call option on Pepsi. The closing stock price was $35.

5. Carefully explain your answers to these questions about assets, options, and risk.

   (a) How does an asset's risk affect the asset's value?

   (b) How does an asset's risk affect the value of an *option* on that asset?

   (c) How does an option's risk affect the option's value?

6. The expression, $C_T = \text{Max}(S_T - E, 0)$, is central to option valuation. Use simple language to explain the meaning of this expression. How does it represent an option's most important characteristic?

7. Samuel Choi wants to purchase a put option with an exercise price of $35 on Harrell Stores common stock. Unfortunately, only $35 call options are presently available.

   (a) Use the put-call parity relationship to show Samuel how to create his own put option.

   (b) Graph Samuel's payoffs on the expiration date to confirm the effect of your transactions. Assume a stock price range of $20 to $50.

8. List the variables that determine a call option's value prior to the expiration date. State whether each variable has a positive or negative effect on the option's value and explain why.

9. The December 19, 1996 issue of *The Wall Street Journal* reported the closing prices for Chrysler's and Micron Technology's common stocks and call options on the stocks shown below. The companies' betas are from the Value Line Investment Survey for Windows.

	Chrysler	Micron
Closing stock price	$32.625	$32.375
Beta	1.30	1.80

Exercise Price	Expiration	Closing Price of Chrysler's Option	Closing Price of Micron's Option
$32.50	January	$1.375	$2.1875
35.00	January	0.500	1.2500
35.00	July	2.250	5.1250

   (a) Which options were in- and out-of-the-money when the markets closed? Why were investors willing to pay *anything* for out-of-the-money call options?

   (b) Why are both companies' January $35 call options worth less than their January $32.50 options?

(c) Why are both companies' July $35 call options worth more than their January $35 options?

(d) Why are Micron's call options worth more than Chrysler's call options?

10. Under normal circumstances, the greater an asset's risk, the lower its value. What is it about options that alters this fundamental relationship?

11. An announcement that Japanese banks intend to buy fewer U.S. Treasury securities sent a shock wave through the stock and bond markets. What happened to option prices?

12. The binomial option pricing model is $C_0 = S_0 \times \Phi_1 - PV(E) \times \Phi_2$. Use simple language to interpret the Φ_1 and Φ_2 terms.

13. The closing prices for call and put options on Best Buy's common stock on June 14, 1996 are shown below. The company's common stock closed at $23.125 that day.

Exercise Price	Expiration	Closing Price of Call Option	Closing Price of Put Option
$20.00	June	$3.25	–
22.50	June	1.00	$0.375
22.50	September	2.625	1.500
25.00	June	0.3125	1.875
25.00	July	0.625	2.25
25.00	September	1.375	3.125

(Source: *The Wall Street Journal*, June 17, 1996, p. C18)

(a) Determine the intrinsic value of each call and put option.

(b) Was any option's closing price *less* than its intrinsic value? Explain.

14. Apache Corporation explores for and produces natural gas. The company's common stock and options are traded on the NYSE. The stock's closing price on June 14, 1996 was $30.00. The closing price of an October call option with a $30.00 exercise price was $2.00 (*The Wall Street Journal*, June 17, 1996, p. C18).

(a) Suppose you have $9,000 to invest in either a common stock or option portfolio on June 14. How many shares of Apache stock can you buy? How many options?

(b) Determine the average rate of return and standard deviation of return of the Apache stock and option portfolios. Use Table 8.3 as a guide and assume the price of Apache's common stock when the options expire can be $20, $25, $30, $35, or $40.

(c) Identify and discuss as many differences between the Apache stock and option portfolios as you can. Is there an alternative to buying options that produces similar differences? Explain your answer.

15. The December 19, 1996 issue of *The Wall Street Journal* reported the following prices for call options on Intel's common stock. The stock's closing price was $135.75.

Exercise Price	Expiration	Closing Price
$125.00	December	$10.875
125.00	January	14.00
125.00	April	20.25

(a) Prepare a graph that shows the minimum and maximum values of these stock options. Use a stock price range of $0 to $150.

(b) Plot the values of the December, January, and April call options on this graph. Do the locations of these call options' values relative to the minimum and maximum values make sense given their characteristics? Explain your answer.

16. Louis Hermann would like to purchase options on Doctor's Medical Supply Corporation's common stock. He prefers an option with an exercise price of $35 but none are available. Consequently, he has decided to create a homemade option by constructing a replica portfolio. The current price of the stock is $30 per share but Louis believes this price will move to $25 or $45 at the end of three months. The riskless rate of return is 4 percent per year.

    (a) What will the value of Louis's homemade option be on the expiration date if the stock price is $25? $45?

    (b) Determine the composition of the levered portfolio that will replicate the expiration date values you computed in part (a).

    (c) What is the value of the levered portfolio at the time it is formed? How much of this value is financed with debt and how much with Louis's own equity?

    (d) Has Louis successfully created a homemade call option? Explain your answer.

17. Consider a call option with an exercise price of $55 on a stock that may be worth $45 or $65 when the option expires.

    (a) Use the appropriate term from the binomial option pricing model to determine this option's hedge ratio.

    (b) Confirm your answer by showing that buying shares of stock and selling call options in this ratio does provide a riskless portfolio.

18. The diagram below describes the current price of a share of common stock and its possible values at the end of four months. A call option on that stock has an exercise price of $20 and expires in four months. The current value of the call option is $2.196. The riskless rate of return over the four-month period is 2 percent.

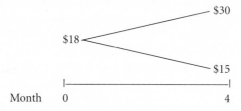

    (a) Calculate the rate of return for each of the following investment alternatives if the stock's value increases to $30 and if it decreases to $15.

        Buying one share of stock.

        Buying one option.

        Constructing the hedge portfolio.

    (b) Use simple language to explain the relationship between risk and return among these investment alternatives.

19. Michael Selphish, the CEO of Alakazam Entertainment Company, received 100,000 options on the company's common stock on December 31, 1996. The common stock's closing price that day was $45. The options have an exercise price of $45 and expire on December 31, 1997 when Michael believes the stock price will be either $40 or $60. The yield on U.S. Treasury strips with one year until maturity on December 31, 1996 was 5.5 percent.

    (a) Use the binomial option pricing model to estimate the market value of Selphish's compensation.

(b) Use the risk neutral form of the binomial option pricing model to confirm your answer to part (a).

(c) On January 1, 1997, Selphish announced the formation of an admittedly risky joint venture to develop Internet-based entertainment sites. The company's stock price fell to $42 per share on analysts' assessments that its end-of-year value could be as high as $80 or as low as $30, depending on the joint venture's success or failure. Recalculate the value of Michael's compensation and explain why he approved this risky joint venture that reduced the owners' wealth.

20. Okie Dokie processes western red cedar trees for use as mulch in gerbil cages. The company's stock price closed at $22.50 on December 15, 1997 but is expected to equal $18 or $24 in 45 days when the results of Christmas sales are known. Helen Franks works in the pet department of a large discount store and believes pet sales are low this year. Consequently, she intends to buy an at-the-money put option on Okie Dokie stock.

(a) Use the risk-neutral form of the binomial option pricing model to determine the price Helen should expect to pay for the put option.

(b) Calculate the value of an at-the-money call option and use put-call parity to confirm your answer to part (a).

21. The December 19, 1996 issue of *The Wall Street Journal* reported the following prices for call options on AMD's common stock on December 18. The stock's closing price was $27.00.

Exercise Price	Expiration	Closing Price
$25.00	January 18	$3.00
27.50	December 21	0.375
27.50	January 18	1.50
30.00	January 18	0.6875

(a) Use each of these option quotations to estimate the standard deviation of the continuously compounded rate of return on AMD's common stock.

(b) Which estimate should you use in subsequent calculations if the riskless rate of return is 5.5 percent per year? Explain your answer.

(c) Use the Black-Scholes option pricing model to estimate the market value of the other three call options.

22. The closing prices of Chrysler's and Micron Technology's common stocks and call options given below are from problem 9. Both call options expire on January 18, 1997 and have an exercise price of $32.50.

	Stock	Call Option
Chrysler	$32.625	$1.375
Micron	32.375	2.1875

(a) Use these option quotations to estimate the standard deviations of the continuously compounded rate of return on Chrysler's and Micron's common stock.

(b) Are the results sensible considering Chrysler's and Micron's betas are 1.30 and 1.80? Explain your answer.

23. The closing prices for call and put options on Microsoft's common stock on December 18, 1996 are shown below. The company's common stock closed at $82.625 that day. The riskless rate of return was 5.5 percent.

Exercise Price	Expiration	Closing Price of Call Option	Closing Price of Put Option
$72.50	January 18	$11.25	$ 0.875
82.50	April 19	7.25	5.75
85.00	July 19	8.25	10.00
90.00	April 19	4.25	11.00

(Source: *The Wall Street Journal*, December 19, 1996, p. C18.)

(a) Use the July 19, $85.00 call option to estimate the standard deviation of the continuously compounded rate of return on Microsoft's common stock.

(b) Use the Black-Scholes option pricing model to estimate the market value of the other three call options. Compare your results to the options' actual market values.

(c) Use put-call parity and your answers to part (b) to estimate the values of the put options on Microsoft's common stock. Compare your results to the options' actual market values.

• A D D I T I O N A L   R E A D I N G

An accessible textbook on options is:

Robert W. Kolb, *Options: An Introduction,* Blackwell Publishers, Cambridge, Massachusetts, 1995.

The article that began the revolution in option pricing and therefore the trading of options and their use to describe many forms of risk management is:

Fischer Black and Myron Scholes, "The Pricing of Options and Corporate Liabilities," *Journal of Political Economy*, May–June 1973, pp. 637–654.

Two articles that derive and describe the binomial option pricing model are:

John C. Cox, Stephen A. Ross, and Mark Rubinstein, "Option Pricing: A Simplified Approach," *Journal of Financial Economics,* 1979, pp. 229–263.

Richard J. Rendleman, Jr. and Brit J. Bartter, "Two-State Option Pricing," *Journal of Finance,* December 1979, pp. 1093–1110.

DERIVATION OF BINOMIAL OPTION PRICING MODEL

To derive the binomial option pricing model, complete the steps necessary to form and value the hedge portfolio using symbols rather than numbers.

1. Write the call option's value on the expiration date in terms of the stock and exercise prices.

$$C_T = \begin{array}{l} S_T^+ - E \text{ If stock price increases} \\ \\ S_T^- - E \text{ If stock price decreases} \end{array}$$

2. Write the replica portfolio's value on the expiration date in terms of the number of shares of stock and amount of debt used to form the portfolio.

$$\text{Portfolio value} = \begin{array}{l} n \times S_T^+ - D_T \text{ If stock price increases} \\ \\ n \times S_T^- - D_T \text{ If stock price decreases} \end{array}$$

3. Equate the call option and portfolio's values in the two states.

$$S_T^+ - E = n \times S_T^+ - D_T \quad \text{If stock price increases}$$
$$S_T^- - E = n \times S_T^- - D_T \quad \text{If stock price decreases}$$

4. Solve these two equations for the number of shares, n, and amount of debt, D_T, used to form the replica portfolio.

$$n = (C_T^+ - C_T^-) / (S_T^+ - S_T^-)$$
$$D_T = n \times S_T^- - C_T^-$$

where

$$C_T^+ = \text{Max}(S_T^+ - E, 0)$$
$$C_T^- = \text{Max}(S_T^- - E, 0)$$

5. Determine the value of the equity in the levered portfolio formed using n shares of stock and $D_T / (1 + r_f)$ debt.

$$\text{Value of equity} = n \times S_0 - D_T / (1 + r_f)$$

where

$$n = (C_T^+ - C_T^-) / (S_T^+ - S_T^-)$$
$$D_T = n \times S_T^- - C_T^-$$

The value of the equity in the levered portfolio equals the value of the call option (C_0) because, as demonstrated in the chapter, the levered portfolio and the call option have identical payoffs. That is,

$$C_0 = n \times S_0 - D_T / (1 + r_f)$$

where
$$n = (C_T^+ - C_T^-) / (S_T^+ - S_T^-)$$
$$D_T = n \times S_T^- - C_T^-.$$

Substituting n and D_T into the equation for C_0 and simplifying gives Equation 8.4 in the text.

$$C_0 = S_0 \times \Phi_1 - PV(E) \times \Phi_2 \qquad [8.4]$$

where
$$S_0 = \text{current stock price}$$
$$PV(E) = E / (1 + r_f)^t$$
$$\Phi_1 = (C_T^+ - C_T^-) / (S_T^+ - S_T^-)$$
$$\Phi_2 = (\Phi_1 \times S_T^- - C_T^-) / E$$

JACKSON FOODS

S arah Jackson left the meeting with her prospective investment bankers, White River Partners, impressed but concerned. William Jefferson, the senior partner, had made a dazzling multimedia presentation that concluded with a proposal to assist Jackson's company with its initial public offering (IPO) of one million shares of common stock. Sarah knew that White River had managed several successful IPOs, but she was still concerned about the company's method of establishing the offer price.

PART A

Upon losing her position teaching high-school nutrition classes in 1990, Sarah Jackson had immediately established a food service company that prepares low-fat, low-cholesterol meals for delivery to business cafeterias. Her skills and timing were excellent, and she rapidly built a business that had more than $15 million of revenue in 1997. In January of 1998, she decided to sell common stock to finance an expansion while reducing the company's reliance on debt.

Sarah's expansion plans are reflected in the actual and projected financial statements in Table 1. Her annual expenditure on fixed assets usually equals current depreciation, but she will spend an additional $4.4 million in 1998 to boost capacity. She expects sales to nearly double in three years.

White River Partners sent two junior analysts to Sarah's office in response to her inquiry about issuing common stock to finance this expansion. They examined her company's financial records, toured the food preparation facilities, and reviewed her business plans. Two weeks later, William Jefferson presented their proposal that the stock be offered at $5.10 per share. Jefferson explained that his analysts arrived at this figure by applying a price/earnings multiple of 5 to the company's 1998 projected earnings per share of $1.02.

Back at her office, Sarah Jackson and her CFO, Richard Stockman, discussed White River's proposal. They were surprised that the analysts didn't ask about their plans for paying dividends or their expectations for years beyond 2000. Sarah and Richard had discussed these issues and planned to pay dividends equal to 25 percent of the cash flows provided by operations each year beginning in 1998. Furthermore, although they hadn't made explicit forecasts for 2001 and beyond, they fully expected that the trends toward healthy eating and outsourcing would enable the business to grow at 4 percent per year indefinitely.

Richard Stockman was especially surprised the investment bankers made no mention of the rate of return investors normally require from this line of business. Stockman knew from his own experience this is a major factor in determining stock

Table 1   JACKSON FOODS PARTIAL FINANCIAL STATEMENTS (thousands)

	Actual		Projected		
	1996	1997	1998	1999	2000
Sales	$14,450	$15,317	$22,000	$25,000	$28,000
Cost of goods sold	10,063	10,722	14,960	17,000	19,040
Gross profit	4,387	4,595	7,040	8,000	8,960
Selling & administrative expenses	2,647	2,604	3,500	3,500	3,500
Depreciation	1,250	1,100	1,600	1,450	1,300
Operating income	490	891	1,940	3,050	4,160
Interest expense	410	528	396	336	228
Pre-tax income	80	363	1,544	2,714	3,932
Taxes	29	131	521	942	1,381
Net income	$ 51	$ 232	$ 1,023	$ 1,772	$ 2,551
Dividends	–	–	501	778	826
Addition to retained earnings	51	232	522	994	1,725
Cash	$ 833	$ 919	$ 1,469	$ 1,639	$ 1,771
Receivables	1,425	1,643	2,420	2,720	3,195
Inventory	1,313	1,697	2,366	2,682	3,078
Current assets	3,571	4,259	6,255	7,041	8,044
Gross fixed assets	6,750	7,850	13,850	15,300	16,600
Accumulated depreciation	2,880	3,980	5,580	7,030	8,330
Net fixed assets	3,870	3,870	8,270	8,270	8,270
Total assets	$ 7,441	$ 8,129	$14,525	$15,311	$16,314
Accruals	$ 325	$ 363	$ 479	$ 631	$ 695
Accounts payable	1,216	1,234	1,691	1,831	1,945

prices and was convinced it could not be neglected. He had been following the stock price of Uncommon Catering, a close competitor, and recently received a briefing on interest rates. Stockman felt sure he could use this information, which is summarized in Table 2, to estimate investors' required rate of return.

Jackson and Stockman had to respond to White River's proposal within two days. Should they accept the offering price of $5.10 per share or could they justify a higher price as a result of a more thorough analysis? Whatever the outcome, they would have more confidence in the price if it was based on sound valuation principles.

PART B

Sarah Jackson and Richard Stockman convinced White River Partners to change the offering price for the IPO and now had to negotiate the banker's fee. William Jefferson proposed two alternatives: Jackson Foods could either pay the company a flat fee of

RICHARD STOCKMAN'S ECONOMIC DATA   **Table 2**

Panel A: Uncommon Catering's Stock Prices

Month	Closing Stock Price	Market Index Rate of Return	Month	Closing Stock Price	Market Index Rate of Return
	$10.000				
January 1996	9.625	−0.35%	January 1997	$15.250	−1.63
February	11.250	−0.53	February	12.000	1.50
March	11.750	−0.94	March	10.375	2.29
April	13.875	1.27	April	12.000	−0.58
May	11.750	−1.14	May	11.500	−0.62
June	14.125	−0.04	June	14.250	1.34
July	15.500	0.27	July	10.125	−1.58
August	10.875	−1.72	August	9.875	−1.88
September	11.625	0.50	September	10.000	1.35
October	12.750	−0.97	October	11.125	−1.05
November	11.125	0.65	November	10.125	1.98
December	16.500	−0.51	December	11.375	−0.62

Panel B: Uncommon Catering's Option Prices on December 31, 1997

Call Option	Days Until Expiration	Exercise Price	Market Value
July 19, 1997	200	$12.50	$1.89
October 18, 1997	291	12.50	2.44

Panel C: Report From Economic Associates

Orders for durable goods were up and unemployment was down in the fourth quarter, prompting many analysts to predict the Federal Reserve will soon raise the benchmark Federal Funds rate by as much as one-half of one percent. The current yields on representative government securities rose approximately 2/10 of 1 percent in anticipation, leveling off at the values reported below.

30-day T-bills	5.80%
180-day T-bills	6.00
1-year T-notes	6.25

$150,000 or give the company options on 100,000 shares of common stock. He recommended the options have 365 days until expiration and an exercise price equal to the agreed-on offering price. Sarah and Richard returned to their office to analyze these alternatives and accept one or make a counterproposal.

INVESTMENTS AND OPERATIONS

Part 1 provided a step-by-step development of the principles managers must use to estimate the values of investment, operating, and financing alternatives. These principles require managers to forecast an alternative's free cash flows, choose a required rate of return appropriate for its unavoidable risk, and estimate its market value using net present value analysis or option pricing. The difference between a decision alternative's market value and its cost measures its effect on the owners' wealth, so managers should choose alternatives for which this difference is positive.

A thorough knowledge of finance valuation principles is a prerequisite to making sound investment, operating, and financing decisions—but it isn't enough. Managers also must understand production, marketing, and human resources management to apply these principles to realistic business decisions. Effective managers combine their knowledge of these business functions in creative ways to make decisions that increase the owners' wealth.

Part 2 demonstrates how to apply finance valuation principles to realistic investment and operating decisions. Chapter 9 describes how to analyze long-term investment proposals and integrates valuation principles with concepts from marketing, production, cost accounting, and international finance to estimate the market values of long-term assets.

Chapters 10 through 12 show how to use finance principles to estimate the market value of routine operating decisions. Chapter 10 sets the stage for this discussion by describing the association between a company's operating policies and its operating cash flows. Chapter 11 then shows how to estimate the market value of production alternatives such as outsourcing and the adoption of lean manufacturing. Chapter 12 uses the same approach to evaluate alternative ways to pay cash to suppliers and collect cash from customers.

Chapter 13 is special because it explains the difference between routine investment and operating decisions and strategic ones that permit managers to take advantage of future opportunities. The latter type of decisions have options attached to them and therefore must be evaluated differently. Chapter 13 describes how to conduct this evaluation, using a variety of investment and operating decisions as illustrations.

Part 2 provides examples and exercises that are representative of the ways you may apply finance principles whether you work in finance or in production, marketing, or human resources management. The information in this part will serve you well throughout your management career because you must apply these principles to the investment and operating decisions that you make to maximize the owners' wealth. If you do, your company is more likely to be competitive and your personal position is more likely to be secure.

C H A P T E R   9

ANALYSIS OF LONG-TERM INVESTMENT PROPOSALS

*F*ortune called U.S. companies' investments in capital equipment "the most important economic event of the decade." The amounts, for individual companies and in total, are staggering. Ford Motor Corporation invested $5.4 billion in North America in 1994, an increase of 25 percent from 1993. MCI spent $2.9 billion on capital equipment in 1994, up 70 percent from 1993. Even small companies made large long-term investments. For example, J&L Specialty Steel, with 1994 sales of $712 million, spent $175 million in 1995 for equipment to expand capacity and reduce processing time.[1]

Exhibit 9.1 shows that the total investment in capital equipment by these and other U.S. companies ranged from $546 billion in 1994 to $590 billion in 1995 with planned increases to $600 billion in 1996. The amounts of money at stake make the analysis of long-term investment proposals a crucial task in most companies.

Of course, the financial market's assessment of the *value* of long-term investments is even more important than their cost. A study of 427 industrial companies that announced increases in their capital budgets between 1975–1981 provided evidence about their importance measured in these terms.[2] This study found that, on average, the total value of these companies' common stock increased by $227 million upon the announcement of increases in their capital budgets that averaged $125 million. In other words, a $1.00 increase in long-term investment spending caused an immediate $1.80 increase in the value of the companies' equity.

The impact on individual companies is sometimes even more dramatic. Enzon, Inc., a biotechnology company, announced they were awarded a U.S. patent for a red-blood-cell substitute on August 11, 1993. Their stock price went from $5.00 per share to $5.875 in two days, an increase in the market value of their equity of $20.6 million.[3] This increase in the owners' wealth was a very tangible reward for the company's investment in an intangible asset—research and development.

---

[1]Joseph Spiers, "The Most Important Economic Event of the Decade," *Fortune*, April 3, 1995, pp. 33–40.

[2]John J. McConnell and Chris J. Muscarella, "Corporate Capital Expenditure Decisions and the Market Value of the Firm," *Journal of Financial Economics*, September 1985, pp. 399–422.

[3]*The Wall Street Journal*, August 11, 1993, p. B2.

Exhibit 9.1

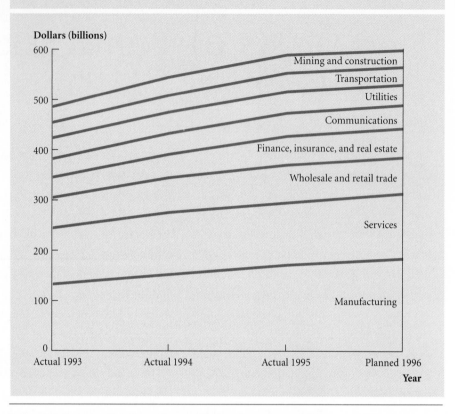

CAPITAL SPENDING BY U.S. COMPANIES

Dollars (billions)

Mining and construction
Transportation
Utilities
Communications
Finance, insurance, and real estate
Wholesale and retail trade
Services
Manufacturing

Actual 1993   Actual 1994   Actual 1995   Planned 1996

Year

Source: U.S. Commerce Department Survey of Business Investment and Plans.

Long-term investment proposals are pervasive and diverse. Some, such as a proposal to expand plant capacity, emerge from a company's strategic plan and require the expenditure of large amounts of money to acquire a tangible asset. Other proposals arise routinely in the normal course of business. Examples include the replacement of worn or obsolete equipment, the purchase of office equipment such as photocopiers and personal computers, and the installation of pollution control equipment mandated by the Environmental Protection Agency. Even contracts for services such as communications, health care, and maintenance are long-term investments if their cash flows extend beyond one year.

Still other long-term investment proposals produce intangible assets that are expected to improve future cash flows by increasing revenues or decreasing costs. Money spent for research and development is a good example because it is expected to produce future cash inflows from the sale of new or improved products and services. Money spent on advertising is a similar example because it creates or enhances a brand name—an intangible asset that is expected to produce future cash inflows by increasing sales. Finally, money spent on training is a long-term investment in human capital. The expected payoff is a higher-skilled workforce that may produce a higher-quality product at a lower cost.

Whatever the motivation, size, and frequency, the analysis of long-term investment decisions involves managers in all areas and at all levels of a company. Business unit managers in research and development, production, marketing, or human relations may provide information for or analyze only a small part of a large, strategic investment and have the authority to approve smaller ones. Senior managers have proportionately larger responsibilities. This means *all* managers, regardless of their position or specialty, must be knowledgeable about the process by which investment proposals are evaluated.

This chapter describes all three stages in the evaluation of long-term investments (origination and classification of proposals, financial analysis, and continuing evaluation); however, the focus is on financial analysis. This stage is an application of the valuation principles we developed in Chapters 2 through 8, so analysts must identify and estimate a project's cash flows, determine its required rate of return, and compute its market value using NPV analysis or option pricing. These topics are addressed in Sections 9.2 through 9.5 of this chapter. Chapter 13 discusses further the use of option pricing to evaluate strategic investments.

9.1 AN OVERVIEW OF THE DECISION PROCESS

Long-term investment proposals routinely pass through three stages of development. These stages are project definition and cash flow estimation, financial analysis, and project implementation and review. We will briefly describe all three stages in this section and focus on the first and second stages in the remainder of the chapter.

Project Definition and Cash Flow Estimation

A long-term investment proposal originates as an idea for improving a company's performance. The first stage of the process that converts this idea into an actual investment is project definition and cash flow estimation. Analysts define a project by describing the relationship between the project and the company's other businesses, deciding how far into the future to predict the project's cash flows, and determining at what level of detail to perform their analysis. They then estimate the project's free cash flows within the limits established by this definition.

The analysts who define projects and estimate cash flows are located throughout corporations. Surveys of capital budgeting practice found that operating personnel, plant managers, or division managers originated 33 percent to 79 percent of investment proposals. These personnel were less likely to originate proposals related to new product lines and more likely to originate proposals to replace existing equipment.[4]

---

[4]David F. Scott, Jr., and J. William Petty II, "Capital Budgeting Practices in Large American Firms: A Retrospective Analysis and Synthesis," *The Financial Review,* March 1984, pp. 111–123.

Financial Analysis

Financial analysis is the second stage through which long-term investment proposals pass. At this stage, analysts estimate the project's required rate of return and use present value analysis or option pricing to determine the market value of its free cash flows. A project will increase the owners' wealth—and therefore is acceptable—if its market value exceeds its cost. Analysts sometimes compare a project's internal rate of return to its required return to determine if its market value exceeds its cost; however, this procedure isn't always reliable.

The analysts who estimate projects' market values were traditionally located in finance departments. For example, one study of capital budgeting practice found that the finance department was responsible for financial analysis of investment proposals in more than 60 percent of the companies surveyed. This practice is changing, however, as companies integrate finance and operations. Review the brief articles on Ford Motor Corporation and DuPont in Chapter 1 for two good examples.

Project Implementation and Review

The final stage through which approved investment proposals pass is project implementation and review. Implementation mostly involves operating managers and may take a few weeks to several years, depending on the project's scale. The review process, sometimes called post-audit, involves both operating and financial managers and should continue throughout the project's life. Post-auditing long-term investment proposals is a common but not universal practice. One study of capital budgeting practices found that 76 percent of the Fortune 500 companies that responded to the survey had formal post-auditing programs.[5]

The two primary objectives of post-auditing an accepted investment proposal are to improve the company's planning procedures and to update the estimate of the project's market value. Process improvements come from normal feedback and from identifying and removing sources of bias in cash flow forecasts. A revised estimate of a project's market value may cause the company to expand, contract, accelerate, delay, or abandon the project. We will discuss the analysis of new information to make expansion, contraction, and abandonment decisions in Chapter 13.

Managers believe project definition and cash flow estimation is the most difficult stage and that sales and costs forecasts are highly important. The weighted average cost of financing (the weighted average cost of capital) is most frequently used as the required rate of return but this is not the unanimous choice. However, there is a very noticeable trend in the adoption of NPV or IRR for valuation.[6] Additional survey results that describe what managers think of the capital budgeting process are summarized in "In the News."

---

[5]Kimberly J. Smith, "Postauditing Capital Investments," *Financial Practice and Education*, Spring/Summer 1994, pp. 129–137.

[6]Binder and Chaput, mentioned "In the News," concluded that more companies used NPV and IRR as opportunity costs and knowledge of these techniques increased. You'll be pleased to know that they used the percentage of the population that had an MBA degree to measure knowledge of NPV and IRR!

SURVEYS OF CAPITAL BUDGETING PRACTICE: WHAT DO MANAGERS THINK?

Which Stage Is Most Critical?*

Stage of Development	% Ranking as	
	Most Difficult	Most Critical
Project definition and cash flow estimation	64.3%	52.0%
Financial analysis	14.9	33.3
Project implementation and review	20.8	14.7

What Factors Are Important for Estimating Cash Flow?†

	% Ranking as Highly Important
Financial Factors	
Tax considerations	77.6%
Project's risk	71.5
Working capital requirements	69.0
Marketing Factors	
Sales forecast	93.5
Competitive strengths	74.6
Product life	51.3
Production Factors	
Operating expenses	90.0
Manufacturing overhead	79.7
Material and supply costs	76.3

How Is the Required Rate of Return Estimated?‡

	% Using Each Approach
Weighted average cost of capital	30–61%
Management determined target	40
Cost of a specific source of capital	17–26
Historical rates of return	10–20

How Is a Project's Market Value Determined?§

Period of Surveys	% Using NPV or IRR
1950s	18%
1960s	40
1970s	65

*Lawrence J. Gitman and John R. Forrester, Jr., "A Survey of Capital Budgeting Techniques Used by Major U.S. Firms," *Financial Management*, Fall 1977, pp. 66–71.

†Randolph A. Pohlman, Emmanuel S. Santiago, and F. Lynn Markel, "Cash Flow Estimation Practices of Large Firms," *Financial Management*, Summer 1988, pp. 71–79.

‡Various capital budgeting surveys summarized in David F. Scott, Jr., and J. William Petty II, "Capital Budgeting Practices in Large American Firms: A Retrospective Analysis and Synthesis," *The Financial Review*, March 1984, pp. 111–123.

§Various capital budgeting surveys summarized in John J. Binder and J. Scott Chaput, "A Positive Analysis of Corporate Capital Budgeting Practices," *Review of Quantitative Finance and Accounting*, May 1996, pp. 245–257.

9.2   DEFINE THE PROJECT

An idea for improving a company's performance does not automatically come with a checklist of cash flows to estimate. Instead, managers and analysts must produce this list by precisely defining the project. They perform this task by determining the breadth and timespan of analysis as well as the level of detail required for each year's cash flow estimates. These managers and analysts, who may be drawn from production and marketing as well as finance, must thoroughly understand the proposal *and* the company's business to place the project in the proper context. Their decisions are crucial because they determine whether the subsequent analysis will provide an accurate assessment of the proposal's incremental value to the company.

Classify the Project

Most companies classify their investment proposals according to their purpose and size to facilitate cash flow estimation. A common classification scheme has four categories: mandatory investments such as pollution control equipment, investments to replace current equipment and reduce costs, investments to expand revenue from existing products, and investments to expand revenue by introducing new products. Proposals in each category are further subdivided according to the size of expenditure required. An investment proposal's classification affects the amount of effort expended to estimate its free cash flows.

Mandatory and replacement investments only require cost forecasts and reliable estimates of these cash flows can be obtained from an engineering analysis of the alternatives. Revenue expansion proposals also require sales forecasts, which are more difficult to obtain and subject to more uncertainty. Companies often require more detailed documentation of the methods used to prepare the cash flow forecasts for revenue expansion proposals because of this uncertainty. Finally, a company may perform only cursory analysis for small expenditures and require detailed analysis and formal approval for larger ones. The objective is to save managers' time while still paying careful attention to proposals that can safeguard or jeopardize the company's future.

An investment proposal's classification also may affect the type of financial analysis to use. We can use net present value analysis to determine the market value of a mandatory investment, such as pollution control equipment, but we must use option pricing to evaluate one that provides flexibility. We will discuss this issue in Section 9.5 and again in Chapter 13 when we discuss the financial analysis of strategic investments.

Determine the Breadth of Analysis[7]

Analysts must define a project broadly enough to encompass its own cash flows plus its impact on the cash flows from the company's existing products or services. The impact is favorable when the new product complements an existing product but is unfavor-

---

[7]This section and the section on the level of detail of analysis are based on articles by Barwise, Marsh, and Wensley and by Day and Fahey, which are listed among the additional readings at the end of this chapter.

able when the new product is a substitute. For example, suppose a company that manufactures equipment and supplies for amateur photographers is considering a proposal to produce and sell a new point-and-shoot camera. Introducing this camera will enhance the company's cash flows from selling photographic film and erode its cash flows from selling its other cameras. Consequently, the breadth of analysis for the point-and-shoot camera proposal must encompass the company's existing photographic film and camera businesses.

Measuring the enhancement and erosion to existing products is not as easy as it may seem. First, the status quo usually cannot be taken as the base case against which to measure these effects because the company's competitors also are making long-term investments and introducing new products. This means the cash flows provided by existing products may be lower than the status quo even if the company does not approve the proposal. Ignoring the actions of its competitors can cause a company to underestimate the amount by which an investment proposal will enhance its complementary products and overestimate the amount by which it will erode its substitute products. Second, the enhanced and eroded products may belong to other business units in the company. Therefore, while one business unit may prosper at the expense of another, the entire company's position may be unchanged or even damaged. Senior managers who have a broad view may have to evaluate these types of proposals to ensure they are sound when viewed from the entire company's perspective.

Determine the Timespan of Analysis

The timespan of analysis must be long enough to include all the future cash flows that will be paid or received if the proposal is approved. This means the timespan must extend beyond the life of the equipment in the current proposal if the underlying venture will be continued using future generations of equipment. Conversely, the timespan must be shorter than the life of the equipment in the current proposal if the venture will be discontinued even though the asset still has economic value. In either case, using a timespan equal to the life of the endeavor will ensure that all relevant future cash flows are evaluated.

Establishing a Study Period A timespan of analysis that extends beyond the life of the equipment in the current proposal presents two problems. One problem is that this timespan is impractical if the venture will be continued indefinitely. Then, it would be necessary to estimate cash flows for a period perhaps as long as 50 years or more. The usual procedure in this situation is to divide the life of the venture into two parts: a relatively short *study period* that begins immediately and the remainder of the periods in the venture's life. The proposal is then evaluated as if the venture's life equaled the study period. The cash flows to be paid or received in periods beyond this time period are not ignored; they are used to estimate the endeavor's residual economic value at the conclusion of the study period.

The advantage of this procedure is simplification. Detailed cash flow estimates are prepared for each year during the study period while simplifying assumptions about subsequent cash flows permit the use of simple estimates of the venture's residual value. This procedure is illustrated by the following example.

Managers of the home products unit of Aqua-Air, Inc. are evaluating a proposal to produce a new solar-heated spa. Cash revenues are expected to be $10 million in 1998 and reach $19.2 million in 2007 with a growth path that follows the classic *product life cycle* (see Exhibit 9.2). Marketing analysts note that the projected annual growth in the spa's cash revenues eventually declines to slightly less than 3 percent per year. Although the analysts are unwilling to forecast the year-by-year cash flows beyond 10 years, they believe that product improvements and an aggressive advertising campaign will enable them to maintain a 2 percent growth rate indefinitely.

Marketing's prediction of constant, perpetual growth beginning in year 11 means we can use the formula for the present value of a growing perpetuity, Equation 3.18, to compute the residual value of the spa's revenues at the end of year 10. Given Aqua-Air's required rate of return of 8 percent, the residual value is

$$\text{Residual value at year 2007} = \frac{C_{11}}{r - g}$$

$$= \frac{\$19.2 \times 1.02}{0.08 - 0.02} = \$326.4 \text{ million.}$$

The year-by-year forecasts for 1998–2007 plus the residual value of $326.4 million at the end of year 2007 completely describe the cash revenues Aqua-Air expects to receive from manufacturing and selling the solar-heated spa in perpetuity.

Exhibit 9.2

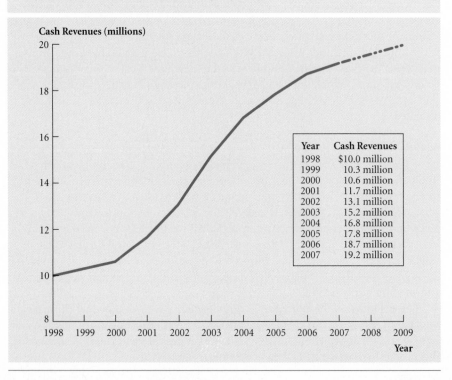

AQUA-AIR'S SOLAR HEATED SPA PROPOSAL

Cash Revenues (millions)

Year	Cash Revenues
1998	$10.0 million
1999	10.3 million
2000	10.6 million
2001	11.7 million
2002	13.1 million
2003	15.2 million
2004	16.8 million
2005	17.8 million
2006	18.7 million
2007	19.2 million

APPLYING THE STUDY PERIOD PROCEDURE

Joe Sass owns the rights to operate AhSo Sushi restaurants in Louisville, Kentucky. His first store will become operational in 1998 and he will add one new location per year in 1999, 2000, and 2001. The free cash flows provided by these locations will grow rapidly with development and then level off at $575,000 per year. Choose a study period for this business and simplify the cash flows Joe must analyze. His required rate of return is 20 percent.

Year	Number of Stores	Free Cash Flow
1998	1	$175,000
1999	2	340,000
2000	3	475,000
2001	4	575,000
2002– ∞	4	575,000

Three years is an appropriate study period because the cash flows are assumed to remain constant at $575,000 beyond this period. Therefore, you can use Equation 3.18, with $g = 0$, to compute the business's residual value at the end of 2000.

Residual value at 2000 = $575,000/(0.20 – 0) = $2,875,000

The simplified cash flows are therefore

Year	Annual Free Cash Flow	Residual Value	Total Free Cash Flows
1998	$175,000	$ 0	$ 175,000
1999	340,000	0	340,000
2000	475,000	2,875,000	3,350,000

The free cash flows at the end of 1998, 1999, and 2000 completely describe Joe's investment opportunity.

The Effect of the Equipment's Life[8]   Another problem that arises when the time-span of analysis extends beyond the life of the equipment in the current proposal is that analysts must estimate the costs of acquiring and operating future generations of equipment. These estimates usually are based on engineering assessment of the rate of deterioration in the equipment's operating efficiency and the rate at which it becomes obsolete. Equipment is often assigned to one of three categories depending on the rate at which these changes take place.

---

[8]The best discussions of asset lives are found in engineering economy textbooks. A classic example is the book by George A. Taylor listed in the additional readings at the end of this chapter.

One type of equipment is replaced when it fails due to sudden, unavoidable, and complete deterioration. Telephone poles are a good example of this type because their lives cannot be prolonged by maintenance and serviceable poles are seldom removed because they are obsolete. Determining the cost of acquiring and operating future generations of this type of equipment requires little more than extending current costs into the future given statistical estimates of the equipment's physical life.

Another type of equipment is replaced when a sudden technological advance makes it totally obsolete. An example is a personal computer. The introduction of PCs with Intel Pentium Pro microprocessors made machines based on earlier microprocessors obsolete for some purposes (e.g., computer-aided design) even though they were still as good as new. Determining when this type of equipment will be replaced and the cost of acquiring and operating the replacements requires an estimate of the pace of technological advance. This is inherently more difficult than estimating physical lives.

Finally, some equipment is subject to gradual deterioration and obsolescence. A lathe operated by a machine-tool company is a good example. The company can continue to operate the lathe indefinitely and thereby avoid the cost of acquiring future generations of equipment. However, these savings are obtained at the expense of higher operating costs because as time passes, the old lathe will require more maintenance and new lathes will have cost-saving innovations. Engineering analysts estimate the acquisition, deterioration, and obsolescence costs for these types of assets and compute the replacement interval or **economic life** that minimizes the sum of these costs. Their estimates should be used to forecast the costs of acquiring and operating future generations of this type of equipment. Consider the following illustration.

Top Hat Roofing has a six-year contract to replace the built-up roofs at a military base. This work requires the use of a gasoline-fired heating pot in which to melt the asphalt. Engineers have determined the heaters have an economic life of only three years, so Top Hat will purchase two pots at $10,000 each over the life of the project. They will have no value at the conclusion of their economic lives. The cost of operating the first heating pot the first year of its life is $4,000; however, this cost will increase by $1,800 each year due to the accumulation of asphalt in the heating chamber. Top Hat expects improved fuel efficiency to reduce the costs of operating the second generation heater by $300 per year compared to the first one. The cash costs of gasoline-fired heating pots for this venture are given in Table 9.1.

Table 9.1   CASH COSTS OF TOP HAT'S GAS-FIRED HEATING POTS

Year	Acquisition Costs	Operating Costs	Total Costs
0	$−10,000	—	$−10,000
1	—	$−4,000	−4,000
2	—	−5,800	−5,800
3	−10,000	−7,600	−17,600
4	—	−3,700	−3,700
5	—	−5,500	−5,500
6	—	−7,300	−7,300

**RECOGNIZING THE COSTS OF OPERATING
FUTURE GENERATIONS OF EQUIPMENT**

A power auger used for digging post holes costs $4,000 and has an economic life of two years. The annual cost of operating the first auger is $800 and $1,150 the first and second years of its life. Improvements in technology will reduce the cost of operating the replacement auger by $100 per year. Prepare the cash flow schedule for acquiring and operating the first auger and its replacement.

Year	Acquisition Cost	Operating Cost	Total Cost
0	$-4,000	$ 0	$-4,000
1	—	-800	-800
2	-4,000	-1,150	-5,150
3	—	-700	-700
4	—	-1,050	-1,050

These cash flows completely describe the cost of acquiring and operating the first auger and its replacement.

Determine the Level of Detail of Analysis

The level of detail of the analysis is determined by the degree a proposal's distinct cash flows are unbundled and separately evaluated. There are three considerations when deciding how far to carry this process. First, the proposal should be unbundled far enough to determine how its cash flow components are associated with the unit's competitive advantages and disadvantages. This will reveal implicit assumptions about a proposal's source of benefits and make it easier to determine whether these assumptions are realistic. Second, the proposal should be unbundled far enough to determine if there are components that can be valued using market prices. Using market values is simpler and more accurate than do-it-yourself valuation and may protect the unit from the questionable assumption that they can operate the asset to obtain a higher value than its current owner. Finally, the proposal should be unbundled far enough to permit an accurate assessment of risk. Some cash flow components can be predicted accurately (such as labor costs under a long-term contract) while others are subject to more uncertainty (such as energy costs). Separating these components permits the analyst to concentrate his or her efforts on those with the greatest amount of risk and assign them a higher required rate of return. The following example illustrates the advantage of estimating the cash flows in sufficient detail.

A local restaurant that owes its success to excellent family recipes and a management process that ensures quality control considered a proposal to open a second location in another city. Unfortunately, the net present value of the expected cash revenues did not cover the cost of building and operating the new restaurant. Analysis of the cash flow components revealed that the proposal was uneconomical because the costs of building and operating the restaurant long-distance were too high, not because the revenues were too low. Given this additional information, the owners decided to license their recipes and management process to an established restauranteur in the target city. This enabled them to exploit their competitive advantage while avoiding the costs and risks of developing property located far away.

Two additional benefits of unbundling are worth mentioning. First, this process prevents managers from naively—or intentionally—using strong projects or project components to subsidize weak ones. Second, continuing evaluation is more accurate and informative when the performance of individual project components can be examined separately.

Decide How to Treat Inflation

There are two ways to treat inflation in your cash flow forecasts. You can forecast real or constant-purchasing-power cash flows and evaluate them using a real required rate of return. This approach excludes the effect of inflation from both the numerator and denominator of the valuation equation so the answer is stated in terms of current dollars. Alternatively, you can forecast nominal cash flows and evaluate them using a nominal required rate of return. This approach incorporates the effect of inflation in both the numerator and denominator of the valuation equation. The effect of inflation cancels in this case, so this method also produces an answer stated in terms of current dollars.

Either approach to inflation is acceptable if applied consistently (real cash flows/real required rate of return or nominal cash flows/nominal required rate of return) because the answer is always stated in current dollar terms. Using nominal cash flows and a nominal required rate of return is probably more convenient, however, because rates of return as they are observed in the financial market already include an inflation premium, as you learned in Chapter 4.

9.3   ESTIMATE THE PROJECT'S FREE CASH FLOWS

Analysts can use either the direct or indirect method to estimate an investment proposal's free cash flows. (Chapter 2 described both procedures.) The indirect method is more widely used, however, perhaps because analysts are familiar with income statements and balance sheets and because these statements are customarily prepared for other parts of financial planning and analysis. Consequently, we will use the indirect method here.

Exhibit 9.3 is a schematic diagram of the process. Analysts begin by preparing detailed worksheets to estimate sales revenues, the costs of goods sold, selling and administrative expenses, fixed assets, and net working capital. They then use these estimates to construct the project's pro forma income statements and balance sheets. Finally, they convert the income statements and balance sheets to free cash flow statements. You may want to refer to Exhibit 9.3 periodically to keep the big picture in mind as we discuss the details.

Exhibit 9.3

ESTIMATING A PROJECT'S FREE CASH FLOWS

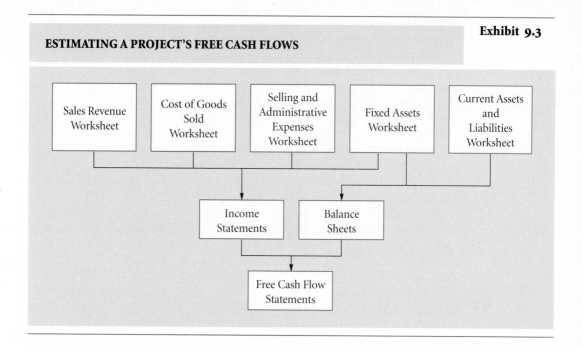

We will use Flav-R-Loc Manufacturing Company's plan to buy new production equipment to illustrate how analysts forecast free cash flow. Flav-R-Loc builds home food dehydrators in a leased manufacturing facility using the company's own equipment. A team of production, marketing, and finance managers is evaluating a proposal to replace this equipment to reduce maintenance and energy costs and to increase the company's production capacity. Because this proposal has both cost reduction and revenue expansion features, Flav-R-Loc will define the project to include the company's entire home food dehydrator business. We will exclusively focus on the new equipment now and compare its cash flows to the cash flows from continuing to operate the old equipment later. By independently examining these alternatives, we can better identify the sources of value in the new equipment proposal.

Sales Revenue Worksheet[9]

Revenue estimates usually are provided by marketing analysts who often use a three-stage procedure similar to that described in the discussion on security analysis in Chapter 7. At the first stage, they forecast conditions in the overall economy considering such factors as the level of employment, inflation, interest rates, and anticipated levels of consumer, business, and government spending. This forecast culminates in a general statement about macroeconomic conditions, perhaps summarized by a prediction about the growth in GNP. General economic forecasts usually are

---

[9]See the Conference Board publication listed among the additional readings at the end of this chapter for a thorough discussion of sales forecasting methods.

prepared at the company level to ensure that all business units operate under a consistent set of assumptions about business conditions.

Analysts predict industry sales at the second stage of this forecast procedure, which is based on anticipated conditions in the macroeconomy. It often is built-up from estimates of the total number of potential buyers, the average number of units each will purchase, and the average price per unit. The typical life-cycle of the product or service may be used to estimate the pattern of these sales over time. An S-shaped curve is a familiar life-cycle pattern; however, there are others depending on whether demand is driven by technology, fashion, or some other product characteristic. The information needed for these estimates is obtained from a variety of sources including industry trade associations, market research firms, surveys of buyer intentions, sales force opinions, test marketing, and statistical forecasting.

Analysts predict the business unit's revenues from the investment proposal at the final stage of this process. This revenue forecast is determined by estimating the unit's share of industry demand as a function of price, quality, service, credit policy, and marketing effort. Competitors' responses must be carefully considered at this stage to avoid overestimating sales.

The revenue estimates for Flav-R-Loc's home food dehydrator are developed in Table 9.2. Marketing managers expect the home food dehydrating fad to last no more than 10 years so the company plans to abandon this line of business at that time. Predicted unit sales over this 10-year period follow the S-shaped product life-cycle and the unit price is forecasted to increase at the anticipated rate of inflation in consumer prices, 3 percent per year.

Cost of Goods Sold Worksheet

Cost of goods sold estimates are provided by analysts familiar with the methods used to produce the investment proposal's product or service. Labor, materials, utilities, and facilities costs are the main components of this cost. Cost of goods sold has both direct and indirect components that should be estimated separately.

Direct Costs   *Direct costs* are the manufacturing costs that are easily and accurately tied to a product. Direct materials cost equals the price-times-quantity of the parts and materials from which the product is constructed. The main direct materials used to manufacture the home food dehydrator are plastic (to produce the housing and trays), a heating element, a fan, and an electronic control module. The cost of these items is Flav-R-Loc's direct materials cost. Direct labor cost equals the wages and benefits of employees who manufacture the product. The employees directly involved in manufacturing the home food dehydrator are mold operators, polishers and finishers, and assemblers. Their wages and benefits are the company's direct labor cost.

Direct material and labor costs are often based on *standard costs*—benchmarks for the quantities and prices of materials and labor required to manufacture the product. Engineers, purchasing managers, human resource managers, and cost accountants provide the information used to establish and revise these standards. Actual direct costs may differ from standard costs, however, because of unexpected changes in prices or efficiency or because the standards are out-of-date. Predictable variances from standard costs should be included in the estimated direct costs.

Table 9.2   HOME FOOD DEHYDRATOR PROPOSAL SALES REVENUE WORKSHEET (Period ending December 31)

Year	1998	1999	2000	2001	2002	2003	2004	2005	2006	2007	2008
Time	0	1	2	3	4	5	6	7	8	9	10
Unit sales	0	11,000	11,110	11,332	11,898	12,968	13,746	13,883	13,188	12,132	10,312
Price per unit	$0.00	$ 50.00	$ 51.50	$ 53.05	$ 54.64	$ 56.28	$ 57.97	$ 59.71	$ 61.50	$ 63.35	$ 65.25
Net sales	$ 0	$550,000	$572,165	$601,163	$650,107	$729,839	$796,856	$828,954	$811,062	$768,562	$672,858

A **learning curve** can sometimes be used to predict the time-pattern of direct labor costs. This curve is a mathematical description of the *time* required to complete a non-routine task as a function of experience or learning. For example, the time required to complete a task with a 95 percent learning curve decreases by 5 percent with each doubling of the number of repetitions.[10]

Here's a lighthearted but realistic application of a learning curve. Suppose it takes a father 5 hours to assemble a bicycle for his eldest daughter on Christmas Eve. Assuming bicycle assembly has an 80 percent learning rate, this father should be able to assemble a bicycle for his second daughter in only 4 hours (5 hours $\times$ 0.80). The father's experience doubles again with the fourth bike, which he should be able to assemble in 3.2 hours (5 hours $\times$ $(0.80)^2$).

Management scientists derived Equation 9.1, which describes the amount of time required to complete the task for any unit, not just the 2nd, 4th, and so on.

$$T_n = T_1 \times n^{[\ln(\text{learning rate})/\ln(2)]} \qquad [9.1]$$

Applying this formula to the hapless father in the preceding example,

$$T_2 = 5 \text{ hours} \times 2^{[\ln(0.80)/\ln(2)]} = 4 \text{ hours}$$
$$T_4 = 5 \text{ hours} \times 4^{[\ln(0.80)/\ln(2)]} = 3.2 \text{ hours}$$
$$T_5 = 5 \text{ hours} \times 5^{[\ln(0.80)/\ln(2)]} = 2.98 \text{ hours.}$$

EXERCISE 9.3

USING THE LEARNING CURVE

Determine how long it will take the father in the preceding example to assemble a bike for his first son who is his seventh child. Applying Equation 9.1,

$$T_n = T_1 \times n^{[\ln(\text{learning rate})/\ln(2)]}$$
$$T_7 = 5 \text{ hours} \times 7^{[\ln(0.80)/\ln(2)]} = 2.67 \text{ hours.}$$

It will take the father 2.67 hours to assemble the seventh bike.

---

[10]See the article by Louis Yelle listed in the end of chapter references for a review of the learning curve.

Exhibit 9.4

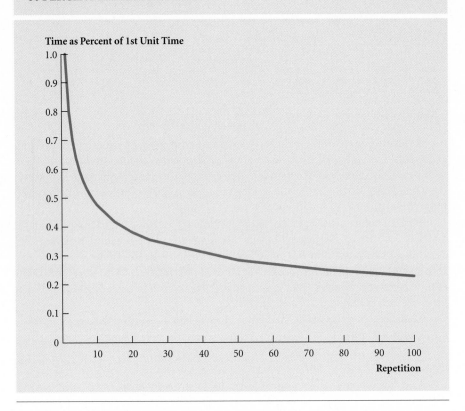

80 PERCENT LEARNING CURVE

Exhibit 9.4 is a graph of the 80 percent learning curve. You can see that the father in our example would have to have a very large number of children to get the assembly time down to a more reasonable one hour per bike.

The amount of time required to complete a task decreases with learning although labor *costs* do not decrease at the same rate as labor time if there are process improvements or wage increases to offset inflation or to reward improvements in productivity. A cost analyst must be familiar with these engineering and human resource management issues to accurately apply the learning curve to his or her company's specific situation.

Indirect Costs   *Indirect costs* or manufacturing overhead are the manufacturing costs not easily and accurately tied to a product. The costs of lighting, heating, and air conditioning are indirect costs that are fixed in the short run while expenditures for lubricants and solvents are indirect materials costs that vary with the level of production. Wages and benefits for personnel in receiving, shipping, and maintenance are indirect labor costs that may have both fixed and variable components. For example, a supervisor's base salary is a fixed cost while her overtime pay varies with the number of direct labor hours she supervises, which depends on the production level.

Indirect costs sometimes are allocated to products in proportion to each product's use of direct labor; however, this practice has fallen out of favor for two reasons. First, indirect costs have increased in both absolute and percentage terms as manufacturers provide customer services not easily associated with a particular product. Examples are providing information for coordinated manufacturing, preparing customized designs, and guaranteeing faster delivery and quality assurance. The increase in these indirect costs makes it more important to allocate them correctly to accurately assess each product's contribution to a company's free cash flows. Second, direct labor is a small percentage of the cost of goods sold for many companies because they use automated processes and buy—rather than make—component parts. The allocation of indirect costs therefore is sensitive to even small changes in the use of direct labor.

Activity-based costing addresses these problems by using activities or transactions in addition to direct labor hours to allocate some indirect costs. The key to this system is identifying the activities that drive or cause each type of indirect cost and then allocating or forecasting the costs accordingly. For example, the receiving and shipping departments' costs probably are more closely related to the number of batches they process than to the number of direct labor hours used to manufacture the product. A product requiring many parts from different vendors therefore must bear a large proportion of the receiving department's costs; a product shipped in many small batches must bear a large proportion of the shipping department's costs. By the same reasoning, maintenance and utilities costs may be allocated to products according to the amount of factory floor space they occupy. The cost of supervising a production facility largely depends on the number of man-hours it operates, so direct labor hours still may be useful for allocating this indirect cost.

Table 9.3 is the cost of goods sold worksheet for Flav-R-Loc's home food dehydrator. Direct labor costs begin at $6.00 per unit and decline by 5 percent with every doubling of *annual* output due to the effect of learning. Wage increases, estimated at 3 percent per year, partially offset this cost reduction. The first doubling of output occurs in year 2, so its direct labor cost per unit is $6.00 \times (1 - 0.05) \times 1.03 = \$5.87$. The next doubling of output occurs in year 4, which has a direct labor cost per unit of $6.00 \times (1 - 0.05)^2 \times (1.03)^3 = \$5.92$.[11] Direct material costs and the variable portion of indirect costs begin at $12.00 and $8.50 per unit and increase at the rate of inflation in producer prices—2.5 percent per year. Other indirect costs are estimated to be $80,000 per year in real terms and are also expected to increase by 2.5 percent per year due to inflation.

Selling and Administrative Expenses Worksheet

That portion of a business unit's selling and administrative expenses attributed to the project proposal should be included in the pro forma income statement. Expenses that may be included are advertising and sales promotion and the costs of general administration, accounting, computing services, etc. The business unit's accounting and finance staff is the most likely source for estimates of these costs.

---

[11]Direct labor costs for intermediate years are approximations.

The home food dehydrator's selling and administrative expenses are the total expenses for this line of business because Flav-R-Loc defined the scope of the project as their entire food dehydrator business. The company's selling and administrative expenses worksheet is given in Table 9.4.

Current Asset and Liability Worksheet

The current asset and liability worksheet describes the amounts of receivables, inventory, payables, and financial slack required to support the long-term investment proposal. Current liabilities unrelated to operations (such as bank loans) are not included in this worksheet because we are not concerned with how the investment project will be financed.

Working Capital Required for Operations   Recall from Chapter 2 that we subtract the change in accounts receivable and inventory and add the change in accounts payable and accruals to net income to compute cash flow provided by operations. These adjustments are necessary to convert accrued revenue into the actual amount of cash collected from customers and cost of goods sold into the actual amount of cash paid to suppliers. Consequently, we must estimate the amount of working capital for operations used by a long-term investment proposal each year.

The amount of working capital an investment project requires depends on several factors, including the product's characteristics and industry practice. For example, some products require a large investment in inventories because they have a lengthy production process or a high cost of stock-outs; other products and all services cannot be inventoried at all. Similarly, companies in some industries provide generous credit terms to their customers to promote sales or facilitate distribution. These companies have a large investment in accounts receivable while others require cash on delivery. Chapters 10, 11, and 12 describe how these and other factors are evaluated to determine the best working capital policy.

Companies often use simple financial ratios to predict working capital levels in lieu of a detailed forecast based on their actual working capital policies. Following this approach, the annual investment in accounts receivable is sometimes estimated from the days'-sales-outstanding (DSO) ratio as shown below.

$$DSO = \frac{\text{Predicted accounts receivable}}{\text{Predicted sales per day}}$$

$$\text{Predicted accounts receivable} = DSO \times (\text{predicted sales per day})$$

As an illustration, suppose the Switzer Piano Company's credit terms are net 45 but that customers usually pay on day 50. The company predicts next year's sales will be $1,500,000 with cost of goods sold of $1,150,000. Then their predicted investment in accounts receivable is

$$\begin{aligned}
\text{Predicted accounts receivable} &= DSO \times (\text{predicted sales per day}) \\
&= 50 \text{ days} \times \$1,500,000/365 \\
&= \$205,479
\end{aligned}$$

Table 9.3 HOME FOOD DEHYDRATOR PROPOSAL COST OF GOODS SOLD WORKSHEET (Period ending December 31)

Year Time	1998 0	1999 1	2000 2	2001 3	2002 4	2003 5	2004 6	2005 7	2006 8	2007 9	2008 10
Unit sales	0	11,000	11,110	11,332	11,898	12,968	13,746	13,883	13,188	12,132	10,312
Variable costs per unit											
Direct labor	$0.00	$ 6.00	$ 5.87	$ 5.87	$ 5.92	$ 5.99	$ 6.09	$ 6.20	$ 6.33	$ 6.46	$ 6.60
Direct materials	0.00	12.00	12.30	12.61	12.93	13.25	13.58	13.92	14.27	14.63	15.00
Indirect costs	0.00	8.50	8.71	8.93	9.15	9.38	9.61	9.85	10.10	10.35	10.61
Total	$0.00	$ 26.50	$ 26.88	$ 27.41	$ 28.00	$ 28.62	$ 29.28	$ 29.97	$ 30.70	$ 31.44	$ 32.21
Total variable costs	$ 0	$291,500	$298,637	$310,610	$333,144	$371,144	$402,483	$416,074	$404,872	$381,430	$332,150
Other indirect costs	0	80,000	82,000	84,050	86,151	88,305	90,513	92,776	95,095	97,472	99,909
Total cost of goods sold	$ 0	$371,500	$380,637	$394,660	$419,295	$459,449	$492,996	$508,850	$499,967	$478,902	$432,059

Table 9.4 HOME FOOD DEHYDRATOR PROPOSAL SELLING AND ADMINISTRATIVE EXPENSES WORKSHEET (Period ending December 31)

Year Time	1998 0	1999 1	2000 2	2001 3	2002 4	2003 5	2004 6	2005 7	2006 8	2007 9	2008 10
Salaries	$0	$45,000	$45,900	$46,818	$47,754	$48,709	$49,683	$50,677	$51,691	$52,725	$53,780
Office furniture lease payments	0	10,000	10,200	10,404	10,612	10,824	11,040	11,261	11,486	11,716	11,950
Advertising and promotion	0	10,000	10,200	10,404	10,612	10,824	11,040	11,261	11,486	11,716	11,950
Total	$0	$65,000	$66,300	$67,626	$68,978	$70,357	$71,763	$73,199	$74,663	$76,157	$77,680

The days'-costs-in-inventory (DCI) and days'-payables-outstanding (DPO) ratios are used similarly to forecast inventory and accounts payable and accruals.

$$DCI = \frac{\text{Predicted inventory}}{\text{Predicted cost of goods sold per day}}$$

$$\text{Predicted inventory} = DCI \times (\text{predicted costs of goods sold per day})$$

$$DPO = \frac{\text{Predicted payables and accruals}}{\text{Predicted cost of goods sold per day}}$$

$$\text{Predicted payables and accruals} = DPO \times (\text{predicted cost of goods sold per day})$$

EXERCISE

9.4   **ESTIMATING WORKING CAPITAL REQUIREMENTS**

The Switzer Piano Company's days'-cost-in-inventory and days'-payables-outstanding are 30 and 40 days. Determine the company's predicted levels of inventory and accounts payable and accruals.

$$\text{Predicted inventory} = DCI \times (\text{predicted costs of goods sold per day})$$
$$= 30 \text{ days} \times \$1,150,000/365$$
$$= \$94,521$$
$$\text{Predicted payables and accruals} = DPO \times (\text{predicted cost of goods sold per day})$$
$$= 40 \text{ days} \times \$1,150,000/365$$
$$= \$126,027$$

The Switzer Piano Company requires \$94,521 of inventory and \$126,027 of payables and accruals.

Flav-R-Loc's materials manager estimated that \$10,000 of inventory will be required at the end of 1998 to begin production. The resulting accounts payable plus a small amount of accrued wages are estimated to total \$11,500. There are no accounts receivable at the end of 1998 because there are no sales. Receivables, inventory, and payables for subsequent years are predicted using the financial ratios described above with DSO = 27 days, DCI = 11 days, and DPO = 15 days. For example, accounts receivable for 1999 = 27 days × \$550,000/365 = \$40,685. Estimated year-by-year receivables, inventory, and payables as well as net working capital (receivables plus inventory minus payables) are given in Table 9.5.[12]

---

[12]Accounts receivable and payable actually are not reduced to zero on December 31, 2008 because some credit sales and purchases near the end of the year are still outstanding then. Nevertheless, we are working with annual cash flows so these collections and payments are assigned to the nearest *year*, 2008.

Table 9.5 HOME FOOD DEHYDRATOR PROPOSAL CURRENT ASSET AND LIABILITY WORKSHEET (Period ending December 31)

Year	1998	1999	2000	2001	2002	2003	2004	2005	2006	2007	2008
Time	0	1	2	3	4	5	6	7	8	9	10
Current operating assets											
Accounts receivable	$ 0	$40,685	$42,325	$44,470	$48,090	$53,988	$58,946	$61,320	$59,996	$56,853	$0
Inventory	10,000	11,196	11,471	11,894	12,636	13,846	14,857	15,335	15,067	14,433	0
Total	$10,000	$51,881	$53,796	$56,364	$60,726	$67,834	$73,803	$76,655	$75,063	$71,286	$0
Current operating liabilities											
Accounts payable and accruals	$11,500	$15,267	$15,643	$16,219	$17,231	$18,881	$20,260	$20,912	$20,547	$19,681	$0
Total	$11,500	$15,267	$15,643	$16,219	$17,231	$18,881	$20,260	$20,912	$20,547	$19,681	$0
Net working capital	$(1,500)	$36,614	$38,153	$40,145	$43,495	$48,953	$53,543	$55,743	$54,516	$51,605	$0
Financial slack	$45,000	$55,000	$57,217	$60,116	$65,011	$72,984	$79,686	$82,895	$81,106	$76,856	$0

Financial Slack   Companies have less free cash flow to distribute to investors when they increase financial slack and vice versa. The amount of slack companies maintain depends on the uncertainty of future cash flows, the cost of obtaining funds from other sources on short notice, and the opportunity cost of holding temporary investments. Chapter 19 describes how companies can balance these factors to determine whether to increase or decrease financial slack. For forecasting purposes, however, many companies estimate the amount of cash and temporary investments they will hold as a simple percent of sales or assets.

Flav-R-Loc's treasurer decided the company should hold $45,000 of cash and temporary investments as financial slack when the project is initiated and maintain a level equal to 10 percent of sales. The year-by-year requirements are given in Table 9.5.

Fixed-Asset Worksheet

The fixed-asset worksheet describes a project's period-by-period investment in property, plant, and equipment. This worksheet requires estimates of two items. First, the analyst must estimate a project's initial cost which may include the costs of purchasing property, building a plant, and acquiring and installing the necessary equipment. This information is obtained from the company's property management department, construction bids and estimates, equipment sales representatives, and the company's engineers and manufacturing managers.

Second, the analyst must prepare depreciation schedules for a project's fixed assets other than land. Depreciation is not a cash flow but it affects taxes, which are cash flows, because depreciation is deducted to determine taxable income. We only are concerned about the effect on taxes, so we must use the depreciation method used for tax purposes rather than the method used for financial reporting to prepare this schedule.

Table 9.6   MODIFIED ACCELERATED COST RECOVERY SYSTEM (Yearly Depreciation Deduction as Percentage of Cost)

		Year							
Type of Equipment	Class Life	1	2	3	4	5	6	7	8
Small tools	3 years	33.33	44.44	14.82	7.41				
Automobiles and office machinery	5 years	20.00	32.00	19.20	11.52	11.52	5.76		
Office furniture, most factory machinery	7 years	14.29	24.49	17.49	12.49	8.93	8.93	8.93	4.45

Companies compute depreciation for U.S. tax purposes using the **Modified Accelerated Cost Recovery System (MACRS),** which was introduced in 1981 and modified by the Tax Reform Act of 1986. Under MACRS, a depreciable asset is assigned to a class that specifies its depreciable life and the proportion of its cost that can be taken as a depreciation deduction each year. Representative asset classes and the allowable depreciation for each class are shown in Table 9.6.

The depreciation deduction for each year is based on the double-declining balance method with a switch to straight-line when the straight-line method provides a faster rate of depreciation. Assets are assumed to be placed in service at mid-year so only half of the first year's depreciation deduction is permitted the year the asset is acquired. The depreciation deduction continues for one year beyond an asset's class life to make up for using only a half-year deduction the first year. The total of the percentages in each asset class equals 100.00 percent; that is, MACRS depreciates an asset to zero book value if the company holds it at least one year longer than its class life. Here's a simple illustration.

O'Grady Motorworks spent $10,000 on hand tools for the service department in 1999. These tools have a class life of three years (according to Table 9.6) so the company's annual depreciation deduction is

Year	MACRS Depreciation Deduction
1999	$10,000 × 0.3333 = $ 3,333
2000	10,000 × 0.4444 = 4,444
2001	10,000 × 0.1482 = 1,482
2002	10,000 × 0.0741 = 741
Total	$10,000

EXERCISE

9.5   COMPUTING MACRS DEPRECIATION

O'Grady's accountant overlooked the fact that the company also paid $2,000 for an elaborate red cabinet for storing these tools. This cabinet also is depreciable, so recompute O'Grady's annual depreciation deduction given its total expenditures for small tools.

Year	MACRS Depreciation Deduction	
1999	$12,000 × 0.3333 =	$ 3,999.60
2000	12,000 × 0.4444 =	5,332.80
2001	12,000 × 0.1482 =	1,778.40
2002	12,000 × 0.0741 =	889.20
Total		$12,000.00

This schedule fully depreciates O'Grady's hand tools and the storage cabinet in four years.

● ———————— ●

Flav-R-Loc's new production equipment will cost $550,000 plus $50,000 for installation and will be placed in service at the end of the company's fiscal year on December 31, 1998. The equipment is expected to be worth $30,000 when the company abandons this line of business on December 31, 2008. This new machinery will be depreciated according to MACRS rules, which specify a class life of seven years.

The new equipment's current depreciation deduction, its accumulated depreciation, and net book value for each year of the project's life are given in Table 9.7. The current depreciation deduction equals the equipment's original cost multiplied by the MACRS depreciation allowance. Accumulated depreciation equal the sum of the depreciation deductions up to that time. Net fixed assets equal gross fixed assets minus accumulated depreciation. All depreciation deductions are exhausted on December 31, 2005 even though the company intends to continue operating the equipment until December 31, 2008.

The Project's Income Statements and Balance Sheets

Companies prepare an investment proposal's income statements and balance sheets for a variety of reasons, including financial planning and control. We will use these statements to prepare indirect format free cash flow statements so we can omit some entries included in complete income statements and balance sheets.

Table 9.7   HOME FOOD DEHYDRATOR PROPOSAL FIXED-ASSET WORKSHEET (Period ending December 31)

Year	1998	1999	2000	2001	2002	2003	2004	2005	2006	2007	2008
Time	0	1	2	3	4	5	6	7	8	9	10
Gross fixed assets	$600,000	—	—	—	—	—	—	—	—	—	—
MACRS depreciation allowance	0.1429	0.2449	0.1749	0.1249	0.0893	0.0893	0.0893	0.0445	0	0	0
Current depreciation deduction	$ 85,740	$146,940	$104,940	$ 74,940	$ 53,580	$ 53,580	$ 53,580	$ 26,700	$ 0	$ 0	$0
Gross fixed assets	$600,000	$600,000	$600,000	$600,000	$600,000	$600,000	$600,000	$600,000	$600,000	$600,000	$0
Accumulated depreciation	85,740	232,680	337,620	412,560	466,140	519,720	573,300	600,000	600,000	600,000	0
Net fixed assets	$514,260	$367,320	$262,380	$187,440	$133,860	$ 80,280	$ 26,700	$ 0	$ 0	$ 0	$0

Income Statements   The main entries for the investment proposal's income statements (sales revenues, cost of goods sold, selling and administrative expenses, and depreciation) are taken directly from the worksheets we've already prepared. We'll discuss the remaining entries now and use the results to construct the home food dehydrator project's income statements.

A common source of other revenue or cost for a new investment proposal is the gain or loss from disposing of the new equipment at the end of its useful life. The amount of a gain or loss on an operating asset is determined by subtracting the asset's book value from its selling price. Gains to the extent of accumulated depreciation are treated as ordinary gains and added to taxable income; losses are treated as ordinary losses and deducted from taxable income. These ordinary gains or losses are therefore taxed at the company's ordinary tax rate. Gains in excess of accumulated depreciation are taxed at the capital gains rate. There currently is no preferential tax rate on capital gains, so all gains are subject to the ordinary tax rate.[13]

EXERCISE   •⎯⎯⎯⎯⎯⎯⎯⎯⎯⎯⎯⎯⎯⎯⎯⎯⎯⎯•

9.6   COMPUTING GAINS AND LOSSES FROM SELLING CAPITAL EQUIPMENT

Webster's Brew Haus has a stainless steel fermenting tank that cost $75,000 and has accumulated depreciation of $15,000. Determine the amount of the company's gain or loss if they sell this tank for $55,000, $60,000, or $70,000.

The tank's book value is $60,000 ($75,000 – $15,000) and the gain or loss equals sales price minus book value. Therefore,

$$\text{Gain or loss} = \$55,000 - \$60,000 = \$-5,000 \text{ loss}$$
$$\text{Gain or loss} = \$60,000 - \$60,000 = \qquad 0$$
$$\text{Gain or loss} = \$70,000 - \$60,000 = \$10,000 \text{ gain.}$$

Webster's Brew Haus can deduct $5,000 from taxable income if they sell the fermenting tank for only $55,000; however, they must add $10,000 to taxable income if they sell it for $70,000.

•⎯⎯⎯⎯⎯⎯⎯•

Flav-R-Loc expects to dispose of the new equipment for $30,000 on December 31, 2008. That equipment will be fully depreciated in 2008, so they will report an ordinary gain of $30,000 as other income then.

Income statements normally include a line for interest expense but it isn't necessary when the ultimate purpose is to forecast free cash flows. This is because the separation principle tells us to evaluate investment decisions separately from financing decisions. Then, the owners can make their own borrowing and lending decisions to arrange an acceptable investment's cash flows into the pattern they prefer. Interest expense and the related cash flows are the result of the *company's* financing decisions

⎯⎯⎯⎯⎯⎯

[13]These tax effects are the more common ones. Companies that acquire or dispose of plant and equipment through an exchange of assets may encounter different tax effects.

and must not be commingled with the investment's cash flows. This is precisely the reason we omitted interest from cash flows provided by operations when we first developed the free cash flow statement in Chapter 2. We won't use any information about how the company will finance the investment; therefore, we don't need to enter interest expense in the income statements.

Finally, the project's taxable income will be added to the company's taxable income, which is taxed at the company's marginal tax rate. Therefore, the investment proposal's taxes should be computed at the company's marginal tax rate. The result is that taxes are assessed against the project when its taxable income is positive, and taxes are credited to the project when its taxable income is negative.

Any tax credits specific to the investment proposal should be subtracted from the project's taxes. For example, the U.S. federal government sometimes offers an **investment tax credit** to encourage long-term investments. This provision permits companies to reduce the taxes they owe by a fraction of the amount they spend on qualifying investments. A 10 percent investment tax credit would permit Flav-R-Loc to reduce its 1998 tax bill by $60,000 in the current example. The investment tax credit is not currently in force although it may be in the future.

The company may have other general tax credits that will reduce its *total* tax bill, but this doesn't change how we compute the investment proposal's contribution to the company's taxes. This is because when the project's taxable income is positive, it increases the actual amount of taxes the company must pay or it consumes an equal amount of the company's tax credits. The incremental effect is the same in both cases.

The home food dehydrator proposal's income statements are given in Table 9.8. The entries for sales revenues, cost of goods sold, selling and administrative expenses, and depreciation were taken directly from the worksheets in Tables 9.2, 9.3, 9.4 and 9.7. Other revenue and expenses were calculated above and taxes were computed at the entire company's marginal tax rate of 38 percent, which includes national, state, and local taxes.

Balance Sheets   The period-by-period balance sheets for the proposal are assembled from Tables 9.5 and 9.7. These balance sheets are given in Table 9.9.

The Project's Free Cash Flow Statements

Finally, the project's free cash flow is determined by using its income statements and balance sheets and their accompanying notes to prepare the operating, investment, and financial slack sections of its cash statements. (This procedure was described in detail in Chapter 2, so only a brief review is given here.)

To compute cash flow from operations, begin with net income and remove any transactions that did not provide or use cash (such as depreciation). Next, adjust revenue for the effect of credit sales and adjust cost of goods sold for the effect of additions to inventory and credit purchases. Subtract the change in accounts receivable and inventory and add the change in accounts payable and accruals to make these adjustments. Alternatively, you can subtract the change in net working capital for operations (accounts receivable plus inventory minus accounts payable) to make these adjustments in a single step. Remove the gains and losses from selling assets so the associated *cash flows* can be accounted for in the investment section. Finally, remove after-tax interest

Table 9.8   **HOME FOOD DEHYDRATOR PROPOSAL INCOME STATEMENTS (Period ending December**

Year	1998	1999	2000	2001
Time	0	1	2	3
Net sales	$ 0	$550,000	$572,165	$601,163
Cost of goods sold	0	371,500	380,637	394,660
Gross profit	0	178,500	191,528	206,503
Selling and administrative expenses	0	65,000	66,300	67,626
Depreciation	85,740	146,940	104,940	74,940
Net operating income	(85,740)	(33,440)	20,288	63,937
Other revenue and costs	0	0	0	0
Interest expense	NA	NA	NA	NA
Taxable income	(85,740)	(33,440)	20,288	63,937
Taxes	(32,581)	(12,707)	7,709	24,296
Net income	$(53,159)	$(20,733)	$ 12,579	$ 39,641

Table 9.9   **HOME FOOD DEHYDRATOR PROPOSAL BALANCE SHEETS (Period ending December 31)**

Year	1998	1999	2000	2001
Time	0	1	2	3
Assets				
Cash	$ 45,000	$ 55,000	$ 57,217	$ 60,116
Accounts receivable	0	40,685	42,325	44,470
Inventory	10,000	11,196	11,471	11,894
Total current assets	$ 55,000	$106,881	$111,013	$116,480
Gross fixed assets	$600,000	$600,000	$600,000	$600,000
Accumulated depreciation	85,740	232,680	337,620	412,560
Net fixed assets	$514,260	$367,320	$262,380	$187,440
Total assets	$569,260	$474,201	$373,393	$303,920
Claims				
Accounts payable and accruals	$ 11,500	$ 15,267	$ 15,643	$ 16,219

expense if it was subtracted to compute net income. These adjustments convert net income into cash flow from operations. Cash flow provided by or used for investment is the amount of cash expended for new equipment. Cash flows provided by or used for financial slack are the planned decreases or increases in the cash balance. An investment proposal's free cash flow is the sum of these amounts:

Cash flow provided by or used for operations

+ Cash flow provided by or used for investments

2002 4	2003 5	2004 6	2005 7	2006 8	2007 9	2008 10
$650,107	$729,839	$796,856	$828,954	$811,062	$768,562	$672,858
419,295	459,449	492,996	508,850	499,967	478,902	432,059
230,812	270,390	303,860	320,104	311,095	289,660	240,799
68,978	70,357	71,763	73,199	74,663	76,157	77,680
53,580	53,580	53,580	26,700	0	0	0
108,254	146,453	178,517	220,205	236,432	213,503	163,119
0	0	0	0	0	0	30,000
NA	NA	NA	NA	NA	NA	NA
108,254	146,453	178,517	220,205	236,432	213,503	193,119
41,137	55,652	67,836	83,678	89,844	81,131	73,385
$ 67,117	$ 90,801	$110,681	$136,527	$146,588	$132,372	$119,734

2002 4	2003 5	2004 6	2005 7	2006 8	2007 9	2008 10
$ 65,011	$ 72,984	$ 79,686	$ 82,895	$ 81,106	$ 76,856	$0
48,090	53,988	58,946	61,320	59,996	56,853	0
12,636	13,846	14,857	15,335	15,067	14,433	0
$125,737	$140,818	$153,489	$159,550	$156,169	$148,142	$0
$600,000	$600,000	$600,000	$600,000	$600,000	$600,000	$0
466,140	519,720	573,300	600,000	600,000	600,000	0
$133,860	$ 80,280	$ 26,700	$ 0	$ 0	$ 0	$0
$259,597	$221,098	$180,189	$159,550	$156,169	$148,142	$0
$ 17,231	$ 18,881	$ 20,260	$ 20,912	$ 20,547	$ 19,681	$0

+   Cash flow provided by or used for financial slack
=   Free cash flow.

Flav-R-Loc's home food dehydrator project's free cash flows are given in Table 9.10. We will use these cash flows in Section 9.5 to determine the proposal's market value and to decide if it's acceptable.

Table 9.10 HOME FOOD DEHYDRATOR PROPOSAL FREE CASH FLOW STATEMENTS (Period ending December 31)

Year	1998	1999	2000	2001	2002	2003	2004	2005	2006	2007	2008
Time	0	1	2	3	4	5	6	7	8	9	10

Cash Flow Provided by (Used for) Operations

	1998	1999	2000	2001	2002	2003	2004	2005	2006	2007	2008
Net income	$(53,159)	$(20,733)	$12,579	$39,641	$67,117	$90,801	$110,681	$136,527	$146,588	$132,372	$119,734
Plus depreciation	85,740	146,940	104,940	74,940	53,580	53,580	53,580	26,700	0	0	0
Minus change in net working capital	(1,500)	38,114	1,539	1,992	3,350	5,458	4,590	2,200	(1,227)	(2,911)	(51,605)
Minus gain on sale of asset	0	0	0	0	0	0	0	0	0	0	30,000
Plus after-tax interest expense	NA	NA	NA	NA	NA	NA	NA	NA	NA	NA	NA
Net cash flow	$ 34,081	$ 88,093	$115,980	$112,589	$117,347	$138,923	$159,671	$161,027	$147,815	$135,283	$141,339

Cash Flow Provided by (Used for) Investment

	1998	1999	2000	2001	2002	2003	2004	2005	2006	2007	2008
Purchase fixed assets	$(600,000)	$ 0	$ 0	$ 0	$ 0	$ 0	$ 0	$ 0	$ 0	$ 0	$ 0
Sell fixed assets	0	0	0	0	0	0	0	0	0	0	0,000
Net cash flow	$(600,000)	$ 0	$ 0	$ 0	$ 0	$ 0	$ 0	$ 0	$ 0	$ 0	$ 30,000

Cash Flow Provided by (Used for) Financial Slack

	1998	1999	2000	2001	2002	2003	2004	2005	2006	2007	2008
Net cash flow	$ (45,000)	$(10,000)	$ (2,217)	$ (2,899)	$ (4,895)	$ (7,973)	$ (6,702)	$ (3,209)	$ 1,789	$ 4,250	$ 76,856
Net Free Cash Flow	$(610,919)	$ 78,093	$113,763	$109,690	$112,452	$130,950	$152,969	$157,818	$149,604	$139,533	$248,195

9.4 ESTIMATE THE PROJECT'S REQUIRED RATE OF RETURN

The next step in the financial analysis of a long-term investment proposal is to determine its required rate of return or discount rate. This required rate of return should be the opportunity cost investors would assign to the project if it was directly available to them in the financial market. Using their opportunity cost as the required rate of return ensures that the company accepts only those investment proposals that cover the cost of the financial resources the investors provide to the project.

There are several ways to determine the required rate of return but many companies compute a weighted average of the costs of the financing provided by the creditors and owners. (This preference was reported in one of the surveys cited earlier.) A discount rate computed this way is called the **weighted average cost of capital**. This method of computing a discount rate is simply a straightforward application of the principle that the required rate of return should be based on the investors' opportunity cost. Importantly, an investment proposal that earns a rate of return greater than or equal to the weighted average cost of capital generates more than enough free cash flow to repay the investors' claims. We easily can see these features by using our definitions of free cash flow and financial cash flow to derive the weighted average cost of capital.

The cash flow identity, described previously by Equation 2.2, is

$$\text{Free cash flow}_t + \text{financial cash flow}_t = 0.$$

Assuming a company finances an investment proposal's cost with a combination of debt and equity, we can rewrite this identity as[14]

$$\text{Free cash flow}_t + \text{Debt}_t + \text{Equity}_t = 0$$

where
Debt_t = cash flow provided by (used for) debt
Equity_t = cash flow provided by (used for) equity.

Investors provide cash to finance a proposal's negative free cash flow so the cash flow identity at time 0 is

$$\text{Free cash flow}_0 + \text{Debt}_0 + \text{Equity}_0 = 0.$$

The company uses a proposal's positive free cash flow to repay the investors. The minimum amount of cash required to repay investors who financed a one-period investment proposal equals their original capital plus a rate of return on this capital computed at their opportunity costs. That is,

$$\text{Minimum free cash flow}_1 = \text{Debt}_0 \times [1 + r_d(1 - T)] + \text{Equity}_0 \times [1 + r_e] \quad [9.2]$$

---

[14]This assumption has the effect of relating the method and cost of financing to the *book* values of the debt and equity rather than to their market values. Some surveys of capital budgeting practice indicate companies use book values for this purpose even though it can cause errors. We will discuss this issue in detail in Chapter 17.

where r_d = opportunity cost of debt
T = company's marginal tax rate
r_e = opportunity cost of equity.

The opportunity cost of debt is multiplied by one minus the tax rate because interest payments on debt are tax-deductible.

Dividing both sides of Equation 9.2 by the free cash flow at time 0 and subtracting 1 expresses this critical value as a rate of return. After simplification, the result is

$$\text{Minimum required rate of return} = \frac{\text{Debt}_0}{\text{Free cash flow}_0} \times r_d(1 - T) + \frac{\text{Equity}_0}{\text{Free cash flow}_0} \times r_e \qquad \textbf{[9.3]}$$

The minimum required rate of return described by this equation is called the weighted average cost of capital because it equals a weighted average of the opportunity costs of the debt and equity used to finance the proposal. The weights are the proportion of capital obtained from each source, $\text{Debt}_0/\text{FCF}_0$ and $\text{Equity}_0/\text{FCF}_0$.

Suppose Flav-R-Loc will obtain the $610,919 needed to finance their home food dehydrator proposal by issuing $350,000 of common stock and $260,919 of bonds. They estimate the required rates of return on the debt and equity are 8 percent and 13 percent. Given the company's marginal tax rate of 38 percent, the weighted average cost of capital (r_{wacc}) for this proposal is

$$r_{\text{wacc}} = \frac{\$260,919}{\$610,919} \times 0.08 \times (1 - .38) + \frac{\$350,000}{\$610,919} \times 0.13$$

$$= 0.096 \text{ or } 9.6\%.$$

There are many complications to using the weighted average cost of capital in practical situations. For example, the investment proposal's own risk may be different from the company's risk, we should use the market values of the debt and equity to compute the weights rather than book values as we did here, and the mix of debt and equity used to finance the project will affect both the risk and return. We will address these issues in Chapter 17.

9.5   DETERMINE THE PROJECT'S MARKET VALUE

Analysts use present value analysis or option pricing to determine a project's market value at the second step of financial analysis and then recommend approval if the project's market value exceeds its cost. They sometimes can deduce that a project is acceptable by comparing its internal rate of return to its required return. Whether or not the project is independent of the company's other investment opportunities determines which of these procedures they can use.

Determining the Value of Independent Investment Projects

An independent investment project does not affect—and is not affected by—current or future investment opportunities. This restrictive definition virtually eliminates all but one-shot proposals unrelated to the company's existing businesses. For example, proposals that require or preclude other investments and proposals that permit but do not require future investments are not independent. Even apparently independent proposals are not actually independent if, by accepting one, the company becomes financially unable to accept others.

Analysts can evaluate a genuinely independent investment proposal by itself because its free cash flows completely describe its costs and benefits. Companies should accept independent investment proposals with positive NPVs because their market values exceed their costs. They should reject the rest.

Some companies prefer to compare an independent project's internal rate of return to its required rate of return to deduce whether its NPV is positive. Chapter 3 demonstrated that this approach is reliable if the project has a simple cash flow pattern (only one change in the sign of its cash flows) but not otherwise. The reason is that a project with a nonsimple cash flow pattern has the characteristics of both an investment and a loan and therefore may have more than one internal rate of return. As a result, a nonsimple investment project may have a negative NPV even though its IRRs are greater than the required rate of return. Here's an illustration.

Martin Resource Development Company can purchase the rights to remove fire-damaged, standing timber from Indian lands in New Mexico for $2.4 million. The company expects to receive free cash flows of $11.5 million when the job is completed in one year. The tribal council will require Martin to spend the following year repairing the fire and logging damage at an expected cost of $10 million. The project's free cash flows are therefore

Year	Free Cash Flows
0	$-2,400,000
1	11,500,000
2	-10,000,000

Martin prefers to use the internal rate of return to analyze investment proposals. Should the company accept this one if its required rate of return is 12 percent?

We must use trial-and-error to determine this nonsimple project's internal rates of return because some financial calculators and spreadsheets do not warn that there are two IRRs, as you learned in Chapter 3. This project has two IRRs, 14.15 percent and 265.02 percent. The project apparently is acceptable because both IRRs are greater than the required rate of return of 12 percent.

Let's check the project's NPV at 12 percent just to be sure. The result is

$$NPV = \$-2,400,000 + \$11,500,000/(1.12) + \$-10,000,000/(1.12)^2$$
$$= \$-104,082.$$

The recovery and reclamation project actually is unacceptable because it reduces the owners' wealth.

Internal rates of return greater than the required rate of return may not imply that a nonsimple, independent project has an NPV greater than zero. Consequently, you must use net present value analysis to evaluate this type of investment.

9.7   MULTIPLE INTERNAL RATES OF RETURN

The Green Belt Waste Management Company has an opportunity to open a landfill site at the end of 1998 at a cost of $3 million. They expect to earn free cash flows of $9 million at the end of 1999 and then close the site at the end of 2000 at a cost of $6.5 million. This project's required rate of return is 30 percent. Compute the project's IRR(s) and determine whether they should accept the project. Verify your conclusion by computing the project's NPV.

By trial-and-error, the project's internal rates of return are 21.13 percent and 78.87 percent. One IRR is less than and one IRR is greater than the required rate of return, so the outcome seems indeterminate. The project's NPV at the required rate of return of 30 percent is

$$\text{NPV} = \$-3,000,000 + \$9,000,000/(1.30) + \$-6,500,000/(1.30)^2$$
$$= \$76,923.$$

Green Belt should accept this proposal because it increases the owners' wealth (even though this is not apparent from its IRRs).

● ———————— ●

Determining the Value of Nonindependent Projects

Nonindependent investment proposals must be evaluated together to properly measure their effect on the owners' wealth. This analysis may be easy or difficult depending on the relationship between the projects.

Prerequisite and Concurrent Investments   Prerequisite and concurrent investments are easy to evaluate. You simply bundle the related projects together and evaluate the resulting super-project as an independent investment proposal. Suppose, for example, that a manufacturer cannot expand its plant's capacity unless it builds a new warehouse. The plant-expansion and warehouse-construction projects are dependent because the company will not invest in one without the other. The analyst should combine these proposals to form a plant-warehouse super-project and then use net present value analysis to accept or reject the combined proposal in its entirety.

Mutually Exclusive Projects   Proposals that preclude investments in other projects (because they are mutually exclusive ways of performing a single task) also must be evaluated together to determine which is best. Using net present value analysis for this purpose is easy. Accept the proposal with the highest net present value (because it adds the greatest amount to the owners' wealth) and reject the rest. Of course, the best proposal must have an NPV greater than zero or the company should reject all of the alternatives.

Flav-R-Loc actually has two mutually exclusive investment alternatives to consider. One alternative is to buy equipment to reduce costs and expand capacity. The other alternative is to continue operating its old equipment. These alternatives are mutually exclusive because the company will not buy the new equipment if it keeps the old and vice versa.

We already have the replacement alternative's free cash flows in Table 9.10. The same process used to estimate these cash flows was used to estimate the cash flows without replacement. Both sets of cash flows are provided in Table 9.11.

The NPVs of these cash flows, computed at the company's weighted average cost of capital of 9.6 percent, also are given in Table 9.11. The net present value of the new equipment is larger so Flav-R-Loc should accept the home food dehydrator proposal.

Many companies prefer to use the IRR rule to evaluate long-term investment proposals; however, it may fail to identify the better mutually exclusive alternative. Look at the cash flows of Flav-R-Loc's mutually exclusive alternatives again. The IRR of buying new equipment is 15.73 percent. The IRR of continuing to operate the old equipment is not a meaningful number, however, because there are no cash outflows. Therefore Flav-R-Loc cannot compare these alternatives' IRRs to determine which is better.

The internal rate of return rule may fail to identify the better alternative even if both have meaningful IRRs. This problem is apparent in the following example.

Sinbad Cruise Line advertises its adventure cruises in a bimonthly travel magazine. A half-page ad costs $95,000 and produces $59,000 of free cash flows the following month. The ad's effect begins to wear off at that point; in the next month, it produces only $43,000 of free cash flows. A full-page ad costs $164,000 and produces larger free cash flows that persist for a longer time—$87,000 per month for two months. Should Sinbad buy a half- or full-page ad if the required rate of return is 15 percent per year or 1.25 percent per month?

FLAV-R-LOC'S MUTUALLY EXCLUSIVE INVESTMENT PROPOSALS   **Table 9.11**

| | | Free Cash Flows | |
| | | Buy New Equipment | Continue to Operate Old Equipment |
Year	Time		
1998	0	$(610,919)	$51,485
1999	1	78,093	46,730
2000	2	113,763	40,150
2001	3	109,690	35,023
2002	4	112,452	21,656
2003	5	130,950	11,461
2004	6	152,969	5,493
2005	7	157,818	3,576
2006	8	149,604	2,542
2007	9	139,533	1,744
2008	10	248,195	7,868
NPV at 9.6%		$202,671	$186,587
IRR		15.73%	—

The net present values of the half- and full-page ads are

$$\text{NPV(half-page)} = \$-95,000 + \$59,000/(1.0125) + \$43,000/(1.0125)^2$$
$$= \$5,216$$
$$\text{NPV(full-page)} = \$-164,000 + \$87,000/(1.0125) + \$87,000/(1.0125)^2$$
$$= \$6,791.$$

Sinbad should purchase the full-page ad because it creates an additional $1,575 ($6,791 − $5,216) of wealth for the owners.

Now let's see if we obtain the same conclusion by choosing the project with the larger internal rate of return. Using a calculator, these projects' IRRs are

$$\text{IRR(half-page)} = 5.15\%$$
$$\text{IRR(full-page)} = 4.04\%.$$

The half-page ad has the larger IRR but not the larger NPV. Therefore, we cannot evaluate these mutually exclusive investment proposals by comparing their internal rates of return.

You can see why this conflict arises by examining the projects' net present value profiles in Exhibit 9.5. The full-page ad has a *size advantage* because it provides more future free cash flows. These additional cash flows are worth waiting for when the opportunity cost is low; therefore, the full-page ad has a higher NPV at low required rates of return. The half-page ad has a *timing advantage* because its cash flows arrive sooner (most are received in the first month). Timing is more important when the opportunity cost is high, so the half-page ad has a higher NPV at high required rates of return.

The IRR method always will select the project with better timing (the half-page ad in this example) even though the larger project may have a higher value at the company's opportunity cost. The simplest way to avoid the possibility of choosing the wrong project is to use net present value analysis to evaluate mutually exclusive investment proposals. If you cannot use the NPV method because your company requires you to base investment decisions on the internal rate of return, then you must modify the IRR method to make it work. Here's how.

First, add each project's free cash flows to determine which proposal is larger. Note that these sums are the vertical intercepts of the projects' net present value profiles.

Second, determine the period-by-period incremental cash flows by subtracting the smaller project's cash flows from the larger project's cash flows. This step removes the effect of size and permits you to evaluate the timing of the incremental cash flows as you would any independent investment proposal.

Third, determine the internal rate of return of the incremental cash flows (IIRR). The incremental investment is acceptable if the IIRR is greater than the required rate of return—but not otherwise. The larger project is better than the smaller project if the incremental investment is acceptable. Otherwise, the smaller project is better.

Fourth, accept the winner from step three if its own IRR is greater than the required rate of return. Reject the winning project and do nothing if its IRR is less than the required rate of return.

Applied to Sinbad's advertising proposals, determine which proposal is larger.

Exhibit 9.5

NPV PROFILES OF MUTUALLY EXCLUSIVE INVESTMENT PROPOSALS

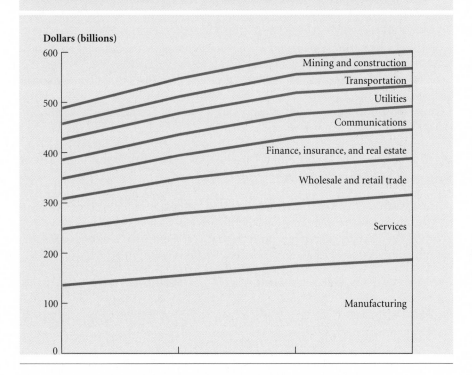

$$\text{Sum of half-page ad's cash flows} = \$-95,000 + \$59,000 + \$43,000$$
$$= \$7,000$$
$$\text{Sum of full-page ad's cash flows} = \$10,000$$

The full-page ad is the larger investment proposal.[15]

Determine the incremental cash flows.

Month	Incremental Cash Flows
0	$-164,000 - \$-95,000 = \$-69,000$
1	$87,000 - \quad 59,000 = \quad 28,000$
2	$87,000 - \quad 43,000 = \quad 44,000$

Calculate the IIRR to determine which proposal is better.

$$\text{NPV} = \$-69,000 + \$28,000/(1 + \text{IIRR}) + \$44,000/(1 + \text{IIRR})^2 = 0$$

---

[15]This step may seem unnecessary to you because it is obvious the full-page ad is the larger project. However, two projects can require the same investment and *still* be of different size—as you will see in Exercise 9.8.

Using a calculator, IIRR = 2.68 percent. The full-page ad is better than the half-page ad because the IIRR is greater than the required rate of return of 1.25 percent.

Calculate the winner's IRR to determine if it is acceptable.

$$NPV = \$-164{,}000 + \$87{,}000/(1 + IRR) + \$87{,}000/(1 + IRR)^2 = 0$$

Using a calculator, IRR = 4.04 percent. Sinbad should place the full-page ad because it is better than the half-page ad *and* acceptable in its own right.

Using the incremental internal rate of return procedure to evaluate mutually exclusive investment proposals is a lot of extra work but it gives you the correct answer. Remember, you can always avoid this work by choosing the investment proposal with the larger net present value.

E X E R C I S E ●─── ●

9.8   THE INCREMENTAL IRR PROCEDURE

Crain Farms has five acres of irrigated land it will plant in strawberries or raspberries. The strawberries mature quickly and produce fruit at a uniform rate for two years. The raspberries do not bear fruit the first year although the second year's harvest is quite valuable. Each alternative's free cash flows are given below.

Year	Strawberries	Raspberries
1998	$-100,000	$-100,000
1999	65,000	0
2000	65,000	140,000

The farm's required rate of return is 14 percent per year. Use the incremental IRR method to determine which fruit they should plant. Verify your conclusion by comparing the alternatives' net present values.

The sum of the cash flows is

Strawberries	$30,000
Raspberries	40,000

The raspberry proposal is larger.

The incremental cash flows are

Year	Raspberries – Strawberries
1998	$ 0
1999	−65,000
2000	75,000

The incremental internal rate of return is

$$NPV = \$0 + \$-65{,}000/(1 + IIRR) + \$75{,}000/(1 + IIRR)^2 = 0.$$

Using a calculator, IIRR = 15.38 percent. This IIRR is greater than the company's required rate of return of 14 percent, so planting raspberries is better than planting strawberries.

The raspberries' internal rate of return is

$$NPV = \$-100,000 + \$0/(1 + IRR) + \$140,000/(1 + IRR)^2 = 0.$$

Using a calculator, IRR = 18.32 percent. Planting raspberries is acceptable, so Crain Farms should proceed with this alternative.

The alternatives' NPVs are

$$NPV(strawberries) = \$-100,000 + \$65,000/(1.14) + \$65,000/(1.14)^2$$
$$= \$7,033$$
$$NPV(raspberries) = \$-100,000 + \$0/(1.14) + \$140,000/(1.14)^2$$
$$= \$7,725.$$

Planting raspberries provides a greater increase in the owners' wealth as indicated by the incremental internal rate of return analysis.

● ———————— ●

Strategic Investments   We cannot use net present value analysis to evaluate proposals that permit—but do not require—future investment decisions. The problem is that net present value analysis assumes projects are take-it-or-leave-it propositions and that managers must live with the outcome no matter what happens. This assumption ignores the managers' abilities to act strategically, that is, to expand or contract, accelerate or delay, or even abandon an investment as new information becomes available. As a result, net present value analysis undervalues strategic investment proposals that provide managers these options. This problem is illustrated by the following example.

Eco-Tech, Inc. advises companies on the use of waste-water treatment equipment and facilities. The company recently learned that a new process was developed and submitted to the Environmental Protection Agency for testing and approval on January 1, 1998. EPA certification takes six months and Eco-Tech estimates the likelihood of approval is 0.50.

Eco-Tech may use the six-month certification period to prepare new seminars that they will sell to clients who adopt the new process. The seminars will provide Eco-Tech with $124,000 at the end of the year if the EPA approves the new process; however, the seminars will be worthless otherwise. The project's expected future cash flow is therefore $62,000 ($124,000 × 0.50 + $0 × 0.50). The cost of developing and producing the notebooks and other instructional materials required for the seminars is $60,000. These free cash flows are summarized in panel A of Table 9.12. The company's required rate of return is 16 percent per year or 8 percent every six months.

Applying the NPV rule to this investment proposal's expected cash flows,

$$NPV = \$-60,000 + \frac{\$62,000}{(1.08)^2} = \$-6,845.$$

This result indicates Eco-Tech should not prepare the new seminars because the NPV is less than zero.

Net present value analysis is not applicable to this proposal, however, if Eco-Tech can defer at least part of the investment until it learns if the new waste-water treatment process is approved. As an illustration, suppose the company must spend $15,000 immediately to train its consultants and can defer the $45,000 needed to produce instruc-

Table 9.12   ECO-TECH, INC.'S INVESTMENT PROPOSAL

Panel A: As Originally Presented

Free Cash Flow

Period	If Approval Granted	If Approval Denied	Expected
0	$–60,000	$–60,000	$–60,000
1	0	0	0
2	124,000	0	62,000

Panel B: Revised to Recognize Managerial Flexibility

Free Cash Flow

Period	If Approval Granted	If Approval Denied
0	$ –15,000	$–15,000
1	–45,000	0
2	124,000	0

tional materials until the EPA's decision is announced on June 30, 1998. The revised cash flow schedule that recognizes this flexibility is presented in panel B of Table 9.12.

The net present values of the company's alternatives on June 30, computed at Eco-Tech's required rate of return, are

$$\text{NPV} = \$–45,000 + \frac{\$124,000}{(1.08)} = \$69,815 \quad \text{if approval granted}$$

$$= \$\,0 \qquad\qquad\qquad\qquad\qquad \text{if approval denied.}$$

Presented this way, management's problem is to decide whether to spend $15,000 now for an option on a project that will be worth $69,815 or $0 in six months.

You may think that we can apply the NPV rule to strategic investments if we carefully describe management's alternatives and compute the net present value of each one. This would work *if* we knew the proper discount rate to apply to the cash flows. Unfortunately, we can't use the weighted average cost of capital because some risks are avoidable when managers have the option to abandon the project. We must use an alternative technique based on option pricing. We will discuss this approach in Chapter 13.

Capital Rationing   Finally, analysts cannot use net present value analysis to evaluate seemingly independent investment proposals if, by accepting one group, the company becomes financially unable to accept others. This situation, called **capital rationing**, arises when companies limit the amount of money they will spend on long-term investments. Even a very simple example illustrates that net present value analysis does not work when capital is rationed.

Division managers of the Weingartner Paint Company submitted the four investment proposals shown below to the board of directors for approval. Each project has a positive NPV at the company's required rate of return but the board decided to limit its capital expenditures to $1 million. Which proposal(s) should the board approve?

Project	Cost	NPV
A	$1,000,000	$120,000
B	500,000	70,000
C	500,000	65,000
D	500,000	50,000

If the board ranks the projects according to NPV and chooses from the top of the list until the capital budget is exhausted, they will approve only project A for a total NPV of $120,000. However, in this simple example, it is clear that they should approve B and C for a total NPV of $135,000.

This example shows that we must know more than the net present values of individual investment proposals to determine which will provide the most wealth when there is a budget constraint. There are techniques, such as mathematical programming, that can be used to maximize net present value subject to a budget constraint but they are beyond the scope of this text. Advanced capital budgeting books discuss these techniques, or you can consult the references listed at the end of this chapter.

9.6 APPLICATION TO INTERNATIONAL INVESTMENT PROPOSALS

The procedures described in Sections 9.2 through 9.5 are applicable to international investment proposals as well as domestic ones.

Estimate the Project's Free Cash Flows

The method to determine free cash flow described in Section 9.3 also can be used for international investment proposals; however, there are three areas in which additional care is required to obtain accurate estimates. First, analysts should use inflation assumptions consistent with the market's consensus estimate of the rate of inflation in the foreign country. We saw in Chapter 4 that purchasing power parity ensures that the ratio of forward-to-spot exchange rates equals the ratio of foreign-to-domestic inflation. That is,

$$\frac{[1 + E(I^d)]}{[1 + E(I^f)]} = \frac{F}{S}. \qquad [4.4]$$

Rewriting this equation, the market's consensus estimate of the rate of inflation in the foreign country is

$$E(I^f) = \frac{S}{F} \times [1 + E(I^d)] - 1. \qquad [9.4]$$

Assuming a different rate of inflation is inconsistent with the market's estimate and therefore questionable. Here's an illustration of how to use Equation 9.4.

On September 13, 1996, the dollar/yen exchange rates were

	U.S. Dollar Equivalent[16]
Japanese yen	
Spot rate	0.009051
90-day forward rate	0.009168
180-day forward rate	0.009289

Assuming the expected 90-day U.S. inflation rate is 0.75 percent, the expected 90-day Japanese inflation rate is

$$E(I^f) = \frac{S}{F} \times [1 + E(I^d)] - 1$$

$$= \frac{0.009051}{0.009168} \times (1.0075) - 1 = -0.0054.$$

These foreign exchange rates imply the market expected Japan to experience *deflation* over the next 90 days.

EXERCISE

9.9

ESTIMATING EXPECTED FOREIGN INFLATION RATES

Determine the expected 180-day Japanese inflation rate if the 180-day expected U.S. inflation rate is 1.5 percent.

$$E(I^f) = \frac{S}{F} \times [1 + E(I^d)] - 1$$

$$= \frac{0.009051}{0.009289} \times (1.015) - 1 = -0.0110$$

The market also expected Japan to experience deflation over the next 180 days.

Second, computing an international investment proposal's net tax liability is a more difficult task. One cause of this difficulty is that many countries have tax treaties with one another that allow companies to apply their foreign tax payments as a credit against their domestic tax liabilities. When the foreign and domestic tax rates are different, companies can shift tax-deductible expenses to the high-tax country to reduce their net tax liability. For example, if the foreign tax rate is higher than the domestic tax rate, the company can increase the price at which it supplies goods and services to the foreign venture and have the venture remit its income as tax-deductible interest payments rather than as dividends. Identifying the best policy and assessing its effect on the proposal's net tax liability is difficult because it requires detailed knowledge of both countries' tax laws.

---

[16]Source: *The Wall Street Journal,* September 16, 1996, p. C21.

Third, the amount of free cash flow a company can obtain from its foreign investment project is affected by the political climate of the foreign country. Tax rates, restrictions on the repatriation of income, and the possibility that all future income will be expropriated are products of political processes that may be quite different from one country to another. Uncertainty about how these processes work and what decisions may emerge from them is termed **political risk.**

Analysts are sometimes tempted to adjust the required rate of return to account for political risk although this is not the preferred approach. After all, capital market theory says that the required rate of return should be based on systematic risk and political risk is unique to each country; that is, it can be diversified away. Adverse political decisions will affect cash flow, however. Consequently, an analyst should adjust an international investment proposal's free cash flows to account for the probability of unfavorable changes in tax rates or repatriation rules and the likelihood of expropriation.

Estimate the Project's Required Rate of Return

The required rate of return for an international investment proposal should be based on the same principle as the required return for a domestic investment. This principle is that the required return should be the opportunity cost investors would assign to the project if it was directly available to them in the financial market. The difficulties of applying this principle to international investment proposals are estimating the project's risk and accounting for the cost of specialized or unique methods of financing.

Determine the Project's Market Value[17]

Any of the discounted cash flow decision rules can be applied to an international investment proposal subject to the restrictions described in Section 9.5. The only additional complication to evaluating an international proposal is that its free cash flows are stated in different currencies. All the analyst must do is convert the free cash flows to a single currency before computing the NPV or IRR. The current spot and expected future spot foreign exchange rates are used for this purpose. We can use interest rate parity to estimate these exchange rates.

We saw in Chapter 4 that interest rate parity ensures that the ratio of forward-to-spot exchange rates equals the ratio of domestic-to-foreign interest rates. That is,

$$\frac{1 + r^d}{1 + r^f} = \frac{F}{S}. \qquad [4.6]$$

Rewriting this equation and assuming the forward rate, F, is an unbiased estimate of the expected future spot rate, $E(S)$,

$$E(S) = S \times (1 + r^d)/(1 + r^f).$$

Applying this logic to successive periods,

---

[17]James S. Ang and Tsong-Yue Lai suggested an alternative procedure that does not require converting a project's cash flows to a domestic currency to value them. See their article listed in the end of chapter references.

Table 9.13   CONVERTING FOREIGN CURRENCY FREE CASH FLOWS

| | | Exchange Rates | | |
| | Free Cash Flow in | Current | Expected | Free Cash Flow |
Year	Deutsche Marks	Spot Rate	Spot Rate	in Dollars
0	−1,000	0.6061		$−606
1	350		0.5997	210
2	425		0.5934	252
3	575		0.5871	338

German riskless interest rate: 4.2%
U.S. riskless interest rate: 3.1%

$$E(S_t) = S_0 \times [(1 + r^d)/(1 + r^f)]^t. \qquad [9.5]$$

This process is illustrated in Table 9.13. The estimated free cash flows for an investment project located in Germany are given in the first column. The second column has the current rate at which deutsche marks can be converted to dollars (0.6061) and the expected future spot rates based on interest rate parity and the current U.S. and German riskless interest rates of 3.1 percent and 4.2 percent. For example, the expected spot exchange rate at the end of year 3 is

$$E(S_t) = S_0 \times [(1 + r^d)/(1 + r^f)]^t$$
$$= 0.6061 \times (1.031/1.042)^3 = 0.5871.$$

This proposal's dollar-denominated free cash flows are obtained by multiplying the deutsche mark–denominated free cash flows by the expected exchange rates. The results are given in the third column. The company can compute the NPV or IRR of these dollar-denominated free cash flows in the standard way using the appropriate U.S. or dollar-based required rate of return.

9.7 SUMMARY

The process by which companies allocate funds to long-term investments has three stages: origination and classification of proposals, financial analysis, and continuing evaluation. Proposals may originate in nearly any of a company's business units and may involve the purchase of tangible assets such as plant and equipment or intangible assets such as advertising and training. These proposals are classified according to purpose and size to ensure subsequent stages of analysis are appropriate for each type. A particularly important distinction is between routine and strategic investments; the latter cannot be evaluated using discounted cash flow decision rules because they provide options.

The financial analysis of a routine investment proposal has three steps: identify and estimate the proposal's free cash flows, determine its required rate of return, and apply a discounted cash flow decision rule. This analysis must encompass the proposal's own cash flows and its impact on the cash flows from existing products. Furthermore, the analysis must be extended into the future if the venture will be continued beyond the life of the equipment in the present proposal.

Free cash flow estimates are obtained from projected financial statements. Information from marketing analysts, production managers, engineers, and accountants are used to forecast income statements and balance sheets that are converted to cash statements using the indirect method.

The weighted average of the cost of capital used to finance the proposal is its required rate of return. Proposals with a positive net present value when discounted at this required rate of return generate more than enough future cash flows to repay the investors who provided the original financing.

The net present value and internal rate of return criteria are the discounted cash flow decision rules that are usually applied to long-term investment proposals. The NPV rule can be used to evaluate any independent investment proposal while the IRR can be used only if the project has a simple cash flow pattern.

Nonindependent proposals must be evaluated together. Proposals that must be undertaken simultaneously are bundled together and evaluated as a single, independent investment proposal. Mutually exclusive investment proposals can be evaluated using the NPV rule but the IRR rule can lead to the wrong decision unless it is applied to the incremental cash flows. Investment proposals that are subject to budget constraints and those that provide options cannot be evaluated using discounted cash flow decision rules. The use of option pricing in capital budgeting is described in Chapter 13.

Finally, the same procedures should be used to analyze international investment proposals, taking care to adjust cash flows for differences in the domestic and foreign economic environments.

- ## KEY TERMS

Economic life *372*	Investment tax credit *387*	Capital rationing *400*
Learning curve *377*	Weighted average cost of	Political risk *403*
Modified Accelerated Cost	capital *391*	
Recovery System		
(MACRS) *384*		

- ## QUESTIONS AND PROBLEMS

1. List and describe the categories companies often use to classify long-term investment proposals. How does a proposal's classification affect its treatment during subsequent stages of analysis?

2. Koma Koffee Company produces and distributes mountain-grown coffee from South America and Hawaii. The company is considering proposals to introduce a line of flavored coffees and a line of flavored coffee creamers. Discuss the issues the projects' sponsors must consider when defining the breadth of these proposals.

3. Your manager wants to put your business school education to work quickly and asks you to revise the procedures manual that describes how to evaluate long-term investment proposals.

She wants you to prepare a brief outline first, however, so she can explain your plan to her manager and colleagues. Prepare an outline of Section I of the procedures manual, *Defining Projects*. Use a few simple sentences to describe the content of each subsection.

4. Your manager liked your plan for revising Section I of the procedures manual (see question 3) and asked you to outline Section II, *Estimating Free Cash Flows*. Prepare this outline, using a few simple sentences to describe the content of each subsection.

5. The managers and analysts who will use your revised procedures manual (see question 3) will not be required to estimate the company's weighted average cost of capital but they must understand the concept. Write a short paragraph for Section III of the manual, *The Weighted Average Cost of Capital*, that explains the economic rationale for using this required rate of return. Use simple, intuitive language.

6. It is time to outline your plan for the last section of the procedures manual that describes how to evaluate long-term investment proposals (see question 3). Prepare an outline of Section IV, *Determining a Project's Market Value*, using a few simple sentences to describe the content of each subsection.

7. Amie Lau Inc. is considering a proposal to market crystal-growing kits for do-it-yourself new-agers. Amie expects to receive $1,200,000 of cash revenue at the end of year 1 with growth of 20 percent and 10 percent for years 2 and 3. The market will be saturated by the end of year 3 so subsequent annual cash revenues will be constant for the foreseeable future.

    (a) Determine the residual value of the future cash revenues at the end of year 3 using Amie's required rate of return of 15 percent.

    (b) Determine the present value of the cash revenues. Should Amie adopt the crystal-growing proposal if the present value of all cash costs is $15,000,000?

8. Robertson Realty is evaluating an opportunity to buy a shopping mall with an expected life of 40 years. The company establishes a study period to evaluate such long-lived projects because analysts believe it is unrealistic to prepare year-by-year cash flow forecasts for the distant future. What factors should the analysts consider when choosing the length of the study period for the shopping mall?

9. Caton Brewers may introduce an ale patterned after a popular New Zealand variety. The company will produce this ale for the foreseeable future but analysts estimated its free cash flows for only the next 10 years. Their estimates are given below.

Year	Free Cash Flow
1998	$100,000,000
1999	112,000,000
2000	122,400,000
2001	130,750,000
2002	136,250,000
2003	138,800,000
2004	140,200,000
2005	141,650,000
2006	143,100,000
2007	144,600,000
And so on.	

The company establishes a study period to evaluate long-lived projects such as this one. A 10-year study period is one possibility but analysts believe a shorter study period also is acceptable given the project's cash flow pattern.

(a) Choose a study period of less than 10 years and explain the reason for your choice. (It may be helpful to graph the project's free cash flows relative to time or to compute the annual percentage change in its free cash flows.)

(b) Use your study period and determine the present value of *all* the proposal's free cash flows given a required rate of return of 12 percent.

10. Deterioration and obsolescence affect the length of time a company can or should employ a productive asset.

(a) What is the difference between deterioration and obsolescence?

(b) How do managers forestall the replacement of equipment subject to deterioration? How do managers forestall the replacement of equipment subject to obsolescence?

11. Give some examples of equipment that is replaced for each of the following reasons.

(a) The accumulation of gradual deterioration.

(b) Sudden, catastrophic deterioration.

(c) The accumulation of gradual obsolescence.

(d) Sudden, catastrophic obsolescence.

(e) The accumulation of gradual deterioration and obsolescence.

12. Analysts sometimes make a like-for-like replacement assumption when estimating the cost of operating future generations of equipment. What is their implicit assumption about the effect of technological advances?

13. Securities analysts examine a company from the outside while marketing and financial analysts examine their company and its investment proposals from the inside.

(a) Describe the similarities and differences between the procedures these analysts use.

(b) What can marketing and financial analysts learn from securities analysts about the sources of risk or uncertainty in their forecasts? (You may want to briefly review Chapter 5's discussion of diversifiable and nondiversifiable risk to answer this question.)

14. Insatsu Electronic Company produces printers for microcomputer applications. The home products division produces an ink-ejection printer that is popular because it provides near-laser quality at a reasonable price. The office products division produces laser printers. The laser printers have always been too expensive for home applications but the division has developed an economical model. This new printer is only slightly more expensive than the ink-ejection model so the managers of the home products division are concerned about its effect on their business. Both printers have a life of only two years due to the pace of technological advance in this field. The relevant free cash flows are given below. The company's required rate of return is 14 percent.

Time	Laser Printer	Ink-ejection Printer	
		Without Laser	With Laser
0	$-5,000,000	$2,400,000	$2,400,000
1	4,000,000	2,000,000	1,100,000
2	3,500,000	1,500,000	800,000

(a) Will the managers of the office products division introduce the new laser printer if they are permitted to make the decision themselves?

(b) How much does the decision to introduce the new laser printer cost the home products division? What should the company do? Explain your answer.

(c) Combine the cash flows given above in a project definition that is broad enough to ensure that the company makes the right decision. How does the NPV of the project you defined compare with your answers to parts (a) and (b)?

15. Which of the following statements is a better explanation for why it is necessary to estimate a project's net working capital to estimate its free cash flows? Explain your answer.

   (a) Companies invest cash in accounts receivable and inventory when they initiate a project and don't get the cash back until they terminate it.

   (b) Companies use the periodic changes in accounts receivable and inventory to adjust for differences between net income and cash flow.

16. Federal tax law recognizes advertising as a tax-deductible expense. This means a company that spends $10,000,000 for advertising in a particular year is permitted to deduct the full amount from its taxable income that year. In contrast, economists argue that advertising is an investment that produces benefits over time. Suppose the U.S. Internal Revenue Service adopted the economists' position and required companies to depreciate advertising expenses using MACRS with a class life of five years.

   (a) Determine the amount of advertising expense a company could deduct from its taxable income each year after spending $10,000,000 for advertising.

   (b) What is the present value of these deductions for advertising expense to a company that has a 6 percent required rate of return?

   (c) How much would this change in IRS policy cost a company that has a 35 percent federal tax rate?

17. Describe the similarities and differences between the analysis of domestic and foreign long-term investment proposals.

18. E.R. Satz Antiques, Inc. is a small company that produces decorative metal signs and boxes from the past for nostalgic customers who are financially challenged. The company currently produces items from the 1930s and 1940s, but management believes it is time to introduce the 1950s product line. Satz must spend $155,000 for a metal press to initiate production of the new items. The company also must spend $15,000 to modify and install the press in a vacant area of their existing plant. Analysts expect the metal press to be worth only $5,000 after eight years when the company ceases production of the 1950s product line.

   Prepare the company's fixed-asset worksheet for this investment using MACRS with a 7-year class-life to compute the annual depreciation deduction.

19. E.R. Satz's assumptions about sales and costs for its 1950s product line (see problem 18) are given below.

	First Year	Annual Rate of Change
Selling price/unit	$ 15.00	4.0%
Direct cost/unit		
Labor	$ 2.25	3.5
Materials	$ 3.00	3.5
Indirect cost/unit	$ 2.50	3.5
Other indirect costs/year	$ 16,000	3.5
Unit sales	11,000 units	
2nd year	—	5.0
3rd year	—	9.0

continued

	First Year	Annual Rate of Change
4th year	—	6.0
5th year	—	−5.0
6th year	—	−8.0
7th year	—	−15.0

(a) Prepare the company's sales revenue worksheet for this investment proposal.

(b) Prepare the company's cost of goods sold worksheet for this project.

20. E. R. Satz's selling and administrative expenses for the 1950s product line (see problem 18) will be $7,000 the first year of production with annual increases of 3.5 percent, the rate of inflation in producers' prices. The company's marginal tax rate is 34 percent. Use this information and the results from problems 18 and 19 to prepare the investment proposal's income statements.

21. Wild Wicks Candle Company plans to expand its line of beeswax candles to increase sales by more than 50 percent in two years. The company's actual results for 1997 and plans for 1998–2001 are shown below. Wild Wicks' managers know that this ambitious sales goal will also increase the company's net working capital requirements even though they plan to continue the company's present accounts receivable, inventory, and accounts payable policies.

	Actual 1997	Planned			
		1998	1999	2000	2001
Net sales	$150	$195	$230	$235	$220
Cost of goods sold	83	108	126	130	122
Accounts receivable	13				
Inventory	15				
Accounts payable	9				

(a) Determine the company's days'-sales-outstanding, days'-cost-in-inventory, and days'-payables-outstanding ratios for 1997.

(b) How much net working capital does the beeswax candle project require each year from 1998 to 2001?

22. Bond Flag Company's marketing division recommended that the company produce and distribute home flagpoles. The equipment required to produce the flagpoles costs $375,000 and will have a salvage value of $20,000 at the end of its useful life in eight years. Production, marketing, and financial analysts prepared the proposal's income statements and balance sheets given in the table on page 410.

(a) Prepare the project's free cash flow statements.

(b) Should Bond Flag Company begin producing home flagpoles if its weighted average cost of capital is 12 percent?

23. Cottonwood Creek Figurines adds a third shift of production workers every July, August, and September to meet the seasonal demand for its ceramic Santas, elves, reindeers, and sleighs. The company pays these workers $6.50 per hour plus benefits valued at $2.50 an hour. The typical new employee can paint the first figurine in 1.5 hours and has a 92 percent learning rate.

TABLE FOR PROBLEM 22

Time

	0	1	2	3	4	5	6	7	8
				Income Statements					
Net sales	$ 0	$ 346,000	$ 359,840	$ 392,225	$ 396,145	$376,340	$ 319,890	$ 303,895	$ 288,700
Cost of goods sold	0	233,700	240,975	255,805	258,380	250,270	227,135	215,775	204,975
Gross profit	0	112,300	118,865	136,420	137,765	126,070	92,755	88,120	83,725
Selling and administrative expenses	0	40,890	42,170	44,765	45,215	43,795	39,750	37,760	35,885
Depreciation	53,588	91,838	65,588	46,838	33,488	33,488	33,488	16,684	0
Net operating income	(53,588)	(20,428)	11,107	44,817	59,062	48,787	19,517	33,676	47,840
Other revenue and costs									20,000
Interest expense	NA	NA	NA	NA	NA	NA	NA	NA	NA
Taxable income	(53,588)	(20,428)	11,107	44,817	59,062	48,787	19,517	33,676	67,840
Taxes	(19,292)	(7,354)	3,999	16,134	21,262	17,563	7,026	12,123	24,422
Net income	($34,296)	($ 13,074)	$ 7,108	$ 28,683	$ 37,800	$ 31,224	$ 12,491	$ 21,553	$ 43,418
				Balance Sheets					
Assets									
Cash	$ 3,000	$ 3,460	$ 3,598	$ 3,922	$ 3,961	$ 3,763	$ 3,199	$ 3,039	$ 0
Accounts receivable	24,000	27,680	28,787	31,378	31,692	30,108	25,592	24,312	0
Inventory	$ 7,000	$ 8,073	$ 8,324	$ 8,836	$ 8,925	$ 8,645	$ 7,846	$ 7,454	$ 0
Total current assets	34,000	39,213	40,709	44,136	44,578	42,516	36,637	34,805	0
Gross fixed assets	$ 375,000	$ 375,000	$ 375,000	$375,000	$375,000	$375,000	$375,000	$375,000	$375,000
Accumulated depreciation	$ 53,588	$ 145,426	$ 211,014	$257,852	$291,340	$324,828	$358,316	$375,000	$375,000
Net fixed assets	321,412	229,574	163,986	117,148	83,660	50,172	16,684	0	0
Total assets	$ 355,412	$ 268,787	$204,695	$161,284	$128,238	$92,688	$ 53,321	$ 34,805	$ 0
Claims									
Accounts payable	$ 11,103	$ 12,805	$ 13,204	$ 14,017	$ 14,158	$ 13,714	$ 12,446	$ 11,824	$ 0

(a) How long does it take a typical employee to paint each of her first 10 figurines? How many figurines can she paint during her first 8-hour shift?

(c) Suppose there is virtually no improvement in efficiency after painting the 100th figurine. What is the direct labor cost per unit produced by an experienced employee? Assume wages and benefits are fixed at $9.00 per hour.

(d) Explain why it is important to measure the effect of learning when estimating an investment proposal's free cash flows.

24. Holiday Fruits and Gifts paid $60,000 for a shrink-wrap packager on September 2, 1995 to wrap its fruit and gift baskets and began depreciating it using MACRS with a class life of five years. The company used the packager for two years, taking two years of depreciation deductions, before selling it to buy a faster one. The gift company's marginal tax rate is 35 percent.

(a) What was the packager's book value at the time of the sale?

(b) What was the company's net cash flow from the sale if the selling price was $25,000? If the selling price was $35,000? Assume the tax-related cash flows are paid or received at the time of the sale.

25. Miles Motor Works uses 40 percent debt and 60 percent equity to finance its long-term investment projects. What is the company's weighted average cost of capital if the required rate of return on debt is 8.5 percent, the required rate of return on equity is 14 percent, and the company's marginal tax rate is 36 percent?

26. The Taggart Tow Company may buy a new tugboat to use in Boston Harbor. The company's target financial structure is 45 percent debt and 55 percent equity and analysts will estimate the cost of these sources of financing from the market price of the company's bonds and the risk of its common stock. Taggart Tow's only long-term bonds are 8.9 percent, $1,000 par value bonds that pay interest once a year. These bonds are due in 20 years and their market price is $1,056. The company's common stock has a beta of 1.10, the rate of return on U.S. Treasury bills is 5.5 percent, and the expected rate of return on the market index is 14.2 percent.

(a) Calculate the yield to maturity on Taggart's bonds and the CAPM required rate of return on its common stock.

(b) What is the company's weighted average cost of capital if its marginal tax rate is 38 percent?

(c) Should Taggart purchase the new tugboat if its internal rate of return is 9.8 percent? Explain your answer.

27. Consider the two mutually exclusive investment projects shown below.

Free Cash Flows

Year	Project 1	Project 2
0	$-6,000	$-3,000
1	2,000	-2,000
2	1,000	1,000
3	2,000	2,000
4	4,000	4,000

(a) Use the incremental internal rate of return procedure to determine which project to accept given a required rate of return of 10 percent.

(b) Confirm your answer to part (a) by comparing the alternatives' net present values.

28. The free cash flows provided by two mutually exclusive investment proposals are shown below.

Free Cash Flows

Year	Project 1	Project 2
0	$-10,000	$-25,000
1	3,000	10,500
2	3,000	5,000
3	3,000	7,000
4	3,000	6,000
5	3,000	6,000

(a) Determine each proposal's internal rate of return.

(b) Plot each proposal's net present value profile on the same graph.

(c) Which proposal is better if the required rate of return is 10 percent? Which is better if the required rate of return is 12 percent? Explain your answer.

(d) Use the incremental internal rate of return procedure to confirm your answers to part (c).

29. Napoli Spice and Vinegar Company is evaluating two alternatives for producing this season's flavored vinegar. Each process produces mildly flavored vinegar after one year of aging and full flavored vinegar after two years. The alternatives' free cash flows are shown below. The company's required rate of return is 12 percent.

Free Cash Flows

Year	Process A	Process B
0	$-100,000	$-98,000
1	57,500	45,000
2	65,000	76,500

(a) Which investment proposal is larger? Compute its incremental free cash flows.

(b) Can you use the incremental internal rate of return procedure to determine which investment proposal is better? What is your alternative for determining which is better? Explain your answers.

(c) Which process should Napoli Spice and Vinegar Company adopt?

30. Narcissus Press is a vanity publishing company that produces art posters drawn or painted by amateur artists. The company uses a four-color copier it purchased several years ago for $80,000 to produce these posters. The free cash flows provided by this copier if the company operates it six more years are given below.

Year	Free Cash Flows from Old Copier
1	$1,500
2	1,500
3	1,650
4	1,650
5	1,350
6	1,100

Narcissus is considering a new copier that is faster than the old one and that produces higher-quality reproductions. This copier costs $100,000, has a useful life of six years, and is depreciable over a five-year life under MACRS. The old copier's salvage value is zero.

The company will use the new copier to produce 2,500 posters per year that will sell for $30 each with inflation at 2 percent per year. The cost of producing the posters is $13.00 each for direct labor but this cost is expected to decline with experience at an 80 percent learning rate. Direct materials will be $5.00 per poster the first year with inflation at 5 percent per year thereafter. Selling and administrative expenses are expected to be $8,000 the first year with annual increases of $750. The company's marginal tax rate is 35 percent and its required rate of return is 15 percent. Narcissus's working capital policies are reflected in the ratios given below.

Days'-sales-outstanding	30 days
Days'-costs-in-inventory	60 days
Days'-payments-outstanding	25 days
Financial slack	3% of sales

(a) Prepare a complete set of worksheets for this investment proposal (sales revenue, cost of goods sold, selling and administrative expenses, current asset and liability, and fixed-asset worksheets).

(b) Prepare the proposal's income statements and balance sheets.

(c) Use the results from parts (a) and (b) to compute the new copier's free cash flows.

(d) Determine the net present values of continuing to operate the old copier and buying the new one. What should Narcissus do?

31. Use the following information to determine the NPV of a machine used to produce carbide-tipped saw blades. The company's marginal tax rate is 35 percent.

Equipment

Cost	$500,000
Useful life	5 years
MACRS life	3 years
Expected salvage value	$ 15,000

Revenues

Unit sales	18,000 the 1st year, 6% annual growth
Price	$30/unit, 3% annual inflation

Costs

Direct labor	$2.00/unit, 90% learning rate
Direct materials	$4.00/unit, 5% annual inflation
Indirect costs	$6.00/unit, 7% annual inflation
Other indirect costs	$30,000/year, 7% annual inflation
Selling and administrative expenses	$60,000/year, 2% inflation

Working Capital Policies

Financial slack	2% of sales
Days'-sales-outstanding	36 days
Days'-costs-in-inventory	45 days
Days'-payables-outstanding	30 days

Capital Structure

Debt	30%
Equity	70%
Common stock beta	0.90

Rates of Return

Riskless rate of return	5.0%
Company's cost of debt	9.0%
Market index rate of return	13.5%

32. Walnut Grove Leather Works is exploring the possibility of producing leather steering wheel covers and gloves in a small town in southern England. The proposal's free cash flows in pounds over a five-year study period are given below. The company's required rate of return for similar domestic projects is 15 percent.

Year	Free Cash Flows in British Pounds
0	–5,760,000
1	844,000
2	957,000
3	1,089,000
4	1,372,000
5	8,600,000

(a) Convert the project's free cash flows to dollars assuming interest rate parity, a spot exchange rate of 0.6100 British pound per dollar, and U.S. and British interest rates of 5.38 percent and 6.13 percent.

(b) Should Walnut Grove accept this investment proposal?

33. Amalgamated International (AI) is planning to build a manufacturing plant in Ireland to produce car parts for sale in France. They must spend 10,000,000 punts (the Irish currency) for the land and to construct a building but the company can buy its equipment in Ireland or the United States. The relevant exchange rates are

	Dollars per Punt	Dollars per Franc
Spot rate	1.6093	.2015
180-day forward rate	1.6098	.2008

(a) Where should the company buy its equipment given the following prices and costs? What is the net cost of the entire investment in U.S. dollars?

	In Punts	In Dollars
Price of equipment	3,000,000	4,500,000
Shipping and licenses	0	250,000

(b) AI expects to receive annual cash inflows and pay annual cash outflows of the following amounts in perpetuity. The managers assume that future exchange rates will remain constant at the level of the current 180-day forward rate.

	In Punts	In Francs
Annual cash inflows	—	34,625,000
Annual cash outflows	2,650,000	

(c) What is the company's expected annual free cash flow in U.S. dollars?

(d) AI's required rate of return, stated in dollars, is 10 percent. Should they accept this investment opportunity?

34. Dennis Huncker owns three acres of vacant property on which he'd like to build a service station and convenience store. The preliminary cost of this project is $5,000 for zoning changes and site preparation. Actual construction costs are $330,000 for a total cost of $335,000. The 20-acre site adjacent to Dennis Huncker's property will be developed as an outlet mall or a gigantic truck stop. Dennis knows the profitability of his investment depends on what happens to this site and prepared the separate estimates of his free cash flows shown below.

Dennis's Free Cash Flow
if Adjacent Property Is:

Year	Outlet Mall	Truck Stop
0	$–335,000	$–335,000
1	50,000	10,000
2	50,000	10,000
3–20	100,000	20,000

(a) Determine the expected free cash flows from Dennis's investment opportunity if the adjacent property is equally likely to be developed as an outlet mall or truck stop.

(b) Should Dennis invest $335,000 now to construct the service station and convenience store if his required rate of return is 15 percent? Explain your answer.

(c) Suppose Dennis can spend $5,000 now for zoning changes and site preparation and delay construction for one year until he knows how the adjacent property will be developed. What is the NPV of his investment opportunity if an outlet mall is built next door? What is the NPV if a truck stop is built next door? Does the investment opportunity look more or less attractive now? Explain your answer.

(d) Why doesn't the NPV of the expected free cash flows reveal the investment's true potential?

● ADDITIONAL READING

Two articles that describe how to define a project are:

> Patrick Barwise, Paul R. Marsh, and Robin Wensley, "Must Finance and Strategy Clash?" *Harvard Business Review*, September–October 1989, pp. 85–90.

> George S. Day and Liam Fahey, "Putting Strategy into Shareholder Value Analysis," *Harvard Business Review*, March–April 1990, pp. 156–162.

Economic life is discussed in the following references:

> George A. Taylor, *Managerial and Engineering Economy*, Van Nostrand Reinhold Company, New York, 1964.

> Gary W. Emery, "Some Guidelines for Evaluating Capital Investment Alternatives with Unequal Lives," *Financial Management*, Spring 1982, pp. 14–19.

A comprehensive discussion of sales forecasting techniques is provided by:

> David L. Hurwood, Elliott S. Grossman, and Earl L. Bailey, *Sales Forecasting*, The Conference Board, Inc., New York, 1978.

See the following article for applications of the product life cycle.

> Jeffrey S. Morrison, "Life-Cycle Approach to New Product Forecasting," *The Journal of Business Forecasting*, Summer 1995, pp. 3–5.

Activity-based costing was proposed in the two articles listed below. The textbook covers this and other managerial accounting topics.

> Jeffrey G. Miller and Thomas E. Vollmann, "The Hidden Factory," *Harvard Business Review*, September–October, 1985, pp. 142–150.

> Robin Cooper and Robert S. Kaplan, "Measure Costs Right: Make the Right Decisions," *Harvard Business Review*, September–October, 1985, pp. 96–103.

> Anthony A. Atkinson, Rajiv D. Banker, Robert S. Kaplan, and S. Mark Young, *Management Accounting*, Prentice Hall, 1995.

The learning curve and its applications are described in:

> Louis E. Yelle, "The Learning Curve: Historical Review and Comprehensive Survey," *Decision Sciences*, April 1979, pp. 302–328.

An authoritative reference on capital rationing is H. Martin Weingartner's dissertation.

> H. Martin Weingartner, *Mathematical Programming and the Analysis of Capital Budgeting Problems*, Kershaw Publishing Company, Ltd., London, 1974.

For a simple approach to evaluating foreign investments, see:

> James S. Ang and Tsong-Yue Lai, "A Simple Rule for Multinational Capital Budgeting," *The Global Finance Journal*, Fall 1989, pp. 71–75.

OTHER INVESTMENT DECISION RULES

T he payback period and accounting rate of return are two popular investment deci-sion rules not based on the discounted value of a proposal's cash flows. These decision rules are not used as frequently as in the past although some compa-nies continue to use them even though they do not account for the time value of money. Investment scholars have suggested they are still used in spite of this deficiency because they are simple and may help mitigate problems that arise when investment analysis is delegated to business unit managers.

We'll use the investment proposal described in Table 9A.1 to illustrate the payback period and accounting rate of return and to compare them to the NPV and IRR rules. Note that this proposal is acceptable because its net present value is greater than zero and its internal rate of return is greater than the required rate of return of 12 percent.

THE PAYBACK PERIOD

The payback period (PB) is the number of periods it takes to recover a proposal's ini-tial investment. This value is computed by counting the number of periods it takes for a proposal's cumulative free cash flow to equal zero. The investment proposal in Table 9A.1 has a payback period of 3.375 years if we assume the cash flow in year four is received uniformly throughout the period.

An independent investment proposal that pays back sooner than required is acceptable; one that pays back later is not. Companies often require faster paybacks from

---

ILLUSTRATION OF NONDISCOUNTED CASH FLOW DECISION RULES   Table 9A.1

Year	Net Income at End of Year	Book Value during Year	Free Cash Flow at End of Year	Cumulative Free Cash Flow
0			$-48,000	$-48,000
1	$-4,600	$50,000	12,000	-36,000
2	-8,200	33,335	14,000	-22,000
3	8,600	11,115	16,000	-6,000
4	12,000	3,705	16,000	10,000
5	12,000	0	12,000	22,000

NPV at 12%	$ 2,241
IRR	13.8%
Average net income	$ 3,960
Average book value	$19,631

riskier investments but there is no precise method for determining this critical value. The absence of an objective technique for establishing the required payback is one of this decision rule's serious deficiencies.

Another deficiency of the PB decision rule is that it disregards the cash flows received beyond the payback period and is not affected by the timing of the cash flows within the payback period. Suppose we change the free cash flows of the investment proposal in Table 9A.1 to: (–$48,000, $0, $0, $42,000, $16,000, $0). Then its NPV equals $–7,937 and its IRR equals 6.0 percent even though its PB is unchanged at 3.375 years. The PB rule cannot distinguish between the original and new versions of this investment proposal even though they have vastly effects on the owners' wealth.

Some investment scholars believe companies continue to use the PB rule despite its limitations because it tends to favor proposals that recover their initial cost quickly. An advantage of this bias is that senior managers can appraise the quality of a business unit's investment decisions quickly. Another advantage is that the company can redirect cash flow from one business unit's projects to another quickly. These advantages may improve the allocation of resources within a company that delegates investment analysis to business unit managers. The obvious disadvantage of the bias in favor of early cost recovery is that it may discourage managers from undertaking strategic investments with distant payoffs that are contingent on events and decisions that take place in the intervening years.

When considering these advantages and disadvantages, don't forget that a company can use the NPV rule and still evaluate managers and redirect resources to their most productive use by conducting thorough continuing evaluations of accepted investment proposals. Using the NPV rule does not eliminate the bias against strategic investment proposals. We'll discuss procedures that address this problem in Chapter 13.

THE ACCOUNTING RATE OF RETURN

The accounting rate of return (ARR) is an investment proposal's return on assets, that is, its net income divided by its book value. Net income and book value are usually averaged over the proposal's life and used to calculate a single, average ARR although year-by-year rates of return can also be computed. The investment proposal in Table 9A.1 has an average ARR = $3,960/$19,631 = 20.2 percent.

Some companies use total net income divided by total assets as the required accounting rate of return. The idea is that, by accepting only investment proposals with ARRs greater than this value, they will improve their overall return on assets. They may improve their return on assets by selecting investments this way; however, this does not necessarily benefit the company or its owners. The reason is that the accounting rate of return ignores the time value of money and risk so it does not indicate how a proposal affects the amount of wealth available to the company and its owners.

These deficiencies are apparent by changing the net income and free cash flow patterns of the investment in Table 9A.1. Suppose year-by-year net income equals ($–16,600, $–8,200, $8,600, $12,000, and $24,000) and free cash flow equals ($–48,000, $0, $14,000, $16,000, $16,000, and $24,000). Then the proposal's NPV equals $–1,664 and IRR equals 10.9 percent even though its ARR is unchanged at 20.2 percent. Once again, the nondiscounted cash flow decision rule cannot distinguish between the two versions of the investment proposal even though they have quite different effects on wealth.

Simplicity and the use of familiar accounting measures of income and value are the only claimed advantages for the accounting rate of return decision rule. These are not compelling reasons for using a decision rule that can cause a company to make poor investment choices.

• QUESTIONS AND PROBLEMS

1. The payback period and accounting rate of return are not based on the discounted value of an investment proposal's free cash flows.

   (a) Define these investment decision rules.

   (b) What advantages are claimed for them?

   (c) What are the disadvantages of these decision rules in comparison to NPV and IRR?

2. Consider the mutually exclusive investment proposals shown below.

Year	Project 1	Project 2
0	$-10,000	$-10,000
1	5,000	1,000
2	5,000	1,000
3	5,000	15,000

   (a) Which proposal is better according to the payback period criterion?

   (b) Which proposal is better according to the NPV criterion if the company's required rate of return is 12 percent?

   (c) Rework parts (a) and (b) if project 2's free cash flow in year 3 is $50,000. How much did its payback period improve? How much did its NPV improve? What deficiency of the payback period criterion does this illustrate? Explain your answer.

3. Consider the mutually exclusive investment proposals shown below.

	Project 1			Project 2		
Year	Net Income	Book Value	Free Cash Flow	Net Income	Book Value	Free Cash Flow
0	—	—	$-10,000	—	—	$-10,000
1	$3,000	$10,000	5,000	$ 500	$10,000	1,000
2	3,000	5,000	5,000	500	8,000	1,000
3	9,000	0	5,000	16,000	0	15,000

   (a) Which proposal is better according to the accounting rate of return criterion?

   (b) Which proposal is better according to the NPV criterion if the company's required rate of return is 12 percent?

   (c) Rework parts (a) and (b) if project 2's free cash flow in year 1 is $15,000 and its free cash flow in year 3 is $1,000. How much did its accounting rate of return improve? How much did its NPV improve? What deficiency of the accounting rate of return criterion does this illustrate? Explain your answer.

C H A P T E R   1 0

INTRODUCTION TO FINANCIAL MANAGEMENT OF OPERATIONS

*F*ortune estimates that, on average, Fortune 500 companies have net working capital equal to 20 percent of sales. For these companies, accounts receivable and inventories exceed accounts payable by approximately $500 billion![1] Money tied up in these seemingly unproductive assets cannot be used to repay debt or to pay interest or dividends. The annual opportunity costs are immense.

Some managers have begun to closely examine their company's investments in these assets. They have discovered that they can reduce opportunity costs and increase the cash flow provided by operations by shortening the amount of time goods are in production or held in inventory. For example, *Fortune* reported that American Standard has been so successful at improving its operations that some of its business segments have *negative* net working capital. Managers who seek similar results must have a thorough knowledge of the relationship between each phase of their company's operations and its use of net working capital.

This chapter describes how to use finance valuation principles to make decisions that affect net working capital. We will describe the cash flows that are paid and received as a company conducts operations and how the timing and amounts of those cash flows are associated with net working capital. You will learn how to value those cash flows and which factors to consider before changing your company's net working capital.

This chapter uses the principles you learned in Chapters 2 through 8 to build skills you will use later. Consequently, we use simple examples to focus on the new applications. The examples are more realistic in Chapters 11 and 12 where you will use the techniques you learn here to evaluate alternative production, payment, and collection policies.

---

[1]Shawn Tully, "Raiding a Company's Hidden Cash," *Fortune*, August 22, 1994, pp. 82–87.

10.1 OVERVIEW OF FINANCIAL MANAGEMENT OF OPERATIONS

The acquisition of materials; the production, sale, and distribution of products or services; and the payment and collection of cash are not instantaneous, seamless activities. These activities, known collectively as the **operating cycle**, take time and none of them can be perfectly coordinated with the others. Companies and business units adapt to the delays and discontinuities in their operating cycles by stocking materials and finished goods, by accepting and issuing *promises* to pay, and by using checks and other payment media in place of currency. Their adaptations are evident as short-term operating assets (inventories and accounts receivable) and short-term operating liabilities (accounts payable and accruals).

The administration of these assets and liabilities is sometimes called *working capital management* or *short-term financial management.* Neither term is accurate, however, because both operating and financial managers make decisions that affect the levels of these accounts. For example, purchasing, materials, production, and sales managers make the major decisions that affect inventory levels but the cost of financing these assets is also an important consideration. Similarly, purchasing and financial managers make decisions that affect the level of accounts payable while sales and financial managers make decisions that affect the level of accounts receivable. The term *financial management of operations* was used in this chapter's title to emphasize this dual nature of short-term asset and liability management.

The purpose of the financial management of operations is to help identify policies that maximize the owners' wealth. This task is accomplished by applying fundamental valuation principles to the periodic cash flows a company pays and receives with each completion of the cycle. Managers can use net present value analysis to evaluate routine operating policies; however, they must use techniques based on option pricing to evaluate strategic policies that provide flexibility. This use of fundamental valuation principles makes the financial management of operations similar to the financial management of long-term investments.

The financial management of operations has one distinguishing characteristic that affects the application of these valuation principles: Cash flows are paid and received on a daily basis as the company conducts operations in collaboration with its suppliers and customers. This peculiarity has three consequences. First, the amount of net working capital a company requires and the timing and amount of its cash flows from operations depend on the length of its operating cycle. Second, managers must be aware of the special problems of contracting with other companies in the presence of asymmetric information to protect the company and reassure its customers. Third, management of the operating cycle requires the coordination and integration of the primary business functions of production, marketing, and finance.

10.2 THE OPERATING CYCLE, NET WORKING CAPITAL, AND CASH FLOW FROM OPERATIONS

The operating cycle comprises the activities a company performs to produce and sell its product or service. The typical operating cycle described by the time line in Exhibit 10.1

Exhibit 10.1

TYPICAL OPERATING CYCLE

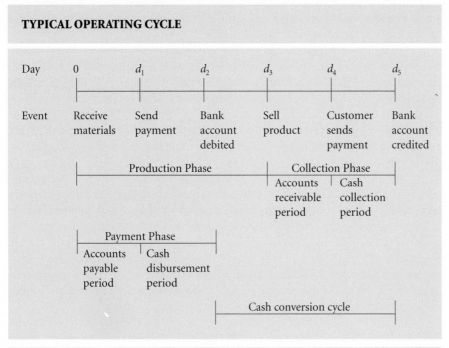

begins when the company receives materials from its supplier on day 0. This initiates the production phase, which continues until the company sells the finished product to a customer.[2] Day 0 also initiates the payment phase of the operating cycle, which has two parts. The first part ends at the conclusion of the supplier's credit period when payment is due. The second part begins at this point and ends when the company's check or other payment medium is presented to its bank and its account is debited. These parts of the payment phase are called the accounts payable and cash disbursement periods.

The collection phase is similar to the payment phase. The accounts receivable period begins when the company sells its finished product to a customer and ends at the conclusion of the company's credit period when payment is due. The cash collection period begins at this point and ends when the company's bank account is credited at the conclusion of the operating cycle. The length of the operating cycle in Exhibit 10.1 is d_5 days.

The Operating Cycle and Net Working Capital

Each phase of the operating cycle is related to a short-term operating asset or liability. The production phase is associated with raw materials, work-in-process, and finished goods inventories. Similarly, the payment phase is related to accounts payable and

---

[2]Manufacturing companies also obtain labor services from their employees during the production phase of the operating cycle. The employees convert the raw materials to work-in-process and finished goods and are paid wages at the conclusion of the pay period. We will include accrued wages with accounts payable to simplify our discussion.

accruals while the collection phase is associated with accounts receivable.[3] We will see that a company has a larger amount of a particular short-term asset or liability the longer the corresponding phase of its operating cycle.

The cash flows depicted on the time line in Exhibit 10.1 are the cash outflow for materials and labor when the company's bank account is debited on day d_2 and the cash inflow from sales when its account is credited on day d_5.[4] The length of time between these cash flows $(d_5 - d_2)$ is the **cash conversion cycle,** which equals the length of the production phase plus the length of the collection phase minus the length of the payment phase. Because these phases are associated with inventory, receivables, and payables, a company has a larger amount of *net* working capital the longer its cash conversion cycle.

A simple numerical example illustrates the connections between a company's operating and cash conversion cycles and its short-term assets and liabilities. The Vanity Business Supply Company purchases designer fountain pens from manufacturers at an average cost of $70 each and distributes them to retailers 60 days later at an average price of $100. The manufacturers offer a 20-day credit period while Vanity permits its customers to pay 30 days after delivery. Vanity and its customers pay by check, causing the cash disbursement and collection periods to be two and three days, respectively. Panel A of Exhibit 10.2 provides a diagram of this operating cycle; panel B computes the lengths of Vanity's operating and cash conversion cycles.

Exhibit 10.3 places Vanity's daily income statements and balance sheets on the time line that describes their operating cycle. These accrual accounting statements record inventory at cost on the day it is acquired and recognize revenues and costs on the day of the sale. Payments and collections are posted to accounts payable and receivable, respectively, when cash is paid and received rather than when checks are issued.[5] Net working capital equals accounts receivable plus inventory minus accounts payable.

The company's average daily investment in net working capital is computed two ways in Exhibit 10.4 to demonstrate the association between the phases of the operating cycle and net working capital. Vanity's daily investment in net working capital is simply averaged in panel A. Exhibit 10.3 shows the company had zero net working capital for 22 days, $70 of net working capital for 38 days (from day 22 to day 60), and $100 of net working capital for 33 days (from day 60 to day 93). The company's time-weighted average investment in net working capital is therefore $64.09.

The length of each phase of the operating cycle is used to compute the average daily amount of short-term operating assets and liabilities in panel B. These calculations show that a company has a larger amount of a particular short-term asset or liability the longer the corresponding phase of its operating cycle. Using the average amounts of the individual accounts in the definition of net working capital gives an answer of $64.08—the same value as calculated in panel A except for rounding.

---

[3]The cash collection and disbursement periods create a discrepancy between the cash balance recorded on a company's books and the cash balance available at its bank. We will discuss this feature of alternative cash collection and cash disbursement policies in Chapter 12.

[4]Other cash flows are omitted for simplicity. We will discuss them later in this section.

[5]This simplification ensures the company's book and bank cash balances are the same.

Exhibit 10.2

VANITY BUSINESS SUPPLY CO.

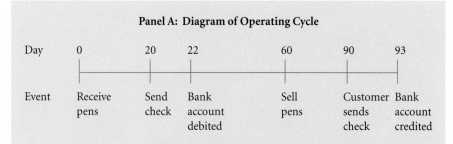

Panel A: Diagram of Operating Cycle

Day	0	20	22	60	90	93
Event	Receive pens	Send check	Bank account debited	Sell pens	Customer sends check	Bank account credited

Panel B: Length of Operating and Cash Conversion Cycles

Production Phase		60 days
Collection Phase		
Accounts receivable period	30	
Cash collection period	3	33
Operating Cycle		93
Payment Phase		
Accounts payable period	20	
Cash disbursement period	2	22
Cash Conversion Cycle		71

The Operating Cycle and Cash Flow from Operations

There also is a clear connection between the operating cycle and the timing and amount of a company's cash flows from operations. This relationship is illustrated in Exhibit 10.5 on page 428 where Vanity's daily direct and indirect cash statements are placed on the time line that describes its operating cycle. The information used to prepare the indirect statements was taken from the company's daily income statements and balance sheets in Exhibit 10.3. As always, the timing and amounts of net cash flows are the same in both types of statements.

The difference between the direct and indirect format cash statements is that the indirect format statements reveal how these periodic cash flows are affected as short-term assets are built up and drawn down with each completion of the operating cycle. The indirect format cash statement is more useful for evaluating alternative operating policies because it describes this association between cash flow from operations and the levels of short-term assets and liabilities.

Exhibit 10.3

VANITY BUSINESS SUPPLY CO. OPERATING CYCLE, BALANCE SHEETS, AND INCOME STATEMENTS

Day	0	20	22	60	90	93
Event	Receive pens	Send check	Bank account debited	Sell pens	Customer sends check	Bank account credited
Income Statements						
Revenue	$ 0	$ 0	$ 0	$100	$ 0	$0
Costs	0	0	0	70	0	0
Profit	$ 0	$ 0	$ 0	$ 30	$ 0	$0
Balance Sheets						
Receivables	$ 0	$ 0	$ 0	$100	$100	$0
Inventory	70	70	70	0	0	0
Payables	70	70	0	0	0	0
Net working capital	$ 0	$ 0	$70	$100	$100	$0

We can use financial ratios to measure a real company's operating cycle. The production phase is associated with inventories so its length is measured by the days'-cost-in-inventory (DCI) ratio.

$$DCI = \frac{Inventory}{Cost\ of\ goods\ sold/365}$$

The lengths of the collection and payment phases are measured similarly using the days'-sales-outstanding (DSO) and days'-payments-outstanding (DPO) ratios.

$$DSO = \frac{Accounts\ receivable}{Sales/365}$$

$$DPO = \frac{Accounts\ payable}{Cost\ of\ goods\ sold/365}$$

The lengths of the operating cycle and cash conversion cycle are therefore

$$Operating\ cycle = DCI + DSO$$

$$Cash\ conversion\ cycle = Operating\ cycle - DPO$$

$$= DCI + DSO - DPO.$$

Exhibit 10.4

VANITY BUSINESS SUPPLY CO. AVERAGE INVESTMENT IN NET WORKING CAPITAL

Panel A: Computed from Average of Daily Investment in Net Working Capital

Daily Investment in Net Working Capital	Number of Days
$ 0	22
70	38
100	33

$$\text{Average net working capital} = \frac{\$0 \times 22 \text{ days} + \$70 \times 38 \text{ days} + \$100 \times 33 \text{ days}}{93 \text{ days}} = \$64.09$$

Panel B: Computed from Operating Cycle Phases

Phase	Length	Associated Balance Sheet Account	Amount	Average Daily Amount
Production	60 days	Inventory	$ 70	$\dfrac{60 \text{ days} \times \$70}{93 \text{ days}} = \$45.16$
Collection	33 days	Accounts receivable	100	$\dfrac{33 \text{ days} \times \$100}{93 \text{ days}} = 35.48$
Payment	22 days	Accounts payable	70	$\dfrac{22 \text{ days} \times \$70}{93 \text{ days}} = 16.56$

Average net working capital = $45.16 + $35.48 – $16.56 = $64.08

Net working capital and the lengths of the operating and cash conversion cycles for three companies are provided in Table 10.1. The results are understandable: McDonald's Corporation has very few inventories, as you'd expect, and collects from its customers more quickly than it pays its suppliers. As a result, it has negative net working capital and a negative cash conversion cycle. Dillards, a large department store chain, has a large amount of inventories *and* receivables. Consequently, its cash conversion cycle is much longer. Boeing, the aircraft manufacturer, has very large inventories and therefore has a long operating cycle. Boeing has a long payment period, however, which makes its cash conversion cycle only slightly longer than Dillards'.

EXERCISE

10.1

CALCULATING OPERATING AND CASH CONVERSION CYCLES

Sonic Corporation's 1995 results are given below. Determine its net working capital and the lengths of its operating and cash conversion cycles.

Exhibit 10.5

VANITY BUSINESS SUPPLY CO. OPERATING CYCLE AND CASH FLOW FROM OPERATIONS

Day	0	20	22	60	90	93
Event	Receive pens	Send check	Bank account debited	Sell pens	Customer sends check	Bank account credited

Panel A: Direct Method

Cash received from customers	$ 0	$0	$ 0	$ 0	$0	$100
Cash paid to suppliers	0	0	(70)	0	0	0
Net cash flow	$ 0	$0	$(70)	$ 0	$0	$100

Panel B: Indirect Method

Net income	$ 0	$0	$ 0	$30	$0	$ 0
Minus change in receivables and inventory	70	0	0	30	0	(100)
Plus change in payables	70	0	(70)	0	0	0
Net cash flow	$ 0	$0	$(70)	$ 0	$0	$100

Sales	$120,700
Cost of sales	92,663
Accounts receivable	5,229
Inventories	1,868
Accounts payable	2,904

$$\text{Net working capital} = \text{receivables} + \text{inventories} - \text{payables}$$
$$= \$5,229 + \$1,868 - \$2,904 = \$4,193$$
$$\text{DCI} = \text{Inventory}/(\text{Cost of sales}/365)$$
$$= \$1,868/(\$92,663/365) = 7.4 \text{ days}$$
$$\text{DSO} = \text{Receivables}/(\text{Sales}/365)$$
$$= \$5,229/(\$120,700/365) = 15.8 \text{ days}$$
$$\text{DPO} = \text{Payables}/(\text{Cost of sales}/365)$$
$$= \$2,904/(\$92,663/365) = 11.4 \text{ days}$$
$$\text{Length of operating cycle} = \text{DCI} + \text{DSO}$$
$$= 7.4 + 15.8 = 23.2 \text{ days}$$
$$\text{Length of cash conversion cycle} = \text{DCI} + \text{DSO} - \text{DPO}$$
$$= 7.4 + 15.8 - 11.4$$
$$= 11.8 \text{ days}$$

Sonic's cash conversion cycle is similar to although not as favorable as McDonald's.

EXAMPLE OPERATING CYCLES   **Table 10.1**

Panel A: Sales, Costs, and Net Working Capital

Results for 1995	McDonald's	Dillards	Boeing
Sales	$6,863.5	$5,918.0	$19,515
Cost of sales	5,547.7	3,893.8	18,613
Inventories	58.0	1,486.0	14,001
Accounts receivable	377.3	1,103.6	1,675
Accounts payable	619.7	559.0	6,634
Net working capital	−184.4	2,030.6	9,042

Panel B: Operating and Cash Conversion Cycles

	McDonald's	Dillards	Boeing
Length of production phase			
Days' cost in inventory	3.8 days	139.3 days	274.6 days
Length of collection phase			
Days' sales outstanding	20.1	68.1	31.3
Length of operating cycle	23.9 days	207.4 days	305.9 days
Length of payment phase			
Days' payables outstanding	40.8	52.4	130.1
Length of cash conversion cycle	−16.9 days	155.0 days	175.8 days

Source for Panel A: Companies' 10-K reports retrieved from the *U.S. Security and Exchange Commission's EDGAR Database of Corporate Information* at http://www.sec.gov/index.html.

10.3 VALUING CASH FLOWS IN THE OPERATING CYCLE

A routine operating policy must have a positive net present value to increase the owners' wealth. Analysts can compute a policy's exact NPV by discounting its free cash flows or its approximate NPV by subtracting an opportunity cost from its accounting profit. The exact method is preferred; however, the approximate method clearly shows the cost of a policy that requires a long operating cycle and a large investment in net working capital.

The Exact NPV

The exact NPV is the sum of the discounted cash flows paid or received during the operating cycle. Each cash flow is discounted to the beginning of the cycle using the company's daily opportunity cost as the discount rate. That is,

$$\text{NPV} = \sum_{t=0}^{n} \frac{\text{CF}_t}{(1+r)^t} \qquad [10.1]$$

where CF_t = cash flow paid or received on day t
         day 0 = beginning of operating cycle

r = company's daily opportunity cost.

Suppose Vanity Business Supply Co.'s opportunity cost is 12 percent per year. Then the exact net present value of the cash flows described in Exhibit 10.5 is

$$NPV = \frac{\$-70}{(1+0.12/365)^{22}} + \frac{\$100}{(1+0.12/365)^{93}} = \$27.49.$$

This positive net present value indicates Vanity's operations contribute to the owners' wealth. Of course, different inventory, payables, or receivables policies may provide an even larger NPV.

An Approximate NPV

Analysts also sometimes use an approximation to the net present value that is computed by subtracting an opportunity or financing cost from profit over the operating cycle. The financing cost equals interest paid or forgone over the length of the operating cycle multiplied by the average amount of net working capital. That is,

$$\text{Approximate NPV} = R - C - (r \times d \times \text{ANWC}) \qquad [10.2]$$

where
R = operating revenue
C = operating cost
r = daily opportunity cost
d = length of the operating cycle in days
ANWC = average net working capital during the operating cycle.

Vanity Business Supply Co.'s operating revenue and costs (from Exhibit 10.3) are $100 and $70. The company's average net working capital (from Exhibit 10.4) was $64.09. Consequently, the approximate net present value of Vanity's operating policies is

$$\text{Approximate NPV} = \$100 - \$70 - \left(\frac{0.12}{365} \times 93 \text{ days} \times \$64.09\right)$$

$$= \$28.04.$$

The approximate NPV is nearly equal to the value we computed using the exact calculation.

The main reason for the difference between the exact and approximate net present values is that Equation 10.1 accounts for the opportunity cost using compound interest while Equation 10.2 uses simple interest. This makes very little difference in the net present values when interest rates are small and the operating cycle is short as was the case in these examples. Nevertheless, the exact NPV is not difficult to calculate and is preferred.

Equation 10.2 is useful, however, because it separately shows how the opportunity cost of money invested in net working capital affects the value of a company's operating policy. Furthermore, it shows that this opportunity cost is larger the longer the company's operating cycle and the larger its investment in net working capital. A company that reduces this opportunity cost by shortening its operating cycle or reducing its investment in net working capital improves its net present value by nearly the same amount if the changes do not affect operating revenues or costs.

Suppose Vanity Business Supply Co. adopts a new inventory policy that reduces the length of the production phase of its operating cycle from 60 days to 30 days. This change reduces the length of its entire operating cycle to 63 days and changes its average investment in inventory, receivables, payables, and net working capital to

$$\text{Average inventory} = \frac{30 \text{ days} \times \$70}{63 \text{ days}} = \$33.33$$

$$\text{Average receivables} = \frac{33 \text{ days} \times \$100}{63 \text{ days}} = \$52.38$$

$$\text{Average payables} = \frac{22 \text{ days} \times \$70}{63 \text{ days}} = \$24.44$$

$$\text{Average net working capital} = \$33.33 + \$52.38 - \$24.44 = \$61.27.$$

The company's new approximate NPV is therefore

$$\text{Approximate NPV} = \$100 - \$70 - \left(\frac{0.12}{365} \times 63 \times \$61.27 \right)$$

$$= \$28.73.$$

This is an improvement of $0.69 ($28.73 – $28.04).

Vanity's exact NPV under the new policy is

$$\text{NPV} = \frac{\$-70}{(1 + 0.12/365)^{22}} + \frac{\$100}{(1 + 0.12/365)^{63}} = \$28.45.$$

This is an improvement of $0.96 ($28.45 – $27.49), close to the amount computed by comparing the approximate net present values.

VALUE OF OPERATING CASH FLOWS

Suppose Dillards has $1,000,000 of sales on March 1 and its variable costs are 65.8 percent of sales. Use the information in Table 10.1 to determine the net present value of these sales as of the beginning of the company's operating cycle assuming an opportunity cost of 14 percent per year.

The company's cash flow time line is

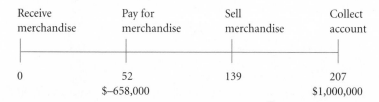

$$\text{NPV} = \frac{\$-658,000}{(1 + 0.14/365)^{52}} + \frac{\$1,000,000}{(1 + 0.14/365)^{207}} = \$278,678.$$

The NPV of the sales at the beginning of the operating cycle is $278,678.

● —————— ●

10.4   RETURN AND RISK OF ALTERNATIVE LEVELS OF NET WORKING CAPITAL

The preceding exercise suggests that a company should minimize its investment in net working capital to maximize the net present value of its operations. This is accomplished by reducing its inventories and accounts receivable and by increasing its accounts payable. You must think this through carefully, however, because these changes may affect revenues and costs. There are two factors to consider.

The Reactions of Customers and Suppliers

A company can reduce accounts receivable by restricting the availability of trade credit, by shortening its credit period, and by requiring its customers to use a payment medium (such as an electronic fund transfer) that is quickly convertible into cash. These changes may reduce the company's cash revenues because the opportunity cost savings are obtained at its customers' expense. Customers denied credit may have to obtain an expensive market loan before they can pay cash or they may become offended and take their current and future business elsewhere. Even customers who are granted credit may take their business elsewhere if other suppliers provide longer credit periods and accept a wider range of payment media. The loss of cash revenue may completely offset the opportunity cost savings in these cases.

A company can decrease its inventories by requiring suppliers to make more frequent deliveries and to deliver the supplies directly to the production line or sales floor. However, this policy transfers inventory costs to the supplier. Suppliers that cannot raise prices or reduce their own costs may decide the company's business is not profitable. Small suppliers may be especially hard-hit (see "In the News").

As another alternative, a company can increase accounts payable by delaying payments to its suppliers and by using a payment medium (such as a paper check) that is not quickly convertible into cash. These changes may increase the company's costs because the opportunity cost savings are obtained at its suppliers' expense. Suppliers who are not paid on a timely basis may react by charging explicit interest on past due accounts. They also may require the company to use its inventory as collateral for trade loans, which entails burdensome administrative costs. Suppliers may even reduce the company's line of credit or require cash payments on delivery or in advance. These responses reduce the amount of financing provided by accounts payable—the exact opposite of the effect a company intends when it delays payments.

The Effect of Uncertainty and Asymmetric Information

A company that reduces its net working capital to the bare minimum required for the expected level of operations has no slack it can use to accommodate surprises. A com-

IN THE NEWS

HOW TO ALIENATE YOUR SUPPLIERS

DEPARTMENT STORES ARE increasingly placing onerous logistical demands on apparel suppliers, saddling them with extra distribution costs and penalizing them when they don't conform to rigid and exacting rules. Take the rules about shipping. Packing labels may be required to include, say, eight specific bits of information. Often the label has to be affixed to a specific place on a particular kind of shipping box. Then the clothes may have to be prepriced and hung, facing a certain way, on special hangers. And stores will accept the goods only on certain days, say, Mondays and Tuesdays.

Because each store chain has different "routing guides," it's nearly impossible for apparel makers to comply with the rules, which can run 50 pages or more. But if the supplier fails to follow them—if a packing label, say, is one-half inch off—it's hit with a "chargeback," or deduction from its payment. For many smaller companies, the price is too high: They take their business elsewhere.

Source: Christina Duff, "Big Stores' Outlandish Demands Alienate Small Suppliers," *The Wall Street Journal,* October 27, 1996, p. B1. Reprinted by permission of *The Wall Street Journal,* © 1996 Dow Jones & Company, Inc. All rights reserved worldwide.

pany in this situation may have higher costs if an unexpected shortage of raw materials forces it to choose between paying a premium for an emergency shipment or leaving employees and equipment idle. The company also may have lower revenues if an unexpected shortage of finished goods causes it to lose sales to customers who will not wait until the product is available. An inability to receive or extend trade credit when the company or its customers are unexpectedly and temporarily out of cash can have a similar effect on costs and revenues.

These costly surprises may be caused by uncertainty or asymmetric information. Unexpected changes in supply and demand and unforeseen disruptions to transportation systems and production processes may affect the availability of raw materials, work-in-process, and finished goods. In addition, suppliers may falsely claim the ability to deliver high-quality raw materials and customers may falsely claim their intention to buy a large quantity of finished goods to induce the company to make costly and perhaps irreversible commitments to them. The random events are unpredictable and suppliers' and customers' claims are difficult to *verify* in advance. Both reduce the reliability of estimates of supply and demand, which affect revenues and costs.

Trade-offs in the Financial Management of Operations

These factors reveal that there is more to the financial management of operations than simply reducing the average investment in net working capital. Reducing net working capital reduces opportunity costs and affects suppliers and customers who may react in ways that decrease a company's revenues and increase its costs. Reducing net working capital also diminishes a company's capacity to respond to surprises caused by uncertainty and asymmetric information, which may decrease the company's revenues, increase its costs, and make its cash flows from operations more risky.

Exhibit 10.6

COSTS OF NET WORKING CAPITAL

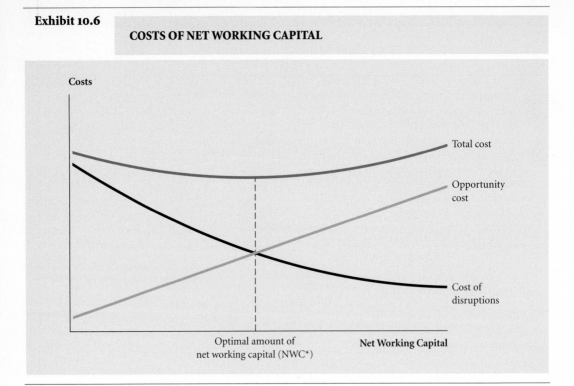

Exhibit 10.6 may help you visualize how these factors affect financial management of operations. In this graph, the opportunity cost increases with the level of net working capital because the company must use more discretionary financing to fund the additional investment. The cost of disruptions to operations caused by customer and supplier ill-will, uncertainty, and asymmetric information decreases with the level of net working capital because the company has more capacity to avoid these disturbances. Total costs first decrease and then increase with a minimum at NWC*. The objective of financial management of operations is to help determine the value of NWC*, which is the amount of net working capital that maximizes the owners' wealth.

10.5   INTEGRATION OF BUSINESS FUNCTIONS IN THE OPERATING CYCLE

Management of the production, payment, and collection phases of the operating cycle requires the cooperation and integration of the primary business functions of production, marketing, and finance. Finance must be integrated with production and marketing because a company's accounts payable and receivable are loans from its suppliers and to its customers. These trade loans are similar to ordinary loans because the borrower pays explicit or implicit transaction costs and interest. This means the cost of purchasing raw materials on credit and the profitability of selling finished goods on credit partly depend on the amount of the imbedded financing charges. Finance specialists are equipped to evaluate these financing charges because they know the costs and benefits of borrowing and lending in the financial market. They therefore can help purchasing and sales managers identify acceptable accounts payable and receivable policies.

Finance must be integrated with production because a company must fund that part of its investment in inventories not financed by its suppliers through trade credit. Consequently, the desirability of holding large inventories partly depends on the cost of obtaining these funds in the financial market or by reducing the amount of money invested elsewhere. Finance specialists know the actual or opportunity cost of obtaining money from these sources and therefore can help production managers identify acceptable inventory policies.

10.6 ADDING REALISTIC FEATURES TO THE CASH FLOW TIME LINES

Important features were omitted from the cash flow time lines in Exhibits 10.1 through 10.5 to simplify the illustrations. Adding other operating cash flows and extending the time horizon convert these simple time lines into ones that more accurately describe a company's operations over the course of a year.

Other Operating Cash Flows

A time line describing a company's actual operations over the course of a year would include several important operating cash flows. For example, cash outflows for indirect costs or manufacturing overhead would be included in the production phase. The more important cash flows in this category are the personnel and facilities costs of purchasing, materials management, and production scheduling and supervision. Cash outflows arising from similar administrative costs would be included in the payment and collection phases. Examples of these cash flows are the costs of evaluating requests for payment or credit, monitoring account balances, and managing the company's banking system.

Indirect and administrative costs also are significant and would typically be included in an actual company's operating cycle. In fact, many companies focus on these areas when they reengineer or redesign their operating processes to reduce costs and improve quality and service. We will include indirect and administrative cash flows when we discuss specific phases of the operating cycle in Chapters 11 and 12. This will permit a comprehensive financial analysis of alternative operating policies.

Extending the Time Horizon

The planning horizon for operations usually is longer than the duration of a single operating cycle. This means a new operating cycle may be initiated each day of the planning horizon as a company receives a new shipment of raw materials, produces a new batch of products, and subsequently sells them. Many companies prepare an annual business plan so their planning horizon encompasses several overlapping operating cycles. As a result, they experience *periodic* changes in their inventories, accounts payable, and accounts receivable and pay and receive *periodic* cash outflows and inflows. In all other respects, their experience is similar to that of Vanity Business Supply, our simplified example company. We will make our analysis more realistic by extending the time horizon used to evaluate alternative operating policies to one year in Chapters 11 and 12.

10.7   SUMMARY

The operating cycle is the period during which a company receives and pays for raw materials, produces and sells its products, and collects cash. These activities are reflected in a company's investment in inventories, its financing from accounts payable, and its investment in accounts receivable. The financial management of this process and the assets and liabilities it creates is fundamentally the same as financial management in any other area of the firm. That is, managers should estimate the cash flows provided by alternative production, payment, and collection policies and adopt the policies with the largest market values because they meet market-wide standards of financial performance.

The timing of these cash flows and the level of inventories, accounts payable, and accounts receivable are related to the lengths of the operating and cash conversion cycles. The length of the operating cycle equals the amount of time goods are held in inventory plus the amount of time credit sales are held as accounts receivable. This means a company must wait a longer time to collect the cash inflows from credit sales and must maintain a larger investment in inventories or accounts receivable the longer its operating cycle. The cash conversion cycle equals the length of the operating cycle minus the amount of time credit purchases are financed by accounts payable. Consequently, a company must pay the cash outflows for raw materials further in advance of collecting cash inflows and must maintain a larger investment in *net* working capital the longer its cash conversion cycle.

Routine policies with operating and cash conversion cycles of different lengths are easily compared using NPV analysis because this method expressly accounts for the timing and amounts of the cash outflows and inflows paid and received during the cycles. In many cases, an approximate NPV calculated by applying an opportunity cost to the average investment in net working capital is an acceptable alternative to the exact NPV. The approximation is not as accurate although it explicitly shows how the investment in net working capital affects the value of a company's operating policies. Strategic operating policies that provide options must be evaluated using option pricing.

Companies that reduce their average investment in net working capital reduce their opportunity costs and may also reduce their revenues, increase their costs, and increase the risk of their operating cash flows. These adverse changes may be caused by the reactions of the company's suppliers and customers and by its impaired ability to absorb the surprises to operations caused by uncertainty and asymmetric information. After considering these additional factors, the truly best operating policies are those with the highest valued cash flows.

- **KEY TERMS**

Operating cycle   *424*
Cash conversion cycle   *426*

- **QUESTIONS AND PROBLEMS**

1. Define the operating and cash conversion cycles. Explain which cycle is more important from a purely financial point of view.

2. Draw and label the operating and cash conversion cycles for a typical
   (a) Manufacturer
   (b) Wholesale distributor or retail store
   (c) Travel agency

3. List the phases of a typical manufacturer's operating cycle and identify the managers primarily responsible for each phase.

4. Why are cash and securities and bank loans omitted when measuring the length of a company's operating and cash conversion cycles?

5. Briefly describe how each of the following changes in operations affects the length of a company's operating and cash conversion cycles.
   (a) Offer credit customers a 2 percent cash discount for early payments.
   (b) Adopt a build-to-order manufacturing policy.
   (c) Pay employees every two weeks rather than once a month.
   (d) Require suppliers to deliver materials directly to the production line.
   (e) Outsource the production of a key component part.
   (f) Mail checks to suppliers from a remote location.

6. Briefly describe how each of the policy changes in question 5 affects the level of a company's net working capital and the timing of its cash flows provided by or used for operations.

7. A summary of Larson Manufacturing's operating results for 1997 is given below.

Annual sales	$7,300,000
Variable cost ratio	65%
Days'-sales-outstanding	30 days
Days'-payables-outstanding	22 days
Days'-cost-in-inventory	20 days

   (a) What was the average amount of sales per day based on a 365-day year? What was the cost of these sales?
   (b) Place the cash flows from a single day's sales and costs on a time line that describes the company's operating and cash conversion cycles.
   (c) Use the exact method to determine the net present value of one completion of the operating cycle. The company's required rate of return is 11 percent per year.

8. Refer to the information about Larson Manufacturing in problem 7 to answer the following questions.

(a) What was the average amount of sales per day based on a 365-day year? What was the cost of these sales?

(b) What was the average level of accounts receivable, accounts payable, and inventories associated with a single day's sales? What was the average level of net working capital?

(c) Use the approximate method to determine the net present value of one completion of the operating cycle. The company's required rate of return is 11 percent per year. Why isn't the result the same as your answer to part (c) of problem 7?

9. Congratulations on your promotion to senior financial analyst. Your first assignment is to present a seminar to operating managers on the relationship between their decisions and the company's free cash flows. Write a short description of your seminar, emphasizing how you will organize it around the indirect format cash statement.

10. Maxwell Weber Construction Company's operating results for 1996 are summarized below.

Annual sales	$1,740,000
Variable cost ratio	62%
Days'-sales-outstanding	63 days
Days'-payables-outstanding	75 days
Days'-cost-in-inventory	131 days

(a) What was the average amount of sales per month? What was the cost of these sales?

(b) What was the average level of accounts receivable, accounts payable, and inventories associated with a single month's sales? What was the average level of net working capital?

(c) Use the approximate method to determine the net present value of one completion of the operating cycle. The company's required rate of return is 15 percent per year.

At the beginning of 1997, Weber adopted an incentive pay system that rewards the construction manager for controlling inventory, rewards the credit manager for controlling accounts receivable, and rewards the payments manager for controlling accounts payable. The company's operating results for 1997 are given below.

Annual sales	$1,734,000
Variable cost ratio	62.5 %
Days'-sales-outstanding	61 days
Days'-payables-outstanding	79 days
Days'-cost-in-inventory	128 days

(d) What was the average amount of sales per month under the new policies? What was the cost of these sales? What are some probable causes of the differences between 1997 and 1996?

(e) What was the average level of accounts receivable, accounts payable, and inventories associated with a single month's sales? What was the average level of net working capital?

(f) Use the approximate method to determine the net present value of one completion of the operating cycle. The company's required rate of return is 15 percent per year.

(g) Did the managers act rationally from their own point of view? From the owners' point of view? What can be done to correct this situation?

11. Work parts (a) through (f) of problem 10 using the exact method to compute the NPV of the old and new policies. Does this method give you more or less information about the effects of the managers' decisions? Explain your answer.

12. Upson Downs supplies duck and goose feathers to companies that manufacture jackets and comforters. Upson's operating cycle is among the longer ones in its industry so the company's managers are attempting to shorten it to reduce opportunity costs. One proposal will reduce the amount of time customers' payments are in the mail from six days to three days while the other will increase the accounts payable period from 10 days to 15 days.

   (a) By how much do these proposals reduce the length of the company's operating cycle? Its cash conversion cycle?

   (b) How much will these proposals reduce Upson's opportunity costs per $1 million of sales if its required rate of return is 15 percent per year and its variable cost ratio is 70 percent?

13. Ageless Aphorisms Incorporated (AAI) produces and distributes desk calendars and appointment books with inspirational messages appropriate to each day of the year. The company's average direct materials cost, for paper and ink, is $3.50 per unit. Direct labor costs are $2.75 per unit. Direct materials and labor costs are added to inventory the day production begins although Ageless doesn't pay them until seven days later. A typical press run is eight days plus four days for packaging and delivery. Customers pay an average of $10.50 for each calendar and appointment book. Ageless records a sale at the time of delivery but gives its customers a 20-day credit period. Both AAI and its customers pay by checks, which take an average of two days to clear.

   (a) Prepare a time line that shows the timing of each event in Ageless Aphorism's operating cycle.

   (b) Determine the length of the production, collection, and payment phases of the company's operating cycle. What is the length of its cash conversion cycle?

   (c) Assume that Ageless receives an order for 1,000 calendars. Place the resulting daily income statements, balance sheets, and indirect format cash statements on the time line to track the order through the operating cycle.

   (d) Determine the company's time-weighted average investment in net working capital.

   (e) Confirm your answer to part (d) by using the length of each phase of the company's operating cycle to calculate its average investment in working capital.

14. Shown below is a time line that describes the events in a company's operating cycle. Also shown is its direct format cash statements.

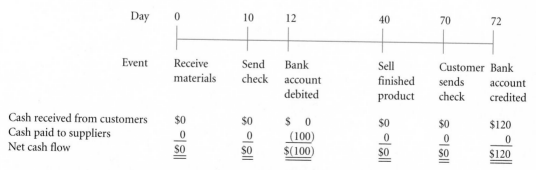

Day	0	10	12	40	70	72
Event	Receive materials	Send check	Bank account debited	Sell finished product	Customer sends check	Bank account credited
Cash received from customers	$0	$0	$ 0	$0	$0	$120
Cash paid to suppliers	0	0	(100)	0	0	0
Net cash flow	$0	$0	$(100)	$0	$0	$120

   (a) Prepare the company's daily income statements, balance sheets, and indirect format cash statements.

   (b) Use the exact method to compute the NPV of the company's cash flows provided by operations. The required rate of return is 14 percent.

(c) Determine the company's average investment in net working capital over the operating cycle and use the result to calculate the approximate NPV of the company's cash flows provided by operations.

15. Wilbur McConnell, CFO of Smith Boiler Works, was concerned about his company's investment in net working capital, which averages $306 million over its 108-day operating cycle. McConnell believed this amount was excessive because sales and the variable portion of cost of goods sold were only $1.019 billion and $710 million. The CFO asked his production, marketing, and financial analysts to determine the impact of reducing the company's investment in inventories and receivables. Their estimates are given below.

Net Working Capital	Length of Operating Cycle	Sales Revenue	Variable Cost Ratio
$306	108 days	$1,019	0.697 (current policy)
244	90	1,016	0.698
229	69	1,010	0.699
195	56	1,000	0.700

The marketing analyst advised against any changes because he expected sales to decline by as much as 2 percent if fewer customers were given credit. The production analyst also advised against any changes because she anticipated that variable costs would actually increase as a percent of sales due to stock-outs, special orders, and supplier ill-will. The financial analyst conceded these points but insisted that opportunity costs be given due consideration. Wilbur McConnell knew he'd have to make the final decision himself to reconcile their conflicting viewpoints.

(a) Use the approximate method to determine the NPV of the alternative operating policies. The company's opportunity cost is 15 percent per year. Which policy should the company adopt?

(b) In the final analysis, who was right—the marketing analyst, the production analyst, or the financial analyst? Explain your answer.

16. Given below are partial 1995 income statements and balance sheets for Dow Jones and Company, publisher of *The Wall Street Journal,* and Campbell's Soup Company. All figures are in millions of dollars.

	Company X	Company Z
Sales	$7,278.000	$2,283.761
Cost of goods sold	4,037.000	1,009.489
Accounts receivable	631.000	272.601
Inventories	755.000	12.752
Accounts payable	556.000	104.597

Source: Standard & Poor's CompuStat PC Plus.

(a) Determine each company's net working capital.

(b) Compute each company's days'-sales-outstanding, days'-costs-in-inventory, and days'-payments-outstanding ratios. Use the results to determine the length of each company's operating and cash conversion cycles.

(c) Is Company X Dow Jones or Campbell's Soup? Explain your reasoning.

FINANCIAL MANAGEMENT AND PRODUCTION

*T*he *Wall Street Journal* reported that the price of a share of IBM common stock fell $2.875 on September 13, 1995 when the company announced shipments of new mainframe computers would be delayed up to four weeks. IBM did not anticipate how quickly its customers would change over to the new computer, which led to a shortage of power supplies that the company buys from a single supplier.[1] IBM had approximately 587.7 million shares of common stock outstanding on September 13, which means the delay cost the owners nearly $1.7 billion ($2.875 × 587.7 million shares).

This costly delay in shipping its new mainframe computers was the result of IBM's production policies. The company did not accurately forecast demand, it outsourced the production of a key component to a single supplier with limited capacity, and it did not make adequate provisions for uncertainty. We do not know how much the delay harmed IBM's relationships with its customers although we do know that the owners suffered a very large loss.

IBM's experience with its new mainframe computers showed that production managers have a significant effect on the owners' wealth. Consequently, they should use finance valuation principles to take this effect into account when they make their decisions. Applying finance principles improves the likelihood that these operating managers will choose production policies that maximize the owners' wealth.

We will use present value analysis to evaluate routine production policies in this chapter. You will see that we can choose the best policy by comparing the present values of the alternatives' direct and indirect cash flows. This approach is flexible as well as simple. We can, for example, evaluate such diverse proposals as how often to order materials, whether to make or buy component parts, and whether to adopt production innovations such as total quality management.

You may think the ideas presented in this chapter do not apply to nonmanufacturing companies but they do. A distribution company's cost of goods sold may com-

---

[1]Laurie Hays, "IBM Shares Fall Nearly 3% Due to Delay in Shipments," *The Wall Street Journal*, September 14, 1995, p. A3.

prise mostly payments for merchandise but the company's managers should still evaluate purchasing and delivery policies by comparing the present value of their costs. Similarly, a service company's operating costs may comprise mostly wages and salaries but managers should use present value analysis to compare staffing and payment policies. Manufacturing companies have more diverse operating costs than either distribution or service companies so we will use a manufacturing company for this chapter's illustrations. You can simply omit the irrelevant cash flow components when you apply these ideas to other types of companies.

11.1   THE AMOUNT AND TIMING OF PRODUCTION COSTS

Production costs are accumulated in inventory and periodically are deducted from a company's revenue as cost of goods sold. The amount of money involved is astonishing. For example, Ford Motor Corporation reported $96.2 billion cost of goods sold for its automobile division in 1994. This figure dwarfs the $8.3 billion the division spent on capital equipment that year.[2]

The cash outflow associated with cost of goods sold is a principal component of cash flow from operations and free cash flow as we saw in previous chapters. We measured these cash outflows on an annual basis in Chapter 9 because a shorter interval is seldom used to evaluate long-term investment decisions. Companies use short decision horizons to manage production and operations, however, so more frequent cash flow estimates are required.

The procedure we'll use to estimate a company's production cash flows is the same as we've used before. We'll apply this procedure after we've described how the characteristics of the company's business and production policies affect the amount and timing of these intra-year cash flows.

Direct and Indirect Production Costs

Recall from Chapter 9 that production costs have both direct and indirect components. Direct costs are the manufacturing costs that are easily and accurately tied to a particular product. Direct materials costs are the costs of the purchased raw materials and component parts from which the product is constructed. The wages and benefits paid to employees who construct the product are direct labor costs. Standard or benchmark costs are used for planning and control although the actual direct cost of manufacturing a product may be more or less than the standard cost because of variations in prices or efficiency.

Indirect costs, sometimes known as manufacturing overhead, are the manufacturing costs not easily and accurately tied to a particular product. Examples of indirect costs are the expenses for purchasing and receiving, materials management, production scheduling, quality control, shipping, and maintenance. These expenses include the wages

---

[2]Ford Motor Corporation's 1994 10-K report (pp. 53 and 79), *U.S. Securities and Exchange Commission EDGAR Database of Corporate Information* at http://www.sec.gov/index.html.

and benefits of personnel employed in these areas as well as the cost of the services, computers, tools, materials, and office equipment and supplies they use.

Indirect costs are allocated to products according to the number of direct labor hours they use or, under the activity based costing system, according to the product's "use" of the activity that generates the cost. For example, a large portion of the costs of purchasing and receiving may be allocated to a product that requires many parts from different vendors.

Measuring and allocating indirect costs correctly is particularly important when evaluating certain production policies. For example, cost-minimization models such as the economic order quantity model consider *only* indirect costs. A subsequent example also will show that indirect costs are the main determinant of the optimal batch size found using present value analysis.

The composition of a company's production costs depends on its production policy. As an example, consider two companies in the same industry, one that purchases component parts and one that purchases materials and builds its own parts. The first company probably spends more on direct materials and less on direct labor than the second company. Furthermore, the company that buys component parts probably has lower indirect costs because less effort is required to coordinate and control production. The company that buys completed parts may even have less risk if delegating some stages of production to an outside source reduces fixed costs.

The Timing of Production Costs

The timing of production costs is partially determined by the availability of raw materials, the nature of the company's manufacturing process, and the demand for its finished goods. Within the constraints imposed by these factors, managers determine the actual timing of production costs when they decide how often to order materials or build parts.

How a Company's Line of Business Affects the Timing of Its Production Costs   The availability of raw materials is one factor that affects the timing of a company's production costs. Companies that use raw materials that are available throughout the year can purchase them as needed for production, which shifts some direct material costs to the future. In contrast, companies that use raw materials that are produced on a seasonal basis (such as fresh salmon) must purchase a large supply when materials are available and store them for future production and sales. They cannot defer the direct cost of these materials until later. The difference in their abilities to defer these costs to the future is reflected in their raw materials inventories; companies that can defer direct materials costs have small raw materials inventories and vice versa.

The duration of a company's manufacturing process is another factor that affects the timing of its production costs. Companies that use short, simple manufacturing processes can defer production costs to the future by purchasing raw materials shortly before they produce the finished goods. Companies that use long, multistep manufacturing processes have fewer opportunities to defer production costs because their raw materials must be on hand to pass through the stages of production. The differences between their opportunities to defer costs is apparent in the difference between their work-in-process inventories; short, simple manufacturing systems hold less work in process than long, multistep ones.

The contrast between bakeries and breweries is a good example. Companies in both industries use grains and yeast as raw materials although bread is produced and delivered to stores in a matter of hours while beer must be aged before it can be bottled and sold. Bakeries don't need raw materials until shortly before they sell their finished goods and can defer their production costs until then. By comparison, breweries must purchase raw materials in advance of sales to initiate their lengthy production process. Consequently, bakeries have no work-in-process inventories while breweries have large ones.

The seasonality of demand also influences the timing of a company's production costs. Companies that sell products for which demand is uniform throughout the year can match production to sales and thereby defer their production costs until then. Companies that sell a seasonal product *can* match production to sales although this may be uneconomical. They probably cannot reverse their investment in fixed assets during the slack period and it may be costly to leave the equipment idle then. In addition, it may be expensive to assemble and dismiss a skilled work force as demand waxes and wanes. A preferable alternative for many companies in this situation is to produce a level amount each period and store finished goods for sale during the peak period. Companies that adopt this response to seasonal demand must pay their production costs sooner and have a larger investment in finished goods inventories than companies that don't.

The Effect of Batch Size   The nature of a company's business establishes constraints on the timing of direct production costs. Nevertheless, managers also affect the timing of these costs when they decide how many parts or finished goods to buy or build in each batch.

Buying or making parts and finished goods in small batches as they are needed for production and sales defers direct costs to the future. For example, a publishing company that uses 156 rolls of newsprint each year can purchase an entire year's supply in January or buy their paper in smaller batches of, say, 13 rolls per month. They must pay the annual cost of direct materials in January under the first policy but defer one-twelfth of this cost until February, one-twelfth until March, and so on under the second policy. The company can defer these direct costs even further into the future by purchasing three rolls of newsprint each week.

Small orders also defer some indirect costs to the future and reduce others. The variable portion of indirect costs are deferred to the future when the associated activities are performed on several small batches rather than one large one. Let's continue the publishing company example by assuming that the variable cost of handling an incoming shipment of newsprint is $3.00 per roll. At this rate, the company pays $468 in indirect costs in January if it orders an entire year's supply then or $39.00 per month if it orders paper 12 times a year.

Small orders reduce other indirect costs by reducing the average amount of inventory on hand. Smaller storage facilities are required and insurance, property taxes, and losses due to deterioration, obsolescence, and theft are lower. The potential cost of obsolescence for inventories of high-tech products, such as computers, can be quite large (see "In the News"). In addition, the costs of moving materials through the produc-

IN THE NEWS

THE COST OF OBSOLESCENCE AT BEST BUY

BEST BUY CO. swung to a loss in its fiscal third quarter, after taking a charge for personal-computer supplies that will become obsolete when new technology arrives next month. Wall Street analysts had forecast a profit of seven cents a share, according to First Call. Best Buy's stock fell 62.5 cents, or 5 percent, to $11.875 in the New York Stock Exchange composite trading.

Best Buy, which operates 272 electronics superstores, said demand for all types of electronic goods was soft in the quarter, extending a slump that began in the spring. But it highlighted intensified pressure to sell PCs to be ready for models coming

in January that will be run by Intel Corp.'s MMX microprocessor.

To spur PC sales, Best Buy and other stores have touted 12-month no-interest financing specials and, with some models, offered free printers or monitors. Best Buy had been forced to delay payments to suppliers earlier this year by high inventories coming out of the 1995 holiday season.

While the quarterly loss placed Best Buy in violation of its bank borrowing terms, the company said it expects a "satisfactory resolution" to talks with lenders, led by First Bank, of Minneapolis.

Source: Evan Ramstad, "Best Buy Posts Fiscal Third-Period Loss on a Charge for PC Supplies Inventory," *The Wall Street Journal*, December 19, 1996, p. B8.

tion process are reduced because the materials are directly transferred from one stage of production to another without being periodically diverted to storage.

The savings from reducing the average amount of inventory on hand depend on the costs of storing the materials in their most stable state. Products that are volatile or perishable when held as raw materials may be easier and cheaper to store when they are converted to work-in-process or finished goods. Examples are ammonia gas, which is used to make fertilizer, and fresh fish, which is canned or frozen. Other commodities become more difficult to store *after* they are converted to finished goods; bread is more perishable than flour and garments are more perishable than cloth because they may go out of style. The savings therefore must be computed relative to the costs of storing the commodity in its least expensive form as raw materials, work-in-process, or finished goods.[3]

Placing several small orders to reduce some costs and defer others to the future reduces the present value of direct costs and some indirect costs. Companies would buy or make parts one unit at a time to maximize these benefits if they were the only effects of changing the order size.

---

[3]The difficulty and expense of storing materials also affects the distribution of inventory between the company, its suppliers, and its customers because one party's finished goods are another's raw materials. For example, the season's supply of salmon is certain to be held by food processors rather than by commercial fishing fleets; the season's supply of grain is certain to be held by elevators and mills as grain and flour rather than by bakers as bread. We will see that trade credit plays a crucial role in the distribution of these inventories between the company, its suppliers, and customers.

Unfortunately, reducing the order size or, equivalently, increasing the number of orders per year, increases other indirect costs. Many of the costs in purchasing and receiving, production scheduling, and shipping depend on the number of *batches* employees process rather than the number of items per batch. Examples are the costs of approving, initiating, receiving, and inspecting an order from an outside vendor; modifying production plans and setting up machines to fulfill an internal order; and the costs of assembling, inspecting, packaging, and shipping a customer's order. These indirect costs are sometimes simply called order costs; their amounts and timing must be considered when trying to determine the order size that provides the lowest present value of all direct and indirect production costs.

11.2   A CASH FLOW MODEL OF PRODUCTION COSTS

The amount and timing of a company's periodic cash outflows for direct and indirect costs are determined by the duration of its manufacturing process, the seasonality of supply and demand, and the amount of parts in each batch that it makes or buys. *Any production policy can be completely described by the pattern of cash costs it requires.* Consequently, we can simply compute the present value of these costs to determine which routine production policy is best.

We will use a very simple description of periodic production costs for the illustrations in this chapter. This will make it easier for you to learn how to model production costs and will reveal the implicit assumptions in some standard approaches to production management. Remember, you must use a more realistic direct and indirect cost structure when you apply the model in reality. We'll revisit this issue in Section 11.3.

Equation 11.1 is our simple model of a company's periodic production costs. It describes the direct and indirect costs of each batch of parts and materials a company makes or buys. Several simplifying assumptions are required to obtain such an uncomplicated equation.

1. Demand for the materials and parts is completely predictable and uniform throughout the year.
2. Direct costs per unit are constant.
3. The indirect cost of placing and processing an order is fixed.
4. The indirect cost of storing the materials is proportional to the average amount of inventory on hand.
5. All direct and indirect costs are paid when a batch is received.

The first two assumptions imply that the direct cost of each batch equals cQ where c is the direct cost of each unit and Q is the number of units in a batch; Q is equal to annual demand, D, divided by the number of batches produced or ordered each year, N. The first assumption also implies the average amount of inventory on hand is $Q/2$. The third assumption means the indirect cost of ordering each batch is a constant, b. Each batch results in an average inventory of $Q/2$ that is on hand only $1/N$th of a year. Therefore, if s represents the annual cost of storing one unit for one year, the indirect cost of storing each batch is $(Q/2) \times (s/N)$. The fifth assumption permits us to simply add the direct cost, order cost, and storage cost together to obtain the total cost of each batch.

$$\text{Periodic production costs} = cQ + b + [(Q/2) \times (s/N)] \qquad \textbf{[11.1]}$$

where

c = direct cost of each unit
Q = number of units in each order
b = order cost
$Q/2$ = average number of units held in inventory
s = storage cost per unit per year
N = number of orders per year, which equals annual demand, D, divided by the number of units in each order, Q

The following example illustrates the use of Equation 11.1.

Quick Switch Manufacturing uses 7,500 microswitches each year to produce safety controls for high-speed machine tools. Each switch costs $8.00 while wages and benefits for the technician who adapts the switches to Quick Switch's use cost an additional $2.20 per switch. The company's accountants have determined that it costs $106.00 to place and process an order while storage costs are $1.53 per switch per year. All costs, including the $2.20 for direct labor, are paid in cash when an order is received. Quick Switch's required rate of return on assets is 12 percent per year. Assuming Quick Switch orders 1,875 switches four times per year, the cost of each order is

Direct costs				
Materials	1,875 ×	$8.00	=	$15,000.00
Labor	1,875 ×	$2.20	=	4,125.00
Indirect costs				
Order cost			=	106.00
Storage costs	$\frac{1,875}{2}$ ×	$\frac{\$1.53}{4}$	=	358.59
Periodic production costs			=	$19,589.59

These periodic cash flows are placed on a time line in panel A of Exhibit 11.1.

● EXERCISE
11.1

CALCULATING PERIODIC PRODUCTION COSTS

What is Quick Switch's periodic production cost if the company orders 1,250 switches six times per year?

Direct costs				
Materials	1,250 ×	$8.00	=	$10,000.00
Labor	1,250 ×	$2.20	=	2,750.00
Indirect costs				
Order cost			=	106.00
Storage costs	$\frac{1,250}{2}$ ×	$\frac{\$1.53}{6}$	=	159.38
Periodic production costs			=	$13,015.38

Ordering more often reduces the cost of each order.

● ——— ●

Exhibit 11.1

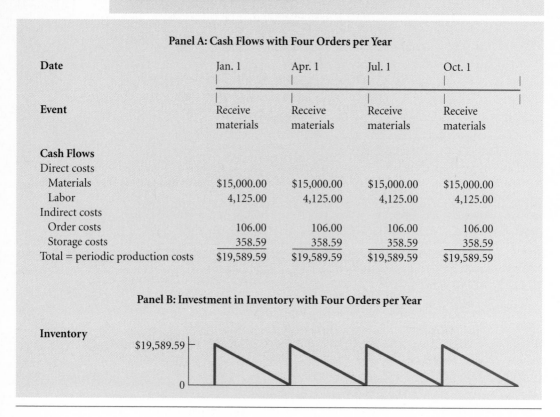

QUICK SWITCH MANUFACTURING COMPANY'S
CASH FLOWS AND INVENTORY

Panel A: Cash Flows with Four Orders per Year

Date	Jan. 1	Apr. 1	Jul. 1	Oct. 1
Event	Receive materials	Receive materials	Receive materials	Receive materials
Cash Flows				
Direct costs				
Materials	$15,000.00	$15,000.00	$15,000.00	$15,000.00
Labor	4,125.00	4,125.00	4,125.00	4,125.00
Indirect costs				
Order costs	106.00	106.00	106.00	106.00
Storage costs	358.59	358.59	358.59	358.59
Total = periodic production costs	$19,589.59	$19,589.59	$19,589.59	$19,589.59

Panel B: Investment in Inventory with Four Orders per Year

Inventory

$19,589.59

0

The total cost of each order determines a company's total investment in inventory and its annual cost of goods sold. Direct and indirect costs are added to inventory when the materials are acquired and subtracted from inventory as sales take place. The amount the item adds to a company's annual cost of goods sold equals the total cost of each order multiplied by the number of orders per year. These values can be used to compute the days'-cost-in-inventory ratio, which equals the length of the production phase of a company's operating cycle.

Quick Switch Manufacturing Company's total investment in inventory is graphed in panel B of Exhibit 11.1. Their investment follows the familiar sawtooth pattern because the $19,589.59 of direct and indirect costs are added to the inventory when an order is received and then depleted to zero at a uniform rate until the next order arrives. Quick Switch's average investment in inventory is simply the total cost of each order divided by two for this reason. That is,

Average investment in inventory = Periodic production costs/2

= $19,589.59/2 = $9,794.80.

The annual cost of goods sold for the switches is simply the cost of each order multiplied by the number of orders per year.

$$\text{Cost of goods sold} = \text{Periodic production costs} \times N$$
$$= \$19,589.59 \times 4 = \$78,358.36$$

The length of the production phase of the company's operating cycle is therefore

$$\text{Days'-cost-in-inventory} = \frac{\text{Average inventory}}{\text{Cost of goods sold per day}}$$

$$= \frac{\$9,794.80}{\$78,358.80/365} = 45.6 \text{ days.}$$

EXERCISE
11.2

CALCULATING THE LENGTH OF THE PRODUCTION PHASE OF THE OPERATING CYCLE

What is the length of the production phase of Quick Switch's operating cycle if the company orders 1,250 switches six times per year? Use the information from Exercise 11.1.

The length of the production phase of the company's operating cycle equals its days'-cost-in-inventory:

$$\text{Days'-cost-in-inventory} = \frac{\text{Average inventory}}{\text{Cost of goods sold per day}}$$

$$\text{Average inventory} = \text{Periodic production costs}/2$$
$$= \$13,015.38/2 = \$6,507.69$$

$$\text{Cost of goods sold} = \text{Periodic production costs} \times N$$
$$= \$13,015.38 \times 6 = \$78,092.28$$

$$\text{Days'-cost-in-inventory} = \frac{\$6,507.69}{\$78,092.28/365} = 30.4 \text{ days.}$$

Ordering more often shortens the production phase of the operating cycle.

The present value of the production costs is the discounted value of the periodic cash flows shown on the cash flow time line in Exhibit 11.1. These orders comprise an annuity due of N periods and the length of each period is one year divided by N. Therefore, the cash flows must be discounted at the company's opportunity cost divided by N. The formula used to calculate the present value of an annuity due of length N was given in Chapter 3. It is

$$\text{PV(annuity due of length } N) = 1 + \text{APVF}_{r,N-1}.$$

Applying this formula to the production costs,

PV(production costs) = Periodic production costs $\times$ [1 + APVF$_{r,N-1}$]   **[11.2]**

where r = company's annual opportunity cost divided by N.

Quick Switch Manufacturing Company's required rate of return on assets is 12 percent per year. The present value of their production costs is therefore

$$
\begin{aligned}
\text{PV(production costs)} &= \text{Periodic production costs} \times [1 + \text{APVF}_{r,N-1}] \\
&= \$19{,}589.59 \times [1 + \text{APVF}_{0.12/4,3}] \\
&= \$19{,}589.59 \times 3.8286 \\
&= \$75{,}000.70.
\end{aligned}
$$

Quick Switch can use this present value as a standard of comparison for evaluating proposals to organize production differently.

EXERCISE

11.3   **THE PRESENT VALUE OF PRODUCTION CASH FLOWS**

What is the present value of Quick Switch's production costs if the company orders 1,250 switches six times per year?

$$
\begin{aligned}
\text{PV(production costs)} &= \text{Periodic production costs} \times [1 + \text{APVF}_{r,N-1}] \\
&= \$13{,}015.38 \times [1 + \text{APVF}_{0.12/6,5}] \\
&= \$13{,}015.38 \times [1 + 4.7135] \\
&= \$74{,}363.37.
\end{aligned}
$$

Ordering more often reduced the present value of production costs; however, you must consider other production policies before concluding that six orders per year is best.

11.3   APPLICATIONS OF THE CASH FLOW MODEL

Managers can use the cash flow model of production costs to evaluate any routine production policy. For example, they can use the model to determine the optimal batch size, to determine whether to make the parts or buy them, or to analyze the effect of adopting innovative production systems. We will apply the model to the batch size and outsourcing in this section and examine innovative production systems later.

Optimal Batch Size

Deciding on the amount of materials or parts to acquire in each order is a pervasive management problem. This decision often is described as an inventory management problem because a company's average investment in inventory depends on the amount of materials it orders each time. This orientation explains why models that focus on inventory costs often are used to determine the optimal batch size.

We know that the problem is broader than this, however, because the amount of materials a company orders affects its direct and indirect cost of goods sold as well as the present value of these costs. Furthermore, the choice of production batch size is imbedded in every other production problem. This is true because a change in costs brought about by buying rather than making parts or by adopting innovative manufacturing techniques is certain to change the optimal batch size. We will use our cash flow model to determine the optimal batch size considering its effect on all these costs. In the process, you will see how the assumptions of traditional inventory management models limit them to a very narrow range of applications.

Applying the Cash Flow Model   The optimal batch size is determined by using Equation 11.2 to compute the present value of production costs for different sized orders. The quantity that provides the lowest present value of annual production costs is best. We will continue to use the Quick Switch Manufacturing Company to illustrate this and other applications of the cash flow model.

The present values of Quick Switch's production costs for alternatively sized orders are given in Table 11.1. You can see that the present value of direct costs and storage costs increases as the order size is increased from 250 to 7,500 switches while the present value of order costs decreases. Consequently, the present value of total costs first decreases then increases with a minimum at $74,093.69. Quick Switch Manufacturing Company's optimal policy is therefore to order 750 microswitches 10 times each year.

Exhibit 11.2 shows how the present value of production costs behaves as Quick Switch increases the order size from 250 to 1,500 switches. The present value of storage costs increases by 600 percent (from $180.60 to $1,094.96), the present value of order

QUICK SWITCH MANUFACTURING COMPANY PRESENT   **Table 11.1**
VALUE OF PRODUCTION COSTS*

Batch Size (# of Switches)	Number of Batches/Year	Present Value of Direct Cost	Order Cost	Storage Cost	Total Cost
250	30	$72,240.68	$3,002.95	$ 180.60	$75,424.23
300	25	72,271.12	2,503.51	216.81	74,991.44
375	20	72,316.76	2,004.07	271.19	74,592.02
500	15	72,392.74	1,504.63	361.96	74,259.33
625	12	72,468.63	1,204.97	452.93	74,126.53
750	**10**	**72,544.42**	**1,005.19**	**544.08**	**74,093.69**
1,250	6	72,846.61	605.63	910.58	74,362.82
1,500	5	72,997.13	505.73	1,094.96	74,597.82
1,875	4	73,222.19	405.83	1,372.92	75,000.94
2,500	3	73,595.41	305.93	1,839.89	75,741.23
3,750	2	74,334.91	206.00	2,787.56	77,328.47
7,500	1	76,500.00	106.00	5,737.50	82,343.50

*The entries for 4 and 6 batches per year differ from the values computed in the text only because of rounding.

Exhibit 11.2

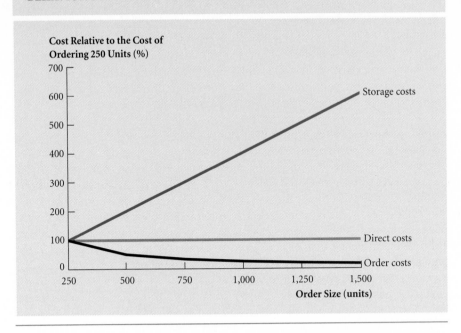

costs decreases by 83 percent (from $3,002.95 to $505.73), and the present value of direct costs increases by about 1 percent (from $72,240.68 to $72,997.13). These results show that changing the batch size primarily affects indirect costs. These relationships explain why companies are concerned about indirect costs and attempt to measure them accurately.

The characteristics of Quick Switch's optimal production policy are summarized in Table 11.2. The length of the production phase of the company's operating cycle when they follow this cost-minimizing policy is 18.3 days.

Relationship to the EOQ Model   The Economic Order Quantity (EOQ) model is a well-known technique for directly calculating the cost-minimizing number of units to order each time. A common form of this model is given by Equation 11.3.[4]

---

[4]Equation 11.3 is derived by finding the minimum of the total cost of inventory, which is the sum of ordering and holding costs.

$$\text{Total cost} = bN + hQ/2$$
$$= bD/Q + hQ/2$$

Setting the first derivative with respect to Q equal to zero gives

$$0 = -bDQ^{-2} + h/2.$$

Solving for $Q = [2bD/h]^{1/2}.$

QUICK SWITCH MANUFACTURING COMPANY CHARACTERISTICS OF PRODUCTION POLICY WITH OPTIMAL ORDER SIZE OF 750 UNITS

Table 11.2

Total cost of each order
  Direct costs
    Materials   750 units × $8.00/unit = $ 6,000.00
    Labor   750 units × $2.20/unit =   1,650.00
  Indirect costs
    Order cost   =   106.00
    Storage costs $\frac{750}{2} \times \frac{\$1.53}{10}$ = 57.38
  Periodic production costs $ 7,813.38

Average investment in inventory $7,813.38/2 = $ 3,906.69
Annual cost of goods sold $7,813.38 × 10 = $78,133.80
Days'-cost-in-inventory $\frac{\$3,906.69}{\$78,133.80/365}$ = 18.3 days
Present value of costs $7,813.38 × [1 + APVF$_{0.12/10,9}$] = $74,093.74*

$$EOQ = [2bD/h]^{1/2} \qquad [11.3]$$

where b = order cost
         D = annual demand
         h = holding cost per unit per year

In this form, the holding cost equals the cost of storing the commodity plus the opportunity cost of the investment in inventory. Using the symbols from Equation 11.1, the storage cost per unit is s and the opportunity cost is $c \times r$. Substituting these terms for h, the revised EOQ model is

$$EOQ = [2bD/(s + cr)]^{1/2} \qquad [11.4]$$

where c = direct cost of each unit of material
         s = storage cost per unit per year
         r = opportunity cost stated in annual terms.

Applying this model to Quick Switch's inventory problem, the opportunity cost, cr, is $1.22 ($10.20 × 0.12) and economic order quantity is

$$EOQ = [2 \times \$106.00 \times 7,500/(\$1.53 + \$1.22)]^{1/2}$$
$$= 760 \text{ units.}$$

According to the EOQ model, Quick Switch should order 760 units approximately 10 times a year for a present value total cost of $74,093.91.

EXERCISE

11.4   **APPLYING THE EOQ MODEL**

Use the EOQ model given by Equation 11.4 to determine Quick Switch's optimal batch size when order costs are $45.90. How many orders should the company place each year in this situation?

$$EOQ = [2bD/(s + cr)]^{1/2}$$
$$= [2 \times \$45.90 \times 7{,}500/(\$1.53 + \$1.22)]^{1/2}$$
$$= 500 \text{ units}$$

Ordering this quantity requires Quick Switch to place 15 orders per year (7,500 units of annual demand/500 units per batch).

The EOQ model results are very close to the results from the cash flow model; the present value of their total costs differs by only $0.22. These results are similar because both models rely on the same simplifying assumptions used to construct Equation 11.1: Demand is uniform, direct costs and order costs are fixed, storage costs and opportunity costs are proportional to the average inventory, and all costs are paid when an order is received. In fact, the EOQ model given by Equation 11.4 can be derived directly from Equation 11.2.[5]

The main reason for comparing the EOQ model to present value analysis is to reveal that it relies on some very unrealistic assumptions about production cash flows. Other cost-minimization models use more realistic assumptions but are still only applicable to the specific problems for which they were designed. You can derive alternative versions of these cost-minimization models to fit more realistic situations; however, this process is difficult and tedious and the resulting equation can be quite complicated.

In contrast, you can use present value analysis to evaluate nearly *any* conceivable structure of direct and indirect costs. You can, for example, analyze production policies that have nonuniform demand, direct costs with quantity discounts, indirect costs with both fixed and variable components, and the prepayment or deferred payment of both direct and indirect costs. This flexibility makes present value analysis a preferred method of applying financial management techniques to the production phase of the operating cycle.

Outsourcing

Many companies have the option to make a component part themselves or buy it from a supplier. Interest in this choice has intensified as managers try to determine which activities to undertake and which to abandon in order to concentrate on their company's competitive advantages. Make or buy decisions have their largest impact on a company's production costs so our cash flow model is ideally suited to the analysis of this choice.

---

[5]See Yong H. Kim, George Philippatos, and Kee H. Chung, "Evaluating Investment in Inventory Policy: A Net Present Value Framework," *Engineering Economist*, Winter 1986, pp. 119–136.

Suppose the firm supplying microswitches to Quick Switch Manufacturing offers to produce switches specifically designed for them at a cost of $10.00 per unit. This proposal increases Quick Switch's direct materials cost from $8 to $10 per unit and reduces its direct labor costs from $2.20 to $0 for a net savings of $0.20 per switch. Suppose also that the $10 per unit price is f.o.b. Quick Switch's factory, which reduces the company's order cost from $106.00 to $56.50. Finally, suppose the elimination of work-in-process inventory permits Quick Switch to reduce its storage costs from $1.53 to $0.90 per unit per year.

Recomputing the entries in Table 11.1 using the new costs reveals Quick Switch's optimal policy is to order 625 completed microswitches 12 times a year. The present value of their total production and inventory costs under this policy is $71,956.38, a savings of $2,137.31. The characteristics of this policy are described in Table 11.3 and the make or buy alternatives are compared in Table 11.4. Most of the savings from obtaining the completed switches from an outside source are produced by the reduced direct costs, order costs, and storage costs described above. However, Quick Switch can maintain a smaller inventory under the new policy and also saves opportunity costs.

The results in Table 11.4 indicate that Quick Switch Manufacturing should buy completed microswitches rather than adapt generic ones to their use. There are some additional considerations, however. First, unions understandably want to make it more costly for a company to outsource production to protect their members' interests. Outsourcing is a central issue in contract negotiations between Chrysler Corporation and the United Auto Workers union (see "In the News").

Second, a company that at least partially produces its own parts stays abreast of developments in the field and maintains the skills needed to fully produce its own parts if that alternative ever becomes profitable. Conserving this knowledge and these skills

---

QUICK SWITCH MANUFACTURING COMPANY CHARACTERISTICS OF PRODUCTION POLICY WITH OUTSOURCING   **Table 11.3**

Total cost of each order
  Direct costs
    Materials   625 units $\times$ $10.00/unit = $ 6,250.00
    Labor   0
  Indirect costs
    Order cost   =   56.50
    Storage costs $\dfrac{625}{2} \times \dfrac{\$0.90}{12}$ =   23.44
  Periodic production costs $ 6,329.94

Average investment in inventory $6,329.94/2 = $ 3,164.97
Annual cost of goods sold $6,329.94 \times 12 = $75,959.28
Days'-cost-in-inventory $\dfrac{\$3,164.97}{\$75,959.28/365}$ =   15.2 days
Present value of costs $6,329.94 \times [1 + \text{APVF}_{0.12/12,11}]$ = $71,956.38

Table 11.4   QUICK SWITCH MANUFACTURING COMPANY COMPARISON OF PRODUCTION COSTS WITH AND WITHOUT OUTSOURCING

	Make Switches	Buy Switches
Number of orders each year	10	12
Total cost of each order		
Direct cost		
Materials	$ 6,000.00	$ 6,250.00
Labor	1,650.00	0
Indirect costs		
Order cost	106.00	56.50
Storage cost	57.38	23.44
Periodic production costs	$ 7,813.38	$ 6,329.94
Average investment in inventory	$ 3,906.69	$ 3,164.97
Annual cost of goods sold	$78,133.80	$75,959.28
Days'-cost-in-inventory	18.3 days	15.2 days
Present value of total costs	$74,093.74	$71,956.38

by continuing to perform some of the work internally provides a valuable option on future production alternatives. The value of this option may more than offset the immediate disadvantage in the net present value of making rather than buying the necessary parts. We will examine this benefit in Chapter 13.

11.4   ACCOMMODATING UNCERTAINTY AND ASYMMETRIC INFORMATION

Managers cannot be certain operations will be carried out as planned. Unforeseeable events may interrupt the supply of raw materials, delay the completion of work-in-process, or interfere with sales and deliveries. Asymmetric information can have similar effects. Companies take precautions to limit the disruptions to operations caused by these factors.

The Costs of Uncertainty and Asymmetric Information

Surprises due to uncertainty and asymmetric information can cause a company to deplete its inventories sooner than expected. This produces unexpected production costs that affect current and future cash flows.

A company must order an emergency shipment or postpone production or sales if raw materials or finished goods of appropriate quality are not available when they are needed. These responses affect a company's current cash flows. An emergency order probably costs more than a normal shipment due to the exceptional circumstances. Similarly, deferred production probably costs more than normal production because

UAW OPPOSES OUTSOURCING

IN INITIAL CONTRACT demands to Chrysler Corp., the United Auto Workers union is seeking provisions that would make it even more costly for the company to lay off union members, and that would bar the company from farming out more work to outside suppliers.

Based on excerpts from the 116-page document made available to this newspaper, the UAW goes right after what it has said is its chief concern in Big Three bargaining this year: "While major gains were made during the 1993 round of bargaining, Chrysler has failed to live up to our expectations and the needs of our members on the matter of sourcing" of automotive parts, the document declares.

The union asks Chrysler to set "a moratorium and prohibition on the outsourcing or contracting out of work we have traditionally performed or could perform." The UAW also requests "the right to strike over sourcing and outside-contracting violations." The current Big Three contracts prohibit strikes over such matters. It has become a sore point as the auto industry has sought to cut costs by assigning more and more parts work to lower-cost outside suppliers.

Says one UAW insider: "Having that right doesn't mean we'll exercise it irresponsibly. We want that right because it will make the company act more responsibly and think out its decision more clearly."

Source: Nichole M. Christian, "UAW Targets Outsourcing and Layoffs," *The Wall Street Journal,* June 20, 1996, p. A2. Reprinted by permission of *The Wall Street Journal,* © 1996 Dow Jones & Company, Inc. All rights reserved worldwide.

some costs are fixed in the short run and it may be necessary to pay employees an overtime premium to catch up when supplies become available. Finally, deferred sales are worth less than normal sales because of the time value of money.

Persistent problems also may imperil a company's future cash flows. Skilled workers who must adjust to periodic idleness and overtime may seek more stable employment elsewhere. By the same reasoning, a company's suppliers and customers may seek more reliable trading partners elsewhere. A company experiencing these changes incurs costs to recruit and train new employees, to locate new suppliers and evaluate their capabilities, and to seek new customers. In addition, the company may not be able to maintain the quality of its products until normal operating conditions are restored. Failure to maintain product quality for these reasons also may reduce cash revenues.

Providing for Uncertainty and Asymmetric Information

Companies sometimes provide for uncertainty and asymmetric information by installing excess production capacity. They also install flexible manufacturing systems that can be switched from one task to another as the need arises. Flexible manufacturing systems provide production options; we will discuss this response in Chapter 13.

Companies also use inventory safety stocks to adapt to uncertainty and asymmetric information. A safety stock isolates a disruption at a particular stage of the operating cycle and permits the other stages to proceed somewhat independently. Raw material and work-in-process safety stocks permit a company to continue normal production when supplies are temporarily unavailable and to continue acquiring or building parts when subsequent stages of production are temporarily suspended. A finished goods safety stock decouples production and sales with a similar effect. Maintaining an inventory safety stock reduces the unexpected production costs caused by uncertainty and asymmetric information.

Maintaining an extra inventory to reduce unexpected production costs is not costless. The company must pay the direct costs to acquire the items held in the safety stock and the indirect cost of storing them. An inventory safety stock also has agency costs. Managers can use the safety stock to hide performance problems such as low quality, poor training, and the lack of maintenance, which shields them from monitoring and control. They also can maintain an excessive safety stock to make their jobs easier and safer than is desirable to the owners.

Companies should hold an inventory safety stock that minimizes the present value of the cost of unexpectedly depleting the inventory and the direct, indirect, and agency costs of the safety stock itself. By following this policy, managers ensure that the company's investment in both ordinary and precautionary inventories conforms to the same market-wide standards of financial performance.

You must estimate the amounts and timing of an inventory safety stock's cash flows to determine the present value of its costs. We will describe these cash flows in general terms here because the specific amounts and timing vary from one type of production process to another. Nevertheless, this general description serves as a guide for estimating the actual cash flows in a specific situation.

First, consider the costs of acquiring the items held in the safety stock. This cost equals the direct materials and labor costs of the items purchased or produced for the precautionary inventory plus the indirect cost of ordering them. The direct cost should be the same as the direct cost of items in the ordinary inventory, and the marginal ordering cost may be zero because ordinary and precautionary orders can be combined. The safety stock must be in place when production is initiated so the cost of acquiring the units in the safety stock occurs at the beginning of the year.

Now consider the indirect cost per unit of storing the safety stock. This cost probably is the same as the indirect cost of storing the ordinary inventory and probably is paid at the same time. The average value of the safety stock will not decline as the ordinary inventory's average value does between orders, however, because the safety stock is not used on a regular basis.

Finally, consider the cost of unexpectedly depleting the inventory. This cost may be simply the cost of placing an emergency order or it may be the cost of an emergency order plus the costs of lost production and sales. These costs may occur at any time during the year but are more likely to occur shortly before a company expects to receive a routine shipment. (This is when the ordinary inventory is at its lowest level and may be exhausted if the anticipated shipment is delayed, if the remaining items in inventory are used more rapidly than expected, or if they are defective.) The probability of a stock-out at any time depends on the likelihood of these surprises and the size of the inventory safety stock; the larger the safety stock, the lower the probability the company will unexpectedly deplete its inventory.

The timing and amounts of the agency costs of inventory are difficult to measure although it is possible to state some guidelines. Low quality is the result of using safety stocks to hide performance problems, which are manifest as the actual costs of inspections, waste, rework, and returns. (These are costs of extra labor and materials and therefore are probably paid at the same time as the direct costs of the ordinary inventory.) In contrast, the leisurely and secure attitude toward work that inventory safety stocks permit produces opportunity costs that are probably best evaluated qualitatively because they cannot be measured precisely.

11.5   INNOVATIVE PRODUCTION SYSTEMS

Many manufacturing and service companies have begun to adopt innovative production systems that use fewer short- and long-term assets and less labor, materials, and time than traditional methods of production. These innovative systems are sometimes called lean production, total quality management (TQM) or, when the focus is on inventories, just-in-time (JIT). Many of these innovations were developed at the Toyota Motor Company in Nagoya, Japan and affected product design and distribution as well as manufacturing. Here, we will focus on the effect on production and inventories.[6]

Key Features of Innovative Production Systems

Most innovative production systems work by reducing the amount of time required to obtain materials from external suppliers and to set up the machinery used to produce parts internally. This improves the availability of raw materials and work-in-process, which reduces the requirement for these inventories. Reducing the amount of time required to switch production from one product to another also makes it economical for a company to match production to sales, which reduces the requirement for finished goods. Stated simply, reducing *order costs* permits a company to reduce its investment in ordinary and safety stock inventories, which shortens the production phase of its operating cycle.

Small inventories are uneconomical if the company remains vulnerable to stock-out costs. Consequently, innovative production systems provide a powerful incentive for reducing uncertainty and asymmetric information—the sources of these costs. This is accomplished by establishing commitments between the company and its suppliers, employees, and customers that enable them to confidently share information that is essential for production planning.

Companies using innovative production systems establish long-term relationships with their suppliers to reduce adverse selection problems and principal–agent conflicts. The company invests time and effort to evaluate potential suppliers and awards long-term contracts that provide reasonable initial profits to the capable ones. This contracting process reduces adverse selection problems because the company is informed and its suppliers do not have to exaggerate their abilities to win competitive bids. Suppliers must share future cost savings with the company. However, they may keep any savings in excess of the amounts specified in the contract. This provision diminishes principal–agent con-

[6]*The Machine That Changed the World* by James P. Womack, Daniel T. Jones, and Daniel Roos, New York: HarperPerennial, 1990, provides an excellent description of the complete Toyota production system.

I N   T H E   N E W S

SUPPLIER COORDINATION AND CONTROL AT CHRYSLER

ONE WAY COMPANIES are fine-tuning the flow of goods in and out of their factories is by fostering tighter relationships with suppliers. At its Jeep plant in Detroit, for example, Chrysler orders the seats for the individual Grand Cherokees being manufactured only after the bodies leave the paint shop and start down the production line. At that time, a message is sent electronically to a Johnson Controls factory—30 minutes away—specifying the color and style of seats needed. The seats are assembled, loaded onto trucks, and delivered within a few hours. The system, which helps Chrysler and Johnson Controls keep inventories at a minimum, requires—and encourages—close cooperation between the two companies. Chrysler, for example, shares its production forecasts with Johnson Controls.

But even just-in-time cannot insulate companies like Chrysler from errant sales estimates. Many businesses that have streamlined their inventory systems still must lock into manufacturing schedules months before assembly begins on the factory floor. And that is where problems often arise. "Inventories," declares Merrill Lynch's Donald Straszheim, "will be less destabilizing to the overall economy in the future, but bad forecasts will continue until the end of time."

Source: "Sitting on Excess Supplies," *U.S. News & World Report*, September 18, 1995, p. 88.

flicts by compensating the company for its long-term commitment while maintaining the suppliers' incentives to improve their own operations.

The company and its suppliers share detailed information about product development and manufacturing as the contract is executed. This is sometimes accomplished by integrating their management information systems to facilitate the exchange of engineering drawings, production schedules, and inventory reports. Some suppliers are even permitted to use this information to initiate a shipment instead of waiting for the company to place an order. The exchange of data is often augmented by exchanging employees who provide additional information and identify and solve problems before they become insurmountable. These information-sharing processes permit the company and its suppliers to plan production with greater certainty and monitor each other to reduce principal–agent conflicts. This reduces the requirement for inventory safety stocks because materials are shipped directly to the factory floor exactly when they are needed without any delays to determine their quality (see "In the News").

Any particular company is a customer in some transactions and a supplier in others. Consequently, a company can use the processes described above to improve its relationships with its customers just as well as to improve its relationships with its suppliers.

Many Japanese companies establish commitments with their employees by providing lifetime employment and paying wages on the basis of seniority. Workers can trust the company because they have permanent employment and the company can trust the workers because they must start over on the pay scale if they leave for another firm.

This makes the company more willing to provide training and the workers more willing to accept flexible work assignments and quickly identify sources of poor quality in the workplace. There is a current debate about whether these innovative employment practices are culturally specific or transferable to Western countries.

Using Present Value Analysis to Evaluate Innovative Production Systems

We can see how innovative production techniques affect the ordinary inventory by examining the standard EOQ model, repeated below for convenience.

$$EOQ = [2bD/(s + cr)]^{1/2}$$
$$= [b]^{1/2} \times [2D/(s + cr)]^{1/2}$$

The rearranged version of Equation 11.4 shows that reducing the order cost (b) to Y proportion of its original value reduces the size of the economic order quantity to the square root of Y of its original size. For example, reducing the order cost to 0.25 of its original value reduces the size of the optimal order to the square root of $0.25 = 0.50$ of its original size.

Suppose that Quick Switch Manufacturing Company adopts a new ordering system that uses a preprinted order form attached to the container that holds the last 50 switches in inventory. A clerk faxes this card to the supplier when technicians begin to use switches from this container and a new shipment of switches is on its way. Order costs under this new system are $9.00. The new order cost is .16 ($9.00/$56.50) of the old order cost. Consequently, the new optimal order size should be approximately the square root of $0.16 = 0.40$ of the original optimal order size, or 250 switches (0.40 × 625 switches).

Table 11.5 shows that 250 units is, in fact, the new cost-minimizing order size. The characteristics of this new policy are summarized in Table 11.6.

Innovative production systems also permit a company to reduce its inventory safety stock by reducing the cost of unexpectedly depleting its inventory. An improved ordering system reduces the cost of placing an emergency shipment while flexible, multiskilled

QUICK SWITCH MANUFACTURING COMPANY PRESENT VALUE OF INVENTORY   Table 11.5 COSTS FOR ALTERNATIVE-SIZED ORDERS WITH PRODUCTION INNOVATIONS

Order Size (# of Switches)	Number of Orders/Year	Present Value of			
		Direct Cost	Order Cost	Storage Cost	Total Cost
240		$70,818.22	$265.57	$101.98	$71,185.77
245		70,821.21	260.16	104.11	71,185.48
250	**30**	**70,824.19**	**254.97**	**106.24**	**71,185.40**
255		70,827.18	249.98	108.37	71,185.53
260		70,830.17	245.18	110.50	71,185.85

Table 11.6   **QUICK SWITCH MANUFACTURING COMPANY CHARACTERISTICS OF OPTIMAL INVENTORY POLICY WITH PRODUCTION INNOVATIONS**

Total cost of each order
  Direct costs
    Materials   250 units $\times$ \$10/unit = \$ 2,500.00
  Indirect costs
    Order cost   =   9.00
    Storage costs $\dfrac{250}{2} \times \dfrac{\$0.90}{30}$ =   3.75

  Periodic production costs   \$ 2,512.75

Average investment in inventory   \$2,512.75/2 = \$ 1,256.38
Annual cost of goods sold   \$2,512.75 $\times$ 30 = \$ 75,382.50
Days'-cost-in-inventory $\dfrac{\$1,256.38}{\$75,382.50/365}$ =   6.1 days
Present value of costs $\$2,512.75 \times [1 + APVF_{0.12/30,29}]$ = \$71,185.40*

*The value differs from the entry in Table 11.5 only because of rounding.

employees can be assigned to other tasks during a stock-out, which reduces the cost of lost production. The probability of a stock-out is reduced as well because orders are more likely to arrive when they are expected and are more likely to have zero defects.

11.6 SUMMARY

Companies use supplies, materials, labor, and energy to produce the products and services they sell to customers. Managers must decide which supplies and materials they need, whether to buy or build these parts, when to buy or build them, and in what quantity and quality. The costs of all the choices the managers make are accumulated in the company's inventories before they are subtracted from revenue as the cost of goods sold. Consequently, the amounts, timing, and risk of the cash flows to acquire, store, and use inventories completely describe a particular production policy.

The objective of financial management in the production phase of the operating cycle is to help managers identify the best production policy. This is accomplished by computing the present value of the alternatives' costs of goods sold. The production policy with the lowest present value cost is best.

This approach to financial management in the production phase of the operating cycle requires a cash flow model of production costs. Analysts can construct a cash flow model of literally *any* production policy, although we used a relatively simple one here for illustration. Importantly, the simplifying assumptions required for our model are identical to those required for the EOQ model, which reveals its limitations.

Cash flow models also are useful for evaluating inventory safety stocks which provide the traditional response to uncertainty and asymmetric information about external and internal supply and demand for inputs and outputs. Given a cost structure, the best safety stock is the one with the lowest present value of costs.

Innovative production policies such as total quality management or just-in-time address the root causes of disruptions to production by reducing uncertainty and asymmetric information. The key to the success of many of these innovations is establishing long-term relationships with suppliers, employees, and customers. Whatever the name or focus of these innovations, they can be evaluated using the same type of cash flow models as we applied to ordinary production management problems.

• QUESTIONS AND PROBLEMS

1. LaRry's Fashion Accessories produces handmade leather purses and bags that are sold in exclusive department stores worldwide. The company's cost of goods sold for the most recent quarter comprised expenses for the following activities and items.

   Rent for garment district warehouse

   Five gallons of sewing machine oil

   Thirty cases of zippers

   Wages of cutters, sewers, and finishers

   Insurance on contents of warehouse

   Twenty cases of assorted brass fasteners and clasps

   Two thousand square yards of leather

   Wages of shipping and receiving employees

   Twenty-five gallons of dye, five gallons of finishing wax

   Payment for warehouse pest control

   Salaries of leather buyer and inspector

   (a) Classify each of these expenses as a direct or indirect cost.

   (b) Which of these costs can LaRry reduce or defer to the future by conducting operations with smaller batch sizes?

2. A company located in Mexico with good access to steer hides and inexpensive labor offered to cut and assemble leather purses and bags for LaRry's Fashion Accessories (see question 1). The Mexican company will manufacture the goods to LaRry's specifications at its plant in Chihuahua, Mexico, and deliver them to a warehouse in Ciudad Juárez, just across the border from El Paso, Texas. LaRry will take possession of the goods in Juárez and transport them to New York where it will apply its patented dyes and attach its distinctive brass fasteners and clasps.

   (a) Which of the costs listed in question 1 can LaRry reduce or eliminate by outsourcing part of the production process to the Mexican leather company? What cost increases or new costs will take their places? Explain your answer.

   (b) Is LaRry likely to conduct operations with smaller or larger batch sizes if it accepts the Mexican leather company's proposal? Why?

   (c) Should LaRry's treasurer plan to finance a larger or smaller investment in net working capital if the company accepts the Mexican leather company's proposal? Explain your answer.

3. Describe how each factor given below affects the timing of a company's production costs and the level of its inventories.

    (a) The availability of raw materials.

    (b) The duration of the manufacturing process.

    (c) The seasonality of demand.

4. A company's line of business may seem to place inflexible constraints on the timing of its production costs and the level of its inventories. Nevertheless, managers can adopt innovations that relax these constraints. Describe some actual or potential innovations that managers can use to change the availability of raw materials, the duration of the manufacturing process, and the seasonality of demand.

5. Describe how the choice of batch size affects the timing and the amount of the following production costs.

    (a) Direct labor and materials costs.

    (b) Indirect costs.

    (c) Agency costs of holding inventories.

6. Maxine's Bike and Skate Shop orders in-line skates 12 times a year on average. Rely on your intuition and understanding of production and finance to answer the following questions about the production phase of the company's operating cycle. Explain each answer.

    (a) What is the approximate length of the production phase of the store's operating cycle?

    (b) Would the owner lengthen or shorten the production phase of the shop's operating cycle if the in-line skate manufacturer closed its regional distribution center?

    (c) Would the owner lengthen or shorten the production phase of the shop's operating cycle if the city levied a tax on business inventories?

    (d) Does Maxine's Bike and Skate Shop require more or less financing as a result of the changes in parts (b) and (c)?

7. Uncertainty and asymmetric information can disrupt production and operations.

    (a) What are the similarities and differences between disruptions caused by these factors? What are the costs?

    (b) Describe some alternatives for reducing the costs of disruptions caused by uncertainty and asymmetric information. In principle, how should managers choose among these alternatives?

8. Maintaining an inventory safety stock substitutes one set of agency costs for another.

    (a) What are the agency costs of inventories?

    (b) How do innovative production systems address the agency costs of inventories?

9. At first glance, innovative production systems such as JIT and TQM seem to affect only the direct and indirect costs of inventories.

    (a) How do these systems affect the agency costs of production and operations?

    (b) How do innovative production systems affect the financial costs of production and operations?

10. The economic order quantity model is widely known but subject to many limitations.

    (a) List and explain the assumptions of the EOQ model.

    (b) Which of the EOQ model's assumptions seems most unrealistic to you? Why?

11. Old Reliable Incorporated uses 3,600 cast aluminum housings each year to produce its backyard barbecue smokers. Each housing costs $50. The company presently orders 300 housings

each month but the purchasing and production managers want to change this policy. The purchasing manager prefers to place only nine orders per year to save ordering costs while the production manager wants to order only 200 housings each time to save storage costs. The costs of the company's present policy are shown below. These costs are based on ordering costs of $200, storage costs of $3 per unit per year, and opportunity cost of 12 percent. All costs are paid when an order is received.

	Present Policy	Purchasing's Proposal	Production's Proposal
Orders/year	12	9	—
Units/order	300	—	200
PV(order costs)	$ 2,274	—	—
PV(direct costs)	$170,514	—	—
PV(storage costs)	$ 426	—	—
PV(total costs)	$173,214	—	—

(a) Complete the table. Whose proposal should Old Reliable adopt?

(b) How can you convince the manager whose proposal was rejected that his suggestion was unacceptable even though he was right about how it would affect ordering or storage costs?

(c) How can you use the days'-costs-in-inventory ratio for monitoring to ensure the best policy was implemented?

12. Riedel Industrial Hand Towel Company produces and distributes bundles of inexpensive cloth hand towels used by mechanics. The company buys rejected rolls of cloth from a bath towel company, cuts the cloth into 12-inch squares, and binds the edges. Each roll costs $300 and yields 6,000 hand towels. Direct labor costs are an additional $900 per roll. Riedel receives two rolls of cloth each week and sells 624,000 towels each year. Order costs are $25 per week while storage costs are $120 per roll per year. All costs are paid weekly.

(a) Compute Riedel's weekly production costs and average investment in inventory.

(b) What amount will the company report for cost of goods on its annual income statement? Is the present value of its production costs less than or greater than the reported figure? Explain your answer.

(c) What is the length of the production phase of the company's operating cycle?

13. Determine the net present value of Riedel Industrial Hand Towel Company's annual production costs. (See problem 12.) The company's required rate of return is 14 percent.

14. Globe Enterprises manufactures floormats for sport-utility vehicles. The company pays $8.50 for a sheet of rubber from which it molds and cuts a set of floormats. Direct labor is $2.50 per set while storage costs are $3.48 per set per year. The cost of placing and processing an order is $100 and all costs are paid when an order is received. Globe produces 24,000 sets of floormats per year at a uniform rate and sells them under a long-term contract to a mail-order automobile accessories dealer. Globe's opportunity cost is 12 percent per year.

(a) Use the EOQ model to determine how many sheets of rubber Globe Enterprises should order each time.

(b) How many orders must the company place per year and what is the cost of each order?

(c) Determine the present value of Globe's annual production costs under this production policy.

15. Use the cash flow model of production costs to re-examine Globe Enterprises' choice of batch size (see problem 14).

(a) Calculate the present value of the company's annual production costs if the company places 20, 24, 25, and 30 orders per year.

(b) How many sheets of rubber should the company order each time according to the cash flow model of production costs? How does this answer compare to the answer you obtained using the EOQ model? Why?

16. The Back 9 Golf Cart Company uses 18,000 wheel assemblies each year to manufacture golf and utility carts. Each assembly costs $17.50. The cost of placing and processing an order is $150 while storage costs are $2.00 per unit per year. Back 9's opportunity cost is 10 percent per year. The timing and amounts of these production costs conform to the assumptions of the economic order quantity model.

(a) Use the EOQ model to determine how many wheel assemblies Back 9 should order each time. What amount do the wheel assemblies contribute to the company's reported annual cost of goods sold? What is the present value of these production costs?

(b) Suppose Back 9's supplier offers the company a quantity discount on wheel assemblies. The new price is $p = \$17.50 - 0.00006 \times Q$. For example, the cost per assembly if the company buys 1,000 units at a time is $p = \$17.50 - 0.00006 \times 1,000 = \$17.44$. How will this change affect the number of wheel assemblies Back 9 should order each time?

(c) Is it possible to modify the EOQ model to fit the new problem? Can *you* do it? Explain your answers.

(d) Incorporate the quantity discount in the cash flow model of production costs. Use this revised model to calculate the present value of production costs for batch sizes of 1,500, 1,800, and 2,250 units.

(e) Which policy should Back 9 adopt to minimize days'-costs-in-inventory? To minimize the price per wheel assembly? To maximize the owners' wealth?

17. Scherr On-Line Training Labs produces and sells compact disks that provide step-by-step instruction in the use of a wide range of statistical techniques. The company buys 36,000 blank CDs each year for $3.00 a piece and produces and records them in its own facilities. Scherr's opportunity cost is 9 percent per year and the cost of placing and processing an order is $260. The company can store up to 4,500 blank disks at an average cost of $0.23 per disk per year. The cost of storing any more disks is higher: $0.24 average cost per disk per year to store up to 6,000 disks and $0.25 average cost per disk per year to store up to 7,200. The timing and amounts of all other production costs conform to the assumptions of the economic order quantity model.

(a) Is it possible to modify the EOQ model to determine how many blank CDs Scheer should order each time? Can *you* do it? Explain your answers.

(b) Incorporate the effect of increasing storage costs in the cash flow model of production costs. Use this revised model to calculate the present value of production costs for batch sizes of 4,500, 6,000, and 7,200 units.

(c) Which policy should Scheer adopt to minimize reported cost of goods sold? To minimize days'-costs-in-inventory? To maximize the owners' wealth?

18. Miraculous Manufacturing Co. (MMC) makes do-it-yourself trophy fish kits that it sells on late night cable TV. Each kit contains a foam fish form and naturally colored paints that anglers use to create replicas of their prize catches. Forms that represent large mouth bass, walleye, and northern pike are available. The direct cost of each form, for the chemical compounds used to produce the foam, and for direct labor is $3.15. MMC produces the forms that represent all three species on a single machine. The cost of switching the machine from producing one type of form to another is $11.95. The cost of storing the chemicals and finished

forms averages $0.45 per form per year. The company's opportunity cost is 11 percent per year. All costs are paid when the forms are produced.

(a) Miraculous sells 12,000 kits of each species each year. How many of one particular type of kit (bass, walleye, or pike) should the company produce before switching production to another species?

(b) What is the present value of the company's production costs for one type of kit?

19. A local company that produces foam boat fenders offered to supply the fish forms to MMC (see problem 18) for $3.00 each. Miraculous's order costs will increase to $16.00 per order because it must coordinate with an external company, but its storage costs will decline to $0.27 because the company will no longer store hazardous chemicals.

(a) How much will outsourcing save the company if it orders kits in the same quantity that it produced internally?

(b) How much will outsourcing save MMC if it adjusts its order size to the costs of buying the forms externally?

• ADDITIONAL READING

The three articles listed below describe other production innovations that should be evaluated using finance valuation principles.

B. Joseph Pine II, Bart Victor, and Andrew C. Boynton, "Making Mass Customization Work," *Harvard Business Review,* September–October 1993, pp. 108–119.

Robert H. Hayes, "Beyond World-Class: The New Manufacturing Strategy," *Harvard Business Review,* January–February 1994, pp. 77–86.

James P. Womack and Daniel T. Jones, "From Lean Production to the Lean Enterprise," *Harvard Business Review,* March–April 1994, pp. 93–103.

FINANCIAL MANAGEMENT OF PAYMENTS AND COLLECTIONS

At one time, IBM's financial subsidiary took from 6–14 days to process a salesperson's request to extend credit to a customer. This delay was in addition to the length of the company's operating cycle that increased its opportunity costs. The delay also may have caused IBM to lose sales to companies that could respond more quickly. IBM managers revised the credit approval process and shortened the company's response time to four *hours,* thereby reducing its net working capital and opportunity costs.

Ford Motor Company changed the way it paid its suppliers. The company began to pay for some parts when it *used* them rather than when it received the parts or was billed for them. This policy lengthened the payment period and reduced Ford's net working capital and opportunity costs. The new policy also was simpler to implement, which allowed the company to reduce employment in the payables department by 75 percent. Both of these effects improved Ford's profitability.[1]

The changes IBM and Ford made to their credit and payables departments reduced opportunity costs and therefore almost certainly increased the owners' wealth. Recognizing and measuring the benefits of these types of changes is what the financial management of payments and collections is all about.

Companies buy raw materials from suppliers and sell finished goods to customers but do not simultaneously pay and receive cash. The trade credit they receive from suppliers and extend to customers causes part of this delay while the use of payment media that is not immediately convertible to cash causes the remainder of the delay.

Companies normally have some choice about the lengths of these delays. Their suppliers may extend trade credit and at the same time provide a cash discount for early payment. They may offer their own customers the same choice. Furthermore, companies can choose payment media to lengthen or shorten the delay until their suppliers are paid

---

[1]IBM's and Ford's experiences are related in Michael Hammer and James Champy, *Reengineering the Corporation,* HarperCollins Publishers, New York, 1993.

and must respond to similar choices by their customers. The objective of financial management of payment and collections is to help make these choices by considering the benefits and costs of delayed payment. This is accomplished by combining a thorough understanding of trade credit and the payment system with the ability to apply fundamental valuation principles.

You learned valuation principles in earlier chapters and this chapter describes the benefits and costs of trade credit and the process by which checks are cleared. You will see how to use this information to estimate the timing and amount of the cash flows paid to suppliers and received from customers. Then, choosing the best payment or collection policy becomes a simple matter of identifying the one with the highest present value of cash flows. This approach is particularly well-suited to evaluating alternative operating policies because it properly reconciles the potentially conflicting interests of sales and financial managers.

12.1   THE BENEFITS AND COSTS OF TRADE CREDIT

Trade credit is pervasive because it provides benefits not easily obtained from other payment arrangements. Perhaps the most widespread benefit is the simple convenience of writing a single check to pay for hundreds of purchases by scores of separate business units spread over several days or weeks. This is a substantial benefit because the cost to prepare, mail, and clear a single paper check may be only slightly more than 1 percent of the cost to prepare, mail, and clear 100 paper checks. The supplier has similar cost savings from receiving and processing one check rather than many.

Specialization is another benefit of trade credit. One form is specialization in the transfer of goods and cash. Delayed payment separates the transfer of goods from the transfer of cash, which permits companies to use specialists to perform each task. Strong workers can be employed to load and unload trucks while knowledgeable and trustworthy workers can be employed to issue and receive payments. The delivery and payment systems these employees use also are highly specialized to provide additional cost savings. The benefits of using trade credit to separate delivery and payment are so important for some products that they are sold *only* on credit. Electricity is a notable example. We simply could not have a modern electrical power distribution system if companies and individuals were required to pay for electricity as they used it.[2]

Trade credit also permits inventory specialization. A company can accept delivery of raw materials and specialize in managing that physical inventory while its supplier accepts delayed payment for the materials and specializes in managing a financial inventory of accounts receivable. This exchange benefits both parties if the customer has lower storage costs (such as a fish canner in comparison to a commercial fishing fleet) and the supplier has lower financial or opportunity costs.[3]

---

[2]See Gary W. Emery, "Positive Theories of Trade Credit," in Yong H. Kim (ed.), *Advances in Working Capital Management Volume 1*, JAI Press, Inc., Greenwich, Connecticut, 1988.
[3]See Gary W. Emery, "An Optimal Financial Response to Variable Demand," *Journal of Financial and Quantitative Analysis*, June 1987, pp. 209–225.

An additional benefit of a trade credit relationship is that it reduces the information asymmetry between a supplier and its customers. The customer obtains information because delayed payment provides the opportunity to determine a shipment's quality before paying for it. This is a valuable opportunity because the Uniform Commercial Code permits buyers to deduct the value of defective items from the amount owed. This recourse to unexpectedly receiving a low-quality shipment is simpler and more effective than requesting a refund *after* paying the bill. Placing control over the refunding process in the hands of the customer makes the seller responsible for defects—even if the customer cannot judge quality in advance. Suppliers may even voluntarily extend trade credit to accept this responsibility and thereby signal their confidence in the quality of their products.[4]

Trade credit transactions also provide information to suppliers because a customer that makes *extensive* use of trade credit may reveal poor access to the financial markets. The supplier therefore may not view the customer as a viable partner in a long-term business relationship.[5]

Finally, trade credit provides financial benefits because these loans are less risky than market loans. There are several reasons. First, the supplier's familiarity with the industry and the customer makes the credit application easier to evaluate. Second, the supplier controls the availability of an essential raw material so the customer is more likely to repay this loan before paying a bank. If you are not sure about this, suppose it is February and you live in northern Minnesota. Would you use your last $200 to pay your heating bill (trade credit) or your credit card bill? Third, if the borrower defaults, the supplier's bad debt losses should be less than a bank's because the supplier can sell the repossessed merchandise through its regular channels while a bank may have to liquidate the goods at distressed sale prices.[6]

Buyers and sellers cannot obtain the benefits of trade credit without cost. Suppliers incur costs to determine which customers are good and bad credit risks. They also incur bad debt costs because they cannot perfectly predict their customers' behaviors. Suppliers even incur costs when they are paid as expected because the delay in receiving the cash flows provided by customers produces an opportunity cost.

The customer's cost of using trade credit is the implicit financing charge built into *every* credit purchase. This cost is present even when the customer receives a discount for early payment—say, within 10 days—because the supplier provides financing until the account is paid. Managers become aware that there is a financing charge for this 10-day loan when they are offered an even larger discount to pay their bill electronically, that is, within 1 day.

---

[4]See Yul W. Lee and John D. Stowe, "Product Risk, Asymmetric Information, and Trade Credit," *Journal of Financial and Quantitative Analysis*, June 1993, pp. 285–300; Michael S. Long, Ileen B. Malitz, and S. Abraham Ravid, "Trade Credit, Quality Guarantees, and Product Marketability," *Financial Management*, Winter 1993, pp. 117–127; and Gary W. Emery and Nandkumar Nayar, "Product Quality and Payment Policy," *Review of Quantitative Finance and Accounting*, forthcoming.

[5]See Janet Smith, "Trade Credit and Informational Asymmetry," *Journal of Finance*, September 1987, pp. 863–872.

[6]See Gary W. Emery, "A Pure Financial Explanation for Trade Credit," *Journal of Financial and Quantitative Analysis*, September 1984, pp. 271–285.

12.2   FINANCIAL MANAGEMENT OF RECEIVABLES

A company must establish a credit policy to manage its investment in receivables. The elements of this policy are the company's credit terms, the standards its customers must meet to receive credit, and the procedures it will use to monitor and control its investment in receivables. Establishing a credit policy appears to be an overwhelming task because of the number of alternatives to consider. However, laws and industry practice impose constraints that limit a company's choices. Furthermore, credit associations and specialized financial service companies collect and disseminate information that helps companies determine industry practice and assess a credit applicant's default risk.

Perhaps the greatest challenge to establishing an acceptable credit policy is the inherent conflict between sales and credit managers. Sales managers often prefer that their company offers lengthy credit terms, adopts permissive credit standards, and is lax at controlling the investment in receivables. Their motivation is that a generous credit policy stimulates sales by reducing the present value of the price the buyer pays for the product and by increasing the population of potential customers. These managers may ignore the fact that a generous credit policy increases the opportunity cost of the investment in accounts receivable and losses due to bad debts, particularly if their performance appraisal and salary are based on sales. Credit managers often have the opposite view and prefer that their company offers short credit terms, adopts strict credit standards, and is conscientious about controlling the investment in receivables. Of course, their motivation is to limit the investment in receivables and losses due to bad debts because their performance appraisal and salary often are based on these factors.

You know by now that the best routine credit policy is the one with the highest net present value. Importantly, a properly conducted present value analysis balances the perspectives of sales and credit managers by including the cash flow consequences of the change in sales, receivables, and bad debts that result from adopting a more or less generous credit policy. We will apply this discounted cash flow approach to the choice of credit terms and the establishment and enforcement of credit standards in this section.

Factors to Consider When Establishing Credit Terms

The first step in establishing credit policy is to specify credit terms. These terms state (1) whether payment is due on delivery or deferred until later, (2) the product's price with delayed payment, and (3) whether the buyer gets a cash discount for early payment. The benefits of trade credit and how these benefits are allocated between the supplier and its customers are largely determined by the choice of these terms.

One factor to consider when establishing credit terms is the amount of processing costs saved by allowing customers to make one payment for purchases spread over several days or weeks. The supplier saves money by processing one payment instead of many and its customers may be willing to pay a slightly higher price for the product because they obtain similar savings of their own. Charging a higher price for credit sales gives the seller a share of its customers' cost savings.

Another factor to consider is the relationship between the company's opportunity cost and its customers' opportunity costs. Lengthening the payment period permits customers to defer paying cash until later, which reduces the present value of the price they pay for the product. This price reduction is costly to the seller who compensates by adding an implicit financing charge to the price of the product. Deferred payment is beneficial to the buyer, however, who therefore is willing to pay a higher credit price.

The minimum credit price acceptable to the seller is the cash price compounded at the seller's opportunity cost for the length of the credit period. At this price, cash and credit sales have the same present value to the seller. The maximum credit price acceptable to the buyer is the cash price compounded at the buyer's opportunity cost for the length of the credit period. At this price, cash and credit sales have the same present value to the buyer. A credit price within this range is feasible because it is acceptable to both seller and buyers. This is illustrated by the following example.

Nebraska Wholesale Tool Company (NWT) sells a concrete saw for $2,700. The company currently requires cash on delivery but may provide credit for 30 days. The seller's opportunity cost, r_s, is 10 percent per year while the buyers' opportunity cost, r_b, is 14 percent per year. Given these values, the minimum and maximum credit prices for the concrete saw are

$$\text{Minimum credit price acceptable to NWT} = \text{Cash price} \times (1 + r_s/365)^t$$
$$= \$2,700 \times (1 + 0.10/365)^{30}$$
$$= \$2,722.28$$

$$\text{Maximum credit price acceptable to buyers} = \text{Cash price} \times (1 + r_b/365)^t$$
$$= \$2,700 \times (1 + 0.14/365)^{30}$$
$$= \$2,731.24.$$

Any credit price greater than or equal to $2,722.28 and less than or equal to $2,731.24 is feasible when the credit period is 30 days and the seller's and buyer's opportunity costs are 10 percent and 14 percent.

● ── ● **EXERCISE**

DETERMINING MINIMUM ACCEPTABLE CREDIT PRICE

12.1

NWT's sales manager wants the company to raise the price of the saw to $2,740 with payment due 60 days after the sale. Are these credit terms feasible?

$$\text{Minimum credit price acceptable to NWT} = \$2,700 \times (1 + 0.10/365)^{60}$$
$$= \$2,744.74$$

These credit terms are *not* feasible. The company must charge at least $2,744.74 for the concrete saw to cover its opportunity cost of 10 percent for 60 days.

● ────────────── ●

The difference between the credit prices acceptable to the seller and buyer is the financial benefit of a credit sale. This benefit arises when the seller is able to assign a low opportunity cost to the trade credit loan because it has fewer problems due to asymmetric information and less risk than a market loan. If the credit price is set at its maximum value, 100 percent of the benefit goes to the seller, and if the credit price is set at its minimum value, 100 percent of the benefit goes to the buyer. Credit prices between the minimum and the maximum divide the benefit between the parties.

Suppose Nebraska Wholesale Tool Company permits its customers to buy the concrete saw for $2,725.00, net 30. Then the present value of a credit sale, from NWT's perspective, is

$$\text{Present value price to NWT} = \text{Credit price}/(1 + r_s/365)^{30}$$
$$= \$2,725.00/(1 + 0.10/365)^{30}$$
$$= \$2,702.70.$$

The present value of a credit sale from NWT's perspective is therefore $2.70 ($2,702.70 − $2,700.00) more than the present value of a cash sale.

These credit terms also benefit NWT's customers.

$$\text{Present value price to buyers} = \text{Credit price}/(1 + r_b/365)^{30}$$
$$= \$2,725.00/(1 + 0.14/365)^{30}$$
$$= \$2,693.83$$

The present value of a credit purchase from the buyer's perspective is therefore $6.17 ($2,700.00 − $2,693.83) less than the present value of a cash purchase. These credit terms benefit both parties because the credit price is *between* $2,722.28 and $2,731.24.

A financial advantage to trade credit may provide other benefits if there is an increase in demand because the present value price is lower. This will happen if demand is price-elastic or if the buyer's storage costs are lower than the seller's. The resulting revenue increase or cost reduction is an operating benefit that is an addition to the implicit interest income, which is the financial benefit of trade credit. Managers must consider the nature of the demand for their product and the buyer's storage costs relative to their own to determine the magnitude of these potential operating advantages.

Sellers also must consider whether buyers rely on the credit period to assess their product's quality. This benefit of trade credit is particularly important if the quality of the seller's product cannot be determined at the time of sale and if the buyer has no other reliable sources of information. Consequently, companies without an established reputation, whose products do not carry strong warranties, or whose products are not certified by independent agencies such as the Society of Automotive Engineers may offer longer credit periods to provide this assurance to their customers.

The incremental cost of administering credit sales is another factor to consider when establishing credit terms. These costs include the expenses of determining which credit applicants are good credit risks, keeping records of credit purchases and payments, and following up on delinquent accounts to obtain payment. Companies that cannot perform these tasks efficiently may not extend trade credit or may delegate some of this activity to a third party such as a secured lender.

The final consideration is a legal one. The Robinson-Patman Act is a U.S. federal law that requires companies to offer the same credit terms to all their credit customers. A violation of this Act is considered a form of price discrimination and is punishable by law. Companies are permitted to deny credit to customers if they are bad risks; however, once a company is approved for credit, it must receive the same terms as all others.

Financial Analysis of Credit Terms

Alternative credit terms are compared by determining the net present value of the cash flows received from customers. The terms establish credit price and payment due date, but customers determine whether they pay then or not at all. Consequently, managers must anticipate their customers' behaviors to accurately determine the amount and timing of cash flows from credit sales. We will examine these issues with a set of increasingly more complicated examples.

Financial Analysis of Net Credit Terms[7]   Country Wood Farm produces mesquite wood chips for barbecuing. The variable cost of production is $5.00 per cubic yard and the company sells the chips to distributors for $12.50 a cubic yard. Costs and revenues are paid and received weekly in cash. The company typically sells 800 cubic yards of chips a week for cash revenues of $10,000 and cash costs of $4,000 per week. Weekly net cash flow is $6,000. Assuming there are 52 weeks of sales each year and that Country's opportunity cost is 9 percent, the present value of a year's cash flows is

$$\text{PV(annual sales)} = \$6,000 \times \text{APVF}_{0.09/52,52}$$
$$= \$6,000 \times 49.6876$$
$$= \$298,126.$$

This value is the standard against which we will compare the value of alternative credit policies.

Country's managers are considering a proposal to extend 30 days of credit to these distributors. They assume the distributors' opportunity cost is 12 percent and will charge the maximum acceptable credit price:

$$\text{Maximum credit price acceptable to distributors} = \text{Cash price} \times (1 + r_b/365)^t$$
$$= \$12.50 \times (1 + 0.12/365)^{30}$$
$$= \$12.62.$$

The present value of this price from the distributors' perspectives equals the cash price, $\$12.62/(1 + 0.12/365)^{30} = \$12.50$, so Country does not expect an increase in the quantity demanded. Neither the seller nor the buyer has an advantage at storing wood chips so adopting these terms will not shift inventory to the distributors either. Finally, anyone can easily determine the condition of wood chips on sight so extending the credit period does not provide an additional quality assurance. Considering these factors, Country expects demand to remain constant at 800 cubic yards per week.

$$\text{Weekly sales} = \$12.62 \times 800 \text{ cubic yards}$$
$$= \$10,096$$
$$\text{Weekly costs} = \$5.00 \times 800 \text{ cubic yards}$$
$$= \$4,000$$

---

[7]The procedure for evaluating credit policy alternatives was first proposed in Ned C. Hill and William L. Sartoris, "Evaluating Credit Policy Alternatives: A Present Value Framework," *Journal of Financial Research*, Winter 1981, pp. 81–89.

Exhibit 12.1

COUNTRY WOOD FARM RESULTS OF A TYPICAL WEEK'S SALES WITH TERMS NET 30

	Day	0	30
Event		Sell chips, pay costs	Collect receivables
Income Statements			
Sales		$ 10,096	$ 0
Costs of sales		4,000	0
Net income		$ 6,096	$ 0
Accounts Receivable			
Beginning balance		$ 0	$ 10,096
Credit sales		10,096	0
Collections		0	10,096
Ending balance		$ 10,096	$ 0
Cash Flow			
Net income		$ 6,096	$ 0
Minus change in accounts receivable		10,096	(10,096)
Net cash flow		$(4,000)	$ 10,096

Accounts receivable immediately increase by the amount of credit sales and fall to zero when the accounts are collected 30 days later. These features of the new policy are placed on a time line in Exhibit 12.1.

The present value of the resulting cash flows, discounted at Country's opportunity cost of 9 percent per year, is

$$\text{PV(single week's sales)} = \frac{\$10,096}{(1 + 0.09/365)^{30}} - \$4,000$$

$$= \$6,022.$$

Assuming the incremental cost of administering the new payment terms is $1,000, the present value of *annual* sales is

$$\text{PV(annual sales)} = \$6,022 \times \text{APVF}_{0.09/52,52} - \$1,000$$

$$= \$298,219.$$

The new policy improved the owners' wealth by $93 after deducting administrative costs.[8]

The company's days'-sales-outstanding over this 30-day interval equals its investment in receivables, $10,096, divided by its sales per day, $336.53.

$$DSO = \$10,096/\$336.53 = 30 \text{ days}^9$$

Applying this value to Country's *annual* sales of $524,992 ($10,096 × 52), its average investment in receivables throughout the year is $43,150 ($524,992 × 30/365).

Accounting for Changes in Demand   The preceding example was simplified by assuming every distributor's opportunity cost was 12 percent. Consequently, the present value of the credit price equaled the cash price for every distributor and none of them changed the quantity of wood chips they were willing to buy. In reality, the distributors may have different opportunity costs because they have different access to the financial markets. Customers with good access to financing may have an opportunity cost less than 12 percent while customers with poor access to financing may have an opportunity cost greater than 12 percent. The former will view a price of $12.62 payable in 30 days as a price increase in comparison to $12.50 cash on delivery while the latter will view these terms as a price decrease.

Suppose 60 percent of the distributors who purchase wood chips from Country have an opportunity cost of 10 percent and the remaining 40 percent have an opportunity cost of 15 percent. The present values of the $12.62 credit price to these customers are

$$PV(\text{to 10\% customers}) = \$12.62/(1 + 0.10/365)^{30}$$
$$= \$12.52 > \$12.50 \text{ (cash price)}$$
$$PV(\text{to 15\% customers}) = \$12.62/(1 + 0.15/365)^{30}$$
$$= \$12.47 < \$12.50 \text{ (cash price)}.$$

Country's low opportunity cost customers interpret the new credit terms as a price increase and its high opportunity cost customers interpret the new terms as a price decrease.

Because of these price changes, Country should expect its low opportunity cost customers to buy a smaller quantity of wood chips and its high opportunity cost customers to buy a larger quantity. The anticipated changes in sales volume and any resulting changes in the costs of producing the product must be incorporated in the cash flow estimates.

The low opportunity cost distributors originally purchased 480 cubic yards of wood chips per week (0.60 × 800 yards) while the high opportunity cost distributors purchased the remaining 320 cubic yards. Suppose sales to low opportunity cost customers

---

[8]You get the same answer by discounting the *change* in the present value of one week's sales and subtracting the administrative costs.

$$\text{Change in PV} = (\$6,022 - \$6,000) \times \text{APVF}_{0.09/52,52} - \$1,000$$
$$= \$22 \times 49.6876 - \$1,000 = \$93$$

[9]You know this value is correct because, with no early payments, late payments, or bad debts, the company's DSO must equal its credit period.

decrease from 480 to 455 cubic yards per week and sales to high opportunity cost customers increase to 340 yards per week. Total sales are therefore 795 cubic yards.

$$\text{Weekly credit sales} = \$12.62 \times 795 \text{ yards} = \$10,033$$

$$\text{Weekly cost of sales} = \$5.00 \times 795 \text{ yards} = \$3,975$$

$$\text{PV(single week's sales)} = \frac{\$10,033}{(1 + 0.09/365)^{30}} - \$3,975$$

$$= \$5,984$$

$$\text{PV(annual sales)} = \$5,984 \times \text{APVF}_{0.09/52,52} - \$1,000$$

$$= \$296,331$$

The net 30 credit terms are not acceptable when Country recognizes that decreased sales to low opportunity cost distributors will reduce the net present value.

Financial Analysis of Cash Discount Credit Terms   Country Wood Farm could improve the net present value *if* it could charge each group a different credit price or if it could provide the new terms to only the high opportunity cost distributors. In the latter case, the low opportunity cost customers would pay a cash price of $12.50 per yard and continue to buy 480 cubic yards per week while the high opportunity cost customers would pay a present value price of $12.47 and buy 340 cubic yards. Unfortunately, the Robinson-Patman Act prohibits either type of discrimination in granting credit.

The company can accomplish the same result by placing the decision to purchase with cash or on credit in the *customers'* hands. Here's how it's done. Country prices its product at $12.62 with payment in 30 days or $12.50 with payment on delivery. The $0.12 difference is a cash discount for early payment. Written in the traditional format, the company's credit terms are $12.62, 1/0 net 30 where the 1 percent cash discount is $0.12/$12.62 and 0 indicates the discounted payment is due on delivery.

You can see how this will work by calculating the financing charge implicit in the credit terms. To do this, place the cash flows on a time line and solve for the internal rate of return. The cash flow on day t is the loan the customer receives by not paying the discounted invoice at that time, $I \times (1 - d)$. The cash flow on day $n(I)$ is the repayment of this loan with interest.

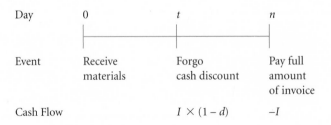

where I = full amount of invoice
d = cash discount
t = due date to obtain cash discount
n = final due date

The internal rate of return of these cash flows is obtained by setting the net present value equal to zero and solving for the rate of return, r.

$$\text{NPV} = 0 = \frac{-I}{(1 + r/365)^{n-t}} + [I \times (1 - d)]$$

Substituting $\{1 + [(n - t) \times r]/365\}$ for $(1 + r/365)^{n-t}$ and rearranging terms gives the approximate value of r.

$$r = \frac{d}{(1 - d)} \times \frac{365}{(n - t)} \qquad [12.1]$$

Applying this expression for the implicit cost of forgoing a cash discount to Country Wood Farm's credit terms, 1/0 net 30, we get

$$r = \frac{0.01}{0.99} \times \frac{365}{30} = .123 \text{ or } 12.3\%.^{10}$$

● —————————————————————————————— ●   EXERCISE

COST OF FORGOING A CASH DISCOUNT   12.2

What effective annual interest rate does a company pay by forgoing a cash discount when the terms are 2/10 net 30?

$$r = \frac{d}{(1 - d)} \times \frac{365}{(n - t)}$$

$$= \frac{0.02}{0.98} \times \frac{365}{20} = .3724 \text{ or } 37.24\%$$

By forgoing the cash discount and paying on day 30, the company borrows money at an implicit interest rate of 37.24 percent per year.

● ————————— ●

Distributors with an opportunity cost less than 12.3 percent will pay cash to avoid borrowing from the supplier at this rate; those with an opportunity cost greater than 12.3 percent will pay on day 30 to take advantage of the favorable interest rate. In Country's case, 60 percent of its customers will pay cash and the remainder will use trade credit. This makes the new credit policy profitable as the continuation of our example shows.

When credit terms are 1/0 net 30, Country's weekly sales and costs are

Weekly cash sales = 12.50×480 yards = \$6,000

Weekly credit sales = 12.62×340 yards = \$4,291

Weekly cost of sales = 5.00×820 yards = \$4,100.

———————

[10]The effective annual interest rate would be exactly 12 percent if not for rounding.

Exhibit 12.2

**COUNTRY WOOD FARM RESULTS OF A TYPICAL
WEEK'S SALES WITH TERMS 1/0 NET 30**

	Day	0	30
Events		Sell chips, pay costs, collect cash sales	Collect receivables

Income Statements

		0	30
Sales		$10,291	$ 0
Costs of sales		4,100	0
Net income		$ 6,191	$ 0

Accounts Receivable

Beginning balance		$ 0	$4,291
Credit sales		4,291	0
Collections		0	4,291
Ending balance		$ 4,291	$ 0

Cash Flow

Net income		$ 6,191	$ 0
Minus change in accounts receivable		4,291	(4,291)
Net cash flow		$ 1,900	$4,291

Cash sales minus cash costs equals the net cash flow of $1,900 on the day of the sale. Credit sales cause accounts receivable to increase to $4,291 that day and remain at this level for 30 days until the accounts are collected. These cash flows are shown in Exhibit 12.2. The present values of these cash flows are

$$PV(\text{single week's sales}) = \$1,900 + \frac{\$4,291}{(1 + 0.09/365)^{30}}$$
$$= \$6,159$$
$$PV(\text{annual sales}) = (\$6,159 \times APVF_{0.09/52,52}) - \$1,000$$
$$= \$305,026.$$

The new credit policy makes the extension of credit profitable by allowing customers with different opportunity costs to select the best credit terms.

The new policy also reduces the company's average investment in receivables and its days'-sales-outstanding ratio because some customers accept the discount and pay early. The level of accounts receivable is constant at $4,291 and sales per day are $343

IN THE NEWS

LATE PAYMENTS CAN SINK A BUSINESS

THE BIG-BUSINESS slowdown in paying suppliers is getting worse, and it is squeezing small business. Lawrence Winters, a Dun & Bradstreet Corporation assistant vice-president, says some large companies are routinely paying their bills as much as 90 days after receiving invoices, routinely due in 30 days. Not all warn vendors.

Earthly Elements Inc. didn't anticipate how much an overdue payment would hurt. When the maker of dried floral gifts and accessories landed a $10,000 order from a national home-shopping service in November, founder Thomas Re says he threw a party. The order represented 20 percent of the start-up's $50,000 in orders for 1993.

But by the end of February, Earthly Elements was no longer rejoicing. Mr. Re says fulfilling the order cost 25 percent more than expected, and then the payment was 30 days overdue. Faced with a worsening cash crunch, Mr. Re delayed paying his own bills and began to lay off employees. Mr. Re, who started the Randolph, N.J., business in March 1993 by borrowing against his house, wasn't willing to borrow more. In March 1994, he closed shop. By the time the customer paid in April, "it was way too late" to revive the company, Mr. Re says.

Source: Michael Selz, "Big Customers' Late Bills Choke Small Suppliers," *The Wall Street Journal*, June 22, 1994, p. B1.

($10,291/30); therefore, days'-sales-outstanding is 12.5 days ($4,291/$343) compared to 30 days when terms were net 30.

The preceding example shows that offering a cash discount permits a company to offer credit terms appropriate for different customers without resorting to illegal forms of discrimination. Another advantage is that the seller may not be able to identify these customers in advance but the credit terms induce them to identify themselves. Consequently, the seller knows which customers have less risk and are more reliable and which have more risk and may not be reliable in the long run. The seller can afford to make commitments to its high-quality customers and vice versa.

Accounting for Late Payments and Bad Debts   Recognizing that all customers may not have the same opportunity cost made our example more realistic. Nevertheless, it is still too simple because we have ignored the possibility that some customers who are given possession of a product before they pay for it may pay late or not at all. This can be a serious problem, especially for small businesses (see "In the News"). Although it is difficult to predict which customers will not pay their trade credit debts when they are due, it is easy to incorporate the predictions in a present value analysis of alternative credit terms.

Late payments and defaults merely change the timing of the cash flows from credit sales. Late payments are received after the stated due date and defaulted payments are never received. These effects are incorporated in the present value analysis by simply distributing the cash flows from credit sales over the days on which they are expected to be collected. The difference between the amount of credit sales and the sum of the collected cash flows equals bad debts. By carefully specifying the timing and amount of the cash flows the company actually collects, an analyst can determine whether the credit policy has a positive NPV even if all customers do not behave as planned. Let's continue our example as an illustration.

Country Wood Farm estimates that 80 percent of its high opportunity cost distributors (those who accept 30 days' credit) will pay on the due date, 10 percent will pay 30 days late, 6 percent will pay 60 days late, and the remaining 4 percent will be written off as uncollectible. Applying these percentages to a typical week's sales,

Weekly cash sales = $12.50 × 480 yards = $6,000

Weekly credit sales = $12.62 × 340 yards = $4,291

Weekly cost of sales = $5.00 × 820 yards = $4,100

Sales receipts

Collected on day 0		= $6,000
Collected on day 30	$4,291 × 0.80 =	3,433
Collected on day 60	4,291 × 0.10 =	429
Collected on day 90	4,291 × 0.06 =	257
Uncollectible	4,291 × 0.04 =	172

These cash flows are placed on a time line in Exhibit 12.3. Cash sales minus cash costs equal the net cash flow of $1,900 on the day of the sale. Adding the present value of the cash flows collected on days 30, 60, and 90 gives the present value of a single week's sales.

$$PV(\text{single week's sales}) = \$1,900 + \frac{\$3,433}{(1 + 0.09/365)^{30}} + \frac{\$429}{(1 + 0.09/365)^{60}}$$
$$+ \frac{\$257}{(1 + 0.09/365)^{90}} = \$5,982$$

The present value of annual sales is the present value of weekly sales discounted as an annuity of 52 weeks.

$$PV(\text{annual sales}) = (\$5,982 \times APVF_{0.09/52,52}) - \$1,000 = \$296,231$$

The new credit terms are unacceptable because late payments and defaults cause the net present value to be less than the net present value of cash on delivery even though total sales have increased by 20 cubic yards per week.

Late payments and bad debts also increase a company's investment in receivables and days'-sales-outstanding ratio. For Country, the new average investment in receivables is

$$\text{Average investment in receivables} = [(\$4,291 \times 30 \text{ days}) + (\$858 \times 30 \text{ days}) +$$
$$(\$429 \times 30 \text{ days})]/90 \text{ days} = \$1,859.$$

Average sales per day over the collection period are $114 ($10,291/90). Days'-sales-outstanding is therefore 16.3 days ($1,859/$114) compared to 12.5 days without late payments and defaults.[11]

---

[11]The fact DSO is longer does not, by itself, indicate the credit policy is unacceptable. This can only be determined by computing present values.

Exhibit 12.3

COUNTRY WOOD FARM RESULTS OF A TYPICAL WEEK'S SALES WHEN SOME CUSTOMERS PAY LATE OR DEFAULT

Day	0	30	60	90
Event	Sell chips, pay costs	Collect receivables	Collect receivables	Collect receivables, write off bad debts

Income Statements

Sales	$10,291	$ 0	$ 0	$ 0
Bad debts	0	0	0	172
Net revenue	10,291	0	0	(172)
Cost of sales	4,100	0	0	0
Net income	$ 6,191	$ 0	$ 0	$(172)

Accounts Receivable

Beginning balance	$ 0	$4,291	$ 858	$ 429
Credit sales	4,291	0	0	0
Collections	0	3,433	429	257
Bad debts written off	0	0	0	172
Ending balance	$ 4,291	$ 858	$ 429	$ 0

Cash Flow

Net income	$ 6,191	$ 0	$ 0	$(172)
Minus change in accounts receivable	4,291	(3,433)	(429)	$(429)
Net cash flow	$ 1,900	$3,433	$ 429	$ 257

EXERCISE

COMPREHENSIVE PROBLEM

12.3

Oklahoma Clay Products Company (OCPC) sells facing brick for $225 per 1,000, cash on delivery. The cost of producing the bricks is $135 per thousand, paid at the time of the sale. The company sells 100,000 bricks each week, which provides operating cash flows of $9,000 [($225 × 100) – ($135 × 100)].

The sales and credit managers are evaluating a proposal to increase the price of the bricks to $230 per 1,000, payable 45 days after delivery; however, the company will give a 2 percent cash discount for payments on the 15th day. The sales manager expects to sell 37,000 bricks to customers who accept the cash discount and 68,000 to customers who use the full credit period. The credit manager expects that 3 percent of the customers who do not pay on the 15th will never pay. Should OCPC adopt the new credit terms if its opportunity cost is 15 percent?

The first step is to compute the cash costs and cash collections.

$$\text{Costs} = \frac{37,000 + 68,000}{1,000} \times \$135 \text{ per } 1,000 = \$14,175$$

$$\begin{array}{l} \text{Amount collected} \\ \text{from customers that} \\ \text{take the discount} \end{array} = \frac{37,000}{1,000} \times \$230 \times (1 - 0.02)$$

$$= \$8,339.80$$

$$\begin{array}{l} \text{Amount collected} \\ \text{from customers that} \\ \text{don't take the discount} \end{array} = \frac{68,000}{1,000} \times \$230 \times (1 - 0.03)$$

$$= \$15,170.80$$

The present value of a single week's cash flows at the company's opportunity cost of 15 percent per year is

$$\text{PV(new policy)} = \$-14,175 + \frac{\$8,339.80}{(1 + 0.15/365)^{15}} + \frac{\$15,170.80}{(1 + 0.15/365)^{45}}$$

$$= \$9,006.44.$$

The present value of the new policy is only slightly higher than the present value of the old policy ($9,006.44 versus $9,000). The additional $6.44 probably does not cover the cost of administering trade credit, so OCPC should continue to sell its bricks for $225, cash on delivery.

● ———————— ●

Establishing and Enforcing Credit Standards

The final example in the last section shows that losses caused by extending credit to customers who pay late or not at all can make an otherwise sound credit policy unacceptable. Companies that can identify these poor credit risks in advance reduce these losses and thereby preserve the benefits of lending money to their creditworthy customers. Companies determine whether a customer is a poor or good credit risk by gathering facts and opinions that reduce the asymmetric information between them. The information they use for this purpose may come from their own experience, from the customer, or from the experience of others. In any case, a company can use fundamental valuation principles to determine the amount of information to acquire and how to interpret it.

Information Required for Credit Analysis   The objective of credit analysis is to determine the likelihood a customer will be willing and able to pay its debts when they are due. A traditional method for assessing this likelihood is to examine the customer's *character, capacity,* and *capital* as well as *conditions* in the economy. These factors are known as the "four Cs of credit" although analysts sometimes add a fifth factor, the availability of *collateral.* The first two factors consider whether the managers are trustworthy and competent while the third considers the company's financial condition. Taking general economic conditions into account may produce a more or less favorable assessment than one based on the company's situation alone.

Some proponents of the four Cs approach to credit analysis apply the method subjectively but this is not necessary or advisable. Although references may be used as the basis for a subjective assessment of character, past payment history provides the basis for an objective assessment. Furthermore, most companies analyze a customer's financial statements to obtain an objective assessment of its capacity and capital. Both simple and elaborate forms of financial statement analysis are used for this purpose, as we will see shortly.

The references, past payment history, and financial statements used for credit analysis may be obtained from a variety of sources. Perhaps the most reliable source of information is a company's own experience with the customer. The customer's credit file typically contains historical financial statements, evaluations and comments by credit and sales managers, a payment history, and a description of its account as current or past due. Companies consider this information such a reliable predictor of future payment behavior that they perform only a cursory analysis of a credit request from existing customers whose accounts are in good standing.

Companies that have no experience with a credit applicant must obtain the information from other sources. Customers are an indispensable source of information but they are likely to describe themselves in the most favorable terms. Consequently, many companies contact a customer's other suppliers and banks to verify and supplement the information the customer provides. These other lenders can legally share factual credit information but are cautious because they must avoid saying anything that might defame the credit applicant or influence the company's credit decision.

Credit reporting agencies compile information about borrowers and sell it to banks and companies that extend trade credit. A typical credit report includes a company's abbreviated financial statements, a summary of its operations and history, a description of its banking relationships, and an assessment of whether it pays its bills promptly or slowly. Some agencies also provide credit ratings analogous to the ratings assigned to a company's commercial paper and long-term debt.

Two prominent credit reporting agencies are The Dun and Bradstreet Corporation, which prepares reports on companies in the United States and other countries, and The Teikoku Databank, which specializes in the Japanese market. Credit managers themselves exchange information about their experiences with customers through the National Association of Credit Management and its affiliates. This association prepares general interest reports that are supplemented by its industry credit groups with reports of interest to specific industries.

Financial Statement Analysis   Most companies perform some type of financial statement analysis to help them assess a customer's ability to pay its debts when they are due. This analysis may be as simple as calculating a few basic financial ratios such as those described in Appendix 2A.

More complicated forms of financial statement analysis use statistical models to identify ratios that explain or predict some characteristic related to credit risk. Lawrence Fisher found that a measure of earnings variability and a market-value debt ratio helped explain the risk premium on corporate bonds.[12] Edward Altman conducted a number of studies on financial distress and found that liquidity, profitability, turnover, and leverage ratios were useful for identifying solvent and insolvent companies.[13]

Companies can use these statistical models or variations of them to compute a customer's *credit score* that is the basis for granting or denying credit or for establishing its credit limit. Alternatively, companies can use these models as a guide for choosing the ratios to compute in their own form of financial statement analysis. In either case, caution is required because financial statements are subject to all the limitations caused by the use of accrual accounting as described in Chapter 2.

Determining the Value of Credit Information   Effective credit analysis distinguishes between customers who will pay their debts when they are due and those who will pay late or not at all. Consequently, a company that spends money on credit analysis should expect an improvement in the timing and amount of cash flows from credit sales. Increasing the intensity of credit analysis enlarges these benefits but also increases the cost. The best level of credit analysis is the one that provides the greatest NPV of benefits over costs. This level of analysis will only coincidentally be the one that produces the smallest investment in accounts receivable or lowest level of bad debts.

Monitoring the Investment in Receivables[14]

Companies monitor their investment in accounts receivable to determine if their employees are following the established credit policy and to determine if their customers are paying their bills when they are due. They may routinely monitor large accounts individually but they usually monitor the status of an entire portfolio of small accounts to save costs. Some companies calculate the days'-sales-outstanding ratio for this purpose and believe a change in its value signals an improvement or deterioration in the quality of credit management.

The DSO ratio is a poor indicator of the quality of credit management, however, because its value is sensitive to changes in sales levels and may indicate a change in payment behavior when no such change has taken place. A better way to monitor this process is simply to determine the proportion of credit sales for a particular period that are paid in subsequent periods. An improvement or deterioration in this payment pattern correctly signals whether customers are paying their accounts earlier or later. This problem is illustrated by the following example.

The treasurer of Johnson Service Company noticed an increase in the company's investment in accounts receivable and asked her financial analyst, Jeff Gallinger, to investigate. Jeff obtained records of the company's credit sales and accounts receivable for the past four months and computed the days'-sales-outstanding ratios in panel A of Table

---

[12] See Lawrence Fisher, "Determinants of Risk Premiums on Corporate Bonds," *Journal of Political Economy*, June 1959, pp. 217–237.

[13]See Edward I. Altman, "Financial Ratios, Discriminant Analysis and the Prediction of Corporate Bankruptcy," *Journal of Finance*, September 1968, pp. 589–609.

[14]For additional information about this method of monitoring accounts receivable, see Wilbur G. Lewellen and Robert W. Johnson, "Better Way to Monitor Accounts Receivable," *Harvard Business Review*, May–June 1972, pp. 101–109.

JOHNSON SERVICE COMPANY ANALYSIS OF INVESTMENT IN RECEIVABLES   **Table 12.1**

Panel A: Calculation of Days'-Sales-Outstanding Ratio

	September	October	November	December
Credit sales				
Total	$1,200	$2,400	$4,800	$6,000
Per day	40	80	160	200
Accounts receivable	$1,200	$2,640	$5,280	$6,960
Days'-sales-outstanding	30.0	33.0	33.0	34.8

Panel B: Calculation of Payment Proportions

	September	October	November	December
Accounts receivable				
Beginning balance	$ 0	$1,200	$2,640	$5,280
Credit sales	$1,200	$2,400	$4,800	$6,000
Collections				
From 1st prior month's credit sales				
Amount (proportion)	$ 0	$ 960 (80%)	$1,920 (80%)	$3,840 (80%)
From 2nd prior month's credit sales				
Amount (proportion)	0	0	240 (20%)	480 (20%)
Total	$ 0	$ 960	$2,160	$4,320
Ending balance	$1,200	$2,640	$5,280	$6,960

12.1 as the basis for his report. The 16 percent increase in days' sales outstanding from 30 to 34.8 days looked alarming.

Jeff checked with the credit manager before finishing his report to the treasurer and was glad he did. The credit manager pointed out that the company had obtained a substantial increase in sales during this time period and therefore should *expect* an increase in receivables. Furthermore, the credit manager used the information in panel B of Table 12.1 to show Jeff that the pattern of payments from credit customers was invariant throughout the period. At the end of 30 days, 80 percent of credit sales were paid and the remaining 20 percent were paid at the end of 60 days. Jeff concluded that the complete absence of any variation in the payment pattern implied the increase in receivables was solely due to the increase in sales even though the company's days'-sales-outstanding during the period increased from 30 to nearly 35 days.

● ─────────────────────────────────────── ●   E X E R C I S E

CALCULATING PAYMENT PROPORTIONS   **12.4**

Johnson Service Company's credit sales and collections for April, May, and June are given below. Did the company's customers' payment behavior change during this period?

	April	May	June
Accounts receivable			
Beginning balance	$4,005	$4,355	$4,355
Credit sales	1,500	1,200	1,245
Collections			
From 1st prior month's sales	700	900	660
From 2nd prior month's sales	$ 450	$ 300	$ 585
Total	1,150	1,200	1,245
Ending balance	$4,355	$4,355	$4,355

There is enough information to compute the proportion of the first prior month's credit sales collected in May and in June. These proportions are

April's credit sales collected in May = $900/$1,500 = 0.60 or 60.0%

May's credit sales collected in June = $660/$1,200 = 0.55 or 55.0%.

The decline in these proportions indicates the company's customers are not paying their accounts as quickly in June as they did in May.

● —————————— ●

12.3   FINANCIAL MANAGEMENT OF PAYABLES

The financial management of payables is similar to the financial management of receivables because both involve trade credit. The difference is that receivables management concerns the trade credit a company provides to its customers while payables management involves the trade credit a company receives from its suppliers. Receiving credit requires less analysis than extending credit because the company simply responds to the credit policies established by others. Nevertheless, we will see that the fundamental valuation principles we used to evaluate alternative credit policies in Section 12.2 also can be used to evaluate alternative payment policies.

Financial Analysis of Payment Policies

A financial analysis of alternative payment policies is performed by computing the present value of the cash payments. From a purely financial point of view, the policy with the lowest present value of costs is best.

Sometimes, you can get an *indication* of which payment policy is best by comparing the implicit or explicit interest rate on trade credit loans to the interest rate at which the company can borrow money elsewhere. For example, Exercise 12.2 showed that when the payment terms are 2/10 net 30, the implicit cost of using trade credit as a source of financing between days 10 and 30 is 37.24 percent. This implicit interest rate suggests that a company with a lower opportunity cost, say 18 percent, should always take the discount and use another method of financing for the period between days 10 and 30. This conclusion is premature, however, because the calculations ignore the costs of processing payments. Considering these costs may narrow the gap between the costs of trade credit and other sources of financing; the only way to be sure is to thoroughly analyze all the payment-related cash flows.

Determining the present value of alternative payment policies is easy in principle but difficult in practice because some of the cash flows are hard to estimate. Consequently, we'll begin with a simple example and add complexities as we go.

The Ajax Painting Company buys 200 gallons of paint for $5.00 per gallon 60 times a year or approximately every six days. The company pays for the paint when it is delivered so the present value of the cost of all 60 orders is

$$\text{Present value of costs} = \$1,000 \times [1 + APVF_{0.12/60,59}] = \$56,600.$$

There are no accounts payable when payment is cash on delivery, which makes the length of Ajax's payables period zero.

Now let's assume that competition from a new paint dealer prompts Ajax's supplier to offer two alternative payment plans that delay payment. The first alternative permits Ajax to pay for each month's purchases on the first day of the following month. Exhibit 12.4 describes the events and cash flows for a typical month under this policy. Accounts payable build up from zero to $5,000 in steps as the company purchases paint on credit. The balance is paid in full on the first of the following month. This pattern is repeated every month so the present value of Ajax's costs are simply

$$\text{Present value of costs} = \$5,000 \times APVF_{0.12/12,12} = \$56,275.$$

The opportunity to pay its bills once a month reduces the present value of Ajax's cost of goods sold by $325 ($56,600 − $56,275). Therefore, the supplier's offer of delayed payment is beneficial.

The average daily balance of Ajax's accounts payable under the new policy is determined by computing the weighted average of the daily balances shown in Exhibit 12.4. The calculations are

$$\begin{aligned} \text{Average accounts payable} &= [(\$1,000 \times 6 \text{ days}) + (\$2,000 \times 6 \text{ days}) + (\$3,000 \\ &\quad \times 6 \text{ days}) + (\$4,000 \times 6 \text{ days}) + (\$5,000 \\ &\quad \times 6 \text{ days})]/30 \text{ days} \\ &= \$90,000/30 \text{ days} \\ &= \$3,000. \end{aligned}$$

This $3,000 is financing that was not available to Ajax when payment was cash on delivery.[15]

Given the average level of the company's accounts payable and annual cost of goods sold, $60,000 ($1,000 × 60 orders), the length of Ajax's payment period, measured by days'-payables-outstanding, is

[15]Note that the $325 difference in the NPV of the two payment policies approximately equals the amount of financing provided by accounts payable, $3,000, multiplied by the company's opportunity cost of 12 percent. The amount of savings computed this way, $360, overstates the actual savings because accounts payable provide less than the average amount of financing early in each month when the present value benefits are higher.

Exhibit 12.4

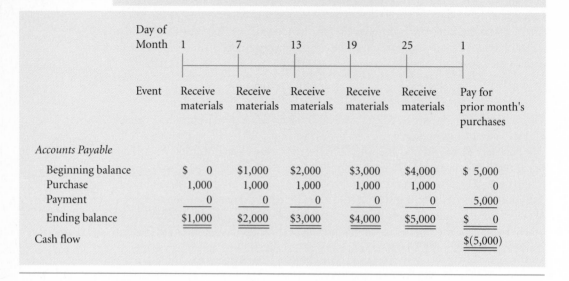

AJAX PAINTING COMPANY ACCOUNTS PAYABLE AND CASH FLOW WITH MONTHLY PAYMENTS

Day of Month	1	7	13	19	25	1
Event	Receive materials	Receive materials	Receive materials	Receive materials	Receive materials	Pay for prior month's purchases
Accounts Payable						
Beginning balance	$ 0	$1,000	$2,000	$3,000	$4,000	$ 5,000
Purchase	1,000	1,000	1,000	1,000	1,000	0
Payment	0	0	0	0	0	5,000
Ending balance	$1,000	$2,000	$3,000	$4,000	$5,000	$ 0
Cash flow						$(5,000)

$$DPO = \frac{\$3,000}{\$60,000/365} = 18.3 \text{ days.}$$

EXERCISE ●────────────────────────────────────●

12.5   PRESENT VALUES OF PAYMENT ALTERNATIVES

Air Movement Corporation manufactures fans and spends $50,000 for electric motors monthly. The supplier's payment terms are 1/10 net 30. Air Movement's opportunity cost is 11 percent per year.

Determine the implicit interest rate the company pays if it forgos the discount and pays on the 30th. Should Air Movement pay on the 10th and accept the discount or pay on the 30th? Confirm your answer by determining the present value of a typical purchase with payment on the 10th or 30th.

$$r = \frac{d}{(1-d)} \times \frac{365}{(n-d)} = \frac{0.01}{0.99} \times \frac{365}{20} = 0.1843 \text{ or } 18.43\%$$

Air Movement should pay on the 10th because the company can borrow elsewhere at less than 18 percent interest.

Present value of cost with payment on 10th = Cost $\times (1-d)/(1+r/365)^{10}$
$$= \$50,000 \times (1-0.01)/(1+0.11/365)^{10}$$
$$= \$49,351$$

Present value of cost with payment on 30th = Cost$/(1+r/365)^{30}$
$$= \$50,000/(1+0.11/365)^{30}$$
$$= \$49,550$$

Exhibit 12.5

**AJAX PAINTING COMPANY ACCOUNTS PAYABLE
AND CASH FLOW WITH WEEKLY PAYMENTS**

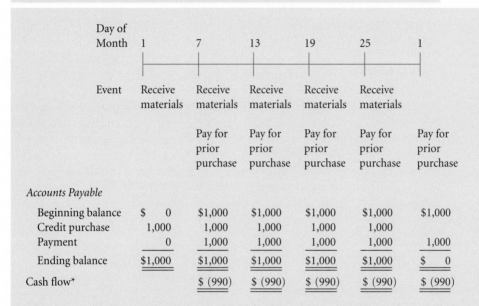

Day of Month	1	7	13	19	25	1
Event	Receive materials	Receive materials	Receive materials	Receive materials	Receive materials	
		Pay for prior purchase	Pay for prior purchase	Pay for prior purchase	Pay for prior purchase	Pay for prior purchase
Accounts Payable						
Beginning balance	$ 0	$1,000	$1,000	$1,000	$1,000	$1,000
Credit purchase	1,000	1,000	1,000	1,000	1,000	
Payment	0	1,000	1,000	1,000	1,000	1,000
Ending balance	$1,000	$1,000	$1,000	$1,000	$1,000	$ 0
Cash flow*		$ (990)	$ (990)	$ (990)	$ (990)	$ (990)

*Cash flow equals 0.99 of the payment credited to Ajax's account because the company receives a 1 percent cash discount for paying early.

Paying on the 10th to earn the 1 percent discount reduces the present value of the cost of each order by $199 ($49,550 − $49,351). The company should pay on the 10th.

• ———————— •

The second payment alternative permits Ajax to defer paying for a particular shipment until the next shipment is received. The supplier will discount the invoice by 1.0 percent as an inducement for Ajax to adopt this policy. Exhibit 12.5 describes the events and cash flows for a typical month under this policy. Accounts payable immediately build up to $1,000 and remain at this level throughout the year because subsequent payments equal purchases.

The full amount of the invoice is credited to Ajax's account although their periodic cash outflow is only $990 because the company receives the cash discount of 1 percent. This cost is paid 60 times each year so the present value of Ajax's costs are

$$\text{Present value of costs} = \$990 \times \text{APVF}_{0.12/60,60} = \$55,922.$$

The average level of accounts payable is $1,000 while cost of goods sold is $59,400 ($990 × 60 orders). Days'-payables-outstanding is therefore

$$\text{DPO} = \frac{\$1,000}{\$59,400/365} = 6.1 \text{ days.}$$

Table 12.2   AJAX PAINTING COMPANY SUMMARY OF PAYMENT POLICIES

	C.O.D.	Pay Monthly	Pay Weekly
Average level of accounts payable	$ 0	$ 3,000	$ 1,000
Days'-payables-outstanding	0	18.3	6.1
Present value of costs	$56,600	$56,275	$55,922

The characteristics of the three payment alternatives are summarized in Table 12.2. Both new policies are preferable to the supplier's current terms because they permit delayed payment or provide a cash discount for early payment. The cash discount policy has the lowest present value of costs, primarily because the company receives a cash discount for early payment. This discount more than makes up for the fact that Ajax obtains less financing from its supplier under these terms.[16] This is the payment policy the company should adopt if all relevant costs are included here.

EXERCISE •

12.6   ACCOUNTS PAYABLE AND DAYS' PAYABLES OUTSTANDING

Refer to Exercise 12.5 where you determined that Air Movement Corporation should pay on the 10th and accept a cash discount. What is the company's average level of accounts payable and days'-payables-outstanding during a typical month if it follows this policy or pays on the 30th? Is it always wise to choose the payment policy that lengthens days'-payables-outstanding?

Payment on 10th

$$\text{Average accounts payable} = [(\$50,000 \times 10 \text{ days}) + (\$0 \times 20 \text{ days})]/30 \text{ days}$$
$$= \$16,667$$
$$\text{Cost of goods sold per day} = \$50,000 \times (1 - 0.01)/30$$
$$= \$1,650$$
$$\text{DPO} = \$16,667/\$1,650 = 10.1 \text{ days}$$

Payment on 30th

$$\text{Average accounts payable} = (\$50,000 \times 30 \text{ days})/30 \text{ days}$$
$$= \$50,000$$
$$\text{Cost of goods sold per day} = \$50,000/30$$
$$= \$1,667$$
$$\text{DPO} = \$50,000/\$1,667 = 30.0 \text{ days}$$

---

[16]The actual net savings under the cash discount policy, $353.62, approximately equals
Amount of the discount: $0.01 \times \$60,000 = \$600$
Minus opportunity cost of less financing: $-0.12 \times (\$3,000 - \$1,000) = \underline{240}$
Net saving: $\$360$

You can't base the decision on the days'-payables-outstanding ratio. Paying on the 30th provides the largest amount of financing from suppliers; paying on the 10th has a lower present value cost.

● ─────────── ●

Other Factors to Consider

Before making this choice, Ajax should consider other costs and benefits of trade credit. First, processing invoices and issuing and clearing checks are costly and the cash discount policy requires the company to process five times as many payments as the monthly policy. Therefore, the company's payables manager must consider the cost of processing payments to determine which policy is actually best (see "In the News").

One way to approach this problem is to determine the cost at which the company is indifferent between the two policies. This is accomplished by solving the following equation for the break-even cost

$$\text{Cost of Monthly Payment} = \text{Cost of Weekly Payment}$$
$$\$56{,}275 + (12 \times P) = \$55{,}922 + (60 \times P)$$

where P = cost of processing an individual payment.[17]

The solution to this equation is $P = \$7.35$. Ajax should pay invoices once a month if the cost of processing payments is greater than $7.35 each and adopt the cash discount policy otherwise.

Second, longer payment periods give a customer more opportunities to discover product defects and request corrective action. This factor seems to favor the monthly payment policy. However, the very fact that the supplier *offers* this alternative may signal its confidence in the paint's quality. Ajax therefore may be able to use the information implicit in the delayed payment policy without paying for it by forgoing the cash discount. We will revisit this problem in Chapter 13 when we look at the opportunity to return a defective product as a put option.

12.4   THE PAYMENT SYSTEM

Money must be used to pay for goods and services. There is no other choice. Nevertheless, advances in technology have broadened our definition of money and provided alternative payment media. The many alternatives available in a modern financial system are based on currency, demand deposit accounts, or credit.

Overview of the Payment System

Currency-based payment systems are simple and familiar; the traders simultaneously exchange the goods or services for currency without the involvement of a third party.

---

[17]This cost should be in present value terms; however, little accuracy is lost by ignoring the time value of money for this part of the problem.

IN THE NEWS

PROCTER & GAMBLE STREAMLINES ITS PAYMENT POLICIES

PROCTER & GAMBLE Co. will tell retailers today it will standardize and streamline the way they pay for and receive shipments of its products. Currently, retailers ordering P&G health and beauty aids qualify for 2 percent cash discounts when they pay the company within 30 days, retailers that order P&G soaps and food and beverages have only 10 days to qualify for the 2 percent discount, and those that order paper goods have 15 days to pay for the goods to receive the 2 percent discount.

Under the new system, there won't be any distinction among these categories. Whether they're ordering Crisco shortening, Crest toothpaste, or Charmin toilet tissue, retailers will have 19 days to qualify for the 2 percent discount. Additionally, the payment clock will start ticking when the retailer receives the merchandise. Currently, it starts when the products leave P&G warehouses. This will give retailers across the board a few more days in which to pay the company. P&G also will move to a shipping system designed to encourage retailers to order full truckloads of its products, a plan that has been under consideration since last fall.

By changing payment and shipping terms, P&G will decrease the number of invoices retailers handle by 25 percent to 75 percent, according to the company. For retailers, the cost of handling each P&G invoice is between $35 and $75, P&G said. P&G estimates that its own savings will be substantial in the long run. The company says that as many as 25 percent of orders, or 27,000 a month, require manual corrections by P&G employees.

Source: Gabriella Stern, "Retailers of P&G to Get New Plan on Bills, Shipments," *The Wall Street Journal*, June 22, 1994, p. A12.

The simplicity of this system also creates problems because currency can be lost or stolen and it is inconvenient for large transactions. In addition, using currency for payment poses problems due to asymmetric information if the buyer cannot determine the quality of the goods at the time the exchange takes place.

A demand deposit or checking account functions as money because it is a store of value that is easily transferred to others. The transfer usually is accomplished by check but debit cards are increasingly an important alternative. Depositors insert these magnetically encoded plastic cards in automatic teller machines (ATMs) to withdraw currency or present them to merchants to pay for purchases. The amount of the withdrawal or purchase is deducted from the owner's checking account. Depositors also can arrange for automatic, direct transfers into and out of their checking accounts by pre-authorizing electronic credits and debits. These transfers are widely used to handle repetitive transactions such as payroll checks and mortgage payments.

Finally, any device that provides direct and convenient access to a person's ability to borrow money can function as a credit-based payment medium. Bank and travel and entertainment credit cards such as MasterCard and the American Express card fully satisfy this criterion because the owner can directly present them to merchants to pay for a wide variety of goods and services. Other credit arrangements such as home mortgages and personal loans do not meet this standard because the principal of the loan must be used to pay for a specific asset or must be converted into currency or a demand deposit before the borrower can spend it.

Demand deposit–and credit-based payment systems have several advantages over a currency-based system. First, there is less risk of loss because checks and credit cards are *claims* to money rather than actual money and safeguards are built into the procedures for transferring these claims (signatures are required, for example). Second, these systems are convenient because the amount of a transfer can be described to the nearest penny. Third, the buyer receives some protection from the hazards of asymmetric information because the product and cash are not exchanged simultaneously. The buyer can stop payment on the check or withhold payment for a credit purchase if a subsequent inspection reveals the product is defective. Some credit card issuers even extend manufacturer's warranties on products purchased with their cards.

Of course, these payment systems have problems of their own. Merchants do not receive cash until the checks or credit card vouchers are collected and card issuers may suffer losses from bad debts if asymmetric information prevents them from identifying good and bad credit risks. Nevertheless, checks and credit cards are the dominant methods of payment in many countries because their advantages far outweigh the disadvantages.

Checks, debit cards, and credit cards instruct a financial intermediary to transfer money from one party to another. The transfer takes place when the item is collected. Checks and vouchers are collected by physically presenting them to a Federal Reserve or privately operated interbank network that nets the claims of member financial institutions. Resulting differences are settled via Fed reserve accounts. Then, the seller's demand deposit account is credited and the purchaser's demand deposit account or credit card balance is debited depending on the payment media used.

Preauthorized credits and debits, intercompany cash transfers, and some corporate-to-corporate payments are settled via an electronic interbank system called the Automated Clearing House (ACH). This system reduces transfer costs because paper checks and vouchers are not transported around the country.

The Length and Composition of the Cash Disbursement Period

The type of payment medium a buyer uses determines the length and composition of its cash disbursement period. No delay occurs between initiating payment and transferring cash from the buyer's account when the buyer pays with currency because currency *is* cash. Similarly, no delay occurs when the buyer wires money to the seller because the buyer's demand deposit account is debited when the transfer is initiated. Other payment media, including checks and electronic fund transfers using the ACH system, involve some delay. Mailed paper checks are the most common form of payment and are subject to the longest delay so we will discuss them first.

Exhibit 12.6 diagrams the process by which cash is transferred from the buyer to the seller when the buyer mails a paper check for payment. The buyer initiates the procedure by preparing and mailing the check and deducting the amount from its cash balance as reflected in its own accounting books; that is, from its **book balance**. Next, a *mail*

Exhibit 12.6

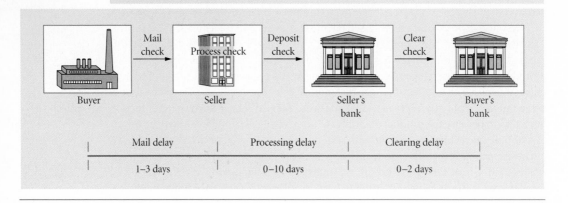

DIAGRAM OF CHECK COLLECTION PROCESS

delay occurs while the postal service delivers the check to the seller. Then, the seller processes the payment and sends the check to its own bank for deposit. The amount of time the seller requires for these tasks is called the *processing delay*. Finally, the seller's bank physically presents the check to the bank on which it was drawn where it is deducted from the **available balance** in the buyer's demand deposit account. The amount of time required for this part of the procedure is called the *clearing delay*. The typical lengths of these stages for checks mailed in the continental United States are 1–3 days for mail delay, 0–10 days for processing delay, and 0–2 days for clearing delay.

Electronic fund transfers using the ACH system reduce all three sources of delay. ACH payments are not mailed and the funds are transferred before the seller credits the buyer's account payable so the mail and processing delays are zero. Furthermore, an ACH transfer is effective the day after it is initiated, that is, its clearing delay is only one day.

12.5   FINANCIAL MANAGEMENT OF CASH DISBURSEMENTS

Section 12.4 described several payment media that buyers can use to pay their accounts payable. These media are currency, checks, and other devices that transfer ownership of their demand deposit accounts, and bank and travel and entertainment cards that provide access to their credit capacity. The main difference among these media and the payment policies based on them is the length of the delay between the time the buyer initiates payment and the time cash is transferred from its account. This delay, the cash disbursement period, increases the amount of financing obtained from trade credit. Consequently, the objective of financial management of cash disbursements is to identify disbursement policies that meet market-wide standards of financial performance without alienating suppliers who expect to receive timely payments on accounts payable.

Alternative Cash Disbursement Policies

The best cash disbursement policy minimizes the present value of the total cost of paying suppliers. Some companies pursue this objective by adopting policies that increase **disbursement float** to obtain opportunity cost savings. Others adopt policies that permit them to accurately estimate when cash will be transferred from their account so they can minimize their idle balances.

Policies That Maximize Disbursement Float   Mailed checks must be used as the payment medium if a company's objective is to maximize disbursement float because currency provides no float and electronic fund transfers clear in one day or less. In addition, a company can do obvious things to lengthen the amount of time it takes for its checks to clear. For example, to lengthen the mail delay, a company can send its checks from distant locations or locations where mail service is periodically interrupted by adverse weather conditions. It also can send checks that are not properly completed or that do not match the invoice. Finally, to lengthen the clearing delay, a company can write checks drawn on distant banks or small banks that do not receive the best service from the clearing system.

These tactics lengthen the cash disbursement period but are costly and may be ineffective. First, it is costly to establish and maintain distant mailing points and extra demand deposit accounts at banks used only for remote disbursing. Second, these tactics are obvious and often met with obvious responses from suppliers. Suppliers can negate the effect of mail delays by insisting that they *receive* the check by the due date. They also can significantly reduce processing delays by requiring the company to send its payment directly to a post office box, known as a **lock-box,** accessible to the supplier's bank. Bank employees remove envelopes from the lock-box several times a day and begin clearing the checks received there *before* the supplier processes the paperwork to credit the customer's account. Lock-boxes also reduce clearing delays because they can be placed near or even at the remote bank on which the checks are drawn. Finally, the Federal Reserve system has taken steps to speed check clearing because the float that arises from clearing delays is an unintended addition to the money supply.

Administrative costs, suppliers' responses, and Federal Reserve policies make the net savings from policies designed to maximize disbursement float smaller and less certain. The net savings after considering these factors may not compensate for the risk of alienating a company's suppliers by creating disbursement float at their expense. For this reason, many companies no longer use disbursement policies intended to maximize disbursement float.

Policies That Permit Accurate Funding of Demand Deposit Accounts   A simpler and more certain way to reduce the present value of the total cost of paying suppliers is to keep the cash in an interest-bearing account until the exact moment it must be transferred to them. This policy is easy to administer when payments are by currency, a wire transfer, or an ACH electronic fund transfer because their clearing times are known with certainty. Payments by currency and wire transfer are effective immediately so cash must be withdrawn from the interest-bearing account when these disbursements are initiated. ACH electronic fund transfers are effective the day after they are initiated so the cash can remain in the interest-bearing account until then.

Exhibit 12.7

HAWK LUMBER YARD'S OPERATING CYCLES

Panel A: Payment with Currency

Day	0		30	

Event	Receive plywood		Withdraw currency, pay Noble	
Income Statements				
Sales	$	0	$	0
Cost of sales		0		0
Net income	$	0	$	0
Accounts Payable	$12,000		$	0
Change to Book Cash Balance				
Net income	$	0	$	0
Plus change in payables		0		(12,000)
Net change	$	0	$(12,000)	
Cash Balance				
Available	$12,000		$	0
Book	12,000			0
Float	$	0	$	0

The amount of time it takes a mailed check to clear is uncertain but banks have developed a cash management product that permits companies to fund their demand deposit account only when a check arrives. This product is called a **zero-balance account (ZBA)**, and it works this way. The company writes checks on a ZBA but keeps no money there. Instead, the bank notifies the company on a daily basis of the amount of checks that have been presented. The company then transfers the exact amount of money needed to cover the checks from an interest-bearing account located in the same or a different bank. Companies can have several ZBAs to account for a wide variety of disbursements without incurring the opportunity cost of idle cash balances.

Financial Analysis of Cash Disbursement Policies

The cash disbursement period lengthens the payment phase of a buyer's operating cycle. This increases the amount of financing provided by accounts payable, which reduces

Exhibit 12.7

HAWK LUMBER YARD'S OPERATING CYCLES (continued)

Panel B: Payment by Check

Day	0	30	36
Event	Receive plywood	Pay Noble by check, deduct cash from book balance	Check clears, bank deducts cash from available balance

Income Statements

Sales	$ 0	$ 0	$0
Cost of sales	0	0	0
Net income	$ 0	$ 0	$0

Accounts Payable	$12,000	$ 0	$0

Change to Book Cash Balance

Net income	$ 0	$ 0	$0
Plus change in payables	0	(12,000)	0
Net change	$ 0	$(12,000)	$0

Cash Balance

Available	$12,000	$ 12,000	$0
Book	12,000	0	0
Float	$ 0	$ 12,000	$0

the amount of net working capital required for operations. Stated differently, a cash disbursement period greater than zero reduces the present value of the cost of purchased supplies and materials. These effects are easier to see in a simple numerical example.

Suppose the Hawk Lumber Yard purchases plywood from the Noble Wood Products Company for $12,000 with payment due in 30 days. Noble considers currency or a check received on the due date as timely methods of payment. The check is not presented to Hawk's bank for collection until six days later because of the cumulative effect of processing and clearing delays. The company's initial book and available cash balances are $12,000. The events and partial financial statements associated with these two disbursement alternatives are given in Exhibit 12.7. Hawk's opportunity is 10 percent.

The present values of the cost of the plywood under the two disbursement alternatives are

Payment with currency

$$PV(\text{cost of plywood}) = \frac{\$12,000}{(1 + 0.10/365)^{30}} = \$11,901.79$$

Payment by check

$$PV(\text{cost of plywood}) = \frac{\$12,000}{(1 + 0.10/365)^{36}} = \$11,882.24.$$

Paying by check reduces the cost of the plywood by $19.55 ($11,901.79 – $11,882.24).

Look closely at both panels of Exhibit 12.7 and notice that the company's available and book cash balances are always equal when they pay with currency but the available balance sometimes exceeds the book balance when they pay by check. The difference between these balances, which arises when the check is issued and persists until the check clears, is caused by processing and clearing delays. This difference between the available and book cash balances is the company's disbursement float. Hawk Lumber Yard has no disbursement float when it pays with currency and it has $12,000 of disbursement float for six days when it pays by check. At the company's opportunity cost of 10 percent per year, the value of this float is

Value of disbursement float = $12,000 × 6 days × 0.10/365 = $19.73.

The increase in value from paying by check approximately equals the reduction in the present value of the cost of the plywood, $19.55.

EXERCISE ●───●

12.7 **VALUE OF DISBURSEMENT ALTERNATIVES**

Lomas Farms trains thoroughbred racing horses at facilities in Oklahoma and California. On February 1, the company bought a promising young racehorse at a Texas auction for $750,000. Payment was due at the time of the sale but Frank Lomas had the choice of writing a check drawn on the company's Oklahoma or California banks. No mail delay occurs and the processing delay is the same for both banks, three days. The clearing delays for the Oklahoma and California checks are one and two days. How much money does Lomas Farms save by writing the check on its California bank? The company's opportunity cost is 12 percent per year.

Value of disbursement float = $750,000 × (5 days – 4 days) × 0.12/365

= $246.58

Using the California bank reduces the cost of the racehorse by approximately $246.58.

Confirm your answer by determining the exact net present value of the disbursement alternatives.

$$\text{Present value using Oklahoma bank} = \frac{\$750,000}{(1 + 0.12/365)^{4}} = \$749,014.51$$

$$\text{Present value using California bank} = \frac{\$750,000}{(1 + 0.12/365)^{5}} = \$748,768.34$$

Using the California bank reduces the present value of the racehorse's cost by $246.17, nearly the value of the disbursement float.

● ——————— ●

12.6   FINANCIAL MANAGEMENT OF CASH COLLECTIONS

Cash disbursements and collections are counterparts of the same process. Section 12.5 described how customers choose payment media to maximize their disbursement float or to make it predictable. This section describes how the companies they pay design systems to reduce this float.

Improving the Timing of Cash Inflows from Customers

From the recipient's perspective, float is called **collection float** but is caused by the same factors as disbursement float. Consequently, the systems companies use to reduce collection float are, for all practical purposes, designed to counteract the factors that increase disbursement float. Mailed checks are the most common payment medium used in the United States so we will examine their effect on the recipient more closely than other payment media.

Cash collection float is caused by mail, processing, and clearing delays. Companies can eliminate some of these delays and reduce others. Suppliers eliminate mail float by requiring that they receive the check by the due date. A simple way to reduce processing delays is to increase the efficiency of the accounts receivable department. For example, checks should be separated from other documents received from customers and deposited as quickly as possible. Large denomination checks probably should get special treatment to expedite processing.

A company with a large enough volume of checks or checks with high monetary value may use a lock-box, which substitutes a bank's check processing facilities for its own. Banks specialize in processing checks and therefore have mail handling and check sorting equipment to speed this operation. Using more than one lock-box reduces the average distance to customers' banks, which reduces clearing delays. That is, it takes less time for the lock-box banks to physically present the checks to the buyers' banks on which they are drawn.

Asking customers to pay electronically rather than by mailed check also is an effective way to reduce or eliminate collection float. This approach may be expensive initially if the company accepts both check and electronic payments and therefore must operate dual cash collection systems. The company also may need to offer an additional cash discount to induce customers to make the switch because they lose disbursement float. The adoption of integrated electronic ordering and payment systems by large companies such as the General Motors Corporation reduces the fixed-cost barriers to electronic payment. This eventually will reduce the requirement for dual payment systems and permit companies to calculate cash discounts for electronic payment that share the float and processing costs between the trading partners.

Exhibit 12.8

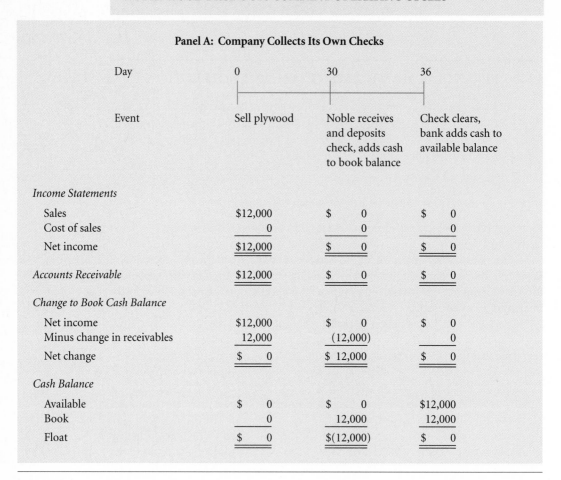

NOBLE WOOD PRODUCTS COMPANY OPERATING CYCLES

Panel A: Company Collects Its Own Checks

Day	0	30	36
Event	Sell plywood	Noble receives and deposits check, adds cash to book balance	Check clears, bank adds cash to available balance
Income Statements			
Sales	$12,000	$ 0	$ 0
Cost of sales	0	0	0
Net income	$12,000	$ 0	$ 0
Accounts Receivable	$12,000	$ 0	$ 0
Change to Book Cash Balance			
Net income	$12,000	$ 0	$ 0
Minus change in receivables	12,000	(12,000)	0
Net change	$ 0	$ 12,000	$ 0
Cash Balance			
Available	$ 0	$ 0	$12,000
Book	0	12,000	12,000
Float	$ 0	$(12,000)	$ 0

Financial Analysis of Cash Collection Policies

The cash inflows from customers are available at different times under alternative collection policies. Furthermore, these policies have different costs that depend on whether the company administers the systems or delegates administration to a bank. We will re-examine the Hawk Lumber Yard example of Section 12.2 from the seller's perspective to see these effects.

Recall that Hawk Lumber Yard purchased plywood from the Noble Wood Products Company for $12,000 and paid by check 30 days later. The funds represented by the check are not available to Noble for an additional six days, however, because of the cumulative effects of processing and clearing delays. A time line that describes the events and cash flows from Noble's perspective is shown in panel A of Exhibit 12.8. The present value of cash flow from the sale at Noble's required rate of return on assets of 10 percent is

Exhibit 12.8

NOBLE WOOD PRODUCTS COMPANY OPERATING CYCLES (continued)

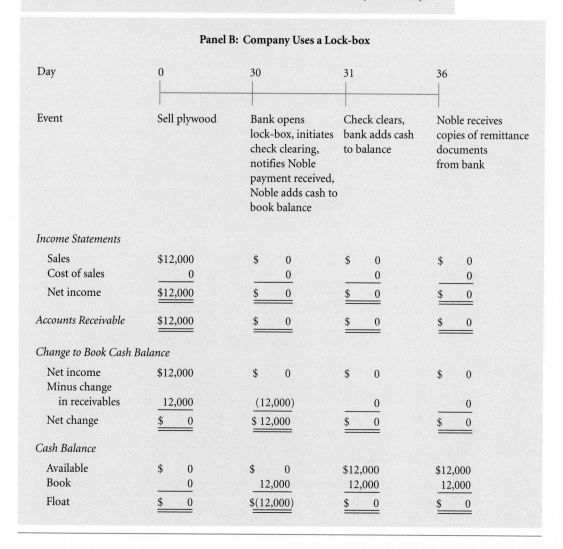

Panel B: Company Uses a Lock-box

Day	0	30	31	36
Event	Sell plywood	Bank opens lock-box, initiates check clearing, notifies Noble payment received, Noble adds cash to book balance	Check clears, bank adds cash to balance	Noble receives copies of remittance documents from bank

Income Statements				
Sales	$12,000	$ 0	$ 0	$ 0
Cost of sales	0	0	0	0
Net income	$12,000	$ 0	$ 0	$ 0

Accounts Receivable	$12,000	$ 0	$ 0	$ 0

Change to Book Cash Balance				
Net income	$12,000	$ 0	$ 0	$ 0
Minus change in receivables	12,000	(12,000)	0	0
Net change	$ 0	$ 12,000	$ 0	$ 0

Cash Balance				
Available	$ 0	$ 0	$12,000	$12,000
Book	0	12,000	12,000	12,000
Float	$ 0	$(12,000)	$ 0	$ 0

PV(cash flow from customers) = $12,000/(1 + 0.10/365)^{36}$ = $11,882.24.

$$\text{PV(cash flow from customers)} = \$12{,}000/(1 + 0.10/365)^{36} = \$11{,}882.24.$$

EXERCISE

12.8

THE COST OF A CASH COLLECTION POLICY

Willard Department Stores' credit customers pay their bills by mailing checks to the company's Arizona headquarters. Willard's accounting staff processes the checks, credits the customers' accounts, and deposits the checks in a local bank that clears them through the Federal Reserve system. Average mail, processing, and clearing delays are 2.5 days,

5 days, and 1.5 days. Average daily collections equal $4.5 million and the company's opportunity cost is 15 percent per year. What is the present value of a typical day's collections measured at the time customers mail their payments? What is the cost of the company's average daily collection float?

Nine days (2.5 + 5 + 1.5) pass between the time customers mail their checks and the funds are available to Willard. Therefore, the present value of a typical day's collections is

$$PV(\text{cash flow from customers}) = \$4,500,000/(1 + 0.15/365)^9$$
$$= \$4,483,390.31$$
$$\text{Cost of collection float} = \$4,500,000 \times 9 \text{ days} \times 0.15/365$$
$$= \$16,643.84.$$

The difference between the amount customers pay and the present value to Willard, $16,609.69 ($4,5000,000 − $4,483,390.31), approximately equals the cost of Willard's collection float.

● ———————— ●

Now suppose Noble establishes a lock-box to process collections from Hawk Lumber and its other customers. This lock-box reduces processing and clearing delays from six days to one day by initiating the clearing process sooner. The $12,000 cash inflow is therefore received on the thirty-first rather than the thirty-sixth day. The present value of the cash flow now is

$$PV(\text{cash flow from customers}) = \$12,000/(1 + 0.10/365)^{31} = \$11,899.$$

This is an improvement in present value of $17.

Exhibit 12.8 also shows Noble's collection float under the two cash collection alternatives. They have $12,000 of float for six days when the company collects the check itself and $12,000 of float for one day when it uses a lock-box. The cost of this collection float under the two alternatives therefore is

Collect Own Checks

$$\text{Cost of collection float} = \$12,000 \times 6 \text{ days} \times 0.10/365 = \$19.73.$$

Use Lock-box

$$\text{Cost of collection float} = \$12,000 \times 1 \text{ day} \times 0.10/365 = \$3.29.$$

The float cost savings from using the lock-box, $16.44 ($19.73 − $3.29), approximately equals the improvement in the present value of the cash flows from Hawk Lumber.

You must consider the annual volume of transactions processed by a lock-box and its annual costs to determine if it is worthwhile. An approximate answer is easily obtained by computing the annual opportunity cost savings and subtracting the annual cost. The lock-box is profitable if the resulting value is positive. Let's continue the Noble Wood Products example for an illustration.

Noble's annual sales equal $33 million. The company's bank charges a fee of $25,000 plus $0.30 per item to operate the lock-box, which reduces collection float by five days. Noble estimates 10,000 items will be sent to the lock-box each year. What are the benefits and costs of using a lock-box?

$$\text{Opportunity cost savings} = \$33,000,000 \times 5 \text{ days} \times 0.10/365 = \$45,205$$

$$\text{Service costs} = \$25,000 + (\$0.30 \times 10,000) = \$28,000$$

Noble's net savings per year are $17,205 ($45,205 – $28,000) so they should implement the lock-box collection system.

VALUE OF A LOCK-BOX COLLECTION SYSTEM

Willard Department Stores from Exercise 12.8 is considering establishing lock-boxes at two banks. The company will route 55 percent of its daily collections to a Los Angeles bank. The funds represented by these checks will be available to Willard two days after customers mail them. The remaining checks will be routed to a Dallas bank and the funds will be available 3.5 days after customers mail the checks. Incremental check-processing costs are $8,000 per month. Determine the cost of Willard's collection float under the new policy. Should they adopt the new system?

Willard's average collection delay using the lock-boxes is

$$\text{Average collection delay} = (0.55 \times 2 \text{ days}) + (0.45 \times 3.5 \text{ days})$$

$$= 2.675 \text{ days.}$$

Therefore the cost of collection float is

$$\text{Cost of collection float} = \$4,500,000 \times 2.675 \text{ days} \times 0.15/365$$

$$= \$4,946.92.$$

The lock-boxes reduce the cost of Willard's collection float by $11,696.92 ($16,643.84 – $4,946.92). The incremental check processing costs are $8,000 so the NPV of the lock-box collection system is $3,696.92 ($11,696.92 – $8,000). Willard should adopt the new cash collection system.

Verify your answer by determining the difference in net present value.

$$\text{NPV of lock-box} = \$4,500,000/(1 + 0.15/365)^{2.675} - \$8,000$$

$$= \$4,487,056.81$$

This is an improvement in present value of $3,666.50 ($4,487,056.81 – $4,483,390.31), nearly the same as the answer based on floatation costs.

Companies are increasingly replacing paper check payment and collection systems with electronic funds transfers, usually through an ACH. Electronic funds transfers reduce processing costs, provide more information, and make the timing of cash receipts and disbursements very predictable (see "In the News").

I N   T H E   N E W S

ELECTRONIC PAYMENTS BECOME MORE POPULAR

IN A RACE to cash checks, three helicopters land in rapid succession at the airport here. Workers scramble to unload hundreds of pounds of bundled checks, hurl them into carts, and run them out to a waiting Learjet. "Shake a leg, Louie," dispatcher Martin Evans shouts. He paces anxiously as shifting winds and incoming air traffic delay flight 401's scheduled 10:30 p.m. takeoff by five minutes. On board are $600 million in checks that must get to banks in 46 cities by 8 a.m. or payment will be delayed a day—a costly proposition.

In contrast, Barbara Woollett, an accountant at Chevron U.S.A. Inc., has no doubt about the delivery time for an $11,637 payment she authorized that same day for parts used in one of the Chevron Corp. unit's oil refineries. Instead of telling her accounts-payable staff to write a check, which might have ended up on that Burbank flight, Ms. Woollett zapped the payment electronically from Chevron's bank to the parts manufacturer's bank.

Companies are souring on checks for a variety of reasons. Some cite increased counterfeiting. Others say the "float" game—keeping your cash in your account while a check you wrote wends its way through the system—isn't so important anymore now that interest rates are low and banking rules have tightened settlement times. Sometimes checks go to the wrong banks. Or worse. Once a batch was found in a dumpster behind the Doggie Diner in San Francisco.

Companies save about 75 cents each time they do not print, handle, and mail checks. And knowing precisely which day payments will be debited and credited gives companies more flexibility in managing their cash. Of even greater interest to corporate treasurers is the precision, thoroughness, and uniformity of remittance information arriving in a standard electronic format.

Susan Rapp, a vice-president of PNC Bank in Pittsburgh, believes that financial EDI is at the explosive stage because of a multiplier effect as more and more large companies pay big suppliers electronically. The federal government—the biggest such buyer—began pressing suppliers in the late 1980s and now sends them electronic payments exceeding $300 billion a year.

Source: Fred R. Bleakley, "Electronic Payments Now Supplant Checks at More Large Firms," *The Wall Street Journal*, April 13, 1994, p. A1.

12.7   SUMMARY

The objective of financial management in the payment and collection phases of the operating cycle is to help identify the best ways to pay cash to suppliers and collect cash from customers. This task is accomplished by using fundamental finance principles to identify the routine policies with the largest present values. Some special knowledge of trade credit and the payment system is all that is needed to apply these finance principles to these phases of the operating cycle.

Analysts must understand why their companies receive and extend trade credit to evaluate alternative accounts payable and receivable policies. Possible reasons are simple convenience, to obtain the gains from giving or receiving a private loan and the cost savings from specialization, and to give or receive credible assurances about product quality. The credit price of the product and the seller's and buyer's opportunity costs determine how these benefits are divided between them; a high price confers more of the benefits to the seller and vice versa.

The benefits of trade credit improve the amount and timing of the buyer's and seller's cash flows. The best accounts payable policy has the lowest present value of cash outflows to suppliers while the best accounts receivable policy has the highest present value of cash inflows from customers. The cash flows that should be included in the analysis are the cash outflows or inflows from buying or selling the product and the cash outflows for administration. The latter category includes the cash costs of processing payments and receipts, evaluating credit applicants, recordkeeping, and monitoring and enforcing credit policy.

Analysts must know how the payment system works to evaluate alternative cash disbursement and collection policies. The cash represented by some payment media is not deducted from the buyer's account or added to the seller's account when the payment order is sent or received. Mailed checks are subject to mail, processing, and clearing delays before the transaction is effective. Other payment media have shorter delays or none at all. The float these delays produce is called disbursement float (buyer's perspective) and collection float (seller's perspective). Disbursement float provides additional financing to the buyer at the seller's expense.

Cash flow management policies improve the timing of the buyer's and seller's cash flows. The best cash disbursement policy has the lowest present value of cash outflows to suppliers; the best collection policy has the highest present value of cash inflows from customers. The cash flows that should be included in the analysis are the cash outflows or inflows from buying or selling the product and the cash outflows for administration. The latter category includes the cash costs of processing payments and receipts and the cost of bank services such as zero balance accounts and lock-boxes.

- ## KEY TERMS

Book balance *495*	Lock-box *497*	Collection float *501*
Available balance *496*	Zero balance account	
Disbursement float *497*	(ZBA) *498*	

- ## QUESTIONS AND PROBLEMS

1. Describe the principal benefit of giving or receiving trade credit in each of the situations listed below.

   (a) An individual extends trade credit to a long-distance telephone service provider by purchasing a prepaid phone card.

   (b) A food processor pays a Louisiana farmer for sugar cane 90 days after the harvest takes place.

   (c) A manufacturer extends trade credit to its best customers in place of purchasing U.S. Treasury bills.

   (d) An individual uses a credit card rather than a money order to buy an unusual product offered on late night cable TV.

(e) A small company that can obtain new financing only from the owners or local banks uses trade credit to fund its sales growth.

(f) An interstate trucking company permits its customers to mail their payments to lock-boxes rather than give a check or cash to the drivers.

(g) A new company with an innovative product extends trade credit to its customers to break into an established market.

2. Credit and sales managers often have conflicting opinions about credit policy.

(a) What are the principal costs of a generous credit policy from a credit manager's perspective?

(b) What are the principal benefits of a generous credit policy from a sales manager's perspective?

(c) How can you reconcile these conflicting opinions to choose the best credit policy from the owners' perspective?

3. Seamoore Farms sells custom-cured hams and bacon to supermarkets on terms of 1/5 net 20. Two of Seamoore's customers apparently are very similar supermarket chains but Atkinson Groceries invariably accepts the 1 percent cash discount and pays on the 5th day while O'Hare Food Stores forgoes the discount and pays on the 20th.

(a) What effective annual interest rate does O'Hare pay by forgoing the 1 percent cash discount?

(b) Discuss some possible operating and financial explanations for O'Hare's payment policy.

(c) Explain why Seamoore Farms may want to treat these apparently similar supermarket chains differently.

4. A paper check is a method of payment that has many similarities to trade credit.

(a) Describe the advantages and disadvantages of paying by check rather than with cash.

(b) Relate the advantages and disadvantages of paying by check to the benefits and costs of trade credit.

(c) Discuss the similarities and differences between the techniques companies use to manage accounts receivable and the techniques they use to manage cash collections.

5. Exhibit 12.6 is a diagram of the collection process for paper checks. Redraw this diagram assuming the seller uses a lock-box.

6. Bernell Hill Enterprises receives 30 days of credit from its major supplier and pays the bill by check, which provides an additional six days of disbursement float. The supplier wants Hill to pay electronically but the company is resisting. Hill's treasurer knows that paying electronically will reduce the company's transaction costs but she values the 36 days of financing provided by accounts payable.

(a) How can the supplier compensate Hill Enterprises for losing the 36 days of financing provided by accounts payable if the company pays electronically?

(b) Alternatively, how can the supplier enable Hill Enterprises to keep the 36 days of financing provided by accounts payable even if it pays electronically?

(c) How should Hill Enterprises and its supplier determine which alternative is better?

7. Fossil Fuel Supply Company presently requires its customers to pay cash on delivery for purchases of #2 fuel oil. The price is $135 per 100 gallons and the company normally sells 500,000 gallons per year.

(a) The sales manager has asked for permission to change the company's terms to net 30. What is the minimum permissible credit price for the fuel oil if Fossil's opportunity cost is 12 percent per year? What is the maximum permissible credit price if the company's typical customer has an opportunity cost of 15 percent per year?

(b) Determine Fossil Fuel's approximate annual benefit from offering the new terms at the maximum permissible credit price. Should the company adopt the new terms if the administrative cost is $2,000 per year? Explain your answers.

8. Nabria Manufacturing Company constructs tanks used to temporarily store oil at the well-head. A typical tank costs $100,000 and most customers pay by check 10 days following delivery. Disbursement and collection float are an additional two days. Nabria's treasurer estimates it costs the company $125 to process each check and assumes it costs customers a similar amount to authorize and issue checks. Nabria and its customers have opportunity costs of 14 percent.

(a) What is the present value of the cost of a tank as of the day it is delivered from a customer's perspective? What is the present value from Nabria's perspective? Assume the transaction costs are paid when a check clears.

(b) Nabria's treasurer would like to collect these funds electronically to save transaction and opportunity costs. Determine the largest percentage discount the company can offer customers to pay electronically one day after delivery if transaction costs are only $25.

(c) Suppose Nabria offers a 0.4 percent discount for electronic payment. Will the typical customer accept these terms and pay one day following delivery if its processing costs also are reduced to $25?

9. Far East Seafood Products received an order for $10,000 of frozen shrimp on terms of net 60 from the Dragon & Phoenix restaurant chain. Far East will buy the shrimp from a distributor for $8,500 on payment terms of net 20 and immediately deliver it to Dragon & Phoenix. What risk of default can Far East accept and still earn its 20 percent annual required rate of return on these operating cash flows?

10. The Wilson Electric Company currently sells 2,500 motors per week for $40 each on terms of net 30. The variable portion of the cost of goods sold for the motors is $30. This cost is paid 15 days following a sale. Eighty percent of sales are collected on time, 18 percent are collected on the 45th day after a sale, and 2 percent are written off as bad debts then.

The company is considering a new credit policy that will provide more generous credit terms but will be more selective about who gets them. Under the new policy, Wilson will charge a price of $40.50, payable on the 45th day with a $0.75 discount for cash on delivery. Of the present sales, 34 percent will be for cash, 65 percent will be on credit, and 1 percent will take their business elsewhere. Ninety-nine percent of the credit sales will be paid on time but the other 1 percent will be written off as bad debts. Wilson's required rate of return for this line of business is 15 percent per year.

(a) What is the NPV of a typical week's sales under the current and new policies?

(b) What is the average days'-sales-outstanding under the current and new policies?

(c) Which policy should Wilson adopt?

11. Cornflower Distributors sells videotapes to rental stores. The company's credit terms are net 30 but late payments and bad debts are recurring problems. A consultant recommended that the company subscribe to a credit reporting service that screens credit applicants and monitors credit accounts. The consultant's estimates of a typical month's sales and collections with and without using the reporting service are given below. A subscription to the credit reporting service costs $6,000 per month, paid at the beginning of each month. Cornflower's opportunity cost is 1.5 percent per month.

	Without Credit Service	With Credit Service
Cash sales	$ 25,000	$ 35,000
Credit sales	320,000	300,000
Percent of credit sales		
Collected on day 30	75%	80%
Collected on day 60	10	10
Collected on day 90	10	8
Written off as bad debts	5	2

(a) Should Cornflower subscribe to the credit reporting service if the variable portion of the company's cost of goods sold is 50 percent of sales? If the variable cost is 55 percent of sales? Assume this cost is paid at the beginning of each month.

(b) Rework part (a) assuming the company's opportunity cost is 2 percent per month.

(c) Given your answers to parts (a) and (b), what type of companies should be especially diligent when performing credit analysis? Explain your answer.

12. Designed 4U Inc. sells a 24-count case of teddy bear motif ceramic picture frames for $108.00 on terms of net 30 to mom-and-pop gift shops, department stores, and super discount centers. The company's sales manager asked for approval to change the terms to net 90 to increase sales revenues. The treasurer agreed with the stipulation that the price be increased to $110.50 to cover the company's opportunity cost.

(a) Determine the present value cost of a case of picture frames to Designed 4U's customers under the old and new policies. The customers' opportunity costs are

Gift shops	18%
Department stores	14
Discount centers	10

(b) How will each group of customers react to the new policy? Is the net result likely to be what the sales manager was looking for when he recommended a change in credit policy? Explain your answer.

(c) What can Designed 4U do to avoid unfavorable reactions to the new credit policy without eliminating favorable reactions or resorting to illegal forms of price discrimination?

13. L.J. Johnson Supply sells sports equipment to small sporting goods stores. The results for a typical month are summarized below.

Day	Event
0	Receive merchandise
10	Receive orders totaling $100,000
	Grant credit on terms 2/10 net 30 to 80%
	Sell for cash on delivery to 20%
20	Collect discounted payments (50% of credit sales)
25	Pay for merchandise (65% of total sales)
40	Collect net payments (40% of credit sales)
70	Collect late payments (8% of credit sales)

(a) Prepare a time line that shows the timing of each event in Johnson's operating cycle. Place the company's daily income statements, balance sheets, and indirect format cash statements on this time line to track a typical month's business through the operating cycle.

(b) Use the approximate method (see Chapter 10) to determine the net present value of the cash flows provided by and used for operations in a typical month. The company's opportunity cost is 16 percent.

(c) Confirm your answer to part (b) by using the exact method to determine the NPV of the cash flows provided by and used for operations in a typical month.

14. Julie Marsh manages an accounts receivable portfolio for Welsh Manufacturing Company. Credit sales and collections for the companies in her portfolio are summarized below.

Julie Marsh's Accounts Receivable Portfolio (in thousands)

	September	October	November	December
Beginning balance	$140.0	$163.2	$114.9	$163.7
Credit sales	$150.0	$100.0	$150.0	$350.0
Collections				
From 1st prior month's sales	$106.8	$136.5	$ 88.0	$126.0
From 2nd prior month's sales	18.0	10.8	12.0	9.0
From 3rd prior month's sales	2.0	1.0	1.2	0.8
Total	$126.8	$148.3	$101.2	$135.8
Ending balance	$163.2	$114.9	$163.7	$377.9

(a) Calculate the days'-sales-outstanding ratio for each month. Assume there are 30 days in a month. In which month does Julie's collection effort seem to be most successful? Least successful? Explain your answer.

(b) Calculate the payment proportions for which there is enough information. In which month does Julie's collection effort seem to be most successful? Least successful? Explain your answer.

(c) Julie must decide which customers to examine more closely in the future. Should she pay more attention to the customers that made credit purchases in September, October, November, or December? Why?

15. Jack Kulsrud, treasurer of Kulsrud Cleaning Supplies, must estimate the amount of cash the company will collect from credit accounts in July and asked the credit manager to prepare the report shown below for this purpose. Credit sales in February and March were $125 and $175. The company writes off bad debts after 60 days.

Kulsrud's Accounts Receivable Portfolio (in thousands)

	April	May	June
Beginning balance	$268.8	$359.5	$344.7
Credit sales	$200.0	$150.0	$125.0
Collections			
From current month's sales	$ 47.3	$ 50.0	$ 39.0
From 1st prior month's sales	60.0	82.3	98.0
From 2nd prior month's sales	2.0	32.5	43.8
Total	$109.3	$164.8	$180.8
Ending balance	$359.5	$344.7	$288.9

(a) On average, what proportion of credit sales are collected in the month of the sale? In each subsequent month? What proportion are written off as bad debts?

(b) The sales manager forecasted $250 of credit sales in July. What is the amount of cash flow the treasurer should expect to collect from credit accounts that month? How many dollars of accounts receivable should he anticipate financing?

(c) Suppose July's results come in and neither of Jack Kulsrud's predictions is correct. Describe some possible explanations for the errors.

16. Clay Dog Manufacturing Co. must pay for its clay three days prior to delivery. The cost of each shipment is $5,500 and the supplier will accept cash or a check. Processing and clearing delays for the check are three days and one day. Clay Dog's opportunity cost is 20 percent per year.

(a) Determine the present value cost of a shipment of clay if the company pays by cash. Determine the present value cost if it pays by check. Measure these values as of the day of delivery. Which method of payment should Clay Dog use? Why?

(b) Determine the values of Clay Dog's disbursement float if the company pays by cash and by check. Are the results consistent with your answer to part (a)? Why or why not?

17. Maier Catalog Sales Company pays its suppliers with checks drawn on remote banks to increase its disbursement float. Vanderweide Jewelry Supply, one of Maier's suppliers, uses lock-boxes to decrease its collection float.

(a) Who are the most likely beneficiaries of their cash management duel?

(b) Describe some ways these companies could cooperatively pay and collect cash to their mutual benefit.

18. Cyclone Electronic Company's annual sales are $17,500,000. The company's customers pay by checks (approximately 250,000 checks per year) that are subject to nine days' collection float on average. Cyclone's bank has offered to operate a lock-box for the company, which will reduce the average collection float to 2.5 days and save the company approximately $0.03 per item for internal processing costs. The bank will charge Cyclone $10,000 plus $0.11 per item to operate the lock-box. Should Cyclone use the lock-box if its opportunity cost is 12 percent per year?

19. Henderson Labs sells mail-order vitamins from its headquarters in Kansas City, Kansas. Customers mail an average of 1 million checks per year to the company's local lock-box bank. The average check is for $35 and is subject to four days of collection float. The bank charges an annual fee of $30,000 plus $0.10 per item to operate the lock-box. Henderson's opportunity cost is 14 percent per year.

(a) Determine the total cost of Henderson's one-bank cash collection system.

(b) Henderson Lab's cash manager is considering replacing the company's single lock-box bank with banks located in Atlanta and Denver. The banks' fees, the allocation of payments to the banks, and their days of collection float are summarized below. Determine the total cost of the two-bank collection system. Should Henderson Lab's make the change?

	Atlanta	Denver
Annual fee	$40,000	$30,000
Per item cost	$ 0.08	$ 0.10
Number of items assigned to bank	600,000	400,000
Days of collection float	2.5	3.0

(c) What would the Atlanta bank's annual fee have to be to change your answer to part (b)? Given these results, explain what prevents companies from placing a lock-box in every city to completely eliminate collection float.

• ADDITIONAL READING

The best source of all-around information about payments and collections is a good working capital management textbook. Two alternatives are:

Ned C. Hill and William L. Sartoris, *Short-Term Financial Management,* Macmillan Publishing Company, New York, 1992.

Terry S. Maness and John T. Zietlow, *Short-Term Financial Management,* West Publishing Company, Minneapolis/St. Paul, 1993.

The Credit Research Foundation, a subsidiary of the National Association of Credit Management, has several publications dealing with credit and collections. The Foundation's handbook is exactly what you'd expect from the title.

George N. Christie and Albert E. Bracuti, *Credit Executives Handbook,* Credit Research Foundation, Columbia, Maryland, 1986.

CHAPTER 13

DETAILED ANALYSIS OF ROUTINE AND STRATEGIC DECISIONS

On October 3, 1996, *The Wall Street Journal* reported that WellPoint Health Networks Incorporated was negotiating with Hancock Mutual Life Insurance Company to buy the latter's health insurance operations.[1] The article noted that profit margins in this business are very thin, suggesting that the acquisition may have a negative net present value. The report went on to state, however, that Hancock's health insurance operations have "enormous strategic value to WellPoint" because they will give the California company access to employers across the country that buy a wide range of health care services. WellPoint's managers apparently believe that this acquisition will provide an *option* to enter the national health-care market that may be valuable later even if it is out-of-the-money now.

WellPoint's managers and the managers of every other company must make investment decisions without knowing for certain whether the results will be favorable or unfavorable. The results they obtain depend partly on the investment project's own payoffs and partly on their responses when these payoffs are better or worse than expected. The decision rules managers use must account for these effects to correctly determine a project's market value.

The net present value rule determines a project's market value by using a risk-adjusted opportunity cost to discount its expected free cash flows. The project is acceptable if its market value is greater than or equal to its cost (that is, if its NPV $\geq$ 0) but not otherwise. This is the approach we developed in the chapters on risk and return (Chapters 5 and 6) and then applied to debt and equity in Chapter 7 and routine investment proposals in Chapters 9 through 12.

Using a risk-adjusted opportunity cost to discount expected free cash flows presumes the investment is a take-it-or-leave-it proposition or that the managers are passive. *All* free cash flows are averaged together on the assumption that the investor does not have the opportunity to minimize the effect of unfavorable outcomes or maximize the effect of favorable ones. This is a reasonable assumption when valuing debt and equity because individual stockholders cannot influence the payoffs they receive.

---

[1]Leslie Scism and Rhonda L. Rundle, "WellPoint Is Close to Deal with Hancock," *The Wall Street Journal*, October 3, 1996, p. A3.

Their only recourse to unfavorable or favorable returns is to sell their securities or buy more of them.

The assumption that an investment is a take-it-or-leave-it proposition also is reasonable for certain routine projects that provide no scope for managerial discretion. For example, a coal-fired electric power plant must have a pollution control system to remain in operation. Managers therefore can choose the system with the lowest present value of expected costs without considering the (unattainable) benefits of scrapping it if costs are higher than they anticipated.

Strategic decisions are different, however, because managers have choices and few if any of them must be made at the outset. They can initiate a project now or later and accelerate or delay implementation as conditions become more or less favorable. They also can implement a project at one scale and increase or decrease its size later as conditions warrant. Finally, they can abandon a project if they learn it is no longer viable in any form. The salient characteristic of strategic decisions bears repeating: *Managers have choices and need not make them in advance.* They simply must be aware of the alternatives and their consequences and be prepared to implement them as the situation dictates.

Of course, managers should make strategic choices by accelerating or expanding a project only if conditions are favorable and by delaying, contracting, or abandoning it only if they are not. This has the effect of amplifying favorable outcomes and dampening unfavorable ones. The result is that a strategic project provides favorable cash flows more frequently and unfavorable cash flows less frequently than an otherwise identical take-it-or-leave-it proposition. Consequently, using a risk-adjusted opportunity cost to discount a strategic project's expected free cash flows underestimates its value because it disregards the effect of management's choices.

This chapter describes how to evaluate strategic decisions (such as WellPoint's decision to enter the national health-care market) to account for the value of active management. We will begin by using event trees and decision trees to describe a decision's outcome and management's choices. Then we will solve the same problems using option pricing models. Developing the similarities and differences between these methods will reveal the strengths of the option pricing approach.

13.1   DESCRIBING A DECISION'S OUTCOMES AND MANAGEMENT'S CHOICES

Event trees and decision trees are effective ways to describe a decision's outcomes. Event trees only represent the effect of uncertainty so they can only be applied to take-it-or-leave-it propositions. Decision trees describe the effects of uncertainty *and* the managers' choices so they can be applied to strategic decisions.

Event Trees and a Project's Value with Passive Management

Ted Parr has the opportunity to buy a field of stripper wells (oil wells that produce less than 10 barrels per day) for $600,000. The field is presently equipped to produce 50,000 barrels of oil per year for two years with operating costs known to be $15.00 per

OIL FIELD PAYOFFS WITH PASSIVE MANAGEMENT **Table 13.1**

1997

Cash flow provided by (used for) investment	$–600,000
Free cash flow	$–600,000

1998

	$18/bbl	$26/bbl
Price of oil	**$18/bbl**	**$26/bbl**
(Probability)	**(0.50)**	**(0.50)**
Cash revenue	$900,000	$1,300,000
Cash costs	750,000	750,000
Cash flow provided by (used for) operations	150,000	550,000
Cash flow provided by (used for) investment	0	0
Free cash flow	$150,000	$ 550,000

1999

	$18/bbl	$26/bbl	$18/bbl	$26/bbl
Price of oil	**$18/bbl**	**$26/bbl**	**$18/bbl**	**$26/bbl**
(Probability)	**(0.80)**	**(0.20)**	**(0.10)**	**(0.90)**
Cash revenue	$900,000	$1,300,000	$900,000	$1,300,000
Cash costs	750,000	750,000	750,000	750,000
Cash flow provided by (used for) operations	150,000	550,000	150,000	550,000
Cash flow provided by (used for) investment	0	0	0	0
Free cash flow	$150,000	$ 550,000	$150,000	$ 550,000

barrel. The project's only uncertainty is whether oil prices will be $18.00 or $26.00 per barrel. Ted believes these prices are equally likely in 1998 but that $18 per barrel of oil that year increases the probability of $18 per barrel of oil in 1999 and vice versa.

Table 13.1 describes the outcomes from Ted's investment opportunity assuming he manages it passively. Under this condition, the investment project's free cash flow is either $150,000 or $550,000 per year, the result completely dependent on oil prices.

Exhibit 13.1 is an **event tree** that summarizes the essential information in Table 13.1. The circles indicate that the subsequent outcomes are produced by chance (are they roulette wheel icons?) rather than by management's choice. Along each line originating at a circle is a description of the uncertain outcome described by that section of the path; $26 per barrel of oil with probability of 0.50, for example. At the end of each line is the resulting free cash flow. The probability that events will follow a particular path equals the product of the probabilities of the sections along the path. The probability that oil prices will be $26 per barrel in 1998 and 1999 (path 1) is 0.50 × 0.90 = 0.45, for example. The four paths that go from start to finish and their probabilities are summarized in Table 13.2.

This project's expected free cash flows provide the best representation of its payoffs if it is a take-it-or-leave-it proposition and Ted Parr will not change its operation in response to changing oil prices. Using the summary information given in Table 3.2, the stripper well's expected free cash flows (FCFs) are

Exhibit 13.1

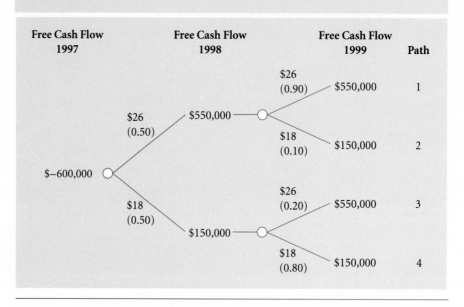

OIL FIELD EVENT TREE

$E(\text{FCF 1997}) = \$-600{,}000$

$E(\text{FCF 1998}) = \$550{,}000 \times 0.45 + \$550{,}000 \times 0.05 + \$150{,}000 \times 0.10$
$\qquad\qquad + \$150{,}000 \times 0.40$

$\qquad\qquad = \$350{,}000$

$E(\text{FCF 1999}) = \$550{,}000 \times 0.45 + \$150{,}000 \times 0.05 + \$550{,}000 \times 0.10$
$\qquad\qquad + \$150{,}000 \times 0.40$

$\qquad\qquad = \$370{,}000.$

Assuming a 10 percent required rate of return, the project's market value and net present value are

$$\text{Market value} = \frac{\$350{,}000}{(1.10)} + \frac{\$370{,}000}{(1.10)^2} = \$623{,}967$$

Net present value = $\$623{,}967 - \$600{,}000 = \$23{,}967.$

The field of stripper wells is an acceptable investment project because it has a positive, albeit small, net present value. (Its internal rate of return is 12.4 percent.) Next, we will see how Ted can increase this value by becoming an active manager and responding in obvious ways to changes in oil prices.

EXERCISE

13.1   NEW PRODUCT INTRODUCTION WITH PASSIVE MANAGEMENT

Dento-Flux has the rights to market a new plaque-fighting toothpaste. The toothpaste has not received FDA approval and the company doesn't know if consumers will like

SUMMARY OF OIL FIELD PAYOFFS WITH PASSIVE MANAGEMENT   Table 13.2

| | | Free Cash Flow | | |
Path	Probability	1997	1998	1999
1	0.45	$–600,000	$550,000	$550,000
2	0.05	–600,000	550,000	150,000
3	0.10	–600,000	150,000	550,000
4	0.40	–600,000	150,000	150,000

the taste. There is a 30 percent probability the FDA will approve the formula and a 50 percent probability consumers will like the taste. The business will be worth $3,850,000 if both outcomes are favorable; $750,000 if the FDA approves the formula but consumers don't like the taste; and $0 if the FDA withholds its approval. All values are measured at the end of one year.

The cost of launching the business is $1,800,000, which includes $50,000 to apply for FDA approval. The required rate of return for this line of business is 8 percent per six months.

Construct an event tree that describes the payoffs from launching the new toothpaste. What is the project's net present value assuming passive management? Should the company proceed with this investment?

Payoffs from New Toothpaste

The table below summarizes the event tree's cash flows.

| | | Free Cash Flow | |
Path	Probability	Time 0	Value in 1 Year
1	0.15	$–1,800,000	$3,850,000
2	0.15	–1,800,000	750,000
3	0.70	–1,800,000	0

Free cash flow at time 0 = $-1,800,000

Expected value in 1 year = $3,850,000 × 0.15 + $750,000 × 0.15 + $0 × 0.70

= $690,000

Market value = $690,000/(1.08)^2 = $591,564

Net present value = $591,564 − $1,800,000

= $-1,208,436

Dento-Flux's managers should not launch the new toothpaste because it reduces the owners' wealth.

● ——————————— ●

Decision Trees and a Project's Value with Active Management

Ted Parr can convert his investment opportunity from a take-it-or-leave-it proposition into a strategic investment project by being prepared to expand or curtail operations when oil prices are favorable or unfavorable. He may not be able to act immediately because he doesn't know which of the four paths oil prices will take. Nevertheless, he can establish action plans to implement as soon as he has better information. This is, after all, the essence of strategic planning. The opportunity—but not the obligation—to make these strategic choices can only increase the project's value.

We will consider two strategic alternatives representative of those most commonly available with investment projects: the opportunity to expand a profitable project and the opportunity to abandon an unsuccessful one. We will examine other strategic choices later after we have considered these fundamental ones.

Evaluating the Opportunity to Expand a Strategic Project   Most projects can be expanded after the initial investment is made. Pharmaceutical companies develop and introduce new medicines that pass through stages including basic research, clinical trials, regulatory approval, and availability to the general population. Consumer goods companies produce small amounts of new products to sell in regional test markets and switch to full-scale production later if the tests are successful. In each case, the decision to move to the next stage is an investment decision that expands the project's scale. Other companies expand output by using production machinery that can be operated in different configurations or at different speeds. However expansion is accomplished, a company should plan to expand or not expand by determining which choice provides the highest value.

Ted Parr has the opportunity to expand operations in the field of stripper wells by installing an advanced recovery system at the end of 1998 for an initial cost of $300,000. This system will increase production to 100,000 barrels per year but will raise the operating cost to $16.25 per barrel. Now we must re-evaluate this investment project given that he will actively manage the oil field and expand the business when it is to his advantage.

We proceed by adding decision points to the tree in Exhibit 13.1, which converts it from an event tree to the **decision tree** shown in Exhibit 13.2. Each decision point is represented by a rectangle to distinguish it from chance events that are represented

Exhibit 13.2

DECISION TREE FOR EXPANSION

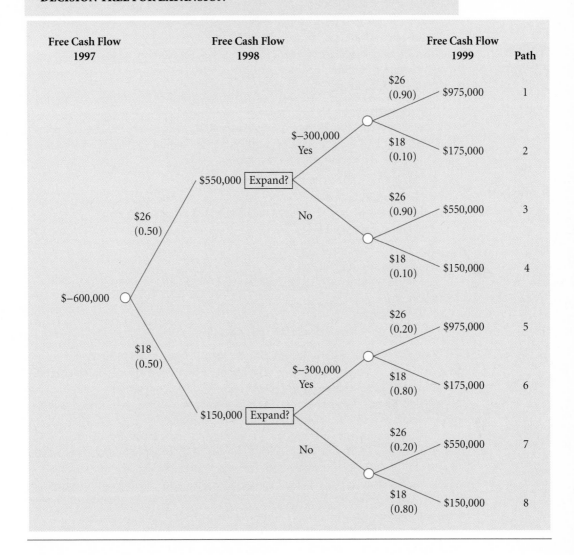

by circles. The lines originating from each rectangle describe the outcomes of the decision: (1) an immediate cash outflow of $300,000 and the chance for $975,000 or $175,000 at the end of 1999 if he does expand operations and (2) the chance for $550,000 or $150,000 at the end of 1999 if he does not.

Ted's choice at each decision point depends on the values of expanding operations or continuing them at their original level. These values at the end of 1998 equal the discounted value of the expected cash flows in 1999. Given $26 per barrel of oil in 1998, they are as follows.

Value of expanding operations if price of oil in 1998 was $26/bbl

$$= \frac{\$975,000 \times 0.90 + \$175,000 \times 0.10}{1.10} - \$300,000$$

$$= \$513,636$$

Value of continuing operations at original level if price of oil in 1998 was $26/bbl

$$= \frac{\$550,000 \times 0.90 + \$150,000 \times 0.10}{1.10}$$

$$= \$463,636$$

If oil was $26 per barrel in 1998, Ted should expand the field because $513,636 is greater than $463,636. This plan eliminates paths 3 and 4 in Exhibit 13.2 from consideration when it is time to determine the oil field's overall value.

We evaluate the other decision point similarly.

Value of expanding operations if price of oil in 1998 was $18/bbl

$$= \frac{\$975,000 \times 0.20 + \$175,000 \times 0.80}{1.10} - \$300,000$$

$$= \$4,545$$

Value of continuing operations at original level if price of oil in 1998 was $18/bbl

$$= \frac{\$550,000 \times 0.20 + \$150,000 \times 0.80}{1.10}$$

$$= \$209,091$$

Expansion is clearly unwarranted if the price of oil was $18 in 1998 because $209,091 is much larger than $4,545. The reason is that low oil prices in 1998 significantly increase the likelihood of low oil prices in 1999, which makes the expansion uneconomical. This plan to not expand the business if prices were low in 1998 eliminates paths 5 and 6 in Exhibit 13.2 from further consideration.

The four paths that go from start to finish given Ted's expansion plans are summarized in Table 13.3. Note that free cash flow in 1998 for paths 1 and 2 is $250,000 to account for the cost of the advanced recovery system ($550,000 − $300,000).

We will discount the expected free cash flows using the market opportunity cost of 10 percent even though we must reconsider this choice for the required rate of return later. The results are

Table 13.3   SUMMARY OF OIL FIELD PAYOFFS WITH EXPANSION

		Free Cash Flow		
Path	Probability	1997	1998	1999
1	0.45	$−600,000	$250,000	$975,000
2	0.05	−600,000	250,000	175,000
7	0.10	−600,000	150,000	550,000
8	0.40	−600,000	150,000	150,000

$E(\text{FCF } 1997) = \$-600,000$

$E(\text{FCF } 1998) = \$250,000 \times 0.45 + \$250,000 \times 0.05 + \$150,000$
$\times 0.10 + \$150,000 \times 0.40$
$= \$200,000$

$E(\text{FCF } 1999) = \$975,000 \times 0.45 + \$175,000 \times 0.05 + \$550,000$
$\times 0.10 + \$150,000 \times 0.40$
$= \$562,500$

$$\text{Market value} = \frac{\$200,000}{(1.10)} + \frac{\$562,500}{(1.10)^2} = \$646,694$$

Net present value = \$646,694 – \$600,000 = \$46,694.

By planning to actively manage the oil field and expand operations when it is advantageous, Ted increased the proposal's value by \$22,727 (\$46,694 – \$23,967).

EXERCISE

13.2

NEW PRODUCT INTRODUCTION WITH ACTIVE MANAGEMENT

Suppose Dento-Flux's managers (from Exercise 13.1) recognize that they can defer part of the cost of launching the company's new toothpaste until they learn the FDA's decision. That is, they can spend \$50,000 immediately to apply for FDA approval and defer the remaining investment, \$1,750,000, for six months until they know the outcome.

Redraw the event tree recognizing management's ability to actively influence the outcome. Should the company spend the \$50,000 to seek FDA approval for the toothpaste?

Payoffs from New Toothpaste with Active Management

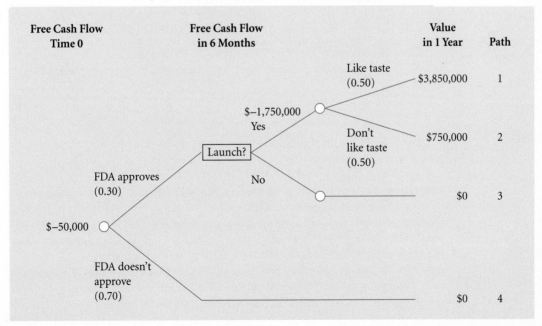

The value of launching the toothpaste at the six-month point if the FDA has approved the formula (derived from paths 1 and 2) is

$$\text{Value of product launch} = \frac{\$3,850,000 \times 0.5 + \$750,000 \times 0.5}{1.08} - \$1,750,000$$

$$= \$379,630.$$

This amount is greater than the value of not launching, $0, so path 3 is dropped from further consideration. The remaining paths are summarized in the following table.

Path	Probability	Time 0	In 6 Months	Value in 1 Year
		Free Cash Flow		
1	0.15	$–50,000	$–1,750,000	$3,850,000
2	0.15	–50,000	–1,750,000	750,000
4	0.70	–50,000	0	0

$$\text{Free cash flow at time } 0 = \${-}50,000$$

$$\text{Expected free cash flow in 6 months} = \${-}1,750,000 \times 0.15 + \${-}1,750,000 \times 0.15$$
$$+ \$0 \times 0.70$$
$$= \${-}525,000$$

$$\text{Expected free cash flow in 1 year} = \$3,850,000 \times 0.15 + \$750,000 \times 0.15$$
$$+ \$0 \times 0.70$$
$$= \$690,000$$

$$\text{Market value} = \$690,000/(1.08)^2 = \$591,564$$

$$\text{Present value of costs} = \${-}50,000 + \${-}525,000/1.08$$
$$= \${-}536,111$$

$$\text{Net present value} = \$591,564 - \$536,111 = \$55,453$$

Dento-Flux should apply for FDA approval for the company's new toothpaste because the NPV is greater than zero. Applying for approval increases the owners' wealth by $55,453.

● ———————— ●

Dento-Flux is a hypothetical company but real companies also must develop products in stages that provide an active role for managers (see "In the News").

Evaluating the Opportunity to Abandon a Strategic Project   Most projects can be terminated before the expected end of their life. Some may be sold to other companies who expect to operate them more profitably and some simply may be sold for their salvage values. Other projects are costly to shut down. For example, labor agreements may require a company to pay a termination settlement to its employees and environmental protection laws require companies to clean up hazardous wastes. Whatever the case, a company should plan to operate or abandon an investment project by determining which choice provides the higher value.

IN THE NEWS

HEARTSTREAM, INC.'S NEW PRODUCT OPTION

HERE ARE SOME of the stages related to the development, testing, certification, and sale of a new medical technology product. The successful completion of each stage gave Heartstream an option to continue its product development at the next stage.

December 16, 1994
After secretively working on its "portable automatic external defibrillator" for more than a year, Seattle-based Heartstream is now acknowledging the outlines of its production plans.

The 31-employee company is testing a defibrillator that should be cheaper, easier to use and sturdier than those made by industry leaders, said Alan Levy, president and CEO. Levy said Heartstream is "in the process of clinical trials now," although he declined to say when the company might seek Food and Drug Administration approval.*

December 8, 1995
Heartstream seeks FDA approval for its automatic-external defibrillator.

January 31, 1996
Heartstream common stock offered at $13 per share in an initial public offering.

September 13, 1996
Heartstream Inc. said the Food and Drug Administration approved a light-weight, easy-to-operate device for treating sudden cardiac arrest, which kills more than 350,000 annually.

Industry analysts had expected FDA approval of Heartstream's device for about a month, yet the company's stock jumped $2.625 to $13.875 in Nasdaq Stock Market trading yesterday.

Heartstream has received an unspecified number of orders in Europe, where it has distribution agreements with several large medical-device makers. It has no distributors for the U.S. market yet. The first units are expected to be shipped by the middle of the fourth quarter, the company said.†

November 17, 1996
American Airlines is expected to announce Tuesday that it will become the first U.S. airline to equip its planes with automatic defibrillators, the portable battery-powered machines that can reverse an otherwise fatal cardiac arrest with a jolt of electricity to the heart.

Airline and industry sources say American has signed an agreement to purchase 300 of the devices from Seattle-based Heartstream Corp., with the first units to be delivered in January and the remainder in time for the airline's busy summer tourist season.‡

---

*Rami Grunbaum, "Heartstream Testing Portable Defibrillator, Sees Big Market," *Puget Sound Business Journal*, December 16–22, 1994, p. 14.

†Ralph T. King, Jr., "Heartstream Says FDA Approves Device for Cardiac Arrest, Boosting Stock 23%," *The Wall Street Journal*, September 13, 1996, p. B5.

‡John Crewdson, "1st Airline in U.S. Adds Heart-Rescue Equipment," *Chicago Tribune*, November 17, 1996, p. 1.

VALUE OF A TRAINING PROGRAM WITH PASSIVE MANAGEMENT   EXERCISE

13.3

HydroArc does underwater welding for the off-shore oil industry. The company hires high school graduates and sends them to diving and welding schools for one year at a cost of $52,000 each. On average, only 10 percent of all new employees become qualified divers and 60 percent of all new employees become qualified welders. The value of the new business these employees produce (measured at the end of their training) depends on their skills. The possibilities are summarized below. The required rate of return for this line of business is 12.5 percent per six months.

Employee's Skills	Value of Business
Can dive, can weld	$500,000
Can dive, can't weld	100,000
Can't dive, can weld	50,000
Can't dive, can't weld	0

Construct the event tree that describes the payoffs from hiring a new employee. What is the present value of hiring a new employee assuming the managers are passive? Should the company hire new employees under these conditions?

Payoffs from Hiring New Employee

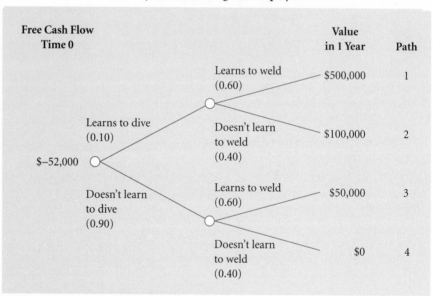

The following table summarizes the event tree's cash flows.

		Free Cash Flow	
Path	Probability	Time 0	Value in 1 Year
1	0.06	$-52,000	$500,000
2	0.04	-52,000	100,000
3	0.54	-52,000	50,000
4	0.36	-52,000	0

Free cash flow at time 0 = $-52,000
Expected value in 1 year = $500,000 × 0.06 + $100,000 × 0.04 + $50,000
   × 0.54 + $0 × 0.36
   = $61,000

Exhibit 13.3

DECISION TREE FOR ABANDONMENT

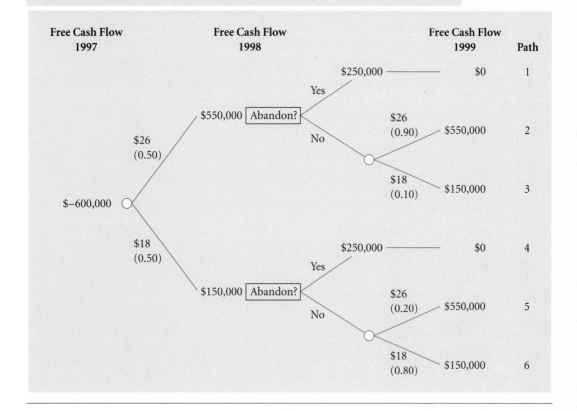

Free Cash Flow 1997	Free Cash Flow 1998	Free Cash Flow 1999	Path

$$\text{Market value} = \$61,000/(1.125)^2 = \$48,198$$
$$\text{NPV} = \$48,198 - \$52,000 = \$-3,802$$

HydroArc should not hire new employees under these conditions because the effect on the owners' wealth is negative.

• ——————— •

Ted Parr would almost certainly have the opportunity to abandon the field of stripper wells if he chooses. Let's suppose he can do so for a net cash inflow of $250,000 from the salvage value of the equipment and the sale of the land. Now we must re-evaluate the investment project given that he will actively manage the oil field and abandon the business when it is to his advantage.

We proceed as before by adding decision points to the tree in Exhibit 13.1 to convert it from an event tree to a decision tree for evaluating the abandonment decision. The result is shown in Exhibit 13.3. The lines originating at each rectangle describe the outcome of the decision: an immediate cash inflow of $250,000 if Ted abandons the project and the chance for $550,000 or $150,000 in 1999 if he doesn't.

Ted's choice at each decision point depends on the values of abandoning or continuing to operate the oil field. The value of abandoning the field at the end of 1998 is $250,000 regardless of what happened to oil prices that year. The value of continuing to operate the field at the end of 1998 equals the discounted value of the expected cash flows in 1999. Given $26 per barrel of oil in 1998, this value is

$$\text{Value of continued operations if price of oil in 1998 was \$26/bbl} = \frac{\$550,000 \times 0.90 + \$150,000 \times 0.10}{1.10}$$

$$= \$463,636$$

$$\text{Value of abandoning the oil field} = \$250,000.$$

If oil was $26 per barrel in 1998, Ted should not abandon the field because $463,636 is greater than $250,000. This plan eliminates path 1 in Exhibit 13.3 from further consideration

We use the same approach to evaluate the other decision point.

$$\text{Value of continued operations if price of oil in 1998 was \$18/bbl} = \frac{\$550,000 \times 0.20 + \$150,000 \times 0.80}{1.10}$$

$$= \$209,091$$

$$\text{Value of abandoning the oil field} = \$250,000$$

Abandoning the oil field has a higher value in this case so Ted should not continue operations if the price of oil was only $18 in 1998. This plan will produce a total cash flow of $400,000 ($150,000 + $250,000) in 1998 and eliminate paths 5 and 6 in Exhibit 13.3 from consideration.

The three paths that go from start to finish given Ted's abandonment plans are summarized in Table 13.4. The expected free cash flows and their discounted value using the 10 percent required rate of return are computed below.

$$E(\text{FCF 1997}) = \$-600,000$$

$$E(\text{FCF 1998}) = \$550,000 \times 0.45 + \$550,000 \times 0.05 + \$400,000 \times 0.50$$
$$= \$475,000$$

$$E(\text{FCF 1999}) = \$550,000 \times 0.45 + \$150,000 \times 0.05 + \$0 \times 0.50$$
$$= \$255,000$$

Table 13.4   SUMMARY OF OIL FIELD PAYOFFS WITH ABANDONMENT

Path	Probability	Free Cash Flow 1997	1998	1999
2	0.45	$-600,000	$550,000	$550,000
3	0.05	-600,000	550,000	150,000
4	0.50	-600,000	400,000	0

$$\text{Market value} = \frac{\$475,000}{(1.10)} + \frac{\$255,000}{(1.10)^2} = \$642,562$$

Net present value = $642,562 − $600,000 = $42,562

By planning to actively manage the oil field and abandon operations when it is advantageous, Ted increased the proposal's value by $18,595 ($42,562 − $23,967).

VALUE OF A TRAINING PROGRAM WITH ACTIVE MANAGEMENT   13.4

HydroArc's managers (from Exercise 13.3) recognized that they can sequence training and dismiss workers who do not become qualified divers. The diving training program lasts six months and costs $9,000. The welding training program also lasts six months and costs the remaining $43,000, but the welding school refunds $40,000 for cancellations.

Redraw the event tree recognizing management's ability to actively manage the training program. Should they hire employees under the new conditions?

Payoffs from Hiring New Employee with Active Management

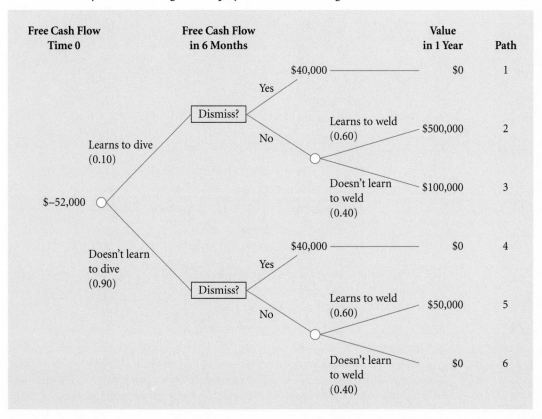

The value of retaining qualified divers at the six-month point, derived from paths 2 and 3, is

$$\text{Value of retaining qualified divers} = \frac{\$500,000 \times 0.60 + \$100,000 \times 0.40}{1.125}$$

$$= \$302,222.$$

This amount is greater than the $40,000 refund from dismissing the divers and cancelling the welding school so path 1 is eliminated from further consideration.

The value of retaining nondivers, derived from paths 5 and 6, is

$$\text{Value of retaining nondivers} = \frac{\$50,000 \times 0.60 + \$0 \times 0.40}{1.125}$$

$$= \$26,667.$$

This amount is less than the $40,000 refund from dismissing the divers and cancelling the welding school, so paths 5 and 6 are eliminated from further consideration. The remaining paths are summarized below.

Path	Probability	Free Cash Flow		Value in 1 Year
		Time 0	In 6 Months	
2	0.06	$–52,000	$ 0	$500,000
3	0.04	–52,000	0	100,000
4	0.90	–52,000	40,000	0

$$\text{Free cash flow at time 0} = \$-52,000$$

$$\text{Expected free cash flow in 6 months} = \$0 \times 0.06 + \$0 \times 0.04 + \$40,000 \times 0.90$$

$$= \$36,000$$

$$\text{Expected free cash flow in 1 year} = \$500,000 \times 0.06 + \$100,000 \times 0.04 + \$0 \times 0.90$$

$$= \$34,000$$

$$\text{Market value} = \$36,000/1.125 + \$34,000/(1.125)^2$$

$$= \$58,864$$

$$\text{NPV} = \$58,864 - \$52,000 = \$6,864$$

The new training program is acceptable because it improves the owners' wealth by $6,864. This is an improvement of $10,666 over the old program which had a NPV of $–3,802 (computed in Exercise 13.3).

• ——————— •

This discussion was phrased in terms of complete abandonment but companies also can scale back projects—the equivalent of partial abandonment. The decision to reduce a project's scale is approached the same way although there are many more alternatives to consider (10 percent abandonment, 20 percent abandonment, etc.). Nevertheless, the results are similar. The opportunity—but not the obligation—to scale back operations can only increase the investment proposal's value.

Summary of the Effect of Active Management   Active management contributed a significant amount to the value of the field of stripper wells. The breakdown of the sources of this asset's value follows.

Value of passive investment	$23,967
Value of expansion opportunity	22,727
Value of abandonment opportunity	18,595
Total value	$65,289

It is perilous for companies to overlook these sources of value by applying net present value analysis to strategic investment opportunities. If they do, they forgo opportunities to create wealth for their owners and they cede important strategic advantages to competitors who recognize them.

Other Strategic Choices   Companies can combine abandonment and expansion alternatives to construct a wide range of strategic choices. As an example, consider the elaboration of Ted Parr's strategic choices described in the following table.

	Production Capacity (bbls)	
Strategy	**1998**	**1999**
A	50,000	50,000
B	50,000	100,000
C	50,000	0
D	0	0
E	0	50,000
F	0	100,000
G	100,000	0
H	100,000	50,000
I	100,000	100,000

We only examined strategies A, B, and C—passive management, expansion, and abandonment. Strategies D, E, and F are implemented by deferring the investment (D is permanent deferral) while G, H, and I require immediate expansion with the possibility of complete or partial abandonment. An even wider array of strategic choices is available for projects that last more than two years. For example, Ted Parr could alternately expand and contract operations as oil prices periodically increase and decrease.

   We will examine some of these other strategic choices later, but first we need a more efficient method of analysis to properly describe the complexity and risk of realistic problems.

Limitations of Decision Tree Analysis   Using decision trees to analyze strategic decisions is an improvement over ordinary NPV analysis because decision trees account for the value created by active managers. However, there are two obstacles to using decision trees to analyze realistic proposals.

The first obstacle is that realistic investment proposals are too complex to be described by manageable decision trees. This complexity arises from the combination of four factors. There are usually *many* (1) years in a project's life, (2) possibilities at each chance event, (3) decisions to be made, and (4) choices at each decision point. Consequently, a very large number of paths may be needed to completely describe even a simple strategic decision.

To see how quickly a decision tree can become unmanageable, consider the relatively simple project described below.

Life:	5 years
Chance events:	1 per year with 3 possible outcomes
Decision points:	1 per year except the last
Choices at each decision point:	3

The decision tree that completely describes this project has 19,683 paths![2] You may object that a computer could analyze this large decision tree very quickly and you'd be right. However, *people* must provide the cash flow and probability estimates for those 19,683 paths and this is what makes large decision trees unmanageable.

The second obstacle to using decision trees to analyze strategic decisions is that we don't know the required rate of return to use for discounting the modified cash flows. The required rate of return for the passively managed project is inappropriate because active management amplifies the project's desirable outcomes and dampens its undesirable ones. This changes the probability distribution of the project's rate of return and therefore changes the covariance between these returns and market returns. Consequently, we need an entirely different required rate of return. Unfortunately, the decision tree approach provides no information that we can use to estimate it.

We overcome these obstacles by using option pricing models to value management's opportunities to modify the payoffs from strategic projects. The Black-Scholes option pricing model permits us to value a project with an infinite number of paths and we don't need to know the required rate of return for the modified cash flows to apply it or the binomial option pricing model. These features allow us to correctly analyze any imaginable strategic decision.

13.2   USING OPTION PRICING MODELS TO EVALUATE STRATEGIC DECISIONS

We can use option pricing models to evaluate strategic decisions because the opportunities to expand, contract, accelerate, delay, and abandon the underlying assets are options. These strategic choices *are* options because managers can implement the ones that become valuable as circumstances change and ignore the others or let them expire worthless (see "In the News"). Furthermore, we can use particular types of options

---

[2]The formula used to compute the number of paths is

$$\text{Paths} = (\text{number of outcomes per chance event})^n \times (\text{number of choices per decision})^{n-1}$$
$$= 3^5 \times 3^4 = 19{,}683.$$

I N   T H E   N E W S

OPTIONAL INVESTING

ALL INVESTMENT CALCULATIONS rely on predicting uncertain future profits. But the traditional theory also assumes, implicitly, that investments are a now-or-never choice. That is unrealistic, say economists. Mostly, managers have some choice about when to invest. Waiting may mean missed opportunities. More often, in an uncertain world, it offers a valuable chance to learn more about the likely fate of the project.

The ability to delay an irreversible investment is like a financial "call option." The firm has the right, but not the obligation, to buy (invest in) an underlying asset (the profits from the project) at a price (the investment cost) at a future time of its choosing. This option has a value. When the firm makes the investment, it exercises (or, in financial-market jargon, "kills") its option.

It follows, then, that the cost of that killed option (the value of waiting for better information) ought to be included when calculating net present value. Before a project goes ahead, the present value of profits should exceed the investment costs by at least the value of keeping the option alive.

The theory will be most useful in areas when the uncertainties are relatively apparent. The sums are already being churned over in the computers of some oil firms, for instance. There is one main risk in developing an oil field—a change in the oil price. Property developers, electric utilities, and drug companies are also investigating how to apply the theory in practice.

Source: "Optional Investing," *The Economist*, January 8, 1994, p. 76. Copyright © 1994, The Economist, Ltd. Distributed by New York Times Special Features/Syndication Sales.

---

and option strategies to almost perfectly represent these opportunities. We'll begin by using the binomial option pricing model to re-examine the opportunities to expand or abandon a project and consider some more complicated strategies later.

Using a Call Option to Represent the Opportunity to Expand a Strategic Project

The opportunity to expand a strategic project, called an **expansion option**, is accurately represented by a call option on the market value of the additional assets. These assets occupy the role of common stock in the option pricing model so you must calculate their market value as if you will manage them passively. That is, you simply discount their expected free cash flows using a required rate of return appropriate for their risk.

The exercise price of this call option is the initial cost of the additional assets. The company will exercise the option and acquire these assets to expand the project if their market value exceeds the exercise price on the expiration date—but not otherwise. Therefore, the value of the expansion option on the expiration date is

$$\text{Value of expansion option at expiration} = \text{Max}(S_T - E, 0)$$

where S_T = market value of additional assets
E = initial cost of additional assets.

Exhibit 13.4

SOURCES OF VALUE IN STRATEGIC DECISIONS

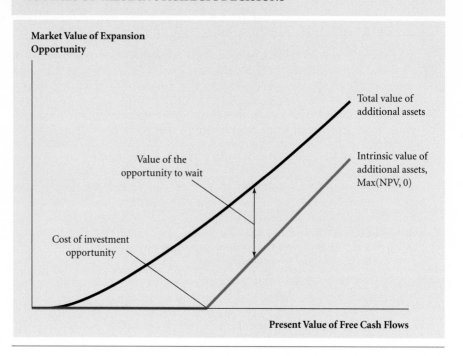

Given the definitions of S_T and E, we also can write the value of the expansion option as

$$\text{Value of expansion option at expiration} = \text{Max}(\text{NPV}, 0).$$

The option's value prior to the expiration date is greater than or equal to this value, as you learned in Chapter 8, because volatility and time increase the likelihood the option will be valuable when it expires. The total value of the opportunity to expand the strategic project therefore equals the intrinsic value of the additional assets plus the value of the right to choose expansion when it is advantageous. These sources of value are diagrammed in Exhibit 13.4.

We will use Ted Parr's opportunity to expand the field of stripper wells to illustrate this approach to evaluating a strategic investment opportunity.

Remember from Section 13.1 that Ted has the opportunity to expand operations in the field of stripper wells by installing an advanced recovery system at the end of 1998 for an initial cost of $300,000. This system will increase 1999's free cash flows from $550,000 to $975,000 or from $150,000 to $175,000, depending on whether oil prices are $26 or $18 per barrel. The free cash flows provided by the additional assets are therefore $425,000 under favorable conditions and $25,000 under unfavorable conditions. These cash flows and the probabilities of the oil prices on which they depend are shown in panel A of Exhibit 13.5.

Exhibit 13.5

EXPANSION OPTION

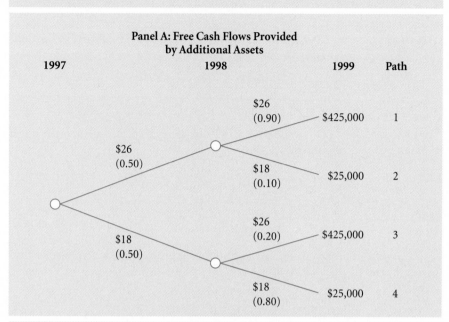

Panel A: Free Cash Flows Provided by Additional Assets

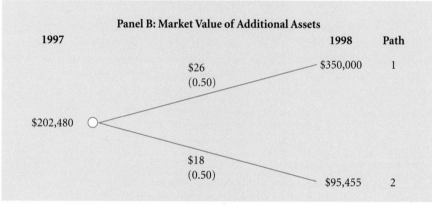

Panel B: Market Value of Additional Assets

The market value of the advanced recovery system equals its expected free cash flows discounted at the market's required rate of return of 10 percent. The possible market values at the end of 1998 are as follows.

1998 Market Value if 1998 Oil Prices Were $26/bbl

$$\text{Market value 1998} = \frac{\$425,000 \times 0.90 + \$25,000 \times 0.10}{1.1}$$

$$= \$350,000$$

1998 Market Value if 1998 Oil Prices Were $18/bbl

$$\text{Market value 1998} = \frac{\$425,000 \times 0.20 + \$25,000 \times 0.80}{1.1}$$

$$= \$95,455$$

The market value of the system at the end of 1997 is computed similarly by discounting 1998's expected market values.

$$\text{Market value 1997} = \frac{\$350,000 \times 0.50 + \$95,455 \times 0.50}{1.1}$$

$$= \$202,480$$

These market values are shown in panel B of Exhibit 13.5. Using the option pricing notation from Chapter 8, the market values are as follows.

$$S_T^+ = \$350,000$$
$$S_T^- = \$95,455$$
$$S_0 = \$202,480$$
$$E = \$300,000$$

The value at the end of 1997 of committing to install the advanced recovery system at the end of 1998 is its intrinsic value at that time, $\text{Max}(S_0 - E, 0)$, which equals zero.

$$\text{Intrinsic value at 1997} = \text{Max}(\$202,480 - \$300,000, \$0)$$
$$= \$0$$

Ted's option does not expire until 1998, however, so its value is greater than or equal to this minimum. He will exercise the option then for a gain of $50,000 ($S_T^+ - E = \$350,000 - \$300,000$) if oil prices were $26 per barrel in 1998 but let it expire worthless otherwise. According to the certainty equivalent form of the binomial option pricing model, the current value of his (call) option to expand the project if r_f equals 6 percent is

$$C_0 = \frac{C_T^+ \times q_T^+ + C_T^- \times (1 - q_T^+)}{1 + r_f}$$

where
$$C_T^+ = \$50,000$$
$$C_T^- = \$0$$
$$u = S_T^+/S_0 = \$350,000/\$202,480 = 1.7286$$
$$d = S_T^-/S_0 = \$95,455/\$202,480 = 0.4714$$
$$q_T^+ = (1 + r_f - d)/(u - d)$$
$$= (1.06 - 0.4714)/(1.7286 - 0.4714) = 0.4682$$
$$C_0 = \frac{\$50,000 \times 0.4682 + \$0 \times 0.5318}{1.06} = \$22,085.$$

Therefore, the right—but not the obligation—to expand the field of stripper wells is worth $22,085 at the end of 1997 even though the intrinsic value of the advanced recovery equipment at that time is zero.

Note that the value of the expansion option is close to but different from the value obtained by analyzing the decision tree. This is due to the fact that we did not impose the 10 percent required rate of return, which is tantamount to assuming the advanced recovery equipment has the same risk as the passively managed oil field. On the contrary, we were able to determine its current value without explicitly considering its risk. In a sense, the expansion opportunity's risk is irrelevant because all we really need to know is that its value is positive. Our ability to compute the value of the expansion option this way overcomes one of the obstacles to using decision tree analysis.

Note also that we obtained the value of the expansion option directly without explicitly analyzing other, irrelevant portions of the decision tree. This is a definite advantage when evaluating realistic strategic decisions that have extremely complicated decision trees.

EXERCISE

13.5

AN OPTION ON A NEW PRODUCT

Use the binomial option pricing model to re-examine Dento-Flux's decision to introduce a new brand of toothpaste. The riskless rate of interest is 5 percent per six months. Begin by drawing the tree that describes the value of the toothpaste business in one year and at the six-month point.

Option Analysis of New Toothpaste

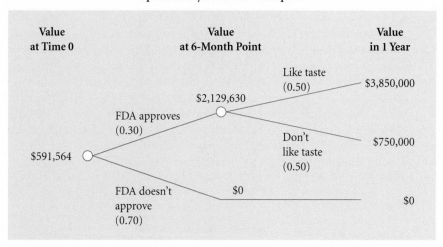

Now use the values in this tree to apply the binomial option pricing model.

$$u = \$2{,}129{,}630/\$591{,}564 = 3.6000$$

$$d = \$0/\$591{,}564 = 0$$

$$q_T^+ = (1.05 - 0)/(3.6000 - 0) = 0.2917$$

$$C_T^+ = \$2{,}129{,}630 - \$1{,}750{,}000 = \$379{,}630$$

$$C_0 = \frac{\$379{,}630 \times 0.2917}{1.05} = \$105{,}465$$

Applying for FDA approval gives Dento-Flux the option of introducing the new toothpaste if the formula is approved. The value of this option is $105,465, which is more than its cost, $50,000, so the company should seek approval for the product.

Using a Put Option to Represent the Opportunity to Abandon a Strategic Project

The opportunity to abandon a strategic project, called an **abandonment option,** is represented by a put option on the market value of the *existing* assets. These assets occupy the role of common stock in the option pricing model so you must calculate their market value as if you will manage them passively. This means you simply discount their expected free cash flows using a required rate of return appropriate for their risk.

The exercise price of the put option is the salvage value of the existing assets. The company will exercise the option and sell the assets to contract or abandon the project if the exercise price exceeds their market value—but not otherwise. Therefore, the value of the abandonment option on the expiration date is

$$\text{Value of abandonment option at expiration} = \text{Max}(E - S_T, 0)$$

where E = salvage value of existing assets
                 S_T = market value of existing assets.

The current worth of the opportunity to abandon the strategic project equals this intrinsic value (of the existing assets) plus the value of the right to sell them when it is advantageous.

Let's return to Ted Parr's field of stripper wells for an illustration. He has the opportunity to abandon operations at the end of 1998 by selling the equipment and land for $250,000 or continue operations to obtain the free cash flows they provide. These cash flows and the probabilities of the oil prices on which they depend are shown in panel A of Exhibit 13.6.

Ted will abandon operations if the market value of the existing assets is less than this $250,000 at the end of 1998—but not otherwise. The market value of these assets equals their expected free cash flows discounted at the market's required rate of return of 10 percent. The possible market values of the existing assets at the end of 1998 are as follows.

1998 Market Value if 1998 Oil Prices Were $26/bbl

$$\text{Market value 1998} = \frac{\$550,000 \times 0.90 + \$150,000 \times 0.10}{1.1}$$
$$= \$463,636$$

1998 Market Value if 1998 Oil Prices Were $18/bbl

$$\text{Market value 1998} = \frac{\$550,000 \times 0.20 + \$150,000 \times 0.80}{1.1}$$
$$= \$209,091$$

The market value of the existing assets at the end of 1997 is computed similarly by discounting 1998's expected market values.

$$\text{Market value 1997} = \frac{\$463,636 \times 0.50 + \$209,091 \times 0.50}{1.1}$$
$$= \$305,785$$

Exhibit 13.6

ABANDONMENT OPTION

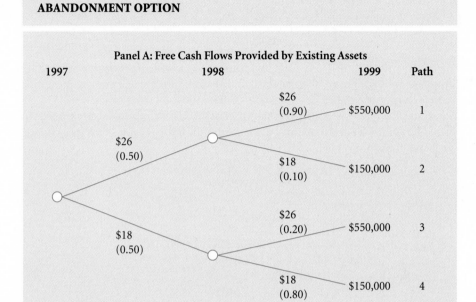

Panel A: Free Cash Flows Provided by Existing Assets

1997	1998	1999	Path
	$26 (0.90)	$550,000	1
$26 (0.50)			
	$18 (0.10)	$150,000	2
	$26 (0.20)	$550,000	3
$18 (0.50)			
	$18 (0.80)	$150,000	4

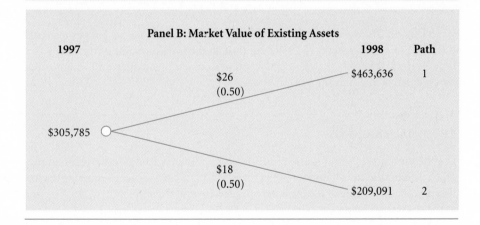

Panel B: Market Value of Existing Assets

1997		1998	Path
	$26 (0.50)	$463,636	1
$305,785			
	$18 (0.50)	$209,091	2

These market values are shown in panel B of Exhibit 13.6. Using the option pricing notation from Chapter 8, the market values are as follows.

$$S_T^+ = \$463,636$$
$$S_T^- = \$209,091$$
$$S_0 = \$305,785$$
$$E = \$250,000$$

The value at the end of 1997 of committing to sell the existing assets at the end of 1998 is its intrinsic value at that time, $\text{Max}(E - S_0, 0)$, which equals zero.

$$\text{Intrinsic value at 1997} = \text{Max}(\$250,000 - \$305,785, \$0)$$
$$= \$0$$

Ted doesn't have to decide what to do until 1998, however, so the value of his abandonment option is greater than or equal to this minimum. He will exercise the option then for a gain of $40,909 ($E - S_T^- = \$250,000 - \$209,091$) if oil prices were $18 per barrel in 1998 but let it expire worthless otherwise. According to the certainty equivalent form of the binomial option pricing model, the current value of his (put) option to abandon the project is

$$P_0 = \frac{P_T^+ \times q_T^+ + P_T^- \times (1 - q_T^+)}{1 + r_f}$$

where

$$P_T^+ = \$0$$
$$P_T^- = \$40,909$$
$$u = S_T^+ / S_0 = \$463,636 / \$305,785 = 1.5162$$
$$d = S_T^- / S_0 = \$209,091 / \$305,785 = 0.6838$$
$$q_T^+ = (1 + r_f - d)/(u - d)$$
$$= (1.06 - 0.6838)/(1.5162 - 0.6838) = 0.4519$$
$$P_0 = \frac{\$0 \times 0.4519 + \$40,909 \times 0.5481}{1.06} = \$21,153.$$

Therefore, the right—but not the obligation—to abandon the field of stripper wells is worth $21,153 at the end of 1997 even though the intrinsic value of the sale at that time is zero. Once again, the value of the option is similar to but different from the value we obtained using decision tree analysis.

E X E R C I S E   • ———————————————————————————————————— •

13.6   OPTIONAL TRAINING

Use the binomial option pricing model to re-examine HydroArc's new training program. The riskless rate of interest is 5 percent per six months. Begin by drawing the tree that describes the value of the business produced by trained employees in one year and at the six-month point.

Now use the values in this tree to apply the binomial option pricing model.

$$u = \$302,222 / \$48,198 = 6.2704$$
$$d = \$26,667 / \$48,198 = 0.5533$$
$$q_T^+ = (1.05 - 0.5533)/(6.2704 - 0.5533) = 0.0869$$
$$P_T^- = \$40,000 - \$26,667 = \$13,333$$
$$P_0 = \frac{\$13,333 \times (1 - 0.0869)}{1.05} = \$11,595.$$

The option to dismiss employees who do not become qualified divers rather than send them to welding school is worth $11,595.

Option Analysis of Training Program

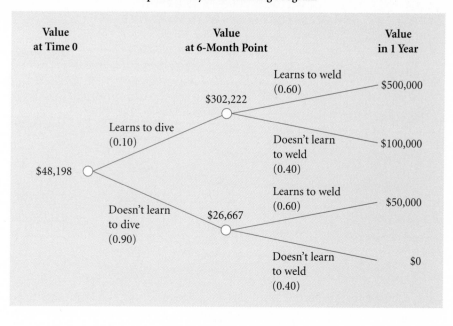

Value at Time 0	Value at 6-Month Point	Value in 1 Year

- $48,198
- Learns to dive (0.10) → $302,222
  - Learns to weld (0.60) → $500,000
  - Doesn't learn to weld (0.40) → $100,000
- Doesn't learn to dive (0.90) → $26,667
  - Learns to weld (0.60) → $50,000
  - Doesn't learn to weld (0.40) → $0

Other Strategic Options

Long-term investment projects are not the only place you will find strategic options. Manufacturing managers have alternative ways to organize production and purchasing, sales, and cash managers have alternative ways to process payments and collections. We will re-examine two issues we discussed in Chapters 11 and 12 to illustrate the importance of recognizing and valuing the options attached to operating decisions.

Outsourcing   We discussed the make-or-buy decision in Chapter 11 where you learned how to determine the present value of production costs. There, we tentatively concluded a company should buy component parts from suppliers if this policy reduces the present value of total costs. The disadvantage of this approach is that it overlooks the value of the knowledge and skills maintained by continuing to perform some of the work internally. Maintaining the ability to produce the parts internally may become valuable and should be incorporated in the analysis. Now, we can re-examine this question using option pricing to measure the potential benefit of maintaining the option to produce parts internally.

There may be several intangible benefits from producing parts internally. First, the production process can be used to train employees to use new technology before entry barriers become insurmountable. The knowledge gained in this way also can be applied to other products even if the company never enters that particular area of production. Second, external sources of supply may be interrupted if, for example, a supplier decides to vertically integrate and compete with one of its customers. Whatever

Table 13.5   **QUICK SWITCH MANUFACTURING COMPANY COMPARISON OF PRODUCTION AND INVENTORY COSTS WITH MAKE OR BUY**

	Make Switches	Buy Switches
Number of orders each year	10	12
Cost of each order		
Direct cost		
Materials	$ 6,000.00	$ 6,250.00
Labor	1,650.00	0
Indirect costs		
Order cost	106.00	56.50
Storage cost	57.38	23.44
Total costs	$ 7,813.38	$ 6,329.94
Present value	$74,093.74	$71,956.38

the benefit, internal production keeps alive an option on future production alternatives that has value. This value must be accounted for when the decision to make or buy a component part is evaluated.

We will use the Quick Switch Manufacturing Company example from Chapter 11 to illustrate this process. That example was summarized by Table 11.4, repeated here as Table 13.5. The annual savings from buying completed microswitches rather than modifying generic ones is $2,137.36 ($74,093.74 − $71,956.38). If we assume this production process continues indefinitely, then these savings comprise a perpetual annuity due with a present value of $19,949 ($2,137.36 + $2,137.36/0.12).

Now let us suppose that Quick Switch foresees the possibility that emerging technology will enable them to offer a new line of special purpose safety controls that employ fuzzy logic. Quick Switch believes its technicians can easily master the new technology if they remain involved in the design process but will have a great deal of difficulty if they become mere assemblers. Consequently, they anticipate they can enter the new market in one year if they continue to adapt microswitches to their own use but not if they buy them ready made. That is, the option to develop and market the new safety controls is attached to the production policy under which they make parts and not to the policy under which they buy them. We must value this option before we conclude it is truly better to buy ready made microswitches from their supplier.

Quick Switch's new product design team estimates it will cost $200,000 and take one year to develop and launch the fuzzy logic safety controls. The market value of this business at the end of 1998 depends on the presence or absence of competition and whether the company's design is successful. The possibilities and their probabilities are depicted in panel A of Exhibit 13.7.

The market values of the new safety controls on June 30, 1998, when Quick Switch must decide whether to proceed with development, equal the expected market values on December 31, 1998, discounted at the company's required rate of return of

Exhibit 13.7

OPTION ATTACHED TO MAKING OWN PARTS

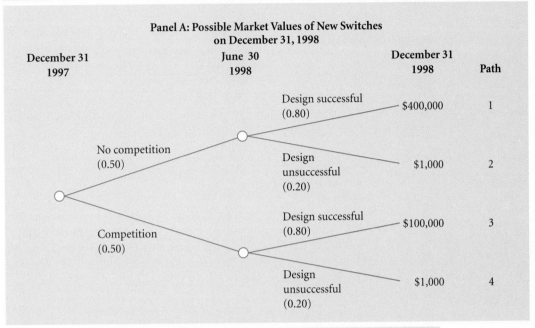

Panel A: Possible Market Values of New Switches
on December 31, 1998

December 31 1997	June 30 1998	December 31 1998	Path

No competition (0.50)

Design successful (0.80) — $400,000 — 1

Design unsuccessful (0.20) — $1,000 — 2

Competition (0.50)

Design successful (0.80) — $100,000 — 3

Design unsuccessful (0.20) — $1,000 — 4

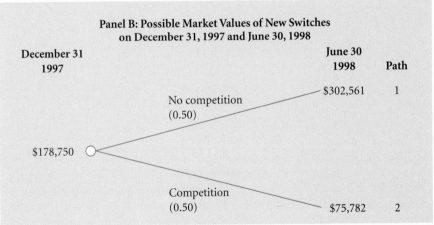

Panel B: Possible Market Values of New Switches
on December 31, 1997 and June 30, 1998

December 31 1997   June 30 1998   Path

$178,750

No competition (0.50) — $302,561 — 1

Competition (0.50) — $75,782 — 2

12 percent per year or 5.83 percent per six months.[3] The possible values on June 30 are as follows.

---

[3]The six-month rate of return that yields an effective annual rate of return of 12 percent is given by

$$(1 + r)^2 = 1.12$$
$$r = 0.0583 \text{ or } 5.83\%.$$

June 1998 Market Value with No Competition

$$\text{Market value June 1998} = \frac{\$400,000 \times 0.80 + \$1,000 \times 0.20}{1.0583}$$

$$= \$302,561$$

June 1998 Market Value With Competition

$$\text{Market value June 1998} = \frac{\$100,000 \times 0.80 + \$1,000 \times 0.20}{1.0583}$$

$$= \$75,782$$

The market value of the new safety controls at the end of 1997 is computed similarly by discounting the expected market values on June 30.

$$\text{Market value December 1997} = \frac{\$302,561 \times 0.50 + \$75,782 \times 0.50}{1.0583}$$

$$= \$178,750$$

You can see that Quick Switch will spend $200,000 on June 30, 1998 to develop and market the new safety controls if no competing products have been introduced—but not otherwise. Therefore, we can use the risk-neutral form of the binomial option pricing model to determine the value of this option. The riskless rate of return is 6 percent per year or 2.96 percent every six months.

$$C_0 = \frac{C_T^+ \times q_T^+ + C_T^- \times (1 - q_T^+)}{1 + r_f}$$

where
$$C_T^+ = \text{Max}(\$302,561 - \$200,000, 0) = \$102,561$$
$$C_T^- = \text{Max}(\$75,782 - \$200,000, 0) = \$0$$
$$u = S_T^+/S_0 = \$302,561/\$178,750 = 1.6926$$
$$d = S_T^-/S_0 = \$75,782/\$178,750 = 0.4240$$
$$q_T^+ = (1 + r_f - d)/(u - d)$$
$$= (1.0296 - 0.4240)/(1.6926 - 0.4240) = 0.4774$$
$$C_0 = \frac{\$102,561 \times 0.4774 + \$0 \times 0.5226}{1.0296} = \$47,555$$

The option to develop and market the new safety controls is worth $47,555 at the end of 1997. Buying ready made microswitches had a value of $19,949 but destroyed the opportunity to enter the new business because Quick Switch's technicians would not keep abreast of new developments. The net value of making their own switches is therefore $27,606 ($47,555 − $19,949), so they should not outsource this production process.

Accept or Forgo a Cash Discount for Early Payment   Many suppliers offer their customers credit terms that provide a cash discount for early payment. The terms 2/10 net 30, which require full payment in 30 days but provide a 2 percent discount for payment within 10 days, are commonplace. You learned in Chapter 12 that these terms may be used to accommodate customers with different opportunity costs or to identify low-risk customers who are worthy of long-term commitments.

Discounts for early payment also may be used to induce customers to accept shipments quickly. This diminishes their opportunity to inspect the goods and make deductions from the amount owed or to return the goods later. Viewed this way, a discount for early payment is the price suppliers are willing to pay to get customers to relinquish their put option and to accept the risk of defective goods. A company should pay early and accept the cash discount if it is larger than the value of this put option—but not otherwise. We will use a numerical example to illustrate how to determine this put option's value.

Burgess Avionics Company buys $130,000 of electronic components per month on terms of 1/10 net 30 and manufactures flight recording equipment that is sold 30 days later for $200,000. There is a 10 percent chance that the company must spend an additional $15,000 to correct defects in each shipment. Burgess's free cash flows each month therefore are $70,000 ($200,000 − $130,000) with probability of 0.90 or $55,000 ($200,000 − $130,000 − $15,000) with probability of 0.10. The expected present value of these cash flows at the beginning of the month using Burgess's opportunity cost of 1 percent per month is

$$\text{Value of flight recorder cash flows} = \frac{\$70,000 \times 0.90 + \$55,000 \times 0.10}{1.01}$$

$$= \$67,822.$$

These end-of-month cash flows and their value at the beginning of a month are diagrammed in Exhibit 13.8.

The companies that supply the electronic components are very good about replacing defective parts if they are returned prior to payment but notoriously uncooperative otherwise. This means Burgess can protect its $70,000 operating profit margin by delaying payment until production is complete or accept the risk of paying for repairs in return for the $1,300 cash discount ($130,000 × 0.01). We can use the risk-neutral form of the binomial option pricing model to determine the value of their put option and compare it to the $1,300 cash discount to decide what they should do.

The underlying asset in this option pricing problem is the production of flight-recording equipment. The current values of this asset and when the put option expires (when payment is due) are given in Exhibit 13.8. They are as follows.

$$S_0 = \$67,822$$
$$S_T^+ = \$70,000$$
$$S_T^- = \$55,000$$

The exercise price of their put option is $70,000 because they can ensure this level of operating profit by returning defective parts to the supplier.

Assuming the riskless rate of return is 0.5 percent per month, the value of Burgess's put option is

Exhibit 13.8

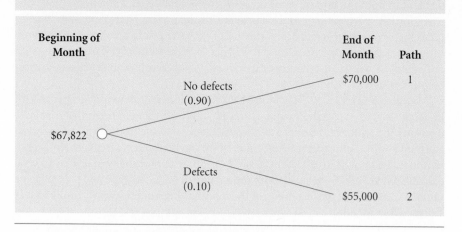

VALUES OF FLIGHT RECORDER SALES

Beginning of Month — $67,822

No defects (0.90) → $70,000 — Path 1

Defects (0.10) → $55,000 — Path 2

End of Month — Path

$$P_0 = \frac{P_T^+ \times q_T^+ + P_T^- \times (1 - q_T^+)}{1 + r_f}$$

where

$$P_T^+ = \text{Max}(E - S_T^+, 0)$$
$$= \text{Max}(\$70,000 - \$70,000, 0) = \$0$$
$$P_T^- = \text{Max}(E - S_T^-, 0)$$
$$= \text{Max}(\$70,000 - \$55,000, 0) = \$15,000$$
$$u = S_T^+ / S_0 = \$70,000/\$67,822 = 1.0321$$
$$d = S_T^- / S_0 = \$55,000/\$67,822 = 0.8109$$
$$q_T^+ = (1 + r_f - d)/(u - d)$$
$$= (1.005 - 0.8109)/(1.0321 - 0.8109) = 0.8775$$
$$P_0 = \frac{\$0 \times 0.8775 + \$15,000 \times 0.1225}{1.005} = \$1,828.$$

Maintaining the ability to return defective parts to the supplier is worth $1,828; therefore, Burgess should not sell its put option by accepting the cash discount of $1,300.

Deciding When to Exercise a Strategic Option

A strategic option should be exercised when doing so provides benefits that exceed the option's market value. You learned in Chapter 8 that this can never happen prior to expiration with an American call option on an asset that does not provide interim benefits even if that option is in-the-money at the time. The reason is that the underlying asset's volatility and the passage of time increase the likelihood the option will be worth even more than its intrinsic value when it expires. You also learned in Chapter 8 that an American call option on an asset that provides interim cash flows may be exercised prior to the expiration date to get those cash flows that are an immediate addition to the option's intrinsic value.

Strategic options often are American options on assets that provide interim cash flows. Therefore, at the end of each period, we must explicitly compare the value of exer-

Exhibit 13.9

FREE CASH FLOWS WITH IMMEDIATE EXPANSION

Free Cash Flow 1997	Free Cash Flow 1998	Free Cash Flow 1999	Path

$26 (0.90) $975,000   1

$26 (0.50) $975,000

$18 (0.10) $175,000   2

$-900,000

$26 (0.20) $975,000   3

$18 (0.50) $175,000

$18 (0.80) $175,000   4

---

cising the option immediately with the value of keeping it open until the end of the next period. You actually already know how to do this. The value of exercising the option immediately is simply the net present value of all its expected free cash flows, that is, its value if it is managed passively. The value of keeping the option open is determined by applying one of our option pricing models. We will return to Ted Parr's field of stripper wells for an illustration.

Remember that we determined the current (1997) value of the option to expand the field of stripper wells at the end of 1998 was $22,085. This amount is the value of Ted Parr's expansion option if it is kept open or alive until 1998. We will compare this value to the payoff from exercising the option immediately.

Ted can exercise the expansion option immediately by expanding the capacity of the field as soon as he purchases it. This strategy requires an immediate cash outflow of $900,000 to buy the oil field and install the advanced recovery system and produces free cash flows of $975,000 or $175,000 each year depending on the level of oil prices. Exhibit 13.9 describes this strategy's payoffs and the expected free cash flows are computed in the following caluculation.

$$E(\text{FCF 1997}) = \$-900,000$$

$$E(\text{FCF 1998}) = \$975,000 \times 0.45 + \$975,000 \times 0.05 + \$175,000 \times 0.10$$
$$+ \$175,000 \times 0.40$$
$$= \$575,000$$

$$E(\text{FCF 1999}) = \$975,000 \times 0.45 + \$175,000 \times 0.05 + \$975,000 \times 0.10$$
$$+ \$175,000 \times 0.40$$
$$= \$615,000$$

Applying Ted's 10 percent required rate of return, the project's market value and net present value are as follows.

$$\text{Market value} = \frac{\$575,000}{(1.10)} + \frac{\$615,000}{(1.10)^2} = \$1,030,992$$

$$\text{Net present value} = \$1,030,992 - \$900,000 = \$130,992$$

The value of the project without expansion was $23,967. Consequently, the value of exercising the expansion option immediately is $107,025 ($130,992 − $23,967). This value is substantially larger than the value of keeping the option alive ($22,085) so Ted should buy the field and install the advanced recovery system immediately.

It was worthwhile for Ted to exercise his strategic option immediately because the additional capacity provided much larger cash flows in 1998. These cash flows more than compensated for the flexibility Ted lost by not being able to choose expansion *after* learning whether 1998's oil prices were high or low. Of course, it could be worthwhile to keep the option open under different circumstances. More volatile oil prices, a longer time until expiration, and the like may increase the option's value and make it worthwhile to defer expansion until later. Whatever the outcome, the method of analysis is the same as demonstrated by this example.

13.3   IDENTIFYING THE FACTORS CRUCIAL TO A DECISION'S SUCCESS

Often one factor, or at most a small number of factors, determines the success of a strategic decision. Potentially crucial factors are the variables that affect the amount, timing, and certainty of the underlying asset's free cash flows. Examples are demand, price, direct labor or materials costs, indirect costs, the rate of production and learning, working capital requirements, and a project's life. The inability to predict the values of the crucial variables with perfect certainty is what makes strategic decisions risky.

Section 13.2 demonstrated that treating strategic decisions as options is a good way to manage this risk. Managers apply this approach by deferring their strategic decision, to expand an investment for example, until they have more information about the value of the crucial variable. Then, they exercise the expansion option if the additional information is favorable but not otherwise. The first example in Section 13.2 had Ted Parr deferring his option to expand the field of stripper wells until he learned whether 1999's oil prices were more likely to be $26 or $18 per barrel.

The price of oil was the crucial variable in Ted's decision because we assumed capacity, production costs, and the life of the field were known with near certainty. Therefore, the success of the oil field with its original capacity and the success of the option to expand its capacity only depended on the uncertain price of oil. This situation is probably rare in reality because the values of most, if not all, of the variables that affect an underlying asset's free cash flows are uncertain at the outset. Furthermore, the sheer number of these variables and the complex way they interact make it difficult to determine which are crucial to a decision's success and which are insignificant.

This section describes sensitivity analysis and simulation, two techniques that can help you identify the factors crucial to a decision's success. The techniques are similar although simulation is usually automated, requires more input information, and provides more detailed results. Both techniques can be used to get a clearer picture of the possible outcomes of routine and strategic decisions.

Sensitivity and Break-Even Analysis

Analysts use **sensitivity analysis** to determine the factors that are crucial to a decision's success. The model is easy to establish and the results usually are easy to interpret.

Establishing the Model   Begin by writing the equation that describes the outcome of the decision in net present value terms. This equation must be written as a function of the variables that affect the underlying asset's free cash flows but it can be as simple or as detailed as you like. A detailed model obviously provides more information about significant and insignificant variables but it *requires* more information as well. A simple model of the outcome of an investment decision is given by Equation (13.1).

$$\text{Net present value} = \sum_{t=1}^{n} \frac{P_t \times Q_t - V_t \times Q_t - F_t - I_t}{(1+r)^t} - I_0 \qquad [13.1]$$

where P_t = cash selling price in year t
Q_t = quantity manufactured and sold in year t
V_t = cash variable cost in year t
F_t = cash fixed cost in year t
I_t = cash provided by or used for investment and financial slack in year t
n = life of the project
r = required rate of return

Next, substitute the most likely value of each of the variables into the model to compute the most likely net present value. This becomes the base case against which the effect of changing the values of the variables that affect free cash flow is measured.

Finally, perform the actual sensitivity analysis by substituting different values for one of the variables, say selling price, while holding the other variables constant at their most likely values. The amount by which the net present value changes indicates whether that variable is significant or not. Repeat this process for each of the other variables in turn and compile the results in a table or graph. Variables that produce a large range in the net present value are more significant or crucial than those that do not.

Table 13.6 describes Enzyme Solution's bottled water project, which we will use to illustrate sensitivity analysis. Panel A contains a simplified model of the project's net present value assuming it is an annuity. Panel B gives the most likely values of the variables that determine its net present value and these are used in panel C to compute its most likely net present value, $14,327.

At this point, we could ask marketing and production managers for estimates of price, variable cost, fixed cost, quantity, life, and so on when circumstances are better or worse than the most likely scenario. This request would be premature, however,

Table 13.6   DESCRIPTION OF ENZYME SOLUTION'S BOTTLED WATER PROJECT

Panel A: Net Present Value Equation

$$NPV = (P \times Q - V \times Q - F) \times APVF_{r,n} - I_0$$

Panel B: Most Likely Values of the Variables

Cash selling price (P)	$ 10
Cash variable cost (V)	$ 5
Cash fixed cost (F)	$ 18,000
Cash provided by or used for investment and financial slack (I_0)	$–150,000
Quantity manufactured and sold (Q)	8,000 bottles
Life (n)	20 years
Required return (r)	12%/year

Panel C: Most Likely Net Present Value

Most likely NPV = ($10 × 8,000 – $5 × 8,000 – $18,000) × $APVF_{0.12,20}$ – $150,000

= $22,000 × 7.4694 – $150,000

= $14,327

because preparing these estimates is a costly and time-consuming task that should not be wasted on insignificant variables. Furthermore, by asking for more information about every variable, we are likely to get less information than we need about the crucial ones and more information than we need about the insignificant ones. Therefore, some pre-screening of the project's sensitivity is warranted.

An easy way to get an initial impression of which variables are significant is to vary each one by a fixed percentage, say plus or minus 20 percent. Only those that produce significant variation in the present value of the underlying asset are selected for additional analysis.

The results of an initial analysis of Enzyme Solution's bottled water project are presented in Table 13.7.[4] You can see that the outcome of the decision is very sensitive to the selling price of the bottled water and insensitive to the life of the investment project. Variable costs have an intermediate effect.

These results are even clearer in Exhibit 13.10, a graph of the project's net present value for changes in the values of the variables between plus and minus 20 percent.[5]

---

[4]Only price, variable cost, and life are included in the table to keep the example simple. Nevertheless, all the variables should be included in the pre-screening to determine which are worthy of further investigation.

[5]The simple structure of our net present value model ensures these functions graph as straight lines. They may not in a realistic situation if, for example, the quantity sold is a function of the selling price.

INITIAL ANALYSIS OF BOTTLED WATER PROJECT'S SENSITIVITY   Table 13.7

Panel A: Sensitivity to Price

Price	Variable Cost	Life	Present Value
$ 8	—	—	$−105,184
10	**$5**	**20 years**	**14,327**
12	—	—	133,837

Panel B: Sensitivity to Variable Cost

	$6	—	$−45,428
$10	**5**	**20 years**	**14,327**
—	4	—	74,082

Panel C: Sensitivity to Life

		16 years	$ 3,428
$10	**$5**	**20 years**	**14,327**
—	—	24 years	21,255

Most likely values are in bold.

This graph confirms our conclusions that the selling price is a crucial variable and that the project's life is not. The graph also tells us the break-even point for each of the variables. Holding the other variables at their most likely values, the selling price can decline by approximately 2.5 percent to $9.75 before the net present value becomes negative. Similarly, variable costs can increase by approximately 5 percent to $5.25 before the net present value becomes negative.

Now that we know the outcome of the decision is sensitive to the selling price and variable cost, we can ask the marketing and production managers for detailed estimates of the probable range of values for these variables. We may phrase the question by asking for pessimistic and optimistic values or by asking for ranges likely to encompass the actual values 99.9 percent of the time. The range of values we obtain by this process need not be symmetric around the most likely values and we should expect a wider range of values for variables that are more difficult to estimate. Needless to say, the validity of the estimates depends on the estimator's knowledge, skill, and diligence.

Sensitivity analysis proceeds by computing the project's net present value for all possible combinations of the high, low, and most likely values of the crucial variables. The results describe the worst and best conceivable net present values as well as the more likely intermediate values. Importantly, these results can be arranged to facilitate treating the strategic decision as an option. We will continue our analysis of Enzyme Solution's bottled water project for an illustration.

Exhibit 13.10

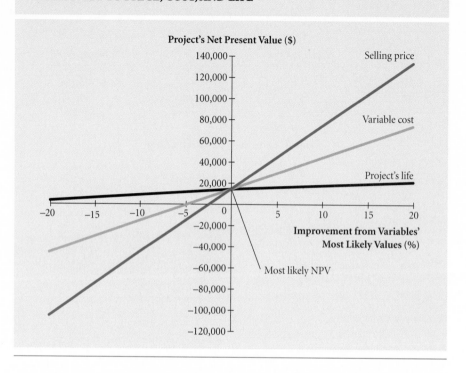

SENSITIVITY TO PRICE, COST, AND LIFE

Let's suppose that Enzyme Solution's marketing manager predicts that the bottled water may sell for as little as $6.00 or for as much as $12.00 per 10-gallon bottle while the production manager forecasts variable costs between $4.50 and $6.00 per bottle. Each range encompasses its respective most likely value but the price range is wider than the variable cost range. This difference indicates that the marketing manager has less confidence in his estimates than the production manager has in hers.

Table 13.8 gives the project's net present value for all combinations of the high, low, and most likely values of the crucial variables. The worst and best conceivable net present values are $–284,449 and $163,715. These values were computed from the extreme estimates of selling price and variable cost so the more probable net present values are those in the neighborhood of the most likely value, $14,327.

The results in Table 13.8 are graphed in Exhibit 13.11. Selling price is plotted on the horizontal axis because we determined it is the more crucial variable while the effect of different variable costs is represented by three separate lines. Each line's horizontal intercept is the break-even price for that level of variable costs. The graph provides essentially the same information as Table 13.8 because it describes the NPV landscape that surrounds the most likely value of $14,327.

Interpreting the Results   How you use the information in Table 13.8 or Exhibit 13.11 depends on the type of decision under consideration. Suppose first that the project is a take-it-or-leave-it proposition. Then the graph tells managers three things. First, they

SENSITIVITY OF BOTTLED WATER PROJECT TO FEASIBLE PRICE/COST COMBINATIONS   Table 13.8

	Price		
Variable Cost	**$6.00**	**$10.00**	**$12.00**
$4.50	$−194,816	$44,204	$163,715
5.00	−224,694	14,327	133,837
6.00	−284,449	−45,428	74,082

Most likely values are in bold.

Exhibit 13.11

SENSITIVITY TO PROBABLE PRICE/COST COMBINATIONS

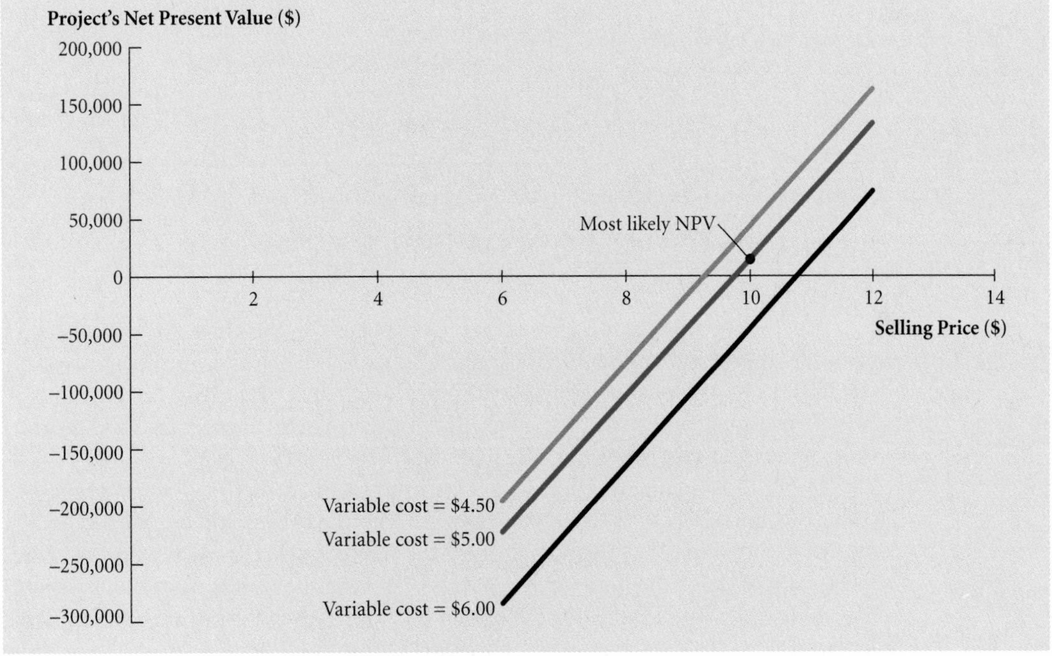

should accept the project because its market value, which equals its most likely present value, exceeds its cost. Second, the managers should be prepared for the possibility that the actual NPV is as low as $−284,449 and as high as $163,715. Finally, they should focus their monitoring and control efforts on the selling price and variable costs to secure a positive net present value.

LOCKHEED CORPORATION

LOCKHEED CORPORATION APPLIED for and received a federal loan guarantee in 1971. One of the issues discussed during the congressional hearings was the economic value of the company's wide-bodied passenger plane, the L-1011.

U. E. Reinhardt, an economics professor at Princeton University, examined the sensitivity of the plane's net present value to several factors, including the number of planes sold, the company's required rate of return, and various costs.* The exhibit presented is adapted from his Figure 1.

Lockheed's managers testified that the company had 178 orders for the plane at the time of the hearings. The graph shows the project's estimated NPV was negative at this sales level no matter what the company's required rate of return. Reinhardt stated that the company expected to sell between 270 and 300 L-1011s but the NPV was still negative at this sales level for any reasonable required rate of return.

Reinhardt concluded that Lockheed would have known the L-1011 project was unacceptable had they applied financial principles. However, he came very close to saying the company may have viewed the L-1011 program as an option on future business in the following quotation:

Lockheed may have viewed the L-1011 program as something akin to a "loss leader," that is, a project designed to reestablish the company in the commercial aircraft market. If so, the program ought not to be evaluated in isolation but instead as an integral part of a much longer-range investment strategy aimed at developing a more diversified set of business activities. Under such a strategy, the L-1011 program might make more sense in spite of its own dubious profit potential.

*U. E. Reinhardt, "Break-Even Analysis for Lockheed's Tri Star: An Application of Financial Theory," *Journal of Finance*, September 1973, pp. 821–838.

Now suppose the project is a strategic investment in the sense that the managers can defer the decision until they have more information. Then, they can accept the project if the selling price and variable cost combination is favorable and decline it otherwise. Their opportunity to exercise this discretion eliminates the negative line segments in Exhibit 13.11 and leaves only the segments for which the NPV is positive.

Don't those remaining line segments look familiar, sort of like the minimum value of a call option? Well, that's exactly what they are because, as you learned earlier, the minimum value of a call option prior to the expiration date is the NPV of the underlying asset at that time. The correspondence between the results of sensitivity analysis and the minimum value of a call option is obvious when the positive line segments are transferred to the separate graph in Exhibit 13.12.

Now the managers can use the results of sensitivity analysis strategically. The value of exercising their call option on the bottled water project immediately by accepting the project now is the most likely net present value, $14,327. The project's market value is greater than this minimum, however, because the passage of time may produce a more favorable selling price and variable cost combination. If they can control their variable costs at $4.50, then they will exercise their option on the expiration date

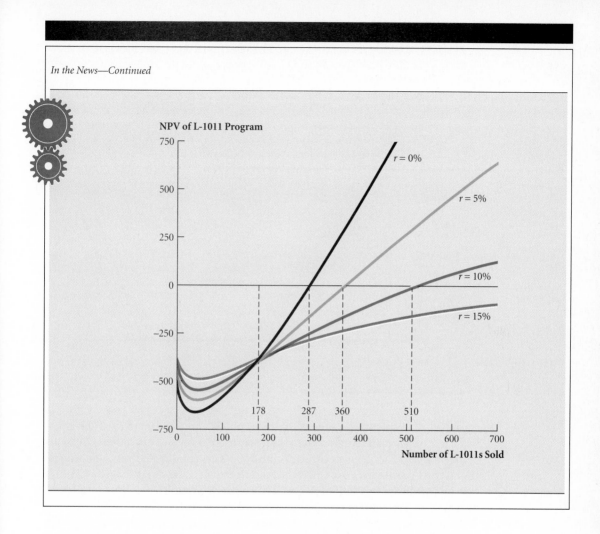

NPV of L-1011 Program

(accept the investment) if the selling price of bottled water is greater than $9.26—but not otherwise. If they cannot reduce their variable costs below $5.00, then the selling price must be greater than or equal to $9.76 on the expiration date or they will not invest. Importantly, we know these minimum values are approximately correct for the next several years because we have determined that the project's NPV is relatively insensitive to its life. See "In the News" for a discussion of the use of sensitivity analysis to evaluate a highly publicized investment that had some of the features of an option.

Simulation

Simulation is an expanded form of sensitivity analysis that uses a computer to examine the effect of a large number of different values for a large number of variables that affect free cash flow. Using a computer permits the analyst to write a very detailed

Exhibit 13.12

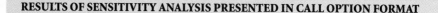

RESULTS OF SENSITIVITY ANALYSIS PRESENTED IN CALL OPTION FORMAT

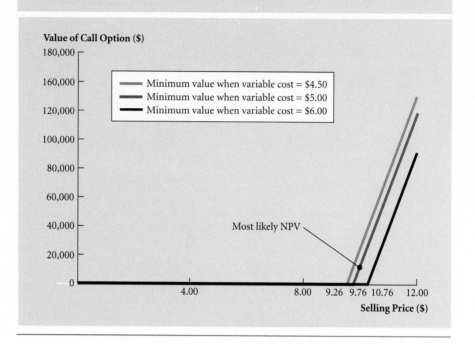

equation to describe the outcome of the decision in net present value terms. This equation can have separate terms for individual sources of revenue from different versions of the product or service, categories of customers, sales regions, and so on. The model also can have separate terms for individual cost elements such as direct labor, direct materials, and various types of indirect costs. The necessity to estimate the values of all these variables is the only limitation on how detailed this model can be.

Using a computer also permits the analyst to examine the effect of more values for each of the variables than merely their worst, best, and most likely values. The additional values for each variable are entered as probability distributions that the computer "samples" to compute the possible outcomes of the decision. The model can be constructed to account for dependencies among these probability distributions. For example, the computer can be forced to sample from the low end of the probability distribution of the number of units sold when it has drawn a sample from the high end of the probability distribution of the price. Using interrelated probability distributions for this purpose not only permits the computer to consider more values for each variable, but also ensures they appear in the summary of the results in proportion to their likelihood of occurrence.

Finally, the computer can compute the results of a large number of trials, say 10,000, very quickly. This provides so much information about the outcome of the decision that it is often summarized as a probability distribution rather than in a table. A graph of the information, similar to Exhibits 13.11 or 13.12, is another possibility.

As noted above, simulation provides a similar but more detailed picture of the outcome of a decision stated in net present value terms. The cost of the additional detail is the effort required to specify the interrelated probability distributions for the values of the variables that affect free cash flow. Simulation provides more information than sensitivity analysis but should be interpreted the same way depending on whether the project is a take-it-or-leave-it proposition or a strategic choice.

13.4 SUMMARY

Managers have the opportunity to influence the outcome of a strategic decision after they learn more about the factors that determine its value. They can expand or accelerate a successful venture and contract, delay, or abandon an unsuccessful one. Ordinary net present value analysis ignores these possibilities and therefore undervalues strategic decisions.

Decision tree analysis is the traditional way to account for management's influence on a decision's outcome. This procedure is applied by determining the best course of action at each decision point given the information available at that time. This strategy increases the likelihood of favorable outcomes, which are selected, and decreases the likelihood of unfavorable ones, which are not. The resulting increase in net present value is the value of active managers.

Decision trees are an improvement over net present value analysis but are impractical. The decision tree for a realistic decision has a large number of paths and we cannot determine the required rate of return to apply to the modified distribution of cash flows.

Option pricing models are a practical alternative to decision trees because management's choices at each decision point *are* options; and, a wide variety of option pricing models and option strategies can be used to represent these choices. The opportunity to expand or abandon a decision can be represented by call and put options, for example. In addition, option pricing models rely on investors' abilities to form replica portfolios so it is unnecessary to estimate a required rate of return to apply them.

Only one or two factors may be crucial to a strategic decision's success. For example, the price of gold may be the only factor that determines whether a mine should be opened or closed. The factors having the greatest effect on more complicated decisions may not be so easy to identify, however. This is particularly true if there is uncertainty about not only price but also costs, demand, the life of the project, and so on. Then, some procedure is needed to determine which factor the decision's value is most sensitive to.

Sensitivity analysis can be used for this purpose. The variables that can affect the project's value are systematically varied and the results recorded to determine which has the greatest influence. Simulation automates this process to permit more complicated analyses. The results of either technique can be presented in option pricing format so managers can see the combination of values that will cause the strategic decision or option to be in-the-money when it expires.

- ● **KEY TERMS**

- ● **QUESTIONS AND PROBLEMS**

1. What is the crucial difference between routine and strategic decisions? Why does this difference make net present value analysis inapplicable to strategic decisions?

2. There is a distinct difference between the payoffs from routine and strategic decisions and a corresponding difference in the techniques we use to represent these payoffs.

   (a) Which factors affect the payoffs from routine decisions: the project's inherent risk, management's subsequent choices, or both? Which factors affect the payoffs from strategic decisions?

   (b) How are the differences between routine and strategic decisions reflected in the differences between event trees and decision trees?

3. Roberts and Smith are wealthy investors with nearly identical amounts of net worth. Roberts invested $100,000 in a company with a market value of $175,000 while Smith invested $100,000 in a company with a market value of $17.5 billion. Did Roberts make a routine or strategic investment? What about Smith? Explain your answers.

4. Explain which company or person in each situation described below has an option. Is it a call or put option? What is the underlying asset?

   (a) One construction company hires carpenters at the union hall as it needs them while another company has its own carpenters.

   (b) One farmer grows corn while another farmer grows corn and raises pigs.

   (c) One school system's teachers can earn tenure while another system's teachers cannot.

   (d) One manufacturer cross-trains all employees while another trains each employee to be a specialist.

   (e) One jewelry company buys the gold it needs for production each day on the spot market while another either buys gold daily or uses the gold it holds in inventory.

   (f) One company goes directly from product development to full-scale production while another conducts test marketing.

   (g) One manager tells his employees exactly how their performance will be evaluated while another is intentionally vague.

   (h) One company uses general purpose production facilities while another uses unique equipment.

5. Decision trees are superior to ordinary net present value analysis for evaluating strategic decisions but they have limitations.

   (a) What are the advantages and disadvantages of using decision trees for this purpose?

   (b) How do option pricing models overcome the disadvantages of decision trees?

6. You are a recent graduate of a prestigious business school and you knew it was bound to happen: Your boss heard about using option pricing models to evaluate long-term investment proposals and asked you to explain the idea to the rest of the staff. Unfortunately for you, no one is familiar with the binomial option pricing model, let alone Black-Scholes. Describe how you can use a simple decision tree to explain the basic idea of using option pricing in capital budgeting without being too complex.

7. Jane and Barry decided it was time to hire an outsider as CEO of their Arizona Egg Nog Company. They began by discussing the position description they would use for recruiting purposes. Jane wanted a very general position description that would give the CEO a great deal of discretion about how to respond to future events. Barry preferred a very detailed and specific position description that would spell out exactly what the CEO must do in every conceivable situation.

   (a) Under which job description is the CEO an administrator? A strategic manager?

   (b) What are the benefits to Jane and Barry of each definition? What are the costs?

   (c) What method of analysis should Jane and Barry use to determine the amount they can pay the new CEO under the general job description? Under the specific job description?

8. A manager of investment planning was overheard to say, "I really like the simplicity of using option pricing for capital budgeting. I don't need to know an investment proposal's required rate of return. I only need to know the riskless interest rate and I can look that up in the newspaper every day." Explain why you agree or disagree with this statement.

9. You cannot make a strategic decision by comparing the NPVs of the alternatives. Nevertheless, you must compute the present value of each alternative's free cash flows as part of the decision process. Explain why these seemingly contradictory statements are true.

10 Three definitions of intrinsic value are given below. In each case, explain the meaning of the term(s) on the right-hand side and whether the entire expression applies to a routine investment, an expansion opportunity, or an abandonment opportunity.

   (a) Intrinsic value $= \text{Max}(E - S, 0)$

   (b) Intrinsic value $= \text{Max}(S - E, 0)$

   (c) Intrinsic value $= \text{NPV}$

11. Macaroni Software produces programs for personal computers. The company continually develops new programs and can introduce them at any time but usually waits until the industry's leader releases a new operating system.

   (a) Is Macaroni's opportunity to introduce new computer programs better described as an American or European call option? Why? What is the expiration date?

   (b) Should Macaroni ever introduce a new program prior to the release of a new operating system? Explain your answer and relate it to the principle that options should not be exercised prior to the expiration date.

12. Describe how managers can use the results of sensitivity analysis and simulation to discover which variables are crucial to an investment proposal's success.

13. Old Time Clock Works makes commemorative grandfather clocks named for past presidents of the United States. The company manufactures each model for two years before withdrawing it from production to enhance its value to collectors. Old Time's first two clocks, the George Washington and the Thomas Jefferson, were very successful models, so the managers are evaluating plans to introduce the third model, the James Madison.

   An investment of $150,000 will permit Old Time to produce 310 Madison clocks each year for two years. Each clock will sell for $3,000. The company contracts with artisans and craftsmen to produce the clocks at a direct labor cost of $1,450 each. Direct material costs comprise $550 for the clock works and miscellaneous hardware plus the cost of decorative hardwood for the case. Wood prices are very volatile and Old Time's managers expect to pay $400 or $800 per clock for the hardwood. The probabilities of these prices for each of the next two years are shown on the next page. Old Time's managers will commit to the entire production run of 620 clocks if they approve the project to avoid unfavorable reactions among collectors.

Cost Year 1	Probability	Cost Year 2	Probability
$400	0.60	$400	0.45
		800	0.55
800	0.40	400	0.20
		800	0.80

(a) Do the company's managers view the Madison clock project as a routine or strategic investment? Explain your answer.

(b) List the possible outcomes given your answer to part (a). Determine the project's free cash flows for each outcome and the probability of each outcome.

(c) Calculate this project's expected free cash flows.

(d) What is the Madison clock project's market value if the company's required rate of return is 15 percent? What is its NPV? Should Old Time Clock Works produce the James Madison grandfather clock?

14. Shown on page 561 is a decision tree for an investment project that can be expanded at the end of the first year. The cost of the expansion is $30,000. The owner's required rate of return is 9 percent.

(a) Determine the value of expanding the project at the end of year 1 if its first year's free cash flow was $40,000. Determine the value of *not* expanding the project in this situation.

(b) What should the owner do with this project at the end of year 1 if its first year's free cash flow was $40,000? Which paths can be eliminated from further consideration?

(c) Determine the value of expanding the project at the end of year 1 if its first year's free cash flow was $20,000. Determine the value of *not* expanding the project in this situation.

(d) What should the owner do with this project at the end of year 1 if its first year's free cash flow was $20,000? Which paths can be eliminated from further consideration?

(e) Calculate the project's expected free cash flows assuming the owner makes the right decision at each opportunity.

(f) What is the project's market value? How much does this project contribute to the owner's wealth? Explain your answer.

15. Bird Houses Unlimited (BHU) received an order to produce wood duck nesting boxes for a federal wetlands area. The cash revenues for this project are fixed but the costs vary according to the availability of unskilled labor in the rural area where the company produces its products. Consequently, its costs are higher the stronger the economy. An event tree that describes the project's potential free cash flows is shown on page 562.

(a) Calculate the project's expected free cash flows assuming it is a take-it-or-leave-it proposition.

(b) Determine the market value and NPV of the wood duck nesting boxes order. Should BHU accept this order? The required rate of return is 11 percent.

16. Before deciding whether to accept the government order, the owner of Bird Houses Unlimited (see problem 15) learned the company will have an opportunity to supply more

Decision Tree for Problem 14

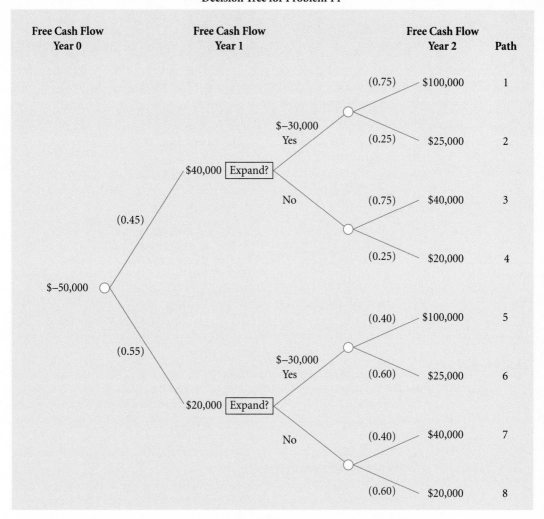

Free Cash Flow Year 0	Free Cash Flow Year 1	Free Cash Flow Year 2	Path

wood duck nesting boxes the second year. BHU will have to spend an additional $6,500 at the end of the first year to gear up for this additional work; however, this investment will increase the company's free cash flows from the nesting boxes at the end of the second year to $35,000 in a weak economy and $20,000 in a strong one. The required rate of return is still 11 percent.

(a) Draw and label the decision tree that describes the wood duck nesting box project with the opportunity for expansion.

(b) Will BHU expand the project if there was a weak economy the first year? Will the company expand the project if there was a strong economy the first year? Support your answers with the appropriate calculations.

(c) Determine the project's market value and NPV assuming the owner makes the right decisions about expansion.

(d) What is the value of the expansion opportunity?

Event Tree for Problem 15

Free Cash Flow Year 0	Free Cash Flow Year 1	Free Cash Flow Year 2	Path

Weak economy (0.70) $25,000   1

Weak economy (0.50) $25,000

Strong economy (0.30) $15,000   2

$−25,000

Weak economy (0.20) $25,000   3

Strong economy (0.50) $15,000

Strong economy (0.80) $15,000   4

17. With a little additional probing, the owner of Bird Houses Unlimited (see problems 15 and 16) also learned the company can break the contract at the end of the first year by paying the government a $2,500 nonperformance penalty. However, this cash outflow will be more than offset by the $20,000 he expects to receive for disposing of the equipment used to produce the nesting boxes.

   (a) Draw and label the decision tree that describes the wood duck nesting box project with the opportunity for abandonment.

   (b) Will BHU abandon the project if there was a weak economy the first year? Will the company abandon the project if there was a strong economy the first year? Support your answers with the appropriate calculations.

   (c) Determine the project's market value and NPV assuming the owner makes the right decisions about abandonment.

   (d) What is the value of the abandonment opportunity?

18. The free cash flows provided by an investment project in three different configurations are described below. The required rate of return is 18 percent.

Project's Free Cash Flows

Time	As Take-It-or-Leave-It Proposition	With Expansion When Justified	With Abandonment When Justified
1	$90,000	$ 25,000	$175,000
2	90,000	140,000	40,000
3	90,000	140,000	40,000

(a) What is the project's market value as a take-it-or-leave-it proposition? With expansion when justified? With abandonment (but no expansion) when justified?

(b) Suppose this project comes up for sale at an auction. Which of the following investors will place the winning bid? What is the maximum amount the winner can afford to pay? Explain your answers.

> Investor A: He will manage the project passively.
>
> Investor B: She will expand the project when justified.
>
> Investor C: She will abandon the project when justified.
>
> Investor D: He will expand or abandon the project when justified.

19. Suppose you must use a decision tree to analyze a strategic investment proposal.

(a) How many paths must you use to describe a project with a two-year life, one chance event per year with three possible outcomes, and one decision point per year except the last with two choices at each decision point?

(b) Verify your answer to part (a) by drawing the entire decision tree.

(c) How many paths must you use to describe a project with a 10-year life, one chance event per year with six possible outcomes, and one decision point per year except the last with four choices at each decision point? (Set your calculator for scientific notation to answer this question!)

(d) Would you like to prepare the decision tree for the relatively simple strategic investment opportunity described in part (c)? What is a better alternative?

20. Patio Gliders International plans to introduce lawn furniture made of wood from black locust trees. The project's initial cost is $150,000 but the company may invest an additional $145,000 at the end of the first year for expansion. A complete description of the possible free cash flows is given below. Patio Glider's required rate of return is 10 percent and the riskless rate of return is 5 percent.

Year 1 Cash Flow	Probability	Expansion	Year 2 Cash Flow	Probability
$175,000	0.50	Yes	$450,000	0.60
175,000	0.50	Yes	175,000	0.40
175,000	0.50	No	175,000	0.60
175,000	0.50	No	100,000	0.40
100,000	0.50	Yes	450,000	0.40
100,000	0.50	Yes	175,000	0.60
100,000	0.50	No	175,000	0.40
100,000	0.50	No	100,000	0.60

(a) Separate the free cash flows that apply to the passive investment from those that apply to the expansion opportunity. What is the NPV of the passive investment? Should Patio Gliders introduce the black locust lawn furniture without considering the possibility of expansion?

(b) Prepare and label an event tree that describes the market value of the expansion opportunity at the end of year 1 and at the present time.

(c) Should the company commit to the expansion plan immediately or wait until the first year's results are known? What is the advantage of waiting? Does waiting for the first year's results make the expansion opportunity more like a passive investment, a call option, or a put option? Explain your answers.

(d) Use the certainty equivalent form of the binomial option pricing model to determine the market value of the expansion opportunity.

(e) What is the total amount by which the black locust lawn furniture increases the owners' wealth?

21. Re-examine Bird Houses Unlimited's wood duck nesting box project (see problems 15–17) using option pricing. The riskless interest rate is 5 percent.

(a) Use the certainty equivalent form of the binomial option pricing model to determine the market value of the expansion opportunity described in problem 16.

(b) Use the certainty equivalent form of the binomial option pricing model to determine the market value of the abandonment opportunity described in problem 17.

(c) Compare your answers to parts (a) and (b) with the answers to problems 16 and 17. Does the similarity between these answers imply that you might as well use decision trees rather than option pricing models to evaluate realistic problems? Explain your answer.

22. Jan's Realty Company sends all its new sales agents to an intensive training program that lasts one month and costs $5,000, paid in advance. Agents who finish the program and stay with the company produce business with a value of $20,000 measured as of the time they complete training. Some new employees do not finish the program, however, while others leave the company as soon as they are trained. The net result is that there is only a 20 percent likelihood that a new employee will produce any income for Jan's Realty Company.

(a) Determine the NPV of hiring a new sales agent under these circumstances if the company's opportunity cost is 1.5 percent per month. Does Jan's Realty Company have a sound employee development program? Explain your answer.

Jan is considering an alternative training and development program under which each new employee will work as a sales assistant for one month. Employees who receive a satisfactory rating during this probationary period will receive the intensive training the following month—the remainder will not. Jan expects that 30 percent of the new employees will qualify for training and that 40 percent of those who qualify will become productive sales agents.

(b) Explain why Jan's new employee development program is similar to an option. Identify the underlying asset and the exercise price.

(c) Use the certainty equivalent form of the binomial option pricing model to determine the market value of Jan's option on a productive sales agent the day a new employee is hired. The riskless rate of return is 1 percent per month. What is the maximum amount Jan can pay each new employee during the month he or she works as a sales assistant?

(d) Suppose Jan pays each new employee $500 to work as a sales assistant. How much better is the new employee development program than the old one?

23. Beach Technology Corporation manufactures silicon rods from which wafers are cut to produce computer memory chips. The cost of manufacturing a rod is $9,500. By agreement with its suppliers, Beach pays this cost at the time of a sale. The company can sell its silicon rods on the spot market or place them in inventory to sell later. Inventory costs are $0. The current spot price of a silicon rod is $10,000. The standard deviation of the continuously compounded change in this price is 30 percent per year. The riskless rate of return is 5 percent per year.

(a) Determine the value of a silicon rod if the company sells it on the spot market today.

(b) Use the Black-Scholes option pricing model to determine the value of a silicon rod if the company places it in inventory for sale in 30 days. Should the company sell the rod now or later?

(c) Rework part (b) if the present value of inventory costs is $200 per rod per month.

(d) What is the break-even level of inventory costs per rod per month? Explain the significance of this value.

24. The Fleeting Fame Furniture Company sells unique home furnishings designed to exploit short-lived fads. The company is about to introduce a plastic armadillo lampshade and the managers know they should be prepared to stop production if fascination with the American Southwest fades quickly. The project's initial cost is $325,000, but the company will recover $190,000 of this cost if it discontinues this product after one year. A complete description of the project's possible free cash flows is given below. Fleeting Fame's required rate of return is 12 percent and the riskless rate of return is 6 percent.

| Year 1 | | | Year 2 | |
Cash Flow	Probability	Abandon	Cash Flow	Probability
$275,000	0.70	Yes	$ 0	
275,000	0.70	No	275,000	0.80
275,000	0.70	No	150,000	0.20
150,000	0.30	Yes	0	
150,000	0.30	No	275,000	0.50
150,000	0.30	No	150,000	0.50

(a) Separate the free cash flows that apply to the passive investment from those that apply to the abandonment opportunity. What is the NPV of the passive investment? Should Fleeting Fame introduce the plastic armadillo lampshade without considering the possibility of abandonment?

(b) Prepare and label an event tree that describes the market value of the abandonment opportunity at the end of year 1 and at the present time.

(c) Should the company commit to the abandonment plan immediately or wait until the first year's results are known? What is the advantage of waiting? Does waiting for the first year's results make the abandonment opportunity more like a passive investment, a call option, or a put option? Explain your answers.

(d) Use the certainty equivalent form of the binomial option pricing model to determine the market value of the abandonment opportunity.

(e) What is the total amount by which the armadillo lampshade project increases the owners' wealth?

25. The Mulligan Machine Works is considering the routine investment opportunity described by the event tree on page 566.

The company can buy this investment and operate it as is or spend an additional $200,000 to increase its scale. This incremental investment will increase the project's subsequent free cash flows under good conditions from $400,000 to $700,000 and under poor conditions from $175,000 to $300,000. Mulligan's required rate of return is 13 percent and the risk-free rate is 5 percent.

(a) Should the company purchase the routine investment project? Explain your answer.

(b) What is the time 0 value of the company's expansion option if it is not exercised then? What is the time 0 value of the company's expansion option if it is exercised immediately? What should the company do? Support your answers with the appropriate calculations.

Event Tree for Problem 25

26. Car Partners Company is planning to produce and sell inflatable life-sized dummies that cus-tomers who fear traveling alone can place in the passenger seats of their automobiles. The most likely values for the variables that determine net present value of this project are given below.

Cash selling price	$ 70
Cash variable cost	$ 30
Cash fixed cost per year	$ 30,000
Cash flow used for investment at time 0	$−750,000
Output per year	5,000 dummies
Project's life	15 years
Required rate of return	15%

(a) Use the most likely values of the parameters to determine this project's market value and NPV. Should Car Partners introduce this product?

(b) Vary the selling price, the variable cost, and the quantity sold per year by plus and minus 25 percent to determine the sensitivity of this project's NPV to the values of these para-meters. Graph the results.

(c) Suppose you are the sponsor of this project. Should you spend your scarce resources to improve the accuracy of your forecast of selling price, variable cost, or quantity sold per year? Explain your answer.

27. Bingo Box and Container Company is considering a proposal to acquire the plant and equip-ment of a competitor that is folding. Bingo's managers have determined that the market value of the additional capacity is sensitive to variable costs and output. A table that summarizes the results of their sensitivity analysis is given on page 567.

	Variable Costs per Unit		
Output	$0.50	$0.75	$1.00
1,000,000	$540,845	$ 310,604	$ 80,362
750,000	248,677	18,435	−211,807
500,000	−43,492	−273,734	−503,976

(a) Prepare a graph of these values that managers can use to evaluate the box plant if they consider it to be a routine investment. Describe how they should interpret the graph for this decision.

(b) Prepare a graph that managers can use to evaluate the box plant if they consider it to be a strategic investment. Describe how they should interpret the graph for this decision.

- ### ADDITIONAL READING

A very accessible discussion of event trees, decision trees, and other valuation topics is:
>   Tom Copeland, Tim Koller, and Jack Murrin, *Valuation,* John Wiley & Sons, Inc., New York, 1994.

There are many recent articles on applying option pricing to capital investment decisions. A few are listed below.
>   Lenos Trigeorgis and Scott P. Masson, "Valuing Managerial Flexibility," *Midland Corporate Finance Journal,* Spring 1987, pp. 14–21.
>   John W. Kensinger, "Adding the Value of Active Management into the Capital Budgeting," *Midland Corporate Finance Journal,* Spring 1987, pp. 31–42.
>   Alan C. Shapiro, "Corporate Strategy and the Capital Budgeting Decision," *Midland Corporate Finance Journal,* Spring 1985, pp. 22–36.
>   Michael J. Brennan and Eduardo S. Schwartz, "A New Approach to Evaluating Natural Resource Investments," *Midland Corporate Finance Journal,* Spring 1985, pp. 37–47.
>   Avinash K. Dixit and Robert S. Pindyck, "The Options Approach to Capital Investment," *Harvard Business Review,* May–June 1995, pp. 105–115.
>   Patrick Barwise, Paul R. Marsh, and Robin Wensley, "Must Finance and Strategy Clash?" *Harvard Business Review,* September–October 1989, pp. 85–90.
>   George S. Day and Liam Fahey, "Putting Strategy into Shareholder Value Analysis," *Harvard Business Review,* March–April 1990, pp. 156–162.

The classic article on simulation analysis of capital budgeting proposals is:
>   David B. Hertz, "Risk Analysis in Capital Investment," *Harvard Business Review,* January–February 1964, pp. 95–106.

The results of sensitivity analysis and simulation must be interpreted with care. These articles give some useful suggestions.
>   Wilbur G. Lewellen and Michael S. Long, "Simulation versus Single-Value Estimates in Capital Expenditure Analysis," in Stewart C. Myers, ed., *Modern Developments in Financial Management,* Praeger Publishers, Inc., New York, 1976.
>   Stewart C. Myers, "Postscript: Using Simulation in Risk Analysis," in Stewart C. Myers, ed., *Modern Developments in Financial Management,* Praeger Publishers, Inc., New York, 1976.

HERMANN FITNESS COMPANY

Hermann Fitness Company produces a highly successful line of exercise equipment for gyms and health clubs. Jeff Hermann, president of the company, believes it is time to produce a compact multifunction exercise machine for home use. The target market comprises health-conscious consumers who don't want to use a public gym but have little exercise space at home.

Jeff formed a project team to study the feasibility of launching the new product, dubbed the Gym-in-a-Box. Team members were Susan Baker from purchasing and production, Lou Ableson from marketing and sales, and Margo Haywood from finance and accounting. Each team member was responsible for obtaining revenue or cost forecasts from his or her area of operations and for assisting with the overall financial analysis. Jeff established the context for the team's work by setting forth the following assumptions.

Target initial selling price (wholesale)	$30.00 per unit
Project life	5 years
Peak capacity required	20,000 units per year
Project's market value must exceed its cost.	

PART A

Susan Baker, Lou Ableson, and Margo Haywood met soon after the Gym-in-a-Box project team was appointed. They agreed to exchange information during the first week of October and meet on October 8 to analyze the project and prepare their recommendation.

INTERDEPARTMENTAL MEMO

TO: Gym-in-a-Box project team
FROM: Susan Baker
DATE: October 2
SUBJECT: Capital and production costs

Our engineers estimate that the installed cost of the equipment needed to produce up to 20,000 units of the Gym-in-a-Box is $275,000 with a salvage value of $15,000. This equipment is mostly hand and bench tools, so we think we can use a MACRS life of three years for depreciation.

Our estimates of the first year's production costs are listed below.

Direct labor	$2.00 per unit
Direct materials	$8.50 per unit
Indirect costs	$1.50 per unit
Other indirect costs	$30,000

We expect direct labor costs to decline by 2.5 percent with each doubling of annual output due to the combined effects of learning and wage inflation. We expect direct materials costs to increase by 5 percent per year and indirect costs to increase by 7 percent per year due to inflation.

We will need $10,000 of inventory to initiate production. Approximately $7,000 of this inventory will be financed by our suppliers as accounts payable. Inventory and payables levels will depend on our operating cycle once production begins. Part of this cycle is described below.

Day	Event
0	Receive materials
32	Bank account debited for payments to suppliers

INTERDEPARTMENTAL MEMO

TO: Gym-in-a-Box project team
FROM: Lou Ableson
DATE: October 2
SUBJECT: Revenues

We believe we are equally likely to sell 10,000 or 12,500 units of the Gym-in-a-Box the first year of production at the target price of $30 per unit. This is a classic fad product for which we forecast +40 percent sales growth the second year and –40 percent each year thereafter. These forecasts assume that we will increase the price of the product by only 3 percent per year in line with the anticipated change in consumer prices. Accounts receivable levels will depend on our operating cycle. Part of this cycle is described below.

Day	Event
40	Receive order, begin order approval process
45	Conclude approval process, ship product
81	Bank account credited with collections equal to sales minus 2 percent bad debts

INTERDEPARTMENTAL MEMO

TO: Gym-in-a-Box project team
FROM: Margo Haywood
DATE: October 2
SUBJECT: Other costs and financial considerations

We expect selling and administration costs to be $5,000 initially with an increase to $50,000 the year sales begin. Subsequent S&A costs are forecast at $50,000 for one additional year before jumping to $60,000 the last three years to sustain acceptable sales level. We will follow company policy and increase our financial slack by 3 percent of sales to support this project. Other company and financial market parameters are given below.

Company's marginal tax rate	37%
Rate of return on U.S. Treasury bills	4.8%
Company's borrowing rate of interest	9.5%
Required rate of return on equity	16%
Percent of financing obtained from debt	40%
Percent of financing obtained from equity	60%

Susan, Lou, and Margo met on October 8 to review their revenue and cost projections and commence their financial analysis of the proposal to develop a compact multifunction exercise machine. Jeff Hermann was CFO before he was appointed president, so the team members knew they'd have to back up their recommendation to accept or reject the proposal with a thorough valuation analysis.

PART B

Jeff Hermann accepted the Gym-in-a-Box project team's recommendation but was convinced that some simple changes in operations could improve the investment proposal's profitability. Accordingly, he asked Susan, Lou, and Margo to search for savings from process improvements in their departments. He asked them to particularly examine the areas where their responsibilities overlapped. The result was the following memo from Lou Ableson and Margo Haywood.

INTERDEPARTMENTAL MEMO

TO:	Gym-in-a-Box project team
FROM:	Lou Ableson and Margo Haywood
DATE:	October 15
SUBJECT:	Order approval process

We have been looking at our order approval process, collection period, and bad debts and think we can do better with no effect on sales. Specifically, we believe we can grant immediate order approval to our current customers, which will give our credit analysts more time to examine new customers. We expect this new process to reduce selling and administrative expenses by $1,200 per year and to reduce bad debts to only 1.0 percent of sales. We should have a smaller investment in receivables *and* inventory because we will be shipping product sooner. Our estimate of the impact on the entire operating cycle is shown below.

Day	Event
0	Receive materials
32	Bank account debited for payments to suppliers
40	Receive orders, ship to current customers (90%)
	Begin order approval process for new customers

Day	Event
50	Conclude approval process, ship to new customers (10%)
70	Bank account credited with collections from current customers equal to sales minus 0.5% bad debts
90	Bank account credited with collections from new customers equal to sales minus 5.5% bad debts

Let's re-examine the Gym-in-a-Box, taking into account the impact of these changes.

PART C

Lou Ableson felt a little more pressure to make the project work than the other team members because his department's inability to accurately forecast the first year's sales was a crucial source of uncertainty. Consequently, he interviewed a marketing research consultant and shared his findings with the Gym-in-a-Box project team in the following memo.

INTERDEPARTMENTAL MEMO

TO: Gym-in-a-Box project team
FROM: Lou Ableson
DATE: October 18
SUBJECT: Market survey

I have met with a marketing consultant and believe we can get a very reliable indication of the reception for this product from a small, focused market survey. The survey will cost $7,500, payable in advance, but when it is finished in three months, we will be able to state with complete confidence whether the first year's sales will be 10,000 or 12,500 units. Let's determine the economic value of commissioning this survey before we decide whether to accept or reject the proposal in its present form.

FINANCIAL POLICY AND PLANNING

Part 1 developed fundamental finance valuation principles. These principles are (1) base decisions on cash flows, (2) choose market-based required rates of return, and (3) use present value analysis or option pricing to estimate market values. Managers maximize the owners' wealth when they apply these principles to their routine and strategic decisions.

Part 2 applied fundamental valuation principles to investment and operating decisions. The outcome of these decisions is a company's investment in long-term assets and net working capital, the excess of accounts receivable, and inventories over accounts payable. In keeping with the separation principle, we did not consider how a company finances these investments in Part 2.

Managers cannot ignore the connection between their investment and operating decisions and the company's financial policies and plans, however, because a company with sound financial policies has flexibility in choosing investments and methods of operations. Conversely, a company that makes sound investment and operating decisions has good access to financing. Managers in every area must understand these connections to contribute to the goal of maximizing the owners' wealth.

Part 3 describes the principles that shape companies' financial policies and the procedures they use to anticipate financing shortages and surpluses. Chapter 14 provides the background for this part by explaining how companies obtain financing from private investors and the public. Chapters 15 and 16 describe the factors companies must consider when choosing the proportion of financing to obtain from retained earnings, debt, and common stock. Chapter 17 explains how companies recognize the effect of this financing choice in investment analysis. Chapters 18 and 19 conclude Part 3 by describing how to use free cash flow and financial cash flow statements for financial planning.

All managers must understand how companies make these financing decisions. Senior finance specialists, especially the treasurer and CFO, may spend the majority of their time on these tasks. Other managers make financing decisions periodically. Some operating managers are authorized to lease equipment, which is a type of financing decision. In addition, managers throughout a company participate in financial planning to justify their requests for investment and operating budgets. These managers can be more effective for their unit, the company, and the owners if they understand the rationale for the company's financial policies and plans.

INTRODUCTION TO FINANCING DECISIONS

U.S. corporations have a huge requirement for financing to pay for the net working capital needed to support operations and to acquire long-term investments. Spending for these purposes by U.S. nonfarm, nonfinancial corporations from 1986–1995 is described in the cash statements in Table 14.1.[1] During this period, these corporations increased their net working capital by $417.0 billion and purchased $3.9 trillion of capital investments. You learned how companies evaluate opportunities to spend money for these purposes in Part 2.

The statements in Table 14.1 also describe how the corporations financed these expenditures. Cash flow from operations before deducting the investment in net working capital provided $5.6 trillion while new debt provided an additional $2.6 trillion. This debt financing was obtained from banks and other financial institutions and creditors who purchased notes, bonds, and mortgages. Dividend payments and repurchases of common stock reduced the amount of financing obtained from the owners by $1.7 trillion.

How did these corporations decide the amount of financing to obtain from operations and from new debt and equity? How did they decide whether to borrow money from banks or bondholders? How did their decisions affect the owners' wealth? These are complex questions that deserve and require careful consideration. We begin to consider these questions in this chapter by describing the financial instruments and markets companies use to meet their financing requirements.

---

[1]Compiled from the Board of Governors of the Federal Reserve System, *Flow of Funds Accounts,* Table F.102, obtained from their Internet site, http://www.bog.frb.fed.us/releases/.

Table 14.1   FREE CASH FLOW AND FINANCIAL CASH FLOW STATEMENTS FOR U.S. NONFARM, NONFINANCIAL CORPORATIONS

	1986	1987	1988	1989
Free Cash Flows				
Cash flows provided by (used for) operations				
Net income	$ 92.8	$ 147.0	$ 178.2	$ 168.0
Depreciation	312.5	323.8	338.0	349.2
Cash flow before deducting changes in net working capital	405.3	470.8	516.2	517.2
Changes in net working capital	(0.9)	64.2	85.9	71.1
Net cash flow	$ 406.2	$ 406.6	$ 430.3	$ 446.1
Cash flows provided by (used for) investments				
Capital expenditures	$(336.8)	$ (328.3)	$(351.6)	$(369.3)
Acquisition of financial assets	(147.8)	(169.1)	(277.9)	(165.6)
Net cash flow	$(484.6)	$ (497.4)	$(629.5)	$(534.9)
Cash flows provided by (used for) financial slack	$ (22.2)	$ (1.6)	$ (14.6)	$ (25.6)
Net free cash flow	$(100.6)	$ (92.4)	$(213.8)	$(114.4)
Financial cash flows				
Cash flows provided by (used for) financing				
New equity financing				
Common stock issued	$ (85.0)	$ (75.5)	$(129.5)	$(124.2)
Dividends paid	(73.4)	(75.7)	(78.6)	(102.8)
Net new equity financing	$(158.4)	$ (151.2)	$(208.1)	$(227.0)
New debt financing				
Bank loans	$ 57.0	$ 4.0	$ 32.8	$ 24.9
Other loans and advances	44.7	38.5	51.0	48.6
Notes and bonds	107.9	79.5	115.2	94.3
Mortgages	26.6	26.7	26.0	15.3
Miscellaneous	36.6	151.3	292.7	269.7
Total new debt financing	$ 272.8	$ 300.0	$ 517.7	$ 452.8
Net financial cash flow	$ 114.4	$ 148.8	$ 309.6	$ 225.8
Reporting discrepancy	$ 13.8	$ 56.4	$ 95.8	$ 111.4

Source: Board of Governors of the Federal Reserve System, *Flow of Funds Accounts*, Table F.102, obtained from their Internet site, http://www.bog.frb.fed.us/releases/.

Companies issue financial instruments or securities in private and public markets to obtain financing for investments and operations. Financial institutions buy these securities and help companies sell them to other investors. Investors subsequently trade securities among themselves when they want their money back to spend or invest elsewhere.

This chapter describes key features of financial instruments and the markets in

1990	1991	1992	1993	1994	1995	10-Year Totals
$ 186.0	$ 179.2	$ 207.6	$ 253.4	$ 286.0	$ 316.8	$ 2,015.0
354.1	362.8	371.0	385.2	413.0	430.1	3,639.7
540.1	542.0	578.6	638.6	699.0	746.9	5,654.7
24.4	(25.9)	(3.6)	44.4	71.0	86.4	417.0
$ 515.7	$ 567.9	$ 582.2	$ 594.2	$ 628.0	$ 660.5	$ 5,237.7
$(389.3)	$(372.1)	$(384.9)	$(405.1)	$ (439.4)	$(509.0)	$(3,885.8)
(97.4)	(111.4)	(106.5)	(276.1)	(129.2)	(210.9)	(1,691.9)
$(486.7)	$(483.5)	$(491.4)	$(681.2)	$ (568.6)	$(719.9)	$(5,577.7)
$ 11.3	$ (24.1)	$ (33.3)	$ (30.5)	$ (42.4)	$ (37.8)	$ (220.8)
$ 40.3	$ 60.3	$ 57.5	$(117.5)	$ 17.0	$ (97.2)	$ (560.8)
$ (63.0)	$ 18.3	$ 27.0	$ 21.3	$ (44.9)	$ (74.2)	$ (529.7)
(117.6)	(123.8)	(132.4)	(151.8)	(160.9)	(175.0)	(1,192.0)
$(180.6)	$ (105.5)	$(105.4)	$(130.5)	$ (205.8)	$(249.2)	$(1,721.7)
$ 2.7	$ (37.8)	$ (19.3)	$ (6.0)	$ 47.4	$ 71.8	$ 177.5
61.2	(54.5)	4.7	(16.4)	43.6	41.6	$ 263.0
56.5	59.2	76.2	85.1	43.2	88.5	$ 805.6
(10.3)	(20.0)	(27.5)	(16.2)	(10.0)	6.7	$ 17.3
113.1	87.0	59.5	111.7	60.4	150.1	$ 1,332.1
$ 223.2	$ 33.9	$ 93.6	$ 158.2	$ 184.6	$ 358.7	$ 2,595.5
$ 42.6	$ (71.6)	$ (11.8)	$ 27.7	$ (21.2)	$ 109.5	$ 873.8
$ 82.9	$ (11.3)	$ 45.7	$ (89.8)	$ (4.2)	$ 12.3	$ 313.0

which they are issued and traded. You will learn about the institutions that help companies obtain financing in these markets and why their services are valuable to companies and investors. You will see that financial instruments, markets, and institutions
apparently are designed to reduce the hazards of investing in the presence of asymmetric
information. This improves the investment opportunities available to owners and
creditors and gives corporations better access to financing.

14.1   DESCRIPTION OF FINANCIAL INSTRUMENTS

Companies use a wide variety of financial instruments to obtain financing. We discussed some of the features of these securities in Chapter 1 and you learned to estimate the market values of debt, equity, and options in Chapters 7 and 8. Now, we will review some of the more important features that distinguish one type of financial instrument from another and relate them to the problems caused by asymmetric information.

Key Features of Financial Instruments

The most important difference between debt, equity, and options is the nature of their claims on a company's future cash flows. Other important differences between debt and equity are the way they are treated for tax purposes, the control rights they provide, and the company's provision for repayment.

Type of Claim   By far the most important feature of any financial instrument is the nature of its claim on the company's future cash flows. Debt holders have a fixed claim that may be paid periodically or in a lump sum when the loan is due. The debt holders' claims have priority because the current amount owed to them must be paid before any profits can be distributed to the owners. The order of priority differs for various types of debt, however. Investors who hold *senior debt*, such as a first mortgage bond, are paid first while those who hold *junior debt*, such as a subordinated bond, are paid last.

Equity holders own the company and have a variable claim that is paid after all other claimants have been paid. Each owner is entitled to a proportionate share of the company's profits that may be paid to them as dividends or reinvested for growth. The owners' claim is variable because a company's profits vary from year to year.

An investor who owns an option has a contingent claim on a company's future cash flows. The investor gains an actual claim on future cash flows by exercising a call option and loses an actual claim on future cash flows by exercising a put option. The underlying asset in either case can be debt or equity.

Other types of financial instruments provide claims that are hybrids of debt, equity, and options. Preferred stock is a debt-equity hybrid. Preferred stockholders expect to receive a fixed dividend that is paid before the owners are paid (a characteristic of debt) but after interest and taxes are paid (a characteristic of equity). Companies are not obligated to pay this dividend so preferred stock is considered to be equity from a legal point of view. A convertible bond is a debt-option hybrid that is issued as a bond and can be converted into common stock at the investor's option.

Tax Treatment   The cash flows paid to creditors and owners are subject to different tax treatments. Interest is a tax-deductible business expense of the company and taxable income to the recipients but there is no tax on the return of the creditor's principal. Therefore, only that portion of a company's income that is paid to creditors as interest is subject to taxes and it is taxed only once at the personal level.

The current dividends and growth the owners receive originate with the net income that remains *after* a company has paid its taxes. In addition, the owners must pay taxes on dividends as they receive them and on the growth in the stock price when they sell their shares. This means payments to the owners are taxed twice—once at the corporate level and again at the personal level. In Chapter 16, you will see that these differences in tax treatment have a significant effect on the decision to use debt or equity as the financing method.

Control Rights   Common stock is the only financial instrument that provides an unconditional right to control the company. An owner of a corporation may exercise this right directly by serving as a manager but is more likely to exercise control indirectly by electing representatives to the board of directors. Owners may vote in person at the corporation's annual meeting or they may use a proxy to temporarily assign their voting rights to others.

Some companies' articles of incorporation grant existing owners the *preemptive right* to buy newly issued shares of stock in amounts that maintain their proportionate ownership in the company. This right protects the owners from dilution of their claims on the company's cash flows and from dilution of control. Sales of stock under this program are called *rights offerings*.

Creditors often have conditional control rights they invoke when the company does not satisfy their claims. Senior creditors may actually become the owners with all their control prerogatives when a company fails and is reorganized. In addition, creditors often exert some control in firms undergoing less serious financial distress and usually are able to limit the owners' rights to control even a healthy firm. The creditors' rights to participate in control are spelled out in **restrictive covenants** that are part of the initial credit agreement or **indenture**. A common example of a restrictive covenant is a limitation on the amount of dividends the company may pay its owners.

Provision for Repayment   Debt obligations have maturity dates so companies must make provisions for repayment. One alternative is to use the cash on hand when the debt matures to repay the loan. This alternative frequently is used to repay short-term debt. Another alternative is to repay the creditors in periodic installments, that is, to amortize the loan. Leases and many bank loans are repaid this way.

Companies also can repay or retire their long-term debt in periodic installments. One method is to purchase the bonds in the open market. Another method is to issue bonds with a call provision that gives the company the right—but not the obligation—to redeem the bonds at a specified price prior to maturity. These securities are callable and are hybrid financial instruments because the call provision has the features of an option. The decision to repay long-term debt prior to maturity is voluntary unless the indenture contains a **sinking fund** provision, a mandatory debt retirement schedule.

Companies needn't make any provisions to repay common and preferred stockholders. These securities have no maturity date and may be outstanding in perpetuity. Some preferred stock is callable, however, and companies can voluntarily repurchase both common and preferred stock in the open market.

The Problems of Asymmetric Information[2]

Using any type of financial instrument to obtain financing is problematic under conditions of asymmetric information. The difficulty is that one of the parties may know more about the details of the transaction than the other and may use this information for personal gain. Asymmetric information creates two impediments to financing.

Adverse Selection   Concern about **adverse selection** is one impediment to obtaining financing in the presence of asymmetric information. Adverse selection is a technical term for an offer's tendency to attract the less desirable portion of the target audience. Perhaps this is what Groucho Marx meant when he said, "Please accept my resignation. I don't care to belong to any club that will accept me as a member."[3]

A restaurant that offers an all-you-can-eat buffet for $6.95 and a la carte service has an adverse selection problem. People who expect to eat more than $6.95 worth of food will choose the buffet while everyone else will order from the menu. This policy suffers from adverse selection because the restaurant's manager does not have enough information to identify the voracious customers in advance. Furthermore, the manager cannot solve the problem by raising the price of the buffet, to $7.95 for example, because this only changes the threshold that separates the avid and ordinary diners.

Voluntary financial transactions may suffer from adverse selection because managers and some owners have inside information about their company's future prospects. Investors otherwise willing to provide financing may be concerned their offer will attract insiders who will try to sell them stocks or bonds that are worth less than their market prices. The mere possibility that this inference is correct will inhibit investors and raise the company's cost of financing.

Principal–Agent Conflicts   Concern about principal–agent conflicts, which we briefly discussed in Chapter 1, is the other impediment to obtaining financing in the presence of asymmetric information. Remember, these conflicts may arise when an agent can secretly take actions to benefit himself at the principal's expense. A principal–agent conflict can arise no matter what type of financial instrument is used to obtain financing.

An owner who sells part of her equity to raise cash but continues as a manager becomes an agent for the new owners who are the principals. Then, she has an incentive to spend the company's money on costly perquisites, such as an elaborately decorated office, because she receives 100 percent of the benefits but pays only a fraction of the cost. Appointed managers have an incentive to spend more time at leisure and less at work for the same reason.

Similarly, an owner who sells debt to raise cash becomes an agent for the creditors who are the principals. Then, contrary to the creditors' interest, the owner may invest the company's money in risky projects in pursuit of high returns. His incentive is that he receives 100 percent of the payoff after the creditors' fixed claims have been paid but shares losses because the owners of corporations have limited liability.

---

[2]An early discussion of these ideas is in Michael C. Jensen and William H. Meckling, "Theory of the Firm: Managerial Behavior, Agency Costs and Ownership Structure," *Journal of Financial Economics,* October 1976, pp. 305–360.

[3]*Bartlett's Familiar Quotations, 16th edition*, Little, Brown and Company, Boston, 1992, p. 693.

Reducing the Problems Caused by Asymmetric Information   One way to reduce the problems caused by asymmetric information is to use observable data to infer the value of an unobservable characteristic such as a person's ability or a business's future prospects. Insurance companies use this technique when they give discounts on automobile insurance to young drivers with good grades. Young drivers do not have driving records and insurers cannot easily observe their true abilities and propensities to take risks. Insurers believe that good grades reveal maturity and responsibility and that these traits are associated with careful driving. They therefore price their policies according to the presence or absence of this observable characteristic.

Sometimes, individuals and companies voluntarily take actions to **signal** their private information to others. Signals are credible and can reduce asymmetric information when they are based on actions that parties with inferior characteristics cannot easily imitate. Suppose a company's founder wants to raise $50,000 by selling stock. The potential investor may be justifiably concerned about adverse selection and the founder's attempts to convey her private information directly may not help. After all, the investor knows the founder has every incentive to present an attractive picture of the business's future. The founder can alleviate the investor's concerns, however, by announcing that *she* will maintain a $100,000 equity investment in the business. This announcement is a credible signal because it is costly for the founder to invest her own money in the venture if she knows it is unsound.[4]

Parties to a financial transaction also can reduce their principal–agent conflicts by writing more complete or stringent financial contracts. A complete contract considers every possible contingency and describes exactly how the agent must respond in every situation. In reality, however, complete contracts are difficult if not impossible to write because it is hard to anticipate every contingency. A more practical alternative is to write a contract that provides incentives for the agent to act in the principal's interest and penalties when he doesn't. This type of contract also must provide a way for the principal to monitor the agent's performance so incentives can be awarded and penalties assessed as appropriate.

Of course, there are fewer problems due to asymmetric information when managers voluntarily refrain from using private information to advance their personal self-interest or the narrowly defined interest of their business unit, that is, when they behave ethically. This behavior may be motivated by altruism or by a belief that unselfishness eventually produces tangible benefits.[5]

Whatever the motivation, companies can foster ethical behavior by (1) adopting an ethical code of conduct; (2) informing managers, employees, customers, etc. of its content; and (3) dispensing rewards and punishments for behaviors that do and do not conform to this code. The results will not always be pleasant because the company may have to reward ethical behavior that harms its short-term interests and vice versa. Nevertheless, many people believe a program to promote ethical behavior by managers is intrinsically worthwhile and others will concede it is worthwhile if agency costs savings more than offset the losses from foregoing opportunistic behavior.

---

[4]See Hayne E. Leland and David H. Pyle, "Information Asymmetries, Financial Structure, and Financial Intermediation," *Journal of Finance*, May 1977, pp. 371–388 for a theoretical development of this idea.

[5]See Eric Noreen, "The Economics of Ethics: A New Perspective on Agency Theory," *Accounting, Organizations and Society*, Number 4, 1988, pp. 359–369.

Features of Financial Instruments and Asymmetric Information   The features of financial instruments described earlier are related to the problems caused by asymmetric information. The owners' control prerogative permits them to elect board members who will replace extravagant managers and change unpopular or unprofitable policies. Furthermore, stockholders can aggregate their votes using the proxy system so that even owners with a small number of shares can be heard.

Owners who are completely dissatisfied with their company's performance can sell their shares and invest their money elsewhere. This may seem so obvious as not worth mentioning but this is a feature of common stock that is not shared by partnerships. The stock price will fall if enough investors sell their shares and may prompt current owners to take corrective action. A falling stock price also may make the company a takeover target that can lead to drastic changes in management and policies.

The features of debt instruments also are related to the problems caused by asymmetric information. The fact that debt has a definite maturity date forces the company and its owners to return to the financial market to renew that debt. This makes them more accountable for their actions and provides periodic opportunities to monitor their performance. Furthermore, short-term debt must be renewed more frequently than long-term debt, which provides more accountability and more opportunities for monitoring. Provisions that require the company to repay a loan in periodic installments have the same effect by shortening the effective maturity of the loan. Requiring companies to periodically repay their debt also reduces the discretionary cash flow available to managers who may use it for their own benefit.

Creditors' conditional control rights also provide them some protection from problems caused by asymmetric information. Restrictive covenants make a loan agreement or bond indenture a more complete contract and provide some measure of control in routine circumstances. Creditors' rights to seize a company's assets when their claims are not satisfied provides protection in extraordinary circumstances.

We will see that some of the financing choices companies and investors make apparently are the result of concern about the problems caused by asymmetric information.

The Markets for Financial Instruments

There are a variety of names for the markets in which financial instruments are issued and traded. Companies issue new securities in the *primary market*. They may sell the securities to a few knowledgeable investors in a *private placement* or to anyone in a *public offering*. The investors who buy the securities may resell them or buy more from other investors in the *secondary market*. The market for long-term financial instruments, such as common stock and bonds, is called the *capital market* while the market for short-term instruments is called the *money market*. Several of these descriptions may apply to a particular transaction. For example, a manufacturing company that obtains financing by issuing bonds to an insurance company has conducted a private placement in the debt sector of the primary capital market.

The remaining sections of this chapter describe the sources of financing that most companies use at one time or another during their development. Accordingly, we will proceed from private to public financing and conclude by discussing the markets in which investors trade securities.

14.2 PRIVATE SOURCES OF FINANCING

Start-up companies have no choice but to use private financing, although many established companies use this source as well. The explanation in both cases may be investors' concerns about asymmetric information.

Financing a New Business

Virtually all companies are initially financed with equity provided by the founders and their friends and relatives. There may be no other way to finance a new business because its viability depends on the quality of the idea and the founders' own abilities, honesty, and willingness to work. These characteristics are unknown to outside investors and it is difficult for the company's founders to credibly reveal this information to them. It also may be hazardous for the founders to reveal this information to outsiders because they may lose their idea without obtaining any financing in return. The conflicting claims of ownership of an idea for a cellular-phone holder (see "In the News" on page 584) is an example of the disputes that can arise in this context. Concerns about asymmetric information on both sides of a transaction may impede financing and leave the founders with no alternative but to sell equity to their acquaintances.

The owners of successful companies eventually exhaust this source of funds and must seek external financing. Their first recourse usually is another private lender such as a bank or venture capitalist.

Governmental Financial Assistance Programs

Some entrepreneurs use governmental assistance programs for help in obtaining external financing. The Small Business Administration (SBA) is an agency of the U.S. government that helps small, independent companies obtain debt financing by guaranteeing their loans from ordinary financial institutions. The SBA also helps small businesses obtain equity financing by licensing privately organized and managed Small Business Investment Companies (SBIC). SBICs qualify for special government financing that they combine with funds from private investors to purchase equity and convertible securities issued by small businesses. A new SBA program to match companies and investors on the Internet (see "In the News" on page 585) will expand the amount of financing provided with governmental assistance.

Some states have their own financial assistance programs modeled on the SBA. All states have economic development agencies that provide advice and that help entrepreneurs locate alternative sources of financing.

Commercial Banks and Other Financial Intermediaries

Many companies turn first to commercial banks and other financial intermediaries for additional financing because they are well-equipped to deal with problems caused by asymmetric information. Banks are private lenders that are more knowledgeable than the average investor and have more direct and frequent contact with the managers. This close relationship gives them access to information not available to the public. For example, bankers can ask managers to describe the company's business strategy and can pursue areas of concern in an ongoing dialogue. This relationship also gives banks more influence and they use this influence to require detailed restrictive covenants when a

I N   T H E   N E W S

T H E   F L I P - P H O N E   F L A P

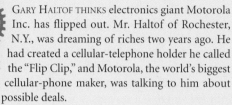

GARY HALTOF THINKS electronics giant Motorola Inc. has flipped out. Mr. Haltof of Rochester, N.Y., was dreaming of riches two years ago. He had created a cellular-telephone holder he called the "Flip Clip," and Motorola, the world's biggest cellular-phone maker, was talking to him about possible deals.

Now Motorola not only says it developed the product but also is trying to squash Mr. Haltof's trademark on the name, claiming that when it comes to cell phones, Motorola owns the word "flip." The flip flap could take years to straighten out. Mr. Haltof, who gave up his work as a design consultant and took out a home-equity loan to pursue his Flip Clip vision, calls the situation tragic. "I'm going to be driven out of business and it's not right," he says.

His story is a cautionary tale for entrepreneurs contemplating deals with big companies. According to Mr. Haltof, Motorola's accessories division was initially keen on the Flip Clip. The plastic cradle is designed to hold the cellular handsets with flip-down mouthpieces advertised as "flip phones"—particularly the kind made by Motorola—inside a car. But last year, Motorola asserted that engineers elsewhere in the company had already drawn up a similar phone cradle, Mr. Haltof says.

"Their general patent counsel called me after I'd showed [the product] around," says Mr. Haltof, who claims that talks had just culminated in Motorola requesting a price for 100,000 Flip Clips. "'Don't talk to us anymore,' [the lawyer] said. 'We think we may have invented your product.'"

Meanwhile, the trademark office did clear "Flip Clip" for Mr. Haltof, apparently deciding that this was a unique term. Motorola filed an opposition to that trademark decision, and Mr. Haltof's lawyer is now battling it out with Motorola's lawyers.

Source: Quentin Hardy, "Inventors Heed Tale of Flip-Phone Flap," *The Wall Street Journal,* August 27, 1996, p. B1. Reprinted by permission of *The Wall Street Journal,* © 1996 Dow Jones & Company, Inc. All rights reserved worldwide.

loan is established and to protect themselves if terms are renegotiated due to financial distress.

Banks often have a noncredit relationship with a borrower, which provides more information and influence. Companies tend to borrow from banks where their checking accounts are located and many banks require companies to establish accounts with them before they will extend a loan. This practice provides two benefits: (1) the bank can monitor activity in the accounts to obtain detailed information about the sources and uses of the company's cash flows, and (2) the bank can seize the money in these accounts and apply it to the loan if the company defaults. These important sources of information and influence are in addition to those available to other private lenders.

The financial market apparently recognizes that banks and other financial intermediaries have better information and are better monitors. Researchers have found that investors are willing to pay a higher price for the common stock of companies that announce they have negotiated a bank credit agreement or a loan.[6] Importantly, they

---

[6]See Christopher James and Peggy Wier, "Are Banks Different? Some Evidence From the Stock Market," *Journal of Applied Corporate Finance,* Summer 1988, pp. 46–54; and Wayne Mikkelson and Megan Partch, "Valuation Effects of Security Offerings and the Issuance Process," *Journal of Financial Economics,* January/February 1986, pp. 31–60.

IN THE NEWS

ANGEL INVESTORS ON THE INTERNET

RICH INDIVIDUALS LOOKING to invest in small companies soon will be able to access an on-line federal matchmaking service, government officials will announce this week.

The service, sponsored by the U.S. Small Business Administration's Office of Advocacy and the Defense Department, is the federal government's first major effort to organize the informal, multibillion-dollar world of so-called angel investing, officials said. Angels are private investors who help finance growing companies.

Would-be angels who sign up for the Angel Capital Electronic Network, or AceNet, will receive a password allowing them to view the names and financial reports of money-seeking enterprises. The businesses pay a fee, which will vary by state, for a listing on the private Internet site.

The SBA decided to spearhead the project as part of its mandate to improve small businesses' access to capital, said Jere Glover, head of the agency's advocacy office. "The idea is to create a whole new generation of angels and a whole new

generation of businesses," added the official, who will announce the service tomorrow.

The SBA estimated that 300,000 businesses are candidates for angel money: They are big enough that they have outgrown traditional capital sources, including the SBA's own loan-guarantee program. But they aren't ready to go public, or even attract venture capital.

Meanwhile, the network could prove to be a real time saver for entrepreneurs, said William E. Wetzel Jr., director emeritus of the Center for Venture Research at the University of New Hampshire. While entrepreneurs generally know where to look to find bank financing or even venture capital, "there are no directories of angels," he said. "It takes entrepreneurs a lot of time to find potentially interested investors."

Although nobody has exact figures, Dr. Wetzel estimated that angels invest $10 billion to $20 billion annually in almost 40,000 different businesses. In contrast, venture-capital funds invested $7.4 billion last year.

Source: Stephanie N. Mehta, "Angel Investors to Get On-Line Service," *The Wall Street Journal*, October 28, 1996, p. B2. Reprinted by permission of *The Wall Street Journal*, © 1996 Dow Jones & Company, Inc. All rights reserved worldwide.

also found that investors take a negative view of private placements used to replace bank debt. This result suggests the market considers financial intermediaries to be better monitors than other private investors.

Venture Capitalists[7]

Entrepreneurs who have made some progress developing their idea into a saleable product or service may obtain additional financing from venture capitalists. These investors accept a new company's substantial risk of failure for the chance to earn an equally substantial rate of return if it is successful. Some venture capitalists are wealthy individuals; others are investment funds that pool monies provided by many separate investors. Even some large, established companies use their business development units to participate in the creation of new technology.

---

[7]The ideas discussed in this section are based on an article by William A. Sahlman, "Aspects of Financial Contracting in Venture Capital," *Journal of Applied Corporate Finance*, Summer 1988, pp. 23–36.

Exhibit 14.1

SOURCES OF VENTURE CAPITAL FINANCING

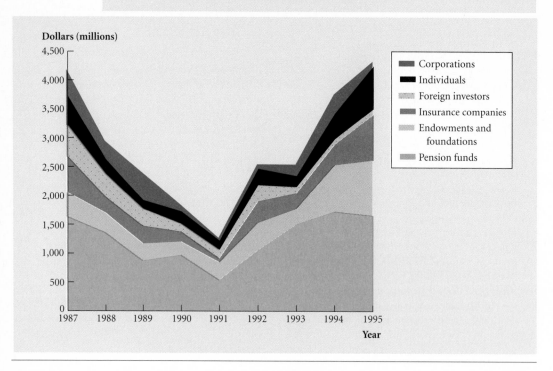

Source: National Venture Capital Association, annual reports for various years.

Exhibit 14.1 shows that pension funds are the dominant source of venture capital in the United States. On average, they accounted for 44 percent of the new funds provided to venture capitalists in the past nine years. Exhibit 14.2 identifies the industries where this money was invested. The money was nearly equally divided among the six industries listed although the software and services and medical and health care industries received slightly more than the others.

What Venture Capitalists Provide   Venture capitalists provide cash in stages to finance a company until it can sell securities to the public. Early stage financing is used for market research, product development, and production facilities. Expansion stage financing is used for working capital to support higher sales, for product improvements, and as bridge financing to sustain the company until it sells securities to other investors. Venture capitalists usually expect to close out their investment in a successful company and obtain their payoff at the conclusion of this final stage. Some venture capital funds also finance acquisitions and provide money to "turnaround" or rescue companies with operating or financial difficulties. Exhibit 14.3 shows that, on average, nearly half of all venture capital financing was used for expansion purposes from 1987–1995. The

Exhibit 14.2

USES OF VENTURE CAPITAL FINANCING

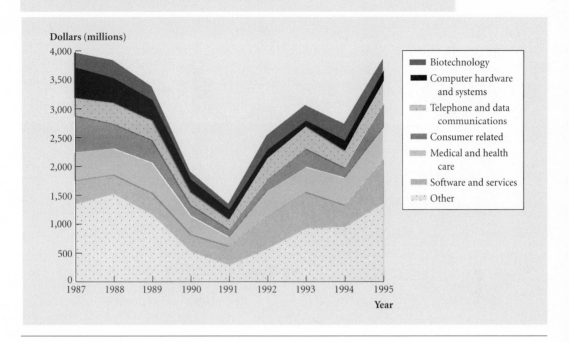

Source: National Venture Capital Association, annual reports for various years.

remainder was about equally split between early stage financing and acquisitions-turnaround financing.

You can easily deduce why the money is provided in stages by thinking about the hazards of investing in the presence of asymmetric information. First, staged financing reduces the amount of discretionary cash available to the company by providing funds as they are needed for each phase. Second, staged financing is like a series of short-term loans that provide periodic opportunities for monitoring the entrepreneur–agent. These monitoring opportunities coincide with the availability of information automatically revealed as the project passes through stages of development. Third, staged financing provides an incentive for the company's owners and managers to work hard to make each phase of the project successful so that subsequent stages will be funded.

Staged financing has another, more subtle, benefit to venture capitalists: It converts the financing of a new venture from a straight investment with an uncertain payoff at the very end into a call option on that payoff. The venture capitalist assesses the information available at each stage and renews this option by financing the next phase of the project if the information is favorable, however, they allow it to expire by refusing to make additional investments otherwise. This provides a great deal of flexibility and is an efficient way to manage the substantial amount of risk inherent in financing a new business.

Exhibit 14.3

NEW VENTURE CAPITAL INVESTMENTS BY STAGE OF FINANCING

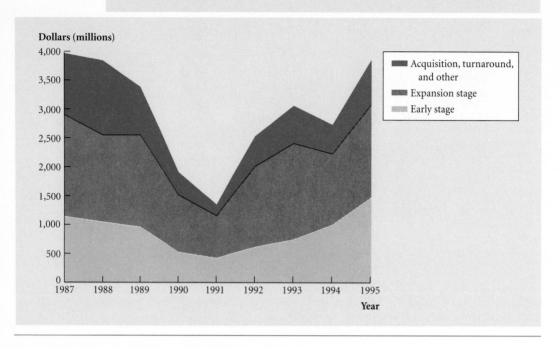

Source: National Venture Capital Association, annual reports for various years.

Staged financing also is beneficial to the entrepreneur because each phase of the project is financed on more favorable terms as information is revealed and uncertainty resolved. This enables the entrepreneur to fund the project without giving up as much future cash flow or control as would be necessary if it were financed all at once.

What Venture Capitalists Want   Venture capitalists want the founders to have a large equity investment in the company. This investment signals the owners' confidence and gives them an incentive to work hard. Venture capitalists also want an equity stake for themselves so they can receive an owner's share of the rewards if the company succeeds. They want their claim to be senior to the owners' claim, however, to protect themselves from exploitation. For these reasons, venture capitalists often hold convertible preferred stock. Its claim is senior to the owners' claim until they convert it into common stock to share in the owners' rewards. Representatives of the venture capital firm often are appointed to the board of directors or key management positions even if their stock is nonvoting.

The Use of Private Financing by Established Companies

Even established companies with publicly traded bonds or common stock sometimes obtain financing in a private placement. These transactions are exempt from regulation, that is, the company does not have to register them or file financial disclosure statements. This saves time and money. In addition, the investors who purchase private placements usually are large financial institutions or wealthy individuals who know what questions to ask and how to interpret the answers. They can therefore obtain better information than the public and can monitor the company more closely.

The advantages of private placements are obtained at the expense of a limited secondary market because the public may be unaware that the securities exist. In addition, restrictions often exist as to whom the original investor can sell the securities. For example, the SEC prohibits the sale of privately placed securities for two years unless the buyer is an institutional investor with at least $100 million invested in securities. This reduced liquidity is thought to be the reason why privately placed debt pays slightly higher returns than similar publicly placed issues.

There are indications that the advantages of a private placement outweigh the disadvantages. Several scholars have found that investors are willing to pay a higher price for the already issued common stock of companies that announce they will sell additional equity or convertible debt in a private placement.[8] Improved monitoring is the apparent benefit of a private placement in these cases because the sample companies were already filing financial disclosure statements for their public offerings.

14.3   ISSUING SECURITIES TO THE PUBLIC

Most successful companies eventually issue securities to the public to replace their start-up financing and to fund subsequent expansions. At that time, the owners and managers must decide whether to issue debt or equity and whether to hire an investment bank for assistance. We will devote Chapter 16 to the choice between debt and equity and concentrate on the other choices companies make here. The sale of securities to the public is governed by federal and state regulations so we will begin with a review of these important provisions.

Regulation of the Securities Business

The objective of regulations that govern the issuance of securities is to ensure that investors have enough information to make an informed decision—not to guarantee the safety of investments. Merely requiring companies to provide information when they issue securities is a valuable objective, however, because investors need data to identify the best investment opportunities and to reduce the hazards of asymmetric information.

---

[8]Karen Wruck, "Equity Ownership Concentration and Firm Value Evidence from Private Equity Financings," *Journal of Financial Economics,* June 1989, pp. 3–28; L. Page Fields and Eric L. Mais, "The Valuation Effects of Private Placements of Convertible Debt," *Journal of Finance,* December 1991, pp. 1925–1932; and William R. McDaniel II and William R. McDaniel III, "The Private Placements of Public Corporations' Common Stock," *Journal of Small Business Finance,* Number 3, 1992, pp. 205–220.

Most security sales in the United States are regulated by the federal government under the authority of the Securities Act of 1933, which is administered by the Securities and Exchange Commission (SEC). This act requires companies to disclose information about their operating and financial condition when they issue new securities in a public or rights offering. Securities sold to any number of accredited investors (such as financial institutions and wealthy individuals) but no more than 35 unsophisticated investors are considered private placements and are exempt from these regulations. They may still be subject to state regulation, however.

Companies subject to federal regulation disclose the required operating and financial information by filing a registration statement with the SEC and by providing a **prospectus** to potential investors. These documents contain current and historical financial statements, management's discussion and analysis of the company's condition, a description of the security's features, and the intended use of the proceeds. They are prepared by the company's management with the assistance of attorneys, accountants, and possibly an investment banker. These parties may be asked to show that they exercised due diligence (were conscientious) when they helped prepare the registration statements if investors allege important information was omitted or misstated.

The prospectus is issued in three forms. A preliminary prospectus or **red herring** (so called because "preliminary" and other cautionary statements are stamped in red ink on the cover) is issued when the registration statements are filed. An abbreviated version, the summary prospectus, is issued at the same time. The preliminary prospectus contains most of the information that will be provided in the final prospectus but is subject to amendment. Neither the preliminary nor summary prospectus gives the price of the securities. The preliminary prospectus is withdrawn and the final prospectus is issued when the SEC approves the registration statement. The final prospectus contains all the operating and financial information in final form plus the price at which the securities are offered for sale. Consequently, the final prospectus is used for both disclosure and marketing purposes.

The traditional registration process requires the company and its investment banker to attempt to sell the entire issue upon approval. The *shelf registration* process, adopted in 1982, is an alternative that permits companies to register an issue and then sell the securities from the shelf as they need the money. This supposedly enables them to reduce registration and investment banking costs and to issue securities at favorable times.

The Securities Act of 1933 also regulates the activities of the company's managers and investment banker during the time periods that surround the sale of securities. First, these parties cannot make announcements intended to pave the way for the sale during the time they are planning the issue and gathering information for the registration statement. Second, they can undertake only limited sales efforts during the approximately 20 days between the time they file the registration forms and obtain SEC approval. Permitted activities are distributing the preliminary and summary prospectuses, placing advertisements, and receiving but not accepting oral offers. Third, the company and its investment banker are permitted to stabilize the price of the securities for a short interval of time once sales begin even though price manipulation is prohibited at any other time.

Companies whose securities are traded on organized exchanges or over-the-counter must meet the continuing disclosure requirements prescribed by the Securities Exchange Act of 1934. This act specifies the form and content of financial and nonfinancial disclosures and requires companies to follow generally accepted accounting principles (GAAP) as described by the Financial Accounting Standards Board. Companies comply with the provisions of this act by submitting annual and quarterly reports to the SEC (the 10-K and 10-Q reports) and their common stockholders. These reports update the information that was contained in the original registration statement. Copies of these reports are available on the SEC's Internet site at http://www.sec.gov/index.html.

Investment Banks

Companies that plan any type of securities sale can hire an **investment bank** for assistance. Investment banks are financial institutions that specialize in the securities business. Among other things, they design and market financial instruments to manage risk, trade securities to earn profits for themselves, arrange mergers and acquisitions, and help companies issue securities to investors. They are different from commercial banks because they do not accept deposits and provide loans in the usual sense. Some countries permit their banks to offer both types of services, however, in the United States, the Glass-Steagall Act of 1933 prohibits investment banks from entering the commercial banking business and vice versa.

Investment banks help companies issue securities by advising them during the planning and registration phase and by distributing the securities upon approval. The issuing company decides how much of these services to purchase when they hire their investment bank. A company that hires an investment bank under a **negotiated agreement** obtains its advice on the type and features of the securities to issue, when to sell them, and whether to distribute them in a public offering, a rights offering, or a private placement. A company that hires an investment bank on a **competitive bid** basis makes its own decisions and awards the job of distributing the securities to the bank that offers the highest net proceeds from the sale.

An investment bank hired under either set of terms can distribute the securities on a **firm commitment** or **best efforts** basis. A bank **underwrites** or guarantees the amount of the net proceeds when it makes a firm commitment. The bank purchases the entire issue from the company at the guaranteed price and then bears the risk of reselling the securities at a profit. Investment banks only promise to do their best when they are hired on a best efforts basis and therefore are paid a simple commission. The lead bank or banks invariably form a syndicate or coalition with other investment banks to share the underwriting risk and enlist other banks and brokerage firms to help sell the securities to their clients.

Table 14.2 describes the activities of the top 10 investment banks in the United States in 1996. These banks managed or led nearly 81 percent of the offerings conducted that year. As a whole, the industry disclosed fees that totaled almost 1 percent of the value of the securities the banks underwrote.

Companies tend to use the more expensive investment banking services such as negotiated, firm commitment offers. Some finance scholars believe they do this to

Table 14.2   TOP UNDERWRITERS OF U.S. DEBT AND EQUITY IN 1996

Manager	Amount (billions)	Market Share	Number of Issues	Disclosed Fees (millions)
Merrill Lynch	$155.9	16.4%	1,113	$1,335.4
Lehman Brothers	100.7	10.6	782	488.2
Goldman, Sachs	98.5	10.3	796	1,204.5
Salomon Brothers	96.2	10.1	623	491.8
Morgan Stanley	83.7	8.8	531	881.6
J. P. Morgan	68.7	7.2	469	249.8
CS First Boston	60.0	6.3	453	422.1
Bear, Stearns	41.7	4.4	NA	NA
Donaldson, Lufkin & Jenrette	34.8	3.6	243	646.8
Smith Barney	29.9	3.1	376	563.6
Top 10	$770.1	80.8%		
Industry total	$953.4	100.0%	8,921	$9,193.1

Source: *The Wall Street Journal,* January 2, 1997, p. R38.

reassure potential investors who are concerned about the hazards of asymmetric information.[9] The problem is that companies enter the financial market to obtain new financing intermittently. Investors therefore may expect them to issue securities when it is in the current owners' and managers' best interests—when the securities are selling for more than they are really worth, for example. Furthermore, investors cannot easily penalize them for this abuse of private information if the company does not issue securities again for several years. The investors' only alternative may be to assume the worst and pay a low price for the securities at the time they are issued.

A company can diminish the perception that it will exploit investors by relinquishing some control over its financing decisions. By choosing the traditional rather than the shelf form of registration, a company limits its opportunity to sell securities when the timing is favorable. Negotiated, firm commitment arrangements similarly require companies to share the responsibility for designing and distributing the securities with their investment bankers. The investment banker thereby stakes its own reputation on the issue and can be expected to monitor the company to protect *itself.* Importantly, investment bankers enter the financial market regularly to obtain financing for their clients and will lose business if investors believe they have been misled. The participation of a well-known investment bank reassures investors who are therefore willing to pay a gross price for the securities that more than compensates for the investment banking fees.

---

[9]For a discussion of these issues and a review of the empirical evidence on the use of investment banking services, see Clifford W. Smith Jr., "Raising Capital: Theory and Evidence," *Midland Corporate Finance Journal,* Spring 1986, pp. 6–22.

I N   T H E   N E W S

NOTHING BUT 'NET FOR GMAC

ON SEPT. 27, General Motors Acceptance Corp. started marketing $500 million in bonds through Chicago Corp. What makes this otherwise mundane bond issue noteworthy is that it is being done on the Internet. That a powerhouse such as GMAC pursued its sizable deal on the Internet speaks volumes for how the Internet is altering the way businesses reach investors and raise money. GMAC says the Internet is ideal for pitching bonds issued by well-known companies to retail customers who don't normally get a crack at such offerings. "We're getting a new marketplace and additional funding," says GMAC director David Walker.

Source: Linda Himelstein and Leah Nathans Spiro, "The Net Hits the Big Time," *Business Week*, October 28, 1996,

The General Motors Acceptance Corporation (GMAC), General Motors' credit company, is a familiar name to investors as it has more than $31 billion of long-term debt outstanding. GMAC's familiarity permitted it to bypass the normal procedures for selling securities to the public with its recent $500 million sale of bonds over the Internet (see "In the News"). Whether less well-known companies can do the same thing remains to be seen.

14.4   THE EXCHANGE OF FINANCIAL INSTRUMENTS

Individuals and financial institutions eventually exchange their securities with other investors in the secondary market. These trades permit them to recover their money to spend or invest elsewhere even though the company that issued the securities is under no obligation to redeem them. The opportunity to trade with other investors provides liquidity and improves the prospect that security prices quickly and accurately reflect the value of new information. Stock exchanges and associations and their member companies are the financial institutions that help investors conduct these trades.

Some secondary markets are *organized exchanges* with a physical location where traders meet to conduct transactions for themselves and their customers. Organized exchanges usually are auction markets in which the traders shout out the prices at which they are willing to buy and sell securities. The apparent pandemonium this produces is often used in news films to depict activity in the financial markets. The New York Stock Exchange (NYSE) is a well-known example of an organized exchange.

Other secondary markets are *virtual* markets with traders who do not meet at a specific place but are connected via telephones, facsimile machines, or a computer network. These are called *over-the-counter (OTC) markets* and most are negotiated markets because the buyers and sellers or their representatives arrange the terms of their trades privately rather than through a public auction. Important examples of OTC markets are the markets for U.S. Treasury securities and the market for bonds and stocks covered by the National Association of Securities Dealers' Automated Quotation (NASDAQ) Service.

Regulation of Secondary Markets

United States secondary markets are regulated by the SEC under the authority of the Securities Exchange Act of 1934 and its amendments. These laws apply to the organized exchanges and the OTC markets and their members, brokers, and dealers. The laws require each market participant and company whose securities are publicly traded to register with the SEC and they require the exchanges to discipline those whose conduct is detrimental to the securities business. The National Association of Securities Dealers and the National Futures Association are organizations that provide self-regulation to the OTC and futures markets.

Price manipulation is one form of detrimental conduct specifically prohibited by the Exchange Act. Manipulation is defined as purchases and sales designed to stabilize a security's price or give the false impression of active trading to induce buying and selling by others. As noted earlier, investment bankers are exempt from the prohibition against price stabilization during the initial period when securities are offered to the public.

Insider trading is another form of conduct regulated by the Exchange Act. Officers, directors, and common stockholders who own at least 10 percent of a company must inform the SEC when they buy and sell their company's stock. The SEC makes these reports public and the company or its shareholders can sue the traders to recover their short-term profits for the company. The basis for these suits is that the traders breached their fiduciary duty by personally profiting from information that belonged to the company and its owners.

Other SEC rules permit charges of fraud based on the illegal use of insider information. Any insider who possesses confidential information and any outsider who improperly acquires confidential information (such as an insider's brother-in-law) must reveal that information or abstain from trading. The person harmed by the trade or the SEC itself can bring charges for violations of this rule. Possible penalties include the assessment of monetary damages, disbarment from the securities business, and a prison sentence. United States courts do not always agree with the SEC about this interpretation of insider trading (see "In the News").

The regulation of insider trading is controversial. Some people argue that insider trading must be prohibited to protect corporations and their shareholders and to maintain investors' faith in the financial system. Others argue that permitting insider trading improves the efficiency of the financial markets by promoting the rapid adjustment of prices to new information. The U.S. position on this issue is among the strictest in the world.

The Federal Reserve Bank and the Commodity Futures Trading Commission (CFTC) also regulate the securities business in the United States. The Fed establishes initial margin requirements (the proportion of a security's price that the investor may borrow at the time of purchase) while the CFTC regulates financial futures contracts and options on futures.

IN THE NEWS

AN INSIDER OR NOT?
THE COURTS WILL DECIDE

JAMES H. O'HAGAN was a lawyer in a Minneapolis firm who learned that a client of the firm planned to make a big takeover offer. So he bought stock and stock options in the target company. He made $4 million.

Does that sound like insider trading to you? It did to a jury that convicted Mr. O'Hagan of securities fraud, and to a judge who sentenced him to 41 months in prison.

But that's not the way the judges on the United States Court of Appeals for the Eighth Circuit saw it. "Such conduct is certainly unethical and immoral and must be condemned, which we make haste to do," wrote Judge David R. Hansen. But, he added, it was not illegal.

That decision, entered last month, has shaken officials at the Securities and Exchange Commission, and it is likely to end up being reviewed by the Supreme Court.

Source: Floyd Norris, "An Insider Gets Rich on Trades and Walks," *The New York Times*, September 8, 1996. Copyright © 1996 by The New York Times Co. Reprinted by permission.

The Operations of Secondary Markets

An important difference between negotiated and auction markets is the method by which security prices are established. In addition, each market has its own rules governing which securities can be traded and who can trade there.

Price-Setting in a Negotiated Market   Dealers who stand ready to buy and sell a security for their own account set its price in a negotiated or dealer market. Dealers post *bid* prices at which they are willing to buy securities and *ask* prices at which they are willing to sell them.

The bid–ask spread compensates dealers for being ready to buy and sell securities on demand. An investor who simply wants to sell a security because she has a cash deficit can search for a buyer who is willing to pay the true value or sell it to a dealer at the bid price. The difference between the true value and bid price is the discount the investor accepts to make a *sale* without delay. Similarly, the difference between the ask price and true value is the premium an investor pays to make a *purchase* without delay.

Competition encourages dealers to set their bid and ask prices near their best estimate of the security's true value given current information. Otherwise, investors and other dealers will make money at their expense by buying from them securities that they priced too low and selling to them securities that they priced too high. Dealers change their prices as new information becomes available to avoid losses due to mispricing.

The bid–ask spread also may protect dealers from losses to investors who obtain new information before they do. This situation is illustrated in Table 14.3 where an informed investor profits at the dealer's expense when the bid–ask spread is $1—but not when it is $2. Note that an informed investor would still make a profit in spite of

Table 14.3   EFFECT OF BID–ASK SPREAD ON INFORMED INVESTOR'S PROFITS

	Initial	With New Information
Security's value	$20.00	$22.00
Panel A: $1 Bid–Ask Spread		
Dealer's quotes		
Bid	$19.50	$21.50
Ask	20.50	22.50
Informed investor's experience		
Purchase price	20.50	
Selling price		21.50
Profit		1.00
Panel B: $2 Bid–Ask Spread		
Dealer's quotes		
Bid	$19.00	$21.00
Ask	21.00	23.00
Informed investor's experience		
Purchase price	21.00	
Selling price		21.00
Profit		0

a $2 bid–ask spread if his information was worth more than $2. If this isn't clear, rework the table when the security's value changes from $20 to $22.10. This means dealers can be expected to increase their bid–ask spreads the more uncertain they are about the security's true value.

Price-Setting in an Auction Market   Brokers representing investors who want to buy or sell a security establish its price by publicly bargaining with one another in an auction market. These brokers shout out their bid and ask prices for market orders, which are executed immediately, and submit a list of bid and ask prices for limit orders, which are executed when the price reaches a specified value. These current orders and inventory of future orders provide competition on both the demand and supply sides of this two-sided auction. The security's price is the price at which at least one trade is executed as a result of this process.

Security prices change in an auction market when supply does not equal demand at the current price, that is, when there is an order imbalance. For example, sell orders may exceed buy orders because of unfavorable new information or because there are more investors with cash deficits than cash surpluses. For either reason, the auction price will fall as brokers with sell orders compete to dispose of their securities to reluctant buyers. The security's new, lower price is established when a trade takes place.

Hybrid Markets   The New York Stock Exchange is a prominent example of a hybrid secondary market. Trades in each security listed on the exchange are conducted at one of 400 trading posts where brokers meet for the two-sided auction. A unique broker–dealer, called a *specialist*, is stationed at each post to facilitate trading. Specialists keep track of and execute limit orders on behalf of others and buy and sell securities for their own account when there are order imbalances. Their trading profits are their compensation for performing these services. Because there is only one specialist for each security traded on the NYSE, they appear to have a monopoly. However, brokers in the crowd at the trading post compete with the specialist as do freelance dealers (known as *registered traders*) who buy and sell securities for their own accounts. The Exchange also monitors specialists to determine if their trades improve liquidity and provide quick and orderly adjustment of prices to new information.

Access to Secondary Markets   Each segment of the secondary market has its own rules for which securities can be traded there. A large segment of the OTC market has no rules other than that someone must be willing to act as a dealer for the security. The company that issued the security may be small, unprofitable, and obscure and the results of trades may not be widely reported but the existence of a dealer means a market exists.

Other segments of the secondary market have criteria restricting which securities can be listed or traded there. Commonly used criteria are measures of size and profitability and indicators of the breadth of investors' interest in the company. In the United States, the least stringent requirements are those that permit an OTC company's stock to be listed in the SmallCap sector of the NASDAQ system. This electronic service reports the bid–ask quotes of the dealers who make a market in the securities listed there. OTC companies that meet more stringent requirements can be included in the NASDAQ National Market System (NMS). The NASDAQ/NMS provides the same information as the basic NASDAQ system plus the results of actual trades. Companies also can apply to have their stock traded on the American or New York Stock Exchanges. Current listing requirements are given in Table 14.4. A recent article reports that more companies have chosen to list their stock on the NYSE or NASDAQ than the American Stock Exchange (AMEX) (see "In The News").

There is some evidence that companies benefit from having their stock traded on an organized exchange.[10] Researchers have found that investors are willing to pay a higher price for the common stock of companies that announce they will move from the OTC to the AMEX or NYSE. Investors apparently anticipate improved liquidity because stocks with low liquidity when they were traded over-the-counter received a higher premium than stocks with high prelisting liquidity. In addition, financial executives have cited higher prestige and visibility as important benefits. Both groups believe these benefits have declined with the introduction of the NASDAQ/NMS, however, because it provides exchange-like information and therefore intensifies competition among dealers.

---

[10]For a review of the research on the effect of changing the location where a company's stock is traded, see H. Kent Baker and Sue E. Meeks, "Research on Exchange Listings and Delistings: A Review and Synthesis," *Financial Practice and Education,* Spring 1991, pp. 57–71.

Table 14.4   LISTING REQUIREMENTS FOR MAJOR U.S. SECONDARY MARKETS

Panel A: Requirements to Be Listed in NASDAQ Reporting Systems

	SmallCap Market	National Market
Net tangible assets	NA	$4,000,000
Total assets	$4,000,000	NA
Total equity	$2,000,000	NA
Net income (2 of last 3 years)	NA	$400,000
Pre-tax earnings (2 of last 3 years)	NA	$750,000
Number of shares outstanding	100,000	500,000
Market value of shares outstanding	$1,000,000	$3,000,000
Minimum bid	$3.00	$10.00
Number of market makers	2	2
Number of stockholders	300	400

Panel B: Requirements to Be Listed on National Organized Exchanges

	AMEX	NYSE
Net tangible assets	NA	$18,000,000
Stockholders' equity	$4,000,000	NA
Pre-tax earnings most recent year	$750,000	$2,500,000
Pre-tax earnings each of 2 preceding years	NA	$2,000,000
Number of shares outstanding	500,000	1,100,000
Market value of shares outstanding	$3,000,000	$18,000,000
Minimum price	$3.00	NA
Average monthly trading volume (shares)	NA	100,000
Number of stockholders	800	2,000

Sources: http://www.nasdaq.com
http://www.amex.com
http://www.nyse.com

Each segment of the secondary market also has rules governing who can trade there. Any person who holds a valid securities license can act as a broker or dealer in the OTC market but only members of the organized exchanges are permitted to trade there. One becomes a member by purchasing a seat on the exchange. Prices for seats in 1995 ranged from $785,000 to $1,050,000.[11] Most seats are held by firms that provide stock brokerage services. These companies (Merrill-Lynch is a familiar example) employ registered representatives who meet with customers in their local offices where stock trades are ini-

[11]New York Stock Exchange, *New York Stock Exchange Fact Book, 1995 Data,* 1996.

I N   T H E   N E W S

COMPANIES JOIN THE LIST AT THE NYSE AND NASDAQ

THE TWO LARGEST markets in the U.S. had a bumper crop of new companies listing with them for the first time during 1996—a year in which record numbers of companies came public for the first time and a roaring bull market enticed scores of foreign companies to U.S. markets.

The New York Stock Exchange, the nation's largest market, added 279 companies' names to its listings, while the No. 2 Nasdaq Stock Market added 1,009 new companies.

Of course, both lost companies as well. On Nasdaq, hundreds of companies were delisted, and a record 97 defected to the Big Board during the year, leaving Nasdaq with 5,576 companies listed on its market at year end, 454 more than the previous year. That fell short of 1993's record of 498 net Nasdaq additions. The Big Board, which has a rule effectively barring most companies from defecting to other markets, ended 1996 with 2,907 listed companies, a net gain of 232 companies.

Nasdaq, true to its reputation as the main home for smaller, start-up companies, attracted the lion's share of newly public small-cap companies. A total of 687 newly public U.S. companies listed on Nasdaq, compared with 117 on the Big Board, which has more-stringent listing standards that may prohibit listing by many less-mature companies. The IPOs listing on Nasdaq had market capitalizations averaging $174 million. The average market cap of all the new companies listing on the Big Board, meanwhile, was around $350 million.

The American Stock Exchange, which has had trouble competing in recent years with the Big Board's global stature for larger stocks and Nasdaq's record in signing up start-up companies, listed only 73 new companies, with an average market cap of $146.3 million. And factoring in companies that left, merged with another company, or were delisted, the Amex ended the year with 18 fewer companies than it started with—although the Amex points out that it lost fewer companies in 1996 than in the year before.

"Nasdaq's growth was heavily in smaller IPOs, while New York saw a mix of very large IPOs and major switches from Nasdaq," says Patrick Healy, president of the Issuer Network, which advises companies on listing issues. At the same time, he says, while the Amex had an increase in new companies listing on its exchange, it "had no real large-trading-volume stocks listing."

Source: Deborah Lohse, "Big Board, Nasdaq Listings Surge," *The Wall Street Journal*, January 2, 1997, p. R4. Reprinted by permission of *The Wall Street Journal*, © 1997 Dow Jones & Company, Inc. All rights reserved worldwide.

tiated and commission brokers who actually execute the trades on the floor of the exchange. Other seats are held by independent floor brokers who assist the commission brokers when trading is heavy and the specialists and registered traders mentioned earlier.

Measures of Secondary Market Performance

Many people watch the day-to-day and long-term performance of securities traded in the secondary financial markets. Economic policymakers use the level of security prices as an indication of their economy's health while investors use market indices as benchmarks against which to assess the performance of their portfolios. Financial managers do the same to evaluate their company's relative performance.

IN THE NEWS

JOINING THE INDEX BOOSTS STOCK PRICES

WHEN THE STANDARD & Poor's 500 stock index adds or drops a stock, index funds—which mirror the index's composition—adjust their holdings accordingly. That process, report economists Anthony W. Lynch of New York University and Richard R. Mendenhall of the University of Notre Dame, can create some nifty profit opportunities. What's behind these rises? The economists estimate that some 16 percent of the shares of companies in the S&P 500 are now tied up in index investments. Thus, being added to the index can cause a big decline in the effective supply of a stock—and a nice jump in its price.

Source: "It Pays to Join the S&P 500," *Business Week*, July 29, 1996, p. 20.

You know that a comprehensive index of market performance plays a crucial role in the measurement and pricing of risk in the Capital Asset Pricing Model. We used the rate of return on the S&P 500 index for that purpose in Chapters 5 and 6 and elsewhere. A recent study found that the stocks of companies that join the index get a price boost because they find a ready market among investment funds that attempt to match the index's performance (see "In the News").

Measures of financial market performance are computed in one of two ways. A price-weighted average is computed by adding the prices of the securities in the index and dividing by a number that accounts for changes in the sample over time. This method of calculation causes high price stocks to have a larger influence on the level of the average than the low price stocks. A value-weighted index is computed by dividing the current market value of all the stocks in the index by their baseline market value and multiplying the result by an arbitrary index number such as 100. The price movements of stocks issued by large companies have the greatest influence on the level of a value-weighted index. Averages and indices represent overall market performance and the performance of particular subgroups such as industrial, utility, financial, or transportation stocks. Some of the more widely watched stock market averages and indices are described in Table 14.5.

14.5   FINANCIAL MARKET EFFICIENCY[12]

The owners expect financial managers to make decisions that maximize the owners' wealth. You have learned that one way managers accomplish this objective is to choose investment and operating alternatives with market values that exceed their costs. A

---

[12]Read a good investments textbook, such as Robert A. Haugen, *Modern Investment Theory*, Prentice-Hall, New Jersey, 1997, or the articles listed in the additional reading at the end of this chapter for more information about financial market efficiency.

MAJOR STOCK MARKET INDICES   Table 14.5

Market Segment	Index	Composition	Type
NYSE stocks	Dow-Jones Industrial Average	30 blue-chip industrial stocks	Price-weighted
NYSE stocks	NYSE Composite Index	All NYSE stocks	Value-weighted
NYSE/OTC* stocks	Standard & Poor's Index of 500 Stocks	400 industrial, 40 utility, 40 financial, and 20 transportation stocks	Value-weighted
AMEX stocks	Market Value Index	All AMEX common stocks and warrants	Value-weighted
OTC stocks	NASDAQ Composite Index	All domestic NASDAQ stocks	Value-weighted
London stocks	Financial Times 100		
Tokyo stocks	Nikkei 225 Index	225 stocks on the First Section of the Tokyo Stock Exchange	Price-weighted

*The S&P 500 index is largely a NYSE index but it does include the stocks of some financial intermediaries that are traded over-the-counter.

natural question to ask at this point is whether managers can choose *financing* alternatives with market values that exceed their costs. The answer depends on how quickly and how accurately information about a company's future prospects is reflected in the market prices of its securities.

Suppose first that market prices adjust to new information immediately and therefore always account for everything there is to know about the company, its industry, and the general economy. Then, a security's market price simply is the present value of its future cash flows because buyers will pay no more and sellers will accept no less. Selling a security at this price is merely an exchange of current for future cash flows, which does not increase the seller's wealth.

Now suppose that market prices adjust slowly to new information. In this case, a security's market price will be greater than the present value of its future cash flows until bad news is fully disseminated. An investor who buys such a security during this interval of time pays too much for it, which transfers some of his or her wealth to the seller. An investor who sells an undervalued security before its price fully adjusts to good news suffers a similar loss.

A financial market in which prices fully reflect available information and in which these wealth transfers cannot take place is called an **efficient market**. No one, including the companies that issue them, can consistently sell securities for more or buy securities for less than they are really worth in an efficient market. In this situation, there are no financing alternatives with market values that exceed their costs, so managers cannot make financing decisions that increase the owners' wealth.

This and other implications of market efficiency are so important that the efficient market hypothesis is one of the more thoroughly studied questions in finance. A brief discussion of these studies will help you appreciate the importance of their implications for financing decisions.

Degrees of Market Efficiency

Market efficiency is not an all-or-nothing concept. Market prices may adjust immediately to some information and slowly to other information. Finance scholars have organized their research of market efficiency by dividing the information the market responds to into three categories.

Weak-Form Market Efficiency   The first category of information contains only past prices. A financial market is *weak-form efficient* if current prices reflect everything that can be learned by studying past prices. Stock price charts and statistical tests, such as time series analysis, are of no use in this situation. The first person who discovers how to use past prices in a novel way to predict future prices may profit from the discovery but his or her own actions will eliminate the value of the discovery. The following example illustrates this idea.

Suppose you learn that anytime you see the following pattern of price changes, you know that the stock price will go up on day 7.

Day:	1	2	3	4	5	6
Price change:	+	+	+	−	−	−

You will, of course, buy the stock on day 6 so you can sell it on day 7 at a profit. However, your purchase on day 6 and subsequent sale on day 7 will cause the stock price to increase and decrease on those days. Your transactions thereby destroy the pattern you rely on for your prediction and your profit. No one can mimic you because your information is reflected in the market prices as a result of your actions.

Finance scholars have tested a large number of trading strategies more complicated than the simple one described above. Nearly all of them are unprofitable after their rates of return are adjusted for the costs of buying and selling securities and for differences in risk. *The Wall Street Journal*'s Investment Dartboard column (see "In the News") is a humorous version of these tests that generally support the conclusion that the stock market is weak-form efficient.

Finance scholars also have conducted statistical tests of security prices. Price changes that contain useful information exhibit trends or reversals, such as the trend and reversal displayed by the six-day pattern in the example above. Price changes that contain no useful information are random or independent of one another. Researchers detect the presence or absence of predictable patterns using correlation analysis and other statistical techniques. The results of these tests also support the conclusion that the stock market is weak-form efficient.

Semi-Strong-Form Market Efficiency   The second category of information that the financial market responds to contains all public information. This category comprises all historical information, including past prices, as well as new information announced to the public. Announcements may originate with the company or elsewhere and may apply to only one company or to several. Examples of information that applies to only one company are the company's own announcement that its quarterly earnings will be less than expected and the publication of a securities analyst's prediction that the company will have lower earnings. An announcement that the Federal Reserve system will raise interest rates to fight inflation is an example of new information that

I N   T H E   N E W S

PROS DON'T WIN EVEN WHEN THEY WIN

FOR JUST OVER five years now, *The Wall Street Journal*'s Investment Dartboard column has pitted investment pros against the forces of change, in the form of darts heaved at the stock listings. One aim has been to provide a lighthearted test of the "efficient-market theory."

On the surface, the results clearly favor the professionals and go against the theory. Since the contest adopted its current rules in 1990, the pros have won 24 times, the darts 17 times. The average six-month gain for the pros, 8.4 percent, has been much better than the 3.3 percent gain achieved by the darts. (Those figures are price changes only, without dividends.)

But Burton Malkiel, an economics professor at Princeton University and a leading exponent of the efficient-market theory, says there's less than meets the eye in the pros' apparent success in the contest.

According to Prof. Malkiel, the pros' favorable showing can be explained by two factors. First, they are picking riskier, more volatile stocks than the darts are. Second, they benefit from a favorable pub-

licity effect on the day the article is published.

With Prof. Malkiel, Gilbert E. Metcalk, an assistant professor of economics at Princeton, recently wrote a paper analyzing the dartboard contests from 1990 through 1992. The professors found that the pros' picks were about 40 percent more volatile—and therefore riskier—than the overall market. The dart stocks were only about 6 percent more volatile than the market.

In other words, the pros' selections tend to move up or down 14 percent for every 10 percent the overall market moves. Once you adjust for risk, the researchers say, the pros' margin shrinks to 0.4 percent, which is not statistically significant.

But that's not all. The researchers say the pros are riding the coattails of a strong "announcement effect" that causes the pros' picks to surge on the day they appear in this newspaper. Take away the announcement effect, they say, and the pros' superiority vanishes altogether.

Source: John R. Dorfman, "Luck or Logic? Debate Rages on Over 'Efficient Market' Theory," *The Wall Street Journal*, November 4, 1993, p. C1. Reprinted by permission of *The Wall Street Journal,* © 1993 Dow Jones & Company, Inc. All rights reserved worldwide.

applies to all companies. No matter where the information comes from or how broad its potential impact, a financial market is *semi-strong-form efficient* if current prices reflect everything that can be learned by studying public information.

Finance scholars have studied market reactions to announcements to assess how quickly market prices adjust to new public information. Among the announcements they have studied are quarterly earnings and dividend announcements, changes in capital structure, analysts' earnings forecasts, and changes in macroeconomic conditions. The results generally support the conclusion that market prices quickly and accurately reflect the value of public information.

Ederington's and Lee's study of market reactions in the interest rate and foreign exchange futures markets is particularly interesting.[13] In their words, "The speed and

---

[13]Louis H. Ederington and Jae Ha Lee, "The Impact of Macroeconomic News on Financial Markets," *Journal of Applied Corporate Finance,* Spring 1996, pp. 41–49.

efficiency with which the markets incorporate this information is amazing. The major adjustment to the information release (and the window for trading profits) lasts about 40 seconds." This is rapid adjustment to new information by any standard.

Strong-Form Market Efficiency   The third and final category of information the financial market responds to contains all relevant information—public or private. Insiders, managers, and other insiders who learn about significant events before the general public does are one source of private information. Professional investors, such as mutual and pension fund managers, are another source. The professional investors have private information in the sense that they use private, carefully guarded methods to obtain unique insights from the public record. Insiders' trading activities are regulated in the United States although professional investors are entitled to use their skills for the benefit of their participants. If these investors are unable to use their private information to generate superior rates of return for their participants, then market prices apparently reflect all private information and the market is *strong-form efficient.*

Finance scholars have studied professional investors and concluded they cannot *consistently* produce superior rates of return. Mutual funds that "beat the market" on a risk-adjusted basis one year are no more likely to do so the following year than any other fund. The results of a recent study of fund performance by Droms and Walker (see "In the News") are representative of this research. Their results and the results of other studies are consistent with a financial market that is strong-form efficient, at least on average.

Anomalies   Studies of market efficiency largely support the conclusion that information about a company's future prospects is quickly and accurately reflected in the market prices of its securities. There are, however, some anomalies that seem to be inconsistent with an efficient market. Small companies appear to provide excess risk-adjusted returns, rates of return are higher in January than in other months, and portfolios formed of companies with low market-to-book ratios seem to outperform portfolios formed of companies with high market-to-book ratios. Researchers are carefully examining these and other anomalies to determine whether we can explain them or must conclude that the financial markets are inefficient in certain respects. This is an ongoing process that you will read about in the news long after you have completed this book and this course.

Implications for Managers

The results of these studies imply that a security's market price usually is a good estimate of the present value of its future cash flows. The sale or purchase of a security at this price is only an exchange of current for future cash flows that does not increase the owners' wealth. This means that managers cannot consistently sell securities (issue them) or make other purely financing decisions to increase the owners' wealth either.

From time to time, managers may be able to increase the owners' wealth by executing a financing transaction that exploits some anomaly, however, these opportunities are unusual. Most of them are rare and fleeting because other managers pursue the

IN   THE   NEWS

LOOKING FOR CONSISTENCY
IN ALL THE WRONG PLACES

IF YOU'RE HUNTING for stock funds that perform consistently well, William Droms and David Walker have some bad news for you.

The two Georgetown University finance professors looked at the performance of the 151 U.S. stock funds that were in existence for the entire 20 years ended 1990. Many funds came and went during this 20-year stretch. These 151 funds survived, one presumes, because they were reasonably successful.

Yet only 40 of these 151 funds managed to beat Standard & Poor's 500 stock index in more than 10 of these 20 calendar years. The picture isn't any better if you look at longer time periods. For instance, if you divide the 20 years into four periods of five years each, you will find that no funds beat the S&P 500 in all four periods and only 15 beat the market in three of these five-year stretches.

Identifying these winners wouldn't have been easy. Buy based on performance? Unfortunately, funds that thrived in the period 1971–80 weren't any more likely than other funds to generate decent returns over the next 10 years.

Other fund-picking strategies also weren't much help. Conventional wisdom, for instance, suggests that larger funds and funds that trade rapidly tend to have poorer performance. But the Georgetown professors found that there was no relationship between investment performance and either portfolio turnover or fund size. "It's kind of discouraging," concludes Mr. Droms.

Source: Jonathan Clements, "By the Numbers: What the Researchers Are Digging Up on Fund Performance," *The Wall Street Journal*, December 24, 1996, p. C1. Reprinted by permission of *The Wall Street Journal*, © 1996 Dow Jones & Company, Inc. All rights reserved worldwide.

anomalies once they are recognized. Other opportunities are so commonplace that the market will take it for granted that managers will arrange the company's financing to exploit the anomaly. The use of debt financing to take advantage of the tax-deductibility of interest is a good example. The result is that managers should view the opportunity to make a great financing decision as serendipitous.

Managers cannot be complacent, however, and assume an efficient market will protect them from making poor financing choices. For example, managers who do not recognize the tax savings associated with a particular financing choice may inadvertently give the savings away in a market transaction. In addition, many of the financing decisions managers make are not *pure* financing decisions. Managers who issue debt may signal to the market their confidence that the company's investments will generate the cash flows needed to repay the debt. This favorable signal may cause the stock price to increase. Conversely, managers who use equity may signal to the market their inside information that investments are performing poorly. This unfavorable signal may cause the stock price to decrease. The net result is financing choices may affect the owners' wealth but not because the company can sell securities for more than they are really worth. We will explore these issues in more detail in the following chapters.

14.6   SUMMARY

Companies issue securities to obtain cash to establish or expand their businesses. The key features of these financial instruments establish the investors' claims on a company's future cash flows, explain their control rights, and describe the company's provisions for repayment.

Issuing securities to obtain financing is difficult because asymmetric information may make the financial market suspicious of the company's motives. Investors cannot easily verify the owners' or managers' claims and may be unwilling to pay what a security is really worth for fear that it is overvalued. A security's features, such as the requirement to make periodic debt payments, helps reduce these problems but does not eliminate them.

New companies usually obtain financing from banks and venture capitalists because these private investors are better equipped than the general public to deal with the problems of asymmetric information. The company and the private investors can exchange information in confidence, the investor can provide financing in stages to avoid its misuse, and private investors can more closely monitor the company's activities.

Most companies hire an investment bank for assistance when they sell securities to the general public. These banks help design, register, and distribute the securities to the public. They often guarantee the success of the sale as well. Investment banks are active in the financial market so their sponsorship of a company's financing transaction helps reduce investors' concerns that the company will take advantage of them.

Secondary financial markets provide a facility for trading securities before they mature. Prices in these markets may be negotiated with a dealer or they may be established in a public, double-sided auction. Empirical evidence indicates that what investors value most about more formalized markets is the additional liquidity they provide for their trades.

Most available evidence indicates that information about a company's future prospects is quickly and accurately reflected in the market prices of its securities. Trading strategies based on the analysis of past prices are not profitable and markets have been shown to respond to new public information in as little as 40 seconds. Furthermore, even professional investors cannot consistently earn a risk-adjusted excess rate of return. These results imply managers should not expect to issue securities for more than they are really worth.

●   K E Y   T E R M S

Restrictive covenants *579*	Prospectus *590*	Firm commitment *591*
Indenture *579*	Red herring *590*	Best efforts *591*
Sinking fund *579*	Investment bank *591*	Underwrite *591*
Adverse selection *580*	Negotiated agreement *591*	Efficient market *601*
Signal *581*	Competitive bid *591*	

• QUESTIONS AND PROBLEMS

1. Describe debt and equity's distinguishing features. Which feature is most important? Why?

2. A company that issues *income bonds* must pay the interest on these bonds only when its income is positive. Is an income bond more like debt or equity? How does an income bond compare to preferred stock?

3. Callable and convertible bonds are debt instruments with options attached.

   (a) What option is attached to a callable bond? Who owns the option?

   (b) What option is attached to a convertible bond? Who owns the option?

   (c) Given what you know about options, do you think a callable bond will sell for more or less than an identical noncallable bond? Do you think a convertible bond will sell for more or less than an identical nonconvertible bond? Explain your answers.

4. What opportunities do creditors have to exercise control over a company to which they have loaned money? Where are their control prerogatives described?

5. How are the following characteristics of financial instruments related to concerns about asymmetric information?

   (a) Common stockholders can vote by proxy.

   (b) A bond issue has a sinking fund provision.

   (c) Preferred stockholders can elect representatives to the board of directors if the company fails to pay preferred stock dividends.

   (d) A bond indenture prohibits the company from obtaining debt financing senior to the present issue.

   (e) A restrictive covenant requires the company to maintain an adequate amount of financial slack.

6. Apogee Appliances sells vacuum cleaners for $275 and offers its noncommercial customers a three-year maintenance contract for an additional $75.

   (a) Does this policy expose the company to any adverse selection problems? Explain your answer.

   (b) Explain the relationship between the company's noncommercial use clause and adverse selection problems.

7. Why does concern about adverse selection make it unlikely you will ever see the following advertisement?

   > You have a friend in the banking business. Come in today and Friendly Bank will lend you $1,000 for one year at 15 percent interest—*no questions asked.*

8. Spending on perquisites, such as a company car, may be an agency cost or it may be part of a manager's compensation. How can we tell which description is correct?

9. Two entrepreneurs with similar business proposals requested financing from a venture capitalist. One had invested her life savings of $50,000 in her business. The other entrepreneur also had invested $50,000 in his business: his life savings of $20,000 plus $30,000 he borrowed using his home as collateral. Suppose the venture capitalist will fund only one of the proposals. Who is more likely to get the financing? Explain your answer.

10. Here is a variation of a question that appeared at the end of Chapter 13 (problem 7). Jane and Barry decided it was time to hire an outsider as CEO of their Arizona Egg Nog Company. They began by discussing the position description they would use for recruiting

purposes. Jane wanted a general position description that would give the CEO a great deal of discretion about how to respond to future events. Barry preferred a detailed and specific position description that would spell out exactly what the CEO must do in every conceivable situation.

(a) Which position description is a more complete contract?

(b) What are the benefits to Jane and Barry of each job description?

(c) What type of agency costs will they incur if they use the position description Jane prefers? The position description Barry prefers?

11. Most members of the medical, legal, and accounting professions are employed as agents. How does this fact explain the adoption of standards of professional conduct and codes of ethics by these professions?

12. New and established businesses use private sources of financing such as bank loans, venture capital, and privately placed bonds and common stock.

(a) Explain why new businesses usually have no alternative to using private sources of financing.

(b) Describe the benefits and costs to an established business of using private sources of financing.

(c) Why does the financial market interpret an established business's use of private financing as a positive signal about its future prospects?

13. Kracaw Stores' common stock is traded over-the-counter. The company is about to modernize its department stores and will borrow $10 million using a five-year term loan. A regional bank known for its careful credit analysis and high-quality loan portfolio offered Kracaw the loan in return for five annual payments of $2,571,000. A volume-oriented national bank priced the loan at 8.85 percent.

(a) Which loan has the better interest rate?

(b) Which loan will provide the better signal about Kracaw's future prospects? Why?

(c) What tangible benefit should the company expect from the signal? How should Kracaw choose between these loans?

14. Staged financing is a hallmark of venture capital financing.

(a) Why is venture capital provided in stages?

(b) Describe some other transactions (financing, purchases, etc.) that are conducted in stages. Are there similar explanations for these practices? Explain your answer.

15. Visit the Securities and Exchange Commission's Internet site at http://www.sec.gov/edgarhp.htm and click on EDGAR Form Definitions. Write a short description of each of the following SEC forms.

(a) Prospectus.

(b) Proxy Solicitation Materials.

(c) 1933 Act Registration Statements Form S-1 and Form S-2.

(d) 1934 Act Registration Statements Form 8-K, Form 10-K, and Form 10-Q.

16. Under which arrangement does an investment bank provide a higher level of service? Explain each answer.

(a) A negotiated agreement or a competitive bid?

(b) Traditional or shelf registration?

(c) Best efforts or firm commitment?

17. Companies are free to choose the level of investment banking services they use to issue securities.

    (a) Why are they thought to use the more expensive investment banking services when they don't have to?

    (b) Why was the General Motors Acceptance Corporation able to sell its bonds on the Internet and avoid these costs?

18. Campbell Vision Products Company's common stock is traded over the counter where its value is approximately 58⅞ dollars per share. The FDA is about to announce whether it will approve the company's new enzyme solution for cleaning contact lenses. A favorable ruling will increase the value of the company's stock by 1½ dollars per share. An unfavorable ruling will have no effect. Suppose you buy the stock shortly before the FDA announces its approval and sell it shortly after.

    (a) What is your profit if the dealers' spread is ½ dollar per share? What is your profit if the dealers' spread is 1¾ dollars per share?

    (b) Given your answers to part (a), when should you expect dealers to increase the bid–ask spread?

19. The national secondary markets located in the United States are the NYSE, AMEX, and NASDAQ.

    (a) Why are secondary markets important to companies if they don't actually obtain financing there?

    (b) What factors should a company consider when choosing the secondary market on which to list its stock?

    (c) What factors seem to be important to investors?

20. Listed below are the closing values of three New York Stock Exchange indexes for December 1994 and each month of 1995.

	Dow Jones Industrial Average	NYSE Composite	S&P 500
Dec. 30, 1994	3,834.44	250.94	459.27
Jan. 31, 1995	3,843.86	255.93	470.42
Feb. 28, 1995	4,011.05	264.65	487.39
Mar. 31, 1995	4,157.69	271.04	500.71
Apr. 28, 1995	4,321.27	277.31	514.71
May 31, 1995	4,465.14	286.44	533.40
June 30, 1995	4,556.10	291.84	544.75
July 31, 1995	4,708.47	301.32	562.06
Aug. 31, 1995	4,610.56	302.00	561.88
Sep. 29, 1995	4,789.08	313.26	584.41
Oct. 31, 1995	4,755.48	309.61	581.50
Nov. 30, 1995	5,074.49	323.59	605.37
Dec. 29, 1995	5,117.12	329.51	615.93

    (a) Calculate the percentage change of each index for each month and for the entire year.

    (b) Calculate the correlation between the percentage changes for the Dow Jones Industrial Average and the NYSE Composite Index, for the Dow Jones Industrial Average and the S&P 500 index, and for the NYSE Composite Index and the S&P 500 index.

(c) Which pair of indexes is most closely related? How can you explain this result?

21. A financial market in which prices fully reflect available information is an efficient market.

(a) What information is reflected in prices when a market is weak-form efficient? Semi-strong-form efficient? Strong-form efficient?

(b) How have finance scholars tested the efficient market hypothesis and what is the general nature of their results?

22. Managers should not expect to become rich and famous by making great financing decisions if the financial markets are efficient.

(a) Does this mean managers can be complacent because there are no adverse consequences of making *bad* financing decisions? Explain your answer.

(b) How can managers use financing decisions to increase the owners' wealth according to modern finance theory?

• A D D I T I O N A L   R E A D I N G

For more information about venture capital financing, see:
  Pratt's Guide to Venture Capital Sources, Venture Economics, Inc., Wesley Hills, Massachusetts, 1995.

Two textbooks that describe financial markets and institutions in more detail are:
  Tim S. Campbell and William A. Kracaw, *Financial Institutions and Capital Markets,* HarperCollins College Publishers, New York, 1993.
  Meir Kohn, *Financial Institutions and Markets,* McGraw-Hill, New York, 1994.

Important review articles on the efficient market hypothesis are:
  Eugene F. Fama, "Efficient Capital Markets: A Review of Theory and Empirical Work," *Journal of Finance,* May 1970, pp. 383–417.
  Eugene F. Fama, "Efficient Capital Markets: II," *Journal of Finance,* December 1991, pp. 1575–1617.
  Ray Ball, "The Theory of Stock Market Efficiency: Accomplishments and Limitations," *Journal of Applied Corporate Finance,* Spring 1995, pp. 4–17.

CHAPTER 15

LONG-TERM FINANCIAL POLICY: DIVIDENDS

On October 28, 1994, McDonnell-Douglas Corporation announced three simultaneous changes in the way it would distribute value to its common stockholders. The company raised its cash dividend 71 percent, split each share of stock into three shares, and described its intention to repurchase 15 percent of the nearly 39.5 million shares of stock outstanding. The financial market reacted very favorably to this announcement, increasing the price of a pre-split share of stock by $15.625 on that day. This single day's price change increased the owners' wealth by $617 million (39.5 million shares × $15.625 per share). McDonnell-Douglas's new policy clearly met with the owners' approval.

The income that remains after a company has paid its operating expenses, financing charges (such as interest and lease payments), and taxes belongs to the owners. The board of directors decides how much of this income to distribute to the owners as dividends and how much to keep as internal equity financing or retained earnings. They also decide whether to pay dividends in cash or in another form such as additional shares of stock.

This chapter describes the factors the board must consider when making these decisions. You will see that a company's dividend policy has no effect on its value in a perfect financial market with symmetric information. You also will see that particular market imperfections and specific consequences of asymmetric information favor higher or lower dividends but we don't know their *precise* effects. Consequently, we cannot make categorical statements about what proportion of earnings a company should pay as dividends. About the best we can do is identify the factors important to consider and associate them with the financial policies companies follow in reality.

15.1 HOW COMPANIES DISTRIBUTE VALUE TO THE OWNERS

A company can distribute part of its value to the owners by paying them a cash dividend, repurchasing some of its common stock, or by paying a stock dividend.

Cash Dividends

Cash is the most common form in which dividends are paid. Consequently, this chapter will focus on cash dividends.

Payment Method   The board of directors decides how much and when to pay cash dividends and announces its decision on the dividend **declaration date**. This dividend is usually a *regular* or *ordinary quarterly dividend* but sometimes an *extra* or *special dividend* is added. The board describes these components separately to discourage investors from expecting the larger dividend on a regular basis.

The board of directors' right to determine the amount of dividend payments often is limited by laws and debt contracts. Most states prohibit companies from paying dividends when they are insolvent or in amounts that exceed current or retained earnings, whichever is larger. Bondholders often place additional restrictions on dividend payments in debt covenants.

Dividends are paid to the owners on the **payment date** that is usually between 30 and 60 days after the declaration date. Stock ownership changes every day as investors trade their shares, so a company must choose a **holder of record date**, the date on which a company examines its records to see who is an owner and entitled to receive the dividend. This date usually is about halfway between the declaration and payment dates.

By common agreement, companies are given four business days to update their ownership records. An investor who purchases stock five days prior to the record date will be identified as an owner and receive a dividend while an investor who purchases stock only four days before the record date will not. This cutoff date four days prior to the holder of record date is called the **ex-dividend date** because the stock begins trading without or *ex-dividend* on that day.

The declaration and ex-dividend dates also have economic significance. The declaration date is significant because the financial market first learns of unexpected dividend changes on this date. Consequently, the company's stock price should increase or decrease on or near the declaration date in response to the favorable or unfavorable information investors infer from the dividend surprise. The ex-dividend date is significant because the stock loses that part of its value contributed by the current dividend on this date. Present value effects are negligible for this nearby payment so the stock price should fall by approximately the amount of the dividend on the ex-dividend date.

Exhibit 15.1 is the time line for the McDonnell-Douglas fourth quarter dividend described at the beginning of this chapter. The announcement of the dividend increase, stock split, and share repurchase was a surprise to the financial market because the stock price increased by $15.625 on that day. This was a very large price change that provided a one-day rate of return of nearly 12.5 percent ($141.00/$125.375 − 1). The stock price fell by $0.625 on the ex-dividend date, a decrease approximately equal to the $0.60 cash dividend—as predicted.

Amount   Most companies pay a cash dividend each year even though it isn't mandatory. Table 15.1 summarizes the experience of the 1,608 companies included in the January 1996 edition of Value Line's Value/Screen III data base. Overall, nearly 75 per-

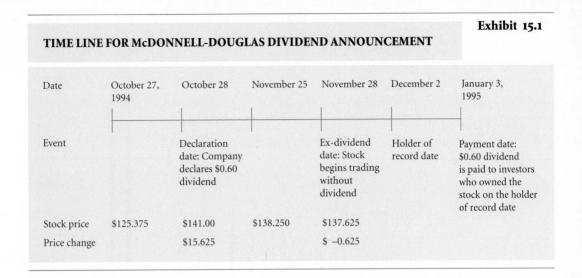

Exhibit 15.1

TIME LINE FOR McDONNELL-DOUGLAS DIVIDEND ANNOUNCEMENT

Date	October 27, 1994	October 28	November 25	November 28	December 2	January 3, 1995
Event		Declaration date: Company declares $0.60 dividend		Ex-dividend date: Stock begins trading without dividend	Holder of record date	Payment date: $0.60 dividend is paid to investors who owned the stock on the holder of record date
Stock price	$125.375	$141.00	$138.250	$137.625		
Price change		$15.625		$ −0.625		

1995 DIVIDEND PAYMENTS BY COMPANIES INCLUDED IN VALUE LINE INVESTMENT SURVEY

Table 15.1

	Total Number of Companies	Percent That Paid a Dividend	Average Dividend Payout Ratio
Entire data base	1,608	74.07%	36.22%
All manufacturing	736	70.79	32.82
Food and kindred products	58	86.21	42.98
Apparel and textiles	28	57.14	35.37
Chemicals and allied products	121	84.30	37.64
Petroleum and coal products	30	96.67	60.98
Industrial machinery	162	49.38	26.53
Electrical equipment	76	59.21	27.01
Retail	129	57.36	32.21

Source: January 1, 1996 edition of Value/Screen III, Value Line Publishing, Inc., copyright 1993.

cent of the companies paid a dividend in 1995, paying out approximately 36 percent of earnings on average.

Exhibit 15.2 shows McDonnell-Douglas's earnings per share and dividend record for the past 15 years. The company's earnings fluctuated widely but dividends were maintained within a comparatively narrow range ($0.15 to $0.47 per share). The company even paid dividends in 1989, 1990, and 1992 when it suffered losses. McDonnell-Douglas's average dividend payout ratio over the entire 15-year period was 28.90 percent.

Most other companies have similar records. They pay a moderate amount of dividends. They keep the dollar amount of dividends stable and allow the payout ratio to

Exhibit 15.2

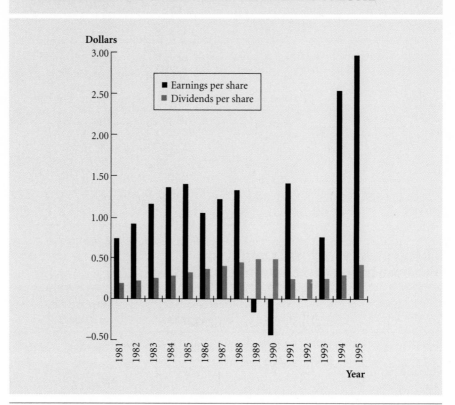

McDONNELL-DOUGLAS'S EARNINGS AND DIVIDENDS RECORD

Source: Value Line Investment Service's October 4, 1996, report on McDonnell Douglas Corporation, Value Line Publishing Company, copyright 1996.

fluctuate as earnings increase and decrease. Companies apparently are reluctant to reduce dividend payments—even in the face of losses—and do not increase these payments until they are confident an increase in earnings is permanent. We will have more to say about these characteristics of dividend policies later.

Share Repurchases

A company also can distribute cash to the owners by offering to repurchase some of its common stock. This policy permits each owner to determine whether he or she receives a current dividend from the company. Stockholders who want a dividend sell some of their shares back to the company; those who don't want a dividend simply keep their shares. The owners who keep their shares of stock, in effect, permit the company to reinvest the cash for them.

Share repurchases have become popular in recent years. McDonnell-Douglas's share repurchase program was described at the beginning of this chapter and Table 15.2 describes some other share repurchase programs initiated by prominent companies.

| | | Announced Buyback | Recent Share |
| **RECENT SHARE REPURCHASES BY PROMINENT COMPANIES** | | | **Table 15.2** |

RECENT SHARE REPURCHASES BY PROMINENT COMPANIES

Company	Amount of Intended Buyback, (billions)	Announced Buyback as Percent of Total Shares Outstanding	Recent Share Price Increase from Date Announced
Phillip Morris	$7.3	14%	$ 74.88 (27%)
General Electric	5.0	6	59.00 (20%)
Walt Disney	3.8	17	58.00 (37%)
Citicorp	3.0	13	65.63 (15%)
IBM	5.0	10	109.63 (53%)
Merck	2.0	4	50.25 (36%)
American Express	1.9	12	38.88 (26%)
BankAmerica	1.9	11	54.63 (19%)

Source: Richard D. Hylton, "Stock Buybacks Are Hot—Here's How to Cash In," *Fortune,* September 4, 1995, pp. 133–134. © 1995 Time, Inc. All rights reserved.

Each announcement was followed by stock price increases. Furthermore, these stock price reactions are typical. Ikenberry, Lakonishok, and Vermaelen studied 1,239 repurchases announced between 1980 and 1990 and found that the price of the average stock increased by 3.5 percent on the day of the announcement.[1]

Boards of directors apparently consider share repurchases equivalent to special dividends because they do not use them as substitutes for regular cash dividends. McDonnell-Douglas announced its share repurchase *and* its increase in its regular dividend on the same day. Since making their initial announcements, the companies listed in Table 15.2 have increased their regular cash dividends per share approximately 20 percent on average.

Stock Dividends and Stock Splits

Companies also pay *in kind* dividends as **stock dividends** or as **stock splits**. Each owner receives one new share of stock for every 10 shares they own when a company declares a 10 percent stock dividend. This transaction could just as easily be called an 11-for-10 stock split but by convention, small distributions (less than approximately a 20 percent dividend or greater than a 6-for-5 split) are called stock dividends while large distributions are called stock splits.[2]

Stock dividends and splits are administered in much the same way as cash dividends. The split is announced on a declaration date, the identity of the owners entitled to receive the new shares is established on the holder of record date that has an associated ex-split date, and the company's shares begin to trade in the new form on the payment date. The financial market's reaction to news of the split should take place on the declaration date

---

[1]David Ikenberry, Josef Lakonishok, and Theo Vermaelen, "Market Underreaction to Open Market Share Repurchases," *Journal of Financial Economics,* October–November 1995, pp. 181–208.

[2]Companies must account for stock dividends and stock splits differently on the balance sheet but the distinction is unimportant from a financial point of view.

Exhibit 15.3

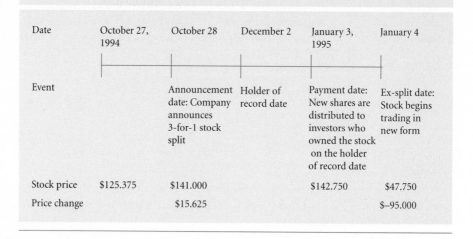

TIME LINE FOR McDONNELL-DOUGLAS STOCK SPLIT ANNOUNCEMENT

Date	October 27, 1994	October 28	December 2	January 3, 1995	January 4
Event		Announcement date: Company announces 3-for-1 stock split	Holder of record date	Payment date: New shares are distributed to investors who owned the stock on the holder of record date	Ex-split date: Stock begins trading in new form
Stock price	$125.375	$141.000		$142.750	$47.750
Price change		$15.625			$–95.000

Table 15.3   **HOW OWNERS MAKE ALTERNATIVE FORMS OF DIVIDENDS EQUIVALENT**

Owner's Preference	If Company Pays a Cash Dividend	If Company Repurchases Shares	If Company Pays a Stock Dividend
Cash dividend	Owner accepts dividend	Owner sells some of original shares to company	Owner sells new shares to other investors
Reinvestment	Owner uses cash to buy more shares	Owner keeps original shares	Owner keeps new shares

and the stock price should adjust to a level appropriate for its new form on the ex-split date.

Exhibit 15.3 is the time line for the McDonnell-Douglas 3-for-1 stock split described at the beginning of this chapter. The $15.625 price increase on October 28 was the market's reaction to all three changes announced that day. The closing stock price on January 4, 1995, the ex-split date, was 33.45 percent of the previous day's closing stock price, very nearly 1/3, as predicted.

In a perfect financial market, share repurchases and stock dividends are equivalent to cash dividends because owners can buy or sell shares of stock to convert one form to another.[3] Table 15.3 describes the possibilities. Because these forms are equivalent, we will focus on cash dividends in the remainder of this chapter and discuss share repurchases and stock dividends and splits only as needed.

---

[3]Remember from earlier chapters that a perfect financial market has no transaction costs or taxes, information is instantaneously and freely available to everyone, securities are infinitely divisible, and the market is competitive, *i.e.,* individual traders cannot affect market prices.

15.2   WHEN DIVIDEND POLICY IS IRRELEVANT

A company's dividend-earnings retention policy does not affect the owners' wealth and therefore is irrelevant in a perfect financial market because investors can accept the company's decision or costlessly reverse its effect on their portfolios by selling or buying shares in the financial market. An investor who does not receive a dividend but prefers one can sell shares of stock to make his own. Conversely, an investor who receives a dividend she does not want can buy shares of stock to reinvest it. *Homemade* dividends and reinvestment are perfect substitutes for dividends and reinvestment undertaken by the company, so the particular policy a company adopts provides no extra value.

Miller and Modigliani proved that dividend policy is irrelevant in an article that is in many ways a companion piece to their famous articles on capital structure.[4] We will use a numerical example to illustrate their conclusions, distinguishing between companies with and without positive net present value investment opportunities.

Irrelevance When There Are No Positive NPV Projects

A company with cash but no positive net present value investment opportunities can hold financial slack or distribute the cash to its stockholders as dividends. Financial slack is a zero-NPV project in a perfect financial market and stockholders have access to the slack whether the company distributes it or not. Consequently, the decision to retain or distribute the cash does not affect the company or the value of its common stock. This result is illustrated by the following example.

Franko International is a Chicago sausage maker with cash flows provided by operations of $100,000 now and $336,000 in one year. The company cannot reinvest the $100,000 in the sausage business because the decline of neighborhood grocery stores has limited the market for their highly specialized products. The company is 100 percent equity financed with 20,000 shares of stock outstanding and the required rate of return for the sausage business is 12 percent. The market value of Franko's assets is therefore the $100,000 cash plus the present value of the cash flows from selling sausages, which is $336,000 discounted at 12 percent.

$$\text{Market value of Franko's assets} = \text{Value of cash} + \text{Value of sausage business}$$
$$= \$100,000 \quad + \quad \frac{\$336,000}{(1.12)}$$
$$= \$100,000 \quad + \quad \$300,000 \quad = \$400,000$$

The market value of claims equals the market value of assets, so the value of a single share of stock is $20 ($400,000/20,000 shares).

Panel A of Table 15.4 gives Franko's free cash flow and financial cash flow statements if they hold the $100,000 cash as financial slack invested in U.S. Treasury securities that earn 10 percent per year. This investment causes them to have zero free cash flow at time 0 but provides additional free cash flow in year 1 when the treasury securities mature and pay principal and interest of $110,000.

---

[4]Merton H. Miller and Franco Modigliani, "Dividend Policy, Growth and the Valuation of Shares," *Journal of Business*, October 1961, pp. 411–433.

Table 15.4   FRANKO'S CASH FLOWS AND BALANCE SHEET

Perfect Financial Market
Has No Positive NPV Investments
Does Not Pay a Current Dividend

Panel A: Cash Flow Statements

	Time 0	Time 1
Free Cash Flow		
Cash flow provided by (used for) operations	$ 100,000	$ 336,000
Cash flow provided by (used for) investment	0	0
Cash flow provided by (used for) financial slack	(100,000)	110,000
Net free cash flow	$ 0	$ 446,000
Financial Cash Flow		
Common stock dividend	$ 0	$(446,000)

Panel B: Market-Value Balance Sheet

Assets		Claims	
Financial slack	$100,000	Debt	$ 0
Fixed assets	300,000	Equity	400,000
Total	$400,000	Total	$400,000

EXERCISE

15.1   DIVIDEND POLICY'S EFFECT ON CASH FLOWS

Mason Electronics Company's cash flows provided by operations are $50,000 at the end of 1998 and $172,500 at the end of 1999. The company will undertake no new investments and the board of directors is considering whether to retain the $50,000 as financial slack or distribute it as cash dividends. Money retained as financial slack is invested in U.S. Treasury securities that earn 6 percent interest. All of 1999's free cash flows will be paid as dividends. Determine the company's net free cash flows and financial cash flows under each alternative.

Company retains financial slack:

	1998	1999
Free Cash Flow		
Cash flow provided by (used for) operations	$ 50,000	$ 172,500
Cash flow provided by (used for) investments	0	0
Cash flow provided by (used for) financial slack	(50,000)	53,000
Net free cash flow	$ 0	$ 225,500

Financial Cash Flow

Common stock dividend	$ 0	$(225,500)

Company Pays a Current Dividend:

	1998	1999
Free Cash Flow		
Cash flow provided by (used for) operations	$ 50,000	$ 172,500
Cash flow provided by (used for) investments	0	0
Cash flow provided by (used for) financial slack	0	0
Net free cash flow	$ 50,000	$ 172,500
Financial Cash Flow		
Common stock dividend	$(50,000)	$(172,500)

The company can pay common stock dividends of $0 and $225,500 or $50,000 and $172,500 in 1998 and 1999 under the two alternatives.

• ———— •

Financial slack is a zero-NPV project in a perfect financial market. Furthermore, retaining cash as financial slack under these circumstances does not change the value of the cash flows provided by operations, so we should expect the value of the sausage business to remain at $300,000. Therefore, Franko's market value should still be $400,000. That is,

Market value of Franko's assets = Value of financial slack + Value of sausage business

$$= \$110,000/1.1 + \$336,000/1.12 = \$400,000.$$

These values are entered on Franko's market-value balance sheet in panel B of Table 15.4. The market value of the Treasury securities equals their cost because their net present value is zero.

We can verify that the market value of the equity equals the market value of the assets by discounting the dividends paid to the common stockholders using the company's required rate of return on equity. This required return is a weighted average of the required returns on the company's assets using the market value of these assets as the weights. That is,

$$r_e = 0.10 \times \frac{\$100,000}{\$400,000} + 0.12 \times \frac{\$300,000}{\$400,000} = 0.115$$

$$\text{Market value of Franko's equity} = \$0 + \frac{\$446,000}{(1.115)} = \$400,000.$$

The value of a single share of stock is still $20.

Table 15.5 shows what happens if the company does not retain the $100,000 cash flow provided by operations as financial slack. Free cash flow at time 0 is $100,000, which is paid to stockholders as a current dividend. The company has no cash *after* paying this dividend, so the market value of its assets simply is the discounted present value of the

Table 15.5   **FRANKO'S CASH FLOWS AND BALANCE SHEET**

Perfect Financial Market
Has No Positive NPV Investments
Pays a Current Dividend

Panel A: Cash Flow Statements

	Time 0	Time 1
Free Cash Flow		
Cash flow provided by (used for) operations	$ 100,000	$ 336,000
Cash flow provided by (used for) investment	0	0
Cash flow provided by (used for) financial slack	0	0
Net free cash flow	$ 100,000	$ 336,000
Financial Cash Flow		
Common stock dividend	$(100,000)	$(336,000)

Panel B: Market-Value Balance Sheet

Assets		Claims	
Financial slack	$ 0	Debt	$ 0
Fixed assets	300,000	Equity	300,000
Total	$300,000	Total	$300,000

cash flows provided by the sausage business ($300,000). This also equals the market value of the common stock because the stockholders receive the $336,000 at time 1. The price of a single share of stock is $15 ($300,000/20,000 shares). Adding the five-dollar cash dividend ($100,000/20,000 shares) accounts for the total value of $20 per share.

EXERCISE

15.2   **DIVIDEND POLICY'S EFFECT ON THE TOTAL VALUE OF AN OWNER'S SHARE**

Mason Electronics Company's market-value balance sheets under each alternative described in Exercise 15.1 are given below. The required rate of return for the electronics business is 15 percent and the company has 100,000 shares of stock outstanding. Discount the dividends per share at the appropriate required rate of return and add the current dividend to determine the total value of an owner's share under each alternative.

The market-value balance sheet if the company retains financial slack is

Assets		Claims	
Financial slack	$ 50,000	Debt	$ 0
Fixed assets	150,000	Equity	200,000
Total	$200,000	Total	$200,000

The market-value balance sheet if the company pays a current dividend is

Assets		Claims	
Financial slack	$ 0	Debt	$ 0
Fixed assets	$150,000	Equity	150,000
Total	$150,000	Total	$150,000

Dividends per share are the amounts computed in Exercise 15.1 divided by 100,000 shares outstanding. The discount rate is a weighted average of the rate of return on U.S. Treasury securities (6 percent) and the required rate of return for the electronics business (15 percent). The weights are obtained from the company's market-value balance sheet.

If Mason retains financial slack, dividends per share in 1998 and 1999 are $0 ($0/100,000) and $2.255 ($225,500/100,000). The required rate of return is

$$r_e = \frac{\$50,000}{\$200,000} \times 0.06 + \frac{\$150,000}{\$200,000} \times 0.15 = 0.1275.$$

Therefore, the total value of an owner's share is

Value of stock	$2.255/1.1275 =	$2.00
Current cash dividend		0
Total value		$2.00

If Mason pays a current dividend, dividends per share in 1998 and 1999 are $0.50 ($50,000/100,000) and $1.725 ($172,500/100,000). The required rate of return, r_e, is

$$r_e = \frac{\$0}{\$150,000} \times 0.06 + \frac{\$150,000}{\$150,000} \times 0.15 = 0.15.$$

Therefore, the total value of an owner's share, including the value of the current dividend, is

Value of stock	$1.725/1.15 =	$1.50
Current cash dividend		0.50
Total value		$2.00

The company's choice of dividend policy does not affect the total value of an owner's share of the company.

● ——————— ●

These examples confirm that a company's decision to retain cash as financial slack or pay a dividend does not affect the value of a share of stock. We must examine the position of a representative stockholder, however, to see if he or she is similarly unaffected.

Kevin Merton is a typical stockholder who owns 240 shares of Franko's common stock that was worth $4,800 ($20 × 240 shares) prior to the company's decision to retain or distribute the $100,000 cash flow provided by operations. Panel A of Table 15.6

describes Kevin's personal portfolio if Franko decides to hold the $100,000 as financial slack. If Kevin accepts the company's decision, 100 percent of his portfolio is allocated to common stock. If he reverses the effect of the company's decision by selling 60 shares of stock to make his own cash dividend of $1,200 (60 shares × $20 per share), 25 percent of his portfolio is allocated to cash and 75 percent is allocated to stock. Importantly, in either case, the total value of his portfolio is $4,800.

Panel B of Table 15.6 describes Kevin's personal portfolio if Franko decides to distribute the $100,000 as dividends. The value of the stock falls to $15 per share, so Kevin's portfolio is 75 percent stock and 25 percent cash if he accepts the company's decision. Alternatively, he can reinvest the dividend by using the $1,200 to buy 80 shares of stock ($1,200/$15 per share) to allocate 100 percent of his wealth to stock. Again, in either case, the value of his portfolio is $4,800.

Table 15.6   VALUE OF KEVIN MERTON'S PERSONAL PORTFOLIO

Perfect Financial Market

Panel A: Franko Holds Financial Slack

		Kevin Accepts Decision		Kevin Sells 60 Shares of Stock for $1,200 Homemade Dividend
Cash			$ 0	$1,200
Stock				
Original number of shares	240		240	
Number sold	0		60	
Total number of shares	240		180	
Price per share	$20		$20	
Value		4,800		3,600
Total		$4,800		$4,800

Panel B: Franko Pays Dividend

		Kevin Accepts Decision		Kevin Buys 80 Shares of Stock to Reinvest $1,200
Cash			$1,200	$ 0
Stock				
Original number of shares	240		240	
Number bought	0		80	
Total number of shares	240		320	
Price per share	$15		$15	
Value		3,600		4,800
Total		$4,800		$4,800

DIVIDEND POLICY'S EFFECT ON AN INDIVIDUAL OWNER

Alex Lightner owns 1,200 shares of Mason Electronics Company's common stock. Use Table 15.6 as a model to show that Alex's personal portfolio is unaffected by the company's choice of dividend policy.

VALUE OF ALEX LIGHTNER'S PERSONAL PORTFOLIO

Perfect Financial Market

Panel A: Mason Retains Financial Slack

	Alex Accepts Decision		Alex Sells 300 Shares of Stock for $600 Homemade Dividend	
Cash		$ 0		$ 600
Stock				
Original number of shares	1,200		1,200	
Number sold	0		300	
Total number of shares	1,200		900	
Price per share	$2.00		$2.00	
Value		2,400		1,800
Total		$2,400		$2,400

Panel B: Mason Pays Dividend

	Alex Accepts Decision		Alex Buys 400 Shares of Stock to Reinvest $600	
Cash		$ 600		$ 0
Stock				
Original number of shares	1,200		1,200	
Number bought	0		400	
Total number of shares	1,200		1,600	
Price per share	$1.50		$1.50	
Value		1,800		2,400
Total		$2,400		$2,400

Alex has $2,400 in cash or stock—no matter what Mason Electronics Company does and no matter what his preference.

Our representative investor was able to obtain a portfolio with any combination of stocks and cash that he preferred. Consequently, the company's decision about which combination to offer through dividend policy is inconsequential. Of course, this conclusion depended on our assumption that stockholders incur no costs to create homemade dividends or reinvestment. Financial market imperfections introduce costs that can change these conclusions. We will consider these costs shortly.

Irrelevance When There Are Positive NPV Projects

You may be surprised to learn that a company's dividend-earnings retention policy is irrelevant in a perfect market even if the company has positive net present value investment opportunities. Companies that do not pay dividends are not affected by this change at all; companies that do pay dividends must simply obtain new financing to replace the cash flows they distribute to the owners. Companies can replace these cash flows at no cost in a perfect financial market, so the decision to reinvest cash flows or pay dividends does not affect the owners' wealth.

Let's continue our example with Franko International. Suppose the company has developed a new beef jerky snack product to sell in Chicago's numerous sports bars. This project requires an investment of $100,000 and will provide operating cash flows of $224,000 next year. At the required rate of return for meat processing of 12 percent, the proposal's net present value is $100,000 ($–100,000 + $224,000/1.12), so Franko should undertake this investment.

Table 15.7 gives Franko's cash flow statements and market-value balance sheet if the company retains the $100,000 cash flow provided by operations to finance this investment project. The project reduces the company's free cash flow at time 0 to $0 and increases its free cash flow at time 1 to $560,000. This beef jerky project has the same required rate of return as the sausage business, so the market value of Franko's assets is

$$\text{Market value of Franko's assets} = \$0 + \frac{\$560,000}{(1.12)} = \$500,000.$$

The company's new market value equals the value of the sausage business, $300,000, plus the value of the beef jerky project, $200,000. The market value of claims equals the market value of assets, therefore the value of a single share of stock is $25 ($500,000/20,000 shares). The value of each share of stock increased by $5—the project's net present value per share ($100,000/20,000 shares).

Just as before, stockholders can accept the company's decision to reinvest the cash flow provided by operations or reverse its effect by selling some stock to create a homemade dividend. The difference is that every stockholder is better off by $5 per share, whatever his or her choice. Kevin Merton has $6,000 (240 shares × $25 per share) rather than $4,800 to allocate between cash and stock, for example.

EXERCISE

15.4   **FINANCIAL CASH FLOWS WITH REINVESTMENT AND NO DIVIDENDS**

Mason Electronics Company can buy a one-year license to produce collision avoidance alarms for people who use in-line skates in public places. The license costs $50,000, payable at the end of 1998, and the product will provide an operating cash flow of $69,000 at the end of 1999. The project's NPV at 15 percent interest is $10,000 ($69,000/1.15 – $50,000), so Mason accepts it.

Determine Mason's net free cash flows and financial cash flows assuming the company uses the $50,000 available in 1998 to purchase the investment project.

	1998	1999
Free Cash Flow		
Cash flow provided by (used for) operations		
From original assets	$ 50,000	$ 172,500
From new investment	0	69,000
Net cash flow	50,000	241,500
Cash flow provided by (used for) investments	(50,000)	0
Cash flow provided by (used for) financial slack	0	0
Net free cash flow	$ 0	$ 241,500
Financial Cash Flow		
Common stock dividend	$ 0	$(241,500)

The company can pay dividends of $0 and $241,500 in 1998 and 1999.

● ——————— ●

FRANKO'S CASH FLOWS AND BALANCE SHEET   **Table 15.7**

Perfect Financial Market
Has Positive NPV Investments
Does Not Pay a Current Dividend

Panel A: Cash Flow Statements

	Time 0	Time 1
Free Cash Flow		
Cash flow provided by (used for) operations		
From original assets	$ 100,000	$ 336,000
From new investment	0	224,000
Net cash flow	100,000	560,000
Cash flow provided by (used for) investment	(100,000)	0
Cash flow provided by (used for) financial slack	0	0
Net free cash flow	$ 0	$ 560,000
Financial Cash Flow		
Common stock dividend	$ 0	$(560,000)

Panel B: Market-Value Balance Sheet

Assets		Claims	
Financial slack	$ 0	Debt	$ 0
Fixed assets	500,000	Equity	500,000
Total	$500,000	Total	$500,000

Table 15.8 describes Franko's situation if it pays the $100,000 cash flow provided by operations as a dividend to the original stockholders and issues new common stock to finance the project. Free cash flow is $0 at time 0 and $560,000 at time 1, the same as if they financed the investment internally. Consequently, the market value of the company's assets and claims is the same, $500,000 ($560,000/1.12).

Net financial cash flow also is the same with internal or external financing, however, now it is divided between the original and new stockholders. There are 20,000 shares of old stock outstanding and the number of new shares (N) Franko must issue equals the amount of money required divided by the price per share (P). That is,

$$N = \$100,000/P.$$

Table 15.8   FRANKO'S CASH FLOWS AND BALANCE SHEET

Perfect Financial Market
Has Positive NPV Investments
Pays a Current Dividend

Panel A: Cash Flow Statements

	Time 0	Time 1
Free Cash Flow		
Cash flow provided by (used for) operations		
From original assets	$ 100,000	$ 336,000
From new investment	0	224,000
Net cash flow	100,000	560,000
Cash flow provided by (used for) investment	(100,000)	0
Cash flow provided by (used for) financial slack	0	0
Net free cash flow	$ 0	$ 560,000
Financial Cash Flow		
Pay dividend to original stockholders	$(100,000)	$(448,000)
Issue new common stock (5,000 shares)	100,000	
Pay dividend to new stockholders	0	(112,000)
Net financial cash flow	$ 0	$(560,000)

Panel B: Market-Value Balance Sheet

Assets		Claims	
Financial slack	$ 0	Debt	$ 0
Fixed assets	500,000	Equity	500,000
Total	$500,000	Total	$500,000

The price of the original and new shares must be the same because they have identical claims on the $560,000 free cash flow at time 1. Therefore, the price per share must equal the market value of the company's equity divided by the total number of shares of stock outstanding. In symbols,

$$P = \frac{\$500,000}{20,000 + N} \; .$$

Solving these two equations for N, we find that Franko must issue 5,000 shares of stock to finance the project externally. There are 20,000 shares of old stock outstanding, so 80 percent or $448,000 of the $560,000 free cash flow at time 1 is paid to the original stockholders while the remaining 20 percent is paid to the new ones. Discounting these dividends at the required rate of return on equity of 12 percent or substituting $N = 5,000$ into either equation given above reveals that the market value of each share of stock is $20.

● ————————————————————————————————— ● EXERCISE

FINANCIAL CASH FLOWS WITH INVESTMENT AND DIVIDENDS

15.5

Rework Exercise 15.4 assuming Mason Electronics Company pays $50,000 of dividends to the original owners and issues new common stock to finance the investment project.

Mason must issue enough shares to obtain the $50,000 needed to purchase the license,

$$N = \$50,000/P.$$

The new and original shares have equal claims on the company's future free cash flows, so the price per share is the present value of the $241,500 divided by the number of shares outstanding,

$$P = \frac{\$241,500/1.15}{100,000 + N} \; .$$

Solving these equations simultaneously, the company must issue 31,250 shares at a price of $1.60 each. The market values of the original and new equity therefore are

Original equity: $1.60 × 100,000 shares = $160,000

New equity: $1.60 × 31,250 shares = $ 50,000.

The original owners therefore receive 76.19 percent ($160,000/$210,000) of the dividends in 1999 while the new owners receive the remainder, 23.81 percent ($50,000/$210,000).

	1998	1999
Free Cash Flow		
Cash flow provided by (used for) operations		
From original assets	$ 50,000	$ 172,500
From new investment	0	69,000
Net cash flow	50,000	241,500
Cash flow provided by (used for) investments	(50,000)	0
Cash flow provided by (used for) financial slack	0	0
Net free cash flow	$ 0	$ 241,500
Financial Cash Flow		
Pay dividend to original stockholders	$(50,000)	$(184,000)
Issue new common stock (31,250 shares)	50,000	0
Pay dividend to new stockholders	0	(57,500)
Net financial cash flow	$ 0	$(241,500)

Mason's net financial cash flow is the same but now it is divided between the original and new stockholders.

● ——————— ●

A little thought will convince you this is the correct price for Franko's common stock. The original stockholders owned the sausage business and the opportunity to invest in the beef jerky project, which had combined market values of $25 per share. These stockholders extracted $5 from the business as a cash dividend, leaving them with stock valued at $20 per share. The new stockholders pay $20 to buy a share of stock and receive a dividend of $22.40 ($112,000/5,000 new shares) at time 1. This provides a 12 percent rate of return that equals the required rate of return on equity.

An original stockholder who wanted the cash dividend is happy and one who didn't can simply buy some of the new shares of stock for homemade reinvestment. The company's dividend-earnings retention policy still is irrelevant even when a company has positive net present value investment opportunities. This is because the company and its investors can use the perfect financial market to costlessly rearrange the timing of cash flows. The company's value is determined by its free cash flows—and nothing else.

EXERCISE ● —————————————————————————————————— ●

15.6   DIVIDEND POLICY'S EFFECT ON THE TOTAL VALUE OF AN OWNER'S SHARE WITH INVESTMENT

Rework Exercise 15.2 assuming Mason Electronic Company invests in the collision alarm project. The company's market-value balance sheets with and without a current dividend are given below.

The market-value balance sheet if the company invests in the new project and does not pay a current dividend is

Assets		Claims	
Financial slack	$ 0	Debt	$ 0
Fixed assets	210,000	Equity	210,000
Total	$210,000	Total	$210,000

The market-value balance sheet if the company invests in the new project and pays a current dividend is

Assets		Claims	
Financial slack	$ 0	Debt	$ 0
Fixed assets	210,000	Original equity	160,000
		New equity	50,000
Total	$210,000	Total	$210,000

If Mason does not pay a current dividend, dividends per share in 1998 and 1999 are $0 ($0/100,000) and $2.415 ($241,500/100,000). The discount rate is the required rate of return for the electronics business, 15 percent. Therefore, the total value of a share of stock is

$$\text{Value of stock } \$2.415/1.15 = \$2.10$$

Current cash dividend	0
Total value	$2.10

If Mason pays a current dividend, dividends per share in 1998 and 1999 are $0.50 ($50,000/100,000) and $1.84 ($241,500/131,250). The required rate of return is 15 percent. Therefore, the total value of a share of stock, including the value of the current dividend, is

$$\text{Value of stock } \$1.84/1.15 = \$1.60$$

Current cash dividend	0.50
Total value	$2.10

The company's choice of dividend policy will not affect the total value of a share of stock owned by an original stockholder.

● ———————— ●

15.3   THE EFFECT OF FINANCIAL MARKET IMPERFECTIONS

Financial market imperfections may change our conclusion that a company's dividend-earnings retention policy has no effect on the company or its investors. Taxes and transaction costs to buy and sell shares reduce the net cash flows paid to investors, which can alter the attractiveness of alternative policies. Once again, we will consider separately a company with and without positive net present value investment opportunities.

Table 15.9   VALUE OF KEVIN MERTON'S PERSONAL PORTFOLIO

Personal Taxes and Transaction Costs

Panel A: Franko Holds Financial Slack

	Kevin Accepts Decision	Kevin Sells 60 Shares of Stock for $1,200 Homemade Dividend
Initial value	$4,800.00	$4,800.00
Brokerage fee to sell 60 shares (1%)	0	12.00
Capital gains tax on proceeds (28%)	0	97.44
Ending value	$4,800.00	$4,690.56

Panel B: Franko Pays Dividend

	Kevin Accepts Decision	Kevin Buys 50.69 Shares of Stock to Reinvest $1,200
Initial value	$4,800.00	$4,800.00
Ordinary tax on dividend (36%)	432.00	432.00
Brokerage fee to buy 50.69 shares (1%)	0	7.60
Ending value	$4,368.00	$4,360.40

The Effect on a Company without Positive NPV Projects

A company with cash flows provided by operations but no positive NPV projects is unaffected by taxes and transaction costs because it doesn't replace the cash paid to stockholders with new financing.[5] The stockholders are affected, however, because they must pay taxes on the dividends they receive or create with financial market transactions and must pay brokerage fees to buy or sell their common stock. Table 15.9 illustrates these effects by recalculating the value of Kevin Merton's personal portfolio when he is subject to these costs.

Panel A of Table 15.9 gives the value of Kevin's personal portfolio if Franko International does not pay a dividend. Kevin's portfolio is worth $4,800 if he accepts the company's decision and does nothing; however, he loses value due to brokerage fees and taxes if he sells shares to create a homemade dividend. His taxable gain is the difference between the selling price and the price he paid for the shares, say $14, minus the 1 percent brokerage fee. At a capital gains tax rate of 28 percent, brokerage fees and taxes reduce the value of Kevin's portfolio to $4,690.56.

[5]This statement isn't strictly true because the company must pay a brokerage fee to buy or sell the securities held as financial slack. The size of these transactions makes these fees insignificant for most companies, however.

Panel B of Table 15.9 gives the value of Kevin's portfolio if the company pays a cash dividend. Taxes on this dividend, computed at the ordinary rate of 36 percent, are $432. The value of his portfolio if he does nothing is $4,368 ($4,800 – $432). Alternatively, he can reinvest his after-tax cash flow, $768 ($1,200 – $432), which will buy 50.69 shares of stock ($768/$15 × 1.01). The brokerage fee is therefore $15 × 50.69 shares × 0.01, or $7.60. The value of his portfolio after reinvesting his dividend is therefore $4,360.40 ($4,800 – $432.00 – $7.60).

Table 15.9 shows that Kevin Merton is better off if Franko does not pay a dividend (holds financial slack), no matter what his preference. This policy gives him a portfolio worth $4,800 if he does not want a dividend in comparison to $4,360.40 if he must reinvest the company's dividends himself. Conversely, this policy allows him to create his own dividend if that's what he wants, and end up with a portfolio worth $4,690.56 rather than $4,368 if the company distributed the cash flow. Given the tax and transaction costs in this example, Franko's dividend-earnings retention policy is no longer irrelevant. Every shareholder would prefer the company pay no dividends to maximize the value of their portfolios.

Investors who want a dividend would feel differently if the ordinary income tax rate was lower, the capital gains tax rate was higher, or brokerage costs were higher. These changes would increase the costs of creating a homemade dividend and reduce the cost of one provided by the company. There is some evidence that investors in lower tax brackets are attracted to or become the "dividend clientele" of companies that pay high dividends for just these reasons.[6] Corporate investors have a lower effective ordinary tax rate on dividends because they can exclude up to 70 percent of the dividends they receive from taxable income. Corporations therefore have a strong preference for receiving dividend income from the common and preferred stock that they hold.

Finally, many companies offer programs that permit owners to use their cash dividends to purchase additional shares of common stock. The stock usually is offered at a price slightly below the market price, which partially compensates stockholders for the tax they pay on ordinary income, and there are no brokerage costs. These dividend reinvestment plans (DRIPs) therefore partially overcome an investor's preference for corporate rather than homemade reinvestment (see "In the News").

You can learn more about DRIPs by visiting the Dividend ReInvestment Plan Guide on the Internet at http://www.cs.cmu.edu/~jdg/drip.html. This site describes DRIPs, explains how they are administered, and has a list of companies offering DRIPs.

The Effect on a Company with Positive NPV Projects

A company's stockholders with positive net present value investment alternatives are subject to all the adverse effects described above if the company pays dividends. In addition, the company must pay transaction costs to obtain the new financing that replaces the cash they distributed to the owners. These floatation costs encourage companies to retain internally generated cash flows to finance new investment opportunities.

---

[6]See Wibur G. Lewellen, Kenneth L. Stanley, Ronald C. Lease, and Gary G. Schlarbaum, "Some Direct Evidence on the Dividend Clientele Phenomenon," *Journal of Finance*, December 1978, pp. 1385–1399.

We have seen that realistic values for tax rates, brokerage costs, and floatation costs suggest that companies should retain cash whether or not they have positive net present value investment opportunities. This policy permits the company to finance its investments at lower cost and permits stockholders to obtain either current income or

EXERCISE ● ———————————————————————————————————— ●

15.7   DIVIDEND POLICY'S EFFECT WITH FINANCIAL MARKET IMPERFECTIONS

Rework Exercise 15.3 assuming Alex Lightner's ordinary tax rate is 36 percent, the capital gains tax rate is 28 percent, and brokerage fees are 1 percent. Assume Alex purchased the shares of stock for $1.80. Use Table 15.9 as an example.

Alex must sell 300 shares of stock ($600/$2.00 per share) to create $600 of homemade dividends if Mason doesn't pay any. Conversely, if Mason pays a $600 dividend, Alex has $384 to reinvest in the company after paying taxes ($600 $\times$ [1 − 0.36]). This $384 will purchase 253.47 shares with brokerage costs of 1 percent ($384/$1.50 $\times$ 1.01). The values of Alex's portfolio after executing these transactions are given below.

VALUE OF ALEX LIGHTNER'S PERSONAL PORTFOLIO

Personal Taxes and Transaction Costs

Panel A: Mason Retains Financial Slack

	Alex Accepts Decision	Alex Sells 300 Shares of Stock for $600 Homemade Dividend
Initial value	$2,400.00	$2,400.00
Brokerage fee to sell 300 shares (1%)	0	6.00
Capital gains tax on proceeds (28%)	0	15.12
Ending value	$2,400.00	$2,378.88

Panel B: Mason Pays Dividend

	Alex Accepts Decision	Alex Buys 253.47 Shares of Stock to Reinvest $600
Initial value	$2,400.00	$2,400.00
Ordinary tax on dividend (36%)	216.00	216.00
Brokerage fee to buy 253.47 shares (1%)	0	3.80
Ending value	$2,184.00	$2,180.20

With these tax rates and transaction costs, Alex is better off if the company does not pay a current dividend.

● ——————————— ●

I N   T H E   N E W S

INVESTING, DRIP BY DRIP

WOULD YOU BUY stock from a drip? Millions of people do, and most of them seem quite happy about it.

The drips in question are *dividend reinvestment plans;* programs that hundreds of large corporations offer to their shareholders. In a classic DRIP, an investor buys one or more shares in a company with a DRIP and signs up for the plan. Thereafter, instead of sending the investor a check when dividends are distributed each quarter, the firm uses the money to buy shares in the investor's name. Generally, the investor gets fractional shares if his or her dividend is less than the share price or if the amounts don't come out even.

It's pretty inexpensive. There are sometimes modest fees for the service but many companies absorb them. In any case, there is no broker's fee. Most DRIPs allow investors to add to their purchases by sending in additional cash, and some even discount the share price for DRIP purchases.

Many of the nation's biggest corporations, including Mobil Corp., offer DRIPs. Mobil's plan "is quite popular" with the company's investors, said Hank Thomassen, Mobil assistant secretary. As of last fall, 55,000 of Mobil's approximately 190,000 shareholdes were enrolled.

Source: Albert B. Crenshaw, "For Shareholders, a 'Drip' Can Generate Quite a Pool," *The Washington Post*, January 28, 1996, p. H1. © 1996 The Washington Post. Reprinted with permission.

reinvestment at lower cost than if the company paid dividends. Consequently, we must look beyond the effect of financial market imperfections to explain the widespread practice of paying regular dividends.

15.4   THE EFFECT OF ASYMMETRIC INFORMATION

Asymmetric information between the managers and either original or new stockholders also can change our conclusion that a company's dividend-earnings retention policy is irrelevant. The problem is that managers know more about the value of the company's assets and their own ability, honesty, and willingness to work than the stockholders do. If the stockholders draw inferences about these characteristics from a company's dividend-earnings retention policy, then that policy can affect the price they are willing to pay for the company's stock. It is helpful to describe these effects as the agency cost of (1) paying dividends and (2) retaining earnings.

The Agency Cost of Paying Dividends

The agency cost of paying dividends arises when investors believe the managers may pay dividends to the original stockholders with the intention of replacing the cash by selling overvalued shares to new stockholders. Managers can play this game when there

Table 15.10   FRANKO'S CASH FLOWS AND BALANCE SHEET

Asymmetric Information
Has Positive NPV Investments
Does Not Pay a Current Dividend

	Time 0	Time 1	
		What the Market Believes	What the Managers Know
Free Cash Flow			
Cash flow provided by (used for) operations			
From original assets	$ 100,000	$ 336,000	$ 280,000
From new investment	0	224,000	224,000
Net cash flow	100,000	560,000	504,000
Cash flow provided by (used for) investment	(100,000)	0	0
Cash flow provided by (used for) financial slack	0	0	0
Net free cash flow	$ 0	$ 560,000	$ 504,000
Financial Cash Flow			
Pay dividend to original stockholders	$ 0	$(560,000)	$(504,000)

is asymmetric information because they learn how well their company's existing assets are performing before outside investors do. Consequently, they are tempted to pay a dividend and sell new common stock when they know the value of the assets will decline in the future. This reduces the impact of the loss in value on the original stockholders because cash is transferred to them from the new stockholders.[7]

Potential new stockholders understand this game and may penalize the company by offering a lower price for the common stock when they suspect the managers know the assets are overvalued. They may even penalize companies when the managers are not playing this game if they cannot easily distinguish between the guilty and innocent. This imposes the agency cost of dividends on the original stockholders who may forgo attractive investment opportunities or be forced to rely on internal financing. We can see these effects clearly by incorporating asymmetric information in our Franko International example.

Table 15.10 shows what happens to the original stockholders if Franko retains the $100,000 cash flow provided by operations to finance the new beef jerky project. The first two columns of numbers repeat the information in Table 15.7; the financial market believes the company's free cash flow at time 1 will be $560,000, so the market price

---

[7]See Stewart C. Myers and Nicholas S. Majluf, "Corporate Financing and Investment Decisions When Firms Have Information That Investors Do Not Have," *Journal of Financial Economics*, June 1984, pp. 187–222.

FRANKO'S CASH FLOWS AND BALANCE SHEET

Asymmetric Information
Has Positive NPV Investments
Pays a Current Dividend

Table 15.11

	Time 0	Time 1	
		What the Market Believes	What the Managers Know
Free Cash Flow			
Cash flow provided by (used for) operations			
From original assets	$ 100,000	$ 336,000	$ 280,000
From new investment	0	224,000	224,000
Net cash flow	100,000	560,000	504,000
Cash flow provided by (used for) investment	(100,000)	0	0
Cash flow provided by (used for) financial slack	0	0	0
Net free cash flow	$ 0	$ 560,000	$ 504,000
Financial Cash Flow			
Pay dividend to original stockholders	$(100,000)	$(448,000)	$(403,200)
Issue new common stock (5,000 shares)	100,000	0	0
Pay dividend to new stockholders	0	(112,000)	$(100,800)
Net financial cash flow	$ 0	$(560,000)	$(504,000)

of each share of stock is $25.00. The third column describes what the managers know: free cash flow will be only $504,000 at time 1 due to poor performance by the sausage business. This reduced cash flow will provide a dividend per share of $25.20 ($504,000/20,000 shares), which supports a common stock value of only $22.50 ($25.20/1.12). The market value of the stock will decline to $22.50 when the managers' information is revealed, causing the original stockholders to suffer a loss of $2.50 per share.

Suppose the managers decide to distribute the $100,000 cash flow provided by operations to the original stockholders and finance the project by selling 5,000 shares of new common stock. Table 15.11 shows the effect. The first two columns of numbers repeat the information in Table 15.8; the financial market believes the company's free cash flow at time 1 will be $560,000, so the market price of the old and new shares is $20.00. (Remember, the original stockholders already received a cash dividend of $5.00 per share.) The managers know dividends per share on the outstanding stock will actually be only $20.16 ($504,000/25,000 shares). The stock therefore will eventually sell for $18.00 per share ($20.16/1.12).

The original stockholders receive a $5.00 dividend and stock worth $18.00 for a total of $23.00 under this dividend payout, external financing plan. They therefore have $0.50 more per share ($23.00 – $22.50) than if Franko finances the new project internally. The extra $0.50 per share (or $10,000 in total) came from the new stockholders who bought 5,000 shares for $20.00 each, $2.00 per share more than they were really worth.

EXERCISE

15.8   **DIVIDEND POLICY'S EFFECT WITH ASYMMETRIC INFORMATION**

The market price of Reilly and Remington's common stock is $11 per share but the managers know this price will fall to $9 when the company's quarterly performance report is released. There are 5,000 shares outstanding. How will the original and new owners be affected by a decision to pay the original owners a dividend of $1 per share financed by selling new common stock?

The financial market believes the new stock is worth $10 per share, its value ex-dividend. Therefore, the company must sell 500 shares of stock to finance the dividend ($5,000/$10 per share). The new stock is sold for $1,000—or $2.00 per share—more than it is really worth, thereby reducing the original owners' losses by $0.20 per share ($1,000/5,000 shares).

Potential new common stockholders, knowing they may be victimized by this game, are likely to revise downward their estimate of the future free cash flows for *any* company that issues new common stock. This is only fair if the company's existing assets have declined in value because then the original stockholders bear their own losses. An adverse market reaction is not fair, however, if the company's assets have not declined in value.

A properly valued company that cannot distinguish itself in some other way can avoid this adverse market reaction only by abstaining from the use of external financing. This is accomplished by forgoing the investment opportunity and losing its net present value or by forgoing the dividend and financing the investment internally. The latter alternative is probably less costly for most companies and their stockholders because the owners can replace a company's dividend with a homemade one but probably cannot create a homemade version of the investment opportunity.

Summarizing our discussion to this point, financial market imperfections and the agency cost of dividends encourage companies to retain cash. A low dividend, high earnings retention policy shields stockholders from ordinary income taxes and brokerage costs and keeps the company from being incorrectly perceived as overvalued. If these concerns are legitimate, then real companies should exhibit a preference for internal rather than external financing and real investors should react negatively (revise the stock price downward) when a company issues new common stock. These are the precise things we see when we examine financing patterns. This evidence has led many finance scholars to conclude that these departures from a perfect financial market are what cause companies to adopt dividend-earnings retention policies that provide a substantial proportion of new financing from internal sources.

I N   T H E   N E W S

WHAT TO DO WITH EXCESS CASH?

MANY EXECUTIVES WHO run America's large corporations are at a crossroads. With profits high, they must decide what to do with all the cash now flowing in. Plow it into the business? Or please many shareholders, perhaps by increasing dividends or buying back stock?

"More and more institutional investors think the best use of the money is for companies to put it into their own shares," says Michael Metz, director of research at Oppenheimer & Co. Recent history warns institutions, he adds, not to let companies "go on egomaniacal empire-building or binges of spending for overcapacity." So, the investors push for buybacks even though many executives pledge to avoid past corporate mistakes.

Corporations already are scrimping on dividend increases. In good times in the past, many paid out 50 percent or more of profits. This year, Standard & Poor's predicts, the payout on the S&P 500 will drop. One reason: Individual investors aren't as eager for dividends as in the past; they prefer stock-market gains, which are taxed at lower rates. Executives, too, are inclined to favor rising stock prices because more of their total compensation is coming in the form of stock options that gain value as share prices rise.

That displeases John Neff, who manages the Vanguard Group's $13.5 billion Windsor fund and likes companies to pay hefty dividends. Although companies tell him that other big investors "are pushing for buybacks, saying the hell with dividends," he says "they should do both at the same time."

Source: Fred R. Bleakley, "Management Problem: Reinvest High Profits or Please Institutions?" *The Wall Street Journal*, October 16, 1995, p. A1. Reprinted by permission of *The Wall Street Journal*, © 1995 Dow Jones & Company, Inc. All rights reserved worldwide.

The Agency Cost of Retaining Earnings

Managers can use internal financing at their discretion with little monitoring or control. This provides them the opportunity to invest the company's excess free cash flows in projects that satisfy their own objectives. For example, they may hold excess financial slack to increase the company's safety and to protect their own jobs. They also may invest in projects that increase sales or earnings per share if their compensation is tied to these variables. The financial market recognizes these possibilities and encourages companies to distribute the cash as dividends or by repurchasing common stock (see "In the News").

Rozeff and others suggested that boards of directors declare dividends to deprive managers of this unsupervised access to internal financing.[8] Companies must enter the financial market and submit to its monitoring to replace these funds, however, this does not inhibit those with good investment opportunities. Rozeff found that companies whose owners were dispersed and therefore had the least abilities to closely monitor managers paid out a higher proportion of earnings as dividends. This finding supports the idea that owners are concerned about the agency costs of retaining earnings.

---

[8]Michael Rozeff, "How Companies Set Their Dividend Payout Ratios," *The Revolution in Corporate Finance*, Joel M. Stern and Donald H. Chew, editors, Basel Blackwell, New York, 1986.

15.5   ESTABLISHING A DIVIDEND PAYOUT–EARNINGS RETENTION POLICY

Finance scholars have not been able to incorporate the conflicting influences of financial market imperfections and agency costs into a dividend policy-earnings retention model that managers can use to select the best policy. This unfortunate situation is best described by the final sentence of Fischer Black's article, "The Dividend Puzzle." He said, "What should the corporation do about dividend policy? We don't know."[9] Managers must act, however, even if they cannot rely on a rigorous economic model for advice. Under the circumstances, the results of Lintner's study and the practices of successful companies whose dividend-earnings retention policies have met the market test may provide the best guidance.

Lintner found that managers gradually increase dividend payments when earnings increase but make no adjustments to temporary earnings changes. They follow the same practice when earnings decrease because they reduce dividends only after it becomes clear that the current level is not sustainable. Managers appear to implement this gradual adjustment policy by pursuing a long-term target payout ratio (dividends per share/earnings per share). This ratio is larger for mature companies with stable earnings and few investment opportunities and smaller for growth companies.[10]

Managers do not routinely pay out anywhere near 100 percent of a company's cash flows as dividends, however. A possible explanation for this restraint is that financial market imperfections and asymmetric information make internal financing less expensive than new external financing. Managers therefore retain some cash as financial slack to fund current and prospective investments.

The financial market reacts to dividend changes by increasing and decreasing the stock price in response to favorable and unfavorable dividend surprises. This reaction and managers' reluctance to increase dividends until the new level can be sustained implies both sides believe unexpected dividend changes convey information about the managers' diligence and the quality of the company's assets that supplements the information in financial statements, auditors' reports, filings with the SEC, etc. McDonnell-Douglas's announcement, described at the beginning of this chapter, and the General Motors and Reebok announcements described in "In the News" illustrate this information effect. Recent research indicates that stock splits convey additional information about the persistence of a company's earnings strength (see the article about Helen of Troy in "In the News").

Under the circumstances, a company probably should adopt a stable dividend policy to reduce the likelihood of conveying incorrect or misleading information to the financial market. These dividends probably should be based on a target payout ratio that takes into account the company's anticipated investment opportunities and

---

[9]Fischer Black, "The Dividend Puzzle," *Journal of Portfolio Management,* Winter 1976, pp. 5–8.

[10]This study is described in John Lintner, "Distribution of Incomes of Corporations Among Dividends, Retained Earnings, and Taxes," *American Economic Review,* May 1956, pp. 97–113. Eugene F. Fama and Harvey Babiak, "Dividend Policy: An Empirical Analysis," *Journal of the American Statistical Association,* December 1968, pp. 1132–1161 conducted an empirical test that confirmed some of the implications of Lintner's partial adjustment model.

I N   T H E   N E W S

DIVIDENDS ARE SIGNALS

A Cash Dividend Increase at General Motors

IN A FURTHER sign of the No. 1 auto maker's financial recovery, the General Motors Corp. board raised its quarterly dividend 33 percent, to 40 cents.

Last week, when GM reported record 1995 earnings of $6.9 billion, or $7.21 a share, some Wall Street analysts predicted that a dividend increase was likely. "They have done a very good job of turning around the company, and [the increase] is a signal of that to investors," says Ken Blaschke, a Dean Witter Reynolds analyst. "It shows that the management at GM is willing to convert some of the turnaround success into shareholder value."

GM Chairman John F. Smith Jr. struck just that note yesterday, declaring, "Our objective is to maximize GM shareholder value over the long term." He added: "We're confident this increase . . . can be sustained over the long term, thanks to fundamental profitability improvements we've been able to achieve as well as the continued strengthening of our balance sheet and ongoing improvement in our cash position."

A Large Share Repurchase at Reebok

Reebok International Ltd., seeking to boost its lagging stock price, said it will offer to repurchase one-third of the company's stock, or 24 million common shares, for as much as $864 million.

Reebok's stock yesterday jumped $3.50, or 11 percent, closing at $34.75 in composite trading on the New York Stock Exchange.

Paul Fireman, who has acknowledged some marketing errors even as he encouraged dissatisfied shareholders to sell, signaled his confidence in the company by promising to keep his money invested. Reebok said Mr. Fireman and his wife, Phyllis, who together own 14.1 percent of the company's shares outstanding, wouldn't be tendering their shares in the offering.

The buyback "is an order of magnitude that's quite breathtaking," said George Wyper, who sold his stake in Reebok last year out of frustration with management. "Paul obviously must see good things happening, or he wouldn't be doing this."

Sources: Rebecca Blumenstein, "GM Raises Dividend 33% to 40 Cents," *The Wall Street Journal*, February 6, 1996, p. A3 and James S. Hirsch, "Reebok Will Offer to Buy Back One-Third of Its Common Shares," *The Wall Street Journal*, June 30, 1996, p. B4. Reprinted by permission of *The Wall Street Journal*, © 1996 Dow Jones & Company, Inc. All rights reserved worldwide.

---

financing requirements. The idea is to adopt a target payout ratio that reduces the company's need to sell new common stock without raising concerns about overretention and misuse of free cash flows. Barclay, Smith, and Watts concluded that concern about this trade-off explained about one-third of the differences in dividend policies among the 6,700 companies in their study.[11]

An industry's average dividend payout ratio is a convenient target, however, it should not be adopted uncritically. A particular company may have different investment opportunities and its owners may have different concerns about taxes and asymmetric information than the average company in its industry. The board of directors and

---

[11]See Michael J. Barclay, Clifford W. Smith, and Ross L. Watts, "The Determinants of Corporate Leverage and Dividend Policies," *Journal of Applied Corporate Finance*, Winter 1995, pp. 4–19.

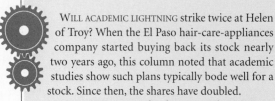

IN THE NEWS

WHAT STOCK SPLITS MEAN

WILL ACADEMIC LIGHTNING strike twice at Helen of Troy? When the El Paso hair-care-appliances company started buying back its stock nearly two years ago, this column noted that academic studies show such plans typically bode well for a stock. Since then, the shares have doubled.

Now comes a new development. The company recently split its stock 2 for 1, increasing the number of shares to 13.6 million. And if academic studies are right again, now might be another good time to pick up Helen of Troy.

A forthcoming research paper indicates that the stocks of companies that undergo 2-for-1 splits typically outperform a portfolio of similar-size companies by 7.94 percent in the first year, and by as much as 12.14 percent over three years.

Why the big moves? Usually because companies are on a roll when they split, says David Ikenberry, a Rice University associate professor and one of three authors of the paper scheduled to be published in the September issue of the *Journal of Financial and Quantitative Analysis*.

Company executives typically consider stock splits only after a company's shares have run up strongly. Managers who don't expect the strength to continue ultimately opt not to split the company's stock, Mr. Ikenberry says, while those that remain optimistic "step up to the plate and go ahead with the split."

And Helen of Troy's management certainly has reason for optimism. The company is coming off a record year for sales and profit in 1995, and recently reported a record first quarter. Sales for the quarter, which ended May 31, surged 31 percent from the year-earlier period to $43.8 million, while net income jumped 43 percent to $2.4 million, or 18 cents a share, adjusted for the split. Aaron Lehmann, an analyst with M. H. Meyerson & Co., a Jersey City, N.J., brokerage firm—and one of only two analysts following the company—expects earnings for fiscal 1997 will increase by 24 percent at about $1.17 a share. "All factors argue for higher sales and earnings," says Mr. Lehmann.

Source: Jeff D. Opdyke, "Double Play: Stock Split May Mean Big Gains for Helen of Troy Shares," *The Wall Street Journal*, July 24, 1996, p. B-T2. Reprinted by permission of *The Wall Street Journal*, © 1996 Dow Jones & Company, Inc. All rights reserved worldwide.

the managers must refer to financial theory to assess the effect of these differences on the desirability of paying more or less dividends than other companies in the industry.

15.6 SUMMARY

A company's dividend policy does not affect its value in a perfect financial market with symmetric information. Miller and Modigliani proved this is true because the owners can create or undo dividends by conducting financial transactions themselves. This frees companies of responsibility for financial decisions and permits them to focus on investment and operating decisions.

The situation is different in reality, however, because market imperfections and asymmetric information produce benefits and costs that affect the value of dividend payments. The existence of taxes favors earnings retention because owners are taxed at a lower rate when they create a homemade dividend by selling shares of stock. Asymmetric information also may favor earnings retention if the financial market believes the company is trying to sell overvalued stock when it replaces the cash paid as dividends. At the same time, asymmetric information may favor the payment of dividends if the financial market believes managers will invest retained earnings unwisely.

We don't know exactly how real companies evaluate these costs and benefits when they establish dividend policies. We do know, however, that most pay a regular, moderate dividend that they are reluctant to change. This behavior suggests managers prefer to use earnings as an internal source of financing but are aware that increases and decreases in dividends convey positive and negative information.

KEY TERMS

Declaration date *612*	Holder of record	Stock dividend *615*
Payment date *612*	date *612*	Stock split *615*
	Ex-dividend date *612*	

QUESTIONS AND PROBLEMS

1. "Emerson Electric Co. said its fiscal fourth-quarter earnings jumped 12 percent, benefiting from overseas sales and improved productivity despite moderate domestic growth. The St. Louis industrial giant also announced a string of investor-friendly actions: a dividend increase, a 2-for-1 stock split, and a stock buyback. The news sent Emerson shares climbing $1.625 to close at $98.625 in New York Stock Exchange composite trading. Emerson said its board voted to increase the quarterly dividend 10.2 percent to 54 cents a share, payable December 10 to stock of record November 22. The stock split is effective March 10, 1997, for stock of record February 21." (Source: Carl Quintanilla, "Emerson Electric's Net Gains 12%; Stock Split, Payout Rise Planned," *The Wall Street Journal*, November 13, 1996, p. B4.)

   (a) Place each date mentioned in this article on a time line and describe its significance. Be sure to include the dividend and stock split ex-dates.

   (b) What is the explanation for the stock price increase on November 12? By what amount do you expect the stock price to change on the other dates on your time line? Explain your answers.

2. The Value Line Investment Service's August 2, 1996 report on Dow Chemical Company reported the following values for the company's earnings per share and dividends per share.

Year	Earnings per Share	Dividends per Share
1980	$2.95	$1.10
1981	2.00	1.20
1982	0.76	1.20
1983	1.00	1.20

Year	Earnings per Share	Dividends per Share
1984	$1.67	$1.20
1985	1.55	1.20
1986	2.58	1.27
1987	4.33	1.43
1988	8.55	1.73
1989	9.20	2.37
1990	5.10	2.60
1991	3.56	2.60
1992	2.10	2.60
1993	2.02	2.60
1994	3.91	—
1995	8.27	—

(a) Prepare a graph of Dow Chemical's earnings per share and dividends per share. Use Exhibit 15.2 as a model.

(b) Describe the distinctive features of your graph. What kind of dividend policy does Dow Chemical seem to follow? How quickly do they adjust dividends per share to changes in earnings per share?

(c) Predict the company's dividends per share for 1994 and 1995 and explain the basis for your predictions.

3. Cash dividends, share repurchases, and in-kind dividends (such as stock dividends and stock splits) are alternative ways for a company to distribute part of its value to the owners.

(a) Why are these alternatives equivalent to one another in a perfect financial market?

(b) Explain how brokerage fees and taxes can make one alternative preferable to the others.

4. More and more companies are providing Dividend ReInvestment Plans (DRIPs) to the owners.

(a) Do these plans make the market for the companies' common stocks more or less perfect? Explain your answer.

(b) What other factors that influence dividend policy may become more important to companies that offer DRIPs?

(c) All other things equal, do you expect companies to pay higher or lower cash dividends after initiating a dividend reinvestment program? Explain your answer.

5. Suppose the financial market is perfect and managers and investors have the same information about a company's future prospects.

(a) Explain why dividend policy is irrelevant to a company without positive net present value investment opportunities.

(b) Is dividend policy still irrelevant if the company develops acceptable investment opportunities? Explain your answer.

6. North Woods Tours ended a great travel season with $1 million temporarily invested in U.S. Treasury bills. The company has no need for this cash during the off-season but expects to buy a resort lodge that will come up for sale in 10 months.

(a) What should the company do with its $1 million of financial slack if the financial market is perfect with no asymmetric information? Explain your answer.

(b) What should the company consider doing with its financial slack if the financial market is perfect but North Woods' managers know more about the travel business than investors do? Explain your answer.

7. Chrysler Corporation held $6.4 billion of cash in 1995, on its way to accumulating $7.5 billion that the managers believed the company needed to weather a possible recession. This cash attracted the attention of Kirk Kerkorian, the company's largest shareholder. He believed the company needed only $2.5 billion of cash and pressed the managers to distribute the excess to the owners. When they refused to do so, he attempted to take over the company so he could distribute the cash himself. (Sources: Steven Lipin and Gabriella Stern, "Chrysler Plans Suggest Firm Has Ample Cash, Even for a Downturn," *The Wall Street Journal*, October 20, 1995, p. A1 and David Woodruff, "Target Chrysler," *Business Week*, April 24, 1995, pp. 34–38.)

(a) Explain why Kerkorian and others may have been concerned about Chrysler's accumulation of what they considered to be excess cash.

(b) Suppose the takeover attempt was successful (it wasn't). How would you expect the new managers to distribute the excess cash to the owners? As an increase in the regular quarterly dividend, as a special dividend, as a share repurchase, or as a stock dividend or stock split? Explain your answer.

8. Zany Films Incorporated (ZFI) was established to produce documentaries for political action committees. The company's assets are $500,000 cash and animated films that will provide $2,280,000 of operating cash flows in one year. The company is all-equity financed with 250,000 shares of stock outstanding. The yield on U.S. Treasury securities is 6 percent and the required rate of return for the film business is 14 percent.

(a) Prepare ZFI's market-value balance sheet assuming the $500,000 cash will be invested in U.S. Treasury securities. What is the value of a share of common stock?

(b) The company will pay all of next year's cash flows to the owners as dividends. Use the dividends per share and the ZFI's required rate of return on equity to determine the value of a share of common stock.

(c) Is the price of the company's stock acceptable to everyone or only patient owners who are willing to wait for one year to receive a cash dividend? Explain your answer.

9. Gimme-a-Break Plaster Company's cash flows from operations are $90,000 now and $297,000 in year 1. The company is all-equity financed with 60,000 shares of stock outstanding. The yield on U.S. Treasury securities is 6 percent and the required rate of return for this line of business is 10 percent. The company has no positive NPV projects available and the financial markets are perfect with no asymmetric information.

(a) Prepare the company's free cash flow and financial cash flow statements assuming the $90,000 cash is invested in U.S. Treasury securities. What is the value of a share of Gimme-a-Break's common stock?

(b) Prepare the company's free cash flow and financial cash flow statements assuming the $90,000 cash is paid as a current dividend. What is the value of a share of common stock excluding the current dividend? Including the current dividend?

(c) Don Paris owns 300 shares of Gimme-a-Break stock. How many shares must he sell for a homemade dividend of $1.50 per share if the company doesn't pay one? How many shares must he buy for homemade reinvestment if the company pays a current dividend of $1.50 per share?

(d) Prepare a table that shows the value and composition of Don Paris's personal portfolio for each situation described below. Does the company's dividend policy affect his wealth?

Company Pays a Dividend	Don Wants a Dividend
No	No
Yes	No
No	Yes
Yes	Yes

10. Ann Vestor owns 180 shares of Feline Learning Toys, Inc. (FLT). The company's market-value balance sheet is shown below. There are 12,000 shares outstanding. FLT has no acceptable investment opportunities and the financial market is perfect.

Assets		Claims	
Cash	$30,000	Debt	$ 0
Fixed assets	60,000	Equity	90,000
Total	$90,000	Total	$90,000

(a) Determine the total amount of money Ann will receive if the company uses its $30,000 cash to pay dividends.

(b) Suppose the board of directors decides not to use the $30,000 to pay dividends. Prepare a table that shows the value and composition of Ann's personal portfolio if she accepts this decision and if she creates a homemade dividend.

(c) Now suppose the board of directors decides to use the $30,000 to pay dividends. Prepare a table that shows the value and composition of Ann's personal portfolio if she accepts this decision and if she reinvests the money in the company herself.

(d) Does the company's dividend policy affect Ann's wealth? Does this outcome depend on the absence of acceptable investment opportunities or the perfect financial market? Explain your answer.

11. CastOff Inc. manufactures marine hardware. The required rate of return for this line of business is 12 percent. The company has 20,000 shares of stock outstanding and its free cash flow statement for the present and next year is given below.

	Year 0	Year 1
Free Cash Flow		
Cash flow provided by (used for) operations	$ 100,000	$ 112,000
Cash flow provided by (used for) investments	0	0
Cash flow provided by(used for) financial slack	0	0
Net free cash flow	$ 100,000	$ 112,000

(a) Determine the dividends per share and price per share of CastOff's common stock.

(b) Place these dividends and stock price on a graph that shows *all* the combinations of year 0 and year 1 cash flows an owner can create with homemade dividends and reinvestment. (See Exhibit 3.6 in Chapter 3 for an example.)

(c) Can the company provide the owners any cash flow patterns that are superior to those shown on your graph if it has no positive NPV investment opportunities and the financial market is perfect? Explain your answer.

(d) Use your graph to explain why the irrelevance of dividend policy in a perfect financial market is merely an example of the separation principle.

12. Suppose CastOff Inc. (see problem 11) has an opportunity to produce titanium winches for an ocean racing yacht. This project requires an investment of $30,000 at year 0, will provide operating cash flows of $56,000 at year 1, and has a required rate of return of 12 percent.

(a) Revise CastOff's free cash flow statements assuming the company finances the project internally.

(b) Determine the dividends per share and price per share of CastOff's common stock with the new investment project. Should the company accept this investment opportunity? Why?

(c) Place the company's original dividends and stock price and its dividends and stock price with the investment on a graph that shows *all* the combinations of year 0 and year 1 cash flows an owner can create with homemade dividends and reinvestment. (See Exhibit 3.7 in Chapter 3 for an example.)

(d) Given that CastOff makes the right investment decision and that the financial market is perfect, can the company provide the owners any cash flow patterns that are superior to those shown on your graph? Explain your answer.

(e) Which of the managers' decisions increased the owners' wealth: the decision to produce the titanium winches or the decision to forgo dividends to finance the project? Explain your answer.

13. Plasti-Chrome Inc. produces reproductions of chrome trim parts for classic automobiles. The company's operating cash flows are $125,000 now and $310,750 in one year. Plasti-Chrome is all-equity financed with 100,000 shares of stock outstanding; the required rate of return for this line of business is 13 percent. The company is considering an opportunity to produce chrome tail-fin trim that will be sold to members of the 1955 Buick Car Club. The project costs $100,000 and will provide operating cash flows of $135,600 in one year. Plasti-Chrome will use its own cash flows to finance the project and pay the remainder as dividends.

(a) Prepare the company's free cash flow and financial cash flow statements with and without the investment project.

(b) Determine Plasti-Chrome's dividends per share and stock price with and without the project. Should the company produce tail-fin trim for 1955 Buicks? Explain your answer.

(c) Now suppose a major investor who owns 20,000 shares calls to tell the chairman of the board she *needs* a current dividend to pay her taxes. Should the chairman change the company's investment or financing decision to accommodate her? Explain your answer.

14. Xymon Food Company's baking operations will provide operating cash flows of $230,000 next year. The company also has an opportunity to produce a high-energy snack bar for competitive walkers. This project costs $42,000 now and will provide additional operating cash flows of $59,800 next year. Xymon will finance the investment by selling new common stock. The company currently has 5,000 shares of stock outstanding and the required rate of return is 15 percent.

(a) Determine the value of a share of Xymon's common stock before the company accepts the investment proposal.

(b) Determine the NPV per share of the investment proposal.

(c) How many new shares must Xymon issue to finance the investment proposal? What is the price per share?

(d) Did the company's decision to accept the snack-bar project increase the wealth of the original stockholders or the new stockholders? Explain your answer.

15. Holiday Magic produces lighting that homeowners use to decorate the exterior of their houses and yards at Christmas. The company's operating cash flows are $400,000 now and $650,000 next year. The company plans to expand its operations by producing lighting for the Halloween season. This project requires an investment of $400,000 and will provide operating cash flows of $460,000 next year. Holiday Magic will use the cash on hand to pay dividends and finance the Halloween lighting project, if it is acceptable, by selling new common stock. The company has no debt, there are 60,000 shares of stock outstanding, and the required rate of return for the holiday lighting business is 11 percent. The financial market is perfect.

(a) Determine the market value of Holiday Magic's common stock without considering the investment proposal.

(b) Determine the NPV of the Halloween lighting project. Should Holiday Magic accept this investment proposal? By what amount will this investment increase the market value of a share of the company's common stock?

(c) Prepare Holiday Magic's free cash flow statements and market-value balance sheet assuming the company accepts the investment proposal.

(d) How many shares of stock must Holiday Magic issue to finance the Halloween lighting project? What is the price per share?

(e) Prepare the company's financial cash flow statements, distinguishing between the dividends paid to the original and new shareholders.

(f) What is the market value of an original owner's share of stock, including the current dividend?

(g) Compare your answer to part (f) with the sum of your answers to parts (a) and (b). Which of the managers' decisions increased the owners' wealth: the decision to produce Halloween lighting or the decision to pay a current dividend and finance the project externally? Explain your answer.

16. Rework problem 15 assuming Holiday Magic uses only $120,000 of its current cash flow to pay dividends and uses the rest to finance the investment project. Does this change in the company's dividend-earnings retention policy change your answer to part (g)? Why or why not?

17. Vinyl Four, Inc., makes plastic souvenirs that are sold at championship basketball games. The company's operating cash flows are $500,000 for 1998 and $580,000 for 1999. Vinyl Four has no debt, there are 250,000 shares of stock outstanding, and the required rate of return for this line of business is 16 percent.

(a) Determine the market price of a single share of Vinyl Four's common stock.

(b) The company has an opportunity to produce the souvenirs for a college track and field championship. This project requires an immediate investment of $250,000 and is expected to provide operating cash flows of $319,000 next year. Should Vinyl Four accept this investment proposal? What is the effect on the market value of a single share of common stock?

Vinyl Four's board of directors and senior financial managers are considering the alternative dividend-earnings retention policies for 1998 described below.

	Policy 1	Policy 2	Policy 3
Free Cash Flow			
Cash flow provided by operations	$ 500,000	$ 500,000	$ 500,000
Cash flow used for investment	(250,000)	(250,000)	(250,000)
Net free cash flow	$ 250,000	$ 250,000	$ 250,000
Financial Cash Flow			
Pay dividend to original owners	$(250,000)	$(400,000)	$(500,000)
Issue new common stock	0	150,000	250,000
Net financial cash flow	$(250,000)	$(250,000)	$(250,000)

(c) Which dividend-earnings retention policy should the company adopt to maximize the owners' wealth if the financial market is perfect? Explain your answer.

(d) Which dividend-earnings retention policy should the company adopt if its investment banker charges a 10 percent fee to issue common stock but the financial market is perfect in all other respects? Explain your answer.

(e) Which dividend-earnings retention policy should the company adopt if the board of directors and senior financial managers believe that investors are concerned about the agency costs of dividends? Explain your answer.

18. Bill McGrew owns 200,000 shares or 20 percent of Longhorn Enterprises. He purchased this stock two years ago for $30 per share. Bill's stake in the company is worth $8 million given the market-value balance sheet shown below.

Assets		Claims	
Cash	$11,000,000	Debt	$ 0
Fixed assets	29,000,000	Equity	40,000,000
Total	$40,000,000	Total	$40,000,000

Longhorn Enterprises's CEO and treasurer are discussing alternative dividend-earnings retention policies and must consider Bill's preferences because he is the company's major stockholder. They know his ordinary income is taxed at the highest rate, 39.6 percent, but that he is subject to only a 28 percent tax rate on capital gains. They also know that his broker charges a 1.5 percent commission for buying and selling stock. They decide to examine the effects of two extreme policies: paying no current dividends and paying all $11 million out as dividends. They chose these two policies because they realized the effect of any other policy would be intermediate between the effects of these two.

(a) Determine the total value of McGrew's stake in Longhorn Enterprises for each of the following scenarios:

Company Pays a Dividend	McGrew Wants a Dividend
No	No
Yes	No
No	Yes
Yes	Yes

(b) Can the CEO and treasurer use the results of part (a) to decide which policy to adopt without consulting McGrew? Explain your answer.

(c) Suppose the CEO and treasurer learn that McGrew does not want to reduce his stake in the business by selling shares of stock. How does this knowledge affect their choice of dividend policy? Explain your answer.

19. SW Oil Properties, Incorporated also owns a large block of Longhorn Enterprises common stock (see problem 18), 150,000 shares in total that were purchased one year ago for $35 per share. The company's ordinary income and capital gains are taxed at the 35 percent rate but 70 percent of the dividends the company receives are tax-exempt. Rework Problem 18 considering SW Oil Properties' situation rather than McGrew's.

20. The CEO of Crain Enterprises gave the following bad news–good news report to the board of directors:

> I am sorry to report that next year our existing businesses are unlikely to provide an operating cash flow of $1,276,000 as we expected when we announced our cost-cutting program. Reducing costs is much more difficult than we expected so we now believe next year's operating cash flow from existing businesses is likely to be around $1,044,000. I have not shared this information with securities analysts. That is the bad news. The good news is that we won the contract to install the sprinkler system in the county's new high school. The project will cost us $300,000 and return $464,000 in one year, providing a rate of return of nearly 55 percent. This rate of return far exceeds our required rate of return of 16 percent. The only remaining issue we must consider at this meeting is how to finance the sprinkler system project. We have $300,000 cash on hand that we can use for financing. Alternatively, we can pay the $300,000 out as dividends and sell new common stock. The decision is, of course, up to the board.

(a) Suppose Crain does not pay a dividend. What is the market price of the company's common stock now and what will it be when the financial market learns the cost-cutting program is not as successful as planned? There are 100,000 shares outstanding.

(b) Suppose Crain pays the $300,000 out as dividends to the original shareholders and sells new common stock. How many shares of new common stock must Crain sell and what price will the company receive for the stock if it is sold before the financial market learns that the cost-cutting program is not as successful as planned? What will the price of the stock be after the market learns the unfavorable information?

(c) What will an original owner's stake be worth (including the current dividend) after the unfavorable information is revealed if the company pays a current dividend? If it does not pay a current dividend?

(d) The board of directors may be tempted to pay a current dividend to reduce the original owners' losses. Explain why the board may want to resist this temptation if the company will ever issue new common stock again.

21. Visit the Dividend ReInvestment Plan Guide on the Internet at http://www.cs.cmu.edu/~jdg/drip.html. Click on List of Companies with DRIPs. Examine the features of some of the DRIP programs listed there.

(a) What are the typical discounts offered on shares bought through DRIPs?

(b) What is the typical minimum number of shares required to join DRIP programs?

(c) What other features do DRIP programs have?

- ## ADDITIONAL READING

The classic article on dividend policy in a perfect financial market is

    Merton H. Miller and Franco Modigliani, "Dividend Policy, Growth and the Valuation of Shares," *Journal of Business,* October 1961, pp. 411–433.

Lintner's description of how companies establish dividend policies and a subsequent test of his predictions are in

    John Lintner, "Distribution of Incomes of Corporations Among Dividends, Retained Earnings, and Taxes," *American Economic Review,* May 1956, pp. 97–113.

    Eugene F. Fama and Harvey Babiak, "Dividend Policy: An Empirical Analysis," *Journal of the American Statistical Association,* December 1968, pp. 1132–1161.

For discussions of what we don't know about dividend policy, see

    Fischer Black, "The Dividend Puzzle," *Journal of Portfolio Management,* Winter 1976, pp. 5–8.

    Peter L. Bernstein, "Dividends: The Puzzle," *Journal of Applied Corporate Finance,* Spring 1996, pp. 16–22.

C H A P T E R   1 6

LONG-TERM FINANCIAL POLICY: CAPITAL STRUCTURE

U.S. nonfarm, nonfinance corporations raised more than $6.5 trillion from 1986–1995 to finance investments in capital equipment, working capital, and financial assets. These companies obtained more than $4.4 trillion of this new money by retaining their own earnings and nearly $2.6 trillion by issuing debt. They didn't issue common stock on a net basis during this period however, they repurchased approximately $500 billion worth.[1] Their year-by-year financing choices are graphed in Exhibit 16.1.

This strong preference for obtaining financing from retained earnings, new debt, and new equity (in that order) also was revealed by a survey sent to the CFOs of the 1986 Fortune 500 companies.[2] Nearly 69 percent of the survey respondents indicated they follow a financing hierarchy when they obtain capital. Table 16.1 summarizes their preferences; retained earnings was their overwhelming first choice followed by straight debt. New common stock was a distant fourth.

Chapter 15 partially explained why companies that need additional financing prefer retained earnings to selling new securities. But why do they usually issue bonds rather than new common stock? And why do some successful companies, such as Microsoft and Merck, use almost no long-term debt in their capital structures? Financial theories provide answers to these questions and guidance to the board of directors and senior managers who must periodically decide how to finance their company's investments and operations.

The choice between debt and equity may be the most important financing decision managers must make. This decision affects the common stockholders' expected rate of return, how their rate of return varies in response to changes in economic conditions, and the risk of financial distress. The debt-equity or capital

---

[1]Board of Governors of the Federal Reserve System, *Flow of Funds Accounts*, Table F.102, obtained from their Internet site, http://www.bog.frb.fed.us/releases.

[2]J. Michael Pinegar and Lisa Wilbricht, "What Managers Think of Capital Structure Theory: A Survey," *Financial Management*, Winter 1989, pp. 82–91.

Exhibit 16.1

FINANCING CHOICES BY U.S. NONFARM NONFINANCIAL CORPORATIONS

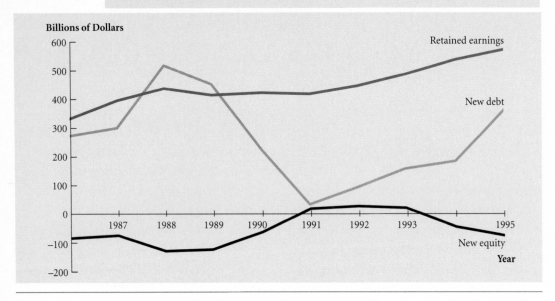

Source: Board of Governors of the Federal Reserve System, *Flow of Funds Accounts,* Table F.102, obtained from their Internet site, http://www.bog.frb.fed.us/releases.

Table 16.1   FINANCING PREFERENCES OF FORTUNE 500 CFOs

Method of Financing	Percent Ranked			
	1st	2nd	3rd	4th
Retained earnings	84.3%	7.4%	2.5%	0.8%
Straight debt	14.9	71.9	5.0	5.0
Convertible debt	0.0	2.5	43.0	31.4
Common stock	0.0	9.9	23.1	19.0

Source: J. Michael Pinegar and Lisa Wilbricht, "What Managers Think of Capital Structure Theory: A Survey," *Financial Management,* Winter 1989, pp. 82–91.

structure decision also affects the creditors because their security is enhanced when the company obtains financing from investors whose position is junior to them and vice versa. Finally, this decision affects managers who may lose their jobs if they choose a capital structure that provides too little return or too much risk. These wealth or poverty consequences have given capital structure decisions a prominent place in finance research and practice.

We will examine the debt-equity choice using much the same organization as we used to examine dividend policy and the choice between internal and external financing. Furthermore, we will draw similar conclusions: the choice between debt and equity has no effect on the company and the market value of its common stock in a perfect financial market with symmetric information, however, it may have an effect under other conditions. Once again, Modigliani and Miller's research played a celebrated role in the development of these ideas.

16.1   WHEN CAPITAL STRUCTURE IS IRRELEVANT[3]

Modigliani and Miller showed that a company's capital structure is irrelevant in a perfect financial market because investors can costlessly accept the company's decision or reverse its effect on their portfolios by borrowing or lending their own money.[4] An investor whose company does not finance its assets with debt can take out a personal loan to create the effects of financial leverage for himself. Conversely, an investor whose company uses too much debt for her taste can lend part of her wealth to "unlever" her personal portfolio. **Homemade leverage** is a perfect substitute for corporate leverage, therefore the particular capital structure a company adopts provides no extra value. Once again, we will demonstrate this principle first with a numerical example and then with equations.

Effect on Firm Value and the Cost of Equity

Durand Displays Inc. manufactures window display units for department stores. Their current situation is described by the cash statements and market-value balance sheet in Table 16.2. The company's pre-tax cash flow provided by operations is expected to be $12,500 per year in perpetuity. There are no taxes in a perfect financial market, so Durand's net cash flow provided by operations is $12,500. We will assume the company does not reinvest its cash flows to hold its size constant, so we can focus on the effect of changing its capital structure. Consequently, cash flow provided by or used for investment is zero. The company's net free cash flow is therefore $12,500. There are 10,000 shares of stock outstanding.

Durand Displays' value when it is operated without leverage, V_U, is given by Equation 16.1.

$$V_U = \frac{\text{Net free cash flow}}{r_a} \qquad [16.1]$$

The discount rate, r_a, is the required rate of return appropriate for the risk of the company's assets. This required rate of return only reflects the company's business risk because it has no debt and therefore no financial risk.

---

[3]The theories described in this section were developed by Franco Modigliani and Merton H. Miller in their path-breaking article, "The Cost of Capital, Corporation Finance and the Theory of Investment," *American Economic Review*, June 1958, pp. 261–297.

[4]Remember from earlier chapters that a perfect financial market has no transaction costs or taxes, information is instantaneously and freely available to everyone, securities are infinitely divisible, and the market is competitive, i.e., individual traders cannot affect market prices.

Table 16.2   DURAND DISPLAYS' CASH FLOWS AND BALANCE SHEET

Perfect Financial Market
No Debt

Panel A: Cash Flow Statements

	Time 1 to ∞
Free Cash Flow	
Cash flow provided by (used for) operations	
Pre-tax cash flow provided by operations	$ 12,500
Taxes	0
After-tax cash flow provided by operations	12,500
Cash flow provided by (used for) investment	0
Cash flow provided by (used for) financial slack	0
Net free cash flow	$ 12,500
Financial Cash Flow	
Pay interest	$ 0
Pay common stock dividends	(12,500)
Net financial cash flow	$(12,500)

Panel B: Market-Value Balance Sheet

Assets		Claims	
Financial slack	$ 0	Debt	$ 0
Fixed assets	125,000	Equity	125,000
Total	$125,000	Total	$125,000

The beta of the window display business is 1.0 and the riskless and market rates of return are 6 percent and 10 percent. The required rate of return and the company's value therefore are

$$r_a = 0.06 + (0.10 - 0.06) \times 1.0 = 0.10$$
$$V_U = \$12,500/0.10 = \$125,000.$$

The market value of claims equals the market value of assets, therefore the value of a single share of stock is $12.50 ($125,000/10,000 shares). This is, of course, the value you would obtain by discounting dividends per share ($1.25), at the required rate of return on equity, which equals the required rate of return on assets because the company has no financial risk.

$$\text{Value of a single share of stock} = \$1.25/0.10 = \$12.50$$

Now suppose the company is considering a change in its capital structure that will be brought about by borrowing $25,000 at 6 percent interest and using the proceeds

---

DURAND DISPLAYS' FINANCIAL CASH FLOWS AND BALANCE SHEET　　　**Table 16.3**

Perfect Financial Market
$25,000 of Debt

Panel A: Cash Flow Statements

	Time 1 to ∞
Net Free Cash Flow (from Table 16.2)	$ 12,500
Financial Cash Flow	
Pay interest	$ (1,500)
Pay common stock dividends	(11,000)
Net financial cash flow	$(12,500)

Panel B: Market-Value Balance Sheet

Assets		Claims	
Financial slack	$ 0	Debt	$ 25,000
Fixed assets	125,000	Equity	100,000
Total	$125,000	Total	$125,000

---

to repurchase common stock. This recapitalization changes the company's financial cash flows—but not its free cash flows—so the market value of its assets remains the same, $125,000. The market value of equity equals the market value of assets minus the market value of debt or $100,000 ($125,000 – $25,000). The debt was used to repurchase 2,000 shares of stock ($25,000/$12.50 per share), which leaves 8,000 shares outstanding. The market value of a single share therefore equals $12.50 ($100,000/8,000 shares). The company's new financial cash flows and balance sheet are shown in Table 16.3.

● ── ●　EXERCISE

THE EFFECT OF LEVERAGE ON CASH FLOWS AND MARKET VALUE　　16.1

Prepare Durand Displays' financial cash flow statement and market-value balance sheet assuming the company borrows $62,500 and uses the proceeds to repurchase common stock.

The company's net free cash flow is $12,500 per year and interest on the debt is $3,750 ($62,500 × 0.06). This leaves $8,750 to pay common stock dividends. The market value of the company's assets is still $125,000 and there is $62,500 of debt outstanding so the value of the equity is $62,500. Therefore, Durand Displays' financial cash flow statement and market-value balance sheet are:

Financial Cash Flows	
Pay interest	$(3,750)
Pay dividends	$(8,750)
Net cash flow	$(12,500)

Market-Value Balance Sheet

Assets	$125,000
Claims	
Debt	62,500
Equity	62,500
Total	$125,000

The creditors have a larger claim on the company's cash flows and assets because more debt is outstanding. Otherwise, the company's value is unchanged.

• ——————— •

To be sure $12.50 is an equilibrium stock price, we must compare the expected rate of return on the common stock to the required rate of return given the addition of financial risk. The expected rate of return is easy to compute: It is simply the amount of dividends the company is expected to pay, $11,000, divided by the value of the equity, $100,000. This return, 11 percent, is higher than if Durand has an all-equity capital structure to compensate the owners for the addition of financial risk.

The required rate of return is only slightly more difficult to compute. We will use the Capital Asset Pricing Model to estimate this return, so we need to know the beta of the equity given the addition of financial risk. Recall from Chapter 6 that the beta of a portfolio is a weighted average of the betas of the assets in the portfolio. Now, a company is a portfolio of its assets or, equivalently, a portfolio of its claims. Therefore, the beta of the company's assets must be a weighted average of the beta of its debt and equity. That is,

$$\beta_a = \beta_d \times \frac{\text{Debt}}{\text{Market value}} + \beta_e \times \frac{\text{Equity}}{\text{Market value}}.$$

Everyone can borrow and lend at the riskless rate of interest in a perfect financial market, therefore $\beta_d = 0$. The equation for the beta of assets simplifies to

$$\beta_a = \beta_e \times \frac{\text{Equity}}{\text{Market value}} = \beta_e \times \frac{\text{Equity}}{\text{Debt + equity}}.$$

Rearranging terms,

$$\beta_e = \beta_a \times (1 + \text{Debt/Equity}). \qquad [16.2]$$

Equation 16.2 says that the risk of a company's common stock equals the risk of its assets if it uses no debt in its capital structure, however, this risk increases linearly with an increase in leverage as measured by the debt/equity ratio.[5] Does this equation look familiar to you? It should. We used a similar equation in Chapter 2 to explain the relationship between the rate of return on a company's equity and the rate of return on its assets. That equation, which was part of the DuPont decomposition of financial ratios, was

$$\text{ROE} = \text{ROA} \times (\text{Assets/Equity}) = \text{ROA} \times (1 + \text{Debt/Equity}).$$

———————

[5]We will have to reconsider this simple adjustment of a company's beta to account for financial risk later.

Now you know that the CAPM lets us use the same approach to decompose the equity risk.

Applying Equation 16.2 to the Durand Displays' example,

$$\beta_e = 1.0 \times (1 + \$25,000/\$100,000) = 1.25.$$

Substituting this value into the Capital Asset Pricing Model with $r_f = 0.06$ and $r_m = 0.10$,

$$r_e = 0.06 + (0.10 - 0.06) \times 1.25 = 0.11.$$

At a market value of $12.50 per share, the stockholders' expected rate of return equals the required rate of return, so this is an equilibrium price. The use of debt in the capital structure increased dividends per share from $1.25 to $1.375 ($11,000/8,000 shares) and increased the risk from a beta of 1.0 to 1.25. The result leaves the common stockholders neither better nor worse off than before.

EXERCISE

16.2

THE EFFECT OF LEVERAGE ON RISK AND THE PRICE PER SHARE

Compare the expected and required rates of return on Durand Displays' common stock assuming the company borrows $62,500 and uses the proceeds to repurchase common stock.

The company will repurchase 5,000 ($62,500 debt/$12.50 per share) shares of stock, leaving 5,000 shares outstanding (10,000 – 5,000). Total dividends are $8,750 (from Exercise 16.1), so dividends per share are $1.75. The expected rate of return is therefore 14.0 percent ($1.75/$12.50).

Durand Displays has $62,500 of debt and $62,500 of equity, so its equity beta is

$$\beta_e = 1.0 \times (1 + \$62,500/\$62,500) = 2.0.$$

Substituting this value into the Capital Asset Pricing Model with $r_f = 0.06$ and $r_m = 0.10$,

$$r_e = 0.06 + (0.10 - 0.06) \times 2.0 = 0.14 \text{ or } 14.0\%.$$

The expected rate of return equals the required rate of return, so $12.50 is an equilibrium stock price.

This example demonstrates that $12.50 *is* the equilibrium price but does not really explain *why*. To understand this, we must examine the position of a representative stockholder.

Jim Westin is a typical stockholder who owns 400 shares (4 percent) of Durand's common stock. The first column of Table 16.4 gives Jim's personal balance sheet and cash statement if he accepts Durand's decision to remain all-equity financed (panel A) or use $25,000 of debt (panel B). The values of Jim's personal assets are the same under either capital structure given the equilibrium market price of $12.50 per share. Jim's portfolio is therefore worth $5,000 ($12.50 × 400 shares).

There are no debt claims against the company's assets or Jim's assets if Jim accepts the company's decision to remain all-equity financed, so his personal debt/equity ratio is zero in this case. There are claims against Jim's assets when the company

---

Table 16.4   JIM WESTIN'S PERSONAL PORTFOLIO AND CASH FLOWS

Perfect Financial Market

Panel A: Durand Uses No Debt

	Jim Accepts Decision		Jim Buys 100 Shares Using $1,250 of Homemade Leverage	
Personal Assets				
Original number of shares	400		400	
Number bought	0		100	
Total number of shares	400		500	
Price per share	$12.50		$12.50	
Total		$5,000		$6,250
Personal Claims				
Proportionate share of company's debt	$ 0		$ 0	
Personal debt	0		1,250	
Financial slack	0		0	
Net debt	0		1,250	
Equity	5,000		5,000	
Total		$5,000		$6,250
Personal Debt/Equity Ratio		0		0.25
Personal Cash Flow				
Dividends	$ 500		$ 625	
Personal interest payment	0		(75)	
Net cash flow		$ 500		$ 550

---

borrows money even if Jim does not because there is no limited liability in a perfect financial market. This means Jim is required to pay his proportionate share of the company's debt if the company defaults. His share is $1,000 or 4 percent of the amount of the company's debt because he owns 4 percent of the company's common stock. Jim's actual equity is therefore only $4,000 and his personal debt/equity ratio is 0.25 ($1,000/$4,000).

The company's dividends are $1.25 per share if it uses no debt and $1.375 per share if it borrows $25,000 to repurchase stock. Jim's net cash flows are therefore either $500 ($1.25 × 400 shares) or $550 ($1.375 × 400 shares). The increase in cash flows come at the expense of an increase in Jim's risk represented by the debt/equity ratio of 0.25.

The second column of Table 16.4 shows that Jim can reverse the effect of the company's decision to remain all-equity financed or use debt by levering or unlevering his personal portfolio. First consider the information in panel A. Jim has a $5,000 equity

Continued **Table 16.4**

Panel B: Durand Uses $25,000 of Debt

	Jim Accepts Decision	Jim Sells 80 Shares and Lends $1,000 for Homemade Unleverage
Personal Assets		
Original number of shares	400	400
Number sold	0	80
Total number of shares	400	320
Price per share	$12.50	$12.50
Total	$5,000	$4,000
Personal Claims		
Proportionate share of company's debt	$1,000	$1,000
Personal debt	0	0
Financial slack	0	1,000
Net debt	1,000	0
Equity	4,000	4,000
Total	$5,000	$4,000
Personal Debt/Equity Ratio	0.25	0
Personal Cash Flow		
Dividends	$ 550	$ 440
Personal interest income	0	60
Net cash flow	$ 550	$ 500

investment in Durand Displays and can obtain exactly the same amount of leverage as the company is considering by personally borrowing $1,250 and using the proceeds to buy 100 shares of stock. The company has no debt but Jim's personal debt is $1,250; Jim's equity of $5,000 gives him a personal debt/equity ratio of 0.25 ($1,250/$5,000), identical to the company's plans.

With an all-equity capital structure, the company's dividends are $1.25 per share and Jim now owns 500 shares of stock, so he receives dividends of $625. The interest on his personal loan is $75 ($1,250 × 0.06), which leaves him with net cash flow of $550. This is exactly the same cash flow with the same level of risk Jim would receive if the company provided the leverage. Because he can obtain the equivalent leverage for himself, Jim will attach no value to the company's leverage choice and will not pay more for the common stock than if the company used no financial leverage at all.

The second column of panel B of Table 16.4 shows that Jim also can remove the effects of leverage if he doesn't want it. The opportunity to do this is equally important because it shows that investors will not punish a company for using leverage.

Jim removes the effect of the leverage by holding financial slack that exactly equals his proportionate share of the company's debt. We already know he is responsible for $1,000 of the company's debt, so he must sell 80 shares of stock at $12.50 per share and invest the proceeds in riskless debt or financial slack.[6] This leaves him with 320 shares of stock worth $4,000 ($12.50 × 320 shares). Jim's net debt is zero because his financial slack exactly offsets his share of the company's debt, therefore his debt/equity ratio is zero. The effect of leverage is removed.

Jim's net cash flow also reflects the complete elimination of the effect of leverage. Durand Displays' dividend when they use debt in their capital structure is $1.375 per share. Jim owns 320 shares, so he receives dividends of $440 ($1.375 × 320 shares). He also receives 6 percent interest on his financial slack or $60 (0.06 × $1,000) for total net cash flow of $500. Again, the amount is exactly the same as if the company had not used leverage. Jim is therefore indifferent between an all-equity firm and one with leverage that he can eliminate with financial market transactions.

EXERCISE   •   ————————————————————————————————   •

16.3   **THE EQUIVALENCE OF CORPORATE AND PERSONAL FINANCIAL TRANSACTIONS**

Gary Willard owns 800 shares of Durand Displays' common stock. Determine his personal net cash flow if the company uses $62,500 of debt and if the company uses no debt but he uses the equivalent amount of personal leverage.

The company has 5,000 shares of stock outstanding and pays $8,750 of dividends if it uses $62,500 of debt (see Exercises 16.1 and 16.2). Gary's share is 16 percent (800 shares/5,000 shares) or $1,400.

Gary's equity in the company when it uses no debt is $10,000 (800 shares × $12.50 per share). He must borrow $10,000 and purchase 800 additional shares to have a personal debt/equity ratio of 1.0, which is the same as the company's. Durand Displays' total dividends are $12,500. Gary's share is 16 percent (1,600 shares/10,000 shares) or $2,000. The interest on his personal debt is $600 ($10,000 × 0.06), leaving him personal net cash flow of $1,400 ($2,000 − $600).

Gary Willard has the same risk, as represented by the debt/equity ratio, and the same net cash flow with corporate or personal financial leverage.

•   ————————————   •

Effect on the Weighted Average Cost of Capital

A general way to show that capital structure does not affect the value of a company and therefore the value of its common stock is to examine the weighted average cost of capital. Remember, this required rate of return can be used to discount free cash flows to

————————

[6]Note that the riskless debt Jim purchases can be U.S. Treasury securities or Durand Displays' own debt because it is riskless in a perfect financial market. It's easy to see that he has removed the effect of leverage in the latter case because he, in effect, owes the money to himself!

determine the value of the associated assets. Discounting an entire company's free cash flows at the weighted average cost of capital therefore gives the company's value. The use of financial leverage does not affect free cash flows in a perfect financial market, so we can conclude that a company's value is similarly unaffected if the weighted average cost of capital does not change.

The weighted average cost of capital, r_{wacc}, equals the required rate of return for each source of financing multiplied by the proportion of financing obtained from each source.

$$r_{wacc} = r_d \times \frac{D}{D+E} + r_e \times \frac{E}{D+E} \qquad [16.3]$$

where r_d = required rate of return on debt
r_e = required rate of return on equity
$r_e = r_f + (r_m - r_f)\beta_e$
D = amount of financing provided by debt
E = amount of financing provided by equity

Debt is riskless in a perfect financial market, so $r_d = r_f$ and $\beta_e = \beta_a \times (1 + D/E)$. Substituting these expressions into the equation for the weighted average cost of capital,

$$r_{wacc} = r_f \times \frac{D}{D+E} + \left[r_f + (r_m - r_f)\beta_a \times \frac{E+D}{E} \right] \times \frac{E}{D+E}.$$

Collecting terms and simplifying,

$$r_{wacc} = r_f + (r_m - r_f)\beta_a. \qquad [16.4]$$

Equation 16.4 says a company's weighted average cost of capital is determined by the risk of its assets and is unaffected by its capital structure.

CALCULATING THE WEIGHTED AVERAGE COST OF CAPITAL

Use Equation 16.3 to calculate Durand Displays' weighted average cost of capital with no debt, $25,000 of debt, and $62,500 of debt. The cost of debt is constant at 6 percent. The market value of Durand's equity and its required rate of return on equity at these debt levels were computed in earlier illustrations and in Exercise 16.2. These values are repeated here for convenience.

Value of Debt	Value of Equity	Equity Required Rate of Return
$ 0	$125,000	10.0%
25,000	100,000	11.0
62,500	62,500	14.0

At $0 debt,

$$r_{wacc} = 6.0\% \times \frac{\$ \qquad 0}{\$125,000} + 10.0\% \times \frac{\$125,000}{\$125,000} = 10.0\%.$$

At $25,000 debt,

$$r_{wacc} = 6.0\% \times \frac{\$ \; 25,000}{\$125,000} + 11.0\% \times \frac{\$100,000}{\$125,000} = 10.0\%.$$

At $62,500 debt,

$$r_{wacc} = 6.0\% \times \frac{\$ \; 62,500}{\$125,000} + 14.0\% \times \frac{\$ \; 62,500}{\$125,000} = 10.0\%.$$

Durand Displays' weighted average cost of capital is 10 percent no matter how much debt the company uses because the financial market is perfect.

● ——————— ●

Now, we can determine Durand Displays' value by discounting its net free cash flows using its weighted average cost of capital. For any amount of debt, r_{wacc} = 10 percent. Therefore, the company's total value, V, is

$$V = \frac{\$12,500}{0.10} = \$125,000.$$

Our conclusion that the required rate of return on equity increases linearly with the use of financial leverage, causing the weighted average cost of capital to remain constant, is graphed in Exhibit 16.2. The use of financial leverage does not affect free cash flow, so the value of the firm remains constant at all levels of debt as shown in Exhibit 16.3.

16.2 THE EFFECT OF TAXES

Taxes change our conclusion that a company's capital structure has no effect on the company or its investors. Corporate taxes reduce the company's free cash flows and personal taxes may further reduce the owners' and creditors' personal cash flows. A company can shelter some of its cash flows from taxes by using debt in its capital structure and investors may be able to shelter some of their income by buying common stock. Under these circumstances, investors may no longer be indifferent to a company's choice of financing.

The Effect When Only Corporate Income Is Taxed

Modigliani and Miller corrected their classic article on capital structure to account for the effect of corporate taxes.[7] They recognized that when the government permits com-

---

[7]Franco Modigliani and Merton H. Miller, "Corporate Income Taxes and the Cost of Capital: A Correction," *American Economic Review*, June 1963, pp. 433–443.

Exhibit 16.2

THE EFFECT OF LEVERAGE ON REQUIRED RATES OF RETURN IN A PERFECT FINANCIAL MARKET

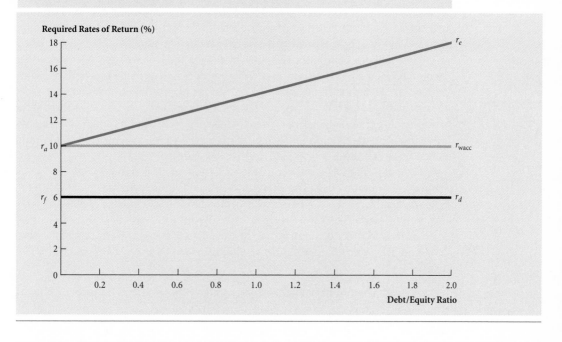

Exhibit 16.3

THE EFFECT OF LEVERAGE ON THE VALUE OF THE FIRM IN A PERFECT FINANCIAL MARKET

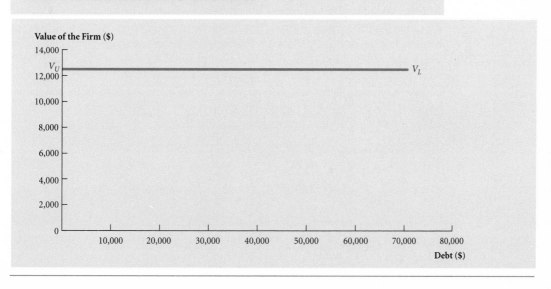

panies to deduct interest from taxable income, the use of debt provides an additional cash flow that equals the amount of the periodic tax-shield. The present value of the cash flows provided by the interest tax-shield is an addition to the company's value. Furthermore, this increase goes directly to the stockholders because the creditors have a fixed claim. Considering only corporate taxes, companies would use large amounts of debt in their capital structures to obtain large tax-shields and therefore large increases in value. To see these effects, we can modify our example of Durand Displays.

Table 16.5 gives Durand's cash flow statements and balance sheet when corporate income is taxed at a 35 percent rate. Taxes on cash flow provided by operations are $4,375. This leaves the company with $8,125 of net free cash flow. Taxes do not change the risk of these cash flows, so their value still is determined by discounting them at the required rate of return on assets, r_a, which equals 10 percent for Durand. The company's value if it is operated without leverage therefore is $81,250 and the value of an individual share of stock is $8.125 ($81,250/10,000 shares).

Table 16.6 describes the company's situation when it uses $25,000 of debt to repurchase common stock. The interest expense on this debt, $1,500 ($25,000 × 0.06) is tax-deductible, so the company's taxable income is only $11,000 ($12,500 − $1,500). Tax on this income is $3,850 ($11,000 × 0.35), so the net cash flow that can be paid to investors is $8,650. This amount is $525 more than the company's free cash flow when it had no debt. The difference is the savings provided by the interest tax-shield, ITS. That is,

$$\text{ITS} = \text{Amount of loan} \times \text{interest rate} \times \text{corporation's tax rate}$$
$$= D \times r_d \times T_c$$
$$= \$25,000 \times 0.06 \times 0.35 = \$525.$$

The interest tax-shield is shown as an adjustment to free cash flow in Table 16.6 to emphasize that its source is different.

We can still discount the company's free cash flow at r_a, however, we must use a different rate of return to discount the interest tax-shield because its risk is different. We can deduce the risk of the interest tax-shield by recognizing that it comprises the periodic interest payment, $1,500 for Durand, and the tax rate, 35 percent. There is no uncertainty about the tax rate (assuming governmental tax policies don't change), and the risk of the periodic interest payment equals the risk of the associated loan. Consequently, the interest tax-shield has the same risk as the company's debt and should be discounted at the same required rate of return, r_d. The present value of the interest tax-shield on Durand's perpetual debt is therefore

$$\text{PV(ITS)} = \frac{D \times r_d \times T_c}{r_d} = D \times T_c$$
$$= \frac{\$25,000 \times 0.06 \times 0.35}{0.06} = \$25,000 \times 0.35 = \$8,750.$$

The company's value when it is operated with leverage, V_L, is its unlevered value, V_U, plus the present value of the interest tax-shield. This value is given by Equation 16.5.

DURAND DISPLAYS' CASH FLOWS AND BALANCE SHEET   **Table 16.5**

Corporate Tax Rate $T_c = 35\%$
No Debt

Panel A: Cash Flow Statements

	Time 1 to ∞
Free Cash Flow	
Cash flow provided by (used for) operations	
Pre-tax cash flow provided by operations	$12,500
Taxes	(4,375)
After-tax cash flow provided by operations	8,125
Cash flow provided by (used for) investment	0
Cash flow provided by (used for) financial slack	0
Net free cash flow	$ 8,125
Adjustments to Free Cash Flow	
Interest tax shield	0
Net Cash Flow Payable to Investors	$ 8,125
Financial Cash Flow	
Pay interest	$ 0
Pay common stock dividends	(8,125)
Net financial cash flow	$ (8,125)

Panel B: Market-Value Balance Sheet

Assets		Claims	
Financial slack	$ 0	Debt	$ 0
Fixed assets	81,250	Equity	81,250
Total	$81,250	Total	$81,250

$$V_L = V_U + D \times T_c \qquad\qquad [16.5]$$

For Durand, this value is

$$V_L = \$81,250 + \$8,750 = \$90,000.$$

The market value of equity equals the market value of the firm minus the market value of the debt or $65,000 ($90,000 − $25,000). The debt was used to repurchase

Table 16.6   DURAND DISPLAYS' FINANCIAL CASH FLOWS AND BALANCE SHEET

Corporate Tax Rate $T_c = 35\%$
$25,000 of Debt

Panel A: Cash Flow Statements

	Time 1 to ∞
Net Free Cash Flow (from Table 16.5)	$ 8,125
Adjustments to Free Cash Flow	
Interest tax-shield	525
Net Cash Flow Payable to Investors	$ 8,650
Financial Cash Flow	
Pay interest	$(1,500)
Pay common stock dividends	(7,150)
Net financial cash flow	$(8,650)

Panel B: Market-Value Balance Sheet

Assets		Claims	
Financial slack	$ 0	Debt	$25,000
Fixed assets	90,000	Equity	65,000
Total	$90,000	Total	$90,000

3,076.92 shares of stock ($25,000/$8.125 per share), which leaves 6,923.08 shares of stock outstanding. The market value of a single share therefore equals $9.389 ($65,000/6,923.08 shares). By using debt, Durand increased the market value of each share of stock by $1.264 ($9.389 – $8.125). This increase is the per share value of the present value of the interest tax-shield ($8,750/6,923.08 shares).

E X E R C I S E

16.5   THE EFFECT OF LEVERAGE WITH CORPORATE TAXES

Prepare Durand Displays' financial cash flow statement and market-value balance sheet assuming the company borrows $62,500 and uses the proceeds to repurchase common stock.

Interest on the company's debt is $3,750 ($62,500 × 0.06). The net cash flow payable to investors equals the company's net free cash flow, $12,500, plus the tax-shield provided by this interest payment, $1,312.50 ($62,500 × 0.06 × 0.35). The total is $9,437.50. Subtracting the interest payment from the total cash flow payable to investors leaves $5,687.50 for common stock dividends.

The present value of the interest tax-shield, $21,875 ($1,312.50/0.06) is added to the value of the company without leverage, $81,250, to determine its total value, $103,125. The value of the equity is therefore $40,625 ($103,125 − $62,500). Durand Displays' financial cash flow statement and market-value balance sheet are:

Financial Cash Flows

Pay interest	$(3,750.00)
Pay dividends	(5,687.50)
Net cash flow	$(9,437.50)

Market-Value Balance Sheet

Assets	$103,125
Claims	
Debt	62,500
Equity	40,625
Total	$103,125

There is more cash that can be paid to investors and the company has a higher value with more debt because its tax-shield is larger.

● ——————— ●

Once again, we must compare the expected and required rates of return to ensure the new common stock price is an equilibrium value. Table 16.6 shows the stockholders are paid $7,150 of dividends or $1.033 per share ($7,150/6,923.08 shares of stock). The expected rate of return is therefore 11 percent ($1.033/$9.389).

The required rate of return is obtained from the CAPM, however, we need a new expression for the equity beta because the tax-deductibility of interest changes the relationship between a company's asset risk and its equity risk. The new equation is

$$\beta_e = \beta_a \times [1 + (1 - T_c) \times D/E].\qquad [16.6]$$

This expression is conceptually the same as Equation 16.2 except it accounts for the fact that debt is not as costly when interest payments are tax-deductible.

Applying Equation 16.6 to Durand's capital structure,

$$\beta_e = 1.0 \times [1 + (1 - 0.35) \times \$25,000/\$65,000] = 1.25.$$

The equity required rate of return is therefore

$$r_e = 0.06 + (0.10 - 0.06) \times 1.25 = 0.11 \text{ or } 11\%.$$

The required rate of return equals the expected rate of return at a market price of $9.389 per share, so this is the equilibrium stock price.

THE EFFECT OF LEVERAGE ON RISK AND THE PRICE PER SHARE

Compare the expected and required rates of return on Durand Displays' common stock assuming the company borrows $62,500 and uses the proceeds to repurchase common stock.

The company will repurchase 7,692.31 ($62,500 debt/$8.125 per share) shares of stock, leaving 2,307.69 shares outstanding (10,000 – 7,692.31). Total dividends and the total value of the equity are $5,687.50 and $40,625 (from Exercise 16.5). Dividing these values by 2,307.69 shares outstanding gives dividends per share and price per share, $2.465 and $17.604. The expected rate of return therefore is 14.0 percent ($2.465/$17.604).

Durand Displays has $62,500 of debt and $40,625 of equity, so its equity beta is

$$\beta_e = 1.0 \times [1 + (1 - 0.35) \times \$62,500/\$40,625] = 2.0.$$

Substituting this value into the Capital Asset Pricing Model with $r_f = 0.06$ and $r_m = 0.10$,

$$r_e = 0.06 + (0.10 - 0.06) \times 2.0 = 0.14 \text{ or } 14.0\%.$$

The expected rate of return equals the required rate of return, so $17.604 is an equilibrium stock price.

The Weighted Average Cost of Capital with Taxes

We can see this result in general terms by examining the effect of debt on the company's weighted average cost of capital. The equation for the weighted average cost of capital is the same as before except the required rate of return on debt is multiplied by one minus the tax rate because the interest payments are tax-deductible. This is the form of the expression for the weighted average cost of capital that we used in Chapter 9.

$$r_{\text{wacc}} = r_d \times (1 - T_c) \times \frac{D}{D + E} + r_e \times \frac{E}{D + E} \qquad [16.7]$$

The debt is riskless, so $r_d = r_f$ and the required rate of return on equity is given by the CAPM with

$$\beta_e = \beta_a \times [1 + (1 - T_c) \times D/E].$$

Substituting these expressions into the equation for the weighted average cost of capital and simplifying,

$$r_{\text{wacc}} = r_a \times \left[1 - T_c \times \frac{D}{D + E} \right]. \qquad [16.8]$$

Equation 16.8 says a company's weighted average cost of capital equals the required rate of return on its assets if it is all-equity financed but that it declines by a factor that depends on the tax rate and the amount of debt in the company's capital structure. A company's free cash flow is unaffected by the use of financial leverage therefore the decline in its weighted average cost of capital produces an increase in its value that belongs to the common stockholders.

CALCULATING THE WEIGHTED AVERAGE COST OF CAPITAL

Use Equation 16.7 to calculate Durand Displays' weighted average cost of capital with no debt, $25,000 of debt, and $62,500 of debt given a corporate tax rate of 35 percent. Confirm your answers using Equation 16.8. The cost of debt is constant at 6 percent. The market value of Durand's equity and its required rate of return on equity at these debt levels were computed in earlier illustrations and in Exercise 16.6. These values are repeated here for convenience.

Value of Debt	Value of Equity	Equity Required Rate of Return
$ 0	$ 81,250	10.0%
25,000	65,000	11.0
62,500	40,625	14.0

At $0 debt,

$$r_{wacc} = r_d \times (1 - T_c) \times \frac{D}{D + E} + r_e \times \frac{E}{D + E}$$

$$= 6.0\% \times (1 - 0.35) \times \frac{\$0}{\$81,250} + 10.0\% \times \frac{\$81,250}{\$81,250} = 10.00\%$$

$$r_{wacc} = r_a \times \left[1 - T_c \times \frac{D}{D + E}\right]$$

$$= 10.0\% \times (1 - 0.35 \times \$0/\$81,250) = 10.00\%.$$

At $25,000 debt,

$$r_{wacc} = 6.0\% \times (1 - 0.35) \times \frac{\$25,000}{\$90,000} + 11.0\% \times \frac{\$65,000}{\$90,000} = 9.03\%$$

$$r_{wacc} = 10.0\% \times (1 - 0.35 \times \$25,000/\$90,000) = 9.03\%.$$

At $62,500 debt,

$$r_{wacc} = 6.0\% \times (1 - 0.35) \times \frac{\$62,500}{\$103,125} + 14.0\% \times \frac{\$40,625}{\$103,125} = 7.88\%$$

$$r_{wacc} = 10.0\% \times (1 - 0.35 \times \$62,500/\$103,125) = 7.88\%.$$

Durand Displays' weighted average cost of capital declines with the use of leverage because interest is tax-deductible.

Now that we have an expression for the weighted average cost of capital that incorporates the effect of the interest tax-shield, we can determine a company's value by using this rate of return to discount its net free cash flow. That is,

$$V_L = \frac{\text{Net free cash flow}}{r_{\text{wacc}}} . \qquad [16.9]$$

We should get the same answer as we did by using Equation 16.5, $V_L = V_U + D \times T_c$.

Assuming Durand uses $25,000 of debt, its weighted average cost of capital is 9.02778 percent (we rounded this number to 9.03 percent above), so its value is

$$V_L = \$8{,}125/0.0902778 = \$90{,}000.$$

Why should this be the same value as we obtained earlier? Equation 16.5 recognizes the value of the interest tax-shield by discounting this cash flow at its own required rate of return. Equation 16.9 recognizes the value of the interest tax-shield by adjusting the required rate of return and using it to discount the net free cash flows. We should obtain the same answer using either method if our adjustments are consistent as they are here. We will have more to say about this issue in Chapter 17.

E X E R C I S E

16.8   USING r_{WACC} TO DETERMINE A COMPANY'S VALUE

Use Equation 16.9 to determine Durand Displays' value if it uses no debt or $62,500 of debt in its capital structure. How do the results compare with the results obtained earlier using Equation 16.5?

With no debt, Durand Displays' weighted average cost of capital is 10 percent, therefore,

$$V_L = \$8{,}125/0.10 = \$81{,}250.$$

With $62,500 debt, the company's weighted average cost of capital is 7.87879 (rounded to 7.88 percent above), therefore,

$$V_L = \$8{,}125/0.0787879 = \$103{,}124.97.$$

These are the same values obtained earlier using Equation 16.5.

Exhibit 16.4 shows how the use of debt affects a company's required rates of return in the presence of corporate taxes. The required rate of return on equity increases linearly with the use of debt, although the rate of increase is reduced by the tax-deductibility of interest. As a result, the company's weighted average cost of capital declines with the use of debt financing. The decrease in the weighted average cost of capital is manifest as an increase in the company's market value, as shown in Exhibit 16.5.

Equation 16.5 and Exhibit 16.5 indicate that a company can increase its value without limit. This implies companies would use a very large amount of debt to obtain the

Exhibit 16.4

THE EFFECT OF LEVERAGE ON REQUIRED RATES OF RETURN WITH CORPORATE TAXES

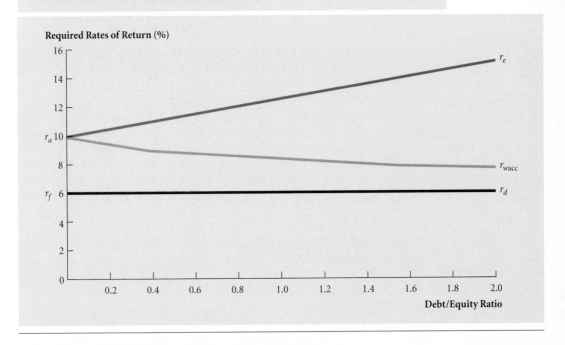

Exhibit 16.5

THE EFFECT OF LEVERAGE ON THE VALUE OF THE FIRM WITH CORPORATE TAXES

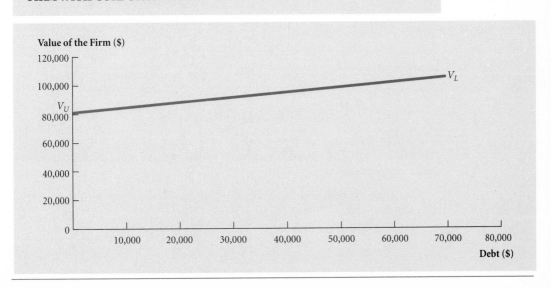

highest possible value. We don't see companies using nearly 100 percent debt in their capital structures, so we must examine other financial market imperfections and the effects of asymmetric information to see what limits the use of debt in reality.

The Effect When Corporate and Personal Income Are Taxed

Subsequent to his early work with Modigliani, Miller made an additional adjustment to capital structure theory to account for the fact that individuals must pay taxes on the income they receive from investing in debt and equity.[8] The most important feature of his model is the recognition that the effective personal tax rate on interest income may be different from the effective personal tax rate on equity income. This difference arises because interest income is recognized and taxed each year while some equity income is deferred to the future when it is paid as a capital gain rather than a current dividend. The time value of money makes the effective tax rate on the deferred income lower even if the statutory tax rates are the same and there may be an additional reduction if capital gains are subject to a preferential tax rate. Everything else constant, investors may prefer to buy stock, which provides a partial tax-shield from personal taxes, rather than bonds, which do not.

Personal taxes make the individual's situation just the opposite of the company's. The company can use debt financing to obtain the corporate interest tax-shield, however, this denies the personal tax-shield to investors. Conversely, the company can relinquish the corporate interest tax-shield and use equity financing to enable investors to shelter their personal income.

Both corporate and personal tax-shields ultimately benefit the investors because *they* receive the company's after-tax cash flows. Consequently, they will want the tax-shield to be placed where it does the most good. This means the company should use equity financing if investors' effective tax rate on equity income is less than their effective tax rate on interest and vice versa. The company's capital structure is irrelevant (again) if these tax rates are equal.

The interaction of corporate and personal tax rates that affects the preference for using debt or equity is easily described. Each dollar of corporate cash flow distributed as interest escapes corporate taxes (because interest is tax-deductible) but is subject to personal taxes at the recipient's tax rate. That is,

$$\text{After-tax cash flow of a dollar distributed as interest} = \$1.00 \times (1 - T_d)$$

where T_d = personal tax rate on income from debt.

Each dollar of corporate cash flow distributed as equity income (paid as dividends or reinvested for growth) is taxed first at the corporate level and again at the personal level at the recipient's tax rate.

$$\text{After-tax cash flow of a dollar distributed as dividends or growth} =$$
$$\$1.00 \times (1 - T_c) \times (1 - T_e)$$

[8]Merton Miller, "Debt and Taxes," *Journal of Finance,* May 1977, pp. 261–275.

where T_c = corporate tax rate

T_e = personal tax rate on income from equity

A company should finance with debt or equity according to which of these values is larger. That is,

Use debt if $(1 - T_d) > (1 - T_c) \times (1 - T_e)$
Use either if $(1 - T_d) = (1 - T_c) \times (1 - T_e)$
Use equity if $(1 - T_d) < (1 - T_c) \times (1 - T_e)$.

After placing both terms on the left-hand side, these conditions become

Use debt if $(1 - T_d) - (1 - T_c) \times (1 - T_e) > 0$
Use either if $(1 - T_d) - (1 - T_c) \times (1 - T_e) = 0$
Use equity if $(1 - T_d) - (1 - T_c) \times (1 - T_e) < 0$.

As an illustration, suppose T_c = 34 percent, T_d = 28 percent, and T_e = 15 percent. Then investors receive $(1 - 0.28) = 0.72$ or 72 percent of each dollar distributed as interest and only $(1 - 0.34) \times (1 - 0.15) = 0.561$ or 56.1 percent of each dollar distributed as dividends or growth. In this situation, the company should use debt financing.

EXERCISE 16.9

THE INTERACTION OF CORPORATE AND PERSONAL TAXES

Do investors receive a larger after-tax cash flow from a dollar distributed as interest or dividends and growth if T_c = 34 percent, T_d = 36 percent, and T_e = 0 percent? Should the company obtain financing by using debt or equity?

After-tax cash flow received by creditors = $1 \times (1 - 0.36) = $0.64

After-tax cash flow received by owners = $1 \times (1 - 0.34) \times (1 - 0.00) = $0.66

Investors receive a larger after-tax cash flow from a dollar distributed as dividends or growth, so the company should obtain financing by using equity.

The present value of a company's interest tax-shield is no longer simply $D \times T_c$, as shown in Equation 16.5, when there are personal taxes. This is because the personal tax rates on income from debt and equity can make the company's tax-shield more or less attractive to investors than their own tax-shields. The revised expression for the value of the tax-shield is given below.

Present value of company's interest tax-shield = $D \times T_n$

where T_n = net tax rate that applies to corporate debt

$$T_n = \frac{(1 - T_d) - (1 - T_c) \times (1 - T_e)}{(1 - T_d)}$$

The revised equation for the value of a levered firm is

$$V_L = V_U + D \times T_n. \qquad [16.10]$$

Note that the numerator of the net tax rate is the condition used above to determine whether investors receive a larger after-tax cash flow from a dollar distributed as debt or equity income. We determined that the company should use debt financing when this term is positive; Equation 16.10 shows that the resulting interest tax-shield increases the value of the firm. Conversely, we determined that the company should not use debt financing if $(1 - T_d) - (1 - T_c) \times (1 - T_e) < 0$. Equation 16.10 shows that the interest tax-shield is negative, confirming the conclusion that the personal tax-shield is more valuable than the corporate tax-shield in this case. Finally, the company can use either debt or equity financing when $(1 - T_d) - (1 - T_c) \times (1 - T_e) = 0$ because investors receive the same after-tax income from both debt and equity and the present value of the interest tax-shield is zero.

Panel A of Table 16.7 shows how personal taxes of 39.6 percent on income from debt and 36 percent on income from equity affect Durand Displays' capital structure decision. The after-tax cash flow received by owners is the company's cash flow provided by operations minus interest payments multiplied by $(1 - T_c) \times (1 - T_e)$. The after-tax cash flow received by creditors is the interest payment multiplied by $(1 - T_d)$. In panel A, these calculations are as follows.

No Debt

After-tax cash flow received by owners $= (\$12,500 - \$0) \times (1 - 0.35) \times (1 - 0.36) = \$5,200$

After-tax cash flow received by creditors $= \$0 \times (1 - 0.396) = \$0$

\$25,000 Debt

After-tax cash flow received by owners $= (\$12,500 - \$1,500) \times (1 - 0.35) \times (1 - 0.36) = \$4,576$

After-tax cash flow received by creditors $= \$1,500 \times (1 - 0.396) = \$906.00$

The total amount of after-tax cash flow investors receive is \$5,200 with no debt and \$5,482 (\$4,576 + \$906) with \$25,000 of debt. Investors receive more after-tax cash flow with debt than without because $(1 - T_d) = 0.604 > (1 - T_c) \times (1 - T_e) = 0.416$. That is, these corporate and personal tax rates favor the use of debt as the method of financing.

The company's value and the price of an individual share of stock are similarly affected. With no debt, the company's value is

$$V_U = \frac{\text{Net free cash flow}}{r_a} = \frac{\$8,125}{0.10} = \$81,250.$$

The value of the equity is the value of the company minus the value of debt or \$81,250 − \$0 = \$81,250. There are 10,000 shares of stock outstanding, so the value of an individual share is \$8.125.

DURAND DISPLAYS' CASH FLOWS AND BALANCE SHEETS

Table 16.7

Corporate Tax Rate $T_c = 35\%$

Panel A:
Personal Tax Rate on Income from Debt $T_d = 39.6\%$
Personal Tax Rate on Income from Equity $T_e = 36.0\%$

	No Debt	$25,000 Debt
After-tax cash flow received by owners	$ 5,200.00	$ 4,576.00
After-tax cash flow received by creditors	0	906.00
Total after-tax cash flow	$ 5,200.00	$ 5,482.00
Value of debt	$ 0	$25,000.00
Value of equity	81,250.00	64,032.50
Value of the company	$81,250.00	$89,032.50
Number of shares outstanding	10,000	6,923.08
Value of 1 share of common stock	$ 8.125	$ 9.249

Panel B:
Personal Tax Rate on Income from Debt $T_d = 39.6\%$
Personal Tax Rate on Income from Equity $T_e = 7.077\%$

	No Debt	$25,000 Debt
After-tax cash flow received by owners	$ 7,550.00	$ 6,644.00
After-tax cash flow received by creditors	0	906.00
Total after-tax cash flow	$ 7,550.00	$ 7,550.00
Value of debt	$ 0	$25,000.00
Value of equity	81,250.00	56,250.00
Value of the company	$81,250.00	$81,250.00
Number of shares outstanding	10,000	6,923.08
Value of 1 share of common stock	$ 8.125	$ 8.125

Panel C:
Personal Tax Rate on Income from Debt $T_d = 39.6\%$
Personal Tax Rate on Income from Equity $T_e = 0\%$

	No Debt	$25,000 Debt
After-tax cash flow received by owners	$ 8,125.00	$ 7,150.00
After-tax cash flow received by creditors	0	906.00
Total after-tax cash flow	$ 8,125.00	$ 8,056.00
Value of debt	$ 0	$25,000.00
Value of equity	81,250.00	54,346.00
Value of the company	$81,250.00	$79,346.00
Number of shares outstanding	10,000	6,923.08
Value of 1 share of common stock	$ 8.125	$ 7.850

With $25,000 debt, the company's value is $V_L = V_U + D \times T_n$. The net tax rate that applies to corporate debt is

$$T_n = \frac{(1 - T_d) - (1 - T_c) \times (1 - T_e)}{(1 - T_d)}$$

$$= \frac{(1 - 0.396) - (1 - 0.35) \times (1 - 0.36)}{(1 - 0.396)} = 0.3113.$$

Therefore, the company's value equals $81,250 + $25,000 × 0.3113 = $89,032.50. The value of the equity is $89,032.50 − $25,000 = $64,032.50. The debt was used to repurchase 3,076.92 shares of stock ($25,000/$8.125), leaving 6,923.08 shares outstanding. Therefore, the value of an individual share of stock is $64,032.50/6,923.08 shares = $9.249.

By using debt, Durand Displays is able to increase the after-tax cash flows paid to investors and the value of a single share of stock because the corporate tax-shield is more valuable than personal tax-shields at these tax rates.

The entries in panels B and C were computed the same way. The difference is that the company may use either source of financing at the tax rates in panel B because $(1 - T_d) = 0.604 = (1 - T_c) \times (1 - T_e)$. The company should remain unlevered at the tax rates in panel C because $(1 - T_d) = 0.604 < (1 - T_c) \times (1 - T_e) = 0.65$.

EXERCISE •————————————————————————————•

16.10   **THE EFFECT OF LEVERAGE WITH CORPORATE AND PERSONAL TAXES**

Determine the after-tax cash flows paid to investors, the value of the company's debt and equity, and the price of a share of stock if Durand Displays borrows $62,500 and uses the proceeds to repurchase common stock. The tax rates are T_c = 35 percent, T_d = 39.6 percent, and T_e = 36 percent. Use Table 16.7 as an example.

The net tax rate that applies to Durand Displays' debt, T_n, was computed above as 31.13 percent.

After-tax cash flow received by owners	$ 3,640.00
After-tax cash flow received by creditors	2,265.00
Total after-tax cash flow	$ 5,905.00
Value of debt	$ 62,500.00
Value of equity	38,206.25
Value of the company	$100,706.25
Number of shares outstanding	2,307.69
Value of 1 share of common stock	$ 16.556

Durand's value is not as large as it was in Exercise 16.5 ($100,706.25 versus $103,125) because personal taxes reduce the net tax rate that applies to the company's debt.

•————— •—————

A problem with this interpretation of the effect of personal taxes is that a company would have an *all*-debt capital structure (panels A and B) or an *all*-equity capital structure (panels B and C) if tax rates are static. A company could choose a mixture of debt and equity if tax rates are as given in panel B, however, there is no reason to do so. Companies actually use a mixture of debt and equity financing, so we must continue our search for the factors that gradually limit the use of debt.[9]

16.3   THE EFFECT OF FINANCIAL DISTRESS

Financial distress is the disruption of normal operating and financial conditions caused by impending insolvency. Any company with fixed costs becomes financially distressed when its cash inflows are insufficient to cover its cash outflows. This means a company with fixed operating costs can become financially distressed even if it has no debt in its capital structure. Conversely, a company without fixed operating costs can become financially distressed if it uses debt financing.[10]

We will take the structure of a company's operating costs as given and assume there are no taxes in this section and focus on how its capital structure affects the likelihood and cost of distress. We will see that the use of debt increases the probability of financial distress and imposes the costs, if any, on the owners. Finally, we will discuss how the characteristics of a company's assets and claims affect the magnitudes of these costs.

The Effect in a Perfect Market

The first fact we must establish is that financial distress does not affect a company's choice of capital structure in a perfect financial market. The reason is that there are no *costs* of distress in this situation, so a company's market value simply is divided among the claimants. This division affects how much the owners and creditors receive—but not the total. Therefore, the company's total value and the value of one share of common stock are the same with and without debt.

We will use another numerical example to illustrate this result. This example will differ from earlier ones because we'll assume owners and creditors are risk-neutral. Remember from Chapter 5 that this means they only care about the expected amount of cash flows they receive and not the risk. Consequently, we can discount the company's expected free cash flows, interest, and dividend payments at the riskless rate of interest to determine the associated market values.[11]

Bean and Blossom Manufacturing Company (BBMC) makes lawn and garden furniture. Buying outdoor furniture is discretionary spending for most families, so

---

[9]The interaction of corporate and personal tax rates could cause companies to initially use one type of financing and then switch to another if these tax rates change. Some finance scholars have argued that a company's effective tax rate declines as it uses more debt in its capital structure because it has other tax-shields that reduce or eliminate the ability to deduct interest payments. See Harry DeAngelo and Ronald Masulis, "Optimal Capital Structure Under Corporate and Personal Taxes," *Journal of Financial Economics*, March 1980, pp. 5–29.

[10]Perhaps these disruptions are called *financial* distress because there is no distress if the cash flow shortages can be covered with new financing.

[11]This is a valuable simplification because debt is not riskless when there are distress costs. This means we would need to develop a model of the required rate of return on risky debt for these illustrations. Doing this would take us far afield but provide no additional understanding so we will avoid this work by assuming investors are risk-neutral.

Table 16.8   BEAN AND BLOSSOM'S CASH FLOWS AND BALANCE SHEET

Costless Financial Distress
No Debt

Panel A: Cash Flow Statements

	Strong	Weak	Expected
		Economic Conditions	
Probability	0.50	0.50	
Free Cash Flow			
Cash flow provided by (used for) operations	$ 54,060	$ 9,540	$ 31,800
Cash flow provided by (used for) investment	0	0	0
Cash flow provided by (used for) financial slack	0	0	0
Net free cash flow	$ 54,060	$ 9,540	$ 31,800
Adjustments to Free Cash Flow			
Distress costs	0	0	0
Net Cash Flow Payable to Investors	$ 54,060	$ 9,540	$ 31,800
Financial Cash Flow			
Pay interest and repay debt	$ 0	$ 0	$ 0
Pay common stock dividends	(54,060)	(9,540)	(31,800)
Net financial cash flow	$(54,060)	$(9,540)	$(31,800)

Panel B: Market-Value Balance Sheet

Assets		Claims	
Financial slack	$ 0	Debt	$ 0
Fixed assets	30,000	Equity	30,000
Total	$30,000	Total	$30,000

BBMC's sales are very sensitive to economic conditions. This sensitivity is reflected in next year's cash flows provided by operations, which will be $54,060 and $9,540 under strong and weak economic conditions. These economic scenarios are equally likely (probability 0.50). The owners will liquidate the company after next year's business is concluded and distribute BBMC's assets to the claimants.

Table 16.8 gives BBMC's cash statements and market-value balance sheets if it is all-equity financed with 3,000 shares of stock outstanding. The value of the company's assets is next year's expected free cash flow, $31,800 (0.5 × $54,060 + 0.5 × $9,540), discounted at the riskless rate of interest, 0.06. This value is $30,000 ($31,800/1.06). The

---

BEAN AND BLOSSOM'S FINANCIAL CASH FLOWS AND BALANCE SHEET   **Table 16.9**

Costless Financial Distress
$10,500 of Debt

Panel A: Cash Flow Statements

| | Economic Conditions | | |
	Strong	Weak	Expected
Probability	0.50	0.50	
Net Free Cash Flow (from Table 16.8)	$ 54,060	$ 9,540	$ 31,800
Adjustments to Free Cash Flow			
Distress costs	0	0	0
Net Cash Flow Payable to Investors	$ 54,060	$ 9,540	$ 31,800
Financial Cash Flow			
Pay interest and repay debt	$(11,130)	$(9,540)	$(10,335)
Pay common stock dividends	(42,930)	0	(21,465)
Net financial cash flow	$(54,060)	$(9,540)	$(31,800)

Panel B: Market-Value Balance Sheet

Assets		Claims	
Financial slack	$ 0	Debt	$ 9,750
Fixed assets	30,000	Equity	20,250
Total	$30,000	Total	$30,000

---

value of the equity is also $30,000, so the value of a single share of stock is $10.00 ($30,000/3,000 shares outstanding).

Table 16.9 gives BBMC's cash statements and market-value balance sheets if the company sells 6 percent bonds with a face value of $10,500 to repurchase shares of stock. The bondholders therefore have a claim of $11,130 ($10,500 × 1.06) on the company's cash flows. The company's free cash flows are the same as if it used no debt, so the market value of its assets is $30,000.

The bondholders are paid in full if the economy is strong but receive only $9,540 if it is weak. The bondholders expect to receive $10,335 (0.5 × $11,130 + 0.5 × $9,540) in one year, so they will pay only $9,750 ($10,335/1.06) for the bonds. Therefore, the value of the equity must be $20,250 ($30,000 – $9,750). You can confirm this value by discounting the stockholders' expected cash flow of $21,465 (0.5 × $42,930 + 0.5 × $0) at 6 percent, which equals $20,250.

The $9,750 was used to repurchase 975 shares of stock at $10 per share, leaving 2,025 shares outstanding. The market value of each share of stock is therefore still $10.00 ($20,250/2,025 shares). The market value of $10 per share with and without debt establishes that financial distress does not affect a company's choice of capital structure in a perfect financial market.

EXERCISE

16.11

FINANCIAL DISTRESS IN A PERFECT MARKET

Prepare BBMC's financial cash flow statement and market-value balance sheet assuming the company borrows $15,000 and uses the proceeds to repurchase common stock. What is the price of an individual share of stock?

The company's expected net cash flow payable to investors is $31,800 (0.5 × $54,060 + 0.5 × $9,540). BBMC owes the bondholders $15,900 ($15,000 × 1.06). The company can pay this amount in full in a strong economy but can pay only $9,540 otherwise. Consequently, the creditors expect to receive $12,720 (0.5 × $15,900 + 0.5 × $9,540). This leaves $19,080 to pay dividends. The creditors will pay only $12,000 ($12,720/1.06) for the bonds when they are issued and the owners will pay only $18,000 ($19,080/1.06) for the stock. The company's market value is the sum of these amounts, $30,000. Therefore BBMC's financial cash flow statement and market-value balance sheet are:

Financial Cash Flows

Pay interest and repay debt	$(12,720)
Pay dividends	(19,080)
Net cash flow	$(31,800)

Market-Value Balance Sheet

Assets	$ 30,000
Claims	
Debt	12,000
Equity	18,000
Total	$ 30,000

BBMC can use the $12,000 proceeds from issuing debt to repurchase 1,200 shares of stock ($12,000 debt/$10.00 per share), leaving 1,800 shares outstanding. These shares are worth $10 each ($18,000/1,800 shares). The use of debt did not affect the value of the company's stock because financial distress is costless.

The Effect in an Imperfect Market

Financial distress is costly in an imperfect financial market. Companies that become distressed may lose sales to stronger competitors and companies that are reorganized or liquidated may be forced to sell assets for less than their economic value. In addition, companies must pay the attorneys, accountants, and trustees who administer and

BEAN AND BLOSSOM'S FINANCIAL CASH FLOWS AND BALANCE SHEET	Table 16.10

Costly Financial Distress
$10,500 of Debt

Panel A: Cash Flow Statements

	Economic Conditions		
	Strong	**Weak**	**Expected**
Probability	0.50	0.50	
Net Free Cash Flow (from Table 16.8)	$ 54,060	$ 9,540	$ 31,800
Adjustments to Free Cash Flow			
Distress costs	0	(4,770)	(2,385)
Net Cash Flow Payable to Investors	$ 54,060	$ 4,770	$ 29,415
Financial Cash Flow			
Pay interest and repay debt	$(11,130)	$(4,770)	$ (7,950)
Pay common stock dividends	(42,930)	0	(21,465)
Net financial cash flow	$(54,060)	$(4,770)	$(29,415)

Panel B: Market-Value Balance Sheet

Assets		Claims	
Financial slack	$ 0	Debt	$ 7,500
Fixed assets	27,750	Equity	20,250
Total	$27,750	Total	$27,750

supervise this process. The cash flows lost for these reasons are the costs of financial distress. These costs ultimately are borne by the owners and can make the use of debt unattractive to them. We can see these effects by incorporating distress cost in our Bean and Blossom Manufacturing Company example. The results are presented in Table 16.10.

Let's suppose BBMC incurs financial distress costs of $4,770 when its cash flows are insufficient to satisfy the bondholders' claims in full. The company does not incur these costs when the economy is strong but does when it is weak. Their net free cash flows after adjusting for distress costs are therefore $54,060 in a strong economy, $4,770 in a weak economy, and $29,415 on average (0.50 × $54,060 + 0.50 × $4,770). The value of the company's assets is therefore $27,750 ($29,415/1.06). Note that the difference between the values of the company's assets without and with distress costs ($30,000 − $27,750) equals the present value of the expected cost of distress ($2,385/1.06).

The creditors own bonds that entitle them to principal and interest of $11,130 ($10,500 × 1.06). They are paid in full in a strong economy but receive only $4,770, the company's free cash flows after subtracting distress costs, in a weak economy. They therefore expect to receive only $7,950 (0.50 × $11,130 + 0.50 × $4,770) when the bonds mature in one year. The market value of the bonds is therefore only $7,500 ($7,950/1.06).

The market value of the equity is the market value of the company's assets minus the market value of the debt, $20,250 ($27,750 − $7,500). You can obtain the same value by discounting the common stockholders' expected dividends, $21,465/1.06.

At first glance, it may appear that the creditors bear the costs of financial distress because the value of the bonds has declined by the present value of the expected costs of distress, $2,250, while the value of the equity has remained the same. This inference is incorrect, however, because the lower market value of the bonds means less money is available to repurchase shares of common stock. The bonds sell for $7,500 with distress costs and provide enough money to repurchase only 750 shares of stock ($7,500/$10 per share). This leaves 2,250 shares outstanding, so the market price per share is $9.00 ($20,250/2,250 shares). The shareholders bear the costs of financial distress because the $1.00 decrease in the stock price exactly equals the present value of the per share costs of financial distress ($2,250/2,250 shares).

Given the choice between no debt and $10,500 of debt in the presence of $4,770 distress costs, the owners of Bean and Blossom Manufacturing Company would prefer to have an all-equity capital structure.

EXERCISE

16.12   FINANCIAL DISTRESS IN AN IMPERFECT MARKET

Prepare BBMC's financial cash flow statement and market-value balance sheet assuming the company borrows $15,000 and uses the proceeds to repurchase common stock. Financial distress costs are $4,770. What is the price of an individual share of stock?

The company's expected net free cash flow is $31,800 (0.5 × $54,060 + 0.5 × $9,540) and its expected distress costs are $2,385 (0.5 × $0 + 0.5 × $4,770). Therefore, the expected net cash flow payable to investors is $29,415 ($31,800 − $2,385). BBMC owes the bondholders $15,900 ($15,000 × 1.06). The company can pay this amount in full in a strong economy but can pay only $4,770 after deducting distress costs if the economy is weak. Consequently, the creditors expect to receive $10,335 (0.5 × $15,900 + 0.5 × $4,770) which leaves $19,080 to pay dividends. The creditors will pay only $9,750 ($10,335/1.06) for the bonds when they are issued and the owners will pay only $18,000 ($19,080/1.06) for the stock. The company's market value is the sum of these amounts, $27,750. Therefore BBMC's financial cash flow statement and market-value balance sheet are

Financial Cash Flows

Pay interest and repay debt	$(10,335)
Pay dividends	(19,080)
Net cash flow	$(29,415)

Market-Value Balance Sheet

Assets	$27,750
Claims	
Debt	9,750
Equity	18,000
Total	$27,750

BBMC can repurchase 975 shares of stock ($9,750 debt/$10.00 per share), leaving 2,025 shares outstanding. These shares are worth $8.889 each ($18,000/2,025 shares). The use of debt reduced the value of each share of stock by $1.111, the present value of the expected cost of distress ($2,385/1.06/2,025 shares outstanding).

● —————— ●

Types of Distress Costs

The costs of financial distress are the actual costs of reorganizing or liquidating a company that fails plus the actual and opportunity costs that arise when suppliers, employees, and customers believe that a financial crisis is imminent. These actual and opportunity costs are called the direct and indirect costs of financial distress.

The **direct costs of financial distress** are the fees paid to accountants, financial consultants, attorneys, and trustees who devise, evaluate, contest, and administer the process by which a company is reorganized or liquidated. Companies may be forced into this situation by their creditors when they are unable to pay their bills or when the value of their liabilities exceeds the value of their assets. Alternatively, they may voluntarily declare bankruptcy to obtain legal protection from their creditors while they work out a survival plan.

Direct costs of financial distress probably differ among similarly sized companies according to the complexity of their claims. Contrast a closely held company that has a loan from a single private lender and a publicly held company that has several private, trade credit, bank, and market loans. The company with a single private loan probably can avoid reorganization or liquidation longer than the company with market loans because private lenders have better information and can protect their interests without resorting to legal remedies. Even if the companies enter bankruptcy, the competing claims should be easier and less costly to sort out when there are a small number of owners and a single lender. After all, the claimants and their attorneys in the first case may be able to sit around a single table to conduct their negotiations while the same parties in the second case may not fit in a large auditorium.

The direct costs of financial distress may be large in dollar terms but usually are small when stated as a percentage of the value of the distressed company. For example, Warner estimated that the direct costs of financial distress in 11 railroad bankruptcies were only 1 percent of the companies' market values seven years prior to the onset of distress.[12] Costs of this magnitude may not have a material effect on a company's choice of capital structure.

---

[12]Jerold B. Warner, "Bankruptcy Costs: Some Evidence," *Journal of Finance,* May 1977, pp. 337–348.

I N   T H E   N E W S

SOME INDIRECT COSTS OF FINANCIAL DISTRESS

The Costs of Losing Supplier Credit

CALDOR CORP., WHICH in September sought protection under Chapter 11 of the U.S. Bankruptcy Code, seems to have succumbed to a "bank run" in modern form. In August, trade creditors got nervous when Caldor announced that sales of garden hoses, toasters, and such were down about 10 percent for the month in stores open at least a year. In particular, its "factors," the tight-lipped and rather dour individuals who finance a portion of inventory, did what nervous lenders always do—they ran. And factors, which in this case included CIT Group Holdings, Republic Factors, and Heller Financial, are the lead steer. When they cut off credit, Caldor's herd of vendors stopped shipping goods. Bingo, Chapter 11.

The Costs of Attracting Good Executives

With a stronger economy producing more job opportunities at healthy companies, business stars now are less eager to join risky situations. To attract talent, sick companies are piling on the incentives. Among them: triple the usual number of stock options; guaranteed bonuses; longer employment contracts; two years instead of one year of severance pay; and financial protection against a possible bankruptcy filing. Coram Healthcare Corp. landed Donald J. Amaral as its $600,000-a-year president and CEO in mid-October by extending him options that represent about 5.4 percent of its outstanding shares. "This is not an easy job," Mr. Amaral said. Coram "is the biggest train wreck I've ever seen."

Sources: Roger Lowenstein, "Lenders' Stampede Tramples Caldor," *The Wall Street Journal*, October 26, 1995, p. C1; and Joann S. Lubin, "Top Jobs at Troubled Companies Go Begging," *The Wall Street Journal*, December 27, 1995, p. 13.

The **indirect costs of financial distress** are the actual and opportunity costs of the disruptions to normal business that occur in anticipation of and during a crisis. These disruptions can affect every aspect of a company's operations including purchasing, production, and sales. The mere hint of financial distress often panics suppliers who may restrict the availability of trade credit as happened to Caldor Corporation (see "In the News"). Employees and customers also may become alarmed and seek more reliable employment and suppliers elsewhere. Distressed companies may have to pay a premium to hire talented managers in these circumstances. These responses are likely to increase the company's costs and reduce its revenues. Furthermore, all three groups may begin to view their relationship to the company as temporary and downgrade or withdraw their long-term commitments. This imposes additional costs because the absence of commitment is what causes moral hazard problems in the presence of asymmetric information.

Companies that encounter severe financial distress often will enter bankruptcy, become liquidated, and incur additional indirect costs if the value of their liquidated assets is much less than their value in a going concern. There are several possible reasons. First, the values of some assets are intangible and not easily transferred to another owner. For example, a company can sell the equipment in its research lab but will receive much less than the value of the laboratory when it is staffed by a team of talented scientists. Second, options on future growth opportunities comprise a large part of the value of many going concerns. Many if not all of these options expire immediately when a company is liquidated. Third, even tangible assets may sell for less than they are really worth due to the urgency of liquidation sales.

The indirect costs of financial distress and liquidation are difficult to measure. Some are insidious and may be present but invisible when there is only a rumor of financial distress. Other costs appear only under the extreme conditions of liquidation when it is difficult to assign costs to categories. Altman concluded that the costs are quite large. He studied the bankruptcies of 19 industrial firms and concluded that the combination of direct and indirect distress costs for these companies was more than 20 percent of their values just prior to the onset of distress.[13] If Altman's estimates are typical, then indirect distress costs are much more likely than direct costs to affect a company's choice of capital structure.

16.4 THE EFFECT OF ASYMMETRIC INFORMATION

The existence of asymmetric information can change our conclusion that a company's debt-equity policy is irrelevant in much the same way as taxes and distress costs. Some factors favor the use of more debt and some favor the use of less. We'll refer to these as the *agency costs of equity* and the *agency costs of debt*.

Agency Costs of Equity

The **agency costs of equity** are the losses in value attributable to the use of equity as the method of financing. There are several ways these costs can arise.

Equity financing imposes few and relatively lenient deadlines for achieving a minimum level of financial performance. A company is never obligated to return an owner's original investment and dividends are not mandatory. Managers of companies primarily financed with equity may become complacent in the absence of these deadlines.

In contrast, debt financing imposes recurrent, inflexible financial deadlines. A company must repay the principal of a loan and interest payments cannot be omitted. In addition, lenders, especially private lenders such as banks, are likely to be more effective monitors than widely dispersed owners. These two features of debt provide a powerful incentive for managers to avoid misusing free cash flow and to focus their attention on their jobs. Venture capitalists understand this incentive and often require owner-managers to mortgage their homes and invest the money in the business so it will have their complete attention.

There is an additional disadvantage to new external equity financing if investors believe it signals the company's stock is overvalued. They will immediately reduce the price they are willing to pay for all the company's shares in this situation, even if their interpretation is incorrect. This response is what we described as the agency costs of dividends in Chapter 15.

---

[13]Edward I. Altman, "A Further Investigation of the Bankruptcy Cost Question," *Journal of Finance*, September 1984, pp. 1067–1089.

New external debt is not as sensitive to asymmetric information about the value of a company's assets because creditors have a fixed claim that is paid before the owners are paid. Consequently, the common stockholders absorb most if not all of the effect of a decline in the value of the company's assets when management's information is revealed.[14] Senior debt such as mortgage bonds is particularly insensitive to this problem because these bondholders are paid first.

The agency costs of equity encourage companies to use more debt in their capital structures. The effect is similar to the effect of corporate taxes although we cannot describe it as precisely as we can describe the present value of the debt tax-shields.

Agency Costs of Debt

The use of debt financing tempts the owners to make different decisions than they would if only their own wealth was at stake. The resulting losses in value are the **agency costs of debt**. Two manifestations of this problem are risk shifting and the failure to invest in positive NPV projects.

Risk Shifting   The use of debt financing tempts the owners to take chances they otherwise might avoid when investing their own money. This problem arises from the combination of two things. First, the creditors have a fixed claim on a company's earnings and assets while the owners have a variable claim, that is, the owners are the ones who benefit from investments that provide large payoffs. Second, owners have limited liability when they invest through a corporation and therefore are not subject to offsetting losses. Consequently, debt financing gives the owners the opportunity to gamble with someone else's money.

Table 16.11 illustrates the owners' incentive to take extra risks when using debt financing. Mountain Magic Inc. will develop and sell its Colorado property in one year. The company can adopt a conservative strategy and develop the property for single-family homes or adopt an aggressive strategy and develop it for resort condominiums. Panel A of Table 16.11 shows the free cash flows from each strategy in a strong and weak economy and the expected value of these cash flows.

Panel B of Table 16.11 gives the company's financial cash flows and market-value balance sheet if it uses no debt in its capital structure and investors are risk-neutral with a required rate of return of 6 percent. Both investment strategies provide the same expected free cash flow, so the value of the equity is $50,000 ($53,000/1.06) no matter how the company develops the property.

Panel C is constructed under the assumption that, when the bonds are issued, the creditors believe the company will develop the property for single-family homes. Consequently, they are willing to pay $15,000 for the bonds with the expectation they will receive $15,900 ($15,000 × 1.06) at maturity. The value of the equity is $35,000 if the owners actually adopt the conservative strategy but is $42,500 if they switch to the aggressive (risky) strategy after the bonds are sold.

---

[14]This may not be true if the company is financially distressed. Then, a decline in the value of the company's assets can completely wipe out the equity and reduce the debt value.

MOUNTAIN MAGIC'S INVESTMENT AND FINANCING CHOICES   **Table 16.11**

Panel A: Free Cash Flow

	Conservative Strategy			Aggressive Strategy		
Economic conditions	**Strong**	**Weak**	**Expected**	**Strong**	**Weak**	**Expected**
Probability	0.50	0.50		0.50	0.50	
Free Cash Flows	$ 84,800	$ 21,200	$ 53,000	$ 106,000	$ 0	$ 53,000

Panel B: Financial Cash Flows and Balance Sheets with No Debt

Financial Cash Flows						
Pay dividends	$(84,800)	$(21,200)	$(53,000)	$(106,000)	$ 0	$(53,000)

Market-Value Balance Sheets						
Debt			$ 0			$ 0
Equity			50,000			50,000
Assets			$ 50,000			$ 50,000

Panel C: Financial Cash Flows and Balance Sheets with $15,000 Debt

Financial Cash Flows						
Pay interest and repay debt	$(15,900)	$(15,900)	$(15,900)	$(15,900)	$ 0	$(7,950)
Pay dividends	(68,900)	(5,300)	(37,100)	(90,100)	0	(45,050)
Net financial cash flow	$(84,800)	$(21,200)	$(53,000)	$(106,000)	$ 0	$(53,000)

Market-Value Balance Sheets						
Debt			$ 15,000			$ 7,500
Equity			35,000			42,500
Assets			$ 50,000			$50,000

The owners' $7,500 increase in wealth comes at the creditors' expense. In a strong economy, the owners get an additional $21,200 ($90,100 − $68,900) while the creditors' get nothing extra because their claim is fixed at $15,900. In a weak economy, the owners lose $5,300 ($0 − $5,300) while the creditors lose $15,900 ($0 − $15,900). The owners receive a higher payoff in a strong economy that offsets their lower payoff in a weak economy but the creditors are not similarly compensated. The result is a transfer of $7,500 of wealth from the creditors to the owners.

$$\text{Change in owners' wealth} = \frac{0.50 \times \$21,200 + 0.50 \times \${-}5,300}{1.06} = \$7,500$$

$$\text{Change in creditors' wealth} = \frac{0.50 \times \$0 + 0.50 \times \$-15{,}900}{1.06} = \$-7{,}500$$

Risk shifting is even more attractive to companies that use more debt because the owners have less to lose if their gamble fails. Exercise 16.13 illustrates this effect.

EXERCISE ●──●

16.13   THE EFFECT OF INCREASING A COMPANY'S RISK

Determine the creditors' losses and the owners' gains if Magic Mountain issues bonds worth $18,000 and then adopts the agressive property development strategy.

The company will owe the creditors $19,080 ($18,000 × 1.06) in one year. Substituting this value in the company's financial cash flow statements produces the results shown below.

MOUNTAIN MAGIC'S FINANCIAL CASH FLOWS AND BALANCE SHEETS WITH $18,000 DEBT

Economic conditions	Conservative Strategy			Aggressive Strategy		
	Strong	**Weak**	**Expected**	**Strong**	**Weak**	**Expected**
Probability	0.50	0.50		0.50	0.50	
Financial Cash Flows						
Pay interest and repay debt	$(19,080)	$(19,080)	$(19,080)	$(19,080)	$ 0	$ (9,540)
Pay dividends	(65,720)	(2,120)	(33,920)	(86,920)	0	(43,460)
Net financial cash flow	$(84,800)	$(21,200)	$(53,000)	$(106,000)	$ 0	$(53,000)

The creditors gain no additional cash flows in a strong economy and lose $19,080 in a weak one so their expected loss, in present value terms is

$$\text{Change in creditors' wealth} = \frac{0.50 \times \$0 + 0.50 \times \$-19{,}080}{1.06} = \$-9{,}000$$

The owners gain $21,200 of additional cash flows in a strong economy ($86,920 − $65,720) and lose only $2,120 ($0 − $2,120) in a weak economy so their gain from increasing the company's risk is

$$\text{Change in owners' wealth} = \frac{0.50 \times \$21{,}200 + 0.50 \times \$-2{,}120}{1.06} = \$9{,}000$$

There is a potential to transfer more wealth from the creditors to the owners when the company uses more debt in its capital structure.

●────────────●

Failure to Invest   The use of debt financing also may prompt the owners to forgo good investment projects. This problem arises when a company is financially distressed

BRINKMAN SHIP COMPANY'S INVESTMENT DECISION   **Table 16.12**

Panel A: Market-Value Balance Sheets without Investment

Economic Conditions

	Strong	Weak	Expected
Probability	0.5	0.5	
Assets	$400,000	$100,000	$250,000
Claims			
Debt	$300,000	$100,000	$200,000
Equity	100,000	0	50,000
Total	$400,000	$100,000	$250,000

Panel B: Market-Value Balance Sheets with Investment

Economic Conditions

	Strong	Weak	Expected
Probability	0.5	0.5	
Assets			
Original assets	$400,000	$100,000	$250,000
Sailboat	200,000	150,000	175,000
Total	$600,000	$250,000	$425,000
Claims			
Debt	$300,000	$250,000	$275,000
Equity	300,000	0	150,000
Total	$600,000	$250,000	$425,000

and a project's payoffs improve the creditors' position without leaving enough to cover the owners' initial cost. The owners reject the project even though it has a positive NPV because it doesn't improve *their* wealth. This outcome is illustrated by the following example.

Brinkman Ship Company restores classic wooden speedboats. Panel A of Table 16.12 gives the company's market-value balance sheet in its present condition assuming investors are risk-neutral. Brinkman's assets will be worth $400,000 if the economy is strong and $100,000 if it is weak. The company will be able to satisfy its $300,000 debt obligation in full in the first case but not the latter. Under these circumstances, the market value of the debt is $200,000 and the market value of the equity is $50,000.

For $125,000, Brinkman can buy and restore an oceangoing sailboat. The company will sell the boat after restoration is complete in one year. The present value of the selling price will be $200,000 if the economy is strong and $150,000 if it is weak. The project's NPV is therefore

$$\text{NPV} = \text{Market value} - \text{cost}$$
$$= (0.50 \times \$200,000 + 0.50 \times \$150,000) - \$125,000$$
$$= \$175,000 - \$125,000 = \$50,000.$$

The sailboat's NPV is positive, so Brinkman should proceed with the investment.

Panel B of Table 16.12 gives Brinkman's market-value balance sheet if it buys and restores the sailboat. The project adds $175,000 to the company's value, as expected, but increases the owners' wealth by only $100,000 ($150,000 – $50,000) because the creditors get all of the payoff in a poor economy. Therefore, the owners will reject this investment project because it costs them $125,000 but will only add $100,000 to their wealth.

The failure to invest in positive NPV projects is only a problem for financially distressed companies because the owners of healthy companies do not share the investment's payoffs with the creditors. Exercise 16.14 illustrates this effect.

EXERCISE

16.14   **THE EFFECT OF FORGOING GOOD INVESTMENTS**

Rework the Brinkman Ship Company example, assuming the company has $100,000 of debt outstanding. Will the owners reject the sailboat investment project in this situation?

The investment opportunity increases the owners' wealth by $175,000 ($325,000 – $150,000)—the full amount of its market value (see the table on page 691). The net increase in the owners' wealth therefore equals the project's NPV, $50,000. The owners will accept the investment project in this case because they are not required to share the investment's payoff with the creditors when the economy is weak.

Creditors understand risk shifting and the owners' reluctance to invest in good projects and they build the costs of these behaviors into the price of the bonds. They also insert restrictive covenants into bond indentures that limit the owners' abilities to increase their risk in specific ways. Covenants may, for example, require a company to maintain a specific level of working capital. These actions impose the agency costs of debt on the owners. Even companies whose owners have no intention of playing these games must bear these costs if they cannot distinguish themselves in some way.

Risk shifting and the failure to invest are more serious problems the more debt a company uses in its capital structure. Consequently, the agency costs of debt probably are insignificant at low levels of debt and become a matter of concern for highly levered companies. This is the same pattern exhibited by distress costs; in reality, it may be difficult to distinguish between them.

BRINKMAN SHIP COMPANY

Panel A: Market-Value Balance Sheets without Investment

	Economic Conditions		
	Strong	**Weak**	**Expected**
Probability	0.5	0.5	
Assets	$400,000	$100,000	$250,000
Claims			
Debt	$100,000	$100,000	$100,000
Equity	300,000	0	150,000
Total	$400,000	$100,000	$250,000

Panel B: Market-Value Balance Sheets with Investment

	Economic Conditions		
	Strong	**Weak**	**Expected**
Probability	0.5	0.5	
Assets			
Original assets	$400,000	$100,000	$250,000
Sailboat	200,000	150,000	175,000
Total	$600,000	$250,000	$425,000
Claims			
Debt	$100,000	$100,000	$100,000
Equity	500,000	150,000	325,000
Total	$600,000	$250,000	$425,000

16.5   THE DEBT-EQUITY CHOICE: TRADE-OFF OR PECKING ORDER?

Stewart Myers articulated two of the prevailing explanations of financing choice that are known as the trade-off and pecking-order theories. These theories emphasize the role of one or more of the costs and benefits of the debt-equity choice that we described earlier.

Exhibit 16.6

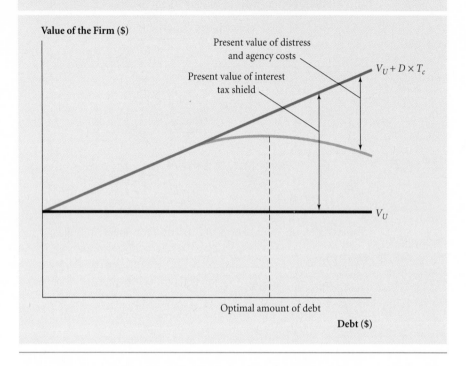

**THE EFFECT OF LEVERAGE ON THE VALUE OF THE FIRM
WITH TAXES, DISTRESS COSTS, AND AGENCY COSTS**

Value of the Firm ($)

Present value of distress
and agency costs

$V_U + D \times T_c$

Present value of interest
tax shield

V_U

Optimal amount of debt

Debt ($)

Companies balance the benefits and costs of debt to arrive at their optimal capital structure according to the **trade-off theory** of financing choice.[15] The benefits, which are primarily to reduce taxes or the agency costs of equity, predominate at low levels of debt. The costs are distress costs, particularly the loss of growth opportunities and agency costs, which become important at high levels of debt. In between the extremes is a debt level at which the marginal benefits equal the marginal costs: A company's optimal debt level according to the trade-off explanation for financing. This explanation is illustrated by adding distress and agency costs to Exhibit 16.5 to obtain Exhibit 16.6.

The **pecking-order theory** of financing choice states that managers prefer to use internal funds to avoid implying their securities are overvalued by selling new debt or common stock.[16] They obtain these funds by simply paying less than 100 percent of their earnings as dividends. The first choice in the pecking order is therefore the complement of the dividend choice we discussed in Chapter 15. Companies must use external financing when internal funds are insufficient, however. The pecking-order theory pre-

_____

[15]Stewart C. Myers, "Determinants of Corporate Borrowing," *Journal of Financial Economics,* March 1977, pp. 146–175.

[16]Stewart C. Myers, "The Capital Structure Puzzle," *Journal of Finance,* July 1984, pp. 575–592.

Exhibit 16.7

LEVERAGE AND MARKET-TO-BOOK RATIOS FOR SELECTED INDUSTRIES

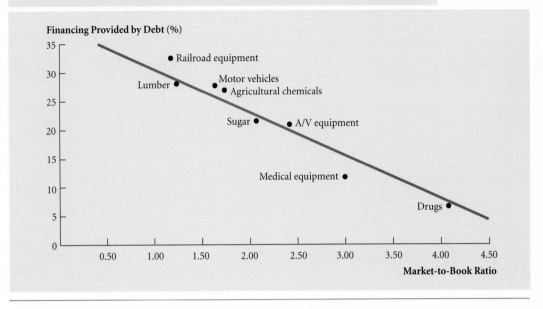

Source: Michael J. Barclay, Clifford W. Smith, and Ross W. Watts, "The Determinants of Corporate Leverage and Dividend Policies," *Journal of Applied Corporate Finance,* Winter 1995, pp. 4–19.

dicts they will issue new debt for this purpose because its use indicates that the managers are confident in the company's future.

The pecking-order theory is consistent with the pattern of financing choices graphed in Exhibit 16.1 and with the results of Pinegar and Wilbricht's survey described at the beginning of this chapter. Nevertheless, recent empirical studies are more supportive of the trade-off theory.

Barclay, Smith, and Watts tested the trade-off theory by examining the association between companies' market-to-book ratios and their use of financial leverage.[17] They reasoned that companies with high market-to-book ratios have more growth options (and therefore more to lose in financial distress) than companies with low market-to-book ratios. The trade-off theory predicts the high market-to-book ratio companies will use less leverage to avoid these distress costs and this is exactly what Barclay, Smith, and Watts found. Their results are summarized in Exhibit 16.7, which was redrawn from one of their figures.

The average market-to-book ratio of companies in the railroad industry is only 1.17 because their values are primarily explained by the worth of the land, track, and rolling stock they own. They may not suffer much from financial distress because these

---

[17]Michael J. Barclay, Clifford W. Smith, and Ross L. Watts, "The Determinants of Corporate Leverage and Dividend Policies," *Journal of Applied Corporate Finance,* Winter 1995, pp. 4–19.

I N   T H E   N E W S

FINANCING CHOICES BY DISTRESSED FIRMS

Two companies, American Healthcare Management and Maxicare, provide an example of how liquidation costs can affect both the amount and kind of debt companies employ when coming out of Chapter 11 bankruptcy. Both these firms have the same three-digit SIC code, and both bankruptcies took place during the period 1988–1990. American Healthcare owns mainly tangible assets, hospital buildings and land, so it should have low liquidation costs. We estimated these costs to be 12 percent of the companies' value. Maxicare, by contrast, owns little tangible property; it is an HMO, which is essentially a network of contracts among physicians, hospitals, and employers for delivery of health care services. A single contract would have little value outside of this network, so Maxicare's liquidation costs should be relatively high, 76 percent of its value according to our estimates.

Given such differences in liquidation costs, we should see differences in the amount and type of debt. And differences we found: Where American Healthcare reorganized with a ratio of long-term debt to assets of 88.8 percent, Maxicare reorganized with long-term debt of 43.5 percent, and where American Healthcare's new debt consisted of 85 percent secured bank debt and 15 percent secured public debt, Maxicare's new debt consisted entirely of unsecured, public debentures.

Source: Michael J. Alderson and Brian L. Betker, "Lessons on Capital Structure from Chapter 11 Reorganizations," *Journal of Applied Corporate Finance*, Winter 1996, pp. 61–72.

assets can easily be transferred to new owners. Therefore, railroads can afford to use more debt than other companies to reduce taxes and the agency cost of equity.

In contrast, the average market-to-book ratio of drug companies is 4.07 because their values are accounted for by the qualities of their research and development programs. The values of these assets may be entirely lost in financial distress if the labs are disbanded and the scientists dispersed to other companies and universities. Therefore, drug companies cannot afford to use as much debt as other companies to reduce taxes and the agency costs of equity.

Alderson and Betker's results are similar.[18] They examined the capital structure choices of companies emerging from bankruptcy and found that those with high liquidation costs used less debt than those with low liquidation costs. Furthermore, the high-liquidation-cost companies used methods of debt financing that preserved their financial flexibility, presumably so they could more easily avoid distress in the future. Two of the cases in their study are described in "In the News."

A synthesis of these results and the theories described earlier is the basis for the following advice to the board of directors and senior managers who must make capital structure decisions.

---

[18]Michael J. Alderson and Brian L. Betker, "Lessons on Capital Structure from Chapter 11 Reorganizations," *Journal of Applied Corporate Finance*, Winter 1996, pp. 61–72.

1. Consider using debt financing to reduce the corporation's taxes. Remember, however, that the net benefit of using debt for this purpose is diminished by the effect of personal taxes. The net benefit may be negative at some tax rates.

2. Consider using debt financing to reduce the agency costs of equity. Debt financing reduces these costs by providing effective monitors, imposing strict deadlines, and reducing the amount of cash flow that can be spent at the managers' discretion.

3. Establish limits on the use of debt financing for these purposes by considering the risk and costs of financial distress. The risk of distress is higher the more variable the income produced by the company's assets; the costs of distress are higher the less tangible the assets and the more complicated the company's capital structure.

4. Apart from these factors, remember that retaining earnings provides internal financing that can be used in lieu of new debt or external equity in normal times and as financial slack when a company has an unexpected requirement for cash. In either case, internal financing permits a company to avoid implying that its securities are overvalued.

16.6 SUMMARY

A company's long-term financial policy does not affect its value in a perfect financial market with symmetric information. Modigliani and Miller proved this is true because the owners can create or undo leverage by conducting the financial transactions themselves. This frees companies of responsibility for financing decisions and permits them to focus on investment and operating decisions.

The situation is different in reality, however, because market imperfections and asymmetric information produce benefits and costs of using internal equity, external equity, or debt. The existence of corporate taxes favors the use of debt for the tax-shield it provides. The existence of personal taxes reduces the value of the corporate tax-shield. The value of the corporate tax-shield may even become negative at some tax rates. Asymmetric information favors the use of internal equity, debt, and external equity (in that order) because investors may suspect that a company's securities are overvalued when it seeks new external financing. Debt is less sensitive to this problem, so it occupies an intermediate position in the pecking order. Finally, distress costs favor the use of equity over debt because the fixed costs of debt increase the probability of financial distress and the owners are more inclined to take desperate actions in these circumstances.

Whether real companies establish their financial policies by balancing these costs and benefits or by following a strict pecking order of preference isn't entirely clear. These are the costs and benefits they consider, however, with the result that most companies use a moderate amount of debt in their capital structures.

- ### KEY TERMS

- ### QUESTIONS AND PROBLEMS

1. Use simple, intuitive language to answer the following questions about long-term financial policy, emphasizing the similarities between dividend policy and capital structure where possible.

   (a) How important are a company's long-term financial policies in a perfect financial market? Explain your answer.

   (b) How important are a company's long-term financial policies when there are corporate and personal taxes? Explain your answer.

   (c) How important are a company's long-term financial policies when there is asymmetric information? Explain your answer.

2. Can a company independently establish its dividend policy and capital structure

   (a) in a perfect financial market? Explain your answer.

   (b) in a financial market that is perfect except for corporate and personal taxes? Explain your answer.

   (c) in a financial market that is perfect except for asymmetric information? Explain your answer.

3. A company's capital structure is irrelevant in a perfect financial market because the owners can use personal financial transactions to accomplish or nullify anything the company can do with corporate financial transactions.

   (a) Explain how the introduction of corporate taxes destroys the symmetry between personal and corporate financial transactions and makes the company's capital structure relevant.

   (b) Explain how the addition of personal taxes can restore the symmetry between personal and corporate financial transactions and make the company's capital structure irrelevant again.

4. Explain why the use of debt in a perfect financial market does not increase the owners' wealth even though it increases their expected rate of return.

5. Betty's Balloons and Party Favors borrowed $50,000 at 12 percent interest. The company makes annual interest payments and will repay the principal of the loan in five years. Determine the present value of the interest tax-shield assuming the company's tax rate is 25 percent.

6. Equations 16.6 and 16.2 describe a levered firm's equity beta in the presence and absence of corporate taxes.

$$\beta_e = \beta_a \times [1 + (1 - T_c) \times D/E] = \beta_a \times [1 + D/E - T_c \times D/E] \qquad [16.6]$$

$$\beta_e = \beta_a \times [1 + D/E] \qquad [16.2]$$

When you compare these equations, it appears that the government accepts part of the company's financial risk when there are corporate taxes. Explain why you agree or disagree with this interpretation of the effect of corporate taxes. It may help to consider the source and variablity of the government's tax receipts.

7. A corporate treasurer was overheard to say, "Capital structure decisions are no-brainers. The interest rate on debt is always lower than the rate of return our owners expect and when you add tax-deductibility, the choice is clear: Bonds are better by far." This treasurer is overlooking what factors that may make the *real* cost of debt much higher than the interest rate on the company's bonds? Explain your answer.

8. Are the direct costs of financial distress likely to be higher for

    (a) a department store that has accounts payable to 250 clothing and appliance vendors or an interstate truck stop that has one account payable to a fuel distributor and three accounts payable to automobile parts suppliers?

    (b) a manufacturer that has two publicly traded bond issues outstanding or a manufacturer that has no publicly traded bonds and loans from four local banks?

    (c) a computer software company that borrows money in its domestic financial market or a computer software company that borrows money internationally?

    Explain each answer.

9. Are the indirect costs of financial distress likely to be higher for

    (a) an Internet access provider or an electric utility?

    (b) a pharmaceutical company or a forest products company?

    (c) a company that manufactures lawn mowers or a company that manufacturers orchestral-quality grand pianos?

10. Milltown Plumbing manufactures metal plumbing fixtures that are used in state and federal correctional facilities. The company's expected net free cash flow is $3.3 million in perpetuity and the beta of the plumbing business is 0.75. John Starr, Milltown's founder and principal stockholder, is very cautious so the company uses no debt in its capital structure. Milltown has 1.5 million shares of stock outstanding and all cash flows are paid to investors. The financial market is perfect with a riskless rate of return of 5 percent and an expected rate of return on the market portfolio of 13 percent.

    (a) Determine Milltown's required rate of return on assets and required rate of return on equity.

    (b) Prepare the company's market-value balance sheet. What is the value of an individual share of common stock?

    (c) Confirm your answers to part (b) by discounting dividends per share and multiplying the result by the number of shares outstanding.

    John's daughter, Melissa Starr, has become more active in the business, working first in metal fabrication and now in the corporate offices as a financial analyst. Melissa is not as cautious as her father and would like the company to issue $10 million of bonds at 5 percent interest and use the proceeds to repurchase common stock. Her objective is to increase the rate of return on the company's common stock and to increase her personal wealth.

    (d) Rework parts (a) through (c) assuming Milltown adopts Ms. Starr's financing proposal.

    (e) Did the change in capital structure accomplish Melissa's objectives? Explain why or why not.

11. Maurice Stanley Glass Company expects free cash flows of $426,000 in perpetuity. The systematic risk of the assets that produce these cash flows is measured by a beta of 0.90.

Stanley has 50,000 shares of common stock and $500,000 of riskless bonds outstanding. The company pays 100 percent of its cash flows to its investors. The financial market is perfect with a riskless rate of return of 7 percent and an expected rate of return on the market portfolio of 15 percent.

(a) Determine Stanley's required rate of return on assets and required rate of return on equity.

(b) Prepare the company's market-value balance sheet. What is the value of an individual share of common stock?

Stanley is considering two alternative capital structures. One alternative is to issue new common stock and use the proceeds to repurchase the $500,000 of bonds outstanding, leaving the company with an all-equity capital structure. The other alternative is to issue an additional $1,000,000 of bonds and use the proceeds to repurchase common stock.

(c) Complete the following table.

Market value of debt	$ 0	$500,000	$1,500,000
Market value of equity			
Market value of assets			
Price per share of common stock			
Debt/equity ratio			
β_e			
r_e			
r_{wacc}			

(d) Graph Stanley's required rates of return (r_d, r_e, and r_{wacc}) as a function of the company's debt/equity ratio. Graph the market value of Stanley's assets as a function of the dollar amount of debt the company uses.

(e) Explain how the shapes of the functions in the required rates of return graph contribute to the shape of the other graph.

(f) Is Stanley's choice of capital structure a crucial decision? Explain your answer.

12. Kelly Lee established the Turkish Carpet Emporium using 100 percent equity financing. After several years of hard work, she built the company into a business that is expected to provide $200,000 of free cash flow per year in perpetuity. There are 20,000 shares of common stock outstanding and the company distributes 100 percent of its cash flows to investors. The beta of the import carpet business is 1.0. Kelly may have the company issue $400,000 of riskless, perpetual debt at 5 percent interest, and use the proceeds to repurchase common stock.

(a) Complete the following table assuming a perfect financial market with an expected rate of return on the market portfolio of 10 percent.

Market value of debt	$ 0	$400,000
Market value of equity		
Market value of assets		
Number of shares outstanding		
Price per share of common stock		
Cash flow paid as interest		
Cash flow paid as dividends		
Dividends per share		
Debt/equity ratio		
β_e		
r_e		

(b) Determine the percentage change in dividends per share and required rate of return on equity. Explain how the amounts of these percentage changes are related to the change in the price per share of common stock.

13. Suppose that Gary Willard, who was introduced in Exercise 16.3, prefers a personal debt/equity ratio of 0.

(a) Prepare his personal balance sheet and personal cash statement assuming that Durand Displays uses no debt in its capital structure.

(b) Rework part (a) assuming that Durand Displays uses $62,500 of debt in its capital structure and that Gary conducts personal financial transactions to unlever the company.

(c) Does the company's decision to use no debt or $62,500 of debt have any effect on Gary's personal financial position? Explain why or why not.

(d) Under these circumstances, will investors pay a premium for the common stock of a company that has a debt policy that exactly meets their preferences? How is your answer related to the conclusion that capital structure is irrelevant in a perfect financial market?

14. Chaput Pizza Company was always 100 percent equity financed with an asset beta of 1.0 and an expected rate of return of 16 percent. However, the company recently replaced 50 percent of its equity with riskless debt.

(a) Plot the owners' original and new positions on the security market line (SML) to illustrate their position before and after the capital structure change. The financial market is perfect with a riskless rate of return of 6 percent and an expected rate of return on the market portfolio of 16 percent.

(b) Lea Alexander has $100,000 to invest. How should she allocate her money between Chaput's common stock and the riskless asset if she prefers an expected rate of return of 31 percent on her personal equity? (You may want to review Section 6.1 of Chapter 6 if you are not sure how to solve this problem.) Plot Lea's portfolio on the SML you drew in part (a).

(c) Ron Schallheim also has $100,000 to invest. How should he allocate his money between Chaput's common stock and the riskless asset if he prefers a beta of 1.0 for his personal portfolio? Plot Ron's portfolio on the SML.

(d) Determine Lea's and Ron's personal debt/equity ratios and use them to calculate their personal equity betas and personal required rates of return. (Don't forget, each is responsible for part of Chaput's debt as modified by their personal financial transactions.) Plot the results on the SML.

(e) How did the results based on allocation, parts (b) and (c), compare with the results based on leverage ratios, part (d)? What does this tell you about the reason capital structure is irrelevant in a perfect financial market?

15. Shank Pharmaceuticals has the right to mine medicinal salts on public land in perpetuity. Shank uses the salt deposits to produce bath products. This business generates after-tax free cash flows of $650,000 per year with a required rate of return of 13 percent. The company pays 100 percent of its cash flows to investors. There are 100,000 shares of stock outstanding and no debt. The company's tax rate is 35 percent and the rate of return on riskless borrowing and lending is 7 percent.

(a) Determine the market value of a single share of Shank's common stock.

The company is considering issuing $2 million of perpetual bonds at 7 percent interest to repurchase common stock.

(b) Determine the amount of the interest tax-shield provided by the $2 million of debt. What is the present value of these tax-shields?

(c) Prepare the company's market-value balance sheet after this recapitalization is completed.

(d) How many shares of stock are outstanding after this change in capital structure? What is the price per share?

(e) What is the per-share value of the interest tax-shield? Add this amount to the company's original stock price and compare the result to your answer to part (d).

(f) Who receives the interest tax-shield, the owners or creditors? Why?

16. Remote Madness produces Internet home pages for alternative music groups. The company's after-tax free cash flows are $640,000 in perpetuity and it pays 100 percent of its cash flows to its investors.

(a) The company recently changed its capital structure to permit the original owners to withdraw some of their wealth to use for other purposes. The table given below describes some aspects of their original and new capital structures. Complete this table assuming the corporate tax rate is 35 percent, the rate of return on riskless borrowing and lending is 8 percent, and the expected rate of return on the market portfolio is 16 percent.

	Original Capital Structure	New Capital Structure
Market value of debt	$ 0	$1,500,000
Market value of equity		
Market value of assets		
Number of shares outstanding	160,000	
Price per share of common stock		
Cash flow paid as interest		
Cash flow paid as dividends		
Dividends per share		
Debt/equity ratio		
β_a	1.0	1.0
β_e		
r_e		

(b) Determine the percentage change in dividends per share and required rate of return on equity. Explain how the magnitudes of these percentage changes are related to the change in the price per share of common stock.

17. Wilson Training and Development Inc.'s multimedia learning centers produce after-tax free cash flows of $600,000 in perpetuity. When all-equity financed, the company had 50,000 shares of stock outstanding with a market price of $80 per share. The company issued $1.92 million of riskless perpetual bonds at 6 percent interest and used the proceeds to repurchase common stock. Wilson's tax rate is 35 percent.

(a) Determine the common stockholders' annual dividends per share after the capital structure change assuming the company pays all its cash flows to investors. What is the rate of return on the company's common stock assuming the stock price increased to $115?

(b) The beta for the training and development business is 1.125 and the expected rate of return on the market portfolio is 14 percent. What is the required rate of return on Wilson's common stock?

(c) Compare your answers to parts (a) and (b). Is $115 the equilibrium price of Wilson's common stock? Can this situation persist? What will happen?

d) Calculate Wilson's stock price after the capital structure change by adding the per share value of the interest tax-shield to its original stock price. Is this value the equilibrium stock price? Explain your answer.

18. For this problem, assume the financial market is perfect although corporate profits are taxed at the rate of 35 percent.

(a) Complete the following table using Equation 16.7 to calculate the weighted average cost of capital.

Value of Debt	r_d	Value of Equity	r_e	Value of Assets	r_{wacc}
$ 0	7%	$500,000	9.0%	$500,000	9.0%
100,000	7		9.3		
200,000	7		9.7		
300,000	7		10.3		
400,000	7		11.2		
500,000	7		12.7		

(b) Recalculate the weighted average cost of capital using Equation 16.8 to confirm your answers.

(c) Graph the company's required rates of return (r_d, r_e, and r_{wacc}) as a function of its debt/equity ratio. Graph the market value of the company's assets as a function of the dollar amount of debt.

(d) Explain how the shapes of the functions in the required rates of return graph contribute to the shape of the other graph.

19. Lovely Home Improvement Corporation has an all-equity capital structure and may issue $10 million of riskless debt to repurchase common stock. The CFO will consider the company's tax rate and the creditors' and owners' tax rates when deciding whether to change the company's capital structure. For each tax scenario described below, determine whether the company should change its capital structure. Explain your answer.

(a) The company's tax rate is 35 percent and the tax rates on personal debt and equity income are 39.6 percent and 31 percent.

(b) The company's tax rate is 35 percent. Individuals, with a marginal tax rate of 39.6 percent, hold the company's bonds and tax-exempt foundations hold its stock.

(c) The company has depreciation tax-shields and tax credits that reduce its effective marginal tax rate to 10 percent and the marginal tax rates on personal debt and equity income are 39.6 percent and 31 percent.

(d) The company's marginal tax rate is 34 percent and the marginal tax rate on personal debt and equity income is 28 percent.

20. Suppose Lovely Home Improvement Corporation issues $10 million of perpetual bonds and uses the proceeds to repurchase common stock (see problem 19).

    (a) Determine the present value of the interest tax-shield provided by these bonds for each tax scenerio described in problem 19.

    (b) Under which tax scenario(s) did the decision to use debt financing increase the value of the company's assets? How do the results compare with your answers to problem 19? Explain your answer.

21. Lovely Home Improvement Corporation (see problems 19 and 20) has net free cash flows in perpetuity of $2.5 million. The cost of debt is 8 percent, the company's market value with all-equity financing is $25 million, and there are 1 million shares outstanding. Suppose the company issues the $10 million of perpetual bonds and uses the proceeds to repurchase common stock.

    (a) Determine the after-tax cash flows received by creditors and owners; the market value of the company's assets, debt, and equity; and the price of a single share of common stock assuming the tax scenario described in part (a) of problem 19.

    (b) Rework part (a) of this problem assuming the tax scenario described in part (b) of problem 19.

    (c) In which case did the change in capital structure increase the owners' wealth? How does this result compare with your answers to problems 19 and 20? Explain your answer.

22. Academy Leasing supplies stadium lights for night television broadcasts of college football games. The company's annual pre-tax free cash flows are $3 million in perpetuity. Academy's value with all-equity financing is $32.5 million and 1,625,000 shares are outstanding. Academy's managers are considering a recapitalization in which they will issue $12 million of perpetual bonds at 7 percent interest and use the proceeds to repurchase common stock. The corporation's tax rate is 35 percent and the personal tax rates on income from debt and equity are 39.6 and 31 percent.

    (a) Determine the after-tax cash flows received by creditors and owners before and after the change in capital structure. Does it appear that the company should issue the bonds and repurchase common stock? Explain your answer.

    (b) Determine the market value of the company's assets, debt, and equity and the price of a single share of common stock. Does the change in capital structure increase the owners' wealth? Why?

23. Big Boy Pocket Knives (BBPK) produces commemorative knives sold at historical celebrations. Next year's model will be the last because it has become too difficult to find skilled craftsmen to carve the handles and engrave the blades. This model will produce net free cash flows of $27,000 in a strong economy and $9,500 in a weak one. The probabilities of a strong and weak economy are 0.40 and 0.60. BBPK will distribute its final cash flows to the company's creditors and owners who are risk-neutral and require a 4 percent rate of return. The financial market is perfect.

    (a) BBPK has 1,000 shares of stock outstanding and no debt. Determine the amount of cash flow the company will pay to the creditors and the amount it will pay to the owners in a strong economy, a weak economy, and on average.

    (b) Prepare the company's market-value balance sheet. What is the market price of an individual share of stock?

    (c) Rework parts (a) and (b) assuming the company issues 4 percent bonds with a face value of $10,000 and uses the proceeds to repurchase common stock.

(d) Did the use of debt financing affect the price of BBPK's common stock? Why or why not? Is the company's choice of capital structure a crucial decision under these circumstances? Explain your answer.

24. Rework problem 23 assuming Big Boy Pocket Knives must pay court costs of $2,000 if it is unable to pay the creditors' claims in full.

25. Cowtown Leather Distributors' net free cash flow next year will be $125,000 in a strong economy and $47,000 in a weak one. These economic conditions are equally likely. Cowtown has ridden the western wear fad as far as it will go and will distribute these cash flows to the company's creditors and owners and go out of business. The company's investors are risk neutral with a required rate of return of 7 percent. The financial market is perfect.

(a) Cowtown has 16,000 shares of stock outstanding and no debt. Determine the amount of cash flow the company will pay to the creditors and the amount it will pay to the owners in a strong economy, a weak economy, and on average.

(b) Prepare the company's market-value balance sheet. What is the market price of an individual share of stock?

(c) Rework parts (a) and (b) assuming the company issues 7 percent bonds with a face value of $50,000 and uses the proceeds to repurchase common stock. Assume also that the managers become so worried about repaying this debt in a weak economy that the company's net free cash flows fall from $47,000 to $32,000. There are no other financial distress costs.

(d) Did the use of debt financing affect the price of Cowtown's common stock? Why or why not? Is the company's choice of capital structure a crucial decision under these circumstances? Explain your answer.

26. Merton Entertainment Inc. has a one-year contract to operate the concession stands at a professional sports stadium. The free cash flows provided by the concessions depend on conditions in the economy as shown below. The company will pay 100 percent of its cash flows to its investors who are risk neutral with a required rate of return of 10 percent.

Economy	Free Cash Flows
Severe recession	$ 900,000
Mild recession	1,000,000
Normal	1,100,000
Modest expansion	1,200,000
Robust expansion	1,300,000

(a) Merton has 110,000 shares of stock outstanding and no debt. Determine the market value of the company's assets on a per share basis and the market price of an individual share of stock for each economic condition. Plot these points on a graph with the market value of the assets on the horizontal axis and the market value of the stock on the vertical axis.

(b) Compare your graph to the graphs in Exhibit 8.2 in Chapter 8. What type of security do the common stockholders own when the company uses no debt in its capital structure?

(c) Suppose Merton issues 10 percent bonds with a face value of $1,000,000 and uses the proceeds to repurchase common stock at a price that equals the average of the prices you computed in part (a). Determine the market value of the company's assets on a per share basis and the market price of an individual share of stock for each economic condition.

Plot these points on a graph with the market value of the assets on the horizontal axis and the market value of the stock on the vertical axis. What is the point at which the value of the common stock switches from zero to a positive number on this graph?

(d) Compare the graph from part (c) to the graphs in Exhibit 8.2 in Chapter 8. What type of security do the common stockholders own when the company uses debt? Describe as many of this security's features as you can.

(e) Use your graphs to explain why owners are tempted to invest in more risky assets once they have obtained debt financing.

27. Passport Ocean Transport's free cash flows and payments to investors one year from today under two investment strategies are shown below. The probabilities of a weak and strong economy are 0.85 and 0.15. There are 1,000 shares of stock outstanding and investors are risk neutral with a required rate of return of 5 percent.

	Conservative Strategy		Aggressive Strategy	
	Weak Economy	Strong Economy	Weak Economy	Strong Economy
Free cash flow	$10,500	$21,000	$ 0	$31,500
Paid to creditors	8,400	8,400	0	8,400
Paid to owners	2,100	12,600	0	23,100
Cash flow per share	2.10	12.60	0	23.10

(a) Determine the owners' expected cash flow per share and the market price of the company's common stock under each investment strategy. Which investment strategy will the owners prefer? Why?

(b) Suppose the company's senior managers own stock options with an exercise price of $7. What is the value of an individual stock option if they elect the conservative investment strategy? If they elect the aggressive investment strategy? Compare their investment preferences to the owners'.

(c) Explain how the presence of a fixed-debt obligation affected the owners' and managers' preferences for a particular investment strategy.

• ADDITIONAL READING

Modigliani and Miller's classic articles, part of the work for which each of them received the Nobel Prize in Economics, are

Franco Modigliani and Merton H. Miller, "The Cost of Capital, Corporation Finance and the Theory of Investment," *American Economic Review,* June 1958, pp. 261–297.

Franco Modigliani and Merton H. Miller, "Corporate Income Taxes and the Cost of Capital: A Correction," *American Economic Review,* June 1963, pp. 433–443.

Merton Miller, "Debt and Taxes," *Journal of Finance,* May 1977, pp. 261–275 or 6.

Two good reviews of capital structure theory are

Stewart C. Myers, "Still Searching for the Optimal Capital Structure," *Journal of Applied Corporate Finance,* Spring 1993, pp. 4–14.

Milton Harris and Artur Raviv, "The Theory of Capital Structure," *Journal of Finance,* March 1991, pp. 297–355.

Aspects of the following paper were discussed in this chapter and in Chapter 15. The entire paper is well worth reading.

Michael J. Barclay, Clifford W. Smith, and Ross L. Watts, "The Determinants of Corporate Leverage and Dividend Policies," *Journal of Applied Corporate Finance,* Winter 1995, pp. 4–19.

A complete set of expressions for beta, required rates of return, and the value of the firm with corporate and personal taxes is provided in

Robert A. Taggart, "Consistent Valuation and Cost of Capital Expressions with Corporate and Personal Taxes," *Financial Management,* Autumn 1991, pp. 8–20.

RECOGNIZING FINANCING EFFECTS IN INVESTMENT ANALYSIS

General Electric Capital Aviation Services (GECAS) buys aircraft from the world's major manufacturers and provides them to other companies under a variety of lease agreements and financing plans. GECAS's fleet of leased aircraft is the largest in the world, accounting for more than 40 percent of the total capacity.[1] The company added to this fleet in 1996 when it placed a $4 billion order for 107 airplanes with Boeing Company. At the same time, it had options to buy as many as 159 more aircraft from Boeing and was negotiating the purchase of 50 planes from Airbus Industrie.[2]

Airlines, package delivery services, and other corporations make a joint investment-financing decision when they acquire these aircraft from GECAS. Obtaining the use of an airplane is the investment component, promising to make future lease or loan payments the financing part. In either case, the customer obtains *debt* financing because its payments to GECAS are fixed, have priority, and are tax-deductible in total or in part. Airlines and other corporations therefore must account for the benefits of the investment and the method of financing when they lease or buy equipment from GECAS and similar financial services companies.

Chapter 16 showed that a company's financial policies can affect the value of its assets in an imperfect market. We saw, for example, that using debt provides interest tax-shields that are an addition to a company's free cash flows. The present value of these tax-shields is an addition to the market value of the company's assets.

Each investment project a company considers has its own financial side effects that contribute to the company's overall value. Projects that can be financed at below-market

---

[1]GE Capital Aviation Services' Internet site at http://www.ge.com/capital/aviation.
[2]Jeff Cole, "Boeing Gets Order for 107 Planes from GE Unit," *The Wall Street Journal,* January 1, 1996, p. B8.

interest rates have a financial side effect that equals the present value of the interest savings. Projects that increase the company's debt capacity provide interest tax-shields. We must determine the value of each of these financial side effects to accurately measure a project's effect on the owners' wealth.

This chapter describes how to measure the values of these and other financial side effects. The methods we will use are analogous to the procedures we used to value an entire company in Chapter 16. We will examine these alternative valuation methods first and then discuss how to estimate the required rates of return needed to implement them.

17.1   THE ADJUSTED PRESENT VALUE METHOD

The adjusted present value (APV) method is applied by discounting each component of cash flow at a separate required rate of return and adding the results. The values of the cash flows provided by financial side effects are the adjustments to the present value of the cash flows provided by operations, investment, and financial slack. The APV method also is the basis for determining an adjusted required rate of return that is used to discount the cash flows provided by operations, investment, and financial slack. Once again, the financial side effects are the sources of these adjustments. We used the weighted average cost of capital as this adjusted required rate of return in Chapter 9, however, we will see this is not always permissible.

An investment project's **adjusted present value (APV)** is the present value of its free cash flows plus the present value of its financial side effects. That is,

$$\text{APV} = \frac{\text{Present value of}}{\text{free cash flows}} + \frac{\text{Present value of}}{\text{financial side effects.}}$$

The first term on the right-hand side of this equation comprises the cash flows you learned how to value in Chapter 9. These cash flows are provided by purchasing and operating and by periodically replacing the company's assets. Consequently, they must be discounted at the required rate of return for assets or, equivalently, the required rate of return appropriate for their business risk, r_a.

The second term in the equation is the present value of the cash flows provided by or used for financial side effects. The three financial side effects we will consider here are interest tax-shields (introduced in Chapter 16), floatation costs, and subsidized financing. We will examine each of these financial side effects in turn, using the Cold-Fit Clothing Company as our example.

An analyst for the Cold-Fit Clothing Company is evaluating a proposal to produce a new line of insulated gloves. The project's free cash flows are shown below. The present value of these free cash flows at Cold-Fit's business risk required rate of return, 15 percent, is $398,480.64. Therefore, the project is acceptable even if we ignore its financial side effects. We must consider them, however, to determine the project's exact effect on the owners' wealth.

Year	Net Free Cash Flow
1997	$-3,060,000
1998	1,962,000
1999	1,471,000
2000	717,000
2001	295,000

Cold-Fit will use $2,000,000 of debt amortized over the life of the project to finance this investment. The company's normal borrowing rate of interest is 12 percent, however, a neighboring county has offered to lend the company the money at 9 percent interest if the production facilities are located there. Floatation costs on this subsidized loan are 1 percent and the company's tax rate is 34 percent. Cold-Fit's project therefore has floatation cost, subsidized financing, and interest tax-shield side effects.

The Value of Floatation Costs

Floatation costs are the fees a company pays to obtain new external financing. These expenses are tax-deductible although they must be allocated to each year in the life of the loan on a straight-line basis. The floatation cost tax-shield for each year of an *n*-year loan therefore is

$$\text{Floatation cost tax-shield} = T_c \times \text{Floatation cost}/n.$$

The present value of floatation costs equals the amount of the immediate cash outflow plus the present value of the future cash inflows from the tax-shields they provide. Once a company pays the floatation costs, the future tax-shields are known with near certainty. We will use the company's after-tax cost of debt financing, r_d, as the discount rate for reasons that we will explain later.

Cold-Fit Clothing Company requires $2,000,000 of debt financing. Floatation costs are 1 percent, so the company must actually borrow $2,020,202 ($2,000,000/0.99) to obtain proceeds of $2,000,000. The cash outflow for floatation costs in 1997 is therefore $20,202. This expense is spread over the life of the loan on a straight-line basis, providing tax-shields of $1,717 (0.34 × $20,202/4) per year from 1998 to 2001. The net present value of the floatation costs at the company's after-tax cost of debt, $0.12 \times (1 - 0.34) = 0.0792$, is therefore

$$\text{NPV(floatation costs)} = \$-20,202 + \$1,717 \times \text{APVF}_{0.0792,4}$$

$$= \$-20,202 + \$1,717 \times 3.3180$$

$$= \$-14,504.99.$$

Floatation costs reduce the project's value by $14,504.99.

THE VALUE OF FLOATATION COSTS

The Mowser Video Game Company will borrow $100,000 for five years to expand its operations. Floatation costs on this loan are 3 percent. What is the present value of the floatation costs if the company's cost of debt is 10 percent and its tax rate is 34 percent?

UNCLE SAM FLOATS SOME LOANS

ALMOST $1 BILLION in new ship construction is pending under a new federal loan guarantee program for U.S. shipyards, the White House said yesterday. The ships will be among the first built in the United States in many years and the first for foreign shipowners to be built in U.S. shipyards in almost 40 years.

Congress passed the "National Shipbuilding Initiative" in November. The act allows government guarantees for up to 87.5 percent of the amount financed for new vessel construction up to 25 years. The loans are obtained from private lenders or bond sales that carry a fixed-interest rate. The act apparently has made U.S. shipyards attractive to foreign buyers. The projects listed yesterday included $726 million pending approval for 30 container ships for a Swiss-based investment concern and $133 million pending approval for four Greek tankers.

Source: Don Phillips, "Financing a Revival in U.S. Shipbuilding," *The Washington Post*, Aug. 3, 1994, p. F1. © 1994 The Washington Post. Reprinted with permission.

$$\text{Amount of loan} = \text{Net proceeds}/(1 - \text{floatation costs})$$
$$= \$100,000/(1 - 0.03) = \$103,093$$
$$\text{Floatation costs} = \$103,093 - \$100,000 = \$3,093$$
$$\text{Tax-shield} = 0.34 \times \$3,093/5 = \$210$$
$$\text{NPV} = \${-}3,093 + \$210 \times \text{APVF}_{0.066,5} = \${-}2,222.66$$

The present value of the company's after-tax floatation costs is $-2,222.66.

The Value of Subsidized Financing

Local, state, and national governments sometimes offer companies financing at below-market interest rates to stimulate investments in particular industries or geographical areas. Governments also guarantee loans, which has the same effect by substituting the guarantor's cost of debt for the borrower's. These subsidies reduce the after-tax payments required to repay the loan in comparison to the payments required to repay a market loan. The present value of the savings at the company's normal after-tax cost of debt is a favorable financial side effect that adds to a project's value, producing the investment incentive governments seek (see "In the News").

You can compute the present value of the savings as described in the preceding paragraph or simply discount the subsidized loan's after-tax cash flows at the company's normal after-tax cost of debt. The answers are the same because the present value of the market loan's after-tax cash flows is zero. This is illustrated by the following numerical example.

Suppose a company can borrow $1,000 for one year at its normal cost of debt, $r_d = 12$ percent, or at a subsidized rate, $r_s = 10$ percent. The company's tax rate is 40 percent, so the after-tax cash flows required to repay the loans are $\$-1,000 + \$-100 \times (1 - 0.40) = \$-1,060$ and $\$-1,072$. The present value of each loan's after-tax payments and the present value of the after-tax interest savings are shown below.

Time	Subsidized Loan	Market Loan	Interest Savings
0	$ 1,000.000	$ 1,000.00	$ 0
1	−1,060.000	−1,072.00	12.000
PV @ 0.072	$ 11.194	$ 0	$11.194

The present value of the subsidized loan equals the present value of the interest savings, so it is unnecessary to compute the interest savings to determine the value of the subsidized financing.

The annual payment on Cold-Fit Clothing Company's subsidized loan is determined by setting the present value of an annuity of four years at 9 percent interest equal to the principal of the loan, $2,020,202. Therefore, the payment is

$$\text{Payment} \times \text{APVF}_{0.09,4} = \$2,020,202$$
$$\text{Payment} \times 3.23972 = \$2,020,202$$
$$\text{Payment} = \$623,573.02.$$

Only the interest portion of each payment is tax-deductible, so we must prepare an amortization table to split each payment into principal and interest. This is shown in Table 17.1.

The subsidized loan's after-tax cash flow at the end of 1997 is the principal of the loan that Cold-Fit receives then. The after-tax cash flow in subsequent years is the amount of each periodic payment applied to principal, which is not tax-deductible, plus the after-tax amount of interest paid. For example, the after-tax cash flow at the end of 1998 equals $\$-441,754.84 + \$-181,818.18 \times (1 - 0.34) = \$-561,754.84$. All of the subsidized loan's after-tax cash flows are given below.

AMORTIZATION OF COLD-FIT'S SUBSIDIZED LOAN **Table 17.1**

Date	Payment	Interest Due	Applied to Principal	Loan Balance
1997	$ 0	$ 0	$ 0	$2,020,202.00
1998	623,573.02	181,818.18	441,754.84	1,578,447.16
1999	623,573.02	142,060.24	481,512.78	1,096,934.38
2000	623,573.02	98,724.09	524,848.93	572,085.45
2001	623,573.14	51,487.69	572,085.45	0

Year	Subsidized Loan's After-tax Cash Flows
1997	$2,020,202.00
1998	−561,754.84
1999	−575,272.54
2000	−590,006.83
2001	−606,067.34

The present value of these cash flows at the company's normal after-tax cost of debt, 7.92 percent, is $89,529.32. By locating its production facilities in the neighboring county to obtain the subsidized loan, Cold-Fit will increase the value of its insulated gloves project by $89,529.32.

EXERCISE ●————————————————————————————●

17.2   **THE VALUE OF SUBSIDIZED FINANCING**

Cleveland County offered Mowser Video Game Company (from Exercise 17.1) a $100,000, five-year loan from its industrial development fund. Interest on this loan, at 8 percent, is paid annually while the principal is repaid at maturity. What is the value of Cleveland County's loan if Mowser's normal borrowing cost is 10 percent and its tax rate is 34 percent?

Mowser receives a cash flow of $100,000 at time 0 and repays the same amount at time 5. The annual after-tax interest payments on this loan are $100,000 × 0.08 × (1 − 0.34) = $5,280. Therefore, the loan's after-tax cash flows are given below.

Time	Subsidized Loan's After-tax Cash Flows
0	$100,000
1	−5,280
2	−5,280
3	−5,280
4	−5,280
5	−105,280

The present value of these cash flows at Mowser's normal after-tax cost of debt, 6.6 percent, is $5,470.72.

●————————————————●

The Value of Interest Tax-Shields

Recall from Chapter 16 that the cash flow provided by an interest tax-shield equals the amount of interest multiplied by the company's tax rate. Stated in general terms, this cash flow is

$$ITS_t = r_d \times D_t \times T_c$$

where ITS_t = interest tax-shield at the end of period t
 r_d = interest rate on debt
 D_t = amount of debt outstanding during period t
 T_c = corporate tax rate.

The interest tax-shields for Cold-Fit Clothing Company's subsidized loan equals the periodic interest payments, given in Table 17.1, multiplied by the company's tax rate. For example, the interest tax-shield for 1998 is $181,818.18 \times 0.34 = \$61,818.18$. The complete schedule of interest tax-shields for the clothing company's insulated gloves project is given below.

Year	Interest Tax Shields
1998	$61,818.18
1999	48,300.48
2000	33,566.19
2001	17,505.81

The rate of return at which to discount these cash flows depends on their risk, which in turn depends on how the company manages the debt used to finance the project. So far, we have assumed that a company determines the *dollar* amount of debt it will use during each year of a project's life at the time the project is accepted. We assumed the amount of debt was constant in perpetuity in Chapter 16, for example, to simplify our discussion of capital structure. For Cold-Fit Clothing Company, we assumed the company set the project's year-by-year debt levels at the amounts implied by the amortization of the four-year loan. Under these circumstances, the risk of the interest tax-shield is completely determined by the risk of the interest payment itself. The company's normal cost of debt, r_d, reflects this risk and is therefore appropriate for discounting the associated tax-shield.

The present value of these interest tax-shields at the company's normal cost of debt, 12 percent, is $128,716.66. The tax-deductibility of interest payments adds $128,716.66 to the value of Cold-Fit's insulated gloves project.

EXERCISE
17.3

THE VALUE OF INTEREST TAX-SHIELDS

Determine the value of the interest tax-shields provided by Mowser Video's 8 percent subsidized loan described in Exercise 17.2.

Mowser's debt level is a constant $100,000 throughout the project's life, so its annual interest tax-shield is

$$ITS = 0.08 \times \$100,000 \times 0.34 = \$2,720.$$

The present value of this five-year annuity at the company's normal cost of debt, 10 percent, is

$$PV(ITS) = \$2,720 \times APVF_{0.10,5}$$
$$= \$2,720 \times 3.7908 = \$10,310.98.$$

The interest tax-shields add $10,310.98 to the value of Mower's expansion project.

● ———————— ●

The Project's Adjusted Present Value

A project's APV equals the value of its net free cash flows plus the value of its financial side effects. For Cold-Fit Clothing Company's insulated gloves proposal, these values are given below.

Value of net free cash flows		$398,480.64
Value of financial side effects		
Floatation costs	$–14,504.99	
Subsidized financing	89,529.32	
Interest tax-shields	$128,716.66	
Total		203,740.99
Adjusted present value		$602,221.63

This project will add $602,221.63 to the wealth of the clothing company's owners.

EXERCISE

17.4   ADJUSTED PRESENT VALUE

The value of the net free cash flows provided by Mowser Video Game Company's expansion project is $–2,500.00. Is the project acceptable considering its financial side effects?

Value of net free cash flows		$–2,500.00
Value of financial side effects		
Floatation costs	$–2,222.66	
Subsidized financing	5,470.72	
Interest tax-shields	$10,310.98	
Total		13,559.04
Adjusted present value		$11,059.04

Mowser's expansion project will add $11,059.04 to the owners' wealth, so it is acceptable.

● ———————— ●

17.2   EVALUATING FINANCIAL LEASES

Companies lease rather than purchase many types of capital equipment. Examples are aircraft, ships and barges, railroad cars, trucks, machine tools, computers, copiers, and other office equipment; the list goes on and on. The company that uses the equipment, the *lessee*, obtains many of the benefits of ownership by paying lease payments to the owner, the *lessor*.

The contract between the lessee and lessor may be a financial or operating lease. The salient characteristics of a **financial lease** are that it is noncancelable and that the lease payments fully amortize the original cost of the equipment. These same characteristics describe the lessee's situation if he borrows money and buys the equipment outright. Consequently, a financial lease is an investment with debt financing.

An **operating lease** is cancelable and the periodic payments do not recover the original cost of the equipment. The term of the lease may be measured in time (years, for example) or the amount of service provided (miles). The lessor expects to recover its costs by leasing the equipment to another company when the lease agreement expires. Lessors usually maintain and insure the asset leased under an operating agreement to preserve its value for the future leasing opportunities.

A simple numerical example highlights the difference between these types of lease contracts. Pretty Good Image Inc. (PGI) manufactures and sells a high-volume office copier with an expected life of three years. The company's opportunity cost is 12 percent per year. PGI's sales and lease terms are described below.

Cash sale:	$50,000
Financial lease:	3 years
	Excludes maintenance and insurance
	$18,587 per year paid in advance
Operating lease:	1 year, 600,000 copies
	Includes maintenance and insurance
	$19,000 per year paid in advance

The lease payment under the financial lease was determined by amortizing the cost of the equipment over three years using the lessor's 12 percent required rate of return. That is,

$$\text{Lease payment} + \text{Lease payment} \times \text{APVF}_{0.12,2} = \$50,000$$
$$\text{Lease payment} = \$50,000/(1 + \text{APVF}_{0.12,2})$$
$$= \$50,000/2.6901 = \$18,587.$$

We will restrict our attention to financial leases because our focus is on the analysis of investment proposals with financing side effects.

APV Analysis of Financial Leases

A financial lease may be the most common type of financing under which a company predetermines the dollar amount of debt it will use during each year of the project's life. This debt, sometimes called the **equivalent loan,** is the debt-like obligation the company incurs when it signs the lease. You will learn how to measure the amount of this obligation later.

The fact that a company predetermines the dollar amount of debt it will use when it signs a financial lease means that the lease should be evaluated using APV analysis. Furthermore, companies usually have the opportunity to borrow money and buy the equipment, so we must determine the APV of this alternative as well. Written in the terms of Section 17.1, we must compare

$$\text{APV(lease)} = \frac{\text{Present value of}}{\text{free cash flows}} + \frac{\text{Present value of financial}}{\text{side effects of leasing}}$$

with

$$\text{APV(purchase)} = \frac{\text{Present value of}}{\text{free cash flows}} + \frac{\text{Present value of financial}}{\text{side effects of purchasing.}}$$

The better course of action is the one with the higher APV (greater than zero). We will compare these two alternatives explicitly first and then look at a shortcut procedure that, in effect, compares only their financial side effects.

Present Value of Free Cash Flows   We must slightly change our procedure for computing net free cash flows when our objective is to compare leasing and purchasing. This change is necessary when evaluating leases because a lessee does not receive the depreciation tax-shield an owner receives. Consequently, we must omit the effect of depreciation from cash flow provided by operations and account for it as a financing adjustment instead.

How you omit depreciation's effect from cash flow provided by operations depends on whether you prepare direct or indirect format cash statements. This is accomplished in a direct format cash statement by computing cash flow provided by operations as follows:

Cash flow provided by operations = (cash revenues – cash costs) $\times$ (1 – T_c).

The indirect format statement begins with net income, which means depreciation has been deducted. Therefore, you must reverse the depreciation deduction by adding the after-tax amount of depreciation to net income. That is,

(Revenue – costs – depreciation) $\times$ (1 – T_c) = Net income,

so

(Revenue – costs) $\times$ (1 – T_c) = Net income + depreciation $\times$ (1 – T_c).

The remaining entries in the indirect format statement are the same as before except you don't add back depreciation; the depreciation tax-shield is recognized in the adjustment section. We'll use Tyson Wagon Works to illustrate this and other steps in the analysis of a financial lease.

Tyson Wagon Works produces scale models of historical western wagons for sale to hobbyists. The company's distributor, acting on requests from retailers, has suggested the company add a model prairie schooner to its product line. Tyson's financial analysts estimate it will cost $80,000 at the end of 1997 for the bench and hand tools needed to produce this product and that the product will be viable for five years. The tools are depreciable over a three-year life under the Modified Accelerated Cost Recovery System. Alternatively, Tyson can lease the tools for five annual payments of $17,500, the first payment due when the lease is signed at the end of 1997. The company's tax rate is 34 percent.

The project's free cash flows are computed in Table 17.2. Cash flow provided by operations, excluding the effect of depreciation, equals net income plus depreciation

TYSON'S WAGON PROJECT—FREE CASH FLOW   **Table 17.2**

Panel A: Net Income

	1997	1998	1999	2000	2001	2002
Cash revenue	$ 0	$48,000	$70,000	$40,000	$27,000	$20,000
Cash operating costs	0	12,100	16,500	21,200	18,900	15,200
Depreciation (MACRS						
3-year life)	26,664	35,552	11,856	5,928	0	0
Net operating income	(26,664)	348	41,644	12,872	8,100	4,800
Taxes (0.34)	(9 066)	118	14,159	4,376	2,754	1,632
Net income	$(17,598)	$ 230	$27,485	$ 8,496	$ 5,346	$ 3,168

Panel B: Free Cash Flow

	1997	1998	1999	2000	2001	2002
Cash flow provided by						
(used for) operations						
Net income	$(17,598)	$ 230	$27,485	$ 8,496	$ 5,346	$ 3,168
Plus depreciation						
$\times$ (1 – 0.34)	17,598	23,464	7,825	3,912	0	0
Net cash flow	0	23,694	35,310	12,408	5,346	3,168
Cash flow provided by						
(used for) investment	(80,000)	0	0	0	0	0
Cash flow provided by						
(used for) financial slack	0	0	0	0	0	0
Net free cash flow	$(80,000)	$23,694	$35,310	$12,408	$ 5,346	$ 3,168

multiplied by one minus the tax rate. This cash flow equals $23,694 for 1998. You would get the same answer by subtracting cash costs from cash revenues and multiplying the result by one minus the tax rate; ($48,000 – $12,100) $\times$ (1 – 0.34) = $23,694. There was no need to add and subtract changes in current operating assets and current operating liabilities because the revenues and costs were stated in cash rather than accrual terms.

The present value of the wagon project's free cash flows at the company's business risk required rate of return, 12 percent, is $–16,669. The wagon project is not acceptable without considering the value of its financial side effects.

APV of Leasing the Equipment   Leasing an asset produces two financial side effects. First, the company avoids paying the cash cost of the asset, which has the effect of a cash inflow at the end of 1997. Second, Tyson pays the after-tax lease payments at the end of years 1997 through 2001. The annual cash flows attributable to these side effects are shown in Table 17.3.

The cash saved by not purchasing the asset, $80,000, is in present value terms while the present value of the after-tax lease payments at the company's cost of debt, 10 percent, is

Table 17.3   TYSON WAGON PROJECT
ADJUSTMENTS TO FREE CASH FLOW IF ASSET LEASED

	1997	1998	1999	2000	2001	2002
Avoidance of initial cost	$80,000	$ 0	$ 0	$ 0	$ 0	$0
After-tax lease payment	(11,550)	(11,550)	(11,550)	(11,550)	(11,550)	0
Total adjustments	$68,450	$(11,550)	$(11,550)	$(11,550)	$(11,550)	$0

$$PV(\text{after-tax lease payments}) = \$11{,}550 \times (1 + APVF_{0.10,4})$$
$$= \$11{,}550 \times 4.1699 = \$48{,}162.$$

Therefore the project's adjusted present value if the company leases the equipment is given below.

Value of net free cash flows	$-16,669
Value of financial side effects of leasing	
Avoidance of initial cost	$80,000
After-tax lease payment	−48,162
Total	31,838
Adjusted present value	$ 15,169

Leasing the tools to produce the prairie schooner is acceptable because it adds $15,169 to the owners' wealth.

EXERCISE ●

17.5   FINANCIAL SIDE EFFECTS OF LEASING

Determine the value of the financial side effects of leasing a portable sandblaster for three years at an annual cost of $7,000 per year, paid in advance. The company's cost of debt and tax rate are 10 percent and 35 percent. The cost to purchase the machine is $20,000.

The adjustments to free cash flow with leasing are given below.

Time	0	1	2
Avoidance of initial cost	$20,000	0	0
After-tax lease payment	−4,550	−4,550	−4,550
Total adjustments	$15,540	$−4,550	$−4,550

Therefore, the value of the financial side effects of leasing is

$$\text{Value of financial side effects of leasing} = \$15{,}450 - \$4{,}550 \times APVF_{0.10,2}$$
$$= \$7{,}553.31.$$

Leasing the sandblaster adds $7,553.31 to the value of the associated project's free cash flows.

● ────────── ●

APV of Borrowing Money and Buying the Equipment   There are different financial side effects from borrowing money and buying the equipment. First, the company owns the asset and is permitted to deduct depreciation when computing taxable income. This deduction provides a depreciation tax-shield that equals the year's depreciation multiplied by the company's tax rate. That is,

$$\text{Depreciation tax-shield}_t = \text{Depreciation}_t \times T_c.$$

Second, although the buyer may or may not use debt to finance the purchase, it must conduct the analysis *as if* it will. This is necessary to make the purchase and lease alternatives comparable because a financial lease is a debt-financed investment. The interest tax-shield provided by the debt that makes leasing and buying comparable is the purchase alternative's other financial side effect.

The amount of debt that makes the two alternatives comparable is the equivalent loan described earlier. We determine the amount of this equivalent loan by applying a simple principle: *The company should use the maximum amount of debt possible without placing additional demands on its free cash flows.* There are three sources of cash flows available to repay the loan given this restriction. First, the after-tax lease payments are available to repay the loan because the company does not lease the asset if it purchases it. Second, the cash flows provided by the depreciation tax-shield are available because the company receives these cash flows as the owner. Third, the debt issued to finance the purchase provides its own interest tax-shield that is available for repaying the loan.

In symbols, the debt service cash flow in year t is

$$\text{Debt service cash flow}_t = L_t \times (1 - T_c) + \text{Depreciation}_t \\ \times T_c + r_d \times D_t \times T_c \qquad [17.1]$$

where
$$L_t \times (1 - T_c) = \text{after-tax lease payment in year } t$$
$$\text{Depreciation}_t \times T_c = \text{depreciation tax-shield in year } t$$
$$r_d \times D_t \times T_c = \text{interest tax-shield in year } t.$$

This amount of cash flow is available for debt service without placing any additional demands on the company's net free cash flows because the after-tax lease payment and the two tax-shields are additional cash flows that are not available under the lease alternative. The present value of these cash flows at the required rate of return on debt is the principal amount of debt, D, that makes the purchase alternative comparable to the lease.

We have a circularity problem with this definition of the amount of cash flow available for debt service. The amount of cash flow available determines the amount of debt the company can issue, however, the amount of debt it issues determines the amount of the interest tax-shield. Fortunately, this circularity is easily removed from the problem by discounting the first two components of the debt service cash flows at the company's *after-tax* required rate of return on debt.[3] That is,

$$D = \sum_{t=0}^{n} \frac{L_t \times (1 - T_c) + \text{Depreciation}_t \times T_c}{[1 + r_d \times (1 - T_c)]^t} \qquad [17.2][4]$$

This method of determining the amount of the loan that makes the purchase comparable to the lease is demonstrated for Tyson Wagon Works in Table 17.4. The debt service cash flows are computed in panel A. The present value of these cash flows at the company's after-tax cost of debt, 6.6 percent, is $76,645. Tyson can repay a loan of this amount using the after-tax lease payment, the depreciation tax-shield, and the loan's own interest tax-shield for funds. This loan is amortized in panel B to determine the amount of each year's interest payment. Note that the principal is reduced each year by cash flows from two sources: the debt service cash flows, computed in panel A, and the loan's own periodic interest tax-shields.

EXERCISE ●──●

17.6   **THE EQUIVALENT LOAN**

Determine the amount of the loan that makes the lease and purchase of the portable sandblaster (first mentioned in Exercise 17.5) equivalent. The company will depreciate the asset in two years using straight-line depreciation if it purchases the machine.

The debt service cash flows equal the after-tax lease payment, from Exercise 17.5, plus the depreciation tax-shield.

$$\text{Annual depreciation tax-shield} = 0.35 \times \$20,000/2$$
$$= \$3,500$$

Time	0	1	2
From after-tax lease payment	$4,550	$4,550	4,550
From depreciation tax-shield	0	3,500	3,500
Total	$4,550	$8,050	$8,050

---

[3]See Richard S. Ruback, "Calculating the Market Value of Riskless Cash Flows," *Journal of Financial Economics*, March 1986, pp. 323–339 for a general treatment of the valuation of riskless cash flows.

[4]This is easiest to see for a one-year loan although it applies to a loan of any maturity. Using Equation 17.1, the debt service cash flow available to repay a one-year loan is

$$\text{Debt service cash flow} = L \times (1 - T_c) + \text{Depreciation} \times T_c + r_d \times D \times T_c.$$

The amount of debt this cash flow will support is

$$D = \frac{L \times (1 - T_c) + \text{Depreciation} \times T_c + r_d \times D \times T_c}{1 + r_d}.$$

Solving for D,

$$D \times (1 + r_d) - D \times r_d \times T_c = L \times (1 - T_c) + \text{Depreciation} \times T_c.$$

Collecting terms and simplifying, we get Equation 17.2.

INTEREST TAX-SHIELD ON COMPARABLE LOAN   Table 17.4

Panel A: Determining the Amount of the Loan

	1997	1998	1999	2000	2001	2002
Cash flows available for debt service						
From after-tax lease payment	$11,550	$11,550	$11,550	$11,550	$11,550	$0
From depreciation tax-shield	9,066	12,088	4,031	2,016	0	0
Total	$20,616	$23,638	$15,581	$13,566	$11,550	$0

Panel B: Loan Amortization

	1997	1998	1999	2000	2001
Payment					
From debt service cash flows	$20,616	$23,638	$15,581	$13,566	$11,550
From interest tax-shield	0	1,905	1,227	778	368
Total	20,616	25,543	16,808	14,344	11,918
Interest due	0	5,603	3,609	2,289	1,083
Applied to principal	20,616	19,940	13,199	12,055	10,835
Loan balance	$56,029	$36,089	$22,890	$10,835	$ 0

The equivalent loan, D, equals the present value of the debt service cash flows at the company's after-tax cost of debt.

$$D = \$4,550 + \$8,050 \times \text{APVF}_{0.065,2}$$
$$= \$19,206.04$$

Signing the lease contract is equivalent to borrowing $19,206.04.

● ——————— ●

The depreciation and interest tax-shields for Tyson's purchase alternative are given in Table 17.5. The depreciation tax-shields equal the periodic depreciation (computed in Table 17.1) multiplied by the company's tax rate. The present value of these cash flows at the company's cost of debt is $24,901. The interest tax-shields are the annual interest expense (from panel B of Table 17.4) multiplied by the company's tax rate. The present value of these cash flows at the cost of debt, 10 percent, is $3,582.

Therefore the project's APV if the company purchases the equipment is given below.

Value of net free cash flows		$–16,669
Value of financial side effects of purchasing		
Depreciation tax-shield	$24,901	
Interest tax-shield	3,582	
Total		28,483
Adjusted present value		$ 11,814

Table 17.5   ADJUSTMENTS TO FREE CASH FLOW IF ASSET PURCHASED

	1997	1998	1999	2000	2001	2002
Depreciation tax-shield	$9,066	$12,088	$4,031	$2,016	$ 0	$0
Interest tax-shield	0	1,905	1,227	778	368	0
Total adjustments	$9,066	13,993	$5,258	$2,794	$368	$0

The adjusted present value of the proposal to produce prairie schooner wagons by purchasing the equipment is $11,814. This is an acceptable approach, however, leasing is better by $3,355 ($15,169 – $11,814), so Tyson should lease the tools and add the wagons to its product line.

EXERCISE •
17.7   **FINANCIAL SIDE EFFECTS OF PURCHASING**

Determine the financial side effects of purchasing the sandblasting equipment described in Exercises 17.5 and 17.6. Is leasing or purchasing better?

The adjustments to free cash flow with purchasing are the depreciation and interest tax-shields. You computed the depreciation tax-shields in Exercise 17.6. The interest tax-shields are based on the amortization of the equivalent loan given below. The loan's beginning balance is $19,206.04, determined in Exercise 17.6.

Time	0	1	2
Payment			
From debt service cash flows	$ 4,550.00	$8,050.00	$8,050.00
From interest tax-shield	0	512.96	264.55
Total	$ 4,550.00	$8,562.96	$8,314.55
Interest due	0	1,465.60	755.86
Applied to principal	4,550.00	7,097.36	7,558.69
Loan balance	$14,656.04	$7,558.69	$ 0

Time	0	1	2
Depreciation tax-shield	$ 0	$3,500.00	$3,500.00
Interest tax-shield	0	512.96	264.55
Total adjustments	$ 0	$4,012.96	$3,764.55

Therefore, the value of the financial side effects of purchasing is

$$\text{Value of financial side effects of purchasing} = \$0 + \frac{\$4,012.96}{1.10} + \frac{\$3,764.55}{(1.10)^2}$$

$$= \$6,759.34.$$

Purchasing the sandblaster adds $6,759.34 to the value of the associated project's free cash flows.

The value of the financial side effects from leasing the sandblaster was $7,553.31. Therefore, leasing is better than purchasing by $793.97 ($7,553.31 − $6,759.34).

● ————————— ●

The Equivalent Loan Method

Now that you know how to evaluate leases using the adjusted present value method, you can appreciate the logic of a convenient shortcut approach. This alternative approach, sometimes called the equivalent loan method, is conceptually and computationally consistent with the APV.

The equivalent loan method compares leasing and purchasing by discounting the incremental cash flows at the company's after-tax required rate of return on debt. Leasing is better if this value is positive; purchasing is better if it is negative. The equivalent loan method does not explicitly consider the net free cash flows, so you must make another calculation to see if the project is acceptable after you have determined the best way to finance it.

You can see the logic of the equivalent loan method clearly by computing the incremental cash flows for a particular year, t. In words,

$$CF_t(\text{lease}) = \text{Net free cash flow}_t - L_t \times (1 - T_c) + \text{Initial cost}_{t=0}$$

$$CF_t(\text{purchase}) = \text{Net free cash flow}_t + \text{Depreciation}_t \times T_c$$
$$+ r_d \times D_t \times T_c$$

$$\text{Incremental cash flow}_t = CF_t(\text{lease}) - CF_t(\text{purchase})$$
$$= -L_t \times (1 - T_c) - \text{Depreciation}_t \times T_c$$
$$- r_d \times D_t \times T_c + \text{Initial cost}_{t=0}. \qquad [17.3]$$

The first three terms on the right-hand side of Equation 17.3 are the cash flows available for debt service (see Equation 17.1). Omitting the interest tax-shield and discounting the after-tax lease payment and the depreciation tax-shield at the company's after-tax cost of debt equals the amount of the equivalent loan (see Equation 17.2). The incremental present value of the lease, sometimes called the net advantage of the lease (NAL), therefore is

$$NPV(\text{lease} - \text{purchase}) = \text{Initial cost} - \sum_{t=1}^{n} \frac{L_t \times (1 - T_c) + \text{Dep}_t \times T_c}{[1 + r_d \times (1 - T_c)]^t}$$

$$NAL = NPV(\text{lease} - \text{purchase}) = \text{Initial cost} - \text{equivalent loan}.$$

The equivalent loan method therefore says the lease is better than the purchase if the value of the asset acquired (the initial cost) is greater than the value of the debt-like obligation the company incurs (the equivalent loan) when it signs the lease.

We have already performed the calculations necessary to apply the equivalent loan method to the Tyson Wagon Works investment proposal. The initial cost of the tools is $80,000 and the value of the equivalent loan is $76,645. The net advantage of the lease therefore is

$$NAL = \text{Initial cost} - \text{equivalent loan}$$
$$= \$80,000 - \$76,645 = \$3,355.$$

This is the same answer we obtained by explicitly applying the APV method to both alternatives. Tyson can acquire the services of assets that cost $80,000 by incurring a debt obligation of only $76,645, so the lease is better than the purchase.

EXERCISE
17.8

THE EQUIVALENT LOAN METHOD

Use the equivalent loan method to determine whether it is better to lease or purchase the sandblaster described in Exercises 17.5 through 17.7.

The cost of the sandblaster is $20,000. The amount of the equivalent loan, from Exercise 17.6, is $19,206.04. Therefore, the net advantage of the lease is

$$NAL = \text{Initial cost} - \text{equivalent loan}$$
$$= \$20,000 - \$19,206.04 = \$793.96.$$

This is the same answer you obtained in Exercise 17.7 by comparing the financing side effects of leasing and purchasing.

Note that the equivalent loan method is an incremental analysis that tells us whether the lease or purchase is better, however, it does not tell us if either is acceptable because the free cash flows were netted from the calculation. Therefore, you must go back and recalculate the value of the winner (the lease in Tyson's case) to be sure that it is acceptable. The APV of the lease is $15,169. Tyson should proceed with this project and lease the equipment because it will increase the owners' wealth by $15,169.

17.3   THE WEIGHTED AVERAGE COST OF CAPITAL METHOD

The adjusted present value method works when a project's interest tax-shields are independent of its free cash flows. This condition is what makes it possible to separately calculate the value of these cash flows and add the results to determine the project's APV. Up until now, we have ensured that these cash flows are independent by assuming that the company predetermines the dollar amount of debt it will use each year of the project's life.

Chapter 16 showed that we also can compute a project's value by using the weighted average cost of capital, r_{wacc}, to discount its free cash flows when the project is a perpetuity. The APV method accounts for the value of the interest tax-shield by adjusting the present value while the weighted average cost of capital method accounts for it by adjusting the required rate of return. Both methods give the same results if the adjustments are done consistently. The consistent definitions of the weighted average cost of capital we developed in Chapter 16 were

$$r_{wacc} = r_d \times (1 - T_c) \times \frac{D}{D + E} + r_e \times \frac{E}{D + E} \qquad [16.7]$$

with

$$r_e = r_f + (r_m - r_f) \times \beta_e$$
$$\beta_e = \beta_a \times [1 + (1 - T_c) \times D/E] \qquad [16.6]$$

or

$$r_{wacc} = r_a - r_a \times T_c \times \frac{D}{D + E}. \qquad [16.8]$$

Companies may not predetermine the dollar amount of debt outstanding. They may, for example, use a larger dollar amount of debt than normal when the project's value is larger than expected and vice versa. This is a familiar policy that individuals follow by using home-equity loans to increase the dollar amount of their indebtedness after their homes have appreciated in value.

An individual or company can administer this policy by predetermining the *leverage ratio* to maintain each year of the investment's life. Banks and mortgage companies often describe their lending policies in these terms. A common example is, "We will lend 90 percent of the home's appraised value."

This simple change in policy makes the adjusted present value method unworkable as are the weighted average cost of capital expressions based on it. Here's the problem: The dollar amount of debt outstanding fluctuates with the project's value when the company predetermines the project's leverage ratio. The amount of debt outstanding the first year of the project's life is determined when the project is accepted although subsequent debt levels and therefore subsequent tax-shields are uncertain then. Furthermore, the amounts of the subsequent tax-shields are perfectly correlated with the project's value. This means that although we can continue to discount the first year's interest tax-shield at the cost of debt, r_d, we must discount the expected future tax-shields in subsequent years at the project's business risk required rate of return, r_a.

Stated succinctly, a project's free cash flows and interest tax-shields are not independent when a company predetermines the project's leverage ratio. This means we cannot separately determine their values and add them together to determine the project's APV. We cannot use the weighted average cost of capital expressions based on the APV then either.

Fortunately, Miles and Ezzell derived analogous weighted average cost of capital equations that apply when a company predetermines a project's leverage ratio.[5] You can use their equations whether the project's free cash flows are a level perpetuity or not. Discounting the free cash flows using their expressions for the weighted average cost of capital correctly accounts for the value of those cash flows and the value of the project's interest tax-shields. Their key equation is

$$r_{wacc} = r_a - r_d \times \frac{(1 + r_a)}{(1 + r_d)} \times T_c \times \frac{D}{D + E}. \qquad [17.4]$$

---

[5]James A. Miles and John R. Ezzell, "The Weighted Average Cost of Capital, Perfect Capital Markets, and Project Life: A Clarification," *Journal of Financial and Quantitative Analysis*, September 1980, pp. 719–730.

Note the similarity between Equations 16.8 and 17.4. Both equations say that a project's weighted average cost of capital is less than its business risk required rate of return, r_a, by a factor that depends on the tax rate and the amount of financial leverage the company uses. The appearance of r_d and $(1 + r_a)/(1 + r_d)$ in the adjustment factor in Equation 17.4 accounts for the fact that, when a company predetermines a project's leverage ratio, interest tax-shields beyond the first year are uncertain and perfectly correlated with the project's value. Here is a simple application.

The William Chalk Decorative Arts Company has an opportunity to produce and sell transparent candles. The company's debt is riskless and the asset beta for this line of business is 0.90. Chalk's tax rate is 35 percent and the company's target debt/value ratio is 40 percent. The riskless interest rate is 6.5 percent and the expected rate of return on the market portfolio is 15 percent. Anticipated net free cash flows are given below.

Time	Net Free Cash Flows
0	$-80,000
1	38,000
2	30,000
3	23,000
4	15,000
5	7,000

The required rate of return for this line of business is

$$r_a = r_f + (r_m - r_f) \times \beta_a$$
$$= 0.065 + (0.150 - 0.065) \times 0.9 = 0.1415.$$

Therefore, the project's weighted average cost of capital is

$$r_{wacc} = r_a - r_d \times \frac{(1 + r_a)}{(1 + r_d)} \times T_c \times \frac{D}{D + E}$$

$$= 0.1415 - 0.065 \times \frac{1.1415}{1.065} \times 0.35 \times 0.40$$

$$= 0.1317 \text{ or } 13.17\%.$$

The net present value of the transparent candle project's free cash flows at this required rate of return is $5,785.60. Chalk should accept the candle project because it adds $5,785.60 to the owners' wealth.

EXERCISE ●

17.9   **THE WEIGHTED AVERAGE COST OF CAPITAL WHEN THE LEVERAGE RATIO IS PREDETERMINED**

Determine the net present value of William Chalk's candle project if the company's target debt/value ratio is 50 percent. What is the source of the project's additional value?

The company's weighted average cost of capital with a target debt/value ratio of 50 percent is

$$r_{wacc} = 0.1415 - 0.065 \times \frac{1.1415}{1.065} \times 0.35 \times 0.50$$

$$= 0.1293 \text{ or } 12.93\%.$$

The project's NPV at this required rate of return is $6,176.23. The extra $390.63 ($6,176.23 – $5,785.60) is the present value of the additional tax-shields provided by using a larger proportion of debt financing.

● ———————— ●

Miles and Ezzell also derived an expression for the beta of a levered project that is analogous to Equation 16.6.[6] By using this equation and the CAPM, an analyst can compute the equity required rate of return and then use Equation 16.7 to determine the weighted average cost of capital. The result will equal the value obtained by using Equation 17.4.

Miles and Ezzell's expression for the beta of a levered project is not repeated here because it is complex and because there is a simpler alternative. The alternative is Equation 16.2, which describes financial leverage's effect on risk in the absence of corporate taxes.

$$\beta_e = \beta_a \times (1 + D/E) \qquad\qquad \text{[16.2]}$$

Harris and Pringle showed that this expression is correct even in the presence of corporate taxes if all the future tax-shields, including the first one, are considered uncertain.[7] In addition, Taggart states that there is no practical difference between using Miles and Ezzell's complicated expression and Harris and Pringle's simple one.[8] Consequently, that is what we will do.

Let's return to the William Chalk Decorative Arts Company for an illustration. Remember, the facts related to this company's project were

$r_m = 15\%$
$r_d = r_f = 6.5\%$
$\beta_a = 0.90$
$r_a = 14.15\%$
$T_c = 35\%$
Debt/value ratio = 40%.

A debt/value ratio of 0.40 corresponds to a debt/equity ratio of 0.667. Therefore, the candle project's equity beta and required rate of return are

---

[6]James A. Miles and John R. Ezzell, "Reformulating Tax-Shield Valuation: A Note," *Journal of Finance,* December 1985, pp. 1485–1492.

[7]Robert S. Harris and John J. Pringle, "Risk-Adjusted Discount Rates—Extensions from the Average Risk Case," *Journal of Financial Research,* Fall 1985, pp. 237–244.

[8]Robert A. Taggart, Jr., "Consistent Valuation and Cost of Capital Expressions with Corporate and Personal Taxes," *Financial Management,* Autumn 1991, pp. 8–20.

$$\beta_e = \beta_a \times (1 + D/E)$$
$$= 0.90 \times 1.667$$
$$= 1.50$$
$$r_e = 0.065 + (0.15 - 0.065) \times 1.50$$
$$= 0.1925.$$

The project's weighted average cost of capital therefore is

$$r_{\text{wacc}} = r_d \times (1 - T_c) \times \frac{D}{D+E} + r_e \times \frac{E}{D+E}$$
$$= 0.065 \times (1 - 0.35) \times 0.40 + 0.1925 \times 0.60$$
$$= 0.1324 \text{ or } 13.24\%.$$

This estimate of the weighted average cost of capital does not equal the value computed from Equation 17.4, 13.17 percent, because we used Harris and Pringle's expression for the beta of a levered project rather than Miles and Ezzell's. The project's NPV at this required rate of return is $5,672.25 rather than $5,785.60, a difference of less than 2 percent. This may be a tolerable error considering the other sources of error in valuing long-term investment projects.

EXERCISE • ————————————————————————————— •

17.10   **THE WEIGHTED AVERAGE COST OF CAPITAL WHEN THE LEVERAGE RATIO IS PREDETERMINED**

Determine the weighted average cost of capital for William Chalk's candle project if the company's target debt/value ratio is 50 percent. Compare your results to Exercise 17.9.

A debt/value ratio of 0.50 corresponds to a debt/equity ratio of 1.0. Therefore, the project's equity beta, equity required rate of return, and weighted average cost of capital are

$$\beta_e = \beta_a \times (1 + D/E)$$
$$= 0.90 \times 2.0$$
$$= 1.80$$
$$r_e = 0.065 + (0.15 - 0.065) \times 1.80$$
$$= 0.2180 \text{ or } 21.80\%$$
$$r_{\text{wacc}} = r_d \times (1 - T_c) \times \frac{D}{D+E} + r_e \times \frac{E}{D+E}$$
$$= 0.065 \times (1 - 0.35) \times 0.50 + 0.2180 \times 0.50$$
$$= 0.1301 \text{ or } 13.01\%.$$

This estimate of the weighted average cost of capital differs from the estimate in Exercise 17.9, 12.93 percent, because we didn't use Miles and Ezzell's equation for the equity beta.

• ——————— •

17.4 CHOOSING THE VALUATION METHOD

You now have two methods of recognizing financing effects in investment analysis: the APV and weighted average cost of capital approaches. We discussed many issues while developing these procedures, and you may have lost sight of the factors to consider when deciding which method to use. The choice, which is described by the roadmap in Exhibit 17.1, is actually very clear. This roadmap was adapted from one in Taggart's article, referred to earlier. His valuation roadmaps also consider the effect of personal taxes.

The company's debt-management policy determines which method of valuation you may use. If the company predetermines the dollar amount of debt outstanding each year of the project's life, then the tax-shields are certain and you must use the APV

Exhibit 17.1

VALUATION ROADMAP

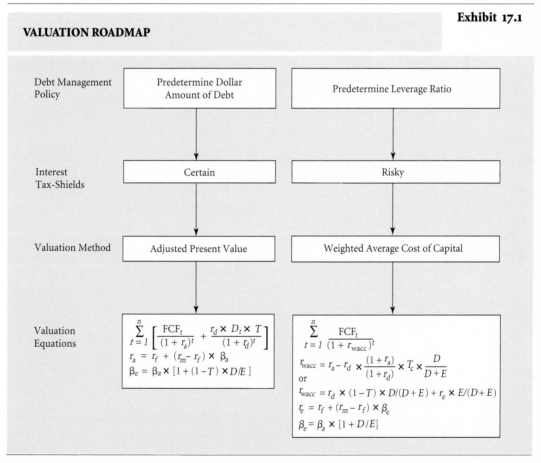

Adapted from Robert A. Taggart, Jr., "Consistent Valuation and Cost of Capital Expressions with Corporate and Personal Taxes," *Financial Management,* Autumn 1991, pp. 8–20.

method. Financial leases conform to this situation very closely. If the company pre-determines the project's leverage ratio, then the tax-shields are risky and you must use the weighted average cost of capital approach. The appropriate valuation equations for each method are summarized in Exhibit 17.1.

17.5   ESTIMATING THE REQUIRED RATES OF RETURN

Estimates of the market's required rates of return on the company's assets, its debt, and its equity are needed to implement these valuation models. The logical starting point for determining these returns is the required rate of return on the company's assets, r_a. This is a good place to start because the value of r_a depends on the business risk of the company's assets and is unaffected by financial risk and financial side effects such as the tax-deductibility of interest.

Estimating the Required Rate of Return on Assets

We will continue to use the Capital Asset Pricing Model (CAPM) to determine the required rate of return on assets although other models, such as the Arbitrage Pricing Theory, are available. The information we need to apply the CAPM to this problem are the expected rates of return on riskless assets and the market portfolio and the invest-ment project's beta. The market interest rates are easy to estimate, but the project's beta requires a little more work.

Estimating Market Interest Rates   You should use the expected yield on U.S. Treasury bills for the market's expected rate of return on riskless assets. T-bills have no default risk, they are the most marketable securities in the world, and they have very little interest rate risk due to their short term to maturity. These characteristics make T-bills the closest thing to a riskless asset that is available in reality.

The *current* T-bill yield may not equal the market's expected rate of return on risk-less assets over an extended period of time, however, because T-bill rates change. Therefore, we must use an interest rate that reflects the market's *long-term* expectations about T-bill yields when our purpose is to estimate the required rate of return for long-lived assets.

The preferred habitat theory of the term structure of interest rates, which you learned about in Chapter 4, tells us how to infer these long-term expectations. This the-ory says that the current yield on long-term financial instruments is an average of expected future short-term yields plus a term or liquidity premium. Consequently, the current yield on long-term Treasury securities minus a term premium is an estimate of average expected future T-bill yields.

Ibbotson Associates found that the average yield on long-term U.S. government bonds exceeded the average yield on T-bills by 1.7 percent from 1926–1995.[9] Interpreting this yield differential as a term premium, the market's expected rate of return on

[9]*Stocks, Bonds, Bills and Inflation, 1996 Yearbook,* Chicago, Ibbotson Associates, 1996.

riskless assets equals the current yield on long-term U.S. government bonds minus 1.7 percent.

$$r_f = \text{Yield on long-term U.S. government bonds} - 0.017$$

The yield on U.S. government bonds with 30 years until maturity averaged 7.9 percent on December 30, 1994. This implies the market's expected rate of return on riskless assets was 6.2 percent (0.079 − 0.017). This compares with the current T-bill yield on that date of 6.5 percent.

Ibbotson Associates' historical rates of return also provide a way to estimate the expected rate of return on the market portfolio. They found that the average rate of return on a portfolio of common stocks exceeded the average yield on T-bills by 8.7 percent from 1926–1995. Assuming their portfolio of 500 common stocks is an acceptable proxy for the market portfolio, this return differential is the market risk premium, $E(r_m) - r_f$.[10]

$$E(r_m) = \text{Expected rate of return on riskless assets} + 0.087$$

Referring to December 30, 1994, the expected rate of return on the market portfolio was 14.9 percent (6.2 percent + 8.7 percent). The CAPM with the required rates of return measured on December 30, 1994 is therefore

$$r_j = r_f + (r_m - r_f) \times \beta$$

$$= 0.062 + (0.149 - 0.062) \times \beta.$$

Estimating a Project's Beta   A project's beta measures the systematic or nondiversifiable risk of its free cash flows before adjustment for financing effects. We could estimate this beta using regression analysis if we could observe the periodic rates of return computed from these cash flows. We would simply relate the asset's rate of return each period to the rate of return on the market portfolio to determine its sensitivity to economic conditions.

We seldom observe an *asset's* periodic cash flows or rates of return, however, because most assets are held in portfolios financed with both debt and equity. Instead, we see only the periodic rates of return the stockholders earn on their investment in the portfolio. We can compute a beta from these rates of return, however, it is an equity beta. This beta does not measure the systematic risk of a particular asset in the portfolio because the stockholders' returns are affected by the performance of all the company's assets as well as the company's capital structure.

Philip Morris Companies provides a good illustration of this problem. The company has two major business segments, tobacco and food, that are financed with both debt and equity. Individual assets within these business segments include Marlboro and Virginia Slims cigarettes and Kraft cheese and Oscar Mayer meat products. The sales and operating profits provided by each business segment and the company's overall capital structure are described in Table 17.6.

---

[10]For an alternative way to use Ibbotson's historical returns to estimate the market risk premium, see Russell J. Fuller and Kent A. Hickman, "A Note on Estimating the Historical Risk Premium," *Financial Practice and Education*, Fall/Winter 1991, pp. 45–48.

**Table 17.6   PHILIP MORRIS COMPANIES, INC.
SEGMENT DATA AND BALANCE SHEETS**

Business Segment	Percent of 1994 Revenues	Percent of 1994 Operating Profits
Tobacco	44%	62%
Food	49	32
Beer	6	4
Financial services	1	2

	Book Values	Market Values*
Total debt	$39,578	$39,578
Common equity	11,627	50,762
Total assets	$51,205	$90,340
Equity beta	1.20	

*The market value of the debt is estimated to equal the book value of the debt because creditors have a fixed claim on the company's assets. The market value of the equity equals the closing price per share on December 31, 1994 multiplied by the number of shares outstanding.

Source: January 1, 1995 edition of Value/Screen III, Value Line Publishing Inc., copyright 1993.

The company's equity beta, equal to 1.20, also is given in the table. This beta, which measures the systematic risk of the company's common stock, is a weighted average of the betas of the individual assets in the various business segments adjusted for the amount of financial leverage the company uses. Determining how much systematic risk an individual asset, such as the meat products business, contributes to this equity beta is difficult, even for a narrowly diversified company such as Phillip Morris.

We overcome the difficulties of using common stock rates of return to measure asset betas in two steps. The first step is to choose a sample of publicly traded companies whose assets are, as nearly as possible, identical to the investment project's assets. The company evaluating the investment proposal may include itself in this sample if it meets this criterion but not otherwise. For example, a diversified consumer products company should not include itself in a sample that it will use to estimate the systematic risk of snack foods. Choosing the sample companies this way eliminates the problem of trying to allocate systematic risk to the different business segments or assets held by a diversified company.

The second step is to remove the effect of financial leverage from each sample company's equity beta. You should use Harris and Pringle's approach, Equation 16.2, for this purpose if you think the interest tax-shields are risky and Equation 16.6 if you believe they are riskless. The result is

$$\beta_a = \beta_e/(1 + D/E)$$

or

$$\beta_a = \beta_e/[1 + (1 - T_c) \times D/E].$$

Let's apply this two-step procedure to companies in the food industry. A diversified consumer products company, like Philip Morris, could use an asset beta estimated this way to measure the systematic risk and required rate of return for assets in its food business segment.

Table 17.7 contains information about a sample of companies drawn from the food industry, SIC 2000. These companies were chosen for the sample because their assets are concentrated in this industry according to the Value Line Investment Survey. Given in Table 17.7 is each company's equity beta and its market value total debt/equity ratio as of December 31, 1994. Equation 16.2 was used to calculate their asset betas. For example, CPC International's asset beta is

$$\beta_a = \beta_e/(1 + D/E)$$
$$= 1.00/1.42$$
$$= 0.70.$$

An unconditional estimate of the systematic risk of the food business is the average of the individual values or 0.70.

CALCULATION OF ASSET BETA FOR FOOD-PROCESSING COMPANIES   **Table 17.7**

Company	Equity Beta	Market Value Debt/Equity	Asset Beta	Major Food Products
CPC International	1.00	0.42	0.70	Knorr soups, Hellmann's mayonnaise, Skippy peanut butter, Mazola products
H.J. Heinz	0.95	0.44	0.66	Heinz products, Ore-Ida potatoes, Star-Kist tuna
Hershey Foods	1.00	0.34	0.75	Hershey chocolate products, American Beauty pasta products
Hormel Foods	0.80	0.26	0.63	Hormel, Dinty Moore, and Top Shelf meat products
Kellogg	1.00	0.19	0.84	Ready-to-eat cereals, convenience and snack foods
Quaker Oats	0.90	0.63	0.55	Ready-to-eat cereals, Rice-A-Roni, Snapple, Gatorade
J.M. Smucker	0.95	0.20	0.79	Jams, jellies, peanut butter
Average	0.94	0.35	0.70	

Source: January 1, 1995 edition of Value/Screen III, Value Line Publishing, Inc., copyright 1993.

This procedure for estimating an asset's beta appears scientific but it involves a lot of art. First, we cannot find sample companies whose assets are identical to an investment project's assets. Even the undiversified companies listed in Table 17.7 produce and sell a wide range of food products and undoubtedly employ a similar wide range of technologies. Using their average asset beta as our estimate diversifies away some of their unique characteristics but we cannot be certain this is the correct estimate for a particular food-related investment project. Second, the factor we used to remove the effect of financial leverage is only approximately correct, as we discussed earlier.

Perhaps the best thing you can do when confronted with these uncertainties is to use your financial intuition to see if the estimate is reasonable. Our estimate that the beta of the food business is 0.70 is reasonable because this line of business is less risky than average; people must buy food whether the economy does well or poorly. Consequently, we know our estimate should be less than 1.0 even though we don't know exactly how much.

The required rate of return for an investment project in the food industry, using the CAPM based on December 30, 1994 required rates of return, is

$$r_a = 0.062 + (0.149 - 0.062) \times 0.70$$
$$= 0.123 \text{ or } 12.3\%.$$

Estimating the Required Rate of Return on Equity

You need an estimate of the required rate of return on equity to use the weighted average cost of capital method for determining an investment proposal's market value. This estimate is easy to obtain once you have determined an asset's beta and the way it will be financed. All you do is use Equation 16.2 to adjust the asset's beta for the amount of financial leverage the project will use and then substitute this beta into the CAPM to obtain the required return. Continuing our food business example, an investment in this line of business by a company with a target debt/equity ratio equal to 0.35 (the average for our proxy companies) has an equity beta and required rate of return of

$$\beta_e = \beta_a \times (1 + D/E)$$
$$= 0.70 \times 1.35$$
$$= 0.94$$
$$r_e = r_f + (r_m - r_f) \times \beta_e$$
$$= 0.062 + (0.149 - 0.062) \times 0.94 = 0.144 \text{ or } 14.4\%.[11]$$

We also should check the reasonableness of this estimate. One reference point is the expected rate of return on common stock implied by the constant growth dividend valuation model that is repeated below for convenience.

$$P_0 = \frac{D_1}{r_e - g} \qquad [7.9]$$

---

[11]You can complete this calculation in a single step by substituting the equation for an equity or levered beta into the equation for the CAPM and simplifying. The result is

$$r_e = r_a + (r_a - r_d) \times D/E.$$

where P_0 = present stock price
              D_1 = next year's dividend
              r_e = rate of return on equity
              g = dividend growth rate

Rearranging terms,

$$r_e = \frac{D_1}{P_0} + g.$$

This equation says that the rate of return on equity is the expected dividend yield plus the expected dividend growth rate.

Table 17.8 gives forecasts of the dividend yield and dividend growth rate for our proxy companies. The average, 12.6 percent, is lower than our estimate of the required rate of return on equity for a similarly financed food asset but the difference is not alarming.

Estimating the Required Rate of Return on Debt

You learned in Chapter 4 that the required rate of return on debt depends on the general level of interest rates, the term to maturity of the loan, and the financial instrument's special features such as its tax status, marketability, default risk, and whether it provides the issuer or investor valuable options. These are the factors you must consider to estimate the required rate of return on the debt used to finance a project or business.

The yields to maturity on U.S. government debt provide a good reference point for determining the level of interest rates and the effect of term to maturity because these factors affect both government and corporate bonds. These yields as of December 30, 1994 are given in panel A of Table 17.9. You can see that the term structure of interest rates was fairly flat at around 8.06 percent.

Treasury securities are highly marketable and have no default risk, so we must estimate the effect of these factors separately. The yields to maturity on corporate debt rated by agencies such as Standard & Poor's provide a useful reference point for this purpose. These agencies evaluate a debt issue's special features and assign it a rating that

---

IMPLIED EQUITY RATES OF RETURN FOR FOOD-PROCESSING COMPANIES   Table 17.8

	Dividend Yield	Dividend Growth	Rate of Return on Equity
CPC International	2.7%	7.0%	9.7%
H.J. Heinz	4.0	11.5	15.5
Hershey Foods	2.7	7.5	10.2
Hormel Foods	2.2	10.0	12.2
Kellogg	2.5	10.5	13.0
Quaker Oats	3.7	10.0	13.7
J.M. Smucker	2.1	11.5	13.6
Average	2.8	9.7	12.6

Table 17.9   YIELDS ON DEBT
December 30, 1994

Panel A: U.S. Government Debt*

Bond Rating	Time to Maturity	Yield to Maturity
N.A.	1 to 10 years	8.04%
N.A.	More than 10 years	8.08
Average		8.06

Panel B: Corporate Bonds Rated by Standard & Poor's**

AAA	Varies	8.28%
AA	Varies	8.50
A	Varies	8.89
Average		8.56

Panel C: Food-Processing Companies**

CPC International			
8.500% debentures	A+	22 years	8.80%
H.J. Heinz			
5.500% notes	AA	3 years	8.00
6.750% notes	AA	5 years	8.19
6.875% notes	AA	9 years	8.21
Hershey Foods			
8.800% debentures	AA–	27 years	8.53
Kellogg			
5.900% notes	AAA	3 years	8.11
Average		12 years	8.31

*The Wall Street Journal, January 3, 1995, p. 33.

**Standard & Poor's Bond Guide, January 1995, various pages.

depends on the company's default risk and the security's marketability and suscepti-bility to being called. The average yield to maturity for each rating class therefore gives an indication of the market's overall concern about these factors. Panel B of Table 17.9 shows that the average yield premiums on corporate debt at the end of 1994 were 0.5 percent (8.56 – 8.06 percent).

The yield on debt issued by a particular company in a particular industry may vary widely from the overall averages depending on the company's unique characteristics. For example, we might expect that food-processing companies' bonds have lower yields than average because their assets are less risky; remember, their average beta was only 0.70. Panel C of Table 17.9 shows this was the case.

The four proxy companies shown in panel C have publicly traded debt with three to 27 years until maturity and ratings of A+ to AAA. All but one (Hershey Foods) have yields to maturity that are less than the averages for their rating classes as we expected. Consequently, their overall average yield to maturity (8.31 percent) is less than the average for all debt rated by Standard & Poor's (8.56 percent). There is some difference in average yields to maturity of the notes and the debentures but this difference is partly attributable to the fact the longer-term loans are the lowest rated in the sample. Given this confounding factor and the fact the term structure for government debt was fairly flat, we will use the proxy companies' overall average yield to maturity (8.3 percent) as our estimate of the cost of debt for food-processing projects and companies.

Estimating the Weighted Average Cost of Capital

Finally, we can use our estimates of r_d and r_e to obtain an approximate value for the weighted average cost of capital. A debt/equity ratio of 0.35 implies the debt/value and equity/value ratios are 0.26 and 0.74. Assuming the proxy companies' marginal tax rate is 35 percent, the weighted average cost of capital for the food business is

$$r_{wacc} = r_d \times (1 - T_c) \times \frac{D}{D + E} + r_e \times \frac{E}{D + E}$$

$$= 0.083 \times (1 - 0.35) \times 0.26 + 0.144 \times 0.74$$

$$= 0.12 \text{ or } 12.1\%.$$

We also should check our estimates to be sure the relationships among them make sense. Think first about the required rate of return on equity, r_e. This return equals r_a if the company uses no debt in its capital structure but is larger than r_a otherwise because of the addition of financial risk. Importantly, this general relationship, that $r_e \geq r_a$, holds even if the CAPM does not.

Now think about the required rate of return on debt, r_d. This required rate of return equals the risk-free rate if financial distress is costless but is larger than r_f otherwise because cash is lost to competitors, attorneys, etc. Nevertheless, the required rate of return on debt cannot be larger than the required rate of return on the company's assets because the creditors have a claim on the more certain cash flows from these assets. Putting these conditions together, we must have $r_f \leq r_d \leq r_a$.

Lastly, the weighted average cost of capital, r_{wacc}, equals r_a for a company that uses no debt in its capital structure, however, this average is reduced by the tax-deductibility of interest. This weighted average cannot be smaller than the cost of debt, however, because this cost is a component (the smallest component) of the average. Therefore, we should expect $r_d \leq r_{wacc} \leq r_a$.

Putting these conditions together, the market's required rates of return must bear the following relationships to one another.

$$r_f \leq r_d \leq r_{\text{wacc}} \leq r_a \leq r_e$$

Substituting our estimates into this inequality,

$$\begin{array}{ccccc} r_f & r_d & r_{\text{wacc}} & r_a & r_e \end{array}$$
$$6.2\% < 8.3\% < 12.1\% < 12.3\% < 14.4\%.$$

Although we cannot be 100 percent certain about the accuracy of our estimates, they do meet our rough-and-ready intuitive tests.

A company considering an investment in the food-processing business could use the rates of return we've estimated to determine the project's market value. The required rate of return on assets, $r_a = 12.3$ percent, and the required rate of return on debt, $r_d = 8.3$ percent, are appropriate for applying the APV method. A company with circumstances that require it to use the weighted average cost of capital approach could use $r_{\text{wacc}} = 12.1$ percent as its required rate of return.

17.6   SUMMARY

The method of financing used for an investment project affects its value in an imperfect financial market. These financial side effects arise in an imperfect market because (1) there are costs to issue securities, (2) it may be possible to obtain financing at subsidized rates, and (3) interest is tax-deductible. We must account for the value of these side effects to determine the project's actual effect on the owners' wealth.

We examined two ways to account for a project's financial side effects. The cash flows attributable to each side effect are discounted at a rate of return appropriate for their risk and the result is added to the value of the project's free cash flows in the adjusted present value method. The APV method is the one to use if the company predetermines the dollar amount of debt it will use each year of the project's life.

Companies incur a debt-like obligation with a predetermined pattern of payments when using a financial lease. This means APV should be used to evaluate the choice between leasing equipment or borrowing money and buying it. A simpler alternative that compares the initial cost of the equipment to the amount of the loan equivalent to the lease obligation gives the same answer, however.

Analysts can refer to market proxy companies in the same line of business to estimate the market required rates of return for an investment project. The proxies' betas are used to compute the required rate of return on assets after they are adjusted for the effect of financial leverage. The proxies' borrowing costs are also useful benchmarks although some adjustments for differences in capital structure, maturity of debt, etc. may be required. These market estimates can be used in the APV or weighted average cost of capital method as appropriate.

• **KEY TERMS**

Adjusted present value (APV) 708	Financial lease *715* Operating lease *715*	Equivalent loan *715*

• QUESTIONS AND PROBLEMS

1. An investment proposal's APV equals the present value of its net free cash flows plus the present value of its financial side effects.

    (a) Why is the business risk required rate of return used to discount its net free cash flows?

    (b) Why is the after-tax cost of debt used to discount the floatation cost side effects?

    (c) Why is the company's normal after-tax cost of debt used to discount a subsidized loan's after-tax cash flows?

    (d) Why is the company's normal cost of debt used to discount the interest tax-shields?

2. The APV method of recognizing financing effects in investment analysis is valid only if the company predetermines the dollar amount of debt outstanding each year of a project's life. Why?

3. What are the principal differences between an operating lease and a financial lease? Refer to these characteristics to explain why signing a financial lease and borrowing money to buy an asset are similar.

4. Why should you use the adjusted present value approach rather than the weighted average cost of capital to evaluate a financial lease?

5. The amount of the loan equivalent to a financial lease obligation equals the after-tax lease payments plus the depreciation tax-shields discounted at the company's after-tax cost of debt.

    (a) Explain why the after-tax lease payments and the depreciation tax-shields are the cash flows used in this calculation.

    (b) Explain why the after-tax cost of debt is the discount rate used in this calculation.

6. Suppose a company uses the equivalent loan method to evaluate a financial lease. Should the company go ahead and lease the asset if the net advantage of the lease is positive or is one more step in the analysis necessary? Explain your answer.

7. The weighted average cost of capital method of recognizing financing effects in investment analysis is valid only if the company predetermines the debt/equity ratio it will maintain each year of a project's life. Why?

8. What is the relationship between β_e and β_a when interest tax-shields are riskless? When they are risky? Give an intuitive explanation for the difference between these cases.

9. Larry's Leather Chairs needs $250,000 to buy vat-dying equipment so it can produce its own upholstery.

    (a) How much money must the company borrow if the floatation costs on the loan are 2.5 percent?

    (b) Determine the present value of the floatation cost side effect assuming the interest rate on the loan is 9 percent, its life is 7 years, and Larry's Leather Chairs' tax rate is 34 percent.

10. Calculate the interest tax-shield for each of the following situations.

	Loan Balance	Interest Rate	Tax Rate
(a)	$1,500,000	10.25%	35%
(b)	985,000	9.50	34
(c)	100,000	8.00	25

11. O'Hare Foods, Inc. requires $400,000 to purchase and install new walk-in freezers. The company will borrow the money at 9.5 percent interest and repay the loan in four equal annual installments. The first payment is due in one year. The bank providing the loan charges a 1.5 percent service fee payable when the loan is initiated. O'Hare's tax rate is 34 percent.

    (a) Determine the total amount of money O'Hare Foods must borrow.

    (b) Determine the value of the service charge side effect.

    (c) Determine the amount of the interest tax-shield provided by this loan each year of its life.

    (d) What required rate of return should O'Hare use to determine the value of the interest tax-shields? Why?

    (e) Compute the value of the interest tax-shields and the total value of the loan's financial side effects.

12. Milton's Medical Supplies will borrow $300,000 to finance start-up costs at a new suburban location. Bank A offered Milton an amortized loan at 12 percent interest. This loan requires three equal annual payments, the first payment due in one year. Bank B offered the company a three-year loan in which interest is paid annually and the principal is paid at maturity. The cost of Bank B's balloon loan is 12.25 percent. Milton's tax rate is 34 percent.

    (a) Determine the present value of the interest tax-shields provided by each loan.

    (b) What part of the difference in the present value of the loans' tax-shields is attributable to the difference in their repayment schedules? What part is attributable to the difference in their interest rates?

    (c) Should Milton simply choose the loan with the higher present value of tax-shields? Explain your answer.

13. The Shawnee County Rural Development Agency offered CenterBoard Boats a 10-year $500,000 loan at 9 percent interest if the company will locate its new warehouse in the county. The loan is repaid at maturity although the interest is paid annually. CenterBoard's tax rate is 34 percent and its normal cost of debt is 11 percent.

    (a) Determine the annual interest savings provided by the subsidized loan. What is the present value of these savings at CenterBoard's normal after-tax cost of debt?

    (b) Determine the present value of the subsidized loan's after-tax cash flows. Compare the result to your answer to part (a). What is the financial side effect of the subsidized loan?

14. Todd High Gaming Corp. was about to construct a bingo parlor in Missouri when a group of Native Americans offered the company a subsidized loan to build the facility on tribal lands just across the border in Oklahoma. The group gave the company two financing alternatives: A five-year $5,000,000 amortized loan at 10 percent interest or a five-year $5,000,000 loan with principal paid at maturity and interest paid annually. The interest rate on this loan is 10.125 percent. The company's tax rate is 35 percent and its normal cost of debt is 13 percent.

    (a) Determine each subsidized loan's value to Todd High Gaming Corp.

    (b) Which subsidized loan has the larger value to Todd High Gaming? Why?

    (c) Should the company automatically choose the alternative with the larger value or consider other factors?

    (d) Todd determined that construction costs in Oklahoma will be about $90,000 higher than in Missouri. Can he commit to building the bingo parlor in Oklahoma before deciding which financing alternative to use? Explain your answer.

15. Cathy Smith, president of Smith Canvas Products, noticed the problems shoppers have with plastic grocery bags and decided to examine the possibility of producing reusable canvas ones. She didn't want the company to be distracted from its core business of manufacturing canvas products for industrial applications, however. Therefore, Cathy instructed the project team to assume the company will take five years to build the business and then sell it to one of several companies that produce canvas products for consumers. The project team's after-tax cash flow forecasts are given below. If it is acceptable, Smith will use a $600,000 term loan to partially finance this investment. The full amount of the principal of the loan is due in five years although interest, at 8 percent, must be paid annually. The systematic risk of the company's assets is 0.85, and the rates of return on riskless assets and the market portfolio are 6 percent and 14 percent. Smith's tax rate is 35 percent.

Cash Flow Provided by (Used for)

Time	Investment	Operations
0	$(750,000)	$ 0
1		−75,000
2		50,000
3		100,000
4		125,000
5	950,000	125,000

Determine the canvas grocery bag project's APV. Should Smith Canvas Products develop and then sell this business?

16. Beauti-Home Wallpaper Co. is considering an expansion of its operations into window treatments, including draperies, blinds, and shades. The project's cash flows provided by and used for investment, operations, and financial slack are given below. A minority business development agency will guarantee a loan of $800,000 to Beauti-Home to partially finance this project. The agency charges a one-time fee of 1.5 percent for this service. The interest rate on the guaranteed loan is 8 percent in comparison to 10 percent for a market loan. The company will use internal equity for the remainder of its financing. Beauti-Home's business risk required rate of return is 13 percent and its tax rate is 34 percent.

Cash Flow Provided by (Used for)

Time	Investment	Operations	Financial Slack
0	$(1,450,000)	$ 0	$(50,000)
1		300,000	0
2		400,000	0
3		500,000	0
4		500,000	0
5		400,000	50,000

(a) Determine the value of the expansion project's net free cash flows. Is this a viable investment without considering its financial side effects?

(b) How much must the company borrow under the guaranteed loan program to obtain proceeds of $800,000?

(c) Determine the value of the initiation fee side effect.

(d) Prepare the loan's amortization schedule.

(e) Determine the value of the loan guarantee.

(f) Determine the value of the interest tax-shield.

(g) Determine the project's adjusted present value. Should Beauti-Home expand its product line?

17. Crain Automotive sells and leases extended cab, 4-wheel drive pickup trucks. Both operating and financial leases are available. A typical truck sells for $25,000.

(a) Which set of the following terms is an operating lease and which is a financial lease? Explain your answer.

	Lease A	Lease B
Term	7 years	3 years
Residual value	$ 0	$12,000
Annual maintenance allowance	0	750
License tag provided	No	Yes

(b) Determine the monthly payment for the financial lease assuming Crain's required rate of return is 12 percent. Lease payments are made in advance.

18. Posen Manufacturing Co. produces personal fitness machines sold through infomercials. Belly Basher, the company's abdominal exercise machine, is no longer profitable so the company is considering production of a new device called the Thigh-B-Gone. This project's expected net free cash flows over its life of four years are given below. The net free cash flow at time zero, $–700,000, is the cost of the equipment. Rather than purchase the equipment, Posen can lease it for four annual payments of $185,000 paid in advance. The company's cost of debt is 9 percent, its business risk required rate of return is 11 percent, and its tax rate is 35 percent.

Time	Net Free Cash Flow
0	$–700,000
1	375,000
2	250,000
3	140,000
4	75,000

(a) Determine the present value of the project's net free cash flows. Is this project acceptable regardless of the method of financing? Explain your answer.

(b) Determine the value of the financial side effects of leasing and the project's APV. Is the project acceptable if Posen leases the equipment?

19. The equipment Posen Manufacturing Co. needs to produce the Thigh-B-Gone has a MACRS life of three years. (Refer to problem 18 for additional information you may need to solve this problem.)

(a) Determine the present value of the project's net free cash flows. Is this project acceptable regardless of the method of financing? Explain your answer.

(b) Determine Posen's annual depreciation tax-shields if the company purchases the equipment. Assume the company receives the first depreciation tax-shield at time 0.

    (c) Determine the yearly cash flows available for debt service.

    (d) Compute the amount of the equivalent loan. What discount rate did you use? Why?

    (e) Determine the value of the financial side effects of purchasing and the project's APV. Is the project acceptable if Posen purchases the equipment?

20. Complete your analysis of Posen Manufacturing Co.'s Thigh-B-Gone project (see problems 18 and 19).

    (a) Determine the net advantage of the lease by comparing the APVs of leasing and purchasing the equipment. What should the company do?

    (b) Determine the net advantage of the lease using the equivalent loan method to confirm your conclusion.

21. Taupin Tow Company can buy a new dockside loading crane for $350,000 or lease it for 10 annual payments of $50,000 each. The crane is depreciable over a seven-year life under MACRS. Taupin's cost of debt is 8 percent and its tax rate is 35 percent.

    (a) Determine the amount of the equivalent loan. Assume the company receives the first year's depreciation tax-shield at time 0.

    (b) What is the net advantage of the lease? Assuming the present value of the crane's free cash flows is positive, should Taupin lease or purchase it? Why?

22. CheckBack, Inc. transports paper checks between banks for private clearing systems. A super-regional bank offered the company a contract to transport checks between its five clearing centers. CheckBack's net free cash flows under the contract will be $16,000 per year for eight years. The company must buy or lease five new vans if it accepts the contract. The vans cost $20,000 each or can be leased for eight years at a cost of $3,000 per van per year, paid in advance. The vans have a class life of five years under MACRS. CheckBack's required rate of return on assets is 14 percent and its cost of debt is 10 percent. The company's tax rate is 35 percent.

    (a) Use the equivalent loan method to determine whether it is better for CheckBack to buy or lease the vans. Assume the company receives the first year's depreciation tax-shield at time 0.

    (b) Compute the APV of CheckBack's project using the financing method you determined was better in part (a). Should CheckBack accept the contract to transport checks for the super-regional bank? Explain your answer.

23. Bingo's Livery Service is planning to purchase or lease a stretch-limo to rent for weddings, graduations, proms, and so on. The model they are considering costs $60,000 or can be leased for six annual payments of $12,000, paid in advance. The limo has a five-year MACRS life. Bingo's business risk required rate of return is 16 percent and its cost of debt is 12 percent. The company's tax rate is 34 percent. Bingo's expected net free cash flows from renting the limo are given below.

Time	Net Free Cash Flow
0	$-60,000
1	27,000
2	23,000
3	18,000
4	12,000
5	6,000
6	6,000

Use the APV method to determine whether Bingo's Livery Service should purchase, lease, or forgo the stretch-limo.

24. The average yield on U. S. Treasury bonds with 30 years until maturity was 7.10 percent on March 27, 1997.

   (a) Use Ibbotson and Associates data to estimate the parameters of the Capital Asset Pricing Model.

   (b) What is the required rate of return on assets for a company in the 35 percent tax bracket that has an equity beta of 1.20 and a debt/equity ratio of 0.80? Assume the company predetermines the dollar amount of debt outstanding.

   (c) Rework part (b) assuming the company predetermines its debt/equity ratio.

   (d) Should you use the result of part (b) or part (c) to compute the present value of a project's net free cash flows when applying the APV method? Explain your answer.

25. The companies listed below are in the 35 percent tax bracket. The rates of return on the riskless asset and the market portfolio are 6 percent and 14 percent.

Company	Asset Beta	Debt/Equity Ratio
Myers Manufacturing Co.	0.86	0.70
Miles Trucking Co	0.59	1.10
Ezzell Electronics Inc.	0.94	0.40

   (a) Compute each company's equity beta and required rate of return on equity assuming its interest tax-shields are riskless.

   (b) Rework part (a) assuming each company's interest tax-shields are risky.

   (c) Should you use the required rate of return on equity from part (a) or part (b) to compute each company's weighted average cost of capital? Explain your answer.

26. A prominent fashion designer approached Rabbits Unlimited with the idea of producing clothing for its exclusive line of stuffed toy animals. Alice Porter, owner of Rabbits Unlimited, is convinced she must use a high cost of capital for this project because she believes that even avid collectors will consider expensive stuffed animal clothing discretionary. Alice observed that companies selling similar luxury goods have an average equity beta of 1.50 and an average debt/equity ratio of 0.20. She will maintain a debt/value ratio of only 0.10 for this project, however, to preserve her company's ability to borrow at 6 percent interest. Rabbits Unlimited's tax rate is 35 percent. The rates of return on the riskless asset and the market portfolio are 6 percent and 14 percent.

   (a) Determine the asset beta and required rate of return on assets for luxury goods. Assume the interest tax shields are risky. What is the project's weighted average cost of capital given Alice's intention to maintain a 0.10 debt/value ratio?

   (b) Determine the equity beta and required rate of return on equity for the stuffed animal clothing project. What is the project's weighted average cost of capital computed from this rate of return and the company's after-tax cost of debt?

   (c) Compare your answers to parts (a) and (b). Explain why the answers are different.

27. Described below are the net free cash flows provided by an investment proposal and the equity betas and debt/equity ratios of three companies in the same line of business. The company

considering this investment opportunity maintains a debt/equity ratio of 0.30 and has a cost of debt of 5.5 percent. Its tax rate is 35 percent. The riskless rate of return and the expected rate of return on the market portfolio are 5.5 percent and 14 percent.

Investment Proposal		Proxy Companies		
Time	Net Free Cash Flows	Company	β_e	Debt/Equity Ratio
	$-1,000,000	A	1.36	0.43
	175,000	B	1.40	0.51
	350,000	C	1.44	0.57
	455,000			
	390,000			
	225,000			

(a) Determine each proxy company's asset beta and use the average of these betas for the investment proposal's business risk. Assume the interest tax shields are risky.

(b) What is the investment proposal's business risk required rate of return? What is its value (ignoring financial side effects)?

(c) Determine the proposal's equity beta to the company considering the investment. What is its required rate of return on equity?

(d) Compute the project's weighted average cost of capital and determine its total value.

(e) What is the value of its financial side effects? Explain your answer.

28. Refer to the Philip Morris Companies example in section 17.4 to work this problem.

(a) Determine the entire company's asset beta assuming it uses the same debt/equity ratio for the tobacco and food businesses. Assume the company's interest tax-shields are risky.

(b) Use the result from part (a) and the beta of the food business, calculated in the example, to estimate the beta of the tobacco business. Remember that the beta of a portfolio equals a weighted average of the betas of the assets in the portfolio. Use the percent of operating profits obtained from each business segment as the portfolio weights.

(c) Determine the required rate of return on equity and the weighted average cost of capital for Philip Morris Companies' tobacco business. Use Philip Morris's debt/value ratio and assume the tobacco and food businesses have the same cost of debt.

(d) How should Philip Morris Companies use these weighted average costs of capital, assuming your answers and the example in the text are correct?

29. Denshi Omocha, Ltd. produces traditional and electronic toys and games and inexpensive personal computers. The company has always used its overall weighted average cost of capital to evaluate investment proposals, but Sam Ono, Omocha's CFO, believes they may have made some serious errors. Consequently, he has decided to be more careful and estimate separate costs of capital for each division.

Sam identified two electronics companies and three toy companies that he will use to estimate the business risk of Omocha's divisions. These proxy companies, their equity betas, the market value of their equity, and the book value of their debt as of December 31, 1996 are given on the next page.

Company	β_e	Book Value of Debt (in millions)	Market Value of Equity (in millions)
Computer Industry			
Dell Computer Corp.	1.40	$1,175.0	$9,467.4
Gateway 2000, Inc.	1.60	568.5	4,102.7
Toy Industry			
Hasbro, Inc.	1.25	1,090.8	3,349.4
Mattel, Inc.	1.30	1,420.3	7,631.3
Tyco Toys, Inc.	1.15	349.8	418.9

Source: Value Line Investment Survey for Windows, Value Line Publishing Company, 1996.

(a) Calculate each company's asset beta and the average for each industry segment. Assume the interest tax-shields are risky.

(b) Calculate r_a and r_e for each division assuming that Omocha maintains a debt/equity ratio of 0.20 for the computer division and 0.40 for the toy division. Assume the company's interest tax-shields are risky. The rate of return on the riskless asset is 5.4 percent and the expected rate of return on the market portfolio is 14.1 percent.

(c) Sam estimates that r_d is 9 percent for the computer division and 8.5 percent for the toy division. Calculate each division's weighted average cost of capital given the company's tax rate of 35 percent.

(d) The company's overall weighted average cost of capital is 15 percent. What type of errors might Sam make when using this required rate of return to evaluate investment proposals submitted by the computer division? The toy division? Explain your answers.

30. Denshi Omocha's computer and toy divisions (see problem 29) submitted the following investment proposals for approval. (Free cash flows are in thousands of dollars.)

	Computer Division			Toy Division		
Time	C1	C2	C3	T1	T2	T3
0	$-235	$-125	$-187	$-95	$-140	$-127
1	115	45	114	34	41	53
2	115	45	114	34	41	53
3	115	45		34	41	53
4		45		34	41	
5					41	

(a) Which investment proposals will be approved and rejected if Omocha's overall weighted average cost of capital is used as the required rate of return?

(b) Which investment proposals will be approved and rejected if each division's own weighted average cost of capital, computed in the preceding problem, is used as the required rate of return?

(c) What is Omocha's actual and opportunity cost of using the wrong required rate of return to evaluate its investment proposals?

• ADDITIONAL READING

For additional information about leasing see

James S. Schallheim, *Lease or Buy?* Harvard Business School Press, Boston, Massachusetts, 1994.

Clifford W. Smith, Jr. and L. Macdonald Wakeman, "Determinants of Corporate Leasing Policy," *Journal of Finance,* July 1985, pp. 895–908.

To learn more about the weighted average cost of capital, see

Michael C. Ehrhardt, *The Search for Value: Measuring a Company's Cost of Capital,* Harvard Business School Press, Boston, Massachusetts, 1994.

Robert A. Taggart, Jr., "Consistent Valuation and Cost of Capital Expressions with Corporate and Personal Taxes," *Financial Management,* Autumn 1991, pp. 8–20.

CHAPTER 18

LONG-TERM FINANCIAL PLANNING

Chrysler Corporation became the target of a hostile takeover attempt in 1995 because its largest shareholder thought its long-term financial plans were inconsistent with its business plan.[1] Kirk Kerkorian, who owned 14 percent of Chrysler at the time, believed the company's economic, sales, and cost reduction assumptions implied it was holding an excess amount of financial slack. He also believed the company could borrow more money and thereby accelerate its program to repurchase common stock. Chrysler's managers success-fully defended themselves from the takeover threat although the dispute forced them to reconsider their assumptions and plans for the future. The dispute probably distracted their attention from managing the company if the amount of attention it received in the business press is any indication of the disruptions it caused. Chrysler's experience reveals that financial planning is more than a mundane accounting exercise without serious strategic consequences.

Financial planning is where theory meets practice. The financial plan itself is a practical instrument that uses pro forma financial statements to summarize a company's operating and financial objectives. Managers use these statements to anticipate cash flow surpluses and shortages and to plan investments and financing to offset them. The predictions and responses embodied in the financial plan must be realistic to reduce potentially costly surprises during the planning horizon.

The financial plan is a practical instrument although its operating, investment, and financing decisions must be based on the best financial theories. This connection is necessary to ensure that each decision meets market-wide performance standards. Then, the company can increase its value by obtaining the financial resources required to carry

---

[1]Steven Lipin and Gabriella Stern, "Chrysler Plans Suggest Firm Has Ample Cash, Even for a Downturn," *The Wall Street Journal*, October 20, 1995, p. A1.

out its plans at the lowest possible cost. Ultimately, this is the best way for the managers to improve their job security.

This chapter and Chapter 19 describe the financial planning process. You will learn how to project financial statements, how to interpret those statements to predict cash flow surpluses and shortages, and how to examine alternatives for eliminating surpluses and shortages.

18.1 OVERVIEW OF FINANCIAL PLANNING

Managers prepare business plans and budgets to coordinate and control a company's activities. Long-range business plans cover the next five to 10 years while short-term or annual business plans cover the coming year. Both types of plans contain similar information although annual business plans are prepared in greater detail to coordinate and control individual departments' monthly or weekly activities.

Short- and long-range **business plans** comprise operating budgets that establish sales and production objectives and set limits for expenditures such as wages, materials, salaries, and advertising. Long-range plans also include an investment schedule or capital budget that describes anticipated purchases of plant and equipment. A business plan therefore describes each unit's service or production goals and the operating and financial resources they will use to achieve those goals.

A **financial plan** comprises pro forma balance sheets, income statements, and cash statements. These statements forecast the assets that managers need to carry out their operating objectives, the methods by which they intend to finance these assets, and the net income and cash flows they expect to produce. Sears uses a financial planning system that updates these forecasts daily (see "In the News").

Pro forma free cash flow and financial cash flow statements (described in Chapter 2) are the most useful components of the financial plan for several reasons. First, analysts can evaluate an individual unit's or investment's free cash flows to see if they meet minimum standards of financial performance. Those with negative NPVs are candidates for contraction or abandonment while those with positive NPVs are candidates for expansion. Of course, abandonment and expansion may be deferred to preserve the related options.

Second, the pro forma free cash flow and financial cash flow statements can be used to anticipate cash flow surpluses and shortages. Senior managers can use a company's statements to estimate how much cash the company can provide to or must obtain from owners and creditors. Senior and subordinate managers can use a business unit's free cash flow and financial cash flow statements to estimate how much cash the company can obtain from or must provide to the unit. In either case, the financial cash flow statement describes the specific financial transactions that are planned to offset anticipated free cash flow surpluses and shortages. The free cash flow and financial cash flow statements in a business plan thereby succinctly describe a company's external financing requirements and the allocation of its financial resources to units given their operating plans.

Third, pro forma cash statements are convenient because unit statements can be added together to obtain a company's cash flow statements. In contrast, individual

A 'SPREADSHEET ON STEROIDS'

To ASSEMBLE AN annual financial plan for its 3,500 U.S. stores, Sears, Roebuck & Co. used to collect data scattered across so many computers that it took a 100-square-foot flow chart to describe the 300-step consolidation process. Now the process is down to just 25 steps, all described on a sheet of 8½-by-11-inch paper. Sears' analysts now have two years' worth of detailed budgets and plans at their fingertips, ready for viewing and analysis on their PCs.

Sears' secret is a homegrown financial system called EPIC, based on Essbase, a program from Arbor Software in Sunnyvale, Calif. Steve Beitler,

senior director for financial processes and systems, calls Essbase "our spreadsheet on steroids." It stores billions of bytes of financial data, along with information about how each item relates to the others. Each day, after being fed the latest figures, it recalculates all forecasts and plans.

Beitler says Essbase has paid for itself many times over, identifying opportunities—not all pursued—to slash $100 million in costs. Says Chief Financial Officer Allan J. Lacy: "We've got a real-time system that's allowing us to focus on some pretty aggressive financial goals."

Source: Reprinted from October 28, 1996, issue of *Business Week* ("A Spreadsheet on Steroids" by John W. Verity) by special permission, copyright © 1996 by The McGraw-Hill Companies, Inc.

balance sheet and income statements cannot be added together because there are complex accounting rules for consolidating these statements.

You can see that the financial plan, particularly the free cash flow and financial cash flow statements, provides a crucial link between a company's operations and the financial market. Managers determine which projects and activities meet market-wide performance standards by applying market-determined opportunity costs to the free cash flows. Under ideal conditions, this process allocates both real and financial resources to their most productive use. Managers determine the amount of money the company may provide to or must obtain from the financial market by aggregating the free cash flows of approved projects and activities. The distribution of these cash flows among investors is shown in a financial cash flow statement. This distribution of cash flows describes the company's financial structure, and, along with the appropriate discount rates, determines the value of its securities. These links between a company's operations and the financial market are illustrated in Exhibit 18.1.

All of a company's managers usually are involved in preparing a business plan. Operating managers must provide sales and cost estimates and describe their requirements for capital equipment. They often must provide this information in the form of completed financial statements, which means they must be familiar with accounting and finance principles. Furthermore, managers must understand the links between their operating goals and the financial market to ensure they propose acceptable projects.

Operating managers may still receive some assistance with financial planning from finance specialists even if their company has reduced staff support. However, both parties must recognize the possibility of having divergent interests. Operating managers may want to obtain financing for their favorite projects whether or not they are

Exhibit 18.1

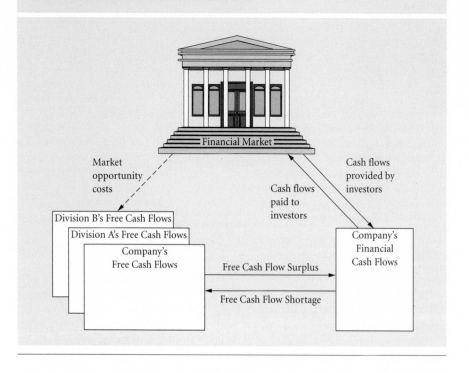

**RELATIONSHIPS BETWEEN COMPANY'S
CASH FLOWS AND FINANCIAL MARKET**

Financial Market

Market opportunity costs

Cash flows paid to investors

Cash flows provided by investors

Division B's Free Cash Flows

Division A's Free Cash Flows

Company's Free Cash Flows

Company's Financial Cash Flows

Free Cash Flow Surplus

Free Cash Flow Shortage

acceptable. Their motivation may be to improve the safety of their jobs or maximize their returns from the company's incentive compensation program. In any case, they may be more concerned with using the financial planning process to serve their own objectives rather than the company's and its owners. Finance specialists may take a narrow, controlling view of their role as custodians of the investors' resources and restrict financing for promising but risky projects. They may view themselves as principals who must control the operating managers' opportunistic behavior.

Of course, the company and its owners suffer real or opportunity losses if either position prevails. These losses, which are agency costs similar to ones we have discussed elsewhere, are reduced if both parties adopt constructive, cooperative attitudes. Finance specialists *must* apply the financial market's performance standards to requests for financing to ensure resources are allocated to their most productive use. Nevertheless, finance specialists also should ensure that operating managers understand the necessity for market-wide performance standards and they should help the managers obtain and use the analytical skills needed to apply them. The operating managers must realize that they must compete for funds because the company has to compete for funds in the financial market. Furthermore, the company may be able to remove some of the controls the unit managers consider burdensome if they conduct their competition ethically.

18.2 PREPARING PRO FORMA FINANCIAL STATEMENTS

A complete set of pro forma financial statements is required for a financial plan. Income statements and balance sheets are needed for rudimentary financial analysis and may be needed to prepare pro forma cash statements if the units' cash statements are not combined to obtain the company's. The pro forma balance sheets also can be used to anticipate cash flow surpluses and shortages although this approach provides less information than using cash statements.

However they are used, the pro forma income statements and balance sheets are obtained by projecting their various components such as revenues, costs, working capital, fixed assets, etc. Chapter 9 described in detail how to forecast these items for individual projects and the same procedures can be used for entire business units and companies. Nevertheless, many companies simplify this process and use financial ratios, management estimates, and company policies to prepare pro forma statements. This is the process we will describe here.

Projecting Sales and Costs

Many financial plans begin with a target sales growth rate, which should be based on a realistic assessment of market demand, the company's market share given competitors' likely responses, and the company's production or service capacity. The company's capacity depends on its present capacity and planned increases described in its capital budget. A company's financial policies also affect its ability to achieve its growth objectives as we will see later. The sales target often is expressed as an annual percentage growth rate that is constant or varies according to the products' life cycles.

Cost of goods sold and selling and administrative expenses often are modeled as a function of sales. The model should approximate the company's actual cost structure that may exhibit economies or diseconomies of scale and may have both fixed and variable cost components. A simple linear model of costs at time t with fixed, a, and variable, b, components is

$$\text{Costs}_t = a + b \times \text{Sales}_t \qquad [18.1]$$

Regression analysis may be applied to a sample of costs and sales to estimate the values of a and b.

The **percent of sales method** is a simple and widely used alternative to Equation 18.1 that assumes fixed costs are 0. The variable costs component, p, is estimated by expressing the costs as a percentage of sales. This model is described by Equation 18.2.

$$\text{Costs}_t = p \times \text{Sales}_t \qquad [18.2]$$

This percentage may be estimated from a single period's costs and sales or from an average of several periods' costs and sales. The following example illustrates the estimation and use of these models.

Beedles Bikes' annual sales and cost of goods sold for the past five years are given on the next page.

Year	Sales	Cost of Goods Sold
1996	$2,160	$1,335
1995	1,800	1,155
1994	1,732	1,125
1993	1,570	1,060
1992	1,398	955
Average	1,732	1,126

Jack Beedles used regression analysis to fit Equation 18.1 to this data. The result was

$$\text{Cost of goods sold}_t = \$279 + 0.489 \times \text{Sales}_t.$$

He also fit Equation 18.2 to this data, using average cost divided by average sales to estimate the value of p.

$$\text{Cost of goods sold}_t = \frac{\$1,126}{\$1,732} \times \text{Sales}_t$$
$$= 0.65 \times \text{Sales}_t$$

Jack Beedles can use these models to predict future cost of goods sold given a sales prediction. Suppose Beedles intends to increase sales by 7 percent to $2,311 ($2,160 × 1.07) in 1997. Then his forecast of cost of goods sold using the two models is

$$\text{Cost of goods sold}_{1997} = \$279 + 0.489 \times \$2,311 = \$1,409$$

and

$$\text{Cost of goods sold}_{1997} = 0.65 \times \$2,311 = \$1,502.$$

These two forecasts differ because the percent of sales method ignores fixed costs. The forecast based on the regression model is better, however, because it accounts for the effect of fixed costs. Consequently, it will be more accurate when sales are different from the value used to estimate the percentage factor (average sales in this example). This is apparent in Exhibit 18.2, which plots the company's actual cost of goods sold and sales and the lines representing the two forecasting models. You can see that the regression forecast is more accurate because it is nearer the points representing the company's actual costs and sales.[2] The percent of sales model is equally accurate only when sales are approximately their average value.

EXERCISE

18.1   **PERCENT OF SALES FORECAST**

Use the information given below to estimate the relationship between sales and selling costs for Beedles Bikes. Use both regression analysis and percent of sales based on average sales and costs. Predict 1997's selling costs given Beedles' sales goal of $2,311.

---

[2]The relative accuracy of the two models is better seen by comparing the standard deviation of their forecast errors. These standard deviations are 7.1 for the regression model and 41.7 for the percent of sales approach.

Exhibit 18.2

COMPARISON OF FORECASTING TECHNIQUES

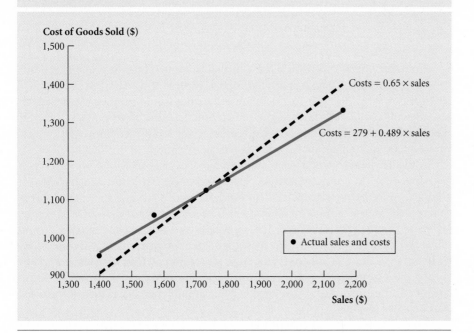

Year	Sales	Selling Costs
1996	$2,160	$380
1995	1,800	326
1994	1,732	324
1993	1,570	299
1992	1,398	281
Average	1,732	322

The models are

$$\text{Selling costs}_t = \$96 + 0.13 \times \text{Sales}_t$$

and

$$\text{Selling costs}_t = \frac{\$322}{\$1,762} \times \text{Sales}_t = 0.19 \times \text{Sales}_t.$$

Predicted selling costs for 1997 are

$$\text{Selling costs}_{1997} = \$96 + 0.13 \times \$2,311 = \$396$$

and

$$\text{Selling costs}_{1997} = 0.19 \times \$2,311 = \$439.$$

Beedles should use $396 as his estimate of 1997's selling costs because the percent of sales method ignores fixed costs.

• ———————— •

Projected interest expense is the anticipated amount of interest paid on debt outstanding each year. This item is difficult to estimate because of circularity. Projected interest expenses affect the pro forma income statements and balance sheets, which determine the amount of financing required. This, in turn, affects projected interest expenses. Furthermore, whether the required financing is obtained from equity, short-term debt, or long-term debt is an additional complication.

Computer-based financial planning models reduce this problem by using feedback loops that make the estimated interest expenses consistent with the financing choices. A simple and effective alternative is to forecast interest expense for *known* discretionary financing and provide for any additional interest expense in the estimated financing requirements. This is the procedure we will use in a subsequent example.

Projected tax payments are determined from the company's taxable income, marginal tax rate, and tax credits such as foreign tax credits and operating losses that will be carried backward or forward. Because detailed estimates can become very complex, taxes often are estimated by simply applying the statutory marginal tax rate to the company's taxable income.

Finally, the statement of retained earnings links a company's income statement to its balance sheet by describing what part of current earnings is distributed to the owners as dividends and what part is held as additional equity financing. Companies often have a target dividend payout ratio, as we saw in Chapter 15, so future dividends are frequently estimated as a simple percent of net income.

Projecting Operating Assets and Claims

A company's operating assets are those used to produce, sell, and distribute its products or services. Property, plant, and equipment are long-term or fixed operating assets while inventories and receivables are short-term ones. The cash balance a company maintains for transactions purposes also can be treated as a short-term operating asset; however, we will incorporate it in financial slack. A company's operating claims are those that are inexorably linked to its operating cycle. Accounts payable and accrued wages and taxes belong to this category because these sources of financing are linked to the purchase of materials and labor and the recognition of profits on sales. These sources of financing arise spontaneously in the normal course of business and are therefore called **spontaneous financing**.

The projected investment in accounts receivable depends on projected sales and the company's credit policies that comprise its credit terms, credit standards, and the forcefulness of its collection efforts. The effect of a company's credit policies is summarized by the amount of time required to collect an account that is measured by the days'-sales-outstanding (DSO) ratio. Similarly, the projected investment in inventories depends on projected sales and the company's inventory policies. Policies regarding the size and frequency of orders and the maintenance of safety stocks determine the average amount of time items remain in inventory, which is summarized by the days'-costs-in-inventory (DCI) ratio. Chapter 9 showed that multiplying DSO and DCI by projected sales per day and projected cost of sales per day provides estimates of the amount of money invested in accounts receivable and inventories. This approach is a variation of the percent of sales method.

The projected gross investment in fixed assets equals the prior period's investment less anticipated sales of assets plus anticipated purchases as described in the capital budget. These transactions also produce predictable changes in a company's depreciation expense given its depreciation policy. Estimates of these items are probably available to the financial planner in the capital budget so it is relatively easy to project the net investment in fixed assets.

Finally, projected accounts payable and accruals depend on the projected level of sales and the company's payment policies. The effect of these policies is summarized by the amount of time required to pay an account, which is measured by the days'-payables-outstanding (DPO) ratio. As noted earlier, Chapter 9 showed that multiplying DPO by the projected cost of sales per day provides an estimate of accounts payable and accruals.

Projecting Requirements for Financial Slack

Financial slack is the amount of uncommitted financial resources available to meet a sudden requirement for cash. Cash balances and marketable securities, such as short-term government debt and high-quality commercial paper, are the main types of financial assets held for this purpose. These assets provide financial slack because the owner can quickly convert them to cash without offering a price discount. Cash and marketable securities often are called liquid assets for this reason.

Projecting requirements for financial slack is a difficult task that we will examine in detail in Chapter 19, which discusses short-term financial planning and policy. For long-term financial planning purposes, many companies simply estimate their investment in cash and securities as a percent of sales, as we did in Chapter 9.

Projecting Existing Discretionary Financing

Discretionary financing includes all sources of debt and equity not directly linked to a company's operating cycle. Discretionary financing must be deliberately arranged in contrast to operating claims, such as accounts payable. Furthermore, discretionary financing may be used for any legitimate business purpose while operating claims are tied to a specific activity such as purchasing raw materials.

Bank loans, term loans, long-term debt, and preferred and common stock are examples of discretionary financing. All companies have existing discretionary financing when they begin financial planning. Even the youngest start-up company must have some equity financing and may have some guaranteed debt financing as described in Chapter 14.

The projected amount of discretionary financing provided by existing debt is easily determined by referring to the loan repayment schedules. Short-term debt, such as notes payable, and the current portion of long-term debt are expected to be paid within one year. Long-term debt may be repaid in installments or with a single payment at maturity. Payments that occur within the financial planning horizon reduce the amount of financing provided by that source.

No change in the amount of financing from preferred and common stock should be projected at this stage. A company may issue or retire stock to offset a cash flow shortage or surplus but its existing discretionary financing must be used to project the amounts of these shortages or surpluses. Of course, additional equity financing is provided by retained earnings, as described earlier.

An Illustrative Financial Plan

We'll use the Ariga Manufacturing Company to demonstrate how to prepare pro forma financial statements. Ariga produces a wide range of consumer electronic products and uses a three-year horizon for long-range financial planning because of the rapid pace of change in its industry. The company's 1997 income statement, statement of retained earnings, and balance sheet provide the starting point for projecting its pro forma financial statements (see Table 18.1).

Ariga's forecast model is described by the equations in Table 18.2. Projected sales are obtained by applying the company's target sales growth rate of 10 percent to the prior period's sales. The cost of sales is approximated by a linear model with fixed and variable components. Selling and administrative costs are assumed to be a constant 24 percent of sales while depreciation expense is taken from the company's depreciation schedule. Interest expense is computed as 7 percent of the amount of debt outstanding at the beginning of the year. The marginal tax rate for corporations, 35 percent, is used to estimate their taxes. Ariga's target dividend payout ratio is 60 percent of net income.

The managers plan to maintain cash at 6.25 percent of sales. Accounts receivable, inventories, and accounts payable and accruals are projected using 1997's days'-sales-outstanding, days'-costs-in-inventory, and days'-payments-outstanding ratios. The gross investment in fixed assets and depreciation are taken from the company's capital budget and its depreciation schedule. The term loan is the only discretionary financing payable during the planning horizon; it is due on December 31, 2000. The pro forma income statements, statements of retained earnings, and balance sheets obtained by applying the company's forecast model to its actual 1997 financial statements are given in Table 18.3.

Table 18.1

ARIGA MANUFACTURING COMPANY'S 1997 FINANCIAL STATEMENTS (THOUSANDS OF DOLLARS)

Panel A: Income Statement

Net sales	$40,000
Cost of goods sold	26,000
Gross profit	14,000
Selling and administrative expenses	9,700
Depreciation	2,000
Operating income	2,300
Interest expense	800
Taxable income	1,500
Taxes	500
Net income	$ 1,000

Panel B: Statement of Retained Earnings

Beginning balance	$ 4,400
Plus net income for the period	1,000
Minus dividends for the period	600
Ending balance	$ 4,800

Panel C: Balance Sheet

Assets

Cash	$ 2,500
Accounts receivable	2,800
Inventories	3,000
Total current assets	8,300
Gross fixed assets	22,000
Accumulated depreciation	9,500
Net fixed assets	12,500
Total assets	$20,800

Claims

Accounts payable and accruals	$ 2,000
Total current liabilities	2,000
Term loan	2,000
Bonds	10,000
Total long-term debt	12,000
Common stock	2,000
Retained earnings	4,800
Total equity	6,800
Total claims	$20,800

Table 18.2   ARIGA MANUFACTURING COMPANY'S FORECAST MODEL

Panel A: Income Statement and Statement of Retained Earnings Equations

$\text{Sales}_t = (1.1) \times \text{Sales}_{t-1}$
$\text{Cost of goods sold}_t = \$4{,}000 + 0.55 \times \text{Sales}_t$
$\text{Selling and administrative expenses}_t = 0.24 \times \text{Sales}_t$
$\text{Depreciation} = \$2{,}500 \ (1998), \$3{,}000 \ (1999), \$3{,}000 \ (2000)$
$\text{Interest expense}_t = 0.07 \times \text{Debt}_{t-1}$
$\text{Taxes}_t = .35 \times \text{Taxable income}_t$
$\text{Dividends}_t = 0.60 \times \text{Net income}$

Panel B: Balance Sheet Equations

$\text{Cash}_t = 0.0625 \times \text{Sales}_t$
$\text{Accounts receivable}_t = \text{DSO}_{1997} \times \text{Sales per day}_t$
$\text{DSO}_{1997} = \$2{,}800/(\$40{,}000/365) = 25.6 \text{ days}$
$\text{Inventories}_t = \text{DCI}_{1997} \times \text{Cost of goods sold per day}_t$
$\text{DCI}_{1997} = \$3{,}000/(\$26{,}000/365) = 42.1 \text{ days}$
$\text{Gross fixed assets}_t = \text{Gross fixed assets}_{t-1} - \text{Sales}_t + \text{Purchases}_t$
$\text{Sales of fixed assets} = 0$
$\text{Purchases of fixed assets} = \$3{,}250 \ (1998), \$4{,}750 \ (1999), \$4{,}500 \ (2000)$
$\text{Accumulated depreciation}_t = \text{Accumulated depreciation}_{t-1} + \text{Depreciation}_t$
$\text{Accounts payable and accruals}_t = \text{DPO}_{1997} \times \text{Cost of goods sold per day}_t$
$\text{DPO}_{1997} = \$2{,}000/(\$26{,}000/365) = 28.1 \text{ days}$
Term loan is due December 31, 2000

Table 18.3   ARIGA MANUFACTURING COMPANY'S PRO FORMA FINANCIAL STATEMENTS (THOUSANDS OF DOLLARS)

Panel A: Income Statements

	Actual 1997	Pro Forma 1998	Pro Forma 1999	Pro Forma 2000	Projection Method
Net sales	$40,000	$44,000	$48,400	$53,240	$(1.1) \times \text{Sales}_{t-1}$
Cost of goods sold	26,000	28,200	30,620	33,282	$\$4{,}000 + 0.55 \times \text{Sales}$
Gross profit	14,000	15,800	17,780	19,958	
Selling and administrative expenses	9,700	10,560	11,616	12,778	$0.24 \times \text{Sales}$
Depreciation	2,000	2,500	3,000	3,000	Depreciation schedule
Operating income	2,300	2,740	3,164	4,180	
Interest expense	800	840	840	840	$0.07 \times \text{Debt}_{t-1}$
Taxable income	1,500	1,900	2,324	3,340	
Taxes	500	665	813	1,169	$0.35 \times \text{Taxable income}$
Net income	$ 1,000	$ 1,235	$ 1,511	$ 2,171	

Table 18.3   Continued

Panel B: Statements of Retained Earnings

Beginning balance	$ 4,400	$ 4,800	$ 5,294	$ 5,898	
Plus net income for the period	1,000	1,235	1,511	2,171	
Minus dividends for the period	600	741	907	1,303	0.60 × Net income
Ending balance	$ 4,800	$ 5,294	$ 5,898	$ 6,766	

Panel C: Balance Sheets

	Actual 1997	Pro Forma 1998	Pro Forma 1999	Pro Forma 2000	Projection Method
Assets					
Cash and securities	$ 2,500	$ 2,750	$ 3,025	$ 3,328	$0.0625 \times$ Sales
Accounts receivable	2,800	3,086	3,395	3,734	$DSO_{1997} \times$ Sales per day
Inventories	3,000	3,253	3,532	3,839	$DCI_{1997} \times$ Cost of goods sold per day
Total current assets	8,300	9,089	9,952	10,901	
Gross fixed assets	22,000	25,250	30,000	34,500	Beginning balance – Sales + Purchases
Accumulated depreciation	9,500	12,000	15,000	18,000	Depreciation schedule
Net fixed assets	12,500	13,250	15,000	16,500	
Total assets	$20,800	$22,339	$24,952	$27,401	
Claims					
Accounts payable and accruals	$ 2,000	$ 2,171	$ 2,357	$ 2,562	$DPO_{1997} \times$ Cost of goods sold per day
Total current liabilities	2,000	2,171	2,357	2,562	
Term loan	2,000	2,000	2,000	0	Note due 12/31/00
Bonds	10,000	10,000	10,000	10,000	
Total long-term debt	12,000	12,000	12,000	10,000	
Common stock	2,000	2,000	2,000	2,000	
Retained earnings	4,800	5,294	5,898	6,766	Statement of retained earnings
Total equity	6,800	7,294	7,898	8,766	
Total claims	$20,800	$21,465	$22,255	$21,328	

18.3 FORECASTING CASH FLOW SURPLUSES AND SHORTAGES

Information in pro forma financial statements can be used in several ways to determine whether a company will have cash flow surpluses or shortages. Each method provides exactly the same forecasts but in slightly different formats. We will examine two methods based on pro forma balance sheets and free cash flow and financial cash flow statements.

Using the Pro Forma Balance Sheets

Perhaps the simplest way to determine whether a company can expect cash flow surpluses or shortages is to subtract projected total assets from projected total claims. A company has excess financing when claims are greater than assets and insufficient financing when they are less. An increase in the amount of excess financing or a reduction in the amount of a financing shortfall from one period to the next implies the company had a cash flow surplus for that period. Conversely, a reduction in the amount of excess financing or an increase in the amount of a financing shortfall implies there was a cash flow shortage.

Ariga Manufacturing's projected financing surpluses and deficits and their implied cash flow surpluses and shortages are computed in Table 18.4. The table shows that Ariga's managers must improve operations, reduce investments, or obtain additional financing to cover the $874,000 deficit projected for 1998. This deficit is expected to increase to $2,697,000 in 1999 and to $6,073,000 by the end of 2000.

Table 18.4 also shows Ariga's cash flow shortages for each period. The cash flow shortage of $874,000 in 1998 produced the company's financing deficit that year. Another cash flow shortage of $1,823,000 the following year increased the financing deficit to $2,697,000 in 1999. We inferred the amounts of these cash flow shortages by taking the difference between the financing deficits in successive years. Next, we will see that the free cash flow and financial cash flow statements compute these cash flow shortages directly.

Table 18.4   ARIGA MANUFACTURING COMPANY'S PROJECTED FINANCING REQUIREMENTS (THOUSANDS OF DOLLARS)

		Projected		
	Actual 1997	**1998**	**1999**	**2000**
Total claims	$20,800	$21,465	$22,255	$21,328
Total assets	20,800	22,339	24,952	27,401
Financing surplus (deficit)		(874)	(2,697)	(6,073)
Cash flow surplus (shortage)	$ 0	$ (874)	$(1,823)	$(3,376)

FINANCING SURPLUS AND DEFICIT

Bagamery Building Supplies' actual and pro forma balance sheets are given below. Determine the amount of the company's financing surplus or deficit and its cash flow surplus or shortage each year.

		Projected	
	1999	2000	2001
Assets	$300,000	$342,500	$355,000
Claims	300,000	319,000	336,000

The company's projected financing surplus or deficit equals its projected claims minus its projected assets.

	1999	2000	2001
Claims	$300,000	$319,000	$336,000
Assets	300,000	342,500	355,000
Financing surplus (deficit)	$ 0	$(23,500)	$(19,000)

Bagamery's cash flow surplus or shortage equals the change in its financing position each year. These amounts are $–23,500 for 2000 ($–23,500 – $0) and $4,500 for 2001 ($–19,000 – $–23,500).

Using Free Cash Flow and Financial Cash Flow Statements

Net free cash flow equals the amount of cash that can be paid to investors or that must be obtained from them. When financial planning begins, net financial cash flow equals the amount of cash provided by or used for existing sources of discretionary financing. Adding net free cash flow and net financial cash flow gives the company's projected cash flow surplus or deficit for the period. The cumulative cash flow shortage equals the financing deficit we computed using the balance sheet.

Ariga Manufacturing Company's free cash flow and financial cash flow statements are given in Table 18.5. The company's pro forma income statements and balance sheets were used to prepare these statements. Cash flow provided by operations equals net income plus depreciation, which did not use cash, minus the change in net working capital to adjust for credit sales and purchases. After-tax interest expense also is added back to net income because it will be assigned to the financing category. The company's only investment cash flows were to purchase fixed assets and it used a small amount of cash to increase its financial slack.

Ariga's financial cash flows are for interest (on an after-tax basis), to repay the term loan, and for dividends. No cash flows from new discretionary financing are shown in Table 18.5 because we will use these statements to determine how much new financing the company requires.

The company's cash flow surplus or shortage equals its net free cash flow plus net financial cash flow. These amounts are shown at the bottom of Table 18.5. Ariga's financing surplus or deficit is its cumulative cash flow surplus or shortage. Note that these are the same values obtained from the pro forma balance sheets.

Table 18.5   **ARIGA MANUFACTURING COMPANY'S PRO FORMA CASH FLOW STATEMENTS (THOUSANDS OF DOLLARS)**

	1998	1999	2000
Free Cash Flow			
Cash flow provided by (used for) operations			
Net income	$ 1,235	$ 1,511	$ 2,171
Plus depreciation	2,500	3,000	3,000
Minus change in net working capital for operations	368	402	441
Plus after-tax interest expense	546	546	546
Net cash flow	$ 3,913	$ 4,655	$ 5,276
Cash flow provided by (used for) investment			
Purchase fixed assets	$(3,250)	$(4,750)	$(4,500)
Cash flow provided by (used for) financial slack	$ (250)	$ (275)	$ (303)
Net free cash flow	$ 413	$ (370)	$ 473
Financial Cash Flow			
Cash flow received from (paid to) creditors			
Interest payments	$ (546)	$ (546)	$ (546)
Payment of term loan			(2,000)
Net cash flow	$ (546)	$ (546)	$(2,546)
Cash flow received from (paid to) owners			
Dividends	$ (741)	$ (907)	$(1,303)
Net financial cash flow	$(1,287)	$(1,453)	$(3,849)
Cash Flow Surplus (Shortage)	$ (874)	$(1,823)	$(3,376)
Financing Surplus (Deficit)	$ (874)	$(2,697)	$(6,073)

EXERCISE ●

18.3   **CASH FLOW SURPLUS AND SHORTAGE**

Bagamery Building Supplies' actual and pro forma free cash flow and financial cash flow statements are given below. Determine the amount of the company's cash flow surplus or shortage and its financing surplus or deficit each year. Compare the results with Exercise 18.2.

	1999	2000	2001
Net free cash flow	$ 9,860	$ 11,250	$ 28,600
Net financial cash flow	(9,860)	(34,750)	(24,100)

The company's projected cash flow surplus or shortage equals free cash flow plus financial cash flow.

	1999	2000	2001
Net free cash flow	$ 9,860	$ 11,250	$28,600
Net financial cash flow	(9,860)	(34,750)	(24,100)
Cash flow surplus (shortage)	$ 0	$(23,500)	$ 4,500

Bagamery's financing surplus or deficit equals its cumulative cash flow surplus or shortage. These amounts are $–23,500 for 2000 ($0 + $–23,500) and $–19,000 for 2001 ($–23,500 + $4,500).

Projected surpluses and deficits are the same using either method.

● ——————— ●

Pro forma balance sheets or cash statements can be used to anticipate a company's cash flow surpluses and shortages and its requirements for additional financing. However, the cash statement has advantages worth repeating. First, a company's free cash flow statement can be linked directly to the cash outflows and inflows from acquiring and operating individual assets. Second, analysts can use the free cash flows to estimate the market value of those assets. Third, the financial cash flows are the basis for determining the market value of the company's securities. These associations provide links between the company's operations and the financial market that are not as readily apparent when the pro forma balance sheets are used for financial planning.

18.4 ANALYZING AND REVISING THE FINANCIAL PLAN

The cash flow surpluses and shortages and the financing requirements projected in the initial financial plan should be considered as tentative amounts that are subject to change. Managers who anticipate cash flow shortages *may* seek additional financing but they also can modify their operating and investment plans to reduce the requirement for external funds. Even managers who anticipate cash flow surpluses must plan to invest the money profitably or to repay it to the company's investors. In either case, managers must re-examine or analyze their operating, investing, and financing policies and plans to determine the most economical way to offset the anticipated cash flow shortages and surpluses.

Planned changes in operations, investments, or financing eliminate projected cash flow surpluses and shortages from the final financial plan. This planning–analyzing–revising process is one of the ways that financial planning links a company's operations and the financial market. Some of the financial ratios described in Chapter 2 are useful for performing the analysis part of this process. Sustainable growth analysis is a particularly effective way to employ these financial ratios.

Sustainable Growth Analysis of a Financial Plan

Recall from Chapter 7 that a company's sustainable growth rate is the annual amount by which it can increase its dividends without changing its operating or financial policies. We derived this growth rate, g_s, in Equation 7.10. This equation is repeated here as Equation 18.3.

$$g_s = ROE \times RET \qquad [18.3]$$

A company's sustainable growth rate is a more comprehensive constraint than you learned in Chapter 7 because it limits the growth in sales, net income, dividends, total assets, debt, and equity. A company that attempts to grow faster than its sustainable growth rate allows will encounter this constraint and *must* sell new common stock,

IN THE NEWS

PAYING FOR GROWTH

I HAD NO concept of the relationship between sales and cash flow when I started my first company. I thought sales were everything. Our sales went from zero to $12.8 million in five years—fast enough to put us on the 1984 *Inc.* 500 list. We had cash flow problems all the way, but I didn't focus on them. I was too busy selling.

What I learned is that you have to look ahead. You have to figure out how you're going to get the cash required to increase your sales at whatever rate you have in mind. If you don't, you run the risk of selling yourself into a corner. I'm talking about losing control of your situation, about decisions being taken away from you, about being forced to

do extreme and unwise things just to stay alive.

You obviously aren't going to turn away good, high-margin business. So you look for ways to generate the additional cash. Maybe you can reduce the collection days on your current accounts. Maybe you can extend your accounts payable by a week or two. Maybe you can make a deal with the new customers to get paid more quickly than usual. Of course, as a last resort, you can always borrow the money, if you don't mind increasing your bank debt and adding to your costs.

In business, you can't be in control if you aren't on top of your cash flow. That's a lesson worth learning as early as possible.

Source: Reprinted with permission from Norm Brodsky, "Paying for Growth," *Inc.* Magazine (October 1996), pp. 29–30. Copyright 1996 by Goldhirsh Group, Inc., 38 Commercial Wharf, Boston, MA 02110.

improve its operations, or change its financing policies to achieve its objective (see "In the News"). Conversely, a company that intends to grow slower than its sustainable growth rate allows has extra financial resources that can be distributed to investors or used in operations.

The easiest way to see how a company's sustainable growth rate limits its growth in assets, sales, and financing is to derive it step-by-step using a slightly different approach than we used in Chaper 7. First, all new equity financing must come from retained earnings because the company will not issue new common stock. The amount of new equity, ΔE, available from this source equals the company's net income multiplied by its earnings retention ratio.

$$\Delta E = \text{NI} \times \text{RET}$$

Second, when combined with additional debt as determined by the company's leverage ratio, this equity will support ΔA of new assets. That is,

$$\Delta A = \Delta E \times \text{LEV}$$
$$= \text{NI} \times \text{RET} \times \text{LEV}$$

Third, the amount of new sales (ΔS) these assets will produce depends on the company's total asset turnover ratio.

$$\Delta S = \Delta A \times \text{TAT}$$
$$= \text{NI} \times \text{RET} \times \text{LEV} \times \text{TAT}$$

Finally, the sustainable percentage growth in sales, g, equals the increase in sales, ΔS, divided by the original sales, S.

LEE ELECTRIC SUPPLY COMPANY'S FINANCIAL STATEMENTS   **Table 18.6**

Panel A: Income Statement

	1997	1998
Sales		$100,000
Costs and taxes		93,000
Net income		$ 7,000

Panel B: Statement of Retained Earnings

Net income	$ 7,000
Dividends	3,150
Addition to retained earnings	$ 3,850

Panel C: Balance Sheets

	1997	1998
Total assets	$56,408	$ 62,500
Claims		
Debt	$20,694	$ 22,936
Equity	35,714	39,564
Total claims	$56,408	$ 62,500

$$g_s = \Delta S/S$$
$$= \frac{NI}{S} \times RET \times LEV \times TAT$$

Net income divided by sales equals the profit margin, PM, so

$$g_s = PM \times LEV \times TAT \times RET \qquad [18.4]$$
$$= ROE \times RET$$

The result is the same as Equation 18.3.

Here's an example that demonstrates that the sustainable growth rate is a comprehensive constraint. The managers of Lee Electric Supply Company want to determine the amount by which the company can grow. They have managed the company successfully and therefore do not plan to change their operating or financial policies. The company's abbreviated financial statements for 1997 and 1998 are given in Table 18.6. Lee's sustainable growth rate as of the end of 1998 is calculated below. Note that ROE is based on the income earned on the equity available at the *beginning* of the period.

$$ROE = NI_t/E_{t-1} = \$7,000/\$35,714 = 0.196$$
$$RET = (NI_t - Dividends_t)/NI_t = (\$7,000 - \$3,150)/\$7,000 = 0.55$$
$$g_s = ROE \times RET = 0.196 \times 0.55 = 0.108 \text{ or } 10.8\%$$

Table 18.7   LEE ELECTRIC SUPPLY COMPANY'S PRO FORMA FINANCIAL STATEMENTS

Panel A: Income Statements

	Actual 1998	Pro Forma 1999	Growth Rate
Sales	$100,000	$110,779	10.8%
Costs and taxes	93,000	103,024	10.8
Net income	$ 7,000	$ 7,755	10.8

Panel B: Statements of Retained Earnings

Net income	$ 7,000	$ 7,755	10.8
Dividends	3,150	3,490	10.8
Addition to retained earnings	$ 3,850	$ 4,265	10.8

Panel C: Balance Sheets

Total assets	$ 62,500	$ 69,237	10.8
Claims			
Debt	$ 22,936	$ 25,408	10.8
Equity	39,564	43,829	10.8
Total claims	$ 62,500	$ 69,237	10.8

Now let's use Lee's operating and financial policies—as represented by its profit margin, total asset turnover, leverage, and retention ratios—to project its 1999 financial statements. We'll use these statements to see how much sales, assets, and financing grow. The value of Lee's key ratios as of the end of 1998 are computed below.

$$\text{PM} = \text{Net income}_t/\text{sales}_t = \$7,000/\$100,000 = 0.07$$
$$\text{TAT} = \text{Sales}_t/\text{total assets}_t = \$100,000/\$62,500 = 1.60$$
$$\text{LEV} = \text{Total assets}_t/\text{equity}_{t-1} = \$62,500/\$35,714 = 1.75$$
$$\text{RET} = 0.55$$

Lee's current and pro forma financial statements are shown in Table 18.7. The $39,564 of equity available at the end of 1998 will support $69,237 of assets in 1999 given the company's leverage ratio of 1.75 ($39,564 × 1.75). Lee's total asset turnover ratio of 1.6 implies that the company will use these assets to generate sales of $110,779 ($69,237 × 1.6). The company's profit margin is 7 percent, so projected net income from the new sales is $7,755 ($110,779 × 0.07). Lee pays 45 percent of its income as dividends and keeps 55 percent as an addition to retained earnings. Dividends and the addition to retained earnings for 1999 therefore are predicted to be $3,490 ($7,755 × 0.45) and $4,265 ($7,755 × 0.55). The company's 1999 equity is therefore $43,829 ($39,564 + $4,265). The remainder of its total assets are financed with debt of $25,408 ($69,237 − $43,829).

Calculate the growth rate for any item in Lee's financial statements and you will see that it equals the company's sustainable growth. For example, the growth rate in retained earnings for 1999 was

Growth in retained earnings = ($4,265/$3,850) − 1 = 0.108 or 10.8%.

Lee cannot increase its sales, income, assets, dividends, or financing by more than 10.8 percent without changing its operating or financial policies.

EXERCISE
18.4

SUSTAINABLE GROWTH CONSTRAINT

Singh Corporation's abbreviated financial statements for 1996 and 1997 are given below. Can the company achieve its target sales level of $5,300 for 1998 without altering its operating and financial policies?

	1996	1997
Income Statement		
Sales	$4,700	$5,000
Costs and taxes	4,277	4,550
Net income	$ 423	$ 450
Statement of Retained Earnings		
Net income	$ 423	$ 450
Dividends	338	360
Addition to retained earnings	$ 85	$ 90
Balance Sheet		
Total assets	$2,350	$2,500
Claims		
Debt	740	800
Equity	1,610	1,700
Total claims	$2,350	$2,500

Singh's target sales growth rate is 6 percent ($5,300/$5,000 − 1). Based on its 1996 and 1997 performance, Singh's sustainable growth rate is

$$\text{ROE} = \text{NI}_{1997}/E_{1996}$$
$$= \$450/\$1,610 = 0.2795$$
$$\text{RET} = (\text{NI}_{1997} - \text{Dividends}_{1997})/\text{NI}_{1997}$$
$$= (\$450 - \$360)/\$450 = 0.20$$
$$g_s = 0.2795 \times 0.20 = 0.0559 \text{ or } 5.59\%.$$

Singh cannot achieve its target sales level without changing its operating or financial policies because its sustainable growth rate, 5.59 percent, is less than its target growth rate, 6 percent.

Ariga's 1996 equity was $6,400 ($4,400 + $2,000). Based on this information and the company's 1997 financial statements (given in Table 18.1), Ariga's sustainable growth rate is

$$PM = \$1,000/\$40,000 = 0.0250$$
$$TAT = \$40,000/\$20,800 = 1.9231$$
$$LEV = \$20,800/\$6,400 = 3.2500$$
$$ROE = 0.025 \times 1.9231 \times 3.2500 = 0.1563$$
$$RET = (\$1,000 - \$600)/\$1,000 = 0.40$$
$$g_s = 0.1563 \times 0.40 = 0.0625 \text{ or } 6.25\%.$$

Ariga must change its policies to overcome the financing deficits identified in the pro forma financial statements because the company's sustainable growth rate, 6.25 percent, is less than its target sales growth rate of 10 percent.

Re-Examine Operating and Financial Plans and Policies

Ariga's managers must change the company's operating or financing policies and Equation 18.4 helps identify their alternatives. An increase in the value of the ratios on the right-hand side of this equation will reduce the amount of funds needed to finance the 10 percent sales growth or increase the amount of internal funds available.

An increase in Ariga's total asset turnover ratio will reduce the amount of funds needed. The company must reduce its investment in assets without reducing its sales to achieve an improvement in this ratio. Sales and credit managers may be asked to offer less generous payment terms to customers to reduce the company's invesment in accounts receivable while production managers may be asked to reduce the company's investment in inventories. Managers also must reconsider the company's long-term investments. A company that anticipates a financing deficit may abandon or sell poorly performing business units if their operations cannot be sufficiently improved. Likewise, marginally acceptable long-term investment proposals may be deferred or scaled back to a level that preserves the company's option to fully enter those lines of business later.

An increase in the profit margin or the retention ratio will increase the amount of funds available from retained earnings. Operating managers may be asked to reduce production costs while marketing managers may be asked to reduce selling costs. Senior financial managers, in consultation with the board of directors, consider whether it is feasible to reduce the company's target dividend payout ratio.

Managers may compare their company's projected financial ratios to historical values or to benchmark companies' ratios when re-examining their operating and financial plans and policies. However, this is the beginning rather than the end of the process. Ultimately, the managers must use sound financial principles to identify the operating, investment, and financing alternatives that do and do not meet market-wide performance standards. These principles are discussed throughout this book.

Prepare the Final Pro Forma Financial Statements

The managers' plans for eliminating cash flow and financing surpluses or shortages must be carefully incorporated into the pro forma financial statements so that they remain internally consistent. Incorporating financing changes is difficult because of the circularity problem described earlier: Issuing debt to eliminate a financing deficit increases interest expense which reduces net income which reduces the amount of financing provided by retained earnings which increases the amount of the deficit. Furthermore, this effect carries over into subsequent years because cumulative retained earnings are entered on the balance sheet. Computerized financial planning models automatically adjust for these effects but you may have to do it by trial-and-error when using simple models.

Ariga Manufacturing Company's final pro forma financial statements are given in Table 18.8 assuming the company issues new debt to eliminate the financing deficits. The amount of new debt required in 1998 equals the amount of the original financing deficit for that year, $874, because the company does not pay interest on this debt until the following year.

The amount of new debt required in 1999 equals the amount of the original financing deficit plus additional financing needed to make up for the reduction in retained earnings caused by the interest payments on prior periods' extra debt. This extra financing equals

$$\text{Extra financing}_t = \Delta\text{Retained earnings}_t + \text{Extra financing}$$
$$\text{required in prior periods}$$

where

$$\Delta\text{Retained earnings}_t = \Delta\text{Net income}_t \times \text{RET}$$
$$= \Delta\text{Interest expense}_t \times (1 - T) \times \text{RET}$$
$$= r_d \times \Delta\text{Debt}_{t-1} \times (1 - T) \times \text{RET}.$$

For Ariga in 1999,

$$\text{Extra financing}_{1999} = 0.07 \times \$874 \times 0.65 \times 0.40 + \$0 = \$16.$$

The company's total new debt in 1999 therefore equals the original financing deficit plus the extra financing, $2,697 + $16 = $2,713.

The change in retained earnings for 2000 is computed similarly and the prior year's extra financing requirement is added due to the cumulative effect of retained earnings. That is,

$$\text{Extra financing}_{2000} = 0.07 \times \$2,713 \times 0.65 \times 0.40 + \$16 = \$65.$$

The total amount of new financing required in 2000 therefore is $6,138 ($6,073 + $65).

Ariga Manufacturing Company's final plan describes the total amount of operating and financial resources the company needs to accomplish its objectives. Managers will use this plan to direct the company's activities and as a benchmark against which to measure the company's actual performance.

Table 18.8   ARIGA MANUFACTURING COMPANY'S FINAL PRO FORMA FINANCIAL STATEMENTS (THOUSANDS OF DOLLARS)

Panel A: Income Statements

		Pro Forma		
	Actual 1997	1998	1999	2000
Net sales	$40,000	$44,000	$48,400	$53,240
Cost of sales	26,000	28,200	30,620	33,282
Gross profit	14,000	15,800	17,780	19,958
Selling and administrative expenses	9,700	10,560	11,616	12,778
Depreciation	2,000	2,500	3,000	3,000
Operating income	2,300	2,740	3,164	4,180
Interest expense	800	840	901	1,030
Taxable income	1,500	1,900	2,263	3,150
Taxes	500	665	792	1,103
Net income	$ 1,000	$ 1,235	$ 1,471	$ 2,047

Panel B: Statements of Retained Earnings

Beginning balance	$ 4,400	$ 4,800	$ 5,294	$ 5,882
Plus net income for the period	1,000	1,235	1,471	2,047
Minus dividends for the period	600	741	883	1,228
Ending balance	$ 4,800	$ 5,294	$ 5,882	$ 6,701

Panel C: Balance Sheets

Assets

Cash and securities	$ 2,500	$ 2,750	$ 3,025	$ 3,328
Accounts receivable	2,800	3,086	3,395	3,734
Inventories	3,000	3,253	3,532	3,839
Total current assets	8,300	9,089	9,952	10,901
Gross fixed assets	22,000	25,250	30,000	34,500
Accumulated depreciation	9,500	12,000	15,000	18,000
Net fixed assets	12,500	13,250	15,000	16,500
Total assets	$20,800	$22,339	$24,952	$27,401

Claims

Accounts payable and accruals	$2,000	$2,171	$2,357	$2,562
Total current liabilities	2,000	2,171	2,357	2,562
Term loan	2,000	2,000	2,000	0
Bonds	10,000	10,000	10,000	10,000
New debt	0	**874**	**2,713**	**6,138**
Total long-term debt	12,000	12,874	14,713	16,138
Common stock	2,000	2,000	2,000	2,000
Retained earnings	4,800	5,294	5,882	6,701
Total equity	6,800	7,294	7,882	8,701
Total claims	$20,800	$22,339	$24,952	$27,401

Changes from preliminary values appear in bold type.

18.5 SUMMARY

Managers use a financial plan to coordinate and control a company's activities. A complete plan includes operating budgets that establish sales, production, and cost goals and capital budgets that describe anticipated purchases of plant and equipment. Pro forma financial statements describe the company's financial condition if operations are conducted as planned.

Financial planners usually begin by forecasting sales. This forecast often is expressed as a target growth rate and must consider the company's competitive position. Costs often are estimated as a function of sales. Interest expense depends on the amount of debt outstanding at the beginning of each period although this may change when the company obtains additional financing to eliminate cash flow deficits. Taxes are based on the company's marginal tax rate and offsetting tax credits.

The pro forma balance sheet describes the resources managers need to accomplish their sales objectives. Some variation of the percent of sales method is frequently used to forecast the amounts of financial slack and accounts receivable, inventory, and accounts payable and accruals that are required. The capital budget contains the information needed to project gross and net fixed assets.

The funding provided by existing discretionary financing should be entered into the projected balance sheet at this point. Retired securities or securities issued to eliminate projected surpluses and deficits are considered later. The amount of funds available from existing discretionary debt (all debt except accounts payable and accruals) equals the debt on the prior period's balance sheet minus scheduled repayments. The amount of funds available from equity equals the change in retained earnings.

Managers can use the pro forma balance sheets directly to forecast financing surpluses and deficits or use them to prepare free cash flow and financial cash flow statements to make identical predictions. The cash statements provide more detailed information and can be used to link financing requirements to the cash flows from acquiring and operating individual assets and business units.

Managers must plan their response to projected cash flow shortages and surpluses. They may plan to issue or retire securities or they may decide to change their operating plans and policies or their financing policies. Determining the company's sustainable growth rate and analyzing the determinants of this rate may suggest areas in which to seek improvements. Of course, the managers must apply sound operating and financial principles to decide which potential change is likely to meet market-wide performance standards. The financial statements in the final plan must reflect all the planned changes in operations and financing and, consequently, must balance with neither cash flow surpluses nor shortages.

• **K E Y   T E R M S**

Business plan *750*	Spontaneous	Discretionary
Financial plan *750*	financing *756*	financing *757*
Percent of sales		
method *753*		

● QUESTIONS AND PROBLEMS

1. Can financial planning be delegated to finance specialists or must managers in operations and administration participate? Explain your answer.

2. Describe the connections between the financial market; a company's investment, operating, and financing decisions; and its financial plan. Refer to these connections to explain why it is essential for operating managers to understand the principles of finance and for financial managers to understand operations.

3. Describe some principal–agent conflicts that may arise during financial planning. What can be done to reduce the impact of these conflicts?

4. Regression analysis and the percent of sales method may be used to estimate costs when preparing pro forma income statements.
   (a) Compare and contrast these forecasting methods.
   (b) Under what conditions will the percent of sales method provide accurate and inaccurate forecasts?

5. Companies often use financial ratios to forecast accounts receivable, inventories, and accounts payable.
   (a) Describe how the DSO, DCI, and DPO ratios are used for these purposes.
   (b) Rewrite the forecasting equations based on these ratios in a form that clearly shows they provide percent of sales forecasts.
   (c) Discuss the limitations of forecasts based on these financial ratios given the results of part (b).

6. What are the differences between spontaneous and discretionary sources of new financing? Give some examples of each. How are these sources treated differently in a preliminary financial plan?

7. Pro forma balance sheets and free cash flow and financial cash flow statements are the main components of a financial plan.
   (a) Describe how to use the preliminary versions of these statements to estimate a company's financing surpluses and deficits and cash flow surpluses and shortages.
   (b) Both methods provide the same estimate of surpluses and shortages. Why is a forecast based on the free cash flow and financial cash flow statements likely to be more useful to a financial planner?

8. Write the expression for sustainable growth in terms of the retention ratio and the financial ratios used in DuPont analysis. Use this expression to explain why a company's sustainable growth rate is a comprehensive constraint that limits its growth in sales, net income, dividends, assets, and financing.

9. Write the expression for sustainable growth in terms of the retention ratio and the financial ratios used in DuPont analysis. Explain how managers can use this expression to identify opportunities for increasing their company's sustainable growth.

10. Sales and costs for two companies are shown below. Each company's cost structure is valid for a wide range of sales.

	Company A	Company B
Sales	$50,000	$50,000
Fixed costs	20,000	3,000
Total costs	35,000	35,000

(a) For each company, develop a percent of sales forecast model and a forecast model that accounts for both fixed and variable costs.

(b) Suppose each company expects sales of $50,000 next year. Which model (percent of sales or fixed and variable cost) is more accurate for Company A? For Company B? Explain your answer.

(c) Suppose each company expects sales of $80,000 next year. Which model (percent of sales or fixed and variable cost) is more accurate for Company A? For Company B? Explain your answer.

11. A budget analyst for Pesky Pest Control Co. must prepare the company's pro forma income statement for 1998 and has compiled the following information about sales, cost of goods sold, and selling and administrative costs.

Year	Sales	Cost of Goods Sold	Selling and Administrative Costs
1988	$2,495	$1,643	$275
1989	2,607	1,663	270
1990	2,679	1,720	286
1991	2,815	1,769	309
1992	2,940	1,818	299
1993	3,000	1,838	313
1994	3,028	1,869	323
1995	3,168	1,921	323
1996	3,296	1,982	342
1997	3,456	2,045	363

(a) Develop forecast models for cost of goods sold using regression analysis and percent of sales based on average sales and costs.

(b) Apply your models to the data from 1988 to 1997 and compute the error terms (actual cost minus predicted cost).

(c) Calculate the standard deviation of the error terms for the regression model and for the percent of sales model. Which is more accurate? Does the accuracy of these models differ very much? Why?

(d) Rework parts (a) through (c) for selling and administrative costs.

(e) Suppose Pesky Pest expects sales of $3,600 in 1998. Use your better forecasting models and compute the company's predicted net operating income.

12. Some information from Pilk Pipe Company's 1997 financial statements is given below.

Sales	$730,000
Cost of goods sold	
Fixed	128,000
Variable	310,000
Total	438,000
Accounts receivable	46,000
Inventories	22,800
Accounts payable	20,400

(a) Determine Pilk's days'-sales-outstanding, days'-costs-in-inventory, and days'-payables-outstanding ratios.

(b) Pilk's target sales growth rate for 1998 is 10 percent. Determine the company's projected investment in accounts receivable and inventories and the projected amount of financing provided by accounts payable.

(c) How much does the company's requirement for net working capital contribute to its need for additional discretionary financing in 1998?

13. Kiefer Klassics restores classic cars that it sells to dealers of classic and exotic cars throughout the country. Sales growth has accelerated with the result that the company seeks additional discretionary financing nearly every year. Kiefer's December 31, 1997, financial statements are given below.

Income Statement

Net sales	$3,200,000
Cost of goods sold	1,920,000
Gross profit	1,280,000
Selling and administrative expenses	849,800
Depreciation	80,000
Net operating income	350,200
Interest expense	80,400
Taxable income	269,800
Taxes	94,430
Net income	$ 175,370

Statement of Retained Earnings

Beginning balance	$ 187,430
Plus net income	175,370
Minus dividends	105,000
Ending balance	$ 257,800

Balance Sheet

Assets	
Cash	$ 70,400
Accounts receivable	220,200
Inventories	460,000
Total current assets	750,600
Gross fixed assets	1,500,000
Accumulated depreciation	610,800
Net fixed assets	889,200
Total assets	$1,639,800

Claims

Accounts payable and accruals	$ 150,300
Total current liabilities	150,300
Term loan	390,100
Bonds	540,700
Total long-term debt	930,800
Common stock	300,900
Retained earnings	257,800
Total equity	558,700
Total claims	$1,639,800

(a) The marketing manager established a target sales growth rate of 8 percent for 1998 and 1999. Kevin Kiefer, president of the company, asked if this ambitious plan would require changes in the company's operating or financing policies. The marketing manager said he didn't think so but Kiefer turned to you for a quick assessment. Calculate the company's 1997 sustainable growth rate and answer Kiefer's question.

(b) Kevin Kiefer trusts your instincts but now wants a detailed description of the sales plan's effect on the company's financial position. Prepare Kiefer Klassic's 1998 and 1999 pro forma financial statements using the company's December 31, 1997 financial statements and the forecast assumptions given below.

Cost of goods sold = $420,000 + 0.47 × Sales
Selling and administrative costs = 0.27 × Sales
Depreciation = $80,000 per year
Interest expense = 0.09 × Long-term debt outstanding at end of previous year
Tax rate = 35%
Dividends = 0.60 × Net income
Cash = 0.025 × Sales
Accounts receivable = DSO × Sales per day
Inventory = DCI × Cost of goods sold per day
Accounts payable = DPO × Cost of goods sold per day
No purchases or sales of fixed assets
Term loan is due December 31, 1998

(c) Determine the amount of the company's projected financing and cash flow surpluses or deficits for 1998 and 1999.

(d) Prepare Kiefer's pro forma free cash flow and financial cash flow statements and use them to confirm your answers to part (b).

14. Use Niarc Corporation's pro forma balance sheets to estimate its projected cash flow surpluses or shortages.

NIARC CORPORATION BALANCE SHEETS

	Actual	Projected	
	Year 0	Year 1	Year 2
Assets			
Cash	$ 10,800	$ 12,350	$ 14,456
Accounts receivable	15,700	18,700	24,200
Inventories	12,000	16,000	18,000
Total current assets	38,500	47,050	56,656
Gross fixed assets	95,000	98,000	98,000
Accumulated depreciation	28,000	39,000	40,000
Net fixed assets	67,000	59,000	58,000
Total assets	$105,500	$106,050	$114,656
Claims			
Accounts payable	$ 15,700	$ 21,001	$ 25,300
Bank loan	9,500	8,500	7,500
Total current liabilities	25,200	29,501	32,800
Term loan	19,000	15,000	11,000
Common stock	49,075	49,075	49,075
Retained earnings	12,225	15,474	19,691
Total equity	61,300	64,549	68,766
Total claims	$105,500	$109,050	$112,566

15. Use Global Enterprises' free cash flow and financial cash flow statements to estimate the company's projected financing and cash flow surpluses and deficits for years 1 and 2.

	Year 1	Year 2
Free Cash Flow		
Cash flow provided by (used for) operations		
Net income	$14,417	$17,615
Plus depreciation expense	6,000	6,000
Minus change in net working capital for operations	4,056	4,417
Plus after-tax interest expense	6,332	3,692
Net cash flow	22,693	22,890
Cash flow provided by (used for) investment		
Purchase fixed assets	0	0
Cash flow provided by (used for) financial slack	(930)	(518)
Net free cash flow	$21,763	$22,372

	Year 1	Year 2
Financial Cash Flow		
Cash received from (paid to) creditors		
After-tax interest payments	$ (6,332)	$ (3,692)
Repayment of term loan	(29,325)	0
Net cash flow	$(35,657)	$ (3,692)
Cash flow received from (paid to) owners		
Dividends	$ (7,209)	$ (8,808)
Net financial cash flow	$(42,866)	$(12,500)

16. Prepare Ariga Manufacturing Company's final pro forma free cash flow and financial cash flow statements. The information you need is in Tables 18.2 and 18.8. Your statements should show that the company's financial plan eliminated its financing and cash flow deficits.

17. Computer Accessories Company's abbreviated 1996 and 1997 financial statements are given below.

Income Statements

	1996	1997
Sales	—	$91,700
Costs and taxes	—	89,951
Net income	—	$ 1,749

Statements of Retained Earnings

Net income	—	$ 1,749
Dividends	—	1,500
Addition to retained earnings	—	$ 249

Balance Sheets

Total assets	$93,500	$99,050
Claims		
Debt	44,200	49,501
Equity	49,300	49,549
Total claims	$93,500	$99,050

(a) Calculate the company's profit margin, total asset turnover ratio, leverage ratio, and retention ratio for 1997.

(b) What is Computer Accessories' sustainable growth rate?

(c) Use the financial ratios from part (a) to project the company's 1998 abbreviated financial statements.

(d) Determine Computer Accessories' growth in sales, net income, dividends, retained earnings, assets, debt, and equity from 1997 to 1998. Explain the relationship between these growth rates and your answer to part (b).

18. Green Glass Bottle and Jar Company's financial ratios are given below.

Profit margin	0.030
Total asset turnover	1.756
Leverage	2.400
Retention	0.700

(a) What is the company's sustainable growth rate?

(b) The company's managers have concluded that opportunities to grow the bottle and jar business are capped at 5 percent. By how much can they reduce the company's leverage ratio and still achieve 5 percent growth? By how much can they increase the company's dividend payout ratio and still achieve 5 percent growth assuming all other ratios remain at their original levels?

(c) Discuss the factors managers should consider when choosing between the alternatives in part (b).

19. Happy Tales Children's Books' pro forma financial statements are given below.

Income Statements

	Actual	Projected	
	Year 0	Year 1	Year 2
Net sales	$692,000	$719,680	$ 748,400
Cost of sales	467,400	481,950	497,600
Gross profit	224,600	237,730	250,800
Selling and administrative expenses	81,780	84,340	87,700
Depreciation	81,211	95,400	98,200
Operating income	61,609	57,990	64,900
Interest expense	25,965	25,965	25,965
Taxable income	35,644	32,025	38,935
Taxes	12,475	11,209	13,627
Net income	$ 23,169	$ 20,816	$ 25,308

Balance Sheets

Assets			
Cash	$ 6,920	$ 7,196	$ 7,484
Accounts receivable	55,360	57,574	59,872
Inventory	16,146	16,648	17,189
Total current assets	78,426	81,418	84,545
Gross fixed assets	750,000	950,000	1,025,000
Accumulated depreciation	107,176	202,576	300,776
Net fixed assets	642,824	747,424	724,224
Total assets	$721,250	$828,842	$ 808,769
Claims			
Accounts payable	$25,610	$26,408	$27,266
Total current liabilities	25,610	26,408	27,266
Long-term debt	288,500	288,500	288,500
Common stock	300,000	300,000	300,000
Retained earnings	107,140	127,956	153,264
Total equity	407,140	427,956	453,264
Total claims	$721,250	$742,864	$ 769,030

Prepare the company's final pro forma financial statements given that the treasurer will borrow money at 9 percent interest to cover any financing deficits. Interest on new debt is paid the following year. The company pays no dividends.

20. Plush + Incorporated manufactures after-market leather upholstery that automobile dealers install in entry-level luxury sedans. The company has done well in recent years and plans to expand sales by 7 percent per year for the next three years. The December 31, 1997 financial statements and forecast assumptions for Plush + are given below.

Income Statement

Net sales	$450,000
Cost of goods sold	271,690
Gross profit	178,310
Selling and administrative expenses	81,000
Depreciation	35,000
Net operating income	62,310
Interest expense	8,850
Taxable income	53,460
Taxes	18,711
Net income	$ 34,749

Statement of Retained Earnings

Beginning balance	$108,610
Plus net income	34,749
Minus dividends	50,000
Ending balance	$ 93,359

Balance Sheet

Assets

Cash	$ 6,025
Accounts receivable	50,707
Inventories	14,280
Total current assets	71,012
Gross fixed assets	603,000
Accumulated depreciation	443,000
Net fixed assets	160,000
Total assets	$231,012

Claims

Accounts payable	$ 22,653
Total current liabilities	22,653
Term loan (9%)	15,000
Bonds (10%)	75,000
Long-term debt	90,000
Common stock	25,000
Retained earnings	93,359
Total equity	118,359
Total claims	$231,012

Forecast Assumptions

Cost of goods sold = $20,000 + 0.50 × Sales
Selling and administrative costs = 0.18 × Sales
Depreciation = $40,000 per year
Interest expense = Interest on term loan and bonds outstanding at end of preceding year
Tax rate = 35%
Dividends = $50,000 for 1998 and $55,000 for 1999 and 2000
Cash = $6,025
DSO = 41 days
DCI = 19 days
DPO = 30 days
Purchases of new capital equipment = $47,000 in 1998, $40,000 in 1999, and $35,000 in 2000
Due date of term loan = December 31, 1999

(a) Determine the amount of Plush +'s projected financing and cash flow surpluses or deficits for 1998, 1999, and 2000.

(b) Can Plush + eliminate its financing deficit by reducing its purchases of new capital equipment? Which financial statement entries will or may be affected by this change? What factors should the company's managers consider before choosing this alternative?

(c) Can Plush + eliminate its financing deficit by reducing its net working capital for operations? Which financial statement entries will or may be affected by this change? What factors should the company's managers consider before choosing this alternative?

(d) Can Plush + eliminate its financing deficit by reducing its common stock dividends or issuing new common stock? What factors should the company's managers consider before choosing one of these alternatives?

21. Ben Thair, Plush + Incorporated's CFO, will take out a one-year bank loan when the company has a financing deficit and will purchase a one-year U.S. Treasury note when it has a surplus. The bank loan costs 12 percent and the Treasury note yields 7 percent. Use the projected financial statements from problem 20 and the CFO's plans to prepare the company's final pro forma financial statements.

• ADDITIONAL READING

A thorough discussion of basic and advanced methods of financial planning is
   Cheng F. Lee, *Financial Analysis and Planning: Theory and Application,* Reading, Massachusetts: Addison Wesley, 1985.

The following article describes a technique for incorporating the effect of borrowing on the requirement for additional funds.
   Daniel T. Winkler, "Financing Costs of Additional Funds Needed: A Modified Equation Approach," *Financial Practice and Education,* Spring/Summer 1994, pp. 149–154.

SHORT-TERM FINANCIAL POLICY AND PLANNING

Chrysler Corporation was preparing for a recession in 1995 by planning to increase inventory turnover, reduce its advertising budget and payments to suppliers, and cut warranty expenses and employment. In addition to these changes in operations, the company was planning financial changes that included increasing its cash and temporary investments to $7.5 billion. Chrysler's managers claimed these precautions were necessary to avoid a repeat of the company's experience in the 1990–1991 recession when it used $4.2 billion of cash, saw its credit rating reduced, and was forced to obtain additional cash from costly sources. The managers drew these conclusions from their forecasts of the company's projected cash position under various economic conditions. These forecasts and Chrysler's planned responses to them had important consequences for the company, its owners, managers, and employees.[1]

Managers use both short- and long-term financial plans to anticipate their company's financial condition and prepare appropriate operating and financial responses. These plans are similar in every respect except the short-term plan covers a shorter forecast horizon, often one year, in greater detail. The key components of each plan are financial statements—particularly cash statements—that managers use to anticipate cash flow surpluses and shortages and to arrange investments and financing to offset them.

The amount and timing of a company's intrayear cash flow surpluses and shortages largely depend on the results of operations although short-term financial policy also has an effect. This policy guides decisions about how much financial slack is required to meet unexpected requirements for cash and decisions about the use of permanent versus temporary financing. These decisions must be based on sound financial

---

[1]Steven Lipin and Gabriella Stern, "Chrysler Plans Suggest Firm Has Ample Cash, Even for a Downturn," *The Wall Street Journal*, October 20, 1995, p. A1.

principles. This means a short-term financial plan must integrate principles and practice just as a long-term financial plan does.

This chapter integrates short-term financial policy into a short-term financial planning process that is directly connected to long-term financial planning. We will continue to use the Ariga Manufacturing Company example from Chapter 18 to emphasize the connections. You will learn the factors to consider when planning the requirements for financial slack, how to estimate a company's monthly cash flow surpluses and shortages, and the advantages and disadvantages of using permanent and temporary financing. You also will learn which financial instruments companies buy with temporary cash surpluses and sell to cover temporary cash shortages.

19.1 ESTIMATING REQUIREMENTS FOR FINANCIAL SLACK

Companies maintain a large amount of financial slack in both absolute and percentage terms. The 1,608 companies covered by Value/Screen III, published by Value Line Publishing, Inc., held an average of $463.9 million of cash and securities in January 1996. This amount was 5.8 percent of the companies' total assets. Exhibit 19.1 shows that large companies in this sample held more cash and securities in dollar terms but less as a percentage of their total assets than small companies.

Exhibit 19.1

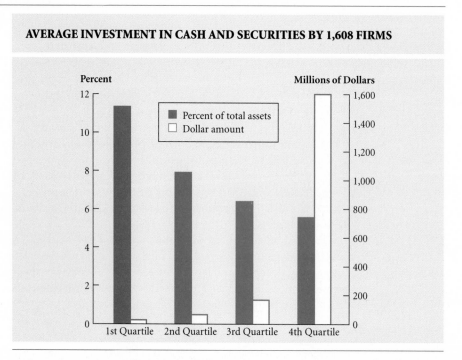

AVERAGE INVESTMENT IN CASH AND SECURITIES BY 1,608 FIRMS

Source: January 1, 1996 edition of Value/Screen III, Value Line Publishing, Inc. copyright 1993.

Managers establish their company's investment in cash and securities by evaluating the benefits and costs of financial slack and by assessing the prospects for financial distress. Their decisions regarding the amount of financial slack to maintain are reflected in the company's short-term financial plan. This section discusses these issues.

The Benefits of Financial Slack

The famed British economist, John Maynard Keynes, said that companies hold cash and other temporary investments as financial slack for transaction, precautionary, and speculative purposes.[2] They use **transaction balances** to provide for expected cash requirements and use **precautionary balances** when cash inflows are less than expected or cash outflows are greater than expected. A company's **speculative balances** provide the capacity to purchase other assets when prices are favorable. Although Keynes did not mention them, companies also hold idle, **compensating balances** in demand deposit accounts to pay banks for credit and noncredit services. Finally, Myers and Majluf suggested companies also maintain financial slack to reduce the hazards of asymmetric information as we discussed in Chapter 15.[3] These balances enable companies to finance their positive-NPV projects internally and avoid inadvertently sending a negative signal.

These motives for holding financial slack seem reasonable and persuasive. However, as we have seen on previous occasions, some care is required to identify the conditions under which they are and are not important.

Suppose first that the financial market is perfect and there is no asymmetric information.[4] Then, the transaction motive for financial slack is unimportant because even very short-term cash surpluses can be distributed to the owners or used to repay debt and be recovered later by selling securities without cost or delay. The precautionary and speculative motives are unimportant for the same reason; a company can costlessly and instantaneously obtain money to cover unexpected cash shortages and make bargain purchases. Financial slack is not required to compensate banks for their services either because companies have no need of a bank's services in a perfect financial market. And, with no asymmetric information, companies don't need to finance projects internally to avoid giving negative signals.

The situation is very different in an imperfect financial market with asymmetric information. Transaction costs make it uneconomical for a company to issue or retire long-term securities to offset a short-term free cash flow shortage or surplus. Registering and distributing long-term securities takes time; therefore, money cannot be obtained from this source quickly enough to cover unexpected cash shortages or make bargain

---

[2] John Maynard Keynes, *The General Theory of Employment, Interest, and Money*, New York, Harcourt, Brace and Company, 1936.

[3] Stewart C. Myers and Nicholas S. Majluf, "Corporate Financing and Investment Decisions When Firms Have Information That Investors Do Not Have," *Journal of Financial Economics*, June 1984, pp. 187–222.

[4] Remember from earlier chapters that a perfect financial market has no transaction costs or taxes, information is instantaneously and freely available to everyone, securities are infinitely divisible, the market is competitive, and there is a single market rate of interest for borrowing and lending.

purchases. Financial institutions help companies overcome the effects of market imperfections and it is sometimes economical to pay them by maintaining compensating balances. Finally, the presence of asymmetric information makes it advantageous to fund projects internally.

The Costs of Financial Slack

Financial slack is useful in an imperfect financial market with asymmetric information but it is not costless. The opportunity cost of financial slack is obvious. Companies incur opportunity costs when they maintain financial slack because they could use that money to buy productive assets or repay long-term financing. The interest they receive on marketable securities reduces but does not eliminate this cost because long-term investments and financing usually are more profitable and costly, respectively.

The agency cost of financial slack is more subtle. Slack shields managers from the market's scrutiny by enabling them to finance investment projects internally. The availability of internal financing reduces the hazards of asymmetric information, as described above, however, managers may abuse these resources in two ways. First, they may use the company's financial slack to finance favorite projects that don't meet market-wide performance standards. Second, they may maintain an excess amount of financial slack to improve the company's safety to protect their own jobs. This misallocation of the company's resources has exactly the same effect as unwarranted company diversification described in Chapter 5.

How Much Slack Is Enough?

Increasing a company's financial slack lowers its transaction costs, distress costs, and signaling costs but raises its opportunity costs and agency costs. The amount of financial slack that minimizes the sum of these costs is optimal. Stating the problem this way makes it apparent that managing financial slack is similar to managing an inventory. Financial slack is the inventoried item, the cost of buying and selling securities are the ordering costs, and the opportunity cost of financial slack is the cost of holding the inventory.

William Baumol recognized these similarities and showed how to use the EOQ model to manage a company's cash position.[5] However, this simple model only is applicable to companies that have uniform, predictable cash inflows or outflows but not both. Merton Miller and Daniel Orr developed a more complicated model that permits both cash inflows and outflows but it imposes other restrictive conditions.[6] The two more important restrictions are that the company's net cash flows must be completely unpredictable and have an expected value of zero.

A treasurer follows Miller and Orr's policy by converting $\$Q^*$ of securities to cash when the cash balance reaches zero and by converting $\$2Q^*$ of cash to securities when the balance reaches $\$3Q^*$. Both transactions restore the cash balance to $\$Q^*$, the opti-

---

[5] William J. Baumol, "The Transactions Demand for Cash: An Inventory Theoretic Approach," *Quarterly Journal of Economics*, November 1952, pp. 545–556.

[6]Merton H. Miller and Daniel Orr, "The Demand for Money by Firms," *Quarterly Journal of Economics*, August 1966, pp. 413–435.

mal return point. The optimal cash return point and the average cash balance for this model are given by Equations 19.1 and 19.2.

$$Q^* = [3b\sigma^2/4r]^{1/3} \qquad\qquad \textbf{[19.1]}$$

$$\text{Average cash balance} = 4Q^*/3 \qquad\qquad \textbf{[19.2]}$$

where b = fixed cost of buying or selling securities
σ^2 = variance of periodic net cash flows
r = opportunity cost of cash balances

As an example, suppose the mean and standard deviation of Ulysses Travel Agency's daily net cash flows are $0 and $2,000. To what level should the company return its cash balance when it becomes too large or too small and what is the average cash balance under this policy? The cost of buying and selling securities is $186 per transaction and the rate of return on securities is 4 percent per year or 0.011 percent per day. Applying Miller and Orr's model,

$$Q^* = [3 \times \$186 \times (\$2,000)^2/(4 \times 0.00011)]^{1/3} = \$17,182$$

$$\text{Average cash balance} = 4 \times \$17,182/3 = \$22,909.$$

EXERCISE
19.1

MILLER AND ORR'S MODEL

Concerns about inflation caused interest rates to increase from 4 percent to 5 percent. How should Ulysses Travel Agency manage cash and what is the resulting average cash balance?

The company's new daily opportunity cost is 0.000137 and its new optimal cash return point, Q^*, is

$$Q^* = [3 \times \$186 \times (\$2,000)^2/(4 \times 0.000137)]^{1/3} = \$15,970.$$

Ulysses should sell $15,970 of marketable securities to obtain cash when the balance reaches zero and buy $31,940 (2 × $15,970) of securities to reduce cash when the balance reaches $47,910 (3 × $15,970). As a result, the company's average cash balance will be $21,293 (4 × $15,970/3).

Ulysses' average cash balance is lower because the opportunity cost of holding cash increased from 4 percent to 5 percent.

Baumol's and Miller and Orr's models are reassuringly precise and therefore seem useful for determining the requirements for financial slack. Nevertheless, they are not widely used for two reasons. First, these models are suitable only in extreme situations—complete certainty or complete uncertainty—while most companies' requirements for financial slack have both predictable and unpredictable components. Second, neither those nor more sophisticated inventory control models provide a way to incorporate the signaling costs of having too little financial slack and the agency costs of having too much. These costs may very well be more important than transaction costs to a large company, so their omission is a serious deficiency.

Inventory control models are useful even though they cannot be used to determine the precise amount of financial slack a company requires. Baumol's and Miller and Orr's models confirm the intuition that a company should maintain more financial slack the larger its size, the larger its cost of buying and selling securities, and the smaller its opportunity cost of holding financial slack. Importantly, both models reveal that the change in the amount of financial slack a company should hold is less than proportional to the change in the values of these parameters. Knowing this simple fact can help managers avoid overreacting to changes in their company's or the economy's situation.

Alternative Measures of Financial Slack

Occasionally, companies have so much money invested in liquid assets that it is tempting to conclude they have sufficient financial slack by any measure. You must be careful, however, because you cannot determine if there is an adequate supply of financial slack until you evaluate the potential demand. Traditional and modern measures of financial slack, or liquidity as it was once called, help with this assessment because they are constructed as ratios of the supply and demand of uncommitted financial resources.

Undoubtedly, the most widely used liquidity measures are the current ratio and the quick ratio, defined by Equations 19.3 and 19.4.

$$\text{Current ratio} = \frac{\text{Current assets}}{\text{Current liabilities}} \qquad [\mathbf{19.3}]$$

$$\text{Quick ratio} = \frac{\text{Current assets} - \text{inventory}}{\text{Current liabilities}} \qquad [\mathbf{19.4}]$$

These ratios use a company's current liabilities as an estimate of its demand for financial slack in the coming year. The current ratio uses current assets to represent the supply of financial slack while the quick ratio excludes inventory because it is not liquid. Many analysts conclude a company has adequate financial slack if its current and quick ratios are at least 2.0 and 1.0. Analysts also examine the trend in these ratios and compare a company's ratios to benchmark companies as described in Chapter 2.

The current and quick ratios are poor measures of financial slack, however, because current assets and liabilities do not accurately represent the supply and demand for financial slack. Current assets exclude important sources of liquidity such as expected cash inflows and the company's borrowing capacity while current liabilities exclude cash outflows expected to arise from future transactions. Excluding a company's cash flows also means there is no provision for incorporating the uncertainty about its requirements for financial slack. As a result, these ratios and their arbitrarily chosen critical values are unreliable indicators of financial slack.

An alternative to the current and quick ratios and other balance sheet measures of financial slack is a cash flow-based ratio, the **lambda index** (λ).[7] This measure of financial slack is defined by Equation 19.5.

---

[7]Gary W. Emery and Kenneth O. Cogger, "The Measurement of Liquidity," *Journal of Accounting Research*, Autumn 1982, pp. 290–303.

$$\lambda = \frac{L + E(\text{NCF})}{\sigma(\text{NCF})} \qquad [19.5]$$

where
L = uncommitted financial resources (cash, marketable securities, and borrowing capacity)
$E(\text{NCF})$ = expected net cash flow during the planning period
$\sigma(\text{NCF})$ = standard deviation of net cash flow during the planning period

Lambda also is a coverage ratio like the current and quick ratios but it uses more comprehensive measures of the supply and demand for financial slack. The supply of financial slack equals a company's investment in cash and marketable securities and its borrowing capacity plus the net cash flow it expects to receive or pay out during the planning period. Positive expected net cash flow augments its financial slack while negative expected net cash flow diminishes it. A company's net expected supply of financial slack must provide for unexpected requirements for cash, represented by the standard deviation of net cash flow.

One of the lambda index's better features is that it can be used to estimate the probability the company will exhaust its financial slack and experience cash insolvency. This is possible because, under the assumption that the company's net cash flows are normally distributed, lambda is a standardized normal random variable or Z-score. Therefore, an analyst can simply look up the lambda value in a standard normal probability table for an estimate of the likelihood of cash insolvency. That is,

$$\text{Probability of cash insolvency} = 1.0 - N(\lambda) \qquad [19.6]$$

where
$N(\lambda)$ = probability that the normally distributed random variable Z is less than or equal to λ.

The ability to estimate this probability gives lambda a natural benchmark that reduces the need for comparison with other companies. The following example illustrates the process.

The Lyons Fuel Oil Company must evaluate a major customer's capacity to withstand adversity next year. This customer, Ram Brothers Distribution Company, has $500,000 of cash and securities and a $2 million credit line at its bank. The company's expected annual net cash flow from operations is $4.2 million with a standard deviation of $2 million. What is Ram Brothers' lambda index and probability of cash insolvency?

$$\lambda = (\$2.5 + \$4.2)/\$2 = 3.35$$

A simple interpretation of this value for the lambda index is that the Ram Brothers have enough financial slack to cover the uncertainty in their cash flow forecast a little more than three and one-third times. The more informative interpretation is obtained by looking up 3.35 in a standard normal probability table such as Table A4 in the appendix.

$$\text{Probability of cash insolvency} = 1 - N(3.35)$$
$$= 0.0004$$

There are four chances out of 10,000 that the Ram Brothers Distribution Company will become cash insolvent next year.

19.2   CALCULATING THE LAMBDA INDEX

Suppose uncertainty about oil prices increases the standard deviation of the Ram Brothers Distribution Company's future net cash flows to $2.25 milllion. What is the company's new lambda value and probability of cash insolvency if all other values remain the same?

$$\lambda = (\$2.5 + \$4.2)/\$2.25 = 2.98$$

$$\text{Probability of cash insolvency} = 1 - N(2.98)$$

$$= 0.0014$$

The additional uncertainty about its future net cash flows increased Ram Brothers' risk of cash insolvency to 14 chances out of 10,000.

Some companies actually solve this problem backwards to determine how much financial slack to maintain given a target probability of cash insolvency.[8] Suppose that after considering transaction, distress, signaling, opportunity, and agency costs, the managers of the Ram Brothers Distribution Company decided they should reduce the company's probability of cash insolvency to 0.0003. How much financial slack is required if their cash flow characteristics remain the same?

The body of a normal probability table reveals that a 0.0003 probability of cash insolvency requires a lambda index of 3.45. Substituting this value and the company's cash flow characteristics in Equation 19.5 and solving for *L*,

$$\lambda = \frac{L + \$4.2}{\$2} = 3.45$$

$$L = 3.45 \times \$2 - \$4.2 = \$2.70 \text{ million.}$$

The Ram Brothers Distribution company must increase its financial slack by $200,000 ($2.7 million – $2.5 million) to achieve the target probability of cash insolvency.

19.3   ESTIMATING THE REQUIREMENT FOR FINANCIAL SLACK

How much financial slack does the Ram Brothers Distribution Company need to reduce the probability of cash insolvency to 0.0002 if its standard deviation of net cash flows is $2.25 million?

According to the normal probability distribution table, a lambda index of 3.49 is required to obtain a probability of cash insolvency of 0.0002. Therefore,

$$\lambda = \frac{L + \$4.2}{\$2.25} = 3.49$$

$$L = 3.49 \times \$2.25 - \$4.2 = \$3.65 \text{ million.}$$

---

[8]Kelly R. Conaster, "Can You Pay the Bills?" *Lotus,* January 1991, pp. 30–34.

Achieving a smaller target probability of cash insolvency with a larger standard deviation requires the company to increase its financial slack by $1.15 million ($3.65 million – $2.5 million).

• ——————— •

19.2   PREPARING MONTHLY CASH STATEMENTS

A company's short-term financial plan accounts for the cash flows provided by and used for financial slack as well as the cash flows provided by and used for operations, investments, and financing. Monthly pro forma financial statements usually are used to account for these cash flows so managers can anticipate cash flow surpluses and shortages within the year and plan temporary investments and financing to offset them. Managers also use the monthly statements throughout the year to measure a company's performance and to identify areas for improvement.

Short-term financial plans usually contain a complete set of financial statements; the cash statement is the centerpiece because it provides the clearest link between a company's planned operations and its anticipated cash flow surpluses and shortages. This statement is invariably called a cash budget but you will recognize it as a pro forma cash statement prepared using the direct method introduced in Chapter 2. We will focus on this statement in this section.

Distributing Annual Sales and Production Across the Months of the Year

Monthly cash statements begin with an estimate of monthly sales because sales affect the amount and timing of cash received from customers. These sales often follow a distinctive seasonal pattern that varies from one industry to another. For example, retail sales of consumer goods exhibit a large peak in December and a smaller peak in the spring or autumn. Sales by distributors who supply these goods to retail stores peak 60 to 90 days earlier.

Monthly sales also affect the amount and timing of cash paid to suppliers unless production exhibits a different seasonal pattern due to the availability of raw materials or production capacity. Most food sales are nearly uniformly distributed over the year but food processors must purchase their raw materials when they are harvested. Conversely, fertilizer sales are concentrated in the spring and summer but chemical companies produce fertilizer year-round and store it for later sale to fully employ their manufacturing facilities. The timing of these companies' payments to suppliers may be virtually independent of the timing of their sales.

Managers can estimate the seasonal pattern of sales or production by using their own company's experience or benchmark companies' experiences to compute the proportion of annual sales or production that occurred each month. Multiplying the annual sales and production in the first year of the long-range business plan by these proportions distributes the annual amounts over the months of the year.

Estimating the Timing and Amounts of Cash Received from Customers and Paid to Suppliers

The timing and amounts of cash received from customers depends on monthly sales and the company's credit policies. The effect of these policies is summarized by the company's days'-sales-outstanding (DSO) ratio that can be directly used to forecast cash receipts. For example, a company with a DSO of 30 days would predict that March's cash receipts from customers will equal February's sales. This simple, direct approach works well if all sales are on credit and there is no seasonal variation in sales. Otherwise, this method produces inaccurate forecasts. This problem is illustrated in the following example.

Dean Lusch, a financial planner for Walton Products, Inc., must forecast cash receipts from customers for the forthcoming quarter. The company's projected sales are given in panel A of Table 19.1. Dean knows that 50 percent of sales are for cash and 50 percent are on credit due in 60 days. Accounts are collected promptly and there are no bad debts so the company's DSO is 30 days (0.50×0 days + 0.50×60 days). Therefore, Dean's DSO-based forecast is that each month's total sales are collected in full 30 days later. This forecast is provided in panel B of the table.

Panel C of Table 19.1 describes the actual amount of cash Walton Products will receive from its customers given their payment pattern. Cash sales are paid for immediately while credit sales are paid for 60 days later. As a result, the cash received in a particular month comprises that month's cash sales plus the second prior month's credit sales.

Table 19.1   WALTON PRODUCTS, INC.'S PROJECTED CASH RECEIPTS FROM CUSTOMERS

Panel A: Monthly Sales

	Actual	Projected			
	February	March	April	May	June
Cash sales	$ 5,000	$ 5,000	$35,000	$ 5,000	$ 5,000
Credit sales	5,000	5,000	35,000	5,000	5,000
Total sales	$10,000	$10,000	$70,000	$10,000	$10,000

Panel B: Forecast Based on DSO = 30 days

			April	May	June
Cash received from customers			$10,000	$70,000	$10,000

Panel C: Forecast Based on Actual Collection Behavior

			April	May	June
Cash received from current month's cash sales			$35,000	$ 5,000	$ 5,000
Cash received from second prior month's credit sales			5,000	5,000	35,000
Total			$40,000	$10,000	$40,000

You can see that the DSO approach underestimates cash receipts when sales increase in April and overestimates cash receipts when sales decrease in May. These inaccurate estimates may cause unanticipated, costly cash surpluses or shortages. Financial planners avoid these forecast errors by using detailed collection information when there are both cash and credit sales and when sales vary over time.

The timing and amounts of cash paid to suppliers depend on monthly production and on the company's inventory and payment policies. The effect of these policies is summarized by the company's days'-costs-in-inventory (DCI) and days'-payables-outstanding (DPO) ratios, which can be directly used to forecast cash payments. For example, a company with a DCI and DPO of 75 days and 45 days purchases materials 75 days prior to a sale and pays for them 45 days later. The cash payments to suppliers associated with a particular sale therefore take place 30 days prior to the sale (45 days − 75 days). If all purchases are not on credit and production varies over time, this method is subject to the same inaccuracies as the DSO approach to forecasting cash collections.

● ———————————————————————————— ●   E X E R C I S E

FORECASTING CASH PAID TO SUPPLIERS

19.4

Walton Products Company's actual and projected purchases of raw materials are given in the following table. The company pays for credit purchases in 90 days. Prepare estimates of the amount of cash paid to suppliers in April using the company's DPO and actual payment pattern.

	Cash Purchases	Credit Purchases	Total Purchases
Actual			
January	$ 6,000	$ 3,000	$ 9,000
February	8,000	4,000	12,000
March	10,000	5,000	15,000
Projected			
April	40,000	20,000	60,000

Two-thirds of Walton's purchases are for cash, so its DPO is 30 days (0.667×0 days $+ 0.333 \times 90$ days). Therefore, the company's DPO-based forecast of cash paid to suppliers in April equals March's purchases, $15,000. The forecast based on the company's actual payment pattern equals April's cash purchases plus payment for January's credit purchases, $40,000 + $3,000 = $43,000. The DPO-based forecast severely underestimates the amount of cash paid to suppliers.

● ——————————— ●

Estimating the Timing and Amounts of Other Cash Flows

The timing and amounts of other cash flows depend on conventions, regulations, and the company's policies rather than on the time pattern of sales or production. Dividends and interest are customarily paid quarterly and semi-annually while the U.S. Internal

Revenue Service requires quarterly tax payments. These items should be entered in the cash statement accordingly. Selling and administrative expenses comprise salaries and facilities costs that often are uniformly distributed over the months of the year. Expenditures for capital equipment are scheduled when it is ordered given the delivery date and the vendor's payment policy. Finally, planned increases and decreases in financial slack may be implemented gradually or abruptly depending on the managers' assessment of when liquidity may be needed.

Application to Ariga Manufacturing Company

We will prepare Ariga Manufacturing Company's monthly pro forma free cash flow and financial cash flow statements for 1998 to illustrate this process. The company's actual pro forma financial statements for 1998, from Chapter 18, are repeated here in Table 19.2.

Ariga's managers will use the company's historical monthly sales pattern to distribute 1998's annual sales and cost of goods sold over the months of the year. This historical pattern is graphed in Exhibit 19.2. The peak in July is mostly due to shipments of big-screen televisions to retailers in advance of the fall football season. The larger peak in

---

Table 19.2   ARIGA MANUFACTURING CO.'S 1998 FINANCIAL STATEMENTS (THOUSANDS OF DOLLARS)

Panel A: Income Statement

Net sales	$44,000
Cost of goods sold	28,200
Gross profit	15,800
Selling and administrative expenses	10,560
Depreciation	2,500
Operating income	2,740
Interest expense	840
Taxable income	1,900
Taxes	665
Net income	$ 1,235

Panel B: Statement of Retained Earnings

Beginning balance	$ 4,800
Plus net income for the period	1,235
Minus dividends for the period	741
Ending balance	$ 5,294

Panel C: Balance Sheet

Assets	
Cash	$2,750
Accounts receivable	3,086
Inventories	3,253
Total current assets	9,089
Gross fixed assets	25,250
Accumulated depreciation	12,000
Net fixed assets	13,250
Total assets	$22,339

Claims	
Accounts payable and accruals	$ 2,171
Total current liabilities	2,171
Term loan	2,000
Bonds	10,000
Total long-term debt	12,000
Common stock	2,000
Retained earnings	5,294
Total equity	7,294
Total claims	$21,465

Exhibit 19.2

ARIGA MANUFACTURING CO.'S MONTHLY SALES PATTERN

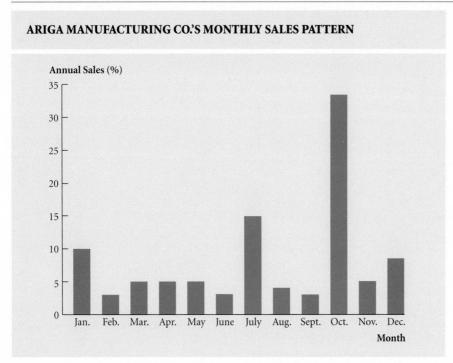

October is due to shipments of both televisions and home entertainment centers to retailers prior to Christmas. Applying these proportions to 1998's projected annual sales of $44,000 and cost of goods sold of $28,200 gives the monthly estimates for these items shown in Table 19.3. Fifteen percent of total sales are for cash and 85 percent are on credit.

The entries for the remaining items in the worksheet follow their own schedules. Anticipated selling and administrative expenses for 1998 are equally divided among all 12 months. Interest is paid every six months while taxes and dividends are paid quarterly. The new fixed assets will be installed in June so they can be used during the peak selling season. Payment is due when installation is complete. The managers will reduce the company's financial slack from $2,500 to $1,000 for the first half of the year when sales and purchases are low and then increase it to $2,750 for the last six months when sales and purchases are higher.

Ariga's free cash flow and financial cash flow statements, given in Table 19.4, are prepared using information from the cash flow worksheet. Cash sales are collected the month of the sale and the company has no bad debts, so credit sales are collected in full the following month. The amount of cash received from customers each month therefore equals that month's cash sales plus the prior month's credit sales.

Ariga's DCI of 42.1 days implies that on average the company purchases raw materials six weeks prior to a sale. We could use a two-week interval for the cash statements but we will simplify and assume that these purchases take place only four weeks prior to a sale. The company's DPO of 28.1 days implies that these purchases are

Table 19.3   ARIGA MANUFACTURING CO.'S CASH FLOW WORKSHEET (THOUSANDS OF DOLLARS)

	Jan.	Feb.	Mar.	Apr.	May	June	July	Aug.	Sept.	Oct.	Nov.	Dec.	Total
Percent of annual sales and cost of goods sold	10.0%	3.0%	5.0%	5.0%	5.0%	3.0%	15.0%	4.0%	3.0%	33.5%	5.0%	8.5%	100%
Net sales													
Cash (15% of total)	$ 660	$ 198	$ 330	$ 330	$ 330	$ 198	$ 990	$ 264	$ 198	$ 2,211	$ 330	$ 561	$ 6,600
Credit (85% of total)	3,740	1,122	1,870	1,870	1,870	1,122	5,610	1,496	1,122	12,529	1,870	3,179	37,400
Total	4,400	1,320	2,200	2,200	2,200	1,320	6,600	1,760	1,320	14,740	2,200	3,740	44,000
Cost of goods sold	2,820	846	1,410	1,410	1,410	846	4,230	1,128	846	9,447	1,410	2,397	28,200
Selling and administrative expenses	880	880	880	880	880	880	880	880	880	880	880	880	10,560
Interest expense	0	0	0	0	0	420	0	0	0	0	0	420	840
Taxes	0	0	166	0	0	166	0	0	166	0	0	167	665
Dividends	0	0	185	0	0	185	0	0	185	0	0	186	741
Purchase fixed assets	0	0	0	0	0	3,250	0	0	0	0	0	0	3,250
Increase (decrease) financial slack	(1,500)	0	0	0	0	1,750	0	0	0	0	0	0	250

paid for four weeks later. The net result is the company pays suppliers an amount that equals its cost of goods sold for the month. To illustrate, materials required for February's sales, valued at $846, are purchased and placed in inventory in January and paid for four weeks later in February. Therefore, cash paid to suppliers in February equals cost of goods sold for February.

Selling and administrative expenses are entered in the free cash flow statements directly from the worksheet. Interest expense is multiplied by one minus the tax rate and entered in the financial cash flow statements. Because we have entered after-tax interest in the financial cash flow statements, we must remove the interest tax-shield from taxes before we enter them in the free cash flow statements. This is accomplished by adding back the interest tax-shield for the year, $294 ($840 × 0.35), and distributing the total, $959 ($665 + $294), across the four quarters in Table 19.4.

Ariga's monthly cash flow provided by operations equals the sum of cash received from customers, cash paid to suppliers, and cash used for selling and administrative expenses and taxes. The company's largest operating cash flow deficit occurs in October when it pays a large amount of cash to suppliers. The largest operating cash flow surplus occurs the following month when Ariga collects a large amount of cash from customers.

Cash in the amount of $3,250 will be used for investment in new fixed assets in June. Reducing financial slack will provide $1,500 of cash flow in January while increasing financial slack will use $1,750 in June.

Net free cash flow equals the sum of the cash flows provided by or used for operations, investment, and financial slack. Ariga's largest net free cash flow deficit and surplus will occur in October and November for the reasons mentioned earlier. Ariga's only financial cash flows are its semi-annual after-tax interest payments and quarterly dividend payments.

The cash flow surplus or shortage for each month equals net free cash flow plus net financial cash flow. The cumulative deficit is the company's monthly financing sur-

ARIGA MANUFACTURING CO.'S MONTHLY CASH STATEMENTS (THOUSANDS OF DOLLARS)   **Table 19.4**

	Jan.	Feb.	Mar.	Apr.	May	June	July	Aug.	Sept.	Oct.	Nov.	Dec.
Free Cash Flow												
Cash flow provided by (used for) operations												
Cash received from customers												
Cash sales	$ 660	$ 198	$ 330	$ 330	$ 330	$ 198	$ 990	$ 264	$ 198	$ 2,211	$ 330	$ 561
Collection of credit sales	2,890	3,740	1,122	1,870	1,870	1,870	1,122	5,610	1,496	1,122	12,529	1,870
Total	3,550	3,938	1,452	2,200	2,200	2,068	2,112	5,874	1,694	3,333	12,859	2,431
Cash paid to suppliers	(2,820)	(846)	(1,410)	(1,410)	(1,410)	(846)	(4,230)	(1,128)	(846)	(9,447)	(1,410)	(2,397)
Selling and administrative expenses	(880)	(880)	(880)	(880)	(880)	(880)	(880)	(880)	(880)	(880)	(880)	(880)
Taxes	0	0	(239)	0	0	(240)	0	0	(240)	0	0	(240)
Net cash flow	(150)	2,212	(1,077)	(90)	(90)	102	(2,998)	3,866	(272)	(6,994)	10,569	(1,086)
Cash flow provided by (used for) investment												
Purchase fixed assets	0	0	0	0	0	(3,250)	0	0	0	0	0	0
Cash flow provided by (used for) financial slack	1,500	0	0	0	0	(1,750)	0	0	0	0	0	0
Net free cash flow	1,350	2,212	(1,077)	(90)	(90)	(4,898)	(2,998)	3,866	(272)	(6,994)	10,569	(1,086)
Financial Cash Flow												
After-tax interest payments	0	0	0	0	0	(273)	0	0	0	0	0	(273)
Dividend payments	0	0	(185)	0	0	(185)	0	0	(185)	0	0	(186)
Net financial cash flow	0	0	(185)	0	0	(458)	0	0	(185)	0	0	(459)
Cash Flow Surplus (Shortage)	1,350	2,212	(1,262)	(90)	(90)	(5,356)	(2,998)	3,866	(457)	(6,994)	10,569	(1,545)
Financing Surplus (Deficit)	$1,350	$3,562	$2,300	$2,210	$2,120	$(3,236)	$(6,234)	$(2,368)	$(2,825)	$(9,819)	$ 750	$(795)

plus or deficit. December's financing deficit, $795, is slightly different from the amount projected in the long-range financial plan, $874, because we didn't use differences in annual working capital accounts to estimate cash flow from operations. The amount shown in the short-term financial plan therefore is more accurate.

The more important information in the short-term financial plan is the company will have recurring intrayear financing deficits much larger than its end of year deficit. December's deficit is not only the *smallest* of the year, it also is less than one-twelfth the size of the maximum requirement of $9,819 in October. Two factors cause these financing deficits. First, Ariga's cash collection cycle requires the company to pay cash for labor and materials approximately 40 days (42.1 days − 28.1 days + 25.6 days = 39.6 days) prior to collecting cash from the sale.[9] The obligation to finance the net working

---

[9]Remember, we rounded 42.1 days to four weeks when we prepared Ariga's monthly cash statements.

capital this cash collection cycle represents contributes to the company's financing deficit. Second, and more significantly, Ariga's sales are highly seasonal; by far the company's largest cash flow deficits occur in the peak sales months of July and October.

Ariga's managers may respond to the projected financing deficits by changing operations to shorten the company's cash collection cycle or reduce the seasonality of sales. They may, for example, apply the principles we discussed in Chapters 11 and 12 to reduce inventories, shorten credit terms, or accelerate the collection of cash from customers. The managers also may be able to persuade the company's suppliers to extend longer payment terms on a temporary basis during the crucial months of June through October. Finally, Ariga's managers may be able to adopt a credit policy that encourages the company's customers to place their orders in advance of the peak sales months to reduce the seasonality of sales. Operating and financial managers must work together to determine which, if any, of these changes are efficient ways to reduce the company's temporary financing deficits.

Ariga's managers must obtain permanent or temporary financing to cover any intrayear deficits that remain after changing the company's operations. We will discuss the choice between permanent and temporary financing next.

19.3   THE CHOICE BETWEEN PERMANENT AND TEMPORARY FINANCING

Ariga Manufacturing Company's monthly cash statements show that their largest financing deficits are due to the net working capital requirements of their seasonal business. In comparison, their plan to purchase $3,250 of capital equipment contributes only a small amount to their requirement for cash. You can see these conclusions more clearly in Exhibit 19.3, which graphs the company's monthly net fixed assets and net working capital (current assets minus current liabilities). The monthly accounts receivable balance equals the beginning balance for the month plus credit sales minus collections. The balances of the other working capital accounts were computed similarly.

Exhibit 19.3 shows that Ariga's net investment in fixed assets is constant except for the $3,250 increase in June. The company's requirement for net working capital is relatively stable at the beginning of the year because sales are relatively stable then. Between June and October, however, net working capital fluctuates as inventories and receivables are built up and drawn down by the seasonal fluctuations in sales.

Most companies face situations similar to Ariga's. They have a permanent investment in assets, which comprises net fixed assets and the net working capital required for baseline sales, plus temporary net working capital required for seasonal sales. Companies use some combination of permanent and temporary financing to finance these permanent and temporary investments. We'll discuss their alternatives by beginning with two extreme financing strategies: a conservative one that has the least risk and an aggressive one that may have the lowest cost. These policies probably are not very practical, however, they illuminate the issues managers must consider when they make this financing choice.

Exhibit 19.3

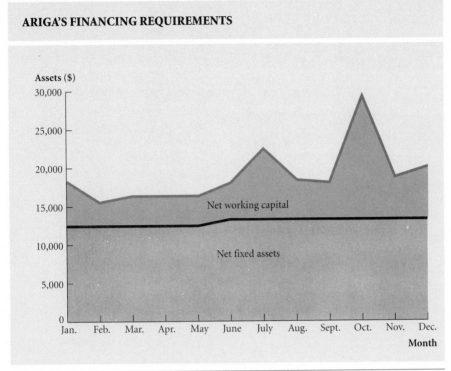

ARIGA'S FINANCING REQUIREMENTS

Conservative and Aggressive Financing Policies

Companies use permanent sources of funds to pay for net fixed assets and both permanent and temporary net working capital under the conservative financing policy. Long-term debt, preferred stock, and common equity are the main sources of permanent financing. Companies that follow this policy have no short-term debt other than the current liabilities, such as accounts payable and accruals, that arise spontaneously from operations. These sources of financing already are accounted for in net working capital.

Exhibit 19.4 applies this policy to Ariga Manufacturing. Slightly less than $30 million of long-term financing is arranged at the beginning of 1998 and fully employed in October when the maximum amount of permanent and temporary assets is required. The excess funds provided by this policy during the remainder of the year are held as temporary investments. The average amount of excess funds held as temporary investments over the entire year is $10.5 million.

Think back to our discussion of financial slack and you will immediately see the benefits and costs of the conservative policy. Companies that follow this policy have low expected transaction, distress, and signaling costs because they are unlikely to unexpectedly enter the financial market for additional funds. They incur high opportunity and agency costs, however, and may attract the attention of investors who believe all

Exhibit 19.4

ARIGA'S CONSERVATIVE FINANCING STRATEGY

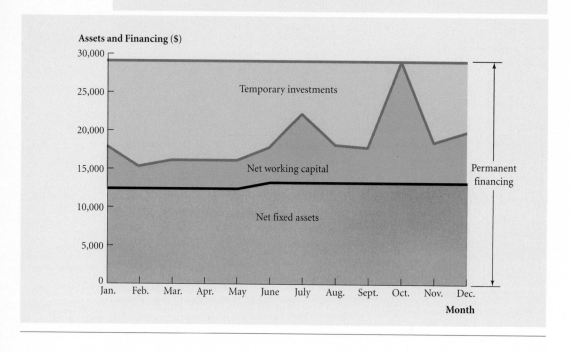

this safety is unwarranted. It is probably for these reasons that extemely conservative financing policies are not widely used.

Companies use permanent sources of financing to fund net fixed assets and temporary debt to fund both permanent and temporary net working capital under the aggressive policy. Commercial paper, bank loans, and secured loans from other financial institutions are the main sources of temporary debt. Companies that follow this policy have both spontaneous and discretionary short-term debt.

Exhibit 19.5 applies this policy to Ariga Manufacturing Company. Ariga begins the year with $12.5 million of long-term financing and increases it to $13.25 million in June to finance the increase in net fixed assets. Short-term debt is initiated and repaid according to the company's need for funds to finance net working capital. The maximum and average amounts of short-term debt outstanding under this policy are $16.2 and $6.0 million. The aggressive policy produces no idle funds, therefore, the company's only temporary investments are those held as financial slack. These temporary investments already are included among the assets that comprise net working capital.

Companies that follow the aggressive policy have lower expected opportunity and agency costs because they have no idle funds. However, they have higher expected transaction, distress, and signaling costs because they must frequently obtain and repay short-term loans. Furthermore, their interest costs may be higher than under the conservative policy if short-term interest rates are volatile. The fact that this policy has higher risk

Exhibit 19.5

ARIGA'S AGGRESSIVE FINANCING STRATEGY

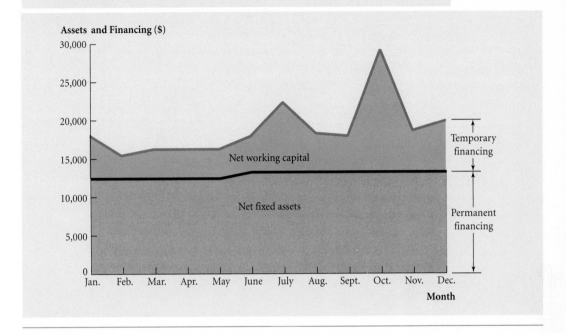

with only a possibility of lower interest costs is probably why few companies adopt an extremely aggressive short-term financing policy.

Moderate Financing Policies

Most companies choose a moderate short-term financing policy to balance expected transaction, distress, and signaling costs with expected opportunity and agency costs. Permanent financing is used for net fixed assets and part of net working capital while temporary financing is used for the rest. Companies that follow a moderate policy have both spontaneous and discretionary short-term debt and may have temporary investments depending on how much permanent financing they use.

Two moderate policies are applied to Ariga Manufacturing in Exhibit 19.6. Panel A illustrates a pure matching policy under which permanent financing is used to fund net fixed assets and permanent net working capital, the part that persists throughout the year. Following this policy, Ariga has no temporary investments but its temporary financing fluctuates from zero in February to $13.2 million in October. Panel B of the exhibit illustrates a conservative matching policy that uses more permanent and less temporary financing. This policy is safer than a pure matching policy because the company has idle funds that are held as temporary investments at the beginning and end of the year when less net working capital is required. Most companies have both temporary debt and temporary investments during the year, that is, they implicitly follow a conservative matching short-term financing policy.

Exhibit 19.6

ARIGA MANUFACTURING CO.'S MATCHING FINANCING STRATEGIES

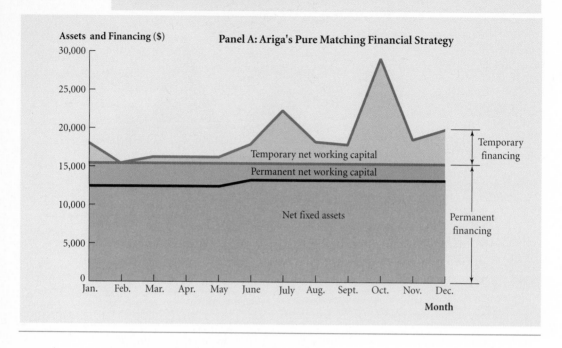

Temporary Financing Alternatives

Companies that follow any short-term financing policy other than the extremely conservative one require some temporary debt. They may obtain these funds from investors indirectly by borrowing from financial intermediaries, such as commercial banks, or directly by selling commercial paper. The differences between indirect and direct loans explains the features and advantages and disadvantages of these alternative sources of temporary financing.

Loans from commercial banks are the primary source of temporary financing for most companies. These obligations usually appear on the balance sheet as a note payable although the underlying credit arrangement may be a line of credit or a revolving credit agreement. There is some variation in what is meant by each of these terms in practice but their most common features are described below.

A company has a **line of credit** when its bank(s) agrees to lend it up to a specified amount of money over a given term, usually one year. Although the money is presumably available on demand, the bank is not legally obligated to honor the request for funds if the company's or its own credit situation deteriorates after the agreement is signed. A **revolving credit agreement (revolver)** is similar to a line of credit except the term may extend beyond one year and the bank makes a legally enforceable commitment to provide the agreed financing. Some revolving credit agreements permit the borrower to convert the outstanding balance to a term loan when the agreement expires, making its effective term even longer.

Exhibit 19.6

(Continued)

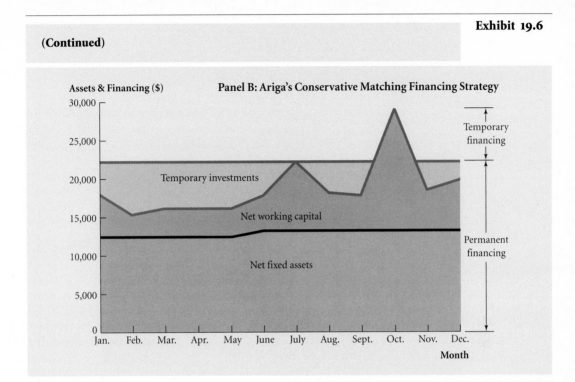

Panel B: Ariga's Conservative Matching Financing Strategy

Financing obtained from these types of bank loans is temporary because the company can increase the amount borrowed when it has a cash flow shortage and reduce the amount borrowed when it has a cash flow surplus. Furthermore, most banks require the borrower to reduce its outstanding loan balance to zero for 30 days during the term of the agreement to ensure the funds are not used for permanent financing.

The cost of a bank loan depends on the stated interest rate and the requirement for fees and compensating balances. Most banks charge their commercial borrowers a variable interest rate that is tied to some benchmark interest rate. The prime rate that major money center banks charge their most creditworthy customers is one such benchmark; the rate at which London banks borrow from one another, the **London Interbank Offer Rate (LIBOR),** is another. A bank's most valuable customers may be able to borrow for less than the prime rate, however, most pay a premium over prime that depends on their perceived credit risk, whether collateral is provided, etc.

Banks sometimes charge fees to initiate a lending agreement and to maintain their commitment to provide financing. These fees are transaction costs analogous to investment banking fees that raise the effective cost of the loan. Banks also often require borrowers to maintain a demand deposit account with them in which the borrowers must keep a compensating balance that averages from 10 percent to 20 percent of the amount of the loan. This requirement serves several purposes. First, the bank can monitor transactions in the account to assess the borrower's risk. Second, the bank can apply these balances to the amount due if the borrower defaults on the loan. Third, the balances raise the effective cost of the loan because companies implicitly borrow this money but cannot use it. The following example demonstrates how fees and compensating balances raise the cost of bank loans.

The Sartoris Hill Fruit Company has applied for a one-year bank loan to cover its $1,000,000 financing deficit. The company's bank has agreed to provide a fixed-rate loan at a stated interest rate of 3 percent over prime or 9 percent per year. The loan initiation fee is 1 percent and the bank requires a 15 percent compensating balance. What is the effective annual interest rate on this loan?

The net proceeds of the loan equal its principal amount, P, minus the fee and compensating balance. The company requires net proceeds of $1,000,000, therefore the principal of the loan must be

$$P - (0.01 \times P) - (0.15 \times P) = \$1,000,000$$
$$P = \$1,000,000/(0.84) = \$1,190,476.$$

The initiation fee and compensating balance equal $11,905 ($0.01 \times \$1,190,476$) and $178,571 ($0.15 \times \$1,190,476$), so the company's net cash flow is $1,000,000. The fee is gone forever but the company gets the compensating balance back when it repays the loan.

The amount due at maturity is the principal plus interest or $1,297,619 ($\$1,190,476 \times 1.09$). Subtracting the compensating balance gives the net cash outflow at maturity, $1,119,048. The effective annual interest rate is the internal rate of return, r, of a single-period loan with net cash flows of $1,000,000 and $-1,119,048 at time zero and time one.

$$\text{NPV} = 0 = \$1,000,000 - \frac{\$1,119,048}{(1 + r)}$$
$$r = (\$1,119,048/\$1,000,000) - 1$$
$$= 0.119 \text{ or } 11.9\%$$

These example terms, which are typical of many bank loans, raise the effective annual interest rate by nearly 3 percent.

EXERCISE ●───●

19.5   EFFECTIVE INTEREST RATE ON A LOAN

A competing bank offered Sartoris Hill Fruit Company a loan at 9.5 percent interest with a 0.5 percent initiation fee and a 12.5 percent compensating balance. Which loan should the company accept based on the effective rate of interest?

The amount the company must borrow is

$$P - (0.005 \times P) - (0.125 \times P) = \$1,000,000$$
$$P = \$1,000,000/(0.87) = \$1,149,425.$$

The net proceeds are $1 million and the amount due at maturity, net of the compensating balance, is

$$(\$1,149,425 \times 1.095) - (0.125 \times \$1,149,425) = \$1,114,942.$$

The effective interest rate on the loan, *r*, therefore is

$$r = (\$1,114,942/\$1,000,000) - 1 = 0.1149 \text{ or } 11.49\%.$$

The loan from a competing bank is less costly even though the stated interest rate is higher.

• ———————— •

Large, well-known companies with impeccable credit ratings can bypass financial intermediaries and obtain temporary financing directly from the financial market. The instrument they use for this purpose is commercial paper, an unsecured promissory note with a term to maturity between 1 and 270 days. Terms to maturity in the neighborhood of 30 days and denominations of around $5 million are most common. Interest usually is computed on a discount basis.

Industrial companies tend to distribute their commercial paper through dealers while finance companies, such as the General Motors Acceptance Corporation, deal directly with investors. This difference is due to the fact that finance companies continually borrow large amounts of money in the commercial paper market. They are therefore familiar to investors and cannot time their issuances to take advantage of privileged information.

Commercial paper is exempt from registration with the Securities and Exchange Commission because its term to maturity is less than nine months. Evaluation by a rating agency (such as Moody's or Standard & Poor's) is, in effect, a substitute for registration because companies that do not receive one of the two highest ratings have virtually no access to the commercial paper market. The highest ratings are assigned to companies whose credit standing is very high or whose commercial paper is backed by a line of credit from a reliable bank.

The effective cost of borrowing by issuing commercial paper usually is lower than the effective interest rate on a bank loan. One reason is that commercial paper loans do not require compensating balances. Another reason is that commercial paper loans do not require intermediation. The lenders usually are large sophisticated investors, such as other corporations and banks, who do not need help analyzing credit risks or diversifying their portfolios. In addition, the borrowers have low risk and the loans are very short-term, so continuous monitoring is unnecessary.

The lower effective cost of borrowing by issuing commercial paper comes at the price of less flexibility and the forgone opportunity to reassure other investors by submitting to monitoring by a bank. Companies with temporary financial problems cannot easily negotiate revised terms with the diverse group of investors who purchased their commercial paper. Nor can they expect the special considerations that a bank's best customers receive when credit is tight. Furthermore, studies have shown that investors are willing to pay more for the common stock of companies that announce they have negotiated a bank credit agreement.[10] At least some of the cost advantages to commercial paper may disappear when its effect on a company's other securities is included.

---

[10]See Christopher James and Peggy Wier, "Are Banks Different? Some Evidence from the Stock Market," *Journal of Applied Corporate Finance,* Summer 1988, pp. 46–54.

Finally, companies sometimes must pledge their accounts receivable as security for their temporary financing. These asset-based loans were once considered a sign of financial weakness but they now are routine in some industries. Properly structured, they provide an efficient way for the company and financial institutions to adopt specialized roles in the process of creating, holding, and collecting trade receivables.[11]

19.4   TEMPORARY INVESTMENT POLICIES

All companies have temporary investments for financial slack. Some companies have additional temporary investments when their permanent financing temporarily exceeds their financing requirements. Temporary investments held for either reason must be convertible into a predictable amount of cash on short notice. Consequently, risk is the primary concern when choosing temporary investments; rate of return is of secondary importance.

Risk Factors for Temporary Investments

There are three factors to consider when assessing the risk of alternative temporary investments. One factor is the risk of default that varies from one issuer to another and may vary with an instrument's term to maturity because more things can go wrong in 30 years than in 30 days. Another risk factor is marketability, which depends on an instrument's features and the size of the secondary market in which it is traded. Actively traded, standardized financial instruments are the most marketable because the owner can quickly convert them to cash without offering a price discount. The final risk factor to consider is interest rate risk, which is determined by an instrument's duration. Short-term financial instruments have the least interest rate risk because their prices are least sensitive to changes in interest rates.

Treasurers manage these risks by investing their company's temporary cash surpluses in money market instruments (see "In the News"). These securities have terms to maturity of one year or less, which limits their interest rate risk, and they are issued by governments and high-quality corporations and financial institutions, thus limiting their default risk. Furthermore, the money markets are among the more active markets in the world, which provides marketability.

Money market instruments are not homogeneous, however, so there are some differences in these risk factors from one type of security and issuer to another. For this reason, most boards of directors require their treasurers to diversify their temporary investment portfolio across types of securities and issuers. About the only exception to this policy is that most treasurers are permitted to invest 100 percent of the portfolio in U.S. Treasury bills. Enforced diversification is necessary to control the agency costs that arise when a treasurer's performance is judged on the basis of return but he or she does not bear the costs of accepting risk.

---

[11]Shehzad L. Mian and Clifford W. Smith, Jr., "Extending Trade Credit and Financing Receivables," *Journal of Applied Corporate Finance*, Spring 1994, pp. 75–84.

IN THE NEWS

CFOS DESCRIBE FINANCIAL SLACK POLICIES

MANAGING CORPORATE CASH is a lot like handling inventory: Although you can't have too little, you don't want too much. In fact, many CFOs are pushing their finance staffs toward "just-in-time" cash management systems in which little or no cash lies idle. Some 40 percent of the 1,600 CFOs recently surveyed said that their companies aggressively utilized corporate cash. Other questions answered by the survey were:

What is the total amount of investable cash assets, on average?

Less than $100 million	65.9%
$100 to $500 million	20.7
$500 million to $1 billion	5.2
More than $1 billion	8.1

What percentage of cash assets is held in

	Demand Deposit Accounts?	U.S. Government Securities?	Commercial Paper?
10% or less	93.3%	60.2%	59.7%
11% to 25%	2.9	17.8	16.0
More than 25%	3.7	22.1	24.4

What is the average maturity of your financial instruments?

Overnight	24.2%
2 to 90 days	56.1
91 to 180 days	6.8
181 to 365 days	4.5
More than 1 year	8.3

Source: "Cash Conundrum," *Institutional Investor*, May 1996, p. 33.

Temporary Investment Alternatives

The most widely held money market instrument is the U.S. Treasury bill. These discount instruments are issued with original terms to maturity of 3 months, 6 months, and 1 year and are traded daily in the secondary market. This market is very active; more than $760 billion of T-bills were outstanding at the end of 1995.[12] The absence of default risk, an active secondary market, and the availability of extremely short terms to maturity permit treasurers to place their company's temporary cash surpluses at no risk by investing in Treasury bills.

Federal agencies, such as the Federal Home Loan bank, also issue short-term financial instruments with most but not all the characteristics of Treasury bills. Agency notes are considered default-free and are available with short terms to maturity, however, they are not as liquid as T-bills because their secondary market is not as active. In addition, the interest income from U.S. Treasury securities is not subject to state taxes although the income from some agency securities is taxable. U.S. federal agency securities provide slightly higher rates of return than U.S. Treasury securities because of these marketability and tax differences.

---

[12] *Federal Reserve Bulletin,* Board of Governors of the Federal Reserve System, May 1996, Table 1.41.

Treasurers also lend money directly to other companies by purchasing their commercial paper. These securities have some default risk and poor marketability because there is no secondary market. Consequently, they provide a slightly higher rate of return than either U.S. Treasury or agency securities.

Large denomination, negotiable certificates of deposit issued by banks also are popular temporary investment alternatives. These certificates are issued directly to investors or through dealers in minimum denominations of $100,000 with maturities that range from 14 to 180 days. Most are sold in $1,000,000 units with at least 30 days until maturity. Certificates of deposit are interest-bearing securities and the interest rate may be fixed or variable. The interest income is subject to both state and federal taxes. Dollar denominated certificates of deposit issued outside the United States are called Eurodollar CDs no matter where they are issued.

Certificates of deposit are liabilities of the issuing bank but they are not insured, so there is a risk of default. They also are less marketable than government securities because their secondary market is smaller and less active. This is particularly true for Eurodollar CDs. Certificates of deposit provide a higher yield than U.S. Treasury and agency securities because the interest income is taxable and they have more risk and less marketability.

19.5   CONTINUAL PLANNING AND ANALYSIS

Short-term financial planning and analysis continue after the annual business plan and its pro forma financial statements are approved and permanent and temporary financing are secured. Managers and analysts compare each month's operating and financial performance to the plan to determine the causes of both favorable and unfavorable variations from their expectations. They use variance analysis, as employed by cost or managerial accountants, to determine whether the differences were caused by errors in estimating the prices, volumes, or costs of outputs and inputs. Managers rely on this information to coordinate and control a company's activities and redirect its resources to their most productive use.

Managers also prepare revised forecasts for the remainder of the year based on their analysis of the variations from their original expectations. The revised forecasts provide new performance standards used for measuring the company's progress toward the revised objectives. Revised forecasts also provide better estimates of the company's cash flow and financing surpluses and deficits, which reduce their financing costs.

19.6   SUMMARY

The annual or short-term financial plan is similar to the long-range financial plan. The main difference is the short-term plan is prepared in greater detail to anticipate intrayear cash flow surpluses and deficits. A company's short-term financial policies affect the size and amounts of these surpluses and deficits and govern the company's planned responses to them.

A company's policy regarding financial slack determines the amount of uncommitted financial resources maintained to meet unexpected requirements for cash.

The requirement for slack depends on the costs of obtaining and repaying emergency loans, the opportunity cost of idle resources, the cost of giving the impression that cash flows are less than expected (signaling cost), and the cost of removing the market's discipline (agency cost). These costs are significant in an imperfect financial market with asymmetric information but not otherwise. Companies must balance these costs to determine the amount of financial slack to maintain.

A cash statement prepared in the direct format is the main financial statement in a short-term financial plan. Financial planners usually prepare this statement by distributing annual sales, production, costs, etc., across the months of the first year in the long-range business plan. The company's actual collection and payment experience should be used to forecast receipts and disbursements to avoid potentially costly errors in predicting the timing of these cash flows.

The month-by-month cash statement will often reveal intrayear cash flow surpluses or shortages that are much larger than end-of-year surpluses or shortages. The timing and amounts of these shortages and surpluses depend on the seasonality of the company's business and its cash collection cycle.

Managers must arrange permanent and temporary financing to fund the requirement for permanent and seasonal or temporary assets. Many companies use a conservative matching short-term financing policy under which net fixed assets and baseline net working capital are funded by permanent sources. Seasonal net working capital is funded by temporary sources such as bank loans and commercial paper. Companies following this policy also have temporary investments that may be held as government securities, commercial paper, and certificates of deposit.

Financial planning and analysis is not a periodic event; it continues throughout the year to measure progress toward the company's goals. Importantly, the entire planning and analysis process is used to redirect resources as soon as it is apparent they can be used more efficiently.

- **KEY TERMS**

Transaction balances *785*	Compensating	Revolving credit agreement
Precautionary	balances *785*	(revolver) *802*
balances *785*	Lambda index (λ) *788*	London Interbank Offer
Speculative balances *785*	Line of credit *802*	Rate (LIBOR) *803*

- **QUESTIONS AND PROBLEMS**

1. Long- and short-term financial plans are "cut from the same cloth."
   (a) Describe the similarities and differences between long- and short-term financial planning.
   (b) What are the relationships between a company's long- and short-term financial plans?
2. Chapters 10, 11, and 12 describe how seasonality in the supply of raw materials and demand for finished goods affect a company's investment in inventories and accounts payable.

(a) How are these seasonal factors reflected in a company's requirement for permanent and temporary assets?

(b) How do these seasonal factors affect a company's choice of permanent and temporary financing?

3. We cannot know the future with perfect certainty, so managers should use the short-term financial planning process to anticipate and prepare for operating and financial surprises.

(a) How can managers incorporate the effects of uncertainty in their short-term financial plans? Explain your answer.

(b) How does their policy regarding financial slack and the choice between permanent and temporary financing affect their ability to respond to these surprises? Explain your answer.

4. Considering the rate of return on marketable securities, financial slack seems to be a zero-NPV investment at best.

(a) Explain why financial slack *is* a zero-NPV investment in a perfect financial market with symmetric information.

(b) Explain why financial slack *may* by valuable in an imperfect financial market with asymmetric information. Distinguish between financial slack held for transaction, precautionary, speculative, and compensating balance purposes.

5. Companies maintain a limited amount of financial slack even though it is valuable because it also is costly. What are the opportunity costs of financial slack? What are the agency costs? Why must managers be mindful of these costs when formulating financial plans?

6. The Miller-Orr model treats cash as an inventoried item and identifies the return point and upper and lower limits that minimize the cost of this "inventory."

(a) What is the holding cost when cash is the inventoried item? What is the order cost? Explain your answers.

(b) How is the demand for cash represented in the Miller-Orr model? Why is this way of representing the demand for cash a limitation of the model? Explain your answer.

7. Managers must measure their own company's financial slack to establish short-term financial policy and they must measure the financial slack of their trading partners to avoid costly surprises.

(a) Why are the traditional ratios, such as the current and quick ratios, poor measures of financial slack?

(b) What are the lambda index's advantages as a measure of financial slack in comparison to the traditional ratios?

8. Which of the variables used in the lambda index probably are difficult for a manager to estimate when measuring her own company's financial slack? When measuring another company's financial slack? Explain your answers.

9. Managers have many alternatives for financing their company's permanent and temporary assets.

(a) What are the expected benefits and costs of a conservative financing strategy? An aggressive financing strategy?

(b) Is the choice between these strategies important in a perfect financial market? In an imperfect financial market? Explain your answers.

10. Review Section 14.2, Private Sources of Financing, and discuss the merits of bank loans and commercial paper.

11. The mean and standard deviation of Millstone Industrial Lubricants Company's daily net cash flows are $0 and $500. The cost of buying and selling marketable securities is $50 per transaction and the yield on marketable securities is 5 percent per year.

    (a) To what level should the treasurer return the cash balance when it becomes too large or too small?

    (b) At what level should the treasurer buy securities to reduce the cash balance? What amount of securities should she buy?

    (c) At what level should the treasurer sell securities to increase the cash balance? What amount of securities should she sell?

    (d) What is Millstone Industrial Lubricants Company's average cash balance and opportunity cost of holding cash rather than marketable securities if the treasurer applies this cash management policy for an entire year?

12. Robert Bernell, treasurer of Stone-Wood Manufacturing Company, would like to use the Miller-Orr model to manage the company's cash balance. He knows from experience that the company pays $25 per transaction to buy and sell marketable securities and that these securities presently yield 7 percent per year. A representative sample of Stone-Wood's daily net cash flows is given below.

Day	Net Cash Flow	Day	Net Cash Flow
1	$-2,451	6	$5,290
2	3,190	7	3,761
3	-4,155	8	-211
4	-1,733	9	-2,860
5	1,098	10	-1,931

    (a) Compute the mean and variance of this sample of Stone-Wood's daily net cash flows. Can Bernell use the Miller-Orr model assuming this sample and his other estimates are representative of what the company will experience in the future? Explain your answer.

    (b) Determine the optimal return point for Stone-Wood's cash balance.

    (c) At what level should Bernell buy securities to reduce the cash balance? What amount of securities should he buy?

    (d) At what level should Bernell sell securities to increase the cash balance? What amount of securities should he sell?

    (e) Bernell began applying his model when the company's cash balance was $2,000. The company net cash flows for the following 10 days are given below. What was the company's closing cash balance each day? What was the average cash balance over this 10-day period?

Day	Net Cash Flow	Day	Net Cash Flow
1	$1,060	6	$2,043
2	-1,613	7	-3,671
3	-1,507	8	4,258
4	4,870	9	2,470
5	-2,853	10	-5,058

13. Partial balance sheets and cash flow forecasts for three companies are given below.

	Company A	Company B	Company C
Cash	$ 6,000	$ 5,000	$ 5,000
Marketable securities	10,000	11,000	12,000
Accounts receivable	15,000	14,000	21,000
Inventories	11,000	11,000	7,000
Total current assets	$42,000	$41,000	$45,000
Total current liabilities	$31,000	$25,000	$30,000
Net cash flow forecast			
Expected value	$35,000	$32,000	$38,000
Standard deviation	17,000	24,000	22,000

(a) Use the current ratio, quick ratio, and lambda index to rank these companies from most liquid to least liquid.

(b) Explain why the companies are ranked differently by each measure of financial slack.

(c) According to the lambda index, which company has the highest probability of cash insolvency? The lowest?

(d) What size lines of credit must the less liquid companies have to match the more liquid company's probability of cash insolvency?

14. Ting-a-Ling Bell Company's partial balance sheet and cash flow forecast are given below.

Cash	$ 1,000
Marketable securities	6,000
Accounts receivable	5,000
Uncommitted lines of credit	13,000
Net cash flow forecast	
Expected value	500
Standard deviation	8,135

(a) Does the company have enough financial slack to provide for the coming year if its target probability of cash insolvency is 0.0022?

(b) Ting-a-Ling's treasurer is considering alternative ways to increase the company's safety. For each alternative listed below, determine the value of the missing variable that will give the company a probability of cash insolvency of 0.0022.

Cash and Securities	Lines of Credit	Expected Cash Flow	Standard Deviation of Cash Flow
$?	$13,000	$500	$8,135
7,000	?	500	8,135
7,000	13,000	?	8,135
7,000	13,000	500	?

(c) In principle, how should the treasurer choose between these alternatives for increasing the company's safety? Explain your answer.

15. Given below is information from the financial statements of Coleco Industries, Inc., a toy company perhaps best known for its Cabbage Patch dolls. The company's financial slack equals its cash, marketable securities, and the uncommitted portion of its lines of credit as reported on its balance sheets. Expected cash flow and standard deviation of cash flow were estimated from the company's actual cash flows provided by or used for operations. Coleco filed Chapter 11 bankruptcy in 1988.

Year	Current Assets	Current Liabilities	Financial Slack	Expected Cash Flow	Standard Deviation of Cash Flow
1982	$250,915	$121,308	$ 89,974	$ 6,654	$ 3,224
1983	407,090	299,313	19,511	−31,756	87,018
1984	325,408	244,098	37,959	−30,722	87,655
1985	305,613	118,295	260,734	6,967	136,485
1986	393,477	287,720	221,745	−40,215	174,115
1987	334,842	311,412	82,533	−56,833	172,440

(a) Compute Coleco's current ratios and plot them on a graph. Can you foresee the company's bankruptcy? Explain your answer.

(b) Compute Coleco's lambda indexes and use them to estimate the probability of cash insolvency. Plot these probabilities on a graph. Cah you foresee the company's bankruptcy? Explain your answer.

(c) Explain why the second graph is more informative than the first one.

16. Collins International's sales were $120,000 each month during the last quarter of 1998. Forecasted sales for 1999 also are $120,000 per month for January through June. One-third of Collins' sales are collected in cash, the remainder are collected in 90 days.

(a) Determine the company's DSO and use it to forecast the cash received from customers in January through June 1998.

(b) Use the customers' actual payment pattern to forecast monthly cash receipts for January through June.

(c) Explain the similarities or differences between the forecasts computed in parts (a) and (b).

17. Retro Necktie Corporation must forecast its cash receipts for the first quarter of 1998. Actual sales in November and December of 1997 were $120,000 and $130,000. Projected sales for January, February, and March 1998 are $60,000, $50,000, and $50,000. One-half of Retro's sales are for cash, the remainder are collected in 60 days.

(a) Compute the company's DSO and use it to forecast cash received from customers in January, February, and March.

(b) Use the customers' actual payment pattern to forecast monthly cash receipts in January, February, and March.

(c) Explain the differences between the forecasts computed in parts (a) and (b).

18. Jayhawk Signs and Signals manufactures outdoor advertising displays and sells repair parts for existing displays. Parts sales, 10 percent of total sales, are for cash. Eighty percent of total sales are new displays sold to commercial customers and 10 percent of total sales are signs

sold to local governments. Commercial customers pay in 30 days while the local governments pay in 60 days. Cost of goods sold is 60 percent of sales. Jayhawk pays 50 percent of its vendors electronically (within the same month as the purchase) and pays the remainder in 60 days. Actual and projected sales are given below.

Actual Total Sales

July	$100,000
August	150,000

Projected Total Sales

September	350,000
October	200,000
November	150,000
December	50,000

(a) Use Jayhawk's DSO and DPO ratios to forecast cash flow provided by operations for September through December. Ignore taxes.

(b) Use the company's and its customers' actual payment patterns to forecast cash flow provided by operations for September through December.

(c) The other entries in Jayhawk's projected cash statements are given below. What problems will the CFO encounter if he relies on the wrong forecast of cash flows provided by operations? Explain your answer.

Cash Flow Provided by (Used for)

	Investment	Financial Slack	Financing
September	$ 0	$ 0	$(35,000)
October	(240,000)	0	(10,000)
November	(40,000)	0	(10,000)
December	0	1,000	(35,000)

19. T & M Clothing produces and sells insulated clothing used by hunters and other winter sports fans. Cash sales are 25 percent of the total and credit sales, collected in 30 days, are 74 percent. Bad debts are 1 percent of sales. The company's projected sales for the last six months of 1997 are given below.

July	$ 900	October	$300
August	1,800	November	200
September	2,400	December	100

T & M's costs of goods sold for fabric, insulation, labor, and so on equal $140 plus 55 percent of sales. These costs are paid the month prior to the sale. Selling and administrative costs are $200 per month. Quarterly tax payments are expected to be $125 in September and December. Financial slack will be reduced by $100 in September to partially cover the $300 cost of new capital equipment that will be purchased and paid for that month. T&M expects to pay quarterly dividends of $49 in September and December. Total sales in June 1997 were $100 and projected sales for January 1998 are $100.

(a) Use direct format free cash flow and financial cash flow statements to forecast T & M's cash flow and financing surpluses and deficits for July through December.

(b) Explain the pattern of the company's financing surpluses and deficits.

(c) Describe some operating alternatives for reducing the seasonality of the company's surpluses and deficits. In principle, how should the managers choose between these alternatives?

20. Kevin Kiefer, president of Kiefer Klassics, asked for a projection of the company's monthly cash flow and financing surpluses and deficits for 1998. This short-term financial plan is to be based on the first year of the company's long-term financial plan prepared in problem 13 in Chapter 18. (You must prepare Kiefer Klassics' 1998 pro forma financial statements to work this problem if you have not already done so.) The monthly pattern of sales and cost of goods sold is given below. Peak sales are in the spring when restored cars are shipped to dealers for summer sales.

January	0%	July	10%
February	5	August	5
March	15	September	5
April	20	October	5
May	15	November	10
June	10	December	0

Twenty percent of sales are for cash and 80 percent are on credit paid the following month. A particular month's costs of goods sold are paid the following month. Selling and administrative expenses are uniformly distributed over the year, interest is paid in June and December, and taxes and dividends are paid quarterly. Kiefer will increase its financial slack in March in anticipation of the peak selling season.

(a) Prepare free cash flow and financial cash flow statements to forecast Kiefer's monthly cash flow and financing surpluses and deficits.

(b) Explain the pattern of the company's surpluses and deficits.

21. Chaput Chaps and Saddles sells saddles, bridles, and other equipment to rodeo contestants. The company's peak sales month is March when riders prepare for the summer's competitions. Chaput's projected 1998 sales are given below. December 1997's sales were $3,000 and January and February 1999's sales are expected to be $3,400 and $7,000.

January	$3,240	July	$3,240
February	6,480	August	2,160
March	16,200	September	2,160
April	9,720	October	2,160
May	3,240	November	1,080
June	3,240	December	1,080

Chaput's partial balance sheet at the end of 1997 was as follows.

Accounts receivable	$ 3,600
Inventory	5,000
Net fixed assets	25,000
Accounts payable	3,000

Chaput's cost of goods sold equals 65 percent of sales. The company acquires these materials and labor 60 days prior to sale and pays for them in 30 days. All sales are on credit on terms net 30 and there are no bad debts. The company will increase net fixed assets by $5,000 at the end of December 1998 to prepare for 1999's higher sales level.

(a) Determine Chaput's monthly accounts receivable, inventory, and accounts payable levels.

(b) Determine Chaput's monthly requirements for net working capital. What is the amount of Chaput's permanent requirement for net working capital? What is the range of the company's temporary requirement for net working capital? What explains this pattern?

(c) Graph Chaput's monthly net asset requirements, distinguishing between net fixed assets and net working capital.

(d) How much permanent financing will the company use if it adopts a conservative financing strategy? An aggressive strategy? A pure matching strategy? A conservative matching strategy that uses permanent financing for 50 percent of temporary net working capital?

22. Wall Avenue Publishers' requirements for net fixed assets and net working capital are described below.

Month	Net Fixed Assets	Net Working Capital
January	$6,000	$2,000
February	6,000	2,000
March	7,500	2,500
April	7,500	3,000
May	7,500	4,000
June	7,500	6,000
July	7,500	5,000
August	8,000	4,000
September	8,000	3,000
October	8,000	2,000
November	8,000	2,000
December	8,000	2,000

(a) Determine the company's monthly levels of permanent financing, temporary financing, and temporary investments for each of the financing strategies described below.

(i)   A conservative strategy.

(ii) A conservative matching strategy with permanent financing equal to net fixed assets plus $4,000.

(iii) A pure matching strategy.

(iv) An aggressive strategy.

(b) What is the company's average level of permanent financing, temporary financing, and temporary investments under each policy described in part (a)? What is the net annual cost of each policy if permanent financing costs 10 percent, temporary financing costs 9 percent, and temporary investments earn 7 percent?

(c) Rank these financing strategies from least costly to most costly. Is this also the order of most to least desirable? What other factors must the managers consider? Explain your answers.

23. Bluegrass Dye Co. expects to have a $120,000 financing deficit next year. The company's bank charges a loan initiation fee of 1.5 percent and requires a 12 percent compensating balance. What amount must the company borrow to cover its $120,000 deficit?

24. Copycat Jerseys Co. expects a financing deficit of $275,000 next year. The company's bank will loan this amount for one year at a fixed rate of 9 percent with a loan initiation fee of 1.5 percent and a compensating balance of 13 percent.

    (a) How much money must the company borrow to cover its financing deficit?

    (b) What are the amounts of the loan initiation fee and compensating balance? What is the company's net cash outflow when the loan matures?

    (c) Determine the effective annual interest rate on the loan.

25. Washington Tree Trimmers needs a $500,000 loan to cover a short-term financing deficit. The bank where the company maintains its demand deposit accounts agreed to provide the financing at a fixed annual rate of 9 percent with no initiation fee and a 10 percent compensating balance requirement. A competing bank offered to lend the money at 8.25 percent interest with a 0.5 percent initiation fee and an 11 percent compensating balance requirement.

    (a) How much money must Washington borrow under each loan agreement assuming it borrows the compensating balances and fees? What are the amounts of the compensating balance requirements and initiation fee for each loan?

    (b) Washington Tree Trimmers uses the Miller-Orr model to manage the cash balances in its demand deposit accounts. The rate of return on marketable securities is 4.4 percent, the cost of buying and selling securities is $35, and the standard deviation of Washington's daily net cash flow is $10,000. What is the average balance in Washington's demand deposit accounts?

    (c) Must the company borrow the money for the compensating balance if it accepts the loan from the bank where it maintains its demand deposit accounts? Explain your answer.

    (d) Determine the effective annual interest rate on each loan given your answer to part (c). Where should Washington borrow the $500,000 assuming cost is the only consideration?

- **ADDITIONAL READING**

See the following textbooks on short-term financial management for additional discussions of short-term financial planning.

> Ned C. Hill and William L. Sartoris, *Short-Term Financial Management,* Macmillan Publishing Company, New York, 1992.
>
> Terry S. Maness and John T. Zietlow, *Short-Term Financial Management,* West Publishing Company, Minneapolis/St. Paul., 1993.

Also see the additional readings at the end of Chapter 18.

TN ENTERPRISES

Tracy Mynatt headed home late Friday afternoon with a heavy briefcase. Ted Nolan, the president of TN Enterprises, asked her to review the company's five-year financial plan, incorporate the newspaper and restaurant divisions' capital spending requests, and forecast the company's financing surpluses and deficits. Most challenging of all, Ted asked her to summarize the advantages and disadvantages of his operating and financial alternatives for meeting TN Enterprises' financing requirements.

TN Enterprises was established in 1938 to publish the *Bartlesville Bugler,* a weekly newspaper that covered Bartlesville, Oklahoma, and surrounding counties. The company gradually acquired the publishers of other local newspapers and a small, family-style restaurant chain. Net income for 1997 was $915,000 on sales of $10 million. Some characteristics of these two industries, benchmark companies in these industries, and the overall financial market are shown in Table 1.

Table 1   INDUSTRY AND MARKET INFORMATION

Panel A: Industry Averages

	Return on Equity	Profit Margin	Total Asset Turnover	Leverage Ratio	Retention Ratio
Weekly newspapers	0.1255	0.0972	0.9478	1.3569	0.6454
Family-style restaurants	0.1046	0.0541	1.5036	1.3034	0.8118

Panel B: Benchmark Companies

	Beta	Market Value of Equity	Book Value of Debt
Newspaper publishers			
Lee Enterprises	0.80	1,169,622,500	95,500,000
McClatchy News	0.85	920,156,250	210,000,000
Family-style restaurants			
Bob Evans Farms	0.85	549,875,000	71,600,000
Ryan's Family Steak Houses	1.00	422,883,750	128,300,000

Panel C: Market Returns

Rate of return on riskless asset	6.0%
Expected rate of return on market portfolio	14.7

Source for panels A and B: Value Line Investment Service, Value Line Publishing Company, 1996.

TN Enterprises seldom issued common stock and had only 500,000 shares outstanding at the end of 1997. This stock is traded over the counter with a market price of around $18 per share. Notes due in 2004 and bonds sold to an Oklahoma-based insurance company comprise the remaining long-term financing. TN Enterprises pays 9 percent interest on the note and the bonds; new debt, however, will cost 10 percent. The company's 1996 and 1997 financial statements are shown in Table 2.

Table 2 also shows an analyst's forecast of the company's pro forma financial statements for 1998–2002. These statements account for the anticipated growth in the company's current businesses; each division's special capital spending requests are described separately in Table 3. TN Enterprises' target debt/equity ratio for these investments is 0.25. The company will not dispose of any fixed assets between 1998 and 2002.

On Saturday morning, Tracy began work on what promised to be a weekend-long project. She would evaluate the divisions' spending requests, incorporate the effect of acceptable projects in the company's financial plan, and estimate the amounts and timing of its financing surpluses and shortages. Tracy would examine the possibility of providing for the financing requirements by delaying or accelerating capital spending, changing the company's operations or dividend policy, or issuing or retiring debt or equity after she completed this analytical work.

TN ENTERPRISES' FINANCIAL STATEMENTS **Table 2**

Panel A: Income Statements

	Actual		Projected				
	1996	1997	1998	1999	2000	2001	2002
Net sales	$9,700	$10,000	$10,800	$11,664	$12,597	$13,605	$14,693
Cost of goods sold	5,900	6,056	6,360	6,749	7,169	7,622	8,112
Gross profit	3,800	3,944	4,440	4,915	5,428	5,983	6,581
Selling expenses	1,425	1,485	1,620	1,750	1,890	2,041	2,204
Depreciation	780	800	530	475	360	360	140
Net operating income	1,595	1,659	2,290	2,690	3,178	3,582	4,237
Interest expense	162	251	207	207	207	207	207
Taxable income	1,433	1,408	2,083	2,483	2,971	3,375	4,030
Taxes	502	493	729	869	1,040	1,181	1,411
Net income	$ 931	$ 915	$ 1,354	$ 1,614	$ 1,931	$ 2,194	$ 2,619

continued

Table 2   CONTINUED

	Actual		Projected				
	1996	**1997**	**1998**	**1999**	**2000**	**2001**	**2002**
	Panel B: Statements of Retained Earnings						
Beginning balance	$ 4,869	$ 5,217	$ 5,549	$ 6,090	$ 6,736	$ 7,509	$ 8,386
Net income	931	915	1,354	1,614	1,931	2,194	2,619
Dividends	583	583	813	968	1,158	1,317	1,571
Ending balance	$ 5,217	$ 5,549	$ 6,090	$ 6,736	$ 7,509	$ 8,386	$ 9,434
	Panel C: Balance Sheets						
Cash	$ 700	$ 750	$ 810	$ 875	$ 945	$ 1,020	$ 1,102
Accounts receivable	915	950	1,026	1,108	1,197	1,292	1,396
Inventories	725	761	799	848	901	958	1,019
Total current assets	2,340	2,461	2,635	2,831	3,043	3,270	3,517
Gross fixed assets	10,542	11,084	12,087	13,063	13,955	14,878	15,616
Accumulated depreciation	2,400	3,200	3,730	4,205	4,565	4,925	5,065
Net fixed assets	8,142	7,884	8,357	8,858	9,390	9,953	10,551
Total assets	$10,482	$10,345	$10,992	$11,689	$12,433	$13,223	$14,068
Accounts payable	$ 675	$ 696	$ 731	$ 776	$ 824	$ 876	$ 932
Total current liabilities	675	696	731	776	824	876	932
Notes payable	990	500	500	500	500	500	500
Bonds	1,800	1,800	1,800	1,800	1,800	1,800	1,800
Total long-term debt	2,790	2,300	2,300	2,300	2,300	2,300	2,300
Common stock	1,800	1,800	1,800	1,800	1,800	1,800	1,800
Retained earnings	5,217	5,549	6,090	6,736	7,509	8,386	9,434
Common equity	7,017	7,349	7,890	8,536	9,309	10,186	11,234
Total claims	$10,482	$10,345	$10,921	$11,612	$12,433	$13,362	$14,466

TN ENTERPRISES' CAPITAL SPENDING REQUESTS   **Table 3**

Free Cash Flow

	1998	1999	2000	2001	2002
Newspaper division					
Project A	$(230,000)	$ 40,000	$ 90,000	$ 150,000	$ 70,000
Project B	(60,000)	90,000	110,000	(165,000)	0
Project C	0	(780,000)	340,000	340,000	340,000
Project D	(620,000)	0	0	0	1,050,000
Restaurant division					
Project A	0	0	(190,000)	110,000	130,000
Project B	(57,000)	17,000	17,000	17,000	17,000
Project C	0	(470,000)	150,000	400,000	70,000

PART 4

RESTRUCTURING

The first three parts of this book described finance valuation principles and their application to routine and strategic decisions. Managers maximize owners' wealth when they follow these principles to continually adjust their company's investments, operations, and financing in response to changes in market conditions.

Part 4 comprises a single chapter that describes how to analyze the opportunity or obligation to make a *substantial* change in a company's assets and claims through an acquisition, divestiture, or reorganization in financial distress. Managers and owners do not need to be convinced that these changes are important because they suddenly create, destroy, or transfer jobs and wealth. The intermittent necessity to make these changes has a large impact, but restructuring decisions are the same as ordinary investment, operating, and financing decisions. Consequently, they should be approached the same way: Use market-determined required rates of return in NPV analysis or option pricing to estimate the value of the decision alternatives.

Chapter 20 applies these finance valuation principles to restructuring decisions, thereby providing a review of Part 1. For a more effective review, you may want to reexamine key portions of Part 1 as you study this chapter. The discussions of free cash flow in Chapter 2 and discounted cash flow and option valuation in Chapters 3 and 8 are especially important.

Although Chapter 20 does not explicitly refer to the topics discussed in Parts 2 and 3 of this book, they clearly apply. Companies that continually make long-term investment decisions using the procedures we discuss in Chapters 9, 13, and 17 are less likely to have restructuring forced upon them than companies that don't use such procedures. Companies that have sound operating policies—discussed in Chapters 10, 11, and 12—and sound financing policies—discussed in Chapters 15 and 16—are in a similar position. Furthermore, these investment, operating, and financing policies are the ones used to improve the performance of restructured companies.

You can see by now that the analysis of restructuring decisions functions as a capstone for the discussion of corporate financial management. The scale is larger and the stakes are higher than for ordinary investment, operating, and financing decisions, but the same principles and practices apply.

RESTRUCTURING A COMPANY'S ASSETS AND CLAIMS

Mergers and acquisitions were conducted at a record pace in 1995 and 1996. A total of $659 billion of mergers, acquisitions, and spinoffs were announced in the United States in 1996, up 27 percent from 1995's record total of $519 billion. The total value of deals conducted world-wide in 1996 was an incredible $1.14 *trillion*. Some of the more prominent transactions in communications, defense, and banking are listed in Table 20.1. In addition, Northrop Grumman Corporation paid Westinghouse Electric Corporation $3 billion for its defense business and Boeing paid Rockwell International $3.2 billion for its defense unit.[1] The companies involved in these transactions dramatically restructured their assets.

Although business failures are not as common among well-known companies as mergers and acquisitions, two familiar companies became bankrupt in 1995 and 1996. Dow Corning Corporation filed for protection under Chapter 11 of U.S. bankruptcy laws on May 15, 1995, to work out a plan for paying damages to women who used its silicone breast implants. Sizzler International Inc. closed 136 steakhouses and filed for Chapter 11 bankruptcy protection on June 4, 1996, so it could void long-term lease contracts on those restaurants.[2] The value of Sizzler's common stock fell by 26 percent on the announcement. These companies used the bankruptcy process to dramatically restructure the *claims* against their assets.

Companies suddenly restructure themselves or have restructuring thrust upon them in transactions that are prominently reported in the business press. Some acquire other companies or are acquired, divest themselves of their own business segments, and are bought out to become privately held. Others enter formal bankruptcy proceedings and are liquidated or go through reorganization to emerge in

---

[1]Steven Lipin, "Gorillas in Our Midst: Megadeals Smash Records as Firms Take Advantage of Favorable Climate," *The Wall Street Journal,* January 2, 1997, p. R8.

[2]Bruce Orwall, "Sizzler Shutters 136 Steakhouses, Files Chapter 11," *The Wall Street Journal,* June 4, 1996, p. B10.

Table 20.1   **PROMINENT MERGERS AND ACQUISITIONS IN 1996**

Industry	Buyer	Acquisition	Value
Communications	Bell Atlantic	Nynex	$21.3 billion
	British Telecom	MCI	21.3
	SBC Communications	Pacific Telesis	16.5
	WorldCom	MFS Communications	13.4
Defense	Boeing	McDonnell-Douglas	14.0
	Lockheed Martin	Loral Corporation	8.8
Banking	Wells Fargo	First Interstate	10.9
	NationsBank	Boatmen's Bancshares	9.5

Source: Steven Lipin, "Gorillas in Our Midst: Megadeals Smash Records as Firms Take Advantage of Favorable Climate," *The Wall Street Journal*, January 2, 1997, p. R8.

---

a new form. These transactions are highly publicized because they affect the companies' customers, employees and managers, creditors, and owners.

Companies also gradually restructure themselves by making routine and strategic investment and financing decisions. Each decision to buy new equipment and replace, expand, or abandon existing equipment is a small restructuring of the company's assets. Similarly, each decision to pay dividends, issue or retire debt and equity, and use a financial lease is a small restructuring of its claims. Companies that are never involved in acquisitions, divestitures, buy-outs, or bankruptcy are gradually restructured by the cumulative effect of these decisions. These gradual restructurings also affect a company's customers, employees and managers, creditors, and owners.

A sudden restructuring, brought about by an acquisition, divestiture, buy-out, or bankruptcy, is necessary when the managers have been unable or unwilling to gradually restructure a company by making the normal business decisions that will keep it competitive. This chapter discusses the reasons for restructuring in this context, describes the forms that are available, and demonstrates how to evaluate them. You will learn the features of acquisitions, divestitures, buy-outs, and reorganizations in financial distress. You also will learn the procedures companies use to implement these restructurings.

20.1   ACQUISITIONS, DIVESTITURES, AND BUY-OUTS

Acquisitions, divestitures, and buy-outs are transactions that transfer ownership of a company or some of its assets from one group of owners to another. The characteristics of the transaction depend on the owners' motives, the form of transfer they select, and the applicable laws and accounting rules.

Motives for Acquisitions, Divestitures, and Buy-Outs

Acquisitions, divestitures, and buy-outs are used to restructure companies that are unable or unwilling to restructure themselves by making the normal business decisions that will keep them competitive. The objective of some of these transactions is to obtain investment synergies; the objective of other transactions is to instill discipline among the managers.

Synergistic Takeovers   Some companies are unable to restructure themselves to stay competitive. Barriers to entry and exit, such as patents and regulations, may prevent companies from developing or expanding profitable businesses and curtailing or abandoning unprofitable ones. Economies of scale in production, distribution, and administration may impose unavoidable costs on smaller companies that make it difficult for them to compete with larger ones. Even something as simple as inexperience may make it unprofitable for companies with new ideas to compete in established markets.

Managers may not be able to overcome these obstacles quickly. Developing successful patent applications and useful experience requires years of work. Developing a *large* business to secure economies of scale also takes time. Governments reform their regulations but the pace often is slow.

Takeovers circumvent these obstacles quickly. Companies with strong product development programs can take over companies with large, effective distribution networks and vice versa. Companies with innovative products or services can take over regulated companies to enter restricted markets. In both cases, the companies probably can eliminate some management functions because there are economies of scale in administration. Takeovers initiated for this purpose are called **synergistic takeovers** because the managers expect the value of the combination to be greater than the sum of its parts.

Disciplinary Takeovers   Some companies are able but *unwilling* to restructure themselves to stay competitive. They may forgo investments with uncertain long-term payoffs (such as research and development), pursue growth for growth's sake and accumulate excess cash, diversify, or avoid debt to reduce risk. Companies also may be unwilling to discontinue unprofitable businesses that established their identity.

The failure to make the normal business decisions that gradually restructure the company is more pronounced when the managers can ignore the owners' interests. The board of directors is supposed to reduce this agency cost but the managers often are able to "capture" the board by recommending the appointment of friendly CEOs from other companies and by serving on or even chairing the board of directors themselves. A recent study by University of Pennsylvania business professors John Core, Robert Holthausen, and David Larcker found that a company's stock performance is weaker when its CEO dominates the board in these ways.[3]

One way the owners can assert their control is to elect a board of directors that will appoint managers who will pursue the owners' interests. The mechanism they use for this purpose is called a **proxy contest** because the leaders of the dissatisfied shareholders vote their own shares and the shares that others have assigned to them by proxy. A proxy contest often is ineffective, however, because it is difficult and expensive for widely dispersed minority owners to accumulate enough proxies to challenge an entrenched board of directors.

---

[3]E. S. Browning, "Wharton Study Connects Strengths and Flaws of Directors to Companies' Financial Returns," *The Wall Street Journal*, April 25, 1997, p. C2.

A takeover is an alternative to a proxy contest. A company that is not managed in the owners' interest has a lower stock price than is possible. This makes the company an attractive target to a new management group that can take it over, replace its old managers, and change its policies. The owners and the new managers who bring about this transformation are rewarded by the resulting increase in the stock price. The old managers may have less responsibility, receive lower pay and perquisites, or even lose their jobs. Takeovers initiated for this purpose are called **disciplinary takeovers** because they punish managers who ignore the owners' interests and correct those managers' mistakes.

Harnischfeger Industries, Inc.'s offer for Giddings & Lewis, Inc. is an example of a disciplinary takeover.[4] Giddings & Lewis is the largest manufacturer of machine tools in the United States. The company's stock was trading at around $12 per share early in 1997, down from about $19 a year earlier. The stock price's decline was attributed to higher costs and to the failure of some of the company's machine tools to work properly for General Motors and Chrysler. Giddings spent more than $64 million in 1996 to fix those tools.

In announcing the offer, Harnischfeger chairman Jeffery T. Grade said he expects to change Giddings's focus from manufacturing machine tools to maintaining and servicing tools made by both companies. The market reacted favorably to the announcement, increasing Giddings's stock price by $6.73 to $20.36. Giddings had 33.2 million shares outstanding, so this price improvement increased the owners' wealth by $223 million ($6.73 × 33.2 million shares).

There are several implications of viewing takeovers as abrupt replacements for the normal business decisions that keep companies competitive. First, some takeovers are likely to be more friendly than others. Synergistic takeovers are likely to be friendly because the objective is to combine businesses with complementary resources. Disciplinary takeovers are likely to be hostile because the objective is to remove the managers of the target firm. Morck, Shleifer, and Vishny found evidence that is consistent with this characterization.[5] Some synergistic takeovers start out friendly but turn hostile when the suitor is rebuffed (see "In the News").

Second, managers are likely to use a method of restructuring that is compatible with the mood they anticipate. Methods based on negotiation are appropriate for friendly restructurings while more aggressive methods may be required if they are hostile. Furthermore, managers should expect their counterparts in the target firm to defend themselves from restructurings they perceive as hostile.

Third, because takeovers are used to suddenly accomplish the same objectives as normal business decisions, we can use the same procedures to value them. These

---

[4]This description of the circumstances surrounding Harnischfeger's offer for Giddings & Lewis is based on the following articles from *The Wall Street Journal:* Carl Quintanilla, "Harnischfeger Unveils Hostile Bid for Giddings," April 28, 1997, p. A3; Richard Gibson and Carl Quintanilla, "Giddings & Lewis's Stock Jumps on Hostile Bid," April 29, 1997, p. A3; and Carl Quintanilla, "Giddings & Lewis Is Standing Firm in Resistance to Harnischfeger Bid," May 1, 1997, p. B4.

[5]Randall Morck, Andrie Shleifer, and Robert Vishny, "Characteristics of Targets of Hostile and Friendly Takeovers," in Alan J. Auerbach, ed., *Takeovers: Causes and Consequences*, University of Chicago Press, Chicago, 1988.

I N   T H E   N E W S

A SYNERGISTIC TAKEOVER
THAT BECAME HOSTILE

HILTON HOTELS CORP. launched a hostile takeover bid for rival ITT Corp. valued at $55 a share in stock and cash, or $6.5 billion, plus the assumption of debt. The $55-a-share bid represents a 29 percent premium over ITT's closing price of $42.625 a share. After the announcement, ITT stock closed in composite trading at $58.50 a share, up $14.75, or 34 percent, on the day.

Stephen F. Bollenbach, Hilton's president and CEO, said that many of ITT's gambling and hotel properties fit precisely into Hilton's plans. The company owns all or part of 72 properties under the Sheraton name. "We want to own those big full-service hotels," Mr. Bollenbach said. "We've made

continuous attempts to contact them. We are hoping that they'll cooperate. But if they don't, we are prepared to take this to their shareholders."

Clearly Hilton is putting the pressure on. It said it would immediately launch a tender offer at $55 a share for roughly half the stock of ITT, to be followed by a stock swap for Hilton shares valued at $55 a share. Hilton also said it would proceed with a proxy battle to oust the board of ITT. Hilton believes the full board of ITT is up for re-election, meaning the entire board can be replaced at the company's annual meeting. The date for the shareholder meeting hasn't been set, but typically it is held in May.

Source: Steven Lipin and Bruce Orwall, "Hilton Launches $6.5 Billion Bid for ITT; Stock Soars After Word of Hostile Offer," *The Wall Street Journal*, January 28, 1997, p. A3. Reprinted by permission of *The Wall Street Journal*, © Dow Jones & Company, Inc. All rights reserved worldwide.

procedures are, of course, NPV analysis for take-it-or-leave-it propositions and option pricing for alternatives that provide strategic choices. Later, we will describe how to apply these valuation principles to acquisition proposals.

Forms and Characteristics

Acquisitions, divestitures, and buy-outs are the basic forms of ownership transfer but there is some variety within each type. This section describes the alternatives and relates them to the takeover motive. Exhibit 20.1 is a diagram of these alternatives.

Mergers   A merger results when two firms are combined and one or both lose their original identity. The board of directors of the merger partners must approve the combination and submit the proposal to the owners for their approval. Some companies require that a simple majority of the owners vote in favor of the merger for it to be approved; others require a super-majority of as much as 80 percent. When a merger is effective, the financial statements of the merger partners are combined according to accounting rules (we will discuss these rules later). Mergers seldom are employed in hostile, disciplinary takeovers because they are easily blocked by the board of directors who simply refuse to submit them to the owners for approval or by strict voting rules.

Exhibit 20.1

METHODS OF TRANSFERRING OWNERSHIP

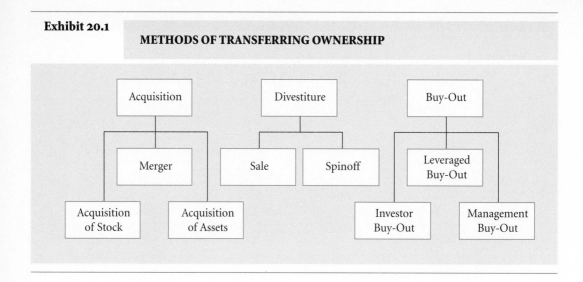

Acquisition of Stock   One company or group of investors, often called the bidder, can take over another company by acquiring the target's common stock. The bidder may first submit the acquisition proposal to the target company's managers to solicit their cooperation or they may appeal directly to the owners in a **tender offer**. This offer invites the owners to tender or sell their shares to the bidding group. No vote is required; owners who approve the offer sell their shares to the bidder; those who don't approve do not.

The acquisition is effective when the bidder gains a controlling interest in the target's common stock. Then, the new owners may permit the target to retain its identity or they may merge the companies to buy out minority shareholders who did not tender their shares. An acquisition of stock may be friendly or hostile, however, a tender offer usually is unfriendly because it is used to bypass recalcitrant managers or the board of directors.

Acquisition of Assets   One company can acquire another company by purchasing its assets rather than by purchasing its stock. The payment is made to the target firm rather than to the target firm's owners. The board of the target firm decides whether to distribute the proceeds of the sale to the owners or to invest it in other assets. Transferring the ownership of assets in this way is more cumbersome but does not leave any minority shareholders whose positions must be consolidated through a merger as an acquisition of stock does.

Sales and Spinoffs   Companies use sales and spinoffs to divest themselves of assets. A sale transfers ownership of specific assets, such as a separate division, to another company or group of investors—usually for cash. The seller may reinvest the cash in the company's remaining assets, repay loans, or distribute it to the owners as a special dividend. A spinoff converts a division or subsidiary into a stand-alone company whose shares are distributed to the parent company's common stockholders. They can hold the shares,

PUTTING A SPIN ON ABC

WALT DISNEY CO. [recently] disclosed plans to explore "its strategic options" for its wildly diverse ABC publishing group: newspapers like the *Fort Worth Star-Telegram*, consumer magazines like *Los Angeles* magazine, trade publications such as *Women's Wear Daily* and *Institutional Investor*, and more prosaic titles like *Kentucky Prairie Farmer*. John Dryer, a company spokesman, said yesterday that the options include an outright sale, or possibly a "swap or spinoff."

Like other entertainment and media giants created by the past five years of megamergers, Disney is under pressure from shareholders to get out of businesses that aren't considered core operations or aren't likely to meet certain targets for return on investment and growth. The ABC network and stations have clear synergies with Disney's entertainment, theme-park, and resort operations. But there are few such links between the publishing properties of the former Capital Cities/ABC and Disney's businesses. "You would like to have some connection to your business focus," says Peter Appert, analyst with Alex Brown & Sons. "I can't imagine Disney publishing *Industrial Safety & Hygiene News* or *Automotive Body Repair News*."

Source: Patrick M. Reilly, "Disney May Sell ABC's Papers and Magazines," *The Wall Street Journal*, January 29, 1997, p. B1. Reprinted by permission of *The Wall Street Journal*, © Dow Jones & Company, Inc. All rights reserved worldwide.

sell them and reinvest the cash in the parent company, or sell them and keep the cash for their own homemade special dividend.

Some sales and spinoffs are prompted by the threat of an acquisition. Managers may sell weak business units to improve their company's stock price when they anticipate a disciplinary takeover attempt and may even sell strong business units to make the company an unattractive takeover candidate. Other divestitures take place after a successful acquisition. New managers may sell specific assets to improve focus and efficiency (see "In the News") or to avoid conflicts with regulators. For example, a U.S. manufacturer may sell a unit that produces products for the military to another U.S. firm when merging with a foreign company.

Buy-Outs   Buy-outs are takeovers in which a company becomes privately held. The buy-out may be initiated by an outside group of investors or by a subset of the company's present managers; in this case, it is called a **management buy-out** (MBO). In either case, the managers of the new, privately held company usually invest a large proportion of their personal wealth in the company's equity. The resulting reduction in agency costs is one of the benefits claimed for this type of takeover. Many buy-outs are financed with a large proportion of debt and are therefore known as **leveraged buy-outs** (**LBOs**). The tax-shield this debt provides is another benefit. The common stock of a company taken private in an LBO is sometimes reissued after the company's performance has improved. Some LBOs are initiated in anticipation of the gains from reissuing the stock; others are initiated in anticipation of a hostile takeover attempt.

Defensive Techniques

Companies have a variety of techniques for defending themselves from unwelcome suitors. Some techniques work continually while others are activated when a threat is perceived. Some impede any type of takeover and others are specifically designed to deter a tender offer. Many of them have colorful names derived from fairy tales.

Charter amendments are takeover defenses that work continually. Common forms of this defense include staggering the terms of the board of directors so a majority are not up for election at one time and requiring that a super-majority of the owners approve a merger. Staggered terms make it impossible for dissident shareholders or a bidder to obtain a majority on the board as the result of a single proxy contest or immediately after completing a successful tender offer. Requiring a super-majority, which is usually invoked only if the majority of the board doesn't approve of a merger, further dilutes the dissident shareholders' power by requiring overwhelming support for a proposal. The mere presence of these provisions can discourage prospective suitors.

Poison pills, white knights, and the crown jewel gambit are takeover defenses activated in response to a hostile tender offer. A **poison pill** gives the owners of the target company the right to buy shares of the combination's common stock at a substantial discount from market value if a hostile takeover is successful. This dilutes the value of the bidder's shares and transfers the value of the acquisition back to the target's shareholders. The target is thereby "poisoned" from the bidder's perspective.

Mylan Laboratories, Incorporated's poison pill gave the owner of each share of common stock the right to purchase 1/1000th of a share of preferred stock.[6] The rights become effective when an outsider launches a tender offer or accumulates 15 percent or more of the company's common stock. Each share of preferred stock will have dividend and voting rights equivalent to 1,000 shares of common stock. This poison pill doubles the number of shares outstanding in the event of an acquisition attempt.

A **white knight** is another company or group of investors willing to acquire the target company in a friendly—rather than a hostile—takeover. A subcommittee of Petrolite Corporation's board of directors advised the company to seek a white knight when it concluded that two offers to buy the company were inadequate.[7] The announcement, which implied the board would hold out for higher offers, sent Petrolite's stock price up by $4.75, an increase of 13 percent. In another case, an association that represents about 40 percent of Pearle Incorporated's franchised optical shops in the United States sought a buyer for the company that will address their concerns for lower royalty fees.[8] Some white knights will even take the job on commission (see "In the News").

Selling a strong business unit to make the company an unattractive takeover candidate is called the **crown jewel gambit**. Commercial Intertech Corporation used a variation of this technique recently to defend itself from an acquisition by United

---

[6] "Board Adopts 'Poison Pill' Involving Preferred Stock," *The Wall Street Journal,* August 26, 1996, p. B4.

[7] Calmetta Y. Coleman, "Special Committee Urges Petrolite to Explore Third-Party Linkup," *The Wall Street Journal,* November 18, 1996, p. B4.

[8] Jeffrey A. Tannenbaum, "Pearl Franchisees Have Intensified a Quest for a White Knight," *The Wall Street Journal,* April 9, 1996, p. B2.

IN THE NEWS

WHITE KNIGHTS FOR SALE

BellSouth's unsuccessful bid to buy Lin Broadcasting is a dramatic example of getting paid to play. Donald Peis, Lin's CEO, wanted BellSouth to enter the bidding for his company. Craig McCaw had made a hostile offer, and Mr. Peis needed some alternatives. The problem was that BellSouth suspected that McCaw would win any bidding contest. So in return for bidding, BellSouth demanded $54 million plus expenses from Lin. BellSouth got what it asked for. As a result of BellSouth's bidding, Lin's stock market value rose by $1 billion. Craig McCaw won in the end, but BellSouth made $54 million with a losing hand. And for Mr. Peis, paying $54 million for $1 billion was a bargain.

Source: Adam Brandenburger and Barry Nalebuff, "Even a Losing Bid Can Pay Off," *The Wall Street Journal*, November 18, 1996, p. A12. Reprinted by permission of *The Wall Street Journal*, © Dow Jones & Company, Inc. All rights reserved worldwide.

Dominion.[9] By spinning off a key division in a tax-free transaction, the company created a tax liability for a potential buyer. "From the point of view of an effective defense, it's probably as good as it gets since it dramatically increases the cost of the deal," said Robert Willens, of Lehman Brothers, Inc.

Managers say they use these defensive tactics to save the company's assets from pillage, however, the suspicion persists that they do so to save their own jobs. The financial market also seems to be suspicious because the adoption of a poison pill reduces a company's stock price.[10]

Procedures

Managers considering an acquisition must (1) be familiar with the legal environment, (2) choose a method of payment, and (3) record the results of the transaction using approved methods of accounting. Managers cannot overlook these procedural issues when contemplating a multi-billion dollar purchase.

The Legal Environment U.S. federal laws prohibit takeovers that will create a monopoly or otherwise result in the restraint of trade. These laws are enforced by the Federal Trade Commission and the U.S. Justice Department, which must be notified when a bidder acquires 15 percent of the target's stock. Other federal agencies, such as the Federal Communications Commission and the Comptroller of the Currency, can block mergers within their areas of jurisdiction on other grounds. The FCC prohibits a single company from dominating broadcast media in a particular market while the Comptroller of the Currency regulates bank mergers.

---

[9]Steven Lipin, "Investing in Mergers Turns Perilous as Deals Collapse," *The Wall Street Journal*, August 6, 1996, p. C1.

[10]See Paul H. Malatesta and Ralph A. Walkling, "Poison Pill Securities: Stockholder Wealth, Profitability, and Ownership Structure," *Journal of Financial Economics*, January/March 1988, pp. 347–376.

State laws sometimes impose additional restrictions. Indiana law requires investors who own more than 20 percent of an Indiana corporation's common stock to obtain the other owners' permission before he or she can vote the shares. The effect of this law is to make a takeover a more time-consuming, two-step process; acquire the shares and then acquire the votes. Wisconsin has an anti-takeover law that can block a hostile takeover for three years. The authors of these and other state laws that lengthen the time required to complete a takeover claim they protect the rights of minority shareholders. These shareholders may feel coerced to accept an initial offer for fear they will receive inferior terms later when the transaction is consolidated. Whatever their intention, states that have enacted these laws have made it more difficult to take over companies incorporated there.

Method of Payment   Cash and stock are the primary methods of payment used in takeovers although companies sometimes use a combination of the two. Each method has its own advantages and disadvantages. One advantage of a cash offer is that it is easier for the target shareholders to evaluate and may be completed more quickly for that reason. Quickness is important if a delay gives other companies time to evaluate the target and prepare a bid. A disadvantage is that the target shareholders' gains are taxable immediately if they sell their shares for cash; however, their gains are deferred if they exchange their shares for stock. This means the bidder may be required to pay a higher price when cash is the method of payment to compensate the target shareholders for this expense. Several scholars have documented a difference between the target shareholders' returns in acquisitions for stock and cash that is partly attributable to the effect of taxes.[11]

The effective price of an acquisition when stock is the method of payment depends on how well the acquisition turns out. The value of the stock increases subsequent to a good acquisition and decreases after a bad one. These price changes raise and lower the price paid for the target firm. Target managers who are willing to accept stock as the method of payment may signal that they believe their stock is currently undervalued. Conversely, bidder managers who insist on stock as the method of payment may signal that they believe their stock is overvalued. Using stock as the method of payment both elicits and conveys possibly adverse information; this characteristic is therefore both an advantage and a disadvantage. On balance, managers seem to prefer cash as the method of payment to avoid giving the impression their own company's common stock is overvalued.[12]

Negotiation and Implementation   Identifying an acquisition target and preparing an offer of cash or stock that provides a positive NPV is only the beginning of the process by which companies seek the benefits of synergistic and disciplinary takeovers. The initial offer may be unsuccessful, prompting the bidder to revise the offer and negotiate in private or in public view. In addition, publicity at this stage may attract the attention of other bidders that become competitors. Their participation lengthens the bidding stage of the process and may raise the cost of the acquisition, which reduces its NPV.

---

[11]See Carla Hayn, "Tax Attributes as Determinants of Shareholder Gains in Corporate Acquisitions," *Journal of Financial Economics*, June 1989, pp. 121–153.

[12]See Tim Loughran and Anand M. Vijh, "Do Long-Term Shareholders Benefit from Corporate Acquisitions?" University of Iowa working paper, 1997.

The difficult work begins after the deal is finalized. Managers at all levels in production, marketing, administration, and finance must eliminate redundant operations and functions and integrate essential ones to obtain the anticipated benefits of a synergistic takeover. Managers in these same areas must be persuaded or forced to make the painful choices required by a disciplinary takeover. These are not simple tasks because these managers are motivated by self-interest and many have private information they can use to their advantage. Simply put, there are myriad agency conflicts. The owners will not receive the expected benefit of the acquisition unless these agency conflicts are resolved.

Accounting for Mergers   Two companies are combined when they merge and must report the results of their operations in a single set of financial statements. These statements are the ones included in 10-K and annual reports and are therefore distinct from the financial statements prepared for tax purposes. The two choices for combining financial statements of merged companies are the purchase and pooling of interest methods of accounting.

The acquired company's assets are recorded in the acquiring company's books at the cost established by the merger under the purchase method of accounting. This cost usually is higher than the assets' book values and the difference is recognized as goodwill. The acquiring company amortizes the goodwill over the life of the assets and deducts the periodic expense, a type of extra depreciation, from reported earnings but not from taxable income. Consequently, using the purchase method of accounting reduces reported earnings per share but has no effect on cash flows.

The book values of the two companies' assets are simply added together under the pooling of interest method of accounting. No goodwill is created and there is no extra depreciation expense; consequently, there is no effect on either cash flows or earnings per share.

Companies are entitled to use pooling of interest when they use stock as the method of payment but must use the purchase method of accounting otherwise. Absent some other motive, the financial analyst is indifferent between these methods of accounting because neither affects cash flows.

20.2   VALUATION OF ACQUISITIONS

The value of an acquisition to the bidding company's owners is the value of the combination created by the transaction, V_C, minus its cost.

$$\text{Value of acquisition} = V_C - \text{Cost}$$

The transaction is acceptable to the bidder's owners if its value is greater than the pre-takeover value of their equity, V_B. That is, an acquisition is acceptable if

$$V_C - \text{Cost} > V_B$$

or if

$$\text{NPV} = V_C - V_B - \text{Cost} > 0.$$

Subtracting the target's pre-takeover value, V_T, from both sides and rearranging terms expresses the inequality in incremental terms.

$$V_C - V_B - V_T > \text{Cost} - V_T \qquad \qquad \textbf{[20.1]}$$

The left-hand side of Inequality 20.1 is the incremental *benefit* of the takeover. This benefit is positive only if the value of the two firms combined is greater than the sum of their values as separate entities. The right-hand side of Inequality 20.1 is the incremental *cost* that equals the amount paid in excess of the target's pre-merger value.

The advantage of using the left-hand side of Inequality 20.1 to describe the benefit of a takeover is that it forces the analyst to think about how the transaction will produce value greater than the value of the separate companies. The advantage of using the right-hand side of this inequality to describe the cost of a takeover is that it expresses this cost explicitly in terms of the premium above market value paid to the target company's shareholders.[13] We'll describe how to measure the incremental benefit and cost next.

Estimating the Incremental Benefit

Inequality 20.1 shows that the benefit of a takeover is the amount by which the value of the combination exceeds the values of the separate companies. This benefit is derived from the options made available by the takeover. A synergistic takeover creates new options not previously available to the managers. They may be able to develop new products and distribution networks, enter new markets, and reduce production or administrative costs because of the synergies provided by the combination. A disciplinary takeover forces managers to exercise the options already available or installs new managers who will exercise them.

Some of the options made available by an acquisition are exercised immediately because the underlying asset provides interim cash flows that make it worthwhile to give up the option's flexibility. The values of these options are their intrinsic values, which are measured by NPV analysis. Other options are not exercised prior to expiration because the flexible response to uncertainty that they provide is more valuable than the interim cash flows. These options' values are measured by an option pricing model. The following example uses NPV analysis and option pricing to estimate the value of an acquisition in the context of Equation 20.1.

The Mercurial Pharmaceutical Company develops patented ethical drugs that doctors prescribe by name. Many of Mercurial's key products are about to lose patent protection. The company's managers would like to sell generic versions of these products rather than lose them to a generic drug distributor but they have no experience in this market. Therefore, they plan to acquire Glixo Industries, a successful generic drug distributor, to obtain the expertise and sales network they need.

Each company's projected net free cash flows are given in Table 20.2. Separate estimates are provided for years 1998–2001 while net free cash flow is assumed to be a level perpetuity for years 2002 and beyond.

---

[13]This procedure for measuring an acquisition's benefits and costs was developed by Stewart C. Myers in "A Framework for Evaluating Mergers," in *Modern Developments in Financial Management*, Stewart C. Myers, ed., Praeger, New York, 1976.

FREE CASH FLOW STATEMENTS (BILLIONS OF DOLLARS)   Table 20.2

Panel A: Mercurial Pharmaceutical Company

	1998	1999	2000	2001	2002 to ∞
Cash flow provided by (used for) operations	$6.775	$7.525	$8.700	$9.400	$9.775
Cash flow provided by (used for) investment	(1.125)	(1.200)	(1.425)	(1.550)	(1.600)
Cash flow provided by (used for) financial slack	(0.060)	(0.060)	(0.070)	(0.085)	(0.075)
Net free cash flow	$5.590	$6.265	$7.205	$7.765	$8.100

Panel B: Glixo Industries

	1998	1999	2000	2001	2002 to ∞
Cash flow provided by (used for) operations	$1.175	$1.400	$1.800	$2.025	$2.150
Cash flow provided by (used for) investment	(0.160)	(0.190)	(0.225)	(0.275)	(0.300)
Cash flow provided by (used for) financial slack	(0.010)	(0.010)	(0.015)	(0.015)	(0.015)
Net free cash flow	$1.005	$1.200	$1.560	$1.735	$1.835

The value of Mercurial's equity equals the present value of its net free cash flows discounted at the weighted average cost of capital minus its debt. Given a weighted average cost of capital of 14 percent, Mercurial's market value at the end of 2002 and 1997 is

$$\text{Mercurial's market value at the end of 2002} = \$8.100/0.14 = \$57.857 \text{ billion}$$

$$\text{Mercurial market value at the end of 1997} = \frac{\$5.590}{(1.14)} + \frac{\$6.265}{(1.14)^2} + \frac{\$7.205}{(1.14)^3} + \frac{\$7.765}{(1.14)^4}$$

$$+ \frac{\$8.100 + \$57.857}{(1.14)^5} = \$53.441 \text{ billion.}$$

Mercurial has $5 billion of debt outstanding so the value of its equity is $48.441 billion ($53.441 − $5.000).

Glixo's weighted average cost of capital is 16 percent and it has $2 billion of debt outstanding, so the value of its equity at the end of 1997 is

$$\text{Glixo's market value at the end of 2002} = \$1.835/0.16 = \$11.469 \text{ billion}$$

$$\text{Glixo's market value at the end of 1997} = \frac{\$1.005}{(1.16)} + \frac{\$1.200}{(1.16)^2} + \frac{\$1.560}{(1.16)^3} + \frac{\$1.735}{(1.16)^4}$$

$$+ \frac{\$1.835 + \$11.469}{(1.16)^5} = \$10.05 \text{ billion}$$

Value of Glixo's equity at the end of 1997 = \$10.05 − \$2.00 = \$8.05 billion.

The additional cash flows Mercurial expects to receive or pay out as a result of the acquisition are given in panel A of Table 20.3. The company expects the initial difficulty of integrating the sales forces to delay any significant improvement in cash revenues until the year 2000. Similarly, Mercurial will incur additional cash costs to integrate operations in 1998 and 1999 and realize savings from eliminating redundant administrative functions beginning in 2000. The additional cash flows used for investment are also expected to be larger initially. The managers expect to reduce the combination's financial slack immediately, however, because of the effect of diversification and because there are economies of scale in holding liquid reserves.

Panel B of Table 20.3 provides the combination's net free cash flows. Each entry in this table is computed by adding the corresponding entries in panels A and B of Table 20.2 and panel A of Table 20.3. For example, the combination's estimated cash flow provided by operations for 1998 is

$$\begin{array}{l}\text{Combination's 1998 cash flow}\\ \text{provided by (used for) operations}\end{array} = \$6.775 + \$1.175 - \$0.500 = \$7.450.$$

Assuming the combination's weighted average cost of capital is 14.5 percent, its market value is

---

Table 20.3   THE ACQUISITION'S EFFECT ON FREE CASH FLOW (BILLIONS OF DOLLARS)

Panel A: Change in Cash Flows from Combining Companies

	1998	1999	2000	2001	2002 to ∞
Cash flow provided by operations					
Change in cash revenues from integrating sales forces	\$ 0	\$ 0.075	\$ 0.150	\$ 0.350	\$ 0.925
Change in cash costs from integrating operations	0.500	0.300	(0.050)	(0.050)	(0.050)
Net increase (decrease)	\$(0.500)	\$(0.225)	\$ 0.200	\$ 0.400	\$ 0.975
Increase (decrease) in cash flow provided by investment	\$(0.215)	\$(0.235)	\$(0.150)	\$(0.150)	\$ (0.150)
Increase (decrease) in cash flow provided by financial slack	\$ 0.007	\$ 0.005	\$ 0.011	\$ 0.010	\$ 0.005

Panel B: Combination's Free Cash Flows

	1998	1999	2000	2001	2002 to ∞
Cash flow provided by (used for) operations	\$ 7.450	\$ 8.700	\$10.700	\$11.825	\$12.900
Cash flow provided by (used for) investment	(1.500)	(1.625)	(1.800)	(1.975)	(2.050)
Cash flow provided by (used for) financial slack	(0.063)	(0.065)	(0.074)	(0.090)	(0.085)
Net free cash flow	\$ 5.887	\$ 7.010	\$ 8.826	\$ 9.760	\$10.765

Combination's market value at the end of 2002 $= \$10.765/0.145 = \$74.241$ billion

Combination's market value at the end of 1997 $= \dfrac{\$5.887}{(1.145)} + \dfrac{\$7.010}{(1.145)^2} + \dfrac{\$8.826}{(1.145)^3} + \dfrac{\$9.760}{(1.145)^4}$

$$+ \dfrac{\$10.765 + \$74.241}{(1.145)^5} = \$65.240 \text{ billion.}$$

Assuming also that Mercurial does not issue or retire any debt as a result of this acquisition, the value of the combination's equity is $58.240 billion ($65.240 − $5.000 − $2.000).

Substituting these equity values into the left-hand side of Inequality 20.1 gives the incremental benefit of the acquisition.

$$\text{Incremental benefit} = V_C - V_B - V_T$$
$$= \$58.240 - \$48.441 - \$8.050$$
$$= \$1.749.$$

The combination is worth $1.749 billion more than the separate companies.

EXERCISE
20.1

BENEFIT OF AN ACQUISITION

Wolf Companies may make a tender offer for the common stock of Sheep Resources. Each company's net free cash flows are shown below. Wolf's managers believe the resulting synergies will provide the changes in net free cash flows (also shown below). Wolf's weighted average cost of capital is 13 percent, Sheep's is 12 percent, and the combination's will be 12.8 percent. Wolf and Sheep have $5.3 and $1.0 million of debt outstanding, and Wolf will neither issue nor retire debt after the acquisition is complete. What is the incremental value of the acquisition?

	Net Free Cash Flow (in millions)		
	1999	**2000**	**2001 to ∞**
Wolf Companies	$1.600	$1.875	$1.750
Sheep Resources	0.450	0.500	0.525
Changes provided by combination	(0.300)	0.100	0.225

The value of each company's equity is as follows.

$$\text{Wolf's market value} = \dfrac{\$1.600}{(1.13)} + \dfrac{\$1.875}{(1.13)^2} + \dfrac{\$1.750 + \$1.750/0.13}{(1.13)^3}$$
$$= \$13.427 \text{ million}$$

$$\text{Wolf's equity value} = \text{Market value} - \text{debt value}$$
$$= \$13.427 - \$5.300 = \$8.127$$

$$\text{Sheep's market value} = \frac{\$0.450}{(1.12)} + \frac{\$0.500}{(1.12)^2} + \frac{\$0.525 + \$0.525/0.12}{(1.12)^3}$$

$$= \$4.288 \text{ million}$$

$$\text{Sheep's equity value} = \$4.288 - \$1.000 = \$3.288 \text{ million}$$

The value of the combination's equity is

$$\text{Combination's market value} = \frac{\$1.750}{(1.128)} + \frac{\$2.475}{(1.128)^2} + \frac{\$2.500 + \$2.500/0.128}{(1.128)^3}$$

$$= \$18.847 \text{ million}$$

$$\text{Combination's equity value} = \$18.847 - \$6.300 = \$12.547 \text{ million.}$$

The incremental benefit of the acquisition is $1.132 million ($12.547 – $8.127 – 3.288).

Mercurial Pharmaceutical Company's managers have another reason to acquire a generic drug distributor. Concerns about the cost of health care and efforts to reform the health care system may diminish the value of Mercurial's patented drugs and enhance the value of generic drugs. By purchasing Glixo and spending an additional $2.15 billion, Mercurial can reorganize into a company well-adapted to the new environment. However, uncertainty about the success of health care reform makes this reorganization currently worth only $2.0 billion. The opportunity to reorganize is an option attached to the acquisition that has value even though it should not be exercised immediately.

Mercurial's managers will use the Black-Scholes option pricing model to determine the value of this opportunity. The current value of the reorganization is $2.0 billion, the option's exercise price is $2.15 billion, and the managers believe this opportunity will be available for three years. The standard deviation of the continuously compounded annual rate of return on the reorganization is 0.30. Then with a riskless interest rate of 6 percent, the value of the option on the reorganization given by the Black-Scholes option pricing model is

$$C_0 = S_0 \times N(d_1) - PV(E) \times N(d_2)$$

where
$$S_0 = \$2.0$$
$$PV(E) = \$2.15/e^{0.06 \times 3} = \$1.80$$
$$d_1 = \ln [S_0/PV(E)]/\sigma \sqrt{t} + (\sigma \sqrt{t})/2$$
$$= \ln[\$2.0/\$1.8]/(0.30 \times 1.73) + (0.30 \times 1.73)/2 = 0.4625$$
$$d_2 = d_1 - \sigma \sqrt{t}$$
$$= 0.4625 - 0.30 \times 1.73 = -0.0565$$
$$N(d_1) = 0.6781$$
$$N(d_2) = 0.4775$$
$$C_0 = \$2.0 \times 0.6781 - \$1.8 \times 0.4775$$
$$= \$0.50 \text{ billion.}$$

The option to respond to health care reform that is attached to the acquisition of Glixo is worth $0.50 billion.

The entire value of the combination is therefore its value as a take-it-or-leave-it proposition, $58.240 billion, plus the value of the option to respond to health care reform, $0.50 billion, or $58.740 billion. Substituting this value into the left-hand side of Inequality 20.1,

$$\text{Incremental benefit} = V_C - V_B - V_T$$
$$= \$58.740 - \$48.441 - \$8.050$$
$$= \$2.249 \text{ billion.}$$

EXERCISE
20.2

OPTION VALUE OF AN ACQUISITION

Wolf Companies (see Exercise 20.1) expects ownership of Sheep Resources to permit it to develop a new line of wool clothing for $3.4 million although the business is not currently viable because its market value is only $3.0 million. What is the value of Wolf's opportunity to enter this business? What is the entire value of the acquisition? The option will expire in one year, the standard deviation of the continuously compounded annual rate of return on the clothing business is 40 percent, and the riskless rate of return is 6 percent.

$$C_0 = S_0 \times N(d_1) - \text{PV}(E) \times N(d_2)$$

where
$$S_0 = \$3.0$$
$$\text{PV}(E) = \$3.4/e^{0.06 \times 1} = \$3.2$$
$$d_1 = \ln[S_0/\text{PV}(E)]/\sigma \sqrt{t} + (\sigma \sqrt{t})/2$$
$$= \ln[\$3.0/\$3.2]/(0.40 \times 1) + (0.40 \times 1)/2 = 0.0387$$
$$d_2 = d_1 - \sigma \sqrt{t}$$
$$= 0.0387 - 0.40 \times 1 = -0.3613$$
$$N(d_1) = 0.5154$$
$$N(d_2) = 0.3589$$
$$C_0 = \$3.0 \times 0.5154 - \$3.2 \times 0.3589$$
$$= \$0.40 \text{ million.}$$

The option to enter the clothing business is worth $0.40 million.

The entire incremental value of the acquisition is its take-it-or-leave-it value plus its option value.

$$\text{Entire incremental value} = \$1.132 + 0.40 = \$1.532$$

Wolf Companies and Sheep Resources are worth $1.532 million more together than separate.

The Cost of an Acquisition

The cost of an acquisition depends on the method of payment. However, ignoring taxes and signaling effects, the bidder can always structure an exchange of shares that has the same anticipated cost as an acquisition for cash.

The Cost of an Acquisition for Cash   The cost of an acquisition for cash is the amount of cash paid. The bidder's owners receive all the acquisition's incremental benefit if this cost equals the target's pre-acquisition market value. For example, if Mercurial Pharmaceutical can acquire Glixo Industries for $8.05 billion, then the NPV of the acquisition to Mercurial's owners is

$$\text{NPV} = V_C - V_B - \text{Cost}$$
$$= \$58.740 - \$48.441 - \$8.050 = \$2.249 \text{ billion.}$$

The NPV equals the incremental benefit of the acquisition because the cost is Glixo's pre-acquisition market value.

The bidder's and target's owners share the benefit of the acquisition when the cost is greater than the target's pre-acquisition market value. The maximum permissible cost from the point of view of the bidder's owners is the cost that makes the NPV equal to zero. That is,

$$\text{NPV} = V_C - V_B - \text{Maximum cost} = 0$$
$$= \$58.740 - \$48.441 - \text{Maximum cost} = \$0$$
$$\text{Maximum cost} = \$10.299 \text{ billion.}$$

At this price, the target's owners receive all the benefits of the acquisition because they are paid $2.249 billion more than the company's pre-acquisition market value. The largest percentage premium Mercurial can pay Glixo's shareholders is therefore 27.9 percent ($2.249/$8.05).

EXERCISE   •   ────────────────────────────────   •

20.3   **DETERMINING THE MAXIMUM PERCENTAGE PREMIUM**

What is the maximum percentage premium Wolf Companies can pay Sheep Industries given the results of Exercise 20.2?

The incremental benefit of the acquisition was $1.532 million and Sheep's pre-acquisition market value was $3.288 million. The maximum percentage premium Wolf can pay Sheep's owners is therefore 46.6 percent ($1.532/$3.288).

•   ───────────   •

The Cost of an Acquisition for Stock   The cost of an acquisition for stock is the number of shares paid multiplied by the *post-acquisition* price per share. Managers determine the number of shares to pay the target's owners by relating the company's post-acquisition value to the amount of money they intend to pay. The process is best seen by example.

A bidder with 100 shares of stock outstanding valued at $50 per share intends to take over a target with 200 shares of stock outstanding valued at $20 per share. The companies' market values are $5,000 and $4,000. Synergies from combining the firms will produce a market value for the combination of $15,000. The incremental value of the acquisition is therefore $6,000 ($15,000 − $5,000 − $4,000).

The bidder intends to pay the target company's shareholders $5,000, a premium of $1,000 or 25 percent. This payment represents one-third of the combination's value

($5,000/$15,000), so the bidder must give the target company's owners one-third of the post-acquisition number of shares outstanding. The bidder currently has 100 shares of stock outstanding, so the target must receive n shares where n is the solution to the following equation.

$$\text{Percentage of shares} = \text{Percentage of value}$$

$$\frac{n}{100 + n} = \frac{\$5,000}{\$15,000}$$

Solving for n, we find that the bidder must issue 50 shares of stock to the target company's owners.

In this example, the target company has 200 shares of stock outstanding, so its owners must exchange four shares of stock for one share of the bidder's stock (200 shares/50 shares). An investor who owned four shares of the target company's stock, valued at $80 prior to the acquisition (4 × $20), will own one share of the bidder's stock valued at $100 after the acquisition, a premium of 25 percent.

Let's use this procedure to determine how many shares of stock Mercurial Pharmaceutical Company must offer Glixo if the company intends to pay a 20 percent premium for the target. Mercurial and Glixo have 750 million and 400 million shares of stock outstanding.

The market value of Glixo Industries common stock was $8.050 billion. Mercurial intends to pay Glixo's owners a 20 percent premium or $9.660 billion ($8.050 × 1.20) for their shares. The value of the combination is $58.740 billion. Therefore, Mercurial must offer Glixo's owners n shares where

$$\frac{n}{0.750 + n} = \frac{\$9.660}{\$58.740}$$

$$n = 0.1476 \text{ billion shares.}$$

Glixo has 400 million shares outstanding, so Mercurial will exchange one share of new stock for every 2.71 shares of Glixo stock outstanding (0.4 billion shares/0.1476 billion shares).

Does each Glixo stockholder receive the 20 percent premium? Yes. Each old Glixo share was worth $20.125 ($8.050/0.400), so 2.71 shares were worth $54.54. Each new share of stock is worth $58.740/(0.750 shares + 0.1476 shares), which equals $65.44. The increase, $10.90, is a 20 percent premium ($10.90/$54.54).

EXERCISE 20.4

DETERMINING THE NUMBER OF SHARES TO OFFER

Wolf Companies and Sheep Resources each have 500,000 shares of stock outstanding. Determine the exchange ratio if Wolf intends to pay Sheep's owners a 25 percent premium for their shares.

Sheep's original value was $3.288 million, so Wolf plans to pay $4.11 million for the shares ($3.288 × 1.25). The value of the combination is expected to be $12.947 million ($12.547 + $0.40). Therefore, Wolf must issue n shares where

$$\frac{n}{0.5 + n} = \frac{\$4.11}{\$12.947}$$

$$n = 0.2325 \text{ million shares.}$$

Sheep has 0.50 million shares outstanding, so the company's owners must exchange 2.15 shares (0.50 shares/0.2325 shares) of Sheep stock for one share of Wolf.

● ———————— ●

The Overpayment Problem   Overpaying for an acquisition appears to be a common problem that is costly to the bidder's owners and may cost the bidder's managers their jobs. Quaker Oats Company's acquisition of Snapple in 1994 is a recent case in point.[14] Quaker paid $1.7 billion for the tea-based fruit-drink producer and immediately encountered problems caused by increased competition and the difficulty of integrating Snapple's distribution system with the distribution system for its own product, Gatorade. Quaker finally sold Snapple in 1997 for a mere $300 million. The sale reduced the book value of the owners' equity by $1.4 billion or $8.15 per share. Quaker Oats' managers also paid a price. The president involuntarily left the company in 1995 and the chairman resigned in 1997.

Quaker Oats' experience may be an extreme example but bidders often pay a high price for their acquisitions. Peterson and Peterson and others studied the rates of return on the bidder and target companies' common stock at the time of an acquisition announcement.[15] They found that bidders receive negative rates of return while targets receive positive rates of return. These results suggest the target companies obtain the majority of the synergy and disciplinary gains from the acquisitions. Roll suggested these outcomes are the result of hubris: The bidder's managers are confident in their assessment of the value of the acquisition and proceed in spite of contradictory evidence.[16]

20.3   RESTRUCTURING IN FINANCIAL DISTRESS

Companies that are unable or unwilling to restructure their assets gradually or suddenly may become financially distressed and be forced to reorganize their claims or be liquidated. The process can be conducted privately or the legal system can be used to mediate, devise, or enforce a plan. In any case, the objective should be to choose the process (private or public) and the outcome (reorganize or liquidate) that provides the most value to the claimants. This section describes these alternatives and the circumstances that make one preferable to the other.

---

[14]This description of Quaker Oats' experience with Snapple is based on the following articles: John Kania, "Why Snapple's Bubble Burst," *The Wall Street Journal*, December 23, 1996, p. A12, Michael J. McCarthy, "Quaker Oats Posts $1.11 Billion Quarterly Loss," *The Wall Street Journal*, April 24, 1997, p. A3, and Zina Moukheiber, "He Who Laughs Last," *Forbes*, January 1, 1996, pp. 42–43.

[15]David R. Peterson and Pamela P. Peterson, "The Medium of Exchange in Mergers and Acquisitions," *The Journal of Banking and Finance*, June 1991, pp. 383–405.

[16]Richard Roll, "The Hubris Hypothesis of Corporate Takeovers," *Journal of Business*, April 1986, pp. 197–216.

OUTBOARD MARINE TRIES
TO STAY AFLOAT

FACED WITH MOUNTING losses and a need for more capital, Outboard Marine Corp. omitted its quarterly dividend and disclosed that its investment banker is exploring strategic options for the company. Those options include finding a major investor, creating a joint venture, or perhaps even securing new ownership that would strengthen its financial footing and give the company more time to implement a likely restructuring. The company also acknowledged that while it is in compliance with lending covenants, a significant loss in the current quarter could trigger a default on its $200 million revolving credit agreement.

The marine-engine and boat maker announced the developments as it reported a fiscal second-quarter loss of $7.3 million or 36 cents a share. Sales for the latest quarter ending March 31 fell 17 percent as demand for its recreational products slipped worldwide. Shares of Outboard Marine, which have lost nearly a third of their value already this year, closed Friday at $12, down 25 cents.

Source: Richard Gibson, "Outboard Marine Omits Dividend, Seeks New Capital," *The Wall Street Journal,* April 28, 1997, p. A8. Reprinted by permission of *The Wall Street Journal,* © Dow Jones & Company, Inc. All rights reserved worldwide.

Types of Financial Distress

Financial distress is an imprecisely defined term but is often used to describe a company that is technically insolvent, actually insolvent, or bankrupt. **Technical insolvency** is a (possibly mild) form of financial distress in which a company is unable to meet its current obligations because it is short of cash or illiquid. A temporary state of technical insolvency is relieved by accelerating cash inflows or delaying cash outflows. The company's managers can unilaterally initiate many of these actions. For example, managers can forgo cash discounts on accounts payable, reduce or omit cash dividends, or delay long-term investments without prior consultation if not without costs (see "In the News"). Chronic technical insolvency may lead to actual insolvency or bankruptcy.

Insolvency is a serious form of financial distress in which the value of a company's debt exceeds the value of its assets. Insolvency is serious because the owners' equity is negative or, equivalently, the creditors' claims cannot be satisfied in full. **Bankruptcy** and insolvency were once considered synonymous but this changed in 1978 when a revision to the U.S. bankruptcy law permitted a solvent company to claim bankruptcy if the value of *all* its obligations exceeds the value of its assets. Companies claiming bankruptcy under the new law have included among their obligations principal and interest payments on debt, product liability judgments owed to consumers, and wages and pension benefits owed to employees. Dow Corning Corporation's declaration of bankruptcy, mentioned earlier, and Johns-Manville's declaration of bankruptcy in 1982 in response to damages attributed to the company's production of asbestos are examples of filings under the new law. No matter what the reason for their distress, insolvent and bankrupt companies must resolve their problems—or fail.

The Resolution of Financial Distress

Insolvency and bankruptcy are resolved by reorganizing a viable company or by liquidating one that is not viable. A company is viable if the value of its assets as a going concern is greater than the value of its assets in liquidation. The owners, creditors, and managers of a company in financial distress have three alternatives for resolving this issue. They can (1) arrange an out-of-court settlement among the claimants, (2) enter formal bankruptcy proceedings, or (3) combine the first two alternatives to obtain some of the benefits of both.

Private Workout   A company meets directly with its creditors to obtain temporary or permanent relief from its obligations in a private workout. The creditors are usually asked to accept a moratorium on the payment of their claims and may be asked to decrease the amounts of their claims by reducing the interest or principal. The objective is to give the company an opportunity to reorganize and become viable.

Creditors may agree to these changes if it is possible to develop a credible reorganization plan that will restore the company's solvency. They may participate in the preparation of both the operating and financing components of this plan, they may impose controls to ensure the plan is implemented, and they may insist that the company install new managers. The creditors also may ask for or be offered junior securities such as preferred or common stock as partial or full compensation for these adjustments. The company's original common stock may become worthless as a result of these changes even if the company eventually emerges from financial distress. Creditors who do not believe a reorganization plan is viable may hold out for full payment or press for liquidation.

Formal Bankruptcy Proceedings   The creditors or the company can transfer the dispute to the courts if a private workout is unsuccessful. A single dissatisfied creditor can file this petition if there are fewer than 12 creditors in total, however, three creditors must sign the petition otherwise. The petitioners' delinquent claims must total at least $5,000. The company also can voluntarily file the bankruptcy petition itself.

A financially distressed company faces the same challenge in or out of bankruptcy: It must develop a viable reorganization plan or fail and be liquidated. The difference is that formal bankruptcy proceedings impose supervision by the courts. Chapters 11 and 7 of the U.S. Federal Bankruptcy Act of 1978 describe the procedures for court-supervised reorganization and liquidation.

Reorganization under Chapter 11 of the federal bankruptcy code gives the company and its creditors 120 days to prepare an acceptable reorganization plan. A moratorium on the repayment of existing debt is imposed during this period. In addition, the company can issue new debt with a claim that has priority over the existing debt. This gives lenders an incentive to provide the financing needed to bridge the reorganization period. The reorganization plan usually must be approved by a majority of the creditors although there are exceptions (see "In the News"). Failure to produce an acceptable plan leads to liquidation.

Chapter 7 of the federal bankruptcy code provides rules for selling a bankrupt company's assets and distributing the proceeds to the claimants. The general procedure is that the creditors elect a trustee who takes possession of the assets and sells them. In

IN THE NEWS

AN UNPALATABLE WORKOUT AT MACY'S

BONDHOLDERS OF R. H. Macy & Co. could end up on the losing end of the retailer's reorganization if senior creditors attempt a "cram down," an often-threatened but little-used maneuver in bankruptcy workouts that crams an unpalatable reorganization plan down the throats of creditors with the least amount of clout.

Ordinarily, when a company emerges from bankruptcy court, senior creditors' claims are paid off at face value, plus accrued interest. Junior creditors, meanwhile, get the bulk of the stock distributed by the reorganized company, which effectively makes them the controlling shareholders.

In Macy's case, however, the banks that hold the company's senior debt have covenants that specify that they must be paid all interest due on their claims since the January 1992 bankruptcy-law filing before bondholders receive a penny. Moreover, the bank creditors actually control a significant portion of Macy bonds.

Senior creditors could use these powers to force through a plan of reorganization that favors them, in effect leaving the bondholders with little or nothing. In practical terms, that means investors who have paid as much as 51 cents on the dollar for Macy senior bonds may face steep losses. For holders of Macy subordinated bonds and zero-coupon bonds, the picture looks even grimmer.

Source: Laura Jereski, "Bondholders of Macy Could Get Hurt if Senior Creditors Try 'Cram Down,'" *The Wall Street Journal,* January 7, 1994, p. A3. Reprinted by permission of *The Wall Street Journal,* © Dow Jones & Company, Inc. All rights reserved worldwide.

principle, the money obtained from the sale is distributed to the claimants in order of strict priority as described in Table 20.4. In practice, the order of priority is often violated with creditors receiving less than they are entitled to and owners receiving more.

Prepackaged Bankruptcy Prepackaged bankruptcy is a recent innovation in which the terms of a reorganization are arranged in a private workout and *then* submitted to a court for its stamp of approval. The company must obtain the agreement of a substantial number of its creditors during the private workout stage and must produce a plan that the bankruptcy court will consider fair and equitable. Bankruptcy courts have been willing to impose the plan on recalcitrant creditors when these conditions are met.

Comparison of the Alternatives Companies can reorganize their claims in a private workout, by filing a Chapter 11 bankruptcy petition, or by combining the two forms to obtain the advantages of both. Gilson found that private workouts are less costly and take less time than Chapter 11 reorganizations.[17] He also found that the value of the equity is higher and that the shareholders are permitted to retain a larger proportion

---

[17]Stuart C. Gilson, "Managing Default: Some Evidence on How Firms Choose between Workouts and Chapter 11," *Journal of Applied Corporate Finance,* Summer 1991, pp. 62–70.

Table 20.4   PRIORITY OF CLAIMS IN BANKRUPTCY

1. Administrative costs of bankruptcy.
2. Claims arising from loans obtained after bankruptcy filing.
3. Wages and salaries earned within 90 days prior to the bankruptcy filing. Maximum per person is $2,000.
4. Contributions to employee benefit plans within 180 days prior to the bankruptcy filing.
5. Consumers' claims such as guarantees and refunds. Maximum per person is $900.
6. Taxes.
7. Unsecured creditors' claims and that part of the secured creditors' claims not covered by the sale of mortgaged assets.
8. Preferred stockholders' claims.
9. Common stockholders' claims.

of the equity in private workouts. These are clear advantages to a private workout from the owners' point of view.

Any creditor can block a private workout, however, by holding out for better terms. Unsecured creditors may hold out on the assumption their small claims are only a nuisance to the other claimants who will pay them in full to obtain an agreement. Secured creditors may hold out for the liquidation of the assets securing their loans. Their objective is to protect the value of these assets that the company may operate without maintenance to maximize cash flows while the company is distressed.

Reorganization under Chapter 11 bankruptcy is more costly and takes more time but there are offsetting advantages. First, the moratorium on payments to creditors and the ability to issue new senior debt provide the company additional cash flows while in reorganization. Second, a reorganization plan approved by a majority of the claimants is imposed on all of them, which reduces the problems caused by holdouts.

Prepackaged bankruptcy provides the benefits of both systems. Money and time are saved by privately negotiating with the major claimants to prepare the reorganization plan. Then, the Chapter 11 petition is filed to obtain court supervision of the plan to prevent holdouts from blocking its implementation. Companies that can obtain approval of a majority of its creditors in private negotiations *and* survive the negotiation period—without a moratorium on debt payments or the ability to issue new senior debt—may find prepackaged bankruptcy preferable.[18]

20.4   THE CHOICE OF REORGANIZATION OR LIQUIDATION

The opportunity to liquidate a company is the opportunity to abandon its entire business. This means we can view liquidation as a put option with the value described below.

$$L \geq \text{Max}(E - S, 0)$$ [20.2]

---

[18]For a discussion of these issues, see John J. McConnell and Henri Servaes, "The Economics of Pre-Packaged Bankruptcy," *Journal of Applied Corporate Finance*, Summer 1991, pp. 93–97.

where L = value of the liquidation put option prior to expiration
E = value of the company in liquidation
S = value of the company as a going concern

The creditors and common stockholders own this option jointly when a company is insolvent or bankrupt because they must collectively decide on reorganization or liquidation. There is an additional owner when a formal bankruptcy petition has been filed because the court also must approve of the plan.[19] We will focus on the determinants of the value of the company in liquidation, E, and the value of the company as a going concern, S, in this section.

The value of a company in liquidation is easy to describe; it is simply the market value of the company's assets as individual items. That is, the liquidation value of a company's assets equals their salvage value. This value presumably is available to anyone who is willing to buy the company's assets or similar assets in the open market.

The value of a company as a going concern is the value of its assets as individual items plus the value of any opportunities created by assembling the assets in a *particular* way to perform a *particular* task. The value of favorable opportunities may depend on the existence of a talented research and development staff or a high-quality, specially trained work force. The value of favorable opportunities also may be derived from patents, trademarks, brand names, and other intangible assets. An effective distribution system and a loyal customer base also provide opportunities that are not available to someone who merely owns the same physical assets as the company. Even tax-shields that can be used in the future are additions to a company's liquidation value. These options, which the company owns, enhance the value of the company as a going concern.

There also may be unfavorable opportunities created by assembling the assets in a particular way. Long-term labor contracts give employees a call option on the company's assets that is paid in installments as wages. A process that produces hazardous products or wastes gives consumers, employees, or agencies of the government a call option on the value of the company's assets that is paid when the courts award damages. These options, which the company has sold, diminish the value of the company as a going concern.

We can see how the value of the liquidation put option is evaluated by incorporating these ideas in Equation 20.2. Let C^+ equal the value of the favorable options a company owns and C^- equal the value of the unfavorable options it has sold. Then, the value of the company as a going concern equals its liquidation value plus the value of these options, or

$$S = E + C^+ - C^-.$$

The value of the liquidation put option is

$$L \geq \text{Max}(E - S, 0)$$
$$\geq \text{Max}(E - (E + C^+ - C^-), 0)$$
$$\geq \text{Max}(C^- - C^+, 0) \qquad\qquad \text{[20.3]}$$

---

[19]The common stockholders of a healthy company own a similar option because they can unilaterally decide to put their company's assets to the creditors by defaulting on the debt. In this case, the value of the company's assets is S and the current debt obligation is the exercise price, E.

where C^- = value of the options a company has sold
C^+ = value of the options a company owns.

In other words, the put option to liquidate a company is in-the-money when the value of the options the company has sold to employees, customers, governmental agencies, etc. exceeds the value of the options it owns.

The claimants receive the put option's intrinsic value, $\text{Max}\,(C^- - C^+, 0)$, if they exercise it when it's in-the-money and liquidate the company. They maintain its option value, L, and receive the cash flows from permitting the company to continue operating if they choose reorganization. Consequently, the decision to liquidate or reorganize the company is based on the inequalities given below:

$$\text{Liquidate if Max}\,(C^- - C^+, 0) > L + \text{Cash flow}$$

$$\text{Reorganize if Max}\,(C^- - C^+, 0) < L + \text{Cash flow}$$

Here is a simple illustration. Rodan Enterprises operates a hazardous waste-processing facility. The company's processing plant is adaptable to a variety of uses but its highly skilled work force is unique: It is valued at $200 million. Unfortunately, Rodan polluted a hazardous waste storage area before it developed its new technology. Environmental Protection Agency fines, cleanup costs, and damage suits by neighbors of the site are valued at $225 million. The value of the liquidation put option therefore is

$$L \geq \text{Max}(\$225 - \$200, 0)$$

$$\geq \$25 \text{ million.}$$

Suppose the liquidation put option is actually worth $26 million because of uncertainty about the outcome of the damage suits. Suppose also that Rodan's cash flows from continuing to operate the processing facility for one year are $1 million. Then the claimants should continue to operate the company because $\text{Max}(C^- - C^+, 0) = \$25$ million is less than $L + \text{cash flow} = \$27$ million.

EXERCISE 20.5

THE LIQUIDATION DECISION

Suppose the value of Rodan's favorable and unfavorable options are $200 million and $225 million, as before. However, an increase in uncertainty about the amount of cleanup costs increased the value of the put option to $30 million. How much cash can the company afford to spend to keep the processing facility open for one more year?

Rodan should continue to operate the waste-processing facility if

$$\text{Max}(C^- - C^+, 0) \leq L + \text{Cash flow}$$

$$\$25 \leq \$30 + \text{Cash flow}$$

$$\text{Cash flow} \geq \$-5 \text{ million.}$$

Rodan can afford to spend up to $5 million operating the waste-processing facility to keep its liquidation put option alive.

We will not develop this approach to choosing between reorganization and liquidation further because the main lessons are clear. An insolvent or bankrupt company may be liquidated if the favorable options it owns are less valuable than the unfavorable options it has sold. However, it should not be liquidated immediately if the value of the put option plus the cash flows from continuing to operate the business exceed the value of the company in liquidation.

20.5 SUMMARY

Companies suddenly restructure themselves or have restructuring thrust upon them when the managers are unable or unwilling to make the normal business decisions that restructure them gradually. Synergistic takeovers remove obstacles and enable managers to pursue options otherwise unavailable to the company. Disciplinary takeovers assert the owners' control and force managers to exercise options they have neglected.

Mergers, which are implemented through negotiation, may be used in synergistic takeovers, but acquisitions of stock are more likely in disciplinary takeovers because they usually are hostile. Sales, spinoffs, and buy-outs may be employed in anticipation of or as a consequence of a synergistic or disciplinary takeover. Some defensive techniques discourage both types of takeovers while others are specifically intended to resist tender offers.

A takeover's benefit equals the value of the options that it creates or frees from a reluctant management's control. The value of an option that will be exercised immediately equals its NPV. Option pricing models must be used to determine the value of options that will not be exercised until later, if at all. A takeover's cost is the amount paid in excess of the target company's market value. Ignoring the effect of taxes, this cost is the same whether the method of payment is cash or stock if the exchange ratio is based on the post-takeover value of the combined companies.

Companies must restructure their claims if the failure to gradually or suddenly restructure their assets causes financial distress. This restructuring in financial distress may be accomplished in a private workout, by filing a formal bankruptcy petition, or with a combination of both. This combination, a prepackaged bankruptcy, saves costs and time and forces holdouts to accept the terms of the reorganization.

Companies that are not viable are liquidated rather than reorganized. The decision to reorganize or liquidate is based on the company's value as a going concern in comparison to its value in liquidation. A going concern owns options that make it worth more than the salvage value of its assets but it also has sold options that may make it worth less. Therefore, a proper treatment of the liquidation decision also requires the valuation of options.

• KEY TERMS

Synergistic takeover   *827*

Proxy contest   *827*

Disciplinary takeover   *828*

Merger   *829*

Tender offer   *830*

Management buy-out
  (MBO)   *831*

Leveraged buy-out
  (LBO)   *831*

Poison pill   *832*

White knight   *832*

Crown jewel gambit   *832*

Technical insolvency   *845*

Insolvency   *845*

Bankruptcy   *845*

• QUESTIONS AND PROBLEMS

1. Describe the decisions that gradually and suddenly restructure a company's assets and claims and discuss their similarities and differences.

2. Define the following terms:

   (a) Merger

   (b) Tender offer

   (c) Spin-off

   (d) Leveraged buy-out

   (e) Poison pill

   (f) White knight

   (g) Crown jewel gambit

3. Compare and contrast synergistic and disciplinary takeovers. What role do options play in each type of restructuring?

4. Is a synergistic or disciplinary acquisition more likely to be friendly? Which type of acquisition is more likely to be accomplished through a merger? Through a tender offer? Explain your answers.

5. Explain how corporate charter amendments make it more difficult to use the proxy mechanism to obtain control of a company.

6. Discuss the advantages and disadvantages of cash and stock as the method of payment in acquisitions.

7. Should a company adopt the purchase or pooling of interest method to account for a merger if the objective is to maximize earnings per share? To maximize cash flow per share? Explain your answers.

8. Financial distress is a general term that encompasses several different forms of difficulty.

   (a) Describe the difference between technical insolvency and actual insolvency.

   (b) Can a company that is neither technically nor actually insolvent become bankrupt? Explain your answer.

9. Companies can obtain protection from their creditors by filing a bankruptcy petition under chapter 7 or 11 of the U.S. federal bankruptcy law.

   (a) What are the differences between a chapter 7 and a chapter 11 bankruptcy petition?

   (b) What type of analysis should a company perform before deciding whether to file a chapter 7 or 11 bankruptcy petition?

10. The resolution of financial distress may or may not involve formal supervision by the courts.

    (a) What are the advantages and disadvantages of using a private workout to resolve financial distress?

(b) What are the advantages and disadvantages of declaring bankruptcy to resolve financial distress?

(c) How does prepackaged bankruptcy combine the advantages of a private workout and a formal declaration of bankruptcy?

11. Chertco Engineering bid $24 a share for 60,000 shares of stock issued by Rhodes and Bridges Construction Company (RBCC). Chertco's managers believe the combined company's equity will be worth $3 million; Chertco's and RBCC's preacquisition values were $1.5 million and $1.2 million.

(a) What is the NPV of the acquisition? What are its incremental benefit and cost?

(b) Suppose this is an acquisition for cash. What proportion of the incremental benefit of the acquisition do Chertco's owners receive? What proportion do RBCC's owners receive?

12. The managers of Illinois Door Company are contemplating the acquisition of Indiana Window and Sash. Each company's partial market value balance sheet is given below. Also given below is an estimate of the combination's free cash flows.

	Illinois Door	**Indiana Window**
Total debt	$125	$175
Total equity	200	275
Total assets	$325	$450

End of Year	**Combination's Free Cash Flows**
1	$ 95 million
2	100
3	110
4	125
5 to ∞	135

(a) Determine the market value of the combination's assets and equity assuming its weighted average cost of capital is 14 percent and that no debt will be issued or retired.

(b) What is the incremental value of the acquisition? What is the NPV of the acquisition if Illinois Door can purchase Indiana Window for $315 million?

13. The managers of Alpha Corp. and Omega Inc. are negotiating a merger that will produce a new company known as Alpha–Omega, Ltd. Information about each company and the combination is given below.

Alpha Corp.   5 million shares outstanding @ $22.50 per share.
Omega, Inc.   8 million shares outstanding @ $28.00 per share.
Alpha–Omega, Ltd.   Anticipated market value of equity $450 million.

(a) Determine the incremental benefit of the merger.

(b) Determine the incremental cost if Alpha's owners are paid $150 million cash for their shares.

(c) What is the NPV of this merger? Should Omega's owners approve the merger? Explain your answer.

14. Bovinia Inc. owns and operates a chain of drive-in movie theaters located in six midwestern states. Competition from cable television, video cassettes, and conventional movie theaters with exceptional sound systems has reduced the value of Bovinia's drive-ins although the real estate is quite valuable. The company's managers are unwilling to close drive-ins and sell the property for development, however, because they "grew up" in the drive-in movie theater business.

(a) Determine the market value of Bovinia's assets and equity as the company is currently operated. The company has no debt outstanding, its cost of capital is 13 percent, and its projected free cash flows, in billions, are shown below.

Bovinia's Free Cash Flows

	Year				
	1	2	3	4	5 to ∞
Cash flow provided by (used for) operations	$0.18	$0.18	$0.18	$0.18	$0.18
Cash flow provided by (used for) investment	(0.02)	(0.02)	(0.02)	(0.02)	(0.02)
Net cash flow	$0.16	$0.16	$0.16	$0.16	$0.16

(b) Terra Max Corporation acquires companies to restructure their assets and free undervalued real estate. Determine the market value of Terra Max's assets and equity. The company has $10.5 billion of debt outstanding and its cost of capital is 10 percent.

Terra Max's Free Cash Flows

	Year				
	1	2	3	4	5 to ∞
Cash flow provided by (used for) operations	$1.42	$1.45	$1.49	$1.51	$1.52
Cash flow provided by (used for) investment	(0.07)	(0.07)	(0.07)	(0.08)	(0.08)
Net cash flow	$1.35	$1.38	$1.42	$1.43	$1.44

(c) Terra Max is evaluating the possibility of acquiring Bovinia through a tender offer. If the offer is successful, Terra Max will close all but the most profitable drive-ins and sell the properties for commercial development. The combination's free cash flows will equal Bovinia's free cash flows plus Terra Max's free cash flows plus the free cash flows shown below. Determine the market value of the combination's assets and equity assuming its weighted average cost of capital will be 10.5 percent and that Terra Max will not issue or retire any debt.

Changes in Combination's Free Cash Flows

	Year				
	1	2	3	4	5 to ∞
Increase (decrease) in cash flow provided by operations	$(0.12)	$(0.12)	$(0.12)	$(0.12)	$(0.12)
Increase (decrease) in cash flow provided by investment	1.75	0.01	0.01	0.01	0.01

(d) Determine the incremental benefit of the acquisition.

(e) Should Terra Max's board of directors approve an offer of $1.4 billion for Bovinia's common stock? Should Bovinia's owners accept the offer if it is extended? Explain your answers.

15. Griffon Stores is considering an acquisition of Linell Merchandise Company. The companies' current operations will be consolidated and existing stores will be operated under the name Griffon–Linell & Company. Griffon may also develop a chain of discount department stores at a cost of $3 billion that will be named GL Discount Club. Estimated market values of the equity in these businesses are given below.

Griffon Stores	$12.0 billion
Linell Merchandise	8.0
Griffon–Linell & Co.	23.0
GL Discount Club	2.0

(a) What is the maximum amount Griffon can pay Linell's owners for the company's current operations? What is the percentage premium over the market value of their equity?

(b) What is the value of the opportunity to develop the GL Discount Club if the standard deviation of its continuously compounded annual rate of return is 0.35, the option is viable for three years, and the riskless rate of return is 7 percent per year?

(c) What is the maximum amount Griffon can pay Linell's owners for the company's current operations plus the expansion option? What is the percentage premium over the market value of their equity?

(d) Suppose Griffon can acquire Linell's equity for $10.5 billion cash. What is the NPV of the acquisition to Griffon's owners? Should the company proceed with the acquisition?

16. Fuller Media Products owns an outstanding library of travel and educational videos that it rents to schools through a mail-order catalogue. The market value of the company's equity is $750 million. Fuller's managers believe the company must develop the capability to deliver its products electronically and is considering the acquisition of Orbtron Incorporated, an Internet video store. Orbtron's owners want $25 million cash for the company.

(a) Combining Fuller's and Orbtron's current operations will create a company with equity worth $770 million. Should Fuller pay Orbtron's owners $25 million for their company if this is the total benefit of the acquisition? Explain your answer.

(b) Fuller's managers believe that if they own Orbtron, they can spend an additional $55 million and develop a new business that fully exploits the potential for delivering videos over the Internet. They estimate that this business is worth only $52 million currently but that the standard deviation of its continuously compounded annual rate of return is 0.50. What is the value of the option to develop this new business if it expires in two years and the riskless rate of return is 6 percent per year?

(c) What is the total value of the acquisition considering the companies' current operations and the expansion opportunity? Should Fuller pay Orbtron's owners $25 million for their company? Explain your answer.

17. Bellhaven Management acquires poorly performing companies, replaces the managers, restructures the assets, and resells the common stock within five years. Bellhaven is examining two companies, code named GO1 and GO2, with the intention of combining them to obtain both synergistic and disciplinary benefits. GO1 is a small company and GO2 is a midsized company in a stable industry. The companies' market value balance sheets, in millions of dollars, are shown below.

	GO1	GO2
Total debt	$ 500	$ 950
Total equity	1,356	2,824
Total assets	$1,856	$3,774

(a) Combining GO1's and GO2's existing operations is expected to provide synergies that produce the additional cash flows (in millions of dollars) shown below. What is the incremental benefit of the restructuring if the combined company's weighted average cost of capital is 12 percent and Bellhaven doesn't issue or retire any debt?

		Year			
	1	2	3	4	5 to ∞
Increase in cash revenues	$20	$70	$90	$90	$ 90
Increase in cash operating costs	10	30	40	40	40

(b) Among GO1's and GO2's assets are some associated with the declining segment of their industry. Bellhaven's managers estimate that these assets are currently worth $150 million, their salvage value is $148 million, and the standard deviation of their continuously compounded annual rate of return is 0.50. The riskless rate of return is 8 percent. What is the additional value provided by the opportunity to abandon these assets as the industry declines in value over the next five years? (Hint: use put-call parity to value this abandonment option.)

(c) What is the entire incremental benefit of acquiring and restructuring these companies? What is the NPV to Bellhaven's owners if the company can buy GO1 and GO2 for $4.3 billion cash?

18. EIO Ltd. has 10 million shares of stock outstanding with a market price of $54 per share and intends to acquire McDonald Farms using stock as the method of payment. The combination will be worth $1.2 billion. McDonald Farms also has 10 million shares outstanding although they are selling for $36 per share. EIO wants to pay McDonald's owners a premium of 25 percent over market value.

(a) What is the incremental benefit of the acquisition?

(b) What is the incremental cost of the acquisition if EIO pays the 25 percent premium? Is the acquisition a positive NPV project for EIO's owners at this cost?

(c) How many shares must EIO issue to McDonald Farms' owners to pay for this acquisition? What is the exchange ratio?

(d) Consider an investor who owned 500 shares of McDonald Farms common stock before the acquisition announcement. How many shares of the combination will she receive when the acquisition is completed? What is the value of each share? Has her wealth increased by 25 percent?

19. Leffe Trucking Corp. intends to acquire Royal Transportation Co. in an exchange of shares. A description of each company's pretakeover condition is given below. Leffe's CEO wants to pay Royal's owners $2.25 million and therefore set the exchange ratio at 1:1.

	Leffe Trucking	Royal Transportation
Number of shares	560,000	100,000
Price per share	$22.50	$15.00
Market value	$12,600,000.00	$1,500,000.00

(a) How much did Leffe Trucking Corp. actually pay Royal's owners if the value of the combination is $18 million? What was the CEO's mistake?

(b) Determine the exchange ratio that will pay Royal's owners exactly $2.25 million if the combination is worth $18 million. Show that a typical owner receives a 50 percent premium for his shares.

20. The pretakeover condition of a bidder company and a target company are described below. The bidder offered the target company's owners one share of the bidder's stock for every two shares of the target's stock they currently own.

	Bidder	Target
Number of shares	700,000	600,000
Price per share	$55.00	$22.75

(a) What is the minimum value of the combination assuming the acquisition is not a negative NPV project?

(b) What is the amount of the dollar premium per share paid to the target company's owners?

21. A declining market for lawn mowers with gasoline engines has placed the AutoClipper Mower Company in financial distress. Should the claimants reorganize or liquidate the company in each of the following situations? Explain your answers.

	Value of Options Company Sold	Value of Options Company Owns	Value of Liquidation Put Option	Cash Flow from Continuing Operations
(a)	$150 million	$200 million	$ 8 million	$10 million
(b)	190	170	23	(5)
(c)	210	160	55	(2)

22. Humboldt Motor Corporation's customers filed a class-action lawsuit alleging that the company's Bodacious Bass Sound System caused hearing losses in teenage drivers. The verdict in the suit will be rendered in one year at which time the company will be worth $3 billion if the verdict is favorable and $1.75 billion if it is not. The liquidation value of the company's assets is $2 billion although their market value at the time the suit was filed was $2.15 billion. The company's weighted average cost of capital is 15 percent and the riskless rate of return is 8 percent.

(a) What is the value of liquidating the company immediately?

(b) What is the value of maintaining the option to liquidate the company? (Hint: use the binomial option pricing model to determine the value of the liquidation put option.) What should the managers do?

(c) Suppose this lawsuit is the only weakness in Humboldt's operating and financial position. Would you expect that a consideration of the company's interim cash flows could change your conclusion about what the managers should do? Explain your answer.

• ADDITIONAL READING

A textbook entirely devoted to reorganizations is:
> J. Fred Weston, Kwang S. Chung, and Susan E. Hoag, *Mergers, Restructuring and Corporate Control,* Prentice Hall, Englewood Cliffs, New Jersey, 1990.

A very readable treatment of valuation with applications to mergers, acquisitions, and buy-outs is:
> Tom Copeland, Tim Koller, and Jack Murrin, *Valuation,* John Wiley & Sons, Inc., New York, 1994.

A law textbook by Ronald Gilson also has an extensive discussion of the financial issues in acquisitions.
> Ronald J. Gilson, *The Law and Finance of Corporate Acquisitions,* Foundation Press, Mineola, New York, 1986.

Edward Altman has written extensively about financial distress and discusses his and others' work in:
> Edward I. Altman, *Corporate Financial Distress,* John Wiley and Sons, New York, 1983.

PRICE STORES

Years of hard work and attention to the owners' interests had paid off handsomely
for Franklin Price. He drew a good salary as chairman and CEO of Price Stores,
the west coast department store chain he established, and had become wealthy
as his shares of the company's common stock increased in value. Consequently, he was
not surprised when two major stockholders of Kelvins Inc. asked him to make a tender offer for the company's common stock.

Kelvins Inc. is an east coast department store chain that had fallen on hard times.
Profitability was declining at the company's urban locations, and the managers were
reluctant to make the hard decisions required to restructure the company's assets and
operations. Consequently, Kelvins' stock price was depressed.

Elizabeth and Rebecca Kelvin, daughters of the company's founder, deplored the
company's situation but had failed to win seats on the board of directors, which was
dominated by the company's senior managers. Nevertheless, they knew enough about
the company's operations to conclude that the managers used outmoded inventory management practices, invested in stores that were not economically viable, and did not use
enough debt in the company's capital structure. Elizabeth and Rebecca were particularly upset when the managers purchased a corporate airplane to avoid traveling on commercial airlines when visiting the company's stores.

Franklin Price agreed to consider making a tender offer for Kelvins' shares and sat
down with his analysts to estimate the value of the acquisition. Their starting point was
an estimate of the combination's net free cash flows prior to making any changes in
Kelvins' operations. These estimates are given in Table 1. The analysts assumed that the
net free cash flow in year 2008 will continue in perpetuity.

COMBINATION'S NET FREE CASH FLOWS PRIOR TO CHANGES (MILLIONS)   **Table 1**

Year	Net Free Cash Flow	Year	Net Free Cash Flow
1998	$1,666.0	2004	$1,960.0
1999	1,733.0	2005	1,980.0
2000	1,793.0	2006	1,999.0
2001	1,847.0	2007	2,009.0
2002	1,893.0	2008	2,020.0
2003	1,931.0		

Franklin's discussions with Elizabeth and Rebecca Kelvin and his own managers led him to consider the following changes in Kelvins' operations and financing.

1. Sell the corporate airplane for $6.0 million in 1998. The sale will reduce the company's cash outflows for selling and administrative expenses by $0.6 million per year beginning in 1999.
2. Combine the companies' accounting, legal, and treasury departments. This restructuring will use $45 million of cash in 1999 and provide $40 million of cash savings in each subsequent year.
3. Use Price Stores' credit scoring model to control the extension of credit to Kelvins' customers. Adopting this policy will provide a one-time reduction in accounts receivable of $200 million in 1999.
4. Require the combination's major vendors to monitor inventory and automatically restock each store. Adopting this policy will provide a one-time reduction in inventory of $1,300 million in 1999. The company will partially compensate the vendors for this service by paying them electronically. This will cause a one-time reduction in accounts payable of $600 million in 1999.
5. Reexamine the major capital expenditures that Kelvins scheduled for 1999 and reject those not acceptable at the combination's cost of capital. These major projects are described in Table 2. The cash flows used and provided by these projects are included in Table 1.
6. Reduce Kelvins' financial slack by $500 million in 1998.
7. Use Prices' debt/equity ratio for the combination's capital structure.

Table 2   FREE CASH FLOWS FOR KELVINS' SCHEDULED CAPITAL EXPENDITURES (MILLIONS)

		Project		
Year	A	B	C	D
1999	$(100)	$(125)	$(225)	$(400)
2000	29	28	41	75
2001	29	28	41	75
2002	29	28	41	75
2003	29	28	41	75
2004	29	28	41	75
2005	0	28	41	75
2006	0	0	41	75
2007	0	0	41	75
2008	0	0	0	75

Project A: update point-of-sale registers
Project B: build a parking garage at the Baltimore store
Project C: remodel two New York City stores

ADDITIONAL FINANCIAL INFORMATION **Table 3**

Panel A: Companies' Market Value Balance Sheets Prior to Acquisition (millions)

	Price Stores	Kelvins Inc.
Total debt	$ 3,518.2	$1,608.8
Equity	7,131.4	4,823.8
Total assets	$10,649.6	$6,432.6
Number of shares outstanding	300.3	357.3
Price per share	$23.75	$ 13.50

Panel B: Market and Industry Data

Riskless rate of return	5.0%
Expected rate of return on the market portfolio	13.5
Department stores' average cost of debt	8.0

Other information Price and his analysts compiled for their work is given in Table 3. They assumed a marginal tax rate of 35 percent and that the combination's interest tax-shields will be risky.

Franklin Price and his analysts sequestered themselves to prepare their estimate of the incremental value of the merger. They intended to work through the weekend to determine how much the acquisition is worth and what factors are crucial to its success.

APPENDIX

Table A.1
FUTURE VALUE FACTORS
$$FVF = (1 + r)^t$$

Rate of Return (r)

Number of Periods (t)	0.01	0.02	0.03	0.04	0.05	0.06	0.07	0.08	0.09	0.10	0.12	0.14	0.16	0.18	0.2	0.24	0.28	0.32	0.36
1	1.0100	1.0200	1.0300	1.0400	1.0500	1.0600	1.0700	1.0800	1.0900	1.1000	1.1200	1.1400	1.1600	1.1800	1.2000	1.2400	1.2800	1.3200	1.3600
2	1.0201	1.0404	1.0609	1.0816	1.1025	1.1236	1.1449	1.1664	1.1881	1.2100	1.2544	1.2996	1.3456	1.3924	1.4400	1.5376	1.6384	1.7424	1.8496
3	1.0303	1.0612	1.0927	1.1249	1.1576	1.1910	1.2250	1.2597	1.2950	1.3310	1.4049	1.4815	1.5609	1.6430	1.7280	1.9066	2.0972	2.3000	2.5155
4	1.0406	1.0824	1.1255	1.1699	1.2155	1.2625	1.3108	1.3605	1.4116	1.4641	1.5735	1.6890	1.8106	1.9388	2.0736	2.3642	2.6844	3.0360	3.4210
5	1.0510	1.1041	1.1593	1.2167	1.2763	1.3382	1.4026	1.4693	1.5386	1.6105	1.7623	1.9254	2.1003	2.2878	2.4883	2.9316	3.4360	4.0075	4.6526
6	1.0615	1.1262	1.1941	1.2653	1.3401	1.4185	1.5007	1.5869	1.6771	1.7716	1.9738	2.1950	2.4364	2.6996	2.9860	3.6352	4.3980	5.2899	6.3275
7	1.0721	1.1487	1.2299	1.3159	1.4071	1.5036	1.6058	1.7138	1.8280	1.9487	2.2107	2.5023	2.8262	3.1855	3.5832	4.5077	5.6295	6.9826	8.6054
8	1.0829	1.1717	1.2668	1.3686	1.4775	1.5938	1.7182	1.8509	1.9926	2.1436	2.4760	2.8526	3.2784	3.7589	4.2998	5.5895	7.2058	9.2170	11.703
9	1.0937	1.1951	1.3048	1.4233	1.5513	1.6895	1.8385	1.9990	2.1719	2.3579	2.7731	3.2519	3.8030	4.4355	5.1598	6.9310	9.2234	12.166	15.917
10	1.1046	1.2190	1.3439	1.4802	1.6289	1.7908	1.9672	2.1589	2.3674	2.5937	3.1058	3.7072	4.4114	5.2338	6.1917	8.5944	11.806	16.060	21.647
11	1.1157	1.2434	1.3842	1.5395	1.7103	1.8983	2.1049	2.3316	2.5804	2.8531	3.4785	4.2262	5.1173	6.1759	7.4301	10.657	15.112	21.199	29.439
12	1.1268	1.2682	1.4258	1.6010	1.7959	2.0122	2.2522	2.5182	2.8127	3.1384	3.8960	4.8179	5.9360	7.2876	8.9161	13.215	19.343	27.983	40.037
13	1.1381	1.2936	1.4685	1.6651	1.8856	2.1329	2.4098	2.7196	3.0658	3.4523	4.3635	5.4924	6.8858	8.5994	10.699	16.386	24.759	36.937	54.451
14	1.1495	1.3195	1.5126	1.7317	1.9799	2.2609	2.5785	2.9372	3.3417	3.7975	4.8871	6.2613	7.9875	10.147	12.839	20.319	31.691	48.757	74.053
15	1.1610	1.3459	1.5580	1.8009	2.0789	2.3966	2.7590	3.1722	3.6425	4.1772	5.4736	7.1379	9.2655	11.974	15.407	25.196	40.565	64.359	100.71
16	1.1726	1.3728	1.6047	1.8730	2.1829	2.5404	2.9522	3.4259	3.9703	4.5950	6.1304	8.1372	10.748	14.129	18.488	31.243	51.923	84.954	136.97
17	1.1843	1.4002	1.6528	1.9479	2.2920	2.6928	3.1588	3.7000	4.3276	5.0545	6.8660	9.2765	12.468	16.672	22.186	38.741	66.461	112.14	186.28
18	1.1961	1.4282	1.7024	2.0258	2.4066	2.8543	3.3799	3.9960	4.7171	5.5599	7.6900	10.575	14.463	19.673	26.623	48.039	85.071	148.02	253.34
19	1.2081	1.4568	1.7535	2.1068	2.5270	3.0256	3.6165	4.3157	5.1417	6.1159	8.6128	12.056	16.777	23.214	31.948	59.568	108.89	195.39	344.54
20	1.2202	1.4859	1.8061	2.1911	2.6533	3.2071	3.8697	4.6610	5.6044	6.7275	9.6463	13.743	19.461	27.393	38.338	73.864	139.38	257.92	468.57
25	1.2824	1.6406	2.0938	2.6658	3.3864	4.2919	5.4274	6.8485	8.6231	10.835	17.000	26.462	40.874	62.669	95.396	216.54	478.90	1033.6	2180.1
30	1.3478	1.8114	2.4273	3.2434	4.3219	5.7435	7.6123	10.063	13.268	17.449	29.960	50.950	85.850	143.37	237.38	634.82	1645.5	4142.1	10143.
35	1.4166	1.9999	2.8139	3.9461	5.5160	7.6861	10.677	14.785	20.414	28.102	52.800	98.100	180.31	328.00	590.67	1861.1	5653.9	16599.	47191.
40	1.4889	2.2080	3.2620	4.8010	7.0400	10.286	14.974	21.725	31.409	45.259	93.051	188.88	378.72	750.38	1469.8	5455.9	19427.	66521.	*
45	1.5648	2.4379	3.7816	5.8412	8.9850	13.765	21.002	31.920	48.327	72.890	163.99	363.68	795.44	1716.7	3657.3	15995.	66750.	*	*
50	1.6446	2.6916	4.3839	7.1067	11.467	18.420	29.457	46.902	74.358	117.39	289.00	700.23	1670.7	3927.4	9100.4	46890.	*	*	*

*FVF > 99,999.

Table A.2
PRESENT VALUE FACTORS
$$PVF = 1/(1 + r)^t$$

Rate of Return (r)

Number of Periods (t)	0.01	0.02	0.03	0.04	0.05	0.06	0.07	0.08	0.09	0.10	0.12	0.14	0.16	0.18	0.2	0.24	0.28	0.32	0.36
1	0.9901	0.9804	0.9709	0.9615	0.9524	0.9434	0.9346	0.9259	0.9174	0.9091	0.8929	0.8772	0.8621	0.8475	0.8333	0.8065	0.7813	0.7576	0.7353
2	0.9803	0.9612	0.9426	0.9246	0.9070	0.8900	0.8734	0.8573	0.8417	0.8264	0.7972	0.7695	0.7432	0.7182	0.6944	0.6504	0.6104	0.5739	0.5407
3	0.9706	0.9423	0.9151	0.8890	0.8638	0.8396	0.8163	0.7938	0.7722	0.7513	0.7118	0.6750	0.6407	0.6086	0.5787	0.5245	0.4768	0.4348	0.3975
4	0.9610	0.9238	0.8885	0.8548	0.8227	0.7921	0.7629	0.7350	0.7084	0.6830	0.6355	0.5921	0.5523	0.5158	0.4823	0.4230	0.3725	0.3294	0.2923
5	0.9515	0.9057	0.8626	0.8219	0.7835	0.7473	0.7130	0.6806	0.6499	0.6209	0.5674	0.5194	0.4761	0.4371	0.4019	0.3411	0.2910	0.2495	0.2149
6	0.9420	0.8880	0.8375	0.7903	0.7462	0.7050	0.6663	0.6302	0.5963	0.5645	0.5066	0.4556	0.4104	0.3704	0.3349	0.2751	0.2274	0.1890	0.1580
7	0.9327	0.8706	0.8131	0.7599	0.7107	0.6651	0.6227	0.5835	0.5470	0.5132	0.4523	0.3996	0.3538	0.3139	0.2791	0.2218	0.1776	0.1432	0.1162
8	0.9235	0.8535	0.7894	0.7307	0.6768	0.6274	0.5820	0.5403	0.5019	0.4665	0.4039	0.3506	0.3050	0.2660	0.2326	0.1789	0.1388	0.1085	0.0854
9	0.9143	0.8368	0.7664	0.7026	0.6446	0.5919	0.5439	0.5002	0.4604	0.4241	0.3606	0.3075	0.2630	0.2255	0.1938	0.1443	0.1084	0.0822	0.0628
10	0.9053	0.8203	0.7441	0.6756	0.6139	0.5584	0.5083	0.4632	0.4224	0.3855	0.3220	0.2697	0.2267	0.1911	0.1615	0.1164	0.0847	0.0623	0.0462
11	0.8963	0.8043	0.7224	0.6496	0.5847	0.5268	0.4751	0.4289	0.3875	0.3505	0.2875	0.2366	0.1954	0.1619	0.1346	0.0938	0.0662	0.0472	0.0340
12	0.8874	0.7885	0.7014	0.6246	0.5568	0.4970	0.4440	0.3971	0.3555	0.3186	0.2567	0.2076	0.1685	0.1372	0.1122	0.0757	0.0517	0.0357	0.0250
13	0.8787	0.7730	0.6810	0.6006	0.5303	0.4688	0.4150	0.3677	0.3262	0.2897	0.2292	0.1821	0.1452	0.1163	0.0935	0.0610	0.0404	0.0271	0.0184
14	0.8700	0.7579	0.6611	0.5775	0.5051	0.4423	0.3878	0.3405	0.2992	0.2633	0.2046	0.1597	0.1252	0.0985	0.0779	0.0492	0.0316	0.0205	0.0135
15	0.8613	0.7430	0.6419	0.5553	0.4810	0.4173	0.3624	0.3152	0.2745	0.2394	0.1827	0.1401	0.1079	0.0835	0.0649	0.0397	0.0247	0.0155	0.0099
16	0.8528	0.7284	0.6232	0.5339	0.4581	0.3936	0.3387	0.2919	0.2519	0.2176	0.1631	0.1229	0.0930	0.0708	0.0541	0.0320	0.0193	0.0118	0.0073
17	0.8444	0.7142	0.6050	0.5134	0.4363	0.3714	0.3166	0.2703	0.2311	0.1978	0.1456	0.1078	0.0802	0.0600	0.0451	0.0258	0.0150	0.0089	0.0054
18	0.8360	0.7002	0.5874	0.4936	0.4155	0.3503	0.2959	0.2502	0.2120	0.1799	0.1300	0.0946	0.0691	0.0508	0.0376	0.0208	0.0118	0.0068	0.0039
19	0.8277	0.6864	0.5703	0.4746	0.3957	0.3305	0.2765	0.2317	0.1945	0.1635	0.1161	0.0829	0.0596	0.0431	0.0313	0.0168	0.0092	0.0051	0.0029
20	0.8195	0.6730	0.5537	0.4564	0.3769	0.3118	0.2584	0.2145	0.1784	0.1486	0.1037	0.0728	0.0514	0.0365	0.0261	0.0135	0.0072	0.0039	0.0021
25	0.7798	0.6095	0.4776	0.3751	0.2953	0.2330	0.1842	0.1460	0.1160	0.0923	0.0588	0.0378	0.0245	0.0160	0.0105	0.0046	0.0021	0.0010	0.0005
30	0.7419	0.5521	0.4120	0.3083	0.2314	0.1741	0.1314	0.0994	0.0754	0.0573	0.0334	0.0196	0.0116	0.0070	0.0042	0.0016	0.0006	0.0002	0.0001
35	0.7059	0.5000	0.3554	0.2534	0.1813	0.1301	0.0937	0.0676	0.0490	0.0356	0.0189	0.0102	0.0055	0.0030	0.0017	0.0005	0.0002	0.0001	*
40	0.6717	0.4529	0.3066	0.2083	0.1420	0.0972	0.0668	0.0460	0.0318	0.0221	0.0107	0.0053	0.0026	0.0013	0.0007	0.0002	0.0001	*	*
45	0.6391	0.4102	0.2644	0.1712	0.1113	0.0727	0.0476	0.0313	0.0207	0.0137	0.0061	0.0027	0.0013	0.0006	0.0003	0.0001	*	*	*
50	0.6080	0.3715	0.2281	0.1407	0.0872	0.0543	0.0339	0.0213	0.0134	0.0085	0.0035	0.0014	0.0006	0.0003	0.0001	*	*	*	*

*PVF < 0.0001

Table A.3
ANNUITY PRESENT VALUE FACTORS

$$APVF = [1/r][1 - 1/(1 + r)^t]$$

Rate of Return (r)

Number of Periods (t)	0.01	0.02	0.03	0.04	0.05	0.06	0.07	0.08	0.09	0.10	0.12	0.14	0.16	0.18	0.2	0.24	0.28	0.32	0.36
1	0.9901	0.9804	0.9709	0.9615	0.9524	0.9434	0.9346	0.9259	0.9174	0.9091	0.8929	0.8772	0.8621	0.8475	0.8333	0.8065	0.7813	0.7576	0.7353
2	1.9704	1.9416	1.9135	1.8861	1.8594	1.8334	1.8080	1.7833	1.7591	1.7355	1.6901	1.6467	1.6052	1.5656	1.5278	1.4568	1.3916	1.3315	1.2760
3	2.9410	2.8839	2.8286	2.7751	2.7232	2.6730	2.6243	2.5771	2.5313	2.4869	2.4018	2.3216	2.2459	2.1743	2.1065	1.9813	1.8684	1.7663	1.6735
4	3.9020	3.8077	3.7171	3.6299	3.5460	3.4651	3.3872	3.3121	3.2397	3.1699	3.0373	2.9137	2.7982	2.6901	2.5887	2.4043	2.2410	2.0957	1.9658
5	4.8534	4.7135	4.5797	4.4518	4.3295	4.2124	4.1002	3.9927	3.8897	3.7908	3.6048	3.4331	3.2743	3.1272	2.9906	2.7454	2.5320	2.3452	2.1807
6	5.7955	5.6014	5.4172	5.2421	5.0757	4.9173	4.7665	4.6229	4.4859	4.3553	4.1114	3.8887	3.6847	3.4976	3.3255	3.0205	2.7594	2.5342	2.3388
7	6.7282	6.4720	6.2303	6.0021	5.7864	5.5824	5.3893	5.2064	5.0330	4.8684	4.5638	4.2883	4.0386	3.8115	3.6046	3.2423	2.9370	2.6775	2.4550
8	7.6517	7.3255	7.0197	6.7327	6.4632	6.2098	5.9713	5.7466	5.5348	5.3349	4.9676	4.6389	4.3436	4.0776	3.8372	3.4212	3.0758	2.7860	2.5404
9	8.5660	8.1622	7.7861	7.4353	7.1078	6.8017	6.5152	6.2469	5.9952	5.7590	5.3282	4.9464	4.6065	4.3030	4.0310	3.5655	3.1842	2.8681	2.6033
10	9.4713	8.9826	8.5302	8.1109	7.7217	7.3601	7.0236	6.7101	6.4177	6.1446	5.6502	5.2161	4.8332	4.4941	4.1925	3.6819	3.2689	2.9304	2.6495
11	10.3676	9.7868	9.2526	8.7605	8.3064	7.8869	7.4987	7.1390	6.8052	6.4951	5.9377	5.4527	5.0286	4.6560	4.3271	3.7757	3.3351	2.9776	2.6834
12	11.2551	10.5753	9.9540	9.3851	8.8633	8.3838	7.9427	7.5361	7.1607	6.8137	6.1944	5.6603	5.1971	4.7932	4.4392	3.8514	3.3868	3.0133	2.7084
13	12.1337	11.3484	10.6350	9.9856	9.3936	8.8527	8.3577	7.9038	7.4869	7.1034	6.4235	5.8424	5.3423	4.9095	4.5327	3.9124	3.4272	3.0404	2.7268
14	13.0037	12.1062	11.2961	10.5631	9.8986	9.2950	8.7455	8.2442	7.7862	7.3667	6.6282	6.0021	5.4675	5.0081	4.6106	3.9616	3.4587	3.0609	2.7403
15	13.8651	12.8493	11.9379	11.1184	10.3797	9.7122	9.1079	8.5595	8.0607	7.6061	6.8109	6.1422	5.5755	5.0916	4.6755	4.0013	3.4834	3.0764	2.7502
16	14.7179	13.5777	12.5611	11.6523	10.8378	10.1059	9.4466	8.8514	8.3126	7.8237	6.9740	6.2651	5.6685	5.1624	4.7296	4.0333	3.5026	3.0882	2.7575
17	15.5623	14.2919	13.1661	12.1657	11.2741	10.4773	9.7632	9.1216	8.5436	8.0216	7.1196	6.3729	5.7487	5.2223	4.7746	4.0591	3.5177	3.0971	2.7629
18	16.3983	14.9920	13.7535	12.6593	11.6896	10.8276	10.0591	9.3719	8.7556	8.2014	7.2497	6.4674	5.8178	5.2732	4.8122	4.0799	3.5294	3.1039	2.7668
19	17.2260	15.6785	14.3238	13.1339	12.0853	11.1581	10.3356	9.6036	8.9501	8.3649	7.3658	6.5504	5.8775	5.3162	4.8435	4.0967	3.5386	3.1090	2.7697
20	18.0456	16.3514	14.8775	13.5903	12.4622	11.4699	10.5940	9.8181	9.1285	8.5136	7.4694	6.6231	5.9288	5.3527	4.8696	4.1103	3.5458	3.1129	2.7718
25	22.0232	19.5235	17.4131	15.6221	14.0939	12.7834	11.6536	10.6748	9.8226	9.0770	7.8431	6.8729	6.0971	5.4669	4.9476	4.1474	3.5640	3.1220	2.7765
30	25.8077	22.3965	19.6004	17.2920	15.3725	13.7648	12.4090	11.2578	10.2737	9.4269	8.0552	7.0027	6.1772	5.5168	4.9789	4.1601	3.5693	3.1242	2.7775
35	29.4086	24.9986	21.4872	18.6646	16.3742	14.4982	12.9477	11.6546	10.5668	9.6442	8.1755	7.0700	6.2153	5.5386	4.9915	4.1644	3.5708	3.1248	2.7777
40	32.8347	27.3555	23.1148	19.7928	17.1591	15.0463	13.3317	11.9246	10.7574	9.7791	8.2438	7.1050	6.2335	5.5482	4.9966	4.1659	3.5712	3.1250	2.7778
45	36.0945	29.4902	24.5187	20.7200	17.7741	15.4558	13.6055	12.1084	10.8812	9.8628	8.2825	7.1232	6.2421	5.5523	4.9986	4.1664	3.5714	3.1250	2.7778
50	39.1961	31.4236	25.7298	21.4822	18.2559	15.7619	13.8007	12.2335	10.9617	9.9148	8.3045	7.1327	6.2463	5.5541	4.9995	4.1666	3.5714	3.1250	2.7778

Table A.4
CUMULATIVE NORMAL PROBABILITIES

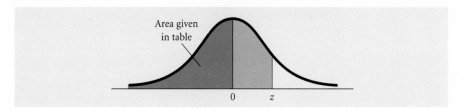

Z	0.00	0.01	0.02	0.03	0.04	0.05	0.06	0.07	0.08	0.09
0.0	.5000	.5040	.5080	.5120	.5160	.5199	.5239	.5279	.5319	.5359
0.1	.5398	.5438	.5478	.5517	.5557	.5596	.5636	.5675	.5714	.5753
0.2	.5793	.5832	.5871	.5910	.5948	.5987	.6026	.6064	.6103	.6141
0.3	.6179	.6217	.6255	.6293	.6331	.6368	.6406	.6443	.6480	.6517
0.4	.6554	.6591	.6628	.6664	.6700	.6736	.6772	.6808	.6844	.6879
0.5	.6915	.6950	.6985	.7019	.7054	.7088	.7123	.7157	.7190	.7224
0.6	.7257	.7291	.7324	.7357	.7389	.7422	.7454	.7486	.7517	.7549
0.7	.7580	.7611	.7642	.7673	.7704	.7734	.7764	.7794	.7823	.7852
0.8	.7881	.7910	.7939	.7967	.7995	.8023	.8051	.8078	.8106	.8133
0.9	.8159	.8186	.8212	.8238	.8264	.8289	.8315	.8340	.8365	.8389
1.0	.8413	.8438	.8461	.8485	.8508	.8531	.8554	.8577	.8599	.8621
1.1	.8643	.8665	.8686	.8708	.8729	.8749	.8770	.8790	.8810	.8830
1.2	.8849	.8869	.8888	.8907	.8925	.8944	.8962	.8980	.8997	.9015
1.3	.9032	.9049	.9066	.9082	.9099	.9115	.9131	.9147	.9162	.9177
1.4	.9192	.9207	.9222	.9236	.9251	.9265	.9279	.9292	.9306	.9319
1.5	.9332	.9345	.9357	.9370	.9382	.9394	.9406	.9418	.9429	.9441
1.6	.9452	.9463	.9474	.9484	.9495	.9505	.9515	.9525	.9535	.9545
1.7	.9554	.9564	.9573	.9582	.9591	.9599	.9608	.9616	.9625	.9633
1.8	.9641	.9649	.9656	.9664	.9671	.9678	.9686	.9693	.9699	.9706
1.9	.9713	.9719	.9726	.9732	.9738	.9744	.9750	.9756	.9761	.9767
2.0	.9772	.9778	.9783	.9788	.9793	.9798	.9803	.9808	.9812	.9817
2.1	.9821	.9826	.9830	.9834	.9838	.9842	.9846	.9850	.9854	.9857
2.2	.9861	.9864	.9868	.9871	.9875	.9878	.9881	.9884	.9887	.9890
2.3	.9893	.9896	.9898	.9901	.9904	.9906	.9909	.9911	.9913	.9916
2.4	.9918	.9920	.9922	.9925	.9927	.9929	.9931	.9932	.9934	.9936
2.5	.9938	.9940	.9941	.9943	.9945	.9946	.9948	.9949	.9951	.9952
2.6	.9953	.9955	.9956	.9957	.9959	.9960	.9961	.9962	.9963	.9964
2.7	.9965	.9966	.9967	.9968	.9969	.9970	.9971	.9972	.9973	.9974
2.8	.9974	.9975	.9976	.9977	.9977	.9978	.9979	.9979	.9980	.9981
2.9	.9981	.9982	.9982	.9983	.9984	.9984	.9985	.9985	.9986	.9986
3.0	.9987	.9987	.9987	.9988	.9988	.9989	.9989	.9989	.9990	.9990
3.1	.9990	.9991	.9991	.9991	.9992	.9992	.9992	.9992	.9993	.9993
3.2	.9993	.9993	.9994	.9994	.9994	.9994	.9994	.9995	.9995	.9995
3.3	.9995	.9995	.9995	.9996	.9996	.9996	.9996	.9996	.9996	.9997
3.4	.9997	.9997	.9997	.9997	.9997	.9997	.9997	.9997	.9997	.9998

GLOSSARY

Abandonment option The opportunity to abandon a strategic project.

Adjusted present value (APV) The present value of an investment project's free cash flow plus the present value of its financial side effects.

Adverse selection An offer's tendency to attract the less desirable portion of the target audience.

Agency costs The losses caused by actual and potential conflicts of interest between a principal and his or her agent.

Agency costs of debt The losses in value, such as risk shifting and failure to invest in positive NPV projects, attributable to the use of debt financing.

Agency costs of equity The losses in value attributable to the use of equity as the method of financing.

Allocation Adjusting the amount of risk a portfolio contains by designating a portion of wealth to risky investments and a portion to safe assets.

American options Options that can be exercised either at the date specified in the option contract, or earlier.

Annuity A series of equal payments made at fixed intervals, over a specified period of time.

Annuity due A series of equal cash flows that are paid or received at the beginning of each time period rather than at the end.

Annuity present value factor (APVF) The sum of the present value factors at r percent for one to n periods.

Arbitrage Pricing Theory (APT) A theory describing the relationship

between risk and return in terms of one or more fundamental economic factors.

Asset pricing models Market-wide models of the relationship between expected rate of return and risk.

Asymmetric information The disparity between the information available to the parties to a transaction.

Available balance The amount of money that is available to be withdrawn from a demand deposit account.

Balance sheet The document that describes a company's assets and how they were financed.

Bankruptcy When a company that cannot meet its financial obligations becomes subject to bankruptcy law and must settle with creditors, enter formal bankruptcy proceedings, or combine the two alternatives.

Best efforts When an investment bank promises to do its best at selling a company's securities, and is thus paid a simple commission.

Beta A measure of the sensitivity of an asset's rate of return to variation in the market index's rate of return.

Book balance The cash balance that is reflected in a company's own accounting books.

Business plan A short- or long-range plan that establishes a company's sales and production objectives and sets limits for expenditures such as wages, materials, salaries, and advertising.

Call option A financial instrument that gives its owner the right to buy an underlying asset at a specified price, within a specified period of time.

Capital Asset Pricing Model (CAPM) A model that states that an asset's expected rate of return must equal the riskless interest rate plus a risk premium determined by the asset's systematic risk.

Capital rationing When companies limit the amount of money they will spend on long-term investments.

Cash conversion cycle The length of time between cash outflow for raw materials and labor, and cash inflow from sales.

Cash statement The financial statement that describes a company's sources and uses of cash.

Characteristic line The regression line that describes the relationship between an asset's rate of return and the market index's rate of return.

Chief financial officer (CFO) The most senior finance specialist in a corporation.

Collection float The amount of money represented by checks received but not yet credited to the payee's account.

Compensating balances Cash balances that a company holds in demand deposit accounts to pay banks for credit and noncredit services.

Competitive bid An agreement under which a company hires the investment bank that offers the highest net proceeds from the sale of its securities.

Compound interest Interest income that is reinvested to earn additional interest.

Continuous compounding The limit of compounding interest that is reached when the compounding period is infinitesimally small.

Controller The senior finance specialist in a corporation who prepares financial statements and administers financial procedures.

Corporation A business with an identity that is distinct from the identities of its owners; the business's assets, liabilities, and income are its own according to law and the U.S. Internal Revenue Service.

Correlation coefficient A quantitative measure of the tendency of two variables, such as the rates of return on two assets, to move together.

Covariance A measure of variability that describes how assets' actual rates of return simultaneously deviate from their respective expected values.

Crown jewel gambit An action in which a company sells a strong business unit to make the company an unattractive takeover candidate.

Decision tree A diagram that describes the possible outcomes of a strategic opportunity.

Declaration date The date on which a company's board of directors announces the amount and schedule of its dividend payments to stockholders.

Direct costs of financial distress The fees paid to accountants, financial consultants, attorneys, and trustees who devise, evaluate, contest, and administer the process by which a company is reorganized or liquidated.

Disbursement float The amount of money represented by checks that have been written but not yet deducted from the payer's account.

Disciplinary takeover A takeover that removes or demotes managers who have previously ignored shareholders' interests and attempts to

correct mistakes made by those managers.

Discretionary financing Financing that includes all sources of debt and equity not directly linked to a company's operating cycle.

Dividend yield A stock's expected dividend, divided by the current price of one share.

Duration A financial instrument's present value–weighted term to maturity.

Earnings/price ratio (E/P) Earnings per share divided by price per share.

Economic life The replacement interval that minimizes the sum of acquisition, deterioration, and obsolescence costs for certain assets.

Effective annual interest rate The *actual* annual rate of return that accounts for the effect of earning interest on interest.

Efficient market A financial market in which prices are considered fair, fully reflecting available information.

Efficient set The set of portfolios that provides the best available or most efficient trade-off between risk and return.

Equivalent loan The debt-like obligation a company incurs when it signs a lease (for items like manufacturing equipment).

European options Options that cannot be exercised until a date specified in the option contract.

Event tree A diagram that describes the possible outcomes of a routine (take-it-or-leave it) opportunity.

Ex-dividend date The cut-off date that is four business days before the holder of record date; an investor who purchases stock after the ex-dividend date does not receive a dividend for that period.

Exercise price The price specified in an option contract.

Exercise the option When an investor takes action on an option, either making a purchase or sale.

Expansion option The opportunity to expand a strategic project.

Expectations theory The theory that forward interest rates equal an average of the spot interest rates that borrowers and lenders anticipate in the future.

Factor model A model of an asset's rate of return that uses several factors to represent economic conditions.

Financial cash flow The financial cash flow to or from investors that offsets free cash flow surpluses or shortages.

Financial lease A contract that is noncancelable and whose payments fully amortize the original cost of the leased item (such as equipment).

Financial plan A plan that contains a company's projected balance sheets, income statements, and cash statements.

Financial slack Planned temporary investments—cash and securities—that a company holds to meet unexpected requirements for funds.

Firm commitment When an investment bank guarantees the amount of net proceeds on the sale of a company's securities, then bears the risk of reselling them at a profit.

Fisher effect The relationship in which a nominal rate of interest equals the real rate of interest plus premiums that compensate for loss of purchasing power on the principal of a loan and on the interest income of a loan.

Foreign exchange rate The rate at which one currency can be exchanged for another.

Forward exchange rates Exchange rates for delivery at a future date.

Forward interest rates   The yields on securities purchased for future delivery.

Free cash flow   Cash flow provided by or used for operations plus cash flow provided by or used for investments plus cash flow provided by or used for financial slack.

Fundamental analysis   A form of security analysis in which the economy and a company's industry are studied in order to predict the company's earnings and cash flows.

Future value (FV)   The amount of cash in the future that is equivalent to an amount of cash paid or received today.

Future value factor   The amount by which one dollar will grow when invested at r percent for t time periods.

Hedge ratio   The number of shares of stock to buy from and call options to sell to a riskless portfolio.

Holder of record date   The date on which a company examines its records to see who is an owner (stockholder) and thus entitled to receive a dividend.

Homemade leverage   The use of personal borrowing and lending to produce the effects of leverage.

In-the-money   An option that provides a gain if it is exercised immediately.

Income statement   The financial statement that describes a company's sources and uses of revenue.

Indenture   A formal credit agreement.

Indirect costs of financial distress   The actual and opportunity costs of the disruptions to normal business that occur in anticipation of and during a crisis.

Insolvency   A serious form of financial distress in which the value of a company's debt exceeds the value of its assets.

Interest rate parity   When identical loans provide the same yield in each of two countries after adjusting for the rate at which one country's currency can be exchanged for the other's.

Interest rate risk   The risk to which borrowers and lenders are exposed due to changing interest rates.

Internal rate of return (IRR)   The discount rate that causes a project's net present value to equal zero.

Investment bank   A financial institution that helps companies issue securities, arrange mergers, and complete other financial transactions.

Investment tax credit   A provision of tax law that allows companies to reduce the taxes they owe by a fraction of the amount they spend on qualifying investments.

Lambda index (λ)   A cash-flow based ratio that measures financial slack.

Learning curve   A mathematical description of the time required to complete a nonroutine task as a function of experience or learning.

Leveraged buy-out (LBO)   A buy-out that is financed with a large proportion of debt.

Line of credit   An arrangement in which a company's bank agrees to lend it up to a specified amount of money over a given time period, usually one year.

Lock-box   A post office box set up by a bank in order to receive collection payments.

London Interbank Offer Rate (LIBOR)   The interest rate at which London banks borrow from one another.

Management buy-out (MBO)   An action in which a company's present managers invest a large proportion of their personal wealth in the company's equity in order to take over the company. The company then becomes privately held.

Market index   A broad-based portfolio of traded assets used as a proxy for the market portfolio.

Market model   A model of an asset's rate of return that uses the performance of a single, large, well-diversified portfolio to represent economic conditions.

Market portfolio   A portfolio that is constructed so that every asset in the economy is included in the portfolio in proportion to its market value.

Market-to-book ratio   The market value per share of common stock divided by the book value per share.

Merger   An action in which two firms are combined and one or both loses its original identity.

Modified Accelerated Cost Recovery System (MACRS)   A system for computing the annual depreciation deduction for business assets.

Negotiated agreement   An agreement under which an investment bank provides advice to a company on the type and features of securities to issue, when to sell them, and what type of offering to make.

Net present value (NPV)   The present value of a decision's future cash flow, plus its cash flow at time 0.

Nominal interest rate   The amount of interest earned in name only, that is, computed from unadjusted cash flows.

Operating cycle   The complete cycle of business operating activities: Acquisition of materials; production, sale, and distribution of goods or services; payment and collection of cash.

Operating lease   A contract that is cancelable and whose periodic payments do not recover the original cost of the item (such as equipment).

Opportunity cost The amount, stated in percentage terms, that an investor loses if he or she cannot take advantage of the next best opportunity.

Option premium The price that an option writer or subsequent owner receives when selling an option.

Partnership A business with two or more owners, and whose identity is inseparable from its owners according to law and the U.S. Internal Revenue Service.

Payment date The date on which dividends are paid to stockholders, usually between 30 and 60 days after the declaration date.

Pecking order theory The theory that states managers prefer to use internal funds to avoid implying their securities are overvalued by selling new debt or common stock.

Percent of sales method A method of forecasting financial requirements that assumes fixed costs are zero and the variable cost component is estimated by expressing the costs as a percentage of sales.

Perpetuity An annuity that goes on forever.

Poison pill A takeover defense that gives owners of the target company the right to buy shares of the combination's common stock at a substantial discount from market value if a hostile takeover is successful.

Political risk Uncertainty about how foreign political processes will affect the cash flows a company can obtain from a foreign investment project.

Portfolio opportunity set The set of all possible portfolios that can be constructed from a particular group of assets.

Precautionary balances The cash balances a company relies on when cash inflows are less than expected or cash outflows are greater than expected.

Preferred habitat theory The assertion that, while investors have maturity preferences, these preferences may be overcome if interest rates include a premium that compensates them for the real and psychological costs of risk.

Present value (PV) The amount of cash today that is equivalent to an amount of cash paid or received in the future.

Present value factor (PVF) The amount by which one dollar is discounted when it cannot be invested at r percent for t time periods.

Prospectus A formal document describing to potential investors a company's financial history and condition, the security's features, intended use of proceeds, and so forth.

Proxy contest An attempt by dissatisfied shareholders to assert control by voting their own shares as well as the shares that other shareholders have assigned to them by proxy.

Purchasing power parity When identical products sell at the same price in two countries after adjusting for the rate at which one country's currency can be exchanged for the other's.

Pure discount instrument A security issued at a discount from face value to provide the investor with implicit interest income in lieu of explicit interest payments.

Put option A financial instrument that gives its owner the right to sell an asset at a specified price, within a specified period of time.

Put-call parity The transactions that make a put and call option equivalent.

Real rate of interest The amount of interest actually earned, taking into consideration a change in purchasing power. The real rate of interest is computed from inflation-adjusted cash flows.

Red herring A preliminary prospectus issued when registration statements are filed with the SEC, containing information that may be subject to amendment in the final prospectus.

Restrictive covenants Provisions in a contract that spell out creditors' rights to participate in the control of a company, especially during financial distress.

Return on assets (ROA) Net income divided by total assets.

Return on equity (ROE) Net income divided by common equity or net worth.

Return on invested capital (ROIC) After-tax operating income divided by total assets.

Revolving credit agreement (revolver) A legally enforceable commitment in which a company's bank provides agreed-upon financing up to a specified amount, during a given time period, often more than one year.

Risk averse Resistant to accepting risk. Risk-averse investors must be paid a higher rate of return on higher-risk investments.

Security Market Line (SML) The equation used to compute the relationship between risk and return in the Capital Asset Pricing Model.

Segmented market theory The assertion that investors' preferences for particular maturities are absolute and cannot be overcome by paying them a risk premium.

Sensitivity analysis A technique used to determine the factors that are crucial to a financial decision's success. The technique indicates how much a net present value will change in response to changes in certain variables.

Signal A credible action taken to reveal private information.

Simple interest Interest paid only on an account's or investment's original principal.

Simulation An expanded form of sensitivity analysis that uses a computer to examine the effect of a large number of different values for a large number of variables that affect free cash flow.

Sinking fund A mandatory debt retirement schedule.

Sole proprietorship A business with an identity that is inseparable from the identity of its individual owner; the business's assets, liabilities, and income are the owner's, according to law and the U.S. Internal Revenue Service.

Speculative balances Balances that provide a company with the capacity to purchase other assets when prices are favorable.

Spot exchange rates Exchange rates for immediate delivery or settlement.

Spot interest rates The yields on securities purchased for immediate delivery.

Stock dividend A dividend that is paid in the form of shares of stock rather than cash.

Stock split An action taken by a company to increase the number of shares of stock that are available to investors, at a lower price. Current stockholders receive a proportionate increase in the number of shares they own.

Sustainable growth rate The annual amount by which a company can grow without issuing new common stock or changing its operating or financial policies.

Synergistic takeover A takeover in which the value of the combination of companies is expected to be greater than the sum of its parts.

Systematic risk A core amount of risk, caused by fluctuations in general economic conditions, that cannot be eliminated through diversification.

Technical analysis The practice of security analysis in which analysts use a security's price history to predict the rise or fall of a security's price.

Technical insolvency A potentially mild form of financial distress in which a company is unable to meet its current obligations because it is short of cash or illiquid.

Tender offer An offer that invites a company's owners (shareholders) to sell their shares to the bidder (another company or group of investors).

Term premium The addition to the interest rate that makes borrowers and lenders indifferent to loans of various maturities.

Term structure of interest rates The relationship between the spot interest rates on financial instruments and their terms to maturity.

Trade-off theory The balancing of benefits and costs of debt in order to arrive at an optimal capital structure.

Transaction balances The cash balances a company relies on to provide for cash requirements, particularly for day-to-day operations.

Treasurer The senior finance specialist in a corporation who obtains new financing, manages cash flow and risk, and makes interest, principal, and dividend payments.

Underwrite When an investment bank guarantees the amount of net proceeds on the sale of a company's securities.

Unsystematic risk The variation in an asset's rate of return that is unrelated to the variations in any other asset's rate of return.

Weighted average cost of capital A method of computing a discount rate by taking the weighted average of component costs of debt, preferred stock, and common equity.

White knight A company or group of investors willing to acquire a target company in a friendly—rather than hostile—takeover.

Yield curve A graph of bonds' yields versus maturity.

Yield to maturity A single interest rate that summarizes the rate of return on a bond over its entire life.

Zero-balance account (ZBA) A checking account that contains no money (zero balance), but when checks are presented against the account, appropriate funds are transferred from a master account in order to cover the checks.

Zero-coupon bond A security issued at a discount from face value to provide the investor with implicit interest income in lieu of explicit interest payments.

ANSWERS TO SELECTED QUESTIONS AND PROBLEMS

CHAPTER 2

11. (a) Cash flow provided by (used for) operations
Cash flow provided by (used for) investments
Cash flow provided by (used for) financing
(b) Net income
Total assets & claims

	January	February	March
	$(31,704)	$ 3,062	$ 2,351
	(6,000)	0	0
	38,982	(18)	(18)
	$ 2,087	$ 1,989	$ 1,706
	41,087	43,076	44,782

13. (a) Cash flow provided by operations = $32,408.
(b) Net free cash flow = $10,408.
(c) Retained earnings = $16,398
Notes payable = $13,052.
(d) Total assets & claims = $80,160.

16. (a) Return on equity = 15.06%   Total asset turnover = 1.379
Profit margin = 6.4%   Leverage = 1.706

CHAPTER 3

2. (a) Opportunity cost = 15%.   (b) Economic profit = $102.50   NPV = $89.13.

7. (a) Cost of bonus to employer = $4,347.83
(b) Value of bonus to you = $4,237.29.
(c) Maximum amount of loan = $4,464.29.

18. (a) Future value @ 9% compounded annually = $15,386.24
Future value @ 9% compounded monthly = $15,656.81.

21. (a) NPV(storage lot) = $3,939.79.

25. (a) Cost of lease = $14,257.22.   (b) Cost of lease = $14,830.33.

26. (a) Projects B and C are investments, project A is a loan.
(b) IRR(A) = 8.25%   IRR(B) = 15.96%   IRR(C) = 13.49%.
(c) A and B are acceptable.

27. (a) Implicit interest rate = 9.75%.

30. Periodic deposit = $8,142.00.

CHAPTER 4

3. One pound is equivalent to 1.5205 dollars.

12. (a) Real rate of return = 2.02%   (b) Forecasted nominal yield = 5.22%.

14. (a) Cost of car in Germany = $45,091.   (b) Maximum shipping costs = $909.   (d) Savings = $114.

15. (b) Exchange-rate-adjusted French interest rate = 5.52%.

17. (a) Implied future one year interest rate = 6.1%.
(b) Expected annual yield = 5.8%.
(c) Actual yield if future rate is 6.3% = 5.9%
Actual yield if future rate is 5.9% = 5.7%.

24. (a) Current two-year spot interest rate = 4.87%.   (b) Decrease in supply, increase in demand.

CHAPTER 5

3. May's holding period rate of return = 1.78%
June's holding period rate of return = −2.82%.

9. Portfolio expected rate of return = 10.50%
Portfolio standard deviation of return = 5.15%.

21. (c)

	$E(r)$	$\sigma(r)$
Dow Jones & Co.	2.46%	4.81%
S&P 500 Index	2.49	1.42

23. (b) Covariance(Safeway, Winn-Dixie) = 0.0014
Correlation(Safeway, Winn-Dixie) = 0.5558.

26. (a) $E(r_{\text{Dow Jones}}|r_I) = -0.002 + r_I \times 1.07$

(c)

	January	$E(r)$	$\sigma(r)$
Market component	2.60%	2.66%	1.52%
Unique component	4.19	−0.002	4.56

28. (a) $E(r_p) = 14.63\%$
$\beta_p = 1.1275$
$\sigma(r_p) = 22.55\%$.

CHAPTER 6

9. (b)

	Allocated to T-Bills	Allocated to Common Stock
Theodore Minneli	$160,000	$40,000
Shawn Robbins	−11,667	41,667

15. (a) NPV = $1,000.   (b) Allocate $21,000 to T-bills.
(c) Net cash flow at time 0 = $−27,000   (d) NPV = $1,000.
Net cash flow at time 1 = $29,960.

17. (a) Maximum bid = $85,339.   (b) NPV = $5,339.

19. (a) Required return for office equipment = 14.0%   (b) Approve fax/scanner
Required return for commuter airline = 16.0%   Reject shopping center and Tulsa–Dallas air service.
Required return for real estate development = 18.0%.

CHAPTER 7

3. (a) Price of one T-bill = $9,880.08. (b) Yield to maturity = 5.15%.

7. (a) Yield to maturity assuming annual interest payments = 6.21%.
(b) Yield to maturity assuming semi-annual interest payments = 6.24%.

9. (a) Ask price = $10,201.22. (b) Ask price = $10,204.07.

11. (a) Duration of installment loan = 2.40 years
Duration of note = 3.58 years
Duration of pure-discount bond = 4.00 years.

15.

	Puget Sound	Cleveland Electric
(a) Market values	$29.78	$112.29
(c) Estimated dividend yield	6.59%	6.59%
Actual dividend yield	7.73	8.97

23. (a) Current stock price = $50.29.
(b) New stock price @ 12% required rate of return = $57.83
New stock price @ 13% required rate of return = $45.05.

27. (a) Current sustainable growth rate = 13.3% (b) Current required rate of return = 12.45%
Sustainable growth rate after changes = 6.70%. Industry average required rate of return = 11.5%.
(c) Stock's estimated value = $21.89.

CHAPTER 8

13. (a)

	Call Option	Put Option
$20.00 June	$3.125	$0
22.50 June	0.625	0
22.50 September	0.625	0
25.00 June	0	1.875
25.00 July	0	1.875
25.00 September	0	1.875

16. (a) Value of homemade option if stock price is $25 = $ 0 (b) Number of shares = 0.50
Value of homemade option if stock price is $45 = $10. Amount of debt = $12.50.
(c) Total value of levered portfolio = $15.00
Amount financed with debt = $12.376
Amount financed with equity = $2.624.

19. (a) Value of compensation = $531,470.
(c) Value of compensation = $949,480.

23. (a) Implied standard deviation = 32.68%. (b) $72.50 January 18 $10.72
(c) $72.50 January 18 $0.26   82.50 April 19 7.01
  82.50 April 19 5.38   90.00 April 19 3.97
  90.00 April 19 9.70

CHAPTER 9

7. (a) Residual value of the cash flows = $10,560,000. (b) Present value of the cash revenues = $10,117,202.

16. (a)

Year	Advertising Expense	Year	Advertising Expense
0	$2,000,000	3	$1,152,000
1	3,200,000	4	1,152,000
2	1,920,000	5	576,000

(b) Present value of deductions for advertising expense = $9,037,815.

(c) Cost of change in IRS policy = $336,765.

23. (a)

Figurine	Time to Paint
1	1.50 hours
2	1.38
3	1.31
4	1.27
5	1.24
6	1.21
7	1.19
8	1.17
9	1.15
10	1.14

New employee can paint approximately 6 figurines during first eight-hour shift.

(b) Average direct labor cost per unit during first eight-hour shift = $12.00.

(c) Average direct labor cost per unit for experienced employee = $7.74.

24. (a) Book value at time of sale = $28,800.

(b) Net cash flow if sold for $25,000 = $26,330
Net cash flow if sold for $35,000 = $32,830.

27. (a) Incremental internal rate of return = 33.33%.

(b) Project 1's NPV = $879
Project 2's NPV = $243.

30. (b)

	Year 0	Year 1	Year 2
Net sales	$ 0	$ 75,000	$ 76,500
Cost of goods sold	0	45,000	39,125
Selling & administrative expenses	0	8,000	8,750
Depreciation	20,000	32,000	19,200
Taxes	(7,000)	(3,500)	3,299
Net income	(13,000)	(6,500)	6,126
Cash	0	2,250	2,295
Accounts receivable	0	6,164	6,288
Inventory	0	7,397	6,432
Accumulated depreciation	20,000	52,000	71,200
Accounts payable	0	3,082	2,680
(c) Cash flow provided by (used for) operations	7,000	15,021	25,765
Cash flow provided by (used for) investment	(100,000)	0	0
Cash flow provided by (used for) financial slack	0	(2,250)	(45)
Net free cash flow	(93,000)	12,771	25,720

32. (a)

Year	Free Cash Flows in Dollars
0	$–9,442,623
1	1,373,829
2	1,546,757
3	1,747,665
4	2,186,273
5	13,607,200

(b) Project's NPV in dollars = $2,085,891.

34. (a)

Year	Expected Free Cash Flows
0	$–335,000
1	30,000
2	30,000
3–20	60,000

(b) Project's NPV = $8,211.
(c) Project's NPV if outlet mall built next door = $207,737.
Project's NPV if truck stop built next door = $–5,000.

CHAPTER 10

7. (a) Sales per day = $20,000
Costs per day = $13,000.
(c) NPV = $6,786.83.

8. (a) Sales per day = $20,000
Costs per day = $13,000.
(c) NPV = $6,827.01.
(b) Average accounts receivable = $12,000
Average accounts payable = $5,720
Average inventories = $5,200
Average net working capital = $11,480.

13. (b) Length of production phase = 12 days
Length of collection phase = 22 days
Length of payment phase = 9 days
Length of cash conversion cycle = 25 days.
(d) Average investment in net working capital = $7,410.29.

CHAPTER 11

12. (a) Weekly production costs = $2,427.31
Average investment in inventory = $1,213.65.
(b) Annual cost of goods sold = $126,220.
(c) Length of production phase of operating cycle = 3.51 days.

13. NPV(annual production costs) = $117,952.

14. (a) Economic order quantity = 1,000 units.
(b) Number of orders per year = 24.

CHAPTER 12

3. (a) Effective annual interest rate = 24.58%.

7. (a) Minimum permissible credit price = $136.34
Maximum permissible credit price = $136.67.
(b) Approximate annual benefit = $–356.

11. (a) NPV without service if variable costs are 50% = $150,617
NPV with service if variable costs are 50% = $150,025.

14. (a)

	September	October	November	December
DSO	32.64	34.47	32.74	32.39
(b) Payment proportions				
1st prior month	—	91.00%	88.00%	84.00%
2nd prior month	—	—	8.00	9.00
3rd prior month	—	—	—	0.53

16. (a) Present value of shipment if pay by cash = $5,509   (b) Disbursement float if pay by cash = $0
Present value of shipment if pay by check = $5,497.   Disbursement float if pay by check = $12.00.

18. Net savings = $7,397 per year.

CHAPTER 13

15. (a)

Year	Expected Cash Flow
0	$–25,000
1	20,000
2	19,500

(b) Market value = $33,845
NPV = $8,845.

16. (b)

	Value of Expanding	Value of Not Expanding
First year economy was weak	$20,977	$19,820
First year economy was strong	14,221	15,315

(c) Market value = $34,366
NPV = $9,366.
(d) Value of expansion opportunity = $521.

17 (b)

	Value of Abandoning	Value of Not Abandoning
First year economy was weak	$17,500	$19,820
First year economy was strong	17,500	15,315

(c) Market value = $34,829
NPV = $9,829.
(d) Value of expansion opportunity = $984.

21. (a) Market value of expansion option = $379.   (b) Market value of abandonment option = $1,479.

25. (a) NPV of routine investment project = $45,967.
(b) Time 0 value of expansion option if not exercised then = $1,073.
Time 0 value of expansion option if exercised then = $167,217.

26. (a) Market value = $994,058
NPV = $244,058.

(b)

Price	Variable Cost	Quantity	NPV
$52.50	$30.00	5,000	$–267,590
70.00	30.00	5,000	244,058
87.50	30.00	5,000	755,706
70.00	22.50	5,000	463,336
70.00	30.00	5,000	244,058
70.00	37.50	5,000	24,781
70.00	30.00	3,750	–48,312
70.00	30.00	5,000	244,058
70.00	30.00	6,250	536,428

CHAPTER 14

13. (a) Cost of regional bank's loan = 9.0%.

18. (a) Profit if dealer's spread is $0.50 per share = $1.00
   Profit if dealer's spread is $1.75 per share = $–0.25.

20. (b) Correlation between Dow Jones Average and S&P 500 = 0.88.

CHAPTER 15

9. (a)

	Now	Year 1
Net free cash flow	$ 0	$ 392,400
Financial cash flow	0	(392,400)

   Value of a share of common stock = $6.00.

   (b)

	Now	Year 1
Net free cash flow	$ 90,000	$ 297,000
Financial cash flow	(90,000)	(297,000)

   Value of a share of common stock excluding current dividend = $4.50
   Value of a share of common stock including current dividend = $6.00.

   (c) Sell 75 shares of stock for homemade dividend.
   Buy 100 shares of stock for homemade reinvestment.

   (d)

Company pays dividend	No	Yes	No	Yes
Don wants dividend	No	No	Yes	Yes
Cash	$ 0	$ 0	$ 450	$ 450
Stock				
Number of shares	300	400	225	300
Price per share	6.00	4.50	6.00	4.50
Value	1,800	1,800	1,350	1,350
Total	$1,800	$1,800	$1,800	$1,800

13. (a)

	Now	Year 1
Without project		
Net free cash flow	$ 125,000	$ 310,750
Financial cash flow	(125,000)	(310,750)
With project		
Net free cash flow	25,000	446,350
Financial cash flow	(25,000)	(446,350)

(b) Stock price without project = $4.00.
   Stock price with project = $4.20.

14. (a) Value of a share of stock without investment = $40.   (b) NPV per share of investment proposal = $2.00.
   (c) Number of shares to issue = 1,000.
   Price per share = $42.

18. (a)

Company Pays Dividend	McGrew Wants Dividend	Value of McGrew's Stake
No	No	$8,000,000.00
Yes	No	7,109,161.50
No	Yes	7,360,240.00
Yes	Yes	7,128,800.00

CHAPTER 16

5. Present value of interest tax shield = $5,407.16.

10. (a) Required rate of return on assets = 11.0%
Required rate of return on equity = 11.0%.
(c) Value of a single share of stock = $20.
(d) Required rate of return on assets = 11.0%
Required rate of return on equity = 14.0%
Total assets = $30,000,000
Total debt = $10,000,000
Common equity = $20,000,000
Value of a single share of stock = $20.

(b) Total assets = $30,000,000
Total debt = $0
Common equity = $30,000,000
Value of a single share of stock = $20.

13. (a) Personal assets

800 shares of Durand stock	$10,000
Personal claims	
Proportionate share of company's debt	$ 0
Personal debt	0
Financial slack	0
Net debt	0
Personal equity	10,000
Total	$10,000

(b) Personal assets

400 shares of Durand stock	$ 5,000
Personal claims	
Proportionate share of company's debt	$ 5,000
Personal debt	0
Financial slack	5,000
Net debt	0
Personal equity	5,000
Total	$ 5,000

15. (a) Value of a single share of stock = $50.
(c) Total assets = $5,700,000
Total debt = $2,000,000
Common equity = $3,700,000.
(e) Per-share value of interest tax shield = $11.67
Original stock price plus interest tax shield = $61.67.

(b) Amount of annual interest tax shield = $49,000
Present value of interest tax shield = $700,000.
(d) Number of shares outstanding = 60,000
Price per share = $61.67.

18. (a)

Value of Debt	r_{wacc}
$100,000	8.4%
200,000	7.9
300,000	7.4
400,000	7.0
500,000	6.7

(b) Answers are the same.

22. (a)

	Original Capital Structure	New Capital Structure
After-tax cash flows received by creditors	$ 0	$507,360
After-tax cash flows received by owners	1,345,500	968,760

(b)

	Original Capital Structure	New Capital Structure
Value of assets	$32,500,000	$35,590,000
Value of debt	0	12,000,000
Value of equity	32,500,000	23,590,000
Price per share of stock	$20.00	$23.01

23. (a)

	Weak Economy	Strong Economy	Average
Amount of cash paid to creditors	$ 0	$ 0	$ 0
Amount of cash paid to owners	9,500	27,000	16,500

(b) Total assets = $15,865.3846
Total debt = $0
Common equity = $15,865.3846.
Price of an individual share of stock = $15.8654.

(c)

	Weak Economy	Strong Economy	Average
Amount of cash paid to creditors	$9,500	$10,400	$9,860
Amount of cash paid to owners	0	16,600	6,640

Total assets = $15,865.3846
Total debt = $9,480.7692
Common equity = $6,384.6154
Price of an individual share of stock = $15.8654.

27. (a)

	Conservative Strategy	Aggressive Strategy
Owners' expected cash flow per share	$3.675	$3.465
Price per share	3.50	3.30
(b) Value of managers' stock option	$0.80	$2.30

CHAPTER 17

9. (a) Amount company must borrow = $256,410.
   (b) Present value of floatation costs = $–4,668.27.

11. (a) Amount of money O'Hare must borrow = $406,091.37.
    (b) Present value of service charge side-effect = $–4,308.29.

(c)

Year	Interest Tax Shield
1	$13,116.75
2	10,269.59
3	7,151.95
4	3,738.13

(d) Required rate of return for interest tax shield = 9.5%.
(e) Present value of interest tax shields = $28,591.18.
   Total value of financial side-effects = $24,282.89.

13. (a) Annual after-tax interest savings = $6,600.
      Present value of after-tax interest savings = $45,803.60.
    (b) Present value of subsidized loan's after-tax cash flows = $45,803.60
      Financial side-effect = $45,803.60.

15. Present value of free cash flows = $–41,650.84
Present value of interest tax shields = $67,077.53
Adjusted present value = $25,426.69.

18. (a) Present value of net free cash flows = $–7,484.94.
(b) Present value of financial side-effects of leasing = $275,361.82
Adjusted present value = $267,876.88.

19. (a) Present value of net free cash flows = $–7,484.94.

Year	(b) Depreciation Tax Shield	(c) Debt Service Cash Flows
0	$ 81,658.50	$201,908.50
1	108,878.00	229,128.00
2	36,309.00	156,559.10
3	18,154.50	138,404.50

(d) Amount of equivalent loan = $674,807.26.
(e) Present value of depreciation tax shields = $226,125.74
Present value of interest tax shields = $24,043.35
Present value of financial side-effects = $250,169.09
Adjusted present value = $242,684.15.

20. (a) Net advantage of leasing = $25,192.73.
(b) Net advantage of leasing = $25,192.74.

25. (a)

	Equity Beta	Required Rate of Return
Myers Manufacturing Co.	1.25	16.00%
Miles Trucking Co.	1.01	14.08
Ezzell Electronics Inc.	1.18	15.44

(b)

	Equity Beta	Required Rate of Return
Myers Manufacturing Co.	1.46	17.68%
Miles Trucking Co.	1.24	15.92
Ezzell Electronics Inc.	1.32	16.56

27. (a)

Company	Asset Beta
A	0.9510
B	0.9272
C	0.9172
Average	0.9318

(b) Business risk required rate of return = 13.42%
Project's value = $93,764.

(c) Project's equity beta = 1.2113
Required rate of return on equity = 15.8%.

(d) Weighted average cost of capital = 12.98%
Project's total value = $106,191.

(e) Value of financial side-effects = $12,427.

CHAPTER 18

13. (a) Sustainable growth rate = 37.55%

(b)

	1998	1999
Net sales	$3,456,000	$3,732,480
Net income	204,612	274,158
Current assets	813,576	870,616
Net fixed assets	809,200	729,200
Total assets	1,622,776	1,599,816
Current liabilities	160,185	170,367
Long-term debt	540,700	540,700
Total equity	640,545	750,208
Total claims	1,341,430	1,461,275

(c)

	1998	1999
Projected deficit	$(281,346)	$(138,541)
Cash flow surplus (shortage)	(281,346)	142,805

(d)

	1998	1999
Cash flow provided by (used for) operations	$ 301,973	$ 345,843
Cash flow provided by (used for) investment	0	0
Cash flow provided by (used for) financial slack	(16,000)	(6,912)
Net free cash flow	$ 285,973	$ 338,931
Cash flow provided by (paid to) creditors	$ (444,552)	$ (31,631)
Cash flow provided by (paid to) owners	(122,767)	(164,495)
Net financial cash flow	$ (567,319)	$ (196,126)
Cash flow surplus (shortage)	$ (281,346)	$ 142,805
Financing surplus (deficit)	$ (281,346)	$ (138,541)

18. (a) Sustainable growth = 8.85%.
(b) Can reduce the leverage ratio from 2.400 to 1.356.
Can increase the dividend payout ratio from 0.30 to 0.604.

19.

	Year 1	Year 2
Interest expense	25,965	33,703
Net income	20,816	20,278
Total assets	828,842	808,769
Long-term debt	374,478	333,269
Retained earnings	127,956	148,234
Total equity	427,956	448,234
Total claims	828,842	808,769

CHAPTER 19

11. (a) The cash return point = $572.36.
(b) Buy $1,144.72 of securities when cash balance = $1,717.08.
(c) Sell $572.36 of securities when cash balance = $0.
(d) Average cash balance = $763.15
Annual opportunity cost of holding cash = $38.16.

13. (a)

Company	Current Ratio	Quick Ratio	Lambda
A	1.35	1.00	3.0
B	1.64	1.20	2.0
C	1.50	1.27	2.5

(c)

Company	Probability of Cash Insolvency
A	0.0013
B	0.0228
C	0.2020

(d) Company B's line of credit must = $24,000
Company C's line of credit must = $11,000.

17. (a) DSO = 30 days

	January	February	March
Forecast cash collections	$130,000	$60,000	$50,000

(b)

	January	February	March
Forecast cash collections	$90,000	$90,000	$55,000

20. (a)

	January	February	March
Free cash flow			
Collection of cash sales	$ 0	$ 34,560	$ 103,680
Collection of credit sales	0	0	138,240
Purchases	0	0	(102,216)
Selling & administrative expenses	(77,760)	(77,760)	(77,760)
Taxes	0	0	(34,870)
Net cash flow provided by (used for) operations	(77,760)	(43,200)	27,074
Cash flow provided by (used for) financial slack	0	0	(16,000)
Net free cash flow	$(77,760)	$ (43,200)	$ 11,074
Financial cash flow			
Pay interest	$ 0	$ 0	$ 0
Repay loan	0	0	0
Pay dividends	0	0	(30,692)
Net financial cash flow	$ 0	$ 0	$ (30,692)
Cash flow surplus (shortage)	$(77,760)	$ (43,200)	$ (19,618)
Financing surplus (deficit)	$(77,760)	$ (120,960)	$(140,578)

22. (a)

	Month	Permanent Financing	Temporary Financing	Temporary Investments
(i)	January	$13,500	$ 0	$5,500
	February	13,500	0	5,500
	March	13,500	0	5,500
(ii)	January	$10,000	0	2,000
	February	10,000	0	2,000
	March	11,500	0	1,500
(iii)	January	$ 8,000	0	0
	February	8,000	0	0
	March	9,500	500	0
(iv)	January	$ 6,000	2,000	0
	February	6,000	2,000	0
	March	7,500	2,500	0

(b)

	Permanent Financing	Average levels of: Temporary Financing	Temporary Investments
Conservative	$13,500.00	$ 0	$2,916.67
Conservative-matching	11,458.33	250.00	1,125.00
Pure-matching	9,458.33	1,125.00	0
Aggressive	7,458.33	3,125.00	0

	Net Annual Cost
Conservative	$1,146
Conservative-matching	1,090
Pure-matching	1,047
Aggressive	1,027

CHAPTER 20

11. (a) NPV of the acquisition = $60,000
    Incremental benefit of the acquisition = $300,000
    Incremental cost of the acquisition = $240,000.
    (b) Chertco's owners receive 20% of the incremental benefit
    RBCC's owners receive 80% of the incremental benefit.

14. (a) Market value of Bovinia's assets and equity = $1.2308 billion.
    (b) Market value of Terra Max's assets = $14.2467 billion
    Market value of Terra Max's equity = $3.7467 billion.
    (c) Market value of the combination's assets = $15.8035 billion.
    Market value of the combination's equity = $5.3035 billion.
    (d) Incremental benefit of the acquisition = $326 million.

16. (a) NPV of the acquisition = $–5.0 million.
    (b) Value of option to develop new business = $15.6 million.
    (c) Total value of the acquisition = $35.6 million.

19. (a) Leffe Trucking actually paid $2,727,272 or $27.27 per share for Royal Transportation Co.
    (b) The correct exchange ratio is 0.80 shares of Leffe stock for every 1.0 share of Royal stock outstanding.

21.

	Value of Liquidating	Value of Continuing
(a)	$ 0	$18
(b)	20	18
(c)	50	53

INDEX

The Addison-Wesley Series in Finance

Campbell/Kracaw
Financial Institutions and Capital Markets

Chambers/Lacey
Modern Corporate Finance: Theory and Practice

Copeland/Weston
Financial Theory and Corporate Policy

Crawford/Sihler
*Financial Service Organizations:
Cases in Strategic Management*

Davis/Pinches
Canadian Financial Management

Dufey/Giddy
Cases in International Finance

Eiteman/Stonehill/Moffett
Multinational Business Finance

Emery
Corporate Finance: Principles and Practice

Eng/Lees/Mauer
Global Finance

Gitman
Foundations of Managerial Finance

Gitman
Principles of Managerial Finance

Gitman
*Principles of Managerial Finance
-Brief Edition*

Gitman/Joehnk
Fundamentals of Investing

Megginson
Corporate Finance Theory

Melvin
International Money and Finance

Mishkin/Eakins
Financial Markets and Institutions

Pinches
Essentials of Financial Management

Pinches
Financial Management

Radcliffe
Investment: Concepts-Analysis-Strategy

Rejda
Principles of Risk Management and Insurance

Rejda/McNamara
Personal Financial Planning

Ritchken
Derivative Markets: Theory, Strategy, and Applications

Sihler
Cases in Applied Corporate Finance

Thygerson
Management of Financial Institutions

Wagner
Financial Management with the Electronic Spreadsheet